POPULAR FICTION

AN ANTHOLOGY

Gary Hoppenstand
Michigan State University

THE LONGMAN LITERATURE AND CULTURE SERIES

General Editor: Charles I. Schuster, University of Wisconsin—Milwaukee

 LONGMAN

An imprint of Addison Wesley Longman, Inc.

New York · Reading, Massachusetts · Menlo Park, California · Harlow, England
Don Mills, Ontario · Sydney · Mexico City · Madrid · Amsterdam

For my wife, Becky, for her steadfast love and gentle kindness, and for my father, David, who introduced me to some great "ripping yarns."

Editor-in-Chief: Patricia Rossi
Senior Editor: Lisa Moore
Associate Editor: Lynn M. Huddon
Supplements Editor: Donna Campion
Text Design: David Munger/DTC
Cover Design: Kay Petronio
Electronic Page Makeup: Karen Milholland/DTC
Manufacturing Manager: Willie Lane/Hilda Koparanian
Printer and Binder: RR Donnelley & Sons Company
Cover Printer: The Lehigh Press, Inc.

For permission to use copyrighted material, grateful acknowledgment is made to the copyright holders on pp. 787–789, which are hereby made part of this copyright page.

Library of Congress Cataloging-in-Publication Data

Popular fiction : an anthology / [compiled by] Gary Hoppenstand.
     p.   cm. -- (The Longman literature and culture series)
  Includes bibliographical references and index.
  ISBN 0-321-01164-3
  1. Popular literature--Great Britain. 2. Popular literature--United States.
3. American fiction. 4. English fiction.
I. Hoppenstand, Gary. II. Series.
PR1309.P67P67 1997
823.008--dc21
                                                                    97–35011
                                                                     CIP

Please visit our Web site at http://longman.awl.com

ISBN: 0-321-01164-3

12345678910—DOC—00999897

CONTENTS

2 ROMANCE FICTION 127

3 SCIENCE FICTION 276

4 DETECTIVE FICTION   441

5 ADVENTURE FICTION   581

Appendix

CRITICAL PERSPECTIVES ON POPULAR FICTION   723

FILMOGRAPHY   783

FOREWORD

If an answer does not give rise
to a new question from itself,
it falls out of the dialogue.
—Mikhail Bakhtin

The volumes in the *Longman Literature and Culture Series* present thoughtful and diverse approaches to the teaching of literature. Each is devoted to a special topic and designed for classes ranging from composition courses with a literature emphasis to introductory courses in literature to literature courses that focus on special topics, American studies, and cultural studies courses. Although the selections in each volume can be considered in terms of their formal literary properties, the power of these works also derives from their ability to induce students to read, re-read, think, sort out ideas, and connect personal views to the explicit and implicit values expressed in the literary works. In this way, the *Longman Literature and Culture Series* teaches critical analysis and critical thinking, abilities that will serve all students well, regardless of their majors.

Popular Fiction focuses on prose fiction through the exploration of many types of fiction not ordinarily studied in the college classroom. *Literature and the Environment, Literature, Culture, and Class, Literature, Race, and Ethnicity,* and *Literature and Gender* are all multigenre, with thematic clusters of readings exploring the central topic of the individual anthologies. These thematic clusters create series of links, allusions, and inflections among a wide variety of texts, and in this way, invite students to read actively and think critically. Meaningful contexts for the readings are provided by an introduction to each volume as well as chapter introductions and headnotes for every selection. An Instructor's Manual is also available for each anthology. These anthologies can be used in combination with each other, individually, and with other texts to suit the focus of the course.

- *Popular Fiction: An Anthology*, by Gary Hoppenstand (Michigan State University), is a collection of historical and contemporary works of prose fiction, including such authors as Edgar Allan Poe, Janet Dailey, Tony Hillerman, Walter Mosely, Stephen King, and Octavia Butler, and representing five popular genres: detective, romance, adventure, horror, and science fiction.

- *Literature and the Environment: A Reader on Culture and Nature*, by Lorraine Anderson, Scott Slovic (University of Nevada, Reno), and John P. O'Grady (Boise State University), is a thematic multigenre anthology that explores our relationship to nature and the role literature can play in shaping a culture responsive to environmental realities. It includes early writers such as John Muir, Henry David Thoreau, and Mary Austin, alongside contemporary voices such as Gary Snyder and Terry Tempest Williams.

- *Literature, Culture, and Class: A Thematic Anthology*, by Paul Lauter (Trinity College) and Ann Fitzgerald (American Museum of Natural History), is a consideration of class in "classless" America, including such authors as Edith Wharton, F. Scott Fitzgerald, Woody Guthrie, Alice Childress, Jimmy Santiago Baca, and Dorothy Allison. The selections allow students to better understand their own economic, political, and psychological contexts through learning about the ways in which social class and "class consciousness" have been experienced and changed over time in America.

- *Literature, Race, and Ethnicity: Contested American Identities*, by Joseph Skerrett (University of Massachusetts, Amherst), invites students to examine the history, depth, and persistence of the complex cultural attitudes toward race and ethnicity in America. The selections span from the late 1700s to the present, including a variety of genres from poems and letters to fiction and autobiography, essays, speeches, advertisements, and historical documents, with works by such writers as Thomas Jefferson, Frederick Douglass, Jacob Riis, Henry James, Langston Hughes, Maxine Hong Kingston, Constantine Panunzio, Lorna Dee Cervantes, Lawson Inada, and Louise Erdrich.

- *Literature and Gender: Thinking Critically Through Fiction, Poetry, and Drama*, by Robyn Wiegman (University of California, Irvine) and Elena Glasberg (California State University), assembles a provocative array of literary texts by such writers as Charlotte Perkins Gilman, Ernest Hemingway, Adrienne Rich, Tobias Wolf, Sherman Alexie, and Rita Dove, which explore the links between cultural beliefs, social institutions, sexual roles, and personal identity.

Although no single anthology, or series for that matter, can address the full complexity of literary expression, these anthologies do hope to engage students in the critical process of analysis by connecting literary texts to current social and cultural debates. In addition, these anthologies frame literature in pedagogically innovative ways, ways that will enable those students who find literature difficult to read, who think meaning is somehow locked inside a text, to critically engage with issues of interpretation, biography, and context. In this way, students begin to see that literature is a cultural expression that emerges from a complex consideration of and response to the world they share with the writers they read.

Very often, literary texts invite discussion on explosive issues in the classroom, provoking students to argue about the sexism of a short story or the racism expressed by a character. These anthologies, however, encourage students to take a step backward so that they can interrogate the cultural contexts of diverse works of literature. This shift away from the personal and toward the cultural should invite thoughtful and considered classroom discussion. Once students perceive this cultural frame, they will be better able to engage with texts, to see them as both profound expressions of the ordinary and eloquent achievements written by real people living in real time.

In addition, no set of anthologies can hope completely to resolve what is intended by the two central terms that anchor this discussion: "literature" and "culture." One of the most exciting contemporary discussions in English departments today centers on the very definition of literature: what it is, what it excludes, and what makes it work. If figuring out what we mean by "the literary" is difficult, determining the definition of "culture" is probably impossible. Like "nature," a term that John Stuart Mill analyzed over a hundred years ago, "culture" seems to designate everything or nothing at all. Is it something we make or does it make us? Is culture a neutral term designating human social activity, or something akin to class and status, a quality that marks you as either refined or vulgar, well-bred or common?

Not that we presume to have the correct answers or even all the appropriate questions. We realize that both the questions and the answers will be tentative and exploratory. Literature, it seems to all of us involved in this series, demands a willingness to maintain uncertainty, to probe multiple possibilities. It invites analysis and demands interpretation. It provokes conversations. This is the intention of the *Longman Literature and Culture Series:* to invite readings and rereadings of texts and contexts, of literature within the cultural and culture within the literary. Rather than answers, these anthologies pose questions and invitations.

Crafted to the vision of the individual editors, *Popular Fiction, Literature and the Environment, Literature, Culture, and Class, Literature, Race, and Ethnicity,* and *Literature and Gender* present an extraordinary range of material in such a way as to unsettle previous readings and provoke new ones. We hope the *Longman Literature and Culture Series* provides a welcoming invitation to all students to see that literature is deeply reflective of the fabric of everyday life.

> CHARLES I. SCHUSTER
> General Editor
> The University of Wisconsin, Milwaukee

ACKNOWLEDGMENTS

As with any project of this magnitude, there are a number of people whose assistance and support were indispensable. I would first like to thank my wonderful editors at Longman, Lynn Huddon and Lisa Moore, who built for me the best safety net possible (for when I sometimes fell off the highwire). I would also like to thank my series editor, Chuck Schuster, for his informed and insightful leadership. I would like to thank Doug Noverr, Acting Chairperson of the Department of American Thought and Language at Michigan State University, for allowing me the time at work to bring this book to completion; without his unerring generosity, you would not be holding this anthology in your hands. Next, I would like to thank the reviewers for *Popular Fiction: An Anthology*—Liahna Babener, Montana State University; Tamara Bolotow, University of Rhode Island—Providence Center; Ray Browne, Bowling Green State University; Bruce Burgett, University of Wisconsin, Madison; Diane Calhoun-French, Jefferson Community College; Curtis Ellison, Miami University; Dennis Hall, University of Louisville; William Hardesty, Miami University; Elyce Rae Helford, Middle Tennessee State University; Carl Holmberg, Bowling Green State University; Marty Knepper, Morningside College; Pamela Marks, University of Rhode Island—Providence Center; Chris Messenger, University of Illinois at Chicago; Michael Oriard, Oregon State University; Garyn Roberts, Northwestern Michigan College; Allison Scott, Bowling Green State University; Jim Smith, Augusta College; Cecelia Tichi, Vanderbilt University; John Trimbur, Worcester Polytechnic Institute; and Lawrence Wharton, University of Alabama at Birmingham—for helping me to direct this book toward publication. Finally, I would like to thank Patricia Julius and Dawn Martin for their kind assistance in the final preparation of the page proofs.

GARY HOPPENSTAND
Michigan State University

INTRODUCTION

Popular culture can encompass every aspect of our lives. It is so pervasive, we may not even notice the influence it can have on the choices we make every day. MTV and VH-1 tell us what music to like. Barbie and Ken dolls tell us how we should look. TV sitcoms tell us how we should act. Daytime talk shows tell us how we should feel. Brand names dictate the clothes we wear (from our Nike shoes, to our Gap jeans, to our Chicago Bulls sports caps), the cars we drive to work (Is your truck "built Ford tough"?), and the foods we eat ("Want a Big Mac with that Coca-Cola?"). Still, at its best, popular culture does two things that Americans seem to love the most: it celebrates commercial success, and it tells a good story. We love to hear the biographies of successful people, especially if they began their life in modest circumstances. We are a nation who adores the triumph of inventors such as Henry Ford and Thomas Edison. We idolize Michael Jordan all the more for the tremendous wealth and fame he has amassed by playing professional basketball. Not only do we enjoy real-life success stories, but we also enjoy reading fictional ones. Following the Civil War, the "American Dream" was packaged and sold in the more than one hundred Horatio Alger, Jr. novels. In all of these highly formulaic stories—the most popular being *Ragged Dick* (published serially in 1867)—a tough but worthy young lad achieves financial success by virtue of his hard work and moral fortitude. Over twenty million copies of Alger's "rags to riches" adventures were purchased by eager parents who wanted to provide their children with a blue-print for becoming successful in business. Readers today get the same information, repackaged and resold to us in the many "self-help" books written by "pop" psychologists. In each of these expressions of the American Dream—from the biographies of real-life inventors and sports heroes, to the fictional biographies of child entrepreneurs—we want to experience the story of hard-won success, or we want to learn how to achieve this success ourselves (and then sell the world our *own* biography).

In our popular culture, one of the most obvious examples of the union between commercial success and storytelling is popular fiction. Americans purchase Mario Puzo's best-selling novel *The Last Don* in the millions of copies, in large part, because it represents the literary expression of the American Dream—and enter-tains at the same time. What we call "popular fiction" can take many forms.

Aficionados of the detective story read Agatha Christie's *Murder on the Orient Express* because they are intrigued by Christie's intricate plotting and by her depiction of the charmingly eccentric Belgian detective, Hercule Poirot. Fans of the horror story read Anne Rice's *Interview with the Vampire* because of Rice's fascinating and richly detailed portrayal of the vampire Louis's search for a meaning to his dark existence. Others who desire a tale of romance and passion read Danielle Steel's *No Greater Love* because of Steel's engaging description of her protagonist Edwina Winfield's quest for happiness following her family's trip on the doomed *Titanic*. Those seeking the thrill of an out-of-this-world adventure read Robert A. Heinlein's *Starship Troopers* because of Heinlein's realistic account of a future high-tech war with an alien race of spiders, as told from an enlisted soldier's point-of-view. Though these five best-selling novels appear to have nothing in common, the one feature that horror fiction, romance fiction, science fiction, detective fiction, and adventure fiction each possesses is the ability to entertain.

"Escapism" is a term that perhaps best expresses how popular fiction functions as entertainment. In *Murder on the Orient Express*, for example, Christie establishes a noticeable distance between the real world and the imaginary world by setting the murder in her detective story on an Istanbul-Calais train coach that is trapped in the snow in Yugoslavia. In such a setting an amateur detective can assume an official capacity that has no equivalent in an actual murder investigation. Poirot, Christie's hero, has no peer on any professional detective force. His impressive powers of observation and deduction cannot be matched by the overworked and underpaid police detective of the real world. Instead of questioning this exaggeration of the truth in her fiction, this "artistic license," Christie's readers expect it. Her readers are anxious to suspend disbelief in the name of entertainment. They want to temporarily escape the day-to-day routine of their lives by climbing on board the Orient Express with the larger-than-life Poirot for a ride into exotic suspense and for the chance to match wits with the great detective's "little grey cells." Christie (like many authors who write popular fiction) understands that her stories must be larger than real life if they are to be more appealing than real life.

This escapist nature of popular fiction may attract readers, but it usually disturbs literary critics. Frequently, popular fiction is attacked as being inferior in quality to elite, or canonical, literature. Critics may consider Herman Melville's *Moby-Dick*, for example, to be artistically superior to Peter Benchley's *Jaws*. Melville's novel is often regarded as a great work of literature—because of Melville's skilled use of metaphor, imagery, social commentary, and character development—while Benchley's novel is typically viewed as a mere "pot-boiler" best-seller. But both of these sea adventure stories, reduced to their basic narrative components, deal with similar fundamental thematic issues. *Moby-Dick* and *Jaws* each illustrate the good and the bad that can be found in human nature, qualities that range in their characters from destructive obsession to courage in the face of great adversity. Benchley's use of language may be less sophisticated than that of Melville (certainly, his writing style is less polished than Melville's), but Benchley basically offers in his novel what Melville offers—an exciting sea adventure story that examines the conflict between the will of the individual and the inexorable forces of nature.

Indeed, popular fiction can have many of the same qualities that we often praise in "respectable" literature—effective use of language, interesting settings, distinctive characterizations, and sophisticated plotting. The spartan, tough-as-nails prose of Ernest Hemingway's *To Have and Have Not*, for example, may be found in

Dashiell Hammett's hard-boiled detective novel *The Maltese Falcon.* The epic scope and grand mythic quality of John Milton's *Paradise Lost* also exist in J. R. R. Tolkien's Lord of the Rings trilogy. The quest for moral self-redemption in Joseph Conrad's *Lord Jim* is mirrored in P. C. Wren's *Beau Geste.*

In practice, all fiction published from the mid-nineteenth century to the present is a mass-produced commodity by virtue of the simple fact that it is manufactured by an industrial system. To condemn the novels of Janet Dailey as being hack work because they are published for the masses smacks a little of hypocrisy, since even F. Scott Fitzgerald's *The Great Gatsby*—hailed by many literary critics as the great American novel of the twentieth century—was manufactured and distributed in a fashion amazingly similar to Dailey's popular romances. Both were edited, revised, designed, typeset, printed, and handled by book retailers in much the same fashion.

If so many similarities exist between fiction read for fun and fiction read for ideas, study, and discussion, what is the difference between popular fiction and other literature? Mere popularity is not enough—it is as important to understand the reasons *why* a particular work, author, or category of fiction is commercially successful. Popular fiction reflects the needs and interests of its readers. If the latest techno-thriller by Michael Crichton achieves best-seller status, then some storytelling quality that strikes a sympathetic chord in its audience must reside in Crichton's work. Crichton's runaway best-seller *Jurassic Park*—a cautionary tale of irresponsible genetic engineering gone dreadfully awry—is popular with today's readers, in part, because of its ability to tap into our collective suspicion of rampant modern technology.

Mass appeal is vital if a story is to succeed commercially, but the same mass appeal carries with it an assortment of negative critical assumptions. Popular fiction is typically chided as being ephemeral. One reason why Thomas Hardy's *Tess of the d'Urbervilles* is considered a great novel is because it has survived in print for over a hundred years. However, many works of popular fiction also demonstrate an appeal over time. Bram Stoker's horror classic *Dracula* is read as much today as when it was first published a hundred years ago, perhaps even more. Popular fiction is also frequently criticized as being too predictable, too formulaic. Yet, while S. S. Van Dine's detective novel *The Bishop Murder Case* is dismissed because it follows a rigid narrative pattern, much great literature is also formulaic. A Shakespearean sonnet is defined by its rigid poetic formula; the medieval or Renaissance tale of courtly love must follow a strict narrative pattern.

Perhaps what best accounts for the current distinction between popular and "serious" (or artistic, or superior) fiction was the development of the high school or college survey of literature course. When the academy established a literary canon of "great works," it in effect created a restricted bookshelf which could accommodate only so many titles. If a new book aspired for a place on this shelf, another book was removed to make room. The teacher, rather than the reader, became the arbiter of quality, and education became one of the few means of accessing literature. Popular fiction's mass appeal—its accessibility—is its undoing in the academic realm. The average reader does not require specialized training to appreciate Scott Turow's *Presumed Innocent* or Margaret Mitchell's *Gone with the Wind.* To approach and understand Geoffrey Chaucer's *The Canterbury Tales,* however, the reader needs a certain amount of formal, academic education. Therefore, since the nineteenth century, when the quality of education became equated with social class, the quality of fiction became equated with the level of one's education; the word *popu-*

lar became a pejorative expression meaning "uneducated" or "inferior." Despite the criticism of its detractors, popular fiction continues to flourish.

Though there may be room for debate about the specific classifications of popular fiction genres, or about what assortment of stories to place in a particular genre, five of the more popular categories include the following: horror fiction, romance fiction, science fiction, detective fiction, and adventure fiction. These genres are represented in the five corresponding chapters of this book. You're probably already familiar with the most commercially successful authors in these five popular genres—their names comprise a "Who's Who" of the national best-seller lists. Stephen King, Dean Koontz, and Anne Rice, for example, are authors who are instantly equated with popular horror fiction. Danielle Steel, Barbara Cartland, and LaVyrle Spencer are easily recognized as popular romance writers. Arthur C. Clarke, Isaac Asimov, and Ursula K. Le Guin are renowned as authors of science fiction. Agatha Christie, Ruth Rendell, and James Lee Burke rank among the most successful detective fiction writers, while Michael Crichton, Tom Clancy, and Louis L'Amour are celebrated adventure fiction authors. Stephen King, in his essay "On Becoming a Brand Name," calls this author/genre association a "brand name" recognition:

> I would define a "brand name author" as one who is known for a certain genre of the popular novel—that is, Robert Ludlum is the Bird's Eye of neo-Nazi spy suspense, Helen MacInnes is the Listerine of ladies' "international intrigue" stories, John Jakes is the General Motors of popular American historical fiction, and I, perhaps, am the Green Giant of what is called the "modern horror story."

For commercially successful authors such as Stephen King, the problem with popular fiction as art is its function as commodity, and the problem with popular fiction as commodity is its function as art. Most best-selling writers—including Ludlum, or MacInnes, or Jakes, or King—attempt to reach as wide an audience as possible. Their motivation to publish is thus inspired, in large part, by their desire to make money. Yet, this purely functional view of popular fiction does not take into account the fact that many of these writers find in their work a satisfactory means of expressing their opinions. Popular fiction *can* embody both art and commerce.

Still, a number of critics argue that literature such as horror fiction's only legitimate quality is its ability to generate a pleasurable response in its readers. While this point may be true to a certain extent—many readers are attracted to a horror story because it offers an enjoyable scare—some may also read horror to examine more fully the boundaries of what is socially acceptable. It is otherwise difficult to understand the pleasures a reader may have while reading the viscerally graphic fiction called "splatterpunk." Do those who purchase Thomas Harris's controversial novel *The Silence of the Lambs* do so only to satisfy some latent sadistic impulses? The horror story (and other genres of popular fiction) may also possess an overt moral intent. Harris's novel, for example, challenges cultural assumptions, such as the belief that a woman is incapable of performing well as an FBI agent—an occupation that has traditionally been a man's job. *The Silence of the Lambs* reinterprets for its reader the limits of social taboos—like murder—and the ability of human dignity and courage to triumph over the worst of nightmares. In a sense, Harris's young female protagonist, the FBI trainee Clarice Starling, is like a hero from classical mythology. Demonstrating great fortitude, she confronts (and in a sense, conquers) the psychopathic monster, "Hannibal the Cannibal" Lecter: she not only thwarts the plans of the serial killer called Buffalo Bill, but during the process of her investigation she also triumphs over her social limitations as a woman working in a so-called man's world. Whether we realize it or not, reading Harris's novel becomes an educating experience which redefines our false assumptions about gender.

Undeniably, popular fiction reflects the society in which it was produced. The horror story describes what happens to that poor individual who transgresses cultural or social taboos. Victor Frankenstein's pursuit of forbidden knowledge in Mary Shelley's famous novel is the cause of his and his family's terrible fate. Robert Louis Stevenson's Dr. Jekyll dares too much when he transforms into Mr. Hyde, and Bram Stoker's Dracula shamelessly indulges his hedonistic desire for blood. The detective story also features a moral conflict between good and evil, but in this category of fiction, notions of right and wrong are defined by the law, and justice is served by the detective's enforcement of the law. As *The Shadow*—a popular pulp magazine and radio vigilante hero during America's Great Depression—often proclaimed in his adventures: "The weed of crime bears bitter fruit. Who knows what evil lurks in the hearts of men? The Shadow knows!" The popular romance story also defines a morality for its reader. The relationships between men and women are socially constructed in the romance's narrative formula. This type of fiction may address issues of marital abuse and female self-definition, for example. The emotionally vulnerable narrator in Daphne du Maurier's novel *Rebecca* is a "good" woman who curbs Maxim de Winter's abusive impulses and eventually discovers a profound inner strength and great courage. In her novel, du Maurier defines what she perceives to be acceptable and unacceptable conduct for women and offers her readers a preferred social code, illustrating the proper way men should treat women.

Popular fiction affects, as well as reflects, society. As an example, witness the extraordinary influence of the nineteenth-century American dime novel frontier story on its readership. During the period between the Civil War to the turn of the twentieth century, the dime novel was a dominant form of mass-media entertainment. It was inexpensively produced, printed on cheap pulpwood paper, and literally sold by train boxcar-loads for a nickel or a dime apiece. The dime novel featured a wide range of fiction—from detective stories to romances—but by far the most popular type of dime novel was the frontier adventure. Books full of appealing nonstop action, featuring larger-than-life frontier heroes like Deadwood Dick and Buffalo Bill, were extremely popular with readers in both America and Europe. Many frontier dime novels imitated James Fenimore Cooper's then famous Leather-Stocking series, including *The Last of the Mohicans* and *The Deerslayer*. However, Cooper's depiction of Native Americans (as being both good and evil) was radically simplified in the frontier dime novel. Native Americans served as a popular dime novel villain—the savage "Red Devil"—and were employed as a convenient foil highlighting the dangerous exploits of the frontier hero. When thousands of working-class readers in the cities of the East Coast read these stories, they thought the overtly racist depictions of Native Americans were accurate. And when a number of these dime novel readers moved west as settlers, they took those prejudices with them. As historian Ray Allen Billington notes in his book, *Land of Savagery Land of Promise: The European Image of the American Frontier in the Nineteenth Century* (1981), even the Europeans of the time, who emigrated to this country and later traveled westward to establish farms or new frontier communities, were profoundly influenced by the negative images of Native Americans presented in the European equivalent of the American dime novel. The dime novel, then, played an unfortunate part in the conflict between native and non-native cultures, planting a destructive prejudice in the minds of its nineteenth-century readers that resulted in unreasoning racial hatred and violence.

Aside from its potentially harmful influences, popular fiction can also give us a better understanding of different world cultures or important knowledge about the past. Best-selling novels or genre stories may help to educate readers about topics they didn't study in school. John Grisham's mega-successful legal thrillers have done more to enlighten the general public about how the law functions than any published law textbook. Similarly, Robert van Gulik's celebrated "Judge Dee" detective novels have done more to instruct readers about ancient Chinese customs than hundreds of university courses on Chinese history.

Although many of us are not fully aware of popular fiction's ability to influence our ideas and actions, we are often all too aware of the guilty pleasure experienced in reading a popular adventure or horror story. We shouldn't feel bad if sometimes we decide to read a Kathleen E. Woodiwiss romance instead of Emily Brontë's *Wuthering Heights*. After all, art and aestheticism can be entirely subjective. The division between high and low literature is, at best, a nebulous one. Shakespeare's plays, before they were co-opted by the college literature professor and defined as high art, were originally produced for the commoner as well as the king. The magnificent novels of Charles Dickens were written for a popular audience in Europe and America during the nineteenth century before they become required reading in the modern-day British literature class.

Today, the literary canon is changing and expanding to include a broader range of ideas and an increased diversity of texts and authors, and this book is part of that ongoing, vibrant metamorphosis. What was once dismissed as "pop fiction" is now being taught in the college classroom in addition to traditional great works of literature. As the bookshelf containing the literary canon continues to expand, both teachers and students will become revitalized by the transformation. If we are openminded, popular fiction can complement our reading of elite fiction, and vice versa. Exclusionism at either end of the literary artistic spectrum is merely reductionism.

In this anthology, the first of its type, I heartily invite you to engage with popular fiction. As you survey the richness and variety of stories contained in this book, you may return to some of the questions articulated in this introduction. How is fiction part of our popular culture? What, for example, does the horror fiction of Edgar Allan Poe say about human psychology? What do the romances of Janet Dailey say about the attitudes of American women? What does the science fiction of Jules Verne say about the views of technology in an industrial Europe? What do the detective stories of Agatha Christie or Dorothy L. Sayers say about the morals of upperclass British society? And what do the westerns of Louis L'Amour say about the American frontier or the notion of rugged individualism? Of course, the generic boundaries and definitions of the many types of popular reading can be debated. Maybe you think the spy story should be included with detective fiction, rather than with adventure fiction. You may even wish to quibble about the authors selected to represent the five genres of popular fiction. Or perhaps you wish to question the distinction between popular fiction and elite literature. Is Jane Austen now a popular writer, since Hollywood has made a number of successful movies and several television series from her novels? Is Charles Dickens an elite writer, since his massive novels today are mainly read in the college literature class and his readers no longer shove one another off the New York City docks to be the first to purchase the latest installment of *The Old Curiosity Shop,* as they did between 1840 and 1841?

All of these are valid questions and can make the discussion of popular fiction a lively and interesting one. What cannot be debated, however, is the fact that millions of people worldwide voraciously read popular fiction and are influenced by what they read. The purpose of this anthology, then, is to introduce Janet Dailey, and Ian Fleming, and C. L. Moore (among many others) to the college classroom, with the hope that students and instructors can be charmed, enlightened, or simply entertained by the richness, variety, and lasting quality of their stories.

1

HORROR FICTION

It seems appropriate that the oldest genre of popular fiction, the horror story, was invented in an author's nightmare. Horace Walpole claimed that he acquired the idea for writing his Gothic novel *The Castle of Otranto* (1764) while having a bad dream. "I thought myself in an ancient castle," Walpole wrote, "(a very natural dream for a head filled like mine with Gothic story) and that on the uppermost banister of a great staircase I saw a gigantic hand in armour. In the evening I sat down and began to write, without knowing in the very least what I intended to say or relate." Indeed, tales of dreams and nightmares literally abound in horror fiction. A "waking dream" supposedly inspired Mary Shelley to begin composing her immortal novel, *Frankenstein* (1818), when she was only eighteen years old. A recurring nightmare also plagued the final years of the great nineteenth-century Irish author of Gothic and supernatural fiction, Joseph Sheridan Le Fanu. Le Fanu, it was said, dreamt a number of times in the later years of his life that an old mansion was about to fall on him. When Le Fanu died on February 7, 1873 of heart disease, his doctor apparently stated: "I feared this—that house fell at last." If these stories about the relationship between horror fiction and nightmares are not true, then they should be, because the popular horror story is a literary expression of individual and societal nightmares, of bad dreams that are given voice and form. Horror fiction, like the horror legends of folklore that provided Walpole with some of his narrative material, is the formal expression of our collective fears.

Freudians may call this expression a subliminal representation of the id; Jungians may call it a collective cultural archetype. Anthropologists have a different definition for this expression, as do comparative mythologists, as do deconstructionist literary critics, as do feminist critics. Yet, whoever is defining the subject of popular horror fiction, they all must recognize one point—the horror story is written and read for the express purpose of experiencing the emotion of fright in order to be entertained, of re-experiencing Mary Shelley's nightmarish "waking dream" sensation.

Horror has existed as long as the narrative tradition in Western culture. Odysseus, for example, visits the land of the dead in Homer's *The Odyssey*. Witches appear in Shakespeare's *Macbeth,* a ghost in Shakespeare's *Hamlet.* The first true horror novel, however, as previously mentioned, was Horace Walpole's *The Castle of Otranto,* which should also be considered the first popular fiction novel. Historically, then, the horror story was the first genre of popular fiction.

Stephen King suggests in his monograph, *Danse Macabre* (1981), which is the single finest examination of the horror genre ever published, that readers are drawn to the fictional horror story so that they can purge the actual horrors experienced in real life. "The great appeal of horror fiction through the ages" King argues in his Foreword to *Night Shift* (1978), "is that it serves as a rehearsal for our own deaths." Certainly, of the various genres of popular fiction, the horror story is the most visceral, the one that makes our skin clammy and our stomachs flutter. But it has survived and flourished because each new generation of writers and readers is able to re-invent the popular horror story to suit its own deeply disturbing anxieties. Simply put, horror fiction is a powerful and pliable metaphor that illuminates the ongoing relationship between life and death.

The selection of stories in this chapter exemplifies the rich history and wide range of formulas that are to be found in popular horror fiction, beginning with Horace Walpole's gothic fairy tale, "The King and His Three Daughters." Both Edgar Allan Poe's "The Tell-Tale Heart" and Joseph Sheridan Le Fanu's "Green Tea" illustrate the early development of psychological horror. Elizabeth Gaskell's "The Old Nurse's Story" typifies the classic nineteenth-century ghost tale, while Ambrose Bierce's "The Damned Thing" and H. P. Lovecraft's "The Call of Cthulhu" embody that formulaic intersection of science fiction and the horror tale that evolved during the late nineteenth and early twentieth centuries in American popular fiction. Bram Stoker's "Dracula's Guest" features, albeit peripherally, one of the most well-known monsters in all of popular culture. Finally, with Stephen King's "Graveyard Shift" and Clive Barker's "Down, Satan!," stories by two of the most famous authors of contemporary horror are included. Indeed, King's and Barker's tremendous success on the best-seller lists proclaims that the horror tale's popularity with readers is both widespread and dynamic.

HORACE WALPOLE

1717-1797

Horace Walpole was born in London, England to Robert Walpole, who was soon to become Great Britain's prime minister, and to Catherine Shorter, the daughter of an affluent merchant. Walpole entered Eton College when he was nine years old and continued his education there until 1734. While at Eton, he formed a society of letters called the Quadruple Alliance. In 1735, Walpole was admitted to King's College at Cambridge, and though he spent nearly four years studying mathematics and other subjects, he never completed his degree. Following his mother's death in 1737, Walpole decided to travel, and from 1739 to 1741, he journeyed with his boyhood friend, Thomas Gray, extensively throughout Europe. In 1749, Walpole's interests turned to architecture. He had just purchased a house— Strawberry Hill, at Twickenham, near the Thames River—and became seriously engaged in expanding and remodeling it, essentially transforming the house into a Gothic castle.

The fascination for Gothic architecture also influenced his prose writing, surfacing in his most famous literary work, The Castle of Otranto, *which, following its initial publication in 1764, eventually became one of Europe's first "best-selling" novels. Except for* The Castle of Otranto, *the majority of Walpole's writings are unknown today, except to the student of eighteenth-century history, but during his lifetime, his prose was influential. Walpole's more important works were his historical biographies—*Memories of the Last Ten Years of the Reign of George the Second *(1822),* Memoirs of the Reign of King George the Third *(1845), and* Journal of the Reign of King George the Third, from the Year 1771 to 1783 *(1859)—which were published after his death.*

"The King and His Three Daughters" originally appeared in Walpole's small anthology, Hieroglyphic Tales, *a volume numbering only a handful of copies which he published at his own expense in 1785 under the Strawberry Hill imprint. The six stories that appear in* Hieroglyphic Tales *reveal Walpole's fascination with the fairy tale structure, and, in fact, help demonstrate that larger narrative process that Walpole was so instrumental in facilitating, where the pre-industrial, popular oral folk tale was transformed into the popular fiction of the industrial era. In addition, the Oriental flavor of the stories in* Hieroglyphic Tales *exemplified both Walpole's and Western Europe's fascination during the late eighteenth century and early nineteenth century with Middle- and Far-Eastern cultures. The fascination, in particular, with Eastern mysticism profoundly influenced the creation and direction of the early popular Gothic narrative, as most easily seen in William Beckford's exotic horror tale,* Vathek *(1786). "The King and His Three Daughters," as an early horror story, illustrates Walpole's use of overtly grotesque, supernatural themes that are also found in* The Castle of Otranto. *In his Gothic tales, Walpole was fond of challenging his reader's expectations; he discarded realism in favor of the horribly fantastic. "The King and His Three Daughters" is a dark fairy tale indeed, where the eldest princess in the story is unborn and her suitor is an Egyptian corpse with three legs.*

THE KING AND HIS THREE DAUGHTERS

There was formerly a king, who had three daughters—that is, he would have had three, if he had had one more, but some how or other the eldest never was born. She was extremely handsome, had a great deal of wit, and spoke French in perfection, as all the authors of that age affirm, and yet none of them pretend that she ever existed. It is very certain that the two other princesses were far from beauties; the second had a strong Yorkshire dialect, and the youngest had bad teeth and but one leg, which occasioned her dancing very ill.

As it was not probable that his majesty would have any more children, being eighty-seven years, two months, and thirteen days old when his queen died, the states of the kingdom were very anxious to have the princesses married. But there was one great obstacle to this settlement, though so important to the peace of the kingdom. The king insisted that his eldest daughter should be married first, and as there was no such person, it was very difficult to fix upon a proper husband for her. The courtiers all approved his majesty's resolution; but as under the best princes there will always be a number of discontented, the nation was torn into different factions, the grumblers or patriots insisting that the second princess was the eldest, and ought to be declared heiress apparent to the crown. Many pamphlets were written pro and con, but the ministerial party pretended that the chancellor's argument was unanswerable, who affirmed, that the second princess could not be the eldest, as no princess-royal ever had a Yorkshire accent. A few persons who were attached to the youngest princess, took advantage of this plea for whispering that *her* royal highness's pretensions to the crown were the best of all; for as there was no eldest princess, and as the second must be the first, if there was no first, and as she could not be the second if she was the first, and as the chancellor had proved that she could not be the first, it followed plainly by every idea of law that she could be nobody at all; and then the consequence followed of course, that the youngest must be the eldest, if she had no elder sister.

It is inconceivable what animosities and mischiefs arose from these different titles; and each faction endeavoured to strengthen itself by foreign alliances. The court party having no real object for their attachment, were the most attached of all, and made up by warmth for the want of foundation in their principles. The clergy in general were devoted to this, which was styled *the first party.* The physicians embraced the second; and the lawyers declared for the third, or the faction of the youngest princess, because it seemed best calculated to admit of doubts and endless litigation.

While the nation was in this distracted situation, there arrived the prince of Quifferiquimini, who would have been the most accomplished hero of the age, if he had not been dead, and had spoken any language but the Egyptian, and had not had three legs. Notwithstanding these blemishes, the eyes of the whole nation were immediately turned upon him, and each party wished to see him married to the princess whose cause they espoused.

The old king received him with the most distinguished honours; the senate made the most fulsome addresses to him; the princesses were so taken with him, that they grew more bitter enemies than ever; and the court ladies and petit-maitres invented a thousand new fashions upon his account—every thing was to be à la Quifferiquimini. Both men and women of fashion left off rouge to look the more cadaverous; their cloaths were embroidered with hieroglyphics, and all the ugly characters they could gather from Egyptian antiquities, with which they were forced to be contented, it being impossible to learn a language that is lost; and all tables, chairs, stools, cabinets and couches, were made with only three legs; the last, however, soon went out of fashion, as being very inconvenient.

The prince, who, ever since his death, had had but a weakly constitution, was a little fatigued with this excess of attentions, and would often wish himself at home in his coffin. But his greatest difficulty of all was to get rid of the youngest princess, who kept hopping after him wherever he went, and was so full of admiration of his three legs, and so modest about having but one herself, and so inquisitive to know how his three legs were set on, that being the best natured man in the world, it went to his heart whenever in a fit of peevishness he happened to drop an impatient word, which never failed to throw her into an agony of tears, and then she looked so ugly that it was impossible for him to be tolerably civil to her. He was not much more inclined to the second princess—In truth, it was the eldest who made the conquest of his affections: and so violently did his passion encrease one Tuesday morning, that breaking through all prudential considerations (for there were many reasons which ought to have determined his choice in favour of either of the other sisters) he hurried to the old king, acquainted him with his love, and demanded the eldest princess in marriage. Nothing could equal the joy of the good old monarch, who wished for nothing but to live to see the consummation of this match. Throwing his arms about the prince-skeleton's neck and watering his hollow cheeks with warm tears, he granted his request, and added, that he would immediately resign his crown to him and his favourite daughter.

I am forced for want of room to pass over many circumstances that would add greatly to the beauty of this history, and am sorry I must dash the reader's impatience by acquainting him, that notwithstanding the eagerness of the old king and youthful ardour of the prince, the nuptials were obliged to be postponed; the archbishop declaring that it was essentially necessary to have a dispensation from the pope, the parties being related within the forbidden degrees; a woman that never was, and a man that had been, being deemed first cousins in the eye of the canon law.

Hence arose a new difficulty. The religion of the Quifferiquiminians was totally opposite to that of the papists. The former believed in nothing but grace; and they had a high-priest of their own, who pretended that he was master of the whole fee-simple of grace, and by that possession could cause every thing to have been that never had been, and could prevent every thing that had been from ever having been. "We have nothing to do," said the prince to the king, "but to send a solemn embassy to the high-priest of grace, with a present of a hundred thousand million of ingots, and he will cause your charming no-daughter to have been, and will prevent my having died, and then there will be no occasion for a dispensation from your old fool at Rome."—How! thou impious, atheistical bag of drybones, cried the old king; dost thou profane our holy religion? Thou shalt have no daughter of mine, thou three-legged skeleton—Go and be buried and be damned, as thou must be; for as thou art dead, thou art past repentance: I would sooner give my child to a baboon, who has one leg more than thou hast, than bestow her on such a reprobate corpse—"You had better give your one-legged infanta to the baboon," said the prince, "they are fitter for one another—As much a corpse as I am, I am preferable to nobody; and who the devil would have married your no-daughter, but a dead body! For my religion, I lived and died in it, and it is not in my power to change it now if I would—but for your part"—a great shout interrupted this dialogue, and the captain of the guard rushing into the royal closet, acquainted his majesty, that the second princess, in revenge of the prince's neglect, had given her hand to a drysalter, who was a common-council-man, and that the city, in consideration of the match, had proclaimed them king and queen, allowing his majesty to retain the title for his life, which they had fixed for the term of six months; and ordering, in respect of his royal birth, that the prince should immediately lie in state and have a pompous funeral.

This revolution was so sudden and so universal, that all parties approved, or were forced to seem to approve it. The old king died the next day, as the courtiers said, for joy; the prince of Quifferiquimini was buried in spite of his appeal to the law of nations; and the youngest princess went distracted, and was shut up in a madhouse, calling out day and night for a husband with three legs.

—1785

EDGAR ALLAN POE
1809-1849

Edgar Allan Poe was a tremendously important figure in the history of popular fiction. He was a significant literary critic of his time, and though his reviews could certainly be cruel, unlike many of his contemporaries, he had the courage to express his honest opinions. In addition, his Gothic horror tales, such as "The Fall of the House of Usher" (1839), were instrumental in successfully transplanting the Gothic narrative formula from Europe to America. Poe was also the inventor of the modern detective story; his "The Murders in the Rue Morgue" (1841) introduced to America and the world the first modern detective hero, C. Auguste Dupin. Poe was instrumental in developing the nineteenth-century science fiction story in America, as evidenced in his "The Unparalleled Adventure of One Hans Pfaall" (1835), and with his only published novel, The Narrative of Arthur Gordon Pym, of Nantucket *(1838), Poe became an important contributor to the sea adventure that was such a fashionable type of story during the mid-nineteenth century.*

Poe was born in Boston, Massachusetts. His parents, David Poe, Jr. and Elizabeth (Arnold) Poe were both actors. Poe's father abandoned his family, and Elizabeth later died in 1811. Poe then was brought into the Richmond home of the prosperous John Allan, but was never legally adopted. He eventually entered the University of Virginia in 1826, but due to gambling problems and other personal financial difficulties, he attended only a single term. Because of the ongoing friction between the young Poe and John Allan, Poe left Richmond for Boston, where he unfortunately had difficulty finding work and subsequently had a brief stint in the Army under the assumed name of Edgar A. Perry.

In 1827, Poe published his first book, a privately printed collection of poetry entitled Tamerlane. *In 1830, he launched a new military career at West Point, but this, too, was short-lived. Poe quarreled again with his godfather, and Allan finally disowned the young man. Between 1829 and 1831, Poe published two more collections of poetry, and after being dismissed from West Point in 1831, he traveled to New York, then to Baltimore, where he began writing and publishing fiction. In 1833, he earned fifty dollars for his tale, "MS. Found in a Bottle." He became editor of the* Southern Literary Messenger *in 1835, greatly improving its circulation. During this period,*

Poe married Virginia Clemm, his thirteen-year-old cousin. (Virginia would later die in 1847 following a lengthy illness.) In 1840, Poe published his first collection of fiction, Tales of the Grotesque and Arabesque, *but it was not commercially successful. In 1843, Poe won a one hundred-dollar first place literary prize for "The Gold Bug," which was published in the June 21 and 28 issues of the* Dollar Newspaper. *Poe moved back to New York City in 1844, and finally achieved wide literary fame with the publication of his poem "The Raven" in 1845. Much troubled during the later years of his life by problems with alcohol, his health, and a public that was, at times, hostile to his recent publications and lectures, Poe died in 1849 in Baltimore. The cause of his death was surrounded, like much of his own fiction, by mysterious circumstances.*

One of Poe's greatest contributions to popular fiction was his skilled use of the psychological tale of horror. Certainly, many of his strongest short stories—"The Pit and the Pendulum" (1842), "The Black Cat" (1843), and "The Cask of Amontillado" (1846)—are literary masterpieces of psychological horror and are among Poe's most enduring creative work. His finest tale of this type, and perhaps his most popular, is "The Tell-Tale Heart," first published in the January 1843 issue of Pioneer, *a Boston periodical.*

THE TELL-TALE HEART

True!—nervous—very, very dreadfully nervous I had been and am! but why *will* you say that I am mad? The disease had sharpened my senses—not destroyed—not dulled them. Above all was the sense of hearing acute. I heard all things in the heaven and in the earth. I heard many things in hell. How, then, am I mad? Hearken! and observe how healthily—how calmly I can tell you the whole story.

It is impossible to say how first the idea entered my brain; but once conceived, it haunted me day and night. Object there was none. Passion there was none. I loved the old man. He had never wronged me. He had never given me insult. For his gold I had no desire. I think it was his eye! yes, it was this! He had the eye of a vulture— a pale blue eye, with a film over it. Whenever it fell upon me, my blood ran cold; and so by degrees—very gradually—I made up my mind to take the life of the old man, and thus rid myself of the eye forever.

Now this is the point. You fancy me mad. Madmen know nothing. But you should have seen *me.* You should have seen how wisely I proceeded—with what caution— with what foresight—with what dissimulation I went to work!

I was never kinder to the old man than during the whole week before I killed him. And every night, about midnight, I turned the latch of his door and opened it— oh, so gently! And then, when I had made an opening sufficient for my head, I put in a dark lantern, all closed, closed, so that no light shone out, and then I thrust in my head. Oh, you would have laughed to see how cunningly I thrust it in! I moved it slowly—very, very slowly, so that I might not disturb the old man's sleep. It took me an hour to place my whole head within the opening so far that I could see him as he lay upon his bed. Ha!—would a madman have been so wise as this? And then, when my head was well in the room, I undid the lantern cautiously—oh, so cautiously—cautiously (for the hinges creaked)—I undid it just so much that a single thin ray fell upon the vulture eye. And this I did for seven long nights—every night just at midnight—but I found the eye always closed; and so it was impossible to do the work; for it was not the old man who vexed me, but his Evil Eye. And every morning, when the day broke, I went boldly into the chamber, and spoke courageously to him, calling him by name in a hearty tone, and inquiring how he had passed the night. So you see he would have been a very profound old man, indeed, to suspect that every night, just at twelve, I looked in upon him while he slept.

Upon the eighth night I was more than usually cautious in opening the door. A watch's minute hand moves more quickly than did mine. Never before that night had I *felt* the extent of my own powers—of my sagacity. I could scarcely contain my feelings of triumph. To think that there I was, opening the door, little by little, and he not even to dream of my secret deeds or thoughts. I fairly chuckled at the idea; and perhaps he heard me; for he moved on the bed suddenly, as if startled. Now you may think that I drew back—but no. His room was as black as pitch with the thick darkness (for the shutters were close fastened, through fear of robbers), and so I knew that he could not see the opening of the door, and I kept pushing it on steadily, steadily.

I had my head in, and was about to open the lantern, when my thumb slipped upon the tin fastening, and the old man sprang up in the bed, crying out—"Who's there?"

I kept quite still and said nothing. For a whole hour I did not move a muscle, and in the meantime I did not hear him lie down. He was still sitting up in the bed listening;—just as I have done, night after night, hearkening to the death watches in the wall.

Presently I heard a slight groan, and I knew it was the groan of mortal terror. It was not a groan of pain or of grief—oh no!—it was the low stifled sound that arises from the bottom of the soul when overcharged with awe. I knew the sound well. Many a night, just at midnight, when all the world slept, it has welled up from my own bosom, deepening, with its dreadful echo, the terrors that distracted me. I say I knew it well. I knew what the old man felt, and pitied him, although I chuckled at heart. I knew that he had been lying awake ever since the first slight noise, when he had turned in the bed. His fears had been ever since growing upon him. He had been trying to fancy them causeless, but could not. He had been saying to himself—"It is nothing but the wind in the chimney—it is only a mouse crossing the floor," or "it is merely a cricket which has made a single chirp." Yes, he has been trying to comfort himself with these suppositions; but he had found all in vain. *All in vain;* because Death, in approaching him, had stalked with his black shadow before him, and enveloped the victim. And it was the mournful influence of the unperceived shadow that caused him to feel—although he neither saw nor heard—to *feel* the presence of my head within the room.

When I had waited a long time, very patiently, without hearing him lie down, I resolved to open a little—a very, very little crevice in the lantern. So I opened it— you cannot imagine how stealthily, stealthily—until, at length, a single dim ray, like the thread of the spider, shot from out the crevice and fell full upon the vulture eye.

It was open—wide, wide open—and I grew furious as I gazed upon it. I saw it with perfect distinctness—all a dull blue, with a hideous veil over it that chilled the very marrow in my bones; but I could see nothing else of the old man's face or person: for I had directed the ray as if by instinct, precisely upon the damned spot.

And now have I not told you that what you mistake for madness is but overacuteness of the senses?—now, I say, there came to my ears a low, dull, quick sound, such as a watch makes when enveloped in cotton. I knew *that* sound well too. It was the beating of the old man's heart. It increased my fury, as the beating of a drum stimulates the soldier into courage.

But even yet I refrained and kept still. I scarcely breathed. I held the lantern motionless. I tried how steadily I could maintain the ray upon the eye. Meantime the hellish tattoo of the heart increased. It grew quicker and quicker, and louder and louder every instant. The old man's terror *must* have been extreme! It grew louder, I say, louder every moment!—do you mark me well? I have told you that I am nervous: so I am. And now at the dead hour of the night, amid the dreadful silence of that old house, so strange a noise as this excited me to uncontrollable terror. Yet, for some minutes longer I refrained and stood still. But the beating grew louder, louder! I thought the heart must burst. And now a new anxiety seized me—the sound would be heard by a neighbor! The old man's hour had come! With a loud yell, I threw open the lantern and leaped into the room. He shrieked once—once only. In an instant I dragged him to the floor, and pulled the heavy bed over him. I then smiled gaily, to find the deed so far done. But, for many minutes, the heart beat on with a muffled sound. This, however, did not vex me; it would not be heard through the wall. At length it ceased. The old man was dead. I removed the bed and examined the corpse. Yes, he was stone, stone dead. I placed my hand upon the heart and held it there many minutes. There was no pulsation. He was stone dead. His eye would trouble me no more.

If still you think me mad, you will think so no longer when I describe the wise precautions I took for the concealment of the body. The night waned, and I worked hastily, but in silence. First of all I dismembered the corpse. I cut off the head and the arms and the legs.

I then took up three planks from the flooring of the chamber, and deposited all between the scantlings. I then replaced the boards so cleverly, so cunningly, that no human eye—not even *his*—could have detected any thing wrong. There was nothing to wash out—no stain of any kind—no blood-spot whatever. I had been too wary for that. A tub had caught all—ha! ha!

When I made an end of these labors, it was four o'clock—still dark as midnight. As the bell sounded the hour, there came a knocking at the street door. I went down to open it with a light heart,—for what had I *now* to fear? There entered three men, who introduced themselves, with perfect suavity, as officers of the police. A shriek had been heard by a neighbor during the night: suspicion of foul play had been aroused; information had been lodged at the police office, and they (the officers) had been deputed to search the premises.

I smiled,—for *what* had I to fear? I bade the gentlemen welcome. The shriek, I said, was my own in a dream. The old man, I mentioned, was absent in the country. I took my visitors all over the house. I bade them search—search *well*. I led them, at length, to *his* chamber. I showed them his treasures, secure, undisturbed. In the enthusiasm of my confidence, I brought chairs into the room, and desired them *here* to rest from their fatigues, while I myself, in the wild audacity of my perfect triumph, placed my own seat upon the very spot beneath which reposed the corpse of the victim.

The officers were satisfied. My *manner* had convinced them. I was singularly at ease. They sat, and while I answered cheerily, they chatted of familiar things. But, ere long, I felt myself getting pale and wished them gone. My head ached, and I fancied a ringing in my ears: but still they sat and still chatted. The ringing became more distinct:—it continued and became more distinct: I talked more freely to get rid of the feeling: but it continued and gained definitiveness—until at length, I found that the noise was *not* within my ears.

No doubt I now grew *very* pale;—but I talked more fluently, and with a heightened voice. Yet the sound increased—and what could I do? It was *a low, dull, quick sound—much such a sound as a watch makes when enveloped in cotton.* I gasped for breath—and yet the officers heard it not. I talked more quickly—more vehemently; but the noise steadily increased. I arose and argued about trifles, in a high key and with violent gesticulations, but the noise steadily increased. Why *would* they not be gone? I paced the floor to and fro with heavy strides, as if excited to fury by the observation of the men—but the noise steadily increased. Oh God! what *could* I do? I foamed—I raved—I swore. I swung the chair upon which I had been sitting, and grated it upon the boards, but the noise arose over all and continually increased. It grew louder—louder—*louder!* And still the men chatted pleasantly, and smiled. Was it possible they heard not? Almighty God!—no, no! They heard!—they suspected!—they *knew!*—they were making a *mockery* of my horror!—this I thought, and this I think. But any thing was better than this agony! Any thing was more tolerable than this derision! I could bear those hypocritical smiles no longer! I felt that I must scream or die!—and now—again!—hark! louder! louder! *louder!*—

"Villains!" I shrieked, "dissemble no more! I admit the deed!—tear up the planks!—here, here!—it is the beating of his hideous heart!"

—1843

E L I Z A B E T H   G A S K E L L
1 8 1 0 - 1 8 6 5

Elizabeth Gaskell was born in London, England. Her father, William Stevenson, though educated as a minister, eventually became a respected author who wrote for the important journals of his time. Her mother, Elizabeth (Holland) Stevenson, died when Gaskell was thirteen months old. She was subsequently raised by her aunt in Knutsford. At age twelve, she was accepted to the Byerley sisters' school at Barford, where she received an excellent liberal arts education. She left school in 1827 to return home to Knutsford. Following the mysterious disappearance of her brother, John Stevenson—while he was in the employ of the East India Company—in 1828 she returned to London to be with her father. William Stevenson had remarried, but Elizabeth did not get along well with her new stepmother. Her father died in 1829 and, once more, she returned home to Knutsford. In 1832, Elizabeth married a Unitarian minister, William Gaskell, and for the next decade and a half devoted herself to home and church. She also experimented with composing different types of poetry during this time, but it was not until after the death of her baby son, in 1845, that she turned to writing full time.

In 1848, she anonymously published her first novel, Mary Barton: A Tale of Manchester Life, *to great public acclaim. After she was identified as* being the author of Mary Barton, she soon began writing for Charles Dickens' periodical, Household Words. As did Dickens, Gaskell frequently published her stories in popular magazines before reprinting them as hardcover books, in order to maximize her income. Over the next five years, from 1850 to 1855, Gaskell wrote prolifically, publishing under her "anonymous" pseudonym both short fiction and novels, including, in book form, The Moorland Cottage (1850), Ruth: A Novel (1853), Cranford (1853), Lizzie Leigh and Other Tales (1855), Hands and Heart and Bessy's Troubles at Home (1855), and North and South (1855). Following the death of her friend Charlotte Brontë in 1855, Gaskell wrote a biography entitled The Life of Charlotte Brontë (1857), which, despite its intelligent treatment of its subject, was soon attacked by some of the people she had discussed in the book. Legal action was even considered, and Gaskell was compelled to publish a revised edition. Gaskell returned to writing fiction, publishing in book form My Lady Ludlow, A Novel (1858), Right at Last, and Other Tales (1860), Lois the Witch and Other Tales (1861), Sylvia's Lovers (1863), A Dark Night's Work (1863), Cousin Phillis: A Tale (1864), and The Grey Woman and Other Tales (1865). Gaskell died before completing the final installment for her last novel, Wives and Daughters: An Every-Day Story, published in book form in 1866.

Gaskell is generally regarded by contemporary literary critics as an important nineteenth-century author of social melodrama, but her most frequently reprinted tale is "The Old Nurse's Story," which has enjoyed continued popularity through the years since its initial 1852 publication in the Christmas Number of Household Words; it was later anthologized in Lizzie Leigh and Other Tales. "The Old Nurse's Story" is also an excellent representative example of the Victorian form of the traditional ghost story. E. F. Benson, who himself was a twentieth-century master of this particular category of horror fiction, offered the following explanation of the appeal of the ghost story:

> [Ghost stories are] written in the hopes of giving some pleasant qualms to their reader, so that, if by chance, anyone may be occupying in their perusal a leisure half-hour before he goes to bed when the night and house are still, he may perhaps cast an occasional glance into the corners and dark places of the room where he sits, to make sure that nothing unusual lurks in the shadow. For this is the avowed object of ghost-stories and such tales as deal with the dim unseen forces which occasionally and perturbingly make themselves manifest.

THE OLD NURSE'S STORY

You know, my dears, that your mother was an orphan, and an only child; and I dare say you have heard that your grandfather was a clergyman up in Westmoreland, where I come from. I was just a girl in the village school, when, one day, your grandmother came in to ask the mistress if there was any scholar there who would do for a nurse-maid; and mighty proud I was, I can tell ye, when the mistress called me up, and spoke to my being a good girl at my needle, and a steady honest girl, and one whose parents were very respectable, though they might be poor. I thought I should like nothing better than to serve the pretty young lady, who was blushing as deep as I was, as she spoke of the coming baby, and what I should have to do with it. However, I see you don't care so much for this part of my story, as for what you think is to come, so I'll tell you at once. I was engaged and settled at the parsonage before Miss Rosamond (that was the baby, who is now your mother) was born. To be sure, I had little enough to do with her when she came, for she was never out of her mother's arms, and slept by her all night long; and proud enough was I sometimes when missis trusted her to me. There never was such a baby before or since, though you've all of you been fine enough in your turns; but for sweet, winning ways, you've none of you come up to your mother. She took after her mother, who was a real lady born; a Miss Furnivall, a granddaughter of Lord Furnivall's, in Northumberland. I believe she had neither brother nor sister, and had been brought up in my lord's family till she had married your grandfather, who was just a curate, son to a shopkeeper in Carlisle—but a clever, fine gentleman as ever was—and one who was as a right-down hard worker in his parish, which was very wide, and scattered all abroad over the Westmoreland Fells. When your mother, little Miss Rosamond, was about four or five years old, both her parents died in a fortnight— one after the other. Ah! that was a sad time. My pretty young mistress and me was looking for another baby, when my master came home from one of his long rides, wet, and tired, and took the fever he died of; and then she never held up her head again, but just lived to see her dead baby, and have it laid on her breast before she sighed away her life. My mistress had asked me, on her death-bed, never to leave Miss Rosamond; but if she had never spoken a word, I would have gone with the little child to the end of the the world.

The next thing, and before we had well stilled our sobs, the executors and guardians came to settle the affairs. They were my poor young mistress's own cousin, Lord Furnivall, and Mr. Esthwaite, my master's brother, a shopkeeper in Manchester; not so well-to-do then as he was afterwards, and with a large family rising about him. Well! I don't know if it were their settling, or because of a letter my mistress wrote on her death-bed to her cousin, my lord; but somehow it was settled that Miss Rosamond and me were to go to Furnivall Manor House, in Northumberland, and my lord spoke as if it had been her mother's wish that she should live with his family, and as if he had no objections, for that one or two more or less could make no difference in so grand a household. So, though that was not the way in which I should have wished the coming of my bright and pretty pet to have been looked at—who was like a sunbeam in any family, be it never so grand—I was well pleased that all the folks in the Dale should stare and admire, when they heard I was as going to be young lady's maid at my Lord Furnivall's at Furnivall Manor.

But I made a mistake in thinking we were to go and live where my lord did. It turned out that the family had left Furnivall Manor House fifty years or more. I could not hear that my poor young mistress had ever been there, though she had been brought up in the family; and I was sorry for that, for I should have liked Miss Rosamond's youth to have passed where her mother's had been.

My lord's gentleman, from whom I asked as many questions as I durst, said that the Manor House was at the foot of the Cumberland Fells, and a very grand place; that an old Miss Furnivall, a great-aunt of my lord's, lived there, with only a few servants; but that it was a very healthy place, and my lord had thought that it would

suit Miss Rosamond very well for a few years, and that her being there might perhaps amuse his old aunt.

I was bidden by my lord to have Miss Rosamond's things ready by a certain day.
He was a stern proud man, as they say all the Lords Furnivall were; and he never
spoke a word more than was necessary. Folk did say he had loved my young mistress; but that, because she knew that his father would object, she would never listen to him, and married Mr. Esthwaite; but I don't know. He never married at any
rate. But he never took much notice of Miss Rosamond; which I thought he might
have done if he had cared for her dead mother. He sent his gentleman with us to
the Manor House, telling him to join him at Newcastle that same evening; so there
was no great length of time for him to make us known to all the strangers before
he, too, shook us off; and we were left, two lonely young things (I was not eighteen),
in the great old Manor House. It seems like yesterday that we drove there. We had
left our own dear parsonage very early, and we had both cried as if our hearts would
break, though we were travelling in my lord's carriage, which I thought so much of
once. And now it was long past noon on a September day, and we stopped to change
horses for the last time at a little smoky town, all full of colliers and miners. Miss
Rosamond had fallen asleep, but Mr. Henry told me to waken her, that she might see
the park and the Manor House as we drove up. I thought it rather a pity; but I did
what he bade me, for fear he should complain of me to my lord. We had left all signs
of a town, or even a village, and were then inside the gates of a large wild park—not
like the parks here in the south, but with rocks, and the noise of running water, and
gnarled thorn-trees, and old oaks, all white and peeled with age.

The road went up about two miles, and then we saw a great and stately house,
with many trees close around it, so close that in some places their branches
dragged against the walls when the wind blew; and some hung broken down; for
no one seemed to take much charge of the place;—to lop the wood, or to keep the
moss-covered carriage-way in order. Only in front of the house all was clear. The
great oval drive was without a weed; and neither tree nor creeper was allowed to
grow over the long, many-windowed front; at both sides of which a wing projected,
which were each the ends of other side fronts; for the house, although it was so
desolate, was even grander than I expected. Behind it rose the Fells, which seemed
unenclosed and bare enough; and on the left hand of the house, as you stood facing it, was a little, old-fashioned flower-garden, as I found out afterwards. A door
opened out upon it from the west front; it had been scooped out of the thick dark
wood for some old Lady Furnivall; but the branches of the great forest trees had
grown and overshadowed it again, and there were very few flowers that would live
there at that time.

When we drove up to the great front entrance, and went into the hall I thought
we should be lost—it was so large, and vast, and grand. There was a chandelier all
of bronze, hung down from the middle of the ceiling; and I had never seen one
before, and looked at it all in amaze. Then, at one end of the hall, was a great fire-
place, as large as the sides of the houses in my country, with massy andirons and
dogs to hold the wood; and by it were heavy old-fashioned sofas. At the opposite
end of the hall, to the left as you went in—on the western side—was an organ built
into the wall, and so large that it filled up the best part of that end. Beyond it, on
the same side, was a door; and opposite, on each side of the fire-place, were also
doors leading to the east front; but those I never went through as long as I stayed
in the house, so I can't tell you what lay beyond.

The afternoon was closing in, and the hall, which had no fire lighted in it, looked dark and gloomy, but we did not stay there a moment. The old servant, who had opened the door for us, bowed to Mr. Henry, and took us in through the door at the further side of the great organ, and led us through several smaller halls and passages into the west drawing-room, where he said that Miss Furnivall was sitting. Poor little Miss Rosamond held very tight to me, as if she were scared and lost in that great place, and as for myself, I was not much better. The west drawing-room was very cheerful-looking, with a warm fire in it, and plenty of good, comfortable furniture about. Miss Furnivall was an old lady not far from eighty, I should think, but I do not know. She was thin and tall, and had a face as full of fine wrinkles as if they had been drawn all over it with a needle's point. Her eyes were very watchful, to make up, I suppose, for her being so deaf as to be obliged to use a trumpet. Sitting with her, working at the same great piece of tapestry, was Mrs. Stark, her maid and companion, and almost as old as she was. She had lived with Miss Furnivall ever since they both were young, and now she seemed more like a friend than a servant; she looked so cold and grey, and stony, as if she had never loved or cared for any one; and I don't suppose she did care for any one, except her mistress; and, owing to the great deafness of the latter, Mrs. Stark treated her very much as if she were a child. Mr. Henry gave some message from my lord, and then he bowed good-bye to us all,—taking no notice of my sweet little Miss Rosamond's outstretched hand—and left us standing there, being looked at by the two old ladies through their spectacles.

I was right glad when they rung for the old footman who had shown us in at first, and told him to take us to our rooms. So we went out of that great drawing-room, and into another sitting-room, and out of that, and then up a great flight of stairs, and along a broad gallery—which was something like a library, having books all down one side, and windows and writing-tables all down the other—till we came to our rooms, which I was not sorry to hear were just over the kitchens; for I began to think I should be lost in that wilderness of a house. There was an old nursery, that had been used for all the little lords and ladies long ago, with a pleasant fire burning in the grate, and the kettle boiling on the hob, and tea-things spread out on the table; and out of that room was the night-nursery, with a little crib for Miss Rosamond close to my bed. And old James called up Dorothy, his wife, to bid us welcome; and both he and she were so hospitable and kind, that by and by Miss Rosamond and me felt quite at home; and by the time tea was over, she was sitting on Dorothy's knee, and chattering away as fast as her little tongue could go. I soon found out that Dorothy was from Westmoreland, and that bound her and me together, as it were; and I would never wish to meet with kinder people than were old James and his wife. James had lived pretty nearly all his life in my lord's family, and thought there was no one so grand as they. He even looked down a little on his wife; because, till he had married her, she had never lived in any but a farmer's household. But he was very fond of her, as well he might be. They had one servant under them, to do all the rough work. Agnes they called her; and she and me, and James and Dorothy, with Miss Furnivall and Mrs. Stark, made up the family; always remembering my sweet little Miss Rosamond! I used to wonder what they had done before she came, they thought so much of her now. Kitchen and drawing-room, it was all the same. The hard, sad Miss Furnivall, and the cold Mrs. Stark, looked pleased when she came fluttering in like a bird, playing and pranking hither and thither, with a continual murmur, and pretty prattle of gladness. I am sure, they were sorry many a time when she flitted away into the kitchen, though they were too proud to ask her to stay with them, and were a little surprised at her taste; though to be sure, as Mrs. Stark said, it was not to be wondered at, remembering what stock her father had come of. The great, old rambling house was a famous place for little Miss Rosamond. She made expeditions all over it, with me at her heels; all, except the east wing, which was never opened, and whither we never thought of going. But in the western and northern part was many a pleasant room; full of things that were curiosities to us, though they might not have been to people who had seen more. The windows were darkened by the sweeping boughs of the trees, and the ivy which had overgrown them: but, in the green gloom, we could manage to see old China jars and carved ivory boxes, and great heavy books, and, above all, the old pictures!

Once, I remember, my darling would have Dorothy go with us to tell us who they all were; for they were all portraits of some of my lord's family, though Dorothy could not tell us the names of every one. We had gone through most of the rooms, when we came to the old state drawing-room over the hall, and there was a picture of Miss Furnivall; or, as she was called in those days, Miss Grace, for she was the younger sister. Such a beauty she must have been! but with such a set, proud look, and such scorn looking out of her handsome eyes, with her eyebrows just a little raised, as if she wondered how any one could have the impertinence to look at her; and her lip curled at us, as we stood there gazing. She had a dress on, the like of which I had never seen before, but it was all the fashion when she was young: a hat of some soft white stuff like beaver, pulled a little over her brows, and a beautiful plume of feathers sweeping round it on one side; and her gown of blue satin was open in front to a quilted white stomacher.

"Well, to be sure!" said I, when I had gazed my fill. "Flesh is grass, they do say; but who would have thought that Miss Furnivall had been such an out-and-out beauty, to see her now?"

"Yes," said Dorothy. "Folks change sadly. But if what my master's father used to say was true, Miss Furnivall, the elder sister, was handsomer than Miss Grace. Her picture is here somewhere; but, if I show it you, you must never let on, even to James, that you have seen it. Can the little lady hold her tongue, think you?" asked she.

I was not so sure, for she was such a little sweet, bold, open-spoken child, so I set her to hide herself; and then I helped Dorothy to turn a great picture, that leaned with its face towards the wall, and was not hung up as the others were. To be sure, it beat Miss Grace for beauty; and, I think, for scornful pride, too, though in that matter it might be hard to choose. I could have looked at it an hour, but Dorothy seemed half frightened at having shown it to me, and hurried it back again, and bade me run and find Miss Rosamond, for that there were some ugly places about the house, where she should like ill for the child to go. I was a brave, high-spirited girl, and thought little of what the old woman said, for I liked hide-and-seek as well as any child in the parish; so off I ran to find my little one.

As winter drew on, and the days grew shorter, I was sometimes almost certain that I heard a noise as if some one was playing on the great organ in the hall. I did not hear it every evening; but, certainly, I did very often; usually when I was sitting with Miss Rosamond, after I had put her to bed, and keeping quite still and silent in the bedroom. Then I used to hear it booming and swelling away in the distance. The first night, when I went down to my supper, I asked Dorothy who had been playing music, and James said very shortly that I was a gowk to take the wind soughing among the trees for music: but I saw Dorothy look at him very fearfully, and Bessy, the kitchen-maid, said something beneath her breath, and went quite white. I saw they did not like my question, so I held my peace till I was with Dorothy alone, when I knew I could get a good deal out of her. So, the next day, I watched my time, and I coaxed and asked her who it was that played the organ; for I knew that it was the organ and not the wind well enough, for all I had kept silence before James. But Dorothy had had her lesson, I'll warrant, and never a word could I get from her. So then I tried Bessy, though I had always held my head rather above her, as I was evened to James and Dorothy, and she was little better than their servant. So she said I must never, never tell; and if I ever told, I was never to say *she* had told me; but it was a very strange noise, and she had heard it many a time, but most of all on winter nights, and before storms; and folks did say, it was the old lord playing on the great organ in the hall, just as he used to do when he was alive; but who the old lord was, or why he played, and why he played on stormy winter evenings in particular, she either could not or would not tell me. Well! I told you I had a brave heart; and I thought it was rather pleasant to have that grand music rolling about the house, let who would be the player; for now it rose above the great gusts of wind, and wailed and triumphed just like a living creature, and then it fell to a softness most complete; only it was always music, and tunes, so it was nonsense to call it the wind. I thought at first that it might be Miss Furnivall who played, unknown to Bessy; but, one day when I was in the hall by myself, I opened the organ and peeped all about it and around it, as I had done to the organ in Crosthwaite Church once before, and I saw it was all broken and destroyed inside, though it looked so brave and fine; and then, though it was noonday, my flesh began to creep a little, and I shut it up, and run away pretty quickly to my own bright nursery; and I did not like hearing the music for some time after that, any more than James and Dorothy did. All this time Miss Rosamond was making herself more and more beloved. The old ladies liked her to dine with them at their early dinner; James stood behind Miss Furnivall's chair, and I behind Miss Rosamond's all in state; and, after dinner, she would play about in a corner of the great drawing-room, as still as any mouse, while Miss Furnivall slept, and I had my dinner in the kitchen. But she was glad enough to come to me in the nursery afterwards; for, as she said, Miss Furnivall was so sad, and Mrs. Stark so dull; but she and I were merry enough; and, by-and-by, I got not to care for that weird rolling music, which did one no harm, if we did not know where it came from.

That winter was very cold. In the middle of October the frosts began, and lasted many, many weeks. I remember, one day at dinner, Miss Furnivall lifted up her sad, heavy eyes, and said to Mrs. Stark, "I am afraid we shall have a terrible winter," in a strange kind of meaning way. But Mrs. Stark pretended not to hear, and talked very loud of something else. My little lady and I did not care for the frost; not we! As long as it was dry we climbed up the steep brows, behind the house, and went up on the Fells, which were bleak, and bare enough, and there we ran races in the fresh, sharp air; and once we came down by a new path that took us past the two old gnarled holly-trees, which grew about halfway down by the east side of the house. But the days grew shorter and shorter; and the old lord, if it was he, played away more and more stormily and sadly on the great organ. One Sunday afternoon,—it must have been towards the end of November—I asked Dorothy to take charge of little Missey when she came out of the drawing-room, after Miss Furnivall had had her nap; for it was too cold to take her with me to church, and yet I wanted to go. And Dorothy was glad enough to promise, and was so fond of the child that all seemed well; and Bessy and I set off very briskly, though the sky hung heavy and black over the white earth, as if the night had never fully gone away; and the air, though still, was very biting and keen.

"We shall have a fall of snow," said Bessy to me. And sure enough, even while we were in church, it came down thick, in great large flakes, so thick it almost darkened the windows. It had stopped snowing before we came out, but it lay soft, thick and deep beneath our feet, as we tramped home. Before we got to the hall the moon rose, and I think it was lighter then,—what with the moon, and what with the white dazzling snow—than it had been when we went to church, between two and three o'clock. I have not told you that Miss Furnivall and Mrs. Stark never went to church: they used to read the prayers together, in their quiet gloomy way; they seemed to feel the Sunday very long without their tapestry-work to be busy at. So when I went to Dorothy in the kitchen, to fetch Miss Rosamond and take her upstairs with me, I did not much wonder when the old woman told me that the ladies had kept the child with them, and that she had never come to the kitchen, as I had bidden her, when she was tired of behaving pretty in the drawing-room. So I took off my things and went to find her, and bring her to her supper in the nursery. But when I went into the best drawing-room, there sat the two old ladies, very still and quiet, drop-ping out a word now and then, but looking as if nothing so bright and merry as Miss Rosamond had ever been near them. Still I thought she might be hiding from me; it was one of her pretty ways; and that she had persuaded them to look as if they knew nothing about her; so I went softly peeping under this sofa, and behind that chair, making believe I was sadly frightened at not finding her.

"What's the matter, Hester?" said Mrs. Stark, sharply. I don't know if Miss Furnivall had seen me, for, as I told you, she was very deaf, and she sat quite still, idly staring into the fire, with her hopeless face. "I'm only looking for my little Rosy-Posy," replied I, still thinking that the child was there, and near me, though I could not see her.

"Miss Rosamond is not here," said Mrs. Stark. "She went away more than an hour ago to find Dorothy." And she too turned and went on looking into the fire.

My heart sank at this, and I began to wish I had never left my darling. I went back to Dorothy and told her. James was gone out for the day, but she and me and Bessy took lights and went up into the nursery first, and then we roamed over the great large house, calling and entreating Miss Rosamond to come out of her hiding-place, and not frighten us to death in that way. But there was no answer; no sound.

"Oh!" said I at last, "Can she have got into the east wing and hidden there?"

But Dorothy said it was not possible, for that she herself had never been in there; that the doors were always locked, and my lord's steward had the keys, she believed; at any rate, neither she nor James had ever seen them: so I said I would go back, and see if, after all, she was not hidden in the drawing-room, unknown to the old ladies; and if I found her there, I said, I would whip her well for the fright she had given me; but I never meant to do it. Well, I went back to the west drawing-room, and I told Mrs. Stark we could not find her anywhere, and asked for leave to look all about the furniture there, for I thought now, that she might have fallen asleep in some warm hidden corner; but no! we looked, Miss Furnivall got up and looked, trembling all over, and she was nowhere there; then we set off again, every one in the house, and looked in all the places we had searched before, but we could not find her. Miss Furnivall shivered and shook so much, that Mrs. Stark took her back into the warm drawing-room; but not before they had made me promise to bring her to them when she was found. Well-a-day! I began to think she never would be found, when I bethought me to look out into the great front court, all covered with snow. I was upstairs when I looked out; but, it was such clear moonlight, I could see, quite plain, two little footprints, which might be traced from the hall door, and round the corner of the east wing. I don't know how I got down, but I tugged open the great, stiff hall door; and, throwing the skirt of my gown over my head for a cloak, I ran out. I turned the east corner, and there a black shadow fell on the snow; but when I came again into the moonlight, there were the little footmarks going up—up to the Fells. It was bitter cold; so cold that the air almost took the skin off my face as I ran, but I ran on, crying to think how my poor little darling must be perished, and frightened. I was within sight of the holly-trees when I saw a shepherd coming down the hill, bearing something in his arms wrapped in his maud. He shouted to me, and asked me if I had lost a bairn; and, when I could not speak for crying, he bore towards me, and I saw my wee bairnie lying still, and white, and stiff, in his arms, as if she had been dead. He told me he had been up the Fells to gather in his sheep, before the deep cold of night came on, and that under the holly-trees (black marks on the hillside, where no other bush was for miles around) he had found my little lady—my lamb—my queen—my darling—stiff and cold, in the terrible sleep which is frost-begotten. Oh! the joy, and the tears of having her in my arms once again! for I would not let him carry her; but took her, maud and all, into my own arms, and held her near my own warm neck and heart, and felt the life stealing slowly back again into her little gentle limbs. But she was still insensible when we reached the hall, and I had no breath for speech. We went in by the kitchen door.

"Bring the warming-pan," said I; and I carried her upstairs and began undressing her by the nursery fire, which Bessy had kept up. I called my little lammie all the sweet and playful names I could think of,—even while my eyes were blinded by my tears; and at last, oh! at length she opened her large blue eyes. Then I put her into her warm bed, and sent Dorothy down to tell Miss Furnivall that all was well; and I made up my mind to sit by my darling's bedside the live-long night. She fell away into a soft sleep as soon as her pretty head had touched the pillow, and I watched by her till morning light; when she wakened up bright and clear—or so I thought at first—and, my dears, so I think now.

She said that she had fancied that she should like to go to Dorothy, for that both the old ladies were asleep, and it was very dull in the drawing-room; and that, as she was going through the west lobby, she saw the snow through the high window falling—falling—soft and steady; but she wanted to see it lying pretty and white on the ground; so she made her way into the great hall; and then, going to the window, she saw it bright and soft upon the drive; but while she stood there, she saw a little girl, not so old as she was, "but so pretty," said my darling, "and this little girl beckoned to me to come out; and oh, she was so pretty and so sweet, I could not choose but go." And then this other little girl had taken her by the hand, and side by side the two had gone round the east corner.

"Now you are a naughty little girl, and telling stories," said I. "What would your good mamma, that is in heaven, and never told a story in her life, say to her little Rosamond, if she heard her—and I dare say she does—telling stories!"

"Indeed, Hester," sobbed out my child, "I'm telling you true. Indeed I am."

"Don't tell me!" said I, very stern. "I tracked you by your footmarks through the snow; there were only yours to be seen: and if you had had a little girl to go hand-in-hand with you up the hill, don't you think the footprints would have gone along with yours?"

"I can't help it, dear, dear Hester," said she, crying, "if they did not; I never looked at her feet, but she held my hand fast and tight in her little one, and it was very, very cold. She took me up the Fell-path, up to the holly trees; and there I saw a lady weeping and crying; but when she saw me, she hushed her weeping, and smiled very proud and grand, and took me on her knee, and began to lull me to sleep; and that's all, Hester—but that is true; and my dear mamma knows it is," said she, crying. So I thought the child was in a fever, and pretended to believe her, as she went over her story—over and over again, and always the same. At last Dorothy knocked at the door with Miss Rosamond's breakfast; and she told me the old ladies were down in the eating parlour, and that they wanted to speak to me. They had both been into the night-nursery the evening before, but it was after Miss Rosamond was asleep; so they had only looked at her—not asked me any questions.

"I shall catch it," thought I to myself, as I went along the north gallery. "And yet," I thought, taking courage, "it was in their charge I left her; and it's they that's to blame for letting her steal away unknown and unwatched." So I went in boldly, and told my story. I told it all to Miss Furnivall, shouting it close to her ear; but when I came to the mention of the other little girl out in the snow, coaxing and tempting her out, and wiling her up to the grand and beautiful lady by the holly-tree, she threw her arms up—her old and withered arms—and cried aloud, "Oh! Heaven, forgive! Have mercy!"

Mrs. Stark took hold of her; roughly enough, I thought; but she was past Mrs. Stark's management, and spoke to me, in a kind of wild warning and authority.

"Hester! keep her from that child! It will lure her to her death! That evil child! Tell her it is a wicked, naughty child." Then Mrs. Stark hurried me out of the room; where, indeed, I was glad enough to go; but Miss Furnivall kept shrieking out, "Oh! have mercy! Wilt Thou never forgive! It is many a long year ago"——

I was very uneasy in my mind after that. I durst never leave Miss Rosamond, night or day, for fear lest she might slip off again, after some fancy or other; and all the more, because I thought I could make out that Miss Furnivall was crazy, from their odd ways about her; and I was afraid lest something of the same kind (which might be in the family, you know) hung over my darling. And the great frost never ceased all this time; and, whenever it was a more stormy night than usual, between the gusts, and through the wind, we heard the old lord playing on the great organ. But, old lord, or not, wherever Miss Rosamond went, there I followed; for my love for her, pretty helpless orphan, was stronger than my fear for the grand and terrible sound. Besides, it rested with me to keep her cheerful and merry, as beseemed her age. So we played together, and wandered together, here and there, and everywhere; for I never dared to lose sight of her again in that large and rambling house. And so it happened, that one afternoon, not long before Christmas Day, we were playing together on the billiard-table in the great hall (not that we knew the right way of playing, but she liked to roll the smooth ivory balls with her pretty hands, and I liked to do whatever she did); and, by-and-by, without our noticing it, it grew dusk indoors, though it was still light in the open air, and I was thinking of taking her back into the nursery, when, all of a sudden, she cried out:

"Look, Hester! look! there is my poor little girl out in the snow!"

I turned towards the long narrow windows, and there, sure enough, I saw a little girl, less than my Miss Rosamond—dressed all unfit to be out-of-doors such a bitter night—crying, and beating against the window-panes, as if she wanted to be let in. She seemed to sob and wail, till Miss Rosamond could bear it no longer, and was flying to the door to open it, when, all of a sudden, and close upon us, the great organ pealed out so loud and thundering, it fairly made me tremble; and all the more, when I remembered me that, even in the stillness of that dead-cold weather, I had heard no sound of little battering hands upon the window-glass, although the Phantom Child had seemed to put forth all its force; and, although I had seen it wail and cry, no faintest touch of sound had fallen upon my ears. Whether I remembered all this at the very moment, I do not know; the great organ sound had so stunned me into terror; but this I know, I caught up Miss Rosamond before she got the hall-door opened, and clutched her, and carried her away, kicking and screaming, into the large bright kitchen, where Dorothy and Agnes were busy with their mince-pies.

"What is the matter with my sweet one?" cried Dorothy, as I bore in Miss Rosamond, who was sobbing as if her heart would break.

"She won't let me open the door for my little girl to come in; and she'll die if she is out on the Fells all night. Cruel, naughty Hester," she said, slapping me; but she might have struck harder, for I had seen a look of ghastly terror on Dorothy's face, which made my very blood run cold.

"Shut the back-kitchen door fast, and bolt it well," said she to Agnes. She said no more; she gave me raisins and almonds to quiet Miss Rosamond: but she sobbed about the little girl in the snow, and would not touch any of the good things. I was thankful when she cried herself to sleep in bed. Then I stole down to the kitchen, and told Dorothy I had made up my mind. I would carry my darling back to my father's house in Applethwaite; where, if we lived humbly, we lived at peace. I said I had been frightened enough with the old lord's organ-playing; but now, that I had seen for myself this little moaning child, all decked out as no child in the neighbourhood could be, beating and battering to get in, yet always without any sound or noise—with the dark wound on its right shoulder; and that Miss Rosamond had known it again for the phantom that had nearly lured her to her death (which Dorothy knew was true); I would stand it no longer.

I saw Dorothy change colour once or twice. When I had done, she told me she did not think I could take Miss Rosamond with me, for that she was my lord's ward, and I had no right over her; and she asked me, would I leave the child that I was so fond of, just for sounds and sights that could do me no harm; and that they had all had to get used to in their turns? I was all in a hot, trembling passion; and I said it was very well for her to talk, that knew what these sights and noises betokened, and that had, perhaps, had something to do with the Spectre-Child while it was alive. And I taunted her so, that she told me all she knew, at last; and then I wished I had never been told, for it only made me more afraid than ever.

She said she had heard the tale from old neighbours, that were alive when she was first married; when folks used to come to the hall sometimes, before it had got such a bad name on the country side: it might not be true, or it might, what she had been told.

The old lord was Miss Furnivall's father—Miss Grace, as Dorothy called her, for Miss Maude was the elder, and Miss Furnivall by rights. The old lord was eaten up with pride. Such a proud man was never seen or heard of; and his daughters were like him. No one was good enough to wed them, although they had choice enough; for they were the great beauties of their day, as I had seen by their portraits, where they hung in the state drawing-room. But, as the old saying is, "Pride will have a fall;" and these two haughty beauties fell in love with the same man, and he no better than a foreign musician, whom their father had down from London to play music with him at the Manor House. For, above all things, next to his pride, the old lord loved music. He could play on nearly every instrument that ever was heard of: and it was a strange thing it did not soften him; but he was a fierce dour old man, and had broken his poor wife's heart with his cruelty, they said. He was mad after music, and would pay any money for it. So he got this foreigner to come; who made such beautiful music, that they said the very birds on the trees stopped their singing to listen. And, by degrees, this foreign gentleman got such a hold over the old lord, that nothing would serve him but that he must come every year; and it was he that had the great organ brought from Holland, and built up in the hall, where it stood now. He taught the old lord to play on it; but many and many a time, when Lord Furnivall was thinking of nothing but his fine organ, and his finer music, the dark foreigner was walking abroad in the woods with one of the young ladies; now Miss Maude, and then Miss Grace.

Miss Maude won the day and carried off the prize, such as it was; and he and she were married, all unknown to any one; and before he made his next yearly visit, she had been confined of a little girl at a farm-house on the Moors, while her father and Miss Grace thought she was away at Doncaster Races. But though she was a wife and a mother, she was not a bit softened, but as haughty and as passionate as ever; and perhaps more so, for she was jealous of Miss Grace, to whom her foreign husband paid a deal of court—by way of blinding her—as he told his wife. But Miss Grace triumphed over Miss Maude, and Miss Maude grew fiercer and fiercer, both with her husband and with her sister; and the former—who could easily shake off what was disagreeable, and hide himself in foreign countries—went away a month before his usual time that summer, and half-threatened that he would never come back again. Meanwhile, the little girl was left at the farm-house, and her mother used to have her horse saddled and gallop wildly over the hills to see her once every week, at the very least—for where she loved, she loved; and where she hated, she hated. And the old lord went on playing—playing on his organ; and the servants thought the sweet music he made had soothed down his awful temper, of which (Dorothy said) some terrible tales could be told. He grew infirm too, and had to walk with a crutch; and his son—that was the present Lord Furnivall's father—was with the army in America, and the other son at sea; so Miss Maude had it pretty much her own way, and she and Miss Grace grew colder and bitterer to each other every day; till at last they hardly ever spoke, except when the old lord was by. The foreign musician came again the next summer, but it was for the last time; for they led him such a life with their jealousy and their passions, that he grew weary, and went away, and never was heard of again. And Miss Maude, who had always meant to have her marriage acknowledged when her father should be dead, was left now a deserted wife—whom nobody knew to have been married—with a child that she dared not own, although she loved it to distraction; living with a father whom she feared, and a sister whom she hated. When the next summer passed over and the dark foreigner never came, both Miss Maude and Miss Grace grew gloomy and sad; they had a haggard look about them, though they looked handsome as ever. But by-and-by Miss Maude brightened; for her father grew more and more infirm, and more than ever carried away by his music; and she and Miss Grace lived almost entirely apart, having separate rooms, the one on the west side, Miss Maude on the east—those very rooms which were now shut up. So she thought she might have her little girl with her, and no one need ever know except those who dared not speak about it, and were bound to believe that it was, as she said, a cottager's child she had taken a fancy to. All this, Dorothy said, was pretty well known; but what came afterwards no one knew, except Miss Grace, and Mrs. Stark, who was even then her maid, and much more of a friend to her than ever her sister had been. But the servants supposed, from words that were dropped, that Miss Maude had triumphed over Miss Grace, and told her that all the time the dark foreigner had been mocking her with pretended love—he was her own husband; the colour left Miss Grace's cheek and lips that very day for ever, and she was heard to say many a time that sooner or later she would have her revenge; and Mrs. Stark was for ever spying about the east rooms.

One fearful night, just after the New Year had come in, when the snow was lying thick and deep, and the flakes were still falling—fast enough to blind any one who might be out and abroad—there was a great and violent noise heard, and the old lord's voice above all, cursing and swearing awfully,—and the cries of a little child,—and the proud defiance of a fierce woman,—and the sound of a blow,—and a dead stillness,—and moans and wailings dying away on the hill-side! Then the old lord summoned all his servants, and told them, with terrible oaths, and words more terrible, that his daughter had disgraced herself, and that he had turned her out of doors,—her, and her child,—and that if ever they gave her help,—or food,—or shelter,—he prayed that they might never enter Heaven. And, all the while, Miss Grace stood by him, white and still as any stone; and when he had ended she heaved a great sigh, as much as to say her work was done, and her end was accomplished. But the old lord never touched his organ again, and died within the year; and no wonder! for, on the morrow of that wild and fearful night, the shepherds, coming down the Fell side, found Miss Maude sitting, all crazy and smiling, under the holly-trees, nursing a dead child,—with a terrible mark on its right shoulder. "But that was not what killed it," said Dorothy; "it was the frost and the cold;—every wild creature was in its hole, and every beast in its fold,—while the child and its mother were turned out to wander on the Fells! And now you know all! and I wonder if you are less frightened now?"

I was more frightened than ever; but I said I was not. I wished Miss Rosamond and myself well out of that dreadful house for ever; but I would not leave her, and I dared not take her away. But oh! how I watched her, and guarded her! We bolted the doors, and shut the window-shutters fast, an hour or more before dark, rather than leave them open five minutes too late. But my little lady still heard the weird child crying and mourning; and not all we could do or say could keep her from wanting to go to her, and let her in from the cruel wind and the snow. All this time, I kept away from Miss Furnivall and Mrs. Stark, as much as ever I could; for I feared them—I knew no good could be about them, with their grey hard faces, and their dreamy eyes, looking back into the ghastly years that were gone. But, even in my fear, I had a kind of pity— for Miss Furnivall, at least. Those gone down to the pit can hardly have a more hopeless look than that which was ever on her face. At last I even got so sorry for her— who never said a word but what was quite forced from her—that I prayed for her; and I taught Miss Rosamond to pray for one who had done a deadly sin; but often when she came to those words, she would listen, and start up from her knees, and say, "I hear my little girl plaining and crying very sad—Oh! let her in, or she will die!"

One night—just after New Year's Day had come at last, and the long winter had taken a turn, as I hoped—I heard the west drawing-room bell ring three times, which was the signal for me. I would not leave Miss Rosamond alone, for all she was asleep—for the old lord had been playing wilder than ever—and I feared lest my darling should waken to hear the spectre child; see her I knew she could not. I had fastened the windows too well for that. So I took her out of her bed and wrapped her up in such outer clothes as were most handy, and carried her down to the drawing-room, where the old ladies sat at their tapestry work as usual. They looked up when I came in, and Mrs. Stark asked, quite astounded, "Why did I bring Miss Rosamond there, out of her warm bed?" I had begun to whisper, "Because I was afraid of her being tempted out while I was away, by the wild child in the snow," when she stopped me short (with a glance at Miss Furnivall), and said Miss Furnivall wanted me to undo some work she had done wrong, and which neither of them could see to unpick. So I laid my pretty dear on the sofa, and sat down on a stool by them, and hardened my heart against them, as I heard the wind rising and howling.

Miss Rosamond slept on sound, for all the wind blew so; and Miss Furnivall said never a word, nor looked round when the gusts shook the windows. All at once she started up to her full height, and put up one hand, as if to bid us listen.

"I hear voices!" said she. "I hear terrible screams—I hear my father's voice!"

Just at that moment my darling wakened with a sudden start: "My little girl is crying, oh, how she is crying!" and she tried to get up and go to her, but she got her feet entangled in the blanket, and I caught her up; for my flesh had begun to creep at these noises, which they heard while we could catch no sound. In a minute or two the noises came, and gathered fast, and filled our ears; we, too, heard voices and screams, and no longer heard the winter's wind that raged abroad. Mrs. Stark looked at me, and I at her, but we dared not speak. Suddenly Miss Furnivall went towards the door, out into the ante-room, through the west lobby, and opened the door into the great hall. Mrs. Stark followed, and I durst not be left, though my heart almost stopped beating for fear. I wrapped my darling tight in my arms, and went out with them. In the hall the screams were louder than ever; they sounded to come from the east wing—nearer and nearer—close on the other side of the locked-up doors—close behind them. Then I noticed that the great bronze chandelier seemed all alight, though the hall was dim, and that a fire was blazing in the vast hearth-place, though it gave no heat; and I shuddered up with terror, and folded my darling closer to me. But as I did so, the east door shook, and she, suddenly struggling to get free from me, cried, "Hester! I must go! My little girl is there; I hear her; she is coming! Hester, I must go!"

I held her tight with all my strength; with a set will, I held her. If I had died, my hands would have grasped her still, I was so resolved in my mind. Miss Furnivall stood listening, and paid no regard to my darling, who had got down to the ground, and whom I, upon my knees now, was holding with both my arms clasped round her neck; she still striving and crying to get free.

All at once the east door gave way with a thundering crash, as if torn open in a violent passion, and there came into that broad and mysterious light, the figure of a tall old man, with grey hair and gleaming eyes. He drove before him, with many a relentless gesture of abhorrence, a stern and beautiful woman, with a little child clinging to her dress.

"O Hester! Hester!" cried Miss Rosamond. "It's the lady! the lady below the holly-trees; and my little girl is with her. Hester! Hester! let me go to her; they are drawing me to them. I feel them—I feel them. I must go!"

Again she was almost convulsed by her efforts to get away; but I held her tighter and tighter, till I feared I should do her a hurt; but rather that than let her go towards those terrible phantoms. They passed along towards the great hall-door, where the winds howled and ravened for their prey; but before they reached that, the lady turned; and I could see that she defied the old man with a fierce and proud defiance; but then she quailed—and then she threw up her arms wildly and piteously to save her child—her little child—from a blow from his uplifted crutch.

And Miss Rosamond was torn as by a power stronger than mine, and writhed in my arms, and sobbed (for by this time the poor darling was growing faint).

"They want me to go with them on to the Fells—they are drawing me to them. Oh, my little girl! I would come, but cruel, wicked Hester holds me very tight." But when she saw the uplifted crutch she swooned away, and I thanked God for it. Just at this moment—when the tall old man, his hair streaming as in the blast of a furnace, was going to strike the little shrinking child—Miss Furnivall, the old woman by my side, cried out, "Oh, father! father! spare the little innocent child!" But just then I saw—we all saw—another phantom shape itself, and grow clear out of the blue and misty light that filled the hall; we had not seen her till now, for it was another lady who stood by the old man, with a look of relentless hate and triumphant scorn. That figure was very beautiful to look upon, with a soft white hat drawn down over the proud brows, and a red and curling lip. It was dressed in an open robe of blue satin. I had seen that figure before. It was the likeness of Miss Furnivall in her youth; and the terrible phantoms moved on, regardless of old Miss Furnivall's wild entreaty,—and the uplifted crutch fell on the right shoulder of the little child, and the younger sister looked on, stony and deadly serene. But at that moment, the dim lights, and the fire that gave no heat, went out of themselves, and Miss Furnivall lay at our feet stricken down by the palsy—death-stricken.

Yes! she was carried to her bed that night never to rise again. She lay with her face to the wall, muttering low but muttering alway: "Alas! alas! what is done in youth can never be undone in age! What is done in youth can never be undone in age!"

—1852

JOSEPH SHERIDAN LE FANU

1814-1873

Joseph Sheridan Le Fanu's influence on nineteenth-century popular supernatural fiction cannot be underestimated. He was an important and prolific Gothic novelist, and his short stories featuring macabre themes represented a high point of the horror genre during this period. The work of other significant horror writers, such as M. R. James, was inspired, in part, by Le Fanu's earlier literary efforts.

Le Fanu was born in Dublin, Ireland. His father, Reverend Thomas Philip Le Fanu, was chaplain at the Royal Hibernian Military School at Phoenix Park during the time of his birth. Le Fanu's family was of French Huguenot origin, and a number of his ancestors were writers. When he was twelve years old, Le Fanu moved with his family from Dublin to nearby

*Abington Rectory in Limerick County. He was educated by his father, and
the young man proved to be an avid reader. In 1833, Le Fanu entered
Trinity College in Dublin, where he was known as a fine debater, and after
receiving his degree, he was admitted to the Irish bar. A career in law, however, did not appeal to him, and he became instead a journalist. Beginning
with his purchase of a Dublin magazine called the* Warder *in 1839 (making
him a co-owner), Le Fanu initiated a series of purchases and investments in
other periodicals which culminated in his directorship of the* Dublin
University Magazine *from 1861 to 1869, a journal that he had earlier contributed to as writer. In 1843, Le Fanu married Susanna Bennett; their marriage lasted fourteen years until her death in 1858. Following his wife's
death, Le Fanu withdrew from Dublin society. His final years were nevertheless productive. He published some of his best fiction during this period—
including the novels* The House by the Churchyard *(1863),* Wylder's Hand:
A Novel *(1864),* Uncle Silas: A Tale of Bartram-Haugh *(1864),* Guy Deverell
(1865), The Wyvern Mystery: A Novel *(1869), and the short story collection,*
In a Glass Darkly *(1872), among other literary works—but he was otherwise
a virtual social recluse, who often worked late into the evenings and who
died in relative isolation.*

*"Green Tea" is one of Le Fanu's finest supernatural tales. The behavior
of the doomed Mr. Jennings, the scholar in the story who describes himself
to Dr. Martin Hesselius as an author who writes "late at night," no doubt
offers a fair description of Le Fanu's own obsessive work habits during the
time "Green Tea" was written. The circumstances surrounding Jennings's
consumption of green tea may also be perceived as an interesting contemporary allusion to the horrors often associated with drug dependency. In
addition, Dr. Hesselius acts as a type of detective in Le Fanu's story and, in
several ways, is similar to Edgar Allan Poe's Auguste Dupin or Arthur
Conan Doyle's Sherlock Holmes; like Dupin and Holmes, Hesselius utilizes
perceptive observation and deductive reasoning to solve mysterious problems. But "Green Tea" is horror fiction, not detective fiction, and Hesselius
ultimately fails to save Jennings's life. "Green Tea" was first published in
1869, between the October 23rd and the November 13th issues of* All the
Year Round, *and was later anthologized in Le Fanu's short story collection,*
In a Glass Darkly.

GREEN TEA

Prologue

Martin Hesselius, the German Physician

Though carefully educated in medicine and surgery, I have never practised either.
The study of each continues, nevertheless, to interest me profoundly. Neither idleness nor caprice caused my secession from the honourable calling which I had just
entered. The cause was a very trifling scratch inflicted by a dissecting knife. This trifle cost me the loss of two fingers, amputated promptly, and the more painful loss
of my health, for I have never been quite well since, and have seldom been twelve
months together in the same place.

In my wanderings I became acquainted with Dr. Martin Hesselius, a wanderer like myself, like me a physician, and like me an enthusiast in his profession. Unlike me in this, that his wanderings were voluntary, and he a man, if not of fortune, as we estimate fortune in England, at least in what our forefathers used to term "easy circumstances." He was an old man when I first saw him; nearly five-and-thirty years my senior.

In Dr. Martin Hesselius, I found my master. His knowledge was immense, his grasp of a case was an intuition. He was the very man to inspire a young enthusiast, like me, with awe and delight. My admiration has stood the test of time and survived the separation of death. I am sure it was well-founded.

For nearly twenty years I acted as his medical secretary. His immense collection of papers he has left in my care, to be arranged, indexed and bound. His treatment of some of these cases is curious. He writes in two distinct characters. He describes what he saw and heard as an intelligent layman might, and when in this style of narrative he had seen the patient either through his own hall-door, to the light of day, or through the gates of darkness to the caverns of the dead, he returns upon the narrative, and in the terms of his art and with all the force and originality of genius, proceeds to the work of analysis, diagnosis and illustration.

Here and there a case strikes me as of a kind to amuse or horrify a lay reader with an interest quite different from the peculiar one which it may possess for an expert. With slight modifications, chiefly of language, and of course a change of names, I copy the following. The narrator is Dr. Martin Hesselius. I find it among the voluminous notes of cases which he made during a tour in England about sixty-four years ago.

It is related in series of letters to his friend Professor Van Loo of Leyden. The professor was not a physician, but a chemist, and a man who read history and metaphysics and medicine, and had, in his day, written a play.

The narrative is therefore, if somewhat less valuable as a medical record, necessarily written in a manner more likely to interest an unlearned reader.

These letters, from a memorandum attached, appear to have been returned on the death of the professor, in 1819, to Dr. Hesselius. They are written, some in English, some in French, but the greater part in German. I am a faithful, though I am conscious, by no means a graceful translator, and although here and there I omit some passages, and shorten others, and disguise names, I have interpolated nothing.

Chapter I

Dr. Hesselius Relates How He Met the Rev. Mr. Jennings

The Rev. Mr. Jennings is tall and thin. He is middle-aged, and dresses with a natty, old-fashioned, high-church precision. He is naturally a little stately, but not at all stiff. His features, without being handsome, are well formed, and their expression extremely kind, but also shy.

I met him one evening at Lady Mary Heyduke's. The modesty and benevolence of his countenance are extremely prepossessing.

We were but a small party, and he joined agreeably enough in the conversation. He seems to enjoy listening very much more than contributing to the talk; but what he says is always to the purpose and well said. He is a great favourite of Lady Mary's, who it seems, consults him upon many things, and thinks him the most happy and blessed person on earth. Little knows she about him.

The Rev. Mr. Jennings is a bachelor, and has, they say sixty thousand pounds in the funds. He is a charitable man. He is most anxious to be actively employed in his sacred profession, and yet though always tolerably well elsewhere, when he goes down to his vicarage in Warwickshire, to engage in the actual duties of his sacred calling, his health soon fails him, and in a very strange way. So says Lady Mary.

There is no doubt that Mr. Jennings' health does break down in, generally, a sudden and mysterious way, sometimes in the very act of officiating in his old and pretty church at Kenlis. It may be his heart, it may be his brain. But so it has happened three or four times, or oftener, that after proceeding a certain way in the service, he has on a sudden stopped short, and after a silence, apparently quite unable to resume, he has fallen into solitary, inaudible prayer, his hands and his eyes uplifted, and then pale as death, and in the agitation of a strange shame and horror, descended trembling, and got into the vestry-room, leaving his congregation, without explanation, to themselves. This occurred when his curate was absent. When he goes down to Kenlis now, he always takes care to provide a clergyman to share his duty, and to supply his place on the instant should he become thus suddenly incapacitated.

When Mr. Jennings breaks down quite, and beats a retreat from the vicarage, and returns to London, where, in a dark street off Piccadilly, he inhabits a very narrow house, Lady Mary says that he is always perfectly well. I have my own opinion about that. There are degrees of course. We shall see.

Mr. Jennings is a perfectly gentlemanlike man. People, however, remark something odd. There is an impression a little ambiguous. One thing which certainly contributes to it, people I think don't remember; or, perhaps, distinctly remark. But I did, almost immediately. Mr. Jennings has a way of looking sidelong upon the carpet, as if his eye followed the movements of something there. This, of course, is not always. It occurs now and then. But often enough to give a certain oddity, as I have said, to his manner, and in this glance travelling along the floor there is something both shy and anxious.

A medical philosopher, as you are good enough to call me, elaborating theories by the aid of cases sought out by himself, and by him watched and scrutinised with more time at command, and consequently infinitely more minuteness than the ordinary practitioner can afford, falls insensibly into habits of observation, which accompany him everywhere, and are exercised, as some people would say, impertinently, upon every subject that presents itself with the least likelihood of rewarding inquiry.

There was a promise of this kind in the slight, timid, kindly, but reserved gentleman, whom I met for the first time at this agreeable little evening gathering. I observed, of course, more than I here set down; but I reserve all that borders on the technical for a strictly scientific paper.

I may remark, that when I here speak of medical science, I do so, as I hope some day to see it more generally understood, in a much more comprehensive sense than its generally material treatment would warrant. I believe the entire natural world is but the ultimate expression of that spiritual world from which, and in which alone, it has its life. I believe that the essential man is a spirit, that the spirit is an organised substance, but as different in point of material from what we ordinarily understand by matter, as light or electricity is; that the material body is, in the most literal sense, a vesture, and death consequently no interruption of the living man's existence, but simply his extrication from the natural body—a process which commences at the moment of what we term death, and the completion of which, at furthest a few days later, is the resurrection "in power."

The person who weighs the consequences of these positions will probably see their practical bearing upon medical science. This is, however, by no means the proper place for displaying the proofs and discussing the consequences of this too generally unrecognized state of facts.

In pursuance of my habit, I was covertly observing Mr. Jennings, with all my caution—I think he perceived it—and I saw plainly that he was as cautiously observing me. Lady Mary happening to address me by my name, as Dr. Hesselius, I saw that he glanced at me more sharply, and then became thoughtful for a few minutes.

After this, as I conversed with a gentleman at the other end of the room, I saw him look at me more steadily, and with an interest which I thought I understood. I then saw him take an opportunity of chatting with Lady Mary, and was, as one always is, perfectly aware of being the subject of a distant inquiry and answer.

This tall clergyman approached me by-and-by; and in a little time we had got into conversation. When two people, who like reading, and know books and places, having travelled, wish to discourse, it is very strange if they can't find topics. It was not accident that brought him near me, and led him into conversation. He knew German and had read my *Essays on Metaphysical Medicine* which suggest more than they actually say.

This courteous man, gentle, shy, plainly a man of thought and reading, who moving and talking among us, was not altogether of us, and whom I already suspected of leading a life whose transactions and alarms were carefully concealed, with an impenetrable reserve from, not only the world, but his best beloved friends—was cautiously weighing in his own mind the idea of taking a certain step with regard to me.

I penetrated his thoughts without his being aware of it, and was careful to say nothing which could betray to his sensitive vigilance my suspicions respecting his position, or my surmises about his plans respecting myself.

We chatted upon indifferent subjects for a time but at last he said:

"I was very much interested by some papers of yours, Dr. Hesselius, upon what you term Metaphysical Medicine—I read them in German, ten or twelve years ago—have they been translated?"

"No, I'm sure they have not—I should have heard. They would have asked my leave, I think."

"I asked the publishers here, a few months ago, to get the book for me in the original German; but they tell me it is out of print."

"So it is, and has been for some years; but it flatters me as an author to find that you have not forgotten my little book, although," I added, laughing, "ten or twelve years is a considerable time to have managed without it; but I suppose you have been turning the subject over again in your mind, or something has happened lately to revive your interest in it."

At this remark, accompanied by a glance of inquiry, a sudden embarrassment disturbed Mr. Jennings, analogous to that which makes a young lady blush and look foolish. He dropped his eyes, and folded his hands together uneasily, and looked oddly, and you would have said, guiltily, for a moment.

I helped him out of his awkwardness in the best way, by appearing not to observe it, and going straight on, I said: "Those revivals of interest in a subject happen to me often; one book suggests another, and often sends me back a wild-goose chase over an interval of twenty years. But if you still care to possess a copy, I shall be only too happy to provide you; I have still got two or three by me—and if you allow me to present one I shall be very much honoured."

"You are very good indeed," he said, quite at his ease again, in a moment: "I almost despaired—I don't know how to thank you."

"Pray don't say a word; the thing is really so little worth that I am only ashamed of having offered it, and if you thank me any more I shall throw it into the fire in a fit of modesty."

Mr. Jennings laughed. He inquired where I was staying in London, and after a little more conversation on a variety of subjects, he took his departure.

Chapter II

The Doctor Questions Lady Mary and She Answers

"I like your vicar so much, Lady Mary," said I, as soon as he was gone. "He has read, travelled, and thought, and having also suffered, he ought to be an accomplished companion."

"So he is, and, better still, he is a really good man," said she. "His advice is invaluable about my schools, and all my little undertakings at Dawlbridge, and he's so painstaking, he takes so much trouble—you have no idea—wherever he thinks he can be of use: he's so good-natured and so sensible."

"It is pleasant to hear so good an account of his neighbourly virtues. I can only testify to his being an agreeable and gentle companion, and in addition to what you have told me, I think I can tell you two or three things about him," said I.

"Really!"

"Yes, to begin with, he's unmarried."

"Yes, that's right—go on."

"He has been writing, that is he *was*, but for two or three years perhaps, he has not gone on with his work, and the book was upon some rather abstract subject—perhaps theology."

"Well, he was writing a book, as you say; I'm not quite sure what it was about, but only that it was nothing that I cared for; very likely you are right, and he certainly did stop—yes."

"And although he only drank a little coffee here to-night, he likes tea, at least, did like it extravagantly."

"Yes, that's *quite* true."

"He drank green tea, a good deal, didn't he?" I pursued.

"Well, that's very odd! Green tea was a subject upon which we used almost to quarrel."

"But he has quite given that up," said I.

"So he has."

"And, now, one more fact. His mother or his father, did you know them?"

"Yes, both; his father is only ten years dead, and their place is near Dawlbridge. We knew them very well," she answered.

"Well, either his mother or his father—I should rather think his father, saw a ghost," said I.

"Well, you really are a conjurer, Dr. Hesselius."

"Conjurer or no, haven't I said right?" I answered merrily.

"You certainly have, and it *was* his father: he was a silent, whimsical man, and he used to bore my father about his dreams, and at last he told him a story about a ghost he had seen and talked with, and a very odd story it was. I remember it particularly, because I was so afraid of him. This story was long before he died—when I was quite a child—and his ways were so silent and moping, and he used to drop in sometimes, in the dusk, when I was alone in the drawing-room, and I used to fancy there were ghosts about him."

I smiled and nodded.

"And now, having established my character as a conjurer, I think I must say good-night," said I.

"But how *did* you find it out?"

"By the planets, of course, as the gipsies do," I answered, and so, gaily we said good-night.

Next morning I sent the little book he had been inquiring after, and a note to Mr. Jennings, and on returning late that evening, I found that he had called at my lodgings, and left his card. He asked whether I was at home, and asked at what hour he would be most likely to find me.

Does he intend opening his case, and consulting me "professionally," as they say? I hope so. I have already conceived a theory about him. It is supported by Lady Mary's answers to my parting questions. I should like much to ascertain from his own lips. But what can I do consistently with good breeding to invite a confession? Nothing. I rather think he meditates one. At all events, my dear Van L., I shan't make myself difficult of access; I mean to return his visit tomorrow. It will be only civil in return for his politeness, to ask to see him. Perhaps something may come of it. Whether much, little, or nothing, my dear Van L., you shall hear.

Chapter III

Dr. Hesselius Picks Up Something in Latin Books

Well, I have called at Blank Street.

On inquiring at the door, the servant told me that Mr. Jennings was engaged very particularly with a gentleman, a clergyman from Kenlis, his parish in the country. Intending to reserve my privilege, and to call again, I merely intimated that I should try another time, and had turned to go, when the servant begged my pardon, and asked me, looking at me a little more attentively than well-bred persons of his order usually do, whether I was Dr. Hesselius; and, on learning that I was, he said, "Perhaps then, sir, you would allow me to mention it to Mr. Jennings, for I am sure he wishes to see you."

The servant returned in a moment, with a message from Mr. Jennings, asking me to go into his study, which was in effect his back drawing-room, promising to be with me in a very few minutes.

This was really a study—almost a library. The room was lofty, with two tall slender windows, and rich dark curtains. It was much larger than I had expected, and stored with books on every side, from the floor to the ceiling. The upper carpet—for to my tread it felt that there were two or three—was a Turkey carpet. My steps fell noiselessly. The bookcases standing out, placed the windows, particularly narrow ones, in deep recesses. The effect of the room was, although extremely comfortable, and even luxurious, decidedly gloomy, and aided by the silence, almost oppressive. Perhaps, however, I ought to have allowed something for association. My mind had connected peculiar ideas with Mr. Jennings. I stepped into this perfectly silent room, of a very silent house, with a peculiar foreboding; and its darkness, and solemn clothing of books, for except where two narrow looking-glasses were set in the wall, they were everywhere, helped this somber feeling.

While awaiting Mr. Jennings' arrival, I amused myself by looking into some of the books with which his shelves were laden. Not among these, but immediately under them, with their backs upward, on the floor, I lighted upon a complete set of Swedenborg's "Arcana Cælestia," in the original Latin, a very fine folio set, bound in the natty livery which theology affects, pure vellum, namely, gold letters, and carmine edges. There were paper markers in several of these volumes, I raised and placed them, one after the other, upon the table, and opening where these papers were placed, I read in the solemn Latin phraseology, a series of sentences indicated by a pencilled line at the margin. Of these I copy here a few, translating them into English.

"When man's interior sight is opened, which is that of his spirit, then there appear the things of another life, which cannot possibly be made visible to the bodily sight." . . . .

"By the internal sight it has been granted me to see the things that are in the other life, more clearly than I see those that are in the world. From these considerations, it is evident that external vision exists from interior vision, and this from a vision still more interior, and so on." . . . .

"There are with every man at least two evil spirits." . . . .

"With wicked genii there is also a fluent speech, but harsh and grating. There is also among them a speech which is not fluent, wherein the dissent of the thoughts is perceived as something secretly creeping along within it."

"The evil spirits associated with man are, indeed from the hells, but when with man they are not then in hell, but are taken out thence. The place where they then are, is in the midst between heaven and hell, and is called the world of spirits—when the evil spirits who are with man, are in that world, they are not in any infernal torment, but in every thought and affection of man, and so, in all that the man himself enjoys. But when they are remitted into their hell, they return to their former state." . . . .

"If evil spirits could perceive that they were associated with man, and yet that they were spirits separate from him, and if they could flow in into the things of his body, they would attempt by a thousand means to destroy him; for they hate man with a deadly hatred." . . . .

"Knowing, therefore, that I was a man in the body, they were continually striving to destroy me, not as to the body only, but especially as to the soul; for to destroy any man or spirit is the very delight of the life of all who are in hell; but I have been continually protected by the Lord. Hence it appears how dangerous it is for man to be in a living consort with spirits, unless he be in the good of faith." . . . .

"Nothing is more carefully guarded from the knowledge of associate spirits than their being thus conjoint with a man, for if they knew it they would speak to him, with the intention to destroy him." . . . .

"The delight of hell is to do evil to man, and to hasten his eternal ruin."

A long note, written with a very sharp and fine pencil, in Mr. Jennings' neat hand, at the foot of the page, caught my eye. Expecting his criticism upon the text, I read a word or two, and stopped, for it was something quite different, and began with these words, *Deus misereatur mei*— "May God compassionate me." Thus warned of its private nature, I averted my eyes, and shut the book, replacing all the volumes as I had found them, except one which interested me, and in which, as men studious and solitary in their habits will do, I grew so absorbed as to take no cognisance of the outer world, nor to remember where I was.

I was reading some pages which refer to "representatives" and "correspondents," in the technical language of Swedenborg, and had arrived at a passage, the substance of which is, that evil spirits, when seen by other eyes than those of their infernal associates, present themselves, by "correspondence," in the shape of the beast *(fera)* which represents their particular lust and life, in aspect direful and atrocious. This is a long passage, and particularises a number of those bestial forms.

Chapter IV

Four Eyes Were Reading the Passage

I was running the head of my pencil-case along the line as I read it, and something caused me to raise my eyes.

Directly before me was one of the mirrors I have mentioned, in which I saw reflected the tall shape of my friend, Mr. Jennings, leaning over my shoulder, and reading the page at which I was busy, and with a face so dark and wild that I should hardly have known him.

I turned and rose. He stood erect also, and with an effort laughed a little, saying:

"I came in and asked you how you did, but without succeeding in awaking you from your book; so I could not restrain my curiosity, and very impertinently, I'm afraid, peeped over your shoulder. This is not your first time of looking into those pages. You have looked into Swedenborg, no doubt, long ago?"

"Oh dear, yes! I owe Swedenborg a great deal; you will discover traces of him in the little book on Metaphysical Medicine, which you were so good as to remember."

Although my friend affected a gaiety of manner, there was a slight flush in his face, and I could perceive that he was inwardly much perturbed.

"I'm scarcely yet qualified, I know so little of Swedenborg. I've only had them a fortnight," he answered, "and I think they are rather likely to make a solitary man nervous—that is, judging from the very little I have read—I don't say that they have made me so," he laughed; "and I'm so very much obliged for the book. I hope you got my note?"

I made all proper acknowledgments and modest disclaimers.

"I never read a book that I go with, so entirely, as that of yours," he continued. "I saw at once there is more in it than is quite unfolded. Do you know Dr. Harley?" he asked, rather abruptly.

In passing, the editor remarks that the physician here named was one of the most eminent who had ever practised in England.

I did, having had letters to him, and had experienced from him great courtesy and considerable assistance during my visit to England.

"I think that man one of the very greatest fools I ever met in my life," said Mr. Jennings.

This was the first time I had ever heard him say a sharp thing of anybody, and such a term applied to so high a name a little startled me.

"Really! and in what way?" I asked.

"In his profession," he answered.

I smiled.

"I mean this," he said: "he seems to me, one half, blind—I mean one half of all he looks at is dark—preternaturally bright and vivid all the rest; and the worst of it is, it seems *wilful.* I can't get him—I mean he won't—I've had some experience of him as a physician, but I look on him as, in that sense, no better than a paralytic mind, an intellect half dead. I'll tell you—I know I shall some time—all about it," he said, with a little agitation. "You stay some months longer in England. If I should be out of town during your stay for a little time, would you allow me to trouble you with a letter?"

"I should be only too happy," I assured him.

"Very good of you. I am so utterly dissatisfied with Harley."

"A little leaning to the materialistic school," I said.

"A *mere* materialist," he corrected me; "you can't think how that sort of thing worries one who knows better. You won't tell any one—any of my friends you know—that I am hippish; now, for instance, no one knows—not even Lady Mary—that I have seen Dr. Harley, or any other doctor. So pray don't mention it; and, if I should have any threatening of an attack, you'll kindly let me write, or, should I be in town, have a little talk with you."

I was full of conjecture, and unconsciously I found I had fixed my eyes gravely on him, for he lowered his for a moment, and he said:

"I see you think I might as well tell you now, or else you are forming a conjecture; but you may as well give it up. If you were guessing all the rest of your life, you will never hit on it."

He shook his head smiling, and over that wintry sunshine a black cloud suddenly came down, and he drew his breath in, through his teeth as men do in pain.

"Sorry, of course, to learn that you apprehend occasion to consult any of us; but, command me when and how you like, and I need not assure you that your confidence is sacred."

He then talked of quite other things, and in a comparatively cheerful way and after a little time, I took my leave.

Chapter V

Dr. Hesselius is Summoned to Richmond

We parted cheerfully, but he was not cheerful, nor was I. There are certain expressions of that powerful organ of spirit—the human face—which, although I have seen them often, and possess a doctor's nerve, yet disturb me profoundly. One look of Mr. Jennings haunted me. It had seized my imagination with so dismal a power that I changed my plans for the evening, and went to the opera, feeling that I wanted a change of ideas.

I heard nothing of or from him for two or three days, when a note in his hand reached me. It was cheerful, and full of hope. He said that he had been for some little time so much better—quite well, in fact—that he was going to make a little experiment, and run down for a month or so to his parish, to try whether a little work might not quite set him up. There was in it a fervent religious expression of gratitude for his restoration, as he now almost hoped he might call it.

A day or two later I saw Lady Mary, who repeated what his note had announced, and told me that he was actually in Warwickshire, having resumed his clerical duties at Kenlis; and she added, "I begin to think that he is really perfectly well, and that there never was anything the matter, more than nerves and fancy; we are all nervous, but I fancy there is nothing like a little hard work for that kind of weakness, and he has made up his mind to try it. I should not be surprised if he did not come back for a year."

Notwithstanding all this confidence, only two days later I had this note, dated from his house off Piccadilly:

DEAR SIR,—I have returned disappointed. If I should feel at all able to see you, I shall write to ask you kindly to call. At present, I am too low, and, in fact, simply unable to say all I wish to say. Pray don't mention my name to my friends. I can see no one. By-and-by, please God, you shall hear from me. I mean to take a run into Shropshire, where some of my people are. God bless you! May we, on my return, meet more happily than I can now write.

About a week after this I saw Lady Mary at her own house, the last person, she said, left in town, and just on the wing for Brighton, for the London season was quite over. She told me that she had heard from Mr. Jennings' niece, Martha, in Shropshire. There was nothing to be gathered from her letter, more than that he was low and nervous. In those words, of which healthy people think so lightly, what a world of suffering is sometimes hidden!

Nearly five weeks had passed without any further news of Mr. Jennings. At the end of that time I received a note from him. He wrote:

"I have been in the country, and have had change of air, change of scene, change of faces, change of everything—and in everything—but *myself.* I have made up my mind, so far as the most irresolute creature on earth can do it, to tell my case fully to you. If your engagements will permit, pray come to me to-day, to-morrow, or the next day; but, pray defer as little as possible. You know not how much I need help. I have a quiet house at Richmond, where I now am. Perhaps you can manage to come to dinner, or to luncheon, or even to tea. You shall have no trouble in finding me out. The servant at Blank Street, who takes this note, will have a carriage at your door at any hour you please; and I am always to be found. You will say that I ought not to be alone. I have tried everything. Come and see."

I called up the servant, and decided on going out the same evening, which accordingly I did.

He would have been much better in a lodging-house, or hotel, I thought, as I drove up through a short double row of sombre elms to a very old-fashioned brick house, darkened by the foliage of these trees, which overtopped, and nearly surrounded it. It was a perverse choice, for nothing could be imagined more triste and silent. The house, I found, belonged to him. He had stayed for a day or two in town, and, finding it for some cause insupportable, had come out here, probably because being furnished and his own, he was relieved of the thought and delay of selection, by coming here.

The sun had already set, and the red reflected light of the western sky illuminated the scene with the peculiar effect with which we are all familiar. The hall seemed very dark, but, getting to the back drawing-room, whose windows command the west, I was again in the same dusky light.

I sat down, looking out upon the richly-wooded landscape that glowed in the grand and melancholy light which was every moment fading. The corners of the room were already dark; all was growing dim, and the gloom was insensibly toning my mind, already prepared for what was sinister. I was waiting alone for his arrival, which soon took place. The door communicating with the front room opened, and the tall figure of Mr. Jennings, faintly seen in the ruddy twilight, came, with quiet stealthy steps, into the room.

We shook hands, and, taking a chair to the window, where there was still light enough to enable us to see each other's faces, he sat down beside me, and, placing his hand upon my arm, with scarcely a word of preface began his narrative.

Chapter VI

How Mr. Jennings Met His Companion

The faint glow of the west, the pomp of the then lonely woods of Richmond, were before us, behind and about us the darkening room, and on the stony face of the sufferer—for the character of his face, though still gentle and sweet, was changed—rested that dim, odd glow which seems to descend and produce, where it touches, lights, sudden though faint, which are lost, almost without gradation, in darkness. The silence, too, was utter: not a distant wheel, or bark, or whistle from without; and within the depressing stillness of an invalid bachelor's house.

I guessed well the nature, though not even vaguely the particulars of the revelations I was about to receive, from that fixed face of suffering that so oddly flushed stood out, like a portrait of Schalken's, before its background of darkness.

"It began," he said, "on the 15th of October, three years and eleven weeks ago, and two days—I keep very accurate count, for every day is torment. If I leave anywhere a chasm in my narrative tell me.

"About four years ago I began a work, which had cost me very much thought and reading. It was upon the religious metaphysics of the ancients."

"I know," said I, "the actual religion of educated and thinking paganism, quite apart from symbolic worship? A wide and very interesting field."

"Yes, but not good for the mind—the Christian mind, I mean. Paganism is all bound together in essential unity, and, with evil sympathy, their religion involves their art, and both their manners, and the subject is a degrading fascination and the Nemesis sure. God forgive me!

"I wrote a great deal; I wrote late at night. I was always thinking on the subject, walking about, wherever I was, everywhere. It thoroughly infected me. You are to remember that all the material ideas connected with it were more or less of the beautiful, the subject itself delightfully interesting, and I, then, without a care."

He sighed heavily.

"I believe, that every one who sets about writing in earnest does his work, as a friend of mine phrased it, *on* something—tea, or coffee, or tobacco. I suppose there is a material waste that must be hourly supplied in such occupations, or that we should grow too abstracted, and the mind, as it were, pass out of the body, unless it were reminded often enough of the connection by actual sensation. At all events, I felt the want, and I supplied it. Tea was my companion—at first the ordinary black tea, made in the usual way, not too strong: but I drank a good deal, and increased its strength as I went on. I never experienced an uncomfortable symptom from it. I began to take a little green tea. I found the effect pleasanter, it cleared and intensified the power of thought so, I had come to take it frequently, but not stronger than one might take it for pleasure. I wrote a great deal out here, it was so quiet, and in this room. I used to sit up very late, and it became a habit with me to sip my tea—green tea—every now and then as my work proceeded. I had a little kettle on my table, that swung over a lamp, and made tea two or three times between eleven o'clock and two or three in the morning, my hours of going to bed. I used to go into town every day. I was not a monk, and, although I spent an hour or two in a library, hunting up authorities and looking out lights upon my theme, I was in no morbid state as far as I can judge. I met my friends pretty much as usual and enjoyed their society, and, on the whole, existence had never been, I think, so pleasant before.

"I had met with a man who had some odd old books, German editions in mediæval Latin, and I was only too happy to be permitted access to them. This obliging person's books were in the City, a very out-of-the-way part of it. I had rather out-stayed my intended hour, and, on coming out, seeing no cab near, I was tempted to get into the omnibus which used to drive past this house. It was darker than this by the time the 'bus had reached an old house, you may have remarked, with four poplars at each side of the door, and there the last passenger but myself got out. We drove along rather faster. It was twilight now. I leaned back in my corner next the door ruminating pleasantly.

"The interior of the omnibus was nearly dark. I had observed in the corner opposite to me at the other side, and at the end next the horses, two small circular reflections, as it seemed to me of a reddish light. They were about two inches apart, and about the size of those small brass buttons that yachting men used to put upon their jackets. I began to speculate, as listless men will, upon this trifle, as it seemed. From what centre did that faint but deep red light come, and from what—glass beads, buttons, toy decorations—was it reflected? We were lumbering along gently, having nearly a mile still to go. I had not solved the puzzle, and it became in another minute more odd, for these two luminous points, with a sudden jerk, descended nearer and nearer the floor, keeping still their relative distance and horizontal position, and then, as suddenly, they rose to the level of the seat on which I was sitting and I saw them no more.

"My curiosity was now really excited, and, before I had time to think, I saw again these two dull lamps, again together near the floor; again they disappeared, and again in their old corner I saw them.

"So, keeping my eyes upon them, I edged quietly up my own side, towards the end at which I still saw these tiny discs of red.

"There was very little light in the 'bus. It was nearly dark. I leaned forward to aid my endeavour to discover what these little circles really were. They shifted position a little as I did so. I began now to perceive an outline of something black, and I soon saw, with tolerable distinctness, the outline of a small black monkey, pushing its face forward in mimicry to meet mine; those were its eyes, and I now dimly saw its teeth grinning at me.

"I drew back, not knowing whether it might not meditate a spring. I fancied that one of the passengers had forgot this ugly pet, and wishing to ascertain something of its temper, though not caring to trust my fingers to it, I poked my umbrella softly towards it. It remained immovable—up to it—*through* it. For through it, and back and forward it passed, without the slightest resistance.

"I can't, in the least, convey to you the kind of horror that I felt. When I had ascertained that the thing was an illusion, as I then supposed, there came a misgiving about myself and a terror that fascinated me in impotence to remove my gaze from the eyes of the brute for some moments. As I looked, it made a little skip back, quite into the corner, and I, in a panic, found myself at the door, having put my head out, drawing deep breaths of the outer air, and staring at the lights and trees we were passing, too glad to reassure myself of reality.

"I stopped the 'bus and got out. I perceived the man look oddly at me as I paid him. I dare say there was something unusual in my looks and manner, for I had never felt so strangely before."

Chapter VII

The Journey: First Stage

"When the omnibus drove on, and I was alone upon the road, I looked carefully round to ascertain whether the monkey had followed me. To my indescribable relief I saw it nowhere. I can't describe easily what a shock I had received, and my sense of genuine gratitude on finding myself, as I supposed, quite rid of it.

"I had got out a little before we reached this house, two or three hundred steps. A brick wall runs along the footpath, and inside the wall is a hedge of yew, or some dark evergreen of that kind, and within that again the row of fine trees which you may have remarked as you came.

"This brick wall is about as high as my shoulder, and happening to raise my eyes I saw the monkey, with that stooping gait, on all fours, walking or creeping, close beside me, on top of the wall. I stopped, looking at it with a feeling of loathing and horror. As I stopped so did it. It sat up on the wall with its long hands on its knees looking at me. There was not light enough to see it much more than in outline, nor was it dark enough to bring the peculiar light of its eyes into strong relief. I still saw, however, that red foggy light plainly enough. It did not show its teeth, nor exhibit any sign of irritation, but seemed jaded and sulky, and was observing me steadily.

"I drew back into the middle of the road. It was an unconscious recoil, and there I stood, still looking at it. It did not move.

"With an instinctive determination to try something—anything, I turned about and walked briskly towards town with askance look, all the time, watching the movements of the beast. It crept swiftly along the wall, at exactly my pace.

"Where the wall ends, near the turn of the road, it came down, and with a wiry spring or two brought itself close to my feet, and continued to keep up with me, as I quickened my pace. It was at my left side, so close to my leg that I felt every moment as if I should tread upon it.

"The road was quite deserted and silent, and it was darker every moment. I stopped dismayed and bewildered, turning as I did so, the other way—I mean, towards this house, away from which I had been walking. When I stood still, the monkey drew back to a distance of, I suppose, about five or six yards, and remained stationary, watching me.

"I had been more agitated than I have said. I had read, of course, as everyone has, something about 'spectral illusions,' as you physicians term the phenomena of such cases. I considered my situation, and looked my misfortune in the face.

"These affections, I had read, are sometimes transitory and sometimes obstinate. I had read of cases in which the appearance, at first harmless, had, step by step, degenerated into something direful and insupportable, and ended by wearing its victim out. Still as I stood there, but for my bestial companion, quite alone, I tried to comfort myself by repeating again and again the assurance, 'the thing is purely disease, a well-known physical affection, as distinctly as small-pox or neuralgia. Doctors are all agreed on that, philosophy demonstrates it. I must not be a fool. I've been sitting up too late, and I daresay my digestion is quite wrong, and, with God's help, I shall be all right, and this is but a symptom of nervous dyspepsia.' Did I believe all this? Not one word of it, no more than any other miserable being ever did who is once seized and riveted in this satanic captivity. Against my convictions, I might say my knowledge, I was simply bullying myself into a false courage.

"I now walked homeward. I had only a few hundred yards to go. I had forced myself into a sort of resignation, but I had not got over the sickening shock and the flurry of the first certainty of my misfortune.

"I made up my mind to pass the night at home. The brute moved close beside me, and I fancied there was the sort of anxious drawing toward the house, which one sees in tired horses or dogs, sometimes as they come toward home.

"I was afraid to go into town, I was afraid of any one's seeing and recognizing me. I was conscious of an irrepressible agitation in my manner. Also, I was afraid of any violent change in my habits, such as going to a place of amusement, or walking from home in order to fatigue myself. At the hall door it waited till I mounted the steps, and when the door was opened entered with me.

"I drank no tea that night. I got cigars and some brandy and water. My idea was that I should act upon my material system, and by living for a while in sensation apart from thought, send myself forcibly, as it were, into a new groove. I came up here to this drawing-room. I sat just here. The monkey then got upon a small table that then stood *there*. It looked dazed and languid. An irrepressible uneasiness as to its movements kept my eyes always upon it. Its eyes were half closed, but I could see them glow. It was looking steadily at me. In all situations, at all hours, it is awake and looking at me. That never changes.

"I shall not continue in detail my narrative of this particular night. I shall describe, rather, the phenomena of the first year, which never varied, essentially. I shall describe the monkey as it appeared in daylight. In the dark, as you shall presently hear, there are peculiarities. It is a small monkey, perfectly black. It had only one peculiarity—a character of malignity—unfathomable malignity. During the first year it looked sullen and sick. But this character of intense malice and vigilance was always underlying that surly languor. During all that time it acted as if on a plan of giving me as little trouble as was consistent with watching me. Its eyes were never off me. I have never lost sight of it, except in my sleep, light or dark, day or night, since it came here, excepting when it withdraws for some weeks at a time, unaccountably.

"In total dark it is visible as in daylight. I do not mean merely its eyes. It is *all* visible distinctly in a halo that resembles a glow of red embers, and which accompanies it in all its movements.

"When it leaves me for a time, it is always at night, in the dark, and in the same way. It grows at first uneasy, and then furious, and then advances towards me, grinning and shaking, its paws clenched, and, at the same time, there comes the appearance of fire in the grate. I never have any fire. I can't sleep in the room where there is any, and it draws nearer and nearer to the chimney, quivering, it seems, with rage, and when its fury rises to the highest pitch, it springs into the grate, and up the chimney, and I see it no more.

"When first this happened, I thought I was released. I was now a new man. A day passed—a night—and no return, and a blessed week—a week—another week. I was always on my knees, Dr. Hesselius, always, thanking God and praying. A whole month passed of liberty, but on a sudden, it was with me again."

Chapter VIII

The Second Stage

"It was with me, and the malice which before was torpid under a sullen exterior, was now active. It was perfectly unchanged in every other respect. This new energy was apparent in its activity and its looks, and soon in other ways.

"For a time, you will understand, the change was shown only in an increased vivacity, and an air of menace, as if it were always brooding over some atrocious plan. Its eyes, as before, were never off me."

"Is it here now?" I asked.

"No," he replied, "it has been absent exactly a fortnight and a day—fifteen days. It has sometimes been away so long as nearly two months, once for three. Its absence always exceeds a fortnight, although it may be but by a single day. Fifteen days having past since I saw it last, it may return now at any moment."

"Is its return," I asked, "accompanied by any peculiar manifestation?"

"Nothing—no," he said. "It is simply with me again. On lifting my eyes from a book, or turning my head, I see it, as usual, looking at me, and then it remains, as before, for its appointed time. I have never told so much and so minutely before to any one."

I perceived that he was agitated, and looking like death, and he repeatedly applied his handkerchief to his forehead; I suggested that he might be tired, and told him that I would call, with pleasure, in the morning, but he said:

"No, if you don't mind hearing it all now. I have got so far, and I should prefer making one effort of it. When I spoke to Dr. Harley, I had nothing like so much to tell. You are a philosophic physician. You give spirit its proper rank. If this thing is real——"

He paused looking at me with agitated inquiry.

"We can discuss it by-and-by, and very fully. I will give you all I think," I answered, after an interval.

"Well—very well. If it is anything real, I say, it is prevailing, little by little, and drawing me more interiorly into hell. Optic nerves, he talked of. Ah! well—there are other nerves of communication. May God Almighty help me! You shall hear.

"Its power of action, I tell you, had increased. Its malice became, in a way, aggressive. About two years ago, some questions that were pending between me and the bishop having been settled, I went down to my parish in Warwickshire, anxious to find occupation in my profession. I was not prepared for what happened, although I have since thought I might have apprehended something like it. The reason of my saying so is this——"

He was beginning to speak with a great deal more effort and reluctance, and sighed often, and seemed at times nearly overcome. But at this time his manner was not agitated. It was more like that of a sinking patient, who has given himself up.

"Yes, but I will first tell you about Kenlis, my parish.

"It was with me when I left this place for Dawlbridge. It was my silent travelling companion, and it remained with me at the vicarage. When I entered on the discharge of my duties, another change took place. The thing exhibited an atrocious determination to thwart me. It was with me in the church—in the reading-desk—in the pulpit—within the communion rails. At last, it reached this extremity, that while I was reading to the congregation, it would spring upon the book and squat there, so that I was unable to see the page. This happened more than once.

"I left Dawlbridge for a time. I placed myself in Dr. Harley's hands. I did everything he told me. He gave my case a great deal of thought. It interested him, I think. He seemed successful. For nearly three months I was perfectly free from a return. I began to think I was safe. With his full assent I returned to Dawlbridge.

"I travelled in a chaise. I was in good spirits. I was more—I was happy and grateful. I was returning, as I thought, delivered from a dreadful hallucination, to the scene of duties which I longed to enter upon. It was a beautiful sunny evening, everything looked serene and cheerful, and I was delighted. I remember looking out of the window to see the spire of my church at Kenlis among the trees, at the point where one has the earliest view of it. It is exactly where the little stream that bounds the parish passes under the road by a culvert, and where it emerges at the road-side, a stone with an old inscription is placed. As we passed this point, I drew my head in and sat down, and in the corner of the chaise was the monkey.

"For a moment I felt faint, and then quite wild with despair and horror. I called to the driver, and got out, and sat down at the road-side, and prayed to God silently for mercy. A despairing resignation supervened. My companion was with me as I re-entered the vicarage. The same persecution followed. After a short struggle I submitted, and soon I left the place.

"I told you," he said, "that the beast has before this become in certain ways aggressive. I will explain a little. It seemed to be actuated by intense and increasing fury, whenever I said my prayers, or even meditated prayer. It amounted at last to a dreadful interruption. You will ask, how could a silent immaterial phantom effect that? It was thus, whenever I meditated praying; It was always before me, and nearer and nearer.

"It used to spring on a table, on the back of a chair, on the chimney-piece, and slowly to swing itself from side to side, looking at me all the time. There is in its motion an indefinable power to dissipate thought, and to contract one's attention to that monotony, till the ideas shrink, as it were, to a point, and at last to nothing—and unless I had started up, and shook off the catalepsy I have felt as if my mind were on the point of losing itself. There are other ways," he sighed heavily; "thus, for instance, while I pray with my eyes closed, it comes closer and closer, and I see it. I know it is not to be accounted for physically, but I do actually see it, though my lids are closed, and so it rocks my mind, as it were, and overpowers me, and I am obliged to rise from my knees. If you had ever yourself known this, you would be acquainted with desperation."

Chapter IX

The Third Stage

"I see, Dr. Hesselius, that you don't lose one word of my statement. I need not ask you to listen specially to what I am now going to tell you. They talk of the optic nerves, and of spectral illusions, as if the organ of sight was the only point assailable by the influences that have fastened upon me—I know better. For two years in my direful case that limitation prevailed. But as food is taken in softly at the lips, and then brought under the teeth, as the tip of the little finger caught in a mill crank will draw in the hand, and the arm, and the whole body, so the miserable mortal who has been once caught firmly by the end of the finest fibre of his nerve, is drawn in and in, by the enormous machinery of hell, until he is as I am. Yes, Doctor, as *I* am, for a while I talk to you, and implore relief, I feel that my prayer is for the impossible, and my pleading with the inexorable."

I endeavoured to calm his visibly increasing agitation, and told him that he must not despair.

While we talked the night had overtaken us. The filmy moonlight was wide over the scene which the window commanded, and I said:

"Perhaps you would prefer having candles. This light, you know, is odd. I should wish you, as much as possible, under your usual conditions while I make my diagnosis, shall I call it—otherwise I don't care."

"All lights are the same to me," he said; "except when I read or write, I care not if night were perpetual. I am going to tell you what happened about a year ago. The thing began to speak to me."

"Speak! How do you mean—speak as a man does, do you mean?"

"Yes; speak in words and consecutive sentences, with perfect coherence and articulation; but there is a peculiarity. It is not like the tone of a human voice. It is not by my ears it reaches me—it comes like a singing through my head.

"This faculty, the power of speaking to me, will be my undoing. It won't let me pray, it interrupts me with dreadful blasphemies. I dare not go on, I could not. Oh! Doctor, can the skill, and thought, and prayers of man avail me nothing!"

"You must promise me, my dear sir, not to trouble yourself with unnecessarily exciting thoughts; confine yourself strictly to the narrative of *facts;* and recollect, above all, that even if the thing that infests you be, you seem to suppose a reality with an actual independent life and will, yet it can have no power to hurt you, unless it be given from above: its access to your senses depends mainly upon your physical condition—this is, under God, your comfort and reliance: we are all alike environed. It is only that in your case, the *'paries,'* the veil of the flesh, the screen, is a little out of repair, and sights and sounds are transmitted. We must enter on a new course, sir,—be encouraged. I'll give to-night to the careful consideration of the whole case."

"You are very good, sir; you think it worth trying, you don't give me quite up; but, sir, you don't know, it is gaining such an influence over me: it orders me about, it is such a tyrant, and I'm growing so helpless. May God deliver me!"

"It orders you about—of course you mean by speech?"

"Yes, yes; it is always urging me to crimes, to injure others, or myself. You see, Doctor, the situation is urgent, it is indeed. When I was in Shropshire, a few weeks ago" (Mr. Jennings was speaking rapidly and trembling now, holding my arm with one hand, and looking in my face), "I went out one day with a party of friends for a walk: my persecutor, I tell you, was with me at the time. I lagged behind the rest: the country near the Dee, you know, is beautiful. Our path happened to lie near a coal mine, and at the verge of the wood is a perpendicular shaft, they say, a hundred and fifty feet deep. My niece had remained behind with me—she knows, of course nothing of the nature of my sufferings. She knew, however, that I had been ill, and was low, and she remained to prevent my being quite alone. As we loitered slowly on together, the brute that accompanied me was urging me to throw myself down the shaft. I tell you now—oh, sir, think of it!—the one consideration that saved me from that hideous death with the fear lest the shock of witnessing the occurrence should be too much for the poor girl. I asked her to go on and walk with her friends, saying that I could go no further. She made excuses, and the more I urged her the firmer she became. She looked doubtful and frightened. I suppose there was something in my looks or manner that alarmed her; but she would not go, and that literally saved me. You had no idea, sir, that a living man could be made so abject a slave of Satan," he said, with a ghastly groan and a shudder.

There was a pause here, and I said, "You *were* preserved nevertheless. It was the act of God. You are in His hands and in the power of no other being: be therefore confident for the future."

Chapter X

Home

I made him have candles lighted, and saw the room looking cheery and inhabited before I left him. I told him that he must regard his illness strictly as one dependent on physical, though *subtle* physical causes. I told him that he had evidence of God's care and love in the deliverance which he had just described, and that I had perceived with pain that he seemed to regard its peculiar features as indicating that he had been delivered over to spiritual reprobation. Than such a conclusion nothing could be, I insisted, less warranted; and not only so, but more contrary to facts, as disclosed in his mysterious deliverance from that murderous influence during his Shropshire excursion. First, his niece had been retained by his side without his intending to keep her near him; and, secondly, there had been infused into his mind an irresistible repugnance to execute the dreadful suggestion in her presence.

As I reasoned this point with him, Mr. Jennings wept. He seemed comforted. One promise I exacted, which was that should the monkey at any time return, I should be sent for immediately; and, repeating my assurance that I would give neither time nor thought to any other subject until I had thoroughly investigated his case, and that to-morrow he should hear the result, I took my leave.

Before getting into the carriage I told the servant that his master was far from well, and that he should make a point of frequently looking into his room.

My own arrangements I made with a view to being quite secure from interruption.

I merely called at my lodgings, and with a travelling-desk and carpet-bag, set off in a hackney carriage for an inn about two miles out of town, called "The Horns," a very quiet and comfortable house, with good thick walls. And there I resolved, without the possibility of intrusion or distraction, to devote some hours of the night, in my comfortable sitting-room, to Mr. Jennings' case, and so much of the morning as it might require.

(There occurs here a careful note of Dr. Hesselius' opinion upon the case, and of the habits, dietary, and medicines which he prescribed. It is curious—some persons would say mystical. But, on the whole, I doubt whether it would sufficiently interest a reader of the kind I am likely to meet with, to warrant its being here reprinted. The whole letter was plainly written at the inn where he had hid himself for the occasion. The next letter is dated from his town lodgings.)

I left town for the inn where I slept last night at half-past nine, and did not arrive at my room in town until one o'clock this afternoon. I found a letter in Mr. Jennings' hand upon my table. It had not come by post, and, on inquiry, I learned that Mr. Jennings' servant had brought it, and on learning that I was not to return until to-day, and that no one could tell him my address, he seemed very uncomfortable, and said his orders from his were that he was not to return without an answer.

I opened the letter and read:

> DEAR DR. HESSELIUS.—It is here. You had not been an hour gone when it returned. It is speaking. It knows all that has happened. It knows every-thing—it knows you, and is frantic and atrocious. It reviles. I send you this. It knows every word I have written—I write. This I promised, and I there-fore write, but I fear very confused, very incoherently. I am so interrupted, disturbed.
>
> Ever yours, sincerely yours,
> ROBERT LYNDER JENNINGS.

"When did this come?" I asked.

"About eleven last night: the man was here again, and has been here three times to-day. The last time is about an hour since."

Thus answered, and with the notes I had made upon his case in my pocket, I was in a few minutes driving towards Richmond, to see Mr. Jennings.

I by no means, as you perceive, despaired of Mr. Jennings' case. He had himself remembered and applied, though quite in a mistaken way, the principle which I lay down in my Metaphysical Medicine, and which governs all such cases. I was about to apply it in earnest. I was profoundly interested, and very anxious to see and examine him while the "enemy" was actually present.

I drove up to the sombre house, and ran up the steps, and knocked. The door, in a little time, was opened by a tall woman in black silk. She looked ill, and as if she had been crying. She curtseyed, and heard my question, but she did not answer. She turned her face away, extending her hand towards two men who were coming down-stairs; and thus having, as it were, tacitly made me over to them, she passed through a side-door hastily and shut it.

The man who was nearest the hall, I at once accosted, but being now close to him, I was shocked to see that both his hands were covered with blood.

I drew back a little, and the man, passing downstairs, merely said in a low tone, "Here's the servant, sir."

The servant had stopped on the stairs, confounded and dumb at seeing me. He was rubbing his hands in a handkerchief, and it was steeped in blood.

"Jones, what is it? what has happened?" I asked, while a sickening suspicion overpowered me.

The man asked me to come up to the lobby. I was beside him in a moment, and, frowning and pallid, with contracted eyes, he told me the horror which I already half guessed.

His master had made away with himself.

I went upstairs with him to the room—what I saw there I won't tell you. He had cut his throat with his razor. It was a frightful gash. The two men had laid him on the bed, and composed his limbs. It had happened, as the immense pool of blood on the floor declared, at some distance between the bed and the window. There was carpet round his bed, and a carpet under his dressing-table, but none on the rest of the floor, for the man said he did not like a carpet on his bedroom. In this sombre and now terrible room, one of the great elms that darkened the house was slowly moving the shadow of one of its great boughs upon this dreadful floor.

I beckoned to the servant, and we went downstairs together. I turned off the hall into an old-fashioned panelled room, and there standing, I heard all the servant had to tell. It was not a great deal.

"I concluded, sir, from your words, and looks, sir, as you left last night, that you thought my master was seriously ill. I thought it might be that you were afraid of a fit, or something. So I attended very close to your directions. He sat up late, till past three o'clock. He was not writing or reading. He was talking a great deal to himself, but that was nothing unusual. At about that hour I assisted him to undress, and left him in his slippers and dressing-gown. I went back softly in about half-an-hour. He was in his bed, quite undressed, and a pair of candles lighted on the table beside his bed. He was leaning on his elbow, and looking out at the other side of the bed when I came in. I asked him if he wanted anything, and he said No.

"I don't know whether it was what you said to me, sir, or something a little unusual about him, but I was uneasy, uncommon uneasy about him last night.

"In another half hour, or it might be a little more, I went up again. I did not hear him talking as before. I opened the door a little. The candles were both out, which was not usual. I had a bedroom candle, and I let the light in, a little bit, looking softly round. I saw him sitting in that chair beside the dressing-table with his clothes on again. He turned round and looked at me. I thought it strange he should get up and dress, and put out the candles to sit in the dark, that way. But I only asked him again if I could do anything for him. He said, No, rather sharp, I thought. I asked him if I might light the candles, and he said, 'Do as you like, Jones.' So I lighted them, and I lingered about the room, and he said, 'Tell me truth, Jones; why did you come again—you did not hear anyone cursing?' 'No, sir,' I said, wondering what he could mean.

"'No,' said he, after me, 'of course, no;' and I said to him, 'Wouldn't it be well, sir, you went to bed? It's just five o'clock;' and he said nothing, but, 'Very likely; good-night, Jones.' So I went, sir, but in less than an hour I came again. The door was fast, and he heard me, and called as I thought from the bed to know what I wanted, and he desired me not to disturb him again. I lay down and slept for a little. It must have been between six and seven when I went up again. The door was still fast, and he made no answer, so I did not like to disturb him, and thinking he was asleep, I left him till nine. It was his custom to ring when he wished me to come, and I had no particular hour for calling him. I tapped very gently, and getting no answer, I stayed away a good while, supposing he was getting some rest then. It was not till eleven o'clock I grew really uncomfortable about him—for at the latest he was never, that I could remember, later than half-past ten. I got no answer. I knocked and called, and still no answer. So not being able to force the door, I called Thomas from the stables, and together we forced it, and found him in the shocking way you saw."

Jones had no more to tell. Poor Mr. Jennings was very gentle, and very kind. All his people were fond of him. I could see that the servant was very much moved.

So, dejected and agitated, I passed from that terrible house, and its dark canopy of elms, and I hope I shall never see it more. While I write to you I feel like a man who has but half waked from a frightful and monotonous dream. My memory rejects the picture with incredulity and horror. Yet I know it is true. It is the story of the process of a poison, a poison which excites the reciprocal action of spirit and nerve, and paralyses the tissue that separates those cognate functions of the senses, the external and the interior. Thus we find strange bed-fellows, and the mortal and immortal prematurely make acquaintance.

Conclusion

A Word for Those Who Suffer

My dear Van L—, you have suffered from an affection similar to that which I have just described. You twice complained of a return of it.

Who, under God, cured you? Your humble servant, Martin Hesselius. Let me rather adopt the more emphasised piety of a certain good old French surgeon of three hundred years ago: "I treated, and God cured you."

Come, my friend, you are not to be hippish. Let me tell you a fact.

I have met with, and treated, as my book shows, fifty-seven cases of this kind of vision, which I term indifferently "sublimated," "precocious," and "interior."

There is another class of affections which are truly termed—though commonly confounded with those which I describe—spectral illusions. These latter I look upon as being no less simply curable than a cold in the head or a trifling dyspepsia.

It is those which rank in the first category that test our promptitude of thought. Fifty-seven such cases have I encountered, neither more nor less. And in how many of these have I failed? In no one single instance.

There is no one affliction of mortality more easily and certainly reducible, with a little patience, and a rational confidence in the physician. With these simple conditions, I look upon the cure as absolutely certain.

You are to remember that I had not even commenced to treat Mr. Jennings' case. I have not any doubt that I should have cured him perfectly in eighteen months, or possibly it might have extended to two years. Some cases are very rapidly curable, others extremely tedious. Every intelligent physician who will give thought and diligence to the task, will effect a cure.

You know my tract on "The Cardinal Functions of the Brain." I there, by the evidence of innumerable facts, prove, as I think, the high probability of a circulation arterial and venous in its mechanism, through the nerves. Of this system, thus considered, the brain is the heart. The fluid, which is propagated hence through one class of nerves, returns in an altered state through another, and the nature of that fluid is spiritual, though not immaterial, any more than, as I before remarked, light or electricity are so.

By various abuses, among which the habitual use of such agents as green tea is one, this fluid may be affected as to its quality, but it is more frequently disturbed as to equilibrium. This fluid being that which we have in common with spirits, a congestion found upon the masses of brain or nerve, connected with the interior sense, forms a surface unduly exposed, on which disembodied spirits may operate: communication is thus more or less effectually established. Between this brain circulation and the heart circulation there is an intimate sympathy. The seat, or rather the instrument of exterior vision, is the eye. The seat of interior vision is the nervous tissue and brain, immediately about and above the eyebrow. You remember how effectually I dissipated your pictures by the simple application of iced eau-de-cologne. Few cases, however, can be treated exactly alike with anything like rapid success. Cold acts powerfully as a repellant of the nervous fluid. Long enough continued it will even produce that permanent insensibility which we call numbness, and a little longer, muscular as well as sensational paralysis.

I have not, I repeat, the slightest doubt that I should have first dimmed and ultimately sealed that inner eye which Mr. Jennings had inadvertently opened. The same senses are opened in delirium tremens, and entirely shut up again when the overaction of the cerebral heart, and the prodigious nervous congestions that attend it, are terminated by a decided change in the state of the body. It is by acting steadily upon the body, by a simple process, that this result is produced—and inevitably produced—I have never yet failed.

Poor Mr. Jennings made away with himself. But that catastrophe was the result of a totally different malady, which, as it were, projected itself upon the disease which was established. His case was in the distinctive manner a complication, and the complaint under which he really succumbed, was hereditary suicidal mania. Poor Mr. Jennings I cannot call a patient of mine, for I had not even begun to treat his case, and he had not yet given me, I am convinced, his full and unreserved confidence. If the patient does not array himself on the side of the disease, his cure is certain.

—1869

AMBROSE BIERCE

1842-1914?

Ambrose Bierce was born in Horse Cave Creek, Ohio, as Marcus Aurelius Bierce's and Laura (Sherwood) Bierce's tenth child. His family moved to Indiana in 1846, and following the outbreak of the Civil War, Bierce enlisted in the Ninth Indiana Infantry. From 1861 to 1865, he participated in some of the bloodiest fighting of the war—including the battles fought at Shiloh, Chickamauga, Lookout Mountain, and Missionary Ridge—and was himself severely wounded in the head at the battle of Kennesaw Mountain in 1864. His experiences with the military and war were to later provide him with material for a number of his finest short stories about the Civil War. Following the war, Bierce worked as an agent for the U.S. Treasury in Alabama. He traveled to Panama and New Orleans in 1865, and joined General William B. Hazen as part of a military expedition that traveled west through Native American territories to San Francisco. Bierce left Hazen in 1867, finding employment at the Sub-Treasury in San Francisco. That same year, he began his career as a journalist that would eventually make him both famous and infamous.

Between 1867 and 1871, Bierce published a variety of short writings—such as poems, essays, and sketches—in several San Francisco-based publications, including the Californian, The Golden Era, *and the* News Letter. *In 1871, he married Mollie Day and also published his first short story in the* Overland Monthly, *the journal made famous by Bret Harte. He published his first two books—*The Fiend's Delight *and* Nuggets and Dust—*in 1873.*

Bierce began his notorious "Prattle" column in 1877 for the San Francisco periodical, The Argonaut. *After a brief period working for the Black Hills Placer Mining Company, Bierce again returned to San Francisco in 1881 to become editor of the* Wasp, *where he quickly resurrected his "Prattle" column. In 1887, he accepted a position with William Randolph Hearsts's San Francisco* Examiner *where he once more wrote his famous "Prattle" column, and from that moment until the mysterious end of his life in 1914(?), his frequently stormy professional relationship with Hearst—as one of Hearst's premier journalists—allowed Bierce to become financially independent. In 1892, he published his first collection of stories,* Tales of Soldiers and Civilians.*

Perhaps Bierce's most noteworthy accomplishment during the later years of his life was when he was sent to Washington, D.C. by Hearst in 1896 to lead the opposition against Collis Huntington's funding bill for the Central and Southern Pacific railroads that was then being considered by Congress. Bierce was primarily responsible for the defeat of this bill. He returned to San Francisco that same year, and later published a collection of humorous sketches entitled Fantastic Fables *in 1899. From 1900 to the end of his life, Bierce lived primarily in Washington, D.C. He traveled to Mexico in November of 1913 to observe firsthand Pancho Villa's revolution and disappeared sometime after December 1913. Some biographers speculate that he died in 1914 at the battle of Ojinaga in Mexico.*

"The Damned Thing," first published in the 1893 Christmas issue of Town Topics, *and anthologized in the collection* Can Such Things Be? *(1893), illustrates an important thematic transition in the development of popular horror fiction. Bierce's utilization of scientificlike empiricism in the tale, as well as his realistic, even naturalistic, portrayal of the invisible creature, anticipated the science fiction-based horror stories of twentieth-century pulp magazine author H. P. Lovecraft.*

THE DAMNED THING

I

One does not always eat what is on the table

By the light of a tallow candle which had been placed on one end of a rough table a man was reading something written in a book. It was an old account book, greatly worn; and the writing was not, apparently, very legible, for the man sometimes held the page close to the flame of the candle to get a stronger light on it. The shadow of the book would then throw into obscurity a half of the room, darkening a number of faces and figures; for besides the reader, eight other men were present. Seven of them sat against the rough log walls, silent, motionless, and the room being small, not very far from the table. By extending an arm any one of them could have touched the eighth man, who lay on the table, face upward, partly covered by a sheet, his arms at his sides. He was dead.

The man with the book was not reading aloud, and no one spoke; all seemed to be waiting for something to occur; the dead man only was without expectation.

From the blank darkness outside came in, through the aperture that served for a window, all the ever unfamiliar noises of night in the wilderness—the long nameless note of a distant coyote; the stilly pulsing thrill of tireless insects in trees; strange cries of night birds, so different from those of the birds of day; the drone of great blundering beetles, and all that mysterious chorus of small sounds that seem always to have been but half heard when they have suddenly ceased, as if conscious of an indiscretion. But nothing of all this was noted in that company; its members were not overmuch addicted to idle interest in matters of no practical importance; that was obvious in every line of their rugged faces—obvious even in the dim light of the single candle. They were evidently men of the vicinity—farmers and woodsmen.

The person reading was a trifle different; one would have said of him that he was of the world, worldly, albeit there was that in his attire which attested a certain fellowship with the organisms of his environment. His coat would hardly have passed muster in San Francisco; his foot-gear was not of urban origin, and the hat that lay by him on the floor (he was the only one uncovered) was such that if one had considered it as an article of mere personal adornment he would have missed its meaning. In countenance the man was rather prepossessing, with just a hint of sternness; though that he may have assumed or cultivated, as appropriate to one in authority. For he was a coroner. It was by virtue of his office that he had possession of the book in which he was reading; it had been found among the dead man's effects—in his cabin, where the inquest was now taking place.

When the coroner had finished reading he put the book into his breast pocket. At that moment the door was pushed open and a young man entered. He, clearly, was not of mountain birth and breeding: he was clad as those who dwell in cities. His clothing was dusty, however, as from travel. He had, in fact, been riding hard to attend the inquest.

The coroner nodded; no one else greeted him.

"We have waited for you," said the coroner. "It is necessary to have done with this business to-night."

The young man smiled. "I am sorry to have kept you," he said. "I went away, not to evade your summons, but to post to my newspaper an account of what I suppose I am called back to relate."

The coroner smiled.

"The account that you posted to your newspaper," he said, "differs, probably, from that which you will give here under oath."

"That," replied the other, rather hotly and with a visible flush, "is as you please. I used manifold paper and have a copy of what I sent. It was not written as news, for it is incredible, but as fiction. It may go as a part of my testimony under oath."

"But you say it is incredible."

"That is nothing to you, sir, if I also swear that it is true."

The coroner was silent for a time, his eyes upon the floor. The men about the sides of the cabin talked in whispers, but seldom withdrew their gaze from the face of the corpse. Presently the coroner lifted his eyes and said: "We will resume the inquest."

The men removed their hats. The witness was sworn.

"What is your name?" the coroner asked.

"William Harker."

"Age?"

"Twenty-seven."

"You knew the deceased, Hugh Morgan?"

"Yes."

"You were with him when he died?"

"Near him."

"How did that happen—your presence, I mean?"

"I was visiting him at this place to shoot and fish. A part of my purpose, however, was to study him and his odd, solitary way of life. He seemed a good model for a character in fiction. I sometimes write stories."

"I sometimes read them."

"Thank you."

"Stories in general—not yours."

Some of the jurors laughed. Against a sombre background humor shows high lights. Soldiers in the intervals of battle laugh easily, and a jest in the death chamber conquers by surprise.

"Relate the circumstances of this man's death," said the coroner. "You may use any notes or memoranda that you please."

The witness understood. Pulling a manuscript from his breast pocket he held it near the candle and turning the leaves until he found the passage that he wanted began to read.

II

What may happen in a field of wild oats

". . . The sun had hardly risen when we left the house. We were looking for quail, each with a shotgun, but we had only one dog. Morgan said that our best ground was beyond a certain ridge that he pointed out, and we crossed it by a trail through the *chaparral*. On the other side was comparatively level ground, thickly covered with wild oats. As we emerged from the *chaparral* Morgan was but a few yards in advance. Suddenly we heard, at a little distance to our right and partly in front, a noise as of some animal thrashing about in the bushes, which we could see were violently agitated.

"'We've started a deer,' I said. 'I wish we had brought a rifle.'

"Morgan, who had stopped and was intently watching the agitated *chaparral*, said nothing, but had cocked both barrels of his gun and was holding it in readiness to aim. I thought him a trifle excited, which surprised me, for he had a reputation for exceptional coolness, even in moments of sudden and imminent peril.

"'O, come,' I said. 'You are not going to fill up a deer with quail-shot, are you?'

"Still he did not reply; but catching a sight of his face as he turned it slightly toward me I was struck by the intensity of his look. Then I understood that we had serious business in hand and my first conjecture was that we had 'jumped' a grizzly. I advanced to Morgan's side, cocking my piece as I moved.

"The bushes were now quiet and the sounds had ceased, but Morgan was as attentive to the place as before.

"'What is it? What the devil is it?' I asked.

"'That Damned Thing!' he replied, without turning his head. His voice was husky and unnatural. He trembled visibly.

"I was about to speak further, when I observed the wild oats near the place of the disturbance moving in the most inexplicable way. I can hardly describe it. It seemed as if stirred by a streak of wind, which not only bent it, but pressed it down—crushed it so that it did not rise; and this movement was slowly prolonging itself directly toward us.

"Nothing that I had ever seen had affected me so strangely as this unfamiliar and unaccountable phenomenon, yet I am unable to recall any sense of fear. I remember—and tell it here because, singularly enough, I recollected it then—that once in looking carelessly out of an open window I momentarily mistook a small tree close at hand for one of a group of larger trees at a little distance away. It looked the same size as the others, but being more distinctly and sharply defined in mass and detail seemed out of harmony with them. It was a mere falsification of the law of aërial perspective, but it startled, almost terrified me. We so rely upon the orderly operation of familiar natural laws that any seeming suspension of them is noted as a menace to our safety, a warning of unthinkable calamity. So now the apparently causeless movement of the herbage and the slow, undeviating approach of the line of disturbance were distinctly disquieting. My companion appeared actually frightened, and I could hardly credit my senses when I saw him suddenly throw his gun to his shoulder and fire both barrels at the agitated grain! Before the smoke of the discharge had cleared away I heard a loud savage cry—a scream like that of a wild animal—and flinging his gun upon the ground Morgan sprang away and ran swiftly from the spot. At the same instant I was thrown violently to the ground by the impact of something unseen in the smoke—some soft, heavy substance that seemed thrown against me with great force.

"Before I could get upon my feet and recover my gun, which seemed to have been struck from my hands, I heard Morgan crying out as if in mortal agony, and mingling with his cries were such hoarse, savage sounds as one hears from fighting dogs. Inexpressibly terrified, I struggled to my feet and looked in the direction of Morgan's retreat; and may Heaven in mercy spare me from another sight like that! At a distance of less than thirty yards was my friend, down upon one knee, his head thrown back at a frightful angle, hatless, his long hair in disorder and his whole body in violent movement from side to side, backward and forward. His right arm was lifted and seemed to lack the hand—at least, I could see none. The other arm was invisible. At times, as my memory now reports this extraordinary scene, I could discern but a part of his body; it was as if he had been partly blotted out—I cannot otherwise express it—then a shifting of his position would bring it all into view again.

"All this must have occurred within a few seconds, yet in that time Morgan assumed all the postures of a determined wrestler vanquished by superior weight and strength. I saw nothing but him, and him not always distinctly. During the entire incident his shouts and curses were heard, as if through an enveloping uproar of such sounds of rage and fury as I had never heard from the throat of man or brute!

"For a moment only I stood irresolute, then throwing down my gun I ran forward to my friend's assistance. I had a vague belief that he was suffering from a fit, or some form of convulsion. Before I could reach his side he was down and quiet. All sounds had ceased, but with a feeling of such terror as even these awful events had not inspired I now saw again the mysterious movement of the wild oats, prolonging itself from the trampled area about the prostrate man toward the edge of a wood. It was only when it had reached the wood that I was able to withdraw my eyes and look at my companion. He was dead."

III

A man though naked may be in rags

The coroner rose from his seat and stood beside the dead man. Lifting an edge of the sheet he pulled it away, exposing the entire body, altogether naked and show-ing in the candle-light a claylike yellow. It had, however, broad maculations of bluish black, obviously caused by extravasated blood from contusions. The chest and sides looked as if they had been beaten with a bludgeon. There were dreadful lacerations; the skin was torn in strips and shreds.

The coroner moved round to the end of the table and undid a silk handkerchief which had been passed under the chin and knotted on the top of the head. When the handkerchief was drawn away it exposed what had been the throat. Some of the jurors who had risen to get a better view repented their curiosity and turned away their faces. Witness Harker went to the open window and leaned out across the sill, faint and sick. Dropping the handkerchief upon the dead man's neck the coroner stepped to an angle of the room and from a pile of clothing produced one garment after another, each of which he held up a moment for inspection. All were torn, and stiff with blood. The jurors did not make a closer inspection. They seemed rather uninterested. They had, in truth, seen all this before; the only thing that was new to them being Harker's testimony.

"Gentlemen," the coroner said, "we have no more evidence, I think. Your duty has been already explained to you; if there is nothing you wish to ask you may go outside and consider your verdict."

The foreman rose—a tall, bearded man of sixty, coarsely clad.

"I should like to ask one question, Mr. Coroner," he said. "What asylum did this yer last witness escape from?"

"Mr. Harker," said the coroner, gravely and tranquilly, "from what asylum did you last escape?"

Harker flushed crimson again, but said nothing, and the seven jurors rose and solemnly filed out of the cabin.

"If you have done insulting me, sir," said Harker, as soon as he and the officer were left alone with the dead man, "I suppose I am at liberty to go?"

"Yes."

Harker started to leave, but paused, with his hand on the door latch. The habit of his profession was strong in him—stronger than his sense of personal dignity. He turned about and said:

"The book that you have there—I recognize it as Morgan's diary. You seemed greatly interested in it; you read in it while I was testifying. May I see it? The public would like—"

"The book will cut no figure in this matter," replied the official, slipping it into his coat pocket; "all the entries in it were made before the writer's death."

As Harker passed out of the house the jury reëntered and stood about the table, on which the now covered corpse showed under the sheet with sharp definition. The foreman seated himself near the candle, produced from his breast pocket a pencil and scrap of paper and wrote rather laboriously the following verdict, which with various degrees of effort all signed:

"We, the jury, do find that the remains come to their death at the hands of a mountain lion, but some of us thinks, all the same, they had fits."

IV

An explanation from the tomb

In the diary of the late Hugh Morgan are certain interesting entries having, possibly, a scientific value as suggestions. At the inquest upon his body the book was not put in evidence; possibly the coroner thought it not worth while to confuse the jury. The date of the first of the entries mentioned cannot be ascertained; the upper part of the leaf is torn away; the part of the entry remaining follows:

". . . would run in a half-circle, keeping his head turned always toward the centre, and again he would stand still, barking furiously. At last he ran away into the brush as fast as he could go. I thought at first that he had gone mad, but on returning to the house found no other alteration in his manner than what was obviously due to fear of punishment.

"Can a dog see with his nose? Do odors impress some cerebral centre with images of the thing that emitted them? . . .

"Sept. 2.—Looking at the stars last night as they rose above the crest of the ridge east of the house, I observed them successively disappear—from left to right. Each was eclipsed but an instant, and only a few at the same time, but along the entire length of the ridge all that were within a degree or two of the crest were blotted out. It was as if something had passed along between me and them; but I could not see it, and the stars were not thick enough to define its outline. Ugh! I don't like this." . . .

Several weeks' entries are missing, three leaves being torn from the book.

"Sept. 27.—It has been about here again—I find evidences of its presence every day. I watched again all last night in the same cover, gun in hand, double-charged with buckshot. In the morning the fresh footprints were there, as before. Yet I would have sworn that I did not sleep—indeed, I hardly sleep at all. It is terrible, insupportable! If these amazing experiences are real I shall go mad; if they are fanciful I am mad already.

"Oct. 3.—I shall not go—it shall not drive me away. No, this is *my* house, *my* land. God hates a coward. . . .

"Oct. 5.—I can stand it no longer; I have invited Harker to pass a few weeks with me—he has a level head. I can judge from his manner if he thinks me mad.

"Oct. 7.—I have the solution of the mystery; it came to me last night—suddenly, as by revelation. How simple—how terribly simple!

"There are sounds that we cannot hear. At either end of the scale are notes that stir no chord of that imperfect instrument, the human ear. They are too high or too grave. I have observed a flock of blackbirds occupying an entire tree-top—the tops of several trees—and all in full song. Suddenly—in a moment—at absolutely the same instant—all spring into the air and fly away. How? They could not all see one another—whole tree-tops intervened. At no point could a leader have been visible to all. There must have been a signal of warning or command, high and shrill above the din, but by me unheard. I have observed, too, the same simultaneous flight when all were silent, among not only blackbirds, but other birds—quail, for example, widely separated by bushes—even on opposite sides of a hill.

"It is known to seamen that a school of whales basking or sporting on the surface of the ocean, miles apart, with the convexity of the earth between, will sometimes dive at the same instant—all gone out of sight in a moment. The signal has been sounded—too grave for the ear of the sailor at the masthead and his comrades on the deck—who nevertheless feel its vibrations in the ship as the stones of a cathedral are stirred by the bass of the organ.

"As with sounds, so with colors. At each end of the solar spectrum the chemist can detect the presence of what are known as 'actinic' rays. They represent colors—integral colors in the composition of light—which we are unable to discern. The human eye is an imperfect instrument; its range is but a few octaves of the real 'chromatic scale.' I am not mad; there are colors that we cannot see.

"And, God help me! the Damned Thing is of such a color!"

—1893

BRAM STOKER
1847-1912

Bram Stoker was born in Dublin, Ireland. His father, Abraham, was an underpaid, yet devoted, civil servant, while his mother, Charlotte, was involved in social welfare causes when she was not raising a family of seven children. Bram Stoker was a sickly child, and his young imagination was shaped by his mother's vivid storytelling ability. Her dark, Irish folktales provided Stoker with narrative material that was later incorporated in his horror and fantasy fiction. In 1864, Stoker was accepted at Trinity College in Dublin, where he graduated, with honors, in 1868. After graduation, Stoker became a civil servant like his father, but quickly tired of this profession. Beginning in 1871, he wrote reviews as a drama critic for the Dublin Mail. *He met the famous nineteenth-century actor Henry Irving in 1876, and a friendship developed. In 1878, Irving offered Stoker the job as acting manager for the Lyceum Theater, and Stoker served in this position for the next twenty-seven years. That year Stoker also married Florence Balcombe. He published an early collection of children's fantasy fiction in 1882 entitled* Under the Sunset. *His first novel was* The Primrose Path, *published in 1875. Stoker's other important fictional works included* The Snake's Pass *(1890),* Miss Betty *(1898),* The Mystery of the Sea *(1902),* The Jewel of the Seven Stars *(1903),* The Man *(1905),* Lady Athlyne *(1908), and* The Lady of the Shroud *(1909). He died the year following the publication of his last novel,* The Lair of the White Worm *(1911). Stoker's most famous novel was* Dracula, *though it received a mixed critical reception upon its initial publication in 1897 and enjoyed only modest commercial success during Stoker's lifetime.* Dracula *became one of the most famous horror stories of all time when Stoker's narrative was translated into the popular cinema. Through the years, the infamous Count Dracula has been portrayed by a variety of actors; the character has been widely interpreted.*

"Dracula's Guest" was originally intended to be the opening chapter of Dracula, *but it was cut from the novel due to concerns about the book's length. The story remained "lost" until it was discovered among Stoker's papers after his death. It subsequently appeared in 1914, some two years following Stoker's death, as the lead story in an anthology of his work bearing the same title as the short story. As an interesting footnote, in celebra-*

tion of the 250th performance of the play Dracula at the Prince of Wales Theater in London, the Dracula's Guest collection was reprinted as a special edition and presented to members of the audience in an envelope requesting that it not be opened before the end of the play's third act. When the theater patrons opened the book, they were greeted by an artificial black bat propelled from the book's pages by elastic.

"Dracula's Guest" stands on its own as a complete short narrative, but when read as an introduction to Dracula, it anticipates, with its vivid description of the narrator's dire encounter with Walpurgis Night, the novel's depiction of the apocalyptic struggle between Abraham Van Helsing and the Count, a struggle that represents (at a metaphoric level) the conflict between good and evil, between God and the Devil, and between the pragmatic, scientific West and the mysterious, exotic East.

DRACULA'S GUEST

When we started for our drive the sun was shining brightly on Munich, and the air was full of the joyousness of early summer. Just as we were about to depart, Herr Delbrück (the maître d'hôtel of the Quatre Saisons, where I was staying) came down, bareheaded, to the carriage and, after wishing me a pleasant drive, said to the coachman, still holding his hand on the handle of the carriage door:

"Remember you are back by nightfall. The sky looks bright but there is a shiver in the north wind that says there may be a sudden storm. But I am sure you will not be late." Here he smiled, and added, "for you know what night it is."

Johann answered with an emphatic, "Ja, mein Herr," and, touching his hat, drove off quickly. When we had cleared the town, I said, after signalling to him to stop:

"Tell me, Johann, what is tonight?"

He crossed himself, as he answered laconically: "Walpurgis Nacht." Then he took out his watch, a great, old-fashioned German silver thing as big as a turnip, and looked at it, with his eyebrows gathered together and a little impatient shrug of his shoulders. I realized that this was his way of respectfully protesting against the unnecessary delay, and sank back in the carriage, merely motioning him to proceed. He started off rapidly, as if to make up for lost time. Every now and then the horses seemed to throw up their heads and sniffed the air suspiciously. On such occasions I often looked round in alarm. The road was pretty bleak, for we were traversing a sort of high, wind-swept plateau. As we drove, I saw a road that looked but little used, and which seemed to dip through a little, winding valley. It looked so inviting that, even at the risk of offending him, I called Johann to stop—and when he had pulled up, I told him I would like to drive down that road. He made all sorts of excuses, and frequently crossed himself as he spoke. This somewhat piqued my curiosity, so I asked him various questions. He answered fencingly, and repeatedly looked at his watch in protest. Finally I said:

"Well, Johann, I want to go down this road. I shall not ask you to come unless you like; but tell me why you do not like to go, that is all I ask." For answer he seemed to throw himself off the box, so quickly did he reach the ground. Then he stretched out his hands appealingly to me, and implored me not to go. There was just enough of English mixed with the German for me to understand the drift of his talk. He seemed always just about to tell me something—the very idea of which evidently frightened him; but each time he pulled himself up, saying, as he crossed himself: "Walpurgis Nacht!"

I tried to argue with him, but it was difficult to argue with a man when I did not know his language. The advantage certainly rested with him, for although he began to speak in English, of a very crude and broken kind, he always got excited and broke into his native tongue—and every time he did so, he looked at his watch. Then the horses became restless and sniffed the air. At this he grew very pale, and, looking around in a frightened way, he suddenly jumped forward, took them by the bridles and led them on some twenty feet. I followed, and asked why he had done this. For answer he crossed himself, pointed to the spot we had left and drew his carriage in the direction of the other road, indicating a cross, and said, first in German, then in English: "Buried him—him what killed themselves."

I remembered the old custom of burying suicides at cross-roads: "Ah! I see, a suicide. How interesting!" But for the life of me I could not make out why the horses were frightened.

Whilst we were talking, we heard a sort of sound between a yelp and a bark. It was far away; but the horses got very restless, and it took Johann all his time to quiet them. He was pale, and said, "It sounds like a wolf—but yet there are no wolves here now."

"No?" I said, questioning him; "isn't it long since the wolves were so near the city?"

"Long, long," he answered, "in the spring and summer; but with the snow the wolves have been here not so long."

Whilst he was petting the horses and trying to quiet them, dark clouds drifted rapidly across the sky. The sunshine passed away, and a breath of cold wind seemed to drift past us. It was only a breath, however, and more in the nature of a warning than a fact, for the sun came out brightly again. Johann looked under his lifted hand at the horizon and said:

"The storm of snow, he comes before long time." Then he looked at his watch again, and, straightaway holding his reins firmly—for the horses were still pawing the ground restlessly and shaking their heads—he climbed to his box as though the time had come for proceeding on our journey.

I felt a little obstinate and did not at once get into the carriage.

"Tell me," I said, "about this place where the road leads," and I pointed down.

Again he crossed himself and mumbled a prayer, before he answered, "It is unholy."

"What is unholy?" I enquired.

"The village."

"Then there is a village?"

"No, no. No one lives there hundreds of years." My curiosity was piqued. "But you said there was a village."

"There was."

"Where is it now?"

Whereupon he burst out into a long story in German and English, so mixed up that I could not quite understand exactly what he said, but roughly I gathered that long ago, hundreds of years, men had died there and been buried in their graves; and sounds were heard under the clay, and when the graves were opened, men and women were found rosy with life, and their mouths red with blood. And so, in haste to save their lives (aye, and their souls!—and here he crossed himself) those who were left fled away to other places, where the living lived, and the dead were dead and not—not something. He was evidently afraid to speak the last words. As he proceeded with his narration, he grew more and more excited. It seemed as if his imagination had got hold of him, and he ended in a perfect paroxysm of fear—white-faced, perspiring, trembling and looking round him, as if expecting that some dreadful presence would manifest itself there in the bright sunshine on the open plain. Finally, in an agony of desperation, he cried:

"Walpurgis Nacht!" and pointed to the carriage for me to get in. All my English blood rose at this, and, standing back, I said:

"You are afraid, Johann—you are afraid. Go home; I shall return alone; the walk will do me good." The carriage door was open. I took from the seat my oak walking stick—which I always carry on my holiday excursions—and closed the door, pointing back to Munich, and said, "Go home, Johann—Walpurgis Nacht doesn't concern Englishmen."

The horses were now more restive than ever, and Johann was trying to hold them in, while excitedly imploring me not to do anything so foolish. I pitied the poor fellow, he was deeply in earnest; but all the same I could not help laughing. His English was quite gone now. In his anxiety he had forgotten that his only means of making me understand was to talk my language, so he jabbered away in his native German. It began to be a little tedious. After giving the direction, "Home!" I turned to go down the crossroad into the valley.

With a despairing gesture, Johann turned his horses towards Munich. I leaned on my stick and looked after him. He went slowly along the road for a while: then there came over the crest of the hill a man tall and thin. I could see so much in the distance. When he drew near the horses, they began to jump and kick about, then to scream with terror. Johann could not hold them in; they bolted down the road, running away madly. I watched them out of sight, then looked for the stranger, but I found that he, too, was gone.

With a light heart I turned down the side road through the deepening valley to which Johann had objected. There was not the slightest reason, that I could see, for his objection; and I daresay I tramped for a couple of hours without thinking of time or distance, and certainly without seeing a person or a house. So far as the place was concerned, it was desolation itself. But I did not notice this particularly till, on turning a bend in the road, I came upon a scattered fringe of wood; then I recognized that I had been impressed unconsciously by the desolation of the region through which I had passed.

I sat down to rest myself, and began to look around. It struck me that it was considerably colder than it had been at the commencement of my walk—a sort of sighing sound seemed to be around me, with, now and then, high overhead, a sort of muffled roar. Looking upwards I noticed that great thick clouds were drifting rapidly across the sky from north to south at a great height. There were signs of coming storm in some lofty stratum of the air. I was a little chilly, and, thinking that it was the sitting still after the exercise of walking, I resumed my journey.

The ground I passed over was now much more picturesque. There were no striking objects that the eye might single out; but in all there was a charm of beauty. I took little heed of time and it was only when the deepening twilight forced itself upon me that I began to think of how I should find my way home. The brightness of the day had gone. The air was cold, and the drifting of clouds high overhead was more marked. They were accompanied by a sort of far-away rushing sound, through which seemed to come at intervals that mysterious cry which the driver had said came from a wolf. For a while I hesitated. I had said I would see the deserted village, so on I went, and presently came on a wide stretch of open country, shut in by hills all around. Their sides were covered with trees which spread down to the plain, dotting, in clumps, the gentler slopes and hollows which showed here and there. I followed with my eye the winding of the road, and saw that it curved close to one of the densest of these clumps and was lost behind it.

As I looked there came a cold shiver in the air, and the snow began to fall. I thought of the miles and miles of bleak country I had passed, and then hurried on to seek the shelter of the wood in front. Darker and darker grew the sky, and faster and heavier fell the snow, till the earth before and around me was a glistening white carpet the further edge of which was lost in misty vagueness. The road was here but crude, and when on the level its boundaries were not so marked, as when it passed through the cuttings; and in a little while I found that I must have strayed from it, for I missed underfoot the hard surface, and my feet sank deeper in the grass and moss. Then the wind grew stronger and blew with ever-increasing force, till I was fain to run before it. The air became icy-cold, and in spite of my exercise I began to suffer. The snow was now falling so thickly and whirling around me in such rapid eddies that I could hardly keep my eyes open. Every now and then the heavens were torn asunder by vivid lightning, and in the flashes I could see ahead of me a great mass of trees, chiefly yew and cypress all heavily coated with snow.

I was soon amongst the shelter of the trees, and there, in comparative silence, I could hear the rush of the wind high overhead. Presently the blackness of the storm had become merged in the darkness of the night. By-and-by the storm seemed to be passing away: it now only came in fierce puffs or blasts. At such moments the weird sound of the wolf appeared to be echoed by many similar sounds around me.

Now and again, through the black mass of drifting cloud, came a straggling ray of moonlight, which lit up the expanse, and showed me that I was at the edge of a dense mass of cypress and yew trees. As the snow had ceased to fall, I walked out from the shelter and began to investigate more closely. It appeared to me that, amongst so many old foundations as I had passed, there might be still standing a house in which, though in ruins, I could find some sort of shelter for a while. As I skirted the edge of the copse, I found that a low wall encircled it, and following this I presently found an opening. Here the cypresses formed an alley leading up to a square mass of some kind of building. Just as I caught sight of this, however, the drifting clouds obscured the moon, and I passed up the path in darkness. The wind must have grown colder, for I felt myself shiver as I walked; but there was hope of shelter, and I groped my way blindly on.

I stopped, for there was a sudden stillness. The storm had passed; and, perhaps in sympathy with nature's silence, my heart seemed to cease to beat. But this was only momentarily; for suddenly the moonlight broke through the clouds, showing me that I was in a graveyard, and that the square object before me was a great massive tomb of marble, as white as the snow that lay on and all around it. With the moonlight there came a fierce sigh of the storm, which appeared to resume its course with a long, low howl, as of many dogs or wolves. I was awed and shocked, and felt the cold perceptibly grow upon me till it seemed to grip me by the heart. Then while the flood of moonlight still fell on the marble tomb, the storm gave further evidence of renewing, as though it was returning on its track. Impelled by some sort of fascination, I approached the sepulchre to see what it was, and why such a thing stood alone in such a place. I walked around it, and read, over the Doric door, in German:

COUNTESS DOLINGEN OF GRATZ
IN STYRIA
SOUGHT AND FOUND DEATH
1801

On the top of the tomb, seemingly driven through the solid marble—for the structure was composed of a few vast blocks of stone—was a great iron spike or stake. On going to the back I saw, graven in great Russian letters:

The dead travel fast.

There was something so weird and uncanny about the whole thing that it gave me a turn and made me feel quite faint. I began to wish, for the first time, that I had taken Johann's advice. Here a thought struck me, which came under almost mysterious circumstances and with a terrible shock. This was Walpurgis Night!

Walpurgis Night, when, according to the belief of millions of people, the devil was abroad—when the graves were opened and the dead came forth and walked. When all evil things of earth and air and water held revel. This very place the driver had specially shunned. This was the depopulated village of centuries ago. This was where the suicide lay; and this was the place where I was alone—unmanned, shivering with cold in a shroud of snow with a wild storm gathering again upon me! It took all my philosophy, all the religion I had been taught, all my courage, not to collapse in a paroxysm of fright.

And now a perfect tornado burst upon me. The ground shook as though thousands of horses thundered across it; and this time the storm bore on its icy wings, not snow, but great hailstones which drove with such violence that they might have come from the thongs of Balearic slingers—hailstones that beat down leaf and branch and made the shelter of the cypresses of no more avail than though their stems were standing-corn. At the first I had rushed to the nearest tree; but I was soon fain to leave it and seek the only spot that seemed to afford refuge, the deep Doric doorway of the marble tomb. There, crouching against the massive bronze door, I gained a certain amount of protection from the beating of the hailstones, for now they only drove against me as they ricocheted from the ground and the side of the marble.

As I leaned against the door, it moved slightly and opened inwards. The shelter of even a tomb was welcome in that pitiless tempest, and I was about to enter it when there came a flash of forked-lightning that lit up the whole expanse of the heavens. In the instant, as I am a living man, I saw, as my eyes were turned into the darkness of the tomb, a beautiful woman, with rounded cheeks and red lips, seemingly sleeping on a bier. As the thunder broke overhead, I was grasped as by the hand of a giant and hurled out into the storm. The whole thing was so sudden that, before I could realize the shock, moral as well as physical, I found the hailstones beating me down. At the same time I had a strange, dominating feeling that I was not alone. I looked towards the tomb. Just then there came another blinding flash, which seemed to strike the iron stake that surmounted the tomb and to pour through to the earth, blasting and crumbling the marble, as in a burst of flame. The dead woman rose for a moment of agony, while she was lapped in the flame, and her bitter scream of pain was drowned in the thunder-crash. The last thing I heard was this mingling of dreadful sound, as again I was seized in the giant-grasp and dragged away, while the hailstones beat on me, and the air around seemed reverberant with the howling of wolves. The last sight that I remembered was a vague, white, moving mass, as if all the graves around me had sent out the phantoms of their sheeted dead, and that they were closing in on me through the white cloudiness of the driving hail.

Gradually there came a sort of vague beginning of consciousness; then a sense of weariness that was dreadful. For a time I remembered nothing; but slowly my senses returned. My feet seemed positively racked with pain, yet I could not move them. They seemed to be numbed. There was an icy feeling at the back of my neck and all down my spine, and my ears, like my feet, were dead, yet in torment; but there was in my breast a sense of warmth which was, by comparison, delicious. It was as a nightmare—a physical nightmare, if one may use such an expression; for some heavy weight on my chest made it difficult for me to breathe.

This period of semi-lethargy seemed to remain a long time, and as it faded away I must have slept or swooned. Then came a sort of loathing, like the first stage of seasickness, and a wild desire to be free from something—I knew not what. A vast stillness enveloped me, as though all the world were asleep or dead—only broken by the low panting as of some animal close to me. I felt a warm rasping at my throat, then came a consciousness of the awful truth, which chilled me to the heart and sent the blood surging up through my brain. Some great animal was lying on me and now licking my throat. I feared to stir, for some instinct of prudence bade me lie still; but the brute seemed to realize that there was now some change in me, for it raised its head. Through my eyelashes I saw above me the two great flaming eyes of a gigantic wolf. Its sharp white teeth gleamed in the gaping red mouth, and I could feel its hot breath fierce and acrid upon me.

For another spell of time I remembered no more. Then I became conscious of a low growl, followed by a yelp, renewed again and again. Then, seemingly very far away, I heard a "Holloa! holloa!" as of many voices calling in unison. Cautiously I raised my head and looked in the direction whence the sound came; but the cemetery blocked my view. The wolf still continued to yelp in a strange way, and a red glare began to move round the grove of cypresses, as though following the sound. As the voices drew closer, the wolf yelped faster and louder. I feared to make either sound or motion. Nearer came the red glow, over the white pall which stretched into the darkness around me. Then all at once from beyond the trees there came at a trot a troop of horsemen bearing torches. The wolf rose from my breast and made for the cemetery. I saw one of the horsemen (soldiers by their caps and their long military cloaks) raise his carbine and take aim. A companion knocked up his arm, and I heard the ball whizz over my head. He had evidently taken my body for that of the wolf. Another sighted the animal as it slunk away, and a shot followed. Then, at a gallop, the troop rode forward—some towards me, others following the wolf as it disappeared amongst the snow-clad cypresses.

As they drew nearer I tried to move, but was powerless, although I could see and hear all that went on around me. Two or three of the soldiers jumped from their horses and knelt beside me. One of them raised my head, and placed his hand over my heart.

"Good news, comrades!" he cried. "His heart still beats!"

Then some brandy was poured down my throat; it put vigor into me, and I was able to open my eyes fully and look around. Lights and shadows were moving among the trees, and I heard men call to one another. They drew together, uttering frightened exclamations; and the lights flashed as the others came pouring out of the cemetery pell-mell, like men possessed. When the further ones came close to us, those who were around me asked them eagerly:

"Well, have you found him?"

The reply rang out hurriedly:

"No! No! Come away quick—quick! This is no place to stay, and on this of all nights!"

"What was it?" was the question, asked in all manner of keys. The answer came variously and all indefinitely as though the men were moved by some common impulse to speak, yet were restrained by some common fear from giving their thoughts.

"It—it—indeed!" gibbered one, whose wits had plainly given out for the moment.

"A wolf—and yet not a wolf!" another put in shudderingly.

"No use trying for him without the sacred bullet," a third remarked in a more ordinary manner.

"Serve us right for coming out on this night! Truly we have earned our thousand marks!" were the ejaculations of a fourth.

"There was blood on the broken marble," another said after a pause—"the lightning never brought that there. And for him—is he safe? Look at his throat! See, comrades, the wolf has been lying on him and keeping his blood warm."

The officer looked at my throat and replied:

"He is all right; the skin is not pierced. What does it all mean? We should never have found him but for the yelping of the wolf."

"What became of it?" asked the man who was holding up my head, and who seemed the least panic-stricken of the party, for his hands were steady and without tremor. On his sleeve was the chevron of a petty officer.

"It went to its home," answered the man, whose long face was pallid, and who actually shook with terror as he glanced around him fearfully. "There are graves enough there in which it may lie. Come, comrades—come quickly! Let us leave this cursed spot."

The officer raised me to a sitting posture, as he uttered a word of command; then several men placed me upon a horse. He sprang to the saddle behind me, took me in his arms, gave the word to advance; and, turning our faces away from the cypresses, we rode away in swift, military order.

As yet my tongue refused its office, and I was perforce silent. I must have fallen asleep; for the next thing I remembered was finding myself standing up, supported by a soldier on each side of me. It was almost broad daylight, and to the north a red streak of sunlight was reflected, like a path of blood, over the waste of snow. The officer was telling the men to say nothing of what they had seen, except that they found an English stranger, guarded by a large dog.

"Dog! That was no dog," cut in the man who had exhibited such fear. "I think I know a wolf when I see one."

The young officer answered calmly: "I said a dog."

"Dog!" reiterated the other ironically. It was evident that his courage was rising with the sun; and, pointing to me, he said, "Look at his throat. Is that the work of a dog, master?'"

Instinctively I raised my hand to my throat, and as I touched it I cried out in pain. The men crowded round to look, some stooping down from their saddles; and again there came the calm voice of the young officer:

"A dog, as I said. If aught else were said we should only be laughed at."

I was then mounted behind a trooper, and we rode on into the suburbs of Munich. Here we came across a stray carriage, into which I was lifted, and it was driven off to the Quatre Saisons—the young officer accompanying me, whilst a trooper followed with his horse, and the others rode off to their barracks.

When we arrived, Herr Delbrück rushed so quickly down the steps to meet me, that it was apparent he had been watching within. Taking me by both hands he solicitously led me in. The officer saluted me and was turning to withdraw, when I recognized his purpose, and insisted that he should come to my rooms. Over a glass of wine I warmly thanked him and his brave comrades for saving me. He replied simply that he was more than glad, and that Herr Delbrück had at the first taken steps to make all the searching party pleased; at which ambiguous utterance the maître d'hôtel smiled, while the officer pleaded duty and withdrew.

"But Herr Delbrück," I enquired, "how and why was it that the soldiers searched for me?"

He shrugged his shoulders, as if in depreciation of his own deed, as he replied:

"I was so fortunate as to obtain leave from the commander of the regiment in which I served, to ask for volunteers."

"But how did you know I was lost?" I asked.

"The driver came hither with the remains of his carriage, which had been upset when the horses ran away."

"But surely you would not send a search party of soldiers merely on this account?"

"Oh, no!" he answered; "but even before the coachman arrived, I had this telegram from the Boyar whose guest you are," and he took from his pocket a telegram which he handed to me, and I read:

> *Bistritz.*
> Be careful of my guest—his safety is most precious to me. Should aught happen to him, or if he be missed, spare nothing to find him and ensure his safety. He is English and therefore adventurous. There are often dangers from snow and wolves and night. Lose not a moment if you suspect harm to him. I answer your zeal with my fortune.—DRACULA.

As I held the telegram in my hand, the room seemed to whirl around me; and, if the attentive maître d'hôtel had not caught me, I think I should have fallen. There was something so strange in all this, something so weird and impossible to imagine, that there grew on me a sense of my being in some way the sport of opposite forces—the mere vague idea of which seemed in a way to paralyze me. I was certainly under some form of mysterious protection. From a distant country had come, in the very nick of time, a message that took me out of the danger of the snow-sleep and the jaws of the wolf.

—1914

H. P. LOVECRAFT

1890-1937

H. P. Lovecraft was an influential writer for the American science fiction and horror pulp magazines, the foremost of which was the long-running Weird Tales. *Indeed, despite his obvious limitations as a writer of fiction— some critics, for example, condemn Lovecraft's excessive use of adjectives in his horror fiction and his sometimes irritating wordiness—Lovecraft was the most startlingly inventive popular horror writer of the early twentieth century. His ground-breaking incorporation of science fiction elements in his writings, as well as his creation of the Cthulhu mythology cycle that functioned as a philosophical and artistic support for a number of his horror tales, make Lovecraft one of the horror genre's most important authors.*

Lovecraft was born in Providence, Rhode Island, where he was to live most of his life. Lovecraft's father, Winfield Scott Lovecraft, died in 1898 when Howard was still a boy. Lovecraft's youth was troubled by health problems, and in 1908 he dropped out of high school. He then devoted much of his time to reading, writing, and other isolated intellectual pursuits, forsaking both the continuation of his formal education and the search for gainful employment. By the early 1920s, he began writing his weird fiction in earnest. Lovecraft married Sonia Greene in 1924, and they moved to Brooklyn. At one point, Lovecraft was offered the editor's position at Weird Tales, *a dark fantasy and horror pulp magazine headquartered at Chicago, which he refused. He returned to Providence in 1926, living near his aunts, and he divorced his wife in 1929. Following his divorce, he traveled frequently, but by 1936, he was plagued by poor health. His death, in 1937, was diagnosed as resulting from intestinal cancer, a condition no doubt exacerbated by a parsimonious lifestyle.*

Lovecraft was a prolific writer, though much of his writing involved a voluminous correspondence with friends and professional associates. He also frequently collaborated with others in writing stories. Unfortunately, because Lovecraft's horror fiction was written for the pulps and because this print medium was ephemeral in nature, much of his work was relatively forgotten until August Derleth helped to resurrect both Lovecraft's stories and his reputation. Derleth created a small press called Arkham House that reprinted Lovecraft's fiction in hardcover, as well as reprinting other horror and fantasy authors' works. In 1939, Arkham House released its first Lovecraft title, The Outsider and Others. *Subsequent Lovecraft titles published by Arkham House include* Marginalia *(1944),* Something About Cats and Other Pieces *(1949),* At the Mountain of Madness and Other Novels *(1964),* Dagon and Other Macabre Tales *(1965),* The Dunwich Horror and Others *(1966), and* The Dark Brotherhood and Other Pieces *(1966). Lovecraft was very knowledgeable about the horror fiction tradition he worked with, as evidenced by his excellent monograph entitled* Supernatural Horror in Literature, *completed as an early draft in 1927 and written for W. Paul Cook's* The Recluse. *The introduction to this lengthy essay offers Lovecraft's often-cited definition of horror.*

"The Call of Cthulhu" is one of Lovecraft's most fully developed tales in the Cthulhu Mythos, a term probably coined by August Derleth. The Cthulhu Mythos was a narrative cycle created by Lovecraft and a handful

of his contemporaries—fellow pulp magazine horror writers like Clark Ashton Smith and Robert Bloch, among others—that featured an invented pantheon of monsters lurking just beyond human perception and understanding. These nightmarish monsters await their opportunity to enter the human sphere and assume a frightful domination of the world. The Cthulhu Mythos actually served as a unique literary dialogue between Lovecraft and his author friends. Lovecraft would sometimes make one of these authors a character in the story, usually a character who dies most hideously by story's end, and, in reply, this honored author would return the favor by making Lovecraft a doomed character in his own story. "The Call of Cthulhu," first published in the February 1928 issue of Weird Tales, reveals Lovecraft's inventive reworking of myth-narrative structures, in particular his reinterpretation of the end-of-the-world myth.

INTRODUCTION TO *SUPERNATURAL HORROR IN LITERATURE*

The oldest and strongest emotion of mankind is fear, and the oldest and strongest kind of fear is fear of the unknown. These facts few psychologists will dispute, and their admitted truth must establish for all time the genuineness and dignity of the weirdly horrible tales as a literary form. Against it are discharged all the crafts of a materialistic sophistication which clings to frequently felt emotions and external events, and of a naively inspired idealism which deprecates the aesthetic motive and calls for a didactic literature to "uplift" the reader toward a suitable degree of smirking optimism. But in spite of all this opposition the weird tale has survived, developed, and attained remarkable heights of perfection; founded as it is on a profound and elementary principle whose appeal, if not always universal, must necessarily be poignant and permanent to minds of the requisite sensitiveness.

The appeal of the spectrally macabre is generally narrow because it demands from the reader a certain degree of imagination and a capacity for detachment from everyday life. Relatively few are free enough from the spell of the daily routine to respond to rappings from outside, and tales of ordinary feelings and events, or of common sentimental distortions of such feelings and events, will always take first place in the taste of the majority; rightly, perhaps, since of course these ordinary matters make up the greater part of human experience. But the sensitive are always with us, and sometimes a curious streak of fancy invades an obscure corner of the very hardest head; so that no amount of rationalisation, reform, or Freudian analysis can quite annul the thrill of the chimney-corner whisper or the lonely wood. There is here involved psychological pattern or tradition as real and as deeply grounded in mental experience as any other pattern or tradition of mankind; coeval with the religious feeling and closely related to many aspects of it, and too much a part of our innermost biological heritage to lose keen potency over a very important, though not numerically great, minority of our species.

Man's first instincts and emotions formed his response to the environment in which he found himself. Definite feelings based on pleasure and pain grew up around the phenomena whose causes and effects he understood, whilst around those which he did not understand—and the universe teemed with them in the early days—were naturally woven such personifications, marvelous interpretations, and sensations of awe and fear as would be hit upon by a race having few and simple ideas and limited experience. The unknown, being likewise the unpredictable, became for our primitive forefathers a terrible and omnipotent source of boons and calamities visited upon mankind for cryptic and wholly extraterrestrial reasons, and thus clearly belonging to spheres of existence whereof we know nothing and wherein we have no part. The phenomenon of dreaming likewise helped to build up the notion of an unreal or spiritual world; and in general, all the conditions of savage dawn-life so strongly conducted toward a feeling of the supernatural, that we need not wonder at the thoroughness with which man's very hereditary essence has become saturated with religion and superstition. That saturation must, as a matter of plain scientific fact, be regarded as virtually permanent so far as the subconscious mind and inner instincts are concerned; for though the area of the unknown has been steadily contracting for thousands of years, an infinite reservoir of mystery still engulfs most of the outer cosmos, whilst a vast residuum of powerful inherited associations clings round all the objects and processes that were once mysterious, however well they may now be explained. And more than this, there is an actual physiological fixation of the old instincts in our nervous tissue, which would make them obscurely operative even were the conscious mind to be purged of all sources of wonder.

Because we remember pain and the menace of death more vividly than pleasure, and because our feelings toward the beneficent aspects of the unknown have from the first been captured and formalised by conventional religious rituals, it has fallen to the lot of the darker and more maleficent side of cosmic mystery to figure chiefly in our popular supernatural folklore. This tendency, too, is naturally enhanced by the fact that uncertainty and danger are always closely allied; thus making any kind of an unknown world a world of peril and evil possibilities. When to this sense of fear and evil the inevitable fascination of wonder and curiosity is superadded, there is born a composite body of keen emotion and imaginative provocation whose vitality must of necessity endure as long as the human race itself. Children will always be afraid of the dark, and men with minds sensitive to hereditary impulse will always tremble at the thought of the hidden and fathomless worlds of strange life which may pulsate in the gulfs beyond the stars, or press hideously upon our own globe in unholy dimensions which only the dead and the moonstruck can glimpse.

With this foundation, no one need wonder at the existence of a literature of cosmic fear. It has always existed, and always will exist; and no better evidence of its tenacious vigour can be cited than the impulse which now and then drives writers of totally opposite leanings to try their hands at it in isolated tales, as if to discharge from their minds certain phantasmal shapes which would otherwise haunt them. Thus Dickens wrote several eerie narratives; Browning, the hideous poem *Childe Roland;* Henry James, *The Turn of the Screw;* Dr. Holmes, the subtle novel *Elsie Venner;* F. Marion Crawford, *The Upper Berth* and a number of other examples; Mrs. Charlotte Perkins Gilman, social worker, *The Yellow Wall Paper;* whilst the humorist, W. W. Jacobs, produced that able melodramatic bit called *The Monkey's Paw.*

This type of fear-literature must not be confounded with a type externally similar but psychologically widely different; the literature of mere physical fear and the mundanely gruesome. Such writing, to be sure, has its place, as has the conventional or even whimsical or humorous ghost story where formalism or the author's knowing wink removes the true sense of the morbidly unnatural; but these things are not the literature of cosmic fear in its purest sense. The true weird tale has something more than secret murder, bloody bones, or a sheeted form clanking chains according to rule. A certain atmosphere of breathless and unexplainable dread of outer, unknown forces must be present; and there must be a hint, expressed with a seriousness and portentousness becoming its subject, of that most terrible conception of the human brain—a malign and particular suspension or defeat of those fixed laws of Nature which are our only safeguard against the assaults of chaos and the daemons of unplumbed space.

Naturally we cannot expect all weird tales to conform absolutely to any theoretical model. Creative minds are uneven, and the best of fabrics have their dull spots. Moreover, much of the choicest weird work is unconscious; appearing in memorable fragments scattered through material whose massed effect may be of a very different cast. Atmosphere is the all-important thing, for the final criterion of authenticity is not the dovetailing of a plot but the creation of a given sensation. We may say, as a general thing, that a weird story whose intent is to teach or produce a social effect, or one in which the horrors are finally explained away by natural means, is not a genuine tale of cosmic fear; but it remains a fact that such narratives often possess, in isolated sections, atmospheric touches which fulfill every condition of true supernatural horror-literature. Therefore we must judge a weird tale not by the author's intent, or by the mere mechanics of the plot; but by the emotional level which it attains at its least mundane point. If the proper sensations are excited, such a "high spot" must be admitted on its own merits as weird literature, no matter how prosaically it is later dragged down. The one test of the really weird is simply this— whether or not there be excited in the reader a profound sense of dread, and of contact with unknown spheres and powers; a subtle attitude of awed listening, as if for the beating of black wings or the scratching of outside shapes and entities on the known universe's utmost rim. And of course, the more completely and unifiedly a story conveys this atmosphere, the better it is as a work of art in the given medium.

—1927

THE CALL OF CTHULHU

(Found Among the Papers of the Late Francis Wayland Thurston, of Boston)

Of such great powers or beings there may be conceivably a survival . . . a survival of a hugely remote period when . . . consciousness was manifested, perhaps, in shapes and forms long since withdrawn before the tide of advancing humanity . . . forms of which poetry and legend alone have caught a flying memory and called them gods, monsters, mythical beings of all sorts and kinds. . . .

—ALGERNON BLACKWOOD

I

The Horror in Clay

The most merciful thing in the world, I think, is the inability of the human mind to correlate all its contents. We live on a placid island of ignorance in the midst of black seas of infinity, and it was not meant that we should voyage far. The sciences, each straining in its own direction, have hitherto harmed us little; but some day the piecing together of dissociated knowledge will open up such terrifying vistas of reality, and of our frightful position therein, that we shall either go mad from the revelation or flee from the deadly light into the peace and safety of a new dark age.

Theosophists have guessed at the awesome grandeur of the cosmic cycle wherein our world and human race form transient incidents. They have hinted at strange survivals in terms which would freeze the blood if not masked by a bland optimism. But it is not from them that there came the single glimpse of forbidden aeons which chills me when I think of it and maddens me when I dream of it. That glimpse, like all dread glimpses of truth, flashed out from an accidental piecing together of separated things—in this case an old newspaper item and the notes of a dead professor. I hope that no one else will accomplish this piecing out; certainly, if I live, I shall never knowingly supply a link in so hideous a chain. I think that the professor, too, intended to keep silent regarding the part he knew, and that he would have destroyed his notes had not sudden death seized him.

My knowledge of the thing began in the winter of 1926–27 with the death of my grand-uncle George Gammell Angell, Professor Emeritus of Semitic Languages in Brown University, Providence, Rhode Island. Professor Angell was widely known as an authority on ancient inscriptions, and had frequently been resorted to by the heads of prominent museums; so that his passing at the age of ninety-two may be recalled by many. Locally, interest was intensified by the obscurity of the cause of death. The professor had been stricken whilst returning from the Newport boat; falling suddenly, as witnesses said, after having been jostled by a nautical-looking negro who had come from one of the queer dark courts on the precipitous hillside which formed a short cut from the waterfront to the deceased's home in Williams Street. Physicians were unable to find any visible disorder, but concluded after perplexed debate that some obscure lesion of the heart, induced by the brisk ascent of so steep a hill by so elderly a man, was responsible for the end. At the time I saw no reason to dissent from this dictum, but latterly I am inclined to wonder—and more than wonder.

As my grand-uncle's heir and executor, for he died a childless widower, I was expected to go over his papers with some thoroughness; and for that purpose moved his entire set of files and boxes to my quarters in Boston. Much of the material which I correlated will be later published by the American Archaeological Society, but there was one box which I found exceedingly puzzling, and which I felt much averse from shewing to other eyes. It had been locked, and I did not find the key till it occurred to me to examine the personal ring which the professor carried always in his pocket. Then indeed I succeeded in opening it, but when I did so seemed only to be confronted by a greater and more closely locked barrier. For what could be the meaning of the queer clay bas-relief and the disjointed jottings, ramblings, and cuttings which I found? Had my uncle, in his latter years, become credulous of the most superficial impostures? I resolved to search out the eccentric sculptor responsible for this apparent disturbance of an old man's peace of mind.

The bas-relief was a rough rectangle less than an inch thick and about five by six inches in area; obviously of modern origin. Its designs, however, were far from modern in atmosphere and suggestion; for although the vagaries of cubism and futurism are many and wild, they do not often reproduce that cryptic regularity which lurks in prehistoric writing. And writing of some kind the bulk of these designs seemed certainly to be; though my memory, despite much familiarity with the papers and collections of my uncle, failed in any way to identify this particular species, or even to hint at its remotest affiliations.

Above these apparent hieroglyphics was a figure of evidently pictorial intent, though its impressionistic execution forbade a very clear idea of its nature. It seemed to be a sort of monster, or symbol representing a monster, of a form which only a diseased fancy could conceive. If I say that my somewhat extravagant imagination yielded simultaneous pictures of an octopus, a dragon, and a human caricature, I shall not be unfaithful to the spirit of the thing. A pulpy, tentacled head surmounted a grotesque and scaly body with rudimentary wings; but it was the *general outline* of the whole which made it most shockingly frightful. Behind the figure was a vague suggestion of a Cyclopean architectural background.

The writing accompanying this oddity was, aside from a stack of press cuttings, in Professor Angell's most recent hand; and made no pretence to literary style. What seemed to be the main document was headed "CTHULHU CULT" in characters painstakingly printed to avoid the erroneous reading of a word so unheard-of. This manuscript was divided into two sections, the first of which was headed "1925— Dream and Dream Work of H. A. Wilcox, 7 Thomas St., Providence, R.I.," and the second, "Narrative of Inspector John R. Legrasse, 121 Bienville St., New Orleans, La., at 1908 A. A. S. Mtg.—Notes on Same, & Prof. Webb's Acct." The other manuscript papers were all brief notes, some of them accounts of the queer dreams of different persons, some of them citations from theosophical books and magazines (notably W. Scott-Elliot's *Atlantis and the Lost Lemuria),* and the rest comments on long-surviving secret societies and hidden cults, with references to passages in such mythological and anthropological source-books as Frazer's *Golden Bough* and Miss Murray's *Witch-Cult in Western Europe.* The cuttings largely alluded to outré mental illnesses and outbreaks of group folly or mania in the spring of 1925.

The first half of the principal manuscript told a very peculiar tale. It appears that on March 1st, 1925, a thin, dark young man of neurotic and excited aspect had called upon Professor Angell bearing the singular clay bas-relief, which was then exceedingly damp and fresh. His card bore the name of Henry Anthony Wilcox, and my uncle had recognised him as the youngest son of an excellent family slightly known to him, who had latterly been studying sculpture at the Rhode Island School of Design and living alone at the Fleur-de-Lys Building near that institution. Wilcox was a precocious youth of known genius but great eccentricity, and had from childhood excited attention through the strange stories and odd dreams he was in the habit of relating. He called himself "psychically hypersensitive," but the staid folk of the ancient commercial city dismissed him as merely "queer." Never mingling much with his kind, he had dropped gradually from social visibility, and was now known only to a small group of aesthetes from other towns. Even the Providence Art Club, anxious to preserve its conservatism, had found him quite hopeless.

On the occasion of the visit, ran the professor's manuscript, the sculptor abruptly asked for the benefit of his host's archaeological knowledge in identifying the hieroglyphics on the bas-relief. He spoke in a dreamy, stilted manner which suggested pose and alienated sympathy; and my uncle shewed some sharpness in replying, for the conspicuous freshness of the tablet implied kinship with anything but archaeology. Young Wilcox's rejoinder, which impressed my uncle enough to make him recall and record it verbatim, was of a fantastically poetic cast which must have typified his whole conversation, and which I have since found highly characteristic of him. He said, "It is new, indeed, for I made it last night in a dream of strange cities; and dreams are older than brooding Tyre, or the contemplative Sphinx, or garden-girdled Babylon."

It was then that he began that rambling tale which suddenly played upon a sleeping memory and won the fevered interest of my uncle. There had been a slight earthquake tremor the night before, the most considerable felt in New England for some years; and Wilcox's imagination had been keenly affected. Upon retiring, he had had an unprecedented dream of great Cyclopean cities of titan blocks and sky-flung monoliths, all dripping with green ooze and sinister with latent horror. Hieroglyphics had covered the walls and pillars, and from some undetermined point below had come a voice that was not a voice; a chaotic sensation which only fancy could transmute into sound, but which he attempted to render by the almost unpronounceable jumble of letters, "*Cthulhu fhtagn.*"

This verbal jumble was the key to the recollection which excited and disturbed Professor Angell. He questioned the sculptor with scientific minuteness; and studied with almost frantic intensity the bas-relief on which the youth had found himself working, chilled and clad only in his night-clothes, when waking had stolen bewilderingly over him. My uncle blamed his old age, Wilcox afterward said, for his slowness in recognising both hieroglyphics and pictorial design. Many of his questions seemed highly out-of-place to his visitor, especially those which tried to connect the latter with strange cults or societies; and Wilcox could not understand the repeated promises of silence which he was offered in exchange for an admission of membership in some widespread mystical or paganly religious body. When Professor Angell became convinced that the sculptor was indeed ignorant of any cult or system of cryptic lore, he besieged his visitor with demands for future reports of dreams. This bore regular fruit, for after the first interview the manuscript records daily calls of the young man, during which he related startling fragments of nocturnal imagery whose burden was always some terrible Cyclopean vista of dark and dripping stone, with a subterrene voice or intelligence shouting monotonously in enigmatical sense-impacts uninscribable save as gibberish. The two sounds most frequently repeated are those rendered by the letters "*Cthulhu*" and "*R'lyeh.*"

On March 23d, the manuscript continued, Wilcox failed to appear; and inquiries at his quarters revealed that he had been stricken with an obscure sort of fever and taken to the home of his family in Waterman Street. He had cried out in the night, arousing several other artists in the building, and had manifested since then only alternations of unconsciousness and delirium. My uncle at once telephoned the family, and from that time forward kept close watch of the case; calling often at the Thayer Street office of Dr. Tobey, whom he learned to be in charge. The youth's febrile mind, apparently, was dwelling on strange things; and the doctor shuddered now and then as he spoke of them. They included not only a repetition of what he had formerly dreamed, but touched wildly on a gigantic thing "miles high" which walked or lumbered about. He at no time fully described this object, but occasional frantic words, as repeated by Dr. Tobey, convinced the professor that it must be identical with the nameless monstrosity he had sought to depict in his dream-sculpture. Reference to this object, the doctor added, was invariably a prelude to the young man's subsidence into lethargy. His temperature, oddly enough, was not greatly above normal; but his whole condition was otherwise such as to suggest true fever rather than mental disorder.

On April 2nd at about 3 P.M. every trace of Wilcox's malady suddenly ceased. He sat upright in bed, astonished to find himself at home and completely ignorant of what had happened in dream or reality since the night of March 22nd. Pronounced well by his physician, he returned to his quarters in three days; but to Professor Angell he was of no further assistance. All traces of strange dreaming had vanished with his recovery, and my uncle kept no record of his night-thoughts after a week of pointless and irrelevant accounts of thoroughly usual visions.

Here the first part of the manuscript ended, but references to certain of the scattered notes gave me much material for thought—so much, in fact, that only the ingrained scepticism then forming my philosophy can account for my continued distrust of the artist. The notes in question were those descriptive of the dreams of various persons covering the same period as that in which young Wilcox had had his strange visitations. My uncle, it seems, had quickly instituted a prodigiously far-flung body of inquiries amongst nearly all the friends whom he could question without impertinence, asking for nightly reports of their dreams, and the dates of any notable visions for some time past. The reception of his request seems to have been varied; but he must, at the very least, have received more responses than any ordinary man could have handled without a secretary. This original correspondence was not preserved, but his notes formed a thorough and really significant digest. Average people in society and business—New England's traditional "salt of the earth"—gave an almost completely negative result, though scattered cases of uneasy but formless nocturnal impressions appear here and there, always between March 23d and April 2nd—the period of young Wilcox's delirium. Scientific men were little more affected, though four cases of vague description suggest fugitive glimpses of strange landscapes, and in one case there is mentioned a dread of something abnormal.

It was from the artists and poets that the pertinent answers came, and I know that panic would have broken loose had they been able to compare notes. As it was, lacking their original letters, I half suspected the compiler of having asked leading questions, or of having edited the correspondence in corroboration of what he had latently resolved to see. That is why I continued to feel that Wilcox, somehow cognisant of the old data which my uncle had possessed, had been imposing on the veteran scientist. These responses from aesthetes told a disturbing tale. From February 28th to April 2nd a large proportion of them had dreamed very bizarre things, the intensity of the dreams being immeasurably the stronger during the period of the sculptor's delirium. Over a fourth of those who reported anything, reported scenes and half-sounds not unlike those which Wilcox had described; and some of the dreamers confessed acute fear of the gigantic nameless thing visible toward the last. One case, which the note describes with emphasis, was very sad. The subject, a widely known architect with leanings toward theosophy and occultism, went violently insane on the date of young Wilcox's seizure, and expired several months later after incessant screamings to be saved from some escaped denizen of hell. Had my uncle referred to these cases by name instead of merely by number, I should have attempted some corroboration and personal investigation; but as it was, I succeeded in tracing down only a few. All of these, however, bore out the notes in full. I have often wondered if all the objects of the professor's questioning felt as puzzled as did this fraction. It is well that no explanation shall ever reach them.

The press cuttings, as I have intimated, touched on cases of panic, mania, and eccentricity during the given period. Professor Angell must have employed a cutting bureau, for the number of extracts was tremendous and the sources scattered throughout the globe. Here was a nocturnal suicide in London, where a lone sleeper had leaped from a window after a shocking cry. Here likewise a rambling letter to the editor of a paper in South America, where a fanatic deduces a dire future from visions he has seen. A despatch from California describes a theosophist colony as donning white robes en masse for some "glorious fulfilment" which never arrives, whilst items from India speak guardedly of serious native unrest toward the end of March. Voodoo orgies multiply in Hayti, and African outposts report ominous mutterings. American officers in the Philippines find certain tribes bothersome about this time, and New York policemen are mobbed by hysterical Levantines on the night of March 22–23. The west of Ireland, too, is full of wild rumour and legendry, and a fantastic painter named Ardois-Bonnot hangs a blasphemous "Dream Landscape" in the Paris spring salon of 1926. And so numerous are the recorded troubles in insane asylums, that only a miracle can have stopped the medical fraternity from noting strange parallelisms and drawing mystified conclusions. A weird bunch of cuttings, all told; and I can at this date scarcely envisage the callous rationalism with which I set them aside. But I was then convinced that young Wilcox had known of the older matters mentioned by the professor.

II

The Tale of Inspector Legrasse

The older matters which had made the sculptor's dream and bas-relief so significant to my uncle formed the subject of the second half of his long manuscript. Once before, it appears, Professor Angell had seen the hellish outlines of the nameless monstrosity, puzzled over the unknown hieroglyphics, and heard the ominous syllables which can be rendered only as *"Cthulhu"*; and all this in so stirring and horrible a connexion that it is small wonder he pursued young Wilcox with queries and demands for data.

This earlier experience had come in 1908, seventeen years before, when the American Archaeological Society held its annual meeting in St. Louis. Professor Angell, as befitted one of his authority and attainments, had had a prominent part in all the deliberations; and was one of the first to be approached by the several outsiders who took advantage of the convocation to offer questions for correct answering and problems for expert solution.

The chief of these outsiders, and in a short time the focus of interest for the entire meeting, was a commonplace-looking middle-aged man who had travelled all the way from New Orleans for certain special information unobtainable from any local source. His name was John Raymond Legrasse, and he was by profession an Inspector of Police. With him he bore the subject of his visit, a grotesque, repulsive, and apparently very ancient stone statuette whose origin he was at a loss to deter-

mine. It must not be fancied that Inspector Legrasse had the least interest in archaeology. On the contrary, his wish for enlightenment was prompted by purely professional considerations. The statuette, idol, fetish, or whatever it was, had been captured some months before in the wooded swamps south of New Orleans during a
raid on a supposed voodoo meeting; and so singular and hideous were the rites connected with it, that the police could not but realise that they had stumbled on a dark
cult totally unknown to them, and infinitely more diabolic than even the blackest of
the African voodoo circles. Of its origin, apart from the erratic and unbelievable
tales extorted from the captured members, absolutely nothing was to be discovered;
hence the anxiety of the police for any antiquarian lore which might help them to
place the frightful symbol, and through it track down the cult to its fountain-head.

Inspector Legrasse was scarcely prepared for the sensation which his offering
created. One sight of the thing had been enough to throw the assembled men of science into a state of tense excitement, and they lost no time in crowding around him
to gaze at the diminutive figure whose utter strangeness and air of genuinely
abysmal antiquity hinted so potently at unopened and archaic vistas. No recognised
school of sculpture had animated this terrible object, yet centuries and even thousands of years seemed recorded in its dim and greenish surface of unplaceable
stone.

The figure, which was finally passed slowly from man to man for close and careful study, was between seven and eight inches in height, and of exquisitely artistic
workmanship. It represented a monster of vaguely anthropoid outline, but with an
octopus-like head whose face was a mass of feelers, a scaly, rubbery-looking body,
prodigious claws on hind and fore feet, and long, narrow wings behind. This thing,
which seemed instinct with a fearsome and unnatural malignancy, was of a somewhat bloated corpulence, and squatted evilly on a rectangular block or pedestal covered with undecipherable characters. The tips of the wings touched the back edge
of the block, the seat occupied the centre, whilst the long, curved claws of the
doubled-up, crouching hind legs gripped the front edge and extended a quarter of
the way down toward the bottom of the pedestal. The cephalopod head was bent
forward, so that the ends of the facial feelers brushed the backs of huge fore paws
which clasped the croucher's elevated knees. The aspect of the whole was abnor-
mally life-like, and the more subtly fearful because its source was so totally
unknown. Its vast, awesome, and incalculable age was unmistakable; yet not one
link did it shew with any known type of art belonging to civilisation's youth—or
indeed to any other time. Totally separate and apart, its very material was a mystery; for the soapy, greenish-black stone with its golden or iridescent flecks and stri-
ations resembled nothing familiar to geology or mineralogy. The characters along
the base were equally baffling; and no member present, despite a representation of
half the world's expert learning in this field, could form the least notion of even
their remotest linguistic kinship. They, like the subject and material, belonged to
something horribly remote and distinct from mankind as we know it; something
frightfully suggestive of old and unhallowed cycles of life in which our world and
our conceptions have no part.

And yet, as the members severally shook their heads and confessed defeat at the
Inspector's problem, there was one man in that gathering who suspected a touch of
bizarre familiarity in the monstrous shape and writing, and who presently told with
some diffidence of the odd trifle he knew. This person was the late William
Channing Webb, Professor of Anthropology in Princeton University, and an explorer

of no slight note. Professor Webb had been engaged, forty-eight years before, in a tour of Greenland and Iceland in search of some Runic inscriptions which he failed to unearth; and whilst high up on the West Greenland coast had encountered a singular tribe or cult of degenerate Esquimaux whose religion, a curious form of devil-worship, chilled him with its deliberate bloodthirstiness and repulsiveness. It was a faith of which other Esquimaux knew little, and which they mentioned only with shudders, saying that it had come down from horribly ancient aeons before ever the world was made. Besides nameless rites and human sacrifices there were certain queer hereditary rituals addressed to a supreme elder devil or *tornasuk;* and of this Professor Webb had taken a careful phonetic copy from an aged *angekok* or wizard-priest, expressing the sounds in Roman letters as best he knew how. But just now of prime significance was the fetish which this cult had cherished, and around which they danced when the aurora leaped high over the ice cliffs. It was, the professor stated, a very crude bas-relief of stone, comprising a hideous picture and some cryptic writing. And so far as he could tell, it was a rough parallel in all essential features of the bestial thing now lying before the meeting.

This data, received with suspense and astonishment by the assembled members, proved doubly exciting to Inspector Legrasse; and he began at once to ply his informant with questions. Having noted and copied an oral ritual among the swamp cult-worshippers his men had arrested, he besought the professor to remember as best he might the syllables taken down amongst the diabolist Esquimaux. There then followed an exhaustive comparison of details, and a moment of really awed silence when both detective and scientist agreed on the virtual identity of the phrase common to two hellish rituals so many worlds of distance apart. What, in substance, both the Esquimau wizards and the Louisiana swamp-priests had chanted to their kindred idols was something very like this—the word-divisions being guessed at from traditional breaks in the phrase as chanted aloud:

"Ph'nglui mglw'nafh Cthulhu R'lyeh wgah'nagl fhtagn."

Legrasse had one point in advance of Professor Webb, for several among his mongrel prisoners had repeated to him what older celebrants had told them the words meant. This text, as given, ran something like this:

"In his house at R'lyeh dead Cthulhu waits dreaming."

And now, in response to a general and urgent demand, Inspector Legrasse related as fully as possible his experience with the swamp worshippers; telling a story to which I could see my uncle attached profound significance. It savoured of the wildest dreams of myth-maker and theosophist, and disclosed an astonishing degree of cosmic imagination among such half-castes and pariahs as might be least expected to possess it.

On November 1st, 1907, there had come to New Orleans police a frantic summons from the swamp and lagoon country to the south. The squatters there, mostly primitive but good-natured descendants of Lafitte's men, were in the grip of stark terror from an unknown thing which had stolen upon them in the night. It was voodoo, apparently, but voodoo of a more terrible sort than they had ever known; and some of their women and children had disappeared since the malevolent tom-tom had begun its incessant beating far within the black haunted woods where no dweller ventured. There were insane shouts and harrowing screams, soul-chilling chants and dancing devil-flames; and, the frightened messenger added, the people could stand it no more.

So a body of twenty police, filling two carriages and an automobile, had set out

in the late afternoon with the shivering squatter as a guide. At the end of the pass-
able road they alighted, and for miles splashed on in silence through the terrible
cypress woods where day never came. Ugly roots and malignant hanging nooses of
Spanish moss beset them, and now and then a pile of dank stones or fragment of a
rotting wall intensified by its hint of morbid habitation a depression which every
malformed tree and every fungous islet combined to create. At length the squatter
settlement, a miserable huddle of huts, hove in sight; and hysterical dwellers ran
out to cluster around the group of bobbing lanterns. The muffled beat of tom-toms
was now faintly audible far, far ahead; and a curdling shriek came at infrequent
intervals when the wind shifted. A reddish glare, too, seemed to filter through the
pale undergrowth beyond endless avenues of forest night. Reluctant even to be left
alone again, each one of the cowed squatters refused point-blank to advance
another inch toward the scene of unholy worship, so Inspector Legrasse and his
nineteen colleagues plunged on unguided into black arcades of horror that none of
them had ever trod before.

The region now entered by the police was one of traditionally evil repute, substantially unknown and untraversed by white men. There were legends of a hidden
lake unglimpsed by mortal sight, in which dwelt a huge, formless white polypous
thing with luminous eyes; and squatters whispered that bat-winged devils flew up
out of caverns in inner earth to worship it at midnight. They said it had been there
before D'Iberville, before La Salle, before the Indians, and before even the wholesome beasts and birds of the woods. It was nightmare itself, and to see it was to die.
But it made men dream, and so they knew enough to keep away. The present voodoo
orgy was, indeed, on the merest fringe of this abhorred area, but that location was
bad enough; hence perhaps the very place of the worship had terrified the squatters
more than the shocking sounds and incidents.

Only poetry or madness could do justice to the noises heard by Legrasse's men
as they ploughed on through the black morass toward the red glare and the muffled
tom-toms. There are vocal qualities peculiar to men, and vocal qualities peculiar to
beasts; and it is terrible to hear the one when the source should yield the other.
Animal fury and orgiastic licence here whipped themselves to daemoniac heights by
howls and squawking ecstasies that tore and reverberated through those nighted
woods like pestilential tempests from the gulfs of hell. Now and then the less organized ululation would cease, and from what seemed a well-drilled chorus of hoarse
voices would rise in sing-song chant that hideous phrase or ritual:

"Ph'nglui mglw'nafh Cthulhu R'lyeh wgah'nagl fhtagn."

Then the men, having reached a spot where the trees were thinner, came suddenly
in sight of the spectacle itself. Four of them reeled, one fainted, and two were
shaken into a frantic cry which the mad cacophony of the orgy fortunately deadened. Legrasse dashed swamp water on the face of the fainting man, and all stood
trembling and nearly hypnotised with horror.

In a natural glade of the swamp stood a grassy island of perhaps an acre's
extent, clear of trees and tolerably dry. On this now leaped and twisted a more indescribable horde of human abnormality than any but a Sime or an Angarola could
paint. Void of clothing, this hybrid spawn were braying, bellowing, and writhing
about a monstrous ring-shaped bonfire; in the centre of which, revealed by occasional rifts in the curtain of flame, stood a great granite monolith some eight feet in
height; on top of which, incongruous in its diminutiveness, rested the noxious carven statuette. From a wide circle of ten scaffolds set up at regular intervals with the

flame-girt monolith as a centre hung, head downward, the oddly marred bodies of the helpless squatters who had disappeared. It was inside this circle that the ring of worshippers jumped and roared, the general direction of the mass motion being from left to right in endless Bacchanal between the ring of bodies and the ring of fire.

It may have been only imagination and it may have been only echoes which induced one of the men, an excitable Spaniard, to fancy he heard antiphonal responses to the ritual from some far and unillumined spot deeper within the wood of ancient legendry and horror. This man, Joseph D. Galvez, I later met and questioned; and he proved distractingly imaginative. He indeed went so far as to hint of the faint beating of great wings, and of a glimpse of shining eyes and a mountainous white bulk beyond the remotest trees—but I suppose he had been hearing too much native superstition.

Actually, the horrified pause of the men was of comparatively brief duration. Duty came first; and although there must have been nearly a hundred mongrel celebrants in the throng, the police relied on their firearms and plunged determinedly into the nauseous rout. For five minutes the resultant din and chaos were beyond description. Wild blows were struck, shots were fired, and escapes were made; but in the end Legrasse was able to count some forty-seven sullen prisoners, whom he forced to dress in haste and fall into line between two rows of policemen. Five of the worshippers lay dead, and two severely wounded ones were carried away on improvised stretchers by their fellow-prisoners. The image on the monolith, of course, was carefully removed and carried back by Legrasse.

Examined at headquarters after a trip of intense strain and weariness, the prisoners all proved to be men of a very low, mixed-blooded, and mentally aberrant type. Most were seamen, and a sprinkling of negroes and mulattoes, largely West Indians or Brava Portuguese from the Cape Verde Islands, gave a colouring of voodooism to the heterogeneous cult. But before many questions were asked, it became manifest that something far deeper and older than negro fetichism was involved. Degraded and ignorant as they were, the creatures held with surprising consistency to the central idea of their loathsome faith.

They worshipped, so they said, the Great Old Ones who lived ages before there were any men, and who came to the young world out of the sky. Those Old Ones were gone now, inside the earth and under the sea; but their dead bodies had told their secrets in dreams to the first men, who formed a cult which had never died. This was that cult, and the prisoners said it had always existed and always would exist, hidden in distant wastes and dark places all over the world until the time when the great priest Cthulhu, from his dark house in the mighty city of R'lyeh under the waters, should rise and bring the earth again beneath his sway. Some day he would call, when the stars were ready, and the secret cult would always be waiting to liberate him.

Meanwhile no more must be told. There was a secret which even torture could not extract. Mankind was not absolutely alone among the conscious things of earth, for shapes came out of the dark to visit the faithful few. But these were not the Great Old Ones. No man had ever seen the Old Ones. The carven idol was great Cthulhu, but none might say whether or not the others were precisely like him. No one could read the old writing now, but things were told by word of mouth. The chanted ritual was not the secret—that was never spoken aloud, only whispered. The chant meant only this: "In his house at R'lyeh dead Cthulhu waits dreaming."

Only two of the prisoners were found sane enough to be hanged, and the rest were committed to various institutions. All denied a part in the ritual murders, and averred that the killing had been done by Black Winged Ones which had come to them from their immemorial meeting-place in the haunted wood. But of those mysterious allies no coherent account could ever be gained. What the police did extract, came mainly from an immensely aged mestizo named Castro, who claimed to have sailed to strange ports and talked with undying leaders of the cult in the mountains of China.

Old Castro remembered bits of hideous legend that paled the speculations of theosophists and made man and the world seem recent and transient indeed. There had been aeons when other Things ruled on the earth, and They had had great cities. Remains of Them, he said the deathless Chinamen had told him, were still to be found as Cyclopean stones on islands in the Pacific. They all died vast epochs of time before men came, but there were arts which could revive Them when the stars had come round again to the right positions in the cycle of eternity. They had, indeed, come themselves from the stars, and brought Their images with Them.

These Great Old Ones, Castro continued, were not composed altogether of flesh and blood. They had shape—for did not this star-fashioned image prove it?—but that shape was not made of matter. When the stars were right, They could plunge from world to world through the sky; but when the stars were wrong, They could not live. But although They no longer lived, They would never really die. They all lay in stone houses in Their great city of R'lyeh, preserved by the spells of mighty Cthulhu for a glorious resurrection when the stars and the earth might once more be ready for Them. But at that time some force from outside must serve to liberate Their bodies. The spells that preserved Them intact likewise prevented Them from making an initial move, and They could only lie awake in the dark and think whilst uncounted millions of years rolled by. They knew all that was occurring in the universe, for Their mode of speech was transmitted thought. Even now They talked in Their tombs. When, after infinities of chaos, the first men came, the Great Old Ones spoke to the sensitive among them by moulding their dreams; for only thus could Their language reach the fleshly minds of mammals.

Then, whispered Castro, those first men formed the cult around small idols which the Great Ones shewed them; idols brought in dim aeras from dark stars. That cult would never die till the stars came right again, and the secret priests would take great Cthulhu from His tomb to revive His subjects and resume His rule of earth. The time would be easy to know, for then mankind would have become as the Great Old Ones; free and wild and beyond good and evil, with laws and morals thrown aside and all men shouting and killing and revelling in joy. Then the liberated Old Ones would teach them new ways to shout and kill and revel and enjoy themselves, and all the earth would flame with a holocaust of ecstasy and freedom. Meanwhile the cult, by appropriate rites, must keep alive the memory of those ancient ways and shadow forth the prophecy of their return.

In the elder time chosen men had talked with the entombed Old Ones in dreams, but then something had happened. The great stone city R'lyeh, with its monoliths and sepulchres, had sunk beneath the waves; and the deep waters, full of the one primal mystery through which not even thought can pass, had cut off the spectral intercourse. But memory never died, and high-priests said that the city would rise again when the stars were right. Then came out of the earth the black spirits of earth, mouldy and shadowy, and full of dim rumours picked up in caverns beneath forgotten sea-bottoms. But of them old Castro dared not speak much. He cut himself off hurriedly, and no amount of persuasion or subtlety could elicit more in this direction. The *size* of the Old Ones, too, he curiously declined to mention. Of the cult, he said that he thought the centre lay amidst the pathless deserts of Arabia, where Irem, the City of Pillars, dreams hidden and untouched. It was not allied to the European witch-cult, and was virtually unknown beyond its members. No book had ever really hinted of it, though the deathless Chinamen said that there were double meanings in the *Necronomicon* of the mad Arab Abdul Alhazred which the initiated might read as they chose, especially the much-discussed couplet:

> *"That is not dead which can eternal lie,*
> *And with strange aeons even death may die."*

Legrasse, deeply impressed and not a little bewildered, had inquired in vain concerning the historic affiliations of the cult. Castro, apparently, had told the truth when he said that it was wholly secret. The authorities at Tulane University could shed no light upon either cult or image, and now the detective had come to the highest authorities in the country and met with no more than the Greenland tale of Professor Webb.

The feverish interest aroused at the meeting by Legrasse's tale, corroborated as it was by the statuette, is echoed in the subsequent correspondence of those who attended; although scant mention occurs in the formal publications of the society. Caution is the first care of those accustomed to face occasional charlatanry and imposture. Legrasse for some time lent the image to Professor Webb, but at the latter's death it was returned to him and remains in his possession, where I viewed it not long ago. It is truly a terrible thing, and unmistakably akin to the dream-sculpture of young Wilcox.

That my uncle was excited by the tale of the sculptor I did not wonder, for what thoughts must arise upon hearing, after a knowledge of what Legrasse had learned of the cult, of a sensitive young man who had *dreamed* not only the figure and exact hieroglyphics of the swamp-found image and the Greenland devil tablet, but had come *in his dreams* upon at least three of the precise words of the formula uttered alike by Esquimau diabolists and mongrel Louisianans? Professor Angell's instant start on an investigation of the utmost thoroughness was eminently natural; though privately I suspected young Wilcox of having heard of the cult in some indirect way, and of having invented a series of dreams to heighten and continue the mystery at my uncle's expense. The dream-narratives and cuttings collected by the professor were, of course, strong corroboration; but the rationalism of my mind and the extravagance of the whole subject led me to adopt what I thought the most sensible conclusions. So, after thoroughly studying the manuscript again and correlating the theosophical and anthropological notes with the cult narrative of Legrasse, I made a trip to Providence to see the sculptor and give him the rebuke I thought proper for so boldly imposing upon a learned and aged man.

Wilcox still lived alone in the Fleur-de-Lys Building in Thomas Street, a hideous Victorian imitation of seventeenth-century Breton architecture which flaunts its stuccoed front amidst the lovely colonial houses on the ancient hill, and under the very shadow of the finest Georgian steeple in America. I found him at work in his rooms, and at once conceded from the specimens scattered about that his genius is indeed profound and authentic. He will, I believe, some time be heard from as one of the great decadents; for he has crystallised in clay and will one day mirror in marble those nightmares and phantasies which Arthur Machen evokes in prose, and Clark Ashton Smith makes visible in verse and in painting.

Dark, frail, and somewhat unkempt in aspect, he turned languidly at my knock and asked me my business without rising. When I told him who I was, he displayed some interest; for my uncle had excited his curiosity in probing his strange dreams, yet had never explained the reason for the study. I did not enlarge his knowledge in this regard, but sought with some subtlety to draw him out. In a short time I became convinced of his absolute sincerity, for he spoke of the dreams in a manner none could mistake. They and their subconscious residuum had influenced his art profoundly, and he shewed me a morbid statue whose contours almost made me shake with the potency of its black suggestion. He could not recall having seen the original of this thing except in his own dream bas-relief, but the outlines had formed themselves insensibly under his hands. It was, no doubt, the giant shape he had raved of in delirium. That he really knew nothing of the hidden cult, save from what my uncle's relentless catechism had let fall, he soon made clear; and again I strove to think of some way in which he could possibly have received the weird impressions.

He talked of his dreams in a strangely poetic fashion; making me see with terrible vividness the damp Cyclopean city of slimy green stone—whose *geometry,* he oddly said, was *all wrong*—and hear with frightened expectancy the ceaseless, half-mental calling from underground: *"Cthulhu fhtagn," "Cthulhu fhtagn."* These words had formed part of that dread ritual which told of dead Cthulhu's dream-vigil in his stone vault at R'lyeh, and I felt deeply moved despite my rational beliefs. Wilcox, I was sure, had heard of the cult in some casual way, and had soon forgotten it amidst the mass of his equally weird reading and imagining. Later, by virtue of its sheer impressiveness, it had found subconscious expression in dreams, in the bas-relief, and in the terrible statue I now beheld; so that his imposture upon my uncle had been a very innocent one. The youth was of a type, at once slightly affected and slightly ill-mannered, which I could never like; but I was willing enough now to admit both his genius and his honesty. I took leave of him amicably, and wish him all the success his talent promises.

The matter of the cult still remained to fascinate me, and at times I had visions of personal fame from researches into its origin and connexions. I visited New Orleans, talked with Legrasse and others of that old-time raiding-party, saw the frightful image, and even questioned such of the mongrel prisoners as still survived. Old Castro, unfortunately, had been dead for some years. What I now heard so graphically at first-hand, though it was really no more than a detailed confirmation of what my uncle had written, excited me afresh; for I felt sure that I was on the track of a very real, very secret, and very ancient religion whose discovery would make me an anthropologist of note. My attitude was still one of absolute materialism, *as I wish it still were,* and I discounted with almost inexplicable perversity the coincidence of the dream notes and odd cuttings collected by Professor Angell.

One thing I began to suspect, and which I now fear I *know,* is that my uncle's death was far from natural. He fell on a narrow hill street leading up from an ancient waterfront swarming with foreign mongrels, after a careless push from a negro sailor. I did not forget the mixed blood and marine pursuits of the cult-members in Louisiana, and would not be surprised to learn of secret methods and poison needles as ruthless and as anciently known as the cryptic rites and beliefs. Legrasse and his men, it is true, have been let alone; but in Norway a certain seaman who saw things is dead. Might not the deeper inquiries of my uncle after encountering the sculptor's data have come to sinister ears? I think Professor Angell died because he knew too much, or because he was likely to learn too much. Whether I shall go as he did remains to be seen, for I have learned much now.

III

The Madness from the Sea

If heaven ever wishes to grant me a boon, it will be a total effacing of the results of a mere chance which fixed my eye on a certain stray piece of shelf-paper. It was nothing on which I would naturally have stumbled in the course of my daily round, for it was an old number of an Australian journal, the *Sydney Bulletin* for April 18, 1925. It had escaped even the cutting bureau which had at the time of its issuance been avidly collecting material for my uncle's research.

I had largely given over my inquiries into what Professor Angell called the "Cthulhu Cult," and was visiting a learned friend in Paterson, New Jersey; the curator of a local museum and a mineralogist of note. Examining one day the reserve specimens roughly set on the storage shelves in a rear room of the museum, my eye was caught by an odd picture in one of the old papers spread beneath the stones. It was the *Sydney Bulletin* I have mentioned, for my friend has wide affiliations in all conceivable foreign parts; and the picture was a half-tone cut of a hideous stone image almost identical with that which Legrasse had found in the swamp.

Eagerly clearing the sheet of its precious contents, I scanned the item in detail; and was disappointed to find it of only moderate length. What it suggested, however, was of portentous significance to my flagging quest; and I carefully tore it out for immediate action. It read as follows:

MYSTERY DERELICT FOUND AT SEA
Vigilant Arrives With Helpless Armed New Zealand Yacht in Tow.
One Survivor and Dead Man Found Aboard. Tale of
Desperate Battle and Deaths at Sea.
Rescued Seaman Refuses
Particulars of Strange Experience.
Odd Idol Found in His Possession. Inquiry
to Follow.

The Morrison Co.'s freighter *Vigilant,* bound from Valparaiso, arrived this morning at its wharf in Darling Harbour, having in tow the battled and disabled but heavily armed steam yacht *Alert* of Dunedin, N.Z., which was sighted April 12th in S. Latitude 34° 21', W. Longitude 152° 17' with one living and one dead man aboard.

The *Vigilant* left Valparaiso March 25th, and on April 2nd was driven considerably south of her course by exceptionally heavy storms and monster waves. On April 12th the derelict was sighted; and though apparently deserted, was found upon boarding to contain one survivor in a half-delirious condition and one man who had evidently been dead for more than a week. The living man was clutching a horrible stone idol of unknown origin, about a foot in height, regarding whose nature authorities at Sydney University, the Royal Society, and the Museum in College Street all profess complete bafflement, and which the survivor says he found in the cabin of the yacht, in a small carved shrine of common pattern.

This man, after recovering his senses, told an exceedingly strange story of piracy and slaughter. He is Gustaf Johansen, a Norwegian of some intelligence, and had been second mate of the two-masted schooner *Emma* of Auckland, which sailed for Callao February 20th with a complement of eleven men. The *Emma,* he says, was delayed and thrown widely south of her course by the great storm of March 1st, and on March 22nd, in S. Latitude 49° 51', W. Longitude 128° 34', encountered the *Alert,* manned by a queer and evil-looking crew of Kanakas and half-castes. Being ordered peremptorily to turn back, Capt. Collins refused; whereupon the strange crew began to fire savagely and without warning upon the schooner with a peculiarly heavy battery of brass cannon forming part of the yacht's equipment. The *Emma*'s men shewed fight, says the survivor, and though the schooner began to sink from shots beneath the waterline they managed to heave alongside their enemy and board her, grappling with the savage crew on the yacht's deck, and being forced to kill them all, the number being slightly superior, because of their particularly abhorrent and desperate though rather clumsy mode of fighting.

Three of the *Emma*'s men, including Capt. Collins and First Mate Green, were killed; and the remaining eight under Second Mate Johansen proceeded to navigate the captured yacht, going ahead in their original direction to see if any reason for their ordering back had existed. The next day, it appears, they raised and landed on a small island, although none is known to exist in that part of the ocean; and six of the men somehow died ashore, though Johansen is queerly reticent about this part of his story, and speaks only of their falling into a rock chasm. Later, it seems, he and one companion boarded the yacht and tried to manage her, but were beaten about by the storm of April 2nd. From that time till his rescue on the 12th the man remembers little, and he does not even recall when William Briden, his companion, died. Briden's death reveals no apparent cause, and was probably due to excitement or exposure. Cable advices from Dunedin report that the *Alert* was well known there as an island trader, and bore an evil reputation along the waterfront. It was owned by a curious group of half-castes whose frequent meetings and night trips to the woods attracted no little curiosity; and it had set sail in great haste just after the storm and earth tremors of March 1st. Our Auckland correspondent gives the *Emma* and her crew an excellent reputation, and Johansen is described as a sober and worthy man. The admiralty will institute an inquiry on the whole matter beginning tomorrow, at which every effort will be made to induce Johansen to speak more freely than he has done hitherto.

This was all, together with the picture of the hellish image; but what a train of ideas it started in my mind! Here were new treasuries of data on the Cthulhu Cult, and evidence that it had strange interests at sea as well as on land. What motive prompted the hybrid crew to order back the *Emma* as they sailed about with their hideous idol? What was the unknown island on which six of the *Emma*'s crew had died, and about which the mate Johansen was so secretive? What had the vice-admiralty's investigation brought out, and what was known of the noxious cult in Dunedin? And most marvellous of all, what deep and more than natural linkage of dates was this which gave a malign and now undeniable significance to the various turns of events so carefully noted by my uncle?

March 1st—our February 28th according to the International Date Line—the earthquake and storm had come. From Dunedin the *Alert* and her noisome crew had darted eagerly forth as if imperiously summoned, and on the other side of the earth poets and artists had begun to dream of a strange, dank Cyclopean city whilst a young sculptor had moulded in his sleep the form of the dreaded Cthulhu. March 23rd the crew of the *Emma* landed on an unknown island and left six men dead; and on that date the dreams of sensitive men assumed a heightened vividness and darkened with dread of a giant monster's malign pursuit, whilst an architect had gone mad and a sculptor had lapsed suddenly into delirium! And what of this storm of April 2nd—the date on which all dreams of the dank city ceased, and Wilcox emerged unharmed from the bondage of strange fever? What of all this—and of those hints of old Castro about the sunken, star-born Old Ones and their coming reign; their faithful cult *and their mastery of dreams?* Was I tottering on the brink of cosmic horrors beyond man's power to bear? If so, they must be horrors of the mind alone, for in some way the second of April had put a stop to whatever monstrous menace had begun its siege of mankind's soul.

That evening, after a day of hurried cabling and arranging, I bade my host adieu and took a train for San Francisco. In less than a month I was in Dunedin; where, however, I found that little was known of the strange cult-members who had lingered in the old sea-taverns. Waterfront scum was far too common for special mention; though there was vague talk about one inland trip these mongrels had made, during which faint drumming and red flame were noted on the distant hills. In Auckland I learned that Johansen had returned *with yellow hair turned white* after a perfunctory and inconclusive questioning at Sydney, and had thereafter sold his cottage in West Street and sailed with his wife to his old home in Oslo. Of his stirring experience he would tell his friends no more than he had told the admiralty officials, and all they could do was to give me his Oslo address.

After that I went to Sydney and talked profitlessly with seamen and members of the vice-admiralty court. I saw the *Alert,* now sold and in commercial use, at Circular Quay in Sydney Cove, but gained nothing from its non-committal bulk. The crouching image with its cuttlefish head, dragon body, scaly wings, and hieroglyphed pedestal, was preserved in the Museum at Hyde Park; and I studied it long and well, finding it a thing of balefully exquisite workmanship, and with the same utter mystery, terrible antiquity, and unearthly strangeness of material which I had noted in Legrasse's smaller specimen. Geologists, the curator told me, had found it a monstrous puzzle; for they vowed that the world held no rock like it. Then I thought with a shudder of what old Castro had told Legrasse about the primal Great Ones: "They had come from the stars, and had brought Their images with Them."

Shaken with such a mental revolution as I had never before known, I now resolved to visit Mate Johansen in Oslo. Sailing for London, I reëmbarked at once for the Norwegian capital; and one autumn day landed at the trim wharves in the shadow of the Egeberg. Johansen's address, I discovered, lay in the Old Town of King Harold Haardrada, which kept alive the name of Oslo during all the centuries that the greater city masqueraded as "Christiania." I made the brief trip by taxicab, and knocked with palpitant heart at the door of a neat and ancient building with plastered front. A sad-faced woman in black answered my summons, and I was stung with disappointment when she told me in halting English that Gustaf Johansen was no more.

He had not long survived his return, said his wife, for the doings at sea in 1925 had broken him. He had told her no more than he had told the public, but had left a long manuscript—of "technical matters" as he said—written in English, evidently in order to safeguard her from the peril of casual perusal. During a walk through a narrow lane near the Gothenburg dock, a bundle of papers falling from an attic window had knocked him down. Two Lascar sailors at once helped him to his feet, but before the ambulance could reach him he was dead. Physicians found no adequate cause for the end, and laid it to heart trouble and a weakened constitution.

I now felt gnawing at my vitals that dark terror which will never leave me till I, too, am at rest; "accidentally" or otherwise. Persuading the widow that my connexion with her husband's "technical matters" was sufficient to entitle me to his manuscript, I bore the document away and began to read it on the London boat. It was a simple, rambling thing—a naive sailor's effort at a postfacto diary—and strove to recall day by day that last awful voyage. I cannot attempt to transcribe it verbatim in all its cloudiness and redundance, but I will tell its gist enough to shew why the sound of the water against the vessel's sides became so unendurable to me that I stopped my ears with cotton.

Johansen, thank God, did not know quite all, even though he saw the city and the Thing, but I shall never sleep calmly again when I think of the horrors that lurk ceaselessly behind life in time and in space, and of those unhallowed blasphemies from elder stars which dream beneath the sea, known and favoured by a nightmare cult ready and eager to loose them on the world whenever another earthquake shall heave their monstrous stone city again to the sun and air.

Johansen's voyage had begun just as he told it to the vice-admiralty. The *Emma,* in ballast, had cleared Auckland on February 20th, and had felt the full force of that earthquake-born tempest which must have heaved up from the sea-bottom the horrors that filled men's dreams. Once more under control, the ship was making good progress when held up by the *Alert* on March 22nd, and I could feel the mate's regret as he wrote of her bombardment and sinking. Of the swarthy cult-fiends on the *Alert* he speaks with significant horror. There was some peculiarly abominable quality about them which made their destruction seem almost a duty, and Johansen shows ingenuous wonder at the charge of ruthlessness brought against his party during the proceedings of the court of inquiry. Then, driven ahead by curiosity in their captured yacht under Johansen's command, the men sight a great stone pillar sticking out of the sea, and in S. Latitude 47° 9', W. Longitude 126° 43' come upon a coast-line of mingled mud, ooze, and weedy Cyclopean masonry which can be nothing less than the tangible substance of earth's supreme terror—the nightmare corpse-city of R'lyeh, that was built in measureless aeons behind history by the vast, loathsome shapes that seeped down from the dark stars. There lay great Cthulhu and his hordes, hidden in green slimy vaults and sending out at last, after cycles incalculable, the thoughts that spread fear to the dreams of the sensitive and called imperiously to the faithful to come on a pilgrimage of liberation and restoration. All this Johansen did not suspect, but God knows he soon saw enough!

I suppose that only a single mountain-top, the hideous monolith-crowned citadel whereon great Cthulhu was buried, actually emerged from the waters. When I think of the *extent* of all that may be brooding down there I almost wish to kill myself forthwith. Johansen and his men were awed by the cosmic majesty of this dripping Babylon of elder daemons, and must have guessed without guidance that it was nothing of this or of any sane planet. Awe at the unbelievable size of the greenish stone blocks, at the dizzying height of the great carven monolith, and at the stupefying identity of the colossal statues and bas-reliefs with the queer image found in the shrine on the *Alert,* is poignantly visible in every line of the mate's frightened description.

Without knowing what futurism is like, Johansen achieved something very close to it when he spoke of the city; for instead of describing any definite structure or building, he dwells only on broad impressions of vast angles and stone surfaces— surfaces too great to belong to any thing right or proper for this earth, and impious with horrible images and hieroglyphs. I mention his talk about *angles* because it suggests something Wilcox had told me of his awful dreams. He had said that the *geometry* of the dream-place he saw was abnormal, non-Euclidean, and loathsomely redolent of spheres and dimensions apart from ours. Now an unlettered seaman felt the same thing whilst gazing at the terrible reality.

Johansen and his men landed at a sloping mud-bank on this monstrous Acropolis, and clambered slipperily up over titan oozy blocks which could have been no mortal staircase. The very sun of heaven seemed distorted when viewed through the polarising miasma welling out from this sea-soaked perversion, and twisted menace and suspense lurked leeringly in those crazily elusive angles of carven rock where a second glance shewed concavity after the first shewed convexity.

Something very like fright had come over all the explorers before anything more definite than rock and ooze and weed was seen. Each would have fled had he not feared the scorn of the others, and it was only half-heartedly that they searched— vainly, as it proved—for some portable souvenir to bear away.

It was Rodriguez the Portuguese who climbed up the foot of the monolith and shouted of what he had found. The rest followed him, and looked curiously at the immense carved door with the now familiar squid-dragon bas-relief. It was, Johansen said, like a great barn-door; and they all felt that it was a door because of the ornate lintel, threshold, and jambs around it, though they could not decide whether it lay flat like a trap-door or slantwise like an outside cellar-door. As Wilcox would have said, the geometry of the place was all wrong. One could not be sure that the sea and the ground were horizontal, hence the relative position of everything else seemed phantasmally variable.

Briden pushed at the stone in several places without result. Then Donovan felt over it delicately around the edge, pressing each point separately as he went. He climbed interminably along the grotesque stone moulding—that is, one would call it climbing if the thing was not after all horizontal—and the men wondered how any door in the universe could be so vast. Then, very softly and slowly, the acre-great panel began to give inward at the top; and they saw that it was balanced. Donovan slid or somehow propelled himself down or along the jamb and rejoined his fellows, and everyone watched the queer recession of the monstrously carven portal. In this phantasy of prismatic distortion it moved anomalously in a diagonal way, so that all the rules of matter and perspective seemed upset.

The aperture was black with a darkness almost material. That tenebrousness was indeed a *positive quality;* for it obscured such parts of the inner walls as ought to have been revealed, and actually burst forth like smoke from its aeon-long imprisonment, visibly darkening the sun as it slunk away into the shrunken and gibbous sky on flapping membraneous wings. The odour arising from the newly opened depths was intolerable, and at length the quick-eared Hawkins thought he heard a nasty, slopping sound down there. Everyone listened, and everyone was listening still when It lumbered slobberingly into sight and gropingly squeezed Its gelatinous green immensity through the black doorway into the tainted outside air of that poison city of madness.

Poor Johansen's handwriting almost gave out when he wrote of this. Of the six men who never reached the ship, he thinks two perished of pure fright in that accursed instant. The Thing cannot be described—there is no language for such abysms of shrieking and immemorial lunacy, such eldritch contradictions of all matter, force, and cosmic order. A mountain walked or stumbled. God! What wonder that across the earth a great architect went mad, and poor Wilcox raved with fever in that telepathic instant? The Thing of the idols, the green, sticky spawn of the stars, had awaked to claim his own. The stars were right again, and what an age-old cult had failed to do by design, a band of innocent sailors had done by accident. After vigintillions of years great Cthulhu was loose again, and ravening for delight.

Three men were swept up by the flabby claws before anybody turned. God rest them, if there be any rest in the universe. They were Donovan, Guerrera, and Ångstrom. Parker slipped as the other three were plunging frenziedly over endless vistas of green-crusted rock to the boat, and Johansen swears he was swallowed up by an angle of masonry which shouldn't have been there; an angle which was acute, but behaved as if it were obtuse. So only Briden and Johansen reached the boat, and pulled desperately for the *Alert* as the mountainous monstrosity flopped down the slimy stones and hesitated floundering at the edge of the water.

Steam had not been suffered to go down entirely, despite the departure of all hands for the shore; and it was the work of only a few moments of feverish rushing up and down between wheel and engines to get the *Alert* under way. Slowly, amidst the distorted horrors of that indescribable scene, she began to churn the lethal waters; whilst on the masonry of that charnel shore that was not of earth the titan Thing from the stars slavered and gibbered like Polypheme cursing the fleeing ship of Odysseus. Then, bolder than the storied Cyclops, great Cthulhu slid greasily into the water and began to pursue with vast wave-raising strokes of cosmic potency. Briden looked back and went mad, laughing shrilly as he kept on laughing at intervals till death found him one night in the cabin whilst Johansen was wandering deliriously.

But Johansen had not given out yet. Knowing that the Thing could surely overtake the *Alert* until steam was fully up, he resolved on a desperate chance; and, setting the engine for full speed, ran lightning-like on deck and reversed the wheel. There was a mighty eddying and foaming in the noisome brine, and as the steam mounted higher and higher the brave Norwegian drove his vessel head on against the pursuing jelly which rose above the unclean froth like the stern of a daemon galleon. The awful squid-head with writhing feelers came nearly up to the bowsprit of the sturdy yacht, but Johansen drove on relentlessly. There was a bursting as of an exploding bladder, a slushy nastiness as of a cloven sunfish, a stench as of a thousand opened graves, and a sound that the chronicler would not put on paper. For an instant the ship was befouled by an acrid and blinding green cloud, and then there was only a venomous seething astern; where—God in heaven!—the scattered plasticity of that nameless sky-spawn was nebulously *recombining* in its hateful original form, whilst its distance widened every second as the *Alert* gained impetus from its mounting steam.

That was all. After that Johansen only brooded over the idol in the cabin and attended to a few matters of food for himself and the laughing maniac by his side. He did not try to navigate after the first bold flight, for the reaction had taken something out of his soul. Then came the storm of April 2nd, and a gathering of the clouds about his consciousness. There is a sense of spectral whirling through liquid gulfs of infinity, of dizzying rides through reeling universes on a comet's tail, and of hysterical plunges from the pit to the moon and from the moon back again to the pit, all livened by a cachinnating chorus of the distorted, hilarious elder gods and the green, bat-winged mocking imps of Tartarus.

Out of that dream came rescue—the *Vigilant,* the vice-admiralty court, the streets of Dunedin, and the long voyage back home to the old house by the Egeberg. He could not tell—they would think him mad. He would write of what he knew before death came, but his wife must not guess. Death would be a boon if only it could blot out the memories.

That was the document I read, and now I have placed it in the tin box beside the bas-relief and the papers of Professor Angell. With it shall go this record of mine— this test of my own sanity, wherein is pieced together that which I hope may never be pieced together again. I have looked upon all that the universe has to hold of horror, and even the skies of spring and the flowers of summer must ever afterward be poison to me. But I do not think my life will be long. As my uncle went, as poor Johansen went, so I shall go. I know too much, and the cult still lives.

Cthulhu still lives, too, I suppose, again in that chasm of stone which has shielded him since the sun was young. His accursed city is sunken once more, for the *Vigilant* sailed over the spot after the April storm; but his ministers on earth still bellow and prance and slay around idol-capped monoliths in lonely places. He must have been trapped by the sinking whilst within his black abyss, or else the world would by now be screaming with fright and frenzy. Who knows the end? What has risen may sink, and what has sunk may rise. Loathsomeness waits and dreams in the deep, and decay spreads over the tottering cities of men. A time will come—but I must not and cannot think! Let me pray that, if I do not survive this manuscript, my executors may put caution before audacity and see that it meets no other eye.

—1928

STEPHEN KING

B. 1947

Stephen King was born in Portland, Maine, to Donald King and Nellie Ruth (Pillsbury) King. When King was two years old, his father, who served in the Merchant Marine during World War II, abandoned the family, which included Stephen, his mother, and the Kings' adopted son, David. In 1958, the King family relocated to Durham, Maine, and a year later, Stephen began submitting fiction to several professional science fiction magazines. After graduating from his high school at Lisbon Falls, Maine, in 1966, he attended the University of Maine at Orono from 1966 to 1970 (graduating with a Bachelor of Science degree in English), and wrote for the school newspaper. King married Tabitha Spruce, a fellow student at college, in 1971. He published his first professional story, "The Glass Floor," in Startling Mystery Stories in 1967. Through the early 1970s, King sold a number of short stories to the "men's magazine" market and continued to write several novels for which he could not find a publisher until years later when they finally appeared under his "Richard Bachman" pseudonym. Between 1971 and 1973 King secured a job as a teacher at Hampden Academy in Maine. He moved with his wife and daughter to Boulder, Colorado in 1974 and finally published his novel, Carrie, in the same year. (Carrie was later to be made into a popular film directed by Brian De Palma in 1976.) Following the release of 'Salem's Lot (1975) and The Shining (1977), King's popularity was assured.

In 1978, King was an English Department writer-in-residence at the University of Maine at Orono, during which time he began developing ideas for his major analysis of the modern horror genre in print, film, television, and radio—a lengthy monograph entitled Danse Macabre (1981). In 1980, King moved to Bangor, Maine, which remains his primary residence. As each successive book appeared in print—The Stand (1978), Night Shift (1978), The Dead Zone (1979), Firestarter (1980), Cujo (1981), The Dark Tower: The Gunslinger (1982), Different Seasons (1982), Christine (1983), Pet Sematary (1983), The Talisman (co-authored with Peter Straub; 1984), Thinner (a "Richard Bachman" novel; 1984), Skeleton Crew (1985), It (1986), The Dark Tower II: The Drawing of the Three (1987), Eyes of the Dragon (1987), Misery (1987), The Tommyknockers (1987), The Dark Half (1989), Four Past Midnight (1990), Dark Tower III: The Waste Lands (1991), Needful Things (1991), Gerald's Game (1992), Dolores Claiborne (1993), Nightmares & Dreamscapes (1993), Insomnia (1994), Rose Madder (1995), The Green Mile (1996), Desperation (1996), and The Regulators (the most recent "Richard Bachman" novel; 1996)—King not only became one of the most financially successful authors of horror fiction, but one of the most commercially successful authors of all time. His work was instrumental in elevating the horror novel to best-seller status, and he has the distinction of placing a number one best-seller on the New York Times' hardcover list and paperback list simultaneously. Perhaps his greatest contribution to modern horror fiction (and the reason for his great success) has been his willingness to deal with such important contemporary social issues as spouse abuse and child victimization in his writing. His stories have been translated into popular motion picture and television adaptations. King himself has written a number of film and television screenplays; in addition, he has both written and directed a 1986 horror movie, Maximum Overdrive.

King's famous essay, "The Horror Market Writer and the Ten Bears," first published in the November 1973 Writer's Digest, nicely outlines what he considers to be the ten most frightening motifs of horror fiction. In one of King's earlier short stories entitled "Graveyard Shift," which first appeared in the October 1970 issue of Cavalier and later was anthologized in Night Shift, he effectively practices what he preaches. The film, Graveyard Shift (1990), directed by Ralph S. Singleton, is loosely based on this tale.

THE HORROR MARKET WRITER
AND THE TEN BEARS

At parties, people usually approach the writer of horror fiction with a mixture of wonder and trepidation. They look carefully into your eyes to make sure there's no overt bloodlust in them, and then ask the inevitable question: "I really liked your last story . . . where do you get your ideas?"

That question is common to any writer who works in a specialized genre, whether it's mystery, crime, western or science fiction. But it's delivered in different tones for different fields. It's directed to the mystery writer with real admiration, the way you'd ask a magician how he sawed the lady in half. It's directed to the science fiction writer with honest respect for a fellow who is so farseeing and visionary. But it is addressed to the horror writer with a sense of fascinated puzzlement—the way a lady reporter might ask mild-mannered Henri Landru how it feels to do away with all those wives. Most of us, you see, look and seem (and *are*) perfectly ordinary. We don't drown houseguests in the bathtub, torture the children, or sacrifice the cat at midnight inside of a pentagram. There are no locked closets or screams from the cellar. Robert Bloch, author of *Psycho,* looks like a moderately successful used car salesman. Ray Bradbury bears an uncomfortable resemblance to Charles M. Schultz, creator of *Peanuts.* And the writer generally acknowledged to be the greatest master of the horror tale in the twentieth century, H. P. Lovecraft, looked like nothing so much as a slightly overworked accountant.

So where do the ideas—the *salable* ideas—come from? For myself, the answer is simple enough. They come from my nightmares. Not the night-time variety, as a rule, but the ones that hide just beyond the doorway that separates the conscious from the unconscious. A good assumption to begin with is what scares you will scare someone else. A psychologist would call these nightmares phobias, but I think there's a better word for our purposes.

Joseph Stefano, who wrote the screenplay for *Psycho* and who produced a mid-sixties television series called *The Outer Limits,* calls these fears "bears." It's a good term for the aspiring writer of horror fiction to use, because it gets across the idea that general phobias have to be focused on concrete plot ideas before you can hope to scare the reader—and that's the name of the game. So before we go any further, let's take a few bears—ones we're all familiar with. You may want to rearrange some of the items on my list, or throw out a few and add some of the skeletons in your own closet. But for purposes of discussion, here is my own top ten.

1. Fear of the dark
2. Fear of squishy things
3. Fear of deformity
4. Fear of snakes
5. Fear of rats
6. Fear of closed-in places
7. Fear of insects (especially spiders, flies, beetles)
8. Fear of death
9. Fear of others (paranoia)
10. Fear *for* someone else

The bears can be combined, too. I took a #1 and #10 and wrote a story called "The Boogeyman," which sold to *Cavalier* magazine. For me, fear of the dark has always focused on a childhood fear: the awful Thing which hides in the closet when you're small, or sometimes curls up under the bed, waiting for you to stick a foot out under the covers. As an adult looking back on those feelings (not that we ever conquer them completely—all those of you out there who don't have a bedroom lamp within reach of your hand please stand up), it seemed to me that the most frightening thing about them was the fact that grown-ups don't understand it very well—they forget how it is. Mother comes in, turns on the light, smiles, opens the closet (the Thing is hiding behind your clothes, well out of sight—it's sly) and says, "See, dear? There's nothing to be afraid of." And as soon as she's gone, the Thing crawls back out of the closet and begins to leap and gibber in the shadows again. I wrote a story about a man who finds out that his three children, who have all died of seemingly natural causes, have been frightened to death by the boogeyman—who is a very real, very frightening monster. The story takes a childhood fear and saddles an adult with it; puts him back into that dreamlike world of childhood where the monsters *don't* go away when you change the channel, but crawl out and hide under the bed.

About two years ago I decided that the scariest things going would be rats—great big #5's, breeding in the darkness under a deserted textile mill. In this case, I began with the fear and built the plot (including the deserted mill) to fit it. The story climaxed with the main character being overwhelmed by these giant rats in the dark and enclosed subcellar of the mill (slyly hedging my main bet by working in a generous dose of #1 and #6). I felt sorry for the poor guy—the thought of being overrun by giant rats frankly made my blood run cold—but I made $250 on the sale and managed to take one of my own pet fears for a walk in the sun at the same time. One of the nice things about working in this field is that, instead of paying a shrink to help you get rid of your fears, a magazine will pay you for doing the same thing.

George Langlahan, a Canadian author, wrote a novelette called *The Fly,* using a #7 bear, made a sale to *Playboy,* and has since seen his bear made into three movies—*The Fly, The Return of the Fly,* and *The Curse of the Fly.* The late John W. Campbell wrote a cracking good horror story in the early 50's called "Who Goes There?" using a #2 bear which turns out to be a sort of walking vegetable from another planet. The story was turned into a classic horror movie called *The Thing.* Hollywood has always understood the principle of working from the bear out—surrounding a basic fear with a plot, rather than the other way around. Edgar Allan Poe wrote the same way, and suggested again and again in his literary essays that the only way to write a short story was to begin with the effect and then work your way out.

The would-be writer of horror stories may be tempted to stop right here and say: That's a lousy list of bears, fella. There isn't a werewolf or a vampire to be had. True enough. Not even an escaped mummy hunting for tanna leaves. My humble advice is to leave these bears to their well-deserved rest. They've been done to death. There are undoubtedly a few twists left in the Old Guard, but not many. Even the endlessly proliferating comics market is turning away from them in favor of more contemporary subjects.

Another caution is in order at this point: Don't think that because you have selected a scary bear, the rest of the story will be a snap. It won't be. Horror isn't a hack market now, and never was. The genre is one of the most delicate known to man, and it must be handled with great care and more than a little love. Some of the greatest authors of all time have tried their hands at things that go bump in the night, including Shakespeare, Chaucer, Hawthorne ("My Kinsman, Major Molinaux" is a particularly terrifying story, featuring a #9 bear), Poe, Henry James, William Faulkner ("A Rose for Emily"), and a score of others.

—1973

GRAVEYARD SHIFT

Two A.M., Friday.

Hall was sitting on the bench by the elevator, the only place on the third floor where a working joe could catch a smoke, when Warwick came up. He wasn't happy to see Warwick. The foreman wasn't supposed to show up on three during the graveyard shift; he was supposed to stay down in his office in the basement drinking coffee from the urn that stood on the corner of his desk. Besides, it was hot.

It was the hottest June on record in Gates Falls, and the Orange Crush thermometer which was also by the elevator had once rested at 94 degrees at three in the morning. God only knew what kind of hellhole the mill was on the three-to-eleven shift.

Hall worked the picker machine, a balky gadget manufactured by a defunct Cleveland firm in 1934. He had only been working in the mill since April, which meant he was still making minimum $1.78 an hour, which was still all right. No wife, no steady girl, no alimony. He was a drifter, and during the last three years he had moved on his thumb from Berkeley (college student) to Lake Tahoe (busboy) to Galveston (stevedore) to Miami (short-order cook) to Wheeling (taxi driver and dishwasher) to Gates Falls, Maine (picker-machine operator). He didn't figure on moving again until the snow fell. He was a solitary person and he liked the hours from eleven to seven when the blood flow of the big mill was at its coolest, not to mention the temperature.

The only thing he did not like was the rats.

The third floor was long and deserted, lit only by the sputtering glow of the fluorescents. Unlike the other levels of the mill, it was relatively silent and unoccupied—at least by the humans. The rats were another matter. The only machine on three was the picker; the rest of the floor was storage for the ninety-pound bags of fiber which had yet to be sorted by Hall's long gear-toothed machine. They were stacked like link sausages in long rows, some of them (especially the discontinued meltons and irregular slipes for which there were no orders) years old and dirty gray with industrial wastes. They made fine nesting places for the rats, huge, fat-bellied creatures with rabid eyes and bodies that jumped with lice and vermin.

Hall had developed a habit of collecting a small arsenal of soft-drink cans from the trash barrel during his break. He pegged them at the rats during times when work was slow, retrieving them later at his leisure. Only this time Mr. Foreman had caught him, coming up the stairs instead of using the elevator like the sneaky sonofabitch everyone said he was.

"What are you up to, Hall?"

"The rats," Hall said, realizing how lame that must sound now that all the rats had snuggled safely back into their houses. "I peg cans at 'em when I see 'em."

Warwick nodded once, briefly. He was a big beefy man with a crew cut. His shirt-sleeves were rolled up and his tie was pulled down. He looked at Hall closely. "We don't pay you to chuck cans at rats, mister. Not even if you pick them up again."

"Harry hasn't sent down an order for twenty minutes," Hall answered, thinking: *Why couldn't you stay the hell put and drink your coffee?* "I can't run it through the picker if I don't have it."

Warwick nodded as if the topic no longer interested him.

"Maybe I'll take a walk up and see Wisconsky," he said. "Five to one he's reading a magazine while the crap piles up in his bins."

Hall didn't say anything.

Warwick suddenly pointed. "There's one! Get the bastard!"

Hall fired the Nehi can he had been holding with one whistling, overhand motion. The rat, which had been watching them from atop one of the fabric bags with its bright buckshot eyes, fled with one faint squeak. Warwick threw back his head and laughed as Hall went after the can.

"I came to see you about something else," Warwick said.

"Is that so?"

"Next week's Fourth of July week." Hall nodded. The mill would be shut down Monday to Saturday—vacation week for men with at least one year's tenure. Layoff week for men with less than a year. "You want to work?"

Hall shrugged. "Doing what?"

"We're going to clean the whole basement level. Nobody's touched it for twelve years. Helluva mess. We're going to use hoses."

"The town zoning committee getting on the board of directors?"

Warwick looked steadily at Hall. "You want it or not? Two an hour, double time on the fourth. We're working the graveyard shift because it'll be cooler."

Hall calculated. He could clear maybe seventy-five bucks after taxes. Better than the goose egg he had been looking forward to.

"All right."

"Report down by the dye house next Monday."

Hall watched him as he started back to the stairs. Warwick paused halfway there and turned back to look at Hall. "You used to be a college boy, didn't you?"

Hall nodded.

"Okay, college boy, I'm keeping it in mind."

He left. Hall sat down and lit another smoke, holding a soda can in one hand and watching for the rats. He could just imagine how it would be in the basement—the sub-basement, actually, a level below the dye house. Damp, dark, full of spiders and rotten cloth and ooze from the river—and rats. Maybe even bats, the aviators of the rodent family. *Gah.*

Hall threw the can hard, then smiled thinly to himself as the faint sound of Warwick's voice came down through the overhead ducts, reading Harry Wisconsky the riot act.

Okay, college boy, I'm keeping it in mind.

He stopped smiling abruptly and butted his smoke. A few moments later Wisconsky started to send rough nylon down through the blowers, and Hall went to work. And after a while the rats came out and sat atop the bags at the back of the long room watching him with their unblinking black eyes. They looked like a jury.

Eleven P.M., Monday.

There were about thirty-six men sitting around when Warwick came in wearing a pair of old jeans tucked into high rubber boots. Hall had been listening to Harry Wisconsky, who was enormously fat, enormously lazy, and enormously gloomy.

"It's gonna be a mess," Wisconsky was saying when Mr. Foreman came in. "You wait and see, we're all gonna go home blacker'n midnight in Persia."

"Okay!" Warwick said. "We strung sixty lightbulbs down there, so it should be bright enough for you to see what you're doing. You guys"—he pointed to a bunch of men that had been leaning against the drying spools—"I want you to hook up the hoses over there to the main water conduit by the stairwell. You can unroll them down the stairs. We got about eighty yards for each man, and that should be plenty. Don't get cute and spray one of your buddies or you'll send him to the hospital. They pack a wallop."

"Somebody'll get hurt," Wisconsky prophesied sourly. "Wait and see."

"You other guys," Warwick said pointing to the group that Hall and Wisconsky were a part of. "You're the crap crew tonight. You go in pairs with an electric wagon for each team. There's old office furniture, bags of cloth, hunks of busted machinery, you name it. We're gonna pile it by the airshaft at the west end. Anyone who doesn't know how to run a wagon?"

No one raised a hand. The electric wagons were battery-driven contraptions like miniature dump trucks. They developed a nauseating stink after continual use that reminded Hall of burning power lines.

"Okay," Warwick said. "We got the basement divided up into sections, and we'll be done by Thursday. Friday we'll chain-hoist the crap out. Questions?"

There were none. Hall studied the foreman's face closely, and he had a sudden premonition of a strange thing coming. The idea pleased him. He did not like Warwick very much.

"Fine," Warwick said. "Let's get at it."

Two A.M., Tuesday.

Hall was bushed and very tired of listening to Wisconsky's steady patter of profane complaints. He wondered if it would do any good to belt Wisconsky. He doubted it. It would just give Wisconsky something else to bitch about.

Hall had known it would be bad, but this was murder. For one thing, he hadn't anticipated the smell. The polluted stink of the river, mixed with the odor of decaying fabric, rotting masonry, vegetable matter. In the far corner, where they had begun, Hall discovered a colony of huge white toadstools poking their way up through the shattered cement. His hands had come in contact with them as he pulled and yanked at a rusty gear-toothed wheel, and they felt curiously warm and bloated, like the flesh of a man afflicted with dropsy.

The bulbs couldn't banish the twelve-year darkness; it could only push it back a little and cast a sickly yellow glow over the whole mess. The place looked like the shattered nave of a desecrated church, with its high ceiling and mammoth discarded machinery that they would never be able to move, its wet walls overgrown with patches of yellow moss, and the atonal choir that was the water from the hoses, running in the half-clogged sewer network that eventually emptied into the river below the falls.

And the rats—huge ones that made those on third look like dwarfs. God knew what they were eating down here. They were continually overturning boards and bags to reveal huge nests of shredded newspaper, watching with atavistic loathing as the pups fled into the cracks and crannies, their eyes huge and blind with the continuous darkness.

"Let's stop for a smoke," Wisconsky said. He sounded out of breath, but Hall had no idea why; he had been goldbricking all night. Still, it was about that time, and they were currently out of sight of everyone else.

"All right." He leaned against the edge of the electric wagon and lit up.

"I never should've let Warwick talk me into this," Wisconsky said dolefully. "This ain't work for a *man*. But he was mad the other night when he caught me in the crapper up on four with my pants up. Christ, was he mad."

Hall said nothing. He was thinking about Warwick, and about the rats. Strange, how the two things seemed tied together. The rats seemed to have forgotten all about men in their long stay under the mill; they were impudent and hardly afraid at all. One of them had sat up on its hind legs like a squirrel until Hall had gotten in kicking distance, and then it had launched itself at his boot, biting at the leather. Hundreds, maybe thousands. He wondered how many varieties of disease they were carrying around in this black sumphole. And Warwick. Something about him—

"I need the money," Wisconsky said. "But Christ Jesus, buddy, this ain't no work for a *man*. Those rats." He looked around fearfully. "It almost seems like they think. You ever wonder how it'd be, if we was little and they were big—"

"Oh, shut up," Hall said.

Wisconsky looked at him, wounded. "Say, I'm sorry, buddy. It's just that . . ." He trailed off. "Jesus, this place stinks!" he cried. "This ain't no kind of *work for a man!*" A spider crawled off the edge of the wagon and scrambled up his arm. He brushed it off with a choked sound of disgust.

"Come on," Hall said, snuffing his cigarette. "The faster, the quicker."

"I suppose," Wisconsky said miserably. "I suppose."

Four A.M., Tuesday.

Lunchtime.

Hall and Wisconsky sat with three or four other men, eating their sandwiches with black hands that not even the industrial detergent could clean. Hall ate looking into the foreman's little glass office. Warwick was drinking coffee and eating cold hamburgers with great relish.

"Ray Upson had to go home," Charlie Brochu said.

"He puke?" someone asked. "I almost did."

"Nuh. Ray'd eat cowflop before he'd puke. Rat bit him."

Hall looked up thoughtfully from his examination of Warwick. "Is that so?" he asked.

"Yeah." Brochu shook his head. "I was teaming with him. Goddamndest thing I ever saw. Jumped out of a hole in one of those old cloth bags. Must have been big as a cat. Grabbed onto his hand and started chewing."

"Jee-*sus*," one of the men said, looking green.

"Yeah," Brochu said. "Ray screamed just like a woman, and I ain't blamin' him. He bled like a pig. Would that thing let go? No sir. I had to belt it three or four times with a board before it would. Ray was just about crazy. He stomped it until it wasn't nothing but a mess of fur. Damndest thing I ever saw. Warwick put a bandage on him and sent him home. Told him to go to the doctor tomorrow."

"That was big of the bastard," somebody said.

As if he had heard, Warwick got to his feet in his office, stretched, and then came to the door. "Time we got back with it."

The men got to their feet slowly, eating up all the time they possibly could stowing their dinner buckets, getting cold drinks, buying candy bars. Then they started down, heels clanking dispiritedly on the steel grillwork of the stair risers.

Warwick passed Hall, clapping him on the shoulder. "How's it going, college boy?" He didn't wait for an answer.

"Come on," Hall said patiently to Wisconsky, who was tying his shoelace. They went downstairs.

Seven A.M., Tuesday.

Hall and Wisconsky walked out together; it seemed to Hall that he had somehow inherited the fat Pole. Wisconsky was almost comically dirty, his fat moon face smeared like that of a small boy who has just been thrashed by the town bully.

There was none of the usual rough banter from the other men, the pulling of shirttails, the cracks about who was keeping Tony's wife warm between the hours of one and four. Nothing but silence and an occasional hawking sound as someone spat on the dirty floor.

"You want a lift?" Wisconsky asked him hesitantly.

"Thanks."

They didn't talk as they rode up Mill Street and crossed the bridge. They exchanged only a brief word when Wisconsky dropped him off in front of his apartment.

Hall went directly to the shower, still thinking about Warwick, trying to place whatever it was about Mr. Foreman that drew him, made him feel that somehow they had become tied together.

He slept as soon as his head hit the pillow, but his sleep was broken and restless: he dreamed of rats.

One A.M., Wednesday.

It was better running the hoses.

They couldn't go in until the crap crews had finished a section, and quite often they were done hosing before the next section was clear—which meant time for a cigarette. Hall worked the nozzle of one of the long hoses and Wisconsky pattered back and forth, unsnagging lengths of the hose, turning the water on and off, moving obstructions.

Warwick was short-tempered because the work was proceeding slowly. They would never be done by Thursday, the way things were going.

Now they were working on a helter-skelter jumble of nineteenth-century office equipment that had been piled in one corner—smashed rolltop desks, moldy ledgers, reams of invoices, chairs with broken seats—and it was rat heaven. Scores of them squeaked and ran through the dark and crazy passages that honeycombed the heap, and after two men were bitten, the others refused to work until Warwick sent someone upstairs to get heavy rubberized gloves, the kind usually reserved for the dye-house crew, which had to work with acids.

Hall and Wisconsky were waiting to go in with their hoses when a sandy-haired bullneck named Carmichael began howling curses and backing away, slapping at his chest with his gloved hands.

A huge rat with gray-streaked fur and ugly, glaring eyes had bitten into his shirt and hung there, squeaking and kicking at Carmichael's belly with its back paws. Carmichael finally knocked it away with his fist, but there was a huge hole in his shirt, and a thin line of blood trickled from above one nipple. The anger faded from his face. He turned away and retched.

Hall turned the hose on the rat, which was old and moving slowly, a snatch of Carmichael's shirt still caught in its jaws. The roaring pressure drove it backward against the wall, where it smashed limply.

Warwick came over, an odd, strained smile on his lips. He clapped Hall on the shoulder. "Damn sight better than throwing cans at the little bastards, huh, college boy?"

"Some little bastard," Wisconsky said. "It's a foot long."

"Turn that hose over there." Warwick pointed at the jumble of furniture. "You guys, get out of the way!"

"With pleasure," someone muttered.

Carmichael charged up to Warwick, his face sick and twisted. "I'm gonna have compensation for this! I'm gonna—"

"Sure," Warwick said, smiling. "You got bit on the titty. Get out of the way before you get pasted down by this water."

Hall pointed the nozzle and let it go. It hit with a white explosion of spray, knocking over a desk and smashing two chairs to splinters. Rats ran everywhere, bigger than any Hall had ever seen. He could hear men crying out in disgust and horror as they fled, things with huge eyes and sleek, plump bodies. He caught a glimpse of one that looked as big as a healthy six-week puppy. He kept on until he could see no more, then shut the nozzle down.

"Okay!" Warwick called. "Let's pick it up!"

"I didn't hire out as no exterminator!" Cy Ippeston called mutinously. Hall had tipped a few with him the week before. He was a young guy, wearing a smut-stained baseball cap and a T-shirt.

"That you, Ippeston?" Warwick asked genially.

Ippeston looked uncertain, but stepped forward. "Yeah. I don't want no more of these rats. I hired to clean up, not to maybe get rabies or typhoid or somethin'. Maybe you best count me out."

There was a murmur of agreement from the others. Wisconsky stole a look at Hall, but Hall was examining the nozzle of the hose he was holding. It had a bore like a .45 and could probably knock a man twenty feet.

"You saying you want to punch your clock, Cy?"

"Thinkin' about it," Ippeston said.

Warwick nodded. "Okay. You and anybody else that wants. But this ain't no unionized shop, and never has been. Punch out now and you'll never punch back in. I'll see to it."

"Aren't you some hot ticket," Hall muttered.

Warwick swung around. "Did you say something, college boy?"

Hall regarded him blandly. "Just clearing my throat, Mr. Foreman."

Warwick smiled. "Something taste bad to you?"

Hall said nothing.

"All right, let's pick it up!" Warwick bawled.

They went back to work.

Two A.M., Thursday.

Hall and Wisconsky were working with the trucks again, picking up junk. The pile by the west airshaft had grown to amazing proportions, but they were still not half done.

"Happy Fourth," Wisconsky said when they stopped for a smoke. They were working near the north wall, far from the stairs. The light was extremely dim, and some trick of acoustics made the other men seem miles away.

"Thanks." Hall dragged on his smoke. "Haven't seen many rats tonight."

"Nobody has," Wisconsky said. "Maybe they got wise."

They were standing at the end of a cozy, zigzagging alley formed by piles of old ledgers and invoices, moldy bags of cloth, and two huge flat looms of ancient vintage. "Gah," Wisconsky said, spitting. "That Warwick—"

"Where do you suppose all the rats got to?" Hall asked, almost to himself. "Not into the walls—" He looked at the wet and crumbling masonry that surrounded the huge foundation stones. "They'd drown. The river's saturated everything."

Something black and flapping suddenly dive-bombed them. Wisconsky screamed and put his hands over his head.

"A bat," Hall said, watching after it as Wisconsky straightened up.

"A bat! A bat!" Wisconsky raved. "What's a bat doing in the cellar? They're supposed to be in trees and under eaves and—"

"It was a big one," Hall said softly. "And what's a bat but a rat with wings?"

"Jesus," Wisconsky moaned. "How did it—"

"Get in? Maybe the same way the rats got out."

"What's going on back there?" Warwick shouted from somewhere behind them. "Where are you?"

"Don't sweat it," Hall said softly. His eyes gleamed in the dark.

"Was that you, college boy?" Warwick called. He sounded closer.

"It's okay!" Hall yelled. "I barked my shin!"

Warwick's short, barking laugh. "You want a Purple Heart?"

Wisconsky looked at Hall. "Why'd you say that?"

"Look." Hall knelt and lit a match. There was a square in the middle of the wet and crumbling cement. "Tap it."

Wisconsky did. "It's wood."

Hall nodded. "It's the top of a support. I've seen some other ones around here. There's another level under this part of the basement."

"God," Wisconsky said with utter revulsion.

Three-thirty A.M., Thursday.

They were in the northeast corner, Ippeston and Brochu behind them with one of the high-pressure hoses, when Hall stopped and pointed at the floor. "There, I thought we'd come across it."

There was a wooden trapdoor with a crusted iron ringbolt set near the center.

He walked back to Ippeston and said, "Shut it off for a minute." When the hose was choked to a trickle, he raised his voice to a shout. "Hey! Hey, Warwick! Better come here a minute!"

Warwick came splashing over, looking at Hall with that same hard smile in his eyes. "Your shoelace come untied, college boy?"

"Look," Hall said. He kicked the trapdoor with his foot. "Sub-cellar."

"So what?" Warwick asked. "This isn't break time, col—"

"That's where your rats are," Hall said. "They're breeding down there. Wisconsky and I even saw a bat earlier."

Some of the other men had gathered round and were looking at the trapdoor.

"I don't care," Warwick said. "The job was the basement, not—"

"You'll need about twenty exterminators, trained ones," Hall was saying. "Going to cost the management a pretty penny. Too bad."

Someone laughed. "Fat chance."

Warwick looked at Hall as if he were a bug under glass. "You're really a case, you are," he said, sounding fascinated. "Do you think I give a good goddamn how many rats there are under there?"

"I was at the library this afternoon and yesterday," Hall said. "Good thing you kept reminding me I was a college boy. I read the town zoning ordinances, Warwick—they were set up in 1911, before this mill got big enough to co-opt the zoning board. Know what I found?"

Warwick's eyes were cold. "Take a walk, college boy. You're fired."

"I found out," Hall plowed on as if he hadn't heard, "I found out that there is a zoning law in Gates Falls about vermin. You spell that v-e-r-m-i-n, in case you wondered. It means disease-carrying animals such as bats, skunks, unlicensed dogs—and rats. Especially rats. Rats are mentioned fourteen times in two paragraphs, Mr. Foreman. So you just keep in mind that the minute I punch out I'm going straight to the town commissioner and tell him what the situation down here is."

He paused, relishing Warwick's hate-congested face. "I think that between me, him, and the town committee, we can get an injunction slapped on this place. You're going to be shut down a lot longer than just Saturday, Mr. Foreman. And I got a good idea what *your* boss is going to say when he turns up. Hope your unemployment insurance is paid up, Warwick."

Warwick's hands formed into claws. "You damned snot-nose, I ought to—" He looked down at the trapdoor, and suddenly his smile reappeared. "Consider yourself rehired, college boy."

"I thought you might see the light."

Warwick nodded, the same strange grin on his face. "You're just so smart. I think maybe you ought to go down there, Hall, so we got somebody with a college education to give us an informed opinion. You and Wisconsky."

"Not me!" Wisconsky exclaimed. "Not me, I—"

Warwick looked at him. "You what?"

Wisconsky shut up.

"Good," Hall said cheerfully. "We'll need three flashlights. I think I saw a whole rack of six-battery jobs in the main office, didn't I?"

"You want to take somebody else?" Warwick asked expansively. "Sure, pick your man."

"You," Hall said gently. The strange expression had come into his face again. "After all, the management should be represented, don't you think? Just so Wisconsky and I don't see *too* many rats down there?"

Someone (it sounded like Ippeston) laughed loudly.

Warwick looked at the men carefully. They studied the tips of their shoes. Finally he pointed at Brochu. "Brochu, go up to the office and get three flashlights. Tell the watchman I said to let you in."

"Why'd you get me into this?" Wisconsky moaned to Hall. "You know I hate those—"

"It wasn't me," Hall said, and looked at Warwick.

Warwick looked back at him, and neither would drop his eyes.

Four A.M., Thursday.

Brochu returned with the flashlights. He gave one to Hall, one to Wisconsky, one to Warwick.

"Ippeston! Give the hose to Wisconsky." Ippeston did so. The nozzle trembled delicately between the Pole's hands.

"All right." Warwick said to Wisconsky. "You're in the middle. If there are rats, you let them have it."

Sure, Hall thought. And if there are rats, Warwick won't see them. And neither will Wisconsky, after he finds an extra ten in his pay envelope.

Warwick pointed at two of the men. "Lift it."

One of them bent over the ringbolt and pulled. For a moment Hall didn't think it was going to give, and then it yanked free with an odd, crunching snap. The other man put his fingers on the underside to help pull, then withdrew with a cry. His hands were crawling with huge and sightless beetles.

With a convulsive grunt the man on the ringbolt pulled the trap back and let it drop. The underside was black with an odd fungus that Hall had never seen before. The beetles dropped off into the darkness below or ran across the floor to be crushed.

"Look," Hall said.

There was a rusty lock bolted on the underside, now broken. "But it shouldn't be underneath," Warwick said. "It should be on top. Why—"

"Lots of reasons," Hall said. "Maybe so nothing on this side could open it—at least when the lock was new. Maybe so nothing on that side could get up."

"But who locked it?" Wisconsky asked.

"Ah," Hall said mockingly, looking at Warwick. "A mystery."

"Listen," Brochu whispered.

"Oh, God," Wisconsky sobbed. "I ain't going down there!"

It was a soft sound, almost expectant; the whisk and patter of thousands of paws, the squeaking of rats.

"Could be frogs," Warwick said.

Hall laughed aloud.

Warwick shone his light down. A sagging flight of wooden stairs led down to the black stones of the floor beneath. There was not a rat in sight.

"Those stairs won't hold us," Warwick said with finality.

Brochu took two steps forward and jumped up and down on the first step. It creaked but showed no sign of giving way.

"I didn't ask you to do that," Warwick said.

"You weren't there when that rat bit Ray," Brochu said softly.

"Let's go," Hall said.

Warwick took a last sardonic look around at the circle of men, then walked to the edge with Hall. Wisconsky stepped reluctantly between them. They went down one at a time. Hall, then Wisconsky, then Warwick. Their flashlight beams played over the floor, which was twisted and heaved into a hundred crazy hills and valleys. The hose thumped along behind Wisconsky like a clumsy serpent.

When they got to the bottom, Warwick flashed his light around. It picked out a few rotting boxes, some barrels, little else. The seep from the river stood in puddles that came to ankle depth on their boots.

"I don't hear them anymore," Wisconsky whispered.

They walked slowly away from the trapdoor, their feet shuffling through the slime. Hall paused and shone his light on a huge wooden box with white letters on it. "Elias Varney," he read, "1841. Was the mill here then?"

"No," Warwick said. "It wasn't built until 1897. What difference?"

Hall didn't answer. They walked forward again. The sub-cellar was longer than it should have been, it seemed. The stench was stronger, a smell of decay and rot and things buried. And still the only sound was the faint, cavelike drip of water.

"What's that?" Hall asked, pointing his beam at a jut of concrete that protruded perhaps two feet into the cellar. Beyond it, the darkness continued and it seemed to Hall that he could now hear sounds up there, curiously stealthy.

Warwick peered at it. "It's . . . no, that can't be right."

"Outer wall of the mill, isn't it? And up ahead . . ."

"I'm going back," Warwick said, suddenly turning around.

Hall grabbed his neck roughly. "You're not going anywhere, Mr. Foreman."

Warwick looked up at him, his grin cutting the darkness. "You're crazy, college boy. Isn't that right? Crazy as a loon."

"You shouldn't push people, friend. Keep going."

Wisconsky moaned. "Hall—"

"Give me that." Hall grabbed the hose. He let go of Warwick's neck and pointed the hose at his head. Wisconsky turned abruptly and crashed back toward the trap-door. Hall did not even turn. "After you, Mr. Foreman."

Warwick stepped forward, walking under the place where the mill ended above them. Hall flashed his light about, and felt a cold satisfaction—premonition fulfilled. The rats had closed in around them, silent as death. Crowded in, rank on rank. Thousands of eyes looked greedily back at him. In ranks to the wall, some fully as high as a man's shin.

Warwick saw them a moment later and came to a full stop. "They're all around us, college boy." His voice was still calm, still in control, but it held a jagged edge.

"Yes," Hall said. "Keep going."

They walked forward, the hose dragging behind. Hall looked back once and saw the rats had closed the aisle behind them and were gnawing at the heavy canvas hos-ing. One looked up and almost seemed to grin at him before lowering his head again. He could see the bats now, too. They were roosting from the roughhewn over-heads, huge, the size of crows or rooks.

"Look," Warwick said, centering his beam about five feet ahead.

A skull, green with mold, laughed up at them. Further on Hall could see an ulna, one pelvic wing, part of a ribcage. "Keep going," Hall said. He felt something burst-ing up inside him, something lunatic and dark with colors. *You are going to break before I do, Mr. Foreman, so help me God.*

They walked past the bones. The rats were not crowding them; their distances appeared constant. Up ahead Hall saw one cross their path of travel. Shadows hid it, but he caught sight of a pink twitching tail as thick as a telephone cord.

Up ahead the flooring rose sharply, then dipped. Hall could hear a stealthy rustling sound, a big sound. Something that perhaps no living man had ever seen. It occurred to Hall that he had perhaps been looking for something like this through all his days of crazy wandering.

The rats were moving in, creeping on their bellies, forcing them forward. "Look," Warwick said coldly.

Hall saw. Something had happened to the rats back here, some hideous muta-tion that never could have survived under the eye of the sun; nature would have for-bidden it. But down here, nature had taken on another ghastly face.

The rats were gigantic, some as high as three feet. But their rear legs were gone and they were blind as moles, like their flying cousins. They dragged themselves for-ward with hideous eagerness.

Warwick turned and faced Hall, the smile hanging on by brute willpower. Hall really had to admire him. "We can't go on, Hall. You must see that."

"The rats have business with you, I think," Hall said.

Warwick's control slipped. "Please," he said. "Please."

Hall smiled. "Keep going."

Warwick was looking over his shoulder. "They're gnawing into the hose. When they get through it, we'll never get back."

"I know. Keep going."

"You're insane—" A rat ran across Warwick's shoe and he screamed. Hall smiled and gestured with his light. They were all around, the closest of them less than a foot away now.

Warwick began to walk again. The rats drew back.

They topped the miniature rise and looked down. Warwick reached it first, and Hall saw his face go white as paper. Spit ran down his chin. "Oh, my God. Dear Jesus."

And he turned to run.

Hall opened the nozzle of the hose and the high-pressure rush of water struck Warwick squarely on the chest, knocking him back out of sight. There was a long scream that rose over the sound of the water. Thrashing sounds.

"Hall!" Grunts. A huge, tenebrous squeaking that seemed to fill the earth.

"HALL, FOR GOD'S SAKE—"

A sudden wet ripping noise. Another scream, weaker. Something huge shifted and turned. Quite distinctly Hall heard the wet snap that a fractured bone makes.

A legless rat, guided by some bastard form of sonar, lunged against him, biting. Its body was flabby, warm. Almost absently Hall turned the hose on it, knocking it away. The hose did not have quite so much pressure now.

Hall walked to the brow of the wet hill and looked down.

The rat filled the whole gully at the far end of that noxious tomb. It was a huge and pulsating gray, eyeless, totally without legs. When Hall's light struck it, it made a hideous mewling noise. Their queen, then, the *magna mater.* A huge and nameless thing whose progeny might someday develop wings. It seemed to dwarf what remained of Warwick, but that was probably just illusion. It was the shock of seeing a rat as big as a Holstein calf.

"Goodbye, Warwick," Hall said. The rat crouched over Mr. Foreman jealously, ripping at one limp arm.

Hall turned away and began to make his way back rapidly, halting the rats with his hose, which was growing less and less potent. Some of them got through and attacked his legs above the tops of his boots with biting lunges. One hung stubbornly on at his thigh, ripping at the cloth of his corduroy pants. Hall made a fist and smashed it aside.

He was nearly three-quarters of the way back when the huge whirring filled the darkness. He looked up and the gigantic flying form smashed into his face.

The mutated bats had not lost their tails yet. It whipped around Hall's neck in a loathsome coil and squeezed as the teeth sought the soft spot under his neck. It wriggled and flapped with its membranous wings, clutching the tatters of his shirt for purchase.

Hall brought the nozzle of the hose up blindly and struck at its yielding body again and again. It fell away and he trampled it beneath his feet, dimly aware that he was screaming. The rats ran in a flood over his feet, up his legs.

He broke into a staggering run, shaking some off. The others bit at his belly, his chest. One ran up his shoulder and pressed its questing muzzle into the cup of his ear.

He ran into the second bat. It roosted on his head for a moment, squealing, and then ripped away a flap of Hall's scalp.

He felt his body growing numb. His ears filled with the screech and yammer of many rats. He gave one last heave, stumbled over furry bodies, fell to his knees. He began to laugh, a high, screaming sound.

Five A.M., Thursday.

"Somebody better go down there," Brochu said tentatively.

"Not me," Wisconsky whispered. "Not me."

"No, not you, jelly belly," Ippeston said with contempt.

"Well, let's go," Brogan said, bringing up another hose. "Me, Ippeston, Dangerfield, Nedeau. Stevenson, go up to the office and get a few more lights."

Ippeston looked down into the darkness thoughtfully. "Maybe they stopped for a smoke, " he said. "A few rats, what the hell."

Stevenson came back with the lights; a few moments later they started down.

—1970

TANITH LEE

B. 1947

Tanith Lee is a prolific and respected author of fantasy, science fiction, and horror. She was born and educated in London and, at one point, worked as a librarian. Among her many interests are music, art, and ancient civilizations. Some of her earliest books were juvenile novels, such as The Dragon Hoard *(1971),* Animal Castle *(1972), and* The Winter Players *(1976). She published her first adult fantasy novel,* The Birthgrave, *in 1975, and it became the first in a series that also features* Vazkor, Son of Vaskor *(1978) and* Quest for the White Witch *(1978). Over the years, Lee has developed a number of fantasy and science fiction series, such as the Tales from the Flat Earth, including* Night's Master *(1978),* Death's Master *(1979),* Delusion's Master *(1981), and* Delirium's Mistress *(1986); the Wars of Vis novels, including* The Storm Lord *(1976),* Anackire *(1983), and* The White Serpent *(1988); the Don't Bite the Sun books, including* Don't Bite the Sun *(1976) and* Drinking Sapphire Wine *(1977); and the Dragonflight novels, including* Black Unicorn *(1991) and* Gold Unicorn *(1994). Lee has also published short story collections, such as* Red as Blood; or, Tales from the Sisters Grimmer *(1983), and* The Gorgon and Other Beastly Tales *(1985). Lee has, in addition, written for both radio and television. She has won the August Derleth Award and the World Fantasy Award.*

Her work, especially her dark fantasy, is notable for its elegant characterization, its use of richly evocative atmosphere, and for its wonderful storytelling quality. Her fiction is somewhat reminiscent of the fantasy of past

*masters of the genre, such as Jack Vance and Lord Dunsany, but Lee is not
an author of mere pastiche. Her imaginative novels and short stories possess
a decidedly post-modern flavor; she frequently challenges (and even under-
mines) traditional formulaic conventions. In this sense, her dark fantasy and
horror fiction are similar to that written by Clive Barker. Lee says about her
work, "I began to write, and continue to write, out of the sheer compulsion to
fantasize . . . I just want to write, can't stop, don't want to stop, and hope I
never shall." Like Anne Rice and Chelsea Quinn Yarbro, Lee has successfully
blended sexual eroticism with horror in her dark fantasy. Her short story,
"Nunc Dimittis," first published in* The Dodd, Mead Gallery of Horror *(1983),
edited by Charles L. Grant, and later collected in the anthology,* Dreams of
Dark and Light: The Great Short Fiction of Tanith Lee *(1986), is an inventive
and sensual reworking of the Dracula myth. Lee, in fact, significantly transforms Bram Stoker's classic story. She modifies the conventions of the traditional vampire tale, thus creating a charming love story in which the vampire is not an evil monster but, instead, is like a princess from a fairy tale who
is compassionately devoted to her "mortal" lovers.*

Nunc Dimittis

The vampire was old, and no longer beautiful. In common with all living things, she
had aged, though very slowly, like the tall trees in the park. Slender and gaunt and
leafless, they stood out there, beyond the long windows, rain-dashed in the grey
morning. While she sat in her high-backed chair in that corner of the room where
the curtains of thick yellow lace and the wine-coloured blinds kept every drop of
daylight out. In the glimmer of the ornate oil-lamp, she had been reading. The lamp
came from a Russian palace. The book had once graced the library of a corrupt pope
named, in his temporal existence, Roderigo Borgia. Now the Vampire's dry hands
had fallen upon the page. She sat in her black lace dress that was one hundred and
eighty years of age, far younger than she herself, and looked at the old man,
streaked by the shine of distant windows.

"You say you are tired, Vassu. I know how it is. To be so tired, and unable to rest.
It is a terrible thing."

"But, Princess," said the old man quietly, "it is more than this. I am dying."

The Vampire stirred a little. The pale leaves of her hands rustled on the page.
She stared, with an almost childlike wonder.

"Dying? Can this be? You are sure?"

The old man, very clean and neat in his dark clothing, nodded humbly.

"Yes, Princess."

"Oh, Vassu," she said, "are you glad?"

He seemed a little embarrassed. Finally he said:

"Forgive me, Princess, but I am very glad. Yes, very glad."

"I understand."

"Only," he said, "I am troubled for your sake."

"No, no," said the Vampire, with the fragile perfect courtesy of her class and
kind. "No, it must not concern you. You have been a good servant. Far better than I
might ever have hoped for. I am thankful, Vassu, for all your care of me. I shall miss

you. But you have earned," she hesitated. She said, "You have more than earned your peace."

"But you," he said.

"I shall do very well. My requirements are small, now. The days when I was a huntress are gone, and the nights. Do you remember, Vassu?"

"I remember, Princess."

"When I was so hungry, and so relentless. And so lovely. My white face in a thousand ballroom mirrors. My silk slippers stained with dew. And my lovers waking in the cold morning, where I had left them. But now, I do not sleep, I am seldom hungry. I never lust. I never love. These are the comforts of old age. There is only one comfort that is denied to me. And who knows. One day, I too . . ." She smiled at him. Her teeth were beautiful, but almost even now, the exquisite points of the canines quite worn away. "Leave me when you must," she said. "I shall mourn you. I shall envy you. But I ask nothing more, my good and noble friend."

The old man bowed his head.

"I have," he said, "a few days, a handful of nights. There is something I wish to try to do in this time. I will try to find one who may take my place."

The Vampire stared at him again, now astonished. "But Vassu, my irreplaceable help—it is no longer possible."

"Yes. If I am swift."

"The world is not as it was," she said, with a grave and dreadful wisdom.

He lifted his head. More gravely, he answered:

"The world is as it has always been, Princess. Only our perceptions of it have grown more acute. Our knowledge less bearable."

She nodded.

"Yes, this must be so. How could the world have changed so terribly? It must be we who have changed."

He trimmed the lamp before he left her.

Outside, the rain dripped steadily from the trees.

The city, in the rain, was not unlike a forest. But the old man, who had been in many forests and many cities, had no special feeling for it. His feelings, his senses, were primed to other things.

Nevertheless, he was conscious of his bizarre and anachronistic effect, like that of a figure in some surrealist painting, walking the streets in clothes of a bygone era, aware he did not blend with his surroundings, nor render them homage of any kind. Yet even when, as sometimes happened, a gang of children or youths jeered and called after him the foul names he was familiar with in twenty languages, he neither cringed nor cared. He had no concern for such things. He had been so many places, seen so many sights; cities which burned or fell in ruin, the young who grew old, as he had, and who died, as now, at last, he too would die. This thought of death soothed him, comforted him, and brought with it a great sadness, a strange jealousy. He did not want to leave her. Of course he did not. The idea of her vulnerability in this harsh world, not new in its cruelty but ancient, though freshly recognised—it horrified him. This was the sadness. And the jealousy . . . that, because he must try to find another to take his place. And that other would come to be for her, as he had been.

The memories rose and sank in his brain like waking dreams all the time he moved about the streets. As he climbed the steps of museums and underpasses, he remembered other steps in other lands, of marble and fine stone. And looking out from high balconies, the city reduced to a map, he recollected the towers of cathedrals, the star-swept points of mountains. And then at last, as if turning over the pages of a book backwards, he reached the beginning.

There she stood, between two tall white graves, the château grounds behind her, everything silvered in the dusk before the dawn. She wore a ball dress, and a long white cloak. And even then, her hair was dressed in the fashion of a century ago; dark hair, like black flowers.

He had known for a year before that he would serve her. The moment he had heard them talk of her in the town. They were not afraid of her, but in awe. She did not prey upon her own people, as some of her line had done.

When he could get up, he went to her. He had kneeled, and stammered something; he was only sixteen, and she not much older. But she had simply looked at him quietly and said: "I know. You are welcome." The words had been in a language they seldom spoke together now. Yet always, when he recalled that meeting, she said them in that tongue, and with the same gentle inflection.

All about, in the small café where he had paused to sit and drink coffee, vague shapes came and went. Of no interest to him, no use to her. Throughout the morning there had been nothing to alert him. He would know. He would know, as he had known it of himself.

He rose, and left the café, and the waking dream walked with him. A lean black car slid by, and he recaptured a carriage carving through white snow—

A step brushed the pavement, perhaps twenty feet behind him. The old man did not hesitate. He stepped on, and into an alleyway that ran between the high buildings. The steps followed him; he could not hear them all, only one in seven, or eight. A little wire of tension began to draw taut within him, but he gave no sign. Water trickled along the brickwork beside him, and the noise of the city was lost.

Abruptly, a hand was on the back of his neck, a capable hand, warm and sure, not harming him yet, almost the touch of a lover.

"That's right, old man. Keep still. I'm not going to hurt you, not if you do what I say."

He stood, the warm and vital hand on his neck, and waited.

"All right," said the voice, which was masculine and young and with some other elusive quality to it. "Now let me have your wallet."

The old man spoke in a faltering tone, very foreign, very fearful. "I have—no wallet."

The hand changed its nature, gripped him, bit.

"Don't lie. I can hurt you. I don't want to, but I can. Give me whatever money you have.

"Yes," he faltered, "yes—yes—"

And slipped from the sure and merciless grip like water, spinning, gripping in turn, flinging away—there was a whirl of movement.

The old man's attacker slammed against the wet grey wall and rolled down it. He lay on the rainy debris of the alley floor, and stared up, too surprised to look surprised.

This had happened many times before. Several had supposed the old man an easy mark, but he had all the steely power of what he was. Even now, even dying, he was terrible in his strength. And yet, though it had happened often, now it was different. The tension had not gone away.

Swiftly, deliberately, the old man studied the young one.

Something struck home instantly. Even sprawled, the adversary was peculiarly graceful, the grace of enormous physical coordination. The touch of the hand, also, impervious and certain—there was strength here, too. And now the eyes. Yes, the eyes were steady, intelligent, and with a curious lambency, an innocence—

"Get up," the old man said. He had waited upon an aristocrat. He had become one himself, and sounded it. "Up. I will not hit you again."

The young man grinned, aware of the irony. The humour flitted through his eyes. In the dull light of the alley, they were the colour of leopards—not the eyes of leopards, but their *pelts*.

"Yes, and you could, couldn't you, granddad."

"My name," said the old man, "is Vasyelu Gorin. I am the father to none, and my nonexistent sons and daughters have no children. And you?"

"My name," said the young man, "is Snake."

The old man nodded. He did not really care about names, either.

"Get up, Snake. You attempted to rob me because you are poor, having no work and no wish for work. I will buy you food, now."

The young man continued to lie, as if at ease, on the ground.

"Why?"

"Because I want something from you."

"What? You're right. I'll do almost anything, if you pay me enough. So you can tell me."

The old man looked at the young man called Snake, and knew that all he said was a fact. Knew that here was one who had stolen and whored, and stolen again when the slack bodies slept, both male and female, exhausted by the sexual vampirism he had practised on them, drawing their misguided souls out through their pores as later he would draw the notes from purse and pocket. Yes, a vampire. Maybe a murderer, too. Very probably a murderer.

"If you will do anything," said the old man, "I need not tell you beforehand. You will do it anyway."

"Almost anything, is what I said."

"Advise me then," said Vasyelu Gorin, the servant of the Vampire, "what you will not do. I shall then refrain from asking it of you."

The young man laughed. In one fluid movement he came to his feet. When the old man walked on, he followed.

Testing him, the old man took Snake to an expensive restaurant, far up on the white hills of the city, where the glass geography nearly scratched the sky. Ignoring the mud on his dilapidated leather jacket, Snake became a flawless image of decorum, became what is always ultimately respected, one who does not care. The old man, who also did not care, appreciated this act, but knew it was nothing more. Snake had learned how to be a prince. But he was a gigolo with a closet full of skins to put on. Now and then the speckled leopard eyes, searching, wary, would give him away.

After the good food and the excellent wine, the cognac, the cigarettes taken from the silver box—Snake had stolen three, but, stylishly overt, had left them sticking like porcupine quills from his breast pocket—they went out again into the rain.

The dark was gathering, and Snake solicitously took the old man's arm. Vasyelu Gorin dislodged him, offended by the cheapness of the gesture after the acceptable one with the cigarettes.

"Don't you like me anymore?" said Snake. "I can go now, if you want. But you might pay for my wasted time."

"Stop that," said Vasyelu Gorin. "Come along."

Smiling, Snake came with him. They walked, between the glowing pyramids of stores, through shadowy tunnels, over the wet paving. When the thoroughfares folded away and the meadows of the great gardens began, Snake grew tense. The landscape was less familiar to him, obviously. This part of the forest was unknown.

Trees hung down from the air to the sides of the road.

"I could kill you here," said Snake. "Take your money, and run."

"You could try," said the old man, but he was becoming weary. He was no longer certain, and yet, he was sufficiently certain that his jealousy had assumed a tinge of hatred. If the young man were stupid enough to set on him, how simple it would be to break the columnar neck, like pale amber, between his fleshless hands. But then, she would know. She would know he had found for her, and destroyed the finding. And she would be generous, and he would leave her, aware he had failed her, too.

When the huge gates appeared, Snake made no comment. He seemed, by then, to anticipate them. The old man went into the park, moving quickly now, in order to outdistance his own feelings. Snake loped at his side.

Three windows were alight, high in the house. Her windows. And as they came to the stair that led up, under its skeins of ivy, into the porch, her pencil-thin shadow passed over the lights above, like smoke, or a ghost.

"I thought you lived alone," said Snake. "I thought you were lonely."

The old man did not answer anymore. He went up the stair and opened the door. Snake came in behind him, and stood quite still, until Vasyelu Gorin had found the lamp in the niche by the door, and lit it. Unnatural stained glass flared in the door panels, and the window-niches either side, owls and lotuses and far-off temples, scrolled and luminous, oddly aloof.

Vasyelu began to walk towards the inner stair.

"Just a minute," said Snake. Vasyelu halted, saying nothing. "I'd just like to know," said Snake, "how many of your friends are here, and just what your friends are figuring to do, and how I fit into their plans."

The old man sighed.

"There is one woman in the room above. I am taking you to see her. She is a Princess. Her name is Darejan Draculas." He began to ascend the stair.

Left in the dark, the visitor said softly:

"What?"

"You think you have heard the name. You are correct. But it is another branch."

He heard only the first step as it touched the carpeted stair. With a bound, the creature was upon him, the lamp was lifted from his hand. Snake danced behind it, glittering and unreal.

"Dracula," he said.

"Draculas. Another branch."

"A vampire."

"Do you believe in such things?" said the old man. "You should, living as you do, preying as you do."

"I never," said Snake, "pray."

"Prey," said the old man. "Prey upon. You cannot even speak your own language. Give me the lamp, or shall I take it? The stair is steep. You may be damaged, this time. Which will not be good for any of your trades."

Snake made a little bow, and returned the lamp.

They continued up the carpeted hill of stair, and reached a landing and so a passage, and so her door.

The appurtenances of the house, even glimpsed in the erratic fleeting of the lamp, were very gracious. The old man was used to them, but Snake, perhaps, took note. Then again, like the size and importance of the park gates, the young thief might well have anticipated such elegance.

And there was no neglect, no dust, no air of decay, or, more tritely, of the grave. Women arrived regularly from the city to clean, under Vasyelu Gorin's stern command; flowers were even arranged in the salon for those occasions when the Princess came downstairs. Which was rarely, now. How tired she had grown. Not aged, but bored by life. The old man sighed again, and knocked upon her door.

Her response was given softly. Vasyelu Gorin saw, from the tail of his eye, the young man's reaction, his ears almost pricked, like a cat's.

"Wait here," Vasyelu said, and went into the room, shutting the door, leaving the other outside it in the dark.

The windows which had shone bright outside were black within. The candles burned, red and white as carnations.

The Vampire was seated before her little harpsichord. She had probably been playing it, its song so quiet it was seldom audible beyond her door. Long ago, nonetheless, he would have heard it. Long ago—

"Princess," he said, "I have brought someone with me."

He had not been sure what she would do, or say, confronted by the actuality. She might even remonstrate, grow angry, though he had not often seen her angry. But he saw now she had guessed, in some tangible way, that he would not return alone, and she had been preparing herself. As she rose to her feet, he beheld the red satin dress, the jewelled silver crucifix at her throat, the trickle of silver from her ears. On the thin hands, the great rings throbbed their sable colours. Her hair, which had never lost its blackness, abbreviated at her shoulders and waved in a fashion of only twenty years before, framed the starved bones of her face with a savage luxuriance. She was magnificent. Gaunt, elderly, her beauty lost, her heart dulled, yet—magnificent, wondrous.

He stared at her humbly, ready to weep because, for the half of one half moment, he had doubted.

"Yes," she said. She gave him the briefest smile, like a swift caress. "Then I will see him, Vassu."

Snake was seated cross-legged a short distance along the passage. He had discovered, in the dark, a slender Chinese vase of the *yang-ts'ai* palette, and held it between his hands, his chin resting on the brim.

"Shall I break this?" he asked.

Vasyelu ignored the remark. He indicated the opened door.

"You may go in now."

"May I? How excited you're making me."

Snake flowed upright. Still holding the vase, he went through into the Vampire's apartment. The old man came into the room after him, placing his black-garbed body, like a shadow, by the door, which he left now standing wide. The old man watched Snake.

Circling slightly, perhaps unconsciously, he had approached a third of the chamber's length towards the woman. Seeing him from the back, Vasyelu Gorin was able to observe all the play of tautening muscles along the spine, like those of something readying itself to spring, or to escape. Yet, not seeing the face, the eyes, was unsatisfactory. The old man shifted his position, edged shadowlike along the room's perimeter, until he had gained a better vantage.

"Good evening," the Vampire said to Snake. "Would you care to put down the vase? Or, if you prefer, smash it. Indecision can be distressing."

"Perhaps I'd prefer to keep the vase."

"Oh, then do so, by all means. But I suggest you allow Vasyelu to wrap it up for you, before you go. Or someone may rob you on the street."

Snake pivoted lightly, like a dancer, and put the vase on a side-table. Turning again, he smiled at her.

"There are so many valuable things here. What shall I take? What about the silver cross you're wearing?"

The Vampire also smiled.

"An heirloom. I am rather fond of it. I do not recommend you should try to take that."

Snake's eyes enlarged. He was naïve, amazed.

"But I thought, if I did what you wanted, if I made you happy—I could have whatever I liked. Wasn't that the bargain?"

"And how would you propose to make me happy?"

Snake went close to her; he prowled about her, very slowly. Disgusted, fascinated, the old man watched him. Snake stood behind her, leaning against her, his breath stirring the filaments of her hair. He slipped his left hand along her shoulder, sliding from the red satin to the dry uncoloured skin of her throat. Vasyelu remembered the touch of the hand, electric, and so sensitive, the fingers of an artist or a surgeon.

The Vampire never changed. She said:

"No. You will not make me happy, my child."

"Oh," Snake said into her ear. "You can't be certain. If you like, if you really like, I'll let you drink my blood."

The Vampire laughed. It was frightening. Something dormant yet intensely powerful seemed to come alive in her as she did so, like flame from a finished coal. The sound, the appalling life, shook the young man away from her. And for an instant, the old man saw fear in the leopard-yellow eyes, a fear as intrinsic to the being of Snake as to cause fear was intrinsic to the being of the Vampire.

And, still blazing with her power, she turned on him.

"What do you think I am," she said, "some senile hag greedy to rub her scaley flesh against your smoothness; some hag you can, being yourself without sanity or fastidiousness, corrupt with the phantoms, the left-overs of pleasure, and then murder, tearing the gems from her fingers with your teeth? Or I am a perverted hag, wanting to lick up your youth with your juices. Am I that? Come now," she said, her fire lowering itself, crackling with its amusement, with everything she held in check, her voice a long, long pin, skewering what she spoke to against the farther wall. "Come now. How can I be such a fiend, and wear the crucifix on my breast? My ancient, withered, fallen, empty breast. Come now. What's in a name?"

As the pin of her voice came out of him, the young man pushed himself away from the wall. For an instant there was an air of panic about him. He was accustomed to the characteristics of the world. Old men creeping through rainy alleys could not strike mighty blows with their iron hands. Women were moths that burnt, but did not burn, tones of tinsel and pleading, not razor blades.

Snake shuddered all over. And then his panic went away. Instinctively, he told something from the aura of the room itself. Living as he did, generally he had come to trust his instincts.

He slunk back to the woman, not close, this time, no nearer than two yards.

"Your man over there," he said, "he took me to a fancy restaurant. He got me drunk. I say things when I'm drunk I shouldn't say. You see? I'm a lout. I shouldn't be here in your nice house. I don't know how to talk to people like you. To a lady. You see? But I haven't any money. None. Ask him. I explained it all. I'll do anything for money. And the way I talk. Some of them like it. You see? It makes me sound dangerous. They like that. But it's just an act." Fawning on her, bending on her the groundless glory of his eyes, he had also retreated, was almost at the door.

The Vampire made no move. Like a marvellous waxwork she dominated the room, red and white and black, and the old man was only a shadow in a corner.

Snake darted about and bolted. In the blind lightlessness, he skimmed the passage, leapt out in space upon the stairs, touched, leapt, touched, reached the open area beyond. Some glint of star-shine revealed the stained-glass panes in the door. As it crashed open, he knew quite well that he had been let go. Then it slammed behind him and he pelted through ivy and down the outer steps, and across the hollow plain of tall wet trees.

So much, infallibly, his instincts had told him. Strangely, even as he came out of the gates upon the vacant road, and raced towards the heart of the city, they did not tell him he was free.

"Do you recollect," said the Vampire, "you asked me, at the very beginning, about the crucifix."

"I do recollect, Princess. It seemed odd to me, then. I did not understand, of course."

"And you," she said. "How would you have it, after—" She waited, then said, "After you leave me."

He rejoiced that his death would cause her a momentary pain. He could not help that, now. He had seen the fire wake in her, flash and scald in her, as it had not done for half a century, ignited by the presence of the thief, the gigolo, the parasite.

"He," said the old man, "is young and strong, and can dig some pit for me."

"And no ceremony?" She had overlooked his petulance, of course, and her tact made him ashamed.

"Just to lie quiet will be enough," he said, "but thank you, Princess, for your care. I do not suppose it will matter. Either there is nothing, or there is something so different I shall be astonished by it."

"Ah, my friend. Then you do not imagine yourself damned?"

"No," he said. "No, no." And all at once there was passion in his voice, one last fire of his own to offer her. "In the life you gave me, I was blessed."

She closed her eyes, and Vasyelu Gorin perceived he had wounded her with his love. And, no longer peevishly, but in the way of a lover, he was glad.

Next day, a little before three in the afternoon, Snake returned.

A wind was blowing, and seemed to have blown him to the door in a scurry of old brown leaves. His hair was also blown, and bright, his face wind-slapped to a ridiculous freshness. His eyes, however, were heavy, encircled, dulled. The eyes showed, as did nothing else about him, that he had spent the night, the forenoon, engaged in his second line of commerce. They might have drawn thick curtains and blown out the lights, but that would not have helped him. The senses of Snake were doubly acute in the dark, and he could see in the dark, like a lynx.

"Yes?" said the old man, looking at him blankly, as if at a tradesman.

"Yes," said Snake, and came by him into the house.

Vasyelu did not stop him. Of course not. He allowed the young man, and all his blown gleamingness and his wretched roué eyes, to stroll across to the doors of the salon, and walk through. Vasyelu followed.

The blinds, a sombre ivory colour, were down, and lamps had been lit; on a polished table hot-house flowers foamed from a jade bowl. A second door stood open on the small library, the soft glow of the lamps trembling over gold-worked spines, up and up, a torrent of static, priceless books.

Snake went into and around the library, and came out.

"I didn't take anything."

"Can you even read?" snapped Vasyelu Gorin, remembering when he could not, a wood-cutter's fifth son, an oaf and a sot, drinking his way or sleeping his way through a life without windows or vistas, a mere blackness of error and unrecognised boredom. Long ago. In that little town cobbled together under the forest. And the château with its starry lights, the carriages on the road, shining, the dark trees either side. And bowing in answer to a question, lifting a silver comfit box from a pocket as easily as he had lifted a coin the day before . . .

Snake sat down, leaning back relaxedly in the chair. He was not relaxed, the old man knew. What was he telling himself? That there was money here, eccentricity to be battened upon. That he could take her, the old woman, one way or another. There were always excuses that one could make to oneself.

When the Vampire entered the room, Snake, practised, a gigolo, came to his feet. And the Vampire was amused by him, gently now. She wore a bone-white frock that had been sent from Paris last year. She had never worn it before. Pinned at the neck was a black velvet rose with a single drop of dew shivering on a single petal: a pearl that had come from the crown jewels of a czar. Her tact, her peerless tact. *Naturally,* the pearl was saying, *this is why you have come back. Naturally. There is nothing to fear.*

Vasyelu Gorin left them. He returned later with the decanters and glasses. The cold supper had been laid out by people from the city who handled such things, paté and lobster and chicken, lemon slices cut like flowers, orange slices like suns, tomatoes that were anemones, and oceans of green lettuce, and cold, glittering ice. He decanted the wines. He arranged the silver coffee service, the boxes of different cigarettes. The winter night had settled by then against the house, and, roused by the brilliantly lighted rooms, a moth was dashing itself between the candles and the coloured fruits. The old man caught it in a crystal goblet, took it away, let it go into the darkness. For a hundred years and more, he had never killed anything.

Sometimes, he heard them laugh. The young man's laughter was at first too eloquent, too beautiful, too unreal. But then, it became ragged, boisterous; it became genuine.

The wind blew stonily. Vasyelu Gorin imagined the frail moth beating its wings against the huge wings of the wind, falling spent to the ground. It would be good to rest.

In the last half hour before dawn, she came quietly from the salon, and up the stair. The old man knew she had seen him as he waited in the shadows. That she did not look at him or call to him was her attempt to spare him this sudden sheen that was upon her, its direct and pitiless glare. So he glimpsed it obliquely, no more. Her straight pale figure ascending, slim and limpid as a girl's. Her eyes were young, full of a primal refinding, full of utter newness.

In the salon, Snake slept under his jacket on the long white couch, its brocaded cushions beneath his cheek. Would he, on waking, carefully examine his throat in a mirror?

The old man watched the young man sleeping. She had taught Vasyelu Gorin how to speak five languages, and how to read three others. She had allowed him to discover music, and art, history and the stars; profundity, mercy. He had found the closed tomb of life opened out on every side into unbelievable, inexpressible landscapes. And yet, and yet. The journey must have its end. Worn out with ecstasy and experience, too tired anymore to laugh with joy. To rest was everything. To be still. Only she could continue, for only she could be eternally reborn. For Vasyelu, once had been enough.

He left the young man sleeping. Five hours later, Snake was noiselessly gone. He had taken all the cigarettes, but nothing else.

Snake sold the cigarettes quickly. At one of the cafés he sometimes frequented, he met with those who, sensing some change in his fortunes, urged him to boast. Snake did not, remaining irritatingly reticent, vague. It was another patron. An old man who liked to give him things. Where did the old man live? Oh, a fine apartment, the north side of the city.

Some of the day, he walked.

A hunter, he distrusted the open veldt of daylight. There was too little cover, and equally too great cover for the things he stalked. In the afternoon, he sat in the gardens of a museum. Students came and went, seriously alone, or in groups riotously. Snake observed them. They were scarcely younger than he himself, yet to him, another species. Now and then a girl, catching his eye, might smile, or make an attempt to linger, to interest him. Snake did not respond. With the economic contempt of what he had become, he dismissed all such sexual encounters. Their allure, their youth, these were commodities valueless in others. They would not pay him.

The old woman, however, he did not dismiss. How old was she? Sixty, perhaps—no, much older. Ninety was more likely. And yet her face, her neck, her hands, were curiously smooth, unlined. At times, she might only have been fifty. And the dyed hair, which should have made her seem raddled, somehow enhanced the illusion of a young woman.

Yes, she fascinated him. Probably she had been an actress. Foreign, theatrical—rich. If she was prepared to keep him, thinking him mistakenly her pet cat, then he was willing, for a while. He could steal from her when she began to cloy and he decided to leave.

Yet, something in the uncomplexity of these thoughts disturbed him. The first time he had run away, he was unsure now from what. Not the vampire name, certainly, a stage name—*Draculas*—what else? But from something—some awareness of fate for which idea his vocabulary had no word, and no explanation. Driven once away, driven thereafter to return, since it was foolish not to. And she had known how to treat him. Gracefully, graciously. She would be honourable, for her kind always were. Used to spending money for what they wanted, they did not baulk at buying people, too. They had never forgotten flesh, also, had a price, since their roots were firmly locked in an era when there had been slaves.

But. But he would not, he told himself, go there tonight. No. It would be good she should not be able to rely on him. He might go tomorrow, or the next day, but not tonight.

The turning world lifted away from the sun, through a winter sunset, into darkness. Snake was glad to see the ending of the light, and false light instead spring up from the apartment blocks, the cafés.

He moved out onto the wide pavement of a street, and a man came and took his arm on the right side, another starting to walk by him on the left.

"Yes, this is the one, the one calls himself Snake."

"Are you?" the man who walked beside him asked.

"Of course it is," said the first man, squeezing his arm. "Didn't we have an exact description? Isn't he just the way he was described?"

"And the right place, too," agreed the other man, who did not hold him. "The right area."

The men wore neat nondescript clothing. Their faces were sallow and smiling, and fixed. This was a routine with which both were familiar. Snake did not know them, but he knew the touch, the accent, the smiling fixture of their masks. He had tensed. Now he let the tension melt away, so they should see and feel it had gone.

"What do you want?"

The man who held his arm only smiled.

The other man said, "Just to earn our living."

"Doing what?"

On either side the lighted street went by. Ahead, at the street's corner, a vacant lot opened where a broken wall lunged away into the shadows.

"It seems you upset someone," said the man who only walked. "Upset them badly."

"I upset a lot of people," Snake said.

"I'm sure you do. But some of them won't stand for it."

"Who was this? Perhaps I should see them."

"No. They don't want that. They don't want you to see anybody." The black turn was a few feet away.

"Perhaps I can put it right."

"No. That's what we've been paid to do."

"But if I don't know—" said Snake, and lurched against the man who held his arm, ramming his fist into the soft belly. The man let go of him and fell. Snake ran. He ran past the lot, into the brilliant glare of another street beyond, and was almost laughing when the thrown knife caught him in the back.

The lights turned over. Something hard and cold struck his chest, his face. Snake realised it was the pavement. There was a dim blurred noise, coming and going, perhaps a crowd gathering. Someone stood on his ribs and pulled the knife out of him and the pain began.

"Is that it?" a choked voice asked some way above him: the man he had punched in the stomach.

"It'll do nicely."

A new voice shouted. A car swam to the kerb and pulled up raucously. The car door slammed, and footsteps went over the cement. Behind him, Snake heard the two men walking briskly away.

Snake began to get up, and was surprised to find he was unable to.

"What happened?" someone asked, high, high above.

"I don't know."

A woman said softly, "Look, there's blood—"

Snake took no notice. After a moment he tried again to get up, and succeeded in getting to his knees. He had been hurt, that was all. He could feel the pain, no longer sharp, blurred, like the noise he could hear, coming and going. He opened his eyes. The light had faded, then came back in a long wave, then faded again. There seemed to be only five or six people standing around him. As he rose, the nearer shapes backed away.

"He shouldn't move," someone said urgently.

A hand touched his shoulder, fluttered off, like an insect.

The light faded into black, and the noise swept in like a tide, filling his ears, dazing him. Something supported him, and he shook it from him—a wall—

"Come back, son," a man called. The lights burned up again, reminiscent of a cinema. He would be all right in a moment. He walked away from the small crowd, not looking at them. Respectfully, in awe, they let him go, and noted his blood trailing behind him along the pavement.

The French clock chimed sweetly in the salon; it was seven. Beyond the window, the park was black. It had begun to rain again.

The old man had been watching from the downstairs window for rather more than an hour. Sometimes, he would step restlessly away, circle the room, straighten a picture, pick up a petal discarded by the dying flowers. Then go back to the window, looking out at the trees, the rain, and the night.

Less than a minute after the chiming of the clock, a piece of the static darkness came away and began to move, very slowly, towards the house.

Vasyelu Gorin went out into the hall. As he did so, he glanced towards the stairway. The lamp at the stairhead was alight, and she stood there in its rays, her hands lying loosely at her sides, elegant as if weightless, her head raised.

"Princess?"

"Yes, I know. Please hurry, Vassu. I think there is scarcely any margin left."

The old man opened the door quickly. He sprang down the steps as lightly as a boy of eighteen. The black rain swept against his face, redolent of a thousand memories, and he ran through an orchard in Burgundy, across a hillside in Tuscany, along the path of a wild garden near St. Petersburg that was St. Petersburg no more, until he reached the body of a young man lying over the roots of a tree.

The old man bent down, and an eye opened palely in the dark and looked at him.

"Knifed me," said Snake. "Crawled all this way."

Vasyelu Gorin leaned in the rain to the grass of France, Italy, and Russia, and lifted Snake in his arms. The body lolled, heavy, not helping him. But it did not matter. How strong he was, he might marvel at it, as he stood, holding the young man across his breast, and turning, ran back towards the house.

"I don't know," Snake muttered, "don't know who sent them. Plenty would like to—How bad is it? I didn't think it was so bad."

The ivy drifted across Snake's face and he closed his eyes.

As Vasyelu entered the hall, the Vampire was already on the lowest stair. Vasyelu carried the dying man across to her, and laid him at her feet. Then Vasyelu turned to leave.

"Wait," she said.

"No, Princess. This is a private thing. Between the two of you, as once it was between us. I do not want to see it, Princess. I do not want to see it with another."

She looked at him, for a moment like a child, sorry to have distressed him, unwilling to give in. Then she nodded. "Go then, my dear."

He went away at once. So he did not witness it as she left the stair, and knelt beside Snake on the Turkish carpet newly coloured with blood. Yet, it seemed to him he heard the rustle her dress made, like thin crisp paper, and the whisper of the tiny dagger parting her flesh, and then the long still sigh.

He walked down through the house, into the clean and frigid modern kitchen full of electricity. There he sat, and remembered the forest above the town, the torches as the yelling aristocrats hunted him for his theft of the comfit box, the blows when they caught up with him. He remembered, with a painless unoppressed refinding, what it was like to begin to die in such a way, the confused anger, the coming and going of tangible things, long pulses of being alternating with deep valleys of non-being. And then the agonised impossible crawl, fingers in the earth itself, pulling him forward, legs sometimes able to assist, sometimes failing, passengers which must be dragged with the rest. In the graveyard at the edge of the estate, he ceased to move. He could go no farther. The soil was cold, and the white tombs, curious petrified vegetation over his head, seemed to suck the black sky into themselves, so they darkened, and the sky grew pale.

But as the sky was drained of its blood, the foretaste of day began to possess it. In less than an hour, the sun would rise.

He had heard her name, and known he would eventually come to serve her. The way in which he had known, both for himself and for the young man called Snake, had been in a presage of violent death.

All the while, searching through the city, there had been no one with that stigma upon him, that mark. Until, in the alley, the warm hand gripped his neck, until he looked into the leopard-coloured eyes. Then Vasyelu saw the mark, smelled the scent of it like singed bone.

How Snake, crippled by a mortal wound, bleeding and semi-aware, had brought himself such a distance, through the long streets hard as nails, through the mossy garden-land of the rich, through the colossal gates, over the watery night-tuned plain, so far, dying, the old man did not require to ask, or to be puzzled by. He, too, had done such a thing, more than two centuries ago. And there she had found him, between the tall white graves. When he could focus his vision again, he had looked and seen her, the most beautiful thing he ever set eyes upon. She had given him her blood. He had drunk the blood of Darejan Draculas, a princess, a vampire. Unique elixir, it had saved him. All wounds had healed. Death had dropped from him like a torn skin, and everything he had been—scavenger, thief, brawler, drunkard, and, for a certain number of coins, *whore*—each of these things had crumbled away. Standing up, he had trodden on them, left them behind. He had gone to her, and kneeled down as, a short while before, she had kneeled by him, cradling him, giving him the life of her silver veins.

And this, all this, was now for the other. Even her blood, it seemed, did not bestow immortality, only longevity, at last coming to a stop for Vasyelu Gorin. And so, many many decades from this night the other, too, would come to the same hiatus. Snake, too, would remember the waking moment, conscious another now endured the stupefied thrill of it, and all that would begin thereafter.

Finally, with a sort of guiltiness, the old man left the hygienic kitchen and went back towards the glow of the upper floor, stealing out into the shadow at the light's edge.

He understood that she would sense him there, untroubled by his presence—had she not been prepared to let him remain?

It was done.

Her dress was spread like an open rose, the young man lying against her, his eyes wide, gazing up at her. And she would be the most beautiful thing that he had ever seen. All about, invisible, the shed skins of his life, husks he would presently scuff uncaringly underfoot. And she?

The Vampire's head inclined towards Snake. The dark hair fell softly. Her face, powdered by the lampshine, was young, was full of vitality, serene vivacity, loveliness. Everything had come back to her. She was reborn.

Perhaps it was only an illusion.

The old man bowed his head, there in the shadows. The jealousy, the regret, were gone. In the end, his life with her had become only another skin that he must cast. He would have the peace that she might never have, and be glad of it. The young man would serve her, and she would be huntress once more, and dancer, a bright phantom gliding over the ballroom of the city, this city and others, and all the worlds of land and soul between.

Vasyelu Gorin stirred on the platform of his existence. He would depart now, or very soon; already he heard the murmur of the approaching train. It would be simple, this time, not like the other time at all. To go willingly, everything achieved, in order. Knowing she was safe.

There was even a faint colour in her cheeks, a blooming. Or maybe, that was just a trick of the lamp.

The old man waited until they had risen to their feet, and walked together quietly into the salon, before he came from the shadows and began to climb the stairs, hearing the silence, their silence, like that of new lovers.

At the head of the stair, beyond the lamp, the dark was gentle, soft as the Vampire's hair. Vasyelu walked forward into the dark without misgiving, tenderly.

How he had loved her.

—1983

CLIVE BARKER

B. 1952

Clive Barker was born to Len and Joan Barker in Liverpool, England, near Penny Lane, the street made famous by the Beatles' hit song. His father, Len, worked in industrial relations, and his mother, Joan, was a school welfare officer. Barker was introduced to fantasy literature, such as J. M. Barrie's Peter Pan *(1904) and Kenneth Grahame's* The Wind in the Willows *(1908), at an early age by his mother, but he was quickly drawn to the horror fiction of Edgar Allan Poe. He also enjoyed horror films, such as George Pal and Byron Haskin's* The War of the Worlds *(1953) and Alfred*

Hitchcock's Psycho *(1960). After studying philosophy and English at the University of Liverpool, Barker moved to London in 1977 where he worked as a graphic artist. He also became involved in London's avant-garde theater, acting in plays that he wrote.*

Barker discovered his early fame, however, in popular horror fiction. When he was about twenty-eight or twenty-nine years old, he began writing the stories that were later to comprise his famous Books of Blood *anthology. In a genre where it is difficult to find commercial success with the short story format, Barker's* Books of Blood *proved the exception to the rule, granting him quick notoriety. His short fiction is distinguished by its ability to parody established horror formulas and by its highly inventive quality. Barker may borrow from such past masters of horror as Edgar Allan Poe ("New Murders in the Rue Morgue") and Gaston Leroux ("Sex, Death and Starshine"), but only to burlesque what has been done before. Indeed, Barker frequently uses his stories in his six-volume* Books of Blood *(1984-1985) as a philosophical vehicle to express his love of imagination— from the grotesque to the wonderful—and his dislike of banality.*

Barker's first novel, The Damnation Game, *was published in 1985, and he also published two short novels—*The Hellbound Heart *and* Cabal—*in 1986 and 1988, respectively. Recently, Barker has left the horror story and has been working with the epic fantasy genre, writing a number of massively popular novels, such as* Weaveworld *(1987),* The Great and Secret Show *(1989),* Imajica *(1991), and* Everville *(1994), that more fully exhibit the diverse range of his imaginative skills. In 1992, he published a dark fantasy novel for children entitled* The Thief of Always. *Barker has enjoyed as much success in movie making as he has in fiction writing. He wrote the screenplays for* Underworld *(1985) and* Rawhead Rex *(1986); he wrote and directed the movies* Hellraiser *(which was based on his short novel,* The Hellbound Heart*) in 1987,* Nightbreed *(which was based on his short novel,* Cabal*) in 1990, and* Lord of Illusions *(which was based on his short story, "The Last Illusion") in 1995. In addition, he has produced the several* Hellraiser *sequels, as well as the 1992 film* Candyman *(based on his short story, "The Forbidden"). Currently, Barker lives and works in Beverly Hills, California. He is one of the most versatile and literate of contemporary best-selling authors of horror and fantasy fiction.*

For Barker, the Faust character—that individual who sells his soul to the devil for wealth, power, or knowledge—is an important mythic protagonist who figures prominently in the development of the popular horror story. Barker offers his own updated and distinctive variant of the Faust archetype in "Down, Satan!," initially published in the fourth volume of Clive Barker's Books of Blood *(titled in the U.S. as* The Inhuman Condition, *1985).*

DOWN, SATAN!

Circumstances had made Gregorius rich beyond all calculation. He owned fleets and palaces; stallions; cities. Indeed he owned so much that to those who were finally charged with enumerating his possessions—when the events of this story reached their monstrous conclusion—it sometimes seemed it might be quicker to list the items Gregorius did *not* own.

Rich he was, but far from happy. He had been raised a Catholic, and in his early years—before his dizzying rise to fortune—he'd found succor in his faith. But he'd neglected it, and it was only at the age of fifty-five, with the world at his feet, that he woke one night and found himself Godless.

It was a bitter blow, but he immediately took steps to make good his loss. He went to Rome and spoke with the Supreme Pontiff; he prayed night and day; he founded seminaries and leper colonies. God, however, declined to show so much as His toenail. Gregorius, it seemed, was forsaken.

Almost despairing, he took it into his head that he could only win his way back into the arms of his Maker if he put his soul into the direst jeopardy. The notion had some merit. Suppose, he thought, I could contrive a meeting with Satan, the Arch-fiend. Seeing me *in extremis,* would not God be obliged to step in and deliver me back into the fold?

It was a fine plot, but how was he to realize it? The Devil did not just come at a call, even for a tycoon such as Gregorius, and his researches soon proved that all the traditional methods of summoning the Lord of Vermin—the defiling of the Blessed Sacrament, the sacrificing of babes—were no more effective than his good works had been at provoking Yahweh. It was only after a year of deliberation that he finally fell upon his master plan. He would arrange to have built a hell on earth— a modern inferno so monstrous that the Tempter would be tempted, and come to roost there like a cuckoo in a usurped nest.

He searched high and low for an architect and found, languishing in a madhouse outside Florence, a man called Leopardo, whose plans for Mussolini's palaces had a lunatic grandeur that suited Gregorius's project perfectly. Leopardo was taken from his cell—a fetid, wretched old man—and given his dreams again. His genius for the prodigious had not deserted him.

In order to fuel his invention the great libraries of the world were scoured for descriptions of hells both secular and metaphysical. Museum vaults were ransacked for forbidden images of martyrdom. No stone was left unturned if it was suspected something perverse was concealed beneath.

The finished designs owed something to de Sade and to Dante, and something more to Freud and Krafft-Ebing, but there was also much there that no mind had conceived of before, or at least ever dared set to paper.

A site in North Africa was chosen, and work on Gregorius's New Hell began. Everything about the project broke the records. Its foundations were vaster, its walls thicker, its plumbing more elaborate than any edifice hitherto attempted. Gregorius watched its slow construction with an enthusiasm he had not tasted since his first years as an empire builder. Needless to say, he was widely thought to have lost his mind. Friends he had known for years refused to associate with him. Several of his companies collapsed when investors took fright at reports of his insanity. He didn't care. His plan could not fail. The Devil would be bound to come, if only out of curiosity to see this leviathan built in his name, and when he did, Gregorius would be waiting.

The work took four years and the better part of Gregorius's fortune. The finished building was the size of half a dozen cathedrals and boasted every facility the Angel of the Pit could desire. Fires burned behind its walls, so that to walk in many of its corridors was almost unendurable agony. The rooms off those corridors were fitted with every imaginable device of persecution—the needle, the rack, the dark—that the genius of Satan's torturers be given fair employ. There were ovens large enough to cremate families; pools deep enough to drown generations. The New Hell was an atrocity waiting to happen; a celebration of inhumanity that only lacked its first cause.

The builders withdrew, and thankfully. It was rumored among them that Satan had long been watching over the construction of his pleasure dome. Some even claimed to have glimpsed him on the deeper levels, where the chill was so profound it froze the piss in your bladder. There was some evidence to support the belief in supernatural presences converging on the building as it neared completion, not least the cruel death of Leopardo, who had either thrown himself or—the superstitious argued—been pitched *through* his sixth-story hotel window. He was buried with due extravagance.

So now, alone in hell, Gregorius waited.

He did not have to wait long. He had been there a day, no more, when he heard noises from the lower depths. Anticipation brimming, he went in search of their source, but found only the roiling of excrement baths and the rattling of ovens. He returned to his suite of chambers on the ninth level and waited. The noises came again; again he went in search of their source; again he came away disappointed.

The disturbances did not abate, however. In the days that followed scarcely ten minutes would pass without his hearing some sound of occupancy. The Prince of Darkness was here, Gregorius could have no doubt of it, but he was keeping to the shadows. Gregorius was content to play along. It was the Devil's party, after all. His to play whatever game he chose.

But during the long and often lonely months that followed, Gregorius wearied of this hide-and-seek and began to demand that Satan show himself. His voice rang unanswered down the deserted corridors, however, until his throat was bruised with shouting. Thereafter he went about his searches stealthily, hoping to catch his tenant unawares. But the Apostate Angel always flitted away before Gregorius could step within sight of him.

They would play a waiting game, it seemed, he and Satan, chasing each other's tails through ice and fire and ice again. Gregorius told himself to be patient. The Devil had come, hadn't he? Wasn't that his fingerprint on the door handle? His turd on the stairs? Sooner or later the Fiend would show his face, and Gregorius would spit on it.

The world outside went on its way, and Gregorius was consigned to the company of other recluses who had been ruined by wealth. His Folly, as it was known, was not entirely without visitors, however. There were a few who had loved him too much to forget him—a few, also, who had profited by him and hoped to turn his madness to their further profit—who dared the gates of the New Hell. These visitors made the journey without announcing their intentions, fearing the disapproval of their friends. The investigations into their subsequent disappearance never reached as far as North Africa.

And in his folly Gregorius still chased the Serpent, and the Serpent still eluded him, leaving only more and more terrible signs of his occupancy as the months went by.

It was the wife of one of the missing visitors who finally discovered the truth and alerted the authorities. Gregorius's Folly was put under surveillance, and finally—

some three years after its completion—a quartet of officers braved the threshold.

Without maintenance the Folly had begun to deteriorate badly. The lights had failed on many of the levels, its walls had cooled, its pitch pits solidified. But as the officers advanced through the gloomy vaults in search of Gregorius they came upon ample evidence that despite its decrepit condition the New Hell was in good working order. There were bodies in the ovens, their faces wide and black. There were human remains seated and strung up in many of the rooms, gouged and pricked and slit to death.

Their terror grew with every door they pressed open, every new abomination their fevered eyes fell upon.

Two of the four who crossed the threshold never reached the chamber at its center. Terror overtook them on their way and they fled, only to be waylaid in some choked passageway and added to the hundreds who had perished in the Folly since Satan had taken residence.

Of the pair who finally unearthed the perpetrator, only one had courage enough to tell his story, though the scenes he faced there in the Folly's heart were almost too terrible to bear relating.

There was no sign of Satan, of course. There was only Gregorius. The master builder, finding no one to inhabit the house he had sweated over, had occupied it himself. He had with him a few disciples whom he'd mustered over the years. They, like him, seemed unremarkable creatures. But there was not a torture device in the building they had not made thorough and merciless use of.

Gregorius did not resist his arrest. Indeed he seemed pleased to have a platform from which to boast of his butcheries. Then, and later at his trial, he spoke freely of his ambition and his appetite; and of how much *more* blood he would spill if they would only set him free to do so. Enough to drown all belief and its delusions, he swore. And still he would not be satisfied. For God was rotting in paradise, and Satan in the abyss, and who was to stop him?

He was much reviled during the trial, and later in the asylum where, under some suspicious circumstances, he died barely two months later. The Vatican expunged all report of him from its records. The seminaries founded in his unholy name were dissolved.

But there were those, even among the cardinals, who could not put his unrepentant malice out of their heads, and—in the privacy of their doubt—wondered if he had not succeeded in his strategy. If, in giving up all hope of angels—fallen or otherwise—he had not become one himself.

Or all that earth could bear of such phenomena.

—1985

CRITICAL BIBLIOGRAPHY

Aguirre, Manuel. *The Closed Space: Horror Literature and Western Symbolism.* Manchester: Manchester UP, 1990.

Barron, Neil, ed. *Horror Literature: A Reader's Guide.* New York: Garland, 1990.

Bataille, Georges. *Literature and Evil.* Trans. Alastair Hamilton. London: Marion Boyars, 1990.

Bayer-Berenbaum, Linda. *The Gothic Imagination: Expansion in Gothic Literature and Art.* Rutherford: Fairleigh Dickinson UP, 1982.

Briggs, Julia. *Night Visitors: The Rise and Fall of the English Ghost Story.* London: Faber, 1977.

Brooke-Rose, Christine. *A Rhetoric of the Unreal: Studies in Narrative and Structure, Especially of the Fantastic.* Cambridge: Cambridge UP, 1981.

Büssing, Sabine. *Aliens in the Home: The Child in Horror Fiction.* New York: Greenwood, 1987.

Carpenter, Lynette, and Wendy K. Kolmar, eds. *Haunting the House of Fiction: Feminist Perspectives on Ghost Stories by American Women.* Knoxville: U of Tennessee P, 1991.

DeLamotte, Eugenia C. *Perils of the Night: A Feminist Study of Nineteenth-Century Gothic.* New York: Oxford UP, 1990.

Docherty, Brian, ed. *American Horror Fiction: From Brockden Brown to Stephen King.* New York: St. Martin's, 1990.

Drake, Douglas. *Horror!* New York: Macmillan, 1966.

Ellis, Kate Ferguson. *The Contested Castle: Gothic Novels and the Subversion of Domestic Ideology.* Urbana: U of Illinois P, 1989.

Frank, Frederick S. *Through the Pale Door: A Guide to and Through the American Gothic.* New York: Greenwood, 1990.

Frost, Brian J. *The Monster with a Thousand Faces: Guises of the Vampire in Myth and Literature.* Bowling Green: BGSU Popular P, 1989.

Haggerty, George E. *Gothic Fiction/Gothic Form.* University Park: Pennsylvania State UP, 1989.

Haining, Peter, ed. *The Penny Dreadful: Or, Strange, Horrid & Sensational Tales!* London: Victor Gollancz, 1976.

Heller, Terry. *The Delights of Terror: An Aesthetics of the Tale of Terror.* Urbana: U of Illinois P, 1987.

Hennessy, Brendan. *The Gothic Novel.* Burnt Mill: Longman, 1978.

Ingebretsen, Edward, J. *Maps of Heaven, Maps of Hell: Religious Terror as Memory from the Puritans to Stephen King.* Armonk: M. E. Sharpe, 1996.

Jackson, Rosemary. *Fantasy: The Literature of Subversion.* London: Methuen, 1981.

Jones, Robert Kenneth. *The Shudder Pulps: A History of the Weird Menace Magazines of the 1930's.* New York: Plume, 1978.

Kerr, Howard, John W. Crowley, and Charles L. Crow, eds. *The Haunted Dusk: American Supernatural Fiction, 1820–1920.* Athens: U of Georgia P, 1983.

MacAndrew, Elizabeth. *The Gothic Tradition in Fiction.* New York: Columbia UP, 1979.

Massé, Michelle A. *In the Name of Love: Women, Masochism, and the Gothic.* Ithaca: Cornell UP, 1992.

Monleón, José B. *A Specter is Haunting Europe: A Sociohistorical Approach to the Fantastic.* Princeton: Princeton UP, 1990.

Penzoldt, Peter. *The Supernatural in Fiction.* New York: Humanities Press, 1965.

Railo, Eino. *The Haunted Castle: A Study of the Elements of English Romanticism.* New York: Dutton, 1927.

Reynolds, David S. *Beneath the American Renaissance: The Subversive Imagination in the Age of Emerson and Melville.* New York: Knopf, 1988.

Ringe, Donald A. *American Gothic: Imagination and Reason in Nineteenth-Century Fiction.* Lexington: U of Kentucky P, 1982.

Sage, Victor, ed. *The Gothick Novel.* Houndmills: Macmillan, 1990.

——. *Horror Fiction in the Protestant Tradition.* Houndmills: Macmillan, 1988.

St. John Barclay, Glen. *Anatomy of Horror: The Masters of Occult Fiction.* London: Weidenfeld and Nicolson, 1978.

Schweitzer, Darrell, ed. *Discovering Modern Horror Fiction.* Mercer Island: Starmont House, 1985.

——, ed. *Discovering Modern Horror Fiction: II.* Mercer Island: Starmont House, 1988.

Sullivan, Jack. *Elegant Nightmares: The English Ghost Story from Le Fanu to Blackwood.* Athens: Ohio UP, 1978.

——, ed. *The Penguin Encyclopedia of Horror and the Supernatural.* New York: Viking, 1986.

Summers, Montague. *The Gothic Quest: A History of the Gothic Novel.* New York: Russell & Russell, 1964.

Tropp, Martin. *Images of Fear: How Horror Stories Helped Shape Modern Culture (1818–1918).* Jefferson: McFarland, 1990.

Varma, Devendra P. *The Gothic Flame.* New York: Russell & Russell, 1966.

Varnado, S. L. Haunted Presence: *The Numinous in Gothic Fiction.* Tuscaloosa: U of Alabama P, 1987.

Wagenknecht, Edward. *Seven Masters of Supernatural Fiction.* New York: Greenwood, 1991.

2

ROMANCE FICTION

At heart (pun intended), the romance features an evolving love relationship between an amorous couple that leads to a permanent, emotional commitment. Among all the major genres of popular fiction, the romance story is the most commercially successful: it accounts for a staggering thirty-five to forty percent of the paperback market. Rita C. Hubbard reports that Harlequin Books—one of the world's leading specialty publishers—accounted for 168 million copies of romance novels sold in 1979 alone.

Despite these impressive sales figures, romance fiction is perhaps the least critically regarded category of popular fiction. Other genres, such as crime fiction or science fiction, have made significant progress toward general critical respectability, yet, as Jayne Ann Krentz states, "Society does not approve of the reading of romance novels. It labels the books as trash and the readers as unintelligent, uneducated, unsophisticated, or neurotic."

The most likely explanation for this seeming contradiction between the popularity of the best-selling romance and its lack of critical appreciation may rest with how the romance is viewed by an uninformed academic and literary establishment. Krentz, who is herself a best-selling writer of romances, suggests those critics who most vehemently attack romance fiction tend to be ignorant of the meaningful social codes communicated between author and reader. By and large, women are both the authors and the readers of romances (some estimates place these figures as high as ninety-nine percent). With women's writings historically undervalued, it makes sense that a popular literary genre written by women for women would be an easy target for socially conservative, elitist critics who fail to understand that the best-selling romance is an effective form of cultural expression. Romance fiction, at one level, encourages numerous women readers to participate in constructive self-definition. At an even more basic level, a number of romance writers claim that romance fiction allows women to flee the drudgery of daily life by engaging in escapist fantasy that provides deep-rooted emotional satisfaction.

Along with horror fiction, science fiction, and crime fiction, the origin of popular romance fiction is found in the eighteenth-century Gothic novel. Although some narrative elements can be traced to poetry, oral folklore, and early fiction, the romance evolved most directly from Horace Walpole's *The Castle of Otranto* (1764). One of Walpole's literary disciples, Ann Radcliffe (1764-1823), successfully adapted Walpole's Gothic story in novels such as *The Mysteries of Udolpho* (1794), subsequently creating a new type of Gothic narrative with a female, rather than a male, protagonist. Emily St. Aubert's trials and tribulations at finding true love in *The Mysteries of Udolpho* are not unlike those encountered by the typical heroine in a Harlequin Romance.

In nineteenth-century Europe and America, the novel of domestic melodrama—a type of romance that explores dramatic conflicts in family relationships—supplanted the Gothic romance in popularity. Domestic melodramas like Charles Dickens's *Nicholas Nickleby* (1838-1839) and *David Copperfield* (1849-1850) enjoyed tremendous popularity. Even today, Dickens is one of the few "popular" nineteenth-century authors whose work is admired equally by readers, literary critics, and the academic community. Conversely, E. D. E. N. Southworth (1819-1899), an American writer of domestic melodrama who was Dickens's equivalent in popularity, is virtually forgotten by the contemporary reader or critic. Her prodigious literary efforts—which include *Retribution* (1849), *Hickory Hall* (1861), *The Fatal Secret* (1877), and *The Rejected Bride* (1894), among numerous other novels—were among the most popular stories published in America during the mid- to late-1800s. Yet, in the majority of modern literary histories, her body of work is censured, or even ignored. For the contemporary reader, the most famous American author of domestic melodrama is Louisa May Alcott (1832-1888), whose stories, in print and in film, continue to be discovered and enjoyed by new audiences.

During the early years of the nineteenth century in Great Britain, Jane Austen (1775-1817) exerted a tremendous influence on the development of domestic melodrama. Her novels, including *Sense and Sensibility* (1811), *Pride and Prejudice* (1813), *Mansfield Park* (1814), and *Emma* (1816), were influential in clarifying the narrative relationship between romantic love and social manners. In recent years, Hollywood has fully embraced Austen's work, successfully translating her elegant novels to film and television. Two of the more important writers of mid-Victorian romance fiction were Emily Brontë (1818-1848), the author of the classic novel of romantic tragedy, *Wuthering Heights* (1847), and her sister Charlotte Brontë (1816-1855), whose novel *Jane Eyre* (1847) helped define the narrative formula of the contemporary romance more than any other. Twentieth-century British writer Daphne du Maurier (1907-1989), in fact, patterned her most famous romantic thriller, *Rebecca* (1938), after Charlotte Brontë's work, reintroducing the popular romance to a fresh and eager generation of readers. Then, a new form found a thriving readership—the historical romance, as perhaps best represented by two best-selling novels, Margaret Mitchell's Pulitzer Prize-winning *Gone with the Wind* (1936) and Kathleen Winsor's *Forever Amber* (1944).

During the mid-twentieth century, paperback specialty publishers like Harlequin Books began to dominate mass-market publishing with highly formulaic and specially packaged romances that tended to follow the *Rebecca* model. These stories featured virginal heroines romanced and won by more powerful, more experienced (and, at times, even threatening) male lovers. Reflecting the social attitudes of its readers, the Harlequin-style romance emphasized heroines who, through the years, became more aggressive, more socially independent, and assumed positions of greater power and authority.

The post-Harlequin period saw an explosion of specialty publishers who sought to capture specialized portions of the paperback romance readership. Some of these publishers feature commercially successful romance series that promote eroticism and near-graphic depictions of lovemaking. In the last twenty years, authors of popular romances have begun to regularly appear on national best-seller lists. Included among the most successful and influential of these best-selling authors are Barbara Cartland (b. 1901), Janet Dailey (b. 1944), Barbara Delinksy (b. 1945), Rosemary Rogers (b. 1932), and Danielle Steel (b. 1947).

As illustrated in this chapter, romance fiction historically has demonstrated a vibrancy and vitality that has rarely, if ever, been surpassed by the other major genres of popular fiction. Louisa May Alcott's "The Sisters' Trial" offers an excellent model of nineteenth-century American domestic melodrama, while Rosamunde Pilcher's "Lalla" nicely exemplifies how contemporary domestic melodrama may be used to examine important issues regarding social definition and self-identity. The novelette, "Jane," which was written by the most popular romance author of the early twentieth century, Mary Roberts Rinehart, shows how the tale of love and humor make a natural match as entertaining fiction. As the romance story dominated the paperback book market in America following the Second World War, Kathleen E. Woodiwiss's novelette, "The Kiss," is a representative example of the type of historical romance that has earned her a devoted international following. Finally, Jayne Ann Krentz's "Connecting Rooms" and Janet Dailey's *The Healing Touch* reveal why these two best-selling authors of contemporary romance currently are among the genre's most widely read.

LOUISA MAY ALCOTT
1832-1888

Louisa May Alcott is today best remembered as the author of the famous children's novel, Little Women; or, Meg, Jo, Beth and Amy *(1868-69), but during her lifetime she was also a prolific writer of diverse fiction and sketches that ranged in subject from Gothic thrillers, to children's stories, to popular domestic melodrama. Born in Germantown, Pennsylvania, Louisa Alcott was the second of Amos Bronson Alcott's and Abigail May Alcott's four daughters. Her youth was spent in genteel poverty, yet her family's connection to the New England Transcendentalists provided the young Alcott with an adequate (if somewhat non-traditional) educational background in literature and philosophy. In 1843, Alcott's father moved his family to Harvard, Massachusetts, in an unsuccessful attempt to establish a utopian community. This failure was indicative of Amos Bronson Alcott's general inability to provide a suitable livelihood for his household, which subsequently resulted in Louisa dedicating herself, at the relatively young age of twelve, to the support of her family.* Little Women, *in fact, provides a revealing fictionalized autobiography of Alcott's childhood. Like her heroine, Jo March, Alcott's youthful ambitions lay in writing, and much of her early work included thrillers and melodramatic fiction that appeared in the popular serial magazines of that era. Following the outbreak of the Civil War, Alcott served as a nurse at a Washington, D.C., hospital, leaving after six weeks when she contracted typhoid fever. She used these experiences as the basis for* Hospital Sketches *(1863), a published collection of her stories that achieved popular success. In 1865, Alcott traveled to Europe, and upon her return to America, was hired as an editor of the Boston-based children's periodical,* Merry's Museum. *During this period, she wrote and published* Little Women; *her income from this novel allowed her to quit her job as editor, and, in 1870, to travel once again to Europe for a year. Toward the end of her life, she was an avid sponsor of women's rights. Alcott published numerous books, including* An Old-Fashioned Girl *(1870),* Little Men: Life at Plumfield with Jo's Boys *(1871),* Eight Cousins; or, The Aunt-Hill *(1875),* Under the Lilacs *(1878), and* Jack and Jill: A Village Story *(1880). She died in 1888.*

"The Sisters' Trial," one of Alcott's early short stories, explores various themes of domestic melodrama, ideas that would later be revised and expanded upon in Little Women. *First published in the January 26, 1856, issue of Boston's* Saturday Evening Gazette, *this tale of four sisters who either succeed or fail at discovering happiness offers an engaging example of Alcott's concept of romantic sentimentality, as illustrated in Leonore's and Walter's emotional reunion at the tale's conclusion.*

THE SISTERS' TRIAL

Four sisters sat together round a cheerful fire on New Year's Eve. The shadow of a recent sorrow lay on the young faces over which the red flames flickered brightly as they lit up every nook of the quiet room, whose simple furniture and scanty decorations plainly showed that Poverty had entered there hand in hand with her sister, Grief.

The deep silence that had lasted long as each sat lost in sad memories of the past, or anxious thought for the future, was at length broken by Leonore, the eldest, a dark haired, dark eyed woman whose proud, energetic face was softened by a tender smile as she looked upon the young girls, saying cheerily:

"Come, sisters, we must not sit brooding gloomily over our troubles when we should be up and doing. To-night you know we must decide what work we will each choose by which to earn our bread, for this home will soon be ours no longer and we must find some other place to shelter us, and some honest labor to maintain ourselves by, that we may not be dependent on the charity of relatives, till our own exertions fail. Tell me what after your separate search you have each decided to do. Agnes, you come first. What among the pursuits left open to us have *you* chosen?"

The color deepened in Agnes' cheek and the restless light burned in her large eyes as she hastily replied, *"I* will be an actress. Nay do not start and look so troubled, Nora. I am fixed, and when you hear all, you will not oppose me, I feel sure. You know this has been the one wish of my life, growing with my growth, strengthening with my strength; haunting my thoughts by day, my dreams by night. I have longed for it, planned for it, studied for it secretly, for years, always hoping a time might come when I could prove to you that it was no idle fancy, but a real desire, and satisfy myself whether I have in truth the power to succeed, or whether I have cherished a false hope and been deluded by my vanity. I have thought of it seriously and earnestly during my search for employment, and see but one thing else that I can do. I *will* not chain myself to a needle and sew my own shroud for a scanty livelihood. Teaching, therefore, is all that remains. I dislike it, am unfitted for it, in every way, and cannot try it till everything else has failed.

"You, Nora, have your pen, Ella her music, Amy her painting; you all *love* them and can support yourselves well by them. *I* have only this one eager longing that haunts me like a shadow and seems to beckon me away to the beautiful brilliant life I feel that I was born to enjoy."

"Set yourself resolutely about some humbler work and this longing will fade away if you do not cherish it," said Leonore earnestly.

"It will not, I have tried in vain and now I will follow it over every obstacle till I have made the trial I desire.

"You are calm and cold, Nora, and cannot understand my feelings, therefore do not try to dissuade me, for an actress I must and *will* be," answered Agnes resolutely.

A look of sudden pain crossed Leonore's face at her sister's words, but it quickly passed and looking into her excited countenance she said gently, "How will you manage this? It is no easy thing for a young and unknown girl to take such a step alone; have you thought of this? and what are your plans?"

"Listen and I will tell you, for all is ready though you seem inclined to doubt it," replied Agnes, meeting her sisters' wondering glances with a look of triumph as she went on.

"Mrs. Vernon, whom our mother loved and respected, (actress though she is,) has known us long and been a friend to us in our misfortunes. I remembered this; after seeking vainly for some employment that I did not hate, I went to her, and telling all my hopes and wishes asked for her advice.

"She listened kindly and after questioning me closely and trying what little skill I have acquired, she said that if you consented she would take me with her to the West, train and teach me, and then try what I can do. There is an opening for me there, and under her protection and motherly care what need I fear? I should have told you this before but you bade us each to look and judge for ourselves before we asked for your advice, making this our first lesson in self-reliance which now is all we can depend on for support and guidance.

"Now what is your answer? Shall I go as I *wish* safely and properly with Mrs. Vernon, or as I *will,* alone and unprotected if you deny me your consent? Ah! do say yes, and you will make my life so beautiful and pleasant that I shall love and bless you forever."

As Agnes spoke, Leonore had thought rapidly of her sister's restless and unsatisfied life. Her unfitness for the drudgery she would be forced to if denied her wish. Of their mother's confidence in the kind friend who would be a faithful guardian to her and looking in the eager imploring face lifted to her own and reading there the real unconquerable passion that filled her sister's heart, she felt that hard experience alone could teach her wisdom, and time only could dispel her dream or fix and strengthen it forever. So she replied simply and seriously. "Yes, Agnes, you may go."

Agnes, prepared for argument and denial seemed bewildered by this ready acquiescence, till meeting Leonore's troubled glance fixed anxiously upon her, she saw there all the silent sorrow and reproach she would not speak, and coming to her side, Agnes said gratefully and with a fond caress, "You never shall have cause to repent your goodness to me, Nora, for I will be true to you and to myself whatever else may happen. So do not fear for me, the memory of *home* and *you,* dear girls, will keep me safe amid the trials and temptations of my future life."

Leonore did not answer but drew her nearer as if to cherish and protect her for the little time they yet could be together, and with dim eyes but a cheerful voice bade Ella tell *her* plans.

"*I,*" said the third sister, turning her placid face from the fire whose pleasant glow seemed shining from it, as if attracted there by kindred light and warmth, "I shall go to the South as governess to three little motherless girls. Aunt Elliott, who told me of it, assured me it would prove a happy home, and with my salary which is large I shall so gladly help you, and mite by mite lay by a little store that may in time grow large enough to buy our dear old home again. This is my future lot and I am truly grateful it is such a pleasant one."

"How can you be content with such a dreary life?" cried Agnes.

"Because it is my duty, and in doing that I know I shall find happiness," replied Ella. "For twenty years I have been shielded from the rough winds that visit so many, I have had my share of rest and pleasure and I trust they have done well their work of sweetening and softening my nature. Now life's harder lessons are to be learned and I am trying to receive them as I ought. Like you I will not be dependent on relatives rich in all but love to us, and so must endeavor to go bravely out into the world to meet whatever fate God sends me."

The light of a pure unselfish heart beamed in the speaker's gentle face and her simple child-like faith seemed to rebuke her sisters' restless doubts and longings.

"I come next," said Amy, a slender graceful girl of eighteen, "and my search has been most successful. While looking for pupils, I met again my dear friend Annie L——, who when she learned my troubles bade me look no farther but come and make my home with her. That I would not do till she agreed that I should take the place of her attendant and companion (for she is lame you know), and go with her to Europe for a year. Think how beautiful it will be to live in those lands I have so longed to see, and pass my days in sketching, painting and taking care of Annie, who is alone in the world and needs an affectionate friend to cheer the many weary hours that must come to one rich, talented, and young, but a cripple for life. I shall thus support myself by my own labor though it is one of love, and gain skill and knowledge in my art in the only school that can give it to me. This is my choice. Have I not done well, sisters?"

"You have indeed, but how can we let you go so far from us, dear Amy?" asked Leonore as they all looked fondly at her for she had been the pet and sunbeam of the household all her life and their hearts clung to her fearing to send her out so young to strive and struggle with the selfish world.

But she met their anxious gaze with a brave smile, saying: "Fear nothing for me, it is what I need, for I shall never know my own strength if it is never tried and with you it will not be, for you cherish me like a delicate flower. Now I shall be blown about and made to think and judge for myself as it's time I should. I shall not seem so far away as you now think for my letters will come to you like my voice from over the sea and it shall always be loving and merry that nothing may be changed as the year rolls on, and I may ever seem your own fond, foolish little Amy.

"Now, Nora, last not least, let us know in what part of the globe you will bestow yourself."

"I shall stay here, Amy," answered Leonore.

"Here!" echoed the sisters. "How can you when the house is sold and the gentleman coming to take possession so soon?"

"Just before our mother died," replied Leonore in a reverent voice, "she said to me in the silence of the night, 'Nora you are the guardian of your sisters now, be a watchful mother to them, and if you separate, as I fear you must, try to secure some little spot, no matter how poor, where you may sometimes meet and feel that you have a *home*. Promise me this, for I cannot rest in peace feeling that all the sweet ties that now bind you tenderly together are broken, and that you are growing up as strangers to each other scattered far apart.'

"I promised her, and this is why I longed so much to have you all remain in B——, that we might often meet and cheer each other on.

"But, as it cannot be, I have decided to remain here, for Mr. Morton is a kind old man, with no family but a maiden sister. They need few apartments, and when I told him how things were, and that I desired to hire one room, he willingly consented, and among those they wished left the rest to me. I chose this one, and here, surrounded by the few familiar things now left us, I shall live and by my pen support myself, or if that fails seek for needlework or teaching.

"It will be a quiet, solitary life, but tidings of *you* all will come to cheer me, and when another New Year shall come round, let us, if we can, meet here again to tell our wanderings and to spend it on the spot where have passed so many happy ones.

"This is my decision, here I shall live, and remember, dear girls, wherever you may be, that there is one nook in the dear old home where in sickness or sorrow you can freely come, ever sure of a joyful welcome, and in this troubled world one heart that is always open to take you in, one friend that can never desert you."

The sisters gathered silently about her as Leonore rose, and taking from a case three delicately painted miniatures of their mother, in a faltering voice, said, as she threw the simply woven chains of her own dark hair about their necks:

"This is my parting gift to you, and may the dear face Amy's hand has given us so freshly, prove a talisman to keep you ever worthy of our mother's love. God bless and bring us all together once again, better and wiser for our first lesson in the school of life."

The fire leaped up with a sudden glow, and from the hearthstone where a tenderly united family once had gathered fell now like a warm, bright blessing on the orphan sisters folded in each other's arms for the last time in the shelter of their home.

The year was gone, and Leonore sat waiting for the wanderers to come with a shadow on her face, and a secret sorrow at her heart.

The once poor room now wore an air of perfect comfort. Flowers bloomed in the deep windows sheltered from the outer cold by the warm folds of graceful curtains, green wreaths framed the picture faces on the walls, and a generous blaze burned red upon the hearth, flashing brightly over old familiar objects beautified and freshened by a tasteful hand.

A pleasant change seemed to have fallen on all but the thoughtful woman, in whose troubled face passion and pride seemed struggling with softer, nobler feelings as she sat there pale and silent in the cheerful room. As the twilight deepened, the inward storm passed silently away, leaving only a slight cloud behind as she paced anxiously to and fro, till well known footsteps sounded without, and Ella and Amy came hastening in.

They had returned a week before, but though much with Leonore in her pleasant home they had playfully refused to answer any questions till the appointed night arrived.

Time seemed to have passed lightly over Ella, for her face was bright and tranquil as of old, while some secret joy seemed measured in her heart, which, though it found no vent in words, shone in the clear light of her quiet eyes, sounded in the music of her voice, and deepened the sweet seriousness of her whole gentle nature.

Amy's single year of travel had brought with its culture and experience fresh grace and bloom to the slender girl who had blossomed suddenly into a lovely woman, frank and generous as ever, but softened and refined by the simple charms of early womanhood.

Gathered in their old places, the sisters, talking cheerfully, waited for Agnes. But at length she came slowly, and faintly her footsteps sounded on the stair, and when she entered such a change had fallen on her they could scarce believe it was the same bright creature who had left them but a year ago.

Worn and wasted, with dim eyes and pallid cheeks, she came back but a shadow of her former self.

Her sisters knew she had been ill, and guessed she had been unhappy, for a gradual change had taken place in her letters; from being full of overflowing hope and happiness, they had grown sad, desponding, and short. But she had never spoken of the cause, and now, though grieved and startled, they breathed not a word of questioning, but, concealing their alarm, tenderly welcomed her, and tried to banish her gloom.

Agnes endeavored with forced gayety to join them, but it soon deserted her, and after the first affectionate greetings, seemed to sink unconsciously into a deep and painful reverie.

The sisters glanced silently and anxiously at one another as they heard her heavy sighs, and saw the feverish color that now burned on her thin cheek as she sat gazing absently into the glowing embers.

None seemed willing to break the silence that had fallen on them till Amy said, with a pleasant laugh:

"As I probably have the least to tell I will begin. My life, since we parted, has been one of rich experience and real happiness; with friends and labor that I loved how could it well be otherwise?

"I have fared better in my trial than I ever hoped to, and have been blessed with health of body and peace of heart to enjoy the many pleasant things about me. A home in Italy more beautiful than I can tell you, a faithful friend in Annie, cultivated minds around me, and time to study and improve myself in all the things that I most love,—all these I have had, and hope I have improved them well. I have gained courage, strength and knowledge, and armed with these I have the will and power to earn with my pencil and brush an honest livelihood, and make my own way in this busy world which has always been a friendly one to me.

"I shall stay with Annie till her marriage with the artist whom we met abroad, about whom I have already told you. Then I shall find some quiet nook, and there sit down to live, love, and labor, while waiting what the future may bring forth for me."

"May it bring you all the happiness you so well deserve, my cheerful-hearted Amy," said Leonore, looking fondly and proudly at her young sister. "Your cheerful courage is a richer fortune to you than money can ever be, while your contented mind will brighten life with the truest happiness for one who can find sunshine everywhere.

"Now, Ella, let us know how you have fared, and what your future is?" continued Leonore.

"The past year has been one of mingled joy and sorrow," answered Ella. "The sorrow was the sudden loss of little Effie, the youngest and dearest of my pupils. It was a heavy grief to us all, and her father mourned most bitterly, till a new love, as strong and pure as that he bore the lost child, came to cheer and comfort him when most he needed it." Here, in the sudden glow on Ella's cheek, and the radiant smile that lit her face with a tenderer beauty, the sisters read the secret she had hidden from them until now, as in a low, glad voice she said:

"The joy I spoke of was that this love, so generous and deep, he offered to the humble girl who had tried to be a mother to his little child, and sorrowed like one when she went. Freely, gratefully did I receive it, for his silent kindness and the simple beauty of his life had long made him very dear to me, and I felt I had the power to be to him a true and loving friend.

"And now, no longer poor and solitary, I shall journey back to fill the place, not of a humble governess, but of a happy wife and mother in my beautiful southern home. Ah, sisters, this has been a rich and blessed year to me, far more than I have deserved."

And Ella bent her head upon her folded hands, too full of happiness for words.

Agnes had been strongly moved while Ella spoke, and when she ceased broke into bitter weeping, while her sisters gathered round her, vainly trying to compose and comfort her. But she did not heed them till her sudden grief had wept itself calm, then speaking like one in a dream, she said, abruptly:

"*My* year has been one of brilliant, bitter sorrow, such another I could not live through.

"When I first began my new life all seemed bright and pleasant to me. I studied hard, learned fast, and at last made the wished for trial, you know how successfully. For awhile I was in a dream of joy and triumph, and fancied all was smooth and sure before me. I had done much, I would do more, and not content to rise slowly and surely, I longed to be at once what years of patient labor alone can make me, I struggled on through the daily trials that thickened round me, often disheartened and disgusted at the selfishness and injustice of those around me, and the thousand petty annoyances that tried my proud, ambitious spirit.

"It was a hard life, and but for the great love I still cherished for the better part of it I should have left it long ago. But there were moments, hours, when I forgot my real cares and troubles in the false ones of the fair creations I was called upon to personate. Then I seemed to move in an enchanted world of my own, and *was* the creature that I *seemed*. Ah! that was glorious to feel that, my power, small as it was, could call forth tears and smiles and fill strange hearts with pity, joy, or fear.

"So time went on, and I was just beginning to feel that at last I was rising from my humble place, lifted by my own power and the kind favor I had won, when between me and my brightening fortune there came a friend, who brought me the happiest and bitterest hours of my whole life."

Here Agnes paused, and putting back her fallen hair from her wet cheek, looked wistfully into the anxious faces around her, and then, after a moment's pause, with an effort and in a hurried voice, went on,

"Among the many friends who admired and respected Mrs. Vernon and often visited her pleasant home, none was more welcome than the rich, accomplished Mr. Butler, (whose name you may remember in my letters). None came oftener, or stayed longer, he was with us at the theatre and paid a thousand kind attentions to my good friend and to me, in whom he seemed to take an interest from the first moment we met. Do not think me weak and vain; how could I help discovering it, when among many who looked coldly on me, or treated me with careless freedom, I found *him* always just, respectful, and ah! how kind? He had read and travelled much, and with his knowledge of the world, he taught, encouraged and advised me, making my hard life beautiful by his generous friendship.

"You know my nature, frank, and quick to love, touched by a gentle word or a friendly deed. I was deeply grateful for his many silent acts of kindness and the true regard he seemed to feel for me, and slowly, half unconsciously, my gratitude warmed into love. I never knew how strong and deep, until I learned too late that it was all in vain.

"One night (how well I can remember its least circumstance!) I was playing one of my best parts, and never had I played it better, for *he* was there, and I thought only of *his* approbation then. Toward the close of the evening I was waiting for my cue, when Mr. Butler and friend passed near the spot where I was standing, partially concealed by a deep shadow; I caught the sound of my own name, and then in a low, pained voice, as if replying to some question, Mr. Butler said,

"'I respect, admire, yes, love her far too deeply, willfully to destroy her peace, but I am of a proud race and cannot make an *actress* my wife. Therefore I shall leave to-morrow before she can discover what I have lately learned, and although we shall never meet again, I shall always be her friend.'

"They passed on and the next moment I was on the stage, laughing merrily with a dizzy brain and an aching heart. Pride nerved me to control my wandering thoughts and to play out mechanically my part in the comedy that had so suddenly become the deepest tragedy to me.

"Actress as I thought myself, it needed all my skill to hide beneath a smiling face the pang that wrung my heart, and but for the many eyes upon us and the false bloom on my cheek I should have betrayed all, when he came to take his leave that night. Little dreaming what I suffered, he kindly, seriously said farewell, and so we parted forever. For days I struggled to conceal the secret grief that preyed upon me until it laid me on a sick bed, from which I rose as you now see me, broken in health and spirit, saddened by the disappointed hopes and dreams that lie in ruins round me, distrustful of myself, and weary of life."

With a desponding sigh Agnes laid her head on Leonore's bosom, as if she never cared to lift it up again.

Ella knew why she had wept so sadly while listening to the story of *her* happy love, and bending over her she spoke gently of the past and cheerfully of the future till the desponding gloom was banished and Agnes looked up with a face brightened by earnest feeling as she said in answer to Leonore's whispered question, "You will stay with us now, dearest?"

"Yes; I shall never tread the stage again, for though I love it with a lingering memory of the many happy hours spent there, the misery of that one night has taught me what a hollow mockery the life I had chosen *may* become. I have neither health nor spirit for it now, and its glare and glitter have lost their charms. I shall find some humble work and quietly pursuing it, endeavor to become what *he* would have me: not an actress, but a simple woman, trying to play well her part in life's great drama. And though we shall never meet again, he may one day learn that, no longer mistaking the shadow for the substance, I have left the fair, false life and taken up the real and true."

"Thank heaven for this change," cried Leonore. "Dear Agnes, this shall henceforth be your home, and here we will lead a cheerful, busy life, sharing joy and sorrow together as in our childhood, and journeying hand in hand thro' light and darkness to a happy, calm old age."

"Leonore, you must tell us your experiences now, or our histories are not complete," said Amy, after a little time.

"I have nothing to relate but what you already know," replied her sister. "My book was well received and made for me a place among those writers who have the power to please and touch the hearts of many. I have earned much with my pen, and have a little store laid by for future need. My life has been a quiet, busy one. I have won many friends whose kindness and affection have cheered my solitude and helped me on. What more can I say but that I heartily rejoice that all has gone so well with us, and we have proved that we possess the power to make our own way in the world and need ask charity of none. Our talismans have kept us safe from harm, and God has let us meet again without one gone."

"Leonore," said Agnes, looking earnestly into her sister's face, "you have not told us *all;* nay, do not turn away, there is some hidden heart-sorrow that you are silent of. I read it in the secret trouble of your eye, the pallor of your cheek, and most of all, in your quick sympathy for me. We have given you our confidence, ah! give us yours as freely, dearest Nora."

"I cannot, do not ask me," murmured Leonore, averting her face.

"Let nothing break the sweet ties that now bind you together, and do not be as strangers to each other when you should be closest friends," whispered Ella from the low seat at her knee.

Leonore seemed to struggle within herself, and many contending emotions swept across her face, but she longed for sympathy and her proud heart melted at the mild echo of her mother's words. So holding Agnes's hand fast in her own, as if their sorrow drew them nearer to each other, she replied with a regretful sigh, "Yes, I will tell you, for your quick eyes have discovered what I hoped to have hidden from your sight forever. It *is* a heart-sorrow, Agnes, deeper than your own, for you can still reverence and trust the friend you have lost, but I can only feel contempt for what I have so truly loved. You well remember cousin Walter, the frank, generous-hearted boy who was our dearest playmate and companion years ago? Soon after we had separated he returned from India with his parents, and though *they* took no heed of me, *he* sought me out, and simply, naturally took the place of friend and brother to me, as of old. I needed help just then, he gave it freely, and by his wise counsel and generous kindness, banished my cares and cheered me when most solitary and forlorn.

"I have always loved him, and pleasant memories of my happy past have kept his image fresh within my heart. Through the long years of his absence I have sighed for his return, longing to know if the promise of a noble manhood I remembered in the boy had been fulfilled. He came at last when I most wished him, and with secret pride and joy I found him all I had hoped, brave, generous, and sincere. Ah! I was very happy then, and as our friendship grew, slowly and silently the frank affection of the girl deepened into the woman's earnest love.

"I knew it was returned, for in every look and deed the sweet, protecting tenderness that had guarded me in my childish days, now showed itself more plainly still, and at length found vent in words, which few and simple as they were seemed to fill my life with a strange happiness and beauty.

"Agnes, you have called me cold, but if you knew the deep and fervent passion that has stirred my heart, softening and sweetening my stern nature, you could never wrong me so again. Unhappy as that love has been, its short experience has made me wiser, and when its first sharp disappointment has passed away, the memory of it will linger like the warm glow of a fire whose brightness has departed.

"Two months ago a change came over Walter; he was kind as ever, coming often to cheer my lonely life, filling my home with lovely things, and more than all with his own dear presence, but a cloud was on him and I could not banish it.

"At length a week passed and he did not come, but in his place a letter from his father saying 'that he disapproved of his son's love for me and had persuaded him to relinquish me for a wife more suited to his rank in life; therefore at his request he wrote to spare us the pain of parting.' I cannot tell what more was in that cold, insulting letter, for I burned it, saving only two faintly written words in Walter's well known hand, 'Farewell Leonore;' that was enough for me; by what magic the great change was wrought I cared not to discover. All I thought or felt was that he had left me without a word of explanation, breaking his plighted word, and like a coward fearing to tell me freely and openly that he no longer loved me.

"I have not seen or heard from him since; though rumors of his approaching marriage, his departure for Europe and a sudden illness, have reached my ears, I believe none of them and struggling sternly to conceal my sorrow, have passed silently on leaving him without one word of entreaty or reproach to the keen regret his cruelty will one day cause him."

A proud indignant light burned in Leonore's eye and flushed her cheek as with a bitter smile she met her sisters' troubled glances saying,

"You need not pity *me, he* wants it most, for money can buy his truth and cast an evil spell on him, and a sordid father has the power to tempt and win him from his duty. None but *you* will ever know the secret sorrow that now bows my spirit but shall never break it; I shall soon banish the tender memories that haunt me, and hiding the deep wound he has caused me, be again the calm, cold Leonore.

"Oh! Walter! Walter! you have made the patient love that should have been the blessing of my life, its heaviest sorrow; may God forgive you as I try to do."

And as these words broke from her lips, Leonore clasped her hands before her face and hot tears fell like rain on Ella's head bent down upon her knee.

Agnes and Amy, blinded by the dimness of their own eyes, had not seen a tall dark man who had entered silently as Leonore last spoke and had stood spell bound till she ceased, then coming to her side the stranger said in a low, eager voice,

"Nora, will you hear me?"

With a quick start Leonore dashed away her tears and rose up pale and stately, looking full into the earnest, manly face before her and plainly reading there all she had doubted. Truth in the frank, reproachful eyes that met her own, tender sorrow in the trembling lips, and over all the light of the faithful, generous love which never had deserted her.

Her stern glance softened as she bowed a silent reply, and fell before his own as standing close beside her and looking steadily into her changing countenance, her cousin Walter laid his thin hand on her own saying in the friendly voice she had so longed to hear,

"Leonore, from the sick bed where I have lain through these long weary weeks, I have come to prove my truth, which had your pride allowed you to inquire into you never would have doubted, knowing me as I fondly hoped you did."

With a sudden motion Leonore drew a little worn and blistered paper from her bosom and laid it in his hand from which she coldly drew her own and fixed a keen look on his face, where not a shadow of shame or fear appeared, as he read it, silently glancing from the tear-stains to the eyes that looked so proudly on him with a quiet smile that brought a hot glow to her cheek as she asked quickly,

"Did *you* write those cruel words?"

"I did; nay, listen patiently before you judge me, Nora," he replied as she turned to leave him.

"Two months ago my father questioned me of *you*. I told him freely that I loved you and soon hoped to gladden his home with a daughter's gentle presence. But his anger knew no bounds and commanding me to beware how I thwarted his wishes, he bade me choose between utter poverty and you, or all his Indian wealth and my cousin Clara; I told him that my choice was already made, but he would not listen to me and bade me consider it well for one whole week and then decide before I saw you again. I yielded to calm his anger and for a week tried to win him to a wiser and kinder course, but all in vain; his will was iron and mine was no less firm, for, high above all selfish doubts and fears, all lures of rank and wealth, rose up my faithful love for you and nothing else could tempt me. That needed no golden fetters to render it more true, no idle show to make it richer, fonder than it is and ever will be.

"It was no virtue in me to resist, for nothing great enough was offered in exchange for that; poverty was wealth with *you* and who would waver between a false, vain girl and a true hearted woman?

"Ah, Nora, you will learn to know me now and see how deep a wrong you have done me. But to finish. When at the week's close I told my father that my purpose was unbroken he bade me leave his house forever and would have cursed me but his passion choked the sinful words ere they were spoken and he is saved that sorrow, when he thinks more kindly of me hereafter.

"I silently prepared to leave his house, which since my own mother's death has never been like home to me, and should have hastened joyfully to you, had not the fever already burning in my veins, augmented by anxiety and grief, laid me on my bed from which I am just risen, and where through those long nights and days I have been haunted even in delirium by your image, and the one longing wish to tell you why I did not come.

"When better, I sent messages and letters, but they never were delivered, for my father thinking sickness might have changed me, was still at my side to watch my actions and to tempt me to revoke my words. I have since learned that he wrote to you and guiding my unconscious hand traced the words that gave you the right to doubt me. But now I am strong again; nothing can separate us more, and I am here to bury the past and win your pardon for the sorrow I could not spare you. Now, Leonore, I am poor and friendless as yourself, with my fortune to make by the labor of my hands as you have done. You once wished this and said you never would receive the wealth I longed to give you; your wish is granted; I have nothing now to offer but a hand to work untiringly for you, and a heart to love and cherish you most tenderly forever. Will you take them, Nora?"

Leonore's proud head had sunk lower and lower as he spoke and when he ceased it rested on his shoulder, and her hand lay with an earnest, loving clasp in his as she whispered in a broken voice,

"Forgive me, Walter, for the wrong I have done you and teach me to be worthy the great sacrifice you have made for me."

The clock struck twelve and as its silvery echoes sounded through the quiet room, the old year with its joys and sorrows, hopes and fears floated away into the shadowing past bearing among its many records the simple one of the Sisters' Trial.

—1856

MARY ROBERTS RINEHART
1876-1958

Mary Roberts Rinehart was born in Pittsburgh, Pennsylvania. She attended the Pittsburgh Training School for Nurses, graduating in 1896; she married Dr. Stanley Rinehart soon thereafter. She lived in the Pittsburgh area until 1920, then moved to Washington, D.C., where she resided for the next twelve years. From 1932 until her death, she called New York City her home. In 1903, because of her family's pressing financial difficulties, Rinehart chose a career as a full-time writer in order to earn money. During the First World War, she became a correspondent in Philadelphia for the Saturday Evening Post. *Much of Rinehart's early fiction appeared in the American pulp magazines, like* Munsey's *and* All-Story. *She published her first (and perhaps most famous) novel,* The Circular Staircase, *in 1908, a book that helped to establish her reputation as a commercially successful author of suspense. In fact, Rinehart invented the "Had I But Known" story, a type of suspense formula in which the heroine becomes embroiled in a mystery where she regrets not having crucial prior information about the crime. Other popular Rinehart novels include* The Man in Lower Ten *(1909),* The Red Lamp *(1925),* The Door *(1930) and* The Wall *(1938). Eleven of Rinehart's books, published between 1908 and 1936, had achieved best-seller status, thus illustrating that she was one of the most popular writers in America for her time. Rinehart also published under the pseudonyms "Elliott Roberts" and "Roberts Rinehart."*

"Jane" first appeared in the May 25, 1912, issue of The Saturday Evening Post *and later was anthologized in the Rinehart short story collection,* Love Stories *(1919). Although "Jane" possesses some fleeting moments of suspense, it is written as a straightforward tale of romance and comedy. "Jane" is a "taming of the shrew" story, narrating the moral transformation of a spoiled young woman into a caring, generous person. It also features several of Rinehart's favorite narrative elements that appear elsewhere in her fiction, such as the use of a hospital setting and protagonists who are medical personnel. In fact, one of Rinehart's most famous literary creations is nurse Hilda Adams (a.k.a. "Miss Pinkerton"), who is featured in the novels*

Miss Pinkerton (1932) and Haunted Lady (1942). In recent years, Rinehart's work has received a mixed critical reception. Some readers recognize in her popular romance fiction an important early attempt to depict strong female protagonists, while others reproach her romances as conforming her female protagonists to traditional social roles. Certainly, "Jane" can either be praised or condemned for these same qualities.

JANE

I

Having retired to a hospital to sulk, Jane remained there. The family came and sat by her bed uncomfortably and smoked, and finally retreated with defeat written large all over it, leaving Jane to the continued possession of Room 33, a pink kimono with slippers to match, a hand-embroidered face pillow with a rose-coloured bow on the corner, and a young nurse with a gift of giving Jane daily the appearance of a strawberry and vanilla ice rising from a meringue of bed linen.

Jane's complaint was temper. The family knew this, and so did Jane, although she had an annoying way of looking hurt, a gentle heart-brokenness of speech that made the family, under the pretence of getting a match, go out into the hall and swear softly under its breath. But it was temper, and the family was not deceived. Also, knowing Jane, the family was quite ready to believe that while it was swearing in the hall, Jane was biting holes in the hand-embroidered face pillow in Room 33.

It had finally come to be a test of endurance. Jane vowed to stay at the hospital until the family on bended knee begged her to emerge and to brighten the world again with her presence. The family, being her father, said it would be damned if it would, and that if Jane cared to live on anæmic chicken broth, oatmeal wafers and massage twice a day for the rest of her life, why, let her.

The dispute, having begun about whether Jane should or should not marry a certain person, Jane representing the affirmative and her father the negative, had taken on new aspects, had grown and altered, and had, to be brief, become a contest between the masculine Johnson and the feminine Johnson as to which would take the count. Not that this appeared on the surface. The masculine Johnson, having closed the summer home on Jane's defection and gone back to the city, sent daily telegrams, novels and hothouse grapes, all three of which Jane devoured indiscriminately. Once, indeed, Father Johnson had motored the forty miles from town, to be told that Jane was too ill and unhappy to see him, and to have a glimpse, as he drove furiously away, of Jane sitting pensive at her window in the pink kimono, gazing over his head at the distant hills and clearly entirely indifferent to him and his wrath.

So we find Jane, on a frosty morning in late October, in triumphant possession of the field—aunts and cousins routed, her father sulking in town, and the victor herself—or is victor feminine?—and if it isn't, shouldn't it be?—sitting up in bed staring blankly at her watch.

Jane had just wakened—an hour later than usual; she had rung the bell three times and no one had responded. Jane's famous temper began to stretch and yawn. At this hour Jane was accustomed to be washed with tepid water, scented daintily with violet, alcohol-rubbed, talcum-powdered, and finally fresh-linened, coifed and manicured, to be supported with a heap of fresh pillows and fed creamed sweet-bread and golden-brown coffee and toast.

Jane rang again, with a line between her eyebrows. The bell was not broken. She could hear it distinctly. This was an outrage! She would report it to the superinten-dent. She had been ringing for ten minutes. That little minx of a nurse was flirting somewhere with one of the internes.

Jane angrily flung the covers back and got out on her small bare feet. Then she stretched her slim young arms above her head, her spoiled red mouth forming a scarlet O as she yawned. In her sleeveless and neckless nightgown, with her hair over her shoulders, minus the more elaborate coiffure which later in the day helped her to poise and firmness, she looked a pretty young girl, almost—although Jane herself never suspected this—almost an amiable young person.

Jane saw herself in the glass and assumed immediately the two lines between her eyebrows which were the outward and visible token of what she had suffered. Then she found her slippers, a pair of stockings to match and two round bits of pink silk elastic of private and feminine use, and sat down on the floor to put them on.

The floor was cold. To Jane's wrath was added indignation. She hitched herself along the boards to the radiator and put her hand on it. It was even colder than Jane.

The family temper was fully awake by this time and ready for business. Jane, sit-ting on the icy floor, jerked on her stockings, snapped the pink bands into place, thrust her feet into her slippers and rose, shivering. She went to the bed, and by dint of careful manœuvring so placed the bell between the head of the bed and the wall that during the remainder of her toilet it rang steadily.

The remainder of Jane's toilet was rather casual. She flung on the silk kimono, twisted her hair on top of her head and stuck a pin or two in it, thus achieving a sort of effect a thousand times more bewildering than she had ever managed with a curl-ing iron and twenty seven hair pins, and flinging her door wide stalked into the hall. At least she meant to stalk, but one does not really stamp about much in number-two, heelless, pink-satin mules.

At the first stalk—or stamp—she stopped. Standing uncertainly just outside her door was a strange man, strangely attired. Jane clutched her kimono about her and stared.

"Did—did you—are you ringing?" asked the apparition. It wore a pair of white-duck trousers, much soiled, a coat that bore the words "furnace room" down the front in red letters on a white tape, and a clean and spotless white apron. There was coal dust on its face and streaks of it in its hair, which appeared normally to be red.

"There's something the matter with your bell," said the young man. "It keeps on ringing."

"I intend it to," said Jane coldly.

"You can't make a racket like that round here, you know," he asserted, looking past her into the room.

"I intend to make all the racket I can until I get some attention."

"What have you done—put a book on it?"

"Look here"—Jane added another line to the two between her eyebrows. In the family this was generally a signal for a retreat, but of course the young man could not know this, and, besides, he was redheaded. "Look here," said Jane, "I don't know who you are and I don't care either, but that bell is going to ring until I get my bath and some breakfast. And it's going to ring then unless I stop it."

The young man in the coal dust and the white apron looked at Jane and smiled.

Then he walked past her into the room, jerked the bed from the wall and released the bell.

"Now!" he said as the din outside ceased. "I'm too busy to talk just at present, but if you do that again I'll take the bell out of the room altogether. There are other people in the hospital besides yourself."

At that he started out and along the hall, leaving Jane speechless. After he'd gone about a dozen feet he stopped and turned, looking at Jane reflectively.

"Do you know anything about cooking?" he asked.

"I know more about cooking than you do about politeness," she retorted, white with fury, and went into her room and slammed the door. She went directly to the bell and put it behind the bed and set it to ringing again. Then she sat down in a chair and picked up a book. Had the red-haired person opened the door she was perfectly prepared to fling the book at him. She would have thrown a hatchet had she had one.

As a matter of fact, however, he did not come back. The bell rang with a soul-satisfying jangle for about two minutes and then died away, and no amount of poking with a hairpin did any good. It was clear that the bell had been cut off outside!

For fifty-five minutes Jane sat in that chair breakfastless, very casually washed and with the aforesaid Billie Burkeness of hair. Then, hunger gaining over temper, she opened the door and peered out. From somewhere near at hand there came a pungent odor of burning toast. Jane sniffed; then, driven by hunger, she made a short sally down the hall to the parlour where the nurses on duty made their headquarters. It was empty. The dismantled bell register was on the wall, with the bell unscrewed and lying on the mantel beside it, and the odour of burning toast was stronger than ever.

Jane padded softly to the odour, following her small nose. It led her to the pantry, where under ordinary circumstances the patients' trays were prepared by a pantrymaid, the food being shipped there from the kitchen on a lift. Clearly the circumstances were not ordinary. The pantrymaid was not in sight.

Instead, the red-haired person was standing by the window scraping busily at a blackened piece of toast. There was a rank odour of boiling tea in the air.

"Damnation!" said the red-haired person, and flung the toast into a corner where there already lay a small heap of charred breakfast hopes. Then he saw Jane.

"I fixed the bell, didn't I?" he remarked. "I say, since you claim to know so much about cooking, I wish you'd make some toast."

"I didn't say I knew much," snapped Jane, holding her kimono round her. "I said I knew more than you knew about politeness."

The red-haired person smiled again, and then, making a deep bow, with a knife in one hand and a toaster in the other, he said: "Madam, I prithee forgive me for my untoward conduct of an hour since. Say but the word and I replace the bell."

"I won't make any toast," said Jane, looking at the bread with famished eyes.

"Oh, very well," said the red-haired person with a sigh. "On your head be it!"

"But I'll tell you how to do it," conceded Jane, "if you'll explain who you are and what you are doing in that costume and where the nurses are."

The red-haired person sat down on the edge of the table and looked at her.

"I'll make a bargain with you," he said. "There's a convalescent typhoid in a room near yours who swears he'll go down to the village for something to eat in his—er—hospital attire unless he's fed soon. He's dangerous, empty. He's reached the cannibalistic stage. If he should see you in that ravishing pink thing, I—I wouldn't answer for the consequences. I'll tell you everything if you'll make him six large slices of toast and boil him four or five eggs, enough to hold him for a while. The tea's probably ready; it's been boiling for an hour."

Hunger was making Jane human. She gathered up the tail of her kimono, and stepping daintily into the pantry proceeded to spread herself a slice of bread and butter.

"Where is everybody?" she asked, licking some butter off her thumb with a small pink tongue.

> Oh, I am the cook and the captain bold,
>   And the mate of the Nancy brig,
> And the bosun tight and the midshipmite,
>   And the crew of the captain's gig.

recited the red-haired person.

"You!" said Jane with the bread halfway to her mouth.

"Even I," said the red-haired person. "I'm the superintendent, the staff, the training school, the cooks, the furnace man and the ambulance driver."

Jane was pouring herself a cup of tea, and she put in milk and sugar and took a sip or two before she would give him the satisfaction of asking him what he meant. Anyhow, probably she had already guessed. Jane was no fool.

"I hope you're getting the salary list," she said, sitting on the pantry girl's chair and, what with the tea inside and somebody to quarrel with, feeling more like herself. "My father's one of the directors, and somebody gets it."

The red-haired person sat on the radiator and eyed Jane. He looked slightly stunned, as if the presence of beauty in a Billie Burke chignon and little else except a kimono was almost too much for him. From somewhere near by came a terrific thumping, as of some one pounding a hairbrush on a table. The red-haired person shifted along the radiator a little nearer Jane, and continued to gloat.

"Don't let that noise bother you," he said; "that's only the convalescent typhoid banging for his breakfast. He's been shouting for food ever since I came at six last night."

"Is it safe to feed him so much?"

"I don't know. He hasn't had anything yet. Perhaps if you're ready you'd better fix him something."

Jane had finished her bread and tea by this time and remembered her kimono.

"I'll go back and dress," she said primly. But he wouldn't hear of it.

"He's starving," he objected as a fresh volley of thumps came along the hall. "I've been trying at intervals since daylight to make him a piece of toast. The minute I put it on the fire I think of something I've forgotten, and when I come back it's in flames."

So Jane cut some bread and put on eggs to boil, and the red-haired person told his story.

"You see," he explained, "although I appear to be a furnace man from the waist up and an interne from the waist down, I am really the new superintendent."

"I hope you'll do better than the last one," she said severely. "He was always flirting with the nurses."

"I shall never flirt with the nurses," he promised, looking at her. "Anyhow I shan't have any immediate chance. The other fellow left last night and took with him everything portable except the ambulance—nurses, staff, cooks. I wish to Heaven he'd taken the patients! And he did more than that. He cut the telephone wires!"

"Well!" said Jane. "Are you going to stand for it?"

The red-haired man threw up his hands. "The village is with him," he declared. "It's a factional fight—the village against the fashionable summer colony on the hill. I cannot telephone from the village—the telegraph operator is deaf when I speak to him; the village milkman and grocer sent boys up this morning—look here." He fished a scrap of paper from his pocket and read:

I will not supply the Valley Hospital with any fresh meats, canned oysters and sausages, or do any plumbing for the hospital until the reinstatement of Dr. Sheets.

T. CASHDOLLAR, BUTCHER.

Jane took the paper and read it again. "Humph!" she commented. "Old Sheets wrote it himself. Mr. Cashdollar couldn't think 'reinstatement,' let alone spell it."

"The question is not who wrote it, but what we are to do," said the red-haired person. "Shall I let old Sheets come back?"

"If you do," said Jane fiercely, "I shall hate you the rest of my life."

And as it was clear by this time that the red-haired person could imagine nothing more horrible, it was settled then and there that he should stay.

"There are only two wards," he said. "In the men's a man named Higgins is able to be up and is keeping things straight. And in the woman's ward Mary O'Shaughnessy is looking after them. The furnaces are the worst. I'd have forgiven almost anything else. I've sat up all night nursing the fires, but they breathed their last at six this morning and I guess there's nothing left but to call the coroner."

Jane had achieved a tolerable plate of toast by that time and four eggs. Also she had a fine flush, a combination of heat from the gas stove and temper.

"They ought to be ashamed," she cried angrily, "leaving a lot of sick people!"

"Oh, as to that," said the red-headed person, "there aren't any very sick ones. Two or three neurasthenics like yourself and a convalescent typhoid and a D.T. in a private room. If it wasn't that Mary O'Shaughnessy——"

But at the word "neurasthenics" Jane had put down the toaster, and by the time the unconscious young man had reached the O'Shaughnessy she was going out the door with her chin up. He called after her, and finding she did not turn he followed her, shouting apologies at her back until she went into her room. And as hospital doors don't lock from the inside she pushed the washstand against the knob and went to bed to keep warm.

He stood outside and apologised again, and later he brought a tray of bread and butter and a pot of the tea, which had been boiling for two hours by that time, and put it outside the door on the floor. But Jane refused to get it, and finished her breakfast from a jar of candied ginger that some one had sent her, and read "Lorna Doone."

Now and then a sound of terrific hammering would follow the steampipes and Jane would smile wickedly. By noon she had finished the ginger and was wondering what the person about whom she and the family had disagreed would think when he heard the way she was being treated. And by one o'clock she had cried her eyes entirely shut and had pushed the washstand back from the door.

II

Now a hospital full of nurses and doctors with a bell to summon food and attention is one thing. A hospital without nurses and doctors, and with only one person to do everything, and that person mostly in the cellar, is quite another. Jane was very sad and lonely, and to add to her troubles the delirium-tremens case down the hall began to sing "Oh Promise Me" in a falsetto voice and kept it up for hours.

At three Jane got up and bathed her eyes. She also did her hair, and thus fortified she started out to find the red-haired person. She intended to say that she was paying sixty-five dollars a week and belonged to a leading family, and that she didn't mean to endure for a moment the treatment she was getting, and being called a neurasthenic and made to cook for the other patients.

She went slowly along the hall. The convalescent typhoid heard her and called.

"Hey, doc!" he cried. "Hey, doc! Great Scott, man, when do I get some dinner?"

Jane quickened her steps and made for the pantry. From somewhere beyond, the delirium-tremens case was singing happily:

> I—love you o—own—ly,
> I love—but—you.

Jane shivered a little. The person in whom she had been interested and who had caused her precipitate retirement, if not to a nunnery, to what answered the same purpose, had been very fond of that song. He used to sing it, leaning over the piano and looking into her eyes.

Jane's nose led her again to the pantry. There was a sort of soupy odour in the air, and sure enough the red-haired person was there, very immaculate in fresh ducks, pouring boiling water into three teacups out of a kettle and then dropping a beef capsule into each cup.

Now Jane had intended, as I have said, to say that she was being outrageously treated, and belonged to one of the best families, and so on. What she really said was piteously:

"How good it smells!"

"Doesn't it!" said the red-haired person, sniffing. "Beef capsules. I've made thirty cups of it so far since one o'clock—the more they have the more they want. I say, be a good girl and run up to the kitchen for some more crackers while I carry food to the convalescent typhoid. He's murderous!"

"Where are the crackers?" asked Jane stiffly, but not exactly caring to raise an issue until she was sure of getting something to eat.

"Store closet in the kitchen, third drawer on the left," said the red-haired man, shaking some cayenne pepper into one of the cups. "You might stop that howling lunatic on your way if you will."

"How?" asked Jane, pausing.

"Ram a towel down his throat, or—but don't bother. I'll dose him with this beef tea and red pepper, and he'll be too busy putting out the fire to want to sing."

"You wouldn't be so cruel!" said Jane, rather drawing back. The red-haired person smiled and to Jane it showed that he was actually ferocious. She ran all the way up for the crackers and down again, carrying the tin box. There is no doubt that Jane's family would have promptly swooned had it seen her.

When she came down there was a sort of after-dinner peace reigning. The convalescent typhoid, having filled up on milk and beef soup, had floated off to sleep. "The Chocolate Soldier" had given way to deep-muttered imprecations from the singer's room. Jane made herself a cup of bouillon and drank it scalding. She was making the second when the red-haired person came back with an empty cup.

"I forgot to explain," he said, "that beef tea and red pepper's the treatment for our young friend in there. After a man has been burning his stomach daily with a quart or so of raw booze——"

"I beg your pardon," said Jane coolly. Booze was not considered good form on the hill—the word, of course. There was plenty of the substance.

"Raw booze," repeated the red-haired person. "Nothing short of red pepper or dynamite is going to act as a substitute. Why, I'll bet the inside of that chap's stomach is of the general sensitiveness and consistency of my shoe."

"Indeed!" said Jane, coldly polite. In Jane's circle people did not discuss the interiors of other people's stomachs. The red-haired person sat on the table with a cup of bouillon in one hand and a cracker in the other.

"You know," he said genially, "it's awfully bully of you to come out and keep me company like this. I never put in such a day. I've given up fussing with the furnace and got out extra blankets instead. And I think by night our troubles will be over." He held up the cup and glanced at Jane, who was looking entrancingly pretty. "To our troubles being over!" he said, draining the cup, and then found that he had used the red pepper again by mistake. It took five minutes and four cups of cold water to enable him to explain what he meant.

"By our troubles being over," he said finally when he could speak, "I mean this: There's a train from town at eight to-night, and if all goes well it will deposit in the village half a dozen nurses, a cook or two, a furnace man—good Heavens, I wonder if I forgot a furnace man!"

It seemed, as Jane discovered, that the telephone wires being cut, he had sent Higgins from the men's ward to the village to send some telegrams for him.

"I couldn't leave, you see," he explained, "and having some small reason to believe that I am *persona non grata* in this vicinity I sent Higgins."

Jane had always hated the name Higgins. She said afterward that she felt uneasy from that moment. The red-haired person, who was not bad-looking, being tall and straight and having a very decent nose, looked at Jane, and Jane, having been shut away for weeks—Jane preened a little and was glad she had done her hair.

"You looked better the other way," said the red-haired person, reading her mind in a most uncanny manner. "Why should a girl with as pretty hair as yours cover it up with a net, anyhow?"

"You are very disagreeable and—and impertinent," said Jane, sliding off the table.

"It isn't disagreeable to tell a girl she has pretty hair," the red-haired person protested—"or impertinent either."

Jane was gathering up the remnants of her temper, scattered by the events of the day.

"You said I was a neurasthenic," she accused him. "It—it isn't being a neurasthenic to be nervous and upset and hating the very sight of people, is it?"

"Bless my soul!" said the red-haired man. "Then what is it?" Jane flushed, but he went on tactlessly: "I give you my word, I think you are the most perfectly"—he gave every appearance of being about to say "beautiful," but he evidently changed his mind—"the most perfectly healthy person I have ever looked at," he finished.

It is difficult to say just what Jane would have done under other circumstances, but just as she was getting her temper really in hand and preparing to launch something, shuffling footsteps were heard in the hall and Higgins stood in the doorway.

He was in a sad state. One of his eyes was entirely closed, and the corresponding ear stood out large and bulbous from his head. Also he was coated with mud, and he was carefully nursing one hand with the other.

He said he had been met at the near end of the railroad bridge by the ex-furnace man and one of the ex-orderlies and sent back firmly, having in fact been kicked back part of the way. He'd been told to report at the hospital that the tradespeople had instituted a boycott, and that either the former superintendent went back or the entire place could starve to death.

It was then that Jane discovered that her much-vaunted temper was not one-two-three to that of the red-haired person. He turned a sort of blue-white, shoved Jane out of his way as if she had been a chair, and she heard him clatter down the stairs and slam out of the front door.

Jane went back to her room and looked down the drive. He was running toward the bridge, and the sunlight on his red hair and his flying legs made him look like a revengeful meteor. Jane was weak in the knees. She knelt on the cold radiator and watched him out of sight, and then got trembly all over and fell to snivelling. This was of course because, if anything happened to him, she would be left entirely alone. And anyhow the D.T. case was singing again and had rather got on her nerves.

In ten minutes the red-haired person appeared. He had a wretched-looking creature by the back of the neck and he alternately pushed and kicked him up the drive. He—the red-haired person—was whistling and clearly immensely pleased with himself.

Jane put a little powder on her nose and waited for him to come and tell her all about it. But he did not come near. This was quite the cleverest thing he could have done, had he known it. Jane was not accustomed to waiting in vain. He must have gone directly to the cellar, half pushing and half kicking the luckless furnace man, for about four o'clock the radiator began to get warm.

At five he came and knocked at Jane's door, and on being invited in he sat down on the bed and looked at her.

"Well, we've got the furnace going," he said.

"Then that was the——"

"Furnace man? Yes."

"Aren't you afraid to leave him?" queried Jane. "Won't he run off?"

"Got him locked in a padded cell," he said. "I can take him out to coal up. The rest of the time he can sit and think of his sins. The question is—what are we to do next?"

"I should think," ventured Jane, "that we'd better be thinking about supper."

"The beef capsules are gone."

"But surely there must be something else about—potatoes or things like that?"

He brightened perceptibly. "Oh, yes, carloads of potatoes, and there's canned stuff. Higgins can pare potatoes, and there's Mary O'Shaughnessy. We could have potatoes and canned tomatoes and eggs."

"Fine!" said Jane with her eyes gleaming, although the day before she would have said they were her three abominations.

And with that he called Higgins and Mary O'Shaughnessy and the four of them went to the kitchen.

Jane positively shone. She had never realised before how much she knew about cooking. They built a fire and got kettles boiling and everybody pared potatoes, and although in excess of zeal the eggs were ready long before everything else and the tomatoes scorched slightly, still they made up in enthusiasm what they lacked in ability, and when Higgins had carried the trays to the lift and started them on their way, Jane and the red-haired person shook hands on it and then ate a boiled potato from the same plate, sitting side by side on a table.

They were ravenous. They boiled one egg each and ate it, and then boiled another and another, and when they finished they found that Jane had eaten four potatoes, four eggs and unlimited bread and butter, while the red-haired person had eaten six saucers of stewed tomatoes and was starting on the seventh.

"You know," he said over the seventh, "we've got to figure this thing out. The entire town is solid against us—no use trying to get to a telephone. And anyhow they've got us surrounded. We're in a state of siege."

Jane was beating up an egg in milk for the D.T. patient, the capsules being exhausted, and the red-haired person was watching her closely. She had the two vertical lines between her eyes, but they looked really like lines of endeavour and not temper.

She stopped beating and looked up.

"Couldn't I go to the village?" she asked.

"They would stop you."

"Then—I think I know what we can do," she said, giving the eggnog a final whisk. "My people have a summer place on the hill. If you could get there you could telephone to the city."

"Could I get in?"

"I have a key."

Jane did not explain that the said key had been left by her father, with the terse hope that if she came to her senses she could get into the house and get her clothes.

"Good girl," said the red-headed person and patted her on the shoulder. "We'll euchre the old skate yet." Curiously, Jane did not resent either the speech or the pat.

He took the glass and tied on a white apron. "If our friend doesn't drink this, I will," he continued. "If he'd seen it in the making, as I have, he'd be crazy about it."

He opened the door and stood listening. From below floated up the refrain:

> I—love you o—own—ly,
> I love—but—you.

"Listen to that!" he said. "Stomach's gone, but still has a heart!"

Higgins came up the stairs heavily and stopped close by the red-haired person, whispering something to him. There was a second's pause. Then the red-haired person gave the eggnog to Higgins and both disappeared.

Jane was puzzled. She rather thought the furnace man had got out and listened for a scuffle, but none came. She did, however, hear the singing cease below, and then commence with renewed vigour, and she heard Higgins slowly remounting the stairs. He came in, with the empty glass and a sheepish expression. Part of the eggnog was distributed over his person.

"He wants his nurse, ma'am," said Higgins. "Wouldn't let me near him. Flung a pillow at me."

"Where is the doctor?" demanded Jane.

"Busy," replied Higgins. "One of the women is sick."

Jane was provoked. She had put some labour into the eggnog. But it shows the curious evolution going on in her that she got out the eggs and milk and made another one without protest. Then with her head up she carried it to the door.

"You might clear things away, Higgins," she said, and went down the stairs. Her heart was going rather fast. Most of the men Jane knew drank more or less, but this was different. She would have turned back halfway there had it not been for Higgins and for owning herself conquered. That was Jane's real weakness—she never owned herself beaten.

The singing had subsided to a low muttering. Jane stopped outside the door and took a fresh grip on her courage. Then she pushed the door open and went in.

The light was shaded, and at first the tossing figure on the bed was only a misty outline of greys and whites. She walked over, expecting a pillow at any moment and shielding the glass from attack with her hand.

"I have brought you another eggnog," she began severely, "and if you spill it——"

Then she looked down and saw the face on the pillow.

To her everlasting credit, Jane did not faint. But in that moment, while she stood staring down at the flushed young face with its tumbled dark hair and deep-cut lines of dissipation, the man who had sung to her over the piano, looking love into her eyes, died to her, and Jane, cold and steady, sat down on the side of the bed and fed the eggnog, spoonful by spoonful, to his corpse!

When the blank-eyed young man on the bed had swallowed it all passively, look-ing at her with dull, incurious eyes, she went back to her room and closing the door put the washstand against it. She did nothing theatrical. She went over to the win-dow and stood looking out where the trees along the drive were fading in the dusk from green to grey, from grey to black. And over the transom came again and again monotonously the refrain:

> I—love you o—own—ly,
> I love—but—you.

Jane fell on her knees beside the bed and buried her wilful head in the hand-embroidered pillow, and said a little prayer because she had found out in time.

III

The full realisation of their predicament came with the dusk. The electric lights were shut off! Jane, crawling into bed tearfully at half after eight, turned the reading light switch over her head, but no flood of rosy radiance poured down on the hand-embroidered pillow with the pink bow.

Jane sat up and stared round her. Already the outline of her dresser was faint and shadowy. In half an hour black night would settle down and she had not even a candle or a box of matches. She crawled out, panicky, and began in the darkness to don her kimono and slippers. As she opened the door and stepped into the hall the convalescent typhoid heard her and set up his usual cry.

"Hey," he called, "whoever that is come in and fix the lights. They're broken. And I want some bread and milk. I can't sleep on an empty stomach!"

Jane padded on past the room where love lay cold and dead, down the corridor with its alarming echoes. The house seemed very quiet. At a corner unexpectedly she collided with some one going hastily. The result was a crash and a deluge of hot water. Jane got a drop on her bare ankle, and as soon as she could breathe she screamed.

"Why don't you look where you're going?" demanded the red-haired person angrily. "I've been an hour boiling that water, and now it has to be done over again!"

"It would do a lot of good to look!" retorted Jane. "But if you wish I'll carry a bell!"

"The thing for you to do," said the red-haired person severely, "is to go back to bed like a good girl and stay there until morning. The light is cut off."

"Really!" said Jane. "I thought it had just gone out for a walk. I daresay I may have a box of matches at least?"

He fumbled in his pockets without success.

"Not a match, of course!" he said disgustedly. "Was any one ever in such an infernal mess? Can't you get back to your room without matches?"

"I shan't go back at all unless I have some sort of light," maintained Jane. "I'm—horribly frightened!"

The break in her voice caught his attention and he put his hand out gently and took her arm.

"Now listen," he said. "You've been brave and fine all day, and don't stop it now. I—I've got all I can manage. Mary O'Shaughnessy is——" He stopped. "I'm going to be very busy," he said with half a groan. "I surely do wish you were forty for the next few hours. But you'll go back and stay in your room, won't you?"

He patted her arm, which Jane particularly hated generally. But Jane had altered considerably since morning.

"Then you cannot go to the telephone?"

"Not to-night."

"And Higgins?"

"Higgins has gone," he said. "He slipped off an hour ago. We'll have to manage to-night somehow. Now will you be a good child?"

"I'll go back," she promised meekly. "I'm sorry I'm not forty."

He turned her round and started her in the right direction with a little push. But she had gone only a step or two when she heard him coming after her quickly.

"Where are you?"

"Here," quavered Jane, not quite sure of him or of herself perhaps.

But when he stopped beside her he didn't try to touch her arm again. He only said:

"I wouldn't have you forty for anything in the world. I want you to be just as you are, very beautiful and young."

Then, as if he was afraid he would say too much, he turned on his heel, and a moment after he kicked against the fallen pitcher in the darkness and awoke a thousand echoes. As for Jane, she put her fingers to her ears and ran to her room, where she slammed the door and crawled into bed with burning cheeks.

Jane was never sure whether it was five minutes later or five seconds when somebody in the room spoke—from a chair by the window.

"Do you think," said a mild voice—"do you think you could find me some bread and butter? Or a glass of milk?"

Jane sat up in bed suddenly. She knew at once that she had made a mistake, but she was quite dignified about it. She looked over at the chair, and the convalescent typhoid was sitting in it, wrapped in a blanket and looking wan and ghostly in the dusk.

"I'm afraid I'm in the wrong room," Jane said very stiffly, trying to get out of the bed with dignity, which is difficult. "The hall is dark and all the doors look so alike——"

She made for the door at that and got out into the hall with her heart going a thousand a minute again.

"You've forgotten your slippers," called the convalescent typhoid after her. But nothing would have taken Jane back.

The convalescent typhoid took the slippers home later and locked them away in an inner drawer, where he kept one or two things like faded roses, and old gloves, and a silk necktie that a girl had made him at college—things that are all the secrets a man keeps from his wife and that belong in that small corner of his heart which also he keeps from his wife. But that has nothing to do with Jane.

Jane went back to her own bed thoroughly demoralised. And sleep being pretty well banished by that time, she sat up in bed and thought things over. Before this she had not thought much, only raged and sulked alternately. But now she thought. She thought about the man in the room down the hall with the lines of dissipation on his face. And she thought a great deal about what a silly she had been, and that it was not too late yet, she being not forty and "beautiful." It must be confessed that she thought a great deal about that. Also she reflected that what she deserved was to marry some person with even a worse temper than hers, who would bully her at times and generally keep her straight. And from that, of course, it was only a step to the fact that red-haired people are proverbially bad-tempered!

She thought, too, about Mary O'Shaughnessy without another woman near, and not even a light, except perhaps a candle. Things were always so much worse in the darkness. And perhaps she might be going to be very ill and ought to have another doctor!

Jane seemed to have been reflecting for a long time, when the church clock far down in the village struck nine. And with the chiming of the clock was born, full grown, an idea which before it was sixty seconds of age was a determination.

In pursuance of the idea Jane once more crawled out of bed and began to dress; she put on heavy shoes and a short skirt, a coat, and a motor veil over her hair. The indignation at the defection of the hospital staff, held in subjection during the day by the necessity for doing something, now rose and lent speed and fury to her movements. In an incredibly short time Jane was feeling her way along the hall and down the staircase, now a well of unfathomable blackness and incredible rustlings and creakings.

The front doors were unlocked. Outside there was faint starlight, the chirp of a sleepy bird, and far off across the valley the gasping and wheezing of a freight climbing the heavy grade to the village.

Jane paused at the drive and took a breath. Then at her best gymnasium pace, arms close to sides, head up, feet well planted, she started to run. At the sundial she left the drive and took to the lawn gleaming with the frost of late October. She stopped running then and began to pick her way more cautiously. Even at that she collided heavily with a wire fence marking the boundary, and sat on the ground for some time after, whimpering over the outrage and feeling her nose. It was distinctly scratched and swollen. No one would think her beautiful with a nose like that!

She had not expected the wire fence. It was impossible to climb and more difficult to get under. However, she found one place where the ground dipped, and wormed her way under the fence in most undignified fashion. It is perfectly certain that had Jane's family seen her then and been told that she was doing this remarkable thing for a woman she had never seen before that day, named Mary O'Shaughnessy, and also for a certain red-haired person of whom it had never heard, it would have considered Jane quite irrational. But it is entirely probable that Jane became really rational that night for the first time in her spoiled young life.

Jane never told the details of that excursion. Those that came out in the paper were only guess-work, of course, but it is quite true that a reporter found scraps of her motor veil on three wire fences, and there seems to be no reason to doubt, also, that two false curls were discovered a week later in a cow pasture on her own estate. But as Jane never wore curls afterward anyhow——

Well, Jane got to her own house about eleven and crept in like a thief to the telephone. There were more rustlings and creakings and rumblings in the empty house than she had ever imagined, and she went backward through the hall for fear of something coming after her. But, which is to the point, she got to the telephone and called up her father in the city.

The first message that astonished gentleman got was that a red-haired person at the hospital was very ill, having run into a wire fence and bruised a nose, and that he was to bring out at once from town two doctors, six nurses, a cook and a furnace man!

After a time, however, as Jane grew calmer, he got it straightened out, and said a number of things over the telephone anent the deserting staff that are quite forbidden by the rules both of the club and of the telephone company. He gave Jane full instructions about sending to the village and having somebody come up and stay with her, and about taking a hot footbath and going to bed between blankets, and when Jane replied meekly to everything "Yes, father," and "All right, father," he was so stunned by her mildness that he was certain she must be really ill.

Not that Jane had any idea of doing all these things. She hung up the telephone and gathered all the candles from all the candlesticks on the lower floor, and started back for the hospital. The moon had come up and she had no more trouble with fencing, but she was desperately tired. She climbed the drive slowly, coming to frequent pauses. The hospital, long and low and sleeping, lay before her, and in one upper window there was a small yellow light.

Jane climbed the steps and sat down on the top one. She felt very tired and sad and dejected, and she sat down on the upper step to think of how useless she was, and how much a man must know to be a doctor, and that perhaps she would take up nursing in earnest and amount to something, and——

It was about three o'clock in the morning when the red-haired person, coming down belatedly to close the front doors, saw a shapeless heap on the porch surrounded by a radius of white-wax candles, and going up shoved at it with his foot. Whereat the heap moved slightly and muttered "Lemme shleep."

The red-haired person said "Good Heavens!" and bending down held a lighted match to the sleeper's face and stared, petrified. Jane opened her eyes, sat up and put her hand over her mutilated nose with one gesture.

"You!" said the red-haired person. And then mercifully the match went out.

"Don't light another," said Jane. "I'm an alarming sight. Would—would you mind feeling if my nose is broken?"

He didn't move to examine it. He just kept on kneeling and staring.

"Where have you been?" he demanded.

"Over to telephone," said Jane, and yawned. "They're bringing everybody in automobiles—doctors, nurses, furnace man—oh, dear me, I hope I mentioned a cook!"

"Do you mean to say," said the red-haired person wonderingly, "that you went by yourself across the fields and telephoned to get me out of this mess?"

"Not at all," Jane corrected him coolly. "I'm in the mess myself."

"You'll be ill again."

"I never was ill," said Jane. "I was here for a mean disposition."

Jane sat in the moonlight with her hands in her lap and looked at him calmly. The red-haired person reached over and took both her hands.

"You're a heroine," he said, and bending down he kissed first one and then the other. "Isn't it bad enough that you are beautiful without your also being brave?"

Jane eyed him, but he was in deadly earnest. In the moonlight his hair was really not red at all, and he looked pale and very, very tired. Something inside of Jane gave a curious thrill that was half pain. Perhaps it was the dying of her temper, perhaps——

"Am I still beautiful with this nose?" she asked.

"You are everything that a woman should be," he said, and dropping her hands he got up. He stood there in the moonlight, straight and young and crowned with despair, and Jane looked up from under her long lashes.

"Then why don't you stay where you were?" she asked.

At that he reached down and took her hands again and pulled her to her feet. He was very strong.

"Because if I do I'll never leave you again," he said. "And I must go."

He dropped her hands, or tried to, but Jane wasn't ready to be dropped.

"You know," she said, "I've told you I'm a sulky, bad-tempered——"

But at that he laughed suddenly, triumphantly, and put both his arms round her and held her close.

"I love you," he said, "and if you are bad-tempered, so am I, only I think I'm worse. It's a shame to spoil two houses with us, isn't it?"

To her eternal shame be it told, Jane never struggled. She simply held up her mouth to be kissed.

That is really all the story. Jane's father came with three automobiles that morning at dawn, bringing with him all that goes to make up a hospital, from a pharmacy clerk to absorbent cotton, and having left the new supplies in the office he stamped upstairs to Jane's room and flung open the door.

He expected to find Jane in hysterics and the pink silk kimono.

What he really saw was this: A coal fire was lighted in Jane's grate, and in a low chair before it, with her nose swollen level with her forehead, sat Jane, holding on her lap Mary O'Shaughnessy's baby, very new and magenta-coloured and yelling like a trooper. Kneeling beside the chair was a tall, red-headed person holding a bottle of olive oil.

"Now, sweetest," the red-haired person was saying, "turn him on his tummy and we'll rub his back. Gee, isn't that a fat back!"

And as Jane's father stared and Jane anxiously turned the baby, the red-haired person leaned over and kissed the back of Jane's neck.

"Jane!" he whispered.

"Jane!!" said her father.

—1912

ROSAMUNDE PILCHER

B. 1924

Rosamunde Pilcher ranks among the finest of contemporary romance authors. She has proven herself adept at writing both short stories for Good Housekeeping *(she is one of the magazine's most popular contributors) and best-selling novels. Born in Lelant, Cornwall, in England, Pilcher was a member of the Women's Royal Navy Service from 1943 to 1946. Her father, Charles Scott, was a commander in the Royal Navy. Following the Second World War, she married Graham Hope Pilcher. Rosamunde's solitary life as a child led to her developing interests in reading and writing. At age six-teen, she submitted a short story to Winnifred Johnson, an editor of women's magazines, for publication. Though Johnson did not buy the story, Pilcher credits the editor's insightful recommendations as greatly benefiting her early writing career. Her first romance novel,* Halfway to the Moon *(1949) was published by Mills and Boon under her pseudonym, "Jane Fraser." She also published other novels under the "Jane Fraser" nom de plume, including* The Brown Fields *(1951),* Young Bar *(1952),* A Family Affair *(1958), and* The Keeper's House *(1963). Under her own name, Pilcher has written a number of novels, such as* A Secret to Tell *(1955),* Sleeping Tiger *(1967),* Snow in April *(1972),* Under Gemini *(1976),* Voices in Summer *(1984),* The Shell Seekers *(1987),* September *(1990), and* Coming Home *(1995).*

Pilcher's work is admired for its exceptional plotting, its use of well-developed characters, and for its intelligent portrayal of romantic love. Pilcher dislikes the generic label of "romantic fiction." She views her stories as "a balance between the out-and-out romantic and the serious woman's writing of today." Pilcher tends to emphasize the importance of family in her writing. She argues that her short stories feature personal relationships that extend beyond the romantic love experienced between a man and a woman, to include the love felt among parents and children, or among sib-lings. In this sense, Pilcher's romances follow the literary example of Louisa May Alcott's Little Women.

"Lalla"—which was anthologized in the collection Love Stories *(1990), edited by Lynn Curtis—ably demonstrates Pilcher's facility for crafting an elegant, yet compact tale of budding romance. Interestingly, Lalla's rite-of-passage in the story appears to parallel Pilcher's discussion concerning her own education about the real meaning of love, as revealed in her autobio-graphical "Introduction" to* Love Stories.

INTRODUCTION TO *LOVE STORIES*

As a schoolgirl, over fifty years ago, I was content in thinking that I knew every-thing that needed to be known about "love." This limitless knowledge of the subject was gleaned from the pages of a magazine called *Peg's Paper*, forbidden to our fam-ily, but which our housemaid took on a regular basis. She would hide it under the cushion of her basket chair in the kitchen, for fear of being reprimanded by my mother for lowering the "moral tone" of the household, but, like a true friend, would smuggle this amorous gazette up to the bedroom of my sister and me under the cover of darkness. Many an eye-opening hour was spent with a torch under the bed-clothes, with only the interruption of either my sister or me having to scramble to the top of the bed for air.

The formula of these stories seldom changed. Boy meets girl, boy loses girl, boy wins girl. Only the characters came from slightly changing backgrounds . . . sometimes they were dukes and duchesses, or hardworking secretaries wearing dark dresses with fresh touches of white at the throat. Sometimes they were girls with high-flying dreams of becoming ballet dancers, but who, having succumbed to the sting of Cupid's arrow, chose a more humdrum future with the boy next door, he being a faultless young man with blunt features and an open expression, so obviously trustworthy that you wondered why the wretched girl had ever considered going on the stage in the first place.

And then I learned, by chance, what a love story really was. For our English Literature examination at school, we were "made" to do an in-depth study of Emily Brontë's *Wuthering Heights*. The books issued to everyone in my class were small school editions with red covers and tiny print. I thought, on opening it for the first time, that the only exciting feature about the book was the crack of the newly glued headband, and the smell of the crisp, white paper . . . Homework that night was to read the first ten pages.

Having eaten my supper, and completed the rest of my prep, I climbed into bed with the book, with every expectation of being asleep by the end of the third page . . . I read through the night, and I think it was five o'clock in the morning before I finally fell asleep. This wasn't English Literature. This was love.

When war broke out, my mother's sister, resident in Philadelphia, decided that she must do her bit for the brave British, and rather than send food parcels or clothes ("My dear, we *must* be more original in our thoughts to help you in your hour of need"), she donated to our household an indefinite subscription to the *Ladies Home Journal.* I don't think that any copy of any publication could have been devoured more avidly than was the *LHJ* in our household.

Apart from going to the pictures, where I sat longing to be Deanna Durbin, or howling over Charles Boyer in *Hold Back The Dawn,* it was the monthly arrival of this magazine that became my greatest comfort in dull and dark wartime Britain, opening windows into other worlds that I had either forgotten, or had never known. A beautifully produced magazine, it ran fiction of the highest quality. I read Daphne du Maurier for the first time in its pages, and Elizabeth Goudge, and was also introduced to some of the very best of American writers.

When I started to write my stories, I am afraid they were more of the *Peg's Paper* type, although, I would hope, a little more enterprising. However, as I grew up, married, had children, and felt myself become more qualified in interpreting relationships and feelings, the stories opened and spread their tentacles, covering all aspects of love and liaisons. The love of parents for children, brothers for sisters, grandparents for grandchildren. The love of old people for youth, of youngsters for age, the love of lovers, the love of marriage, the love that isn't love at all, but a mutual respect and affection.

Love does not necessarily have a happy ending, but it can change the colour of the world.

—1990

LALLA

There was a Before and After. Before was before our father died, when we lived in London, in a tall narrow house with a little garden at the back. When we went on family ski-ing holidays every winter and attended suitable—and probably very expensive—day schools.

Our father was a big man, outgoing and immensely active. We thought he was immortal, but then most children think that about their father. The worst thing was that Mother thought he was immortal too, and when he died, keeling over on the pavement between the insurance offices where he worked, and the company car into which he was just about to climb, there followed a period of ghastly limbo. Bereft, uncertain, lost, none of us knew what to do next. But after the funeral and a little talk with the family lawyer, Mother quietly pulled herself together and told us.

At first we were horrified. "Leave London? Leave school?" Lalla could not believe it. "But I'm starting 'O' levels next year."

"There are other schools," Mother told her.

"And what about Jane's music lessons?"

"We'll find another teacher."

"I don't mind about leaving school," said Barney. "I don't much like my school anyway."

Mother gave him a smile, but Lalla persisted in her inquisition. "But where are we going to *live?*"

"We're going to Cornwall."

And so it was After. Mother sold the lease of the London house and a removals firm came and packed up all the furniture and we travelled, each silently thoughtful, by car to Cornwall. It was spring, and because Mother had not realised how long the journey would take, it was dark by the time we found the village and, finally, the house. It stood just inside a pair of large gates, backed by tall trees. When we got out of the car, stiff and tired, we could smell the sea and feel the cold wind.

"There's a light in the window," observed Lalla.

"That'll be Mrs. Bristow," said Mother, and I knew she was making a big effort to keep her voice cheerful. She went up the little path and knocked at the door, and then, perhaps realising it was ludicrous to be knocking at her own door, opened it. We saw someone coming down the narrow hallway towards us—a fat and bustling lady with grey hair and a hectically flowered pinafore.

"Well, my dear life," she said, "what a journey you must have had. I'm all ready for you. There's a kettle on the hob and a pie in the oven."

The house was tiny compared to the one we had left in London, but we all had rooms to ourselves, as well as an attic for the dolls' house, the books, bricks, model cars and paint-boxes we had refused to abandon, and a ramshackle shed alongside the garage where we could keep our bicycles. The garden was even smaller than the London garden, but this didn't matter because now we were living in the country and there were no boundaries to our new territory.

We explored, finding a wooded lane which led down to a huge inland estuary where it was possible to fish for flounder from the old sea wall. In the other direction, a sandy right-of-way led past the church and over the golf links and the dunes to another beach—a wide and empty shore where the ebb tide took the ocean out half a mile or more.

The Roystons, father, mother and two sons, lived in the big house and were our landlords. We hadn't seen them yet, though Mother had walked, in some trepidation, up the drive to make the acquaintance of Mrs. Royston, and to thank her for letting us have the house. But Mrs. Royston hadn't been in, and poor Mother had had to walk all the way down the drive again with nothing accomplished.

"How old are the Royston boys?" Barney asked Mrs. Bristow.

"I suppose David's thirteen and Paul's about eleven." She looked at us. "I don't know how old you lot are."

"I'm seven," said Barney, "and Jane's twelve and Lalla's fourteen."

"Well," said Mrs. Bristow. "That's nice. Fit in nicely, you would."

"They're far too young for me," said Lalla. "Anyway, I've seen them. I was hanging out the washing for Mother and they came down the drive and out of the gate on their bicycles. They didn't even look my way."

"Come now," said Mrs. Bristow, "they're probably shy as you are."

"We don't particularly want to know them," said Lalla.

"But . . ." I started, and then stopped. I wasn't like Lalla. I wanted to make friends. It would be nice to know the Royston boys. They had a tennis court; I had caught a glimpse of it through the trees. I wouldn't mind being asked to play tennis.

But for Lalla, of course, it was different. Fourteen was a funny age, neither one thing nor the other. And as for the way that Lalla looked! Sometimes I thought that if I didn't love her, and she wasn't my sister, I should hate her for her long, cloudy brown hair, the tilt of her nose, the amazing blue of her eyes, the curve of her pale mouth. During the last six months she seemed to have grown six inches.

I was short and square and my hair was too curly and horribly tangly. The awful bit was, I couldn't remember Lalla ever looking the way I looked, which made it fairly unlikely that I should end up looking like her.

A few days later Mother came back from shopping in the village to say that she had met Mrs. Royston in the grocer's and we had all been asked for tea.

Lalla said, "I don't want to go."

"Why not?" asked Mother.

"They're just little boys. Let Jane and Barney go."

"It's just for tea," pleaded Mother.

She looked so anxious that Lalla gave in. She shrugged and sighed, her face closed in resignation.

We went, and it was a failure. The boys didn't want to meet us any more than Lalla wanted to meet them. Lalla was at her coolest, her most remote. I knocked over my teacup, and Barney, who usually chatted to everybody, was silenced by the superiority of his hosts. When tea was over Lalla stayed with the grown-ups, but Barney and I were sent off with the boys.

"Show Jane and Barney your tree-house," Mrs. Royston told them as we trailed out of the door.

They took us out into the garden and showed us the tree-house. It was a marvellous piece of construction, strong and roomy. Barney's face was filled with longing. "Who built it?" he asked.

"Our cousin Godfrey. He's eighteen. He can build anything. It's our club, and you're not members."

They whispered together and went off, leaving us standing beneath the forbidden tree-house.

When the summer holidays came, Mother appeared to have forgotten about our social debt to the Royston boys and we were careful not to remind her. So their names were never raised, and we never saw them except at a distance, cycling off to the village or down to the beach. Sometimes on Sunday afternoons they had guests and played tennis on their court. I longed to be included, but Lalla, deep in a book, behaved as though the Roystons didn't exist. Barney had taken up gardening, and, with his usual single-mindedness, was concentrating on digging himself a vegetable patch. He said he was going to sell lettuces, and Mother said that maybe he was the one who was going to make our fortune.

It was a hot summer, made for swimming. Lalla had grown out of her old swim-suit, so Mother made her a cotton bikini out of scraps. It was pale blue, just right for her tan and her long, pale hair. She looked beautiful in it, and I longed to look just like her. We went to the beach most days, and often saw the Royston boys there. But the beach was so vast that there was no necessity for social contact, and we all avoided each other.

Until one Sunday. The tide came in during the afternoon that day, and Mother packed us a picnic so we could set off after lunch. When we got to the beach, Lalla said she was going to swim right away, but Barney and I decided we would wait. We took our spades and went down to where the outgoing tide had left shallow pools in the sand. There we started the construction of a large and complicated harbour. Absorbed in our task, we lost track of time, and never noticed the stranger approaching. Suddenly a long shadow fell across the sparkling water.

I looked up, shading my eyes against the sun. He said "Hello," and squatted down to our level.

"Who are you?" I asked.

"I'm Godfrey Howard, the Roystons' cousin. I'm staying with them."

Barney suddenly found his tongue. "Did you build the tree-house?"

"That's right."

"How *did* you do it?"

Godfrey began to tell him. I listened and wondered how any person apparently so nice could have anything to do with those hateful Royston boys. It wasn't that he was particularly good-looking. His hair was mousey, his nose too big and he wore spectacles. He wasn't even very tall. But there was something warm and friendly about his deep voice and his smile.

"Did you go up and look at it?"

Barney went back to his digging. Godfrey looked at me. I said, "They wouldn't let us. They said it was a club. They didn't like us."

"They think you don't like them. They think you come from London and that you're very grand."

This was astonishing. "Grand? *Us?*" I said indignantly. "We never even pretended to be grand." And then I remembered Lalla's coolness, her pale, unsmiling lips. "I mean—Lalla's older—it's different for her." His silence at this was encouraging. "I wanted to make friends," I admitted.

He was sympathetic. "It's difficult sometimes. People are shy." All at once he stopped, and looked over my shoulder. I turned to see what had caught his attention, and saw Lalla coming towards us across the sand. Her hair lay like wet silk over her shoulders, and she had knotted her red towel around her hips like a sarong. As she approached, Godfrey stood up. I said, introducing them the way Mother introduced people, "This is Lalla."

"Hello, Lalla," said Godfrey.

"He's the Roystons' cousin," I went on quickly. "He's staying with them."

"Hello," said Lalla.

Godfrey said, "David and Paul are wanting to play cricket. It's not much good playing cricket with just three people and I wondered if you'd come and join us?"

"Lalla won't want to play cricket," I told myself. "She'll snub him and then we'll never be asked again."

But she didn't snub him. She said, uncertainly, "I don't think I'm much good at cricket."

"But you could always try?"

"Yes." She began to smile. "I suppose I could always try."

And so we all finally got together. We played a strange form of beach cricket invented by Godfrey, which involved much lashing out at the ball and hysterical running. When we were too hot to play any longer, we swam. The Roystons had a couple of wooden surf boards and they let us have turns, riding in on our stomachs on the long, warm breakers of the flood tide. By five o'clock we were ready for tea, and we collected our various baskets and haversacks and sat around in a circle on the sand. Other people's picnics are always much nicer than one's own, so we ate the Royston sandwiches and chocolate biscuits, and they ate Mother's scones with loganberry jam in the middle.

We had a last swim before the tide turned, and then gathered up our belongings and walked slowly home together. Barney and the two Roystons led the way, planning the next day's activities, and I walked with Godfrey and Lalla. But gradually, in the natural manner of events, they fell behind me. Plodding up and over the springy turf of the golf course, I listened to their voices.

"Do you like living here?"

"It's different from London."

"That's where you lived before?"

"Yes, but my father died and we couldn't afford to live there any more."

"I'm sorry, I didn't know. Of course, I envy your living here. I'd rather be at Carwheal than anywhere else in the world."

"Where do you live?"

"In Bristol."

"Are you at school there?"

"I've finished with school. I'm starting college in September. I'm going to be a vet."

"A vet?" Lalla considered this. "I've never met a vet before."

He laughed. "You haven't actually met one yet."

I smiled to myself in satisfaction. They sounded like two grown-ups talking. Perhaps a grown-up friend of her own was all that Lalla had needed. I had a feeling that we had crossed another watershed. After today, things would be different.

The Roystons were now our friends. Our relieved mothers—for Mrs. Royston, faced with our unrelenting enmity, had been just as concerned and conscience-stricken as Mother—took advantage of the truce, and after that Sunday we were never out of each other's houses. Through the good offices of the Roystons, our social life widened, and Mother found herself driving us all over the county to attend various beach picnics, barbecues, sailing parties and teenage dances. By the end of the summer we had been accepted. We had dug ourselves in. Carwheal was home. And Lalla grew up.

She and Godfrey wrote to each other. I knew this because I would see his letters to her lying on the table in the hall. She would take them upstairs to read them in secret in her room, and we were all too great respecters of privacy ever to mention them. When he came to Carwheal, which he did every holiday, to stay with the Roystons, he was always around first thing in the morning on the first day. He said it was to see us all, but we knew it was Lalla he had come to see.

He now owned a battered second-hand car. A lesser man might have scooped Lalla up and taken her off on her own, but Godfrey was far too kind, and he would drive for miles, to distant coves and hilltops, with the whole lot of us packed into his long-suffering car, and the boot filled with food and towels and snorkels and other assorted clobber.

But he was only human, and often they would drift off on their own, and walk away from us. We would watch their progress and let them go, knowing that in an hour or two they would be back—Lalla with a bunch of wild flowers or some shells in her hand, Godfrey sunburned and tousled—both of them smiling and content in a way that we found reassuring and yet did not wholly understand.

Lalla had always been such a certain person, so positive, so unveering from a chosen course, that we were all taken by surprise by her vacillating indecision as to what she was going to do with her life. She was nearly eighteen, with her final exams over and her future spread before her like a new country observed from the peak of some painfully climbed hill.

Mother wanted her to go to university.

"Isn't it rather a waste of time if I don't know what I'm going to do at the end of it? How can I decide now what I'm going to do with the rest of my life? It's inhuman. Impossible."

"But darling, what do you want to do?"

"I don't know. Travel, I suppose. Of course, I could be really original and take a typing course."

"It might at least give you time to think things over."

This conversation took place at breakfast. It might have continued forever, reaching no satisfactory conclusion, but the post arrived as we sat there over our empty coffee cups. There was the usual dull bundle of envelopes, but, as well, a large square envelope for Lalla. She opened it idly, read the card inside and made a face. "Goodness, how grand, a proper invitation to a proper dance."

"How nice," said Mother, trying to decipher the butcher's bill. "Who from?"

"Mrs. Menheniot," said Lalla.

We were all instantly agog, grabbing at the invitation in order to gloat over it. We had once been to lunch with Mrs. Menheniot, who lived with Mr. Menheniot and a tribe of junior Menheniots in a beautiful house on the Fal. For some unspecified reason they were very rich, and their house was vast and white with a pillared portico and green lawns which sloped down to the tidal inlets of the river.

"Are you going to go?" I asked.

Lalla shrugged. "I don't know."

"It's in August. Perhaps Godfrey will be here and you can go with him."

"He's not coming down this summer. He has to earn money to pay his way through college."

She would not make up her mind whether or not she would go to Mrs. Menheniot's party, and probably never would have come to any decision if it had not been for the fact that, before very long, I had been invited too. I was really too young, as Mrs. Menheniot's booming voice pointed out over the telephone when she rang Mother, but they were short of girls and it would be a blessing if I could be there to swell the numbers. When Lalla knew that I had been asked as well, she said of course we would go. She had passed her driving test and we would borrow Mother's car.

We were then faced with the problem of what we should wear, as Mother could not begin to afford to buy us the sort of evening dresses we wanted. In the end she sent away to Liberty's for yards of material, and she made them for us, beautifully, on her sewing machine. Lalla's was pale blue lawn and in it she looked like a goddess—Diana the Huntress perhaps. Mine was a sort of tawny-gold and I looked quite presentable in it, but of course not a patch on Lalla.

When the night of the dance came, we put on our dresses and set off together in Mother's Mini, giggling slightly with nerves. But when we reached the Menheniots' house, we stopped giggling because the whole affair was so grand as to be awesome. There were floodlights and car parks and hundreds of sophisticated-looking people all making their way towards the front door.

Indoors, we stood at the foot of the crowded staircase and I was filled with panic. We knew nobody. There was not a single familiar face. Lalla whisked a couple of glasses of champagne from a passing tray and gave me one. I took a sip, and at that very moment a voice rang out above the hubbub. "Lalla!" A girl was coming down the stairs, a dark girl in a strapless satin dress that had very obviously not been made on her mother's sewing machine.

Lalla looked up. "Rosemary!"

She was Rosemary Sutton from London. She and Lalla had been at school together in the old days. They fell into each other's arms and embraced as though this was all either of them had been waiting for. "What are you doing? I never thought I'd see you here. How marvellous. Come and meet Allan. You remember my brother Allan, don't you? Oh, this is exciting."

Allan was so good-looking as to be almost unreal. Fair as his sister was dark, impeccably turned out. Lalla was tall but he was taller. He looked down at her, and his rather wooden features were filled with both surprise and obvious pleasure. He said, "But of course I remember." He smiled and laid down his glass. "How could I forget? Come and dance."

I scarcely saw her again all evening. He took her away from me and I was bereft, as though I had lost my sister for ever. At one point I was rescued by Mrs. Menheniot herself, who dragooned some young man into taking me to supper, but after supper even he melted away. I found an empty sofa in a deserted sitting-out room, and collapsed into it. It was half-past-twelve and I longed for my bed. I wondered what people would think if I put up my feet and had a little snooze.

Somebody came into the room, and then withdrew again. I looked up and saw his retreating back view. I said, "Godfrey." He turned back. I got up off the sofa, back on to my aching feet.

"What are you doing here? Lalla said you were working."

"I am, but I wanted to come. I drove down from Bristol. That's why I'm so late." I knew why he had wanted to come. To see Lalla. "I didn't expect to see you."

"They were short of girls, so I got included."

We gazed glumly at each other, and my heart felt very heavy. Godfrey's dinner jacket looked as though he had borrowed it from some larger person, and his bow tie was crooked. I said, "I think Lalla's dancing."

"Why don't you come and dance with me, and we'll see."

I thought this a rotten idea, but didn't like to say so. Together we made our way towards the ballroom. The ceiling lights had been turned off and the disco lights now flashed red and green and blue across the smoky darkness. Music thumped and rocked an assault on our ears, and the floor seemed to be filled with an unidentifiable confusion of people, of flying hair and arms and legs. Godfrey and I joined in at the edge, but I could tell that his heart wasn't in it. I wished that he had never come. I prayed that he would not find Lalla.

But of course, he saw her, because it was impossible not to. It was impossible to miss Allan Sutton as well. They were both so tall, so beautiful. Godfrey's face seemed to close up.

"Who's she with?" he asked.

"Allan Sutton. He and his sister have come down from London. Lalla used to know them."

I couldn't say any more. I couldn't tell Godfrey to go and claim her for himself. I wasn't even certain by then what sort of a reception she would have given him. And anyway, as we watched them, Allan stopped dancing and put his arm around Lalla, drawing her towards him, whispering something into her ear. She slipped her hand into his, and they moved away towards the open french window. The next moment they were lost to view, swallowed into the darkness of the garden beyond.

At four o'clock in the morning Lalla and I drove home in silence. We were not giggling now. I wondered sadly if we would ever giggle together again. I ached with exhaustion and I was out of sympathy with her. Godfrey had never even spoken to her. Soon after our dance he had said goodbye and disappeared, presumably to make the long, lonely journey back to Bristol.

She, on the other hand, had an aura of happiness about her that was almost tangible. I glanced at her and saw her peaceful, smiling profile. It was hard to think of anything to say.

It was Lalla who finally broke the silence. "I know what I'm going to do. I mean, I know what I'm going to do with my life. I'm going back to London. Rosemary says I can live with her. I'll take a secretarial course or something, then get a job."

"Mother will be disappointed."

"She'll understand. It's what I've always wanted. We're buried down here. And there's another thing; I'm tired of being poor. I'm tired of home-made dresses and never having a new car. We've always talked about making our fortunes, and as I'm the eldest I might as well make a start. If I don't do it now, I never will."

I said, "Godfrey was there this evening."

"Godfrey?"

"He drove down from Bristol."

She did not say anything and I was angry. I wanted to hurt her and make her feel as bad as I felt. "He came because he wanted to see you. But you didn't even notice him."

"You can scarcely blame me," said Lalla, "for that."

And so she went back to London, lived with Rosemary, and took a secretarial course, just as she said she would. Later, she got a job on the editorial staff of a fashionable magazine, but it was not long before one of the photographers spied her potential, seduced her from her typewriter, and started taking pictures of her. Soon her lovely face smiled at us from the cover of the magazine.

"How does it feel to have a famous daughter?" people asked Mother, but she never quite accepted Lalla's success, just as she never quite accepted Allan Sutton. Allan's devotion to Lalla had proved unswerving and he was her constant companion.

"Let's hope he doesn't marry her," said Barney, but of course eventually, inevitably, they decided to do just that. "We're engaged!" Lalla rang up from London to tell us. Her voice sounded, unnervingly, as though she was calling from the next room.

"Darling!" said Mother, faintly.

"Oh, do be pleased. Please be pleased. I'm so happy and I couldn't bear it if you weren't happy, too."

So of course Mother said that she was pleased, but the truth was that none of us really liked Allan very much. He was—well—spoilt. He was conceited. He was too rich. I said as much to Mother, but Mother was loyal to Lalla. She said, "*Things* mean a lot to Lalla. I think they always have. I mean, possessions and security. And perhaps someone who truly loves her."

I said, "Godfrey truly loved her."

"But that was when they were young. And perhaps Godfrey couldn't give her love."

"He could make her laugh. Allan never makes her laugh."

"Perhaps," said Mother sadly, "she's grown out of laughter."

And then it was Easter. We hadn't heard from Lalla for a bit, and didn't expect her to come to Carwheal for the spring holiday. But she rang up, out of the blue, and said that she hadn't been well and was taking a couple of weeks off. Mother was delighted, of course, but concerned about her health.

By now we were all more or less grown-up. David was studying to be a doctor, and Paul had a job on the local newspaper. I had achieved a place at the Guildhall School of Music, and Barney was no longer a little boy but a gangling teenager with an insatiable appetite. Still, however, we gathered for the holidays, and that Easter Godfrey abandoned his sick dogs and ailing cows to the ministrations of his partner and joined us.

It was lovely weather, almost as warm as summer. The sort of weather that makes one feel young again—a child. There was scented thyme on the golf links and the cliff walks were starred with primroses and wild violets. In the Roystons' garden the daffodils blew in the long grass beneath the tree-house, and Mrs. Royston put up the tennis net and swept the cobwebs out of the summer house.

It was during one of these sessions that Godfrey and I talked about Lalla. We were in the summer house together, sitting out while the others played a set.

"Tell me about Lalla."

"She's engaged."

"I know. I saw it in the paper." I could think of nothing to say. "Do you like him, Allan Sutton, I mean."

I said "Yes," but I was never much good at lying.

Godfrey turned his head and looked at me. He was wearing old jeans and a white shirt, and I thought that he had grown older in a subtle way. He was more sure of himself, and somehow more attractive.

He said, "That night of the Menheniots' dance, I was going to ask her to marry me."

"Oh, Godfrey."

"I hadn't even finished my training, but I thought perhaps we'd manage. And when I saw her, I knew that I had lost her. I'd left it too late."

On the day that Lalla was due to arrive, I took Mother's old car into the neighbouring town to do some shopping. When the time came to return home, the engine refused to start. After struggling for a bit, I walked to the nearest garage and persuaded a kindly, oily man to come and help me. But he told me it was hopeless.

We walked back to the garage and I telephoned home. But it wasn't Mother who answered the call, it was Godfrey.

I explained what had happened. "Lalla's train is due at the junction in about half-an-hour and we said someone would meet her."

There was a momentary hesitation, then Godfrey said, "I'll go. I'll take my car."

When I finally reached home, exhausted from carrying the laden grocery bags from the bus stop, Godfrey's car was nowhere to be seen.

A short time later the telephone rang. But it wasn't Lalla, explaining where they were, it was a call from London and it was Allan Sutton.

"I have to speak to Lalla."

His voice sounded frantic. I said cautiously, "Is anything wrong?"

"She's broken off our engagement. I got back from the office and found a letter from her and my ring. She said she was coming home. She doesn't want to get married."

I found it in my heart to be very sorry for him. "But Allan, you must have had *some* idea."

"None. Absolutely none. It's just a bolt from the blue. I know she's been a bit off-colour lately, but I thought she was just tired."

"She must have her reasons, Allan," I told him, as gently as I could.

"Talk to her, Jane. Try to make her see sense."

He rang off at last. I put the receiver back on the hook and stood for a moment, gathering my wits about me and assessing this new and startling turn of events. I found myself caught up in a tangle of conflicting emotions. Enormous sympathy for Allan; a reluctant admiration for Lalla who had had the courage to take this shattering decision; but, as well, a sort of rising excitement.

Godfrey. Godfrey and Lalla. Where were they? I knew then that I could not face Mother and Barney before I had found out what was going on. Quietly, I opened the door and went out of the house, through the gates, down the lane. As soon as I turned the corner at the end of the lane, I saw Godfrey's car parked on the patch of grass outside the church.

It was a marvellously warm, benign sort of evening. I took the path that led past the church and towards the beach. Before I had gone very far, I saw them, walking up over the golf links towards me. The wind blew Lalla's hair over her face. She was wearing her London high-heeled boots so was taller than Godfrey. They should have appeared ill-assorted, but there was something about them that was totally right. They were a couple, holding hands, walking up from the beach as they had walked innumerable times, together.

I stopped, suddenly reluctant to disturb their intimacy. But Lalla had seen me. She waved, and then let go of Godfrey's hand and began to run towards me, her arms flailing like windmills. "Jane!" I had never seen her so exuberant. "Oh, Jane." I ran to meet her. We hugged each other, and for some stupid reason my eyes were full of tears.

"Oh, darling Jane . . ."

"I had to come and find you."

"Did you wonder where we were? We went for a walk. I had to talk to Godfrey. He was the one person I could talk to."

"Lalla, Allan's been on the phone."

"I had to do it. It was all a ghastly mistake."

"But you found out in time. That's all that matters."

"I thought I was going after what I wanted. I thought I had what I wanted, and then I found out that I didn't want it at all. Oh, I've missed you all so much. There wasn't anybody I could talk to."

Over her shoulder I saw Godfrey coming, tranquilly, to join us. I let go of Lalla and went to give him a kiss. I didn't know what they had been discussing as they paced the lonely beach, and I knew that I never would. But still, I had the feeling that the outcome could be nothing but good for all of us.

I said, "We must go back. Mother and Barney don't know about anything. They'll be thinking that I've dissolved into thin air, as well as the pair of you."

"In that case," said Godfrey, and he took Lalla's hand in his own once more, "perhaps we'd better go and tell them."

And so we walked home; the three of us. In the warm evening, in the sunshine, in the fresh wind.

—1990

JAYNE ANN KRENTZ
B. 1948

Jayne Ann Krentz writes in her introduction to Dangerous Men and Adventurous Women: Romance Writers on the Appeal of the Romance— *"The fact that so many women persist in reading and enjoying romance novels in the face of generations of relentless hostility says something profound not only about women's courage but about the appeal of the books." A prolific, best-selling author of series romances, Krentz is also a persuasive defender of romance formula. Her perceptive analysis of romance fiction in her essay, "Trying to Tame the Romance: Critics and Correctness," also published in* Dangerous Men and Adventurous Women *(1992), reveals her understanding of popular romance fiction as social and political ideology.*

Born in San Diego, California, Krentz earned her B.A. (with honors) from the University of California at Santa Cruz and her M.A. in librarianship from San Jose State University. She has worked as a librarian, and currently lives in the Pacific Northwest. Krentz is among the most popular of contemporary romance writers. A recently published blurb states she is the author of sixteen consecutive New York Times *best-sellers and that over twenty million copies of her books have appeared in print. Her work has been featured in a number of major romance series—such as Harlequin and Silhouette—and she has written over one hundred novels under a variety of pseudonyms. Krentz published* Whirlwind Courtship *in 1979 as "Jayne Taylor." In the same year, as "Jayne Bently," she published* A Moment Past Midnight, *and as "Jayne Castle" she published* Vintage of Surrender. *Her first novel as "Stephanie James" was* A Passionate Business *(1981), and as "Amanda Quick" was* Seduction *(1990).*

Krentz often includes suspense in her romances, and she is noted for her use of self-confident and strong-willed protagonists. For example, in her novella, "Connecting Rooms," first published in the romance anthology Everlasting Love *(1995), the story's hero and heroine are both equally matched romantic partners. Owen Sweet is a headstrong, yet skilled, private investigator who proceeds with his investigations at his own pace, while Amy Comfort is an independent businesswoman (and romance writer) working as a real estate agent. Krentz also demonstrates in this tale how the romance can incorporate, as part of its larger narrative frame, other types of popular formulas. She successfully employs the hard-boiled detective story as the basic plot for "Connecting Rooms" (which includes traces of Dashiell Hammett's screwball mystery,* The Thin Man), *without diminishing the novella's impact as a romance.*

TRYING TO TAME THE ROMANCE:
CRITICS AND CORRECTNESS

Don't think that there hasn't been a lot of pressure exerted to make romance writers and romance fiction more politically correct. During the past few years, even as romance novels have commanded a spectacular share of the publishing market there has been an unrelenting effort to change them.

Much of this effort was exerted by a wave of young editors fresh out of East Coast colleges who arrived in New York to take up their first positions in publishing. (The editing of romance novels has traditionally been viewed as an entry-level job in the industry.) These young women (and most of them were women) didn't read romances themselves and so didn't understand why they appealed to readers. But they did understand that romance novels are held in contempt or at the very least considered politically incorrect by scholars and intellectuals and even by much of the publishing hierarchy which makes billions of dollars from them. And so they set about trying to make romances respectable. They looked for new authors who shared their views of what a respectable romance should be and they tried to change the books being written by the established, successful authors they inherited.

The first target of these reforming editors was what has come to be known in the trade as the alpha male. These males are the tough, hard-edged, tormented heroes that are at the heart of the vast majority of bestselling romance novels. These are the heroes who made Harlequin famous. These are the heroes who carry off the heroines in historical romances. These are the heroes feminist critics despise.

What is it with those of us who write romance? We are intelligent women. We're flexible. We learn fast. Surely those who sought to lead us in the paths of politically correct romance writing ought to have succeeded in their goal of straightening us out by now. Why did we dig in our heels and resist the effort to turn our hard-edged, dangerous heroes into sensitive, right-thinking modern males?

We did it for the same reason a mystery writer sticks to the outcast hero, the same reason a western writer clings to the paladin figure. We did it because, in the romance genre, the alpha male is the one that works best in the fantasy.

And the reason he works so well is because in a romance the hero must play two roles. He is not only the hero, he is also the villain.

To understand what the romance novel is, it is important to understand first what it is not. A romance novel plot does not focus on women coping with contemporary social problems and issues. It does not focus on the importance of female bonding. It does not focus on adventure. A romance novel may incorporate any or all of these elements in its plot, but they are never the primary focus of the story. In a romance novel, the relationship between the hero and the heroine *is* the plot. It is the primary focus of the story, just as solving the crime is the primary focus of a mystery.

Given that conflict is a requirement of all good fiction, especially good genre fiction, and given that the conflict must arise out of the primary focus of the story, it is understandable that in a romance novel conflict must exist between the hero and heroine.

The hero in a romance is the most important challenge the heroine must face and conquer. The hero is her real problem in the book, not whatever trendy issue or daring adventure is also going on in the subplot. In some way, shape, or form, in some manner either real or perceived on the heroine's part, the hero must be a source of emotional and, yes, sometimes physical risk. He must present a genuine threat.

The hero must be part villain or else he won't be much of a challenge for a strong woman. The heroine must put herself at risk with him if the story is to achieve the level of excitement and the particular sense of danger that only a classic romance can provide.

And the flat truth is that you don't get much of a challenge for a heroine from a sensitive, understanding, right-thinking "modern" man who is part therapist, part best friend, and thoroughly tamed from the start. You don't get much of a challenge for her from a neurotic wimp or a good-natured gentleman-saint who never reveals a core of steel.

And it is that core of steel at the center of a good romance hero that makes it all worth while.

Any woman who, as a little girl, indulged herself in books featuring other little girls taming wild stallions knows instinctively what makes a romance novel work. Those much-loved tales of brave young women taming and gentling magnificent, potentially dangerous beasts are the childhood version of the adult romance novel. The thrill and satisfaction of teaching that powerful male creature to respond only to your touch, of linking with him in a bond that transcends the physical, of communicating with him in a manner that goes beyond mere speech—that thrill is deeply satisfying. It is every bit as powerful as the satisfaction readers get from seeing the outcast hero solve the crime and mete out justice in a good mystery. But to get the thrill, you have to take a few risks. The hard-boiled detective must go down a few dark, dangerous alleys and the romance heroine must face a man who is a genuine challenge.

The second target of those who attempted to change romance novels was another familiar convention in the books: the aggressive seduction of the heroine by the hero. Most of the time this seduction is portrayed as intense and unrelentingly sensual; occasionally it is so forceful that it has been mislabeled rape by critics. Either way it is a convention that is universally condemned by those who sit in judgment on the romance novel. It is not politically correct for a woman to fantasize about being aggressively seduced.

It is odd that the romance genre is singled out for this particular criticism, because the aggressive seduction of the protagonist is an extremely common convention in most of the other genres. Mysteries, a field notable for its plethora of both male writers and male protagonists, routinely use this approach to dealing with sex.[1] Many hard-boiled private-eye heroes get themselves seduced by their female clients or suspects in the course of the story. The seducing client or suspect is frequently portrayed as potentially threatening and as having a strong aura of aggressive sexuality, a description that nicely fits romance heroes. In mysteries the private eye very seldom initiates the seduction and, indeed, often appears surprisingly passive about the whole thing. Some put up a token resistance not unlike that put up by the heroines of some romance novels. This aggressive seduction of hard-boiled private investigators could conceivably be mislabeled as rape, but critics rarely even bother to mention it.

Aggressive seduction of the protagonist occurs in other genres as well. The male heroes of thrillers and men's action-adventure novels[2] are frequently swept off their feet and into bed by mysterious, exotic, powerful women. It is only when the tables are turned as they are in the romance genre, when the female protagonist is seduced by a mysterious, exotic, powerful male, that critics become alarmed.

It would seem to be more accurate and more honest simply to acknowledge that the fantasy of being aggressively seduced within the safe, controlled environment of a work of fiction is a popular one shared by men and women alike. And why not? It's very pleasant to enter into a fantasy where one is the treasure rather than the treasure hunter.

It is interesting to note that in the romance novel this fantasy often takes on a complex and fascinating twist. Through the use of male viewpoint, a technique often employed either directly or indirectly, the reader is allowed to experience the seduction from the hero's point of view as well as that of the heroine. The reader gets to enjoy the fantasy of being *simultaneously* the one who seduces and the one who is seduced.

This twist on the basic seduction fantasy is not a simple matter of the writer structuring the scene so that the reader switches back and forth between viewpoints. It cannot be summed up or explained by saying that the seduction is witnessed first through the heroine's eyes and then through those of the hero. In a really good romance, the experience for the reader is that of being in both the heroine's mind and the hero's *at the same time.* The reader knows what each character is feeling, what each is sensing, how each is being affected. She is also profoundly aware of the transcendent quality of the experience, of how it will alter the course of both the hero's and the heroine's life. The whole thing is incredibly complex, exciting, and difficult to describe. I suspect it is almost unique to the romance novel.

Perhaps it is this indefinable richness of the seduction fantasy that makes romance novels so threatening to critics of the genre. But just because one does not have the vocabulary fully to explain the experience does not mean it is a negative one. It does not even make it politically incorrect. The truth is that women who read romance novels never describe themselves as feeling threatened by the fantasy of being seduced, just as men who read hard-boiled detective fiction never appear to feel threatened by the sexually aggressive client or suspect.

The third target of those who sought to make romance novels respectable was the convention of the heroine's virginity. There is no denying that the most popular romances, both contemporary and historical, frequently feature heroines who are virgins. This fact is readily acknowledged by writers such as myself, who have compared royalty statements with other writers. It is also substantiated by an examination of the bestseller lists.

This virginal quality has nothing to do with making the heroine a "trophy" for the hero. Nor is it used as a moral issue. It has everything to do with creating a metaphor for the qualities of female power, honor, generosity, and courage with which the heroine is imbued. Virginity has been the stuff of legends, of stories of kings and queens, bloody wars and patched-up alliances, territorial feuds and historical consequences since the dawn of time. There is an heroic quality about a woman's virginity that is truly powerful when used to its fullest potential in fiction.

There is also the underlying assumption in most romance novels that the heroine is smart enough to choose the right man. It is to this man that she gives the gift of her love and her virginity. Part of being the hero of such a romance novel means appreciating the gift of the heroine's virginity. *She* is never the same again. Perhaps even more important, *he* is never the same, either.

In a romance novel the heroine allows herself to be seduced not by just any male but by one particular male, a larger-than-life hero. She takes a risk, and at the end of the story it pays off. She has chosen the right man. She has tamed the magnificent wild stallion. She has awed and gentled him with the generous gift of herself. She has also forced him to acknowledge her power as a woman as well as the womanly honor she uses to control and channel that power.

Men represent to women one of the greatest sources of risk they will ever encounter in their lives. Taking risks and winning out against all odds is one of the great pleasures of fantasy. In a romance novel the heroines put everything on the line and they win. Virginity is symbolic of the high stakes involved.[3]

The fourth target of the reforming editors was the genre's frequent use of certain core stories. It has often been pointed out that there are only a handful of plots available to the mystery genre and only a few basic stories in westerns or science fiction or horror. This limitation on plot devices is not considered a sin in those genres, but for some reason critics view it as such in romance.

At the core of each of the genres lie a group of ancient myths unique to that genre. The most popular writers in those genres continually mine those ancient myths and legends for the elements that make their particular genre work. Westerns and mysteries incorporate the old chivalric tales. The horror genre relies on the gut-wrenching myths of the supernatural that have been around since the days when people lived in caves. Science fiction uses the myths of exploration and the fear of the "other" that have long fascinated an aggressive species bent on conquering new territory. At the heart of the romance novel lie the ancient myths that deal with the subject of male-female bonding.

Stories become myths because they embody values that are crucially important to the survival of the species. There is no subject more imperative to that survival than the creation of a successful pair bond. The romance novel captures the sense of importance and the sheer excitement of that elemental relationship as no other genre can.

Women, who have traditionally had the primary responsibility for making that bond work, have always responded to the basic myths and legends around which romance is built. I suspect they will continue to do so as long as the current method of reproduction is in use and as long as the family unit is the cornerstone of civilization.

Some of the basic myths and legends that animate the romance genre include the tale of Persephone (echoed in a thousand stories involving a woman being carried off by a mysterious, powerful male who is in turn enthralled and brought to his knees by her). Another popular one is the story of Beauty and the Beast (often portrayed in childhood tales of little girls taming large stallions and in adult stories of women taming dangerous men). Then there is the familiar battle of the sexes, or the Taming of the Shrew story. This one is especially piquant for women because in these tales the man is the one who, for once, is forced to find a way to make the relationship work.

There are other basic stories of romance, all of which have deep roots in ancient myths and legends. In the romance novel the elements of those myths and legends that speak most powerfully to women are preserved and retold.

Romance novels are tales of brave women taming dangerous men. They are stories that capture the excitement of that most mysterious of relationships, the one between a woman and a man. They are legends told to women by other women, and they are as powerful and as endlessly fascinating to women as the legends that lie at the heart of all the other genres.

The effort to make romance novels respectable has been a resounding failure. The books that exemplify the "new breed" of politically correct romances, the ones featuring sensitive, unaggressive heroes and sexually experienced, right-thinking heroines in "modern" stories dealing with trendy issues, have never become the most popular books in the genre.

Across the board, from series romance to single title release, it is the writers who have steadfastly resisted the efforts to reform the genre whose books consistently outsell all others. And the readers have demonstrated where their hearts are by routinely putting the romances that incorporate the classic elements on the bestseller lists.[4]

Notes

1. The propensity of the heroes of mystery novels toward getting themselves aggressively seduced is readily seen in many of the books throughout the genre. From the novels of Raymond Chandler and Dashiell Hammett to the books written by such popular contemporary authors as Dick Francis, Loren D. Estleman, Scott Turow, and Andrew Vachss, it is almost always the woman who does the seducing.

2. In the quintessential men's action adventure series, *The Executioner,* the hero, Mack Bolan, is a man who is certainly aggressive when it comes to dealing out a violent kind of justice to the bad guys. But when it comes to women he is politely aloof, almost reluctant. It is the women in the stories who pursue and sometimes manage to seduce him, not vice versa.

3. I am indebted to romance writer Suzanne Simmons Guntrum for many of the ideas and much of the language I have used in this discussion of virginity.

4. An examination of any of the romance novels written by the following *New York Times* bestselling authors will prove this point: Judith McNaught, Sandra Brown, Johanna Lindsey, Catherine Coulter, Karen Robards, Julie Garwood, Amanda Quick. For more names, check the latest edition of the *New York Times* bestseller lists.

−1992

CONNECTING ROOMS

1

No one ever said that the devil couldn't have a rose garden, Amy Comfort thought. It just seemed a trifle out of character. On the other hand, the rose garden of the old Draycott place was no ordinary one. And Owen Sweet, Amy had decided, was no ordinary gardener.

"Are you, or are you not, a private investigator?" Amy demanded.

"Depends," Owen Sweet answered. With the lethal precision of a fencer, he used a pair of garden shears on a clotted mass of evil-looking vines.

"What does it depend on?"

"On whether or not I feel like working at it." Owen took hold of the severed vines with heavily gloved hands. He ripped the old vegetation away from the window with a single, powerful motion. "I'm a little busy at the moment."

"Yes, I can see that."

Owen took no notice of her sarcasm. He seized another tangle of vines and dispatched them with ease.

Amy watched, morosely fascinated. She couldn't help it. She liked watching Owen Sweet.

The vegetation he was attacking with such diligence had grown so thickly over the windows of the old house that it had effectively blocked all sunlight from reaching some of the rooms.

Not that sunlight was a common commodity here on Misplaced Island, Amy thought. The forgotten little patch of land located off the coast of Washington sat squarely in the middle of a rain shadow. A perpetual mist shrouded the island on good days. Dense rain poured down the rest of the time.

The local joke was that the island had earned its name when its original discoverer had temporarily misplaced it in the fog. Whatever the truth of that story, there was no doubt but that one had to be determined to find Misplaced Island.

And, Amy thought, one had to have either a powerful motivation or an extremely odd sense of whimsy to make one's home here. She wondered which of those two possibilities applied to Owen Sweet.

"Owen, this garden went wild years ago, just like the house." Amy was growing increasingly exasperated. Time was running out, and she needed Owen Sweet. "It can wait a few more days before you tame it."

Owen paused briefly to look at her. His sea-green eyes gleamed in the misty gray light. "I'm in the mood to do it now."

Sweet was definitely a misnomer, Amy reflected, not for the first time. As far as she had been able to discern, Owen was anything but sweet, in either nature or temperament. She suspected he was yet another result of a baby having been switched at birth. Happened all the time, they said. Amy wondered what Sweet's parents had thought when they discovered that they had been given a little green-eyed, black-haired demon to raise.

He was proving to be stubborn and thoroughly irritating, but there was something about the man that fascinated Amy. She did not know him very well, even though she had sold him the Draycott place. No one on the island really knew Owen Sweet.

He had moved to Misplaced Island two months ago. Amy had met him when he walked into the real estate office she operated out of the parlor of her cliffside cottage. She had been stunned by her reaction to him. Hunger and longing and a singing sense of joyous discovery barely began to describe it.

She had tried to squelch the feelings. True, she was a struggling romance novelist on the side, but Amy was far too pragmatic to believe in love at first sight. On the other hand, she trusted her own instincts when it came to people. They had stood her in good stead in the real estate business, and she saw no reason to discount them when dealing with members of the opposite sex. One thing was for certain. Those instincts had never reacted with such overwhelming intensity to any of the handful of men she had dated.

Owen had appeared oblivious of her carefully concealed response to him. He had announced without preamble that he'd already toured the island on his own and had checked out the available properties. He had decided to buy the Draycott place.

Amy had been horrified. Everyone on the island knew that the old Draycott house, a Victorian monstrosity, was a disaster from foundation to roof. She had dutifully done her best to steer Owen toward other real estate opportunities, but he had refused to listen to her advice. In the end a sale was a sale. Amy had reluctantly written up the deal.

The only good part about the transaction, she had told herself, was that Misplaced Island was a very small community. She would see Owen Sweet again. She could only hope it wouldn't be in the course of a lawsuit over the Draycott sale. Some buyers tended to blame the real estate agent when they discovered they had made a bad bargain.

But Owen had appeared to be content with his new home when, to her secret delight, Amy had begun to encounter him with increasing regularity at the post office, in the checkout line at the island's only grocery store, and at the tiny bookshop. One of the few facts that she had gleaned concerning him was that he was a voracious reader. At the rate he ordered books from Mrs. Akers, the owner of the bookshop, he would single-handedly keep her small store in the black during the coming winter.

But last week had been the real turning point. After running into her at the post office, Owen had invited Amy to join him in a cup of coffee at the town's one and only cafe. The conversation had concerned such riveting matters as the weather, the latest novels they had each read, and the limited ferry schedule. Amy had walked on air all the way back to her cottage. Hope had bloomed within her.

She stifled a small, wistful sigh as she watched Owen free another window from its shroud of clinging vines. There was a lean, supple strength about him that captivated her senses. While it was true that, objectively speaking, Owen's grim features could have been created by someone who would have been equally adept at designing junkyard dogs, Amy found him strangely compelling. Which probably said far too much about the limited social life on Misplaced Island, she told herself.

Then again, she had not even been aware of a lack of a social life until Owen had arrived.

She watched him now with brooding determination. This was the first time she had paid a call on Owen Sweet since he had moved into his crumbling abode. She had come on business, not for social reasons. She needed this man. She needed him badly.

It wasn't as if she had a lot of choice. The small sign on the front door of the old Victorian ruin Owen called home said it all. It read SWEET INVESTIGATIONS.

Owen Sweet was the only private investigator on Misplaced Island. There was not a lot of call for his type of work in the small community. Amy was quite certain that since his arrival he had yet to get a single case. She had naively believed that he would be thrilled to have work. Obviously, she had been mistaken.

Amy braced one hand against the garden's stone wall and drummed her fingers with simmering impatience. Unaware or uncaring of her irritation, Owen Sweet went about his work among the grotesquely tangled rosebushes which clogged the garden.

The roses had been abandoned along with the crumbling ruin of a house years ago. Instead of dying off in a bittersweet, genteel manner, they had gone wild, with a vengeance. They climbed the garden walls as though bent on escaping a prison. They formed impenetrable thickets across the cracked paths, choked the empty fishpond, and had apparently been intent on marching up the steps and into the sunporch. Owen Sweet had arrived in the nick of time.

"Can I take it from your attitude that you are not interested in working for me?" Amy asked bluntly.

"Yeah." Sleek muscles moved easily beneath Owen's black T-shirt as he shifted an armload of defeated vines to a growing pile in the center of the garden. "You can draw that conclusion."

"Very well then, you leave me no choice." Amy removed her hand from the stone wall and straightened in resignation. "I shall have to find someone else."

Owen's mouth curved slightly. "Good luck. The last time I looked in the phone book, I was the only PI on the island."

Amy brushed her hands together and started toward the sagging gate. "I had hoped to give my business to someone local because I believe in supporting the local economy. But since you're not interested, I'm sure I can find someone in Seattle who will be happy to take my money."

"Seattle?"

Amy was aware that Owen had gone very still behind her. She did not turn around. "If I hurry, I can catch the afternoon ferry."

"Damn. Hold on just a minute."

Satisfaction surged through Amy. She had been in real estate long enough to sense when a buyer had undergone a quick change of heart. She paused at the gate to smile at Owen with polite inquiry.

"Was there something you wanted, Owen?"

He scowled ferociously, an expression which did nothing to soften his harsh face. "Yeah. Some answers."

"Sorry, I don't have time to chat. The ferry leaves in a couple of hours and I haven't finished packing."

"Let's get real here." Owen stripped off his gloves as he strode toward her along the garden walk. "What does a woman like you need with a private investigator?"

"'A woman like me'?"

"No offense, Amy, but you're hardly the type to have the sort of problems that require the services of someone in my line of work."

"What would you know about my problems?"

Owen came to a halt in front of her and planted his fists on his hips. "You're not exactly a mystery woman. You've been living on Misplaced Island for nearly a year. During that time you've opened a real estate agency and published a romance novel. Before you came here, you worked the condominium market in Seattle. You aren't exactly rich, but you did all right in your own real estate investments."

Amy was taken back. "Good grief. How did you—"

"Everyone on the island seems very fond of you," Owen continued ruthlessly. "I seriously doubt that you have any enemies around these parts. You are thirty years old and have never been married. You do not flirt with married men, so the local women have no reason to dislike you. You are not dating anyone at present, so you have no reason to employ an investigator to tail an errant boyfriend."

Amy gazed at him with mingled anger and amazement. "Are you quite finished?"

"No, not quite. You appear to live like a cloistered nun, Ms. Comfort. Therefore, I find it difficult to believe that you have got yourself into a situation which requires an investigator."

"You seem to have done a fairly thorough job investigating me. May I ask why?"

Owen wiped his sweat-dampened forehead with the back of one muscular bare arm. "That should be sort of obvious."

"Well, it's not obvious to me."

He gripped the top of the drooping gate and contemplated her with narrowed eyes. "No, I can see that."

"I don't know what this is all about, nor do I have the time to find out. If you're not going to accept my case, I've got to find someone else. Please excuse me."

Amy tried to open the gate. Owen took no notice of her effort. Instead, he leaned heavily back against it and folded his arms across his chest. He looked annoyed but resigned.

"Okay, tell me about it," he said.

"Tell you about what?"

"This problem of yours. The one that requires an investigator."

Amy fixed him with a frosty glare. "It's a confidential matter. I see no reason to discuss it with someone who is not going to be working for me."

"Hell, I'll take the case. Now tell me what's got you in such an uproar."

"I don't think that I care for your unprofessional manner."

"Sorry, it's the only manner I've got." He considered her thoughtfully for a few seconds. Then he came away from the gate and took her arm. "Come on, let's go inside. I'll make you a cup of coffee and you can tell me all your problems."

"I'm no longer sure that I want you handling my case."

"Don't be silly. A few minutes ago you were practically begging me to take your precious case."

"I was not begging you. And furthermore, I've changed my mind."

"So have I."

Amy thought about digging in her heels, but her options were extremely limited. It would take time to hunt up an investigator in Seattle. And money. She did not possess unlimited quantities of either. She allowed Owen to lead her up the steps.

The interior of the house was as run-down and abandoned-looking as the garden, but at least nothing appeared to be actually growing on the walls or springing up through the floorboards.

Threadbare velvet curtains that had faded to a peculiar shade of maroon flanked the grimy windows. An atmosphere of gloom and decay hovered over the front parlor. Several pieces of heavy, claw-footed furniture clustered near the black-marble fireplace. There was very little paint left on the walls and the wooden floors were raw and scarred.

A pang of guilt went through Amy, temporarily erasing her irritation. "I did try to warn you that this was a fixer-upper."

"A fixer-upper?" Owen gave her a derisive look. "It's a life sentence. Wiring's shot. Plumbing's rusted out. Roof needs repair. I'll have to replace the furnace before winter sets in, along with all the appliances."

"Don't you dare blame me. I made you read every single word on the seller's disclosure statement. You knew what you were getting into when you bought this place."

"Did I? That's debatable." But Owen appeared perversely satisfied with his purchase. "Have a seat." Not ungently, he pushed her toward a high-backed, velvet-covered sofa. "I'll get the coffee."

Amy sat down gingerly and surveyed the shabby interior of the parlor. She shook her head in amazement. It was true that she had sold him the house, but she had no idea what he was doing here in it. Why had he come here to Misplaced Island, she wondered.

Owen reappeared a few minutes later carrying a tray laden with a French press coffeepot and two cups. He set his burden down on the battered old coffee table.

"All right, tell me what this is all about." He sank into the depths of one of the massive wingback chairs.

"It's a very straightforward case," Amy said crisply. "My aunt, Bernice Comfort, has recently announced her engagement. I want you to investigate her fiancé, Arthur Crabshaw."

Owen looked up as he poured coffee. "Why?"

"Because there's something about Crabshaw that I don't quite trust. I met him a couple of weeks ago, and I have the distinct feeling that he's hiding something. He appeared out of nowhere a few months after her husband, Uncle Morty, died, and immediately swept Aunt Bernice off her feet."

"You write romance novels, don't you? I would have thought you'd have approved of Crabshaw's technique."

"If you're not going to take this case seriously, please tell me now so that I can find another investigator."

"I'm serious. You have no idea just how serious."

She glowered at him. "What's that supposed to mean?"

"Forget it. Why are you suspicious of Crabshaw?"

"My aunt was left quite comfortably well off after Uncle Morty died two years ago," Amy said carefully. "She lives in a small town on the coast. Villantry, Washington. Know it?"

"I've heard of it."

"It's the sort of town where everyone knows everyone else. Crabshaw lived there himself at one time, but he left the place some thirty years ago. Now he's back."

"And you think he returned because he heard that your wealthy aunt is available?"

"Let's just say that there's something about Crabshaw's appearance on the scene which smacks of opportunism," Amy said.

"What exactly is it about Crabshaw that worries you?"

"It's hard to explain." Amy frowned. "He seems nice enough, and Aunt Bernice is obviously mad about him. But I sensed something a bit shifty beneath the surface."

"Shifty."

"Yes."

"Shifty is a rather vague term, Amy."

"I can't be any more specific. I just know that there's something not quite right about that man. I have very good people instincts, you know."

"Is that a fact?"

"Yes, it is," Amy retorted. "Look, I'm going to drive to Villantry this afternoon. Just a social visit, as far as Aunt Bernice is concerned. I'll be staying at the Villantry Inn for a couple of days, because my aunt is having her house remodeled. I want you to come with me."

Owen looked baffled. "What the hell do you expect me to do?"

"Check out Arthur Crabshaw, of course. Surely you don't need me to tell you how to conduct a simple investigation."

"You'd be amazed at what I need."

Amy scowled. "I want you to rummage around in Crabshaw's background. Find out if he's on the level. But I don't want my aunt to realize what you're doing. If he's legit, I'd rather she didn't know that I hired you. It would be embarrassing and awkward."

"Embarrassing and awkward." Owen nodded sagely. "That's me."

Amy blushed. "I didn't mean that as a personal remark."

"Right." Owen leaned back in his chair and stuck out his legs. He crossed his booted feet and regarded Amy with a truculent expression. "I'm supposed to go to Villantry with you, but no one is supposed to know who I am or what I'm doing there, is that it?"

Amy gave him an approving look. "Precisely."

"Villantry is a very small town. I'm not going to be able to hide very easily."

"I don't intend to keep you hidden."

"Just how do you plan to explain my presence?"

Amy smiled a trifle smugly. "Don't worry, I've got it all worked out. I'll pass you off as my fiancé."

2

That evening Owen sat next to Amy in the restaurant of the Villantry Inn and wondered what the hell had come over him. But the question was strictly rhetorical. He knew the answer. Amy Comfort had come over him. Or, to be more precise, he sincerely hoped that their acquaintance would develop to the point where that eventuality became a distinct possibility.

He'd wanted Amy Comfort from the first moment he'd seen her. He would never forget that shattering instant of acute knowledge. He had walked into her parlor office, intent on purchasing the old Draycott place. The moldering pile of timber and stone had appealed to him on sight. He had determined to possess it, regardless of the price.

He'd felt the same way about Amy, although there was nothing moldering about her. Just the opposite. She was fresh and vital and alive. Her chin-length hair was the color of honey and her intelligent eyes were a mesmerizing shade of ultramarine blue.

She was not beautiful in the classic sense, but there was an appealing quality in her firm chin, high cheekbones, and straight little nose. There was something else there, too, an indefinable essence that he suspected an older generation would have labeled strength of character.

She reminded Owen of the wild roses in his garden. She would not fade when the going got tough, the way his first wife had. Amy would endure and flourish, just as the flowers in the Draycott garden had endured and flourished. Owen was not sure how he knew that, but he was very certain of it.

The extent of his desire for Amy had astounded him, because he'd assumed that he was well past the point when passion and desire could dazzle his senses and shake up his world. He was within spitting distance of forty, after all, and he had not got this far the easy way. One broken marriage and a checkered career that included a stint in the military and later as a private investigator had taught him that the world was painted in shades of gray.

But the day he had met Amy, Owen had started viewing life in living color again for the first time in years.

He had decided upon his goal in a heartbeat, but years of training had taken over at that juncture. He was, by nature, a careful, methodical man. He had told himself that he had to approach Amy in a subtle manner. Misplaced Island was a very small community. If he moved too quickly, there would be gossip. Amy might be embarrassed. The last thing he wanted to do was scare her off.

It was clear to Owen that she led a busy, but largely solitary life. He had established immediately that she had not dated anyone since her arrival on the island. That meant the path was clear for him.

He was no ladies' man, but he had determined to woo her with all the finesse at his command. Carefully planned trips to the post office, the grocery store, and the bookshop had netted him a series of seemingly casual encounters. He had told himself that she was getting used to him. She certainly seemed happy enough to run into him several times a week.

He had been encouraged with the results of his invitation to coffee last week. He had been consumed with plotting a dinner invitation when she'd blindsided him with the offer of a job this afternoon.

He had been dumbfounded when she had strolled into his wild garden and offered him a case. He had also been chagrined to learn that weeks of cautious maneuvering had been for naught. After all his painstaking efforts, she apparently viewed him only as a man who happened to have a useful expertise. She wanted to do business with him, not go to bed with him.

Owen stifled a silent groan. His only hope now lay in the fact that he had managed to get connecting rooms here at the Villantry Inn. There was something about adjoining rooms which created a sense of intimacy, he told himself.

To hell with delicacy and masculine finesse. It was obvious to Owen that the time had come to take a more aggressive approach to the business of courting Amy Comfort. Subtlety was lost on the woman.

"I do wish you two could have stayed with me," Bernice said for the fourth time. "But what with the remodeling and all, there's just no place to put you. The house is a mess, isn't it, Arthur?"

"Afraid so," Arthur Crabshaw, a sturdy man with gray hair and friendly eyes, smiled at Amy. "You know how things are during a remodel. Chaos and destruction. And I don't have room at my place."

"The Inn is perfect for us," Amy said quickly. "Isn't that right, Owen?"

"Yeah. Fine." Owen was vividly conscious of the fact that the curve of Amy's thigh, demurely draped in a flowing hunter-green silk skirt, was less than six inches from his leg. Wistfully, he considered the connecting rooms one flight above. "Perfect."

Arthur Crabshaw forked up a fried oyster with gusto. "The Inn's got the best food in town." He winked fondly at Bernice. "With the exception of Bernice's cooking, that is. Nothing compares to that."

Bernice, a robust, athletic-looking woman in her mid-fifties with lively eyes and short, upswept hair that had been dyed a pale gold, blushed. Her eyes sparkled as she smiled at Owen.

"Amy's quite a gourmet cook herself," Bernice confided to Owen. "But I'm sure you've already discovered that."

Owen felt Amy stiffen next to him. He slid her a sidelong glance and was amused to see the barely veiled panic in her gaze. She was apparently not accustomed to subterfuge. She was on the verge of coming unglued at the first mild probe into their relationship. Gallantly, he stepped in to fill the breach.

"So far I've done all the cooking," he said, thinking of the pot of coffee he'd made that afternoon.

"Oh, then you must be a vegetarian also," Bernice said brightly.

Owen heard Amy's fork clatter loudly on the wooden table. He glanced down at the chunk of halibut which sat squarely in the middle of his plate. "I make an exception for fish. Health reasons."

"Well, Amy eats fish on occasion, too." Bernice waved that aside, as if it were common knowledge. "Now, then, the two of you must tell us everything. How did you meet? I swear, Amy, when you told me that you were going to move to that little dinky island, I was extremely worried about your social life."

"I know you were, Aunt Bernice," Amy said.

"I realized you were burned out after that dreadful incident last year," Bernice continued. "And I knew you wanted peace and quiet so that you could devote more time to your writing. But I never thought you'd be happy for long in such a small, isolated community."

Amy shot Owen a quick, unreadable glance. "Misplaced Island suits me. I've been very happy there."

"So I see." Bernice bubbled with enthusiasm "Imagine, after all these years, you've finally discovered the man of your dreams on Misplaced Island."

Amy turned pink. "Uh, yes, well, you know what they say. Love is where you find it."

"The name of the island says it all," Owen said dryly. "I guess Amy and I weren't fated to find each other until we both got ourselves misplaced in the same place."

"I'm not so sure it's any harder to find love in a small town than it is in a big city." Crabshaw chuckled. "Just look at Bernice and me. If I hadn't come back to Villantry after all these years, I never would have found her."

"What made you return to Villantry, Arthur?" Amy asked boldly.

Owen winced at her less than casual tone. But Crabshaw did not seem to mind the pointed question.

"I got tired of the desert," Arthur said. "After thirty years of Arizona sunshine, I realized I missed the rainy Northwest. The only thing I miss about Phoenix is the year-round golf."

"Arthur loves golf," Bernice explained. "He plays every chance he gets, don't you, dear?"

Arthur smiled. "I do, indeed. Got a game scheduled for tomorrow morning, in fact. The Villantry Golf Course is not exactly world-class and the rain has a way of canceling out a lot of games, but I figure that's a small price to pay to live here."

"Life is so unpredictable," Bernice said. "What a coincidence, eh, Amy? You and I both finding true love where we least expected it."

Amy began to look anxious again. "Right. Hey, what's all the excitement about here in Villantry? We saw banners hanging over the main street. Something about fireworks in the park on Saturday evening."

"Didn't you know?" Arthur popped another oyster into his mouth. "The town is going to dedicate the new wing of the Raymond C. Villantry Memorial Public Library on Saturday. Big event. Madeline Villantry and her son, Raymond Junior, are pulling out all the stops."

"The new library wing is really a very generous gift to the community," Bernice said politely.

Amy raised her brows. "Do I detect a note of dutiful peasant gratitude?"

Bernice made a face. "Sorry about that. The Villantrys are nice enough in their own way, and Lord knows they've done a lot for this town. But they never forget for one minute that they are the leading family in Villantry. Very conscious of their position, if you know what I mean. Madeline is quite good in the role of Lady Bountiful."

Owen grinned briefly. "But the noblesse oblige stuff from the lady of the manor gets to be a bit thick at times, I take it?"

Bernice rolled her eyes. "I'm afraid so. Then, too, even though we're all adults now, I suppose a part of me can't quite forget that when we were in high school together, Madeline was the acknowledged beauty of the town. She got every boyfriend she wanted, including one or two of mine."

Arthur shifted uneasily in his chair and cleared his throat. "Villantry Fishing built this town. Most of the jobs here are connected to the company. I worked for Villantry myself years ago, before I went off to Arizona."

"What did you do in Arizona?" Owen asked easily. He pretended not to notice Amy's sharp glance.

"Started a construction company. Got lucky. Hit the building boom in Phoenix. Always thought I'd retire there, but after my wife died I felt restless. Did some traveling and then, on a whim, I decided to see what had happened to my hometown."

"We met in the library," Bernice said with a rueful laugh. "So I suppose one could say that we owe the Villantrys."

Arthur paused with the fork halfway to his mouth. "Speaking of Villantrys," he murmured, "here comes the lady of the manor herself, and Junior. He runs the business now, you know. Took over when his old man died three years ago."

Owen glanced up to see a handsome woman in her fifties moving regally down the aisle between a row of tables. She was followed by a man in his early thirties who looked as if he was on the wrong coast. He wore a pale yellow sweater tied around his neck and a bored look that spoke of having grown up with a sense of entitlement.

The dining room hostess trotted deferentially ahead of the pair, as though to make certain no rude serfs lumbered into their path. Madeline paused briefly at various tables to greet people with heavy-handed graciousness. Raymond Junior paused with her. He was not so gracious, however. He appeared impatient.

A moment later the entourage halted beside the table where Owen and the others sat. Owen and Arthur got to their feet. Madeline acknowledged their chivalry with an aloof inclination of her head. The nod said more plainly than words could have that such good manners were only expected.

"Do sit down, both of you." Madeline's smile was polite, but her voice was laced with a certain pinched quality. Her gaze touched Arthur briefly before sliding away. "Bernice, Arthur, I'm so glad we ran into each other here tonight. I heard about your engagement, and I want to congratulate both of you."

"Thank you, Madeline." Bernice gestured toward Owen and Amy. "I'd like you to meet my niece, Amy Comfort, and her fiancé, Owen Sweet. They're visiting."

"How do you do," Madeline said. "This is my son, Raymond."

Raymond gave Owen a curt nod. "Our table's ready, Mother."

A fleeting frown of disapproval flickered across Madeline's noble features, and then it was gone. "Yes, of course. You will excuse us?"

"Enjoy your dinner," Bernice said cheerfully.

"Thank you." Madeline glanced once more at Arthur and then she was gone.

Something in Arthur Crabshaw's gaze caught Owen's attention. In spite of his opinion of the crazy case and the fact that he had more important things on his mind at that moment than solving it, his instincts went on yellow alert.

Not red alert, Owen noticed, just yellow. But a warning light had definitely flashed. He felt Amy go very still beside him. He wondered if she had sensed the same thing he had.

No doubt about it: Arthur Crabshaw and Madeline Villantry had a history.

Two hours later Owen sat in a chair near the window of his darkened room and contemplated the closed door that stood between him and Amy.

He had been studying the door for nearly twenty minutes, ever since he and Amy had returned from dinner and coffee in the lounge.

After due consideration, Owen had finally concluded that the logical approach was the obvious one. He would simply knock on the connecting door. When Amy opened it from her side, he would tell her that he wanted to discuss the case. It was as clever an excuse as any.

Having considered and determined upon a course of action, he gripped the padded arms of the chair and started to get to his feet. An authoritative knock from Amy's side of the door stopped him in midrise.

"Owen? Are you in there?" Her voice was muffled, but the excited urgency in it was unmistakable. She knocked again, this time with a bit more insistence.

Owen told himself not to get his hopes up. The odds were against the likelihood that Amy had fallen for him sometime during dinner and now wanted to share a passionate good-night embrace.

Nevertheless, he walked across the room with enthusiasm and opened the door with anticipation.

Amy stood there, her hand raised for another peremptory knock. Her honey-colored hair was pinned in a frothy knot on top of her head. She was wearing a heavy, quilted bathrobe that rendered the average nun's habit scandalous in comparison. Owen smiled at the sight of her. She looked freshly scrubbed, and he was willing to bet that she had already brushed her teeth.

"I thought you might want to discuss the case," she said eagerly.

Owen's enthusiasm and anticipation vanished in a puff of smoke. So much for his fond dream of having Amy fall into his arms. Back to Plan A. "I was afraid of that."

Her brows snapped together. "What?"

"Never mind." Owen stepped aside and swept his hand out to invite her into his room. "Come on in and have a seat. I'm at your service. Hell, I'm even willing to unlock the little refrigerator over there and open one of those itsy-bitsy bottles of wine."

Amy scowled. "Those tiny bottles are horribly overpriced for what you get."

"No problem. I'll just put it on my expense account."

Amy halted midway into the room. Alarm flared in her eyes. "Expense account?"

"Sure. That's how this PI business works, you know." He closed the connecting door and strolled to the small refrigerator. He used the small key to open the door. "I bill you by the hour and then tack on all the little extras. Adds up nicely."

"Good heavens. I hadn't realized. That could get rather pricey."

"Yes, indeed." Owen removed a minuscule bottle of brandy and paused to examine the label. "Name of the game, I'm afraid."

"Maybe we should have discussed your fees in more detail."

"Too late." Owen splashed the brandy into two glasses. "I'm already on the job. And once I start something, I always finish it."

Her expression relaxed. "You're teasing me."

"Am I?"

"Yes." She took one of the glasses from his hand. "You know, you've been acting a little weird since you agreed to take this case."

"Maybe that's because the case is a little weird." He took a sip from his glass.

"First time I ever went undercover as a client's fake fiancé. By the way, you want some advice?"

She looked immediately wary. "What advice?"

"Try not to get that deer-caught-in-the-headlights expression in your eyes whenever someone makes a reference to our engagement. Sooner or later you'll blow our cover."

Her mouth fell open in shock. "Good grief. I'm that bad?"

He stared at her full, parted lips. "Maybe you just need to loosen up a bit."

"Loosen up?"

"Mellow out. Get into the role." He closed the distance between them with long, slow strides. "Try to become more comfortable with the idea of having a relationship with me."

She nibbled on her lower lip. "Relationship?"

"It should feel natural." He stopped in front of her. "Otherwise you're going to panic whenever someone says the magic word, *engagement.*"

"Don't be ridiculous. I'm not going to panic."

"No?" He put his hands on her shoulders. "How will you react if, for the sake of maintaining the deception, I do something like this?"

He bent his head and covered her mouth with his own.

3

Amy froze beneath the impact of Owen's kiss. *Just like a deer caught in a car's headlights,* she thought. Owen had been right. The concept of an intimate relationship with him did strange things to her nerves.

But the rest of her body seemed to have no problem with the idea. Owen was kissing her. After all these weeks of her wondering and fantasizing, he was actually kissing her.

Hot excitement flashed through Amy, erasing the momentary paralysis. With an awkward, slightly jerky movement, she wrapped her arms around Owen's neck and kissed him back with all the bottled-up passion she had been concealing for nearly two months.

Her response appeared to take Owen by surprise. He staggered a little under the gentle assault. But he did not release her. He recovered his balance immediately and began to rain kisses on her throat.

"Amy?"

"Oh, my God, this is amazing."

"You can say that again." Owen scooped her up in his arms and carried her across the room to the bed. "When I think of all the time we've wasted."

"Yes, yes, I know what you mean."

He set her down on the bed and fell on top of her. Her bathrobe had been a faithful friend for years, but it had not been designed to defend its wearer from such treatment. It promptly separated. One of Owen's jeaned legs found its way between Amy's thighs.

"Owen."

"Damn," he whispered. "This is incredible. You're incredible."

Amy was dazed by the waves of passion that were coursing through her. She felt deliciously crushed beneath Owen's not inconsiderable weight. The heat of his body triggered a series of lightning strikes within her. She could feel the fires they ignited.

The flames burned most intensely in her lower body, liquefying all that they touched.

Owen found the pins in her hair and tore them free. "Like honey in my hands." He seized a fistful of the stuff and buried his nose in it. "You smell so good."

"So do you." The realization astonished her. She had never before noticed a man's smell unless she happened to be standing downwind of one who had failed to use deodorant.

But this unique scent that belonged to Owen was different. Enticing. Enthralling. It did crazy things to her senses. She wanted more of it. More of him.

"Hang on, let me get you out of this thing." Owen levered himself up on one elbow and tugged at the sash of her robe.

Amy gazed at him, fascinated by the passion that blazed in his eyes. Wonderingly, she touched his hard jaw. "I can't believe this is happening."

"The delay was my fault. I was going for the subtle approach." He put a heavy, warm hand on the bodice of the soft cotton gown. His fingers closed gently around one breast. "Don't ask me why."

"You feel so good." She flattened her palm against his chest, delighting in the strength of him.

"So do you." He bent his head to kiss a nipple. His mouth dampened the fabric of her gown. She gave a small, muffled cry and clutched at his shoulders.

Owen began to tug the nightgown downward. "Amy, you don't know what you're doing to me."

Realization burst through Amy's dazzled senses. "Oh, my God, you're right. This is all my fault."

"Huh?"

"It's the case." She clutched wildly at her sliding nightgown and struggled to sit up. "Don't you see? It's the situation we're in that's causing you to act like this."

"What the hell?" Owen fell to the side as Amy squirmed out from underneath him.

"I thought this was all very sudden." Amy tugged the lapels of her robe together and grabbed for the sash. Her hands were shaking.

"Sudden?"

"Well, it's not as though you've shown any great interest in me until tonight."

"Amy, for God's sake, listen to me. You've got this all wrong."

"I don't think so." She glowered at him as she scooted to the edge of the bed. "We've known each other for several weeks and you've never once indicated that you felt anything other than sort of friendly toward me."

"Sort of friendly?" Owen was beginning to look mildly dangerous.

Amy was mortified. "It's worse than I thought. You weren't even feeling particularly friendly, were you? That was just my imagination."

"Amy, I think we have a small problem here," he began in an ominous tone.

"Please, it's all right. I understand exactly what's happening."

"I'm glad one of us does."

"Well, they do say that women are more inclined to analyze situations."

"Hell."

"I've read about this sort of thing," she said defensively. "But I should have thought that since you're the expert in these matters, you'd have been alert for just this type of unprofessional occurrence."

"Unprofessional?"

She was suddenly outraged by his obstinacy. "Don't look at me as if you don't know what I'm talking about. I'm sure that as a private investigator, you've faced this sort of situation hundreds of times."

Owen reached out to clamp a hand around her wrist. "For the benefit of this non-analytical, slow-witted investigator, would you kindly explain what the hell you're talking about?"

Amy flushed. "You know what I mean. A situation like this, where two people are thrown together in close confines. A situation in which they face a threat of danger. Why, it's bound to generate a heightened sense of intimacy. Intimacy often breeds passion. Especially when the two people involved are single and of the opposite sex."

"Hold it." Owen put his fingers against her lips to silence her. "Stop right there. Let's take this from the top. First, I have been an investigator for over ten years, and I can assure you that I have never, ever made love to a client. Until now, that is."

Amy stared at him. "I see."

"Furthermore, although I will admit that the situation in which we find ourselves has a built-in degree of intimacy, thanks to the cover story you invented for us, I see absolutely no danger here. Therefore, I think we can discount its impact on our sex lives."

Amy frowned. "I'm not so sure about that. We really don't know what we're facing yet. There could definitely be some risk involved."

"No," Owen said authoritatively. "There is no threat involved in this damn-fool situation. A certain amount of idiocy on the part of the PI, perhaps. An amazing imagination on the part of the client, definitely. But no threat. Unless you count the threat to my sanity."

"Owen, we don't know that for certain." Amy got up quickly and tied the sash of her robe. "You haven't even begun to investigate Arthur Crabshaw. The possibility of danger must be present somewhere in the back of your mind. You're a trained investigator, after all."

Owen flopped back against the pillows and threw one arm over his eyes. "You'd never know it."

Amy bit her lip. "Please, I didn't mean to upset you like this. I should never have knocked on your door tonight. If I'd had any sense, I would have recognized the volatile nature of the situation and waited until morning to discuss the case."

"Yeah, right."

Amy edged back toward the connecting door. "I'm sorry."

"Uh-huh."

"It's the adrenaline and hormones and things like that at work. Not genuine emotion."

"Uh-huh."

"But you're right about my imagination," she added sadly.

He removed his arm from his eyes and stared at her with sudden intensity. "What?"

"I do have an overactive imagination. I suppose it's an occupational hazard for a writer."

Owen sat up slowly. "So you admit there's no real danger involved in this loony case?"

She shook her head decisively. "No, I still think we mustn't discount the very real possibility that Arthur Crabshaw is not what he seems. Did you see the way he reacted to Madeline Villantry tonight?"

Owen hesitated. "Okay, I'll admit that there may be some kind of connection between them."

Amy brightened. "I got the exact same impression. This is amazing, Owen. We're on the same wavelength here."

"That's a matter of opinion." Owen sat up on the edge of the bed. A thoughtful expression began to replace the combination of irritation and passion that had burned in his gaze a moment earlier. "Don't get carried away with your brilliant deduction, Amy. It makes sense that Madeline and Arthur knew each other at some point in the past. It's a small town, after all, and Crabshaw told us that he worked for Villantry before he went off to Arizona to make his fortune."

"The thing is, Madeline Villantry and Arthur Crabshaw would have been worlds apart socially in those days. After all, she was married to the town's leading citizen. Arthur worked for her husband. But tonight I got the feeling that there was something more intimate between them."

"Maybe there was." Owen stood and began to pace the room. "But whatever happened occurred over thirty years ago. It doesn't mean anything now."

"Then why did Crabshaw get that funny look in his eyes when Madeline stopped by our table tonight?"

Owen came to a halt and swung around to face her. "I don't know."

Amy was momentarily sidetracked by the sight of him. His dark hair was tousled. His denim shirt had come free of his jeans. All in all, there was a tantalizing, seductive look about him that made her pulse begin to pound once more.

"Something wrong?" Owen asked.

"Uh, no. I was just trying to think this thing through."

"If you can think clearly at the moment, you're way ahead of me." Owen ran his fingers through his hair. "Look, it's late. Go to bed. In the morning I'll call some people I know. Have them check into Crabshaw's Arizona background. I can at least make sure that he doesn't have a criminal record and that he's financially solvent."

"That sounds like a good start."

"Thanks. I do try to give satisfaction."

Aware that he was in a strange mood, Amy backed meekly toward the door. She was almost through it when Owen stopped her with another question.

"Amy, what did you mean a few minutes ago when you said you had an overactive imagination?"

She paused in the doorway, clutched the lapels of her robe very tightly, and gave him her best real estate saleswoman smile. "Nothing. Nothing at all."

"Have I told you that you're a very bad liar?"

"Don't ask me any questions if you don't like my answers," she flared.

Owen raised his eyes briefly to the ceiling in a beseeching expression. Then he fixed her with a look of dogged patience. "Amy, the relationship between a private investigator and his client is founded on mutual trust and confidentiality. If I don't feel that I can rely upon your answers, I won't be able to work for you."

"Oh." She frowned.

He took a deliberate step toward her. "I think we need to get this relationship back on track. The fastest way to do that is to be completely honest with each other."

"What do you want from me?" she asked.

He spread his hands. "I'll get right to the bottom line. Did you really kiss me a few minutes ago because you were driven into a paroxysm of violent passion by the close confines and threat of incredible danger that we face together?"

"Well, no. At least, I don't think so."

"So why did you kiss me?"

She gripped the edge of the door and lifted her chin proudly. "If you must know, I kissed you because I've been wanting to kiss you ever since I sold you that Victorian horror of a house. There. Are you satisfied?"

He stared at her as if he'd just walked into a brick wall. *"Amy."*

"Good night, Owen. I'll meet you downstairs for breakfast. I shall want a complete status report on this case and a detailed outline of your plans for the remainder if this investigation by eight o'clock tomorrow morning. We have no time to waste."

Amy slammed the connecting door behind her and hurried into her room. She took a deep breath. After a few seconds she opened the door again. Owen was still standing in the middle of the room, staring at the door. "Why did you kiss me?" she asked.

His mouth quirked and a sexy gleam appeared in his eyes. "Same reason. Been wanting to do it since I bought the house."

Amy felt her insides turn to jelly. "Oh."

"See you in the morning."

"Right." Amy closed the door again, this time very quietly. Then she snapped off the light, removed her robe, and threw herself down onto the bed.

She contemplated the shadowed ceiling for a very long while before she finally went to sleep.

4

Owen used a copy of the *Villantry Gazette* to shield his gaze as he watched Amy walk toward him. The no-nonsense impact of her determined stride across the Inn's coffee shop was severely undercut by the pink in her cheeks and the shyness in her eyes.

It took a lot to make a real estate agent turn shy, Owen reflected with some satisfaction. Last night's events had obviously had an unsettling effect on Amy. He took that as a good sign and set about composing his strategy for the day.

She was self-conscious about what had happened between them, preferring to blame it on adrenaline and hormones. He would act as if nothing at all out of the ordinary had occurred. He would be businesslike and professional. That might help her relax.

The important thing was that now, after weeks of shilly-shallying around with the subtle approach, he finally knew for certain that she was anything but indifferent to him. She might have concocted a ludicrous reason to explain away the white-hot desire that had flashed between them, but she was definitely not indifferent.

"Good morning." He put down the paper and lazily got to his feet as Amy reached the table.

"Hi." She gave him a practiced real estate agent's smile as he pulled out her chair, but her eyes reflected far less certainty. "How are things going?"

Owen blanked at the question. He seriously doubted that she was inquiring about how he had survived a night complicated by an erection the likes of which he had not endured since his late teens.

"What things?" Owen asked cautiously.

"The investigation, of course. You said you were going to make some calls this morning."

"Oh, yeah, right. The investigation." Owen tried a businesslike smile of his own as he resumed his seat. "It's going just fine. I made my calls before I came downstairs. Should know something by this afternoon."

"Great." Amy opened her menu with a snap. "What about the next step?"

Owen cleared his throat. He did not delude himself into thinking that she was referring to the next step in their relationship. "We'll have to see what sort of information comes in from my contacts before we can make concrete plans."

"In that case, why don't we go to the library later this morning."

He shrugged. "Why not? There's not much else to do until I get some response to my calls. We can take a look at this fancy new wing the town plans to dedicate on Friday."

Amy looked up from the menu with a small frown. She glanced hurriedly around the room and then leaned forward and lowered her voice. "I meant that we should go to the library to do some research, not to kill time."

"Research on what?"

"On Arthur Crabshaw."

"In the *library?*"

"For Pete's sake, you're supposed to be the trained investigator here. Why am I having to do all the work?"

"Because you have a natural aptitude for it?" he suggested with bland innocence.

"Stop teasing me. You know perfectly well why I suggested the library."

"I do?"

"Of course. We might be able to learn something about Crabshaw if we look through old newspapers from the time when he worked for Villantry."

"You know something, Amy? You have a one-track mind. I suppose you need it in the real estate business, though, don't you? What do you do? Sink your teeth into a client and refuse to let go until he signs on the dotted line?"

She gave him a puzzled look. "I'm just trying to keep you focused on the job at hand. Are you always this vague about your work? Does the pressure get to you or something? Is that what went wrong in Portland?"

Owen drummed his fingers on the table. "Amy, you are not going to find anything of interest on Crabshaw in thirty-year-old editions of the *Villantry Gazette.*"

"What makes you so sure of that?"

Owen swore under his breath. "Think about it. If Crabshaw had been involved in an old scandal or if he had left town under a cloud, do you honestly believe that Madeline Villantry would have been so polite and gracious to him last night?"

"Hmm. I hadn't thought about that."

"She went out of her way to congratulate him and your aunt on their engagement. This is a small town, and the Villantrys have obviously ruled it for years. If Crabshaw had done anything thirty years ago that was considered the least bit unsavory, Madam Villantry would not have stopped at our table."

"I suppose you have a point."

"Thank you. I like to think that I'm not completely unsuited to my work."

"Still, it won't hurt to look in the old papers, will it?" Amy continued brightly. "As you said, it's not as if we have anything better to do this morning."

Owen narrowed his eyes. "Is this why you had to quit your high-powered real estate career in Seattle? In your zeal to close a big deal did you finally manage to push one of your clients a little too far?"

To his amazement, Amy paled. "That question does not deserve an answer." She took a deep breath and returned her full attention to the menu.

An hour later Owen found himself reluctantly ensconced in front of a microfilm reader. He was supposed to be perusing the headlines of the old issues of the *Villantry Gazette* that were rolling slowly past his gaze, but his real attention was on Amy. She sat at the machine next to him, her attention on another reel of the *Gazette.*

Owen was still berating himself for the unwitting crack about her real estate tactics. He had obviously stumbled into awkward territory. It didn't take Sherlock Holmes to deduce that something bad had happened in Seattle. He recalled a remark Bernice had made at dinner. Something about Amy being burned out after "that dreadful incident last year."

At the time, Owen had concluded that Bernice had been referring to an affair that had gone sour. He hadn't paid much attention to the comment because whatever it was, it was in the past. He was only concerned with Amy's future.

"Find anything interesting?" Amy asked in a muted tone.

"Interesting?" Owen paused to read the headlines that were moving slowly across the screen. "Let's see. 'Villantry Eagles Break Six-Game Losing Streak.' How does that sound?"

"About as exciting as 'Raymond C. Villantry Dedicates New Library.'"

Owen glanced around. "I guess that would be the old library now. The one we're in."

The Raymond C. Villantry Memorial Public Library, a sturdy structure in the tradition of old-fashioned municipal buildings, was surprisingly busy for a small library on a Friday morning, Owen thought. As a book lover himself, he took a certain pleasure from that fact.

In one corner a gaggle of pre-school-age children had assembled to listen to fairy tales read by a librarian. Their shouts of glee and shrieks of horror drifted across the cavernous main room. The children's mothers, no doubt grateful for the respite in parental duties, perused the display of new books.

The janitor, a balding, middle-aged man in coveralls, set up a sign in front of the women's room and disappeared inside with his wheeled bucket and well-used mop.

Three elderly men sat at tables in the newspaper section poring over copies of the *Wall Street Journal.* Two librarians and a small group of what appeared to be concerned citizens hovered near the entrance to the new wing. They were apparently making final arrangements for Saturday's dedication ceremony. As Owen watched, they were joined by Raymond Villantry Jr., who strode through the door wearing a business suit. When he appeared, there was a chorus of respectful greetings. Then the entire group disappeared into a conference room and closed the door.

"Look, here's a picture of Madeline Villantry standing next to her husband." Amy leaned closer to the screen. "I'll bet she was prom queen, homecoming queen, and head cheerleader."

"You can tell all that from a photo?"

"See for yourself."

More than willing to take advantage of the offer to move closer to Amy, Owen shifted position to get a better view of her screen. "Right. Definitely prom queen."

The old black-and-white photo was grainy and blurred, but there was no hiding the fact that Madeline Villantry had been a beautiful woman in her younger days. She stood beside her husband, the late Raymond C. Villantry Sr., who was holding forth from a lectern in front of the library.

Amy wrinkled her nose. "He looks like a politician."

"Yeah. Junior is a dead ringer for his old man, isn't he?"

"Yes." Amy frowned at the photo. "I'll bet that was not a happy marriage."

Owen glanced at her in surprise. "What makes you say that?"

"I'm not sure. Something about the expression on Madeline Villantry's face. Poised. Gracious. Aloof. Dutiful. Anything but happy."

"I think you're trying to read a little too much into a thirty-year-old photo."

"Maybe." Amy shrugged. "Not that it matters to us. Aunt Bernice said that Raymond C. Villantry Sr. died three years ago."

"And young Raymond Junior took over the company. Wonder how he likes being called Junior."

"Between you and me, he doesn't look any nicer than his father."

"I don't think that being nice is a job requirement for running a company the size of Villantry." Owen took advantage of the situation to lean in just a little closer.

He caught a whiff of the flowery fragrance of Amy's hair and inhaled deeply. Along with it came a more intriguing scent. Warm, female, and deliciously spicy. He did not think he would ever be able to get enough of it. Of her.

"Owen," Amy hissed.

"Sorry, I was just trying to get a better look at the picture."

"Never mind that. Look."

"At what?"

"Arthur Crabshaw. He just walked into the library. See? Over there by the magazine rack."

Owen straightened reluctantly and turned to look at the racks. Sure enough, Crabshaw was leafing through a new copy of *Newsweek*. "So what?"

"What's he doing here?"

"Reading a magazine?"

"That isn't funny. Owen, he told us that he was going to play golf this morning." Amy scowled impatiently. "It's not raining, so why did he cancel his game?"

"Why don't we ask him?"

"Don't be silly. He's up to something. I know it. I told you there was something shifty about that man."

"Amy, the first rule in the investigation business is not to jump to conclusions. Crabshaw simply dropped into the library to scan a few magazines. Don't make a federal case out of it."

"He's leaving the magazine rack. Don't let him see you."

"Why not?"

"Because we want to keep an eye on him. We need to find out where he's going."

"I think he's headed for the men's room," Owen said.

"Oh."

Owen rested one arm over the back of the hard wooden library chair and watched Arthur Crabshaw disappear into the men's rest room. Amy looked severely disappointed.

"Cheer up," Owen said. "Maybe he'll do something really suspicious when he comes out of the john."

"You think this is amusing, don't you."

"I think you're overreacting," he said gently. "Why are you so determined to prove that Arthur Crabshaw is up to no good?"

"I told you, I don't want him to take advantage of Aunt Bernice."

"Just because he happened to return to Villantry a few months after your uncle died doesn't mean he's out to marry Bernice for her money."

"I still say the timing is very suspect. Be careful, he's coming out."

Owen dutifully retreated a little farther behind the shelter of the microfilm reader. Arthur Crabshaw emerged from the men's room and headed swiftly toward the front door of the library.

"He seems to be in a big hurry all of a sudden," Amy observed.

Owen chewed on that for a while. He hated to admit it, but there was something about Crabshaw's behavior this morning that was at odds with the genial man who had entertained them at dinner last night. Whatever it was, it reminded Owen of the look that had been in Crabshaw's eyes last night when he had chatted with Madeline Villantry.

Owen reached a decision.

"Wait here, I'll be right back."

He got to his feet and walked casually toward the men's room. He passed the three elderly men bent over their financial papers. None of them bothered to look up from the stock market listings. The janitor, whose name tag read E. TREDGETT, had finished mopping the women's room. He started off toward the new wing with his clanking wheeled bucket.

Raymond suddenly emerged from the conference room, apparently intent on heading toward the rest room. He walked out just as the janitor went past the door. The toe of Villantry's Italian leather shoe struck the bucket. Sudsy water sloshed over the edge.

"Damn it, Eugene, watch where you're going."

"Sorry, sir." Eugene Tredgett seemed to fold in on himself. He hurriedly used his mop to clean up the spill.

Raymond appeared to realize that Owen was watching the small incident. He scowled and then apparently changed his mind about his destination. With a disgusted shrug, he turned back into the conference room and closed the door.

Owen gave the janitor a sympathetic smile. Tredgett acknowledged it with a wan nod and trundled on with his bucket and mop.

Owen went through the swinging door of the men's room.

The gleaming, white-tiled facility was empty. Owen dismissed the two urinals with a glance and then considered the two stalls. Amy would never forgive him if he didn't make a thorough search of the premises.

He walked into the first cubicle and lifted the tank lid. There was nothing inside the tank except water and the usual float-ball assembly.

He went into the second stall and tried again.

A sealed envelope was taped beneath the lid.

5

"Take it easy, Amy," Owen said. "Calm down. This may have nothing to do with Crabshaw. I need time to think. I've got to get more information before I can decide what to do next."

Amy scowled at him across the picnic table. It wasn't easy. Every time she looked at Owen a flood of memories washed over her. She could still feel the heat of his mouth on hers. She was certain that his arms had left permanent impressions on her body. But his stubbornly slow, methodical approach to his work was going to drive her crazy.

"Are you nuts?" she demanded. "It's got everything to do with Crabshaw. There's a thousand dollars inside that envelope and Crabshaw was the last man to go into that rest room before you. He must have been the one who left the money under the tank lid."

"It could have been left by someone earlier this is morning."

"Hah. What are the odds?"

"Okay," he muttered, "I'll grant you that a coincidence like this is something of a long shot."

"That's putting it mildly." Amy threw up her hands, exasperated. "Who else would have left that money inside a toilet tank? I think it's safe to say that there aren't that many people here in Villantry who could come up with that kind of cash."

"Amy, that envelope could have been taped inside the lid at any time during the past week, or even the past month. Hell, it could have been left there sometime during the past year, for all we know. No one checks the inside of a toilet tank unless the toilet acts up."

"You're going to be difficult about this, aren't you."

"I'm going to be careful. Methodical. I'm going to take it one step at a time. That's the way I do things, Amy."

"Hmm." Amy folded her arms on the picnic table and glumly surveyed Villantry Park. She and Owen had come here to discuss their next move, but so far all they had done was argue about it.

They were seated at a table located near a magnificent mass of rhododendron bushes. The stately Raymond C. Villantry Memorial Public Library was at the far end of the park. The Villantry Inn was on the opposite side. There was a bandstand in the center.

A pond, complete with ducks and a couple of geese, added eye appeal to the attractive setting. Banners announcing fireworks hung over the entrance of the park.

Amy was frustrated by Owen's approach to this startling new development in the case. On the other hand, she had to admit that he was the expert.

"All right. Hypothetically speaking," she said, making an effort to sound reasonable, "what sort of scenario do we construct to explain that envelope you found?"

Owen raised one black brow. "Hypothetically speaking, I'd say that it looks as if Arthur Crabshaw is being blackmailed."

"Blackmail." Amy tasted the word with a sense of dreadful wonder. "Holy cow."

Owen fingered the envelope in his hand. "It's conceivable that he's been told to leave the money in the men's room of the library. Think about it. Anyone can go into a public library at any time when it's open. A person can hang around for hours, a whole day even, without anyone taking much notice. The victim can leave the money at any time. The blackmailer can pick up the payoff whenever he feels like it."

Amy peered at him as she digested that. "You do realize what this means."

"Why do I have the impression that you're about to enlighten me?"

She ignored that. "It means Crabshaw really does have some deep, dark secret. Something he's hiding from my aunt. Something that is worth paying blackmail to conceal."

"Maybe."

"What do you mean, maybe?"

"It's a possibility," Owen conceded. "That's all I'm willing to admit at this point. I will, however, add the simple observation that the blackmailer is probably male. Which does eliminate approximately half the people in town."

"Male? Oh, yes, of course. The payoffs are being left in the men's rest room. So whoever goes in to retrieve them is probably of the masculine persuasion. Right. Good thinking."

"I try," Owen said.

"All right, Mr. Hotshot PI, what do we do next?"

"We follow Plan A."

"Which is?"

"We wait for some of my morning phone calls to be returned. I want a little more information in hand before I confront Crabshaw."

Amy's mouth went dry. "You're going to confront him?"

"Sometimes a surprise frontal assault is the quickest way to get an answer. I'll pin him down this afternoon."

Amy hesitated. "Shouldn't we go to the cops or something?"

"With what? A handful of money that we happened to find in the men's room? There's no way in hell to prove that it's a blackmail payoff. They'd probably put an ad in the *Villantry Gazette* inviting someone to claim it."

"I see what you mean," Amy said. "But confronting Crabshaw could be dangerous. If he's so desperate to protect his secret that he's willing to pay blackmail, he won't take kindly to your questions. He might become violent."

Owen smiled slightly. "I don't believe this. Are you actually worried about me?"

"Yes, of course I am. I've hired you to solve this case. I would feel terrible if something happened to you."

Owen's green eyes darkened with irritation. "Have a little faith, Ms. Comfort. I realize that I no doubt appear to be downwardly mobile, professionally speaking, but I think I'm still capable of dealing with the likes of Arthur Crabshaw."

Amy flushed. "I didn't mean to insult you. And I don't think you're downwardly mobile just because you gave up your business in Portland and moved to Misplaced Island. Heck, I did the same thing."

"True."

Silence fell on the picnic table. Amy was suddenly acutely conscious of the chattering of a pair of ravens, the distant shouts of youngsters playing on the swings, and a large, furry dog that was pointing one of the ducks on the pond.

"So why did you move to Misplaced Island?" she finally asked very softly.

Owen shrugged. "Got burned out, I guess. After I got out of the military, I got my PI ticket."

"Somehow I don't see you in the military. I'll bet you don't take orders well."

Owen smiled wryly. "You're right. It wasn't a good career path for me. But I had married young. No education to speak of. I needed a job, and the military provided a way to support a wife. She left me after I got out of the service. Said she couldn't take the unstable income. She fell for someone else while I was working to get my business up and running. After the divorce I worked harder. Spent the last ten years doing other people's dirty work."

"Dirty work?"

"Staking out people who try to defraud insurance companies. Trapping embezzlers. Finding missing persons. That kind of thing."

"And you got tired of it?"

"Let's just say I woke up one morning and realized I didn't like my clients any more than the people they paid me to catch. The insurance company executives spent their time trying to avoid paying legitimate claims. The corporate executives were more cold-blooded than the embezzlers who stole from them, and the missing persons usually had very good reasons for not wanting to be found."

Amy smiled sympathetically. "Nothing was black-and-white, huh?"

"Just shades of gray. A lot of gray. I had made some money on the side by buying fixer-uppers, doing the repairs myself in my spare time and reselling the houses at a nice profit. I decided to invest some of the money and use the rest of it to fix up my own life."

"On Misplaced Island."

"That's it." Owen looked at her. "What about you?'"

"Me?"

"What made you decide to move to Misplaced Island?"

"Seattle real estate is hard on a body. I worked the downtown condo market. There was a lot of pressure. I guess I burned out, too. Also, I wanted more time to write. And then something happened last year."

"Your aunt called it a 'dreadful incident.'"

Amy grimaced. "I still get occasional nightmares."

"What happened?"

"Most people don't realize it, but real estate agents tend to lead adventurous lives. They never know what they're going to find when they open the door of what is supposed to be an empty house or condo. I've had a variety of surprises."

"Somehow, knowing you, that does not amaze me."

She smiled wryly. "I once showed a condo to a staid, elderly couple. I'd finished the tour of the front room, kitchen, and bedrooms. We walked into the master bath and found two people making love in the jetted tub. They were so involved in what they were doing that they never even heard us."

Owen grinned briefly. "Make the sale?"

"Yes, I did, as a matter of fact. It was the jetted tub that clinched the deal. The elderly couple couldn't wait to try it out themselves."

"I take it that was not the 'dreadful incident' that made you decide you'd shown one condo too many."

"No." Amy propped her elbows on the table and rested her chin on her hands. "Walking in on a murder in progress did that."

"Murder."

"Uh-huh. I came through the front door just after a respected businessman named Bernard Gordon had shot his partner. A little dispute over investment capital, apparently. Gordon was on his way out of the condo just as I arrived. We collided in the front hall."

Owen's gloriously unhandsome features shaped themselves into an ominous mask. "You could have been killed."

"Gordon tried to do just that. He knew I could identify him. Fortunately, he was already rattled because of the first killing. His shot went wild. I had a chance to hurl my cellular phone at him. He instinctively ducked. I ran back the way I had come and headed for the emergency stairwell. I didn't dare wait for the elevators."

Owen closed his eyes briefly. "My God."

"Gordon tried to chase me down the stairwell. But he stumbled on one of the steps." Amy shuddered. "He fell to the bottom. Broke his neck."

Owen exhaled heavily. "Damn." He reached across the table and took one of her hands in his. He crushed her fingers gently in his own.

Silence descended once more. Amy and Owen watched the ducks on the pond for a long while.

"Nothing. Nada. Zilch." Owen glanced at the notes he had made during his last phone call. He flipped the small notebook shut and tossed it onto the bedside table. He looked at Amy, who was lounging, arms folded beneath her breasts, in the connecting doorway. "Arthur Crabshaw is as clean as you can expect a fifty-five-year-old businessman to be."

"No scandals while down in Arizona?"

"No. At least not that my sources could determine in such a limited period of time. I suppose it's possible that Crabshaw left a few bodies buried under one of his strip malls, but I don't think it's very likely."

Amy tapped her toe, thinking. "The blackmail arrangement we witnessed this morning seemed fairly amateurish, didn't it?"

"Yes." Owen walked to the window and looked out at the park. "A toilet tank lid in a library rest room. Definitely the work of an amateur. And a local amateur, at that."

"Local?"

"Crabshaw was told to leave the money in the public library. The implication is that he's being blackmailed by someone here in Villantry."

"Okay, that makes sense. But he's been gone for thirty years."

"And that means that his deep, dark secret, whatever it is, probably dates back thirty years," Owen said softly.

"To the time when he worked for Raymond C. Villantry?"

"Yes." Owen turned away from the window. "I think it's time I paid a call on Arthur Crabshaw."

"I'll get my purse."

"You will stay right here in this room," Owen said.

"I'm paying your tab, remember? That means I can make executive decisions."

"When I'm on a case, I give the orders."

"You need me to help analyze his reactions," Amy said persuasively. "I'm very good at that kind of thing. It's my real estate sales experience, you see. I'm what you might call an amateur practicing psychologist."

"Forget it, Amy. I'm handling this alone."

Arthur Crabshaw looked momentarily nonplussed to see Amy and Owen on his doorstep. Amy was sure she saw evidence of tension around his eyes. But he recovered with alacrity. He smiled genially and ushered them into his front room.

"Well, well, well." He closed the door. "This is a surprise. What can I do for you two?"

"How was the golf game this morning?" Owen asked softly.

Arthur's smile slipped for only an instant. He quickly got it back in place. "Fine. Just fine. Shot a three over par. Although I have to admit that on the Villantry Golf Course that's not saying a great deal."

"Must have been a fast round," Owen said.

Arthur's gaze turned wary. "Why do you say that?"

Amy held her breath as Owen removed the incriminating envelope from his pocket.

"Because you finished in time to visit the library, didn't you?" Owen said.

Arthur stared at the envelope. Then he raised his eyes to meet Owen's unrelenting gaze. His expression crumbled into weary despair. "How did you find out?"

"Amy and I were in the library at the time. We saw you go into the rest room. I went in after you and found this." Owen glanced at the envelope. "I thought maybe you'd like to talk about it."

"There's not much to say now, is there?" Arthur sank down heavily into an armchair. "If you've got the money, that means the blackmailer didn't get his payoff. He'll reveal the truth, just as he threatened to do in his first note."

Owen went to stand in front of Arthur. "What happens if he does reveal the truth, Crabshaw?"

"Madeline Villantry will be humiliated in front of her family and the entire town." Arthur sighed. "And I seriously doubt that Bernice will marry me when she discovers that Madeline and I once had an affair. Bernice is such a sensitive woman. Bad enough that Madeline used to steal her boyfriends back in high school. How will she feel if she finds out that I was once Madeline's lover?"

6

"I think you'd better start from the beginning," Owen said.

"I worked for Madeline's husband, Raymond C. Villantry." Arthur massaged his temples. "Just like almost everyone else did at the time. I was young. Couldn't afford college. But I was determined to make something of myself."

"At Villantry?" Amy asked.

"No, I had my sites set a lot higher. But Villantry was a start, and a good one. I knew who Madeline was, of course. Everyone in Villantry did. Her family was as rich as the Villantrys. I didn't move in Madeline's circles in those days, though." Arthur grimaced. "Only the Villantrys did."

"Go on," Owen said.

"Madeline married Raymond Villantry right out of college. Everyone said it was a perfect match. I honestly believe that she was wildly in love with him in the beginning. But Villantry just took her for granted. He was accustomed to getting whatever he wanted. Then, after he got it, he lost interest. The only exception was the company. He was passionate about it."

"What happened?" Amy asked gently.

"I was doing well at Villantry." Arthur leaned his head back against the chair. "Had a flair for business. Madeline and I were thrown together on a number of occasions because she was on the planning commission for the original library building. Civic duty and all that."

"Why did that bring the two of you together?" Amy asked.

"Villantry's firm had expanded beyond fishing by then. It was into construction. It was going to build the library. I was assigned to act as a liaison between the planning commission and the company. Raymond Villantry had better things to do with his time than fuss with the library that was to he named in his honor."

"Such as?" Owen asked. He was aware that Amy's gaze was softening rapidly. He was not surprised. He recalled their conversation regarding his move to Misplaced Island. He'd suspected all along that she had a soft heart.

Arthur's mouth twisted. "Such as making a number of trips to Seattle. Villantry was having an affair in the city. A lot of people were aware of it, but of course no one actually said anything to Madeline. No one thought she knew. I came across her one day after a committee meeting. She was sitting all alone in a conference room, crying her heart out."

Amy looked at him with sympathetic eyes. "And you comforted her?"

Arthur nodded. "One thing led to another. She wasn't in love with me, nor I with her. But she needed someone, and she was a lovely woman. And so very brave." He moved his hands in a vague gesture. "What can I say? We had an affair."

"What ended it?" Owen demanded. "Did her husband discover what was going on?"

"Oh, no." Arthur frowned. "No one ever discovered us. At least, I thought no one knew. We were very, very careful. Madeline had her reputation and her family to consider. She was so terrified of being caught that she ended the affair after a couple of months."

Amy frowned. "Why?"

"She said she had to consider the future of her two young children. She didn't want to jeopardize their inheritance by risking a divorce. And she had her parents to think of, too. She was their only child. She was afraid that they would be humiliated if we were found out."

"Hmm." Amy said.

Owen glanced at her. He was starting to recognize that tone in her voice. "Yes? Did you have something you wanted to share with the rest of the class?"

Amy shrugged. "Not really. It just occurred to me that Madeline made a very financially astute decision."

"It was a very brave decision," Arthur corrected gallantly. "For which she paid a great price. She endured an unhappy marriage for years in order to salvage her children's inheritance and to protect her family from humiliation."

"There is that," Amy agreed.

It occurred to Owen that Amy had already deduced the truth about Madeline Villantry's marriage from the photo she had seen in the old edition of the *Villantry Gazette.* He turned to Crabshaw. "How many blackmail payments have you made?"

"Two. Or, rather, one. I got the first note a few weeks ago, right after Bernice and I announced our engagement." Arthur nodded glumly at the envelope Owen had placed on the table. "The thousand in there was supposed to be the second payment."

"So the blackmail is recent?" Owen asked sharply. "You weren't bothered by any demands until a few weeks ago?"

"No." Arthur dropped his head into his hands. "I thought there would only be the one payment. Then, two days ago, there was a second demand."

"There always is," Owen said.

"But it hasn't been made, because you took the envelope," Arthur whispered hoarsely. "Now it will all come out into the open. Madeline's reputation will be ruined. Bernice will be crushed. And all because of me."

"No." Amy stepped forward quickly and patted him on the shoulder. "Don't worry, Arthur. Owen will take care of everything. He'll find out who the blackmailer is and stop him before anything else happens."

Owen stared at her. "I will?"

She gave him a bracing smile. "Of course you will."

Owen narrowed his eyes. She had apparently forgotten that she had hired him to discover Arthur Crabshaw's secrets. He had done precisely that. Nothing had been said about saving Crabshaw's rear. "Uh, Amy maybe we'd better discuss this out on the porch."

"Later, Owen. Right now we need to figure out how to keep the blackmailer silent."

"The quickest way to pull the blackmailer's teeth is to call his bluff," Owen said.

"I can't risk it," Arthur whispered.

"Of course not," Amy murmured. "Owen will handle this."

Arthur sighed heavily. "What can Sweet do? It's too late to replace the money. I left that envelope in the rest room shortly after ten this morning. It's nearly five. By now the blackmailer will have checked the toilet lid and realized that I didn't follow his instructions. He'll be furious."

"Don't fret about it, Crabshaw," Owen said. "There will definitely be a second chance. And a third and fourth chance, as well. If we allow this thing to go on that long."

"Which we won't," Amy said confidently.

Owen raised his brows but offered no comment. He didn't need a weather report to tell him that Amy had recently undergone a sea change.

Arthur lifted his head and gave Owen a quizzical look. "What do you mean there will be a second chance? The blackmailer said in his note that he would reveal everything if I didn't make the payments."

Owen smiled grimly. "You're a businessman, Crabshaw. Look at this from the blackmailer's point of view. If he reveals the truth, it's all over for him. He can't expect his victim to make any more payments once the secrets are out in the open."

The anguish and frustration faded in Arthur's eyes. Intelligent perception replaced it. "Good point. I hadn't thought of that."

"The only way the blackmailer can make money is to keep quiet and apply more pressure on you," Owen said.

Amy searched his face. "That makes sense. He's got nothing to gain by revealing the truth, and everything to lose. I'd say he definitely has a strong incentive to try to persuade Arthur to continue with the payments. And when he does, we'll be ready for him, won't we."

"It's beginning to look that way."

Arthur stared at Owen with dawning hope. "You're going to help me?"

Owen looked at Amy, who gave him a glowing smile. He was briefly dazzled by it. He wondered if it was her sign-here-and-you've-got-yourself-a-house smile. He'd never actually seen that smile because when he'd bought the Draycott place from her, he'd almost had to type up the papers himself. She had tried to talk him out of the deal right up until the ink was dry. He had to admit the smile was very effective.

"Something tells me I don't have a lot of choice," Owen said.

Owen waited until he heard the shower stop in Amy's room. He killed a few more minutes pacing his room and then strode to the connecting door. He knocked peremptorily.

"Come in, I'm decent," Amy called.

That was unfortunate, Owen thought wistfully. He yanked open the door. "I want to talk to you."

"Yes?" Amy met his gaze in the mirror. She was dressed in a pair of blue silk trousers and a matching silk tunic that turned her eyes into jewels.

For a few seconds Owen just stood there, transfixed by the sight of her putting a gold earring on one delicate ear. Desire swept through him, hot, unexpected, and laced with longing. Damn. This was getting bad, he thought. Very, very bad.

"Is something wrong?" Amy prompted.

Owen took refuge in righteous irritation. He braced one hand against the doorframe. "Mind telling me what happened in Crabshaw's living room this afternoon?"

"What do you mean?" She finished attaching the earring and turned to face him. "We're going to help Arthur. What's so complicated about that?"

"Amy, you told me you wanted to prove he was concealing something. Okay, I proved it. Case closed."

Her eyes widened. "For heaven's sake, Owen, we can't stop there. Bernice loves him, and this afternoon I finally concluded that he loves her. We have to help him."

"I had a feeling you were going to say that. What the hell made you decide that Arthur is a good guy after all?"

"Intuition. And the fact that he's trying to play the gentleman for Madeline's and Bernice's sake."

"The gentleman?"

"A man who cares about a lady's reputation and who doesn't want to see anyone hurt, even thirty years after the affair, must have a strong sense of honor. A man like that will do right by my aunt."

"Sometimes I forget that you write romance novels in addition to selling real estate," Owen muttered.

She smiled. "Ready to go down to dinner?"

Two hours later Owen stood with Amy on the veranda that ran the length of the Villantry Inn and contemplated night-shrouded Villantry Park. The summer evening was cool but not cold. The tang of the sea was in the air. Bernice and Arthur had left the Inn after dinner. Owen finally had Amy to himself.

Amy and her case, he amended silently.

"Want to take a walk?" he asked.

Amy nodded. "Sounds lovely."

He took her arm, and together they went down the steps and strolled into the park. The globes of the tall, old-fashioned lamps that lit the paths cast a warm glow. The Friday night band concert had just concluded its performance. People streamed out of the park.

By the time Owen had got Amy as far as the pond, the crowd had dwindled to a handful. Owen studied the library through the trees and rhododendron bushes. It was closed for the day, but the lights were on inside.

Everything about this case seemed to center on the library.

"Looks like someone's working late tonight," he said, indicating the building on the far side of the park.

"Maybe some of the people in charge of the dedication ceremonies are holding a last-minute meeting."

"Let's see what's going on." Drawn by the force of his curiosity, Owen steered Amy along the path that meandered toward the library.

Amy glanced at him speculatively. "Are we going to look for clues?"

"Have I ever told you that you have an overactive imagination?"

"I believe you've mentioned it once or twice. So, what are we going to do?"

"I'm not sure. I just want to have a look around. It occurs to me that even though the public library rest room is not a bad choice on the part of the blackmailer, it is a little unusual. Whoever he is, he must feel quite comfortable there."

"A librarian?"

"Maybe."

The path that led to the library was deserted. The trees and shrubs that grew in this portion of the grounds were among the oldest in Villantry Park. They blocked the light from the tall lamps and deepened the already thick shadows on the graveled walk.

Owen and Amy had almost reached the library when the front door opened. Voices floated out into the night. Several people appeared in the entrance. Owen brought Amy to a halt in the shadows.

"You were right," he said softly. "Looks like a committee meeting breaking up."

They watched the small group cluster for a few minutes on the broad steps in front of the building, exchanging pleasantries. Madeline Villantry appeared in the doorway. Raymond Junior was with her. Raymond appeared terminally bored, as usual.

"Is everything taken care of inside, Betty?" Madeline asked.

"Yes, I think so, Madeline." A silver-haired matron paused on the steps. "Eugene will turn off the lights and lock up."

"I'll see you all tomorrow evening at the ceremony, then," Madeline said. "Good night, everyone. And thank you once again for your time and effort."

The committee members moved off in various directions. Most headed toward the small parking lot on the far side of the park.

Madeline and Raymond started along the path that would take them past Owen and Amy.

Owen automatically started to pull Amy into the bushes, then realized belatedly that the rhodies were impenetrable and opted for another means of concealment.

He drew Amy into a passionate embrace in the shadows.

"What are you doing?" Amy hissed, startled.

"Don't want 'em to see us," Owen muttered. "Kiss me. Make it look good."

She hesitated only briefly, more out of surprise than anything else, Owen realized. And then she was kissing him back. Her arms locked around his neck. Her mouth opened for him.

Owen's priorities shifted in a heartbeat. The problem of Madeline and Raymond suddenly dwindled dramatically in importance. All that mattered was the taste and feel of Amy.

He folded her close, hungry for the essence of her, frustrated by clothing, location, and a possible audience. Amy's mouth was warm and moist and inviting. The gentle curves of her breasts were crushed against his chest. Her soft, muffled whimper of excitement threatened to make him lose control.

The scrape of shoes on gravel, a mildly disapproving murmur, and a soft masculine chuckle brought Owen back to reality. Madeline and Raymond were passing directly behind him now. They had obviously seen the couple in the shadows. Owen hoped that the darkness and the manner in which he was enveloping Amy combined to provide effective concealment.

"Some people have no sense of propriety," Madeline said coolly.

"Some people have all the luck," Raymond drawled.

The sound of footsteps on gravel receded into the distance. Owen waited until he was sure Madeline and Raymond were gone and then raised his head. He looked down at Amy, aware that his pulse was still beating heavily and his insides were clenched.

Amy regarded him with eyes that were pools of unfathomable promise. Her lips were still slightly parted.

Owen thought optimistically of the connecting rooms that awaited them back at the Inn. He took a deep breath and released Amy. "We'll get back to this a little later."

"We will?" She sounded pleased.

"First things first," he said manfully. "I want to check out the library's back door."

He took her hand and started around the building. There were no tall lamps in the drive behind the library. The only light was from the moon and a weak yellow bulb set above the library's service entrance. A row of city utility trucks was lined up on the far side of the drive. The graveled area apparently served as a parking lot for Villantry's service vehicles.

"Why are we going to look at the back door of the library?" Amy asked.

"Because I like to know all the entrances and exits in a situation such as this. I wouldn't be surprised if the next blackmail note Crabshaw gets instructs him to make the payment tomorrow night."

"During the dedication festivities?" Amy glanced at him in surprise as she hurried to keep pace with him. "Why then?"

"Think about it. The library will be swarming with people. That means there will be a steady stream of traffic in and out of the rest rooms. Perfect cover for the blackmailer."

"I get it," Amy said enthusiastically. "You're going to stake out the men's room, right?"

"Right. I'll bet you can see now why I became a big-time private eye."

"Because of the thrilling excitement?"

"Just think about it. Staking out a men's room. Got to be the fulfillment of every young man's dreams of swashbuckling adventure."

"Yes, of course. I envy you."

"From what you've told me, real estate has its moments, too."

"Don't remind me." Amy smiled briefly. Then she frowned in the shadows. "But, Owen, I don't see how you can be so certain that the note—" She broke off suddenly as one of the city trucks roared to life. "What in the world?"

Across the drive, a set of headlights flashed on at full beam, blinding Owen. He realized that he and Amy were pinned in the glare. And to think he had accused Amy of looking like a deer caught in headlights. This was the real thing, Owen thought. He couldn't see what was happening. But he could hear all too well.

Tires screeched as the big vehicle shot forward. The truck bore down on Owen and Amy with deadly intent.

7

Amy had barely registered the blinding light when she heard Owen suck in his breath.

"Damn," he whispered.

In the next instant she felt his arm wrap around her waist with the force of a steel band. He lifted her off her feet and hauled her up the three steps that led to the library's back entrance.

The truck engine thundered.

"Owen."

"In here. Move. He may have a gun."

Owen half-pulled, half-carried her into the shadows of the small alcove that concealed the doorway. Then he shoved her hard against the stone wall and held her there. She gasped for breath, dimly aware that he was shielding her with his body.

The city truck came so close to the steps that Amy was almost convinced it would plow straight through the back door of the library.

But at the last possible instant, it veered aside. With an angry howl it lumbered off into the night, a ravenous beast deprived of its prey.

Owen did not move as the sound of the truck engine receded into the darkness. Amy was pressed so tightly against the cold stone she could feel the grit on her cheek.

"You okay?" Owen finally asked. His voice was curiously flat.

"Yes. I think so."

He slowly stepped back, releasing her. "Son of a bitch." There was no emotion in the phrase. "He was aiming for us. You could have been hurt. Killed."

Amy hugged herself. The unnaturally even tone in Owen's voice was somehow more frightening than the near miss. This was a whole new side to the man. A dangerous side.

"An accident," she said, grasping for a more reasonable explanation than the one Owen had concocted. "Some kid taking a joyride in a city truck."

"Maybe, but I doubt it. I have a hunch that it was attempted murder."

Amy was dazed. "You think that the blackmailer was behind the wheel?"

"I think there's a very high probability of that, yes."

"But how could he know that you're a threat to him? As far as everyone in town is concerned, you're just my fiancé."

"My guess is that he doesn't know I'm out to trap him," Owen said quietly. "It's more likely that he's figured out that I took Crabshaw's money before he could get to it. I told you that I thought he was in the library yesterday, watching the payoff. He saw me go into the rest room after Crabshaw left. And when he went to make the pickup there was no envelope."

"So he leaped to the conclusion that you had gotten to it ahead of him. But following that logic, how does he think you learned of the payoffs and where they were made?"

Owen frowned. "Maybe he figures that I accidentally discovered the envelope. Or he may think that Crabshaw confided in me. Who knows? He probably believes that you and I are in this together."

"Perhaps he was simply trying to frighten us away from Villantry," Amy suggested slowly.

"It's possible that was his goal." Owen took her hand.

"Where are we going?"

"To wake the local chief of police."

Amy instantly dug in her heels. "But, Owen, if you tell him about this, you'll have to tell him everything. I don't want to betray Arthur's confidence unless we must."

"Don't worry. I'm a professional, remember? I know how to talk to a cop."

Amy looked at him. "What does that mean?"

"Don't ask. It's a trade secret."

"Some joyridin' kid, no doubt." George P. Hawkins, chief of police of Villantry, poured himself a cup of coffee.

Amy smiled weakly. "That's what I said."

"Or a drunken transient." Hawkins carried the cup back to his desk and lowered his considerable bulk into the chair. "Happens once in a while. Come mornin' we'll find the truck abandoned outside of town or in a ditch. You'll see."

Owen lounged against the wall near the office window and studied Hawkins with brooding speculation. "Whoever was behind the wheel aimed directly for us. If we hadn't made it up the steps and into the alcove, we wouldn't be here talking to you now."

Hawkins squinted at Owen. "Which brings up an interestin' point. Mind tellin' me just what you two were doin' out there behind the library at this hour of the night?"

Amy caught Owen's eye and held her breath. She could hardly blame him if he told Hawkins the whole story, but a part of her still wanted to protect Arthur Crabshaw.

Owen shrugged. "Amy and I took a walk in the park after the band concert."

"The park I can understand," Hawkins said. "But what the hell were you doin' behind the library buildin'?"

"Looking for privacy," Owen said smoothly. "We got there just as some meeting was ending. We went around the corner to avoid the crowd."

Hawkins gave him a man-to-man look. "You two want privacy, you better leave Villantry. This is a small town. Everyone knows everyone else's business here."

"Is that a fact?" Owen asked politely.

"It's a fact, all right."

Owen straightened away from the wall "Then it shouldn't take too long to find out who was behind the wheel of that city truck, should it? If and when you do find out who nearly ran us down tonight you can reach us at the Villantry Inn."

Hawkins glowered at him. "I know where you're stayin'."

Owen smiled coldly. "Right. This is a small town. You know everything."

"Yep. I also know you two got connectin' rooms at the Villantry Inn. Try usin' them next time, instead of takin' a walk in the park."

"What a rude man," Amy said as they walked into the Inn lobby a short while later.

"Hawkins is a cop," Owen said with a surprisingly philosophical air. "Rudeness is a job requirement."

"I fail to see why."

"You wouldn't if you ever took a job as a cop."

The front desk clerk, a thin young man with thick glasses, smiled tentatively at Owen. "Mr. Sweet, there's a message for you. From Arthur Crabshaw. He wants you to call him."

"Thanks." Owen paused at the front desk to collect the slip of paper.

Amy was aware of the tension in his hand as he guided her toward the stairs. She said nothing as they walked up the one flight to their rooms. When they started down the hall, she slanted a questioning glance at Owen's set face.

"What is it?"

"I won't know for sure until I return Crabshaw's call. But I can make a guess."

"Oh, my God, you don't think—"

"Shush." Owen opened the door of her room and ushered her inside.

Amy turned, expecting him to go next door to his own room. Instead, he stepped through her door and closed it behind him. She raised her brows.

Owen smiled faintly as he switched on a light. "No point being coy, is there? We're supposed to be engaged. Hell, even the local chief of police knows we've got connecting rooms."

Amy flushed. "Yes, I know, but—"

"When you go undercover, you've got to make it look real or it won't work."

"I keep forgetting you're the professional here," Amy muttered.

"I've noticed." He went to the table, picked up the phone, and dialed the number on the slip of paper.

"Arthur? This is Owen Sweet. Yeah, I got your message. What's up?" Owen fell silent, listening for a moment. "I hear you. Calm down."

Amy watched anxiously.

"Right. Tomorrow night," Owen said. "Just as I thought. Follow instructions exactly. We're going to nail the bastard this time. I'm not in the mood to give him any more rope. He just tried to run us down. No, I'm not joking. Amy could have been killed." Owen paused. "Yes, I'm sure it was him. A kid? That's what Amy thinks, too, but I'm not a great believer in coincidences."

Amy waited until he had hung up the phone. "Another blackmail note?"

Owen nodded. "Arthur says it arrived earlier this evening. He's to leave the money in the library rest room tomorrow night."

"Just as you suspected." Amy was impressed. "But why would the blackmailer use the same location over and over again?"

"He probably can't think of a safer place. The rest room is still the one spot where any man in town can be seen with no questions asked. And as I told you, it will be busier than usual tomorrow night because of the crowd."

Amy nibbled thoughtfully on her lower lip. "If the blackmailer suspects that you know about the payoffs, he'll be nervous when he sees you at the dedication ceremonies tomorrow evening."

"Not necessarily. He realizes that although he knows who I am, I don't know who he is. He can go in and out of the men's room just as freely as I or any other man in the crowd can. But he won't take any chances this time. He'll make it a point to get in there right after Crabshaw. He won't know that I know about the drop-off. He'll think it's safe to go in as soon as he can."

"Before you have a chance to grab the money?"

"Right."

Amy listened to the silence from the adjoining room for long time before she couldn't stand it any longer. She could almost hear Owen's brain grinding away in solitude.

It struck her that he had probably spent a lot of his life alone. The very nature of his chosen profession indicated that he was accustomed to relying solely on himself. There was a core of strength in Owen Sweet that rarely developed in those who relied on other people.

He possessed an old-fashioned, Wild West sort of character, she thought. He was the kind of man who, a century earlier, would have ridden into town alone, cleaned out the bad guys, and then left without a backward glance.

She pushed aside the covers, got out of bed, and padded to the closed door that linked the two rooms. She put her ear against the wooden panel and listened. Still no sound. But she was certain that he was not asleep.

She knocked once, very softly. Owen opened the door immediately.

Almost as if he had been waiting for her.

She smiled tremulously up at him. "You're not in bed."

"I'm thinking."

"I know." She shivered. "I can't sleep, either. I keep seeing those headlights coming straight toward us."

"Amy." He drew her into his arms. "I'm sorry."

Amy felt something inside her begin to relax. She rested her head on his shoulder. "It's all my fault. I'm the one who should be sorry."

"For what?"

"For getting you into this mess. I swear, I never had any idea that this would get so complicated."

He framed her face in his powerful hands. His eyes gleamed in the shadows. "You don't have a clue just how complicated things have gotten, do you?"

Before she could answer, his mouth was on hers.

His kiss was different this time. Instead of reckless eagerness and hot passion, there was gentleness and a tender warmth. Amy gave herself up to the sweet persuasion without a single qualm.

"Amy?" His voice was ragged but under control.

"Yes," she whispered. "Yes, yes, yes."

"Thank God," Owen whispered against her throat. "I thought I was going to go crazy."

He picked her up and carried her through the doorway into his room, then set her down amid the turned-back sheets of his bed. She looked up at him with dawning wonder as he stripped off his shirt and jeans.

She loved him.

The realization came with quiet certainty, not as a bolt out of the blue. Amy knew that she had recognized the truth deep inside weeks ago. She reached up to take him into her arms.

Owen came to her then.

His body was heavy with desire. Amy felt him shudder at her touch. His hands trembled slightly as he eased aside her quilted robe.

"I've never wanted anything so much in my life," he said against her mouth.

He kissed her throat as he undressed her. And then he lowered his mouth to her breasts. Heat flooded Amy's body. Owen's hand slid upward along her leg, squeezing gently. His fingers moved to the inside of her thigh. Amy gasped.

Owen covered her mouth once more, drinking in the small sound she made. He cupped her softness and then probed, opening her to his intimate touch. She gave another muffled cry and clutched at his shoulders. A frantic sense of urgency stormed through her.

Owen continued the tender torment, stoking the flames within Amy until she could not stand it any longer. She twisted on the sheets.

"Owen, please." She parted her legs and fought to pull him to her. "Please."

"I think I've been waiting for this forever." Owen leaned across Amy to open a drawer in the bedside table.

The movement brought his broad, strong chest directly over Amy's face. She kissed one flat, male nipple and ran her fingers through the curling hair that surrounded it. Then she reached down between their damp bodies to stroke him. It was like touching warm steel. Owen was utterly rigid with his need. Hard and hot and throbbing. When her fingertips moved on him he shuddered. Amy's body responded with another tidal wave of heat.

A moment later Owen was ready. He moved between her thighs, braced himself on his elbows, and looked down at her with burning eyes. He held her gaze as he pushed slowly, carefully, deliberately into her. Amy drew in a sharp breath as her small muscles stretched to accommodate him.

And then he was inside, filling her completely.

"Amy." There was a world of wonder and need in the single word.

Owen began to move. Amy took flight. Mindlessly, she gave herself up to the delicious, spiraling tension. It was unlike anything she had ever experienced. She heard her own voice calling Owen's name over and over again.

And then, without warning, her climax exploded in a series of rippling vibrations that sent pleasure to every nerve in her body. Amy was breathless. All she could do was cling to Owen as the world whirled around her.

She was vaguely aware of his fierce, hoarse shout of masculine satisfaction. He surged into her one last time. She felt every muscle in him tighten.

After a long, long moment, Owen shuddered and collapsed along the length of her. Together they drifted in the darkness, locked in each other's arms.

A long while later, she stirred beside Owen. She stretched languidly, aware of a sense of joyous satisfaction. Before she could even begin to savor her newfound love, a thought struck her. She sat bolt upright in bed.

"Good grief, Owen."

"What's the matter?" Owen sounded like a sleepy lion that had recently been very well fed.

"I just thought of something." She turned to look down at him. "If you're right in thinking that it was the blackmailer who tried to run us down tonight, then that means that it was a . . . what do you call it?"

"A crime of opportunity?"

"Right, exactly. A crime of opportunity. After all, he couldn't have known we'd be walking behind the library at that hour. He must have followed us."

"Maybe." Owen sounded unconvinced.

"You think there's another possibility?"

"Amy, there are lots of possibilities. It could have been one of the people who attended that meeting in the library tonight or someone who was wandering around in the park after the band concert. Whoever it was, he saw us and recognized us, in spite of the fact that we were wrapped up in each other's arms."

"No great trick, I suppose, when you think about it. This is a town in which everyone knows everyone else. We must stand out like sore thumbs, even in the dark."

"Yeah."

Amy had a sudden vision of Madeline Villantry's son. She recalled his comment as he had walked past Amy and Owen. "You don't think Raymond Junior is behind this, do you? I think he might have recognized us tonight."

"We'll find out tomorrow night." Owen tugged her down on top of him. "In the meantime, I've got better things to do.

She smiled demurely. "I suppose you want to get some sleep."

"Hell, no. Us private eyes can go for days without a good night's sleep. It's in the genes."

8

". . . And so I am proud to dedicate the new wing of the Raymond C. Villantry Memorial Public Library." Madeline Villantry's cultured tones rang out from the speaker's podium that had been set up in the center of the library. "We should all be proud of our community's commitment to literacy. A free nation cannot exist without such a commitment. I thank you, friends and neighbors. I salute all of you who helped make our fine library what it is today."

Enthusiastic applause broke out from the large crowd gathered in the library. Madeline Villantry smiled graciously from the lectern.

Owen leaned toward Amy, who was standing next to him in the throng. "You get the feeling she really means all that talk about progress and literacy?"

"Yes, I do," Amy said resolutely. "I know she looks like she's trying out for the role of Queen of Villantry, but Aunt Bernice and Arthur believe that Madeline is honestly committed to this town's welfare. I think they're right."

"Maybe. But I'm not so sure about Raymond Junior over there. I have a hunch he's not the altruistic sort."

"I won't argue that point." Amy scrutinized Raymond, who was following his mother down from the small speaker's stand. "But who knows? Maybe he'll learn."

"I won't hold my breath." Owen stopped clapping. He kept his eyes on the door of the men's room as the crowd broke up and began to mill around.

Amy stood on tiptoe in an effort to see over the heads of the people swarming in front of her. "What's happening?"

"Crabshaw went inside the men's room a few minutes ago. He just came back out. Now he's headed outside to join your aunt at the punch table."

"Darn, I can't see a thing."

"I can," Owen assured her.

There had been a light but steady stream of males coming and going through the swinging men's room door during the past hour. Tredgett, the janitor, had been busy as he made a heroic effort to keep up with the demands that had been placed upon the facilities. As Owen watched, Tredgett emerged from the women's room, removed the small sign he had temporarily placed in the doorway, and wheeled his bucket and mop next door to the men's room.

Raymond Junior followed the janitor inside.

Amy peered at Owen. "So? What do you see?"

"Someone who's bent on cleaning up," Owen said softly.

"What the heck does that mean?"

"It means that this is case is almost concluded." He gave her a repressive look, aware that he had to be forceful and authoritative if he wanted Amy to follow orders. She didn't seem to take them any better than he did. "Wait right here. I'll be back in a few minutes."

Amy's eyes widened. "Where are you going? Did you spot the blackmailer?"

"Yeah."

"I'll come with you."

"No, you will not. You will do as you're told. I'm not taking any more chances with your neck."

"But, Owen, what can possibly happen here?"

"That's what I said to myself last night when we made that little detour behind the library," he muttered. "Stay put."

Without glancing over his shoulder to see if Amy had obeyed him, Owen slipped away from her side and began to ease through the crowd. The conversations ebbed and flowed around him.

In a few minutes it would all be over, Owen thought as he made his way toward the men's room. The identity of the blackmailer was obvious. It should have been from the beginning, but Owen admitted to himself that he'd been distracted by more personal considerations.

It was time to confront the culprit, wrap up the case, and get back to worrying about the more important dilemma he faced. Nabbing a blackmailer was simple compared with the problem of trying to figure out if Amy loved him.

He'd been sweating that out since he had awakened to an empty bed this morning. His initial response to the discovery that Amy was not lying beside him had been a surge of emotion that he knew came very close to something that could be labeled fear. For a terrible instant his sleep-fogged brain had registered an anguished sense of loss. Amy was gone.

Reality had returned with the sound of the shower in her room. She had not left him in the middle of the night. She had merely risen to take her morning bath.

Owen had taken a deep breath and regained his usually unshakable sense of control. But he had not been able to shake the memory of the unnerving sensation he had experienced when he had found himself alone in the bed.

The door of the men's room swung open. Raymond Junior strolled out. He paused for a moment to search the crowd. His gaze fell on Owen. He nodded sternly and then turned to walk toward the knot of people gathered around his mother.

Owen propped one shoulder against the wall and watched the swinging door. He did not have to wait long. It soon opened again.

Tredgett, the janitor, emerged, dragging his bucket behind him. Without looking at anyone, he trundled off toward a door at the far side of the central gallery.

Owen followed at a leisurely pace. When he reached the door, he went through it quietly. He found himself in a dimly lit storage room. Stacks of aging magazines and newspapers lined one wall. The shelves on the opposite wall were filled with dusty books that looked as if they were awaiting repair.

There was no sign of the janitor, but a sliver of light gleamed beneath a closed closet door. Owen smiled humorlessly. He went toward the closet and opened the door. He found himself gazing into a small space filled with mops, sponges, and other assorted janitorial equipment.

Tredgett was inside the closet. He was busy counting the bills he had just removed from a plain white envelope. He jumped at the sight of Owen.

"Busy day," Owen observed.

Panic and rage lit Tredgett's eyes. He clutched the money in one fist. "Damn you," he whispered. "Who the hell are you, anyway? Why have you been nosing around in my business?"

"I'm the naturally curious type."

Tredgett's face worked furiously. "Bastard. I warned you last night. If you and your lady friend think I'm going to share this money with you, you're crazy."

"The janitor," Amy murmured from the shadows behind Owen. "Of course. The one man who is always going in and out of rest rooms."

Owen groaned. "Amy, I told you to wait outside."

"I couldn't let you finish this alone."

Tredgett's desperate gaze shifted wildly from Owen to Amy and back again. "Leave me alone or I'll tell all." He picked up a jar of cleaning solvent and hurled it at Owen.

Owen easily sidestepped the jar. Unfortunately, in the process, he collided with Amy, who had come up behind him. She yelped as she fetched up against a row of metal bookshelves. The shelves shuddered beneath the impact. Several tattered volumes cascaded down from the top shelf.

Owen whirled around at the sound of the toppling books. "Amy, look out."

She reacted instantly, leaping aside. Two heavy volumes struck the floor at her feet, barely missing her head.

Tredgett seized the opportunity. He burst out of the janitorial closet and made for the back door.

"You okay?" Owen asked Amy.

"I'm okay. Owen, be careful."

He whirled around and sprinted after Tredgett, who was already at the back door.

It wasn't much of a contest. Tredgett was twenty years older and thirty pounds overweight. Owen caught him just outside the door. He pinned the janitor to the wall of the alcove.

"I'll tell everyone about the affair between Crabshaw and Mrs. Villantry," Tredgett blustered. "I swear I will."

"And go to jail for blackmail?" Owen asked pleasantly. "Now, why would you want to do that?"

"Crabshaw will never press charges. He'll never admit that he's been paying blackmail. You can't prove a damn thing."

"I wouldn't be too certain of that." Madeline Villantry emerged from the storage room. She was followed by Arthur and Bernice and Raymond Junior. "Arthur finally told me what was going on this morning. I informed him that if his private investigator discovered the identity of the blackmailer, I would insist that he press charges. One simply cannot tolerate this sort of thing."

"Now, Mother," Raymond began. "I think we should talk about this before we make any decisions."

"There is nothing to discuss," Madeline assured him.

Tredgett jerked furiously in Owen's grasp. "Private investigator?" He stared at Owen and then looked helplessly at Arthur Crabshaw. "You hired this damned PI?"

"I hired the damned PI," Amy said briskly. "And he's solved the case brilliantly."

"Thank you," Owen said.

"He certainly has." Bernice smiled warmly at Owen. "Arthur also told me everything. It was very gallant of him to try to protect Madeline and me, but entirely unnecessary. Arthur's relationship with Madeline is thirty years in the past. Who cares about it now?"

"Precisely," Madeline murmured. "My parents are dead and my children are adults. There is no one left to protect."

Arthur looked at Owen. "You were right. The best way to pull the blackmailer's teeth was to tell everyone involved what was going on."

"It's usually the easiest way to put a stop to this kind of thing," Owen said.

Raymond Junior scowled in confusion. "For God's sake, Mother, are you telling me that you and Arthur Crabshaw had an affair thirty years ago? And that the janitor knew about it?"

"Eugene Tredgett used to work for Villantry," Madeline explained. She gave Tredgett a disgusted look. "Apparently he saw something that was none of his business."

"No one ever notices the janitor," Tredgett muttered.

"Good God." Raymond looked scandalized. "I can't believe this."

"Don't worry about it, Raymond." Madeline turned to go back into the library. "It's none of your business, either. These things sometimes happen, even in the best of families. Now, stop blathering on about it. We have our civic duty to perform this evening."

"But, Mother . . ." Raymond hurried after Madeline. The pair vanished into the shadows.

Arthur took Bernice's hand. He looked at Owen. "I owe you."

"No you don't," Owen said. "Amy is the one who hired me. She's already taken care of the bill."

Shock and pain replaced the admiration that had lit Amy's eyes a moment earlier. Too late, Owen realized that she had misinterpreted his words. She thought he meant that he had taken last night's lovemaking as payment for services rendered.

Police Chief Hawkins lumbered out of the storage room gloom. "What the hell's going on? Mrs. Villantry said I was needed out here." He paused when he caught sight of Owen. "Damn. Shoulda guessed that this would involve you, Sweet. You know something? We've had more trouble in the forty-eight hours you've been in town than we've had in a year."

"Just doing my civic duty, Chief."

"Sure." Hawkins squinted at the defeated Tredgett. "Any chance you'll do it somewhere else in the future?"

"Count on it," Owen said.

Owen stood on his side of the doorway that linked the two Inn rooms and watched Amy as she packed her suitcase. This was the first opportunity he'd had to speak to her in private since Eugene Tredgett had been taken into custody earlier in the evening. He'd been waiting for this moment for hours. Now that it was here, he couldn't seem to find the right words.

Amy had been determinedly cheerful and aggressively polite while they had been in the company of others. It seemed to Owen that she had chattered on about everything under the sun except their relationship. She had finally fallen silent when they had climbed the stairs to the connecting rooms.

"Amy . . ."

"I'm almost packed," she assured him as she stuffed a pair of jeans into the suitcase. "I know you want to be on the road first thing in the morning. We'll be able to leave right after breakfast."

"Forget it. I'm not worried about leaving on time." Owen shoved his hands into his back pockets. "Amy, I want to talk to you."

"I'm listening." She disappeared into the bathroom to check for any items she might have left on the sink.

Irritation replaced some of Owen's uneasiness. "I'm trying to have a relationship discussion out here," he called.

She emerged from the bathroom with her quilted robe over her arm. "Good thing I checked the hook on the door. I almost forgot my robe."

Owen gazed at the robe with a shattering sense of longing. "Amy, I think you misunderstood something I said tonight. When I told Crabshaw that you had paid for my services, I didn't mean it the way I think you think I meant it."

"Really?" She came to a halt in the middle of the room. "How did you mean it?"

"I just meant that you and I had a separate understanding."

She stood very still, clutching her robe. "Do we?"

"I thought so."

"What sort of 'understanding' do we have, Owen?"

Owen began to feel desperate. He was no good at this kind of thing. "For God's sake, didn't last night mean anything to you?"

"Everything."

"I realize we haven't known each other very long." Owen shoved a hand through his hair. "I had planned to take it slow. I wanted you to get to know me. I wanted you to—" He broke off abruptly. "What did you say?"

"I said that last night meant everything to me." Amy's eyes were brilliant. "What about you?"

A joyous hope welled up inside him. He was dazzled by the brilliant colors that suddenly lit his world. "It meant everything to me, too. Amy, I love you."

"I love you, Owen." Amy dropped the robe and opened her arms.

Owen gathered her close and kissed her for a very long time. "Something tells me we're not going to get much sleep tonight," he said eventually. "Maybe we'd better not try to get that early-morning start after all."

"If we don't check out before noon, they'll charge us for an extra night," Amy warned him.

"Don't worry about it." Owen picked her up and carried her through the connecting door into his room. "I'll just put the extra night on my expense account."

—1995

KATHLEEN E. WOODIWISS

B. 1939

Kathleen E. Woodiwiss is among the most successful and influential of modern-day romance writers. She helped to reestablish the popularity of the historical love story, and she frequently is credited with being the first to introduce explicit depictions of sex in this particular category of romance fiction. Born Kathleen Erin Hogg in Alexandria, Louisiana, to Charles Wingrove, Sr., and Gladys (Coker) Hogg, Woodiwiss was educated in Alexandria and worked as a fashion model in Tokyo, Japan. In 1956, she married Ross Woodiwiss, a major in the United States Air Force.

Woodiwiss published her first novel, The Flame and the Flower, *in 1972, and the book's impact was immediate. During the early 1970s, the popular romance was dominated by the Gothic variant that found its distant origins in the work of Ann Radcliffe. Woodiwiss considerably expanded the length of the typical romance novel in* The Flame and the Flower, *while utilizing a historical setting for her plot (the story takes place in England and in the American South at the beginning of the nineteenth century). Perhaps most importantly, in* The Flame and the Flower, *Woodiwiss made the relationship between the hero and heroine more sexually explicit, although she disputes the contention that her fiction is "erotic." Woodiwiss argues: "I'm insulted when my books are called erotic. I don't think people who say that have read my books. I believe I write love stories. With a little spice." Nevertheless, Woodiwiss's fiction helped to inspire an entire generation of imitations, popular historical romances that are pejoratively termed "bodice-rippers."*

Following her initial success with The Flame and the Flower, *Woodiwiss went on to publish a number of other best-selling romances, including* The

Wolf and the Dove (1974), Shanna (1977), Ashes in the Wind (1979), A Rose in Winter (1982), Come Love a Stranger (1984), So Worthy My Love (1989), and Forever in Your Embrace (1992). Feminist literary critic Janice Radway suggests that Woodiwiss's romance fiction was influenced by the feminist movement during the 1970s; Woodiwiss herself claims her heroines are not submissive, and instead are independent women demanding an equal partnership with men.

Her novelette, "The Kiss," first published in the romance omnibus Three Weddings and a Kiss *(1995), illustrates both Woodiwiss's fondness for historical settings (Oakley Plantation near antebellum Charleston) and strongminded heroines (the feisty nineteen-year-old, Raelynn Barrett).*

THE KISS

The milliner's face glowed with cheerful enthusiasm as she handed a large, ribbon-bedecked hatbox to the tall, dark-haired man. "I hope Miss Heather will be pleased with her new bonnet, Mr. Jeffrey. I'm convinced it's one of my finest creations."

"You've certainly outdone yourself this time, Mrs. Brewster," Jeff Birmingham agreed. "'Tis nigh impossible for me to imagine my sister-in-law looking less than radiant in any gift of clothing I buy her, but you always create something exceptional for me to give her for her birthday. I'm indebted to you."

"As I should be to you, Mr. Jeffrey, for what you and your lovely family have done for me. Miss Heather looks so exquisite in my bonnets, every time she's seen wearing one of them in public, my shop overflows with women wanting something just as fetching. Why, since you've been buying gifts for Miss Heather here, my hats have been selling faster than Mrs. Thompson's peach pies."

Jeff laughed with an amiable ease that was contagious. "I'm delighted to have been of some benefit, Mrs. Brewster, though there's no question in my mind that your talent is the real reason for your success. I wouldn't be here today if I hadn't been tempted by the display of beautiful hats in your shop window so long ago."

Thelma Brewster vividly recalled the day two years past when he had come into her shop, looking for all the world like the handsomest man who had ever been born. He had been on much the same quest then and, after carefully perusing her available stock, had described exactly the kind of bonnet he had been looking for, an intricately embellished piece he had seen in a Parisian fashion plate. Though she had advised him of the cost involved, certainly more than she had once considered realistic for the area, he had nevertheless ordered the hat. She had dared more extravagant designs after that, and as a result, her struggling business began to thrive. In spite of his refusal to take any credit for her success, she gave it anyway, knowing she would never have risked venturing beyond her humdrum efforts without having first been challenged by the man.

Since then, she had learned much about Jeff Birmingham, his fine tastes, and his fondness for his family. She was perceptive enough to realize that anyone who doted on his sister-in-law as much as he did would likely coddle his wife as well. That is, if the handsome rake could ever settle his sights on a young lady he wanted to marry. No doubt her business would receive an even greater boost if the future

Mrs. Jeffrey Birmingham happened to be as winsome as the present mistress of Harthaven, which seemed a far-fetched feat indeed.

Mrs. Brewster bustled along behind as Jeff made his way toward the door. "You know, Mr. Jeffrey, sometimes I think Miss Heather makes it terribly difficult for you, her being so beautiful and all."

Pausing short of the portal, Jeff turned and raised a dubious brow, somewhat taken aback by her statement. "Your pardon, Mrs. Brewster. I don't think I quite follow you."

The woman lifted her plump shoulders in an innocent shrug. "You're the handsomest bachelor left in these parts, Mr. Jeffrey." She politely refrained from adding, "And also the richest." "So you must be aware of the tizzy you've created, keeping the whole countryside on tenterhooks. People are simply abuzz with conjecture, trying to guess which one of our fair young ladies you'll eventually be choosing for a bride. Personally, I think you'll have a tall order, finding one as rare and as beautiful as Miss Heather. She and Mr. Brandon are a sight to behold when they come into town, and now, with Miss Heather carrying their second child, you'll have absolutely no chance to catch up with your brother, even if you could find a wife to compare."

Jeff smiled in relief, thankful the woman hadn't started to imagine that he was coveting his brother's wife. A few gossips had been rude enough to insinuate such a thing, and he never failed to be appalled by the suggestion that his love for Heather went beyond the boundaries of a deep brotherly affection. "I'm in no hurry, Mrs. Brewster, and believe me, I'm not trying to surpass my brother. In fact," he lowered his tone as if confiding a well-kept secret, prompting the woman to lean forward in anticipation, "I've been far too busy of late to even think of settling down with a wife, much less lend any consideration to starting a family."

Mrs. Brewster was horrified at the thought of the man remaining unattached. "Oh, Mr. Jeffrey, you just can't let Oakley Plantation go without a mistress now that you've finished refurbishing it," she protested. "Your warehouses and lumber mills will grow mighty tiresome in time if you don't have something better to come home to than a big, ol' empty house."

"I'll consider your advice, Mrs. Brewster," Jeff responded, smiling jauntily as he settled a tall beaver hat over his black, neatly cropped hair. Holding the large hatbox aside, he pulled open the door of the millinery shop and winked at the woman as he paused on the threshold. "But I'm afraid I've come to accept my lot as a confirmed bachelor."

"Oh, tish!" Mrs. Brewster waved away his remark. "I'll believe that, you handsome young devil, when I see you laid in your grave with no widow to mourn your passing. Now, I'll bid a good day to you, sir, before I set my sights on you myself, lonely widow that I am."

Tipping his hat in a debonair manner, Jeff gave her a rakish grin as he stepped back to the boardwalk. "And what a tempting wife you'd mak—*Oooff!*"

His last words were jolted from him as a slender, raggedly clad form crashed into him, nearly knocking him back upon his heels and sending his hat and the milliner's box flying helter-skelter. A frightened screech, definitely of a feminine origin, squelched his startled oath as he struggled to regain his balance and, at the same time, assist the young woman who was teetering precariously toward him on her toes. He straightened to his full height, clasped her narrow waist, and stood her safely upright as he mentally prepared a tactful apology. Then he found himself staring down into the widest, most vivid blue-green eyes he had ever seen in his entire life. A copious wealth of deep auburn hair tumbled in unrestrained confusion around a tear-stained, dirt-streaked face, the sublime beauty of which Mrs. Brewster had just been doubting the existence of.

He was momentarily awestruck as an old familiar dream came winging back to him, one wherein he found himself running across a rolling meadow, chasing the love of his life. Though he had often been haunted by that recurring fantasy, he had never glimpsed the woman's face . . . until now. It was as if he stood once again on the very brink of that same illusion and looked down upon a visage he had both desired and cherished for at least half a lifetime.

"I beg your pardon, Miss . . . ?" He waited expectantly, hoping she would supply her name, for he was certain it had to be something superlative to do justice to the bearer of it, but his words seemingly fell on deaf ears as the girl tossed an anxious glance over her shoulder. Her eyes widened even more as a giant of a man rounded a distant corner at a run and spied them.

"Hold that girl!" the man bellowed, raising an arm to command their attention. "She's a runaway!"

The girl bolted past Jeff, putting wings to her feet as she leaped over the hatbox and raced into the street, oblivious of an oncoming four-in-hand as she looked back at the man.

Mrs. Brewster screamed and quickly clasped her hands over her eyes to keep from seeing the girl trodden beneath the horses' hooves, but Jeff was already on the run, sprinting behind the fleeing female and, with his long legs, overtaking her.

The girl's breath left her abruptly in surprise as two very capable arms swept her upward against a male form and bore her at a breakneck run toward the far side of the thoroughfare. For a fleeting moment, the din of thundering hooves drowned her outraged protests, but she was determined to berate the man soundly for his improper advances just as soon as she could be heard. Then she glanced over a wide, manly shoulder and gulped as she focused her gaze on a swiftly passing coach and the four horses racing ahead of it. The conveyance was so close, the breeze from its passage flung dust and grit in her astounded face. She immediately decided she was very fortunate to be alive.

"My goodness!" she murmured breathlessly in awe. "You saved my life!"

The tall gentleman set her to her feet once again, commanding her full attention as he grinned down at her. It was the most dazzling smile she had envisioned since she had given up childish reveries of knights in shining armor.

"I was reluctant to lose you so soon after I found you," Jeff answered glibly, convinced that she had stepped out of his dreams. "What were you running away from in such a panic?"

"*From Me!*"

The shout completely disrupted the girl's tenuous composure, and she would have whirled and fled if not for a large, thick-fingered hand reaching out to seize her upper arm in an unyielding vise.

"Ye're not goin' anywhere, Raelynn Barrett!" the huge man roared ominously. His voice was naturally deep, and though he softened his tone a meager degree as he continued, it still seemed to rock them with its volume. "*Not after I've promised ye to another!*"

"Unhand that girl, you ruffian!" Thelma Brewster demanded as she marched up to them. "This is Charleston, for heaven's sake! No man in his right senses would ever think of accosting a young lady on these streets without fear of being taken to task by our menfolk. You, *sir,* must be a stranger here to be so vile."

Jeff placed a hand upon the elder woman's arm and cocked a warning brow at her, bidding her to hold her silence. He had no idea what kin the man was to the girl, but if the fellow had authority to arrange her life, Jeff could only conclude that he was her father or guardian.

"Perhaps you'd like to step over to Mrs. Brewster's shop and discuss this matter privately," Jeff suggested, briefly indicating the place across the way. His goal was to first try and calm the man with the hope that he would be more reasonable with the girl. A handful of patrons had already gathered from nearby shops, and more were hurrying toward them from across the street and along the boardwalk. "We seem to be *attracting* a lot of attention here on the street."

"I don't give a blasted hoot who hears me! The little wench is comin' wit' me!"

"Oh, please!" Raelynn sobbed, trying to pry his beefy fingers from her arm. "Please don't sell me to that brute! I've done you no hurt! And you swore on my mother's deathbed that you'd watch over me until I was properly wed. Is this how you keep your promises?"

"Gustav said he'd wed ye when he got around ta it," the man rumbled. "An' that's good enough for me."

"You sold me!" Raelynn railed in a panic. "As soon as our ship touched shore, you went out and sold me to the first buffoon with money enough to suit your purposes." Her voice lowered to a rasping snarl. "I curse the day you came into our lives claiming to be my mother's long lost brother! You took what little wealth we had remaining after my father's death and squandered it buying passage on the first ship sailing from England. You might as well have killed my mother yourself! Instead, you let her die of starvation and disease in that rat-infested hold, all for your love of money and gain." Her ire strengthened. "Well, a pox on you, Cooper Frye! I won't be sold to the likes of Gustav Fridrich for two hundred—or even *two thousand* Yankee dollars!"

"Ye've no choice in the matter, missy," Cooper stated emphatically, drawing the girl relentlessly toward him. "Ye're comin' wit' me right now!"

Jeff had felt his hackles rise even before Mrs. Brewster nudged him sharply in the ribs. He laid a restraining hand upon the other man's wrist and stepped between him and the girl. "Wait a minute, will you?"

"Stay outa this!" Cooper flung the words with enough venom to make Mrs. Brewster stumble back in sudden consternation, but Jeff never wavered before the other's menacing glare. "'Tain't none o' yer affair! This is me niece, an' no other but me own bloomin' self will be decidin' what'll happen to her."

"Well, I'm making it my business . . ." Jeff said almost pleasantly.

Cooper issued a loud, derisive snort and stepped closer threateningly, pushing his bewhiskered face forward until his broad nose nearly met the thinner, much more noble one. "Per'aps, stranger, ye'd like to taste me fist in yer mouth."

Jeff refused to retreat before the glowering red eyes that bore into him at very close range, or the foul breath that reeked of a fetid stench like that of one who had passed the night swilling strong rum. They were the same height, Cooper Frye easily outweighing him twice over, but Jeff knew how to handle himself in a fight if it came to that. "You'd be wise to listen to my proposal, Mr. Frye," he cautioned. "If you truly want to sell the girl, then I am offering to buy her."

Mrs. Brewster's startled gasp came a fraction of an instant before Raelynn Barrett caught her own breath in surprise. It remained frozen in her chest as she stared in amazement at the tall, splendidly garbed man who had come into her life only a few moments ago. Why would he want to buy her? With his good looks and polished manners he had no need to lay out coins for a woman, and certainly not such a sorry-looking one as herself. What could he possibly see in her?

A calculating gleam began to shine in Cooper Frye's gray eyes as he considered the expensively garbed man. The dark blue frock coat and gray breeches had obviously been tailored by one of superior reputation in the trade, for the cut was crisp and impeccable. The tall, fashionable riding boots sported turn-down cuffs of gray above polished black leather and, like the smooth-fitting breeches, seemed to mold the lean, muscular shape of the long legs. Cooper was doubtful that he had ever seen such costly clothes before, even on the streets of London.

"Why would ye be wantin' ta buy the wench?" For once, Cooper's voice was mellow enough to be tolerable. "Ye got an itch ta 'ide her away from yer wife an' take yer ease wit' her when ye've got nothin' better to do?"

"For shame, you cod-faced lout!" Mrs. Brewster exclaimed in outrage. "Mr. Birmingham would never dream of doing such a thing!"

Jeff had no wish to destroy the woman's unswerving confidence in him by admitting that he was extremely interested in the girl, at least enough to want to rescue her from this oaf and to see her gowned in clothes as fine as those that Brandon was wont to buy for Heather. The dull brown, threadbare dress Raelynn presently wore did little justice to her uncommon beauty.

"What is the price you'll take for her?" Jeff asked tersely. "Name it, and let this matter be done. The whole town is here to observe this event."

Cooper Frye scratched his bristly chin reflectively and flicked a glance across the wall of faces that was pressing in close around them. "Well, now," he drawled, wondering if his intended lie was too extravagant for the other's purse. He decided to leave some room for haggling. "Gustav Fridrich was willing ta pay a bloody five hundred o' yer Yankee dollars ta have her. I've got to have at least that much and maybe a hundred more ta be able ta face that ornery German and tell him I've sold the chit ta someone else."

Jeff made sure his offer was far more generous than the stranger could have expected. "Seven hundred fifty should give you enough courage to do the deed."

Cooper's mottled tongue flicked across his wide, gaping mouth as he gawked at the other man. "Seven hundred fifty?" he repeated, staggered by the thought of such an extravagant sum. "For the girl here?"

"We have witnesses." Jeff stated the obvious, nodding toward the ever-growing crowd. "Most of these people know me and can attest that my word is true."

"I can vouch for his integrity better than anyone here," a nearby clothier heartily declared, pushing his tall, broad-shouldered bulk through the mass of onlookers until he faced Cooper Frye. "In fact, if Mr. Birmingham isn't presently carrying such a sum on his person, I'd be only too happy to send one of the clerks into my shop here and fetch it for him. So if I were you, Cooper Frye, I'd listen carefully to what my friend has to say. He has other friends in this crowd who are equally loyal and who'll be glad to report this event to any interested parties."

"Thank you, Farrell," Jeff murmured. He accepted the man's offer of a temporary loan and, after receiving a leather pouch filled with gold coins from his friend, returned his attention to Cooper Frye and counted out the necessary amount. "Now, Mr. Frye, I'd advise you to heed my words carefully. Before receiving this pouch, you must sign a bill of receipt pledging that you'll never interfere with me or the girl again. If you should do so, then you'll forfeit what you get here today, either by returning it to the last coin or, if you cannot pay, hiring yourself out to me as a servant until the sum is repaid in full. Do you understand?"

"Where's the receipt?" Cooper inquired bluntly.

Jeff accepted a quill from Farrell, who had been astute enough to foresee the need, and quickly rewrote a lading bill to conform to the requirements of the contract. "Sign at the bottom if you're able to write your name," he instructed Cooper. "Otherwise, make your mark."

"I can write me name," the huge man boasted, swaggering a bit before the crowd, but when he applied the quill to the parchment, he bent over the top of a nearby cask and painstakingly scratched out his name in simple letters.

Rolling up the contract, he handed it back to Jeff, who scanned it quickly, then delivered the bag of coins.

"Remember what you've promised," Jeff cautioned. "If you bother us, you'll forfeit the money."

"I heard ye the first time," Cooper answered sharply. Then, with a leering smirk, he faced Raelynn, who stood in stoic silence before him. "Now that ye'll be takin' yerself a rich lover, I don't suppose I'll be seein' ye 'round where I'll be."

Raelynn's eyes flared with fiery rage at his affront; then, as she took command of her temper, they narrowed into cold, icy shards that pierced him where he stood. "'Twill gratify my most fervent wish, Cooper Frye, if I never, *ever* see you again as long as I may live."

"What's this now?" Cooper queried in feigned surprise. "Ye'll not be showin' ol' Uncle Coop a bit o' fondness afore we part? After all I've done for ye?"

"Be on your way," Jeff advised the man curtly. "If Raelynn hasn't had enough of your antics, then I certainly have."

"I'm goin'! I'm goin'!" Cooper assured him. Chortling to himself, he turned and, tossing the bag of coins in his hand, strolled back across the street from whence he had come.

Raelynn breathed a sigh of relief at his going, but her feeling of contentment was brief, to say the least. Though she was not necessarily averse to the idea of being owned by Mr. Birmingham, she was certainly not blind to the dangers of such a relationship. His unparalleled good looks and easy charm could pose a dire threat to a virtuous maid who had no knowledge of men. Whether they were roués or gallant gentlemen, her experience with them was seriously lacking. For that reason she could not be content with the current situation. Despite what Cooper Frye thought, she was not made of ice.

Stepping beside Jeff, she gazed up at his lean profile as he watched the departing figure of Cooper Frye, and mentally affirmed her admiration of all that she saw. Her heart fluttered unnaturally as the elusive, manly scent of his cologne wafted through her senses, making her realize just how crucial it was for her to establish a code of conduct between them before they were ever alone together. He affected her so strongly that she could not be sure she would be able to stand steadfast and stoically deny him that which he might ask of her.

"Mr. Birmingham"—her voice quavered oddly as she spoke—"'tis most urgent that I speak with you in private."

Any satisfaction Jeff derived from seeing the last of Cooper Frye dwindled rapidly as he looked down into the smudged and troubled face of Raelynn Barrett. That was when the full import of his actions hit him broadside. Had he taken her to an inn and shared a room with her for all the world to see, he could not have done more to destroy her reputation than what he had just accomplished by buying her. If the thought hadn't taken root on its own, then Cooper's taunt had certainly set the seed in fertile soil. Before nightfall, word would spread throughout the area that he had bought himself a young woman, one who was likely destined to become his mistress. How could he have been so blind as not to see what crime he was committing against her? Usually he was far more perceptive than that. What could he possibly do now to restore her honor?

Coming to himself, he realized that Mrs. Brewster was offering the use of her shop. "And perhaps you'd like some tea while you talk."

The milliner hurried back to her shop, scooping up the hatbox and Jeff's beaver as she went. Ushering them in, she led the way to her small apartment in the back, where she made tea as the couple settled at her small table and faced each other rather apprehensively across its surface. Raelynn waited for the woman to excuse herself, but in her haste to set out her best teapot, cups, and a variety of sweetcakes on porcelain plates, Thelma completely forgot the girl's request for privacy.

Jeff also felt the need to talk with Raelynn alone and drew Thelma aside to ask a favor of her, having settled his mind on the only option open to him. "As you can see for yourself, Mrs. Brewster, the girl is in desperate need of some clothes to wear. Would it be too much of an imposition if I asked you to go back to Farrell's and see what he has available in the way of women's clothing that would fit Raelynn—perhaps some gowns and other essentials that were ordered but never picked up?"

"I'd be delighted to, Mr. Jeffrey, but how shall I know what you want to spend for her? Farrell's seamstresses are the best in the area, and I know some of their gowns can be quite elaborate and costly."

"If you're unsure about anything, ask Farrell to help you. He knows me well enough to be able to lend you whatever advice you might need. Otherwise, Mrs. Brewster, I will entrust the decisions to you and your excellent taste."

"Should I bring the clothes back here, then?"

"I rode my stallion into town today, so ask Farrell to have the packages loaded in a hired livery, then send the driver here to await our departure to Oakley."

Jeff escorted the milliner to the front door and watched as she scurried across the street. Then he made his way once more to her private quarters. In his brief absence, Raelynn had washed her face and smoothed her hair, presenting a neater demeanor as she poured him a cup of tea. Watching him from beneath long silky lashes, she daintily sipped from her own cup.

"You're no doubt curious about what I have in mind," Jeff began forthrightly.

Raelynn inclined her head in a slow nod. "I have no idea whether you are married or single, Mr. Birmingham, so you can perhaps understand that I am completely bemused as to what I should expect. Will your wife be my mistress? Or are you my one and only master?"

"I do not consider myself your master, Raelynn," he said with a smile. "And you'll have no mistress, either. I am a bachelor."

"I hope you'll understand, sir, if I tell you that that fact gives me cause to worry," Raelynn admitted candidly. "I have only just met you, and yet suddenly I find myself your solitary possession. I dare not allow myself to think what your intentions may be. To be sure, sir, though you are neatly attired and handsome beyond a mere girl's dreams, I am no more disposed toward becoming your plaything than I was willing to accept Gustav Fridrich's plans for me."

" 'Tis difficult to tell you what has been on my mind since I first saw you," Jeff replied haltingly. "Perhaps I was too intrigued by your beauty to realize that I was acting irrationally, inadvertently doing you more harm than good. I fear you might think me a fool, Raelynn, but I feel as if I've known you the whole of my adult life. . . ."

Raelynn eyed him curiously. "I would never think you a fool, Mr. Birmingham."

"I'm a man in my early thirties, and I've come this far through life never having been tempted to ask for a lady's hand. You may think my proposal completely outrageous, especially since we've just met, but I can think of no better solution to disarm the gossips who'll be wont to talk about this incident for weeks or even months to come."

Though perplexed, Raelynn grew increasingly more attentive as the moments sped by. "I am listening, sir."

"You have need of a protector, Raelynn, and I am in want of a wife to still the wagging tongues that have given me no peace for several years now. They are set to clacking without provocation, even going so far as to spread the sordid rumor that I yearn after my brother's wife. 'Tis a lie I've longed to serve quick death to, but not at the cost of squandering my freedom by taking to wife some woman I cannot tolerate. I know you are young . . ."

"Ten and nine, to be exact, sir," she stated softly.

"Very young," he mumbled pensively behind his cup as he raised it to take a sip.

Raelynn was hanging onto his every word and did not allow his reply to pass without acknowledgment. "That depends, sir, on what you have in mind. I'm far too old to be considered a child, and if 'tis your desire to become my guardian, I would then advise you to consider the gossips and their wagging tongues. In England, I knew several ladies younger than I who had wed doddering ancients, but they were soon widowed and, much to their delight, bequeathed enough wealth to marry whom they would. A pair of them selected young, handsome pups who had to be mothered like children, and my friends soon became exasperated with them. As for me, sir, I would rather wed one who is mature enough to know his own mind and yet young enough to give me a brood of children and be with me 'til I am ancient, too."

It was Jeff's turn to stare at her in awe. "Raelynn, do you truly comprehend what I am suggesting?"

She was reluctant to answer for fear she might be wrong. "And what is that, sir? Tell me outright, so I may not be mistaken."

"I am proposing that we be married posthaste," he said simply.

A smile softly curved her lips. "Then I was not mistaken, sir. And though we've only just met, I am willing to accept your offer of marriage . . . if you might lend some thought that we are, after all, strangers and need some time to come to know each other ere we share a bed together as man and wife."

It was some hours later when Jeff Birmingham and his bride-to-be arrived at Oakley. It seemed he had not long to wait before a carriage came smartly up the lane, and a moment later, Kingston, the butler, showed his brother and sister-in-law into the drawing room where Jeff was awaiting them. Considering all the townspeople who'd witnessed his purchase of Raelynn, he'd known the news would reach Brandon at the lumber mill before traveling on to Harthaven and Heather, and that there would be no need to send a request for their presence, for they'd be concerned enough to come at once. During the long ride home, he had assured Raelynn of his honorable intentions, but upon seeing Heather's face, he wondered if he might have to repeat them to her as well.

His housekeeper, Cora, had answered his summons and now stood in the doorway, awaiting his instructions. Her wide grin told him that the black woman was taking everything in and enjoying the whole affair.

Raelynn had retreated several steps to stand near Jeff, as if for protection, and watched the two newcomers hesitantly. It was not hard for Raelynn to discern that this was the sister-in-law whom the gossips had avowed Jeff was in love with, for she was beautiful beyond belief. Still, the fact that Heather was at least six months along with child should have deterred such talk.

Heather's heart went out to the young woman who, in spite of her shabby garments, held herself with a subdued and natural grace. She seemed wary of them, as if doubtful of being graciously received, which Heather could totally understand, having experienced similar qualms when Brandon brought her home from England to meet his friends and family.

The expression of curiosity that Brandon bestowed upon his brother motivated Jeff to lend his immediate attention to Raelynn, giving the elder no opportunity to take sweet revenge for all the needling Jeff had once done. When he had learned that Brandon had been forced to marry Heather after mistaking her for a woman of the streets, Jeff had been unrelenting in his efforts to get his sibling to realize what a great treasure he had unwittingly stumbled onto in Heather. The greatest obstacle had been Brandon's pride, but since he had already fallen head over heels in love with his wife, it had only been a matter of time before Brandon came around to conceding that she was the best thing that had ever happened to him.

Jeff hurried on with the introductions. "Raelynn, this is my brother, Brandon, and his wife, Heather. Brandon . . . Heather . . . this is Raelynn Barrett."

"Your pardon," Raelynn murmured demurely, sensing the other woman's discomfiture. "My presence here must confound you. I would have stayed in Charleston, but Mr. Birmingham insisted that I come with him and meet his family. No doubt you have much to discuss and need some privacy."

"I think we do," Heather responded gently, greatly heartened by the softly spoken and refined eloquence of the young woman. At least Jeff had not been taken in by some unschooled hoyden, though that possibility had seemed remote.

Jeff gestured to Cora. "Show our guest to the blue room upstairs and help her bathe and dress for dinner. Kingston has already taken several packages upstairs, and you'll find everything she'll need in them. Another guest will be arriving shortly, and he'll want to meet her as soon as possible."

The black woman gave him a toothy grin. "Yo' means yo' want her back here lickety-split, Mr. Jeff?"

"Faster than that, Cora," he urged with more truth than humor, drawing a gleeful cackle from the servant.

Beckoning for Raelynn to follow, Cora hurried into the hall, chattering all the while as she led the Englishwoman upstairs. "Mr. Jeff's done turned this big ol' house into a showplace. Jes' wait 'til yo' see this here bedroom I'm takin' yo' to."

In the absence of Raelynn, the three family members faced one another in indecision. Feeling a need to mentally organize his planned announcement before airing it, Jeff crossed the room and, taking a decanter and a crystal snifter from an imported cabinet, poured a small draught of brandy into the glass. Joining the couple again, he handed the snifter to Brandon.

"News of my purchase traveled fast," Jeff commented. "I was sure I'd have to wait at least another half hour before I saw your face."

Brandon savored a tiny sip of the brew as he returned his brother's grin. "I was at the lumber mill when I heard about the incident in town. I thought it best to return to Harthaven before someone took a notion to ride out and tell Heather."

Heather was, in fact, near tears as she settled onto the settee. "Jeff, how could you take advantage of that poor girl's dilemma and buy her like a slave off a block? Raelynn will not be able to hold up her head for all the slander that is bound to be said about her. Despite your good intentions in saving her from her uncle's greedy plans, you've become as much a culprit by bringing her into your house without a proper chaperon."

Jeff came and squatted down in front of her. Gathering her slender hands in his, he spoke as gently as he could. "My dearest Tory," he murmured, using his pet name for her, "will you trust me enough to believe that I would not knowingly bring shame to any lady or any member of my family?"

"Jeff, you've always been so sensible," she assured him through the threat of new tears, "but I'm afraid in this case you've not thought of the consequences your gallantry may have invited."

"Actually, I've considered a great number of things since my confrontation with Raelynn's uncle," Jeff stated slowly, as if allowing her time to digest his words, "and I've also come to some conclusions. The only way I can be certain that Cooper Frye can never interfere . . ."

Hoofbeats sounded in the lane outside the house, drawing Jeff's immediate attention. In a rush now, he quickly gave his excuses, disappeared into the hallway, and after a muted exchange with Kingston, leaped up the stairs two at a time, leaving the servant to answer the door. A moment later Kingston led Reverend Parsons into the drawing room.

Heather exchanged a quick, worried glance with her husband, who responded with an almost imperceptible shrug before he strode quickly forward to clasp the other man's hand in greeting.

"So good to see you, Reverend," he said affably. "We missed you while you were away."

"'Tis good to be back with my flock and reassure myself of their good health. You and Heather are certainly looking well." He paused as he glanced around in search of his host. "But where is Jeffrey?"

"I think he took flight when he heard you coming," Brandon quipped, then tried to curb his grin as his young wife looked around, seeming completely disconcerted by his statement.

"Aye," the reverend answered wryly. "I heard about the commotion in Charleston. It makes me wonder if some of my flock have taken on different coats in my absence, although I can't imagine Jeffrey being a wolf in sheep's clothing."

Brandon smiled with droll humor. "Whatever the precise cut of his coat, Jeff certainly has a way of calling attention to himself."

Heather rolled her eyes heavenward in disbelief, wondering how her husband could make light of this dreadful situation with Reverend Parsons present.

"Jeff was just being chivalrous, Reverend Parsons," she assured him, ready to defend her brother-in-law with unswerving loyalty.

Reverend Parsons chortled as he accepted a glass of lemonade from Kingston. "Now, Heather, don't get your pretty feathers ruffled. Jeff and I are old friends. Why,

I've known him about as long as anybody has, excepting Brandon here. His gallantry is unquestionable . . . uh . . . for the most part, that is."

While the two men exchanged amused glances, Heather took up a lacy handkerchief and began to fan her flushed face. She wished fervently that she would suddenly awake and find that this whole incident had been nothing more than a bad dream.

Eyeing his agitated wife closely, Brandon acquiesced and came to sit beside her on the settee. A fleeting moment of cherished intimacy passed between them as he lifted her slender fingers to his lips and looked at her with warmly glowing green eyes, winning a soft and loving smile from her lips in response.

Reverend Parsons settled into a chair across from them. "What does your son think about his parents acquiring a new baby? Is he hoping for a sister or perhaps a brother to play with?"

"Our black housekeeper swears we'll be having a little girl this time." Heather smiled as Brandon threaded his fingers through hers. "Hatti deciphers the signs so well, we've considered telling Beau that he'll be getting a new sister named Suzanne Elizabeth in the next couple of months."

"And if it turns out to be a boy?" the reverend inquired.

Brandon chuckled. "We'll just have to tell him Hatti made a mistake and let her explain it away."

Manly footsteps were heard accompanying those of a more delicate tread, and all eyes became riveted on the parlor entrance as the footfalls approached the drawing room. Then Jeff slid back the panel doors and, holding Raelynn's hand, led her into view, prompting the two gentleman guests to rise in appreciation of her stirring beauty. Her rich auburn hair had been swept high on her head and intricately woven with a corded ribbon that matched her gown of silver blue satin. Elegantly coifed and regally gowned, Raelynn Barrett was lovelier than any cherished dream.

An aura of warmth swept Heather as she stared at the couple, and it came to her that she had never seen Jeff looking quite so proud or handsome. His shirt and stock of flawless white seemed to gleam beneath his meticulously cut black silk frockcoat. Narrow breeches, waistcoat, silk stockings and low shoes, all of the same hue, completed the sleek, manly costume.

"Gentlemen." Jeff dipped his head forward slightly as he gave verbal recognition to the men. Then he clicked his heels in a crisp, shallow bow as he faced Heather. "My lady." He swept a hand to acknowledge the splendid beauty who stood beside him. "I would like to present Raelynn Barrett, the woman who is to become my bride."

For a moment the occupants of the room could only stare in amazement. Heather felt her heart swell with unbelievable gladness. Confident now that all was well in the family, she slipped her hand into Brandon's, which clasped and held it lovingly. Together they turned as Reverend Parsons beckoned the couple into the center of the room. Raelynn accepted Jeff's proffered arm and seemed to glide effortlessly beside him.

"Is the lady consenting?" Reverend Parsons queried with careful concern.

Raelynn lifted her gaze to Jeff and smiled as she gazed into his shining green eyes. "I could not have hoped for a more chivalrous champion had I spent the last ten years of my life searching for him. In the short time I've known him, I've come to realize that he's incredibly kind and tender, and I am honored that he has asked me to become his wife."

Jeff faced the man and lent further insight behind their motivation. "We've discussed the matter at some length," Jeff avouched. "Raelynn is in desperate need of a protector, and marriage is the only way we can strip Cooper Frye of his claims as her only kin. I sent for you tonight, Reverend, so you could perform the ceremony for us here in the privacy of my home. Are *you* consenting?"

The man looked to Brandon as the elder Birmingham. "You know your brother better than anyone. Can you name a reason why I should delay the nuptials?"

Brandon spoke with unswerving confidence. "Jeff has always been clear about what he wants out of life, Reverend. He's acted with a great deal more certainty than I've been able to lay claim to at certain times. If he says this marriage should take place, then I am one to believe him."

Reverend Parsons nodded as he accepted Brandon's vote of approval; then he peered questioningly at Heather. "Have you anything to say, my dear?"

"Only to lend my heartfelt endorsement," she murmured with a radiant smile.

The reverend slid a small black book from inside his coat and began to leaf through the pages. "When I was summoned here by Jeffrey's servant, the man advised me to come prepared to perform a wedding ceremony. Little did I know then that it would be for my host." He smiled at the couple. "Now if you will stand before me, Raelynn and Jeffrey, I will speak the words to unite you in marriage."

The moments sped past as the muted voices melded in a ritual nearly as old as time itself. Jeff drew a simple gold band from his pocket and slipped it on Raelynn's finger as he repeated the words:

"With this ring I thee wed. . . ."

His voice was strong and steady, attesting to his unwavering confidence in the decision he had made. When Reverend Parsons spoke the final words of the ceremony unifying the couple, Jeff faced Raelynn and was amazed to see her translucent eyes awash in mistiness.

"You may kiss the bride," the reverend invited.

Raelynn blushed as she lifted her face to accommodate the tall stranger whom she had just married, feeling rather forward doing so. A peck on the cheek was certainly all that she was expecting since Jeff had agreed to give her time to get acquainted with him before pressing her to become his wife in actuality. When she felt the first light brush of his mouth on hers, she was startled by the warm, sweetly moist contact and was hardly aware of her own lips opening in surprise. Her breath stilled in waiting suspense of her first kiss. Then, as lightly as thistledown being borne along on a gentle breeze, his lips moved upon hers, parting ever so slightly to conform to the suppleness of hers.

When Jeff finally drew back, Raelynn swayed weakly against him, realizing with some astonishment that his kiss had sapped the strength from her limbs and been far more potent than she had ever imagined anything could be. Considering that mere minutes ago she had asked for separate rooms, how could she now tell him that she yearned for more of that blissfully sweet nectar?

Jeff laid his arm across the small of her back and drew her closer still, lending her needed support as he whispered, "Are you all right?"

Raelynn nodded slowly as she sought to calm the frantic pounding of her heart and dull her senses to the breathtaking reality that she was in the arms of this tall, handsome man and he was her husband. She was entranced by his nearness and vividly aware of the casual pressure of his manly form. Had she been able to command her wishes into existence, she entertained no doubt that Jeff Birmingham would have been exactly where he was at that precise moment in her life.

Gathering some remnant of her scattered poise, Raelynn managed to face the other occupants of the room. "I beg your forgiveness for my faintness. 'Tis been some time since I last took food."

Heather was there immediately to give her an affectionate hug. "I'm so happy for you both. I'm sure that if Jeff had searched the wide world over, he could not have made a better choice for a bride. And whether you know it or not, my dear, your husband ranks among the best."

Reverend Parsons took his leave shortly after bestowing his blessings and good wishes on the couple. Having other visits to make before retiring to home and to bed, he declined their invitation to stay and partake of the wedding supper. Instead, waving farewell, he rode away, leaving the small clan of Birminghams to gather in the main dining room.

The elegant table was long enough to sit twelve or more easily, but no rigid formality was on display tonight. Jeff had long ago pooh-poohed the idea of the master and mistress of the house sitting at opposite ends of a long table unless they were entertaining a large crowd. Tonight the settings were cozily arranged near one end. A place had been provided on Jeff's right for his young bride and, close on his left, one for Heather, leaving Brandon to take the chair beside his wife.

"All I can say, brother," Brandon commented with puckish humor as he considered the table setting, "is that you're true to your mold. You haven't changed a whit since I first brought Heather home to Harthaven."

"Nary a mite," Jeff agreed. "'Tis certain I'm still the friendlier of us two and have no penchant for isolating myself, as you have been known to do."

Brandon sought to shrug away his brother's waggish gibe with a chuckle, but for a moment his humor was poorly contrived. Because of his own stubborn arrogance, he had once endured the torturous separation of not only a long, formal table between himself and his young wife but different bedrooms as well. In retrospect, he mentally likened the pain of his lengthy abstinence to that which a roué might have suffered had he been imprisoned in a cell right across from a woman whose beauty and form he could see but not touch. Though Heather had come into his house as his wife and been close under his hand, he had found himself beset in much the same way. Even now, the memory of his own foolishness made Brandon squirm uncomfortably in his chair.

"No one's infallible where pride is concerned, Jeff," he replied, having learned that truth the hard way. "In fact, you might be surprised to realize where you are susceptible."

Laughter twinkled in Jeff's green eyes. "I've tried to learn from your example, brother, and refrain from making any rash vows that I'll later regret."

Heather sensed Jeff's pointed glance as the two men made subtle reference to the torment Brandon had suffered while trying to hold her at arm's length. Reaching out, she squeezed her husband's hand reassuringly and conveyed her loving devotion with a warm, gentle smile. "We should all be willing to learn from other's mistakes, Jeff," she responded gaily, glancing toward her brother-in-law, "but sometimes when we make them ourselves, we're better able to grasp the full import of the lesson."

Jeff leaned back in his chair and sipped his wine. He thought of his own recent pledge to wait before claiming his conjugal rights with Raelynn and hoped he could be as strong-willed as his brother had been in controlling his manly desires, yet perhaps not quite as stubborn so that he could quickly discern a warming in his wife.

"'Tis strange how similar circumstances seem to follow in a family," Jeff said. "I may find the pigeons coming home to roost after all."

Brandon elevated a brow in curious question, then glanced at Raelynn as he began to understand Jeff's quandary. In view of the fact that they had wed in haste, he could imagine his brother being gallant enough to agree to a gentlemanly wait before reaping the pleasures of a marriage bed.

Raelynn seemed confused by the brothers' repartee. "Is something amiss?"

Heather dispelled the very idea. "Oh, you needn't fret that it's anything serious, Raelynn. The Birmingham men take great pleasure in sharpening their wit on each other's hide. They're about as tough-skinned as a pair of ol' mules, and it's always a challenge for them to see which one gets the last word in. Still, I've never known two who are closer friends."

It was some time later when Raelynn and Jeff stood on the portico of Oakley and bade farewell to the other couple. The night was still and warm with the faint scent of jasmine in the air. The kind of evening made for lovers, Jeff mused as his young wife strolled along the porch and looked out on the moonlit grounds and huge trees that raised their lofty canopied heads into the belly of the starlit sky.

"There were recent times in England when I yearned to look out and see something besides the squalor of London," Raelynn reminisced in a soft, murmuring tone. "You see, my father, who was once a wealthy lord, was falsely accused of treason against the crown. Everything was taken from him except for a wee bit of money he managed to hide for us. Later, he died in prison, though he claimed his innocence with his last breath. When my uncle found my mother a few months ago, he said we could start a new life here in the Carolinas where no one would lay the title of traitor to our name. During the voyage, my mother discovered that my uncle had spent the last of our money. She died during the crossing, and upon landing my uncle set about providing for himself. He brought Gustav Fridrich to look me over, and the man promised him a purse once Cooper Frye delivered me to his house, but on the way I managed to escape. Now all that seems an eternity ago and a whole continent away. Little did I dream when I woke this morning that I would be married before the evening was over and living amid such splendor. It seems, Jeffrey, that I owe you much more than my life. Indeed, I cannot imagine how I can ever repay you for saving me from a miserable existence and bringing me to this safe, beautiful haven."

"No payment is required beyond the vows we exchanged, Raelynn." Jeff's gaze was nourished by his wife's fluid grace as she came across the porch toward him. When she stood close, he gazed down into her shadowed face and lifted his lean knuckles to lightly brush a loose tendril from her cheek. "And I am patient."

Raelynn sighed as her eyes searched his. "Do you mean that?"

"We have certainly done this whole thing wrong-about, Raelynn. We have put the sail abaft the mast or, if you will, the cart before the horse, but I would have you consider this, madam. The most serious vow was given first, and now we must take into account all the rest." He cupped her chin and stared into her liquid eyes. When he continued, his voice was soft and husky. "It seems I've known you for a thousand years and have only awaited your coming, yet with trembling breath I shall tarry even longer 'til you know the full extent of my honor, as well as my failings, and choose to come to me of your own free will."

"We are strangers. . . ." she whispered breathlessly.

"We are married," Jeff countered gently. "And you are everything I desire. I knew that the moment I saw you."

"Please take me in, Jeff," Raelynn pleaded faintly.

"Your wish is my command, my lady." He took her arm and gallantly complied, then accompanied her upstairs in silence as she made a slow, measured ascent. Escorting her to the entrance of the bedroom adjoining his, he reached out to push the door open and waited for her to leave him. She did not.

Blushing lightly, Raelynn faced her handsome husband. "Would you think me forward, Jeffrey, if I asked to be kissed?"

He stepped close, and she reached parted lips up toward his in anticipation, eager to receive his gently questing kiss. Her senses quivered crazily as Jeff's arms tightened about her and pulled her fully against his long frame. His eyes flamed as he searched her face, seeming to stare into her very soul, demanding answers she was too embarrassed to give.

Jeff was rather amazed that she did not pull away, for the sensual pleasure of holding her against him had affected him in ways he was sure his young wife could not ignore. But instead of pulling back, Raelynn yielded completely to him, leaning into him and raising on tiptoe to accommodate his height.

Desiring her more than he had any woman, Jeff was bold enough to forge ahead, though a part of him waited apprehensively for that moment when she might show some resistance. Lowering his head, he seized her lips with a greedy fervor that made Raelynn catch her breath in delight, and she clung to him with a fevered passion she had not even known she was capable of.

No denials came, and Jeff bent to sweep Raelynn in his arms. He bore her to the bed, pausing only to thrust the door shut with his heel.

—1995

JANET DAILEY

B. 1944

Janet Dailey is advertised as being the top-selling woman writer in America and one of the top three best-selling authors in the world. With over 300 million copies of her books published in some nineteen languages, the prolific Dailey (who, in her Janet Dailey Americana series, wrote a romance novel set in every one of the fifty states in America) is certainly an undisputed master of the contemporary romance. "I consider myself to be a teller of stories about the interrelationships of people," she says of her fiction, "whether it be in the multi-character form of my major novels or the one-on-one, man/woman relationships of my romance stories."

Dailey was born in Storm Lake, Iowa, and attended Independence High School. Before becoming a full-time writer, she worked as a secretary in Omaha, Nebraska, from 1962 to 1974. She did not begin her career as a professional author until she was nearly thirty years old, when her husband, William Dailey, sold his construction company, and, together, they began touring the country in a travel trailer. She used her free time to write romance fiction, telling her husband she could produce better romances than the ones she had been reading. In 1974, Dailey released her first novel,

No Quarter Asked, *becoming the first American author to publish with Mills and Boon of London. Included among her many popular books are the Calder series—*The Calder Sky *(1981),* This Calder Range *(1982),* Stands a Calder Man *(1983), and* Calder Born, Calder Bred *(1983)—as well as other best-selling novels, such as* The Glory Game *(1985),* Heiress *(1987),* Rivals *(1989), and* Tangled Vines *(1992), among others.*

Dailey does not view romances as a second-class fiction. Instead, she sees the genre as offering readers escapist fiction that is "uplifting." She also identifies strongly with her readers, stating they are, like herself, "work-oriented women" who need an occasional escape from the stress of day-to-day life. Although Dailey's short novel, The Healing Touch *(which first appeared in 1995 in the paperback collection* Santa's Little Helpers*), reveals her skill at devising escapist fiction (the major protagonists are beautiful people, after all), it also reveals her ability at writing a romance that possesses genuine emotional power as her characters attempt to deal with the death of loved ones.*

THE HEALING TOUCH

1

"I'm sorry to bother you at this time of night, Dr. Barclay. But we have an emergency here at Casa Colina." The male voice on the phone had a gentle Irish brogue, but not gentle enough to soften the blow. Rebecca Barclay groaned as the words sank into her half-asleep brain. *No . . . no more emergencies tonight, please!* Rolling over in bed, she peered at the clock on her nightstand. Three o'clock in the morning.

"What seems to be the problem, Mr. O'Brien?" she asked, hoping it would be something simple. Normally, Rebecca would have been pleased to hear from Neil O'Brien, one of her favorite people. He was quite proficient at animal husbandry himself, and Rebecca knew he would never call her unless he truly needed her services. She just didn't want to be needed . . . at least not for the rest of the night.

"I've got myself a fine little nanny goat here who's tryin' to deliver her first kid," the Irishman replied. "But surely, somethin's amiss. She's been at it for hours, and she's made no headway at all."

A birthing. *A goat* birthing. Rebecca groaned again. Something simple, huh? Wishful, but naive thinking on her part. It was some sort of cruel cosmic rule that no call was ever simple at three o'clock in the morning.

With an effort she forced a note of cheer into her voice. False, perhaps, but cheerful all the same. "I'd be glad to come out, Mr. O'Brien. I'll be there as quickly as I can."

There's no rest for the weary, Rebecca thought as she hung up the phone and heaved her aching body out of bed. She had only been asleep for an hour. One lousy hour since the last emergency.

At midnight she had been wakened by a frantic phone call—a distraught cat owner who lived across town and far out in the country. As she had tried to find her way in the darkness, Rebecca had decided that the area was so rural it could be considered a suburb of the boondocks.

Weighing in at almost thirty pounds, sleek and shiny black, the feline named Butch had more closely resembled a panther than a common house cat. Her next two hours had been spent reassembling the tomcat's mangled ears. Having lost a skirmish with an even bigger and meaner male, Butch had been in a foul mood. Rebecca's hands and arms still stung from his scratches, and her left thumb bore several holes where he had sunk his cute little fangs into her flesh.

Unfortunately, Rebecca was the only veterinarian in the small town of San Carlos who was willing to do house calls. As a result, she could count on being hauled out of bed several times a week . . . at least.

Exactly why did I want to be a vet? she asked herself as she pulled on her jeans and a plaid flannel shirt that she had only recently draped over a chair nearby. *Wasn't it something about helping animals . . . relieving suffering, healing the wounded?*

Ugh! Altruistic reasons aside, right now she didn't want to see another furry face for at least a month.

Grabbing a favorite old woolen sweater and her case full of pharmaceuticals and surgical instruments, she hurried out to her ancient, battered pickup.

For a brief moment she allowed herself the luxury of pausing to breathe in the sweet smell of the California night. The delicate scent of the star jasmine planted beside her door blended with the heady perfume of the orange blossoms in a nearby grove.

The night air was silent and unusually cool for summer. Her breath frosted, white puffs in the moonlight, as she pulled the sweater more tightly around her and climbed into the truck.

Not a single headlight shone on the highway that ran in front of her house. The town of San Carlos was asleep . . . except for her and Neil O'Brien . . . and, of course, that poor little nanny who was struggling to deliver her first baby.

"I'll be right there, sweetie," Rebecca whispered as she pulled the old jalopy out of her driveway, grinding a gear or two in the process. "Just hang on. Help is on the way."

Ten minutes later, Rebecca arrived at Casa Colina, a lavish estate on the northern edge of town. The enormous house gleamed blue-white in the moonlight, an old-fashioned Spanish hacienda with a red-tiled roof and graceful arches covered with climbing roses.

Rebecca knew the place well. As a child, she had spent many happy hours playing on the estate, exploring the nooks and crannies of the old house, the gardens, barns and orchards. The Flores family had five daughters and she had been friends with them all.

But over the years, the girls had grown up, gone to college, established careers and gotten married. Finally, even the youngest, Gabriella, had left home. Last winter, feeling lost and alone on such a large property, Jose and Rosa Flores had sold Casa Colina and moved to an apartment in town.

Rebecca had been told that the new owners were private people, but she had heard little else about them. Even the standard town gossips seemed in the dark and hungry for tidbits of information about their reclusive neighbors.

She had been pleased to hear that they had chosen to keep Neil O'Brien as their caretaker, and his wife, Bridget, as their housekeeper. After working for the Flores family for twenty years, Neil and Bridget knew more about running Casa Colina than anyone. Rebecca felt a great deal of affection for the couple and enjoyed their company. She admired Neil's skill and compassion with the animals in his care, and he always seemed to have a big smile and a corny joke for everyone he met. Bridget was equally friendly, graciously offering a cup of Irish breakfast tea and queen cakes, as she called her special cupcakes, to visitors at Casa Colina.

Having paid many social calls to the property, Rebecca was intimately familiar with its layout. She didn't bother to go to the house first; Neil would be in the barn with the goat and Bridget would probably be sleeping. So she drove around the front of the house and toward a series of outbuildings in the back.

With her bag in hand, she climbed out of the truck and headed for the stables, where a light shone from one dusty-paned window, throwing a golden glow across the lawns. She rushed inside, hoping she wasn't too late.

O'Brien was kneeling beside a small white nanny goat, who lay on her side in a pile of straw. She was a Nubian, Rebecca's favorite breed of goat, known for its friendly, playful disposition and long, floppy ears. The animal was panting hard, straining with the contractions. But, in spite of her efforts, there was no sign of a new arrival.

With her attention focused on her patient, Rebecca didn't notice the little girl who sat huddled in the corner of a stall. She was hugging her knees, which were drawn up to her chest, her big blue eyes filled with tears.

"How long has she been in hard labor?" Rebecca asked. Kneeling beside the goat, she ran her hand over its bloated belly. She could feel the animal shivering with fear and fatigue; the goat couldn't take much more. But Rebecca felt something else, which gave her hope—the movement of the kid inside. There was still a chance of a positive outcome for both mother and baby.

"She's been at it since yesterday morning," Neil replied, pulling a red kerchief from the pocket of his coveralls. He wiped his brow, which was wet with sweat, despite the coolness of the night. "As you can see for yourself, nothing's happened. I'm thinkin' that somethin' must be tangled up in there."

Rebecca opened her bag and pulled out a tube of antiseptic, lubricating cream. "I believe you're right."

"Since I called you, she's been goin' downhill fast," Neil said, his ruddy, freckled face registering his concern. He looked exhausted, and for the first time, the thought occurred to Rebecca that Neil O'Brien was growing older. When had those lines appeared on his face? When had he lost his youthful vigor? He brushed back a lock of his curly red hair from his forehead—red that was mixed with more silver than Rebecca remembered. "Hilda's a nice little goat," he added, stroking the Nubian's long silky ears. "I'd hate to lose her."

Rebecca heard a sob from the far corner of the barn. Turning around, she peered into the shadows and saw the girl for the first time.

"Hilda's going to die . . . isn't she, Doctor?" the child asked, tears rolling down her cheeks. "I knew something awful was going to happen. And I was right, it is."

Rebecca walked over to the girl and dropped to one knee beside her in the pile of straw. "My name is Rebecca," she told her. "What's yours?"

"Katie," she said with a sniff.

"Well, Katie, I don't think you need to worry so much about Hilda," Rebecca said, reaching out and gently touching one of the girl's shining black curls, which lay on her shoulder. "I run into this sort of problem all the time. It usually works out just fine."

"Really?" The girl choked back her sobs. "You do it all the time?"

"Ten times yesterday," Rebecca replied with a teasing smile.

The child laughed through her tears. "I don't think it happens *that* much," she said.

"I think you're right. But I think Hilda's going to be fine. You'll see."

Having comforted the child, Rebecca returned to Neil and the goat. She rolled up her sleeves and smeared the antiseptic cream from her fingertips to her elbows. Then she pulled on a pair of long, surgical gloves.

"I'll check and see what's going in there," she said. "We need to know what we're dealing with."

As Rebecca examined her patient, the animal lay still, too weak to resist. After only a couple of minutes, she had her answer.

"Well, we have twins," she said. "And the first one is a big fellow. He's the one who's holding up the works."

"What are you going to do?" Neil asked.

"I'm going to turn him a bit to get him in the proper position. Then I can ease him out."

As gently as she could, Rebecca performed her task. Hilda seemed to sense that something had changed and, encouraged, she began to bear down again and push with a vengeance.

In only a few minutes, Rebecca delivered the first kid. As she had predicted, he was huge with an especially large head. But he didn't seem any the worse for having gone through his ordeal. He snorted his disapproval as Rebecca aspirated his nose and mouth and wiped his face with a towel.

Grabbing a handful of straw, Neil began to give the youngster a brisk rubdown. Hilda bleated and craned her neck around to get a better look at her newly arrived offspring.

From the corner of her eye, Rebecca watched as Katie slowly left her spot by the wall and inched toward them.

"Is it a boy or a girl?" the child asked. Her tears had evaporated, but her blue eyes were still big and round with wonder.

"It's a billy," Rebecca said. "A fine, strapping fellow. I certainly won't want to fool around with him in another year or so."

Katie looked disappointed. "Oh . . . I was hoping for a girl."

Neil laughed as he pushed the kid toward his mother's face. She sniffed him curiously, then began to give him his first tongue bath. "Poor Katie," he said, "I promised her she could have one of the kids for a pet if it was a nanny."

"Well, there's one more left in there," Rebecca said. "And we'll know soon whether it's your nanny or this billy's brother."

Katie lost her shyness as she scrambled to Rebecca's side and knelt on the straw. Reaching out her small hand, she stroked the goat's belly. "You're okay, Hilda," she said in a soft, soothing voice. "The nice doctor is going to take care of you."

"Yes," said a deep voice from behind them, "it looks like everything is under control."

Rebecca glanced over her shoulder and caught her breath. The man who stood in the doorway was the most knock-down-dead gorgeous guy she had ever seen. With his shining black hair and blue eyes, it was obvious that he was Katie's father. He almost filled the doorway with his broad shoulders, and the room seemed to vibrate with his presence.

But Rebecca didn't have time to think about a handsome man at the moment. As attractive as he was, she had work to do. With its oversize brother no longer an obstruction, the second kid was on its way into the world.

She felt a pang of concern when she saw the baby. It was much smaller than the first, and it seemed limp and lifeless as she eased it out and onto the straw.

Quickly she cleared its nose and mouth, then began to rub its body with the towel. Neil understood the urgency and did the same to its legs.

"Come on, little one," she whispered. "Let's get you going. Breathe for me . . . come on . . ."

She noticed that it was a female and her heart sank. Katie would be crushed if she didn't live.

Just when Rebecca was about to give her CPR, the tiny animal shuddered. She gasped for air, and kicked her hind legs.

"There she goes," Neil said, his face splitting with a wide grin. "You did it, Doc!" Jumping to his feet, he grabbed Katie, lifted her and gave her a bear hug.

"And it's a girl!" Katie said when he set her back on her feet. "It's a little nanny . . . for *me!*"

"That's right, Katie," Neil said. "A bonny nanny for a bonny lassie."

Hilda bleated and sniffed the second kid as Rebecca presented it to her. The mother wore a relieved and contented expression on her face, her long Nubian ears flopping as she bathed her twins.

Finally, both kids snuggled close to their mother, nuzzling her, seeking her warm milk.

Rebecca sat down in the straw and enjoyed the scene. Moments like this one made it all worthwhile. She had done her job well. Hilda was relieved of her burden. The kids were safe and cozy. Katie and Neil were thrilled with the new arrivals. And Katie's father . . .

Rebecca turned to see if he was enjoying this warm scene as much as they were, but, to her surprise, he wore a frown on his handsome face.

He took a couple of steps closer to them, studying the second nanny. "That goat is obviously a runt," he said. "I don't think it will make an appropriate pet for a child."

"She is too an appropra . . . approp . . . a good pet. I want her!" Katie said. She glared up at her father, her blue eyes angry, but pleading. "And she's *not* a *runt* . . . whatever that is. If it's bad, she's not one!"

Rebecca had to fight to control her temper. What was wrong with this man? Didn't he have a heart? How could he ruin such a beautiful, happy moment?

"A runt is an animal that is born small and unhealthy," he told his daughter. "They often have things wrong with them, and they're hard to care for. And you don't even know if she'll live."

Rebecca couldn't stay quiet any longer. "Excuse me, Mr.—"

"Stafford," he said. "Michael Stafford."

"Mr. Stafford . . . I understand your concern about having a healthy pet for your child. But even though this nanny is a bit small, there's no reason to assume she won't live."

"Oh, really?" His blue eyes were cold and angry as he stared down at her. Apparently, he resented her offering her opinion without being asked. "And can you guarantee that, Doctor?" he snapped.

Rebecca couldn't understand the bitter tone of his voice. Why was he reacting this way? "Of course I can't guarantee the animal will stay healthy, Mr. Stafford," she said. "Life doesn't offer guarantees like that."

"It certainly doesn't," he said.

Again Rebecca heard the anger in his voice. What had happened to this man to make him so cold?

Looking down at Katie, Rebecca could see the same pain mirrored in her blue eyes. It seemed to run in the family.

"Mr. Stafford," she said, trying again to sound more patient and understanding than she felt. "I truly believe this goat is healthy, in spite of her small size. If you'll let Katie have her as a pet, I promise to help all I can. I'll teach your daughter how to take care of the goat. If anything goes wrong, all you have to do is call me, and I'll be here right away."

"Please, Daddy?" Katie pleaded. She ran to her father and, grabbing his hand in both of hers, she said, "Dr. Rebecca thinks it's okay. Let me have her. Please, please, please."

Michael Stafford said nothing for a long time as he looked down at his daughter, who was tugging at his hand. Rebecca couldn't understand how he could resist those big blue eyes. *She* certainly couldn't.

He couldn't either. Gently, he pulled his hand away from hers and turned toward the door. "Well," he said as he walked away, "if the good doctor thinks it's okay, it must be okay. I'm sure she knows more about these things than I do. I only hope she's right this time."

Rebecca wished he hadn't sounded so sarcastic, but as long as he had given his permission and Katie had her baby goat, that was all that counted.

Neil helped her as she gathered her things and placed them in her bag. Her work here was finished. At least, for the moment.

Having said her goodbyes, she turned to leave, but paused at the door to take one more look at Hilda and her kids, Katie and Neil. Katie had her arms around the baby nanny's neck and was saying sweet things in her ear.

Yes, Rebecca thought, *I knew there was some reason why I became a vet. And this is it.*

The moment Rebecca stepped through the door of the Hair Affair beauty salon, she was accosted by a furry missile named Twinkle. Twinkle had been white the last time Rebecca had visited, but this morning the dog's coat was a strange shade of lavender.

Rebecca had seen a lot of animals in her career, but she had never seen a purple Pekinese. She had her first clue as to what might have caused the mysterious skin irritation that Twinkle's mistress had described earlier on the telephone.

"Oh, Twink," Rebecca said as she dropped to one knee and stroked the dog's ears, "what has Betty Sue done to you now?"

The dog simply whined in reply and rolled her eyes pitifully.

"I know, I know . . ." Rebecca accepted the wet kiss on her cheek. "I've tried, Twink, but you know how Betty Sue is. By the way, where is your mistress?" she added, looking around the empty salon.

A door in the back of the salon swung open and a young woman in a hot-pink uniform entered, bringing with her the smell of permanent wave solution and nail polish. For some reason, Rebecca wasn't surprised to see that Betty Sue had dyed her own bleached, platinum blond hair the same shade of lavender. Nothing about Betty Sue shocked Rebecca anymore. But Betty had been born and raised in the heart

of Hollywood, so Rebecca tried to take that into consideration. The poor girl probably couldn't help herself.

"Hi there, sweet thing," she exclaimed, hurrying over to give Rebecca a warm
hug. "It's our very favorite doctor, huh, Twinkle Toes. . . ."

"Don't give me that 'favorite doctor' bull," Rebecca said, shaking her head in mock
disgust. "You're just trying to butter me up because you know I'm upset with you."

"Upset?" Betty Sue batted her false lashes. "You're upset with me? Whatever
for?"

"You didn't hear a thing I said when I was here last time."

"Why, that's not true. Of course I heard you. I—"

"Then you didn't listen. I told you to stop doing weird things to this poor innocent creature."

"But . . . but I . . ." she stammered. "I'd never do anything to Twinkle Toes that I
wouldn't do to myself."

Rebecca looked Betty Sue up and down, taking in the multiprocessed hair, the
porcelain nails, the pounds of trowel-applied makeup. Betty wasn't what you'd call
a natural beauty. That list of things she "wouldn't do" to herself or her long-suffering pet must be pretty short.

"Betty Sue, you have to stop this nonsense. I'm tired of coming over here to treat
problems that *you* have caused. You airbrushed this dog's toenails and—"

"But she liked that. She was having fun."

"She was *high,* Betty Sue. Twinkle was buzzing on the fumes! And remember
when you gave her corn-rows down her back with those beads and feathers?"

"Well, I thought—"

"I had to cut them out. I had to shave the poor little thing. She ran around looking like a scalped rat for an entire winter."

"But I knitted her a little sweater to wear."

"You didn't finish it until spring."

"My heart was in the right place."

Rebecca stifled a smile. "Then maybe you'd better start thinking with your head."
She bent down and picked up the dog. Running her hand backward over her fur,
Rebecca exposed the red, irritated skin. "Look at that! It's a reaction to that stupid
purple dye you used."

"I did a patch test first, just like it said in the instructions!" Betty whined, refusing to meet Rebecca's eyes. "I really did, and it turned out fine."

"Those instructions were for a *person,* Betty Sue, not a Pekinese. I'm not kidding,
you have to *stop* doing this, or I'm going to turn you in for cruelty to animals."

Betty Sue's chin began to quiver slightly, and her lower lip protruded in a pout.
Rebecca felt a wave of relief; finally, she might have gotten through to her.

"I'll give you some shampoo that's medicated. It'll help stop the itching and keep
the skin from getting infected. She won't smell very nice afterward, but—"

"Don't worry," Betty interjected, "I won't put perfume on her. No matter how
much I want to. I'll resist."

"Attagirl."

As Rebecca took the medication from her bag and wrote her instructions on the
label, Betty Sue held Twinkle and cooed into her ear.

"Does her love her mommy?" she asked the dog in a nauseatingly sweet tone.
"Yes, yes, her does. Her knows Mommy was just trying to make her look beautiful.
Twinkle Toes lo-o-o-oves her mommy."

Betty Sue set the dog on the floor and took the bottle from Rebecca. "By the way," she said, a smile on her perfectly outlined, carefully blotted crimson lips, "I heard something . . . but I don't know if it's true."

"What's that?" Rebecca asked, trying to look uninterested as she snapped her bag shut. Betty Sue was a hopeless gossip, and like most people, Rebecca found the idea of gossip appalling and the reality fascinating.

"I heard you've been spending a lot of time at Casa Colina lately . . . with that hunk widower, Michael Stafford."

"Then you heard wrong," Rebecca said, trying to stifle her irritation. Gossip that was about *her* wasn't nearly so fascinating. "I was out there *one* night, and it was business, not pleasure. Believe me. I had my hand in a goat's rear end, up to my elbow. That's not what I call a good time."

"Oh . . . I . . . oh."

Rebecca was pleased to see that she had finally managed to shock even Betty Sue Wilcox. She considered it quite an accomplishment to shock someone from Hollywood.

"But, you *did* meet Michael Stafford, didn't you?" Betty was still trying to squeeze something juicy from the rather dry story.

"Yes, I met him. I saw him with my own two eyes. I gazed, spellbound, upon his handsome face for . . . heck . . . probably all of three or four minutes."

Betty Sue brightened. "And is it true, what they say? Is he really that good-looking?"

"He's stunning, he's breathtakingly gorgeous." She picked up her bag and slung it under her arm. "He's also very cranky, and, personally, I didn't like him . . . not one little bit."

Without another word, Rebecca spun around on her heel and marched out the door, leaving Betty Sue with her mouth hanging open.

But Betty soon recovered and scooped Twinkle up. "I just don't think I believes her, does you?" she asked in a singsong, baby voice. "Mommy thinks Dr. Rebecca likes Mr. Michael more than she's letting on. Don't you think so, too, Twinkle? Yes . . . Mommy knows true love when she sees it."

Betty Sue watched until the decrepit pickup had disappeared around the corner. "There, there, she's all gone. Now, let's go try out that new tooth-whitener stuff Mommy bought at the drugstore. Your little choppers have been looking pretty yellow lately. Yes, they have. And we can't have that, can we, sweetie pie? No, sirree. It worked really great on Mommy's teeth. See. . . ."

2

For the next week, Rebecca couldn't stop thinking about Katie, her father and the baby goat. Finally, she gave in to her worries and dropped by Casa Colina.

The warm sun made her feel lazy as she got out of her pickup and walked up to the house. It was the perfect morning to just sit in the sun and sip ice tea.

She sighed to herself. No such luck. The busy life of a vet didn't offer her much time to be lazy.

She found Katie and the kid romping in the backyard. Playing a game of tag, they seemed to be enjoying each other's company.

"Hi, Dr. Rebecca!" Katie shouted as she ran toward her.

"Hello, Katie." Rebecca reached down to pet the goat. It lowered its tiny head and butted against her fist. "I see you've been teaching her bad habits," Rebecca teased.

"I didn't have to teach her that," Katie said with a giggle. "She seemed to know it all by herself."

"Yes, goats are little rascals. You have to teach them to behave. How is she doing?"

"Oh, fine," Katie said. "I named her Rosebud. But I call her Rosie."

"Rosie . . . um . . ." Rebecca said thoughtfully. She studied the little goat, its silky white coat, its long floppy ears, blue eyes and pink nose. "Rosebud. Yes, I like that name. It's perfect for her."

Katie beamed at the praise. "I'm out of school now for the summer," she said. "We play all the time. She's my best friend."

Rebecca looked around for any sign of another human being. In the distance, Neil was digging in the garden, and his wife, Bridget, stood in the kitchen window.

But Katie's father was nowhere in sight. And Rebecca was sorry to see that Katie had no other children to play with.

"So, it's just you and Rosie?" she asked the girl. "No people friends to play with?"

The girl looked sad for a moment, then shook her head. Her black curls bounced and shone in the sunlight. "Nope. Just me and Rosie. I don't have any other friends."

"Don't you ever invite the girls from school to come over?" Rebecca asked. She thought of all the wonderful times she had shared with the Flores girls here at the Casa.

"I used to have friends over to play," Katie said. She wouldn't look up at Rebecca as she bent to scratch behind Rosie's ear. "But that was before. You know . . . when we lived in Los Angeles and my mommy was still alive."

An unexpectedly sharp pain shot through Rebecca. The pain of loss that was always so close to her heart. About the time she dared to hope the wound might have healed a bit, something pricked it, and the pain returned as deep and searing as ever.

"I'm sorry, Katie," she said. She stroked the girl's shining hair. "It's hard to lose someone you love. Believe me, I know."

Katie looked up at her with curious eyes. "Really? Did someone you love die, too?"

Closing her eyes for a moment against the memories, Rebecca found them there, playing on the screen of her mind. The emergency call in the middle of the night—a dog at the Humane Society, hit by a car, in need of immediate attention. Tim volunteering to go. "You've had a tough day, Becky. I'll take care of it. Just go back to sleep." Hours later, the other call—from the Highway Patrol.

"Yes," she said, opening her eyes. "I lost my husband. He was a veterinarian, too. We had a practice together. We'd only been married two years."

"Was he sick for a long time?" Katie asked.

So, Rebecca thought, *that's how her mother died. A long illness.*

"No," she said. "He was in a car accident."

"Oh . . ." Katie nodded in understanding. "That must have been awful. You didn't even get to say goodbye."

"No, I didn't," Rebecca agreed. "I think that was the worst part."

Katie looked away, as though remembering. "My daddy told me to tell my mommy goodbye," she said. "But I cried, and I wouldn't do it. I was just a dumb seven-year-old. Now I'm eight, and I'm a lot more grown-up."

"Yes, I can see that," Rebecca said with a smile. "But you shouldn't blame yourself. Everyone finds it hard to tell someone they love goodbye. I don't think you were a dumb seven-year-old. I think you were just really scared, that's all."

Katie's eyes brimmed with tears, but she smiled up at Rebecca. "That's nice," she said. "Maybe that's all it was."

"I'm sure of it."

"Want to see something really neat?" Katie asked, suddenly lighthearted.

"Sure, what is it?" Rebecca said, happy to change the subject.

"Just wait until you see this. It's really funny."

The girl ran away to a nearby plum tree and picked a piece of the fruit. Rebecca had a feeling she knew what the "something" was. But she didn't say so.

"Watch this!" Katie said as she held out the plum to Rosebud.

Rebecca had seen goats eat peaches and plums before. She knew what was coming.

The goat took the fruit and rolled it around in her mouth for a couple of seconds. Then she spat out the seed . . . perfectly clean. As the pit sailed through the air, Katie cackled with glee.

"Did you see that?" she said. "She gets *all* the plum off the seed and spits it really far!"

"Most impressive," Rebecca agreed. "A lot of boys I know would love to be able to spit like that."

Katie giggled again, and Rebecca thought what a beautiful child she was. Why didn't her father take more of an interest in her?

"So, has your dad seen this?" Rebecca asked.

Katie's smile disappeared. "No. He's almost never around. He works a lot at his car place in Los Angeles."

"Car place?"

"Yeah. He sells really expensive cars that he gets from Europe." Katie looked away, as though remembering again. "He used to be home a lot. He used to play with me and Mommy and make us pancakes in the morning. But now he just works all the time."

Rebecca recalled the months after her husband's accident, the long hours of trying to escape into her job. It hadn't worked. Sooner or later, she had to stop working and go to bed. Alone. And then she couldn't help remembering.

"I miss my mom," Katie said. "But I miss my dad, too. I wish he was around more."

Rebecca felt a rush of anger toward the man who could neglect this child. When Tim had died, she had been so lonely. If Tim had only left her with a beautiful reminder of himself . . . like Katie, she certainly wouldn't have deserted the child, no matter how much pain she had suffered.

"Have you told your father how you feel?" Rebecca asked.

"No." Katie shrugged her small shoulders. "I don't want to make him feel bad. He's sad enough already."

"Maybe you should tell him," Rebecca said gently. "Perhaps he doesn't know that you're feeling sad, too. It always helps if you have someone to feel sad with."

Katie considered her words for a moment. Then she shook her head. "No. I'll just talk to Rosebud. She doesn't have as much to worry about as my dad does."

Rebecca glanced at her watch. She had another call to make. "I have to go now, Katie. But I'll come by again soon to check on you two."

Katie seemed disappointed, but she nodded. "Okay. Thanks for coming over." She blushed and stared down at her purple and pink sneakers. "I mean . . . Rosie likes you and she was glad to see you."

"I like her, too," Rebecca replied. "Very much."

Rebecca said her goodbyes and walked around to the front of the house. Just as she was about to step into her pickup, a late-model, dark green Jaguar XJ12 pulled into the drive.

Michael Stafford climbed out, looking as striking as he had the other night. He wore a charcoal designer suit and a white silk shirt. His dark hair was combed back. But one lock had escaped and hung boyishly over his forehead.

The look in his blue eyes was anything but boyish. He gave her a curt nod of his head, but no smile of greeting.

"Good morning, Mr. Stafford," Rebecca said. Her tone was much more friendly than she felt.

"What's wrong?" he asked. "Has something happened to the goat?"

"No, not at all," she assured him. "I was just dropping by to say hello to Katie."

He looked relieved, but still angry. "I haven't changed my mind, Dr. Barclay. I believe it was a mistake to let her keep that mangy goat," he said. "My daughter is obsessed with the thing. If it were to get sick or . . ."

"Yes?" she asked, her temper rising.

"Or die, she would be crushed. And I can tell you now, Doctor, I'll blame you if it happens."

That did it. Rebecca could no longer control her tongue. She knew she was about to say things she would regret later.

"Mr. Stafford," she said, gritting her teeth, "your daughter needs a living being to love. Maybe she wouldn't be so obsessed with a goat if her father spent a little time with her."

She turned and stomped back to her truck. "And by the way," she added as she climbed in and slammed the door behind her, "Rosie isn't mangy. *None* of *my* patients have mange, thank you!"

"And *I*, Dr. Barclay . . ." he shouted back ". . . am not *cranky!*"

Oh, Lord, she thought, *someone told him what I said!* She only hoped they hadn't told him the rest. The last thing she wanted was for him to think she found him at all attractive. She'd get Betty Sue for this.

Tires squealing, she pulled away. In her rearview mirror she could see him standing in a cloud of dust . . . *her* dust, his mouth hanging open.

"So there, Mr. Stafford!" she said, still embarrassed, but satisfied with her dramatic exit. "Just put *that* in your pipe and smoke it!"

Michael slammed his desk drawer closed, caught the end of his thumb in the handle and yelled out a curse. Instantly, there was silence in the showroom, the conversation between his secretary and a salesman coming to an abrupt halt.

A second later, Mrs. Abernathy peeked around the corner into his office, a look of concern on her face. "Have you hurt yourself . . . again, Michael?" she asked in a soft, grandmotherly voice. Usually, he would have been flattered by the attention, but her words had a distinctly sarcastic undertone. And, judging by the ever-so-slight smirk she was wearing, she must have been thinking he was a child who had just injured himself while throwing a temper tantrum.

Where the hell would she have gotten an idea like that?

"I'm fine, Mrs. Abernathy," he replied with equally saccharine sweetness. "I just flattened the better part of my thumb. I had two major deals fall through before noon. My pastrami on rye was soggy and dripping with Dijon mustard. I hate Dijon mustard. And I just had the pleasure of informing Mr. Hillman that we can't find the parts we need to repair the brakes on his Silver Ghost. He intends to sue us. But, other than that, I'm having a perfectly *wonderful* day. Thank you for asking."

Instead of turning around and leaving, as he was hoping she would, she walked into his office and sat on one of the overstuffed chairs beside his desk. She adjusted her glasses, cleared her throat and folded her hands demurely in her lap—the picture of feminine grace.

How deceiving, he thought. *Here it comes. She's going to give it to me with both barrels.*

Mrs. Abernathy had worked for Michael for the past five years, and he knew all of her maneuvers. Not that the knowledge did him any good. With Mrs. Abernathy, forewarned wasn't necessarily forearmed. She always initiated, directed and won these little debates of theirs. Sometimes he wondered who worked for whom.

"Okay, what's the matter with you?" she asked, peering at him over the top of her wire frames.

"Excuse me?"

"Don't give me that. You know exactly what I'm talking about. All day you've been acting like a cantankerous grizzly bear, hibernating here in your cave and growling at anybody who gets within ten yards of you. I'm not surprised your deals fell through, you smashed your thumb and alienated Mr. Hillman. I'd sue you, too, if I were him."

He stared at her for a moment, his mouth working up and down as he searched for a suitable retort. "And I suppose the sandwich was my fault, too?"

She shrugged. "Hey, it's karma. You're sending all that negativity out into the universe and—"

"Oh, give me a break. Do you really think that the great cosmos cares if I yell at a few people? Do you really think that some yokel at the deli smearing Dijon mustard on my sandwich is an act of divine retribution? Get real."

She shook her head sadly. "See what I mean? Negative vibes. You're radiating all this hostility and—"

"I'm tired," he snapped. "And . . . and maybe I'm sick. I'm just having a bad day, okay?"

"Well, I'm tired and sick, too. Sick and tired of you being so grouchy. And, thanks to you, *everyone* here at Le Concours d'Excellence is having a bad day. Enough already."

Her authoritative tone didn't leave much room for argument. It was all he could do not to duck his head and blubber, "Yes, ma'am, sorry, ma'am."

Instead, he assumed a semiapologetic look and said, "Okay, point taken. I'll work on it."

Her face softened. "Thanks," she said. Leaning across the desk, she rested one hand on his forearm. "Come on, Mike, what is it? What's wrong . . . really?"

Warming to the genuine concern in her voice, he found himself opening up a bit. She was a feisty old broad, but she was also a sweetheart and a good listener. During his wife's sickness, and afterward, she had been there for him. Every day and some long, dark nights. She was truly a good friend.

"I had a run-in with this veterinarian yesterday," he said. "The one I told you about before."

"The woman who delivered your goats? The one you said filled out her jeans nicely but was difficult?"

"Yeah, that's the one."

Had he really told Abernathy that bit about the jeans? He didn't think so. He could recall saying it to one of his mechanics. Maybe she had been eavesdropping. Wouldn't be the first time.

"So, what were you two fighting about yesterday?" she asked.

"She just said some things that she had no right to say. Stuff about Katie and me . . . and . . ."

"And?"

"And about how I don't spend enough time with her."

"Mmm-mmm." She nodded solemnly.

For once, Mrs. Abernathy seemed noncommittal in her response. Michael wasn't sure what to make of it. Usually, she was disturbingly forthright with her opinion.

"She said that Katie was obsessed with the little goat because she needs a living being to love. Can you believe that? She thinks my child's life is so empty that she's got to look to some scrawny little goat for affection."

"And what do you think, Mike?" Mrs. Abernathy said softly as she stared down at her hands, which were still folded demurely in her lap.

"I think that vet's got a big mouth," he replied without thinking.

Mrs. Abernathy said nothing, and her silence was far more telling than any of her lectures.

"And what she said is really bothering me," he added, although the admission cost him dearly, "because . . . I'm afraid . . . I'm afraid she's right."

Mrs. Abernathy patted his hand, then squeezed it. "I know you're afraid, Mike. I know what you've been through that made you that way. And I know how much you love Katie. You have a battle going on inside, fear versus love. I'm sure your love for your little girl will win in the end."

Michael was thankful that she had the sensitivity to rise from her seat and walk over to the door. He didn't want her to see the moisture in his eyes, and she knew it. Good ol' Abernathy. She knew when to make a graceful exit.

"Abby," he said, "I hope you're right. Thanks."

"No problem." She paused at the door, bared her teeth, and growled at him. "Don't come out until you're in a better mood," she said.

He nodded.

Sitting alone, staring at the picture of his beautiful daughter in its silver frame on his desk, Michael allowed the emotions to wash over him: the fear, the guilt, the love. She looked so much like her mother. So much.

He reached out and with one finger traced the soft line of her cheek. "Oh, Katie," he whispered. "I need you, too, sweetheart."

But the moment he uttered the words, the anxiety rose in him, building until he felt it would squeeze his throat and suffocate him.

He needed her. That was the problem. After losing her mother, he was so afraid. He needed her far too much. That was why he had to guard his heart. Michael Stafford knew his own limitations all too well. And he knew he could never stand to love and lose like that again . . . *never* again.

Autumn arrived in its usual California fashion. Except for the dry Santa Ana winds, the occasional brushfire and the calendar on her wall, Rebecca couldn't tell it was fall. The month of September and the Christmas holidays were the only times of the year when she wished she lived somewhere other than Southern California. In September she found herself longing for a New England autumn, the brightly colored foliage and the smell of burning leaves scenting the crisp air. At Christmas she wished she could see the elaborate decorations on Fifth Avenue in New York City and skate at the foot of the giant tree in Rockefeller Center.

But most of the time, she was perfectly content with her lot in life and the quaint little oceanside town of San Carlos. It felt like home.

One community tradition that she particularly enjoyed was the county fair. As the local vet, she was always asked to judge the dog, cat and rabbit shows. Handing out the blue ribbons was the high point of her year.

She arrived at the fair early on Saturday morning and stood in the center of the hustling, bustling activity, soaking in the unique ambiance. Sheep, cows, pigs and goats protested loudly with grunts, groans and bleats as children herded them down gangways and into their pens. Women scurried from tent to tent, carrying prize flowers, cakes and pies and needlework of all kinds, many bearing ribbons of distinction.

In the Quonset hut, some of the local men displayed their woodworking and leather crafts, miniature train sets, and homegrown vegetables of outrageous proportions.

Seeing dozens of familiar faces, Rebecca greeted almost everyone she met. In a town as small and intimate as San Carlos, most of the citizens knew one another— by reputation, if not by name. The gossip grapevine kept everyone informed.

Just as Rebecca was nearing the livestock area, she spotted a particularly endearing and familiar face. Katie Stafford was clinging to the end of a small, white, leather bridle. At the other end was a transformed Rosebud. The little nanny was decked out with pink ribbons, silver bells and pale blue bows in her tail and around her neck. The goat was behaving quite well—for a goat—as she pranced proudly along behind her mistress.

But most surprising of all, Rebecca saw Michael Stafford walking beside his daughter and her pet, looking almost as proud as they did. Wearing a broad, carefree smile, he appeared more relaxed and at peace with himself than Rebecca had ever seen him.

"Hey, Dr. Rebecca! Doctor, over here!" Katie shouted across the way as she bounced up and down and waved her free arm enthusiastically. She turned to her father. "Look, Daddy, over there! It's Dr. Rebecca!"

"So it is," Michael said. He gave Rebecca a dazzling smile that nearly stopped her heart. "How are you today, Doctor?"

"Ah . . . fine, thank you," Rebecca replied, feeling suddenly, inexplicably, shy and awkward.

"See what we won!" Katie said as she held up a bright red ribbon and waved it under Rebecca's nose. "See! See! Rosie won second place!"

"A red ribbon! Good for you, Katie." Rebecca leaned down and scratched the top of the nanny's head. Many animals seemed to be embarrassed when their masters and mistresses "dressed them up" in ribbons and fluff. But Rosie appeared to love being the center of attention. "You deserve a red ribbon," she told Katie. "Rosebud looks *beautiful* today! You did a wonderful job of grooming her."

"Daddy helped." Katie beamed up at her father. "She wouldn't hold still when I was giving her a bath. So he helped me chase her around. She got more water and soap on *us* than we did on *her*. But it was fun."

Rebecca turned to Michael and their eyes met over the top of Katie's head.

For a moment he seemed embarrassed, then he shrugged. "A red ribbon isn't too bad," he said with a silly half grin, "for a mangy runt. Huh, Doc?"

"Not bad at all," Rebecca replied.

Michael looked down at Katie and patted her shoulder. "Why don't you and Rosebud go on ahead without me," he said. "I want to talk to Dr. Barclay for a minute. I'll be right there."

Katie looked from her father to Rebecca and back. A smirk played across her face. "Sure, Dad. No problem," she said knowingly.

As soon as Katie and the goat were gone, Michael seemed even more nervous than before.

"I . . . ah . . ." he began. He paused to clear his throat.

She leaned closer to him. "Yes, Mr. Stafford?"

"I wanted to thank you for what you said the other day," he blurted, as though afraid to lose his momentum and courage. "I don't mind telling you, I was furious with you then. But I thought about it, and I decided you were right. I *have* been neglecting Katie."

He drew a deep breath, and Rebecca could see the pain in his eyes. This man was no coward, but he had been deeply hurt. That much was obvious, in his face, his voice, even his body language. Usually, he stood with his arms crossed over his chest, as though guarding his heart.

It was ineffectual armor, Rebecca knew. Unfortunately, there was no way to shield the soul from life's cruelest arrows. She remembered Tim and how she had felt the first year after he died. Yes, she knew all about having your heart pierced when you least expected it. A wound like that took a long, long time to heal, if it ever totally did.

"I was married once," she said, "and I lost my husband, too. I've felt some of what you're going through, and I know it's a really tough time for you."

"Yes, it is. But that doesn't excuse the way I acted about the little goat." He stared down at the ground, unable to meet her eyes. "I don't know why I said what I did and . . ."

His voice trailed away, and Rebecca could see the depth of his guilt on his handsome face. Who would have thought that a face that looked so strong could reflect so much doubt? So much self-condemnation?

"I was afraid for Katie," he admitted, "because I truly thought the goat was unhealthy. I didn't want her to lose something else she loved . . . not so soon after . . ." He paused to gather the rest of his thoughts. "I know I overreacted, but the poor kid has already lost so much."

"I understand." Rebecca stood there, wondering if she should say what was on her mind. She would risk making him angry again, but she felt she should be honest with him.

"Mr. Stafford," she said. "I don't claim to know everything you're feeling, everything you've experienced. But if you overreacted, I think it's only because you love your daughter so much."

"Yes, I do," he said. "And her mother's death was very hard for her."

Rebecca nodded. "I know you're afraid of her suffering another loss, and you don't want her to love something else that could die."

"That's true," he said, obviously touched that she understood. "Living things are just so . . . so . . . fragile."

"I know they are. Believe me, in my line of work I know that all too well. But Katie can't close her heart, not even to protect it. She has far too much love to give. And so do you," she added quietly.

He said nothing, but stared down at the sawdust on the ground.

She continued, "To love a living being is to risk getting hurt, because we all die, sooner or later. But there is one thing that's worse than losing someone you love. It's not having anyone to love in the first place."

She couldn't tell how her words had affected him, because he continued to look down at the toes of his boots.

"I know you're afraid to feel your love for Katie," she ventured, knowing she was going too far. But if she was going to upset him, she might as well go all the way. "You know, Michael, there are lots of ways to lose someone . . . besides death, that is. We can lose someone we love, even though we see them every day . . . if we allow our fear to get in the way."

He cleared his throat and nodded curtly. "Yes. Of course you're right, Dr. Barclay. But I have to get going. Katie needs help loading Rosebud into the trailer."

Before she could reply, he was gone.

"Way to go, Rebecca," she muttered. "You sure have a great way with people. The true gift of gab. Maybe, in the future, you'd better confine your conversation to fuzzy faced critters who can't talk."

3

"Would you like another cup of tea, dear?" Bridget took the cobalt blue china teapot from under its knitted cozy and offered it to Rebecca. "Why don't you finish this one off and I'll brew another."

The offer was too tempting to resist. Bridget made the finest cup of tea in town—claimed it was a special County Kerry blend—and Rebecca had managed only three hours of sleep the night before. A little caffeine was exactly what she needed to get her over the midafternoon slump, and sipping tea here in Bridget's homey kitchen was a great way to infuse.

Besides, Rebecca had never been able to deny Bridget anything. Something about those bright green eyes, the translucent skin and the open, friendly smile made her irresistible. Twenty years ago, when Rebecca first met her, Bridget had been young and beautiful. In spite of the passage of two decades, she was still youthful in spirit and more beautiful than ever.

"Oh, okay," Rebecca said, twisting her own arm behind her back. "If I must, I must."

Bridget placed a plate, which was covered with an ornate silver lid, in the middle of the table. With elegance and flourish, she swept the lid aside, revealing a dozen or so of her famous queen cakes. Rebecca remembered the first time she had ever eaten this particular delicacy. She had been ten years old, visiting the Flores girls, and Bridget had treated them all to a formal afternoon tea.

Dressed in old-fashioned clothes garnered from the attic trunks, the six girls had glided into the dining room, nearly falling off their oversize high heels, tripping on the long hems, dripping with costume jewelry. On their heads they wore an assortment of wide-brimmed bonnets, sporting plumed feathers, silk flowers, satin ribbons and, in Rebecca's case, a rhinestone brooch.

Apparently, Bridget was remembering too. She wiped her hands on her snowy apron, sat across the table from Rebecca and helped herself to the plate of goodies.

"You girls always loved my queen cakes," she said. "You were so cute all decked out in those fine old clothes. I miss havin' you around."

"But now you have Katie." Rebecca bit into the cake, which looked like a simple cupcake without frosting, but tasted divine. One bite and you could tell that Bridget didn't spare the butter, fresh eggs or cream. Rebecca tried not to think about the fact that she could almost hear her arteries hardening with every swallow.

"Yes, I have little Katie, and a darlin' child she is, too," Bridget said, a smile softening the lines that had begun to develop around her eyes and mouth. "Have you ever seen eyes so blue . . . outside of ol' Ireland, that is?"

"No, I haven't. Her eyes are a beautiful color, but I see a lot of sadness in them, too."

Bridget nodded and took a sip of her tea. "Aye, 'tis true. She still grieves so for that dear mother of hers—may she rest in the arms of the angels," she added, crossing herself.

"Did you know Mrs. Stafford?" Rebecca felt a bit guilty for trying to get information out of Bridget. If she wanted to know details, she should probably just ask Michael. But the few encounters she'd had with him had proved that they were neither one particularly good at communicating with the other.

"No, I never laid eyes upon the departed lady," Bridget said, "but I'm sure she must have been a saint, considering the love her husband and daughter still have for her."

"Yes, I'm sure." Rebecca felt a tiny stab of jealousy toward the woman for having been adored by such a wonderful child as Katie and a man like . . .

No, that didn't bear thinking about. She pushed the thoughts aside, feeling horribly guilty for entertaining them even for a moment.

"When does Katie get home from school?" Rebecca asked, glancing up at the cuckoo clock on the wall.

"Any minute now. I'd say your timing was just about right," Bridget said with a knowing grin. "Unless you dropped by to see Mr. Michael. I don't expect to see him for hours yet."

Blushing violently, Rebecca searched her mind for an appropriately adamant denial. Nothing came, so she found herself stammering like an idiot. "Ah . . . no . . . I . . . I never wanted . . . I don't even . . . no!"

"Oh, I see." Bridget raised one eyebrow and patted her every-hair-in-place blond French roll. "You haven't taken a fancy to him then?"

"Certainly not."

"Hmmm . . . now I would have thought . . . oh well, never mind."

The squeak and whoosh of school bus brakes outside relieved the tension of the moment, and Rebecca silently blessed its arrival.

"Why, there's the darlin' lass now," Bridget said as they both watched through the kitchen window while Katie climbed down from the bus.

"She doesn't look very happy," Rebecca commented, noting how slowly Katie was walking and how her shoulders slumped.

"No, 'tis a terrible shame." Bridget clucked her tongue and shook her head sadly. "A wee thing like that should have someone to play with after school. I try to give her as much attention as I can, but I have my other duties and . . ."

"You know," Rebecca said, thinking aloud, "I'm not all that busy this afternoon. Do you think she'd enjoy going down to our old swimming hole? The weather's pretty warm."

"Oh, aye! I'm sure she would. What a lovely idea, dear. She's very fond of you. I know she'd be pleased to spend some time with you."

"Do you think it would be okay with Mr. Stafford?" Rebecca was reluctant to mention his name, for fear of more teasing, but he seemed so definite about certain things. She didn't want to find herself locking horns again with him any time soon.

"Well, I don't see why not," Bridget said thoughtfully. "You're a trustworthy adult. And you'll be right here on the property. I think he'd be grateful that you paid attention to her."

The back door opened, and Katie shuffled in. Without looking up, she tossed her books on the counter and placed her Beauty and the Beast lunch pail in the sink.

"Hi, Mrs. Bridget," she said listlessly.

"Welcome home, love," Bridget replied. "Look who's here."

The instant Katie saw Rebecca, she was transformed into a bouncy, animated eight-year-old, a bright smile lighting her face. "Dr. Rebecca!" she shouted, running across the room to the table where Rebecca sat.

For a moment Rebecca thought she was going to receive a hug, but at the last moment, shyness seemed to intervene. Katie stopped abruptly a few feet away and stood with her hands behind her back, awkward but happy.

"Hi, Katie. It's nice to see you again."

Katie blushed and shuffled her scuffed lavender and pink sneakers. Then a look of horror crossed her face. "Oh, no, you're not here because of Rosie, are you? Is she okay? Are Hilda and Pepe all right?"

"The goats are just fine," she said. Reaching out, she placed her hand on the girl's shoulder. "I came to see you."

"Really?" She looked relieved and happy, but a tad dubious.

"Really, really." Rebecca waited as the hint of a frown melted. "But who's Pepe?"

"He's Hilda's other baby . . . the boy. You know, Rosebud's brother. He's a *lot* bigger than Rosie. Mr. Neil won't let me play with him. He says Pepe's too rough."

"I'm sure he's right." Rebecca donned a businesslike face. "What I'd like to know is this—do you have plans for the next couple of hours? Because if you don't . . ."

"Wow, this is really neat!"

Rebecca could tell by the glow on Katie's face and the enthusiasm in her voice that the secret swimming hole was a success.

"The Flores girls and I spent hours here," Rebecca said as she led Katie through the narrow gap between two rocky cliffs toward the natural pool that lay nestled in the tiny arroyo. "On a hot afternoon, it's the perfect place to cool off."

Large smooth rocks surrounded the basin, which collected the meager runoff from nearby hills. In recent drought years, the water level had dropped considerably, but the pool still contained enough clear, clean water to splash around. Old oak trees spread their gnarled limbs over the far end, shading the deepest part of the water.

Various species of water bugs danced along the surface, causing tiny, rippling rings. A dragonfly buzzed among some reeds, its wings nature's most delicate filigree, its body teal blue luminance in the sunshine.

In the distance they could hear the cawing of a crow and nearby the rustling of other smaller birds in the surrounding scrub brush. The air smelled of dust and earth and growing things, a scent that evoked a hundred fond memories for Rebecca.

"We used to bring along a picnic lunch," she told Katie. "Usually peanut butter and jelly sandwiches that we made ourselves . . . or some of Bridget's queen cakes, like today." She held up the brown paper sack that Bridget had packed for their little excursion. Fortunately for them, the Irishwoman lived in constant dread that someone, somewhere might faint from lack of nourishment. And she believed it was her mission in life to make certain that such an awful thing never happened to anyone she knew.

"Are there fish or creepy things in there?" Katie asked as she climbed up onto one of the rocks and peered down into the water.

"One great white shark, two Loch Ness monsters, three electric eels and four stingrays," Rebecca answered promptly. "That's all."

Katie gave her a dubious look. "No partridge in a pear tree?"

"Nope, afraid not."

They both giggled. Rebecca set the sack of goodies on top of one of the boulders and slipped off her socks and sneakers, then removed her denim shirt. Wearing only her T-shirt and shorts, she slid down the rock and into the water with a clumsy splash.

"That was a lot easier when I was your age," she called up to Katie as she shook the water from her hair. Droplets flew, bits of glittering crystal in the sunshine. The pool was fairly shallow, just deep enough for her to tread water.

Katie laughed as she watched her. "Is it cold?"

"Of course it's cold. This is no sissy, heated whirlpool, kiddo. This here is the real thing. So, the question is, are you woman enough to jump in here, too?"

Katie's smile faded and she fumbled with one of her shoelaces. "I . . . uh . . . I can't."

"You can't what?"

"I can't swim."

Rebecca was shocked. She had never known anyone who couldn't swim. The child lived in Southern California, for heaven's sake.

"Didn't one of your parents teach you?" she asked.

"My mom was going to, that summer, but she got sick. And after she . . . left us . . . my dad was afraid for me to go near the water. I think he was scared that I'd die, too."

Rebecca bit back the sarcastic comments that rushed to her tongue. She found it terribly sad that Michael Stafford was so consumed by fear, but it was even worse that he had passed that anxiety on to his daughter. In Katie's eyes, Rebecca could see the uncertainty, the lack of self-confidence as she stood on the edge of the rock and stared down into the water.

"I can understand why your dad might have been worried about you learning to swim," Rebecca said, choosing her words carefully. The last thing this child needed was to have someone speak ill of her father. "Water is something we have to respect. It can be wonderful, but it can be very dangerous if we aren't careful."

Katie crept a bit closer to the edge. "I wish I knew how to swim . . . just a little . . . so that the kids at school wouldn't laugh at me."

"They laugh at you? How do they know that you don't swim?"

"I was invited to a beach party. One of my friends was having her birthday there. My dad wouldn't let me go, 'cause he was afraid I'd try to go in the water and drown. He said, 'The water near the beach has a severe undertow.' I didn't know what that meant, but it sounded awful. It's okay." She shrugged. "I didn't really want to go anyway."

One look at that slightly protruding lower lip and the moisture welling up in those beautiful blue eyes told Rebecca that Katie wasn't being honest with herself. Being excluded for any reason from a friend's birthday party was an emotional trauma for a girl her age.

"Well, you don't have to worry about undertows here in the swimming hole," she said, trying to change the subject. "I can absolutely guarantee you that there's never been a single undertow in this pond."

"Since the beginning of time?" Katie asked with a grin.

"Since *before* the beginning of time."

The girl mulled that information over for a while, looking wistfully down at the water.

"Katie, do you really want to learn how to swim?" Rebecca asked gently.

"Well, yes, but . . . I don't think my dad would let me."

Good point, she thought. She certainly didn't want to go against any parent's wishes where their child was concerned. Especially Michael Stafford. But, on the other hand, the girl really needed to know how to swim and was still young enough to learn quickly.

"Did your father ever tell you that you *couldn't* take lessons or try to learn in any way?" she asked.

"Umm-m-m-m . . . I don't think he said I couldn't learn. He just said he didn't want to teach me and he wouldn't let me go to the beach party."

Rebecca decided to take the chance. The child had enough to fear in her life, without having to be afraid of water.

"Then, why don't I give you a little, bitty swimming lesson. This pool isn't very deep at all, and it's nice and still. I promise I won't let you drown, no matter what."

For several long moments, Rebecca watched as the girl tried to decide. Her pretty face registered her internal battle: her nervousness versus her trust in the woman who had saved Rosebud's life.

Finally, the trusting side of her nature won, and she reached down to remove her sneakers.

"So, it's pretty cold, huh?" she asked as she neatly folded her socks and tucked them into her shoes. "Do you suppose there are any polar bears around?"

"Nope, no polar bears," Rebecca replied, reaching her arms up to ease the child off the rock and into the shallowest part of the pool.

"Are you sure?" As Katie slipped into the water she shivered with excitement.

"Absolutely positive." Rebecca tried to remember back to those days at the YWCA where she had learned. What came first? "Relax, kiddo, there are no polar bears in Southern California. I guarantee it. They all hang out up in the San Francisco Bay area."

When Michael turned his Jaguar XJ12 down the gravel driveway to his home and saw the battered and distinctive pickup parked in front of his house, he felt a flash of pleasure, quickly eclipsed by a bigger rush of irritation. What now? Why was *she* here?

For a second, he entertained the dark thought that something might have happened to one of the goats. But as he drove around the side of the house and into the garage he could see all three of them, romping around in their pen, the picture of health and exuberance.

So, *she* had better have a darned good reason for coming around uninvited and unannounced. That was the problem with a small town, people took liberties with your privacy, just dropping by for no good reason any time of the day or night.

As he crawled out of the car, he quickly checked his reflection in the window.

His hair looked like hell. Great. He ran his fingers through the unruly mess but, as always, it had a mind of its own and refused to lie in any sort of order.

She could have at least waited until he had jumped into the shower and changed clothes to inflict her presence on him.

"Where is she?" he demanded as he trudged through the back door and into the kitchen.

Bridget stood at the sink, peeling potatoes for the evening meal. She turned to him with too wide, too innocent eyes. "And whoever might you be speakin' of?" she asked.

"You know who." He walked over to the refrigerator and grabbed himself a beer. "That pesky vet."

"Oh, it's Rebecca you mean." Bridget tossed the peeled potatoes into a colander and rinsed them at the faucet. "She offered to entertain your Katie for me, while I got some extra work done around here."

"Entertain Katie?" He didn't really like the sound of that. "What are you talking about? How is she entertaining her?"

"Took her out on a hike, she did. Meant to show her a bit of your property that she hasn't seen before."

"You mean they're just roaming around, God knows where?" His irritation and anxiety levels were rising by the minute. Not only had she dropped by uninvited, but she had absconded with his kid, too. The nerve of that woman!

"Ah . . . I wouldn't be worryin' if I were you, Mr. Michael," Bridget said, wiping her hands on a kitchen towel, embroidered with violets and daisies. "Rebecca used to come here all the time when she was a wee lass. Knows the place like the back of her own hand, she does. I'm sure they won't lose their way."

"Did you give your permission for this . . . excursion?" he asked.

She turned and flashed him one of her famous smiles. "I did, indeed. Thought it was the very thing for the little miss. She needs a friend or two, she does, to do things with."

"Well . . . I . . ." He didn't know exactly what to say, so he tilted his beer bottle and chugalugged the first third. Common sense told him that he was overreacting. Bridget was right. Katie did need a friend. And Rebecca was a responsible adult; at least, she appeared to be. So he probably had nothing at all to worry about.

He just wasn't comfortable not knowing exactly where his child was and what she was doing. Anything could happen to her, and he wouldn't know.

"In the future," he said, "I'd like for Katie to stay at home when I'm away, unless I've given my permission."

Bridget looked surprised and a bit hurt, but she nodded agreeably. "I beg your forgiveness, Mr. Michael," she said. "But I thought, as long as she was here on your property, with Rebecca to watch over her, it would be—"

"Yes, yes," he said, holding up one hand. "I understand. I'm not angry with you. I just wanted to make my wishes clear."

"Oh, they are, sir. Very clear, indeed."

Michael heard halting footsteps on the back porch and the sound of voices. Katie's and Rebecca's.

"See there," Bridget said. "Back, safe and sound, the both of them."

Michael crossed the kitchen to open the door for them. But when he looked outside, he saw something that made his heart nearly stop.

His Katie wasn't safe and sound after all. Rebecca was carrying the girl in her arms, and there was blood all over them both.

He threw open the door, rushed out onto the porch and grabbed Katie away from Rebecca. "What the hell did you do to her?" he shouted as he searched his daughter for the source of the blood. She felt cold and her clothing was wet, but she wasn't crying and didn't appear to be particularly upset.

"She's all right, Mr. Stafford," Rebecca replied. "It looks much worse than it is. She has a small cut on her foot, and it bled quite a bit at first. But it's stopped now and it isn't serious."

"Where my daughter is concerned, I'll be the judge of what's serious or not." Michael didn't like the woman's nonchalance. So everything was fine, huh? Easy for her to say; it wasn't her kid who had blood smeared all over her.

"I'm okay, Daddy," Katie said, wrapping her arms around his neck. "I stepped on a sharp rock and cut myself, but Dr. Rebecca wrapped my socks around it and carried me all the way back so that I wouldn't get dirt in the ow-wwie."

Michael looked down at the bloody sock wrapped around his daughter's foot and felt a sick, dizzying sensation of being out of control. Good God, anything could have happened and he wouldn't have been there.

Turning around, he carried Katie into the house, nearly colliding with Bridget, who looked equally distressed.

"Poor little lass," she murmured. "Lay her on the sofa, Mr. Michael, and I'll fetch a cold compress right away."

"No, we're not going to waste time with that," he snapped. "I'll take her straight to the hospital."

Rebecca caught up with him at the front door. "Mr. Stafford, if you want to take her to a doctor, that's certainly your choice. But I assure you that the wound isn't that serious. It isn't even big enough to require a stitch. I had intended to bring her back, clean the cut and close it with a butterfly bandage. I'd still be glad to do that, if you like."

"Let her do it, Daddy," Katie said, holding her foot up to Rebecca. "Please, let Dr. Rebecca take care of me. I don't want to go to the hospital. I don't like hospitals."

Michael didn't have to ask his daughter why. They had both spent too many heartbreaking hours in hospitals. He decided it wasn't fair to force her to return if it wasn't necessary.

"All right. If that's what you want." He turned to Rebecca, reluctant to ask her for assistance. Just on principle, he was still angry with her for taking off with his daughter without permission. And, even worse, getting her hurt. "Go ahead, Dr. Barclay," he said, his voice sounding brusque even to his own ears.

"Thank you," she replied with a softness that made him feel like a bigger jerk than ever.

"Bridget, if you would, please, my bag is in my truck cab. . . ."

"I'll fetch it straightaway," she said, heading for the door.

Rebecca sat on the end of the sofa at Katie's feet and pulled the injured foot onto her lap. "Let's see what we have here," she said as she carefully unwound the bloody sock. "Ah . . . just as I thought . . . you're developing a pretty serious case of creeping cruditis."

Katie's eyebrows pulled together over her pert nose. "The creeping what? What's that? It sounds awful."

"Oh, it is. That's why we have to use some very special treatments to make sure it doesn't turn into *acute* creeping cruditis."

"What kind of treatments?"

Michael could tell by the half grin on Katie's face that she knew she was being teased. He also noticed that Rebecca's chatter was keeping Katie's mind off the fact that she was examining the cut. Okay, so she was good with kids. So what?

"The special treatment," Rebecca said thoughtfully. "Well, let me see. . . . Oh, yes, I remember now. We have to make a poultice for it. Do you know what that is?"

"Isn't it a name for chickens and turkeys and geese and stuff like that?"

Rebecca laughed, and so did Michael, in spite of himself.

"No," she said, "that's poultry, not poultice. A poultice is a mixture of stuff that you make and spread it on a wound to help it heal."

"What kind of stuff?"

At that moment Bridget entered the living room, Rebecca's medical bag in hand. "Here you go, dear," she said, handing it to Rebecca.

"Tell me, Bridget—" Rebecca reached into the bag and pulled out cotton, antiseptic, gauze and tape "—do you have onions in the kitchen?"

Bridget looked puzzled. "Yes, of course I do, but—"

"And hot mustard?"

Again Bridget nodded. "Why do you—"

"We need to throw this stuff in the blender and then smear it on Katie's foot. How about garlic and chili peppers?"

Bridget grinned. "Aye, we've got lots of those."

"How about raw liver?"

Katie's self-control reached the end of its tether. "No! Yuck, no liver! I don't want slippery, slimy liver on my foot!"

"And, of course, you have to wear it to school, every day for a month."

By the time Katie had recovered from the shock of wearing such a disgusting and smelly poultice to school, Rebecca had disinfected and bandaged the small cut.

"There you go, kiddo," she said, gently patting the child's foot. "Good as new. Almost."

Michael felt a stab of jealousy when he saw the look of adoration in his daughter's eyes as she gazed at the vet, spellbound and brimming with affection. Besides, he was the only one who called her "kiddo."

In a small corner of his brain, he knew he was being petty, but the rest of him didn't care. This woman was trying to usurp his position with his daughter and he didn't like it one bit.

Rebecca looked up and their eyes met. He could tell that she was angry with him, too. But, probably out of consideration for the child, she wasn't saying so.

She was pretty, in a down-homey sort of way. No makeup, but then she didn't really need it. She wore her chestnut hair in a simple, no-nonsense cut—shoulder length and blunt. Her slightly damp T-shirt and shorts were covered by a plain denim shirt. Not exactly a fashion plate, but then, businesslike attire wouldn't have been practical for her line of work.

Too bad she wasn't more pleasant.

"Thank you, Dr. Barclay," he said, rising from his chair. "I appreciate what you did. May I see you out now?"

There. That had been pretty blunt. Surely she would get the idea that he wanted her gone.

"No, thank you," she said, standing up and collecting her things into the bag. "I can find my way out alone."

"But I insist," he replied, following after her as she headed for the door.

"Goodbye, Katie." She bent over the girl and placed a quick kiss on her forehead. "I'm sorry you got hurt, but you did a wonderful job with your swimming lesson. I'll drop by to give you another one soon."

She nodded a goodbye to Bridget, then headed out the door. He followed at her heels.

"Just a minute, Dr. Barclay," he called to her as she was about to climb into her pickup. "I'd like to have a word with you."

"Well, *I* don't think that *I* want to have a word with *you*. Unless, of course, you're going to offer me an apology for your rudeness."

"Not on your life! What do you mean 'apology'? You're the one who took off with my kid without asking me first. You're the one who got her hurt. And what's this about you teaching her to swim? You've got a hell of a nerve, Doctor. But you'd just better back off when it comes to my daughter."

"Mr. Stafford . . ." She drew a deep breath. *"You* are acting like a first-rate jerk. I haven't known you very long, so I can't tell if it's because you *are* a first-rate jerk, or maybe it's just a temporary lapse in your social skills due to indigestion, a painful hangnail or constipation. For Katie's sake, I'm going to assume the latter."

She spun on her heel and climbed into the pickup. He tried to think of some great, smart-aleck retort, but he was so mad that his mind was blank.

"I suggest," she said, "that you take a big healthy dose of castor oil and sleep with a coat hanger in your mouth. Maybe you'll wake up tomorrow morning with a load off your mind and a smile on your face."

He sputtered. He fumed. He thought of a perfect rebuttal. Scathing, insulting, crude . . . almost vile. Absolutely perfect.

But, unfortunately, by then Dr. Rebecca Barclay was five miles down the road and long out of sight.

4

"Are you mad at me, kiddo?" Michael studied his daughter's bent head as they helped themselves to the last two pieces of Double, Double, Cheese and Trouble pizza on the platter.

He had taken Katie to her favorite eatery in an effort to cheer her up, but so far it wasn't working. She had been unnaturally quiet during the meal and had turned down an offer to play video games with him in the adjoining arcade.

Something had to be wrong. And Michael had a sinking feeling that he knew what it was.

"Well, are you?" he asked again when she didn't answer.

He reached across the table and tweaked a lock of her hair.

"No," she said, so softly he could hardly hear her.

Her tone was anything but convincing.

"I think you are. It's okay, Katie. We can talk about whatever is bothering you."

She looked up at him with those beautiful blue eyes that constantly broke his heart, and he could see that she was much more than just angry; she was deeply hurt.

"Is it about what happened this afternoon?"

She nodded.

"What did I do wrong?" he asked, dreading the answer. Why were the members of the male gender forever messing up with the females in their lives? If a man wasn't disappointing his mother, it was his girlfriend, sister, wife or daughter. A guy just couldn't win with a woman, no matter what age.

"You were mean to Dr. Rebecca," she said, her lower lip quivering.

He reached out and touched it with his fingertip. For the thousandth time he reflected on the fact that she was so soft, so sweet, and that he was so lucky to have her in his life.

"Do you really think I was mean?" he asked.

Again, she nodded.

"I guess I came down on her pretty hard, but I was worried about you. I was mad that she took you without asking me. I was upset that she let you get hurt."

"But that wasn't her fault. We didn't see the rock through the water. And it wasn't a big deal anyway. It hardly hurt at all. Dr. Rebecca was being nice to me, and we were having a really good time until . . ."

"Until I messed it up?"

"Yeah," Katie admitted, hanging her head again. "I was looking forward to coming home and telling you how good I did on the swimming stuff. But then . . ."

"So, tell me now. How did you do?"

Her eyes brightened and she wriggled in her seat with excitement. "I did *great!* Dr. Rebecca said I was very brave. First I did the mouth part—you know, sticking my mouth under the water and blowing bubbles. Then I did my nose, then I floated on my back and did my ears. That was really weird and it sorta tickled. And *then* . . . and *then* . . . I did *the eyes!* I stuck my *whole* head under the water! All the way! I did it three times, and the last time I even opened my eyes. Right there, under the water, I opened them and looked around. I could see Dr. Rebecca. She was under the water, too, making a funny face and waving to me!"

Michael's heart warmed to see her so excited. She truly had enjoyed the afternoon, thanks to Rebecca Barclay. And the experience had obviously been worth a little cut on the foot.

He *had* been a first-rate jerk.

"I'm sorry, kiddo. Really, I am."

"Thanks, Dad. But you shouldn't tell *me,*" she said. "Dr. Rebecca is the one you yelled at."

His stomach tied into a ball at the mere thought of approaching that woman and offering an apology. But what was a guy to do? He was wrong. His daughter knew he was wrong. They both knew he owed the doctor a heartfelt apology. Maybe he should kiss her ring and oil her feet while he was at it.

"Okay, okay, I'll tell her I'm sorry, but—"

"When?"

"When . . . ah, yes, well . . ."

"Tomorrow."

"Tomorrow? I have a lot of things to do tomorrow, and I don't think I'll have a chance to . . ."

Thick, dark lashes batted over brilliant blue eyes; the rosebud mouth began to tremble again.

"All right, all right. Tomorrow."

Katie grinned, satisfied, and licked the last bit of sauce from her fingers. "You know," she added slyly, "you *could* ask her out on a date—a nice romantic dinner, a movie, a little mo-oo-onlight dancing."

He growled and tossed a piece of crust at her. "Watch it, kiddo. You *could* have to weed that flower bed beside the driveway."

"The one with all the dandelions and crabgrass?"

"That's the one."

She considered for a moment, then said, "Okay, just buy her a double-decker ice cream cone, and we'll call it even."

"I've been instructed to buy you ice cream. A lot of it."

Startled, Rebecca looked up from her examining table where she was clipping the right wing feathers of a parrot named Frederick. Michael Stafford was standing in her doorway. He wore an off-white linen shirt, just-right-tight jeans and a smile on his face that reminded her of the grins worn by a few sheep she had treated in her career.

Fred squawked and flapped, obviously irritated by her hesitation.

"What?" she asked, unable to believe what she had heard.

"I said . . ." He hesitated. "I'd like to buy you some ice cream, as a way of saying that you were right and I was a jerk. Or so I've been told by my eight-year-old daughter."

"I see." She paused to comfort Frederick, who had decided that the examination and feather clipping had gone on long enough. Fortunately, she was nearly finished, close enough to agree with him.

Stroking the bird's head and tickling the back of his neck, she coaxed him into his portable cage. His owner, Marge, would be by to get him soon.

She walked over to the sink and washed her hands, trying to decide how to react to this less than enthusiastic invitation. Half of her wanted to accept—okay, more than half—but the rest wanted to stomp across the room and slap him silly.

"Katie thinks you were a jerk, huh?" she asked as she turned toward him and stood with arms crossed over her chest and a defiant look on her face. "So do I. But the important thing, Mr. Stafford, is what *you* think."

He sighed and walked into the room. Looking weary and frustrated, he sat on one of the stools beside the examining table. "First, please stop calling me Mr. Stafford. People only call me that when they're mad at me or trying to sell me something. Just call me Michael."

"I'm not trying to *sell* you anything, Mr. Stafford," she said.

"Secondly," he continued, ignoring her subtext, "I agree with my daughter—and with you—or I wouldn't be here. I might buy ice cream on command, but I only apologize when it's from the heart."

He took a deep breath and looked her square in the eyes, causing her pulse to pound hard enough to lower her cholesterol level for six months.

"I was unfair to you yesterday," he said. "I was rude, insensitive and stubborn. I don't blame you for being mad at me. I'm mad at me, too, possibly more than you and Katie combined. To be honest, I was feeling guilty that *I* hadn't taken the time to teach her to swim, that *I* hadn't shown her the swimming hole, that *I* hadn't been there when she was hurt. And I took it out on you. I'm truly sorry. Will you forgive me?"

For a moment she saw that same beguiling expression in his eyes that she had seen in Katie's. And, as with the daughter, she couldn't resist it.

"Yes, all forgiven, all forgotten," she said. "You don't even have to buy me ice cream if you don't want to."

"Oh, no, I *have* to do the ice cream bit or Katie will go on strike and not clean that grungy room of hers for two weeks. How do you feel about banana splits?"

After eating the first third of her ice cream and spending twenty minutes in conversation with Michael Stafford, Rebecca decided that she loved banana splits. Funny, she couldn't recall one tasting this good before.

The ice cream parlor was one of the most charming food establishments in town. Its stained glass lamps gave the dining room a cozy glow. In traditional, turn-of-the-century style, the tables and chairs were ornate filigree of white wrought iron with marble tops. A miniature train circled the room on a narrow shelf just below the copper tiled ceiling, puffing smoke and whistling when it passed the front door.

"This was a good idea," she said, dipping into a bit of whipped cream stained pink from the maraschino cherry juice. "Tell Katie I like it when she takes charge of her father."

"No way. The kid's got me under her control too much already. There's no point in encouraging tyranny."

Rebecca couldn't help noticing, not for the first time, that Michael Stafford had a breathtaking smile. And she couldn't deny the way she felt when he flashed it in her direction. Did he know the effect he had on women? More specifically, on her?

Probably, she decided. Most gorgeous men were all too aware of their attractiveness. Rebecca had never found herself drawn to that type—at least, not for more than a few minutes. She found their vanity diluted their overall appeal.

But Michael didn't seem vain. Guarded, maybe a bit sarcastic at times, deeply hurt, but not conceited.

"Tell me about your business," she said, fishing for an impersonal line of conversation. Her heart seemed to be leading her mind down paths that were best left unexplored.

"We import specialty automobiles from Europe," he said, seeming pleased that she would ask. "Usually, we have an interested customer first, then we use our contacts to locate what they want and bring it in for them. I've been in business for seven years, and I make a pretty decent living at it. What else would you like to know?"

"What do you like best about what you do?" she asked, hoping the answer would tell her something new about this man who kept himself so closed off from the rest of the world.

He thought for a moment before answering. "The challenge, I suppose, of finding exactly the right car, of being able to fulfill a lifelong dream for someone. Many of these people have been saving for years in hopes of owning that one special car. Besides, most of our cars are vintage classics, and some are in really bad condition when we get them. It's wonderful to rescue an old Rolls-Royce Silver Ghost from a scrap pile in Britain and bring it back to life."

"You like to take something old and worn-out and make it young again," she observed. "I wish I could do that for some of my patients. What do you like least?"

"Sometimes I'm not fulfilling a lifetime dream. Some customers are just spoiled and the car is nothing but another expensive toy to them. I still get paid, but it isn't as satisfying."

Silently, Rebecca digested this information. She had thought him a materialistic workaholic, spending long hours in search of the almighty buck. But he didn't seem to care that much about money. So why did he work so hard?

She didn't have to think too long about that one. He threw himself into his work because he was a man running scared. Scared of his own emotions, scared of loving, scared of losing and hurting.

She knew the feeling.

When they had finished their splits, he ordered a cup of coffee for each of them, then settled back to drink it. "Tell me about your work," he said. "What do you like and what do you hate?"

"I suppose it sounds pretty sappy, but I really do love the animals. I enjoy helping them, relieving their pain when I can, preventing it sometimes."

She looked into his eyes to see if he found her silly or overly sentimental. But she saw something unexpected in those blue depths—respect.

"You have that special gift, Dr. Rebecca," he said. "I've always admired someone who has the healing touch. Being a healer, of man or beast, must be a wonderful way to spend your life."

Rebecca started to reply but was interrupted by a buzzing vibration against her ribs. She sighed as she reached down and unsnapped her pager from her belt.

"This," she said as she pressed the button to display the telephone number, "is what I *don't* enjoy about being a vet. I seldom get to eat or sleep without being interrupted at least once."

When she saw the number and the 911 suffix, her heart sank. Instantly, she knew who was calling and why.

"Is something wrong?" Michael asked.

"Yes, I'm afraid so. It's the Rileys, an old couple with an ancient golden retriever named Midas. He hasn't been doing very well lately." She replaced the pager on her belt and grabbed her purse. "They live only a few blocks away. Would you mind terribly dropping me off there? They'll give me a ride home."

"Of course." He tossed some bills onto the table and followed her to the door. "But when I take a lady out—even for ice cream—I also take her home. I'll give you a lift there, but I'll wait while you do your doctoring thing."

"Thank you," she said, grateful for his company. But as they walked across the restaurant parking lot to the Jaguar, she recalled the details of Midas's condition and had some misgivings. "I appreciate your offer, but I don't know if you'll want to be along on this one, Michael. Not all of a vet's stories have happy endings."

He thought for a moment, then nodded solemnly. "I understand. But if it's going to be a difficult call, wouldn't it be easier to have a friend along?"

"Yes," she said, not caring what the implication might be, what a comforting, male presence might mean, how the events of this afternoon might complicate her life. Against her will, she thought of Tim and how much she missed having someone go with her on these difficult calls. "It would make it a lot easier," she heard herself saying. "Thank you, Michael."

Beatrice and Jack Riley had each other, pretty good health for their seventy-plus years, a small house with a rainproof roof, a 1956 Chevrolet that they had bought new and Midas.

In dog years, the golden retriever was older than either of them, and Rebecca had been called out several times in the past few months to address his various aches and ills.

But the last time she had been to the little house on Cleveland Avenue, she had suspected that Midas wasn't long for this world.

Her suspicion was confirmed the moment she stepped through their doorway and saw him lying on his blanket in front of the fireplace. No matter how sick he had been before, he had always rushed to the door to greet her. But now, he simply lay there, the only sign of life his chest barely rising and falling.

Beatrice Riley ushered Rebecca and Michael inside and closed the door behind them. Rebecca briefly introduced Michael to her, then turned her full attention to the dog.

"He seemed kind of under the weather last night," Beatrice said. "More than usual, that is. And this morning, he couldn't get up. He hasn't moved or eaten all day and he's been whimpering constantly. I know he's in pain. That's why I called you."

"Yes, of course, Bea," Rebecca replied. "Don't worry. You did the right thing."

The retriever was lying on his left side, his nose pointed toward the fire. As she knelt beside him on the floor, his tail gave a faint thump of recognition.

"Yes, Midas, it's me," she said, stroking the once beautiful golden coat that had lost its luster. "It's that mean woman who sticks needles and thermometers in you and makes you take rotten-tasting medicines."

Gently, Rebecca ran her hand along his spine, searching for the growth that she had discovered on her last visit. There it was, next to the vertebrae, at least twice the size it had been only a few weeks before.

The dog whined more loudly as she palpated the area around the lump. "I'm sorry, Midas," she said, stroking his ears instead. "I didn't mean to hurt you anymore, old boy. Is it pretty bad? Yes . . . I thought so."

Looking up at Beatrice, Rebecca saw the anxiety, the sorrow in her eyes. Michael stood behind her, wearing a similar expression. They both knew. Rebecca had only to speak the words, but they were the most difficult words she had to utter in the course of her work.

"The tumor has invaded his spine, Bea," she said softly. "That's the reason for his paralysis. There's nothing we can do about that. As I told you before, it's too involved for surgery."

Beatrice said nothing but nodded, her eyes filling with tears.

"Where is Jack?" Rebecca asked, looking around, hoping Bea wouldn't have to endure this experience alone.

"He's gone to Orange County, to visit his sister. She hasn't been feeling well either."

Rebecca wished she could wait for Jack's return, but Midas deserved better than that. "Well, I wish I didn't have to tell you this, but you were right, Midas is in a lot of pain. We have to think about what's best for him. I don't think it's fair to let him go on suffering when we can help him."

"You mean . . . put him down? Now?"

"Yes, that's what I mean. You've given him a wonderful life, he's sixteen years old, and I believe he's finished and ready to leave. We'll just be easing him on his way. It's a very gentle passing, I promise."

Rebecca watched as the fear rose in the woman's eyes. In her years as a veterinarian, Rebecca had found a pet's owner far more afraid of death than the animal.

"I can't," Beatrice said, backing away. "I mean, I'll let you do it, if you think it's best, but I can't watch." She burst into tears. "I'm sorry. I feel like a traitor, but I just can't help you do it."

Rebecca rose, walked over to the woman and put her arms around her. "Please don't feel guilty, Beatrice. Many owners can't watch their pets be put to sleep.

There's no reason to put yourself through it if you'd rather not. I'll take care of it all."

"Will you . . . will you talk to him and pet him when you . . . ?"

"Of course I will."

Michael stepped forward and placed a hand on Beatrice's forearm. "Mrs. Riley, why don't you let me take you out into your backyard. Some fresh air will do you good."

He turned to Rebecca and lowered his voice. "I'll be back in a minute or two to help you."

"Thank you, but I'll be fine. You just take care of Bea for me," she replied, silently blessing him for his compassion.

She waited until she heard the back door close, then she returned to her patient.

Sitting beside him, she slowly, carefully lifted his head into her lap and began to stroke his ears. The big, brown eyes opened for a moment, and she knew, despite the pain, he was enjoying the attention.

She pulled her bag toward her and reached into it for the syringe and necessary medication. Laying her supplies aside, she petted him again, speaking soft, soothing words. "There, there, Midas. It's going to stop hurting very soon. You've been such a good dog, guarding the house all these years, chasing those pesky mailmen and meter readers. You put up with Bea's bunko parties, and Jack's snoring and those noisy grandkids. You fetched all those sticks and took Jack for all those walks. But now your work is done and you get to rest."

Quickly and efficiently, Rebecca administered the necessary dosage. The dog barely even flinched when her needle found the vein. He truly was tired and ready to leave.

Relief came within seconds; Rebecca felt him relax in her arms and his tail thumped once more. She continued to stroke his ears and speak to him until she felt the essence that had been Midas Riley leave the worn-out body.

"How can you stand it?" Michael asked as he turned the Jaguar onto the main highway that led back to Rebecca's home. "How can you deal with that sort of sadness on a regular basis? I wouldn't be able to take it."

He wasn't the first to ask that question; Rebecca had asked her own heart the same thing many times. So she gave him the answer that she had always received.

"Sadness isn't necessarily a bad thing," she said, watching as the landscape swept by her window. "It's just part of the fabric of life. So is death. Souls come into the world, souls leave."

"Are you telling me that Midas is in heaven now?" he asked with a half-sarcastic smirk.

"I don't think he's sitting on a cloud somewhere, sprouting wings and a halo and playing a harp, if that's what you mean. But I've held enough living creatures in my arms at the moment of their deaths, and I do know one thing . . . they leave, they don't just stop."

He was silent for a long time, and she could feel the impact that her words had on him. She wasn't sure why.

Pulling off the highway, he guided the car up the drive to her house. He parked in front and turned off the ignition.

"I wish I could believe you," he said softly, staring straight ahead . . . and into the past.

Rebecca said nothing but waited, knowing that he needed to continue.

"I wasn't there when my wife died." His expression and the tone of his voice suggested that he was making a confession of the most difficult kind. "I left the hospital twenty minutes before . . ."

She noticed that he was gripping the seat with fingers that trembled. Reaching down, she covered his hand with hers. "If you'd known, you would have stayed," she said. "Your wife knew your heart. I'm sure she understood."

"I hope so. Were you there, with your husband when he . . . ?"

"No. He was killed instantly in the accident."

"Does it feel strange to you that you weren't there, that you didn't share something so important with your mate after going through so many other things together?"

"Yes, very strange."

Neither of them spoke as he waited for the flood of emotion to subside. Finally, he said, "How long does it take, Dr. Rebecca, for a heart to heal? At least enough that you can stand the pain?"

"I suppose that depends on the person and the circumstances. But for me, the hurt began to fade when I began to let go of it."

He turned to her, puzzled. "What do you mean? Why would anyone hang on to a pain that hurts so much?"

She shrugged and gave his hand a squeeze. "Maybe to punish themselves because of some sort of misplaced guilt."

Rebecca knew that her words had struck home by the way he winced, then pulled his hand away from hers.

"Thanks for having ice cream with me, Dr. Rebecca," he said, making it clear that he considered the social amenities over. "I'll walk you to your door."

His abrupt dismissal surprised and hurt her. One moment they seemed close, almost friends, but the next instant the intimacy was broken. She felt as though she had reached out to him and he had pushed her away.

"You don't need to escort me," she said as she opened the car door. "It's still daylight. I can find my own way."

"Rebecca, wait," he said, reaching for her. His hand closed around her forearm, his touch imparting his warmth and particular male vitality. "Thank you for what you said. You're right. But I have to think about it before I can . . . you know . . ."

"Yes, of course. I understand."

As Rebecca watched him drive away, she realized that she understood him much better than she wanted to. His heart had suffered a blow from which he would probably never fully recover. So had hers. He was afraid to love that deeply again, to risk losing again. So was she.

And, judging by the look in his eyes when he had told her goodbye, he was terrified that continued contact with her might cause his heart to open up again, might make him vulnerable to loving and maybe losing.

Oh, yes, Rebecca understood all too well. She was terrified, too.

It was always so much easier to see what someone else needed to do, to give advice and expect them to accept it gracefully. But it was quite another to take your own words to heart, she decided as she walked into her house, which seemed more empty, more silent than before.

In spite of all the wonderful things in her life, Rebecca knew there was an emptiness, a void in her heart. It had been there since Tim's death.

The silence . . . the heavy, oppressive silence was always there to remind her of all she had lost.

Her heart didn't seem to be speaking to her much anymore.

Or, maybe, somewhere along the line, she had simply stopped listening.

5

"Well, how did it go? What happened, Daddy? Huh? What did you do? Where did you take her?" Katie bounced up and down on the front porch, unable to wait until her father had entered the house.

"For heaven's sake, kiddo, let me get my foot in the door before you interrogate me."

Katie gave him one of those female know-all-and-see-all looks. Damn, she was good at that and she was only eight. He pitied the poor guy who was to be his son-in-law someday. She propped her hands on her waist and planted her tiny sneakers apart, blocking his entrance.

"Did you guys have another fight?" she demanded. "You did! You were rude to her again, weren't you?"

He slipped his hands under her arms, lifted her and set her aside, out of his way. "No, we didn't have a fight. Good grief, you make it sound like we're heavyweights, going fifteen rounds. I don't *fight* women."

"Were you mean to Dr. Rebecca?" She followed him inside, slamming the door behind her. "Did you yell at her again?"

He reached the living room and collapsed into his favorite easy chair, suddenly exhausted. Patting his knee, he invited his daughter to sit on his lap. He knew he was in trouble when she shook her head. Having always been an affectionate child, Katie never refused the opportunity to cuddle.

"I'll stand, thank you," she said with cool formality and dignity far beyond her years.

He stifled a chuckle. "Katie, I did *not* yell at your dear Dr. Rebecca. I was not rude to her. You will be pleased to hear that I even refrained from chewing my nails, scratching my armpits and picking my nose in front of Dr. Rebecca."

"No burping?" she asked without cracking a smile, hands still on her hips.

"No burping. No bodily expulsions of *any* kind."

She continued to give him the deadpan stare. "I'm so very proud of you," she replied flatly.

"Thank you."

Dropping the indignant act, she climbed happily onto his lap and gave him a hug and a peck on the cheek.

"So, tell me all about it," she said. "I want to know everything. Did you kiss her?"

He drew back and stared at her, eyebrows raised in shock. "Katherine Stafford! How could you suggest such a thing? I'm a gentleman!"

"Nah," she said, pinching his cheek, "just because you didn't burp or pick your nose doesn't make you *that* much of a gentleman. Did you kiss her or not?"

"Not! I took her out for a banana split, and I *didn't* kiss her, didn't serenade her, didn't tango with her in the moonlight, didn't—"

"Okay, okay. Then tell me one more thing, but it has to be the truth. You can't fib at all, promise?"

"Yeah, I guess so. I promise."

"You didn't kiss her, huh?"

"Katie!"

She leaned forward until the tip of her nose was touching his, her blue eyes filling his vision. "Did you *want* to?"

Did he want to?

Hell, yes, he had wanted to. It was all Michael could think about as he sat at his desk the next day, pretending to be working, pretending to be doing anything except fantasizing about Rebecca Barclay.

She had looked so cute, sitting there across from him in the ice cream parlor, a couple of yellow and blue fluffs of feather in her hair, compliments of Frederick the parrot. And later, the kindness she had shown the old dog and his owner had touched Michael's heart, whether he had wanted it to or not.

"Michael, I'm going home now. Michael . . ."

The soft voice reached into his reverie, pulling him back to the present. Mrs. Abernathy stood in his office doorway, purse and keys in hand.

"Oh, yes, good night. See you tomorrow."

She gave him a crooked smile and shook her head. "I don't think so."

"Why? Are you taking the day off? Did I forget your dentist appointment again?"

"No, Michael," she said, "I'm not going to the dentist, because he's taking the day off tomorrow, too. The whole country is taking off. It's Thanksgiving, you nitwit."

Briefly, Michael wondered how he had ever hired an employee who would call him a nitwit to his face. Then he realized she was right. How could he have forgotten Thanksgiving?

"Oh, well sure. I knew that."

She laughed and shook her head. "I assume this means that you and Katie don't have plans for dinner."

"Ah . . . not solid plans."

Her face softened. "I'm sorry, Michael. I'd love to have you come to my house, but I'm not cooking this year. I'm going to visit my daughter in the valley."

"No problem, Abernathy, really. We'll be fine. See you on Monday."

After a couple more apologies, Mrs. Abernathy left, and Michael decided to do the same. Without her there, and with the salesmen and mechanics gone, the place seemed too quiet. Tonight he wasn't in the mood for quiet. Aware now that it was the day before Thanksgiving, he felt more lonely than ever.

Each holiday since his wife's death, he had tried to celebrate with Katie, but it was difficult. Beverly had always done the decorating, the cooking, the shopping, and he had taken her efforts for granted. He didn't seem to have that knack for making occasions special for Katie. Or for himself, either.

A multitude of plans raced through his head as he walked through the elegant showroom with its restored classics, turning lights off and alarms on. Bridget and Neil would be leaving at sunrise tomorrow morning to go to her mother's home in San Francisco. Weeks ago, they had asked for the days off and he had gladly granted them. He had assured Bridget that he would make Thanksgiving dinner plans on his own, that she didn't need to leave a full meal in the refrigerator.

Which left him with a dilemma: What should he do for Katie?

He could take her out to a restaurant, try to cook a bird himself—fat chance he could pull that one off—or get a bucket of chicken somewhere and pretend it was turkey. Maybe he could fake her out with some of those deluxe microwave dinners.

No, she was a little too sharp for that. He could see it now, Katie hauling the empty boxes out of the garbage and shoving them under his nose.

A restaurant was probably the best bet. He wondered what might be open. In this small, family-oriented community, most businesses closed on the holidays.

When he stepped outside the back door, locking it behind him, he heard a strange sound that interrupted his frantic planning session. A tiny, high-pitched whimper, coming from the garage area.

Curious, he took a flashlight from his trunk and followed the sound, trying to find its source. It didn't take long.

There, shivering beneath the Dumpster, was a tiny black puppy. The pup yelped with fright as Michael reached down and picked it up.

"Hey, what are you doing under there? Where's Mom and the other kids?"

Michael looked around but saw no sign of any more dogs. He called out and whistled, but the alley was silent except for the puppy's snuffling against his chest.

"Here you go," he said, tucking the dog inside his jacket. The pup nuzzled its cold nose against him. Its paws and belly were also chilled. Michael realized that if he hadn't found it when he had, the pup would have died. Eyes barely open, it was much too young to be weaned from its mother.

Michael took the puppy to his Jaguar, climbed inside and turned on the heater and the overhead dome lamp.

"Let's take a look at you," he said, pulling the puppy out and examining it. The dog was male and appeared to be a mixed breed, but mostly Labrador. A mutt, perhaps, but handsome, nevertheless. Considering the size of his paws, he was going to grow up to be a big boy, a fine pet and watchdog for someone.

Finding Michael's little finger, the pup latched on to the end, sucking hard in hopes of finding milk

"Sorry, Bruiser," he said, "but you're barking up the wrong tree."

He had to feed him . . . soon. But what? How?

Michael didn't have a clue. But he did know who would, and all he needed was an excuse—any excuse—to see her again.

Whether he could kiss her or not.

Rebecca answered the door, expecting some terrible calamity. Usually, when they came directly to her door, it was an emergency, often an accident with a vehicle.

In the past few years she had grown to hate cars and what they did to innocent animals unfortunate enough to come under their wheels. Those were, by far, the worst cases she had to handle, traumatic for her, the animals and the owners.

But when she had pulled her robe around her and opened the door she found, not some poor mangled cat or dog, but Michael Stafford. He was standing there, whole and handsome, with a giant grin on his face.

"Oh, hi," she mumbled. "I . . . I wasn't expecting you." She tied the robe more tightly, suddenly feeling very underdressed. Beneath the terry cloth, she was wearing only a thin T-shirt and panties, her usual sleeping garb. If she had known he was coming over, she would have put on something more appropriate. Like a satin robe and matching chemise.

Stop that, she thought. *A chemise, indeed.*

"I'm sorry for just dropping by like this," he said. "I suppose I should have called first, but I have a new patient for you."

She glanced down at the ground to see if he were leading something on a leash. "A patient? Where? I don't see anything."

At that moment she heard the distinct whimper of a young puppy, coming from somewhere inside Michael's jacket.

"I've got him in here," he said, pointing to his chest. "He was cold."

"Mmm-hmm . . . I see. You'd better bring him in—sounds serious. I've heard of a hot dog, but a cold pup?"

He groaned. "That was awful, Dr. Rebecca."

"Well, Mr. Stafford," she said, pulling him into the house, "call next time and let me know you're on your way. I'll have someone write me some better material."

Half an hour later, Michael sat on the end of Rebecca's sofa, holding the puppy in his lap, a tiny baby bottle stuck into its puckered mouth. "He's slobbering all over my hand," he said. "It's running down on to my leg."

Rebecca sat at the other end, watching, laughing at Michael's clumsiness. The puppy didn't seem to mind at all as he slurped hungrily at the rubber nipple.

"What am I going to do with him?" he said, dabbing the milk off the pup's face with the soft white towel that Rebecca had given him. "I can't take him home. Katie will claim him right away."

Rebecca shrugged. "Let her have him."

"I'd like to, but she has enough responsibility right now, caring for Rosebud. Rosie is her first pet. I don't want to overload her with too much too fast."

"I understand, but that does leave you with a problem. He's going to need a lot of care, especially for the next few weeks. Middle-of-the-night feedings, all that."

"Not interested in having a dog, are you?" He gave her a beguiling smile and held the puppy out to her. "Here, I'll give him to you for a birthday present. Happy birthday, Rebecca! Don't ever say I never gave you anything."

She laughed and shook her head. "Nice try, but my birthday was four months ago."

"Happy Thanksgiving? Merry Christmas, maybe?"

The puppy was cute and the offer tempting. But Rebecca had learned long ago that she couldn't adopt every cute, four-legged creature that needed a home. "Nope," she said. "You found him. *You* are responsible for him. I'm sure you'll find him an excellent home."

"But how? I'm new in town. I don't know anyone."

"Gee, what a great opportunity to meet your neighbors!"

He scowled at her and raised one eyebrow. "I'm learning something about you, Rebecca Barclay. You are not a nice lady."

"I'm a very nice lady. But I'm not going to puppy-sit for you."

Rebecca enjoyed watching the wheels turning in his head. He was in a difficult position, to be sure, but she didn't intend to help him out of it. So many times she had witnessed the power of a small, whimpery fur ball to melt a heart encased in ice. Nothing broke down the barriers faster than the disarming innocence and charm of a puppy or kitten.

Michael Stafford needed this pup more than the dog needed him, whether he knew it or not. Even if only for a few hours.

"Take him home with you, hide him in your room so that Katie doesn't see him, and by tomorrow morning you'll probably have a great plan."

Michael sighed and tucked the dog back inside his jacket. "Yeah, sure. Tomorrow is Thanksgiving Day. Unless I can truss him up like a turkey, no one is going to be interested."

She stood, handed him a bag full of puppy formula and ushered him to the door.

"Hey, wait a minute! I know what you can do!" she said brightly.

He perked up instantly, gullible and hopeful. "What? What can I do?"

"He's already black. Just stick a white collar on him and pass him off as a pilgrim."

6

Michael hung up the telephone and flopped back on his bed, exhausted. Beneath the covers he could feel a soft wet nose, sniffing at his ankle. The tiny lump under the blanket slowly moved up his pajama leg to his knee.

"Don't tell me . . . you're hungry again?" He reached between the sheets and pulled the pup out by the loose scruff of his neck. He held the animal up to his face and looked him in the eye. "I just fed you at seven, and six, and five, and four, and . . . no wonder I'm tired. I don't remember Katie being this much trouble when we first brought her home."

Michael had to admit that she might have been this difficult, but he wouldn't have known. Those were the old days when he and a lot of other men believed that parenting young children was a pastime only for women. Beverly had been the one to roll out of bed at all hours of the day and night for feedings, changings, fanny pattings and lullabies.

Now, looking back, Michael wasn't particularly proud of his record. He could have helped a bit more. Who was he kidding? He could have helped a *lot* more.

Reaching for the miniature baby bottle, which he had wrapped in a heating pad to keep it warm, he wondered if that had been such a great idea. Last night it had seemed brilliant, but he had been half-asleep. This morning the concept seemed dubious, maybe even dangerous.

"Here you go, Bruiser," he said, popping the nipple into the dog's mouth. "Chugalug. At least *somebody* will get to eat today."

He had spent the past hour on the phone, calling around for a reservation at a restaurant for Thanksgiving dinner. But he had found only three establishments that were open and serving, and they were all booked solid. Even thinly veiled bribes to the maître d' had done no good.

Grocery stores were closed, even the convenience stores. So much for the fancy microwave dinners bit. He was in trouble. Katie wasn't going to take this well at all.

A knock on the door startled him. "Daddy, can I talk to you?"

He pulled the bottle from the puppy's mouth and tucked both it and the dog under the blankets again. "Sure, come on in."

The door opened and Katie appeared, wearing her pajamas, her beautiful black curls tousled. "Whatcha doin'?" she asked, her voice still bed-drowsy.

"Doing? Ah . . . nothing. Why do you ask?"

She gave him a suspicious once-over. "No reason," she said slowly. "I was just making conversation. But now that you mention it, what *are* you doing? You look guilty."

"Guilty? Why would I look guilty?"

The puppy, unhappy about having had his breakfast interrupted, let out a loud squeak. The blanket did little to muffle the protest. Katie's eyes widened, and she was instantly alert.

"What was that?" she said, hurrying to the side of his bed.

"What was what?"

"That noise. It sounded like . . . like . . ."

"I coughed, okay? It came out wrong."

"No way. Not even you can make a sound like that. It's something little. Something cute. I can tell."

She got down on her hands and knees and searched under the bed. Michael used the opportunity to peek beneath the covers and find the pup. Hoping to appease it, he stuck the tip of his finger into its mouth. But the dog had quickly learned the difference between a nipple that would give milk and a finger that wouldn't. He promptly spit it out and began to squeak again.

This time Katie had no problem identifying the source. Michael grabbed her hand just before she yanked back the covers.

"Now, you have to understand, Katie, that we're only baby-sitting. We can't keep this for our own, so don't even think about it. Okay?"

"Okay," she replied, straining to see under the blanket.

"Katie, I mean it. You already have a pet and—"

"Ooo-ooh, it's ado-o-rable!" She lifted the pup gently and kissed the top of his head. "You got me a puppy for Thanksgiving! Thank you, Daddy!"

"No, that's not it at all! I discovered him in the alley behind the showroom last night. I'm going to find a home for him, a really good home, today."

Her face fell, her smile evaporated. "Oh."

He felt like an ogre, the worst father on the face of the earth. But what could he do? With Rosebud, Katie really didn't need a dog. She was too young to take responsibility for both animals, and he was far too busy.

"So," she said, "are we going to take him to his new home before or after we eat our turkey dinner?"

"Turkey dinner . . . ah . . . well . . ."

"We *are* going to have turkey, aren't we, Daddy? And pumpkin pie? We *always* have pumpkin pie. It's my favorite."

"Don't worry, kiddo," he said with far more assurance than he felt. "I have something special planned."

She cocked her head and gave him a scrutinizing look that made him want to crawl under the covers. "Do you really?" she said. "Or did you just forget all about Thanksgiving?"

"Forget? Do you really think I'd forget Thanksgiving?"

She nodded.

"Well," he replied indignantly. "Now I know what you think of *me*. Forget all about Thanksgiving, really. . . ." He reached for the dog and popped the bottle into its perpetually hungry mouth. "Boy, are you going to feel bad when you see what I have planned! Forget, indeed."

She gave him another probing look, then turned and slowly left the room.

Michael groaned. "Bruiser, ol' pal, we've certainly stepped in it this time."

Michael could have sworn the dog gave him a look that was very similar to the one on Katie's face.

"All right, all right," he said with a sigh. "You had nothing to do with it. I'm in there all by myself."

Since the other vets in town had families, Rebecca always offered to be the one on call when a holiday rolled around. Holidays were just like any other day to her, she had decided, and there was no point in depriving others of the opportunity to be with their spouses and children.

Somebody had to be available. Unfortunately, accidents and illnesses didn't take time off just because someone had declared a national holiday.

"Just another day," she whispered as she stood at her living room window, wearing her terry-cloth robe and slippers, and holding her coffee cup.

It would be so easy to simply sit at home, missing Tim, and feeling sorry for herself. But she had learned long ago that handling the situation in that way wasn't to her advantage. If she did, it took her days to crawl up out of her depression. Trial and error had taught her that it was better to avoid slipping down into that emotional mire in the first place.

With a pager, she wasn't confined to the house, but as always, she faced the dilemma of where to go. Stores and amusement facilities were closed. Her friends were visiting with their own families. Tim's relatives and her own lived on the East Coast, too far away to consider dropping by for a turkey drumstick.

"What to do, where to go?" she whispered.

Suddenly, she thought of Michael Stafford and his new charge. How were they getting along? Had they made it through the night?

Of course, they had. But she decided she had to go out to Casa Colina and check on them. After all, it was the only neighborly thing to do.

"Chinese food, for Thanksgiving? *This* is your special surprise? Oh, Daddy, you really blew it this time."

Katie stared down at her chicken chow mein and sweet and sour chicken, both of which Michael had tried in vain to convince her were turkey. The kid had pretty sensitive taste buds and wasn't that easily fooled.

In fact, he didn't believe he had fooled her about anything today. She knew exactly what had happened, and his pretending otherwise had only made the situation worse.

"Come on, kiddo," he said, reaching across the table for her small hand. "It isn't what we eat, is it? Thanksgiving is supposed to be a day when we count our blessings. We can do that whether we're eating turkey, or hamburgers, or chow mein. Right?"

She nodded.

"Then let's think of some things we're thankful for."

"I'm thankful for Rosie, and Mrs. Bridget and Mr. Neil, and you, of course, and Dr. Rebecca."

Michael named off his list which included Katie and all of her favorite people as well as Mrs. Abernathy.

The ritual took less than five minutes, and with the traditional stuff out of the way, Michael was at a loss as to how to proceed with the festivities. Katie was obviously still upset with him, and he wasn't naive enough to think it had anything to do with the lack of pumpkin pie on the table.

Inside his jacket, which he had refused to remove, Bruiser had wakened from his nap and was beginning to wriggle around. Michael certainly hadn't wanted to bring a puppy into a restaurant, but what else could he do? The little guy was too young to be left at home for that long, and the weather had turned chilly, so he couldn't leave him in the car.

Glancing around at the red, black and gold decor, and the tables—all empty, except theirs—Michael felt another rush of shame. He loved his daughter so much. Why hadn't he arranged a traditional Thanksgiving for her? All in all, he considered himself a responsible sort. He never forgot a shipment or delivery date at work. Never. So how could he overlook something like this?

"Daddy," Katie said, "can I ask you something?"

"Sure, kiddo." He braced himself because he could tell by the sadness in her eyes that it was something painful.

"Now that Mom's gone . . ." She paused and swallowed hard. "I guess we're not like a real family anymore, right?"

Braced or not, he was thrown for an emotional loop by her question. He couldn't blame her for asking such a thing, but her words still stung.

"Sure we are, Katie," he replied. "I mean, we aren't the all-American family with a mom and dad, three kids and a dog. But we live together, we love each other, we try to do what's best for each other. I think that makes us a family, even if there's only two of us."

When she didn't reply, he nudged her under the table with his foot. "What do *you* think?"

After a long hesitation, she said, "I don't think we really are, 'cause we don't do the things that a real family does together."

"Like what? Besides eating turkey on Thanksgiving, that is."

"Like going on vacations, going to Disneyland, playing games at home on Saturday night, camping out, you know . . . stuff like that."

"Stuff like we used to do before Mom got sick, right?"

She nodded. "You don't even make your pineapple pancakes on Sunday morning anymore. I really liked those."

Tears welled up in her eyes and seemed to spill over into his. The chow mein was suddenly difficult to swallow.

Pineapple pancakes. He had made them for Beverly on their first weekend together and had won her heart forever. They were a Sunday treat every week for as long as they had been together. Until she had gone to the hospital that last time. He hadn't even thought of them since.

"Katie, I'm so sorry. I can see I have some explaining to do." He thought for a moment, then continued, "What would you do if you found yourself face-to-face with something that really, really frightened you?"

"Something really scary?"

"Well, let's just say it's something that scares *you*."

She bit her lower lip, concentrating, trying to come up with the right answer. "I guess I'd either hide or try to run away."

"Me, too," Michael replied. "When you were born, I thought I was always going to have a wife to help me raise you. I was really worried that I wouldn't be a good dad. But your mom helped me learn, and after a while, I relaxed and began to really enjoy being a father. But then she got sick, and she died, and I was really scared."

"Of what? Of me?"

He laughed softly. "No, sweetheart, not of you. I was afraid I wouldn't do a good job of raising you, of providing a good home for you, of making a real family with you. I love you so much, and I was afraid I would blow it."

"Really?" Her blue eyes showed that she was astonished at this revelation of her father: He was afraid of something, something having to do with her.

"Yes, Katie. I was scared then, and I'm still scared now. I'm afraid I won't do it right, so sometimes I try to hide from it, or run from it. Not very courageous, I'll admit. But . . . do you understand any of this?"

She nodded thoughtfully. "I guess it's like when I was scared to go bowling with Sandra and her friends. I was afraid that I'd do it bad and they'd laugh at me. Is it kinda like that?"

"Kinda, but I care a lot more what you think of me than you do what Sandra thinks of you. Whether or not I do a good job with you is the most important thing in my life. I suppose that's why it's so scary for me."

A small, shy smile brightened Katie's eyes and a corner of his heart. "I don't think you need to be so scared, Daddy," she said. "You're a really good dad. Turkey and pie aren't all that big a deal. I just wanted to know that . . . you know."

"That I love you?"

She nodded and bent her head, staring down at her still full plate.

He reached across the table and cupped her chin in his palm, causing her to look up at him. "Katie Stafford, I couldn't possibly love you more," he said, feeling her chin quiver against his fingers. "But I could be a heck of a lot better at showing it."

At that moment, the restaurant owner appeared, bearing a pot of fresh jasmine tea. With no one else eating in the restaurant, he had apparently sent his staff home and was running the show himself.

"You like food?" he asked, pointing to their plates, which had hardly been touched. "Something wrong?"

"No, nothing's wrong," Katie piped up. "Me and my dad have just been talking about important family stuff."

"I see." He nodded politely as be poured her another cup. "And you, you like food?" he asked Michael.

Michael opened his mouth to answer, but all anyone heard was a distinct and plaintive howl from inside his coat.

He cleared his throat, trying to cover the sound. But the puppy had decided that he had been ignored and imprisoned long enough. With another piteous yowl he demanded to see the warden.

The restaurant owner nearly dropped the teapot. "What that?" he asked, glaring at Michael. "What make that sound?"

"Nothing, nothing important," Michael said, mentally searching for some reasonable excuse. He had never been skilled at making up lies under pressure. Inevitably, the truth always came blurting out before he could think of anything good enough to use.

The dog howled again, even louder than before. Katie gasped and clapped her hand over her mouth to stifle a giggle.

"Animal!" the restaurant owner shouted, his face turning dark with anger. "You have animal in coat!"

"Just one little bitty dog," Michael began, reaching into his jacket. "He isn't hurting anything, he's just—"

"No! No animal! No dog in restaurant! Inspector see dirty dog, take license!" He reached over and snatched both of their chopsticks out of their hands. "Out! You, out of Lee's restaurant with dog!"

Michael's temper soared. "Wait a minute, buddy! We haven't even finished eating yet!"

"You lucky. You no pay. Out!"

A moment later, Michael, Katie and the offending canine stood outside the restaurant as Lee slammed and locked the door behind them.

"I can't believe this," Michael said, shaking his head, "eighty-sixed from a Chinese restaurant. What a Thanksgiving this has turned out to be!"

He looked down, expecting to see Katie's woebegone little face. But, instead, she was snickering, still holding her hand over her mouth.

"Well," she said through her laughter, "it's one we won't forget. Not *ever!*"

Rebecca thought she recognized Michael's car as she turned down Cleveland Avenue. How many dark green Jaguar XJ12s could there be in town?

But why was he heading in that direction, the exact opposite of his home or office?

She decided to follow him and try to get his attention. Soon her question was answered as the Jaguar came to a stop in front of Beatrice and Jack Riley's house.

Of course, she thought as she watched Michael and Katie walk, hand in hand, up to the door. She should have thought of it herself. The Rileys were the perfect couple to adopt the new pup. The dog would do as much to heal their hearts as they would do for him.

"Good choice, Michael," she whispered as she turned her pickup down a side street.

Michael and Katie were doing a kind and generous deed on Thanksgiving Day . . . together . . . and this just wasn't the time to intrude.

Yuletide had arrived in Southern California. But, once again, Rebecca had to rely on the calendar and shop window displays to tell her so, not the weather. Houses strung with colored lights reflected their owners' personalities. Some had been carefully hung with every bulb lit and pointing in the same direction, while others had been tossed haphazardly and with gay abandon on any exterior surface of the house.

A strange weather pattern seemed to have dumped several feet of "real" snow on the rear parking lot of the local mall. Rebecca thought of the massive snows in upstate New York where she had been raised. Gladly, she would have imported a foot or so from her past to the present so that California kids could know what it was like to build an honest-to-goodness snowman.

Four days before Christmas, she was strolling down the center of the mall, looking for those last few gifts. Every year a plethora of goodies arrived on her doorstep from her patients and their grateful owners—everything from chocolates to bubble bath to eight-by-twelve "autographed" photos of various furry and feathered creatures. Rebecca tried to give something in return, even if it was only a new squeaky toy for a dog, a sack of catnip for a feline or a mirror for a parakeet's cage.

She had done well and was considering calling it a day. As she left the mall and walked into the parking lot where a gaggle of children were pelting one another with snowballs, she spotted Beatrice Riley, standing on the sidelines, cheering on her favorites. At her feet on the end of a bright red leash sat the black Labrador puppy. Several of the smaller children had gathered around him and were taking turns petting his glossy head.

"Dr. Rebecca," Beatrice called, waving to her. "Merry Christmas!"

"To you, too," Rebecca replied as she crossed the lot to join her. "My goodness, how that dog has grown in only a few weeks."

"I know. I think that Mr. Stafford of yours lied to me when he said it was a puppy. I'm beginning to think it's a colt! You wouldn't believe how much he eats!"

"He isn't exactly *my* Mr. Stafford," Rebecca said. "He's just a friend."

"Hmm, he certainly thinks a lot of you. Talked about you the whole time he was there . . . the day he gave us the puppy, that is."

Rebecca bent down to pet the dog, trying not to look interested. "Really? What did he say?"

Beatrice's sly smile showed that she hadn't bought the nonchalance routine. "He said you had taught him a lot about letting go after a loss and moving ahead."

"He said that?"

Beatrice nodded. "I didn't want the puppy at first. I didn't want to go through having to put another animal down. That was so hard with Midas."

"I know. He was a member of your family."

"Yes, he was. And I told Mr. Stafford that no one could take Midas's place. But he told me that the puppy wouldn't be a replacement for Midas. He was a new little someone who needed me. Nothing could ever fill the void that Midas had left, but Mr. Stafford showed me that I had enough love in my heart to care for another dog, even if it would mean losing him, too, someday."

"I'm so glad, Beatrice," Rebecca said, patting the woman's back. "Michael was right. This little guy couldn't have found a better home."

After they had, once again, exchanged the season's greetings, Rebecca walked back to the pickup, a lightness in her step that was more than just holiday cheer.

Michael had listened to her after all. And he had heard—with his heart as well as his ears.

People could learn, grow and change. In a season of hope and love, it seemed that miracles were still happening.

"Oh, no! Katie, what have you done to your goat?" Rebecca stood behind Casa Colina, staring at the vision before her: a Nubian nanny goat with something that resembled a small, badly pruned tree tied to her head. Her pink nose had been transformed into a red monstrosity, smeared with crimson lipstick. Around her scrawny neck hung a plastic holly wreath.

Katie stood by, grinning broadly, extremely proud of herself. "It's Christmas Eve," she explained, "and I thought Rosie would make a great reindeer. Daddy helped me make the antlers. Aren't they great?"

Rebecca gulped. "Ah . . . yes . . . wonderful!"

Rosie seemed equally delighted with her new persona. She pranced from one end of the yard to the other, tail wagging, head high.

"Rosie the Reindeer. Now I've seen everything." Rebecca turned her attention back to Katie. "It looks like you are definitely in the Christmas spirit."

"Oh, yeah. Me and Daddy—whoops, my father and I—went out the other night to one of those places where you get to cut down your own Christmas tree. And we found the ornaments and lights and stuff in the garage and put them all on it." She rattled on breathlessly. "Then we went out and bought a new box of really pretty balls, four of them, and I got to pick them. They're pink and purple. And Daddy said we could buy some new ones every year because every Christmas is new and special."

Rebecca smiled. "Your father is a very wise man."

"And we're going to have turkey tomorrow, and dressing and pumpkin pie. Mrs. Bridget gave Daddy lessons on how to make it because she's going to leave tonight to go see her mom."

"Sounds great!" She glanced around, hoping to see some sign of Michael, but his Jaguar was gone. "Is your dad around?" She tried not to sound too eager.

"Nope, he had to go get a can of cranberry sauce. He forgot it the other day. And when he gets back, we're going to go down and listen to the carolers in the park, you know, the ones that hold candles and walk around like this. . . ."

She gave a good impression of one of the dignified and somber chorale members who performed in the candlelight service every Christmas Eve in a small park downtown.

"Are you going to go, Dr. Rebecca? Are you? It's really neat."

"Yes, I had planned to. I know a lot of the people in the choir and I really enjoy hearing the old carols."

"Then maybe we could go together."

A Christmas Eve candlelight service, together, the three of them. Part of Rebecca's heart leapt at the thought, but the other part seized up, paralyzed by fear.

She couldn't do something like that. Never.

Although, at the moment she couldn't recall exactly why.

"I don't think so, Katie," she said, "but thank you for the offer. Here—" She reached into her purse and pulled out a small gift. "I just dropped by to give you something. Actually, it's for Rosie."

"For Rosie? Really?" Her eyes brightened as she unwrapped the bright gold and red paper to find a tiny silver bell.

"It's to go on her collar. All of her relatives back in Switzerland wear them, so I thought she should have one, too."

"Thank you, Dr. Rebecca," the girl said as she rang the bell and delighted in its delicate, silvery tones. "It's bea-uuu-tiful. Come here, Rosie, and see what the doctor brought for you."

A minute later, Rosie pranced by again, prouder than ever, with the tiny bell dangling from her thick, leather collar, tinkling with every step.

"I have to go now, Katie." Rebecca stooped to give her a hug. "Merry Christmas to you and your dad. I'll be thinking of you tomorrow."

"Me, too. I wish you could come over for dinner."

"Thank you, but I'd better stick around the house, in case somebody's dog decides to eat their Christmas tree."

"Ah, you're just teasing. That doesn't really happen."

"You'd be surprised, Katie Stafford. At this time of year, *anything* could happen."

7

Rebecca saw them that night at the candlelight vigil. Michael and Katie stood almost directly across from her as the carolers filed down the road that bisected the park and led to the old mission up the hill. Katie waved furiously, hopping up and down with excitement. Michael simply smiled and mouthed the words, "Merry Christmas."

Lifting her hand, Rebecca gave a quick wave in return, but even that was a tremendous effort.

She knew she should have been touched by the attention. She should have responded with genuine warmth, rather than forced civility, affection rather than fear. What was wrong with her?

Don't do it, her heart told her. *Don't get too close. You know what will happen.*

Yeah, so what's going to happen? she silently asked herself. *You might get to truly know and love a great guy and a fantastic kid. Wouldn't that be a tragedy?*

Yes, her heart replied. *It could be. It was before.*

Rebecca turned and disappeared into the crowd. For the moment, she had enjoyed as much of the holiday season and its beauty, peace and love as she could stand.

Rebecca lay in bed, dreaming that she could hear a ship's horn echoing across a foggy sea. One, two, three deep-throated blasts. Then she realized the sound wasn't that deep. In fact, it was annoyingly shrill.

It wasn't a ship at all. It was the darned telephone.

Another call in the middle of the night.

"Maybe it's Santa," she muttered as she fumbled for the phone, "and his reindeer won't fly. Yes?" she asked, trying to mentally shake herself awake.

"Rebecca, this is Michael Stafford. I know it's Christmas Eve, and I hated to call you, but I'm afraid it can't wait."

She sat up in bed, instantly alert. Even in her half-asleep state she realized that he had called her by her first name without "Doctor" preceding it. And from the worried tone of his voice, she knew that something was very wrong.

"That's okay, Michael," she said. "What's going on?"

"Rosebud is sick. I don't know what's wrong with her, but I think it's bad. Neil and Bridget left this evening for the holidays, and Katie . . . well . . . Katie is terribly upset."

"I'll be right there."

As Rebecca jumped out of bed and threw on her clothes, dread—icy and paralyzing—rose in her chest. With an effort, she pushed it down. This wasn't the time to panic.

"Not Rosie, not on Christmas Eve," she whispered as she hurried out the door and climbed into her truck. "Please, not Rosie. Katie really needs her."

The child had lost too much already. Even a heart as buoyant as hers would have a difficult time bouncing back from another tragedy so soon after the last. Rebecca was determined to do everything she could to make certain that didn't happen.

She only prayed her efforts would be enough.

The moment Rebecca entered the stable, she saw that Rosebud was even worse than she had expected. She lay on her side, bleating pitifully, Rebecca's bell still attached to her collar, smudges of lipstick still staining her nose.

As she knelt beside Michael in the straw and examined her patient, Rebecca's heart sank. The little goat's stomach was badly swollen and she was obviously in a lot of pain.

"What's wrong with her?" Katie said, as tears ran down her cheeks. "Is she going to die?"

Rebecca wanted to tell her everything was going to be fine, as she had before, but she wouldn't lie to the child. This time she wasn't sure at all. She didn't even know what was wrong.

She asked the usual questions, and Katie and Michael supplied the appropriate answers, but none of those replies gave her the information she needed.

Quickly Rebecca ran the symptoms through her head, trying to match them with an illness or injury that she had studied.

"Wait a minute," she said at last. "Do you still have avocado trees on the property? Back there behind the grape arbor?"

Katie and Michael looked at each other and nodded in unison.

"Could Rosebud have eaten any of the leaves today after I was here?" Rebecca asked Katie.

"Well . . . when we went to the park to hear the choir, I left her in the backyard. I guess she could have eaten some then."

"I need to know for sure," Rebecca said.

Michael jumped to his feet. "I'll check," he said.

A moment later he returned, holding a half-eaten avocado and some munched leaves. "I'm afraid you were right," he said. "Is that bad?"

Rebecca couldn't bring herself to tell them that she had lost several horses this way. Avocado leaves were deadly for animals. She felt sick with guilt. Why hadn't she warned Katie before about the avocados?

"The problem is—Rosie can't digest the leaves," she told them. "They say a goat can eat anything, and that's true . . . almost. But even a goat's stomach can't handle avocado leaves."

"What can we do?" Michael asked.

"We have to help her get rid of them," Rebecca said, "even if it takes all night."

"How do we do that?" Katie asked.

Rebecca smiled down at the girl. "You may think this is silly," she said, "but the old-fashioned way is the best. Do you guys have a turkey baster?"

"A *turkey baster?*" Michael asked. "Yes, Bridget just showed me how to use it the other day."

"Good, that's what I need."

"I'll go get it."

Rebecca rolled up her sleeves, then reached down to touch the little red nose as she waited for Michael to return. "Poor baby," she said. "I guess Santa will have to make his run without Rosie the Reindeer tonight."

"Do you really think this is going to help?" Michael asked as be watched Rebecca fill the baster again with a mixture of mineral oil and milk of magnesia. Gently he held the nanny's mouth open as Rebecca squeezed it in. Rosie swallowed weakly, then began to cry again.

For the past five hours they had been taking turns giving her the medicine. But so far, there had been no results.

"I don't know yet," Rebecca said, laying the baster aside and sitting in the straw beside the goat. "If we can just get enough into her, it may all work out . . . in the end," she added, pointing to Rosie's tail.

"A bad pun, Dr. Rebecca," Michael said with a tired smile as he sank onto the hay next to her.

"Hey, at six o'clock in the morning that's as good as it gets."

Rebecca looked over at Katie, who was sleeping in the corner, curled into a ball in the straw. Michael's leather jacket was draped over her small shoulders.

"She finally gave it up, huh?" Rebecca said.

"Yes, and I'm glad," Michael replied. "There was no reason for her to be up all night worrying. A hell of a way for a kid to spend Christmas Eve."

He gazed at the child for a long time, then he turned back to Rebecca. "You were right. I am afraid I'm going to lose her, too. I wake up in the middle of the night, sweating, worrying about it."

Rebecca nodded. "I'm not surprised, considering all that's happened to you. I felt the same way after Tim's accident, but as time passed it got easier. It will for you, too."

"Do you think so?" He looked at her with a light of hope in his blue eyes that were so much like his daughter's.

"Yes, I promise. The first two years are the worst. Then it gets easier."

Michael ran his hand over the kid's swollen belly. Rebecca noticed that his fingers were shaking slightly, and her heart went out to him. She wondered how she could ever have considered him cold and uncaring.

"When I think of Beverly," he said, "I only remember her death . . . the fact that I wasn't there. I remember the last time I saw her. She was so sick and helpless—she didn't even know me. Beverly was always a strong, proud woman. She wouldn't want me to remember her that way. *I* don't want to think of her that way."

"Time will help you with that, too," Rebecca said, laying a comforting hand on his broad shoulder. "The day will come when you'll remember her life—the happy times, her strength, her laughter, her beauty—more than the sad circumstances of her death."

To her surprise, he reached out, grabbed her by the shoulders and pulled her to him. For a long time, he held her tightly against his chest, his face buried in her hair, saying nothing.

Her arms went around his waist, and she allowed herself the wonderful luxury of melting into another human being. The embrace was the first intimate contact she had experienced since before Tim's death. And she couldn't believe how much she needed it or how good it felt to hold someone and to be held in return.

Finally, he released her and she was shocked to see the depth of emotion in his eyes. What she saw there was a mirror image of what she was feeling.

"You've done so much for us, Rebecca, for *me,*" he said as his hand slipped lightly down her cheek. His fingertips were so warm, so gentle as he brushed a stray curl away from her temple. "In the time I've known you, you've shown me how important it is to reach out to others."

After a quick glance at his sleeping daughter, he leaned toward her and tenderly kissed her cheek. The sensations of acute desire and equally sharp fear shot through her at the contact. Suddenly, she felt as though she couldn't breathe, couldn't speak.

"I want to reach out to you, Rebecca," he said. His fingers twined in the hair at the nape of her neck, sending shivers of pleasures down her back. "If I do . . . if I find the courage to reach out . . . will you be there?"

A hundred replies raced through Rebecca's mind as she sat there in the straw, looking into the eyes of a man she could easily love. A man she already loved. Her heart could only allow her to give one reply, "Michael . . . I—"

Her words were cut off by a loud bleat as Rosie began to thrash around, struggling to stand.

"Hey, hey," Rebecca said, setting issues of romance aside for the moment, "this looks promising."

"Here," he said, rising from his seat on the straw, "let me help her up."

Carefully, he lifted the nanny, his arms under her belly and supported her for a minute or so. When he released her, she stood on wobbly legs, but, shaky or not, she *was* standing. And that was what mattered at the moment.

"Now we wait again," Rebecca said. "She seems to be ready to do something."

A few minutes later, the medicine had finally worked, and the little animal had rid herself of most of her burden. She wasn't crying any longer, and her tiny tail had even begun to wag a bit.

"What a good girl!" Rebecca said. She dropped to her knees and hugged the goat around the neck. "Your mistress will be so proud of you when she wakes up."

"Should I tell her?" Michael said, nodding toward Katie.

"I wouldn't yet," Rebecca said. "In another hour or two, Rosie will be feeling even better and ready to celebrate Christmas. Why don't you let Katie sleep until then."

Michael walked over to his daughter and tucked the jacket more snugly around her shoulders and neck. "You were right about something else," he said. "Even if I lose Katie someday, I wouldn't have missed having her in my life. She's given me so much joy."

"I can imagine," Rebecca said.

"I was so afraid to love her the way I had her mother," he said. "But just look at her. How could I help it?"

Rebecca smiled. "I know what you mean. She has a beautiful spirit. I fell in love with her right away."

"Well, that feeling seems to be mutual," he said. "All the way around."

His eyes met hers and the affection she saw there went straight to her heart, bringing a rush of happiness, quickly followed by the ever-present wave of anxiety.

It never went away completely . . . the fear of loving . . . of losing.

But something in his eyes gave her the courage to push it away. At least for the moment. She stood and looked out the window at the sun, which was rising in a cloudless sky. "Merry Christmas, Michael," she said.

"Merry Chr—" He gasped. "Oh, no! Santa hasn't come! And he's spent the past month shopping and buying decorations and food to try to make up for the Thanksgiving Day Massacre."

She laughed and waved a hand toward the door. "Go, see to it that Santa takes care of business. We're fine here."

"Gee, thanks for reminding me." He hurried to the door. "Boy, if I'd blown this one, I'd have been on Katie's bad side for the next ten years."

"Katie?" a small voice piped up from the corner. "Somebody call me?"

Michael groaned. "Too late. I'm dead."

Katie sprang up from her bed in the straw, looking sleepy and tired, but delighted. "Rosebud!" she shouted. "You're standing! You're not crying anymore!"

She threw her father's jacket aside and ran to her pet. The goat's tail began to wag as she nuzzled her mistress.

"You made her well!" the child cried as she hugged the animal. "Dr. Rebecca, you fixed her! Thank you! Thank you *so* much!"

"You're welcome, Katie," Rebecca replied. "But I couldn't have done it alone. I had a lot of help." She nodded toward Michael.

Katie glowed with pride as she looked at her father. Clearly he had risen to the status of "Hero Extraordinaire" in her eyes. She bounded over to him and threw her arms around his waist. "Thanks, Daddy," she said. "This is the *best* Christmas present in the world!"

"You're welcome, kiddo." He returned her hug, then tugged on one of her curls. "But, speaking of Christmas . . ." He paused to clear his throat. "You see, Katie, I've been so busy with Rosebud, that I . . . I didn't . . . I haven't had the chance to . . ."

"Let me guess," she said, rolling her eyes heavenward, "the guy with the beard hasn't shown up, right?"

"Uh . . . I haven't been in the house yet, but I strongly suspect you're right."

Katie's eyes softened as she looked up at her father, then at Rosebud, who was becoming more like her frisky self by the moment.

"It isn't important, Daddy," she said. "Rosie's all that really matters. You made her better, and that's what I care about." She paused. "Rosie and pumpkin pie, that is."

Michael laughed and kissed the top of his daughter's head. "Katie, I'll have you know there are *three* pumpkin pies in that refrigerator and gobs of whipped cream to go on them. There's a great big turkey—which I'd better get into the oven—dressing, cranberry sauce, the works. You can eat and eat to your voracious little stomach's delight."

"You won't want to overdo it," Rebecca warned, "or you'll end up like Rosebud and we'll have to chase you around with a turkey baster full of mineral oil."

"Oo-ooo, yuck."

"I have a better suggestion," Michael said, walking over to the corner to retrieve his jacket. "I was just about to ask Rebecca if she wants to have pancakes with us this morning."

"Really?" Katie's smile grew even wider. "Your special pancakes?"

"With pineapple and pecans and maple syrup," he said, looking at Rebecca. "Then, of course, you're invited to hang around for my first, experimental Christmas dinner. No guarantees."

"Sounds great!" she agreed. "I accept."

Katie hurried over to Rebecca and motioned for her to lean down. Placing her lips against her ear, the girl whispered, "He doesn't make his special pancakes for just anybody. I think he really likes you."

"Hmm . . . that's nice," was all Rebecca could say. She felt the blood rushing to her cheeks, turning them nearly as red as the lipstick on Rosie's nose.

"What are you two whispering about?" Michael asked.

"Nothing." Katie giggled and gave Rosebud a hug. "I'll go put the syrup in the microwave," she told Rebecca. "That's *my* job when he makes pancakes."

She bounded away and out the door, running and skipping toward the house.

"Thanks for making me look good with the kid," he said when Katie was out of earshot.

"No problem," she replied. "But I do charge more for that. It'll be on my bill."

"So, I'll owe you, huh, Doc?" He lifted one eyebrow.

"Big time."

He held his hand out to her, a look of affection and apprehension in his eyes. She knew what the gesture symbolized.

"I'm here, Michael," she said, giving him her heart's answer. She took his hand and squeezed it. "Right here."

A second later she was in his arms again, but this time it wasn't a hug between friends; it was a lovers' embrace.

His kiss was warm, soft and gentle, but it conveyed a depth of passion that surprised and thrilled her. Feelings, long dormant, rose and spread deliciously through her body, reminding her that she was still very much a woman.

He gave her another, and then another. She didn't even think of resisting. Why should she, when it felt so natural, so right?

Finally, when both of them were breathless, he led her and Rosebud out of the stable and over to the goat's pen. "Considering the size of my debt," he said, carefully securing the gate, "I might have to pay you off in pancakes."

Again, he took her hand and escorted her toward the house.

"Pineapple pancakes . . . huh?" She bit her bottom lip, contemplating the offer.

"Maybe every Sunday morning for the rest of your life . . . if you like pancakes that much."

She held on to his hand, afraid that she was going to fall off this whirling carousel of happiness any moment. "I like pancakes," she said. "Actually, I love them."

He paused in the middle of the lawn to give her another kiss.

"What about Katie?" she asked, nodding toward the house with its many windows.

"She's going to figure it out pretty quick anyway," he said before he gave her another one that made her weak in the knees.

"Okay," she said, struggling for breath, "the pancakes sound great. Let's call it a down payment."

−1995

CRITICAL BIBLIOGRAPHY

Anderson, Rachel. *The Purple Heart Throbs: The Sub-Literature of Love*. London: Hodder and Stoughton, 1974.

Baym, Nina. *Woman's Fiction: A Guide to Novels By and About Women in America, 1820–1870*. Ithaca: Cornell UP, 1978.

Brown, Herbert Ross. *The Sentimental Novel in America, 1789–1860*. Durham: Duke UP, 1940.

Cecil, Mirabel. *Heroines in Love, 1750–1974*. London: Michael Joseph, 1974.

Cornillion, Susan Koppelman, ed. *Images of Women in Fiction: Feminist Perspectives*. Bowling Green: BGSU Popular P, 1972.

Falk, Kathryn. *How to Write a Romance and Get It Published: With Intimate Advice from the World's Most Popular Romantic Writers*. New York: Crown, 1983.

Fallon, Eileen. *Love's Leading Ladies*. New York: Pinnacle, 1982.

——. *Words of Love: A Complete Guide to Romance Fiction*. New York: Garland, 1984.

Frenier, Mariam Darce. *Good-Bye Heathcliff: Changing Heroes, Heroines, Roles, and Values in Women's Category Romances*. New York: Greenwood, 1988.

Hardwick, Elizabeth. *Seduction and Betrayal: Women and Literature*. New York: Random House, 1974.

Hazen, Helen. *Endless Rapture: Rape, Romance, and the Female Imagination*. New York: Scribner's, 1983.

Henderson, Lesley, ed. *Twentieth-Century Romance and Historical Writers*. 2nd Edition. Chicago: St. James Press, 1990.

Juhasz, Suzanne. *Reading from the Heart: Women, Literature, and the Search for True Love*. New York: Viking, 1994.

Kiely, Robert. *The Romantic Novel in England*. Cambridge: Harvard UP, 1972.

Krentz, Jayne Ann, ed. *Dangerous Men and Adventurous Women: Romance Writers on the Appeal of the Romance*. Philadelphia: U of Pennsylvania P, 1992.

Mann, Peter H. *The Romantic Novel: A Survey of Reading Habits*. London: Mills and Boon, 1969.

Modleski, Tania. *Loving with a Vengeance: Mass Produced Fantasies for Women*. Hamden: Archon Books, 1982.

Moers, Ellen. *Literary Women*. Garden City: Doubleday, 1976.

Mussell, Kay. *Fantasy and Reconciliation: Contemporary Formulas of Women's Romance Fiction*. Westport: Greenwood, 1984.

——. *Women's Gothic and Romantic Fiction: A Reference Guide*. Westport: Greenwood, 1981.

Radcliffe, Elsa J. *Gothic Novels of the Twentieth Century: An Annotated Bibliography*. Metuchen: Scarecrow Press, 1979.

Radway, Janice A. *Reading the Romance: Women, Patriarchy, and Popular Literature*. Chapel Hill: U of North Carolina P, 1984.

Showalter, Elaine. *The Female Tradition in the English Novel: From Charlotte Brontë to Doris Lessing*. Princeton: Princeton UP, 1976.

Thurston, Carol. *The Romance Revolution: Erotic Novels for Women and the Quest for a New Sexual Identity*. Urbana: U of Illinois P, 1987.

Vasudevan, Aruna, ed. *Twentieth-Century Romance and Historical Writers*. 3rd ed. Detroit: St. James Press, 1994.

Weibel, Kathryn. *Mirror, Mirror: Images of Women Reflected in Popular Culture*. Garden City: Doubleday Anchor, 1977.

3

SCIENCE FICTION

Noted critic and author of science fiction, Brian W. Aldiss, argues in what is perhaps the finest book-length study of the genre, *Billion Year Spree: The True History of Science Fiction* (1973), that science fiction found its origins in Gothic literature. Aldiss defines science fiction, in the broadest terms, as humanity's search in the universe for definition and knowledge (or science). Specifically, Aldiss cites Mary Shelley's classic Gothic thriller *Frankenstein; or, The Modern Prometheus* (1818) as the first major science fiction work. Certainly, Shelley's dark tale about Victor Frankenstein's god-like quest to create a new form of "human" life, and the subsequent disasters that befall him after he brings to life his monster, expresses as had no other story of the time a distrust of an unbridled passion for "forbidden" knowledge and of vainglorious scientists. Indeed, whether the young Shelley realized it or not, she wrote the first (and best) dystopian science fiction adventure. Her novel spoke to a generation fearful of the rapid industrialization of British society and the advent of perplexing new technologies.

Since the publication of *Frankenstein*, the larger genre of science fiction has generally divided itself into two major categories—utopian science fiction and dystopian science fiction—each attempting to confront or explain the benefits and the consequences of the Industrial Revolution. Much of the science fiction published in the late nineteenth century and early twentieth century, for example, regarded the acquisition of scientific knowledge and the development of new technology as being highly desirable, while science fiction published after the Second

World War (and following the development of the atom bomb) perceived scientific knowledge as being potentially destructive, and thus problematic.

The writers of the so-called scientific romance, led by the popular nineteenth-century French author, Jules Verne, frequently duplicated the scientific process itself in their speculative fiction, by constructing a thesis as the focus of their narrative, and then extrapolating the results of their thesis during the course of the story. This type of science fiction generally asked: "What if?" Jules Verne articulated the "What if?" question in his science fiction novel, *Vingt mille lieues sous les mers* (1869-1870; translated as *Twenty Thousand Leagues Under the Sea):* "What would happen if a ship could be built to navigate the ocean's depths?" Verne's contemporary, the British writer H. G. Wells, also asked the "What if?" question: "What would happen if a person invented a time machine that could travel to the future?" His answer appeared in his science fiction novel *The Time Machine: An Invention* (1895), a tale that presents a bleak vision of a far distant time when people are divided into two sub-human groups, the docile Eloi and the brutish Morlocks. Indeed, Wells alerted readers to the dire consequences of technology (which can be simply defined as the application of scientific knowledge) in his science fiction, even as Verne promoted in his science fiction the opportunities that technology can provide.

As seen in these two classic tales, science fiction may view science (and the various representations of science in the past, present, and future) either as something wonderful (the magnificence of Frankenstein's achievement in the creation of his monster) or as something terrible (the horror resulting from Frankenstein's violation of Nature's laws). Therefore, to illustrate further this point, science fiction can show us a utopian future in which technology can benefit our lives, in stories like Isaac Asimov's charming "Robbie" (1940), or show us a dystopian future in which technology may harm us, in tales like William Gibson's chilling "Johnny Mnemonic" (1981).

Science fiction is popular, then, because it defines for its readers both the opportunities and the problems of living in a post-industrial, technological society. Science fiction can also isolate and discuss (in a unique way) certain fundamental issues of our existence—such concerns as the quality of courage, the conflict between life and death, and our search for identity. These are the reasons why the "epic" narrative works so well as science fiction. Isaac Asimov's Foundation novels, for example, are among the most popular and critically acclaimed science fiction adventures of all time, because Asimov offers us a technological reworking of the archetypal journey found in our classic literature—a journey that begins in ancient times in the wooden ships of Homer's *The Odyssey,* and that progresses in our contemporary science fiction to magnificent spaceships traveling to distant stars.

The following selection includes the work of some of the most popular and influential authors of science fiction. From Mary Shelley's "The Mortal Immortal," to Jules Verne's "An Express of the Future," to H. G. Wells's "The Star," the evolution of science fiction in Europe during the nineteenth century is well represented by these three seminal authors. And from the early decades of the twentieth century, C. L. Moore's "Shambleau" offers a superior example of American pulp magazine science fiction. Because of stories like Isaac Asimov's "Robbie," Robert A. Heinlein's "Space Jockey," and Ray Bradbury's "Usher II," science fiction, as a literary genre, achieved critical legitimation during the 1940s and 1950s. The "New Wave" revolution of the 1960s is exemplified by Harlan Ellison's "'Repent, Harlequin!' Said the Ticktockman" and Samuel R. Delany's "Time Considered as a Helix of Semi-Precious Stones."

Ursula K. Le Guin's "Vaster Than Empires and More Slow" epitomizes that period in the evolution of science fiction when women were beginning to claim equal authorship of the genre with their male counterparts, while William Gibson's "Johnny Mnemonic" and Octavia E. Butler's "Speech Sounds" typify the current prosperous state of the genre.

MARY SHELLEY

1797-1851

Mary Wollstonecraft Shelley is often credited with inventing the science fiction story in her famous Gothic thriller, Frankenstein; or, The Modern Prometheus *(1818). Certainly,* Frankenstein *articulated, as had no story before it, both the wonder and the fear associated with discovering previously uncharted realms of knowledge. Indeed, Shelley's novel became a powerful Faustian metaphor for the Industrial Revolution in Europe, a cautionary tale that warned against the unfettered and radical development of new science and technology. Shelley's portrayal of Victor Frankenstein's subversion of natural order in his quest to create artificial human life provided a compelling dystopian view of the limitations of human ambition.*

Mary Shelley was born in London, England, to William Godwin, a prominent intellectual who was a defender of the underprivileged, and Mary Wollstonecraft, an advocate for women's rights. Wollstonecraft died shortly after giving birth to her daughter, Mary, and Godwin later remarried. Although the young Mary received no formal schooling, she was provided with a home that supported reading and intellectual development. In 1814, she fell in love with a friend of her father's, Percy Bysshe Shelley. Even though Percy was married at the time, Mary eloped with him, traveling to France, Switzerland, Germany, and Holland along with Jane Clairmont, the daughter of Mary's stepmother. This experience became the basis for her book, History of a Six Weeks' Tour *(1817). Upon her return to England, Shelley found herself the target of gossip and controversy. Personal tragedy also plagued her. Her half-sister, Fanny Imlay, committed suicide, as did Percy's wife, Harriet Westbrook Shelley. In addition, Mary's infant daughter, Clara, died in 1818, and her young son, William, died in 1819. Following Harriet's death, Percy legally married Mary in 1816, but he perished in a boating accident in the Gulf of Spezia just before his thirtieth birthday, thus adding to Mary's growing list of misfortunes. When she returned to England in 1823, she discovered herself to be something of a literary sensation. Her first novel,* Frankenstein, *was being dramatized, and her second novel, a historical romance entitled* Valperga: or, The Life and Adventures of Castruccio, Prince of Lucca *(1823), was gathering an interested readership. Her third novel,* The Last Man *(1826)—which is set during the twenty-first century and recounts how humanity is laid waste by a worldwide plague— became another important contribution to the early development of speculative fiction. Following Percy's death, Shelley remained a widow the remainder of her life.*

Shelley's "The Mortal Immortal," first published in 1834, continues the theme she first explored in Frankenstein: *the notion that dire consequences await those who thirst for an artificial or supernatural power that resides beyond human limitations.*

THE MORTAL IMMORTAL

July 16, 1833—This is a memorable anniversary for me; on it I complete my three hundred and twenty-third year!

The Wandering Jew?—certainly not. More than eighteen centuries have passed over his head. In comparison with him, I am a very young Immortal.

Am I, then, immortal? This is a question which I have asked myself, by day and night, for now three hundred and three years, and yet cannot answer it. I detected a grey hair amidst my brown locks this very day—that surely signifies decay. Yet it may have remained concealed there for three hundred years—for some persons have become entirely whiteheaded before twenty years of age.

I will tell my story, and my reader shall judge for me. I will tell my story, and so contrive to pass some few hours of a long eternity, become so wearisome to me. Forever! Can it be? to live forever! I have heard of enchantments, in which the victims were plunged into a deep sleep, to awake, after a hundred years, as fresh as ever: I have heard of the Seven Sleepers—thus to be immortal would not be so burdensome: but, oh! the weight of never-ending time—the tedious passage of the still-succeeding hours! How happy was the fabled Nourjahad!—But to my task.

All the world has heard of Cornelius Agrippa. His memory is as immortal as his arts have made me. All the world has also heard of his scholar, who, unawares, raised the foul fiend during his master's absence, and was destroyed by him. The report, true or false, of this accident, was attended with many inconveniences to the renowned philosopher. All his scholars at once deserted him—his servants disappeared. He had no one near him to put coals on his ever-burning fires while he slept, or attend to the changeful colors of his medicines while he studied. Experiment after experiment failed, because one pair of hands was insufficient to complete them: the dark spirits laughed at him for not being able to retain a single mortal in his service.

I was then very young—very poor—and very much in love. I had been for about a year the pupil of Cornelius, though I was absent when this accident took place. On my return, my friends implored me not to return to the alchemist's abode. I trembled as I listened to the dire tale they told; I required no second warning; and when Cornelius came and offered me a purse of gold if I would remain under his roof, I felt as if Satan himself tempted me. My teeth chattered—my hair stood on end—I ran off as fast as my trembling knees would permit.

My failing steps were directed whither for two years they had every evening been attracted—a gently bubbling spring of pure living water, beside which lingered a dark-haired girl, whose beaming eyes were fixed on the path I was accustomed each night to tread. I cannot remember the hour I did not love Bertha; we had been neighbors and playmates from infancy—her parents, like mine, were of humble life, yet respectable—our attachment had been a source of pleasure to them. In an evil hour, a malignant fever carried off both her father and mother, and Bertha became an orphan. She would have found a home beneath my paternal roof, but, unfortunately, the old lady of the near castle, rich, childless, and solitary, declared her intention to adopt her. Henceforth Bertha was clad in silk—inhabited a marble palace—and was looked on as being highly favored by fortune. But in her new situation among her new associates, Bertha remained true to the friend of her humbler days; she often visited the cottage of my father, and when forbidden to go thither, she would stray towards the neighboring wood, and meet me beside its shady fountain.

She often declared that she owed no duty to her new protectress equal in sanctity to that which bound us. Yet still I was too poor to marry, and she grew weary of being tormented on my account. She had a haughty but an impatient spirit, and grew angry at the obstacles that prevented our union. We met now after an absence, and she had been sorely beset while I was away; she complained bitterly, and almost reproached me for being poor. I replied hastily,—

"I am honest, if I am poor!—were I not, I might soon become rich!"

This exclamation produced a thousand questions. I feared to shock her by owning the truth, but she drew it from me; and then casting a look of disdain on me, she said,—

"You pretend to love, and you fear to face the Devil for my sake!"

I protested that I had only dreaded to offend her;—while she dwelt on the magnitude of the reward that I should receive. Thus encouraged—shamed by her—led on by love and hope, laughing at my late fears, with quick steps and a light heart, I returned to accept the offers of the alchemist, and was instantly installed in my office.

A year passed away. I became possessed of no insignificant sum of money. Custom had banished my fears. In spite of the most painful vigilance, I had never detected the trace of a cloven foot; nor was the studious silence of our abode ever disturbed by demoniac howls. I still continued my stolen interviews with Bertha, and Hope dawned on me—Hope—but not perfect joy: for Bertha fancied that love and security were enemies, and her pleasure was to divide them in my bosom. Though true of heart, she was somewhat of a coquette in manner; and I was jealous as a Turk. She slighted me in a thousand ways, yet would never acknowledge herself to be in the wrong. She would drive me mad with anger, and then force me to beg her pardon. Sometimes she fancied that I was not sufficiently submissive, and then she had some story of a rival, favored by her protectress. She was surrounded by silk-clad youths—the rich and gay. What chance had the sad-robed scholar of Cornelius compared with these?

On one occasion, the philosopher made such large demands upon my time, that I was unable to meet her as I was wont. He was engaged in some mighty work, and I was forced to remain, day and night, feeding his furnaces and watching his chemical preparations. Bertha waited for me in vain at the fountain. Her haughty spirit fired at this neglect; and when at last I stole out during the few short minutes allotted to me for slumber, and hoped to be consoled by her, she received me with disdain, dismissed me in scorn, and vowed that any man should possess her hand rather than he who could not be in two places at once for her sake. She would be revenged! And truly she was. In my dingy retreat I heard that she had been hunting, attended by Albert Hoffer. Albert Hoffer was favored by her protectress, and the three passed in cavalcade before my smoky window. Methought that they mentioned my name; it was followed by a laugh of derision, as her dark eyes glanced contemptuously towards my abode.

Jealousy, with all its venom and all its misery, entered my breast. Now I shed a torrent of tears, to think that I should never call her mine; and, anon, I imprecated a thousand curses on her inconstancy. Yet, still I must stir the fires of the alchemist, still attend on the changes of his unintelligible medicines.

Cornelius had watched for three days and nights, nor closed his eyes. The progress of his alembics was slower than he expected: in spite of his anxiety, sleep weighed upon his eyelids. Again and again he threw off drowsiness with more than human energy; again and again it stole away his senses. He eyed his crucibles wistfully. "Not ready yet," he murmured; "will another night pass before the work is accomplished? Winzy, you are vigilant—you are faithful—you have slept, my boy—you slept last night. Look at that glass vessel. The liquid it contains is of a soft rose-color: the moment it begins to change its hue, awaken me—till then I may close my eyes. First, it will turn white; and then emit golden flashes; but wait not till then; when the rose-color fades, rouse me." I scarcely heard the last words, muttered, as they were, in sleep. Even then he did not quite yield to nature. "Winzy, my boy," he again said, "do not touch the vessel—do not put it to your lips; it is a philter—a philter to cure love; you would not cease to love your Bertha—beware to drink!"

And he slept. His venerable head sunk on his breast, and I scarce heard his regular breathing. For a few minutes I watched the vessels—the rosy hue of the liquid remained unchanged. Then my thoughts wandered—they visited the fountain, and dwelt on a thousand charming scenes never to be renewed—never! Serpents and adders were in my heart as the word "Never!" half formed itself on my lips. False girl! False and cruel! Nevermore would she smile on me as that evening she smiled on Albert. Worthless, detested woman! I would not remain unrevenged—she should see Albert expire at her feet—she should die beneath my vengeance. She had smiled in disdain and triumph—she knew my wretchedness and her power. Yet what power had she?—the power of exciting my hate—my utter scorn—my—oh, all but indifference! Could I attain that—could I regard her with careless eyes, transferring my rejected love to one fairer and more true, that were indeed a victory!

A bright flash darted before my eyes. I had forgotten the medicine of the adept; I gazed on it with wonder: flashes of admirable beauty, more bright than those which the diamond emits when the sun's rays are on it, glanced from the surface of the liquid; an odor the most fragrant and grateful stole over my sense; the vessel seemed one globe of living radiance, lovely to the eye, and most inviting to the taste. The first thought, instinctively inspired by the grosser sense, was, I will—I must drink. I raised the vessel to my lips. "It will cure me of love—of torture!" Already I had quaffed half of the most delicious liquor ever tasted by the palate of man, when the philosopher stirred. I started—I dropped the glass—the fluid flamed and glanced along the floor, while I felt Cornelius's grip at my throat, as he shrieked aloud, "Wretch! you have destroyed the labor of my life!"

The philosopher was totally unaware that I had drunk any portion of his drug. His idea was, and I gave a tacit assent to it, that I had raised the vessel from curiosity, and that, frightened at its brightness, and the flashes of intense light it gave forth, I had let it fall. I never undeceived him. The fire of the medicine was quenched—the fragrance died away—he grew calm, as a philosopher should under the heaviest trials, and dismissed me to rest.

I will not attempt to describe the sleep of glory and bliss which bathed my soul in paradise during the remaining hours of that memorable night. Words would be faint and shallow types of my enjoyment, or of the gladness that possessed my bosom when I woke. I trod air—my thoughts were in heaven. Earth appeared heaven, and my inheritance upon it was to be one trace of delight. "This is to be cured of love," I thought; "I will see Bertha this day, and she will find her lover cold and regardless; too happy to be disdainful, yet how utterly indifferent to her!"

The hours danced away. The philosopher, secure that he had once succeeded, and believing that he might again, began to concoct the same medicine once more. He was shut up with his books and drugs, and I had a holiday. I dressed myself with care; I looked in an old but polished shield, which served me for a mirror; methought my good looks had wonderfully improved. I hurried beyond the precincts of the town, joy in my soul, the beauty of heaven and earth around me. I turned my steps towards the castle—I could look on its lofty turrets with lightness of heart, for I was cured of love. My Bertha saw me afar off, as I came up the avenue. I know not what sudden impulse animated her bosom, but at the sight, she sprung with a light fawn-like bound down the marble steps, and was hastening toward me. But I had been perceived by another person. The old high-born hag, who called herself her protectress, and was her tyrant, had seen me also; she hobbled, panting, up the terrace; a page, as ugly as herself, held up her train, and fanned her as she hurried along, and stopped my fair girl with a "How, now, my bold mistress? Whither so fast? Back to your cage—hawks are abroad!"

Bertha clasped her hands—her eyes were still bent on my approaching figure. I saw the contest. How I abhorred the old crone who checked the kind impulses of my Bertha's softening heart. Hitherto, respect for her rank had caused me to avoid the lady of the castle; now I disdained such trivial consideration. I was cured of love, and lifted above all human fears; I hastened forwards, and soon reached the terrace. How lovely Bertha looked! Her eyes flashing fire, her cheeks glowing with impatience and anger, she was a thousand times more graceful and charming than ever. I no longer loved—oh no! I adored—worshiped—idolized her!

She had that morning been persecuted, with more than usual vehemence, to consent to an immediate marriage with my rival. She was reproached with the encouragement that she had shown him—she was threatened with being turned out of doors with disgrace and shame. Her proud spirit rose in arms at the threat; but when she remembered the scorn that she had heaped upon me, and how, perhaps, she had thus lost one whom she now regarded as her only friend, she wept with remorse and rage. At that moment I appeared. "Oh, Winzy!" she exclaimed, "take me to your mother's cot; swiftly let me leave the detested luxuries and wretchedness of this noble dwelling—take me to poverty and happiness."

I clasped her in my arms with transport. The old dame was speechless with fury, and broke forth into invective only when we were far on our road to my natal cottage. My mother received the fair fugitive, escaped from a gilt cage to nature and liberty, with tenderness and joy; my father, who loved her, welcomed her heartily; it was a day of rejoicing, which did not need the addition of the celestial potion of the alchemist to steep me in delight.

Soon after this eventful day, I became the husband of Bertha. I ceased to be the scholar of Cornelius, but I continued his friend. I always felt grateful to him for having, unawares, procured me that delicious draught of a divine elixir, which, instead of curing me of love (sad cure! solitary and joyless remedy for evils which seem blessings to the memory), had inspired me with courage and resolution, thus winning for me an inestimable treasure in my Bertha.

I often called to mind that period of trance-like inebriation with wonder. The drink of Cornelius had not fulfilled the task for which he affirmed that it had been prepared, but its effects were more potent and blissful than words can express. They had faded by degrees, yet they lingered long—and painted life in hues of splendor. Bertha often wondered at my lightness of heart and unaccustomed gaiety; for, before, I had been rather serious, or even sad, in my disposition. She loved me the better for my cheerful temper, and our days were winged by joy.

Five years afterwards I was suddenly summoned to the bedside of the dying Cornelius. He had sent for me in haste, conjuring my instant presence. I found him stretched on his pallet, enfeebled even to death; all of life that yet remained animated his piercing eyes, and they were fixed on a glass vessel, full of a roseate liquid.

"Behold," he said, in a broken and inward voice, "the vanity of human wishes! A second time my hopes are about to be crowned, a second time they are destroyed. Look at that liquor—you remember five years ago I prepared the same, with the same success—then, as now, my thirsting lips expected to taste the immortal elixir—you dashed it from me! And at present it is too late."

He spoke with difficulty, and fell back on his pillow. I could not help saying,—

"How, revered master, can a cure for love restore you to life?"

A faint smile gleamed across his face as I listened earnestly to his scarcely intelligible answer.

"A cure for love and for all things—the Elixir of Immortality. Ah! if now I might drink, I should live forever!"

As he spoke, a golden flash gleamed from the fluid; a well-remembered fragrance stole over the air; he raised himself, all weak as he was—strength seemed miraculously to reenter his frame—he stretched forth his hand—a loud explosion startled me—a ray of fire shot up from the elixir, and the glass vessel which contained it was shivered to atoms! I turned my eyes towards the philosopher; he had fallen back—his eyes were glassy—his features rigid—he was dead!

But I lived, and was to live forever! So said the unfortunate alchemist, and for a few days I believed his words. I remembered the glorious intoxication that had followed my stolen draught. I reflected on the change I had felt in my frame—in my soul. The bounding elasticity of the one—the buoyant lightness of the other. I surveyed myself in a mirror, and could perceive no change in my features during the space of the five years which had elapsed. I remembered the radiant hues and grateful scent of that delicious beverage—worthy the gift it was capable of bestowing—I was, then IMMORTAL!

A few days after I laughed at my credulity. The old proverb, that "a prophet is least regarded in his own country," was true with respect to me and my defunct master. I loved him as a man—I respected him as a sage—but I derided the notion that he could command the powers of darkness, and laughed at the superstitious fears with which he was regarded by the vulgar. He was a wise philosopher, but had no acquaintance with any spirits but those clad in flesh and blood. His science was simply human; and human science, I soon persuaded myself, could never conquer nature's laws so far as to imprison the soul forever within its carnal habitation. Cornelius had brewed a soul-refreshing drink—more inebriating than wine—sweeter and more fragrant than any fruit: it possessed probably strong medicinal powers, imparting gladness to the heart and vigor to the limbs; but its effects would wear out; already were they diminished in my frame. I was a lucky fellow to have quaffed health and joyous spirits, and perhaps long life, at my master's hands; but my good fortune ended there: longevity was far different from immortality.

I continued to entertain this belief for many years. Sometimes a thought stole across me—Was the alchemist indeed deceived? But my habitual credence was, that I should meet the fate of all the children of Adam at my appointed time—a little late, but still at a natural age. Yet it was certain that I retained a wonderfully youthful look. I was laughed at for my vanity in consulting the mirror so often, but I consulted it in vain—my brow was untrenched—my cheeks—my eyes—my whole person continued as untarnished as in my twentieth year.

I was troubled. I looked at the faded beauty of Bertha—I seemed more like her son. By degrees our neighbors began to make similar observations, and I found at last that I went by the name of the Scholar bewitched. Bertha herself grew uneasy. She became jealous and peevish, and at length she began to question me. We had no children; we were all in all to each other; and though, as she grew older, her vivacious spirit became a little allied to ill-temper, and her beauty sadly diminished, I cherished her in my heart as the mistress I had idolized, the wife I had sought and won with such perfect love.

At last our situation became intolerable: Bertha was fifty—I twenty years of age. I had, in very shame, in some measure adopted the habits of a more advanced age; I no longer mingled in the dance among the young and gay, but my heart bounded along with them while I restrained my feet; and a sorry figure I cut among the Nestors of our village. But before the time I mentioned, things were altered—we were universally shunned; we were—at least, I was—reported to have kept up an iniquitous acquaintance with some of my former master's supposed friends. Poor Bertha was pitied, but deserted. I was regarded with horror and detestation.

What was to be done? We sat by our winter fire—poverty had made itself felt, for none would buy the produce of my farm; and often I had been forced to journey twenty miles, to some place where I was not known, to dispose of our property. It is true, we had saved something for an evil day—that day was come.

We sat by our lone fireside—the old-hearted youth and his antiquated wife. Again Bertha insisted on knowing the truth; she recapitulated all she had ever heard said about me, and added her own observations. She conjured me to cast off the spell; she described how much more comely grey hairs were than my chestnut locks; she descanted on the reverence and respect due to age—how preferable to the slight regard paid to mere children: could I imagine that the despicable gifts of youth and good looks outweighed disgrace, hatred, and scorn? Nay, in the end I should be burnt as a dealer in the black art, while she, to whom I had not deigned to communicate any portion of my good fortune, might be stoned as my accomplice. At length she insinuated that I must share my secret with her, and bestow on her like benefits to those I myself enjoyed, or she would denounce me—and then she burst into tears.

Thus beset, methought it was the best way to tell the truth. I revealed it as tenderly as I could, and spoke only of a *very long life,* not of immortality—which representation, indeed, coincided best with my own ideas. When I ended, I rose and said,—

"And now, my Bertha, will you denounce the lover of your youth? You will not, I know. But it is too hard, my poor wife, that you should suffer from my ill-luck and accursed arts of Cornelius. I will leave you—you have wealth enough, and friends will return in my absence. I will go; young as I seem, and strong as I am, I can work and gain my bread among strangers, unsuspected and unknown. I loved you in youth; God is my witness that I would not desert you in age, but that your safety and happiness require it."

I took my cap and moved towards the door; in a moment Bertha's arms were round my neck, and her lips were pressed to mine. "No, my husband, my Winzy," she said, "you shall not go alone—take me with you; we will remove from this place, and, as you say, among strangers we shall be unsuspected and safe. I am not so very old as quite to shame you, my Winzy; and I daresay the charm will soon wear off, and, with the blessing of God, you will become more elderly-looking, as is fitting; you shall not leave me."

I returned the good soul's embrace heartily. "I will not, my Bertha; but for your sake I had not thought of such a thing. I will be your true, faithful husband while you are spared to me, and do my duty by you to the last."

The next day we prepared secretly for our emigration. We were obliged to make great pecuniary sacrifices—it could not be helped. We realized a sum sufficient, at least, to maintain us while Bertha lived; and, without saying adieu to any one, quitted our native country to take refuge in a remote part of western France.

It was a cruel thing to transport poor Bertha from her native village, and the friends of her youth, to a new country, new language, new customs. The strange secret of my destiny rendered this removal immaterial to me; but I compassioned her deeply, and was glad to perceive that she found compensation for her misfortunes in a variety of little ridiculous circumstances. Away from all telltale chroniclers, she sought to decrease the apparent disparity of our ages by a thousand feminine arts—rouge, youthful dress, and assumed juvenility of manner. I could not be angry. Did not I myself wear a mask? Why quarrel with hers, because it was less successful? I grieved deeply when I remembered that this was my Bertha, whom I had loved so fondly and won with such transport—the dark-eyed, dark-haired girl, with smiles of enchanting archness and a step like a fawn—this mincing, simpering, jealous old woman. I should have revered her grey locks and withered cheeks; but thus! It was my work, I knew; but I did not the less deplore this type of human weakness.

Her jealousy never slept. Her chief occupation was to discover that, in spite of outward appearances, I was myself growing old. I verily believe that the poor soul loved me truly in her heart, but never had woman so tormenting a mode of displaying fondness. She would discern wrinkles in my face and decrepitude in my walk, while I bounded along in youthful vigor, the youngest-looking of twenty youths. I never dared address another woman. On one occasion, fancying that the belle of the village regarded me with favoring eyes, she brought me a grey wig. Her constant discourse among her acquaintances was, that though I looked so young, there was ruin at work within my frame; and she affirmed that the worst symptom about me was my apparent health. My youth was a disease, she said, and I ought at all times to prepare, if not for a sudden and awful death, at least to awake some morning white-headed and bowed down with all the marks of advanced years. I let her talk—I often joined in her conjectures. Her warnings chimed in with my never-ceasing speculations concerning my state, and I took an earnest, though painful, interest in listening to all that her quick wit and excited imagination could say on the subject.

Why dwell on these minute circumstances? We lived on for many long years. Bertha became bedridden and paralytic; I nursed her as a mother might a child. She grew peevish, and still harped upon one string—of how long I should survive her. It has ever been a source of consolation to me, that I performed my duty scrupulously towards her. She had been mine in youth, she was mine in age; and at last, when I heaped the sod over her corpse, I wept to feel that I had lost all that really bound me to humanity.

Since then how many have been my cares and woes, how few and empty my enjoyments! I pause here in my history—I will pursue it no further. A sailor without rudder or compass, tossed on a stormy sea—a traveler lost on a widespread heath, without landmark or stone to guide him—such have I been: more lost, more hopeless than either. A nearing ship, a gleam from some far cot, may save them; but I have no beacon except the hope of death.

Death! Mysterious, ill-visaged friend of weak humanity! Why alone of all mortals have you cast me from your sheltering fold? Oh, for the peace of the grave! The deep silence of the iron-bound tomb! That thought would cease to work in my brain, and my heart beat no more with emotions varied only by new forms of sadness!

Am I immortal? I return to my first question. In the first place, is it not more probable that the beverage of the alchemist was fraught rather with longevity than eternal life? Such is my hope. And then be it remembered, that I only drank *half* of the potion prepared by him. Was not the whole necessary to complete the charm? To have drained half the Elixir of Immortality is but to be half-immortal—my Forever is thus truncated and null.

But again, who shall number the years of the half of eternity? I often try to imagine by what rule the infinite may be divided. Sometimes I fancy age advancing upon me. One grey hair I have found. Fool! Do I lament? Yes, the fear of age and death often creeps coldly into my heart; and the more I live, the more I dread death, even while I abhor life. Such an enigma is man—born to perish—when he wars, as I do, against the established laws of his nature.

But for this anomaly of feeling surely I might die: the medicine of the alchemist would not be proof against fire—sword—and the strangling waters. I have gazed upon the blue depths of many a placid lake, and the tumultuous rushing of many a mighty river, and have said, peace inhabits those waters; yet I have turned my steps away, to live yet another day. I have asked myself, whether suicide would be a crime in one to whom thus only the portals of the other world could be opened. I have done all, except presenting myself as a soldier or duelist, an objection of destruction to my—no *not* my fellow-mortals, and therefore I have shrunk away. They are not my fellows. The inextinguishable power of life in my frame, and their ephemeral existence, places us wide as the poles asunder. I could not raise a hand against the meanest or the most powerful among them.

Thus I have lived on for many a year—alone, and weary of myself—desirous of death, yet never dying—a mortal immortal. Neither ambition nor avarice can enter my mind, and the ardent love that gnaws at my heart, never to be returned—never to find an equal on which to expend itself—lives there only to torment me.

This very day I conceived a design by which I may end all—without self-slaughter, without making another man a Cain—an expedition, which mortal frame can never survive, even endued with the youth and strength that inhabits mine. Thus I shall put my immortality to the test, and rest forever—or return, the wonder and benefactor of the human species.

Before I go, a miserable vanity has caused me to pen these pages. I would not die, and leave no name behind. Three centuries have passed since I quaffed the fatal beverage; another year shall not elapse before, encountering gigantic dangers—warring with the powers of frost in their home—beset by famine, toil, and tempest—I yield this body, too tenacious a cage for a soul which thirsts for freedom, to the destructive elements of air and water; or, if I survive, my name shall be recorded as one of the most famous among the sons of men; and, my task achieved, I shall adopt more resolute means; and, by scattering and annihilating the atoms that compose my frame, set at liberty the life imprisoned within, and so cruelly prevented from soaring from this dim earth to a sphere more congenial to its immortal essence.

—1834

JULES VERNE
1828-1905

No other author had as important an influence on the development of science fiction during the late nineteenth and early twentieth centuries as did the French writer, Jules Verne. Verne was born in Nantes, France, to a father who was an attorney and a mother who was related to an important ship-owning family. As a child, Verne did well with his studies, which included music and classical languages. But, his greatest obsessions were the sea and machines, two passions that would later manifest themselves in his science fiction. Verne's father wanted him to pursue a career in law, and, in 1848, he began his legal studies in Paris. Verne, however, felt he was ill-suited to be a lawyer. His imaginative nature, coupled with his flair for the literary, eventually led him to his career as a writer. Verne's early work involved poetry, some short fiction, and drama composed for the French theater, where he found modest success. He then turned to writing short stories and scientific sketches for periodicals. His first novel, Cinq Semaines en ballon: Voyages de découvertes en Afrique *(1863; translated as* Five Weeks in a Balloon, *1869), led him to a category of popular fiction (which Verne himself helped to invent) that blended adventure with scientific speculation. Verne called this new literary genre the "novel of science," a type of story that eventually became one of the foundations of modern science fiction. Verne's most famous novels of science include* Voyage au centre de la Terre *(1864; translated as* A Journey to the Center of the Earth, *1872),* De La terre à la lune: Trajet direct en 97 heures *(1865; translated as* From the Earth to the Moon, *1869), and* Vingt Mille Lieues sous les mers *(1869–1870; translated as* Twenty Thousand Leagues Under the Sea, *1873). Collectively, Verne's prolific body of work—his* Voyages extraordinaires, *published between 1863 and 1910—was unmatched by any other author of the period in charting the terrain of nineteenth century speculative fiction.*

"An Express of the Future," published in the January 1895 issue of the Strand Magazine, *illustrates Verne's fascination with technology and the extrapolation of known science. This brief tale's "surprise" ending, though it is somewhat contrived, also illustrates an ironically practical side to Verne's perceptions of the limitations of known science.*

An Express of the Future

"Take care!" cried my conductor, "there's a step!"

Safely descending the step thus indicated to me, I entered a vast room, illuminated by blinding electric reflectors, the sound of our feet alone breaking the solitude and silence of the place.

Where was I? What had I come there to do? Who was my mysterious guide? Questions unanswered. A long walk in the night, iron doors opened and reclosed with a clang, stairs descending, it seemed to me, deep into the earth—that is all I could remember. I had, however, no time for thinking.

"No doubt you are asking yourself who I am?" said my guide: "Colonel Pierce, at your service. Where are you? In America, at Boston—in a station."

"A station?"

"Yes, the starting-point of the 'Boston to Liverpool Pneumatic Tubes Company.'"

And, with an explanatory gesture, the Colonel pointed out to me two long iron cylinders, about a metre and a half in diameter, lying upon the ground a few paces off.

I looked at these two cylinders, ending on the right in a mass of masonry, and closed on the left with heavy metallic caps, from which a cluster of tubes were carried up to the roof; and suddenly I comprehended the purpose of all this.

Had I not, a short time before, read, in an American newspaper, an article describing this extraordinary project for linking Europe with the New World by means of two gigantic submarine tubes? An inventor had claimed to have accomplished the task; and that inventor, Colonel Pierce, I had before me.

In thought I realized the newspaper article.

Complaisantly the journalist entered into the details of the enterprise. He stated that more than 3,000 miles of iron tubes, weighing over 13,000,000 tons, were required, with the number of ships necessary, for the transport of this material—200 ships of 2,000 tons, each making thirty-three voyages. He described this Armada of science bearing the steel to two special vessels, on board of which the ends of the tubes were joined to each other, and incased in a triple netting of iron, the whole covered with a resinous preparation to preserve it from the action of the seawater.

Coming at once to the question of working, he filled the tubes—transformed into a sort of pea-shooter of interminable length—with a series of carriages, to be carried with their travellers by powerful currents of air, in the same way that despatches are conveyed pneumatically round Paris.

A parallel with the railways closed the article, and the author enumerated with enthusiasm the advantages of the new and audacious system. According to him, there would be, in passing through these tubes, a suppression of all nervous trepidation, thanks to the interior surface being of finely polished steel; equality of temperature secured by means of currents of air, by which the heat could be modified according to the seasons; incredibly low fares, owing to the cheapness of construction and working expenses—forgetting, or waving aside, all considerations of the question of gravitation and of wear and tear.

All that now came back to my mind.

So, then, this "Utopia" had become a reality, and these two cylinders of iron at my feet passed thence under the Atlantic and reached to the coast of England!

In spite of the evidence, I could not bring myself to believe in the thing having been done. That the tubes had been laid I could not doubt; but that men could travel by this route—never!

"Was it not impossible even to obtain a current of air of that length?"—I expressed that opinion aloud.

"Quite easy, on the contrary!" protested Colonel Pierce; "to obtain it, all that is required is a great number of steam fans similar to those used in blast furnaces. The air is driven by them with a force which is practically unlimited, propelling it at the speed of 1,800 kilometres an hour—almost that of a cannon-ball!—so that our carriages with their travellers, in the space of two hours and forty minutes, accomplish the journey between Boston and Liverpool."

"Eighteen hundred kilometres an hour!" I exclaimed.

"Not one less. And what extraordinary consequences arise from such a rate of speed! The time at Liverpool being four hours and forty minutes in advance of ours, a traveller starting from Boston at nine o'clock in the morning, arrives in England at 3.53 in the afternoon. Isn't that a journey quickly made? In another sense, on the contrary, our trains, in this latitude, gain over the sun more than 900 kilometres an hour, beating that planet hand over hand: quitting Liverpool at noon, for example, the traveller will reach the station where we now are at thirty-four minutes past nine in the morning—that is to say, earlier than he started! Ha! ha! I don't think one can travel quicker than *that!*"

I did not know what to think. Was I talking with a madman?—or must I credit these fabulous theories, in spite of the objections which rose in my mind?

"Very well, so be it!" I said. "I will admit that travellers may take this madbrained route, and that you can obtain this incredible speed. But, when you have got this speed, how do you check it? When you come to a stop, everything must be shattered to pieces!"

"Not at all," replied the Colonel, shrugging his shoulders. "Between our tubes— one for the out; the other for the home journey—consequently worked by currents going in opposite directions—a communication exists at every joint. When a train is approaching, an electric spark advertises us of the fact; left to itself, the train would continue its course by reason of the speed it had acquired; but, simply by the turning of a handle, we are able to let in the opposing current of compressed air from the parallel tube, and, little by little, reduce to nothing the final shock or stopping. But what is the use of all these explanations? Would not a trial be a hundred times better?"

And, without waiting for an answer to his questions, the Colonel pulled sharply a bright brass knob projecting from the side of one of the tubes: a panel slid smoothly in its grooves, and in the opening left by its removal I perceived a row of seats, on each of which two persons might sit comfortably side by side.

"The carriage!" exclaimed the Colonel. "Come in."

I followed him without offering any objection, and the panel immediately slid back into its place.

By the light of an electric lamp in the roof I carefully examined the carriage I was in.

Nothing could be more simple: a long cylinder, comfortably upholstered, along which some fifty arm-chairs, in pairs, were ranged in twenty-five parallel ranks. At either end a valve regulated the atmospheric pressure, that at the farther end allowing breathable air to enter the carriage, that in front allowing for the discharge of any excess beyond a normal pressure.

After spending a few moments on this examination, I became impatient.

"Well," I said, "are we not going to start?"

"Going to start?" cried the Colonel. "We *have* started!"

Started—like that—without the least jerk, was it possible? I listened attentively, trying to detect a sound of some kind that might have guided me.

If we had really started—if the Colonel had not deceived me in talking of a speed of eighteen hundred kilometres an hour—we must already be far from any land, under the sea; above our heads the huge, foam-crested waves; even at that moment, perhaps—taking it for a monstrous sea-serpent of an unknown kind—whales were battering with their powerful tails our long, iron prison!

But I heard nothing but a dull rumble, produced, no doubt, by the passage of our carriage, and, plunged in boundless astonishment, unable to believe in the reality of all that had happened to me, I sat silently, allowing the time to pass.

At the end of about an hour a sense of freshness upon my forehead suddenly aroused me from the torpor into which I had sunk by degrees.

I raised my hand to my brow: it was moist.

Moist! Why was that? Had the tube burst under pressure of the waters—a pressure which could not but be formidable, since it increases at the rate of "an atmosphere" every ten metres of depth? Had the ocean broken in upon us?

Fear seized upon me. Terrified, I tried to call out—and—and I found myself in my garden, generously sprinkled by a driving rain, the big drops of which had awakened me. I had simply fallen asleep while reading the article devoted by an American journalist to the fantastic projects of Colonel Pierce—who also, I much fear, has only dreamed.

—1895

H . G . WELLS
1866-1946

Herbert George Wells was born in Bromley, Kent, England, to a working-class family enduring financial hardships. His father's shop, for example, never made a substantial income, and his mother labored as a domestic housekeeper to help make ends meet when his father's health deteriorated. Wells, himself, served as an apprentice at several different trades, but by age sixteen he began attending the Midhurst Grammar School, where he enjoyed considerable success with his studies. In 1884, Wells received a scholarship to the Normal School of Science in South Kensington, London. During this period, he nurtured a growing interest in writing, contributing work to the student magazine, The Science School Journal. *Wells left school in 1887 (without receiving a degree) and began a career in teaching. His first job was at a private school in Wales. However, because of serious health problems, he did not hold this position for very long. Wells then taught at Henley House School close to London. After he received his college degree in 1890, he worked as a tutor for the University Correspondence College, publishing two textbooks in 1893. Wells soon discovered success as a writer of short stories, sketches, book reviews, and scientific articles. He published his first major science fiction novel,* The Time Machine: An Invention, *in 1895. Some of Wells's best speculative fiction appeared over the next several years:* The Island of Doctor Moreau *(1896),* The Invisible Man: A Grotesque Romance *(1897),* The War of the Worlds *(1898), and* The First Men in the Moon *(1901). In fact, in just half a decade, he established a reputation as a leading author of science fiction, rivaling that of the French master, Jules Verne. Wells went on to publish many books on a wide range of topics, from philosophy and politics to history, but most critics consider his greatest work to be his early "scientific romances."*

"The Star," first appearing in the 1897 Christmas issue of The Graphic *and anthologized in the collection* Tales of Space and Time *(1899), was published during Wells's most productive period as a science fiction writer. It is an apocalyptic tale describing the near-destruction of the earth. "The Star" anticipates a number of later end-of-the-world science fiction classics, such as Edwin Balmer's and Philip Wylie's* When Worlds Collide *(1933).*

THE STAR

It was on the first day of the new year that the announcement was made, almost simultaneously from three observatories, that the motion of the planet Neptune, the outermost of all the planets that wheel about the sun, had become very erratic. Ogilvy had already called attention to a suspected retardation in its velocity in December. Such a piece of news was scarcely calculated to interest a world the greater portion of whose inhabitants were unaware of the existence of the planet Neptune, nor outside the astronomical profession did the subsequent discovery of a faint remote speck of light in the region of the perturbed planet cause any very great excitement. Scientific people, however, found the intelligence remarkable enough, even before it became known that the new body was rapidly growing larger and brighter, that its motion was quite different from the orderly progress of the planets, and that the deflection of Neptune and its satellite was becoming now of an unprecedented kind.

Few people without a training in science can realise the huge isolation of the solar system. The sun with its specks of planets, its dust of planetoids, and its impalpable comets, swims in a vacant immensity that almost defeats the imagination. Beyond the orbit of Neptune there is space, vacant so far as human observation has penetrated, without warmth or light or sound, blank emptiness, for twenty million times a million miles. That is the smallest estimate of the distance to be traversed before the very nearest of the stars is attained. And, saving a few comets more unsubstantial than the thinnest flame, no matter had ever to human knowledge crossed this gulf of space, until early in the twentieth century this strange wanderer appeared. A vast mass of matter it was, bulky, heavy, rushing without warning out of the black mystery of the sky into the radiance of the sun. By the second day it was clearly visible to any decent instrument, as a speck with a barely sensible diameter, in the constellation Leo near Regulus. In a little while an opera glass could attain it.

On the third day of the new year the newspaper readers of two hemispheres were made aware for the first time of the real importance of this unusual apparition in the heavens. "A Planetary Collision," one London paper headed the news, and proclaimed Duchaine's opinion that this strange new planet would probably collide with Neptune. The leader writers enlarged upon the topic. So that in most of the capitals of the world, on January 3rd, there was an expectation, however vague, of some imminent phenomenon in the sky; and as the night followed the sunset round the globe, thousands of men turned their eyes skyward to see—the old familiar stars just as they had always been.

Until it was dawn in London and Pollux setting and the stars overhead grown pale. The Winter's dawn it was, a sickly filtering accumulation of daylight, and the light of gas and candles shone yellow in the windows to show where people were astir. But the yawning policeman saw the thing, the busy crowds in the markets stopped agape, workmen going to their work betimes, milkmen, the drivers of news-carts, dissipation going home jaded and pale, homeless wanderers, sentinels on their beats, and in the country, labourers trudging afield, poachers slinking home, all over the dusky quickening country it could be seen—and out at sea by seamen watching for the day—a great white star, come suddenly into the westward sky!

Brighter it was than any star in our skies; brighter than the evening star at its brightest. It still glowed out white and large, no mere twinkling spot of light, but a small round clear shining disc, an hour after the day had come. And where science has not reached, men stared and feared, telling one another of the wars and pestilences that are foreshadowed by these fiery signs in the Heavens. Sturdy Boers, dusky Hottentots, Gold Coast Negroes, Frenchmen, Spaniards, Portuguese, stood in the warmth of the sunrise watching the setting of this strange new star.

And in a hundred observatories there had been suppressed excitement, rising almost to shouting pitch, as the two remote bodies had rushed together, and a hurrying to and fro, to gather photographic apparatus and spectroscope, and this appliance and that, to record this novel astonishing sight, the destruction of a world. For it was a world, a sister planet of our earth, far greater than our earth indeed, that had so suddenly flashed into flaming death. Neptune it was, had been struck, fairly and squarely, by the strange planet from outer space and the heat of the concussion had incontinently turned two solid globes into one vast mass of incandescence. Round the world that day, two hours before the dawn, went the pallid great white star, fading only as it sank westward and the sun mounted above it. Everywhere men marvelled at it, but of all those who saw it none could have marvelled more than those sailors, habitual watchers of the stars, who far away at sea had heard nothing of its advent and saw it now rise like a pigmy moon and climb zenithward and hang overhead and sink westward with the passing of the night.

And when next it rose over Europe everywhere were crowds of watchers on hilly slopes, on house-roofs, in open spaces, staring eastward for the rising of the great new star. It rose with a white glow in front of it, like the glare of a white fire, and those who had seen it come into existence the night before cried out at the sight of it. "It is larger," they cried. "It is brighter!" And, indeed the moon a quarter full and sinking in the west was in its apparent size beyond comparison, but scarcely in all its breadth had it as much brightness now as the little circle of the strange new star.

"It is brighter!" cried the people clustering in the streets. But in the dim observatories the watchers held their breath and peered at one another. *"It is nearer,"* they said. *"Nearer!"*

And voice after voice repeated, "It is nearer," and the clicking telegraph took that up, and it trembled along telephone wires, and in a thousand cities grimy compositors fingered the type. "It is nearer." Men writing in offices, struck with a strange realisation, flung down their pens, men talking in a thousand places suddenly came upon a grotesque possibility in those words, "It is nearer." It hurried along awakening streets, it was shouted down the frost-stilled ways of quiet villages; men who had read these things from the throbbing tape stood in yellow-lit doorways shouting the news to the passers-by. "It is nearer." Pretty women, flushed and glittering, heard the news told jestingly between the dances, and feigned an intelligent interest they did not feel. "Nearer! Indeed. How curious! How very, very clever people must be to find out things like that!"

Lonely tramps faring through the wintry night murmured those words to comfort themselves—looking skyward. "It has need to be nearer, for the night's as cold as charity. Don't seem much warmth from it if it *is* nearer, all the same."

"What is a new star to me?" cried the weeping woman kneeling beside her dead.

The schoolboy, rising early for his examination work, puzzled it out for himself—with the great white star, shining broad and bright through the frost-flowers of his window. "Centrifugal, centripetal," he said, with his chin on his fist. "Stop a planet in its flight, rob it of its centrifugal force, what then? Centripetal has it, and down it falls into the sun! And this—!"

"Do *we* come in the way? I wonder—"

The light of that day went the way of its brethren, and with the later watches of the frosty darkness rose the strange star again. And it was now so bright that the waxing moon seemed but a pale yellow ghost of itself, hanging huge in the sunset. In a South African city a great man had married, and the streets were alight to welcome his return with his bride. "Even the skies have illuminated," said the flatterer. Under Capricorn, two Negro lovers, daring the wild beasts and evil spirits, for love of one another, crouched together in a cane brake where the fire-flies hovered. "That is our star," they whispered, and felt strangely comforted by the sweet brilliance of its light.

The master mathematician sat in his private room and pushed the papers from him. His calculations were already finished. In a small white phial there still remained a little of the drug that had kept him awake and active for four long nights. Each day, serene, explicit, patient as ever, he had given his lecture to his students, and then had come back at once to this momentous calculation. His face was grave, a little drawn and hectic from his drugged activity. For some time he seemed lost in thought. Then he went to the window, and the blind went up with a click. Half way up the sky, over the clustering roofs, chimneys and steeples of the city, hung the star.

He looked at it as one might look into the eyes of a brave enemy. "You may kill me," he said after a silence. "But I can hold you—and all the universe for that matter—in the grip of this little brain. I would not change. Even now."

He looked at the little phial. "There will be no need of sleep again," he said. The next day at noon, punctual to the minute, he entered his lecture theatre, put his hat on the end of the table as his habit was, and carefully selected a large piece of chalk. It was a joke among his students that he could not lecture without that piece of chalk to fumble in his fingers, and once he had been stricken to impotence by their hiding his supply. He came and looked under his grey eyebrows at the rising tiers of young fresh faces, and spoke with his accustomed studied commonness of phrasing. "Circumstances have arisen—circumstances beyond my control," he said and paused, "which will debar me from completing the course I had designed. It would seem, gentlemen, if I may put the thing clearly and briefly, that—Man has lived in vain."

The students glanced at one another. Had they heard aright? Mad? Raised eyebrows and grinning lips there were, but one or two faces remained intent upon his calm grey-fringed face. "It will be interesting," he was saying, "to devote this morning to an exposition, so far as I can make it clear to you, of the calculations that have led me to this conclusion. Let us assume—"

He turned towards the blackboard, meditating a diagram in the way that was usual to him. "What was that about 'lived in vain?'" whispered one student to another. "Listen,'" said the other, nodding towards the lecturer.

And presently they began to understand.

That night the star rose later, for its proper eastward motion had carried it some way across Leo towards Virgo, and its brightness was so great that the sky became a luminous blue as it rose, and every star was hidden in its turn, save only Jupiter near the zenith, Capella, Aldebaran, Sirius and the pointers of the Bear. It was very white and beautiful. In many parts of the world that night a pallid halo encircled it about. It was perceptibly larger; in the clear refractive sky of the tropics it seemed as if it were nearly a quarter the size of the moon. The frost was still on the ground in England, but the world was as brightly lit as if it were midsummer moonlight. One could see to read quite ordinary print by that cold clear light, and in the cities the lamps burnt yellow and wan.

And everywhere the world was awake that night, and throughout Christendom a sombre murmur hung in the keen air over the country side like the belling of bees in the heather, and this murmurous tumult grew to a clangour in the cities. It was the tolling of the bells in a million belfry towers and steeples, summoning the people to sleep no more, to sin no more, but to gather in their churches and pray. And overhead, growing larger and brighter, as the earth rolled on its way and the night passed, rose the dazzling star.

And the streets and houses were alight in all the cities, the shipyards glared, and whatever roads led to high country were lit and crowded all night long. And in all the seas about the civilised lands, ships with throbbing engines, and ships with bellying sails, crowded with men and living creatures, were standing out to ocean and the north. For already the warning of the master mathematician had been telegraphed all over the world, and translated into a hundred tongues. The new planet and Neptune, locked in a fiery embrace, were whirling headlong, ever faster and faster towards the sun. Already every second this blazing mass flew a hundred miles, and every second its terrific velocity increased. As it flew now, indeed, it must pass a hundred million of miles wide of the earth and scarcely affect it. But near its destined path, as yet only slightly perturbed, spun the mighty planet Jupiter and his moons sweeping splendid round the sun. Every moment now the attraction between the fiery star and the greatest of the planets grew stronger. And the result of that attraction? Inevitably Jupiter would be deflected from its orbit into an elliptical path, and the burning star, swung by his attraction wide of its sunward rush, would "describe a curved path" and perhaps collide with, and certainly pass very close to, our earth. "Earthquakes, volcanic outbreaks, cyclones, sea waves, floods, and a steady rise in temperature to I know not what limit"—so prophesied the master mathematician.

And overhead, to carry out his words, lonely and cold and livid, blazed the star of the coming doom.

To many who stared at it that night until their eyes ached, it seemed that it was visibly approaching. And that night, too, the weather changed, and the frost that had gripped all Central Europe and France and England softened towards a thaw.

But you must not imagine because I have spoken of people praying through the night and people going aboard ships and people fleeing towards mountainous country that the whole world was already in a terror because of the star. As a matter of fact, use and wont still ruled the world, and save for the talk of idle moments and the splendour of the night, nine human beings out of ten were still busy at their common occupations. In all the cities the shops, save one here and there, opened and closed at their proper hours, the doctor and the undertaker plied their trades, the workers gathered in the factories, soldiers drilled, scholars studied, lovers sought one another, thieves lurked and fled, politicians planned their schemes. The presses of the newspapers roared through the nights, and many a priest of this church and that would not open his holy building to further what he considered a foolish panic. The newspapers insisted on the lesson of the year 1000—for then, too, people had anticipated the end. The star was no star—mere gas—a comet; and were it a star it could not possibly strike the earth. There was no precedent for such a thing. Common sense was sturdy everywhere, scornful, jesting, a little inclined to persecute the obdurate fearful. That night, at seven-fifteen by Greenwich time, the star would be at its nearest to Jupiter. Then the world would see the turn things would take. The master mathematician's grim warnings were treated by many as so much mere elaborate self-advertisement. Common sense at last, a little heated by argument, signified its unalterable convictions by going to bed. So, too, barbarism and savagery, already tired of the novelty, went about their nightly business, and save for a howling dog here and there, the beast world left the star unheeded.

And yet, when at last the watchers in the European States saw the star rise, an hour later it is true, but no larger than it had been the night before, there were still plenty awake to laugh at the master mathematician—to take the danger as if it had passed.

But hereafter the laughter ceased. The star grew—it grew with a terrible steadiness hour after hour, a little larger each hour, a little nearer the midnight zenith, and brighter and brighter, until it had turned night into a second day. Had it come straight to the earth instead of in a curved path, had it lost no velocity to Jupiter, it must have leapt the intervening gulf in a day, but as it was it took five days altogether to come by our planet. The next night it had become a third the size of the moon before it set to English eyes, and the thaw was assured. It rose over America near the size of the moon, but blinding white to look at, and *hot;* and a breath of hot wind blew now with its rising and gathering strength, and in Virginia, and Brazil, and down the St. Lawrence valley, it shone intermittently through a driving reek of thunder-clouds, flickering violet lightning, and hail unprecedented. In Manitoba was a thaw and devastating floods. And upon all the mountains of the earth the snow and ice began to melt that night, and all the rivers coming out of high country flowed thick and turbid, and soon—in their upper reaches—with swirling trees and the bodies of beasts and men. They rose steadily, steadily in the ghostly brilliance, and came trickling over their banks at last, behind the flying population of their valleys.

And along the coast of Argentina and up the South Atlantic the tides were higher than had ever been in the memory of man, and the storms drove the waters in many cases scores of miles inland, drowning whole cities. And so great grew the heat during the night that the rising of the sun was like the coming of a shadow. The earthquakes began and grew until all down America, from the Arctic Circle to Cape Horn, hillsides were sliding, fissures were openings, and houses and walls crumbling to destruction. The whole side of Cotopaxi slipped out in one vast convulsion, and a tumult of lava poured out so high and broad and swift and liquid that in one day it reached the sea.

So the star, with the wan moon in its wake, marched across the Pacific, trailed the thunderstorms like the hem of a robe, and the growing tidal wave that toiled behind it, frothing and eager, poured over island and island and swept them clear of men. Until that wave came at last—in a blinding light and with the breath of a furnace, swift and terrible it came—a wall of water, fifty feet high, roaring hungrily, upon the long coasts of Asia, and swept inland across the plains of China. For a space the star, hotter now and larger and brighter than the sun in its strength, showed with pitiless brilliance the wide and populous country; towns and villages with their pagodas and trees, roads, wide cultivated fields, millions of sleepless people staring in helpless terror at the incandescent sky; and then, low and growing, came the murmur of the flood. And thus it was with millions of men that night—a flight nowhither, with limbs heavy with heat and breath fierce and scant, and the flood like a wall swift and white behind. And then death.

China was lit glowing white, but over Japan and Java and all the islands of Eastern Asia the great star was a ball of dull red fire because of the steam and smoke and ashes the volcanoes were spouting forth to salute its coming. Above was the lava, hot gases and ash, and below the seething floods, and the whole earth swayed and rumbled with the earthquake shocks. Soon the immemorial snows of Tibet and the Himalaya were melting and pouring down by ten million deepening converging channels upon the plains of Burmah and Hindostan. The tangled summits of the Indian jungles were aflame in a thousand places, and below the hurrying waters around the stems were dark objects that still struggled feebly and reflected the blood-red tongues of fire. And in a rudderless confusion a multitude of men and women fled down the broad river-ways to that one last hope of men— the open sea.

Larger grew the star, and larger, hotter, and brighter with a terrible swiftness now. The tropical ocean had lost its phosphorescence, and the whirling steam rose in ghostly wreaths from the black waves that plunged incessantly, speckled with storm-tossed ships.

And then came a wonder. It seemed to those who in Europe watched for the rising of the star that the world must have ceased its rotation. In a thousand open spaces of down and upland the people who had fled thither from the floods and the falling houses and sliding slopes of hill watched for that rising in vain. Hour followed hour through a terrible suspense, and the star rose not. Once again men set their eyes upon the old constellations they had counted lost to them forever. In England it was hot and clear overhead, though the ground quivered perpetually, but in the tropics, Sirius and Capella and Aldebaran showed through a veil of steam. And when at last the great star rose near ten hours late, the sun rose close upon it, and in the centre of its white heart was a disc of black.

Over Asia it was the star had begun to fall behind the movement of the sky, and then suddenly, as it hung over India, its light had been veiled. All the plain of India from the mouth of the Indus to the mouths of the Ganges was a shallow waste of shining water that night, out of which rose temples and palaces, mounds and hills, black with people. Every minaret was a clustering mass of people, who fell one by one into the turbid waters, as heat and terror overcame them. The whole land seemed a-wailing, and suddenly there swept a shadow across that furnace of despair, and a breath of cold wind, and a gathering of clouds, out of the cooling air. Men looking up, near blinded, at the star, saw that a black disc was creeping across the light. It was the moon, coming between the star and the earth. And even as men cried to God at this respite, out of the East with a strange inexplicable swiftness sprang the sun. And then star, sun and moon rushed together across the heavens.

So it was that presently, to the European watchers, star and sun rose close upon each other, drove headlong for a space and then slower, and at last came to rest, star and sun merged into one glare of flame at the zenith of the sky. The moon no longer eclipsed the star but was lost to sight in the brilliance of the sky. And though those who were still alive regarded it for the most part with that dull stupidity that hunger, fatigue, heat and despair engender, there were still men who could perceive the meaning of these signs. Star and earth had been at their nearest, had swung about one another, and the star had passed. Already it was receding, swifter and swifter, in the last stage of its headlong journey downward into the sun.

And then the clouds gathered, blotting out the vision of the sky, the thunder and lightning wove a garment round the world; all over the earth was such a downpour of rain as men had never before seen, and where the volcanoes flared red against the cloud canopy there descended torrents of mud. Everywhere the waters were pouring off the land, leaving mud-silted ruins, and the earth littered like a storm-worn beach with all that had floated, and the dead bodies of the men and brutes, its children. For days the water streamed off the land, sweeping away soil and trees and houses in the way, and piling huge dykes and scooping out Titanic gullies over the country side. Those were the days of darkness that followed the star and the heat. All through them, and for many weeks and months, the earthquakes continued.

But the star had passed, and men, hunger-driven and gathering courage only slowly, might creep back to their ruined cities, buried granaries, and sodden fields. Such few ships as had escaped the storms of that time came stunned and shattered and sounding their way cautiously through the new marks and shoals of once familiar ports. And as the storms subsided men perceived that everywhere the days were hotter than of yore, and the sun larger, and the moon, shrunk to a third of its former size, took now fourscore days between its new and new.

But of the new brotherhood that grew presently among men, of the saving of laws and books and machines, of the strange change that had come over Iceland and Greenland and the shores of Baffin's Bay, so that the sailors coming there presently found them green and gracious, and could scarce believe their eyes, this story does not tell. Nor of the movement of mankind now that the earth was hotter, northward and southward towards the poles of the earth. It concerns itself only with the coming and the passing of the Star.

The Martian astronomers—for there are astronomers on Mars, although they are very different beings from men—were naturally profoundly interested by these things. They saw them from their own standpoint of course. "Considering the mass and temperature of the missile that was flung through our solar system into the sun," one wrote, "it is astonishing what a little damage the earth, which it missed so narrowly, has sustained. All the familiar continental markings and the masses of the seas remain intact, and indeed the only difference seems to be a shrinkage of the white discoloration (supposed to be frozen water) round either pole." Which only shows how small the vastest of human catastrophes may seem, at a distance of a few million miles.

—1897

C. L. MOORE

1911-1987

*Catherine L. Moore was an important and popular author of pulp maga-
zine fantasy and science fiction during those years when women rarely
published speculative fiction. She was born in Indianapolis, Indiana, to Otto
Newman and Maude Estelle (Jones) Moore. Experiencing persistent illness as
a child, Moore developed a love for the fantasy and adventure fiction of
Edgar Rice Burroughs and L. Frank Baum. It was during her adolescent
years that she also developed an interest in writing, eventually attending
Indiana University as an English major. Because of the Depression, she had
to leave the university to attend business school, but she persisted with her
writing. Moore eventually returned to college, graduating with a B.A. in
1956 and a M.A. in 1964 from the University of Southern California.*

*In 1933, Moore submitted her first story, "Shambleau," to editor
Farnsworth Wright, which he accepted for publication in the November
1933 issue of the pulp magazine,* Weird Tales. *"Shambleau" introduced
Moore's intrepid spaceman hero, Northwest Smith, a character who
appeared in twelve more stories (including ten published in* Weird Tales). *
Moore also created a female "swords and sorcery" heroine, Jirel of Joiry,
who was featured in six stories for* Weird Tales. *In 1940, Moore married science fiction author Henry Kuttner, and much of her work during the 1940s
and 1950s was written in collaboration with her husband. These collabora-
tions, co-authored under Kuttner's and Moore's "Lewis Padgett" pseudonym, include* The Brass Ring *(1946),* A Gnome There Was *(1950),* Robots
Have No Tails *(1952),* Mutant *(1953), and* Beyond Earth's Gates *(1954).
Following Kuttner's death in 1958, Moore left science fiction to write for
television and film.*

When "Shambleau" was published in Weird Tales, *it became an instant
favorite among the magazine's readers, perhaps because Moore's story
effectively combined two popular science fiction formulas. On the one hand,
"Shambleau" is "space opera," a category of science fiction that is quite similar to the American western "horse opera" (merely substitute rocket ships
for horses and ray guns for six-shooters). It emphasizes slam-bang action
above all else. Space opera typically features planet-destroying ray guns,
star-jumping space ships, scantily-clad damsels-in-distress, and intrepid
square-jawed heroes combating bug-eyed monsters bent on humanity's
destruction. Space opera was popularized during the 1920s and 1930s by
the American pulp magazines, which were constantly developing new types
of action-oriented fiction to satisfy an ever growing adolescent readership
in search of escapism. (In fact, some historians of the genre argue that modern science fiction was invented, in 1926, by editor and writer Hugo
Gernsback in the pulp,* Amazing Stories.) *The masters of pulp magazine
space opera included E. E. "Doc" Smith, the author of the Skylark and
Lensmen series, and Edmond Hamilton, the author of the Captain Future
and the Starwolf series. On the other hand, "Shambleau" is a science fiction
horror story of the type later perfected by John W. Campbell, Jr.'s "Who
Goes There?" (1938), which became the basis for the classic 1951 film,* The
Thing (from Another World).

SHAMBLEAU

Man has conquered space before. You may be sure of that. Somewhere be- takes *yond the Egyptians, in that dimness out of which come echoes of half-* place on *mythical names—Atlantis, Mu—somewhere back of history's first begin-* Mars-- *nings there must have been an age when mankind, like us today, built cities* colony *of steel to house its star-roving ships and knew the names of the planets in their own native tongues—heard Venus' people call their wet world "Shaardol" in that soft, sweet, slurring speech and mimicked Mars' guttural "Lakkdiz" from the harsh tongues of Mars' dryland dwellers. You may be sure of it. Man has conquered Space before, and out of that conquest faint, faint echoes run still through a world that has forgotten the very fact of a civilization which must have been as mighty as our own. There have been too many myths and legends for us to doubt it. The myth of the Medusa, for instance, can never have had its roots in the soil of Earth. That tale of the snake-haired Gorgon whose gaze turned the gazer to stone never origi- nated about any creature that Earth nourished. And those ancient Greeks who told the story must have remembered, dimly and half believing, a tale of antiquity about some strange being from one of the outlying planets their remotest ancestors once trod.*

"Shambleau! Ha . . . Shambleau!" The wild hysteria of the mob rocketed from wall to wall of Lakkdarol's narrow streets and the storming of heavy boots over the slag-red pavement made an ominous undernote to that swelling bay, "Shambleau! Shambleau!"

Northwest Smith heard it coming and stepped into the nearest doorway, laying a wary hand on his heat-gun's grip, and his colorless eyes narrowed. Strange sounds were common enough in the streets of Earth's latest colony on Mars—a raw, red lit- tle town where anything might happen, and very often did. But Northwest Smith, whose name is known and respected in every dive and wild outpost on a dozen wild planets, was a cautious man, despite his reputation. He set his back against the wall and gripped his pistol, and heard the rising shout come nearer and nearer.

Then into his range of vision flashed a red running figure, dodging like a hunted hare from shelter to shelter in the narrow street. It was a girl—a berry-brown girl in a single tattered garment whose scarlet burnt the eyes with its brilliance. She ran wearily, and he could hear her gasping breath from where he stood. As she came into view he saw her hesitate and lean one hand against the wall for support, and glance wildly around for shelter. She must not have seen him in the depths of the doorway, for as the bay of the mob grew louder and the pounding of feet sounded almost at the corner she gave a despairing little moan and dodged into the recess at his very side.

When she saw him standing there, tall and leather-brown, hand on his heat-gun, she sobbed once, inarticulately, and collapsed at his feet, a huddle of burning scar- let and bare, brown limbs.

Smith had not seen her face, but she was a girl, and sweetly made and in dan- ger; and though he had not the reputation of a chivalrous man, something in her hopeless huddle at his feet touched that chord of sympathy for the underdog that stirs in every Earthman, and he pushed her gently into the corner behind him and jerked out his gun, just as the first of the running mob rounded the corner.

It was a motley crowd, Earthmen and Martians and a sprinkling of Venusian swampmen and strange, nameless denizens of unnamed planets—a typical Lakkdarol mob. When the first of them turned the corner and saw the empty street before them there was a faltering in the rush and the foremost spread out and began to search the doorways on both sides of the street.

"Looking for something?" Smith's sardonic call sounded clear above the clamor of the mob.

They turned. The shouting died for a moment as they took in the scene before them—tall Earthman in the space-explorer's leathern garb, all one color from the burning of savage suns save for the sinister pallor of his no-colored eyes in a scarred and resolute face, gun in his steady hand and the scarlet girl crouched behind him, panting.

The foremost of the crowd—a burly Earthman in tattered leather from which the Patrol insignia had been ripped away—stared for a moment with a strange expression of incredulity on his face overspreading the savage exultation of the chase. Then he let loose a deep-throated bellow, "Shambleau!" and lunged forward. Behind him the mob took up the cry again, "Shambleau! Shambleau! Shambleau!" and surged after.

Smith, lounging negligently against the wall, arms folded and gun-hand draped over his left forearm, looked incapable of swift motion, but at the leader's first forward step the pistol swept in a practiced half-circle and the dazzle of blue-white heat leaping from its muzzle seared an arc in the slag pavement at his feet. It was an old gesture, and not a man in the crowd but understood it. The foremost recoiled swiftly against the surge of those in the rear, and for a moment there was confusion as the two tides met and struggled. Smith's mouth curled into a grim curve as he watched. The man in the mutilated Patrol uniform lifted a threatening fist and stepped to the very edge of the deadline, while the crowd rocked to and fro behind him.

"Are you crossing that line?" queried Smith in an ominously gentle voice.

"We want that girl!"

"Come and get her!" Recklessly Smith grinned into his face. He saw danger there, but his defiance was not the foolhardy gesture it seemed. An expert psychologist of mobs from long experience, he sensed no murder here. Not a gun had appeared in any hand in the crowd. They desired the girl with an inexplicable bloodthirstiness he was at a loss to understand, but toward himself he sensed no such fury. A mauling he might expect, but his life was in no danger. Guns would have appeared before now if they were coming out at all. So he grinned in the man's angry face and leaned lazily against the wall.

Behind their self-appointed leader the crowd milled impatiently, and threatening voices began to rise again. Smith heard the girl moan at his feet.

"What do you want with her?" he demanded.

"She's Shambleau! Shambleau, you fool! Kick her out of there—we'll take care of her!"

"I'm taking care of her," drawled Smith.

"She's Shambleau, I tell you! Damn your hide, man, we never let those things live! Kick her out here!"

The repeated name had no meaning to him, but Smith's innate stubbornness rose defiantly as the crowd surged forward to the very edge of the arc, their clamor growing louder. "Shambleau! Kick her out here! Give us Shambleau! Shambleau!"

Smith dropped his indolent pose like a cloak and planted both feet wide, swinging up his gun threateningly. "Keep back!" he yelled. "She's mine! Keep back!"

He had no intention of using that heat-beam. He knew by now that they would not kill him unless he started the gunplay himself, and he did not mean to give up his life for any girl alive. But a severe mauling he expected, and he braced himself instinctively as the mob heaved within itself.

To his astonishment a thing happened then that he had never known to happen before. At his shouted defiance the foremost of the mob—those who had heard him clearly—drew back a little, not in alarm but evidently surprised. The ex-Patrolman said, "Yours! She's *yours?*" in a voice from which puzzlement crowded out the anger.

Smith spread his booted legs wide before the crouching figure and flourished his gun.

"Yes," he said. "And I'm keeping her! Stand back there!"

The man stared at him wordlessly, and horror, disgust and incredulity mingled on his weather-beaten face. The incredulity triumphed for a moment and he said again,

"*Yours!*"

Smith nodded defiance.

The man stepped back suddenly, unutterable contempt in his very pose. He waved an arm to the crowd and said loudly, "It's—his!" and the press melted away, gone silent, too, and the look of contempt spread from face to face.

The ex-Patrolman spat on the slag-paved street and turned his back indifferently. "Keep her, then," he advised briefly over one shoulder. "But don't let her out again in this town!"

Smith stared in perplexity almost open-mouthed as the suddenly scornful mob began to break up. His mind was in a whirl. That such bloodthirsty animosity should vanish in a breath he could not believe. And the curious mingling of contempt and disgust on the faces he saw baffled him even more. Lakkdarol was anything but a puritan town—it did not enter his head for a moment that his claiming the brown girl as his own had caused that strangely shocked revulsion to spread through the crowd. No, it was something more deeply rooted than that. Instinctive, instant disgust had been in the faces he saw—they would have looked less so if he had admitted cannibalism or *Pharol*-worship.

And they were leaving his vicinity as swiftly as if whatever unknowing sin he had committed were contagious. The street was emptying as rapidly as it had filled. He saw a sleek Venusian glance back over his shoulder as he turned the corner and sneer, "Shambleau!" and the word awoke a new line of speculation in Smith's mind. Shambleau! Vaguely of French origin, it must be. And strange enough to hear it from the lips of Venusians and Martian drylanders, but it was their use of it that puzzled him more. "We never let those things live," the ex-Patrolman had said. It reminded him dimly of something . . . an ancient line from some writing in his own tongue . . . "Thou shalt not suffer a witch to live." He smiled to himself at the similarity, and simultaneously was aware of the girl at his elbow.

She had risen soundlessly. He turned to face her, sheathing his gun, and stared at first with curiosity and then in the entirely frank openness with which men regard that which is not wholly human. For she was not. He knew it at a glance, though the brown, sweet body was shaped like a woman's and she wore the garment of scarlet—he saw it was leather—with an ease that few unhuman beings achieve toward clothing. He knew it from the moment he looked into her eyes, and a shiver of unrest went over him as he met them. They were frankly green as young grass, with

we first think Shambleau is helpless

slit-like, feline pupils that pulsed unceasingly, and there was a look of dark, animal wisdom in their depths—that look of the beast which sees more than man.

There was no hair upon her face—neither brows nor lashes, and he would have sworn that the tight scarlet turban bound around her head covered baldness. She had three fingers and a thumb, and her feet had four digits apiece too, and all sixteen of them were tipped with round claws that sheathed back into the flesh like a cat's. She ran her tongue over her lips—a thin, pink, flat tongue as feline as her eyes—and spoke with difficulty. He felt that that throat and tongue had never been shaped for human speech.

"Not—afraid now," she said softly, and her little teeth were white and pointed as a kitten's.

"What did they want you for?" he asked her curiously. "What had you done? Shambleau . . . is that your name?"

"I—not talk your—speech," she demurred hesitantly.

"Well, try to—I want to know. Why were they chasing you? Will you be safe on the street now, or hadn't you better get indoors somewhere? They looked dangerous."

"I—go with you." She brought it out with difficulty.

"Say you!" Smith grinned. "What are you, anyhow? You look like a kitten to me."

"Shambleau." She said it somberly.

"Where d'you live? Are you a Martian?"

"I come from—from far—from long ago—far country——"

"Wait!" laughed Smith. "You're getting your wires crossed. You're not a Martian?"

She drew herself up very straight beside him, lifting the turbaned head, and there was something queenly in the poise of her.

"Martian?" she said scornfully. "My people—are—are—you have no word. Your speech—hard for me."

"What's yours? I might know it—try me."

She lifted her head and met his eyes squarely, and there was in hers a subtle amusement—he could have sworn it.

"Some day I—speak to you in—my own language," she promised, and the pink tongue flicked out over her lips, swiftly, hungrily.

Approaching footsteps on the red pavement interrupted Smith's reply. A dry-land Martian came past, reeling a little and exuding an aroma of *segir*-whisky, the Venusian brand. When he caught the red flash of the girl's tatters he turned his head sharply, and as his *segir*-steeped brain took in the fact of her presence he lurched toward the recess unsteadily, bawling, "Shambleau, by *Pharol!* Shambleau!" and reached out a clutching hand.

Smith struck it aside contemptuously.

"On your way, drylander," he advised.

The man drew back and stared, blear-eyed.

"Yours, eh?" he croaked. "*Zut!* You're welcome to it!" And like the ex-Patrolman before him he spat on the pavement and turned away, muttering harshly in the blasphemous tongue of the drylands.

Smith watched him shuffle off, and there was a crease between his colorless eyes, a nameless unease rising within him.

"Come on," he said abruptly to the girl. "If this sort of thing is going to happen we'd better get indoors. Where shall I take you?"

"With—you," she murmured.

He stared down into the flat green eyes. Those ceaselessly pulsing pupils disturbed him, but it seemed to him, vaguely, that behind the animal shallows of her gaze was a shutter—a closed barrier that might at any moment open to reveal the very deeps of that dark knowledge he sensed there.

Roughly he said again, "Come on, then," and stepped down into the street.

She pattered along a pace or two behind him, making no effort to keep up with his long strides, and though Smith—as men know from Venus to Jupiter's moons—walks as softly as a cat, even in spacemen's boots, the girl at his heels slid like a shadow over the rough pavement, making so little sound that even the lightness of his footsteps was loud in the empty street.

Smith chose the less frequented ways of Lakkdarol, and somewhat shamefacedly thanked his nameless gods that his lodgings were not far away, for the few pedestrians he met turned and stared after the two with that by now familiar mingling of horror and contempt which he was as far as ever from understanding.

The room he had engaged was a single cubicle in a lodging-house on the edge of the city. Lakkdarol, raw camp-town that it was in those days, could have furnished little better anywhere within its limits, and Smith's errand there was not one he wished to advertise. He had slept in worse places than this before, and knew that he would do so again.

There was no one in sight when he entered, and the girl slipped up the stairs at his heels and vanished through the door, shadowy, unseen by anyone in the house. Smith closed the door and leaned his broad shoulders against the panels, regarding her speculatively.

She took in what little the room had to offer in a glance—frowsy bed, rickety table, mirror hanging unevenly and cracked against the wall, unpainted chairs—a typical camp-town room in an Earth settlement abroad. She accepted its poverty in that single glance, dismissed it, then crossed to the window and leaned out for a moment, gazing across the low roof-tops toward the barren countryside beyond, red slag under the late afternoon sun.

"You can stay here," said Smith abruptly, "until I leave town. I'm waiting here for a friend to come in from Venus. Have you eaten?"

"Yes," said the girl quickly. "I shall—need no—food for—a while."

"Well—" Smith glanced around the room. "I'll be in sometime tonight. You can go or stay just as you please. Better lock the door behind me."

With no more formality than that he left her. The door closed and he heard the key turn, and smiled to himself. He did not expect, then, ever to see her again.

He went down the steps and out into the late-slanting sunlight with a mind so full of other matters that the brown girl receded very quickly into the background. Smith's errand in Lakkdarol, like most of his errands, is better not spoken of. Man lives as he must, and Smith's living was a perilous affair outside the law and ruled by the ray-gun only. It is enough to say that the shipping-port and its cargoes outbound interested him deeply just now, and that the friend he awaited was Yarol the Venusian, in that swift little Edsel ship the *Maid* that can flash from world to world with a derisive speed that laughs at Patrol boats and leaves pursuers floundering in the ether far behind. Smith and Yarol and the *Maid* were a trinity that had caused the Patrol leaders much worry and many gray hairs in the past, and the future looked very bright to Smith himself that evening as he left his lodging-house.

Lakkdarol roars by night, as Earthmen's camp-towns have a way of doing on every planet where Earth's outposts are, and it was beginning lustily as Smith went down among the awakening lights toward the center of town. His business there does not concern us. He mingled with the crowds where the lights were brightest, and there was the click of ivory counters and the jingle of silver, and red *segir* gurgled invitingly from black Venusian bottles, and much later Smith strolled homeward under the moving moons of Mars, and if the street wavered a little under his feet now and then—why, that is only understandable. Not even Smith could drink red *segir* at every bar from the *Martian Lamb* to the *New Chicago* and remain entirely steady on his feet. But he found his way back with very little difficulty—considering—and spent a good five minutes hunting for his key before he remembered he had left it in the inner lock for the girl.

He knocked then, and there was no sound of footsteps from within, but in a few moments the latch clicked and the door swung open. She retreated soundlessly before him as he entered, and took up her favorite place against the window, leaning back on the sill and outlined against the starry sky beyond. The room was in darkness.

Smith flipped the switch by the door and then leaned back against the panels, steadying himself. The cool night air had sobered him a little, and his head was clear enough—liquor went to Smith's feet, not his head, or he would never have come this far along the lawless way he had chosen. He lounged against the door now and regarded the girl in the sudden glare of the bulbs, blinding a little as much at the scarlet of her clothing as at the light.

"So you stayed," he said.

"I—waited," she answered softly, leaning farther back against the sill and clasping the rough wood with slim, three-fingered hands, pale brown against the darkness.

"Why?"

She did not answer that, but her mouth curved into a slow smile. On a woman it would have been reply enough—provocative, daring. On Shambleau there was something pitiful and horrible in it—so human on the face of one half-animal. And yet . . . that sweet brown body curving so softly from the tatters of scarlet leather—the velvety texture of that brownness—the white-flashing smile. . . . Smith was aware of a stirring excitement within him. After all—time would be hanging heavy now until Yarol came. . . . Speculatively he allowed the steel-pale eyes to wander over her, with a slow regard that missed nothing. And when he spoke he was aware that his voice had deepened a little. . . .

"Come here," he said.

She came forward slowly, on bare clawed feet that made no sound on the floor, and stood before him with downcast eyes and mouth trembling in that pitifully human smile. He took her by the shoulders—velvety soft shoulders, of a creamy smoothness that was not the texture of human flesh. A little tremor went over her, perceptibly, at the contact of his hands. Northwest Smith caught his breath suddenly and dragged her to him . . . sweet yielding brownness in the circle of his arms . . . heard her own breath catch and quicken as her velvety arms closed about his neck. And then he was looking down into her face, very near, and the green animal eyes met his with the pulsing pupils and the flicker of—something—deep behind their shallows—and through the rising clamor of his blood, even as he stooped his lips to hers, Smith felt something deep within him shudder away—inexplicable, instinctive, revolted. What it might be he had no words to tell, but the very touch of her was suddenly loathsome—so soft and velvet and unhuman—and it might have been an animal's face that lifted itself to his mouth—the dark knowledge looked hungrily from the darkness of those slit pupils—and for a mad instant he knew that same wild, feverish revulsion he had seen in the faces of the mob. . . .

"God!" he gasped, a far more ancient invocation against evil than he realized, then or ever, and he ripped her arms from his neck, swung her away with such a force that she reeled half across the room. Smith fell back against the door, breathing heavily, and stared at her while the wild revolt died slowly within him.

She had fallen to the floor beneath the window, and as she lay there against the wall with bent head he saw, curiously, that her turban had slipped—the turban that he had been so sure covered baldness—and a lock of scarlet hair fell below the binding leather, hair as scarlet as her garment, as unhumanly red as her eyes were unhumanly green. He stared, and shook his head dizzily and stared again, for it seemed to him that the thick lock of crimson had moved, *squirmed* of itself against her cheek.

At the contact of it her hands flew up and she tucked it away with a very human gesture and then dropped her head again into her hands. And from the deep shadow of her fingers he thought she was staring up at him covertly.

Smith drew a deep breath and passed a hand across his forehead. The inexplicable moment had gone as quickly as it came—too swiftly for him to understand or analyze it. "Got to lay off the *segir*," he told himself unsteadily. Had he imagined that scarlet hair? After all, she was no more than a pretty brown girl-creature from one of the many half-human races peopling the planets. No more than that, after all. A pretty little thing, but animal. . . . He laughed a little shakily.

"No more of that," he said. "God knows I'm no angel, but there's got to be a limit somewhere. Here." He crossed to the bed and sorted out a pair of blankets from the untidy heap, tossing them to the far corner of the room. "You can sleep there."

Wordlessly she rose from the floor and began to rearrange the blankets, the uncomprehending resignation of the animal eloquent in every line of her.

Smith had a strange dream that night. He thought he had awakened to a room full of darkness and moonlight and moving shadows, for the nearer moon of Mars was racing through the sky and everything on the planet below her was endued with a restless life in the dark. And something . . . some nameless, unthinkable *thing* . . . was coiled about his throat . . . something like a soft snake, wet and warm. It lay loose and light about his neck . . . and it was moving gently, very gently, with a soft, caressive pressure that sent little thrills of delight through every nerve and fiber of him, a perilous delight—beyond physical pleasure, deeper than joy of the mind. That warm softness was caressing the very roots of his soul with a terrible intimacy. The ecstasy of it left him weak, and yet he knew—in a flash of knowledge born of this impossible dream—that the soul should not be handled. . . . And with that knowledge a horror broke upon him, turning the pleasure into a rapture of revulsion, hateful, horrible—but still most foully sweet. He tried to lift his hands and tear the dream-monstrosity from his throat—tried but half-heartedly; for though his soul was revolted to its very deeps, yet the delight of his body was so great that his hands all but refused the attempt. But when at last he tried to lift his arms a cold shock went over him and he found that he could not stir . . . his body lay stony as marble beneath the blankets, a living marble that shuddered with a dreadful delight through every rigid vein.

The revulsion grew strong upon him as he struggled against the paralyzing dream—a struggle of soul against sluggish body—titanically, until the moving dark was streaked with blankness that clouded and closed about him at last and he sank back into the oblivion from which he had awakened.

Next morning, when the bright sunlight shining through Mars' clear thin air awakened him, Smith lay for a while trying to remember. The dream had been more vivid than reality, but he could not now quite recall . . . only that it had been more sweet and horrible than anything else in life. He lay puzzling for a while, until a soft sound from the corner aroused him from his thoughts and he sat up to see the girl lying in a catlike coil on her blankets, watching him with round, grave eyes. He regarded her somewhat ruefully.

"Morning," he said. "I've just had the devil of a dream. . . . Well, hungry?"

She shook her head silently, and he could have sworn there was a covert gleam of strange amusement in her eyes.

He stretched and yawned, dismissing the nightmare temporarily from his mind.

"What am I going to do with you?" he inquired, turning to more immediate matters. "I'm leaving here in a day or two and I can't take you along, you know. Where'd you come from in the first place?"

Again she shook her head.

"Not telling? Well, it's your own business. You can stay here until I give up the room. From then on you'll have to do your own worrying."

He swung his feet to the floor and reached for his clothes.

Ten minutes later, slipping the heat-gun into its holster at his thigh, Smith turned to the girl. "There's food-concentrate in that box on the table. It ought to hold you until I get back. And you'd better lock the door again after I've gone."

Her wide, unwavering stare was his only answer, and he was not sure she had understood, but at any rate the lock clicked after him as before, and he went down the steps with a faint grin on his lips.

The memory of last night's extraordinary dream was slipping from him, as such memories do, and by the time he had reached the street the girl and the dream and all of yesterday's happenings were blotted out by the sharp necessities of the present.

Again the intricate business that had brought him here claimed his attention. He went about it to the exclusion of all else, and there was a good reason behind everything he did from the moment he stepped out into the street until the time when he turned back again at evening; though had one chosen to follow him during the day his apparently aimless rambling through Lakkdarol would have seemed very pointless.

He must have spent two hours at the least idling by the space-port, watching with sleepy, colorless eyes the ships that came and went, the passengers, the vessels lying at wait, the cargoes—particularly the cargoes. He made the rounds of the town's saloons once more, consuming many glasses of varied liquors in the course of the day and engaging in idle conversation with men of all races and worlds, usually in their own languages, for Smith was a linguist of repute among his contemporaries. He heard the gossip of the spaceways, news from a dozen planets of a thousand different events. He heard the latest joke about the Venusian Emperor and the latest report on the Chino-Aryan war and the latest song hot from the lips of Rose Robertson, whom every man on the civilized planets adored as "the Georgia Rose." He passed the day quite profitably, for his own purposes, which do not concern us now, and it was not until late evening, when he turned homeward again, that the thought of the brown girl in his room took definite shape in his mind, though it had been lurking there, formless and submerged, all day.

He had no idea what comprised her usual diet, but he bought a can of New York roast beef and one of Venusian frog-broth and a dozen fresh canal-apples and two pounds of that Earth lettuce that grows so vigorously in the fertile canal-soil of Mars. He felt that she must surely find something to her liking in this broad variety of edibles, and—for his day had been very satisfactory—he hummed *The Green Hills of Earth* to himself in a surprisingly good baritone as he climbed the stairs.

The door was locked, as before, and he was reduced to kicking the lower panels gently with his boot, for his arms were full. She opened the door with that softness that was characteristic of her and stood regarding him in the semi-darkness as he stumbled to the table with his load. The room was unlit again.

"Why don't you turn on the lights?" he demanded irritably after he had barked his shin on the chair by the table in an effort to deposit his burden there.

"Light and—dark—they are alike—to me," she murmured.

"Cat eyes, eh? Well, you look the part. Here, I've brought you some dinner. Take your choice. Fond of roast beef? Or how about a little frog-broth?"

She shook her head and backed away a step.

"No," she said. "I can not—eat your food."

Smith's brows wrinkled. "Didn't you have any of the food tablets?"

Again the red turban shook negatively.

"Then you haven't had anything for—why, more than twenty-four hours! You must be starved."

"Not hungry," she denied.

"What can I find for you to eat, then? There's time yet if I hurry. You've got to eat, child."

"I shall—eat," she said softly. "Before long—I shall—feed. Have no—worry."

She turned away then and stood at the window, looking out over the moonlit landscape as if to end the conversation. Smith cast her a puzzled glance as he opened the can of roast beef. There had been an odd undernote in that assurance that, undefinably, he did not like. And the girl had teeth and tongue and presumably a fairly human digestive system, to judge from her human form. It was nonsense for her to pretend that he could find nothing that she could eat. She must have had some of the food concentrate after all, he decided, prying up the thermos lid of the inner container to release the long-sealed savor of the hot meat inside.

"Well, if you won't eat you won't," he observed philosophically as he poured hot broth and diced beef into the dishlike lid of the thermos can and extracted the spoon from its hiding-place between the inner and outer receptacles. She turned a little to watch him as he pulled up a rickety chair and sat down to the food, and after a while the realization that her green gaze was fixed so unwinkingly upon him made the man nervous, and he said between bites of creamy canal-apple, "Why don't you try a little of this? It's good."

"The food—I eat is—better," her soft voice told him in its hesitant murmur, and again he felt rather than heard a faint undernote of unpleasantness in the words. A sudden suspicion struck him as he pondered on that last remark—some vague memory of horror-tales told about campfires in the past—and he swung round in the chair to look at her, a tiny, creeping fear unaccountably arising. There had been that in her words—in her unspoken words, that menaced. . . .

She stood up beneath his gaze demurely, wide green eyes with their pulsing pupils meeting his without a falter. But her mouth was scarlet and her teeth were sharp. . . .

"What food do you eat?" he demanded. And then, after a pause, very softly, "Blood?"

She stared at him for a moment, uncomprehending; then something like amusement curled her lips and she said scornfully, "You think me—vampire, eh? No—I am Shambleau!"

Unmistakably there were scorn and amusement in her voice at the suggestion, but as unmistakably she knew what he meant—accepted it as a logical suspicion—vampires! Fairy tales—but fairy tales this unhuman, outland creature was most familiar with. Smith was not a credulous man, nor a superstitious one, but he had seen too many strange things himself to doubt that the wildest legend might have a basis of fact. And there was something namelessly strange about her. . . .

He puzzled over it for a while between deep bites of the canal-apple. And though he wanted to question her about a great many things, he did not, for he knew how futile it would be.

He said nothing more until the meat was finished and another canal-apple had followed the first, and he had cleared away the meal by the simple expedient of tossing the empty can out of the window. Then he lay back in the chair and surveyed her from half-closed eyes, colorless in a face tanned like saddle-leather. And again he was conscious of the brown, soft curves of her, velvety—subtle arcs and planes of smooth flesh under the tatters of scarlet leather. Vampire she might be, unhuman she certainly was, but desirable beyond words as she sat submissive beneath his low regard, her red-turbaned head bent, her clawed fingers lying in her lap. They sat very still for a while, and the silence throbbed between them.

She was so like a woman—an Earth woman—sweet and submissive and demure, and softer than soft fur, if he could forget the three-fingered claws and the pulsing eyes—and that deeper strangeness beyond words. . . . (Had he dreamed that red lock of hair that moved? Had it been *segir* that woke the wild revulsion he knew when he held her in his arms? Why had the mob so thirsted for her?) He sat and stared, and despite the mystery of her and the half-suspicions that thronged his mind—for she was so beautifully soft and curved under those revealing tatters—he slowly realized that his pulses were mounting, became aware of a kindling within . . . brown girl-creature with downcast eyes . . . and then the lids lifted and the green flatness of a cat's gaze met his, and last night's revulsion woke swiftly again, like a warning bell that clanged as their eyes met—animal, after all, too sleek and soft for humanity, and that inner strangeness. . . .

Smith shrugged and sat up. His failings were legion, but the weakness of the flesh was not among the major ones. He motioned the girl to her pallet of blankets in the corner and turned to his own bed.

From deeps of sound sleep he awoke much later. He awoke suddenly and completely, and with that inner excitement that presages something momentous. He awoke to brilliant moonlight, turning the room so bright that he could see the scarlet of the girl's rags as she sat up on her pallet. She was awake, she was sitting with her shoulder half turned to him and her head bent, and some warning instinct crawled coldly up his spine as he watched what she was doing. And yet it was a very ordinary thing for a girl to do—any girl, anywhere. She was unbinding her turban. . . .

He watched, not breathing, a presentiment of something horrible stirring in his brain, inexplicably. . . . The red folds loosened, and—he knew then that he had not dreamed—again a scarlet lock swung down against her cheek . . . a hair, was it? a lock of hair? . . . thick as a thick worm it fell, plumply, against that smooth cheek . . . more scarlet than blood and thick as a crawling worm . . . and like a worm it crawled.

Smith rose on an elbow, not realizing the motion, and fixed an unwinking stare with a sort of sick, fascinated incredulity, on that—that lock of hair. He had not dreamed. Until now he had taken it for granted that it was the *segir* which had made it seem to move on that evening before. But now . . . it was lengthening, stretching, moving of itself. It must be hair, but it *crawled;* with a sickening life of its own it squirmed down against her cheek, caressingly, revoltingly, impossibly. . . . Wet, it was, and round and thick and shining. . . .

She unfastened the fast fold and whipped the turban off. From what he saw then Smith would have turned his eyes away—and he had looked on dreadful things before, without flinching—but he could not stir. He could only lie there on his elbow staring at the mass of scarlet, squirming—worms, hairs, what?—that writhed over her head in a dreadful mockery of ringlets. And it was lengthening, falling, somehow growing before his eyes, down over her shoulders in a spilling cascade, a mass that even at the beginning could never have been hidden under the skull-tight turban she had worn. He was beyond wondering, but he realized that. And still it squirmed and lengthened and fell, and she shook it out in a horrible travesty of a woman shaking out her unbound hair—until the unspeakable tangle of it—twisting, writhing, obscenely scarlet—hung to her waist and beyond, and still lengthened, an endless mass of crawling horror that until now, somehow, impossibly, had been hidden under the tight-bound turban. It was like a nest of blind, restless red worms . . . it was—it was like naked entrails endowed with an unnatural aliveness, terrible beyond words.

Smith lay in the shadows, frozen without and within in a sick numbness that came of utter shock and revulsion.

She shook out the obscene, unspeakable tangle over her shoulders, and somehow he knew that she was going to turn in a moment and that he must meet her eyes. The thought of that meeting stopped his heart with dread, more awfully than anything else in this nightmare horror; for nightmare it must be, surely. But he knew without trying that he could not wrench his eyes away—the sickened fascination of that sight held him motionless, and somehow there was a certain beauty. . . .

Her head was turning. The crawling awfulnesses rippled and squirmed at the motion, writhing thick and wet and shining over the soft brown shoulders about which they fell now in obscene cascades that all but hid her body. Her head was turning. Smith lay numb. And very slowly he saw the round of her cheek foreshorten and her profile come into view, all the scarlet horrors twisting ominously, and the profile shortened in turn and her full face came slowly round toward the bed— moonlight shining brilliantly as day on the pretty girl-face, demure and sweet, framed in tangled obscenity that crawled. . . .

The green eyes met his. He felt a perceptible shock, and a shudder rippled down his paralyzed spine, leaving an icy numbness in its wake. He felt the goose-flesh rising. But that numbness and cold horror he scarcely realized, for the green eyes were locked with his in a long, long look that somehow presaged nameless things—not altogether unpleasant things—the voiceless voice of her mind assailing him with little murmurous promises. . . .

For a moment he went down into a blind abyss of submission; and then somehow the very sight of that obscenity in eyes that did not then realize they saw it, was dreadful enough to draw him out of the seductive darkness . . . the sight of her crawling and alive with unnameable horror.

She rose, and down about her in a cascade fell the squirming scarlet of—of what grew upon her head. It fell in a long, alive cloak to her bare feet on the floor, hiding her in a wave of dreadful, wet, writhing life. She put up her hands and like a swimmer she parted the waterfall of it, tossing the masses back over her shoulders to reveal her own brown body, sweetly curved. She smiled exquisitely, and in starting waves back from her forehead and down about her in a hideous background writhed the snaky wetness of her living tresses. And Smith knew that he looked upon Medusa.

The knowledge of that—the realization of vast backgrounds reaching into misted history—shook him out of his frozen horror for a moment, and in that moment he met her eyes again, smiling, green as glass in the moonlight, half hooded under drooping lids. Through the twisting scarlet she held out her arms. And there was something soul-shakingly desirable about her, so that all the blood surged to his head suddenly and he stumbled to his feet like a sleeper in a dream as she swayed toward him, infinitely graceful, infinitely sweet in her cloak of living horror.

And somehow there was beauty in it, the wet scarlet writhings with moonlight sliding and shining along the thick, worm-round tresses and losing itself in the masses only to glint again and move silvery along writhing tendrils—an awful, shuddering beauty more dreadful than any ugliness could be.

But all this, again, he but half realized, for the insidious murmur was coiling again through his brain, promising, caressing, alluring, sweeter than honey; and the green eyes that held his were clear and burning like the depths of a jewel, and behind the pulsing slits of darkness he was staring into a greater dark that held all things. . . . He had known—dimly he had known when he first gazed into those flat animal shallows that behind them lay this—all beauty and terror, all horror and delight, in the infinite darkness upon which her eyes opened like windows, paned with emerald glass.

Her lips moved, and in a murmur that blended indistinguishably with the silence and the sway of her body and the dreadful sway of her—her hair—she whispered—very softly, very passionately, "I shall—speak to you now—in my own tongue—oh, beloved!"

And in her living cloak she swayed to him, the murmur swelling seductive and caressing in his innermost brain—promising, compelling, sweeter than sweet. His flesh crawled to the horror of her, but it was a perverted revulsion that clasped what it loathed. His arms slid round her under the sliding cloak, wet, wet and warm and hideously alive—and the sweet velvet body was clinging to his, her arms locked about his neck—and with a whisper and a rush the unspeakable horror closed about them both.

In nightmares until he died he remembered that moment when the living tresses of Shambleau first folded him in their embrace. A nauseous, smothering odor as the wetness shut around him—thick, pulsing worms clasping every inch of his body, sliding, writhing, their wetness and warmth striking through his garments as if he stood naked to their embrace.

All this in a graven instant—and after that a tangled flash of conflicting sensation before oblivion closed over him. For he remembered the dream—and knew it for nightmare reality now, and the sliding, gently moving caresses of those wet, warm worms upon his flesh was an ecstasy above words—that deeper ecstasy that strikes beyond the body and beyond the mind and tickles the very roots of the soul with unnatural delight. So he stood, rigid as marble, as helplessly stony as any of Medusa's victims in ancient legends were, while the terrible pleasure of Shambleau thrilled and shuddered through every fiber of him; through every atom of his body and the intangible atoms of what men call the soul, through all that was Smith the dreadful pleasure ran. And it was truly dreadful. Dimly he knew it, even as his body answered to the root-deep ecstasy, a foul and dreadful wooing from which his very soul shuddered away—and yet in the innermost depths of that soul some grinning traitor shivered with delight. But deeply, behind all this, he knew horror and revulsion and despair beyond telling, while the intimate caresses crawled obscenely in the secret places of his soul—knew that the soul should not be handled—and shook with the perilous pleasure through it all.

And this conflict and knowledge, this mingling of rapture and revulsion all took place in the flashing of a moment while the scarlet worms coiled and crawled upon him, sending deep, obscene tremors of that infinite pleasure into every atom that made up Smith. And he could not stir in that slimy, ecstatic embrace—and a weakness was flooding that grew deeper after each succeeding wave of intense delight, and the traitor in his soul strengthened and drowned out the revulsion—and something within him ceased to struggle as he sank wholly into a blazing darkness that was oblivion to all else but that devouring rapture. . . .

The young Venusian climbing the stairs to his friend's lodging-room pulled out his key absent-mindedly, a pucker forming between his fine brows. He was slim, as all Venusians are, as fair and sleek as any of them, and as with most of his countrymen the look of cherubic innocence on his face was wholly deceptive. He had the face of a fallen angel, without Lucifer's majesty to redeem it; for a black devil grinned in his eyes and there were faint lines of ruthlessness and dissipation about his mouth to tell of the long years behind him that had run the gamut of experiences and made his name, next to Smith's, the most hated and the most respected in the records of the Patrol.

He mounted the stairs now with a puzzled frown between his eyes. He had come into Lakkdarol on the noon liner—the *Maid* in her hold very skillfully disguised with paint and otherwise—to find in lamentable disorder the affairs he had expected to be settled. And cautious inquiry elicited the information that Smith had not been seen for three days. That was not like his friend—he had never failed before, and the two stood to lose not only a large sum of money but also their personal safety by the inexplicable lapse on the part of Smith. Yarol could think of one solution only: fate had at last caught up with his friend. Nothing but physical disability could explain it.

Still puzzling, he fitted his key in the lock and swung the door open.

In that first moment, as the door opened, he sensed something very wrong. . . . The room was darkened, and for a while he could see nothing, but at the first breath he scented a strange, unnameable odor, half sickening, half sweet. And deep stirrings of ancestral memory awoke him—ancient swamp-born memories from Venusian ancestors far away and long ago. . . .

Yarol laid his hand on his gun, lightly, and opened the door wider. In the dimness all he could see at first was a curious mound in the far corner. . . . Then his eyes grew accustomed to the dark, and he saw it more clearly, a mound that somehow heaved and stirred within itself. . . . A mound of—he caught his breath sharply—a mound like a mass of entrails, living, moving, writhing with an unspeakable aliveness. Then a hot Venusian oath broke from his lips and he cleared the door-sill in a swift stride, slammed the door and set his back against it, gun ready in his hand, although his flesh crawled—for he *knew.* . . .

"Smith!" he said softly, in a voice thick with horror. "Northwest!"

The moving mass stirred—shuddered—sank back into crawling quiescence again.

"Smith! Smith!" The Venusian's voice was gentle and insistent, and it quivered a little with terror.

An impatient ripple went over the whole mass of aliveness in the corner. It stirred again, reluctantly, and then tendril by writhing tendril it began to part itself and fall aside, and very slowly the brown of a spaceman's leather appeared beneath it, all slimed and shining.

"Smith! Northwest!" Yarol's persistent whisper came again, urgently, and with a dreamlike slowness the leather garments moved . . . a man sat up in the midst of the writhing worms, a man who once, long ago, might have been Northwest Smith. From head to foot he was slimy from the embrace of the crawling horror about him. His face was that of some creature beyond humanity—dead-alive, fixed in a gray stare, and the look of terrible ecstasy that overspread it seemed to come from somewhere far within, a faint reflection from immeasurable distances beyond the flesh. And as there is mystery and magic in the moonlight which is after all but a reflection of the everyday sun, so in that gray face turned to the door was a terror unnameable and sweet, a reflection of ecstasy beyond the understanding of any who have known only earthly ecstasy themselves. And as he sat there turning a blank, eyeless face to Yarol the red worms writhed ceaselessly about him, very gently, with a soft, caressive motion that never slacked.

"Smith . . . come here! Smith . . . get up . . . Smith, Smith!" Yarol's whisper hissed in the silence, commanding, urgent—but he made no move to leave the door.

And with a dreadful slowness, like a dead man rising, Smith stood up in the nest of slimy scarlet. He swayed drunkenly on his feet, and two or three crimson tendrils came writhing up his legs to the knees and wound themselves there, supportingly, moving with a ceaseless caress that seemed to give him some hidden strength, for he said then, without inflection,

"Go away. Go away. Leave me alone." And the dead ecstatic face never changed.

"Smith!" Yarol's voice was desperate. "Smith, listen! Smith, can't you hear me?"

"Go away," the monotonous voice said. "Go away. Go away. Go—"

"Not unless you come too. Can't you hear? Smith! Smith! I'll—"

He hushed in mid-phrase, and once more the ancestral prickle of race-memory shivered down his back, for the scarlet mass was moving again, violently, rising. . . .

Yarol pressed back against the door and gripped his gun, and the name of a god he had forgotten years ago rose to his lips unbidden. For he knew what was coming next, and the knowledge was more dreadful than any ignorance could have been.

The red, writhing mass rose higher, and the tendrils parted and a human face looked out—no, half human, with green cat-eyes that shone in that dimness like lighted jewels, compellingly. . . .

Yarol breathed "Shar!" again, and flung up an arm across his face, and the tingle of meeting that green gaze for even an instant went thrilling through him perilously.

"Smith!" he called in despair. "Smith, can't you hear me?"

"Go away," said that voice that was not Smith's. "Go away."

And somehow, although he dared not look, Yarol knew that the—the other—had parted those worm-thick tresses and stood there in all the human sweetness of the brown, curved woman's body, cloaked in living horror. And he felt the eyes upon him, and something was crying insistently in his brain to lower that shielding arm. . . . He was lost—he knew it, and the knowledge gave him that courage which comes from despair. The voice in his brain was growing, swelling, deafening him with a roaring command that all but swept him before it—command to lower that arm—to meet the eyes that opened upon darkness—to submit—and a promise, murmurous and sweet and evil beyond words, of pleasure to come. . . .

But somehow he kept his head—somehow, dizzily, he was gripping his gun in his upflung hand—somehow, incredibly, crossing the narrow room with averted face, groping for Smith's shoulder. There was a moment of blind fumbling in emptiness, and then he found it, and gripped the leather that was slimy and dreadful and wet—and simultaneously he felt something loop gently about his ankle and a shock of repulsive pleasure went through him, and then another coil, and another, wound about his feet. . . .

Yarol set his teeth and gripped the shoulder hard, and his hand shuddered of itself, for the feel of that leather was slimy as the worms about his ankles, and a faint tingle of obscene delight went through him from the contact.

That caressive pressure on his legs was all he could feel, and the voice in his brain drowned out all other sounds, and his body obeyed him reluctantly—but somehow he gave one heave of tremendous effort and swung Smith, stumbling, out of that nest of horror. The twining tendrils ripped loose with a little sucking sound, and the whole mass quivered and reached after, and then Yarol forgot his friend utterly and turned his whole being to the hopeless task of freeing himself. For only a part of him was fighting, now—only a part of him struggled against the twining obscenities, and in his innermost brain the sweet, seductive murmur sounded, and his body clamored to surrender. . . .

"Shar! Shar y'danis . . . Shar mor'la-rol—" prayed Yarol, gasping and half unconscious that he spoke, boy's prayers that he had forgotten years ago, and with his back half turned to the central mass he kicked desperately with his heavy boots at the red, writhing worms about him. They gave back before him, quivering and curling themselves out of reach, and though he knew that more were reaching for his throat from behind, at least he could go on struggling until he was forced to meet those eyes. . . .

He stamped and kicked and stamped again, and for one instant he was free of the slimy grip as the bruised worms curled back from his heavy feet, and he lurched away dizzily, sick with revulsion and despair as he fought off the coils, and then he lifted his eyes and saw the cracked mirror on the wall. Dimly in its reflection he could see the writhing scarlet horror behind him, cat face peering out with its demure girl-smile, dreadfully human, and all the red tendrils reaching after him. And remembrance of something he had read long ago swept incongruously over him, and the gasp of relief and hope that he gave shook for a moment the grip of the command in his brain.

Without pausing for a breath he swung the gun over his shoulder, the reflected barrel in line with the reflected horror in the mirror, and flicked the catch.

In the mirror he saw its blue flame leap in a dazzling spate across the dimness, full into the midst of that squirming, reaching mass behind him. There was a hiss and a blaze and a high, thin scream of inhuman malice and despair—the flame cut a wide arc and went out as the gun fell from his hand, and Yarol pitched forward to the floor.

Northwest Smith opened his eyes to Martian sunlight streaming thinly through the dingy window. Something wet and cold was slapping his face, and the familiar fiery sting of *segir*-whisky burnt his throat.

"Smith!" Yarol's voice was saying from far away. "N. W.! Wake up, damn you! Wake up!"

"I'm—awake," Smith managed to articulate thickly. "Wha's matter?"

Then a cup-rim was thrust against his teeth and Yarol said irritably, "Drink it, you fool!"

Smith swallowed obediently and more of the fire-hot *segir* flowed down his grateful throat. It spread a warmth through his body that awakened him from the numbness that had gripped him until now, and helped a little toward driving out the all-devouring weakness he was becoming aware of slowly. He lay still for a few minutes while the warmth of the whisky went through him, and memory sluggishly began to permeate his brain with the spread of the *segir*. Nightmare memories . . . sweet and terrible . . . memories of—

"God!" gasped Smith suddenly, and tried to sit up. Weakness smote him like a blow, and for an instant the room wheeled as he fell back against something firm and warm—Yarol's shoulder. The Venusian's arm supported him while the room steadied, and after a while he twisted a little and stared into the other's black gaze.

Yarol was holding him with one arm and finishing the mug of *segir* himself, and the black eyes met his over the rim and crinkled into sudden laughter, half hysterical after that terror that was passed.

"By *Pharol!*" gasped Yarol, choking into his mug. "By *Pharol*, N. W.! I'm never gonna let you forget this! Next time you have to drag me out of a mess I'll say—"

"Let it go," said Smith. "What's been going on? How—"

"Shambleau." Yarol's laughter died. "Shambleau! What were you doing with a thing like that?"

"What was it?" Smith asked soberly.

"Mean to say you didn't know? But where'd you find it? How—"

"Suppose you tell me first what you know," said Smith firmly. "And another swig of that *segir,* too, please. I need it."

"Can you hold the mug now? Feel better?"

"Yeah—some. I can hold it—thanks. Now go on."

"Well—I don't know just where to start. They call them Shambleau—"

"Good God, is there more than one?"

"It's a—a sort of race, I think, one of the very oldest. Where they come from nobody knows. The name sounds a little French, doesn't it? But it goes back beyond the start of history. There have always been Shambleau."

"I never heard of 'em."

"Not many people have. And those who know don't care to talk about it much."

"Well, half this town knows. I hadn't any idea what they were talking about, then. And I still don't understand, but—"

"Yes, it happens like this, sometimes. They'll appear, and the news will spread and the town will get together and hunt them down, and after that—well, the story doesn't get around very far. It's too—too unbelievable."

"But—my God, Yarol!—what was it? Where'd it come from? How—"

"Nobody knows just where they come from. Another planet—maybe some undiscovered one. Some say Venus—I know there are some rather awful legends of them handed down in our family—that's how I've heard about it. And the minute I opened that door, awhile back—I—I think I knew that smell. . . ."

"But—what *are* they?"

"God knows. Not human, though they have the human form. Or that may be only an illusion . . . or maybe I'm crazy. I don't know. They're a species of the vampire— or maybe the vampire is a species of—of them. Their normal form must be that— that mass, and in that form they draw nourishment from the—I suppose the life-forces of men. And they take some form—usually a woman form, I think, and key you up to the highest pitch of emotion before they—begin. That's to work the life-force up to intensity so it'll be easier. . . . And they give, always, that horrible, foul pleasure as they—feed. There are some men who, if they survive the first experience, take to it like a drug—can't give it up—keep the thing with them all their lives—which isn't long—feeding it for that ghastly satisfaction. Worse than smoking *ming* or—or 'praying to *Pharol.'*"

"Yes," said Smith. "I'm beginning to understand why that crowd was so surprised and—and disgusted when I said—well, never mind. Go on."

"Did you get to talk to—to it?" asked Yarol.

"I tried to. It couldn't speak very well. I asked it where it came from and it said— 'from far away and long ago'—something like that."

"I wonder. Possibly some unknown planet—but I think not. You know there are so many wild stories with some basis of fact to start from, that I've sometimes wondered—mightn't there be a lot more of even worse and wilder superstitions we've never even heard of? Things like this, blasphemous and foul, that those who know have to keep still about? Awful, fantastic things running around loose that we never hear rumors of at all!

"These things—they've been in existence for countless ages. No one knows when or where they first appeared. Those who've seen them, as we saw this one, don't talk about it. It's just one of those vague, misty rumors you find half hinted at in old books sometimes. . . . I believe they are an older race than man, spawned from ancient seed in times before ours, perhaps on planets that have gone to dust, and so horrible to man that when they are discovered the discoverers keep still about it—forget them again as quickly as they can.

"And they go back to time immemorial. I suppose you recognized the legend of Medusa? There isn't any question that the ancient Greeks knew of them. Does it mean that there have been civilizations before yours that set out from Earth and explored other planets? Or did one of the Shambleau somehow make its way into Greece three thousand years ago? If you think about it long enough you'll go off your head! I wonder how many other legends are based on things like this—things we don't suspect, things we'll never know.

"The Gorgon, Medusa, a beautiful woman with—with snakes for hair, and a gaze that turned men to stone, and Perseus finally killed her—I remembered this just by accident, N. W., and it saved your life and mine—Perseus killed her by using a mirror as he fought to reflect what he dared not look at directly. I wonder what the old Greek who first started that legend would have thought if he'd known that three thousand years later his story would save the lives of two men on another planet. I wonder what that Greek's own story was, and how he met the thing, and what happened. . . .

"Well, there's a lot we'll never know. Wouldn't the records of that race of—of *things*, whatever they are, be worth reading! Records of other planets and other ages and all the beginnings of mankind! But I don't suppose they've kept any records. I don't suppose they've even any place to keep them—from what little I know, or anyone knows about it, they're like the Wandering Jew, just bobbing up here and there at long intervals, and where they stay in the meantime I'd give my eyes to know! But I don't believe that terribly hypnotic power they have indicates any superhuman intelligence. It's their means of getting food—just like a frog's long tongue or a carnivorous flower's odor. Those are physical because the frog and the flower eat physical food. The Shambleau uses a—a mental reach to get mental food. I don't quite know how to put it. And just as a beast that eats the bodies of other animals acquires with each meal greater power over the bodies of the rest, so the Shambleau, stoking itself up with the life-forces of men, increases its power over the minds and the souls of other men. But I'm talking about things I can't define—things I'm not sure exist.

"I only know that when I felt—when those tentacles closed around my legs—I didn't want to pull loose, I felt sensations that—that—oh, I'm fouled and filthy to the very deepest part of me by that—pleasure—and yet—"

"I know," said Smith slowly. The effect of the *segir* was beginning to wear off, and weakness was washing back over him in waves, and when he spoke he was half meditating in a low voice, scarcely realizing that Yarol listened. "I know it—much better than you do—and there's something so indescribably awful that the thing emanates, something so utterly at odds with everything human—there aren't any words to say it. For a while I was a part of it, literally, sharing its thoughts and memories and emotions and hungers, and—well, it's over now and I don't remember very clearly, but the only part left free was that part of me that was all but insane from the—the obscenity of the thing. And yet it was a pleasure so sweet—I think there must be some nucleus of utter evil in me—in everyone—that needs only the proper stimulus to get complete control; because even while I was sick all through from the touch of those—things—there was something in me that was—was simply gibbering with delight. . . . Because of that I saw things—and knew things—horrible, wild things I can't quite remember—visited unbelievable places, looked backward through the memory of that—creature—I was one with, and saw—God, I wish I could remember!"

"You ought to thank your God you can't," said Yarol soberly.

His voice roused Smith from the half-trance he had fallen into, and he rose on his elbow, swaying a little from weakness. The room was wavering before him, and he closed his eyes, not to see it, but he asked, "You say they—they don't turn up again? No way of finding—another?"

Yarol did not answer for a moment. He laid his hands on the other man's shoulders and pressed him back, and then sat staring down into the dark, ravaged face with a new, strange, undefinable look upon it that he had never seen there before—whose meaning he knew, too well.

"Smith," he said finally, and his black eyes for once were steady and serious, and the little grinning devil had vanished from behind them, "Smith, I've never asked your word on anything before, but I've—I've earned the right to do it now, and I'm asking you to promise me one thing."

Smith's colorless eyes met the black gaze unsteadily. Irresolution was in them, and a little fear of what that promise might be. And for just a moment Yarol was looking, not into his friend's familiar eyes, but into a wide gray blankness that held all horror and delight—a pale sea with unspeakable pleasures sunk beneath it. Then the wide stare focused again and Smith's eyes met his squarely and Smith's voice said, "Go ahead. I'll promise."

"That if you ever should meet a Shambleau again—ever, anywhere—you'll draw your gun and burn it to hell the instant you realize what it is. Will you promise me that?"

There was a long silence. Yarol's somber black eyes bored relentlessly into the colorless ones of Smith, not wavering. And the veins stood out on Smith's tanned forehead. He never broke his word—he had given it perhaps half a dozen times in his life, but once he had given it, he was incapable of breaking it. And once more the gray seas flooded in a dim tide of memories, sweet and horrible beyond dreams. Once more Yarol was staring into blankness that hid nameless things. The room was very still.

The gray tide ebbed. Smith's eyes, pale and resolute as steel, met Yarol's levelly. "I'll—try," he said. And his voice wavered.

—1933

ISAAC ASIMOV

1920-1992

Isaac Asimov was born in Petrovichi, U.S.S.R., and immigrated to the United States in 1923. His family settled in Brooklyn, New York, and the young Asimov became a naturalized citizen in 1928. His experiences working in his father's candy store helped to develop several important qualities in his adult personality, including his adherence to hard work and his prudent management of time. Following his graduation from high school, Asimov wanted to apply to medical school, but as an immigrant Jew, he was subject to the enrollment restrictions then placed upon Jewish applicants. He eventually graduated with both a B.S. in 1939 and an M.A. in chemistry in 1941 from Columbia University. World War II interrupted his Ph.D. studies; he worked during the war as a chemist at the U.S. Navy Yard in Philadelphia. Following the war, he returned to Columbia, where he graduated with his terminal degree in 1948 and later accepted a teaching position in biochemistry at the Boston University School of Medicine.

Though Asimov proved himself to be a prodigious scholar (much of his vast body of knowledge, in fact, was self-taught), his greatest passion was writing science fiction. As a young man, Asimov voraciously read science fiction (although his father did not approve of his son reading pulp maga-zines), and in 1938 he met John W. Campbell, Jr., the editor of Astounding Science-Fiction *who nurtured his early writing efforts. Asimov's first published story was "Marooned Off Vesta," appearing in the March 1939 issue of the pulp magazine* Amazing Stories. *In 1959, he quit teaching and turned his attention to full-time writing. Like Robert A. Heinlein, Asimov* *brought "science" to science fiction and thus helped to legitimize the genre. He went on to become one of its most admired writers, as well as a highly productive and versatile author of nearly five hundred books on topics as diverse as Shakespeare, the Bible, mystery fiction, and the history of Constantinople. Asimov also established himself as a popular author of science, writing numerous articles and books that made technical concepts in the hard sciences understandable to the average reader. His most successful work in science fiction includes his Foundation trilogy (which won the Hugo Award in 1966 as the "Best All-Time Series")—*Foundation *(1951),* Foundation and Empire *(1952), and* Second Foundation *(1953)—and his Robot stories—featured in the anthology* I, Robot *(1950), in the novels* The Caves of Steel *(1954) and* The Naked Sun *(1957), and in the omnibus edition,* The Rest of the Robots *(1964). During the 1980s, Asimov published a number of best-selling novels that returned to (and connected) his Foundation and Robot series, and they are* Foundation's Edge *(1982), which also won a Hugo Award,* The Robots of Dawn *(1983),* Robots and Empire *(1985),* Foundation and Earth *(1986), and* Prelude to Foundation *(1988).*

"Robbie" is one of Asimov's earliest tales, written when he was only nineteen years old. It was originally published under the title "Strange Playfellow" in the September 1940 issue of Super Science Stories *and was later anthologized in Asimov's first book,* I, Robot. *Chronologically, "Robbie" is the first story in Asimov's Robot series. Arguably, no other author of science fiction contributed more to the perceptions of robots in contemporary popular culture than did Asimov.*

ROBBIE

"Ninety-eight—ninety-nine—*one hundred.*" Gloria withdrew her chubby little forearm from before her eyes and stood for a moment, wrinkling her nose and blinking in the sunlight. Then, trying to watch in all directions at once, she withdrew a few cautious steps from the tree against which she had been leaning.

She craned her neck to investigate the possibilities of a clump of bushes to the right and then withdrew farther to obtain a better angle for viewing its dark recesses. The quiet was profound except for the incessant buzzing of insects and the occasional chirrup of some hardy bird, braving the midday sun.

Gloria pouted, "I bet he went inside the house, and I've told him a million times that that's not fair."

With tiny lips pressed together tightly and a severe frown crinkling her forehead, she moved determinedly toward the two-story building up past the driveway.

Too late she heard the rustling sound behind her, followed by the distinctive and rhythmic clump-clump of Robbie's metal feet. She whirled about to see her triumphing companion emerge from hiding and make for the home-tree at full speed.

Gloria shrieked in dismay. "Wait, Robbie! That wasn't fair, Robbie! You promised you wouldn't run until I found you." Her little feet could make no headway at all against Robbie's giant strides. Then, within ten feet of the goal, Robbie's pace slowed suddenly to the merest of crawls, and Gloria, with one final burst of wild speed, dashed pantingly past him to touch the welcome bark of home-tree first.

Gleefully, she turned on the faithful Robbie, and with the basest of ingratitude, rewarded him for his sacrifice, by taunting him cruelly for a lack of running ability.

"Robbie can't run," she shouted at the top of her eight-year-old voice. "I can beat him any day. I can beat him any day." She chanted the words in a shrill rhythm.

Robbie didn't answer, of course—not in words. He pantomimed running, instead, inching away until Gloria found herself running after him as he dodged her narrowly, forcing her to veer in helpless circles, little arms outstretched and fanning at the air.

"Robbie," she squealed, "stand still!"—And the laughter was forced out of her in breathless jerks.

—Until he turned suddenly and caught her up, whirling her round, so that for her the world fell away for a moment with a blue emptiness beneath, and green trees stretching hungrily downward toward the void. Then she was down in the grass again, leaning against Robbie's leg and still holding a hard, metal finger.

After a while, her breath resumed. She pushed uselessly at her disheveled hair in vague imitation of one of her mother's gestures and twisted to see if her dress were torn.

She slapped her hand against Robbie's torso, "Bad boy! I'll spank you!"

And Robbie cowered, holding his hands over his face so that she had to add, "No, I won't, Robbie. I won't spank you. But anyway, it's my turn to hide now because you've got longer legs and you promised not to run till I found you."

Robbie nodded his head—a small parallelepiped with rounded edges and corners attached to a similar but much larger parallelepiped that served as torso by means of a short, flexible stalk—and obediently faced the tree. A thin, metal film descended over his glowing eyes and from within his body came a steady, resonant ticking.

"Don't peek now—and don't skip any numbers," warned Gloria, and scurried for cover.

With unvarying regularity, seconds were ticked off, and at the hundredth, up went the eyelids, and the glowing red of Robbie's eyes swept the prospect. They rested for a moment on a bit of colorful gingham that protruded from behind a boulder. He advanced a few steps and convinced himself that it was Gloria who squatted behind it.

Slowly, remaining always between Gloria and home-tree, he advanced on the hiding place, and when Gloria was plainly in sight and could no longer even theorize to herself that she was not seen, he extended one arm toward her, slapping the other against his leg so that it rang again. Gloria emerged sulkily.

"You peeked!" she exclaimed, with gross unfairness. "Besides I'm tired of playing hide-and-seek. I want a ride."

But Robbie was hurt at the unjust accusation, so he seated himself carefully and shook his head ponderously from side to side.

Gloria changed her tone to one of gentle coaxing immediately, "Come on, Robbie. I didn't mean it about the peeking. Give me a ride."

Robbie was not to be won over so easily, though. He gazed stubbornly at the sky, and shook his head even more emphatically.

"Please, Robbie, please give me a ride." She encircled his neck with rosy arms and hugged tightly. Then, changing moods in a moment, she moved away. "If you don't, I'm going to cry," and her face twisted appallingly in preparation.

Hard-hearted Robbie paid scant attention to this dreadful possibility, and shook his head a third time. Gloria found it necessary to play her trump card.

"If you don't," she exclaimed warmly, "I won't tell you any more stories, that's all. Not one—"

Robbie gave in immediately and unconditionally before this ultimatum, nodding his head vigorously until the metal of his neck hummed. Carefully, he raised the little girl and placed her on his broad, flat shoulders.

Gloria's threatened tears vanished immediately and she crowed with delight. Robbie's metal skin, kept at a constant temperature of seventy by the high resistance coils within felt nice and comfortable, while the beautifully loud sound her heels made as they bumped rhythmically against his chest was enchanting.

"You're an air-coaster, Robbie, you're a big, silver air-coaster. Hold out your arms straight.—You *got* to, Robbie, if you're going to be an air-coaster."

The logic was irrefutable. Robbie's arms were wings catching the air currents and he was a silver 'coaster.

Gloria twisted the robot's head and leaned to the right. He banked sharply. Gloria equipped the 'coaster with a motor that went "Br-r-r" and then with weapons that went "Powie" and "Sh-sh-shshsh." Pirates were giving chase and the ship's blasters were coming into play. The pirates dropped in a steady rain.

"Got another one. —Two more," she cried.

Then "Faster, men," Gloria said pompously, "we're running out of ammunition." She aimed over her shoulder with undaunted courage and Robbie was a blunt-nosed spaceship zooming through the void at maximum acceleration.

Clear across the field he sped, to the patch of tall grass on the other side, where he stopped with a suddenness that evoked a shriek from his flushed rider, and then tumbled her onto the soft, green carpet.

Gloria gasped and panted, and gave voice to intermittent whispered exclamations of "That was *nice!*"

Robbie waited until she had caught her breath and then pulled gently at a lock of hair.

"You want something?" said Gloria, eyes wide in an apparently artless complexity that fooled her huge "nursemaid" not at all. He pulled the curl harder.

"Oh, I know. You want a story."

Robbie nodded rapidly.

"Which one?"

Robbie made a semi-circle in the air with one finger.

The little girl protested, *"Again?* I've told you Cinderella a million times. Aren't you tired of it?—It's for babies."

Another semi-circle.

"Oh, well," Gloria composed herself, ran over the details of the tale in her mind (together with her own elaborations, of which she had several) and began:

"Are you ready? Well—once upon a time there was a beautiful little girl whose name was Ella. And she had a terribly cruel stepmother and two very ugly and *very* cruel step-sisters and—"

Gloria was reaching the very climax of the tale—midnight was striking and everything was changing back to the shabby originals lickety-split, while Robbie listened tensely with burning eyes—when the interruption came.

"Gloria!"

It was the high-pitched sound of a woman who has been calling not once, but several times; and had the nervous tone of one in whom anxiety was beginning to overcome impatience.

"Mamma's calling me," said Gloria, not quite happily. "You'd better carry me back to the house, Robbie."

Robbie obeyed with alacrity for somehow there was that in him which judged it best to obey Mrs. Weston, without as much as a scrap of hesitation. Gloria's father was rarely home in the daytime except on Sunday—today, for instance—and when he was, he proved a genial and understanding person. Gloria's mother, however, was a source of uneasiness to Robbie and there was always the impulse to sneak away from her sight.

Mrs. Weston caught sight of them the minute they rose above the masking tufts of long grass and retired inside the house to wait.

"I've shouted myself hoarse, Gloria," she said, severely. "Where were you?"

"I was with Robbie," quavered Gloria. "I was telling him Cinderella, and I forgot it was dinner-time."

"Well, it's a pity Robbie forgot, too." Then, as if that reminded her of the robot's presence, she whirled upon him. "You may go, Robbie. She doesn't need you now." Then, brutally, "And don't come back till I call you."

Robbie turned to go, but hesitated as Gloria cried out in his defense, "Wait, Mamma, you got to let him stay. I didn't finish Cinderella for him. I said I would tell him Cinderella and I'm not finished."

"Gloria!"

"Honest and truly, Mamma, he'll stay so quiet, you won't even know he's here. He can sit on the chair in the corner, and he won't say a word,—I mean he won't *do* anything. Will you, Robbie?"

Robbie, appealed to, nodded his massive head up and down once.

"Gloria, if you don't stop this at once, you shan't see Robbie for a whole week."

The girl's eyes fell, "All right! But Cinderella is his favorite story and I didn't finish it.—And he likes it so much."

The robot left with a disconsolate step and Gloria choked back a sob.

George Weston was comfortable. It was a habit of his to be comfortable on Sunday afternoons. A good, hearty dinner below the hatches; a nice, soft, dilapidated couch on which to sprawl; a copy of the *Times;* slippered feet and shirtless chest;—how could anyone *help* but be comfortable?

He wasn't pleased, therefore, when his wife walked in. After ten years of married life, he still was so unutterably foolish as to love her, and there was no question that he was always glad to see her—still Sunday afternoons just after dinner were sacred to him and his idea of solid comfort was to be left in utter solitude for two or three hours. Consequently, he fixed his eye firmly upon the latest reports of the Lefebre-Yoshida expedition to Mars (this one was to take off from Lunar Base and might actually succeed) and pretended she wasn't there.

Mrs. Weston waited patiently for two minutes, then impatiently for two more, and finally broke the silence.

"George!"

"Hmpph?"

"George, I say! *Will* you put down that paper and look at me?"

The paper rustled to the floor and Weston turned a weary face toward his wife, "What is it, dear?"

"You know what it is, George. It's Gloria and that terrible machine."

"What terrible machine?"

"Now don't pretend you don't know what I'm talking about. It's that robot Gloria calls Robbie. He doesn't leave her for a moment."

"Well, why should he? He's not supposed to. And he certainly isn't a terrible machine. He's the best darn robot money can buy and I'm damned sure he set me back half a year's income. He's worth it, though—darn sight cleverer than half my office staff."

He made a move to pick up the paper again, but his wife was quicker and snatched it away.

"You listen to *me,* George. I won't have my daughter entrusted to a machine—and I don't care how clever it is. It has no soul, and no one knows what it may be thinking. A child just isn't *made* to be guarded by a thing of metal."

Weston frowned, "When did you decide this? He's been with Gloria two years now and I haven't seen you worry till now."

"It was different at first. It was a novelty; it took a load off me, and—and it was a fashionable thing to do. But now I don't know. The neighbors—"

"Well, what have the neighbors to do with it. Now, look. A robot is infinitely more to be trusted than a human nursemaid. Robbie was constructed for only one purpose really—to be the companion of a little child. His entire 'mentality' has been created for the purpose. He just can't help being faithful and loving and kind. He's a machine—*made so.* That's more than you can say for humans."

"But something might go wrong. Some—some—" Mrs. Weston was a bit hazy about the insides of a robot, "some little jigger will come loose and the awful thing will go berserk and—and—" She couldn't bring herself to complete the quite obvious thought.

"Nonsense," Weston denied, with an involuntary nervous shiver. "That's completely ridiculous. We had a long discussion at the time we bought Robbie about the First Law of Robotics. You *know* that it is impossible for a robot to harm a human being; that long before enough can go wrong to alter that First Law, a robot would be completely inoperable. It's a mathematical impossibility. Besides I have an engineer from U.S. Robots here twice a year to give the poor gadget a complete overhaul. Why, there's no more chance of anything at all going wrong with Robbie than there is of you or I suddenly going looney—considerably less, in fact. Besides, how are you going to take him away from Gloria?"

He made another futile stab at the paper and his wife tossed it angrily into the next room.

"That's just it, George! She won't play with anyone else. There are dozens of little boys and girls that she should make friends with, but she won't. She won't go *near* them unless I make her. That's no way for a little girl to grow up. You want her to be normal, don't you? You want her to be able to take her part in society."

"You're jumping at shadows, Grace. Pretend Robbie's a dog. I've seen hundreds of children who would rather have their dog than their father."

"A dog is different, George. We *must* get rid of that horrible thing. You can sell it back to the company. I've asked, and you can."

"You've *asked?* Now look here, Grace, let's not go off the deep end. We're keeping the robot until Gloria is older and I don't want the subject brought up again." And with that he walked out of the room in a huff.

Mrs. Weston met her husband at the door two evenings later. "You'll have to listen to this, George. There's bad feeling in the village."

"About what?" asked Weston. He stepped into the washroom and drowned out any possible answer by the splash of water.

Mrs. Weston waited. She said, "About Robbie."

Weston stepped out, towel in hand, face red and angry, "What are you talking about?"

"Oh, it's been building up and building up. I've tried to close my eyes to it, but I'm not going to any more. Most of the villagers consider Robbie dangerous. Children aren't allowed to go near our place in the evenings."

"We trust *our* child with the thing."

"Well, people aren't reasonable about these things."

"Then to hell with them."

"Saying that doesn't solve the problem. I've got to do my shopping down there. I've got to meet them every day. And it's even worse in the city these days when it comes to robots. New York has just passed an ordinance keeping all robots off the streets between sunset and sunrise."

"All right, but they can't stop us from keeping a robot in our home.—Grace, this is one of your campaigns. I recognize it. But it's no use. The answer is still, no! We're keeping Robbie!"

And yet he loved his wife—and what was worse, his wife knew it. George Weston, after all, was only a man—poor thing—and his wife made full use of every device which a clumsier and more scrupulous sex has learned, with reason and futility, to fear.

Ten times in the ensuing week, he cried, "Robbie stays,—and that's *final!*" and each time it was weaker and accompanied by a louder and more agonized groan.

Came the day at last, when Weston approached his daughter guiltily and suggested a "beautiful" visivox show in the village.

Gloria clapped her hands happily, "Can Robbie go?"

"No, dear," he said, and winced at the sound of his voice, "they won't allow robots at the visivox—but you can tell him all about it when you get home." He stumbled all over the last few words and looked away.

Gloria came back from town bubbling over with enthusiasm, for the visivox had been a gorgeous spectacle indeed.

She waited for her father to maneuver the jet-car into the sunken garage, "Wait till I tell Robbie, Daddy. He would have liked it like anything.—Especially when Francis Fran was backing away so-o-o quietly, and backed right into one of the Leopard-Men and had to run." She laughed again, "Daddy, are there really Leopard-Men on the Moon?"

"Probably not," said Weston absently. "It's just funny make-believe." He couldn't take much longer with the car. He'd have to face it.

Gloria ran across the lawn. "Robbie. —Robbie!"

Then she stopped suddenly at the sight of a beautiful collie which regarded her out of serious brown eyes as it wagged its tail on the porch.

"Oh, what a nice dog!" Gloria climbed the steps, approached cautiously and patted it. "Is it for me, Daddy?"

Her mother had joined them. "Yes, it is, Gloria. Isn't it nice—soft and furry. It's very gentle. It *likes* little girls."

"Can he play games?"

"Surely. He can do any number of tricks. Would you like to see some?"

"Right away. I want Robbie to see him, too. —*Robbie!*" She stopped, uncertainly, and frowned, "I'll bet he's just staying in his room because he's mad at me for not taking him to the visivox. You'll have to explain to him, Daddy. He might not believe me, but he knows if you say it, it's so."

Weston's lips grew tighter. He looked toward his wife but could not catch her eye.

Gloria turned precipitously and ran down the basement steps, shouting as she went, "Robbie— Come and see what Daddy and Mamma brought me. They brought me a dog, Robbie."

In a minute she had returned, a frightened little girl. "Mamma, Robbie isn't in his room. Where is he?" There was no answer and George Weston coughed and was suddenly extremely interested in an aimlessly drifting cloud. Gloria's voice quavered on the verge of tears, "Where's Robbie, Mamma?"

Mrs. Weston sat down and drew her daughter gently to her, "Don't feel bad, Gloria. Robbie has gone away, I think."

"Gone *away?* Where? Where's he gone away, Mamma?"

"No one knows, darling. He just walked away. We've looked and we've looked and we've looked for him, but we can't find him."

"You mean he'll never come back again?" Her eyes were round with horror.

"We may find him soon. We'll keep looking for him. And meanwhile you can play with your nice new doggie. Look at him! His name is Lightning and he can—"

But Gloria's eyelids had overflown, "I don't want the nasty dog—I want Robbie. I want you to find me Robbie." Her feelings became too deep for words, and she spluttered into a shrill wail.

Mrs. Weston glanced at her husband for help, but he merely shuffled his feet morosely and did not withdraw his ardent stare from the heavens, so she bent to the task of consolation, "Why do you cry, Gloria? Robbie was only a machine, just a nasty old machine. He wasn't alive at all."

"He was *not* no machine!" screamed Gloria, fiercely and ungrammatically. "He was a *person* just like you and me and he was my *friend.* I want him back. Oh, Mamma, I want him back."

Her mother groaned in defeat and left Gloria to her sorrow.

"Let her have her cry out," she told her husband. "Childish griefs are never lasting. In a few days, she'll forget that awful robot ever existed."

But time proved Mrs. Weston a bit too optimistic. To be sure, Gloria ceased crying, but she ceased smiling, too, and the passing days found her ever more silent and shadowy. Gradually, her attitude of passive unhappiness wore Mrs. Weston down and all that kept her from yielding was the impossibility of admitting defeat to her husband.

Then, one evening, she flounced into the living room, sat down, folded her arms and looked boiling mad.

Her husband stretched his neck in order to see her over his newspaper, "What now, Grace?"

"It's that child, George. I've had to send back the dog today. Gloria positively couldn't stand the sight of him, she said. She's driving me into a nervous breakdown."

Weston laid down the paper and a hopeful gleam entered his eye, "Maybe— Maybe we ought to get Robbie back. It might be done, you know. I can get in touch with—"

"No!" she replied, grimly. "I won't hear of it. We're not giving up that easily. My child shall *not* be brought up by a robot if it takes years to break her of it."

Weston picked up his paper again with a disappointed air. "A year of this will have me prematurely gray."

"You're a big help, George," was the frigid answer. "What Gloria needs is a change of environment. Of course she can't forget Robbie here. How can she when every tree and rock reminds her of him? It is really the *silliest* situation I have ever heard of. Imagine a child pining away for the loss of a robot."

"Well, stick to the point. What's the change in environment you're planning?"

"We're going to take her to New York."

"The city! In August! Say, do you know what New York is like in August. It's unbearable."

"Millions do bear it."

"They don't have a place like this to go to. If they didn't have to stay in New York, they wouldn't."

"Well, *we* have to. I say we're leaving now—or as soon as we can make the arrangements. In the city, Gloria will find sufficient interests and sufficient friends to perk her up and make her forget that machine."

"Oh, Lord," groaned the lesser half, "those frying pavements!"

"We have to," was the unshaken response. "Gloria has lost five pounds in the last month and my little girl's health is more important to me than your comfort."

"It's a pity you didn't think of your little girl's health before you deprived her of her pet robot," he muttered—but to himself.

Gloria displayed immediate signs of improvement when told of the impending trip to the city. She spoke little of it, but when she did, it was always with lively anticipation. Again, she began to smile and to eat with something of her former appetite.

Mrs. Weston hugged herself for joy and lost no opportunity to triumph over her still skeptical husband.

"You see, George, she helps with the packing like a little angel, and chatters away as if she hadn't a care in the world. It's just as I told you—all we need do is substitute other interests."

"Hmpph," was the skeptical response, "I hope so."

Preliminaries were gone through quickly. Arrangements were made for the preparation of their city home and a couple were engaged as housekeepers for the country home. When the day of the trip finally did come, Gloria was all but her old self again, and no mention of Robbie passed her lips at all.

In high good-humor the family took a taxi-gyro to the airport (Weston would have preferred using his own private 'gyro, but it was only a two-seater with no room for baggage) and entered the waiting liner.

"Come, Gloria," called Mrs. Weston. "I've saved you a seat near the window so you can watch the scenery."

Gloria trotted down the aisle cheerily, flattened her nose into a white oval against the thick clear glass, and watched with an intentness that increased as the sudden coughing of the motor drifted backward into the interior. She was too young to be frightened when the ground dropped away as if let through a trap-door and she herself suddenly became twice her usual weight, but not too young to be mightily interested. It wasn't until the ground had changed into a tiny patch-work quilt that she withdrew her nose, and faced her mother again.

"Will we soon be in the city, Mamma?" she asked, rubbing her chilled nose, and watching with interest as the patch of moisture which her breath had formed on the pane shrank slowly and vanished.

"In about half an hour, dear." Then, with just the faintest trace of anxiety, "Aren't you glad we're going? Don't you think you'll be very happy in the city with all the buildings and people and things to see. We'll go to the visivox every day and see shows and go to the circus and the beach and—"

"Yes, Mamma," was Gloria's unenthusiastic rejoinder. The liner passed over a bank of clouds at the moment, and Gloria was instantly absorbed in the unusual spectacle of clouds underneath one. Then they were over clear sky again, and she turned to her mother with a sudden mysterious air of secret knowledge.

"*I* know why we're going to the city, Mamma."

"Do you?" Mrs. Weston was puzzled. "Why, dear?"

"You didn't tell me because you wanted it to be a surprise, but *I* know." For a moment, she was lost in admiration at her own acute penetration, and then she laughed gaily. "We're going to New York so we can find Robbie, aren't we?—With detectives."

The statement caught George Weston in the middle of a drink of water, with disastrous results. There was a sort of strangled gasp, a geyser of water, and then a bout of choking coughs. When all was over, he stood there, a red-faced, water-drenched and very, very annoyed person.

Mrs. Weston maintained her composure, but when Gloria repeated her question in a more anxious tone of voice, she found her temper rather bent.

"Maybe," she retorted, tartly. "Now sit and be still, for Heaven's sake."

New York City, 1998 A.D., was a paradise for the sight-seer more than ever in its history. Gloria's parents realized this and made the most of it.

On direct orders from his wife, George Weston arranged to have his business take care of itself for a month or so, in order to be free to spend the time in what he termed "dissipating Gloria to the verge of ruin." Like everything else Weston did, this was gone about in an efficient, thorough, and business-like way. Before the month had passed, nothing that could be done had not been done.

She was taken to the top of the half-mile tall Roosevelt Building, to gaze down in awe upon the jagged panorama of rooftops that blended far off in the fields of Long Island and the flatlands of New Jersey. They visited the zoos where Gloria stared in delicious fright at the "real live lion" (rather disappointed that the keepers fed him raw steaks, instead of human beings, as she had expected), and asked insistently and peremptorily to see "the whale."

The various museums came in for their share of attention, together with the parks and the beaches and the aquarium.

She was taken halfway up the Hudson in an excursion steamer fitted out in the archaism of the mad Twenties. She travelled into the stratosphere on an exhibition trip, where the sky turned deep purple and the stars came out and the misty earth below looked like a huge concave bowl. Down under the waters of the Long Island Sound she was taken in a glass-walled sub-sea vessel, where in a green and wavering world, quaint and curious sea-things ogled her and wiggled suddenly away.

On a more prosaic level, Mrs. Weston took her to the department stores where she could revel in another type of fairyland.

In fact, when the month had nearly sped, the Westons were convinced that everything conceivable had been done to take Gloria's mind once and for all off the departed Robbie—but they were not quite sure they had succeeded.

The fact remained that wherever Gloria went, she displayed the most absorbed and concentrated interest in such robots as happened to be present. No matter how exciting the spectacle before her, nor how novel to her girlish eyes, she turned away instantly if the corner of her eye caught a glimpse of metallic movement.

Mrs. Weston went out of her way to keep Gloria away from all robots.

And the matter was finally climaxed in the episode at the Museum of Science and Industry. The Museum had announced a special "children's program" in which exhibits of scientific witchery scaled down to the child mind were to be shown. The Westons, of course, placed it upon their list of "absolutely."

It was while the Westons were standing totally absorbed in the exploits of a powerful electro-magnet that Mrs. Weston suddenly became aware of the fact that Gloria was no longer with her. Initial panic gave way to calm decision and, enlisting the aid of three attendants, a careful search was begun.

Gloria, of course, was not one to wander aimlessly, however. For her age, she was an unusually determined and purposeful girl, quite full of the maternal genes in that respect. She had seen a huge sign on the third floor, which had said, "This Way to the Talking Robot." Having spelled it out to herself and having noticed that her parents did not seem to wish to move in the proper direction, she did the obvious thing. Waiting for an opportune moment of parental distraction, she calmly disengaged herself and followed the sign.

The Talking Robot was a *tour de force,* a thoroughly impractical device, possessing publicity value only. Once an hour, an escorted group stood before it and asked questions of the robot engineer in charge in careful whispers. Those the engineer decided were suitable for the robot's circuits were transmitted to the Talking Robot.

It was rather dull. It may be nice to know that the square of fourteen is one hundred ninety-six, that the temperature at the moment is 72 degrees Fahrenheit, and the air-pressure 30.02 inches of mercury, that the atomic weight of sodium is 23, but one doesn't really need a robot for that. One especially does not need an unwieldy, totally immobile mass of wires and coils spreading over twenty-five square yards.

Few people bothered to return for a second helping, but one girl in her middle teens sat quietly on a bench waiting for a third. She was the only one in the room when Gloria entered.

Gloria did not look at her. To her at the moment, another human being was but an inconsiderable item. She saved her attention for this large thing with the wheels. For a moment, she hesitated in dismay. It didn't look like any robot she had ever seen.

Cautiously and doubtfully she raised her treble voice, "Please, Mr. Robot, sir, are you the Talking Robot, sir?" She wasn't sure, but it seemed to her that a robot that actually talked was worth a great deal of politeness.

(The girl in her mid-teens allowed a look of intense concentration to cross her thin, plain face. She whipped out a small notebook and began writing in rapid pot-hooks.)

There was an oily whir of gears and a mechanically-timbred voice boomed out in words that lacked accent and intonation, "I—am—the—robot—that—talks."

Gloria stared at it ruefully. It *did* talk, but the sound came from inside somewheres. There was no *face* to talk to. She said, "Can you help me, Mr. Robot, sir?"

The Talking Robot was designed to answer questions, and only such questions as it could answer had ever been put to it. It was quite confident of its ability, therefore, "I—can—help—you."

"Thank you, Mr. Robot, sir. Have you seen Robbie?"

"Who—is Robbie?"

"He's a robot, Mr. Robot, sir." She stretched to tip-toes. "He's about so high, Mr. Robot, sir, only higher, and he's very nice. He's got a head, you know. I mean you haven't, but he has, Mr. Robot, sir."

The Talking Robot had been left behind, "A—robot?"

"Yes, Mr. Robot, sir. A robot just like you, except he can't talk, of course, and—looks like a real person."

"A—robot—like—me?"

"Yes, Mr. Robot, sir."

To which the Talking Robot's only response was an erratic splutter and an occasional incoherent sound. The radical generalization offered it, i.e., its existence, not as a particular object, but as a member of a general group, was too much for it. Loyally, it tried to encompass the concept and half a dozen coils burnt out. Little warning signals were buzzing.

(The girl in her mid-teens left at that point. She had enough for her Physics-1 paper on "Practical Aspects of Robotics." This paper was Susan Calvin's first of many on the subject.)

Gloria stood waiting, with carefully concealed impatience, for the machine's answer when she heard the cry behind her of "There she is," and recognized that cry as her mother's.

"What are you doing here, you bad girl?" cried Mrs. Weston, anxiety dissolving at once into anger. "Do you know you frightened your mamma and daddy almost to death? Why did you run away?"

The robot engineer had also dashed in, tearing his hair, and demanding who of the gathering crowd had tampered with the machine. "Can't anybody read signs?" he yelled. "You're not allowed in here without an attendant."

Gloria raised her grieved voice over the din, "I only came to see the Talking Robot, Mamma. I thought he might know where Robbie was because they're both robots." And then, as the thought of Robbie was suddenly brought forcefully home to her, she burst into a sudden storm of tears, "And I *got* to find Robbie, Mamma. I *got* to."

Mrs. Weston strangled a cry, and said, "Oh, good Heavens. Come home, George. This is more than I can stand."

That evening, George Weston left for several hours, and the next morning, he approached his wife with something that looked suspiciously like smug complacence.

"I've got an idea, Grace."

"About what?" was the gloomy, uninterested query.

"About Gloria."

"You're not going to suggest buying back that robot?"

"No, of course not."

"Then go ahead. I might as well listen to you. Nothing *I've* done seems to have done any good."

"All right. Here's what I've been thinking. The whole trouble with Gloria is that she thinks of Robbie as a *person* and not as a *machine.* Naturally, she can't forget him. Now if we managed to convince her that Robbie was nothing more than a mess of steel and copper in the form of sheets and wires with electricity its juice of life, how long would her longings last. It's the psychological attack, if you see my point."

"How do you plan to do it?"

"Simple. Where do you suppose I went last night? I persuaded Robertson of U.S. Robots and Mechanical Men, Inc. to arrange for a complete tour of his premises tomorrow. The three of us will go, and by the time we're through, Gloria will have it drilled into her that a robot is *not* alive."

Mrs. Weston's eyes widened gradually and something glinted in her eyes that was quite like sudden admiration, "Why, George, that's a *good* idea."

And George Weston's vest buttons strained. "Only kind I have," he said.

Mr. Struthers was a conscientious General Manager and naturally inclined to be a bit talkative. The combination, therefore, resulted in a tour that was fully explained, perhaps even over-abundantly explained, at every step. However, Mrs. Weston was not bored. Indeed, she stopped him several times and begged him to repeat his statements in simpler language so that Gloria might understand. Under the influence of this appreciation of his narrative powers, Mr. Struthers expanded genially and became ever more communicative, if possible.

George Weston, himself, showed a gathering impatience.

"Pardon me, Struthers," he said, breaking into the middle of a lecture on the photo-electric cell, "haven't you a section of the factory where only robot labor is employed?"

"Eh? Oh, yes! Yes, indeed!" He smiled at Mrs. Weston. "A vicious circle in a way, robots creating more robots. Of course, we are not making a general practice out of it. For one thing, the unions would never let us. But we can turn out a very few robots using robot labor exclusively, merely as a sort of scientific experiment. You see," he tapped his pince-nez into one palm argumentatively, "what the labor unions don't realize—and I say this as a man who has always been very sympathetic with the labor movement in general—is that the advent of the robot, while involving some dislocation to begin with, will, inevitably—"

"Yes, Struthers," said Weston, "but about that section of the factory you speak of—may we see it? It would be very interesting, I'm sure."

"Yes! Yes, of course!" Mr. Struthers replaced his pince-nez in one convulsive movement and gave vent to a soft cough of discomfiture. "Follow me, please."

He was comparatively quiet while leading the three through a long corridor and down a flight of stairs. Then, when they had entered a large well-lit room that buzzed with metallic activity, the sluices opened and the flood of explanation poured forth again.

"There you are!" he said with pride in his voice. "Robots only! Five men act as overseers and they don't even stay in this room. In five years, that is, since we began this project, not a single accident has occurred. Of course, the robots here assembled are comparatively simple, but . . ."

The General Manager's voice had long died to a rather soothing murmur in Gloria's ears. The whole trip seemed rather dull and pointless to her, though there *were* many robots in sight. None were even remotely like Robbie, though, and she surveyed them with open contempt.

In this room, there weren't any people at all, she noticed. Then her eyes fell upon six or seven robots busily engaged at a round table halfway across the room. They widened in incredulous surprise. It was a big room. She couldn't see for sure, but one of the robots looked like—looked like—*it was!*

"*Robbie!*" Her shriek pierced the air, and one of the robots about the table faltered and dropped the tool he was holding. Gloria went almost mad with joy. Squeezing through the railing before either parent could stop her, she dropped lightly to the floor a few feet below, and ran toward her Robbie, arms waving and hair flying.

And the three horrified adults, as they stood frozen in their tracks, saw what the excited little girl did not see,—a huge, lumbering tractor bearing blindly down upon its appointed track.

It took split-seconds for Weston to come to his senses, and those split-seconds meant everything, for Gloria could not be overtaken. Although Weston vaulted the railing in a wild attempt, it was obviously hopeless. Mr. Struthers signalled wildly to the overseers to stop the tractor, but the overseers were only human and it took time to act.

It was only Robbie that acted immediately and with precision.

With metal legs eating up the space between himself and his little mistress he charged down from the opposite direction. Everything then happened at once. With one sweep of an arm, Robbie snatched up Gloria, slackening his speed not one iota, and, consequently, knocking every breath of air out of her. Weston, not quite comprehending all that was happening, felt, rather than saw, Robbie brush past him, and came to a sudden bewildered halt. The tractor intersected Gloria's path half a second after Robbie had, rolled on ten feet further and came to a grinding, long-drawn-out stop.

Gloria regained her breath, submitted to a series of passionate hugs on the part of both her parents and turned eagerly toward Robbie. As far as she was concerned, nothing had happened except that she had found her friend.

But Mrs. Weston's expression had changed from one of relief to one of dark suspicion. She turned to her husband, and, despite her disheveled and undignified appearance, managed to look quite formidable, "*You* engineered this, *didn't* you?"

George Weston swabbed at a hot forehead with his handkerchief. His hand was unsteady, and his lips could curve only into a tremulous and exceedingly weak smile.

Mrs. Weston pursued the thought, "Robbie wasn't designed for engineering or construction work. He couldn't be of any use to them. You had him placed there deliberately so that Gloria would find him. You know you did."

"Well, I did," said Weston. "But, Grace, how was I to know the reunion would be so violent? And Robbie has saved her life; you'll have to admit that. You *can't* send him away again."

Grace Weston considered. She turned toward Gloria and Robbie and watched them abstractedly for a moment. Gloria had a grip about the robot's neck that would have asphyxiated any creature but one of metal, and was prattling nonsense in half-hysterical frenzy. Robbie's chrome-steel arms (capable of bending a bar of steel two inches in diameter into a pretzel) wound about the little girl gently and lovingly, and his eyes glowed a deep, deep red.

"Well," said Mrs. Weston, at last, "I guess he can stay with us until he rusts."

—1940

ROBERT A. HEINLEIN
1907-1988

Often regarded as the "dean of modern American science fiction" by his many fans, Robert A. Heinlein was one of the first authors to incorporate the hard sciences (such as physics, chemistry, and astronomy) as an important element in the writing of "science" fiction. Born in Butler, Missouri (near Kansas City), Heinlein graduated from Kansas City Central High School in 1924. He then enrolled at the University of Missouri, leaving after a year to attend the U.S. Naval Academy at Annapolis. Heinlein graduated in 1929 and served as a gunnery officer on several ships, including the USS Lexington. In 1934, he was forced to leave the Navy after contracting tuberculosis. While searching for a new career, Heinlein attended graduate school at the University of California at Los Angeles for a brief period (researching mathematics and physics) and tried his hand at several different occupations, including real estate work and politics. In 1939, he published his first story, "Life-Line," in the pulp magazine Astounding Science-Fiction, *and his lucrative career as one of science fiction's top authors was launched.*

Heinlein was "discovered" by John W. Campbell Jr., who, in his capacity as the visionary editor of Astounding, *had nurtured the early writings of other soon-to-be masters of science fiction, including Isaac Asimov. Heinlein's most impressive achievement as a yet "unseasoned" writer, was the development of his Future History series, a collection of loosely connected stories that chart humanity's scientific progress. These early stories were anthologized in the books* The Man Who Sold the Moon *(1950),* The Green Hills of Earth *(1951), and* Revolt in 2100 *(1953), and were collectively assembled in the omnibus edition,* The Past Through Tomorrow *(1967).*

As with Andre Norton, Heinlein's early book-length science fiction (published by Scribner's) was intended primarily for an adolescent readership. These novels—including the early juveniles Rocket Ship Galileo *(1947),* Space Cadet *(1948), and* Red Planet: A Colonial Boy on Mars *(1949), and the later juveniles* Time for the Stars *(1956),* Citizen of the Galaxy *(1957), and* Have Space Suit–Will Travel *(1958)—feature some of his most popular work. His controversial vision of futuristic warfare,* Starship Troopers *(1959), initiated his "mature" phase as an author of science fiction, a period that ranges from his epic* Stranger in a Strange Land *(1961), a landmark science fiction novel adopted by the American counter-culture movement during the 1960s, to his more recent national best-sellers,* The Number of the Beast *(1980),* Job: A Comedy of Justice *(1984), and* The Cat Who Walks through Walls *(1985). Over the years, Heinlein's fiction has won a number of literary awards: four Hugo Awards, for* Double Star *(in 1956),* Starship Troopers *(in 1960),* Stranger in a Strange Land *(in 1962), and* The Moon Is a Harsh Mistress *(in 1967), as well as the Science Fiction Writers of America Grand Master Award in 1975. In addition, Heinlein co-authored the screenplay to the classic George Pal/Irving Pichel science fiction film* Destination Moon *(1950), which is based on the novel* Rocket Ship Galileo.

Heinlein wrote science fiction for both the pulp markets and the "slick" magazines. "Space Jockey," for example, was first published in the April 26,

1947, issue of the Saturday Evening Post *(and later anthologized in* The Green Hills of Earth*). This Future History tale nicely illustrates Heinlein's narrative extrapolation of late-1940s astrophysics, which he employs as a crucial motif in the plot. The story also illustrates Heinlein's traditional view of male/female gender roles.*

SPACE JOCKEY

Just as they were leaving the telephone called his name. "Don't answer it," she pleaded. "We'll miss the curtain."

"Who is it?" he called out. The viewplate lighted; he recognized Olga Pierce, and behind her the Colorado Springs office of Trans-Lunar Transit.

"Calling Mr. Pemberton. Calling—Oh, it's you, Jake. You're on. Flight 27, Supra-New York to Space Terminal. I'll have a copter pick you up in twenty minutes."

"How come?" he protested. "I'm fourth down on the call board."

"You *were* fourth down. Now you are standby pilot to Hicks—and he just got a psycho down-check."

"Hicks got psychoed? That's silly!"

"Happens to the best, chum. Be ready. 'Bye now."

His wife was twisting sixteen dollars worth of lace handkerchief to a shapeless mass. "Jake, this is ridiculous. For three months I haven't seen enough of you to know what you look like."

"Sorry, kid. Take Helen to the show."

"Oh, Jake, I don't care about the show; I wanted to get you where they couldn't reach you for once."

"They would have called me at the theater."

"Oh, no! I wiped out the record you'd left."

"Phyllis! Are you trying to get me fired?"

"Don't look at me that way." She waited, hoping that he would speak, regretting the side issue, and wondering how to tell him that her own fretfulness was caused, not by disappointment, but by gnawing worry for his safety every time he went out into space.

She went on desperately, "You don't have to take this flight, darling; you've been on Earth less than the time limit. Please, Jake!"

He was peeling off his tux. "I've told you a thousand times: a pilot doesn't get a regular run by playing space-lawyer with the rule book. Wiping out my follow-up message—why did you do it, Phyllis? Trying to ground me?"

"No, darling, but I thought just this once—"

"When they offer me a flight I take it." He walked stiffly out of the room.

He came back ten minutes later, dressed for space and apparently in good humor; he was whistling: "—the caller called Casey at ha' past four; he kissed his—" He broke off when he saw her face, and set his mouth. "Where's my coverall?"

"I'll get it. Let me fix you something to eat."

"You know I can't take high acceleration on a full stomach. And why lose thirty bucks to lift another pound?"

Dressed as he was, in shorts, singlet, sandals, and pocket belt, he was already good for about minus-fifty pounds in weight bonus; she started to tell him the weight penalty on a sandwich and a cup of coffee did not matter to them, but it was just one more possible cause for misunderstanding.

Neither of them said much until the taxicab clumped on the roof. He kissed her goodbye and told her not to come outside. She obeyed—until she heard the helicopter take off. Then she climbed to the roof and watched it out of sight.

The traveling-public gripes at the lack of direct Earth-to-Moon service, but it takes three types of rocket ships and two space-station changes to make a fiddling quarter-million-mile jump for a good reason: Money.

The Commerce Commission has set the charges for the present three-stage lift from here to the Moon at thirty dollars a pound. Would direct service be cheaper?— a ship designed to blast off from Earth, make an airless landing on the Moon, return and make an atmosphere landing, would be so cluttered up with heavy special equipment used only once in the trip that it could not show a profit at a thousand dollars a pound! Imagine combining a ferry boat, a subway train, and an express elevator—

So Trans-Lunar uses rockets braced for catapulting, and winged for landing on return to Earth to make the terrific lift from Earth to our satellite station Supra-New York. The long middle lap, from there to where Space Terminal circles the Moon, calls for comfort—but no landing gear. The *Flying Dutchman* and the *Philip Nolan* never land; they were even assembled in space, and they resemble winged rockets like the *Skysprite* and the *Firefly* as little as a Pullman train resembles a parachute.

The *Moonbat* and the *Gremlin* are good only for the jump from Space Terminal down to Luna . . . no wings, cocoon-like acceleration-and-crash hammocks, fractional controls on their enormous jets.

The change-over points would not have to be more than air-conditioned tanks. Of course Space Terminal is quite a city, what with the Mars and Venus traffic, but even today Supra-New York is still rather primitive, hardly more than a fueling point and a restaurant-waiting room. It has only been the past five years that it has even been equipped to offer the comfort of one-gravity centrifuge service to passengers with queasy stomachs.

Pemberton weighed in at the spaceport office, then hurried over to where the *Skysprite* stood cradled in the catapult. He shucked off his coverall, shivered as he handed it to the gateman, and ducked inside. He went to his acceleration hammock and went to sleep; the lift to Supra-New York was not his worry—his job was deep space.

He woke at the surge of the catapult and the nerve-tingling rush up the face of Pikes Peak. When the *Skysprite* went into free flight, flung straight up above the Peak, Pemberton held his breath; if the rocket jets failed to fire, the ground-to-space pilot must try to wrestle her into a glide and bring her down, on her wings.

The rockets roared on time; Jake went back to sleep.

When the *Skysprite* locked in with Supra-New York, Pemberton went to the station's stellar navigation room. He was pleased to find Shorty Weinstein, the computer, on duty. Jake trusted Shorty's computations—a good thing when your ship, your passengers, and your own skin depend thereon. Pemberton had to be a better than average mathematician himself in order to be a pilot; his own limited talent made him appreciate the genius of those who computed the orbits.

"Hot Pilot Pemberton, the Scourge of the Spaceways—Hi!" Weinstein handed him a sheet of paper.

Jake looked at it, then looked amazed. "Hey, Shorty—you've made a mistake."

"Huh? Impossible. Mabel can't make mistakes." Weinstein gestured at the giant astrogation computer filling the far wall.

"*You* made a mistake. You gave me an easy fix—'Vega, Antares, Regulus.' You make things easy for the pilot and your guild'll chuck you out." Weinstein looked sheepish but pleased. "I see I don't blast off for seventeen hours. I could have taken the morning freight." Jake's thoughts went back to Phyllis.

"UN canceled the morning trip."

"Oh—" Jake shut up, for he knew Weinstein knew as little as he did. Perhaps the flight would have passed too close to an A-bomb rocket, circling the globe like a policeman. The General Staff of the Security Council did not give out information about the top secrets guarding the peace of the planet.

Pemberton shrugged. "Well, if I'm asleep, call me three hours minus."

"Right. Your tape will be ready."

While he slept, the *Flying Dutchman* nosed gently into her slip, sealed her airlocks to the Station, discharged passengers and freight from Luna City. When he woke, her holds were filling, her fuel replenished, and passengers boarding. He stopped by the post office radio desk, looking for a letter from Phyllis. Finding none, he told himself that she would have sent it to Terminal. He went on into the restaurant, bought the facsimile *Herald-Tribune*, and settled down grimly to enjoy the comics and his breakfast.

A man sat down opposite him and proceeded to plague him with silly questions about rocketry, topping it by misinterpreting the insignia embroidered on Pemberton's singlet and miscalling him "Captain." Jake hurried through breakfast to escape him, then picked up the tape from his automatic pilot, and went aboard the *Flying Dutchman.*

After reporting to the Captain he went to the control room, floating and pulling himself along by the handgrips. He buckled himself into the pilot's chair and started his check off.

Captain Kelly drifted in and took the other chair as Pemberton was finishing his checking runs on the ballistic tracker. "Have a Camel, Jake."

"I'll take a rain check." He continued; Kelly watched him with a slight frown. Like captains and pilots on Mark Twain's Mississippi—and for the same reasons—a spaceship captain bosses his ship, his crew, his cargo, and his passengers, but the pilot is the final, legal, and unquestioned boss of how the ship is handled from blast-off to the end of the trip. A captain may turn down a given pilot—nothing more. Kelly fingered a slip of paper tucked in his pouch and turned over in his mind the words with which the Company psychiatrist on duty had handed it to him.

"I'm giving this pilot clearance, Captain, but you need not accept it."

"Pemberton's a good man. What's wrong?"

The psychiatrist thought over what he had observed while posing as a silly tourist bothering a stranger at breakfast. "He's a little more anti-social than his past record shows. Something on his mind. Whatever it is, he can tolerate it for the present. We'll keep an eye on him."

Kelly had answered, "Will you come along with him as pilot?"

"If you wish."

"Don't bother—I'll take him. No need to lift a deadhead."

Pemberton fed Weinstein's tape into the robot-pilot, then turned to Kelly. "Control ready, sir."

"Blast when ready, Pilot." Kelly felt relieved when he heard himself make the irrevocable decision.

Pemberton signaled the Station to cast loose. The great ship was nudged out by an expanding pneumatic ram until she swam in space a thousand feet away, secured by a single line. He then turned the ship to its blast-off direction by causing a flywheel, mounted on gymbals at the ship's center of gravity, to spin rapidly. The ship spun slowly in the opposite direction, by grace of Newton's Third Law of Motion.

Guided by the tape, the robot-pilot tilted prisms of the pilot's periscope so that Vega, Antares, and Regulus would shine as one image when the ship was headed right; Pemberton nursed the ship to that heading . . . fussily; a mistake of one minute of arc here meant two hundred miles at destination.

When the three images made a pinpoint, he stopped the flywheels and locked in the gyros. He then checked the heading of his ship by direct observation of each of the stars, just as a salt-water skipper uses a sextant, but with incomparably more accurate instruments. This told him nothing about the correctness of the course Weinstein had ordered—he had to take that as Gospel—but it assured him that the robot and its tape were behaving as planned. Satisfied, he cast off the last line.

Seven minutes to go—Pemberton flipped the switch permitting the robot-pilot to blast away when its clock told it to. He waited, hands poised over the manual controls, ready to take over if the robot failed, and felt the old, inescapable sick excitement building up inside him.

Even as adrenaline poured into him, stretching his time sense, throbbing in his ears, his mind kept turning back to Phyllis.

He admitted she had a kick coming—spacemen shouldn't marry. Not that she'd starve if he messed up a landing, but a gal doesn't want insurance; she wants a husband—minus six minutes.

If he got a regular run she could live in Space Terminal.

No good—idle women at Space Terminal went bad. Oh, Phyllis wouldn't become a tramp or a rum bum; she'd just go bats.

Five minutes more—he didn't care much for Space Terminal himself. Nor for space! "The Romance of Interplanetary Travel"—it looked well in print, but he knew what it was: A job. Monotony. No scenery. Bursts of work, tedious waits. No home life.

Why didn't he get an honest job and stay home nights?

He knew! Because he was a space jockey and too old to change.

What chance has a thirty-year-old married man, used to important money, to change his racket? (Four minutes) He'd look good trying to sell helicopters on commission, now, wouldn't he?

Maybe he could buy a piece of irrigated land and—Be your age, chum! You know as much about farming as a cow knows about cube root! No, he had made his bed when he picked rockets during his training hitch. If he had bucked for the electronics branch, or taken a GI scholarship—too late now. Straight from the service into Harriman's Lunar Exploitations, hopping ore on Luna. That had torn it.

"How's it going, Doc?" Kelly's voice was edgy.

"Minus two minutes some seconds." Damnation—Kelly knew better than to talk to the pilot on minus time.

He caught a last look through the periscope. Antares seemed to have drifted. He unclutched the gyro, tilted and spun the flywheel, braking it savagely to a stop a moment later. The image was again a pinpoint. He could not have explained what he did: it was virtuosity, exact juggling, beyond textbook and classroom.

Twenty seconds . . . across the chronometer's face beads of light trickled the seconds away while he tensed, ready to fire by hand, or even to disconnect and refuse the trip if his judgment told him to. A too-cautious decision might cause Lloyds' to cancel his bond; a reckless decision could cost his license or even his life—and others.

But he was not thinking of underwriters and licenses, nor even of lives. In truth he was not thinking at all; he was feeling, feeling his ship, as if his nerve ends extended into every part of her. Five seconds . . . the safety disconnects clicked out. Four seconds . . . three seconds . . . two seconds . . . . one——

He was stabbing at the hand-fire button when the roar hit him.

Kelly relaxed to the pseudo-gravity of the blast and watched. Pemberton was soberly busy, scanning dials, noting time, checking his progress by radar bounced off Supra-New York. Weinstein's figures, robot-pilot, the ship itself, all were clicking together.

Minutes later, the critical instant neared when the robot should cut the jets. Pemberton poised a finger over the hand cut-off, while splitting his attention among radarscope, accelerometer, periscope, and chronometer. One instant they were roaring along on the jets; the next split second the ship was in free orbit, plunging silently toward the Moon. So perfectly matched were human and robot that Pemberton himself did not know which had cut the power.

He glanced again at the board, then unbuckled. "How about that cigarette, Captain? And you can let your passengers unstrap."

No co-pilot is needed in space and most pilots would rather share a toothbrush than a control room. The pilot works about an hour at blast off, about the same before contact, and loafs during free flight, save for routine checks and corrections. Pemberton prepared to spend one hundred and four hours eating, reading, writing letters, and sleeping—especially sleeping.

When the alarm woke him, he checked the ship's position, then wrote to his wife. "Phyllis my dear," he began, "I don't blame you for being upset at missing your night out. I was disappointed, too. But bear with me, darling, I should be on a regular run before long. In less than ten years I'll be up for retirement and we'll have a chance to catch up on bridge and golf and things like that. I know it's pretty hard to—"

The voice circuit cut in. "Oh, Jake—put on your company face. I'm bringing a visitor to the control room."

"No visitors in the control room, Captain."

"Now, Jake. This lunkhead has a letter from Old Man Harriman himself. 'Every possible courtesy—' and so forth."

Pemberton thought quickly. He could refuse—but there was no sense in offending the big boss. "Okay, Captain. Make it short."

The visitor was a man, jovial, oversize—Jake figured him for an eighty pound weight penalty. Behind him a thirteen-year-old male counterpart came zipping through the door and lunged for the control console. Pemberton snagged him by the arm and forced himself to speak pleasantly. "Just hang on to that bracket, youngster. I don't want you to bump your head."

"Leggo me! Pop—make him let go."

Kelly cut in. "I think he had best hang on, Judge."

"Umm, uh—very well. Do as the Captain says, Junior."

"Aw, gee, Pop!"

"Judge Schacht, this is First Pilot Pemberton," Kelly said rapidly. "He'll show you around."

"Glad to know you, Pilot. Kind of you, and all that."

"What would you like to see, Judge?" Jake said carefully.

"Oh, this and that. It's for the boy—his first trip. I'm an old spacehound myself—probably more hours than half your crew." He laughed. Pemberton did not.

"There's not much to see in free flight."

"Quite all right. We'll just make ourselves at home—eh, Captain?"

"I wanna sit in the control seat," Schacht Junior announced.

Pemberton winced. Kelly said urgently, "Jake, would you mind outlining the control system for the boy? Then we'll go."

"He doesn't have to show me anything. I know all about it. I'm a Junior Rocketeer of America—see my button?" The boy shoved himself toward the control desk.

Pemberton grabbed him, steered him into the pilot's chair, and strapped him in. He then flipped the board's disconnect.

"Whatcha doing?"

"I cut off power to the controls so I could explain them."

"Aintcha gonna fire the jets?"

"No." Jake started a rapid description of the use and purpose of each button, dial, switch, meter, gimmick, and scope.

Junior squirmed. "How about meteors?" he demanded.

"Oh, that—maybe one collision in half a million Earth-Moon trips. Meteors are scarce."

"So what? Say you hit the jackpot? You're in the soup."

"Not at all. The anti-collision radar guards all directions five hundred miles out. If anything holds a steady bearing for three seconds, a direct hook-up starts the jets. First a warning gong so that everybody can grab something solid, then one second later—*Boom!*—We get out of there fast."

"Sounds corny to me. Lookee, I'll show you how Commodore Cartwright did it in *The Comet Busters*—"

"Don't touch those controls!"

"You don't own this ship. My pop says—"

"Oh, Jake!" Hearing his name, Pemberton twisted, fish-like, to face Kelly.

"Jake, Judge Schacht would like to know—" From the corner of his eye Jake saw the boy reach for the board. He turned, started to shout—acceleration caught him, while the jets roared in his ear.

An old spacehand can usually recover, catlike, in an unexpected change from weightlessness to acceleration. But Jake had been grabbing for the boy, instead of for anchorage. He fell back and down, twisted to try to avoid Schacht, banged his head on the frame of the open air-tight door below, and fetched up on the next deck, out cold.

Kelly was shaking him. "You all right, Jake?"

He sat up. "Yeah. Sure." He became aware of the thunder, the shivering deck-plates. "The jets! Cut the power!"

He shoved Kelly aside and swarmed up into the control room, jabbed at the cut-off button. In sudden ringing silence, they were again weightless.

Jake turned, unstrapped Schacht Junior, and hustled him to Kelly. "Captain, please remove this menace from my control room."

"Leggo! Pop—he's gonna hurt me!"

The elder Schacht bristled at once. "What's the meaning of this? Let go of my son!"

"Your precious son cut in the jets."

"Junior—did you do that?"

The boy shifted his eyes. "No, Pop. It . . . it was a meteor."

Schacht looked puzzled. Pemberton snorted. "I had just told him how the radar-guard can blast to miss a meteor. He's lying."

Schacht ran through the process he called "making up his mind", then answered, "Junior never lies. Shame on you, a grown man, to try to put the blame on a help-less boy. I shall report you, sir. Come, Junior."

Jake grabbed his arm. "Captain, I want those controls photographed for fingerprints before this man leaves the room. It was not a meteor; the controls were dead, until this boy switched them on. Furthermore the anti-collision circuit sounds an alarm."

Schacht looked wary. "This is ridiculous. I simply objected to the slur on my son's character. No harm has been done."

"No harm, eh? How about broken arms—or necks? And wasted fuel, with more to waste before we're back in the groove. Do you know, Mister 'Old Spacehound,' just how precious a little fuel will be when we try to match orbits with Space Terminal—if we haven't got it? We may have to dump cargo to save the ship, cargo at $60,000 a ton on freight charges alone. Fingerprints will show the Commerce Commission whom to nick for it."

When they were alone again Kelly asked anxiously, "You won't really have to jetti-son? You've got a maneuvering reserve."

"Maybe we can't even get to Terminal. How long did she blast?"

Kelly scratched his head. "I was woozy myself."

"We'll open the accelerograph and take a look."

Kelly brightened. "Oh, sure! If the brat didn't waste too much, then we just swing ship and blast back the same length of time."

Jake shook his head. "You forgot the changed mass-ratio."

"Oh . . . oh, yes!" Kelly looked embarrassed. Mass-ratio . . . under power, the ship lost the weight of fuel burned. The thrust remained constant; the mass it pushed shrank. Getting back to proper position, course, and speed became a complicated problem in the calculus of ballistics. "But you can do it, can't you?"

"I'll have to. But I sure wish I had Weinstein here."

Kelly left to see about his passengers; Jake got to work. He checked his situation by astronomical observation and by radar. Radar gave him all three factors quickly but with limited accuracy. Sights taken of Sun, Moon, and Earth gave him position, but told nothing of course and speed, at that time—nor could he afford to wait to take a second group of sights for the purpose.

Dead reckoning gave him an estimated situation, by adding Weinstein's predic-tions to the calculated effect of young Schacht's meddling. This checked fairly well with the radar and visual observations, but still he had no notion of whether or not he could get back in the groove and reach his destination; it was now necessary to calculate what it would take and whether or not the remaining fuel would be enough to brake his speed and match orbits.

In space, it does no good to reach your journey's end if you flash on past at miles per second, or even crawling along at a few hundred miles per hour. To catch an egg on a plate—don't bump!

He started doggedly to work to compute how to do it using the least fuel, but his little Marchant electronic calculator was no match for the tons of IBM computer at Supra-New York, nor was he Weinstein. Three hours later he had an answer of sorts. He called Kelly. "Captain? You can start by jettisoning Schacht & Son."

"I'd like to. No way out, Jake?"

"I can't promise to get your ship in safely without dumping. Better dump now, before we blast. It's cheaper."

Kelly hesitated; he would as cheerfully lose a leg. "Give me time to pick out what to dump."

"Okay." Pemberton returned sadly to his figures, hoping to find a saving mistake, then thought better of it. He called the radio room. "Get me Weinstein at Supra-New York."

"Out of normal range."

"I know that. This is the Pilot. Safety priority—urgent. Get a tight beam on them and nurse it."

"Uh . . . aye aye, sir. I'll try."

Weinstein was doubtful. "Cripes, Jake, I can't pilot you."

"Dammit, you can work problems for me!"

"What good is seven-place accuracy with bum data?"

"Sure, sure. But you know what instruments I've got; you know about how well I can handle them. Get me a better answer."

"I'll try." Weinstein called back four hours later. "Jake? Here's the dope: You planned to blast back to match your predicted speed, then made side corrections for position. Orthodox but uneconomical. Instead I had Mabel solve for it as one maneuver."

"Good!"

"Not so fast. It saves fuel but not enough. You can't possibly get back in your old groove and then match Terminal without dumping."

Pemberton let it sink in, then said, "I'll tell Kelly."

"Wait a minute, Jake. Try this. Start from scratch."

"Huh?"

"Treat it as a brand-new problem. Forget about the orbit on your tape. With your present course, speed, and position, compute the cheapest orbit to match with Terminal's. Pick a new groove."

Pemberton felt foolish. "I never thought of that."

"Of course not. With the ship's little one-lung calculator it'd take you three weeks to solve it. You set to record?"

"Sure."

"Here's your data." Weinstein started calling it off.

When they had checked it, Jake said, "That'll get me there?"

"Maybe. *If* the data you gave me is up to your limit of accuracy; *if* you can follow instructions as exactly as a robot, *if* you can blast off and make contact so precisely that you don't need side corrections, then you might squeeze home. Maybe. Good luck, anyhow." The wavering reception muffled their goodbyes.

Jake signaled Kelly. "Don't jettison, Captain. Have your passengers strap down. Stand by to blast. Minus fourteen minutes."

"Very well, Pilot."

The new departure made and checked, he again had time to spare. He took out his unfinished letter, read it, then tore it up.

"Dearest Phyllis," he started again, "I've been doing some hard thinking this trip and have decided that I've just been stubborn. What am I doing way out here? I like my home. I like to see my wife.

"Why should I risk my neck and your peace of mind to herd junk through the sky? Why hang around a telephone waiting to chaperon fatheads to the Moon—numbskulls who couldn't pilot a rowboat and should have stayed at home in the first place?

"Money, of course. I've been afraid to risk a change. I won't find another job that will pay half as well, but, if you are game, I'll ground myself and we'll start over. All my love,

"Jake"

He put it away and went to sleep, to dream that an entire troop of Junior Rocketeers had been quartered in his control room.

The closeup view of the Moon is second only to the space-side view of the Earth as a tourist attraction; nevertheless Pemberton insisted that all passengers strap down during the swing around to Terminal. With precious little fuel for the matching maneuver, he refused to hobble his movements to please sightseers.

Around the bulge of the Moon, Terminal came into sight—by radar only, for the ship was tail foremost. After each short braking blast Pemberton caught a new radar fix, then compared his approach with a curve he had plotted from Weinstein's figures—with one eye on the time, another on the 'scope, a third on the plot, and a fourth on his fuel gages.

"Well, Jake?" Kelly fretted. "Do we make it?"

"How should I know? You be ready to dump." They had agreed on liquid oxygen as the cargo to dump, since it could be let boil out through the outer valves, without handling.

"Don't say it, Jake."

"Damn it—I won't if I don't have to." He was fingering his controls again; the blast chopped off his words. When it stopped, the radio maneuvering circuit was calling him.

"*Flying Dutchman,* Pilot speaking," Jake shouted back.

"Terminal Control—Supro reports you short on fuel."

"Right."

"Don't approach. Match speeds outside us. We'll send a transfer ship to refuel you and pick up passengers."

"I think I can make it."

"Don't try it. Wait for refueling."

"Quit telling me how to pilot my ship!" Pemberton switched off the circuit, then stared at the board, whistling morosely. Kelly filled in the words in his mind: *"Casey said to the fireman 'Boy, you better jump, cause two locomotives are agoing to bump!'"*

"You going in the slip anyhow, Jake?"

"Mmm—no, blast it. I can't take a chance of caving in the side of Terminal, not with passengers aboard. But I'm not going to match speeds fifty miles outside and wait for a piggyback."

He aimed for a near miss just outside Terminal's orbit, conning by instinct, for Weinstein's figures meant nothing by now. His aim was good; he did not have to waste his hoarded fuel on last minute side corrections to keep from hitting

Terminal. When at last he was sure of sliding safely on past if unchecked, he braked once more. Then, as he started to cut off the power, the jets coughed, sputtered, and quit.

The *Flying Dutchman* floated in space, five hundred yards outside Terminal, speeds matched.

Jake switched on the radio. "Terminal—stand by for my line. I'll warp her in."

He had filed his report, showered, and was headed for the post office to radiostat his letter, when the bullhorn summoned him to the Commodore-Pilot's office. Oh, oh, he told himself, Schacht has kicked the Brass—I wonder just how much stock that bliffy owns? And there's that other matter—getting snotty with Control.

He reported stiffly. "First Pilot Pemberton, sir."

Commodore Soames looked up. "Pemberton—oh, yes. You hold two ratings, space-to-space and airless-landing."

Let's not stall around, Jake told himself. Aloud he said, "I have no excuses for anything this last trip. If the Commodore does not approve the way I run my control room, he may have my resignation."

"What are you talking about?"

"I, well—don't you have a passenger complaint on me?"

"Oh, that!" Soames brushed it aside. "Yes, he's been here. But I have Kelly's report, too—and your chief jetman's, and a special from Supra-New York. That was crack piloting, Pemberton."

"You mean there's no beef from the Company?"

"When have I failed to back up my pilots? You were perfectly right; I would have stuffed him out the air lock. Let's get down to business: You're on the space-to-space board, but I want to send a special to Luna City. Will you take it, as a favor to me?"

Pemberton hesitated; Soames went on, "That oxygen you saved is for the Cosmic Research Project. They blew the seals on the north tunnel and lost tons of the stuff. The work is stopped—about $130,000 a day in overhead, wages, and penalties. The *Gremlin* is here, but no pilot until the *Moonbat* gets in—except you. Well?"

"But I—look, Commodore, you can't risk people's necks on a jet landing of mine. I'm rusty; I need a refresher and a check-out."

"No passengers, no crew, no captain—your neck alone."

"I'll take her."

Twenty-eight minutes later, with the ugly, powerful hull of the *Gremlin* around him, he blasted away. One strong shove to kill her orbital speed and let her fall toward the Moon, then no more worries until it came time to "ride 'er down on her tail."

He felt good—until he hauled out two letters, the one he had failed to send, and one from Phyllis, delivered at Terminal.

The letter from Phyllis was affectionate—and superficial. She did not mention his sudden departure; she ignored his profession completely. The letter was a model of correctness, but it worried him.

He tore up both letters and started another. It said, in part: "—never said so outright, but you resent my job.

"I have to work to support us. You've got a job, too. It's an old, old job that women have been doing a long time—crossing the plains in covered wagons, waiting for ships to come back from China, or waiting around a mine head after an explosion—kiss him goodbye with a smile, take care of him at home.

"You married a spaceman, so part of your job is to accept my job cheerfully. I think you can do it, when you realize it. I hope so, for the way things have been going won't do for either of us.

Believe me, I love you.
Jake"

He brooded on it until time to bend the ship down for his approach. From twenty miles altitude down to one mile he let the robot brake her, then shifted to manual while still falling slowly. A perfect airless-landing would be the reverse of the take-off of a war rocket—free fall, then one long blast of the jets, ending with the ship stopped dead as she touches the ground. In practice a pilot must feel his way down, not too slowly; a ship could burn all the fuel this side of Venus fighting gravity too long.

Forty seconds later, falling a little more than 140 miles per hour, he picked up in his periscopes the thousand-foot static towers. At 300 feet he blasted five gravities for more than a second, cut it, and caught her with a one-sixth gravity, Moon-normal blast. Slowly he eased this off, feeling happy.

The *Gremlin* hovered, her bright jet splashing the soil of the Moon, then settled with dignity to land without a jar.

The ground crew took over; a sealed runabout jeeped Pemberton to the tunnel entrance. Inside Luna City, he found himself paged before he finished filing his report. When he took the call, Soames smiled at him from the viewplate. "I saw that landing from the field pick-up, Pemberton. You don't need a refresher course."

Jake blushed. "Thank you, sir."

"Unless you are dead set on space-to-space, I can use you on the regular Luna City run. Quarters here or Luna City? Want it?"

He heard himself saying, "Luna City. I'll take it."

He tore up his third letter as he walked into Luna City post office. At the telephone desk he spoke to a blonde in a blue moonsuit. "Get me Mrs. Jake Pemberton, Suburb six-four-oh-three, Dodge City, Kansas, please."

She looked him over. "You pilots sure spend money."

"Sometimes phone calls are cheap. Hurry it, will you?"

Phyllis was trying to phrase the letter she felt she should have written before. It was easier to say in writing that she was not complaining of loneliness nor lack of fun, but that she could not stand the strain of worrying about his safety. But then she found herself quite unable to state the logical conclusion. Was she prepared to face giving him up entirely if he would not give up space? She truly did not know . . . the phone call was a welcome interruption.

The viewplate stayed blank. "Long distance," came a thin voice. "Luna City calling."

Fear jerked at her heart. "Phyllis Pemberton speaking."

An interminable delay—she knew it took nearly three seconds for radio waves to make the Earth-Moon round trip, but she did not remember it and it would not have reassured her. All she could see was a broken home, herself a widow, and Jake, beloved Jake, dead in space.

"Mrs. Jake Pemberton?"

"Yes, yes! Go ahead." Another wait—had she sent him away in a bad temper, reckless, his judgment affected? Had he died out there, remembering only that she fussed at him for leaving her to go to work? Had she failed him when he needed her? She knew that her Jake could not be tied to apron strings; men—grown-up men, not mammas' boys—had to break away from mother's apron strings. Then why had she tried to tie him to hers?—she had known better, her own mother had warned her not to try it.

She prayed.

Then another voice, one that weakened her knees with relief: "That you, honey?"

"Yes, darling, yes! What are you doing on the Moon?"

"It's a long story. At a dollar a second it will keep. What I want to know is—are you willing to come to Luna City?"

It was Jake's turn to suffer from the inevitable lag in reply. He wondered if Phyllis were stalling, unable to make up her mind. At last he heard her say, "Of course, darling. When do I leave?"

"When—say, don't you even want to know *why?*"

She started to say that it did not matter, then said, "Yes, tell me." The lag was still present but neither of them cared. He told her the news, then added, "Run over to the Springs and get Olga Pierce to straighten out the red tape for you. Need my help to pack?"

She thought rapidly. Had he meant to come back anyhow, he would not have asked. "No. I can manage."

"Good girl. I'll radiostat you a long letter about what to bring and so forth. I love you. 'Bye now!"

"Oh, I love you, too. Goodbye, darling."

Pemberton came out of the booth whistling. Good girl, Phyllis. Staunch. He wondered why he had ever doubted her.

−1947

RAY BRADBURY

B. 1920

Ray Bradbury is considered by many to be the poet laureate of science fiction. His numerous short stories and handful of novels have brought him international critical acclaim for their deft manipulation of language and skilled use of profound literary metaphor. Bradbury has never alleged an expertise in writing about new technology. Instead, he is more concerned with how humanity acts and interacts with itself when confronted by developing science. Thus, his "science fiction" possesses strong elements of fantasy; it focuses more on the allegorical rather than on speculation about future technological innovations.

Born in Waukegan, Illinois, the young Bradbury was profoundly influenced by his mother's passion for movies. While growing up, he cultivated a love for the classics of fantasy, including the Oz books and the fiction of Edgar Rice Burroughs. He also developed an infatuation for adventurous comic strips, such as Buck Rogers, Flash Gordon, and Prince Valiant. In

1932, Bradbury's family moved to Tucson, Arizona, where he landed a part-time job at a local radio station; he thus was able to indulge his growing interests in acting. After leaving Tucson and returning to Waukegan, in in 1934 his family again moved west to Los Angeles, California. Bradbury graduated from Los Angeles High School in 1938, and shortly thereafter he was selling stories to the pulps. During the early 1940s, Bradbury's fiction appeared regularly in Weird Tales, *and by 1945 he had broken into the "slick" magazine markets, like* Collier's *and* Mademoiselle. *Bradbury's first book,* Dark Carnival, *a collection of weird fantasy tales, was published by the specialty press,* Arkham House, *in 1947. His next two books—The* Martian Chronicles *(1950) and* The Illustrated Man *(1951), both thematically connected short story collections published by Doubleday—would eventually help to establish his reputation as one of the most important authors of speculative fiction during the 1950s and 1960s. Other important Bradbury anthologies include* The Golden Apples of the Sun *(1953),* A Medicine for Melancholy *(1959),* R is for Rocket *(1962),* The Machineries of Joy *(1964),* S is for Space *(1966),* I Sing the Body Electric! *(1969),* Long After Midnight *(1976), and* Quicker Than the Eye *(1996). Though not a prolific novelist, Bradbury nevertheless produced some memorable longer fiction, such as* Fahrenheit 451 *(1953),* Dandelion Wine *(1957),* Something Wicked This Way Comes *(1962),* The Halloween Tree *(1972),* Death Is a Lonely Business *(1985),* A Graveyard for Lunatics *(1990), and* Green Shadows, White Whale: A Novel *(1992). Bradbury's work has frequently been adapted for film and television.*

A major theme in Bradbury's early science fiction involves censorship. His first novel, Fahrenheit 451 *(which is based on his story, "The Fireman," published some three years earlier in* Galaxy), *was written, in part, as a literary response to McCarthyism in America during the early 1950s. But as Bradbury points out in his essay "Coda," which appeared as an afterword in recent printings of* Fahrenheit 451, *censorship of ideas and of books is not limited to the right side of the political spectrum. Censorship of imagination is at the heart of Bradbury's "Usher II." Initially appearing under the title "Carnival of Madness" in the April 1950 issue of* Thrilling Wonder Stories *(and later anthologized in* The Martian Chronicles), *"Usher II" offers a "revenge" story rivaling in quality anything written by Edgar Allan Poe himself.*

CODA

About two years ago, a letter arrived from a solemn young Vassar lady telling me how much she enjoyed reading my experiment in space mythology, *The Martian Chronicles.*

But, she added, wouldn't it be a good idea, this late in time, to rewrite the book inserting more women's characters and roles?

A few years before that I got a certain amount of mail concerning the same Martian book complaining that the blacks in the book were Uncle Toms and why didn't I "do them over"?

Along about then came a note from a Southern white suggesting that I was prejudiced in favor of the blacks and the entire story should be dropped.

Two weeks ago my mountain of mail delivered forth a pipsqueak mouse of a letter from a well-known publishing house that wanted to reprint my story "The Fog Horn" in a high school reader.

In my story, I had described a lighthouse as having, late at night, an illumination coming from it that was a "God-Light." Looking up at it from the viewpoint of any sea-creature one would have felt that one was in "the Presence."

The editors had deleted "God-Light" and "in the Presence."

Some five years back, the editors of yet another anthology for school readers put together a volume with some 400 (count 'em) short stories in it. How do you cram 400 short stories by Twain, Irving, Poe, Maupassant and Bierce into one book?

Simplicity itself. Skin, debone, demarrow, scarify, melt, render down and destroy. Every adjective that counted, every verb that moved, every metaphor that weighed more than a mosquito—out! Every simile that would have made a sub-moron's mouth twitch—gone! Any aside that explained the two-bit philosophy of a first-rate writer—lost!

Every story, slenderized, starved, bluepenciled, leeched and bled white, resembled every other story. Twain read like Poe read like Shakespeare read like Dostoevsky read like—in the finale—Edgar Guest. Every word of more than three syllables had been razored. Every image that demanded so much as one instant's attention—shot dead.

Do you begin to get the damned and incredible picture?

How did I react to all of the above?

By "firing" the whole lot.

By sending rejection slips to each and every one.

By ticketing the assembly of idiots to the far reaches of hell.

The point is obvious. There is more than one way to burn a book. And the world is full of people running about with lit matches. Every minority, be it Baptist/ Unitarian, Irish/Italian/Octogenarian/Zen Buddhist, Zionist/Seventh-day Adventist, Women's Lib/Republican, Mattachine/Four Square Gospel feels it has the will, the right, the duty to douse the kerosene, light the fuse. Every dimwit editor who sees himself as the source of all dreary blanc-mange plain porridge unleavened literature, licks his guillotine and eyes the neck of any author who dares to speak above a whisper or write above a nursery rhyme.

Fire-Captain Beatty, in my novel *Fahrenheit 451*, described how the books were burned first by minorities, each ripping a page or a paragraph from this book, then that, until the day came when the books were empty and the minds shut and the libraries closed forever.

"Shut the door, they're coming through the window, shut the window, they're coming through the door," are the words to an old song. They fit my lifestyle with newly arriving butcher/censors every month. Only six weeks ago, I discovered that, over the years, some cubby-hole editors at Ballantine Books, fearful of contaminating the young, had, bit by bit, censored some 75 separate sections from the novel. Students, reading the novel which, after all, deals with censorship and book-burning in the future, wrote to tell me of this exquisite irony. Judy-Lynn Del Rey, one of the new Ballantine editors, is having the entire book reset and republished this summer with all the damns and hells back in place.

A final test for old Job II here: I sent a play, *Leviathan 99*, off to a university theater a month ago. My play is based on the "Moby Dick" mythology, dedicated to Melville, and concerns a rocket crew and a blind space captain who venture forth to encounter a Great White Comet and destroy the destroyer. My drama premieres as an opera in Paris this autumn. But, for now, the university wrote back that they hardly dared do my play—it had no women in it! And the ERA ladies on campus would descend with ball-bats if the drama department even tried!

Grinding my bicuspids into powder, I suggested that would mean, from now on, no more productions of *Boys in the Band* (no women), or *The Women* (no men). Or, counting heads, male and female, a good lot of Shakespeare that would never be seen again, especially if you count lines and find that all the good stuff went to the males!

I wrote back maybe they should do my play one week, and *The Women* the next. They probably thought I was joking, and I'm not sure that I wasn't.

For it is a mad world and it will get madder if we allow the minorities, be they dwarf or giant, orangutan or dolphin, nuclear-head or water-conversationalist, pro-computerologist or Neo-Luddite, simpleton or sage, to interfere with aesthetics. The real world is the playing ground for each and every group, to make or unmake laws. But the tip of the nose of my book or stories or poems is where their rights end and my territorial imperatives begin, run and rule. If Mormons do not like my plays, let them write their own. If the Irish hate my Dublin stories, let them rent typewriters. If teachers and grammar school editors find my jawbreaker sentences shatter their mushmilk teeth, let them eat stale cake dunked in weak tea of their own ungodly manufacture. If the Chicano intellectuals wish to re-cut my "Wonderful Ice Cream Suit" so it shapes "Zoot," may the belt unravel and the pants fall.

For, let's face it, digression is the soul of wit. Take philosophic asides away from Dante, Milton or Hamlet's father's ghost and what stays is dry bones. Laurence Sterne said it once: Digressions, incontestably, are the sunshine, the life, the soul of reading! Take them out and one cold eternal winter would reign in every page. Restore them to the writer—he steps forth like a bridegroom, bids them all-hail, brings in variety and forbids the appetite to fail.

In sum, do not insult me with the beheadings, finger-choppings or the lung-deflations you plan for my works. I need my head to shake or nod, my hand to wave or make into a fist, my lungs to shout or whisper with. I will not go gently onto a shelf, degutted, to become a non-book.

All you umpires, back to the bleachers. Referees, hit the showers. It's my game. I pitch, I hit, I catch. I run the bases. At sunset I've won or lost. At sunrise, I'm out again, giving it the old try.

And no one can help me. Not even you.

—1979

USHER II

"'During the whole of a dull, dark, and soundless day in the autumn of the year, when the clouds hung oppressively low in the heavens, I had been passing alone, on horseback, through a singularly dreary tract of country, and at length found myself, as the shades of evening drew on, within view of the melancholy House of Usher. . . .'"

Mr. William Stendahl paused in his quotation. There, upon a low black hill, stood the House, its cornerstone bearing the inscription 2005 A.D.

Mr. Bigelow, the architect, said, "It's completed. Here's the key, Mr. Stendahl."

The two men stood together silently in the quiet autumn afternoon. Blueprints rustled on the raven grass at their feet.

"The House of Usher," said Mr. Stendahl with pleasure. "Planned, built, bought, paid for. Wouldn't Mr. Poe be *delighted?*"

Mr. Bigelow squinted. "Is it everything you wanted sir?"

"Yes!"

"Is the color right? Is it *desolate* and *terrible?*"

"*Very* desolate, *very* terrible!"

"The walls are—*bleak?*"

"Amazingly so!"

"The tarn, is it 'black and lurid' enough?"

"Most incredibly black and lurid."

"And the sedge—we've dyed it, you know—is it the proper gray and ebon?"

"Hideous!"

Mr. Bigelow consulted his architectural plans. From these he quoted in part: "Does the whole structure cause an 'iciness, a sickening of the heart, a dreariness of thought'? The House, the lake, the land, Mr. Stendahl?"

"Mr. Bigelow, it's worth every penny! My God, it's beautiful!"

"Thank you. I had to work in total ignorance. Thank the Lord you had your own private rockets or we'd never have been allowed to bring most of the equipment through. You notice, it's always twilight here, this land, always October, barren, sterile, dead. It took a bit of doing. We killed everything. Ten thousand tons of DDT. Not a snake, frog, or Martian fly left! Twilight always, Mr. Stendahl; I'm proud of that. There are machines, hidden, which blot out the sun. It's always properly 'dreary.'"

Stendahl drank it in, the dreariness, the oppression, the fetid vapors, the whole "atmosphere," so delicately contrived and fitted. And that House! That crumbling horror, that evil lake, the fungi, the extensive decay! Plastic or otherwise, who could guess?

He looked at the autumn sky. Somewhere above, beyond, far off, was the sun. Somewhere it was the month of April on the planet Mars, a yellow month with a blue sky. Somewhere above, the rockets burned down to civilize a beautifully dead planet. The sound of their screaming passage was muffled by this dim, sound-proofed world, this ancient autumn world.

"Now that my job's done," said Mr. Bigelow uneasily, "I feel free to ask what you're going to do with all this."

"With Usher? Haven't you guessed?"

"No."

"Does the name Usher mean nothing to you?"

"Nothing."

"Well, what about *this* name: Edgar Allan Poe?"

Mr. Bigelow shook his head.

"Of course." Stendahl snorted delicately, a combination of dismay and contempt. "How could I expect you to know blessed Mr. Poe? He died a long while ago, before Lincoln. All of his books were burned in the Great Fire. That's thirty years ago— 1975."

"Ah," said Mr. Bigelow wisely. "One of *those!*"

"Yes, one of those, Bigelow. He and Lovecraft and Hawthorne and Ambrose Bierce and all the tales of terror and fantasy and horror and, for that matter, tales of the future were burned. Heartlessly. They passed a law. Oh, it started very small. In 1950 and '60 it was a grain of sand. They began by controlling books of cartoons and then detective books and, of course, films, one way or another, one group or another, political bias, religious prejudice, union pressures; there was always a minority afraid of something, and a great majority afraid of the dark, afraid of the future, afraid of the past, afraid of the present, afraid of themselves and shadows of themselves."

"I see."

"Afraid of the word 'politics' (which eventually became a synonym for Communism among the more reactionary elements, so I hear, and it was worth your life to use the word!), and with a screw tightened here, a bolt fastened there, a push, a pull, a yank, art and literature were soon like a great twine of taffy strung about, being twisted in braids and tied in knots and thrown in all directions, until there was no more resiliency and no more savor to it. Then the film cameras chopped short and the theaters turned dark, and the print presses trickled down from a great Niagara of reading matter to a mere innocuous dripping of 'pure' material. Oh, the word 'escape' was radical, too, I tell you!"

"Was it?"

"It was! Every man, they said, must face reality. Must face the Here and Now! Everything that was *not so* must go. All the beautiful literary lies and flights of fancy must be shot in mid-air! So they lined them up against a library wall one Sunday morning thirty years ago, in 1975; they lined them up, St. Nicholas and the Headless Horseman and Snow White and Rumplestiltskin and Mother Goose—oh, what a wailing!—and shot them down, and burned the paper castles and the fairy frogs and old kings and the people who lived happily ever after (for of course it was a fact that *nobody* lived happily ever after!), and Once Upon A Time became No More! And they spread the ashes of the Phantom Rickshaw with the rubble of the Land of Oz; they filleted the bones of Glinda the Good and Ozma and shattered Polychrome in a spectroscope and served Jack Pumpkinhead with meringue at the Biologists' Ball! The Beanstalk died in a bramble of red tape! Sleeping Beauty awoke at the kiss of a scientist and expired at the fatal puncture of his syringe. And they made Alice drink something from a bottle which reduced her to a size where she could no longer cry 'Curiouser and curiouser,' and they gave the Looking Glass one hammer blow to smash it and every Red King and Oyster away!"

He clenched his fists. Lord, how immediate it was! His face was red and he was gasping for breath.

As for Mr. Bigelow, he was astounded at this long explosion. He blinked and at last said, "Sorry. Don't know what you're talking about. Just names to me. From what I hear, the Burning was a good thing."

"Get out!" screamed Stendahl. "You've done your job, now let me alone, you idiot!"

Mr. Bigelow summoned his carpenters and went away.

Mr. Stendahl stood alone before his House.

"Listen here," he said to the unseen rockets. "I came to Mars to get away from you Clean-Minded people, but you're flocking in thicker every day, like flies to offal. So I'm going to show you. I'm going to teach you a fine lesson for what you did to Mr. Poe on Earth. As of this day, beware. The House of Usher is open for business!"

He pushed a fist at the sky.

The rocket landed. A man stepped out jauntily. He glanced at the House, and his gray eyes were displeased and vexed. He strode across the moat to confront the small man there.

"Your name Stendahl?"

"Yes."

"I'm Garrett, Investigator of Moral Climates."

"So you finally got to Mars, you Moral Climate people? I wondered when you'd appear."

"We arrived last week. We'll soon have things as neat and tidy as Earth." The man waved an identification card irritably toward the House. "Suppose you tell me about that place, Stendahl?"

"It's a haunted castle, if you like."

"I don't like, Stendahl, I *don't* like. The sound of that word 'haunted.'"

"Simple enough. In this year of our Lord 2005 I have built a mechanical sanctuary. In it copper bats fly on electronic beams, brass rats scuttle in plastic cellars, robot skeletons dance; robot vampires, harlequins, wolves, and white phantoms, compounded of chemical and ingenuity, live here."

"That's what I was afraid of," said Garrett, smiling quietly. "I'm afraid we're going to have to tear your place down."

"I knew you'd come out as soon as you discovered what went on."

"I'd have come sooner, but we at Moral Climates wanted to be sure of your intentions before we moved in. We can have the Dismantlers and Burning Crew here by supper. By midnight your place will be razed to the cellar. Mr. Stendahl, I consider you somewhat of a fool, sir. Spending hard-earned money on a folly. Why, it must have cost you three million dollars——"

"Four million! But, Mr. Garrett, I inherited twenty-five million when very young. I can afford to throw it about. Seems a dreadful shame, though, to have the House finished only an hour and have you race out with your Dismantlers. Couldn't you possibly let me play with my Toy for just, well, twenty-four hours?"

"You know the law. Strict to the letter. No books, no houses, nothing to be produced which in any way suggests ghosts, vampires, fairies, or any creature of the imagination."

"You'll be burning Babbitts next!"

"You've caused us a lot of trouble, Mr. Stendahl. It's in the record. Twenty years ago. On Earth. You and your library."

"Yes, me and my library. And a few others like me. Oh, Poe's been forgotten for many years now, and Oz and the other creatures. But I had my little cache. We had our libraries, a few private citizens, until you sent your men around with torches and incinerators and tore my fifty thousand books up and burned them. Just as you put a stake through the heart of Halloween and told your film producers that if they made anything at all they would have to make and remake Ernest Hemingway. My God, how many times have I seen *For Whom the Bell Tolls* done! Thirty different versions. All realistic. Oh, realism! Oh, here, oh, now, oh hell!"

"It doesn't pay to be bitter!"

"Mr. Garrett, you must turn in a full report, mustn't you?"

"Yes."

"Then, for curiosity's sake, you'd better come in and look around. It'll take only a minute."

"All right. Lead the way. And no tricks. I've a gun with me."

The door to the House of Usher creaked wide. A moist wind issued forth. There was an immense sighing and moaning, like a subterranean bellows breathing in the lost catacombs.

A rat pranced across the floor stones. Garrett, crying out, gave it a kick. It fell over, the rat did, and from its nylon fur streamed an incredible horde of metal fleas.

"Amazing!" Garrett bent to see.

An old witch sat in a niche, quivering her wax hands over some orange-and-blue tarot cards. She jerked her head and hissed through her toothless mouth at Garrett, tapping her greasy cards.

"Death!" she cried.

"Now *that's* the sort of thing I mean," said Garrett. "Deplorable!"

"I'll let you burn her personally."

"Will you, really?" Garrett was pleased. Then he frowned. "I must say you're taking this all so well."

"It was enough just to be able to create this place. To be able to say I did it. To say I nurtured a medieval atmosphere in a modern, incredulous world."

"I've a somewhat reluctant admiration for your genius myself, sir." Garrett watched a mist drift by, whispering and whispering, shaped like a beautiful and nebulous woman. Down a moist corridor a machine whirled. Like the stuff from a cotton-candy centrifuge, mists sprang up and floated, murmuring, in the silent halls.

An ape appeared out of nowhere.

"Hold on!" cried Garrett.

"Don't be afraid." Stendahl tapped the animal's black chest. "A robot. Copper skeleton and all, like the witch. See?" He stroked the fur, and under it metal tubing came to light.

"Yes." Garrett put out a timid hand to pet the thing. "But why, Mr. Stendahl, why all *this?* What obsessed you?"

"Bureaucracy, Mr. Garrett. But I haven't time to explain. The government will discover soon enough." He nodded to the ape. "All right. *Now.*"

The ape killed Mr. Garrett.

"Are we almost ready, Pikes?"

Pikes looked up from the table. "Yes, sir."

"You've done a splendid job."

"Well, I'm paid for it, Mr. Stendahl," said Pikes softly as he lifted the plastic eyelid of the robot and inserted the glass eyeball to fasten the rubberoid muscles neatly. "There."

"The spitting image of Mr. Garrett."

"What do we do with him, sir?" Pikes nodded at the slab where the real Mr. Garrett lay dead.

"Better burn him, Pikes. We wouldn't want two Mr. Garretts, would we?"

Pikes wheeled Mr. Garrett to the brick incinerator. "Good-by." He pushed Mr. Garrett in and slammed the door.

Stendahl confronted the robot Garrett. "You have your orders, Garrett?"

"Yes, sir." The robot sat up. "I'm to return to Moral Climates. I'll file a complementary report. Delay action for at least forty-eight hours. Say I'm investigating more fully."

"Right, Garrett. Good-by."

The robot hurried out to Garrett's rocket, got in, and flew away.

Stendahl turned. "Now, Pikes, we send the remainder of the invitations for tonight. I think we'll have a jolly time, don't you?"

"Considering we waited twenty years, quite jolly!"

They winked at each other.

Seven o'clock. Stendahl studied his watch. Almost time. He twirled the sherry glass in his hand. He sat quietly. Above him, among the oaken beams, the bats, their delicate copper bodies hidden under rubber flesh, blinked at him and shrieked. He raised his glass to them. "To our success." Then he leaned back, closed his eyes, and considered the entire affair. How he would savor this in his old age. This paying back of the antiseptic government for its literary terrors and conflagrations. Oh, how the anger and hatred had grown in him through the years. Oh, how the plan had taken a slow shape in his numbed mind, until that day three years ago when he had met Pikes.

Ah yes, Pikes. Pikes with the bitterness in him as deep as a black, charred well of green acid. Who was Pikes? Only the greatest of them all! Pikes, the man of ten thousand faces, a fury, a smoke, a blue fog, a white rain, a bat, a gargoyle, a monster, that was Pikes! Better than Lon Chaney, the father? Stendahl ruminated. Night after night he had watched Chaney in the old, old films. Yes, better than Chaney. Better than that other ancient mummer? What was his name? Karloff? Far better! Lugosi? The comparison was odious! No, there was only one Pikes, and he was a man stripped of his fantasies now, no place on Earth to go, no one to show off to. Forbidden even to perform for himself before a mirror!

Poor impossible, defeated Pikes! How must it have felt, Pikes, the night they seized your films, like entrails yanked from the camera, out of your guts, clutching them in rolls and wads to stuff them up a stove to burn away? Did it feel as bad as having some fifty thousand books annihilated with no recompense? Yes. Yes. Stendahl felt his hands grow cold with the senseless anger. So what more natural than they would one day talk over endless coffeepots into innumerable midnights, and out of all the talk and the bitter brewings would come—the House of Usher.

A great church bell rang. The guests were arriving.

Smiling, he went to greet them.

Full grown without memory, the robots waited. In green silks the color of forest pools, in silks the color of frog and fern, they waited. In yellow hair the color of the sun and sand, the robots waited. Oiled, with tube bones cut from bronze and sunk in gelatin, the robots lay. In coffins for the not dead and not alive, in planked boxes, the metronomes waited to be set in motion. There was a smell of lubrication and lathed brass. There was a silence of the tomb yard. Sexed but sexless, the robots. Named but unnamed, and borrowing from humans everything but humanity, the robots stared at the nailed lids of their labeled F.O.B. boxes, in a death that was not even a death, for there had never been a life. And now there was a vast screaming of yanked nails. Now there was a lifting of lids. Now there were shadows on the boxes and the pressure of a hand squirting oil from a can. Now one clock was set in motion, a faint ticking. Now another and another, until this was an immense clock shop, purring. The marble eyes rolled wide their rubber lids. The nostrils winked. The robots, clothed in hair of ape and white of rabbit, arose: Tweedledum following Tweedledee, Mock-Turtle, Dormouse, drowned bodies from the sea compounded of salt and whiteweed, swaying; hanging blue-throated men with turned-up, clam-flesh eyes, and creatures of ice and burning tinsel, loam-dwarfs and pepper-elves, Tik-Tok, Ruggedo, St. Nicholas with a self-made snow flurry blowing on before him, Bluebeard with whiskers like acetylene flame, and sulphur clouds from which green fire snouts protruded, and, in scaly and gigantic serpentine, a dragon with a furnace in its belly reeled out the door with a scream, a tick, a bellow, a silence, a rush, a wind. Ten thousand lids fell back. The clock shop moved out into Usher. The night was enchanted.

A warm breeze came over the land. The guest rockets, burning the sky and turning the weather from autumn to spring, arrived.

The men stepped out in evening clothes and the women stepped out after them, their hair coiffed up in elaborate detail.

"So *that's* Usher!"

"But where's the door?"

At this moment Stendahl appeared. The women laughed and chattered. Mr. Stendahl raised a hand to quiet them. Turning, he looked up to a high castle window and called:

"Rapunzel, Rapunzel, let down your hair."

And from above, a beautiful maiden leaned out upon the night wind and let down her golden hair. And the hair twined and blew and became a ladder upon which the guests might ascend, laughing, into the House.

What eminent sociologists! What clever psychologists! What tremendously important politicians, bacteriologists, and neurologists! There they stood, within the dank walls.

"Welcome, all of you!"

Mr. Tryon, Mr. Owen, Mr. Dunne, Mr. Lang, Mr. Steffens, Mr. Fletcher, and a double-dozen more.

"Come in, come in!"

Miss Gibbs, Miss Pope, Miss Churchil, Miss Blunt, Miss Drummond, and a score of other women, glittering.

Eminent, eminent people, one and all, members of the Society for the Prevention of Fantasy, advocators of the banishment of Halloween and Guy Fawkes, killers of bats, burners of books, bearers of torches; good clean citizens, every one, who had waited until the rough men had come up and buried the Martians and cleansed the cities and built the towns and repaired the highways and made everything safe. And then, with everything well on its way to Safety, the Spoil-Funs, the people with mercurochrome for blood and iodine-colored eyes, came now to set up their Moral Climates and dole out goodness to everyone. And they were his friends! Yes, carefully, carefully, he had met and befriended each of them on Earth in the last year!

"Welcome to the vasty halls of Death!" he cried.

"Hello, Stendahl, what *is* all this?"

"You'll see. Everyone off with their clothes. You'll find booths to one side there. Change into costumes you find there. Men on this side, women on that."

The people stood uneasily about.

"I don't know if we should stay," said Miss Pope. "I don't like the looks of this. It verges on—blasphemy."

"Nonsense, a *costume* ball!"

"Seems quite illegal." Mr. Steffens sniffed about.

"Come off it." Stendahl laughed. "Enjoy yourselves. Tomorrow it'll be a ruin. Get in the booths!"

The House blazed with life and color; harlequins rang by with belled caps and white mice danced miniature quadrilles to the music of dwarfs who tickled tiny fiddles with tiny bows, and flags rippled from scorched beams while bats flew in clouds about gargoyle mouths which spouted down wine, cool, wild, and foaming. A creek wandered through the seven rooms of the masked ball. Guests sipped and found it to be sherry. Guests poured from the booths, transformed from one age into another, their faces covered with dominoes, the very act of putting on a mask revoking all their licenses to pick a quarrel with fantasy and horror. The women swept about in red gowns, laughing. The men danced them attendance. And on the walls were shadows with no people to throw them, and here or there were mirrors in which no image showed. "All of us vampires!" laughed Mr. Fletcher. "Dead!"

There were seven rooms, each a different color, one blue, one purple, one green, one orange, another white, the sixth violet, and the seventh shrouded in black velvet. And in the black room was an ebony clock which struck the hour loud. And through these rooms the guests ran, drunk at last, among the robot fantasies, amid the Dormice and Mad Hatters, the Trolls and Giants, the Black Cats and White Queens, and under their dancing feet the floor gave off the massive pumping beat of a hidden and telltale heart.

"Mr. Stendahl!"

A whisper.

"Mr. Stendahl!"

A monster with the face of Death stood at his elbow. It was Pikes. "I must see you alone."

"What is it?"

"Here." Pikes held out a skeleton hand. In it were a few half-melted, charred wheels, nuts, cogs, bolts.

Stendahl looked at them for a long moment. Then he drew Pikes into a corridor. "Garrett?" he whispered.

Pikes nodded. "He sent a robot in his place. Cleaning out the incinerator a moment ago, I found these."

They both stared at the fateful cogs for a time.

"This means the police will be here any minute," said Pikes. "Our plan will be ruined."

"I don't know." Stendahl glanced in at the whirling yellow and blue and orange people. The music swept through the misting halls. "I should have guessed Garrett wouldn't be fool enough to come in person. But wait!"

"What's the matter?"

"Nothing. There's nothing the matter. Garrett sent a robot to us. Well, we sent one back. Unless he checks closely, he won't notice the switch."

"Of course!"

"Next time he'll come *himself.* Now that he thinks it's safe. Why, he might be at the door any minute, in *person!* More wine, Pikes!"

The great bell rang.

"There he is now, I'll bet you. Go let Mr. Garrett in."

Rapunzel let down her golden hair.

"Mr. Stendahl?"

"Mr. Garrett. The *real* Mr. Garrett?"

"The same." Garrett eyed the dank walls and the whirling people. "I thought I'd better come see for myself. You can't depend on robots. Other people's robots, especially. I also took the precaution of summoning the Dismantlers. They'll be here in one hour to knock the props out from under this horrible place."

Stendahl bowed. "Thanks for telling me." He waved his hand. "In the meantime, you might as well enjoy this. A little wine?"

"No, thank you. What's going on? How low can a man sink?"

"See for yourself, Mr. Garrett."

"Murder," said Garrett.

"Murder most foul," said Stendahl.

A woman screamed. Miss Pope ran up, her face the color of a cheese. "The most horrid thing just happened! I saw Miss Blunt strangled by an ape and stuffed up a chimney!"

They looked and saw the long yellow hair trailing down from the flue. Garrett cried out.

"Horrid!" sobbed Miss Pope, and then ceased crying. She blinked and turned. "Miss Blunt!"

"Yes," said Miss Blunt, standing there.

"But I just saw you crammed up the flue!"

"No," laughed Miss Blunt. "A robot of myself. A clever facsimile!"

"But, but . . ."

"Don't cry, darling. I'm quite all right. Let me look at myself. Well, so there I *am!* Up the chimney. Like you said. Isn't that funny?"

Miss Blunt walked away, laughing.

"Have a drink, Garrett?"

"I believe I will. That unnerved me. My God, what a place. This *does* deserve tearing down. For a moment there . . ."

Garrett drank.

Another scream. Mr. Steffens, borne upon the shoulders of four white rabbits, was carried down a flight of stairs which magically appeared in the floor. Into a pit went Mr. Steffens, where, bound and tied, he was left to face the advancing razor steel of a great pendulum which now whirled down, down, closer and closer to his outraged body.

"Is that me down there?" said Mr. Steffens, appearing at Garrett's elbow. He bent over the pit. "How strange, how odd, to see yourself die."

The pendulum made a final stroke.

"How realistic," said Mr. Steffens, turning away.

"Another drink, Mr. Garrett?"

"Yes, please."

"It won't be long. The Dismantlers will be here."

"Thank God!"

And for a third time, a scream.

"What now?" said Garrett apprehensively.

"It's my turn," said Miss Drummond. "Look."

And a second Miss Drummond, shrieking, was nailed into a coffin and thrust into the raw earth under the floor.

"Why, I remember *that,*" gasped the Investigator of Moral Climates. "From the old forbidden books. The Premature Burial. And the others. The Pit, the Pendulum, and the ape, the chimney, the Murders in the Rue Morgue. In a book I burned, yes!"

"Another drink, Garrett. Here, hold your glass steady."

"My lord, you *have* an imagination, haven't you?"

They stood and watched five others die, one in the mouth of a dragon, the others thrown off into the black tarn, sinking and vanishing.

"Would you like to see what we have planned for you?" asked Stendahl.

"Certainly," said Garrett. "What's the difference? We'll blow the whole damn thing up, anyway. You're nasty."

"Come along then. This way."

And he led Garrett down into the floor, through numerous passages and down again upon spiral stairs into the earth, into the catacombs.

"What do you want to show me down here?" said Garrett.

"Yourself killed."

"A duplicate?"

"Yes. And also something else."

"What?"

"The Amontillado," said Stendahl, going ahead with a blazing lantern which he held high. Skeletons froze half out of coffin lids. Garrett held his hand to his nose, his face disgusted.

"The what?"

"Haven't you ever heard of the Amontillado?"

"No!"

"Don't you recognize this?" Stendahl pointed to a cell.

"Should I?"

"Or this?" Stendahl produced a trowel from under his cape smiling.

"What's that thing?"

"Come," said Stendahl.

They stepped into the cell. In the dark, Stendahl affixed the chains to the half-drunken man.

"For God's sake, what are you doing?" shouted Garrett, rattling about.

"I'm being ironic. Don't interrupt a man in the midst of being ironic, it's not polite. There!"

"You've locked me in chains!"

"So I have."

"What are you going to do?"

"Leave you here."

"You're joking."

"A very good joke."

"Where's my duplicate? Don't we see him killed?"

"There is no duplicate."

"But the *others!*"

"The others are dead. The ones you saw killed were the real people. The duplicates, the robots, stood by and watched."

Garrett said nothing.

"Now you're supposed to say, 'For the love of God, Montresor!'" said Stendahl. "And I will reply, 'Yes, for the love of God.' Won't you say it? Come on. Say it."

"You fool."

"Must I coax you? Say it. Say 'For the love of God, Montresor!'"

"I won't, you idiot. Get me out of here." He was sober now.

"Here. Put this on." Stendahl tossed in something that belled and rang.

"What is it?"

"A cap and bells. Put it on and I might let you out."

"Stendahl!"

"Put it on, I said!"

Garrett obeyed. The bells tinkled.

"Don't you have a feeling that this has all happened before?" inquired Stendahl, setting to work with trowel and mortar and brick now.

"What're you doing?"

"Walling you in. Here's one row. Here's another."

"You're insane!"

"I won't argue that point."

"You'll be prosecuted for this!"

He tapped a brick and placed it on the wet mortar, humming.

Now there was a thrashing and pounding and a crying out from within the darkening place. The bricks rose higher. "More thrashing, please," said Stendahl. "Let's make it a good show."

"Let me out, let me out!"

There was one last brick to shove into place. The screaming was continuous.

"Garrett?" called Stendahl softly. Garrett silenced himself. "Garrett," said Stendahl, "do you know why I've done this to you? Because you burned Mr. Poe's books without really reading them. You took other people's advice that they needed burning. Otherwise you'd have realized what I was going to do to you when we came down here a moment ago. Ignorance is fatal, Mr. Garrett."

Garrett was silent.

"I want this to be perfect," said Stendahl, holding his lantern up so its light penetrated in upon the slumped figure. "Jingle your bells softly." The bells rustled. "Now, if you'll please say, 'For the love of God, Montresor,' I might let you free."

The man's face came up in the light. There was a hesitation. Then grotesquely the man said, "For the love of God, Montresor."

"Ah," said Stendahl, eyes closed. He shoved the last brick into place and mortared it tight. *Requiescat in pace,* dear friend."

He hastened from the catacomb.

In the seven rooms the sound of a midnight clock brought everything to a halt.

The Red Death appeared.

Stendahl turned for a moment at the door to watch. And then he ran out of the great House, across the moat to where a helicopter waited.

"Ready, Pikes?"

"Ready."

"There it goes!"

They looked at the great House, smiling. It began to crack down the middle, as with an earthquake, and as Stendahl watched the magnificent sight he heard Pikes reciting behind him in a low, cadenced voice:

"'. . . my brain reeled as I saw the mighty walls rushing asunder—there was a long tumultuous shouting sound like the voice of a thousand waters—and the deep and dank tarn at my feet closed sullenly and silently over the fragments of the House of Usher.'"

The helicopter rose over the steaming lake and flew into the west.

—1950

Harlan Ellison

B. 1934

A writer for film and television, a respected essayist, a ground-breaking editor, a champion of social causes, and the winner of more major science fiction and fantasy awards than any other author of speculative fiction, Harlan Ellison is also revered as the undisputed master of the fantasy and science fiction short story. Born in Cleveland, Ohio, Ellison published his first tale by age thirteen in the Cleveland News, *and by age sixteen he established the Cleveland Science-Fiction Society. He attended Ohio State University from 1951 to 1953 but left school to work an assortment of jobs before serving in the army from 1957 to 1959. After leaving military duty, he became an editor for* Rogue *magazine and founded Regency Books. During the 1960s, Ellison wrote successfully for television, including the popular TV programs* The Alfred Hitchcock Hour, The Outer Limits, *and* Star Trek. *He published his first novel,* Rumble, *in 1958. His first short story collection,* The Deadly Streets, *also appeared in 1958. Listed among Ellison's numerous anthologies are* Ellison Wonderland *(1962),* I Have No Mouth and I Must Scream *(1967),* The Beast That Shouted Love at the Heart of the World *(1969),* Deathbird Stories: A Pantheon of Modern Gods *(1975),* Shatterday *(1980), and* Angry Candy *(1988).*

His work as editor of Dangerous Visions: 33 Original Stories *(1967) heralded the "New Wave" movement in science fiction during the 1960s, a postmodern literary crusade that emphasized human interest over technological gimmickry. As Ellison states, "I talk about the things people have always talked about in stories: pain, hate, truth, courage, destiny, friendship, responsibility, growing old, growing up, falling in love, all of these things. I don't write about far-flung galactic civilizations; I don't write about crazed robots; I don't write gimmick stories."*

Like his British counterpart, Michael Moorcock, Ellison is uncomfortable with inflexible genre distinctions. He has argued against the pitfalls of formulaic science fiction, and has even argued against science fiction itself. "'Repent, Harlequin!' Said the Ticktockman," originally appearing in the December 1965 issue of Galaxy, *offers a dystopian vision of a human society that has become enslaved by its own use of time management. The story's mischievously defiant protagonist—the Harlequin, Everett C. Marm—is certainly representative of Ellison's own persona as nonconformist, as science fiction's most famous (and infamous) rebel with a cause. "'Repent, Harlequin!' Said the Ticktockman" won for Ellison the first of his many Hugo Awards.*

"Repent, Harlequin!"
Said the Ticktockman

There are always those who ask, what is it all about? For those who need to ask, for those who need points sharply made, who need to know "where it's at," this:

The mass of men serve the state thus, not as men mainly, but as machines, with their bodies. They are the standing army, and the militia, jailors, constables, posse comitatus, etc. In most cases there is no free exercise whatever of the judgment or of the moral sense; but they put themselves on a level with wood and earth and stones; and wooden men can perhaps be manufactured that will serve the purpose as well. Such command no more respect than men of straw or a lump of dirt. They have the same sort of worth only as horses and dogs. Yet such as these even are commonly esteemed good citizens. Others—as most legislators, politicians, lawyers, ministers, and officeholders—serve the state chiefly with their heads; and, as they rarely make any moral distinctions, they are as likely to serve the Devil, without intending it, as God. A very few, as heroes, patriots, martyrs, reformers in the great sense, and men, *serve the state with their consciences also, and so necessarily resist it for the most part; and they are commonly treated as enemies by it.*

HENRY DAVID THOREAU
Civil Disobedience

That is the heart of it. Now begin in the middle, and later learn the beginning; the end will take care of itself.

But because it was the very world it was, the very world they had allowed it to *become,* for months his activities did not come to the alarmed attention of The Ones Who Kept The Machine Functioning Smoothly, the ones who poured the very best butter over the cams and mainsprings of the culture. Not until it had become obvious that somehow, someway, he had become a notoriety, a celebrity, perhaps even a hero for (what Officialdom inescapably tagged) "an emotionally disturbed segment of the populace," did they turn it over to the Ticktockman and his legal machinery. But by then, because it was the very world it was, and they had no way to predict he would happen—possibly a strain of disease long-defunct, now, suddenly, reborn in a system where immunity had been forgotten, had lapsed—he had been allowed to become too real. Now he had form and substance.

He had become a *personality,* something they had filtered out of the system many decades before. But there it was, and there *he* was, a very definitely imposing personality. In certain circles—middle-class circles—it was thought disgusting. Vulgar ostentation. Anarchistic. Shameful. In others, there was only sniggering: those strata where thought is subjugated to form and ritual, niceties, proprieties. But down below, ah, down below, where the people always needed their saints and sinners, their bread and circuses, their heroes and villains, he was considered a Bolivar; a Napoleon; a Robin Hood; a Dick Bong (Ace of Aces); a Jesus; a Jomo Kenyatta.

And at the top—where, like socially-attuned Shipwreck Kellys, every tremor and vibration threatening to dislodge the wealthy, powerful and titled from their flagpoles—he was considered a menace; a heretic; a rebel; a disgrace; a peril. He was known down the line, to the very heart-meat core, but the important reactions were high above and far below. At the very top, at the very bottom.

So his file was turned over, along with his time-card and his cardioplate, to the office of the Ticktockman.

The Ticktockman: very much over six feet tall, often silent, a soft purring man when things went timewise. The Ticktockman.

Even in the cubicles of the hierarchy, where fear was generated, seldom suffered, he was called the Ticktockman. But no one called him that to his mask.

You don't call a man a hated name, not when that man, behind his mask, is capable of revoking the minutes, the hours, the days and nights, the years of your life. He was called the Master Timekeeper to his mask. It was safer that way.

"That is *what* he is," said the Ticktockman with genuine softness, "but not *who* he is. This time-card I'm holding in my left hand has a name on it, but it is the name of *what* he is, not *who* he is. The cardioplate here in my right hand is also named, but not *whom* named, merely *what* named. Before I can exercise proper revocation, I have to know *who* this *what* is."

To his staff, all the ferrets, all the loggers, all the finks, all the commex, even the mineez, he said, "Who is this Harlequin?"

He was not purring smoothly. Timewise, it was jangle.

However, it *was* the longest speech they had ever heard him utter at one time, the staff, the ferrets, the loggers, the finks, the commex, but not the mineez, who usually weren't around to know, in any case. But even they scurried to find out.

Who is the Harlequin?

High above the third level of the city, he crouched on the humming aluminum-frame platform of the air-boat (foof! air-boat, indeed! swizzleskid is what it was, with a tow-rack jerry-rigged) and he stared down at the neat Mondrian arrangement of the buildings.

Somewhere nearby, he could hear the metronomic left-right-left of the 2:47 P.M. shift, entering the Timkin roller-bearing plant in their sneakers. A minute later, precisely, he heard the softer right-left-right of the 5:00 A.M. formation, going home.

An elfin grin spread across his tanned features, and his dimples appeared for a moment. Then, scratching at his thatch of auburn hair, he shrugged within his motley, as though girding himself for what came next, and threw the joystick forward, and bent into the wind as the air-boat dropped. He skimmed over a slidewalk, purposely dropping a few feet to crease the tassels of the ladies of fashion, and—inserting thumbs in large ears—he stuck out his tongue, rolled his eyes and went wugga-wugga-wugga. It was a minor diversion. One pedestrian skittered and tumbled, sending parcels everywhichway, another wet herself, a third keeled slantwise and the walk was stopped automatically by the servitors till she could be resuscitated. It was a minor diversion.

Then he swirled away on a vagrant breeze, and was gone. Hi-ho.

As he rounded the cornice of the Time-Motion Study Building, he saw the shift, just boarding the slidewalk. With practiced motion and an absolute conservation of movement, they sidestepped up onto the slow-strip and (in a chorus line reminiscent of a Busby Berkeley film of the antediluvian 1930s) advanced across the strips ostrich-walking till they were lined up on the expresstrip.

Once more, in anticipation, the elfin grin spread, and there was a tooth missing back there on the left side. He dipped, skimmed, and swooped over them; and then, scrunching about on the air-boat, he released the holding pins that fastened shut the ends of the home-made pouring troughs that kept his cargo from dumping prematurely. And as he pulled the trough-pins, the air-boat slid over the factory workers and one hundred and fifty thousand dollars' worth of jelly beans cascaded down on the expresstrip.

Jelly beans! Millions and billions of purples and yellows and greens and licorice and grape and raspberry and mint and round and smooth and crunchy outside and soft-mealy inside and sugary and bouncing jouncing tumbling clittering clattering skittering fell on the heads and shoulders and hardhats and carapaces of the Timkin workers, tinkling on the slidewalk and bouncing away and rolling about underfoot and filling the sky on their way down with all the colors of joy and childhood and holidays, coming down in a steady rain, a solid wash, a torrent of color and sweetness out of the sky from above, and entering a universe of sanity and metronomic order with quite-mad coocoo newness. Jelly beans!

The shift workers howled and laughed and were pelted, and broke ranks, and the jelly beans managed to work their way into the mechanism of the slidewalks after which there was a hideous scraping as the sound of a million fingernails rasped down a quarter of a million blackboards, followed by a coughing and a sputtering, and then the slidewalks all stopped and everyone was dumped thisawayandthataway in a jackstraw tumble, still laughing and popping little jelly bean eggs of childish color into their mouths. It was a holiday, and a jollity, an absolute insanity, a giggle. But . . .

The shift was delayed seven minutes.

They did not get home for seven minutes.

The master schedule was thrown off by seven minutes.

Quotas were delayed by inoperative slidewalks for seven minutes.

He had tapped the first domino in the line, and one after another, like chik chik chik, the others had fallen.

The System had been seven minutes' worth of disrupted. It was a tiny matter, one hardly worthy of note, but in a society where the single driving force was order and unity and equality and promptness and clocklike precision and attention to the clock, reverence of the gods of the passage of time, it was a disaster of major importance.

So he was ordered to appear before the Ticktockman. It was broadcast across every channel of the communications web. He was ordered to be *there* at 7:00 dammit on time. And they waited, and they waited, but he didn't show up till almost ten-thirty, at which time he merely sang a little song about moonlight in a place no one had ever heard of, called Vermont, and vanished again. But they had all been waiting since seven, and it wrecked *hell* with their schedules. So the question remained: Who is the Harlequin?

But the *unasked* question (more important of the two) was: how did we get *into* this position, where a laughing, irresponsible japer of jabberwocky and jive could disrupt our entire economic and cultural life with a hundred and fifty thousand dollars' worth of jelly beans . . .

Jelly for God's sake *beans!* This is madness! Where did he get the money to buy a hundred and fifty thousand dollars' worth of jelly beans? (They knew it would have cost that much, because they had a team of Situation Analysts pulled off another assignment, and rushed to the slidewalk scene to sweep up and count the candies, and produce findings, which disrupted *their* schedules and threw their entire branch at least a day behind.) Jelly beans! Jelly . . . *beans?* Now wait a second— a second accounted for—no one has manufactured jelly beans for over a hundred years. Where did he get jelly beans?

That's another good question. More than likely it will never be answered to your complete satisfaction. But then, how many questions ever are?

The middle you know. Here is the beginning. How it starts:

A desk pad. Day for day, and turn each day. 9:00—open the mail. 9:45—appointment with planning commission board. 10:30—discuss installation progress charts with J. L. 11:45—pray for rain. 12:00—lunch. *And so it goes.*

"I'm sorry, Miss Grant, but the time for interviews was set at 2:30, and it's almost five now. I'm sorry you're late, but those are the rules. You'll have to wait till next year to submit application for this college again." *And so it goes.*

The 10:10 local stops at Cresthaven, Galesville, Tonawanda Junction, Selby and Farnhurst, but not at Indiana City, Lucasville and Colton, except on Sunday. The 10:35 express stops at Galesville, Selby and Indiana City, except on Sundays & Holidays, at which time it stops at . . . *and so it goes.*

"I couldn't wait, Fred. I had to be at Pierre Cartain's by 3:00, and you said you'd meet me under the clock in the terminal at 2:45, and you weren't there, so I had to go on. You're always late, Fred. If you'd been there, we could have sewed it up together, but as it was, well, I took the order alone . . ." *And so it goes.*

Dear Mr. and Mrs. Atterley: In reference to your son Gerold's constant tardiness, I am afraid we will have to suspend him from school unless some more reliable method can be instituted guaranteeing he will arrive at his classes on time. Granted he is an exemplary student, and his marks are high, his constant flouting of the schedules of this school makes it impractical to maintain him in a system where the other children seem capable of getting where they are supposed to be on time *and so it goes.*

YOU CANNOT VOTE UNLESS YOU APPEAR AT 8:45 A.M.

"I don't care if the script is *good,* I need it Thursday!"

CHECK-OUT TIME IS 2:00 P.M.

"You got here late. The job's taken. Sorry."

YOUR SALARY HAS BEEN DOCKED FOR TWENTY MINUTES TIME LOST.

"God, what time is it, I've gotta run!"

And so it goes. And so it goes. And so it goes. And so it goes goes goes goes goes tick tock tick tock tick tock and one day we no longer let time serve us, we serve time and we are slaves of the schedule, worshippers of the sun's passing, bound into a life predicated on restrictions because the system will not function if we don't keep the schedule tight.

Until it becomes more than a minor inconvenience to be late. It becomes a sin. Then a crime. Then a crime punishable by this:

EFFECTIVE 15 JULY 2389 12:00:00 midnight, the office of the Master Timekeeper will require all citizens to submit their time-cards and cardioplates for processing. In accordance with Statute 555-7-SGH-999 governing the revocation of time per capita, all cardioplates will be keyed to the individual holder and—

What they had done was devise a method of curtailing the amount of life a person could have. If he was ten minutes late, he lost ten minutes of his life. An hour was proportionately worth more revocation. If someone was consistently tardy, he might find himself, on a Sunday night, receiving a communiqué from the Master Timekeeper that his time had run out, and he would be "turned off" at high noon on Monday, please straighten your affairs, sir, madame, or bisex.

And so, by this simple scientific expedient (utilizing a scientific process held dearly secret by the Ticktockman's office) the System was maintained. It was the only expedient thing to do. It was, after all, patriotic. The schedules had to be met. After all, there *was* a war on!

But, wasn't there always?

"Now that is really disgusting," the Harlequin said, when Pretty Alice showed him the wanted poster. "Disgusting and *highly* improbable. After all, this isn't the Day of the Desperado. A *wanted* poster!"

"You know," Pretty Alice noted, "you speak with a great deal of inflection."

"I'm sorry," said the Harlequin, humbly.

"No need to be sorry. You're always saying 'I'm sorry.' You have such massive guilt, Everett, it's really *very* sad."

"I'm sorry," he said again, then pursed his lips so the dimples appeared momentarily. He hadn't wanted to say that at all. "I have to go out again. I have to *do* something."

Pretty Alice slammed her coffee-bulb down on the counter. "Oh for God's *sake*, Everett, can't you stay home just *one* night! Must you always be out in that ghastly clown suit, running around an*noy*ing people?"

"I'm—" he stopped, and clapped the jester's hat onto his auburn thatch with a tiny tingling of bells. He rose, rinsed out his coffee-bulb at the spray, and put it into the dryer for a moment. "I have to go."

She didn't answer. The faxbox was purring, and she pulled a sheet out, read it, threw it toward him on the counter. "It's about you. Of course. You're ridiculous."

He read it quickly. It said the Ticktockman was trying to locate him. He didn't care, he was going out to be late again. At the door, dredging for an exit line, he hurled back petulantly, "Well, *you* speak with inflection, *too!*"

Pretty Alice rolled her pretty eyes heavenward. "You're ridiculous." The Harlequin stalked out, slamming the door, which sighed shut softly, and locked itself.

There was a gentle knock, and Pretty Alice got up with an exhalation of exasperated breath, and opened the door. He stood there. "I'll be back about ten-thirty, okay?"

She pulled a rueful face. "Why do you tell me that? Why? You *know* you'll be late! You *know* it! You're *always* late, so why do you tell me these dumb things?" She closed the door.

On the other side, the Harlequin nodded to himself. *She's right. She's always right. I'll be late. I'm always late. Why do I tell her these dumb things?*

He shrugged again, and went off to be late once more.

He had fired off the firecracker rockets that said: I will attend the 115th annual International Medical Association Invocation at 8:00 P.M. precisely. I do hope you will all be able to join me.

The words had burned in the sky, and of course the authorities were there, lying in wait for him. They assumed, naturally, that he would be late. He arrived twenty minutes early, while they were setting up the spiderwebs to trap and hold him. Blowing a large bullhorn, he frightened and unnerved them so, their own moisturized encirclement webs sucked closed, and they were hauled up, kicking and shrieking, high above the amphitheater's floor. The Harlequin laughed and laughed, and apologized profusely. The physicians, gathered in solemn conclave, roared with laughter, and accepted the Harlequin's apologies with exaggerated bowing and posturing, and a merry time was had by all, who thought the Harlequin was a regular foofaraw in fancy pants; all, that is, but the authorities, who had been sent out by the office of the Ticktockman; they hung there like so much dockside cargo, hauled up above the floor of the amphitheater in a most unseemly fashion.

(In another part of the same city where the Harlequin carried on his "activities," totally unrelated in every way to what concerns us here, save that it illustrates the Ticktockman's power and import, a man named Marshall Delahanty received his turn-off notice from the Ticktockman's office. His wife received the notification from the gray-suited minee who delivered it, with the traditional "look of sorrow" plastered hideously across his face. She knew what it was, even without unsealing it. It was a billet-doux of immediate recognition to everyone these days. She gasped, and held it as though it were a glass slide tinged with botulism, and prayed it was not for her. Let it be for Marsh, she thought, brutally, realistically, or one of the kids, but not for me, please dear God, not for me. And then she opened it, and it *was* for Marsh, and she was at one and the same time horrified and relieved. The next trooper in the line had caught the bullet. "Marshall," she screamed, "Marshall! Termination, Marshall! OhmiGod, Marshall, whattl we do, whattl we do, Marshall, omigodmarshall . . ." and in their home that night was the sound of tearing paper and fear, and the stink of madness went up the flue and there was nothing, absolutely nothing they could do about it.

(But Marshall Delahanty tried to run. And early the next day, when turn-off time came, he was deep in the Canadian forest two hundred miles away, and the office of the Ticktockman blanked his cardioplate, and Marshall Delahanty keeled over, running, and his heart stopped, and the blood dried up on its way to his brain, and he was dead that's all. One light went out on the sector map in the office of the Master Timekeeper, while notification was entered for fax reproduction, and Georgette Delahanty's name was entered on the dole roles till she could remarry. Which is the end of the footnote, and all the point that need be made, except don't laugh, because that is what would happen to the Harlequin if ever the Ticktockman found out his real name. It isn't funny.)

The shopping level of the city was thronged with the Thursday-colors of the buyers. Women in canary yellow chitons and men in pseudo-Tyrolean outfits that were jade and leather and fit very tightly, save for the balloon pants.

When the Harlequin appeared on the still-being-constructed shell of the new Efficiency Shopping Center, his bullhorn to his elfishly-laughing lips, everyone pointed and stared, and he berated them:

"Why let them order you about? Why let them tell you to hurry and scurry like ants or maggots? Take your time! Saunter a while! Enjoy the sunshine, enjoy the breeze, let life carry you at your own pace! Don't be slaves of time, it's a helluva way to die, slowly, by degrees . . . down with the Ticktockman!"

Who's the nut? most of the shoppers wanted to know. Who's the nut oh wow I'm gonna be late I gotta run . . .

And the construction gang on the Shopping Center received an urgent order from the office of the Master Timekeeper that the dangerous criminal known as the Harlequin was atop their spire, and their aid was urgently needed in apprehending him. The work crew said no, they would lose time on their construction schedule, but the Ticktockman managed to pull the proper threads of governmental webbing, and they were told to cease work and catch that nitwit up there on the spire; up there with the bullhorn. So a dozen and more burly workers began climbing into their construction platforms, releasing the a-grav plates, and rising toward the Harlequin.

After the debacle (in which, through the Harlequin's attention to personal safety, no one was seriously injured), the workers tried to reassemble, and assault him again, but it was too late. He had vanished. It had attracted quite a crowd, however, and the shopping cycle was thrown off by hours, simply hours. The purchasing needs of the system were therefore falling behind, and so measures were taken to accelerate the cycle for the rest of the day, but it got bogged down and speeded up and they sold too many float-valves and not nearly enough wegglers, which meant that the popli ratio was off, which made it necessary to rush cases and cases of spoiling Smash-O to stores that usually needed a case only every three or four hours. The shipments were bollixed, the transshipments were misrouted, and in the end, even the swizzleskid industries felt it.

"Don't come back till you have him!" the Ticktockman said, very quietly, very sincerely, extremely dangerously.

They used dogs. They used probes. They used cardioplate crossoffs. They used teepers. They used bribery. They used stiktytes. They used intimidation. They used torment. They used torture. They used finks. They used cops. They used search&seizure. They used fallaron. They used betterment incentive. They used fingerprints. They used the Bertillon system. They used cunning. They used guile. They used treachery. They used Raoul Mitgong, but he didn't help much. They used applied physics. They used techniques of criminology.

And what the hell: they caught him.

After all, his name was Everett C. Marm, and he wasn't much to begin with, except a man who had no sense of time.

"Repent, Harlequin!" said the Ticktockman.

"Get stuffed!" the Harlequin replied, sneering.

"You've been late a total of sixty-three years, five months, three weeks, two days, twelve hours, forty-one minutes, fifty-nine seconds, point oh three six one one one microseconds. You've used up everything you can, and more. I'm going to turn you off."

"Scare someone else. I'd rather be dead than live in a dumb world with a bogeyman like you."

"It's my job."

"You're full of it. You're a tyrant. You have no right to order people around and kill them if they show up late."

"You can't adjust. You can't fit in."

"Unstrap me, and I'll fit my fist into your mouth."

"You're a nonconformist."

"That didn't used to be a felony."

"It is now. Live in the world around you."

"I hate it. It's a terrible world."

"Not everyone thinks so. Most people enjoy order."

"I don't, and most of the people I know don't."

"That's not true. How do you think we caught you?"

"I'm not interested."

"A girl named Pretty Alice told us who you were."

"That's a lie."

"It's true. You unnerve her. She wants to belong; she wants to conform; I'm going to turn you off."

"Then do it already, and stop arguing with me."

"I'm not going to turn you off."

"You're an idiot!"

"Repent, Harlequin!" said the Ticktockman.

"Get stuffed."

So they sent him to Coventry. And in Coventry they worked him over. It was just like what they did to Winston Smith in NINETEEN EIGHTY-FOUR, which was a book none of them knew about, but the techniques are really quite ancient, and so they did it to Everett C. Marm; and one day, quite a long time later, the Harlequin appeared on the communications web, appearing elfin and dimpled and bright-eyed, and not at all brainwashed, and he said he had been wrong, that it was a good, a very good thing indeed, to belong, and be right on time hip-ho and away we go, and everyone stared up at him on the public screens that covered an entire city block, and they said to themselves, well, you see, he was just a nut after all, and if that's the way the system is run, then let's do it that way, because it doesn't pay to fight city hall, or in this case, the Ticktockman. So Everett C. Marm was destroyed, which was a loss, because of what Thoreau said earlier, but you can't make an omelet without breaking a few eggs, and in every revolution a few die who shouldn't, but they have to, because that's the way it happens, and if you make only a little change, then it seems to be worthwhile. Or, to make the point lucidly:

"Uh, excuse me, sir, I, uh, don't know how to uh, to uh, tell you this, but you were three minutes late. The schedule is a little, uh, bit off."

He grinned sheepishly.

"That's ridiculous!" murmured the Ticktockman behind his mask. "Check your watch." And then he went into his office, going *mrmee, mrmee, mrmee, mrmee.*

—1965

SAMUEL R. DELANY

B. 1942

Samuel Ray Delany, Jr., one of a handful of African-American authors of speculative fiction, is admired as perhaps the finest literary talent to have appeared during the so-called New Wave movement in science fiction during the 1960s. He was born in Harlem, New York City, and his father was a successful funeral director. Delany thus enjoyed a prosperous childhood, attending at age five the private Dalton School in New York. The socio-economic contrast between his friends in Harlem and his friends at Dalton impressed upon the young Delany the striking cultural division between working class black society and upper class white society. Delany suffered from dyslexia, yet early in his life he was interested in writing fiction. When he was a student at the Bronx High School of Science, he co-edited the school's literary magazine, Dynamo. *Delany attended the City College of New York during the early 1960s. In 1975, he became the Butler Professor*

*of English at the State University of New York at Buffalo. He was awarded
prestigious senior fellowships at the University of Wisconsin at Milwaukee
and Cornell University. In 1988, he became a professor of comparative literature at the University of Massachusetts at Amherst.*

*Following his high school graduation, Delany's future wife, Marilyn
Hacker, who was then an editor for the science fiction publisher, Ace Books,
encouraged him to publish his first science fiction novel,* The Jewels of
Aptor, *in 1962. Delany went on to become one of the genre's most talented
and critically praised authors. His most notable work includes* Babel-17
(1966), The Einstein Intersection *(1967),* Nova *(1968),* Dhalgren *(1975),* The
Tales of Nevèrÿon *(1979), the first book in his Return to Nevèrÿon fantasy
series, and his* The Fall of the Towers *omnibus (1970), containing the trilogy* Out of the Dead City *(originally appearing in 1963 under the title*
Captives of the Flame*),* The Towers of Toron *(1964), and* City of a
Thousand Suns *(1965). Delany is also regarded as a superb science fiction
literary critic. His first collection of essays,* The Jewel-Hinged Jaw: Notes on
the Language of Science Fiction, *was published in 1977.*

*Delany's speculative fiction is notable for its complexity and sense of
experimentation. His stories favor sophisticated narrative style over plodding narrative structure. In a genre that has historically been savaged by
the mainstream literary community, Delany's writing illustrates that rare
exception in science fiction in which popularity intersects with critical and
scholarly respect. One of Delany's most highly regarded short stories is
"Time Considered as a Helix of Semi-Precious Stones," which won both the
Hugo Award and Nebula Award following its initial appearance in 1968 in
issue no. 186 of the British science fiction magazine* New Worlds *(it was
reprinted in Delany's first short story collection,* Driftglass, *in 1971). Several
themes that connect Delany's larger body of imaginative fiction also appear
in this tale, including, specifically, his examination of the relationship
between the purpose of the artist and the power of art in society.*

TIME CONSIDERED AS A HELIX
OF SEMI-PRECIOUS STONES

Lay ordinate and abscissa on the century. Now cut me a quadrant. Third quadrant
if you please. I was born in 'fifty. Here it's 'seventy-five.

At sixteen they let me leave the orphanage. Dragging the name they'd hung me
with (Harold Clancy Everet, and me a mere lad—how many monickers have I had
since; but don't worry, you'll recognize my smoke) over the hills of East Vermont, I
came to a decision:

Me and Pa Michaels, who had belligerently given me a job at the request of *The
Official* (looking) *Document* with which the orphanage sends you packing, were running Pa Michaels' dairy farm, i.e., thirteen thousand three hundred sixty-two piebald
Guernseys all asleep in their stainless coffins, nourished and drugged by pink liquid
flowing in clear plastic veins (stuff is sticky and messes up your hands), exercised
with electric pulsers that make their muscles quiver, them not half-awake, and the
milk just a-pouring down into stainless cisterns. Anyway. The Decision (as I stood
there in the fields one afternoon like the Man with the Hoe, exhausted with three

hard hours of physical labor, contemplating the machinery of the universe through the fog of fatigue): With all of Earth, and Mars, and the Outer Satellites filled up with people and what-all, there had to be something more than this. I decided to get some.

So I stole a couple of Pa's credit cards, one of his helicopters, and a bottle of white lightning the geezer made himself, and took off. Ever try to land a stolen helicopter on the roof of the Pan Am building, drunk? Jail, schmail, and some hard knocks later I had attained to wisdom. But remember this o best beloved: I have done three honest hours on a dairy farm less than ten years back. And nobody but nobody has ever called me Harold Clancy Everet again.

Hank Culafroy Eckles (red-headed, a bit vague, six-foot-two) strolled out of the baggage room at the spaceport, carrying a lot of things that weren't his in a small briefcase.

Beside him the Business Man was saying, "You young fellows today upset me. Go back to Bellona, I say. Just because you got into trouble with that little blonde you were telling me about is no reason to leap worlds, come on all glum. Even quit your job!"

Hank stops and grins weakly: "Well . . ."

"Now I admit, you have your real needs, which maybe we older folks don't understand, but you have to show some responsibility toward . . ." He notices Hank has stopped in front of a door marked MEN. "Oh. Well. Eh." He grins strongly. "I've enjoyed meeting you, Hank. It's always nice when you meet somebody worth talking to on these damned crossings. So long."

Out same door, ten minutes later, comes Harmony C. Eventide, six-foot even (one of the false heels was cracked, so I stuck both of them under a lot of paper towels), brown hair (not even my hairdresser knows for sure), oh so dapper and of his time, attired in the bad taste that is oh so tasteful, a sort of man with whom no Business Men would start a conversation. Took the regulation 'copter from the port over to the Pan Am building (Yeah. Really. Drunk), came out of Grand Central Station, and strode along Forty-Second towards Eighth Avenue, with a lot of things that weren't mine in a small briefcase.

The evening is carved from light.

Crossed the plastiplex pavement of the Great White Way—I think it makes people look weird, all that white light under their chins—and skirted the crowds coming up in elevators from the subway, the sub-sub-way, and the sub-sub-sub (eighteen and first week out of jail, I hung around here, snatching stuff from people—but daintily, daintily, so they never knew they'd been snatched), bulled my way through a crowd of giggling, goo-chewing school girls with flashing lights in their hair, all very embarrassed at wearing transparent plastic blouses which had just been made legal again (I hear the breast has been scene [as opposed to obscene] on and off since the seventeenth century) so I stared appreciatively; they giggled some more. I thought, Christ, when I was that age, I was on a God-damn dairy farm, and took the thought no further.

The ribbon of news lights looping the triangular structure of Communication, Inc., explained in Basic English how Senator Regina Abolafia was preparing to begin her investigation of Organized Crime in the City. Days I'm so happy I'm disorganized I couldn't begin to tell.

Near Ninth Avenue I took my briefcase into a long, crowded bar. I hadn't been in New York for two years, but on my last trip through ofttimes a man used to hang out here who had real talent for getting rid of things that weren't mine profitably, safely, fast. No idea what the chances were I'd find him. I pushed among a lot of guys drinking beer. Here and there were a number of well escorted old bags wearing last month's latest. Scarfs of smoke gentled through the noise. I don't like such places. Those there younger than me were all morphadine heads or feeble-minded. Those older only wished more younger ones would come. I pried my way to the bar and tried to get the attention of one of the little men in white coats.

The lack of noise behind me made me glance back.

She wore a sheath of veiling closed at the neck and wrists with huge brass pins (oh so tastefully on the border of taste); her left arm was bare, her right covered with chiffon like wine. She had it down a lot better than I did. But such an ostentatious demonstration of one's understanding of the finer points was absolutely out of place in a place like this. People were making a great show of not noticing.

She pointed to her wrist, blood-colored nail indexing a yellow-orange fragment in the brass claw of her wristlet. "Do you know what this is, Mr. Eldrich?" she asked; at the same time the veil across her face cleared, and her eyes were ice; her brows, black.

Three thoughts: (One) She is a lady of fashion, because coming in from Bellona I'd read the Delta coverage of the "fading fabrics" whose hue and opacity were controlled by cunning jewels at the wrist. (Two) During my last trip through, when I was younger and Harry Calamine Eldrich, I didn't do anything *too* illegal (though one loses track of these things); still I didn't believe I could be dragged off to the calaboose for anything more than thirty days under that name. (Three) The stone she pointed to . . .

". . . Jasper?" I asked.

She waited for me to say more; I waited for her to give me reason to let on I knew what she was waiting for (when I was in jail, Henry James was my favorite author. He really was).

"Jasper," she confirmed.

"—Jasper . . ." I reopened the ambiguity she had tried so hard to dispel.

". . . Jasper—" But she was already faltering, suspecting I suspected her certainty to be ill-founded.

"Okay, Jasper." But from her face I knew she had seen in my face a look that had finally revealed I knew she knew I knew.

"Just whom have you got me confused with, ma'am?"

Jasper, this month, is the Word.

Jasper is the pass/code/warning that the Singers of the Cities (who last month sang "Opal" from their divine injuries; and on Mars I'd heard the Word and used it thrice, along with devious imitations, to fix possession of what was not rightfully my own; and even there I pondered Singers and their wounds) relay by word of mouth for that loose and roguish fraternity with which I have been involved (in various guises) these nine years. It goes out new every thirty days; and within hours every brother knows it, throughout six worlds and worldlets. Usually it's grunted at you by some blood-soaked bastard staggering into your arms from a dark doorway; hissed at you as you pass a shadowed alley; scrawled on a paper scrap pressed into your palm by some nasty-grimy moving too fast through the crowd. And this month, it was: Jasper.

Here are some alternate translations:

Help!

or

I need help!

or

I can help you!

or

You are being watched!

or

They're not watching now, so *move!*

Final point of syntax: If the Word is used properly, you should never have to think twice about what it means in a given situation. Fine point of usage: Never trust anyone who uses it improperly.

I waited for her to finish waiting.

She opened a wallet in front of me. "Chief of Special Services Department Maudline Hinkle," she read without looking at what it said below the silver badge.

"You have that very well," I said, "Maud." Then I frowned. "Hinkle?"

"Me."

"I know you're not going to believe this, Maud. You look like a woman who has no patience with her mistakes. But my name is Eventide. Not Eldrich. Harmony C. Eventide. And isn't it lucky for all and sundry that the Word changes tonight?" Passed the way it is, the Word is no big secret to the cops. But I've met policemen up to a week after change date who were not privy.

"Well, then: Harmony. I want to talk to you."

I raised an eyebrow.

She raised one back and said, "Look, if you want to be called Henrietta, it's all right by me. But you listen."

"What do you want to talk about?"

"Crime, Mr. . . . ?"

"Eventide. I'm going to call you Maud, so you might as well call me Harmony. It really *is* my name."

Maud smiled. She wasn't a young woman. I think she even had a few years on Business Man. But she used make-up better than he did. "I probably know more about crime than you do," she said. "In fact I wouldn't be surprised if you hadn't even heard of my branch of the police department. What does Special Services mean to you?"

"That's right, I've never heard of it."

"You've been more or less avoiding the Regular Service with alacrity for the past seven years."

"Oh, Maud, really—"

"Special Services is reserved for people whose nuisance value has suddenly taken a sharp rise . . . a sharp enough rise to make our little lights start blinking."

"Surely I haven't done anything so dreadful that—"

"We don't look at what you do. A computer does that for us. We simply keep checking the first derivative of the graphed-out curve that bears your number. Your slope is rising sharply."

"Not even the dignity of a name—"

"We're the most efficient department in the Police Organization. Take it as bragging if you wish. Or just a piece of information."

"Well, well, well," I said. "Have a drink?" The little man in the white coat left us two, looked puzzled at Maud's finery, then went to do something else.

"Thanks." She downed half her glass like someone stauncher than that wrist would indicate. "It doesn't pay to go after most criminals. Take your big-time rack-eteers, Farnesworth, The Hawk, Blavatskia. Take your little snatch-purses, small-time pushers, housebreakers, or vice-impresarios. Both at the top and the bottom of the scale, their incomes are pretty stable. They don't really upset the social boat. Regular Services handles them both. They think they do a good job. We're not going to argue. But say a little pusher starts to become a big-time pusher; a medium-sized vice-impresario sets his sights on becoming a full-fledged racketeer; that's when you get problems with socially unpleasant repercussions. That's when Special Services arrive. We have a couple of techniques that work remarkably well."

"You're going to tell me about them, aren't you?"

"They work better that way," she said. "One of them is hologramic information storage. Do you know what happens when you cut a hologram plate in half?"

"The three dimensional image is . . . cut in half?"

She shook her head. "You get the whole image, only fuzzier, slightly out of focus."

"Now I didn't know that."

"And if you cut in half again, it just gets fuzzier still. But even if you have a square centimeter of the original hologram, you still have the whole image—unrec-ognizable but complete."

I mumbled some appreciative *m*'s.

"Each pinpoint of photographic emulsion on a hologram plate, unlike a photo-graph, gives information about the entire scene being hologrammed. By analogy, hologramic information storage simply means that each bit of information we have—about you, let us say—relates to your entire career, your overall situation, the complete set of tensions between you and your environment. Specific facts about specific misdemeanors or felonies we leave to Regular Services. As soon as we have enough of our kind of data, our method is vastly more efficient for keeping track—even predicting—where you are or what you may be up to."

"Fascinating," I said. "One of the most amazing paranoid syndromes I've ever run up against. I mean, just starting a conversation with someone in a bar. Often, in a hospital situation, I've encountered stranger—"

"In your past," she said matter-of-factly, "I see cows and helicopters. In your not too distant future, there are helicopters and hawks."

"And tell me, oh Good Witch of the West, just how—" Then I got all upset inside. Because nobody is supposed to know about that stint with Pa Michaels save thee and me. Even the Regular Service, who pulled me, out of my head, from that whirli-bird bouncing towards the edge of the Pan Am, never got that one from me. I'd eaten the credit cards when I saw them waiting, and the serial numbers had been filed off everything that could have had a serial number on it by someone more competent than I: good Mister Michaels had boasted to me, my first lonely, drunken night at the farm, how he'd gotten the thing in hot from New Hampshire.

"But why,"—it appalls me the clichés to which anxiety will drive us—"are you telling me all this?"

She smiled, and her smile faded behind her veil. "Information is only meaning-ful when shared," said a voice that was hers from the place of her face.

"Hey, look, I—"

"You may be coming into quite a bit of money soon. If I can calculate right, I will have a helicopter full of the city's finest arriving to take you away as you accept it into your hot little hands. That is a piece of information . . ." She stepped back. Someone stepped between us.

"Hey, Maud—"

"You can do whatever you want with it."

The bar was crowded enough so that to move quickly was to make enemies. I don't know—I lost her and made enemies. Some weird characters there: with greasy hair that hung in spikes, and three of them had dragons tattooed on their scrawny shoulders, still another with an eye patch, and yet another raked nails black with pitch at my cheek (we're two minutes into a vicious free-for-all, case you missed the transition. I did) and some of the women were screaming. I hit and ducked, and then the tenor of the brouhaha changed. Somebody sang "Jasper!" the way she is supposed to be sung. And it meant the heat (the ordinary, bungling Regular Service I had been eluding these seven years) were on their way. The brawl spilled into the street. I got between two nasty-grimies who were doing things appropriate with one another, but made the edge of the crowd with no more wounds than could be racked up to shaving. The fight had broken into sections. I left one and ran into another that, I realized a moment later, was merely a ring of people standing around somebody who had apparently gotten really messed.

Someone was holding people back.

Somebody else was turning him over.

Curled up in a puddle of blood was the little guy I hadn't seen in two years who used to be so good at getting rid of things not mine.

Trying not to hit people with my briefcase, I ducked between the hub and the bub. When I saw my first ordinary policeman, I tried very hard to look like somebody who had just stepped up to see what the rumpus was.

It worked.

I turned down Ninth Avenue and got three steps into an inconspicuous but rapid lope—

"Hey, wait! Wait up there . . ."

I recognized the voice (after two years, coming at me just like that, I recognized it) but kept going.

"Wait. It's me, Hawk!"

And I stopped.

You haven't heard his name before in this story; Maud mentioned *the* Hawk, who is a multi-millionaire racketeer basing his operations on a part of Mars I've never been to (though he has his claws sunk to the spurs in illegalities throughout the system) and somebody else entirely.

I took three steps back towards the doorway.

A boy's laugh there: "Oh, man. You look like you just did something you shouldn't."

"Hawk?" I asked the shadow.

He was still the age when two years' absence means an inch or so taller.

"You're still hanging around here?" I asked.

"Sometimes."

He was an amazing kid.

"Look, Hawk, I got to get out of here." I glanced back at the rumpus.

"Get." He stepped down. "Can I come, too?"

Funny. "Yeah." It makes me feel very funny, him asking that. "Come on."

By the street lamp half a block down, I saw his hair was still pale as split pine. He could have been a nasty-grimy: very dirty black denim jacket, no shirt beneath; very ripe pair of black-jeans—I mean in the dark you could tell. He went barefoot; and the only way you can tell on a dark street someone's been going barefoot for days in New York is to know already. As we reached the corner, he grinned up at me under the street lamp and shrugged his jacket together over the welts and furrows marring his chest and belly. His eyes were very green. Do you recognize him? If by some failure of information dispersal throughout the worlds and worldlets you haven't, walking beside me beside the Hudson was Hawk the Singer.

"Hey, how long have you been back?"

"A few hours," I told him.

"What'd you bring?"

"Really want to know?"

He shoved his hands into his pockets and cocked his head. "Sure."

I made the sound of an adult exasperated by a child. "All right." We had been walking the waterfront for a block now; there was nobody about. "Sit down." So he straddled the beam along the siding, one filthy foot dangling above the flashing black Hudson. I sat in front of him and ran my thumb around the edge of the brief-case.

Hawk hunched his shoulders and leaned. "Hey . . ." He flashed green questioning eyes at me. "Can I touch?"

I shrugged. "Go ahead."

He grubbed among them with fingers that were all knuckle and bitten nail. He picked two up, put them down, picked up three others. "Hey!" he whispered. "How much are all these worth?"

"About ten times more than I hope to get. I have to get rid of them fast."

He glanced down past his toes. "You could always throw them in the river."

"Don't be dense. I was looking for a guy who used to hang around that bar. He was pretty efficient." And half the Hudson away a water-bound foil skimmed above the foam. On her deck were parked a dozen helicopters—being ferried up to the Patrol Field near Verrazano, no doubt. But for moments I looked back and forth between the boy and the transport, getting all paranoid about Maud. But the boat *mmmm*ed into the darkness. "My man got a little cut up this evening."

Hawk put the tips of his fingers in his pockets and shifted his position.

"Which leaves me uptight. I didn't think he'd take them all, but at least he could have turned me on to some other people who might."

"I'm going to a party later on this evening—" he paused to gnaw on the wreck of his little fingernail—"where you might be able to sell them. Alexis Spinnel is having a party for Regina Abolafia at Tower Top."

"Tower Top . . . ?" It had been a while since I palled around with Hawk. Hell's Kitchen at ten; Tower Top at midnight—

"I'm just going because Edna Silem will be there."

Edna Silem is New York's eldest Singer.

Senator Abolafia's name had ribboned above me in lights once that evening. And somewhere among the endless magazines I'd perused coming in from Mars, I remembered Alexis Spinnel's name sharing a paragraph with an awful lot of money.

"I'd like to see Edna again," I said offhandedly. "But she wouldn't remember me." Folk like Spinnel and his social ilk have a little game, I'd discovered during the first leg of my acquaintance with Hawk. He who can get the most Singers of the City under one roof wins. There are five Singers of New York (a tie for second place with Lux on Iapetus). Tokyo leads with seven. "It's a two Singer party?"

"More likely four . . . if I go."

The inaugural ball for the mayor gets four.

I raised the appropriate eyebrow.

"I have to pick up the Word from Edna. It changes tonight."

"All right," I said. "I don't know what you have in mind, but I'm game." I closed the case.

We walked back towards Times Square. When we got to Eighth Avenue and the first of the plastiplex, Hawk stopped. "Wait a minute," he said. Then he buttoned his jacket up to his neck. "Okay."

Strolling through the streets of New York with a Singer (two years back I'd spent much time wondering if that were wise for a man of my profession) is probably the best camouflage possible for a man of my profession. Think of the last time you glimpsed your favorite Tri-D star turning the corner of Fifty-seventh. Now be honest. Would you really recognize the little guy in the tweed jacket half a pace behind him?

Half the people we passed in Times Square recognized him. With his youth, funereal garb, black feet and ash pale hair, he was easily the most colorful of Singers. Smiles; narrowed eyes; very few actually pointed or stared.

"Just exactly who is going to be there who might be able to take this stuff off my hands?"

"Well, Alexis prides himself on being something of an adventurer. They might just take his fancy. And he can give you more than you can get peddling them in the street."

"You'll tell him they're all hot?"

"It will probably make the idea that much more intriguing. He's a creep."

"You say so, friend."

We went down into the sub-sub. The man at the change booth started to take Hawk's coin, then looked up. He began three or four words that were unintelligible through his grin, then just gestured us through.

"Oh," Hawk said, "thank you," with ingenuous surprise, as though this were the first, delightful time such a thing had happened. (Two years ago he had told me sagely, "As soon as I start looking like I expect it, it'll stop happening." I was still impressed by the way he wore his notoriety. The time I'd met Edna Silem, and I'd mentioned this, she said with the same ingenuousness, "But that's what we're chosen for.")

In the bright car we sat on the long seat. Hawk's hands were beside him; one foot rested on the other. Down from us a gaggle of bright-bloused goo-chewers giggled and pointed and tried not to be noticed at it. Hawk didn't look at all, and I tried not to be noticed looking.

Dark patterns rushed the window.

Things below the gray floor hummed.

Once a lurch.

Leaning once, we came out of the ground.

Outside, the city tried on its thousand sequins, then threw them away behind the trees of Ft. Tryon. Suddenly the windows across from us grew bright scales. Behind them girders reeled by. We got out on the platform under a light rain. The sign said TWELVE TOWERS STATION.

By the time we reached the street, however, the shower had stopped. Leaves above the wall shed water down the brick. "If I'd known I was bringing someone, I'd have had Alex send a car for us. I told him it was fifty-fifty I'd come."

"Are you sure it's all right for me to tag along then?"

"Didn't you come up here with me once before?"

"I've even been up here once before that," I said. "Do you still think it's . . ."

He gave me a withering look. Well; Spinnel would be delighted to have Hawk even if he dragged along a whole gang of real nasty-grimies—Singers are famous for that sort of thing. With one more or less presentable thief, Spinnel was getting off light. Beside us rocks broke away into the city. Behind the gate to our left the gardens rolled up towards the first of the towers. The twelve immense, luxury apartment buildings menaced the lower clouds.

"Hawk the Singer," Hawk the Singer said into the speaker at the side of the gate. *Clang* and tic-tic-tic and *Clang*. We walked up the path to the doors and doors of glass.

A cluster of men and women in evening dress were coming out. Three tiers of doors away they saw us. You could see them frowning at the guttersnipe who'd somehow gotten into the lobby (for a moment I thought one of them was Maud because she wore a sheath of the fading fabric, but she turned; beneath her veil her face was dark as roasted coffee); one of the men recognized him, said something to the others. When they passed us, they were smiling. Hawk paid about as much attention to them as he had to the girls on the subway. But when they'd passed, he said, "One of those guys was looking at you."

"Yeah. I saw."

"Do you know why?"

"He was trying to figure out whether we'd met before."

"Had you?"

I nodded. "Right about where I met you, only back when I'd just gotten out of jail. I told you I'd been here once before."

"Oh."

Blue carpet covered three-quarters of the lobby. A great pool filled the rest in which a row of twelve foot trellises stood, crowned with flaming braziers. The lobby itself was three stories high, domed and mirror-tiled.

Twisting smoke curled towards the ornate grill. Broken reflections sagged and recovered on the walls.

The elevator door folded about us its foil petals. There was the distinct feeling of not moving while seventy-five stories shucked down around us.

We got out on the landscaped roof garden. A very tanned, very blond man wearing an apricot jump-suit, from the collar of which emerged a black turtleneck dicky, came down the rocks (artificial) between the ferns (real) growing along the stream (real water; phony current).

"Hello! Hello!" Pause. "I'm terribly glad you decided to come after all." Pause. "For a while I thought you weren't going to make it." The Pauses were to allow Hawk to introduce me. I was dressed so that Spinnel had no way of telling whether I was a miscellaneous Nobel laureate that Hawk happened to have been dining with, or a varlet whose manners and morals were even lower than mine happen to be.

"Shall I take your jacket?" Alexis offered.

Which meant he didn't know Hawk as well as he would like people to think. But I guess he was sensitive enough to realize from the little cold things that happened in the boy's face that he should forget his offer.

He nodded to me, smiling—about all he could do—and we strolled toward the gathering.

Edna Silem was sitting on a transparent inflated hassock. She leaned forward, holding her drink in both hands, arguing politics with the people sitting on the grass before her. She was the first person I recognized (hair of tarnished silver; voice of scrap brass). Jutting from the cuffs of her mannish suit, her wrinkled hands about her goblet, shaking with the intensity of her pronouncements, were heavy with stones and silver. As I ran my eyes back to Hawk, I saw half a dozen whose names/faces sold magazines, music, sent people to the theater (the drama critic for *Delta*, wouldn't you know), and even the mathematician from Princeton I'd read about a few months ago who'd come up with the "quasar/quark" explanation.

There was one woman my eyes kept returning to. On glance three I recognized her as the New Fascistas' most promising candidate for president, Senator Abolafia. Her arms were folded, and she was listening intently to the discussion that had narrowed to Edna and an overly gregarious younger man whose eyes were puffy from what could have been the recent acquisition of contact lenses.

"But don't you feel, Mrs. Silem, that—"

"You must remember when you make predictions like that—"

"Mrs. Silem, I've seen statistics that—"

"You *must* remember—" her voice tensed, lowered till the silence between the words was as rich as the voice was sparse and metallic—"that if everything, *every-thing* were known, statistical estimates would be unnecessary. The science of probability gives mathematical expression to our ignorance, not to our wisdom," which I was thinking was an interesting second installment to Maud's lecture, when Edna looked up and exclaimed, "Why, Hawk!"

Everyone turned.

"I *am* glad to see you. Lewis, Ann," she called: there were two other Singers there already (he dark, she pale, both tree-slender; their faces made you think of pools without drain or tribute come upon in the forest, clear and very still; husband and wife, they had been made Singers together the day before their marriage seven years ago), "he hasn't deserted us after all!" Edna stood, extended her arm over the heads of the people sitting, and barked across her knuckles as though her voice were a pool cue. "Hawk, there are people here arguing with me who don't know nearly as much as you about the subject. You'd be on my side, now wouldn't you—"

"Mrs. Silem, I didn't mean to—" from the floor.

Then her arms swung six degrees, her fingers, eyes, and mouth opened. "You!" Me. "My dear, if there's anyone I never expected to see here! Why it's been almost two years, hasn't it?" Bless Edna; the place where she and Hawk and I had spent a long, beery evening together had more resembled that bar than Tower Top. "Where have you been keeping yourself?"

"Mars, mostly," I admitted. "Actually I just came back today." It's so much fun to be able to say things like that in a place like this.

"Hawk—both of you—" (which meant either she had forgotten my name, or she remembered me well enough not to abuse it) "come over here and help me drink up Alexis' good liquor." I tried not to grin as we walked towards her. If she remembered anything, she certainly recalled my line of business and must have been enjoying this as much as I was.

Relief spread over Alexis' face: he knew now I was *someone* if not *which* someone I was.

As we passed Lewis and Ann, Hawk gave the two Singers one of his luminous grins. They returned shadowed smiles. Lewis nodded. Ann made a move to touch his arm, but left the motion unconcluded; and the company noted the interchange.

Having found out what we wanted, Alex was preparing large glasses of it over crushed ice when the puffy-eyed gentleman stepped up for a refill. "But, Mrs. Silem, then what do you feel validly opposes such political abuses?"

Regina Abolafia wore a white silk suit. Nails, lips and hair were one color; and on her breast was a worked copper pin. It's always fascinated me to watch people used to being the center thrust to the side. She swirled her glass, listening.

"I oppose them," Edna said. "Hawk opposes them. Lewis and Ann oppose them. We, ultimately, are what you have." And her voice had taken on that authoritative resonance only Singers can assume.

Then Hawk's laugh snarled through the conversational fabric.

We turned.

He'd sat cross-legged near the hedge. "Look . . ." he whispered.

Now people's gazes followed his. He was looking at Lewis and Ann. She, tall and blonde, he, dark and taller, were standing very quietly, a little nervously, eyes closed (Lewis' lips were apart).

"Oh," whispered someone who should have known better, "they're going to . . ."

I watched Hawk because I'd never had a chance to observe one Singer at another's performance. He put the soles of his feet together, grasped his toes, and leaned forward, veins making blue rivers on his neck. The top button of his jacket had come loose. Two scar ends showed over his collarbone. Maybe nobody noticed but me.

I saw Edna put her glass down with a look of beaming anticipatory pride. Alex, who had pressed the autobar (odd how automation has become the upper crust's way of flaunting the labor surplus) for more crushed ice, looked up, saw what was about to happen, and pushed the cut-off button. The autobar hummed to silence. A breeze (artificial or real, I couldn't tell you) came by, and the trees gave us a final *shush*.

One at a time, then in duet, then singly again, Lewis and Ann sang.

Singers are people who look at things, then go and tell people what they've seen. What makes them Singers is their ability to make people listen. That is the most magnificent over-simplification I can give. Eighty-six-year-old El Posado in Rio de Janeiro saw a block of tenements collapse, ran to the Avenida del Sol and began improvising, in rhyme and meter (not all that hard in rhyme-rich Portuguese), tears runneling his dusty cheeks, his voice clashing with the palm swards above the sunny street. Hundreds of people stopped to listen; a hundred more; and another hundred. And they told hundreds more what they had heard. Three hours later, hundreds from among them had arrived at the scene with blankets, food, money, shovels, and more incredibly, the willingness and ability to organize themselves and work within that organization. No Tri-D report of a disaster has ever produced that sort of reaction. El Posado is historically considered the first Singer. The second was Miriamne in the roofed city of Lux, who for thirty years walked through the metal streets, singing the glories of the rings of Saturn—the colonists can't look at them without aid because of the ultraviolet the rings set up. But Miriamne, with her strange cataracts, each dawn walked to the edge of the city, looked, saw, and came back to sing of what she saw. All of which would have meant nothing except that during the days she did not sing—through illness, or once she was on a visit to another city to which her fame had spread—the Lux Stock Exchange would go down, the number of violent crimes rise. Nobody could explain it. All they could do was proclaim her

Singer. Why did the institution of Singers come about, springing up in just about every urban center throughout the system? Some have speculated that it was a spontaneous reaction to the mass media which blanket our lives. While Tri-D and radio and newstapes disperse information all over the worlds, they also spread a sense of alienation from first-hand experience. (How many people still go to sports events or a political rally with their little receivers plugged into their ears to let them know that what they see is really happening?) The first Singers were proclaimed by the people around them. Then, there was a period where anyone could proclaim himself who wanted to, and people either responded to him or laughed him into oblivion. But by the time I was left on the doorstep of somebody who didn't want me, most cities had more or less established an unofficial quota. When a position is left open today, the remaining Singers choose who is going to fill it. The required talents are poetic, theatrical, as well as a certain charisma that is generated in the tensions between the personality and the publicity web a Singer is immediately snared in. Before he became a Singer, Hawk had gained something of a prodigious reputation with a book of poems published when he was fifteen. He was touring universities and giving readings, but the reputation was still small enough so that he was amazed that I had ever heard of him, that evening we encountered in Central Park. (I had just spent a pleasant thirty days as a guest of the city, and it's amazing what you find in the Tombs Library.) It was a few weeks after his sixteenth birthday. His Singership was to be announced in four days, though he had been informed already. We sat by the lake till dawn while he weighed and pondered and agonized over the coming responsibility. Two years later, he's still the youngest Singer in six worlds by half a dozen years. Before becoming a Singer, a person need not have been a poet, but most are either that or actors. But the roster through the system includes a longshoreman, two university professors, an heiress to the Silitax millions (Tack it down with Silitax), and at least two persons of such dubious background that the ever-hungry-for-sensation Publicity Machine itself has agreed not to let any of it past the copy editors. But wherever their origins, these diverse and flamboyant living myths sang of love, of death, of the changing of seasons, social classes, governments, and the palace guard. They sang before large crowds, small ones, to an individual laborer coming home from the city's docks, on slum street corners, in club cars of commuter trains, in the elegant gardens atop Twelve Towers, to Alex Spinnel's select soirée. But it has been illegal to reproduce the "Songs" of the Singers by mechanical means (including publishing the lyrics) since the institution arose, and I respect the law, I do, as only a man in my profession can. I offer the explanation then in place of Lewis and Ann's song.

They finished, opened their eyes, stared about with expressions that could have been embarrassment, could have been contempt.

Hawk was leaning forward with a look of rapt approval. Edna was smiling politely. I had the sort of grin on my face that breaks out when you've been vastly moved and vastly pleased. Lewis and Ann had sung superbly.

Alex began to breathe again, glancing around to see what state everybody else was in, saw, and pressed the autobar, which began to hum and crush ice. No clapping, but the appreciative sounds began; people were nodding, commenting, whispering. Regina Abolafia went over to Lewis to say something. I tried to listen until Alex shoved a glass into my elbow.

"Oh, I'm sorry . . ."

I transferred my briefcase to the other hand and took the drink, smiling. When Senator Abolafia left the two Singers, they were holding hands and looking at one another a little sheepishly. They sat down again.

The party drifted in conversational groups through the gardens, through the groves. Overhead clouds the color of old chamois folded and unfolded across the moon.

For a while I stood alone in a circle of trees, listening to the music: a de Lassus two-part canon programmed for audio-generators. Recalled: an article in one of last week's large-circulation literaries, stating that it was the only way to remove the feel of the bar lines imposed by five centuries of meter on modern musicians. For another two weeks this would be acceptable entertainment. The trees circled a rock pool; but no water. Below the plastic surface, abstract lights wove and threaded in a shifting lumia.

"Excuse me . . . ?"

I turned to see Alexis, who had no drink now or idea what to do with his hands. He *was* nervous.

". . . but our young friend has told me you have something I might be interested in."

I started to lift my briefcase, but Alexis' hand came down from his ear (it had gone by belt to hair to collar already) to halt me. Nouveau riche.

"That's all right. I don't need to see them yet. In fact, I'd rather not. I have something to propose to you. I would certainly be interested in what you have if they are, indeed, as Hawk has described them. But I have a guest here who would be even more curious."

That sounded odd.

"I know that sounds odd," Alexis assessed, "but I thought you might be interested simply because of the finances involved. I am an eccentric collector who would offer you a price concomitant with what I would use them for: eccentric conversation pieces—and because of the nature of the purchase I would have to limit severely the people with whom I could converse."

I nodded.

"My guest, however, would have a great deal more use for them."

"Could you tell me who this guest is?"

"I asked Hawk, finally, who you were, and he led me to believe I was on the verge of a grave social indiscretion. It would be equally indiscreet to reveal my guest's name to you." He smiled. "But indiscretion is the better part of the fuel that keeps the social machine turning, Mr. Harvey Cadwaliter-Erickson . . ." He smiled knowingly.

I have *never* been Harvey Cadwaliter-Erickson, but then Hawk was always an inventive child. Then a second thought went by, viz., the tungsten magnates, the Cadwaliter-Ericksons of Tythis on Triton. Hawk was not only inventive, he was as brilliant as all the magazines and newspapers are always saying he is.

"I assume your second indiscretion will be to tell me who this mysterious guest is?"

"Well," Alex said with the smile of the canary-fattened cat, "Hawk agreed with me that *the* Hawk might well be curious as to what you have in there," (he pointed) "as indeed he is."

I frowned. Then I thought lots of small, rapid thoughts I'll articulate in due time. *"The* Hawk?"

Alex nodded.

I don't think I was actually scowling. "Would you send our young friend up here for a moment?"

"If you'd like." Alex bowed, turned. Perhaps a minute later, Hawk came up over the rocks and through the trees, grinning. When I didn't grin back, he stopped.

"*Mmmm . . .*" I began.

His head cocked.

I scratched my chin with a knuckle. ". . . Hawk," I said, "are you aware of a department of the police called Special Services?"

"I've heard of them."

"They've suddenly gotten very interested in me."

"Gee," he said with honest amazement. "They're supposed to be pretty effective."

"*Mmmm,*" I reiterated.

"Say," Hawk announced, "how do you like that? My namesake is here tonight. Wouldn't you know."

"Alex doesn't miss a trick. Have you any idea *why* he's here?"

"Probably trying to make some deal with Abolafia. Her investigation starts tomorrow."

"Oh." I thought over some of those things I had thought before. "Do you know a Maud Hinkle?"

His puzzled look said "no" pretty convincingly.

"She bills herself as one of the upper echelon in the arcane organization of which I spoke."

"Yeah?"

"She ended our interview earlier this evening with a little homily about hawks and helicopters. I took our subsequent encounter as a fillip of coincidence. But now I discover that the evening has confirmed her intimations of plurality." I shook my head. "Hawk, I am suddenly catapulted into a paranoid world where the walls not only have ears, but probably eyes and long, claw-tipped fingers. Anyone about me—yea, even very you—could turn out to be a spy. I suspect every sewer grating and second-story window conceals binoculars, a tommygun, or worse. What I just can't figure out is how these insidious forces, ubiquitous and omnipresent though they be, induced you to lure me into this intricate and diabolical—"

"Oh, cut it out!" He shook back his hair, "I didn't lure—"

"Perhaps not consciously, but Special Services has Hologramic Information Storage, and their methods are insidious and cruel—"

"I said cut it out!" And all sorts of hard little things happened again. "Do you think I'd—" Then he realized how scared I was, I guess. "Look, the Hawk isn't some small-time snatch-purse. He lives in just as paranoid a world as you're in now, only all the time. If he's here, you can be sure there are just as many of his men—eyes and ears and fingers—as there are of Maud Hickenlooper's."

"Hinkle."

"Anyway, it works both ways. No Singer's going to—Look, do you really think *I* would—"

And even though I knew all those hard little things were scabs over pain, I said, "Yes."

"You did something for me once, and I—"

"I gave you some more welts. That's all."

All the scabs pulled off.

"Hawk," I said. "Let me see."

He took a breath. Then he began to open the brass buttons. The flaps of his jacket fell back. The lumia colored his chest with pastel shiftings.

I felt my face wrinkle. I didn't want to look away. I drew a hissing breath instead, which was just as bad.

He looked up. "There're a lot more than when you were here last, aren't there?"

"You're going to kill yourself, Hawk."

He shrugged.

"I can't even tell which are the ones I put there anymore."

He started to point them out.

"Oh, come on," I said too sharply. And for the length of three breaths, he grew more and more uncomfortable till I saw him start to reach for the bottom button. "Boy," I said, trying to keep despair out of my voice, "why do you do it?" and ended up keeping out everything. There is nothing more despairing than a voice empty.

He shrugged, saw I didn't want that, and for a moment anger flickered in his green eyes. I didn't want that either. So he said: "Look . . . you touch a person softly, gently, and maybe you even do it with love. And, well, I guess a piece of information goes on up to the brain where something interprets it as pleasure. Maybe something up there in my head interprets the information all wrong . . ."

I shook my head. "You're a Singer. Singers are supposed to be eccentric, sure; but—"

Now he was shaking his head. Then the anger opened up. And I saw an expression move from all those spots that had communicated pain through the rest of his features and vanish without ever becoming a word. Once more he looked down at the wounds that webbed his thin body.

"Button it up, boy. I'm sorry I said anything."

Halfway up the lapels, his hands stopped. "You really think I'd turn you in?"

"Button it up."

He did. Then he said, "Oh." And then, "You know, it's midnight."

"So?"

"Edna just gave me the new Word."

"Which is?"

"Agate."

I nodded.

He finished closing his collar. "What are you thinking about?"

"Cows."

"Cows?" Hawk asked. "What about them?"

"You ever been on a dairy farm?"

He shook his head.

"To get the most milk, you keep the cows practically in suspended animation. They're fed intravenously from a big tank that pipes nutrients out and down, branching into smaller and smaller pipes until it gets to all those high-yield semi-corpses."

"I've seen pictures."

"People."

". . . and cows?"

"You've given me the Word. And now it begins to funnel down, branching out, with me telling others and them telling still others, till by midnight tomorrow . . ."

"I'll go get the—"

"Hawk?"

He turned back. "What?"

"You say you don't think I'm going to be the victim of any hanky-panky with the mysterious forces that know more than we. Okay, that's your opinion. But as soon as I get rid of this stuff, I'm going to make the most distracting exit you've ever seen."

Two little lines bit down Hawk's forehead. "Are you sure I haven't seen this one before?"

"As a matter of fact I think you have." Now I grinned.

"Oh," Hawk said, then made a sound that had the structure of laughter but was all breath. "I'll get the Hawk."

He ducked out between the trees.

I glanced up at the lozenges of moonlight in the leaves.

I looked down at my briefcase.

Up between the rocks, stepping around the long grass, came the Hawk. He wore a gray evening suit; a gray silk turtleneck. Above his craggy face, his head was completely shaved.

"Mr. Cadwaliter-Erickson?" He held out his hand.

I shook: small sharp bones in loose skin. "Does one call you Mr. . . . ?"

"Arty."

"Arty the Hawk?" I tried to look like I wasn't giving his gray attire the once-over.

He smiled. "Arty the Hawk. Yeah. I picked that name up when I was younger than our friend down there. Alex says you got . . . well, some things that are not exactly yours. That don't belong to you."

I nodded.

"Show them to me."

"You were told what—"

He brushed away the end of my sentence. "Come on, let me see."

He extended his hand, smiling affably as a bank clerk. I ran my thumb around the pressure-zip. The cover went *tsk.* "Tell me," I said, looking up at his head still lowered to see what I had, "what does one do about Special Services? They seem to be after me."

The head came up. Surprise changed slowly to a craggy leer. "Why, Mr. Cadwaliter-Erickson!" He gave me the up and down openly. "Keep your income steady. Keep it steady, that's one thing you can do."

"If you buy these for anything like what they're worth, that's going to be a little difficult."

"I would imagine. I could always give you less money—"

The cover went *tsk* again.

"—or, barring that, you could try to use your head and outwit them."

"You must have outwitted them at one time or another. You may be on an even keel now, but you had to get there from somewhere else."

Arty the Hawk's nod was downright sly. "I guess you've had a run-in with Maud. Well, I suppose congratulations are in order. And condolences. I always like to do what's in order."

"You seem to know how to take care of yourself. I mean I notice you're not out there mingling with the guests."

"There are two parties going on here tonight," Arty said. "Where do you think Alex disappears off to every five minutes?"

I frowned.

"That lumia down in the rocks—" he pointed towards my feet—"is a mandala of shifting hues on our ceiling. Alex," he chuckled, "goes scuttling off under the rocks where there is a pavilion of Oriental splendor—"

"And a separate guest list at the door?"

"Regina is on both. I'm on both. So's the kid, Edna, Lewis, Ann—"

"Am I supposed to know all this?"

"Well, you came with a person on both lists. I just thought . . ." He paused.

I was coming on wrong. Well. A quick change artist learns fairly quick that the verisimilitude factor in imitating someone up the scale is your confidence in your unalienable right to come on wrong. "I'll tell you," I said. "How about exchanging these—" I held out the briefcase—"for some information."

"You want to know how to stay out of Maud's clutches?" He shook his head. "It would be pretty stupid of me to tell you, even if I could. Besides, you've got your family fortunes to fall back on." He beat the front of his shirt with his thumb. "Believe me, boy. Arty the Hawk didn't have that. I didn't have anything like that." His hands dropped into his pockets. "Let's see what you got."

I opened the case again.

The Hawk looked for a while. After a few moments he picked a couple up, turned them around, put them down, put his hands back in his pockets. "I'll give you sixty thousand for them, approved credit tablets."

"What about the information I wanted?"

"I wouldn't tell you a thing." He smiled. "I wouldn't tell you the time of day."

There are very few successful thieves in this world. Still less on the other five. The will to steal is an impulse towards the absurd and tasteless. (The talents are poetic, theatrical, a certain reverse charisma . . .) But it is a will, as the will to order, power, love.

"All right," I said.

Somewhere overhead I heard a faint humming.

Arty looked at me fondly. He reached under the lapel of his jacket and took out a handful of credit tablets—the scarlet-banded tablets whose slips were ten thousand apiece. He pulled off one. Two. Three. Four.

"You can deposit this much safely—"

"Why do you think Maud is after me?"

Five. Six.

"Fine," I said.

"How about throwing in the briefcase?" Arty asked.

"Ask Alex for a paper bag. If you want, I can send them—"

"Give them here."

The humming was coming closer.

I held up the open case. Arty went in with both hands. He shoved them into his coat pockets, his pants pockets; the gray cloth was distended by angular bulges. He looked left, right. "Thanks," he said. "Thanks." Then he turned and hurried down the slope with all sorts of things in his pockets that weren't his now.

I looked up through the leaves for the noise, but I couldn't see anything.

I stooped down now and laid my case open. I pulled apart the back compartment where I kept the things that did belong to me and rummaged hurriedly through.

Alex was just offering Puffy-eyes another Scotch, while the gentleman was saying, "Has anyone seen Mrs. Silem? What's that humming overhead—?" when a large woman wrapped in a veil of fading fabric tottered across the rocks, screaming.

Her hands were clawing at her covered face.

Alex sloshed soda over his sleeve, and the man said, "Oh, my God! Who's that?"

"No!" the woman shrieked. "Oh, no! Help me!" waving her wrinkled fingers, brilliant with rings.

"Don't you recognize her?" That was Hawk whispering confidentially to someone else. "It's Henrietta, Countess Effingham."

And Alex, overhearing, went hurrying to her assistance. The Countess, however, ducked between two cacti and disappeared into the high grass. But the entire party followed. They were beating about the underbrush when a balding gentleman in a black tux, bow tie and cummerbund coughed and said in a very worried voice, "Excuse me, Mr. Spinnel?"

Alex whirled.

"Mr. Spinnel, my mother . . ."

"Who are *you?*" The interruption upset Alex terribly.

The gentleman drew himself up to announce: "The Honorable Clement Effingham," and his pants leg shook for all the world as if he had started to click his heels. But articulation failed. The expression melted on his face. "Oh, I . . . my mother, Mr. Spinnel. We were downstairs at the other half of your party when she got hysterical. She ran up here—oh, I told her not to! I knew you'd be upset. But you must help me!" and then looked up.

The others looked, too.

The helicopter blacked the moon, bobbing and settling below its hazy twin parasols.

"Oh, please . . ." the gentleman said. "You look over there! Perhaps she's gone back down. I've got to—" looking quickly both ways—"find her." He hurried in one direction while everyone else hurried in others.

The humming was suddenly syncopated with a crash. Roaring now, as plastic fragments from the transparent roof clattered down through the branches, clattered on the rocks . . .

I made it into the elevator and had already thumbed the edge of my briefcase clasp, when Hawk dove between the unfolding foils. The electric-eye began to swing them open. I hit DOOR CLOSE full fist.

The boy staggered, banged shoulders on two walls, then got back breath and balance. "Hey, there's police getting out of that helicopter!"

"Hand-picked by Maud Hinkle herself, no doubt." I pulled the other tuft of white hair from my temple. It went into the case on top of the plastiderm gloves (wrinkled, thick blue veins, long carnelian nails) that had been Henrietta's hands, lying in the chiffon folds of her sari.

Then there was the downward tug of stopping. The Honorable Clement was still half on my face when the door opened.

Grey and grey, with a downright dismal expression, the Hawk swung through the doors. Behind him people were dancing in an elaborate pavilion festooned with Oriental splendor (and a mandala of shifting hues on the ceiling.) Arty beat me to DOOR CLOSE. Then he gave me an odd look.

I just sighed and finished peeling off Clem.

"The police are up there?" the Hawk reiterated.

"Arty," I said, buckling my pants, "it certainly looks that way." The car gained momentum. "You seem almost as upset as Alex." I shrugged the tux jacket down my arms, turning the sleeves inside out, pulled one wrist free, and jerked off the white starched dicky with the black bow tie and stuffed it into the briefcase with all my other dickies; swung the coat around and slipped on Howard Calvin Evingston's good gray herringbone. Howard (like Hank) is a redhead (but not as curly).

The Hawk raised his bare brows when I peeled off Clement's bald pate and shook out my hair.

"I noticed you aren't carrying around all those bulky things in your pockets any more."

"Oh, those have been taken care of," he said gruffly. "They're all right."

"Arty," I said, adjusting my voice down to Howard's security-provoking, ingenuous baritone, "it must have been my unabashed conceit that made me think that those Regular Service police were here just for me—"

The Hawk actually snarled. "They wouldn't be that unhappy if they got me, too."

And from his corner Hawk demanded, "You've got security here with you, don't you, Arty?"

"So what?"

"There's one way you can get out of this," Hawk hissed at me. His jacket had come half-open down his wrecked chest. "That's if Arty takes you out with him."

"Brilliant idea," I concluded. "You want a couple of thousand back for the service?"

The idea didn't amuse him. "I don't want anything from you." He turned to Hawk. "I need something from you, kid. Not him. Look, I wasn't prepared for Maud. If you want me to get your friend out, then you've got to do something for me."

The boy looked confused.

I thought I saw smugness on Arty's face, but the expression resolved into concern. "You've got to figure out some way to fill the lobby up with people, and fast."

I was going to ask why, but then I didn't know the extent of Arty's security. I was going to ask how, but the floor pushed up at my feet and the door swung open. "If you can't do it," the Hawk growled to Hawk, "none of us will get out of here. None of us!"

I had no idea what the kid was going to do, but when I started to follow him out into the lobby, the Hawk grabbed my arm and hissed, "Stay here, you idiot!"

I stepped back. Arty was leaning on DOOR OPEN.

Hawk sprinted towards the pool. And splashed in.

He reached the braziers on their twelve-foot tripods and began to climb.

"He's going to hurt himself!" the Hawk whispered.

"Yeah," I said, but I don't think my cynicism got through. Below the great dish of fire, Hawk was fiddling. Then something under there came loose. Something else went *Clang!* And something else spurted out across the water. The fire raced along it and hit the pool, churning and roaring like hell.

A black arrow with a golden head: Hawk dove.

I bit the inside of my cheek as the alarm sounded. Four people in uniforms were coming across the blue carpet. Another group were crossing in the other direction, saw the flames, and one of the women screamed. I let out my breath, thinking carpet and walls and ceilings would be flame-proof. But I kept losing focus on the idea before the sixty-odd infernal feet.

Hawk surfaced on the edge of the pool in the only clear spot left, rolled over on to the carpet, clutching his face. And rolled. And rolled. Then, came to his feet.

Another elevator spilled out a load of passengers who gaped and gasped. A crew came through the doors now with fire-fighting equipment. The alarm was still sounding.

Hawk turned to look at the dozen-odd people in the lobby. Water puddled the carpet about his drenched and shiny pants legs. Flame turned the drops on his cheek and hair to flickering copper and blood.

He banged his fists against his wet thighs, took a deep breath, and against the roar and the bells and the whispering, he Sang.

Two people ducked back into two elevators. From a doorway half a dozen more emerged. The elevators returned half a minute later with a dozen people each. I realized the message was going through the building, there's a Singer Singing in the lobby.

The lobby filled. The flames growled, the fire fighters stood around shuffling, and Hawk, feet apart on the blue rug by the burning pool, Sang, and Sang of a bar off Times Square full of thieves, morphadine-heads, brawlers, drunkards, women too old to trade what they still held out for barter, and trade just too nasty-grimy; where earlier in the evening a brawl had broken out, and an old man had been critically hurt in the fray.

Arty tugged at my sleeve.

"What . . . ?"

"Come on," he hissed.

The elevator door closed behind us.

We ambled through the attentive listeners, stopping to watch, stopping to hear. I couldn't really do Hawk justice. A lot of that slow amble I spent wondering what sort of security Arty had:

Standing behind a couple in bathrobes who were squinting into the heat, I decided it was all very simple. Arty wanted simply to drift away through a crowd, so he'd conveniently gotten Hawk to manufacture one.

To get to the door we had to pass through practically a cordon of Regular Service policemen, who I don't think had anything to do with what might have been going on in the roof garden; they'd simply collected to see the fire and stayed for the Song. When Arty tapped one on the shoulder—"Excuse me please"—to get by, the policeman glanced at him, glanced away, then did a Mack Sennet double-take. But another policeman caught the whole interchange, touched the first on the arm, and gave him a frantic little headshake. Then both men turned very deliberately back to watch the Singer. While the earthquake in my chest stilled, I decided that the Hawk's security complex of agents and counter-agents, maneuvering and machinating through the flaming lobby, must be of such finesse and intricacy that to attempt understanding was to condemn oneself to total paranoia.

Arty opened the final door.

I stepped from the last of the air-conditioning into the night.

We hurried down the ramp.

"Hey, Arty . . ."

"You go that way." He pointed down the street. "I go this way."

"Eh . . . what's that way?" I pointed in my direction.

"Twelve Towers sub-sub-subway station. Look. I've got you out of there. Believe me, you're safe for the time being. Now go take a train someplace interesting. Goodbye. Go on now." Then Arty the Hawk put his fists in his pockets and hurried up the street.

I started down, keeping near the wall, expecting someone to get me with a blow-dart from a passing car, a deathray from the shrubbery.

I reached the sub.

And still nothing had happened.

Agate gave way to Malachite:

Tourmaline:

Beryl (during which month I turned twenty-six):

Porphyry:

Sapphire (that month I took the ten thousand I hadn't frittered away and invested it in The Glacier, a perfectly legitimate ice cream palace on Triton—the first and only ice cream palace on Triton—which took off like fireworks; all investors were returned eight-hundred percent, no kidding. Two weeks later I'd lost half of those earnings on another set of preposterous illegalities and was feeling quite depressed, but The Glacier kept pulling them in. The new Word came by):

Cinnabar:

Turquoise:

Tiger's Eye:

Hector Calhoun Eisenhower finally buckled down and spent three months learning how to be a respectable member of the upper middle class underworld. That is a long novel in itself. High finance; corporate law; how to hire help: Whew! But the complexities of life have always intrigued me. I got through it. The basic rule is still the same: observe carefully, imitate effectively.

Garnet:

Topaz (I whispered that word on the roof of the Trans-Satellite Power Station, and caused my hirelings to commit two murders. And you know? I didn't feel a thing):

Taafite:

We were nearing the end of Taafite. I'd come back to Triton on strictly Glacial business. A bright pleasant morning it was: the business went fine. I decided to take off the afternoon and go sight-seeing in the Torrents.

". . . two hundred and thirty yards high," the guide announced, and everyone around me leaned on the rail and gazed up through the plastic corridor at the cliffs of frozen methane that soared through Neptune's cold green glare.

"Just a few yards down the catwalk, ladies and gentlemen, you can catch your first glimpse of the Well of This World, where over a million years ago, a mysterious force science still cannot explain caused twenty-five square miles of frozen methane to liquefy for no more than a few hours during which time a whirlpool twice the depth of Earth's Grand Canyon was caught for the ages when the temperature dropped once more to . . ."

People were moving down the corridor when I saw her smiling. My hair was black and nappy, and my skin was chestnut dark today.

I was just feeling overconfident, I guess, so I kept standing around next to her. I even contemplated coming on. Then she broke the whole thing up by suddenly turning to me and saying perfectly deadpan: "Why, if it isn't Hamlet Caliban Enobarbus!"

Old reflexes realigned my features to couple the frown of confusion with the smile of indulgence. *Pardon me, but I think you must have mistaken . . .* No, I didn't say it. "Maud," I said, "have you come here to tell me that my time has come?"

She wore several shades of blue with a large blue brooch at her shoulder, obviously glass. Still, I realized as I looked about the other tourists, she was more inconspicuous amidst their finery than I was. "No," she said. "Actually I'm on vacation. Just like you."

"No kidding?" We had dropped behind the crowd. "You are kidding."

"Special Services of Earth, while we cooperate with Special Services on other worlds, has no official jurisdiction on Triton. And since you came here with money, and most of your recorded gain in income has been through The Glacier, while Regular Services on Triton might be glad to get you, Special Services is not after you as yet." She smiled. "I haven't been to The Glacier. It would really be nice to say I'd been taken there by one of the owners. Could we go for a soda, do you think?"

The swirled sides of the Well of This World dropped away in opalescent grandeur. Tourists gazed, and the guide went on about indices of refraction, angles of incline.

"I don't think you trust me," Maud said.

My look said she was right.

"Have you ever been involved with narcotics?" she asked suddenly.

I frowned.

"No, I'm serious. I want to try and explain something . . . a point of information that may make both our lives easier."

"Peripherally," I said. "I'm sure you've got down all the information in your dossiers."

"I was involved with them a good deal more than peripherally for several years," Maud said. "Before I got into Special Services, I was in the Narcotics Division of the regular force. And the people we dealt with twenty-four hours a day were drug users, drug pushers. To catch the big ones we had to make friends with the little ones. To catch the bigger ones, we had to make friends with the big. We had to keep the same hours they kept, talk the same language, for months at a time live on the same streets, in the same buildings." She stepped back from the rail to let a youngster ahead. "I had to be sent away to take the morphadine detoxification cure twice while I was on the narc squad. And I had a better record than most."

"What's your point?"

"Just this. You and I are traveling in the same circles now, if only because of our respective chosen professions. You'd be surprised how many people we already know in common. Don't be shocked when we run into each other crossing Sovereign Plaza in Bellona one day, then two weeks later wind up at the same restaurant for lunch at Lux on Iapetus. Though the circles we move in cover worlds, they *are* the same, and not that big."

"Come on." I don't think I sounded happy. "Let me treat you to that ice cream." We started back down the walkway.

"You know," Maud said, "if you do stay out of Special Services' hands here and on Earth long enough, eventually you'll be up there with a huge income growing on a steady slope. It might be a few years, but it's possible. There's no reason now for us to be *personal* enemies. You just may, someday, reach that point where Special Services loses interest in you as quarry. Oh, we'd still see each other, run into each other. We get a great deal of our information from people up there. We're in a position to help you, too, you see."

"You've been casting holograms again."

She shrugged. Her face looked positively ghostly under the pale planet. She said, when we reached the artificial lights of the city, "I did meet two friends of yours recently, Lewis and Ann."

"The Singers?"

She nodded.

"Oh, I don't really know them well."

"They seem to know a lot about you. Perhaps through that other Singer, Hawk."

"Oh," I said again. "Did they say how he was?"

"I read that he was recovering about two months back. But nothing since then."

"That's about all I know, too," I said.

"The only time I've ever seen him," Maud said, "was right after I pulled him out."

Arty and I had gotten out of the lobby before Hawk actually finished. The next day on the news-tapes I learned that when his Song was over, he shrugged out of his jacket, dropped his pants, and walked back into the pool.

The fire-fighter crew suddenly woke up; people began running around and screaming: he'd been rescued, seventy percent of his body covered with second- and third-degree burns. I'd been industriously trying not to think about it.

"*You* pulled him out?"

"Yes. I was in the helicopter that landed on the roof," Maud said. "I thought you'd be impressed to see me."

"Oh," I said. "How did you get to pull him out?"

"Once you got going, Arty's security managed to jam the elevator service above the seventy-first floor, so we didn't get to the lobby till after you were out of the building. That's when Hawk tried to—"

"But it was you who actually saved him, though?"

"The firemen in that neighborhood hadn't had a fire in twelve years! I don't think they even know how to operate the equipment. I had my boys foam the pool, then I waded in and dragged him—"

"Oh," I said again. I had been trying hard, almost succeeding, these eleven months. I wasn't there when it happened. It wasn't my affair. Maud was saying:

"We thought we might have gotten a lead on you from him, but when I got him to the shore, he was completely out, just a mass of open, running—"

"I should have known the Special Services uses Singers, too," I said. "Everyone else does. The Word changes today, doesn't it? Lewis and Ann didn't pass on what the new one is?"

"I saw them yesterday, and the Word doesn't change for another eight hours. Besides, they wouldn't tell me, anyway." She glanced at me and frowned. "They really wouldn't."

"Let's go have some ice-cream sodas," I said. "We'll make small talk and listen carefully to each other while we affect an air of nonchalance; you will try to pick up things that will make it easier to catch me; I will listen for things you let slip that might make it easier for me to avoid you."

"Um-hm." She nodded.

"Why did you contact me in that bar, anyway?"

Eyes of ice: "I told you, we simply travel in the same circles. We're quite likely to be in the same bar on the same night."

"I guess that's just one of the things I'm not supposed to understand, huh?"

Her smile was appropriately ambiguous. I didn't push it.

It was a very dull afternoon. I couldn't repeat one exchange from the nonsense we babbled over the cherry-peaked mountains of whipped cream. We both exerted so much energy to keep up the appearance of being amused, I doubt either one of us could see our way to picking up anything meaningful—if anything meaningful was said.

She left. I brooded some more on the charred phoenix.

The Steward of The Glacier called me into the kitchen to ask about a shipment of contraband milk (The Glacier makes all its own ice cream) that I had been able to wangle on my last trip to Earth (it's amazing how little progress there has been in dairy farming over the last ten years; it was depressingly easy to horn-swoggle that bumbling Vermonter) and under the white lights and great plastic churning vats, while I tried to get things straightened out, he made some comment about the Heist Cream Emperor; that didn't do *any* good.

By the time the evening crowd got there, and the moog was making music, and the crystal walls were blazing; and the floor show—a new addition that week—had been cajoled into going on anyway (a trunk of costumes had gotten lost in shipment [or swiped, but I wasn't about to tell *them* that]), and wandering through the tables I, personally, had caught a very grimy little girl, obviously out of her head on morph, trying to pick up a customer's pocketbook from the back of a chair—I just caught her by the wrist, made her let go, and led her to the door daintily, while she blinked at me with dilated eyes and the customer never even knew—and the floor show, having decided what the hell, were doing their act *au naturel,* and everyone was having just a high old time, I was feeling really bad.

I went outside, sat on the wide steps, and growled when I had to move aside to let people in or out. About the seventy-fifth growl, the person I growled at stopped and boomed down at me, "I thought I'd find you, if I looked hard enough! I mean if I really looked."

I looked at the hand that was flapping at my shoulder, followed the arm up to a black turtleneck where there was a beefy, bald, grinning head. "Arty," I said, "what are . . .?" But he was still flapping and laughing with impervious *gemütlichkeit.*

"You wouldn't believe the time I had getting a picture of you, boy. Had to bribe one out of the Triton Special Services Department. That quick change bit: great gimmick. Just great!" The Hawk sat down next to me and dropped his hand on my knee. "Wonderful place you got here. I like it, like it a lot." Small bones in veined dough. "But not enough to make you an offer on it yet. You're learning fast there, though. I can tell you're learning fast. I'm going to be proud to be able to say I was the one who gave you your first big break." His hand came away, and he began to knead it into the other. "If you're going to move into the big time, you have to have at least one foot planted firmly on the right side of the law. The whole idea is to make yourself indispensable to the good people; once that's done, a good crook has the keys to all the treasure houses in the system. But I'm not telling you anything you don't already know."

"Arty," I said, "do you think the two of us should be seen together here . . . ?"

The Hawk held his hand above his lap and joggled it with a deprecating motion. "Nobody can get a picture of us. I got my men all around. I never go anywhere in public without my security. Heard you've been looking into the security business yourself," which was true. "Good idea. Very good. I like the way you're handling yourself."

"Thanks. Arty, I'm not feeling too hot this evening. I came out here to get some air . . ."

Arty's hand fluttered again. "Don't worry, I won't hang around. You're right. We shouldn't be seen. Just passing by and wanted to say hello. Just hello." He got up. "That's all." He started down the steps.

"Arty?"

He looked back.

"Sometime soon you will come back; and that time you will want to buy out my share of The Glacier, because I'll have gotten too big; and I won't want to sell because I'll think I'm big enough to fight you. So we'll be enemies for a while. You'll try to kill me. I'll try to kill you."

On his face, first the frown of confusion; then the indulgent smile. "I see you've caught on to the idea of hologramic information. Very good. Good. It's the only way to outwit Maud. Make sure all your information relates to the whole scope of the situation. It's the only way to outwit me, too." He smiled, started to turn, but thought of something else. "If you can fight me off long enough and keep growing, keep your security in tiptop shape, eventually, we'll get to the point where it'll be worth both our whiles to work together again. If you can just hold out, we'll be friends again. Someday. You just watch. Just wait."

"Thanks for telling me."

The Hawk looked at his watch. "Well. Goodbye." I thought he was going to leave finally. But he glanced up again. "Have you got the new Word?"

"That's right," I said. "It went out tonight. What is it?"

The Hawk waited till the people coming down the steps were gone. He looked hastily about, then leaned towards me with hands cupped at his mouth, rasped, "Pyrite," and winked hugely. "I just got it from a gal who got it direct from Colette," (one of the three Singers of Triton). Then he turned, jounced down the steps, and shouldered his way into the crowds passing on the strip.

I sat there mulling through the year till I had to get up and walk. All walking does to my depressive moods is add the reinforcing rhythm of paranoia. By the time I was coming back, I had worked out a dilly of a delusional system: The Hawk had already begun to weave some security-ridden plot about me, which ended when we were all trapped in some dead-end alley, and trying to get aid I called out, "Pyrite!" which would turn out not to be the Word at all but served to identify me for the man in the dark gloves with the gun/grenade/gas.

There was a cafeteria on the corner. In the light from the window, clustered over the wreck by the curb was a bunch of nasty-grimies (à la Triton: chains around the wrist, bumblebee tattoo on cheek, high-heel boots on those who could afford them). Straddling the smashed headlight was the little morph-head I had ejected earlier from The Glacier.

On a whim I went up to her. "Hey?"

She looked at me from under hair like trampled hay, eyes all pupil.

"You get the new Word yet?"

She rubbed her nose, already scratch red. "Pyrite," she said. "It just came down about an hour ago."

"Who told you?"

She considered my question. "I got it from a guy, who says he got it from a guy, who came in this evening from New York, who picked it up there from a Singer named Hawk."

The three grimies nearest made a point of not looking at me. Those further away let themselves glance.

"Oh," I said. "Oh. Thanks."

Occam's Razor, along with any real information on how security works, hones away most such paranoia. Pyrite. At a certain level in my line of work, paranoia's just an occupational disease. At least I was certain that Arty (and Maud) probably suffered from it as much as I did.

The lights were out on The Glacier's marquee. Then I remembered what I had left inside and ran up the stairs.

The door was locked. I pounded on the glass a couple of times, but everyone had gone home. And the thing that made it worse was that I could *see* it sitting on the counter of the coat-check alcove under the orange bulb. The steward had probably put it there, thinking I might arrive before everybody left. Tomorrow at noon Ho Chi Eng had to pick up his reservation for the Marigold Suite on the Interplanetary Liner *The Platinum Swan,* which left at one-thirty for Bellona. And there behind the glass doors of The Glacier, it waited with the proper wig, as well as the epicanthic folds that would halve Mr. Eng's sloe eyes of jet.

I actually thought of breaking in. But the more practical solution was to get the hotel to wake me at nine and come in with the cleaning man. I turned around and started down the steps; and the thought struck me, and made me terribly sad, so that I blinked and smiled just from reflex; it was probably just as well to leave it there till morning, because there was nothing in it that wasn't mine anyway.

—1968

URSULA K. LE GUIN
B. 1929

Prominent essayist, popular author of children's fiction, and critically her-
alded voice of contemporary speculative fiction, Ursula K. Le Guin is a major
literary talent. Her award-winning science fiction helped to define a new
movement in the genre away from the "hard" sciences (as was appearing in
the work of Robert A. Heinlein and Isaac Asimov) and toward the "soft," or
social, sciences, like cultural anthropology and psychology. Le Guin was
born in Berkeley, California, to a father who was an anthropologist and a
mother who became a writer. She attended Radcliffe College, receiving an
A.B. in 1951, and Columbia University, receiving an A.M. in 1952. During
the mid-1950s, Le Guin taught French at Mercer University in Macon,
Georgia, and she also taught at the University of Idaho in Moscow. Portland
State University, the University of California (San Diego), the University of
Reading (Great Britain), Kenyon College, Tulane University, and the First
Australian Workshop in Speculative Fiction are listed among the institutions
where she served as a visiting lecturer and writer-in-residence. She has
received numerous distinguished honors for her fiction, the most prominent
being the Hugo Award and the Nebula Award in 1970 for her novel The Left
Hand of Darkness, *the National Book Award for Children's Books in 1973*
for The Farthest Shore, *and the Hugo Award, Nebula Award, Jupiter Award,*
and Jules Verne Award in 1975 for her novel The Dispossessed: An
Ambiguous Utopia. *Le Guin has demonstrated her mastery of the science fic-*
tion genre in her non-fiction writing as well as in her fiction. Her essay,
"Myth and Archetype in Science Fiction," initially appearing in Parabola 1

(Fall 1976), for example, reveals Le Guin's understanding of the complex relationship between science fiction and mythology.

Le Guin published her first story, "An die Musik," in the Summer 1961 issue of Western Humanities Review. *Her first novel,* Rocannon's World, *appeared in 1966, followed by* Planet of Exile *(1966) and* City of Illusions *(1967). Her most famous science fiction includes* The Left Hand of Darkness *(1969) and* The Dispossessed: An Ambiguous Utopia *(1974). Le Guin is also the author of one of the most beloved fantasy series in children's literature, the Earthsea adventures, which is featured in the novels* A Wizard of Earthsea *(1968),* The Tombs of Atuan *(1971),* The Farthest Shore *(1972), and* Tehanu: The Last Book of Earthsea *(1990).*

Part of Le Guin's Hainish cycle of stories, "Vaster Than Empires and More Slow" was first published in Robert Silverberg's New Dimensions 1 *(1971). When Le Guin reprinted this tale in her anthology,* The Wind's Twelve Quarters *(1975), in her introduction to the story she noted her preference for psychological insight over physical adventure in science fiction. "Vaster Than Empires and More Slow" provides a fine example of Le Guin's skill at exploring what she terms "inner space," even though the story is set on an alien planet in outer space. Her title is taken from Andrew Marvell's poem, "To His Coy Mistress:" "Our vegetable love should grow / Vaster than empires, and more slow. . . ."*

MYTH AND ARCHETYPE
IN SCIENCE FICTION

"Science fiction is the mythology of the modern world." It's a good slogan, and a useful one when you're faced with people ignorant and contemptuous of science fiction, for it makes them stop and think. But like all slogans it's a half-truth, and when used carelessly, as a whole truth, can cause all kinds of confusion.

Where care must be taken is with that complex word "mythology." What is a myth?

"Myth is an attempt to explain, in rational terms, facts not yet rationally understood." That is the definition provided by the reductive, scientistic mentality of the first half of the twentieth century and still accepted by many. According to this definition, the god Apollo "is merely" an inadequate effort made by primitive minds to explain and systematize the nature and behavior of the Sun. As soon as the Sun is rationally understood to be a ball of fire much larger than the Earth, and its behavior has been described by a system of scientific laws, the old mythological pseudo-explanation is left empty. The fiery horses and the golden chariot vanish, the god is dethroned, and his exploits remain only a pretty tale for children. According to this view, the advance of science is a progressive draining dry of the content of mythology.[1] And, in so far as the content of myth is rational and the function of myth is explanatory, this definition is suitable. However, the rational and explanatory is only one function of the myth. Myth is an expression of one of the several ways the human being, body/psyche, perceives, understands and relates to the world. Like science, it is a product of a basic human mode of apprehension. To pretend that it can be replaced by abstract or quantitative cognition is to assert that the human being is, potentially or ideally, a creature of pure reason, a disembodied Mind. It might, indeed, be nice if we were all little bubbles of pure reason floating on the stream of time; but we aren't. We are rational beings, but we are also sensual, emotional, appetitive, ethical beings, driven by needs and reaching out for satisfactions which the intellect alone cannot provide. Where these other modes of being and doing are inadequate, the intellect should prevail. Where the intellect fails, and must always fail, unless we become disembodied bubbles, then one of the other modes must take over. The myth, mythological insight, is one of these. Supremely effective in its area of function, it needs no replacement. Only the schizoid arrogance of modern scientism pretends that it ought to be replaced, and that pretension is pretty easily deflated. For example, does our scientific understanding of the nature and behavior of the Sun explain (let alone explain away) Apollo's remarkable sex life, or his role as the god of music and of the divine harmony? No, it has nothing whatever to do with all that; it has nothing to do with sex, or music, or harmony, or divinity; nor *as science,* did it ever pretend to—only scientism made the claim. Apollo is not the Sun, and never was. The Sun, in fact, "is merely" one of the names of Apollo.

Reductionism cuts both ways, after all.

So long, then, as we don't claim either that the science in science fiction replaces the "old, false" mythologies, or that the fiction in science fiction is a mere attempt to explain what science hasn't yet got around to explaining, we can use the slogan. Science fiction is the mythology of the modern world—or one of its mythologies— even though it is a highly intellectual form of art, and mythology is a nonintellectual mode of apprehension. For science fiction does use the mythmaking faculty to apprehend the world we live in, a world profoundly shaped and changed by science and technology, and its originality is that it uses the mythmaking faculty on new material.

But there's another catch to look out for. The presence of mythic material in a story does not mean that the mythmaking faculty is being used.

Here is a science fiction story: its plot is modeled directly upon that of an ancient myth, or there are characters in it modeled upon certain gods or heroes of legend. Is it, therefore, a myth? Not necessarily; in fact, probably not. No mythmaking is involved: just theft.

Theft is an integral function of a healthy literature. It's much easier to steal a good plot from some old book than to invent one. Anyhow, after you've sweated to invent an original plot, it very often turns out to be a perfect parallel to one of the old stories (more on this curious fact later). And since there are beautiful and powerful stories all through world legendry, and since stories need retelling from generation to generation, why not steal them? I'm certainly not the one to condemn the practice; parts of my first novel were lifted wholesale from the Norse mythos (Brisingamen, Freya's necklace, and episodes in the life of Odin). My version isn't a patch on the original, of course, but I think I did the gods of Asgard no harm, and they did my book some good. This sort of pilfering goes on all the time, and produces many pleasant works of art, though it does not lead to any truly new creations or cognitions.

There is a more self-conscious form of thievery which is both more destructive and more self-destructive. In many college English courses the words "myth" and "symbol" are given a tremendous charge of significance. You just ain't no good unless you can see a symbol hiding, like a scared gerbil, under every page. And in many creative writing courses the little beasts multiply, the place swarms with them. What does this Mean? What does that Symbolize? What is the Underlying Mythos? Kids come lurching out of such courses with a brain full of gerbils. And they sit down and write a lot of empty pomposity, under the impression that that's how Melville did it.*

Even when they begin to realize that art is not something produced for critics, but for other human beings, some of them retain the overintellectualizing bent. They still do not realize that a symbol is not a sign of something known, but an indicator of something not known and not expressible otherwise than symbolically. They mistake symbol (living meaning) for allegory (dead equivalence). So they use mythology in an arrogant fashion, rationalizing it, condescending to it. They take plots and characters from it, not in the healthily furtive fashion of the literary sneakthief, but in a posturing, showy way. Such use of myth does real disservice to the original, by trivializing it, and no good at all to the story. The shallowness of its origin is often betrayed either by an elaborate vocabulary and ostentatiously cryptic style, or by a kind of jocose, chatty discomfort in the tone. Watch me up here on Olympus, you peasants, being fresh with Aphrodite. Look at me juggling symbols, folks! We sophisticates, we know how to handle these old archetypes.

But Zeus always gets 'em. ZAP!

So far I have been talking as if all mythologies the writer might use were dead— that is, not believed in with some degree of emotion, other than aesthetic appreciation, by the writer and his community. Of course, this is far from being the case. It's easy to get fresh with Aphrodite. Who believes in some old Greek goddess, anyhow? But there are living mythologies, after all. Consider the Virgin Mary; or the State.

For an example of the use in science fiction of a living religious mythos one may turn to the work of Cordwainer Smith, whose Christian beliefs are evident, I think, all through his work, in such motifs as the savior, the martyr, rebirth, the "underpeople." Whether or not one is a Christian, one may admire wholeheartedly the strength and passion given the works by the author's living belief. In general, however, I think the critics' search for Christian themes in science fiction is sterile and misleading. For the majority of science fiction writers, the themes of Christianity are dead signs, not living symbols, and those who use them do so all too often in order to get an easy emotional charge without working for it. They take a free ride on the crucifix, just as many now cash in cynically on the current occultist fad. The difference between this sort of thing and the genuine, naïve mysticism of an Arthur Clarke, struggling to express his own, living symbol of rebirth, is all the difference in the world.

Beyond and beneath the great living mythologies of religion and power there is another region into which science fiction enters. I would call it the area of Submyth: by which I mean those images, figures and motifs which have no religious resonance and no intellectual or aesthetic value, but which are vigorously alive and powerful, so that they cannot be dismissed as mere stereotypes. They are shared by all of us; they are genuinely collective. Superman is a submyth. His father was Nietzsche and his mother was a funnybook, and he is alive and well in the mind of every ten-year-old—and millions of others. Other science-fictional submyths are the blond heroes of sword and sorcery, with their unusual weapons; insane or self-deifying computers; mad scientists; benevolent dictators; detectives who find out who done it; capitalists who buy and sell galaxies; brave starship captains and/or troopers;

---

*Note (1989). In fact, part of the time, he did. A good deal of Melville is pompously self-conscious.

evil aliens; good aliens; and every pointy-breasted brainless young woman who was ever rescued from monsters, lectured to, patronized or, in recent years, raped, by one of the aforementioned heroes.

It hurts to call these creatures mythological. It is a noble word, and they are so grotty. But they are alive, in books, magazines, pictures, movies, advertising, and our own minds. Their roots are the roots of myth, are in our unconscious—that vast dim region of the psyche and perhaps beyond the psyche, which Jung called "collective" because it is similar in all of us, just as our bodies are basically similar. The vigor comes from there, and so they cannot be dismissed as unimportant. Not when they can help motivate a world movement such as fascism!—But neither can they furnish materials useful to art. They have no element of the true myth except its emotive, irrational "thereness." Writers who deliberately submit to them have forfeited the right to call their work science fiction; they're just popcultists cashing in.

True myth may serve for thousands of years as an inexhaustible source of intellectual speculation, religious joy, ethical inquiry and artistic renewal. The real mystery is not destroyed by reason. The fake one is. You look at it and it vanishes. You look at the Blond Hero—really look—and he turns into a gerbil. But you look at Apollo, and he looks back at you.

The poet Rilke looked at a statue of Apollo about fifty years ago, and Apollo spoke to him. "You must change your life," he said.

When the genuine myth rises into consciousness, that is always its message. You must change your life.

The way of art, after all, is neither to cut adrift from the emotions, the senses, the body, etc., and sail off into the void of pure meaning, nor to blind the mind's eye and wallow in irrational, amoral meaninglessness—but to keep open the tenuous, difficult, essential connections between the two extremes. To connect. To connect the idea with value, sensation with intuition, cortex with cerebellum.

The true myth is precisely one of these connections.

Like all artists, we science fiction writers are trying to make and use such a connection or bridge between the conscious and the unconscious—so that our readers can make the journey too. If the only tool we use is the intellect, we will produce only lifeless copies or parodies of the archetypes that live in our own deeper mind and in the great works of art and mythology. If we abandon intellect, we're likely to submerge our own personality and talent in a stew of mindless submyths, themselves coarse, feeble parodies of their archetypal origins. The only way to the truly collective, to the image that is alive and meaningful in all of us, seems to be through the truly personal. Not the impersonality of pure reason; not the impersonality of "the masses," but the irreducibly personal—the self. To reach the others, artists go into the self. Using reason, they deliberately enter the irrational. The farther they go into the self, the closer they come to the other.

If this seems a paradox it is only because our culture overvalues abstraction and extroversion. Pain, for instance, can work the same way. Nothing is more personal, more unshareable, than pain; the worst thing about suffering is that you suffer alone. Yet those who have not suffered, or will not admit that they suffer, are those who are cut off in cold isolation from their fellow men. Pain, the loneliest experience, gives rise to sympathy, to love: the bridge between self and other, the means of communion. So with art. The artist who goes inward most deeply—and it is a painful journey—is the artist who touches us most closely, speaks to us most clearly.

Of all the great psychologists, Jung best explains this process, by stressing the existence, not of an isolated "id," but a "collective unconscious." He reminds us that the region of the mind/body that lies beyond the narrow, brightly lit domain of consciousness is very much the same in all of us. This does not imply a devaluing of consciousness or of reason. The achievement of individual consciousness, which Jung calls "differentiation," is to him a great achievement, civilization's highest achievement, the hope of our future. But the tree grows only from deep roots.

So it would seem that true myth arises only in the process of connecting the conscious and the unconscious realms. I won't find a living archetype in my bookcase or my television set. I will find it only in myself: in that core of individuality lying in the heart of the common darkness. Only the individual can get up and go to the window, and draw back the curtains, and look out into the dark.

Sometimes it takes considerable courage to do that. When you open curtains you don't know what may be out there in the night. Maybe starlight; maybe dragons; maybe the secret police. Maybe the grace of God; maybe the horror of death. They're all there. For all of us.

Writers who draw not upon the words and thoughts of others but upon their own thoughts and their own deep being will inevitably hit upon common material. The more original the work, the more imperiously *recognizable* it will be. "Yes, of course!" say I, the reader recognizing myself, my dreams, my nightmares. The characters, figures, images, motifs, plots, events of the story may be obvious parallels, even seemingly reproductions, of the material of myth and legend. There will be—openly in fantasy, covertly in naturalism—dragons, heroes, quests, objects of power, voyages at night and under sea, and so forth. In narrative, as in painting, certain familiar patterns will become visible.

This again is no paradox, if Jung is right, and we all have the same kind of dragons in our psyche, just as we all have the same kind of heart and lungs in our body. It does imply that nobody can invent an archetype by taking thought, any more than we can invent a new organ in our body. But this is no loss; rather a gain. It means that we can communicate, that alienation isn't the final human condition, since there is a vast common ground on which we can meet, not only rationally, but aesthetically, intuitively, emotionally.

A dragon, not a dragon cleverly copied or mass-produced, but a creature of evil who crawls up, threatening and inexplicable, out of the artist's own unconscious, is alive: terribly alive. It frightens little children, and the artist, and the rest of us. It frightens us because it is part of us, and the artist forces us to admit it. We have met the enemy, as Pogo remarked, and he is us.

"What do you mean? There aren't any dragons in my living room, dragons are extinct, dragons aren't real . . ."

"Look out of the window . . . Look into the mirror . . ."

The artist who works from the center of being will find archetypal images and release them into consciousness. The first science fiction writer to do so was Mary Shelley. She let Frankenstein's monster loose. Nobody has been able to shut him out again, either. There he is, sitting in the corner of our lovely modern glass and plastic living room, right on the tubular steel contour chair, big as life and twice as ugly. Edgar Rice Burroughs did it, though with infinitely less power and originality—Tarzan is a true myth-figure, though not a particularly relevant one to modern ethical/emotional dilemmas, as Frankenstein's monster is. Capek did it, largely by *naming* something (a very important aspect of archetypizing): "Robots," he called them.

They have walked among us ever since. Tolkien did it; he found a ring, a ring which we keep trying to lose . . .

Scholars can have great fun, and can strengthen the effect of such figures, by showing their relationship to other manifestations of the archetype in myth, legend, dogma and art.[2] These linkages can be highly illuminating. Frankenstein's monster is related to the Golem; to Jesus; to Prometheus. Tarzan is a direct descendant of the Wolfchild/Noble Savage on one side, and every child's fantasy of the Orphan-of-High-Estate on the other. The robot may be seen as the modern ego's fear of the body, after the crippling division of "mind" and "body," "ghost" and "machine," enforced by post-Renaissance mechanistic thought. In "The Time Machine" there is one of the great visions of the End, an archetype of eschatology comparable to any religious vision of the day of judgment. In "Nightfall" there is the fundamental opposition of dark and light, playing on the fear of darkness that we share with our cousins the great apes. Through Philip K. Dick's work one can follow an exploration of the ancient themes of identity and alienation, and the sense of the fragmentation of the ego. In Stanislaw Lem's works there seems to be a similarly complex and subtle exploration of the archetypal Other, the alien.

Such myths, symbols, images do not disappear under the scrutiny of the intellect, nor does an ethical, or aesthetic, or even religious examination of them make them shrink and vanish. On the contrary: the more you look, the more there they are. And the more you think, the more they mean.

On this level, science fiction deserves the title of a modern mythology.

Most science fiction doesn't, of course, and never will. There are never very many artists around. No doubt we'll continue most of the time to get rewarmed leftovers from Babylon and Northrop Frye served up by earnest snobs, and hordes of brawny Gerbilmen ground out by hacks. But there will be mythmakers, too. Even now—who knows?—the next Mary Shelley may be lying quietly in her tower-top room, just waiting for a thunderstorm.

Notes

1. This schema is reproduced in Freudian psychology, where the myth or symbol is considered to be a disguise, and the raising into consciousness of unconscious contents leads to a progressive emptying or draining dry of the unconscious; in contrast to the schema followed by Jung and others, where the emphasis is on the irreducibility of symbol, and the compensatory, mutually creative relationship between the conscious and the unconscious.

2. Note that a manifestation is all we ever get; the archetype itself is beyond the reach of reason, art, or even madness. It is not a thing, an object, but is rather, Jung guessed, a psychic modality, a function comparable to a function/limitation such as the visual range of the human eye, which, by limiting our perception of electromagnetic vibrations to a certain range, enables us to see. The archetypes "do not in any sense represent things as they are in themselves, but rather the forms in which things can be perceived and conceived." They are *a priori* structural forms of the stuff of consciousness" (Jung: *Memories, Dreams, Reflections,* p. 347).

−1976

VASTER THAN EMPIRES AND MORE SLOW

It was only during the earliest decades of the League that the Earth sent ships out on the enormously long voyages, beyond the pale, over the stars and far away. They were seeking for worlds which had not been seeded or settled by the Founders on Hain, truly alien worlds. All the Known Worlds went back to the Hainish Origin, and the Terrans, having been not only founded but salvaged by the Hainish, resented this. They wanted to get away from the family. They wanted to find somebody new. The Hainish, like tiresomely understanding parents, supported their explorations, and contributed ships and volunteers, as did several other worlds of the League.

All these volunteers to the Extreme Survey crews shared one peculiarity: they were of unsound mind.

What sane person, after all, would go out to collect information that would not be received for five or ten centuries? Cosmic mass interference had not yet been eliminated from the operation of the ansible, and so instantaneous communication was reliable only within a range of 120 lightyears. The explorers would be quite isolated. And of course they had no idea what they might come back to, if they came back. No normal human being who had experienced time-slippage of even a few decades between League worlds would volunteer for a round trip of centuries. The Surveyors were escapists, misfits. They were nuts.

Ten of them climbed aboard the ferry at Smeming Port, and made varyingly inept attempts to get to know one another during the three days the ferry took getting to their ship, *Gum*. Gum is a Cetian nickname, on the order of Baby or Pet. There were two Cetians on the team, two Hainishmen, one Beldene, and five Terrans; the Cetian-built ship was chartered by the Government of Earth. Her motley crew came aboard wriggling through the coupling tube one by one like apprehensive spermatozoa trying to fertilize the universe. The ferry left, and the navigator put *Gum* underway. She flittered for some hours on the edge of space a few hundred million miles from Smeming Port, and then abruptly vanished.

When, after 10 hours 29 minutes, or 256 years, *Gum* reappeared in normal space, she was supposed to be in the vicinity of Star KG-E-96651. Sure enough, there was the gold pinhead of the star. Somewhere within a four-hundred-million-kilometer sphere there was also a greenish planet, World 4470, as charted by a Cetian mapmaker. The ship now had to find the planet. This was not quite so easy as it might sound, given a four-hundred-million-kilometer haystack. And *Gum* couldn't bat about in planetary space at near lightspeed; if she did, she and Star KG-E-96651 and World 4470 might all end up going bang. She had to creep, using rocket propulsion, at a few hundred thousand miles an hour. The Mathematician/Navigator, Asnanifoil, knew pretty well where the planet ought to be, and thought they might raise it within ten E-days. Meanwhile the members of the Survey team got to know one another still better.

"I can't stand him," said Porlock, the Hard Scientist (chemistry, plus physics, astronomy, geology, etc.), and little blobs of spittle appeared on his mustache. "The man is insane. I can't imagine why he was passed as fit to join a Survey team, unless this is a deliberate experiment in noncompatibility, planned by the Authority, with us as guinea pigs."

"We generally use hamsters and Hainish gholes," said Mannon, the Soft Scientist (psychology, plus psychiatry, anthropology, ecology, etc.), politely; he was one of the

Hainishmen. "Instead of guinea pigs. Well, you know, Mr. Osden is really a very rare case. In fact, he's the first fully cured case of Render's Syndrome—a variety of infantile autism which was thought to be incurable. The great Terran analyst Hammergeld reasoned that the cause of the autistic condition in this case is a supernormal empathic capacity, and developed an appropriate treatment. Mr. Osden is the first patient to undergo that treatment, in fact he lived with Dr. Hammergeld until he was eighteen. The therapy was completely successful.

"Successful?"

"Why, yes. He certainly is not autistic."

"No, he's intolerable!"

"Well, you see," said Mannon, gazing mildly at the saliva-flecks on Porlock's mustache, "the normal defensive-aggressive reaction between strangers meeting—let's say you and Mr. Osden just for example—is something you're scarcely aware of; habit, manners, inattention get you past it; you've learned to ignore it, to the point where you might even deny it exists. However, Mr. Osden, being an empath, feels it. Feels his feelings, and yours, and is hard put to say which is which. Let's say that there's a normal element of hostility towards any stranger in your emotional reaction to him when you meet him, plus a spontaneous dislike of his looks, or clothes, or handshake—it doesn't matter what. He feels that dislike. As his autistic defense has been unlearned, he resorts to an aggressive-defense mechanism, a response in kind to the aggression which you have unwittingly projected onto him." Mannon went on for quite a long time.

"Nothing gives a man the right to be such a bastard," Porlock said.

"He can't tune us out?" asked Harfex, the Biologist, another Hainishman.

"It's like hearing," said Olleroo, Assistant Hard Scientist, stooping over to paint her toenails with fluorescent lacquer. "No eyelids on your ears. No Off switch on empathy. He hears our feelings whether he wants to or not."

"Does he know what we're *thinking?*" asked Eskwana, the Engineer, looking round at the others in real dread.

"No," Porlock snapped. "Empathy's not telepathy! Nobody's got telepathy."

"Yet," said Mannon, with his little smile. "Just before I left Hain there was a most interesting report in from one of the recently rediscovered worlds, a hilfer named Rocannon reporting what appears to be a teachable telepathic technique existent among a mutated hominid race; I only saw a synopsis in the HILF Bulletin, but—" He went on. The others had learned that they could talk while Mannon went on talking; he did not seem to mind, nor even to miss much of what they said.

"Then why does he hate us?" Eskwana said.

"Nobody hates you, Ander honey," said Olleroo, daubing Eskwana's left thumbnail with fluorescent pink. The engineer flushed and smiled vaguely.

"He acts as if he hated us," said Haito, the Coordinator. She was a delicate-looking woman of pure Asian descent, with a surprising voice, husky, deep, and soft, like a young bullfrog. "Why, if he suffers from our hostility, does he increase it by constant attacks and insults? I can't say I think much of Dr. Hammergeld's cure, really, Mannon; autism might be preferable. . . ."

She stopped. Osden had come into the main cabin.

He looked flayed. His skin was unnaturally white and thin, showing the channels of his blood like a faded road map in red and blue. His Adam's apple, the muscles that circled his mouth, the bones and ligaments of his wrists and hands, all stood out distinctly as if displayed for an anatomy lesson. His hair was pale rust, like long-dried blood. He had eyebrows and lashes, but they were visible only in certain lights; what one saw was the bones of the eye sockets, the veining of the lids, and the colorless eyes. They were not red eyes, for he was not really an albino, but they were not blue or grey; colors had cancelled out in Osden's eyes, leaving a cold water-like clarity, infinitely penetrable. He never looked directly at one. His face lacked expression, like an anatomical drawing, or a skinned face.

"I agree," he said in a high, harsh tenor, "that even autistic withdrawal might be preferable to the smog of cheap secondhand emotions with which you people surround me. What are you sweating hate for now, Porlock? Can't stand the sight of me? Go practice some auto-eroticism the way you were doing last night, it improves your vibes. Who the devil moved my tapes, here? Don't touch my things, any of you. I won't have it."

"Osden," said Asnanifoil in his large slow voice, "why *are* you such a bastard?"

Ander Eskwana cowered and put his hands in front of his face. Contention frightened him. Olleroo looked up with a vacant yet eager expression, the eternal spectator.

"Why shouldn't I be?" said Osden. He was not looking at Asnanifoil, and was keeping physically as far away from all of them as he could in the crowded cabin. "None of you constitute, in yourselves, any reason for my changing my behavior."

Harfex, a reserved and patient man, said, "The reason is that we shall be spending several years together. Life will be better for all of us if—"

"Can't you understand that I don't give a damn for all of you?" Osden said, took up his microtapes, and went out. Eskwana had suddenly gone to sleep. Asnanifoil was drawing slipstreams in the air with his finger and muttering the Ritual Primes. "You cannot explain his presence on the team except as a plot on the part of the Terran Authority. I saw this almost at once. This mission is meant to fail," Harfex whispered to the Coordinator, glancing over his shoulder. Porlock was fumbling with his fly-button; there were tears in his eyes. I did tell you they were all crazy, but you thought I was exaggerating.

All the same, they were not unjustified. Extreme Surveyors expected to find their fellow team members intelligent, well-trained, unstable, and personally sympathetic. They had to work together in close quarters and nasty places, and could expect one another's paranoias, depressions, manias, phobias and compulsions to be mild enough to admit of good personal relationships, at least most of the time. Osden might be intelligent, but his training was sketchy and his personality was disastrous. He had been sent only on account of his singular gift, the power of empathy: properly speaking, of wide-range bioempathic receptivity. His talent wasn't species-specific; he could pick up emotion or sentience from anything that felt. He could share lust with a white rat, pain with a squashed cockroach, and phototropy with a moth. On an alien world, the Authority had decided, it would be useful to know if anything nearby is sentient, and if so, what its feelings towards you are. Osden's title was a new one: he was the team's Sensor.

"What is emotion, Osden?" Haito Tomiko asked him one day in the main cabin, trying to make some rapport with him for once. "What is it, exactly, that you pick up with your empathic sensitivity?"

"Muck," the man answered in his high, exasperated voice. "The psychic excreta of the animal kingdom. I wade through your faeces."

"I was trying," she said, "to learn some facts." She thought her tone was admirably calm.

"You weren't after facts. You were trying to get at me. With some fear, some curiosity, and a great deal of distaste. The way you might poke a dead dog, to see the maggots crawl. Will you understand once and for all that I don't want to be got at, that I want to be left alone?" His skin was mottled with red and violet, his voice had risen. "Go roll in your own dung, you yellow bitch!" he shouted at her silence.

"Calm down," she said, still quietly, but she left him at once and went to her cabin. Of course he had been right about her motives; her question had been largely a pretext, a mere effort to interest him. But what harm in that? Did not that effort imply respect for the other? At the moment of asking the question she had felt at most a slight distrust of him; she had mostly felt sorry for him, the poor arrogant venomous bastard, Mr. No-Skin as Olleroo called him. What did he expect, the way he acted? Love?

"I guess he can't stand anybody feeling sorry for him," said Olleroo, lying on the lower bunk, gilding her nipples.

"Then he can't form any human relationship. All his Dr. Hammergeld did was turn an autism inside out. . . ."

"Poor frot," said Olleroo. "Tomiko, you don't mind if Harfex comes in for a while tonight, do you?"

"Can't you go to his cabin? I'm sick of always having to sit in Main with that damned peeled turnip."

"You do hate him, don't you? I guess he feels that. But I slept with Harfex last night too, and Asnanifoil might get jealous, since they share the cabin. It would be nicer here."

"Service them both," Tomiko said with the coarseness of offended modesty. Her Terran subculture, the East Asian, was a puritanical one; she had been brought up chaste.

"I only like one a night," Olleroo replied with innocent serenity. Beldene, the Garden Planet, had never discovered chastity, or the wheel.

"Try Osden, then," Tomiko said. Her personal instability was seldom so plain as now: a profound self-distrust manifesting itself as destructivism. She had volunteered for this job because there was, in all probability, no use in doing it.

The little Beldene looked up, paintbrush in hand, eyes wide. "Tomiko, that was a dirty thing to say."

"Why?"

"It would be vile! I'm not attracted to Osden!"

"I didn't know it mattered to you," Tomiko said indifferently, though she did know. She got some papers together and left the cabin, remarking, "I hope you and Harfex or whoever it is finish by last bell; I'm tired."

Olleroo was crying, tears dripping on her little gilded nipples. She wept easily. Tomiko had not wept since she was ten years old.

It was not a happy ship; but it took a turn for the better when Asnanifoil and his computers raised World 4470. There it lay, a dark-green jewel, like truth at the bottom of a gravity well. As they watched the jade disc grow, a sense of mutuality grew among them. Osden's selfishness, his accurate cruelty, served now to draw the others together. "Perhaps," Mannon said, "he was sent as a beating-gron. What Terrans call a scapegoat. Perhaps his influence will be good after all." And no one, so careful were they to be kind to one another, disagreed.

They came into orbit. There were no lights on nightside, on the continents none of the lines and clots made by animals who build.

"No men," Harfex murmured.

"Of course not," snapped Osden, who had a viewscreen to himself, and his head inside a polythene bag. He claimed that the plastic cut down on the empathic noise he received from the others. "We're two lightcenturies past the limit of the Hainish Expansion, and outside that there are no men. Anywhere. You don't think Creation would have made the same hideous mistake twice?"

No one was paying him much heed; they were looking with affection at that jade immensity below them, where there was life, but not human life. They were misfits among men, and what they saw there was not desolation, but peace. Even Osden did not look quite so expressionless as usual; he was frowning.

Descent in fire on the sea; air reconnaissance; landing. A plain of something like grass, thick, green, bowing stalks, surrounded the ship, brushed against extended viewcameras, smeared the lenses with a fine pollen.

"It looks like a pure phytosphere," Harfex said. "Osden, do you pick up anything sentient?"

They all turned to the Sensor. He had left the screen and was pouring himself a cup of tea. He did not answer. He seldom answered spoken questions.

The chitinous rigidity of military discipline was quite inapplicable to these teams of mad scientists; their chain of command lay somewhere between parliamentary procedure and peck-order, and would have driven a regular service officer out of his mind. By the inscrutable decision of the Authority, however, Dr. Haito Tomiko had been given the title of Coordinator, and she now exercised her prerogative for the first time. "Mr. Sensor Osden," she said, "please answer Mr. Harfex."

"How could I 'pick up' anything from outside," Osden said without turning, "with the emotions of nine neurotic hominids pullulating around me like worms in a can? When I have anything to tell you, I'll tell you. I'm aware of my responsibility as Sensor. If you presume to give me an order again, however, Coordinator Haito, I'll consider my responsibility void."

"Very well, Mr. Sensor. I trust no orders will be needed henceforth." Tomiko's bullfrog voice was calm, but Osden seemed to flinch slightly as he stood with his back to her, as if the surge of her suppressed rancor had struck him with physical force.

The biologist's hunch proved correct. When they began field analyses they found no animals even among the microbiota. Nobody here ate anybody else. All life-forms were photosynthesizing or saprophagous, living off light or death, not off life. Plants: infinite plants, not one species known to the visitors from the house of Man. Infinite shades and intensities of green, violet, purple, brown, red. Infinite silences. Only the wind moved, swaying leaves and fronds, a warm soughing wind laden with spores and pollens, blowing the sweet pale-green dust over prairies of great grasses, heaths that bore no heather, flowerless forests where no foot had ever walked, no eye had ever looked. A warm, sad world, sad and serene. The Surveyors, wandering like picnickers over sunny plains of violet filicaliformes, spoke softly to each other. They knew their voices broke a silence of a thousand million years, the silence of wind and leaves, leaves and wind, blowing and ceasing and blowing again. They talked softly; but being human, they talked.

"Poor old Osden," said Jenny Chong, Bio and Tech, as she piloted a helijet on the North Polar Quadrating run. "All that fancy hi-fi stuff in his brain and nothing to receive. What a bust."

"He told me he hates plants," Olleroo said with a giggle.

"You'd think he'd like them, since they don't bother him like we do. "

"Can't say I much like these plants myself," said Porlock, looking down at the purple undulations of the North Circumpolar Forest. "All the same. No mind. No change. A man alone in it would go right off his head."

"But it's all alive," Jenny Chong said. "And if it lives, Osden hates it."

"He's not really so bad," Olleroo said, magnanimous. Porlock looked at her side-long and asked, "You ever slept with him, Olleroo?"

Olleroo burst into tears and cried, "You Terrans are obscene!"

"No she hasn't," Jenny Chong said, prompt to defend. "Have you, Porlock?"

The chemist laughed uneasily: ha, ha, ha. Flecks of spittle appeared on his mustache.

"Osden can't bear to be touched," Olleroo said shakily. "I just brushed against him once by accident and he knocked me off like I was some sort of dirty . . . thing. We're all just things, to him."

"He's evil," Porlock said in a strained voice, startling the two women. "He'll end up shattering this team, sabotaging it, one way or another. Mark my words. He's not fit to live with other people!"

They landed on the North Pole. A midnight sun smouldered over low hills. Short, dry, greenish-pink bryoform grasses stretched away in every direction, which was all one direction, south. Subdued by the incredible silence, the three Surveyors set up their instruments and set to work, three viruses twitching minutely on the hide of an unmoving giant.

Nobody asked Osden along on runs as pilot or photographer or recorder, and he never volunteered, so he seldom left base camp. He ran Harfex's botanical taxonomic data through the onship computers, and served as assistant to Eskwana, whose job here was mainly repair and maintenance. Eskwana had begun to sleep a great deal, twenty-five hours or more out of the thirty-two-hour day, dropping off in the middle of repairing a radio or checking the guidance circuits of a helijet. The Coordinator stayed at base one day to observe. No one else was home except Poswet To, who was subject to epileptic fits; Mannon had plugged her into a therapy-circuit today in a state of preventive catatonia. Tomiko spoke reports into the storage banks, and kept an eye on Osden and Eskwana. Two hours passed.

"You might want to use the 860 microwaldoes in sealing that connection," Eskwana said in his soft, hesitant voice.

"Obviously!"

"Sorry. I just saw you had the 840's there—"

"And will replace them when I take the 860's out. When I don't know how to proceed, Engineer, I'll ask your advice."

After a minute Tomiko looked round. Sure enough, there was Eskwana sound asleep, head on the table, thumb in his mouth.

"Osden."

The white face did not turn, he did not speak, but conveyed impatiently that he was listening.

"You can't be unaware of Eskwana's vulnerability."

"I am not responsible for his psychopathic reactions."

"But you are responsible for your own. Eskwana is essential to our work here, and you're not. If you can't control your hostility, you must avoid him altogether."

Osden put down his tools and stood up. "With pleasure!" he said in his vindictive, scraping voice. "You could not possibly imagine what it's like to experience

Eskwana's irrational terrors. To have to share his horrible cowardice, to have to cringe with him at everything!"

"Are you trying to justify your cruelty towards him? I thought you had more self-respect." Tomiko found herself shaking with spite. "If your empathic power really makes you share Ander's misery, why does it never induce the least compassion in you?"

"Compassion," Osden said. "Compassion. What do you know about compassion?"

She stared at him, but he would not look at her.

"Would you like me to verbalize your present emotional affect regarding myself?" he said. "I can do so more precisely than you can. I'm trained to analyze such responses as I receive them. And I do receive them."

"But how can you expect me to feel kindly towards you when you behave as you do?"

"What does it matter how I *behave,* you stupid sow, do you think it makes any difference? Do you think the average human is a well of loving-kindness? My choice is to be hated or to be despised. Not being a woman or a coward, I prefer to be hated."

"That's rot. Self-pity. Every man has—"

"But I am not a man," Osden said. "There are all of you. And there is myself. I am *one.*"

Awed by that glimpse of abysmal solipsism, she kept silent a while; finally she said with neither spite nor pity, clinically, "You could kill yourself, Osden."

"That's your way, Haito," he jeered. "I'm not depressive, and *seppuku* isn't my bit. What do you want me to do here?"

"Leave. Spare yourself and us. Take the aircar and a data-feeder and go do a species count. In the forest; Harfex hasn't even started the forests yet. Take a hundred-square-meter forested area, anywhere inside radio range. But outside empathy range. Report in at 8 and 24 o'clock daily."

Osden went, and nothing was heard from him for five days but laconic all-well signals twice daily. The mood at base camp changed like a stage-set. Eskwana stayed awake up to eighteen hours a day. Poswet To got out her stellar lute and chanted the celestial harmonies (music had driven Osden into a frenzy). Mannon, Harfex, Jenny Chong, and Tomiko all went off tranquillizers. Porlock distilled something in his laboratory and drank it all by himself. He had a hangover. Asnanifoil and Poswet To held an all-night Numerical Epiphany, that mystical orgy of higher mathematics which is the chief pleasure of the religious Cetian soul. Olleroo slept with everybody. Work went well.

The Hard Scientist came towards base at a run, laboring through the high, fleshy stalks of the graminiformes. "Something—in the forest—" His eyes bulged, he panted, his mustache and fingers trembled. "Something big. Moving, behind me. I was putting in a bench-mark, bending down. It came at me. As if it was swinging down out of the trees. Behind me." He stared at the others with the opaque eyes of terror or exhaustion.

"Sit down, Porlock. Take it easy. Now wait, go through this again. You *saw* something—"

"Not clearly. Just the movement. Purposive. A—an—I don't know what it could have been. Something self-moving. In the trees, the arboriformes, whatever you call 'em. At the edge of the woods."

Harfex looked grim. "There is nothing here that could attack you, Porlock. There are not even microzoa. There *could not* be a large animal."

"Could you possibly have seen an epiphyte drop suddenly, a vine come loose behind you?"

"No," Porlock said. "It was coming down at me, through the branches, fast. When I turned it took off again, away and upward. It made a noise, a sort of crashing. If it wasn't an animal, God knows what it could have been! It was big—as big as a man, at least. Maybe a reddish color. I couldn't see, I'm not sure."

"It was Osden," said Jenny Chong, "doing a Tarzan act." She giggled nervously, and Tomiko repressed a wild feckless laugh. But Harfex was not smiling.

"One gets uneasy under the arboriformes," he said in his polite, repressed voice. "I've noticed that. Indeed that may be why I've put off working in the forests. There's a hypnotic quality in the colors and spacing of the stems and branches, especially the helically-arranged ones; and the spore-throwers grow so regularly spaced that it seems unnatural. I find it quite disagreeable, subjectively speaking. I wonder if a stronger effect of that sort mightn't have produced a hallucination . . . ?"

Porlock shook his head. He wet his lips. "It was there," he said. "Something. Moving with purpose. Trying to attack me from behind."

When Osden called in, punctual as always, at 24 o'clock that night, Harfex told him Porlock's report. "Have you come on anything at all, Mr. Osden, that could substantiate Mr. Porlock's impression of a motile, sentient life-form, in the forest?"

Ssss, the radio said sardonically. "No. Bullshit," said Osden's unpleasant voice.

"You've been actually inside the forest longer than any of us," Harfex said with unmitigable politeness. "Do you agree with my impression that the forest ambiance has a rather troubling and possibly hallucinogenic effect on the perceptions?"

Ssss. "I'll agree that Porlock's perceptions are easily troubled. Keep him in his lab, he'll do less harm. Anything else?"

"Not at present," Harfex said, and Osden cut off.

Nobody could credit Porlock's story, and nobody could discredit it. He was positive that something, something big, had tried to attack him by surprise. It was hard to deny this, for they were on an alien world, and everyone who had entered the forest had felt a certain chill and foreboding under the "trees." ("Call them trees, certainly," Harfex had said. "They really are the same thing, only, of course, altogether different.") They agreed that they had felt uneasy, or had had the sense that something was watching them from behind.

"We've got to clear this up," Porlock said, and he asked to be sent as a temporary Biologist's Aide, like Osden, into the forest to explore and observe. Olleroo and Jenny Chong volunteered if they could go as a pair. Harfex sent them all off into the forest near which they were encamped, a vast tract covering four-fifths of Continent D. He forbade side-arms. They were not to go outside a fifty-mile half-circle, which included Osden's current site. They all reported in twice daily, for three days. Porlock reported a glimpse of what seemed to be a large semi-erect shape moving through the trees across the river; Olleroo was sure she had heard something moving near the tent, the second night.

"There are no animals on this planet," Harfex said, dogged.

Then Osden missed his morning call.

Tomiko waited less than an hour, then flew with Harfex to the area where Osden had reported himself the night before. But as the helijet hovered over the sea of purplish leaves, illimitable, impenetrable, she felt a panic despair. "How can we find him in this?"

"He reported landing on the riverbank. Find the aircar; he'll be camped near it, and he can't have gone far from his camp. Species-counting is slow work. There's the river."

"There's his car," Tomiko said, catching the bright foreign glint among the vegetable colors and shadows. "Here goes, then."

She put the ship in hover and pitched out the ladder. She and Harfex descended. The sea of life closed over their heads.

As her feet touched the forest floor, she unsnapped the flap of her holster; then glancing at Harfex, who was unarmed, she left the gun untouched. But her hand kept coming back up to it. There was no sound at all, as soon as they were a few meters away from the slow, brown river, and the light was dim. Great boles stood well apart, almost regularly, almost alike; they were soft-skinned, some appearing smooth and others spongy, grey or greenish-brown or brown, twined with cable-like creepers and festooned with epiphytes, extending rigid, entangled armfuls of big, saucer-shaped, dark leaves that formed a roof-layer twenty to thirty meters thick. The ground underfoot was springy as a mattress, every inch of it knotted with roots and peppered with small, fleshy-leaved growths.

"Here's his tent," Tomiko said, cowed at the sound of her voice in that huge community of the voiceless. In the tent was Osden's sleeping bag, a couple of books, a box of rations. We should be calling, shouting for him, she thought, but did not even suggest it; nor did Harfex. They circled out from the tent, careful to keep each other in sight through the thick-standing presences, the crowding gloom. She stumbled over Osden's body, not thirty meters from the tent, led to it by the whitish gleam of a dropped notebook. He lay face down between two huge-rooted trees. His head and hands were covered with blood, some dried, some still oozing red.

Harfex appeared beside her, his pale Hainish complexion quite green in the dusk. "Dead?"

"No. He's been struck. Beaten. From behind." Tomiko's fingers felt over the bloody skull and temples and nape. "A weapon or a tool . . . I don't find a fracture."

As she turned Osden's body over so they could lift him, his eyes opened. She was holding him, bending close to his face. His pale lips writhed. A deathly fear came into her. She screamed aloud two or three times and tried to run away, shambling and stumbling into the terrible dusk. Harfex caught her, and at his touch and the sound of his voice, her panic decreased. "What is it? What is it?" he was saying.

"I don't know," she sobbed. Her heartbeat still shook her, and she could not see clearly. "The fear—the . . . I panicked. When I saw his eyes."

"We're both nervous. I don't understand this—"

"I'm all right now, come on, we've got to get him under care."

Both working with senseless haste, they lugged Osden to the riverside and hauled him up on a rope under his armpits; he dangled like a sack, twisting a little, over the glutinous dark sea of leaves. They pulled him into the helijet and took off. Within a minute they were over open prairie. Tomiko locked onto the homing beam. She drew a deep breath, and her eyes met Harfex's.

"I was so terrified I almost fainted. I have never done that."

"I was . . . unreasonably frightened also," said the Hainishman, and indeed he looked aged and shaken. "Not so badly as you. But as unreasonably."

"It was when I was in contact with him, holding him. He seemed to be conscious for a moment."

"Empathy? . . . I hope he can tell us what attacked him."

Osden, like a broken dummy covered with blood and mud, half lay as they had bundled him into the rear seats in their frantic urgency to get out of the forest.

More panic met their arrival at base. The ineffective brutality of the assault was sinister and bewildering. Since Harfex stubbornly denied any possibility of animal life they began speculating about sentient plants, vegetable monsters, psychic projections. Jenny Chong's latent phobia reasserted itself and she could talk about nothing except the Dark Egos which followed people around behind their backs. She and Olleroo and Porlock had been summoned back to base; and nobody was much inclined to go outside.

Osden had lost a good deal of blood during the three or four hours he had lain alone, and concussion and severe contusions had put him in shock and semi-coma. As he came out of this and began running a low fever he called several times for "Doctor," in a plaintive voice: "Doctor Hammergeld . . ." When he regained full consciousness, two of those long days later, Tomiko called Harfex into his cubicle.

"Osden: can you tell us what attacked you?"

The pale eyes flickered past Harfex's face.

"You were attacked," Tomiko said gently. The shifty gaze was hatefully familiar, but she was a physician, protective of the hurt. "You may not remember it yet. Something attacked you. You were in the forest—"

"Ah!" he cried out, his eyes growing bright and his features contorting. "The forest—in the forest—"

"What's in the forest?"

He gasped for breath. A look of clearer consciousness came into his face. After a while he said, "I don't know."

"Did you see what attacked you?" Harfex asked.

"I don't know."

"You remember it now."

"I don't know."

"All our lives may depend on this. You must tell us what you saw!"

"I don't know," Osden said, sobbing with weakness. He was too weak to hide the fact that he was hiding the answer, yet he would not say it. Porlock, nearby, was chewing his pepper-colored mustache as he tried to hear what was going on in the cubicle. Harfex leaned over Osden and said, "You *will* tell us—" Tomiko had to interfere bodily.

Harfex controlled himself with an effort that was painful to see. He went off silently to his cubicle, where no doubt he took a double or triple dose of tranquillizers. The other men and women, scattered about the big frail building, a long main hall and ten sleeping-cubicles, said nothing, but looked depressed and edgy. Osden, as always, even now, had them all at his mercy. Tomiko looked down at him with a rush of hatred that burned in her throat like bile. This monstrous egotism that fed itself on others' emotions, this absolute selfishness, was worse than any hideous deformity of the flesh. Like a congenital monster, he should not have lived. Should not be alive. Should have died. Why had his head not been split open?

As he lay flat and white, his hands helpless at his sides, his colorless eyes were wide open, and there were tears running from the corners. He tried to flinch away. "Don't," he said in a weak hoarse voice, and tried to raise his hands to protect his head. "Don't!"

She sat down on the folding-stool beside the cot, and after a while put her hand on his. He tried to pull away, but lacked the strength.

A long silence fell between them.

"Osden," she murmured, "I'm sorry. I'm very sorry. I will you well. Let me will you well, Osden. I don't want to hurt you. Listen, I do see now. It was one of us. That's right, isn't it. No, don't answer, only tell me if I'm wrong; but I'm not. . . . Of course there are animals on this planet. Ten of them. I don't care who it was. It doesn't matter, does it. It could have been me, just now. I realize that. I didn't understand how it is, Osden. You can't see how difficult it is for us to understand. . . . But listen. If it were love, instead of hate and fear . . . Is it never love?"

"No."

"Why not? Why should it never be? Are human beings all so weak? That is terrible. Never mind, never mind, don't worry. Keep still. At least right now it isn't hate, is it? Sympathy at least, concern, well-wishing. You do feel that, Osden? Is it what you feel?"

"Among . . . other things," he said, almost inaudibly.

"Noise from my subconscious, I suppose. And everybody else in the room . . . Listen, when we found you there in the forest, when I tried to turn you over, you partly wakened, and I felt a horror of you. I was insane with fear for a minute. Was that your fear of me I felt?"

"No."

Her hand was still on his, and he was quite relaxed, sinking towards sleep, like a man in pain who has been given relief from pain. "The forest," he muttered; she could barely understand him. "Afraid."

She pressed him no further, but kept her hand on his and watched him go to sleep. She knew what she felt, and what therefore he must feel. She was confident of it: there is only one emotion, or state of being, that can thus wholly reverse itself, polarize, within one moment. In Great Hainish indeed there is one word, *ontá,* for love and for hate. She was not in love with Osden, of course, that was another kettle of fish. What she felt for him was *ontá,* polarized hate. She held his hand and the current flowed between them, the tremendous electricity of touch, which he had always dreaded. As he slept the ring of anatomy-chart muscles around his mouth relaxed, and Tomiko saw on his face what none of them had ever seen, very faint, a smile. It faded. He slept on.

He was tough; next day he was sitting up, and hungry. Harfex wished to interrogate him, but Tomiko put him off. She hung a sheet of polythene over the cubicle door, as Osden himself had often done. "Does it actually cut down your empathic reception?" she asked, and he replied, in the dry, cautious tone they were now using to each other, "No."

"Just a warning, then."

"Partly. More faith-healing. Dr. Hammergeld thought it worked. . . . Maybe it does, a little."

There had been love, once. A terrified child, suffocating in the tidal rush and battering of the huge emotions of adults, a drowning child, saved by one man. Taught to breathe, to live, by one man. Given everything, all protection and love, by one man. Father/Mother/God: no other. "Is he still alive?" Tomiko asked, thinking of Osden's incredible loneliness, and the strange cruelty of the great doctors. She was shocked when she heard his forced, tinny laugh. "He died at least two and a half centuries ago," Osden said. "Do you forget where we are, Coordinator? We've all left our little families behind. . . ."

Outside the polythene curtain the eight other human beings on World 4470 moved vaguely. Their voices were low and strained. Eskwana slept; Poswet To was in therapy; Jenny Chong was trying to rig lights in her cubicle so that she wouldn't cast a shadow.

"They're all scared," Tomiko said, scared. "They've all got these ideas about what attacked you. A sort of ape-potato, a giant fanged spinach, I don't know. . . . Even Harfex. You may be right not to force them to see. That would be worse, to lose confidence in one another. But why are we all so shaky, unable to face the fact, going to pieces so easily? Are we really all insane?"

"We'll soon be more so."

"Why?"

"There *is* something." He closed his mouth, the muscles of his lips stood out rigid.

"Something sentient?"

"A sentience."

"In the forest?"

He nodded.

"What is it, then—?"

"The fear." He began to look strained again, and moved restlessly. "When I fell, there, you know, I didn't lose consciousness at once. Or I kept regaining it. I don't know. It was more like being paralyzed."

"You were."

"I was on the ground. I couldn't get up. My face was in the dirt, in that soft leaf mold. It was in my nostrils and eyes. I couldn't move. Couldn't see. As if I was in the ground. Sunk into it, part of it. I knew I was between two trees even though I never saw them. I suppose I could feel the roots. Below me in the ground, down under the ground. My hands were bloody, I could feel that, and the blood made the dirt around my face sticky. I felt the fear. It kept growing. As if they'd finally *known* I was there, lying on them there, under them, among them, the thing they feared, and yet part of their fear itself. I couldn't stop sending the fear back, and it kept growing, and I couldn't move, I couldn't get away. I would pass out, I think, and then the fear would bring me to again, and I still couldn't move. Any more than they can."

Tomiko felt the cold stirring of her hair, the readying of the apparatus of terror. "They: who are they, Osden?"

"They, it—I don't know. The fear."

"What is he talking about?" Harfex demanded when Tomiko reported this conversation. She would not let Harfex question Osden yet, feeling that she must protect Osden from the onslaught of the Hainishman's powerful, over-repressed emotions. Unfortunately this fueled the slow fire of paranoid anxiety that burned in poor Harfex, and he thought she and Osden were in league, hiding some fact of great importance or peril from the rest of the team.

"It's like the blind man trying to describe the elephant. Osden hasn't seen or heard the . . . the sentience, any more than we have."

"But he's felt it, my dear Haito," Harfex said with just-suppressed rage. "Not empathically. On his skull. It came and knocked him down and beat him with a blunt instrument. Did he not catch *one* glimpse of it?"

"What would he have seen, Harfex?" Tomiko asked, but he would not hear her meaningful tone; even he had blocked out that comprehension. What one fears is alien. The murderer is an outsider, a foreigner, not one of us. The evil is not in me!

"The first blow knocked him pretty well out," Tomiko said a little wearily, "he didn't see anything. But when he came to again, alone in the forest, he felt a great fear. Not his own fear, an empathic effect. He is certain of that. And certain it was nothing picked up from any of us. So that evidently the native life-forms are not all insentient."

Harfex looked at her a moment, grim. "You're trying to frighten me, Haito. I do not understand your motives." He got up and went off to his laboratory table, walking slowly and stiffly, like a man of eighty not of forty.

She looked round at the others. She felt some desperation. Her new, fragile, and profound interdependence with Osden gave her, she was well aware, some added strength. But if even Harfex could not keep his head, who of the others would? Porlock and Eskwana were shut in their cubicles, the others were all working or busy with something. There was something queer about their positions. For a while the Coordinator could not tell what it was, then she saw that they were all sitting facing the nearby forest. Playing chess with Asnanifoil, Olleroo had edged her chair around until it was almost beside his.

She went to Mannon, who was dissecting a tangle of spidery brown roots, and told him to look for the pattern-puzzle. He saw it at once, and said with unusual brevity, "Keeping an eye on the enemy."

"What enemy? What do *you* feel, Mannon?" She had a sudden hope in him as a psychologist, on this obscure ground of hints and empathies where biologists wells astray.

"I feel a strong anxiety with a specific spatial orientation. But I am not an empath. Therefore the anxiety is explicable in terms of the particular stress-situation, that is, the attack on a team member in the forest, and also in terms of the total stress-situation, that is, my presence in a totally alien environment, for which the archetypical connotations of the word 'forest' provide an inevitable metaphor."

Hours later Tomiko woke to hear Osden screaming in nightmare; Mannon was calming him, and she sank back into her own dark-branching pathless dreams. In the morning Eskwana did not wake. He could not be roused with stimulant drugs. He clung to his sleep, slipping farther and farther back, mumbling softly now and then until, wholly regressed, he lay curled on his side, thumb at his lips, gone.

"Two days; two down. Ten little Indians, nine little Indians . . ." That was Porlock.

"And you're the next little Indian," Jenny Chong snapped. "Go analyze your urine, Porlock!"

"He is driving us all insane," Porlock said, getting up and waving his left arm. "Can't you feel it? For God's sake, are you all deaf and blind? Can't you feel what he's doing, the emanations? It all comes from him—from his room there—from his mind. He is driving us all insane with fear!"

"Who is?" said Asnanifoil, looming precipitous and hairy over the little Terran.

"Do I have to say his name? Osden, then. Osden! Osden! Why do you think I tried to kill him? In self-defense! To save all of us! Because you won't see what he's doing to us. He's sabotaged the mission by making us quarrel, and now he's going to drive us all insane by projecting fear at us so that we can't sleep or think, like a huge radio that doesn't make any sound, but it broadcasts all the time, and you can't sleep, and you can't think. Haito and Harfex are already under his control but the rest of you can be saved. I had to do it!"

"You didn't do it very well," Osden said, standing half-naked, all rib and bandage, at the door of his cubicle. "I could have hit myself harder. Hell, it isn't me that's scaring you blind, Porlock, it's out there—there, in the woods!"

Porlock made an ineffectual attempt to assault Osden; Asnanifoil held him back, and continued to hold him effortlessly while Mannon gave him a sedative shot. He was put away shouting about giant radios. In a minute the sedative took effect, and he joined a peaceful silence to Eskwana's.

"All right," said Harfex. "Now, Osden, you'll tell us what you know and all you know."

Osden said, "I don't know anything."

He looked battered and faint. Tomiko made him sit down before he talked.

"After I'd been three days in the forest, I thought I was occasionally receiving some kind of affect."

"Why didn't you report it?"

"Thought I was going spla, like the rest of you."

"That, equally, should have been reported."

"You'd have called me back to base. I couldn't take it. You realize that my inclusion in the mission was a bad mistake. I'm not able to coexist with nine other neurotic personalities at close quarters. I was wrong to volunteer for Extreme Survey, and the Authority was wrong to accept me."

No one spoke; but Tomiko saw, with certainty this time, the flinch in Osden's shoulders and the tightening of his facial muscles, as he registered their bitter agreement.

"Anyhow, I didn't want to come back to base because I was curious. Even going psycho, how could I pick up empathic affects when there was no creature to emit them? They weren't bad, then. Very vague. Queer. Like a draft in a closed room, a flicker in the corner of your eye. Nothing really."

For a moment he had been borne up on their listening: they heard, so he spoke. He was wholly at their mercy. If they disliked him he had to be hateful; if they mocked him he became grotesque; if they listened to him he was the storyteller. He was helplessly obedient to the demands of their emotions, reactions, moods. And there were seven of them, too many to cope with, so that he must be constantly knocked about from one to another's whim. He could not find coherence. Even as he spoke and held them, somebody's attention would wander: Olleroo perhaps was thinking that he wasn't unattractive, Harfex was seeking the ulterior motive of his words, Asnanifoil's mind, which could not be long held by the concrete, was roaming off towards the eternal peace of number, and Tomiko was distracted by pity, by fear. Osden's voice faltered. He lost the thread. "I . . . I thought it must be the trees," he said, and stopped.

"It's not the trees," Harfex said. "They have no more nervous system than do plants of the Hainish Descent on Earth. None."

"You're not seeing the forest for the trees, as they say on Earth," Mannon put in, smiling elfinly; Harfex stared at him. "What about those root-nodes we've been puzzling about for twenty days—eh?"

"What about them?"

"They are, indubitably, connections. Connections among the trees. Right? Now let's just suppose, most improbably, that you knew nothing of animal brain-structure. And you were given one axon, or one detached glial cell, to examine. Would you be likely to discover what it was? Would you see that the cell was capable of sentience?"

"No. Because it isn't. A single cell is capable of mechanical response to stimulus. No more. Are you hypothesizing that individual arboriformes are 'cells' in a kind of brain, Mannon?"

"Not exactly. I'm merely pointing out that they are all interconnected, both by the root-node linkage and by your green epiphytes in the branches. A linkage of incredible complexity and physical extent. Why, even the prairie grass-forms have those root-connectors, don't they? I know that sentience or intelligence isn't a thing, you can't find it in, or analyze it out from, the cells of a brain. It's a function of the connected cells. It is, in a sense, the connection: the connectedness. It doesn't exist. I'm not trying to say it exists. I'm only guessing that Osden might be able to describe it."

And Osden took him up, speaking as if in trance. "Sentience without senses. Blind, deaf, nerveless, moveless. Some irritability, response to touch. Response to sun, to light, to water, and chemicals in the earth around the roots. Nothing comprehensible to an animal mind. Presence without mind. Awareness of being, without object or subject. Nirvana."

"Then why do you receive fear?" Tomiko asked in a low voice.

"I don't know. I can't see how awareness of objects, of others, could arise: an unperceiving response . . . But there was an uneasiness, for days. And then when I lay between the two trees and my blood was on their roots—" Osden's face glittered with sweat. "It became fear," he said shrilly, "only fear."

"If such a function existed," Harfex said, "it would not be capable of conceiving of a self-moving, material entity, or responding to one. It could no more become aware of us then we can 'become aware' of Infinity."

"'The silence of those infinite expanses terrifies me,'" muttered Tomiko. "Pascal was aware of Infinity. By way of fear."

"To a forest," Mannon said, "we might appear as forest fires. Hurricanes. Dangers. What moves quickly is dangerous, to a plant. The rootless would be alien, terrible. And if it is mind, it seems only too probable that it might become aware of Osden, whose own mind is open to connection with all others so long as he's conscious, and who was lying in pain and afraid within it, actually inside it. No wonder it was afraid—"

"Not 'it,'" Harfex said. "There is no being, no huge creature, no person! There could at most be only a function—"

"There is only a fear," Osden said.

They were all still a while, and heard the stillness outside.

"Is that what I feel all the time coming up behind me?" Jenny Chong asked, subdued.

Osden nodded. "You all feel it, deaf as you are. Eskwana's the worst off, because he actually has some empathic capacity. He could send if he learned how, but he's too weak, never will be anything but a medium."

"Listen, Osden," Tomiko said, "you can send. Then send to it—the forest, the fear out there—tell it that we won't hurt it. Since it has, or is, some sort of affect that translates into what we feel as emotion, can't you translate back? Send out a message, We are harmless, we are friendly."

"You must know that nobody can emit a false empathic message, Haito. You can't send something that doesn't exist."

"But we don't intend harm, we are friendly."

"Are we? In the forest, when you picked me up, did you feel friendly?"

"No. Terrified. But that's—it, the forest, the plants, not my own fear, isn't it?"

"What's the difference? It's all you felt. Can't you see," and Osden's voice rose in exasperation, "why I dislike you and you dislike me, all of you? Can't you see that I retransmit every negative or aggressive affect you've felt towards me since we first met? I return your hostility, with thanks. I do it in self-defense. Like Porlock. It is self-defense, though; it's the only technique I developed to replace my original defense of total withdrawal from others. Unfortunately it creates a closed circuit, self-sustaining and self-reinforcing. Your initial reaction to me was the instinctive antipathy to a cripple; by now of course it's hatred. Can you fail to see my point? The forest-mind out there transmits only terror, now, and the only message I can send it is terror, because when exposed to it I can feel nothing except terror!"

"What must we do, then?" said Tomiko, and Mannon replied promptly, "Move camp. To another continent. If there are plant-minds there, they'll be slow to notice us, as this one was; maybe they won't notice us at all."

"It would be a considerable relief," Osden observed stiffly. The others had been watching him with a new curiosity. He had revealed himself, they had seen him as he was, a helpless man in a trap. Perhaps, like Tomiko, they had seen that the trap itself, his crass and cruel egotism, was their own construction, not his. They had built the cage and locked him in it, and like a caged ape he threw filth out through the bars. If, meeting him, they had offered trust, if they had been strong enough to offer him love, how might he have appeared to them?

None of them could have done so, and it was too late now. Given time, given solitude, Tomiko might have built up with him a slow resonance of feeling, a consonance of trust, a harmony; but there was no time, their job must be done. There was not room enough for the cultivation of so great a thing, and they must make do with sympathy, with pity, the small change of love. Even that much had given her strength, but it was nowhere near enough for him. She could see in his flayed face now his savage resentment of their curiosity, even of her pity.

"Go lie down, that gash is bleeding again," she said, and he obeyed her.

Next morning they packed up, melted down the sprayform hangar and living quarters, lifted *Gum* on mechanical drive and took her halfway round World 4470, over the red and green lands, the many warm green seas. They had picked out a likely spot on Continent G: a prairie, twenty thousand square kilos of windswept graminiformes. No forest was within a hundred kilos of the site, and there were no lone trees or groves on the plain. The plant-forms occurred only in large species-colonies, never intermingled, except for certain tiny ubiquitous saprophytes and spore-bearers. The team sprayed holomeld over structure forms, and by evening of the thirty-two-hour day were settled in to the new camp. Eskwana was still asleep and Porlock still sedated, but everyone else was cheerful. "You can breathe here!" they kept saying.

Osden got on his feet and went shakily to the doorway; leaning there he looked through twilight over the dim reaches of the swaying grass that was not grass. There was a faint, sweet odor of pollen on the wind; no sound but the soft, vast sibilance of wind. His bandaged head cocked a little, the empath stood motionless for a long time. Darkness came, and the stars, lights in the windows of the distant house of Man. The wind had ceased, there was no sound. He listened.

In the long night Haito Tomiko listened. She lay still and heard the blood in her arteries, the breathing of sleepers, the wind blowing, the dark veins running, the dreams advancing, the vast static of stars increasing as the universe died slowly, the sound of death walking. She struggled out of her bed, fled the tiny solitude of her cubicle. Eskwana alone slept. Porlock lay straitjacketed, raving softly in his obscure native tongue. Olleroo and Jenny Chong were playing cards, grim-faced. Poswet To was in the therapy niche, plugged in. Asnanifoil was drawing a mandala, the Third Pattern of the Primes. Mannon and Harfex were sitting up with Osden.

She changed the bandages on Osden's head. His lank, reddish hair, where she had not had to shave it, looked strange. It was salted with white, now. Her hands shook as she worked. Nobody had yet said anything.

"How can the fear be here too?" she said, and her voice rang flat and false in the terrific silence.

"It's not just the trees; the grasses too . . ."

"But we're twelve thousand kilos from where we were this morning, we left it on the other side of the planet."

"It's all one," Osden said. "One big green thought. How long does it take a thought to act from one side of your brain to the other?"

"It doesn't think. It isn't thinking," Harfex said, lifelessly. "It's merely a network of processes. The branches, the epiphytic growths, the roots with those nodal junctures between individuals: they must all be capable of transmitting electrochemical impulses. There are no individual plants, then, properly speaking. Even the pollen is part of the linkage, no doubt, a sort of windborne sentience, connecting overseas. But it is not conceivable. That all the biosphere of a planet should be one network of communications, sensitive, irrational, immortal, isolated. . . ."

"Isolated," said Osden. "That's it! That's the fear. It isn't that we're motile, or destructive. It's just that we are. We are other. There has never been any other."

"You're right," Mannon said, almost whispering. "It has no peers. No enemies. No relationship with anything but itself. One alone forever."

"Then what's the function of its intelligence in species-survival?"

"None, maybe," Osden said. "Why are you getting teleological, Harfex? Aren't you a Hainishman? Isn't the measure of complexity the measure of the eternal joy?"

Harfex did not take the bait. He looked ill. "We should leave this world," he said.

"Now you know why I always want to get out, get away from you," Osden said with a kind of morbid geniality. "It isn't pleasant, is it—the other's fear . . . ? If only it were an animal intelligence. I can get through to animals. I get along with cobras and tigers; superior intelligence gives one the advantage. I should have been used in a zoo, not on a human team. . . . If I could get through to the damned stupid potato! If it wasn't so overwhelming . . . I still pick up more than the fear, you know. And before it panicked it had a—there was a serenity. I couldn't take it in, then, I didn't realize how big it was. To know the whole daylight, after all, the whole night. All the winds and lulls together. The winter stars and the summer stars at the same time. To have roots, and no enemies. To be entire. Do you see? No invasion. No others. To be whole . . ."

He had never spoken before, Tomiko thought.

"You are defenseless against it, Osden," she said. "Your personality has changed already. You're vulnerable to it. We may not all go mad, but you will, if we don't leave."

He hesitated, then he looked up at Tomiko, the first time he had ever met her eyes, a long, still look, clear as water.

"What's sanity ever done for me?" he said, mocking. "But you have a point, Haito. You have something there."

"We should get away," Harfex muttered.

"If I gave in to it," Osden mused, "could I communicate?"

"By 'give in,'" Mannon said in a rapid, nervous voice, "I assume that you mean, stop sending back the empathic information which you receive from the plant-entity: stop rejecting the fear, and absorb it. That will either kill you at once, or drive you back into total psychological withdrawal, autism."

"Why?" said Osden. "Its message is *rejection*. But my salvation is rejection. It's not intelligent. But I am."

"The scale is wrong. What can a single human brain achieve against something so vast?"

"A single human brain can perceive pattern on the scale of stars and galaxies," Tomiko said, "and interpret it as Love."

Mannon looked from one to the other of them; Harfex was silent.

"It'd be easier in the forest," Osden said. "Which of you will fly me over?"

"When?"

"Now. Before you all crack up or go violent."

"I will," Tomiko said.

"None of us will," Harfex said.

"I can't," Mannon said. "I . . . I am too frightened. I'd crash the jet."

"Bring Eskwana along. If I can pull this off, he might serve as a medium."

"Are you accepting the Sensor's plan, Coordinator?" Harfex asked formally.

"Yes."

"I disapprove. I will come with you, however."

"I think we're compelled, Harfex," Tomiko said, looking at Osden's face, the ugly white mask transfigured, eager as a lover's face.

Olleroo and Jenny Chong, playing cards to keep their thoughts from their haunted beds, their mounting dread, chattered like scared children. "This thing, it's in the forest, it'll get you—"

"Scared of the dark?" Osden jeered.

"But look at Eskwana, and Porlock, and even Asnanifoil—"

"It can't hurt you. It's an impulse passing through synapses, a wind passing through branches. It is only a nightmare."

They took off in a helijet, Eskwana curled up still sound asleep in the rear compartment, Tomiko piloting, Harfex and Osden silent, watching ahead for the dark line of forest across the vague grey miles of starlit plain.

They neared the black line, crossed it; now under them was darkness.

She sought a landing place, flying low, though she had to fight her frantic wish to fly high, to get out, get away. The huge vitality of the plant-world was far stronger here in the forest, and its panic beat in immense dark waves. There was a pale patch ahead, a bare knoll-top a little higher than the tallest of the black shapes around it; the not-trees; the rooted; the parts of the whole. She set the helijet down in the glade, a bad landing. Her hands on the stick were slippery, as if she had rubbed them with cold soap.

About them now stood the forest, black in darkness.

Tomiko cowered and shut her eyes. Eskwana moaned in his sleep. Harfex's breath came short and loud, and he sat rigid, even when Osden reached across him and slid the door open.

Osden stood up; his back and bandaged head were just visible in the dim glow of the control panel as he paused stooping in the doorway.

Tomiko was shaking. She could not raise her head. "No, no, no, no, no, no, no," she said in a whisper. "No. No. No."

Osden moved suddenly and quietly, swinging out of the doorway, down into the dark. He was gone.

I am coming! said a great voice that made no sound.

Tomiko screamed. Harfex coughed; he seemed to be trying to stand up, but did not do so.

Tomiko drew in upon herself, all centered in the blind eye in her belly, in the center of her being; and outside that there was nothing but the fear.

It ceased.

She raised her head; slowly unclenched her hands. She sat up straight. The night was dark, and stars shone over the forest. There was nothing else.

"Osden," she said, but her voice would not come. She spoke again, louder, a lone bullfrog croak. There was no reply.

She began to realize that something had gone wrong with Harfex. She was trying to find his head in the darkness, for he had slipped down from the seat, when all at once, in the dead quiet, in the dark rear compartment of the craft, a voice spoke. "Good," it said.

It was Eskwana's voice. She snapped on the interior lights and saw the engineer lying curled up asleep, his hand half over his mouth.

The mouth opened and spoke. "All well," it said.

"Osden—"

"All well," said the soft voice from Eskwana's mouth.

"Where are you?"

Silence.

"Come back."

A wind was rising. "I'll stay here," the soft voice said.

"You can't stay—"

Silence.

"You'd be alone, Osden!"

"Listen." The voice was fainter, slurred, as if lost in the sound of wind. "Listen. I will you well."

She called his name after that, but there was no answer. Eskwana lay still. Harfex lay stiller.

"Osden!" she cried, leaning out the doorway into the dark, wind-shaken silence of the forest of being. "I will come back. I must get Harfex to the base. I will come back, Osden!"

Silence and wind in leaves.

They finished the prescribed survey of World 4470, the eight of them; it took them forty-one days more. Asnanifoil and one or another of the women went into the forest daily at first, searching for Osden in the region around the bare knoll, though Tomiko was not in her heart sure which bare knoll they had landed on that night in the very heart and vortex of terror. They left piles of supplies for Osden, food enough for fifty years, clothing, tents, tools. They did not go on searching; there was no way to find a man alone, hiding, if he wanted to hide, in those unending labyrinths and dim corridors vine-entangled, root-floored. They might have passed within arm's reach of him and never seen him.

But he was there; for there was no fear any more.

Rational, and valuing reason more highly after an intolerable experience of the immortal mindless, Tomiko tried to understand rationally what Osden had done. But the words escaped her control. He had taken the fear into himself, and, accepting, had transcended it. He had given up his self to the alien, an unreserved surrender, that left no place for evil. He had learned the love of the Other, and thereby had been given his whole self. —But this is not the vocabulary of reason.

The people of the Survey team walked under the trees, through the vast colonies of life, surrounded by a dreaming silence, a brooding calm that was half aware of them and wholly indifferent to them. There were no hours. Distance was no matter. Had we but world enough and time . . . The planet turned between the sunlight and the great dark; winds of winter and summer blew fine, pale pollen across the quiet seas.

Gum returned after many surveys, years, and lightyears, to what had several centuries ago been Smeming Port. There were still men there, to receive (incredulously) the team's reports, and to record its losses: Biologist Harfex, dead of fear, and Sensor Osden, left as a colonist.

—1971

WILLIAM GIBSON

B. 1948

William Gibson was born in Conway, South Carolina, to William Ford Gibson, a contractor, and Otey (Williams) Gibson. He moved to Canada in 1968, and to Vancouver in 1972, the year he married Deborah Thompson, a language teacher. He attended the University of British Columbia, graduating with a B.A. in 1977. During this period, Gibson also sold his first science fiction story, "Fragments of a Hologram Rose," to Unearth. *After publishing a number of short stories in the early 1980s—garnering a Nebula Award nomination in 1983 for his tale, "Burning Chrome"—he released his first novel,* Neuromancer, *in 1984 to great critical acclaim, winning the Nebula and Hugo Awards for best novel, as well as the Philip K. Dick Award for best U.S. original paperback.* Neuromancer *is the first in the Cyberspace trilogy, which includes* Count Zero *(1986) and* Mona Lisa Overdrive *(1988). With Bruce Sterling, Gibson also wrote a novel entitled* The Difference Engine *(1990).*

Gibson is one of the major innovators of "cyberpunk," a science fiction movement which evolved during the 1980s. Cyberpunk depicts a high-tech near future (literally, the day-after-tomorrow) and features characters who are outsiders, lowlifes, or anti-heroes. Cyberpunk generally envisions a globalized, dystopian world, but a dystopia that sees both wonder and horror in our rapidly-evolving technology. In the short story collection, Mirrorshades: The Cyberpunk Anthology *(1986), Bruce Sterling defines the term: "Cyberpunk comes from the realm where the computer hacker and the rocker overlap . . . technology is visceral. It is not the bottled genie of remote Big Science boffins; it is pervasive, utterly intimate. Not outside us, but next to us. Under our skin; often, inside our minds."*

For authors of cyberpunk fiction, such as Gibson, technology is realistically portrayed and entirely within the probability of existence. Cyberpunk high-tech is often shown to be personalized, biologically invasive, and dehumanizing. In Gibson's "Johnny Mnemonic," for example, the information-smuggler protagonist of the story has no identity of his own. He exists only to provide a service for others, to house and transport other people's information, knowledge of which he is totally ignorant. He is merely a walking computer storage system possessing no sense of self. Even his very name, "Johnny," indicates a lack of individuality. Johnny's quest for his own identity results in his transformation from a high-tech information courier to a "Lo Tek" rebel. First published in the May 1981 issue of Omni*—and later anthologized in Gibson's 1986 short story collection* Burning Chrome*— "Johnny Mnemonic" is indeed populated by a bizarre assortment of supporting characters, misfits and outsiders who either succumb to the power of technology or who resist it. In both cases, humanity is redefined by Gibson in a way that is utterly alien, yet entirely recognizable. "Johnny Mnemonic" was made into a film in 1995, starring Keanu Reeves.*

JOHNNY MNEMONIC

I put the shotgun in an Adidas bag and padded it out with four pairs of tennis socks, not my style at all, but that was what I was aiming for: If they think you're crude, go technical; if they think you're technical, go crude. I'm a very technical boy. So I decided to get as crude as possible. These days, though, you have to be pretty technical before you can even aspire to crudeness. I'd had to turn both these twelve-gauge shells from brass stock, on a lathe, and then load them myself; I'd had to dig up an old microfiche with instructions for hand-loading cartridges; I'd had to build a lever-action press to seat the primers—all very tricky. But I knew they'd work.

The meet was set for the Drome at 2300, but I rode the tube three stops past the closest platform and walked back. Immaculate procedure.

I checked myself out in the chrome siding of a coffee kiosk, your basic sharp-faced Caucasoid with a ruff of stiff, dark hair. The girls at Under the Knife were big on Sony Mao, and it was getting harder to keep them from adding the chic suggestion of epicanthic folds. It probably wouldn't fool Ralfi Face, but it might get me next to his table.

The Drome is a single narrow space with a bar down one side and tables along the other, thick with pimps and handlers and an arcane array of dealers. The Magnetic Dog Sisters were on the door that night, and I didn't relish trying to get out past them if things didn't work out. They were two meters tall and thin as grey-hounds. One was black and the other white, but aside from that they were as nearly identical as cosmetic surgery could make them. They'd been lovers for years and were bad news in a tussle. I was never quite sure which one had originally been male.

Ralfi was sitting at his usual table. Owing me a lot of money. I had hundreds of megabytes stashed in my head on an idiot/savant basis, information I had no conscious access to. Ralfi had left it there. He hadn't, however, come back for it. Only Ralfi could retrieve the data, with a code phrase of his own invention. I'm not cheap to begin with, but my overtime on storage is astronomical. And Ralfi had been very scarce.

Then I'd heard that Ralfi Face wanted to put out a contract on me. So I'd arranged to meet him in the Drome, but I'd arranged it as Edward Bax, clandestine importer, late of Rio and Peking.

The Drome stank of biz, a metallic tang of nervous tension. Muscle-boys scattered through the crowd were flexing stock parts at one another and trying on thin, cold grins, some of them so lost under superstructures of muscle graft that their outlines weren't really human.

Pardon me. Pardon me, friends. Just Eddie Bax here, Fast Eddie the Importer, with his professionally nondescript gym bag, and please ignore this slit, just wide enough to admit his right hand.

Ralfi wasn't alone. Eighty kilos of blond California beef perched alertly in the chair next to his, martial arts written all over him.

Fast Eddie Bax was in the chair opposite them before the beef's hands were off the table. "You black belt?" I asked eagerly. He nodded, blue eyes running an automatic scanning pattern between my eyes and my hands. "Me, too," I said. "Got mine here in the bag." And I shoved my hand through the slit and thumbed the safety off. Click. "Double twelve-gauge with the triggers wired together."

"That's a gun," Ralfi said, putting a plump, restraining hand on his boy's taut blue nylon chest. "Johnny has an antique firearm in his bag." So much for Edward Bax.

I guess he'd always been Ralfi Something or Other, but he owed his acquired surname to a singular vanity. Built something like an overripe pear, he'd worn the once-famous face of Christian White for twenty years—Christian White of the Aryan Reggae Band, Sony Mao to his generation, and final champion of race rock. I'm a whiz at trivia.

Christian White: classic pop face with a singer's high-definition muscles, chiseled cheekbones. Angelic in one light, handsomely depraved in another. But Ralfi's eyes lived behind that face, and they were small and cold and black.

"Please," he said, "let's work this out like businessmen." His voice was marked by a horrible prehensile sincerity, and the corners of his beautiful Christian White mouth were always wet. "Lewis here," nodding in the beefboy's direction, "is a meatball." Lewis took this impassively, looking like something built from a kit. "You aren't a meatball, Johnny."

"Sure I am, Ralfi, a nice meatball chock-full of implants where you can store your dirty laundry while you go off shopping for people to kill me. From my end of this bag, Ralfi, it looks like you've got some explaining to do."

"It's this last batch of product, Johnny." He sighed deeply. "In my role as broker—"

"Fence," I corrected.

"As broker, I'm usually very careful as to sources."

"You buy only from those who steal the best. Got it."

He sighed again. "I try," he said wearily, "not to buy from fools. This time, I'm afraid, I've done that." Third sigh was the cue for Lewis to trigger the neural disruptor they'd taped under my side of the table.

I put everything I had into curling the index finger of my right hand, but I no longer seemed to be connected to it. I could feel the metal of the gun and the foam-pad tape I'd wrapped around the stubby grip, but my hands were cool wax, distant and inert. I was hoping Lewis was a true meatball, thick enough to go for the gym bag and snag my rigid trigger finger, but he wasn't.

"We've been very worried about you, Johnny. Very worried. You see, that's Yakuza property you have there. A fool took it from them, Johnny. A dead fool."

Lewis giggled.

It all made sense then, an ugly kind of sense, like bags of wet sand settling around my head. Killing wasn't Ralfi's style. Lewis wasn't even Ralfi's style. But he'd got himself stuck between the Sons of the Neon Chrysanthemum and something that belonged to them—or, more likely, something of theirs that belonged to someone else. Ralfi, of course, could use the code phrase to throw me into idiot/savant, and I'd spill their hot program without remembering a single quarter tone. For a fence like Ralfi, that would ordinarily have been enough. But not for the Yakuza. The Yakuza would know about Squids, for one thing, and they wouldn't want to worry about one lifting those dim and permanent traces of their program out of my head. I didn't know very much about Squids, but I'd heard stories, and I made it a point never to repeat them to my clients. No, the Yakuza wouldn't like that; it looked too much like evidence. They hadn't got where they were by leaving evidence around. Or alive.

Lewis was grinning. I think he was visualizing a point just behind my forehead and imagining how he could get there the hard way.

"Hey," said a low voice, feminine, from somewhere behind my right shoulder, "you cowboys sure aren't having too lively a time."

"Pack it, bitch," Lewis said, his tanned face very still. Ralfi looked blank.

"Lighten up. You want to buy some good free base?" She pulled up a chair and quickly sat before either of them could stop her. She was barely inside my fixed field of vision, a thin girl with mirrored glasses, her dark hair cut in a rough shag. She wore black leather, open over a T-shirt slashed diagonally with stripes of red and black. "Eight thou a gram weight."

Lewis snorted his exasperation and tried to slap her out of the chair. Somehow he didn't quite connect, and her hand came up and seemed to brush his wrist as it passed. Bright blood sprayed the table. He was clutching his wrist white-knuckle tight, blood trickling from between his fingers.

But hadn't her hand been empty?

He was going to need a tendon stapler. He stood up carefully, without bothering to push his chair back. The chair toppled backward, and he stepped out of my line of sight without a word.

"He better get a medic to look at that," she said. "That's a nasty cut."

"You have no idea," said Ralfi, suddenly sounding very tired, "the depths of shit you have just gotten yourself into."

"No kidding? Mystery. I get real excited by mysteries. Like why your friend here's so quiet. Frozen, like. Or what this thing here is for," and she held up the little control unit that she'd somehow taken from Lewis. Ralfi looked ill.

"You, ah, want maybe a quarter-million to give me that and take a walk?" A fat hand came up to stroke his pale, lean face nervously.

"What I want," she said, snapping her fingers so that the unit spun and glittered, "is work. A job. Your boy hurt his wrist. But a quarter'll do for a retainer."

Ralfi let his breath out explosively and began to laugh, exposing teeth that hadn't been kept up to the Christian White standard. Then she turned the disruptor off.

"Two million," I said.

"My kind of man," she said, and laughed. "What's in the bag?"

"A shotgun."

"Crude." It might have been a compliment.

Ralfi said nothing at all.

"Name's Millions. Molly Millions. You want to get out of here, boss? People are starting to stare." She stood up. She was wearing leather jeans the color of dried blood.

And I saw for the first time that the mirrored lenses were surgical inlays, the silver rising smoothly from her high cheekbones, sealing her eyes in their sockets. I saw my new face twinned there.

"I'm Johnny," I said. "We're taking Mr. Face with us."

He was outside, waiting. Looking like your standard tourist tech, in plastic zoris and a silly Hawaiian shirt printed with blowups of his firm's most popular microprocessor; a mild little guy, the kind most likely to wind up drunk on sake in a bar that puts out miniature rice crackers with seaweed garnish. He looked like the kind who sing the corporate anthem and cry, who shake hands endlessly with the bartender. And the pimps and the dealers would leave him alone, pegging him as innately conservative. Not up for much, and careful with his credit when he was.

The way I figured it later, they must have amputated part of his left thumb, somewhere behind the first joint, replacing it with a prosthetic tip, and cored the stump, fitting it with a spool and socket molded from one of the Ono-Sendai diamond analogs. Then they'd carefully wound the spool with three meters of monomolecular filament.

Molly got into some kind of exchange with the Magnetic Dog Sisters, giving me a chance to usher Ralfi through the door with the gym bag pressed lightly against the base of his spine. She seemed to know them. I heard the black one laugh.

I glanced up, out of some passing reflex, maybe because I've never got used to it, to the soaring arcs of light and the shadows of the geodesics above them. Maybe that saved me.

Ralfi kept walking, but I don't think he was trying to escape. I think he'd already given up. Probably he already had an idea of what we were up against.

I looked back down in time to see him explode.

Playback on full recall shows Ralfi stepping forward as the little tech sidles out of nowhere, smiling. Just a suggestion of a bow, and his left thumb falls off. It's a conjuring trick. The thumb hangs suspended. Mirrors? Wires? And Ralfi stops, his back to us, dark crescents of sweat under the armpits of his pale summer suit. He knows. He must have known. And then the joke-shop thumbtip, heavy as lead, arcs out in a lightning yo-yo trick, and the invisible thread connecting it to the killer's hand passes laterally through Ralfi's skull, just above his eyebrows, whips up, and descends, slicing the pear-shaped torso diagonally from shoulder to rib cage. Cuts so fine that no blood flows until synapses misfire and the first tremors surrender the body to gravity.

Ralfi tumbled apart in a pink cloud of fluids, the three mismatched sections rolling forward onto the tiled pavement. In total silence.

I brought the gym bag up, and my hand convulsed. The recoil nearly broke my wrist.

It must have been raining; ribbons of water cascaded from a ruptured geodesic and spattered on the tile behind us. We crouched in the narrow gap between a surgical boutique and an antique shop. She'd just edged one mirrored eye around the corner to report a single Volks module in front of the Drome, red lights flashing. They were sweeping Ralfi up. Asking questions.

I was covered in scorched white fluff. The tennis socks. The gym bag was a ragged plastic cuff around my wrist. "I don't see how the hell I missed him."

"'Cause he's fast, so fast." She hugged her knees and rocked back and forth on her bootheels. "His nervous system's jacked up. He's factory custom." She grinned and gave a little squeal of delight. "I'm gonna get that boy. Tonight. He's the best, number one, top dollar, state of the art."

"What you're going to get, for this boy's two million, is my ass out of here. Your boyfriend back there was mostly grown in a vat in Chiba City. He's a Yakuza assassin."

"Chiba. Yeah. See, Molly's been Chiba, too." And she showed me her hands, fingers slightly spread. Her fingers were slender, tapered, very white against the polished burgundy nails. Ten blades snicked straight out from their recesses beneath her nails, each one a narrow, double-edged scalpel in pale blue steel.

I'd never spent much time in Nighttown. Nobody there had anything to pay me to remember, and most of them had a lot they paid regularly to forget. Generations of sharpshooters had chipped away at the neon until the maintenance crews gave up. Even at noon the arcs were soot-black against faintest pearl.

Where do you go when the world's wealthiest criminal order is feeling for you with calm, distant fingers? Where do you hide from the Yakuza, so powerful that it owns comsats and at least three shuttles? The Yakuza is a true multinational, like ITT and Ono-Sendai. Fifty years before I was born the Yakuza had already absorbed the Triads, the Mafia, the Union Corse.

Molly had an answer: you hide in the Pit, in the lowest circle, where any outside influence generates swift, concentric ripples of raw menace. You hide in Nighttown. Better yet, you hide *above* Nighttown, because the Pit's inverted, and the bottom of its bowl touches the sky, the sky that Nighttown never sees, sweating under its own firmament of acrylic resin, up where the Lo Teks crouch in the dark like gargoyles, black-market cigarettes dangling from their lips.

She had another answer, too.

"So you're locked up good and tight, Johnny-san? No way to get that program without the password?" She led me into the shadows that waited beyond the bright tube platform. The concrete walls were overlaid with graffiti, years of them twisting into a single metascrawl of rage and frustration.

"The stored data are fed in through a modified series of microsurgical contraautism prostheses." I reeled off a numb version of my standard sales pitch. "Client's code is stored in a special chip; barring Squids, which we in the trade don't like to talk about, there's no way to recover your phrase. Can't drug it out, cut it out, torture it. I don't *know* it, never did."

"Squids? Crawly things with arms?" We emerged into a deserted street market. Shadowy figures watched us from across a makeshift square littered with fish heads and rotting fruit.

"Superconducting quantum interference detectors. Used them in the war to find submarines, suss out enemy cyber systems."

"Yeah? Navy stuff? From the war? Squid'll read that chip of yours?" She'd stopped walking, and I felt her eyes on me behind those twin mirrors.

"Even the primitive models could measure a magnetic field a billionth the strength of geomagnetic force; it's like pulling a whisper out of a cheering stadium."

"Cops can do that already, with parabolic microphones and lasers."

"But your data's still secure." Pride in profession. "No government'll let their cops have Squids, not even the security heavies. Too much chance of interdepartmental funnies; they're too likely to watergate you."

"Navy stuff," she said, and her grin gleamed in the shadows. "Navy stuff. I got a friend down here who was in the navy, name's Jones. I think you'd better meet him. He's a junkie, though. So we'll have to take him something."

"A junkie?"

"A dolphin."

He was more than a dolphin, but from another dolphin's point of view he might have seemed like something less. I watched him swirling sluggishly in his galvanized tank. Water slopped over the side, wetting my shoes. He was surplus from the last war. A cyborg.

He rose out of the water, showing us the crusted plates along his sides, a kind of visual pun, his grace nearly lost under articulated armor, clumsy and prehistoric. Twin deformities on either side of his skull had been engineered to house sensor units. Silver lesions gleamed on exposed sections of his gray-white hide.

Molly whistled. Jones thrashed his tail, and more water cascaded down the side of the tank.

"What is this place?" I peered at vague shapes in the dark, rusting chain link and things under tarps. Above the tank hung a clumsy wooden framework, crossed and recrossed by rows of dusty Christmas lights.

"Funland. Zoo and carnival rides. 'Talk with the War Whale.' All that. Some whale Jones is. . . ."

Jones reared again and fixed me with a sad and ancient eye.

"How's he talk?" Suddenly I was anxious to go.

"That's the catch. Say 'hi,' Jones."

And all the bulbs lit simultaneously. They were flashing red, white, and blue.

```
RWBRWBRWB
RWBRWBRWB
RWBRWBRWB
RWBRWBRWB
RWBRWBRWB
```

"Good with symbols, see, but the code's restricted. In the navy they had him wired into an audiovisual display." She drew the narrow package from a jacket pocket. "Pure shit, Jones. Want it?" He froze in the water and started to sink. I felt a strange panic, remembering that he wasn't a fish, that he could drown. "We want the key to Johnny's bank, Jones. We want it fast. "

The lights flickered, died.

"Go for it, Jones!"

```
        B
BBBBBBBBB
        B
        B
        B
```

Blue bulbs, cruciform.

Darkness.

"Pure! It's *clean.* Come on, Jones."

```
WWWWWWWWW
WWWWWWWWW
WWWWWWWWW
WWWWWWWWW
WWWWWWWWW
```

White sodium glare washed her features, stark monochrome, shadows cleaving from her cheekbones.

```
R    RRRRR
R    R
RRRRRRRRR
        R    R
RRRRR    R
```

The arms of the red swastika were twisted in her silver glasses. "Give it to him," I said. "We've got it."

Ralfi Face. No imagination.

Jones heaved half his armored bulk over the edge of his tank, and I thought the metal would give way. Molly stabbed him overhand with the Syrette, driving the needle between two plates. Propellant hissed. Patterns of light exploded, spasming across the frame and then fading to black.

We left him drifting, rolling languorously in the dark water. Maybe he was dreaming of his war in the Pacific, of the cyber mines he'd swept, nosing gently into their circuitry with the Squid he'd used to pick Ralfi's pathetic password from the chip buried in my head.

"I can see them slipping up when he was demobbed, letting him out of the navy with that gear intact, but how does a cybernetic dolphin get wired to smack?"

"The war," she said. "They all were. Navy did it. How else you get 'em working for you?"

"I'm not sure this profiles as good business," the pirate said, angling for better money. "Target specs on a comsat that isn't in the book—"

"Waste my time and you won't profile at all," said Molly, leaning across his scarred plastic desk to prod him with her forefinger.

"So maybe you want to buy your microwaves somewhere else?" He was a tough kid, behind his Maojob. A Nighttowner by birth, probably.

Her hand blurred down the front of his jacket, completely severing a lapel without even rumpling the fabric.

"So we got a deal or not?"

"Deal," he said, staring at his ruined lapel with what he must have hoped was only polite interest. "Deal."

While I checked the two recorders we'd bought, she extracted the slip of paper I'd given her from the zippered wrist pocket of her jacket. She unfolded it and read silently, moving her lips. She shrugged. "This is it?"

"Shoot," I said, punching the RECORD studs of the two decks simultaneously.

"Christian White," she recited, "and his Aryan Reggae Band."

Faithful Ralfi, a fan to his dying day.

Transition to idiot/savant mode is always less abrupt than I expect it to be. The pirate broadcaster's front was a failing travel agency in a pastel cube that boasted a desk, three chairs, and a faded poster of a Swiss orbital spa. A pair of toy birds with blown-glass bodies and tin legs were sipping monotonously from a Styrofoam cup of water on a ledge beside Molly's shoulder. As I phased into mode, they accelerated gradually until their Day-Glo-feathered crowns became solid arcs of color. The LEDS that told seconds on the plastic wall clock had become meaningless pulsing grids, and Molly and the Mao-faced boy grew hazy, their arms blurring occasionally in insect-quick ghosts of gesture. And then it all faded to cool gray static and an endless tone poem in an artificial language.

I sat and sang dead Ralfi's stolen program for three hours.

The mall runs forty kilometers from end to end, a ragged overlap of Fuller domes roofing what was once a suburban artery. If they turn off the arcs on a clear day, a gray approximation of sunlight filters through layers of acrylic, a view like the prison sketches of Giovanni Piranesi. The three southernmost kilometers roof Nighttown. Nighttown pays no taxes, no utilities. The neon arcs are dead, and the geodesics have been smoked black by decades of cooking fires. In the nearly total darkness of a Nighttown noon, who notices a few dozen mad children lost in the rafters?

We'd been climbing for two hours, up concrete stairs and steel ladders with perforated rungs, past abandoned gantries and dust-covered tools. We'd started in what looked like a disused maintenance yard, stacked with triangular roofing segments. Everything there had been covered with that same uniform layer of spray-bomb graffiti: gang names, initials, dates back to the turn of the century. The graffiti followed us up, gradually thinning until a single name was repeated at intervals. LO TEK. In dripping black capitals.

"Who's Lo Tek?"

"Not us, boss." She climbed a shivering aluminum ladder and vanished through a hole in a sheet of corrugated plastic. "'Low technique, low technology.'" The plastic muffled her voice. I followed her up, nursing my aching wrist. "Lo Teks, they'd think that shotgun trick of yours was effete."

An hour later I dragged myself up through another hole, this one sawed crookedly in a sagging sheet of plywood, and met my first Lo Tek.

"'S okay," Molly said, her hand brushing my shoulder. "It's just Dog. Hey, Dog."

In the narrow beam of her taped flash, he regarded us with his one eye and slowly extruded a thick length of grayish tongue, licking huge canines. I wondered how they wrote off tooth-bud transplants from Dobermans as low technology. Immunosuppressives don't exactly grow on trees.

"Moll." Dental augmentation impeded his speech. A string of saliva dangled from his twisted lower lip. "Heard ya comin'. Long time." He might have been fifteen, but the fangs and a bright mosaic of scars combined with the gaping socket to present a mask of total bestiality. It had taken time and a certain kind of creativity to assemble that face, and his posture told me he enjoyed living behind it. He wore a pair of decaying jeans, black with grime and shiny along the creases. His chest and feet were bare. He did something with his mouth that approximated a grin. "Bein' followed, you."

Far off, down in Nighttown, a water vendor cried his trade.

"Strings jumping, Dog?" She swung her flash to the side, and I saw thin cords tied to eyebolts, cords that ran to the edge and vanished.

"Kill the fuckin' light!"

She snapped it off.

"How come the one who's followin' you's got no light?"

"Doesn't need it. That one's bad news, Dog. Your sentries give him a tumble, they'll come home in easy-to-carry sections."

"This a *friend* friend, Moll?" He sounded uneasy. I heard his feet shift on the worn plywood.

"No. But he's mine. And this one," slapping my shoulder, "he's a friend. Got that?"

"Sure," he said, without much enthusiasm, padding to the platform's edge, where the eyebolts were. He began to pluck out some kind of message on the taut cords.

Nighttown spread beneath us like a toy village for rats; tiny windows showed candlelight, with only a few harsh, bright squares lit by battery lanterns and carbide lamps. I imagined the old men at their endless games of dominoes, under warm, fat drops of water that fell from wet wash hung out on poles between the plywood shanties. Then I tried to imagine him climbing patiently up through the darkness in his zoris and ugly tourist shirt, bland and unhurried. How was he tracking us?

"Good," said Molly. "He smells us."

"Smoke?" Dog dragged a crumpled pack from his pocket and prized out a flattened cigarette. I squinted at the trademark while he lit it for me with a kitchen match. Yiheyuan filters. Beijing Cigarette Factory. I decided that the Lo Teks were black marketeers. Dog and Molly went back to their argument, which seemed to revolve around Molly's desire to use some particular piece of Lo Tek real estate.

"I've done you a lot of favors, man. I want that floor. And I want the music."

"You're not Lo Tek. . . ."

This must have been going on for the better part of a twisted kilometer, Dog leading us along swaying catwalks and up rope ladders. The Lo Teks leech their webs and huddling places to the city's fabric with thick gobs of epoxy and sleep above the abyss in mesh hammocks. Their country is so attenuated that in places it consists of little more than holds for hands and feet, sawed into geodesic struts.

The Killing Floor, she called it. Scrambling after her, my new Eddie Bax shoes slipping on worn metal and damp plywood, I wondered how it could be any more lethal than the rest of the territory. At the same time I sensed that Dog's protests were ritual and that she already expected to get whatever it was she wanted.

Somewhere beneath us, Jones would be circling his tank, feeling the first twinges of junk sickness. The police would be boring the Drome regulars with questions about Ralfi. What did he do? Who was he with before he stepped outside? And the Yakuza would be settling its ghostly bulk over the city's data banks, probing for faint images of me reflected in numbered accounts, securities transactions, bills for utilities. We're an information economy. They teach you that in school. What they don't tell you is that it's impossible to move, to live, to operate at any level without leaving traces, bits, seemingly meaningless fragments of personal information. Fragments that can be retrieved, amplified . . .

But by now the pirate would have shuttled our message into line for blackbox transmission to the Yakuza comsat. A simple message: Call off the dogs or we wideband your program.

The program. I had no idea what it contained. I still don't. I only sing the song, with zero comprehension. It was probably research data, the Yakuza being given to advanced forms of industrial espionage. A genteel business, stealing from Ono-

Sendai as a matter of course and politely holding their data for ransom, threatening to blunt the conglomerate's research edge by making the product public.

But why couldn't any number play? Wouldn't they be happier with something to sell back to Ono-Sendai, happier than they'd be with one dead Johnny from Memory Lane?

Their program was on its way to an address in Sydney, to a place that held letters for clients and didn't ask questions once you'd paid a small retainer. Fourth-class surface mail. I'd erased most of the other copy and recorded our message in the resulting gap, leaving just enough of the program to identify it as the real thing.

My wrist hurt. I wanted to stop, to lie down, to sleep. I knew that I'd lose my grip and fall soon, knew that the sharp black shoes I'd bought for my evening as Eddie Bax would lose their purchase and carry me down to Nighttown. But he rose in my mind like a cheap religious hologram, glowing, the enlarged chip on his Hawaiian shirt looming like a reconnaissance shot of some doomed urban nucleus.

So I followed Dog and Molly through Lo Tek heaven, jury-rigged and jerry-built from scraps that even Nighttown didn't want.

The Killing Floor was eight meters on a side. A giant had threaded steel cable back and forth through a junkyard and drawn it all taut. It creaked when it moved, and it moved constantly, swaying and bucking as the gathering Lo Teks arranged themselves on the shelf of plywood surrounding it. The wood was silver with age, polished with long use and deeply etched with initials, threats, declarations of passion. This was suspended from a separate set of cables, which lost themselves in darkness beyond the raw white glare of the two ancient floods suspended above the Floor.

A girl with teeth like Dog's hit the Floor on all fours. Her breasts were tattooed with indigo spirals. Then she was across the Floor, laughing, grappling with a boy who was drinking dark liquid from a liter flask.

Lo Tek fashion ran to scars and tattoos. And teeth. The electricity they were tapping to light the Killing Floor seemed to be an exception to their overall aesthetic, made in the name of . . . ritual, sport, art? I didn't know, but I could see that the Floor was something special. It had the look of having been assembled over generations.

I held the useless shotgun under my jacket. Its hardness and heft were comforting, even though I had no more shells. And it came to me that I had no idea at all of what was really happening, or of what was supposed to happen. And that was the nature of my game, because I'd spent most of my life as a blind receptacle to be filled with other people's knowledge and then drained, spouting synthetic languages I'd never understand. A very technical boy. Sure.

And then I noticed just how quiet the Lo Teks had become.

He was there, at the edge of the light, taking in the Killing Floor and the gallery of silent Lo Teks with a tourist's calm. And as our eyes met for the first time with mutual recognition, a memory clicked into place for me, of Paris, and the long Mercedes electrics gliding through the rain to Notre Dame; mobile greenhouses, Japanese faces behind the glass, and a hundred Nikons rising in blind phototropism, flowers of steel and crystal. Behind his eyes, as they found me, those same shutters whirring.

I looked for Molly Millions, but she was gone.

The Lo Teks parted to let him step up onto the bench. He bowed, smiling, and stepped smoothly out of his sandals, leaving them side by side, perfectly aligned, and then he stepped down onto the Killing Floor. He came for me, across that shifting trampoline of scrap, as easily as any tourist padding across synthetic pile in any featureless hotel.

Molly hit the Floor, moving.

The Floor screamed.

It was miked and amplified, with pickups riding the four fat coil springs at the corners and contact mikes taped at random to rusting machine fragments. Somewhere the Lo Teks had an amp and a synthesizer, and now I made out the shapes of speakers overhead, above the cruel white floods.

A drumbeat began, electronic, like an amplified heart, steady as a metronome.

She'd removed her leather jacket and boots; her T-shirt was sleeveless, faint telltales of Chiba City circuitry traced along her thin arms. Her leather jeans gleamed under the floods. She began to dance.

She flexed her knees, white feet tensed on a flattened gas tank, and the Killing Floor began to heave in response. The sound it made was like a world ending, like the wires that hold heaven snapping and coiling across the sky.

He rode with it, for a few heartbeats, and then he moved, judging the movement of the Floor perfectly, like a man stepping from one flat stone to another in an ornamental garden.

He pulled the tip from his thumb with the grace of a man at ease with social gesture and flung it at her. Under the floods, the filament was a refracting thread of rainbow. She threw herself flat and rolled, jackknifing up as the molecule whipped past, steel claws snapping into the light in what must have been an automatic rictus of defense.

The drum pulse quickened, and she bounced with it, her dark hair wild around the blank silver lenses, her mouth thin, lips taut with concentration. The Killing Floor boomed and roared, and the Lo Teks were screaming their excitement.

He retracted the filament to a whirling meter-wide circle of ghostly polychrome and spun it in front of him, thumbless hand held level with his sternum. A shield.

And Molly seemed to let something go, something inside, and that was the real start of her mad-dog dance. She jumped, twisting, lunging sideways, landing with both feet on an alloy engine block wired directly to one of the coil springs. I cupped my hands over my ears and knelt in a vertigo of sound, thinking Floor and benches were on their way down, down to Nighttown, and I saw us tearing through the shanties, the wet wash, exploding on the tiles like rotten fruit. But the cables held, and the Killing Floor rose and fell like a crazy metal sea. And Molly danced on it.

And at the end, just before he made his final cast with the filament, I saw something in his face, an expression that didn't seem to belong there. It wasn't fear and it wasn't anger. I think it was disbelief, stunned incomprehension mingled with pure aesthetic revulsion at what he was seeing, hearing—at what was happening to him. He retracted the whirling filament, the ghost disk shrinking to the size of a dinner plate as he whipped his arm above his head and brought it down, the thumbtip curving out for Molly like a live thing.

The Floor carried her down, the molecule passing just above her head; the Floor whiplashed, lifting him into the path of the taut molecule. It should have passed harmlessly over his head and been withdrawn into its diamond-hard socket. It took his hand off just behind the wrist. There was a gap in the Floor in front of him, and he went through it like a diver, with a strange deliberate grace, a defeated kamikaze on his way down to Nighttown. Partly, I think, he took the dive to buy himself a few seconds of the dignity of silence. She'd killed him with culture shock.

The Lo Teks roared, but someone shut the amplifier off, and Molly rode the

Killing Floor into silence, hanging on now, her face white and blank, until the pitching slowed and there was only a faint pinging of tortured metal and the grating of rust on rust.

We searched the Floor for the severed hand, but we never found it. All we found was a graceful curve in one piece of rusted steel, where the molecule went through. Its edge was bright as new chrome.

We never learned whether the Yakuza had accepted our terms, or even whether they got our message. As far as I know, their program is still waiting for Eddie Bax on a shelf in the back room of a gift shop on the third level of Sydney Central-5. Probably they sold the original back to Ono-Sendai months ago. But maybe they did get the pirate's broadcast, because nobody's come looking for me yet, and it's been nearly a year. If they do come, they'll have a long climb up through the dark, past Dog's sentries, and I don't look much like Eddie Bax these days. I let Molly take care of that, with a local anesthetic. And my new teeth have almost grown in.

I decided to stay up here. When I looked out across the Killing Floor, before he came, I saw how hollow I was. And I knew I was sick of being a bucket. So now I climb down and visit Jones, almost every night.

We're partners now, Jones and I, and Molly Millions, too. Molly handles our business in the Drome. Jones is still in Funland, but he has a bigger tank, with fresh seawater trucked in once a week. And he has his junk, when he needs it. He still talks to the kids with his frame of lights, but he talks to me on a new display unit in a shed that I rent there, a better unit than the one he used in the navy.

And we're all making good money, better money than I made before, because Jones's Squid can read the traces of anything that anyone ever stored in me, and he gives it to me on the display unit in languages I can understand. So we're learning a lot about all my former clients. And one day I'll have a surgeon dig all the silicon out of my amygdalae, and I'll live with my own memories and nobody else's, the way other people do. But not for a while.

In the meantime it's really okay up here, way up in the dark, smoking a Chinese filtertip and listening to the condensation that drips from the geodesics. Real quiet up here—unless a pair of Lo Teks decide to dance on the Killing Floor.

It's educational, too. With Jones to help me figure things out, I'm getting to be the most technical boy in town.

—1981

OCTAVIA E. BUTLER

B. 1947

Octavia Estelle Butler was born in Pasadena, California. Her father died when she was quite young, and she was raised in the Southern California area by her mother, grandmother, and other family members. She was a shy and precocious child who preferred older acquaintances to those her own age. Butler received an A.A. from Pasadena City College in 1968, and attended both California State University at Los Angeles (taking classes in English, anthropology, and history) and the University of California at Los Angeles. Her association with the Writers Guild of America, West, brought her into contact with authors like Harlan Ellison, who provided the essential professional support a young writer often needs. In 1970, Ellison introduced Butler to the Clarion Science Fiction Writer's Workshop, and the resulting six weeks of seminars—where she worked with top-flight science fiction authors like Fritz Leiber, Kate Wilhelm, and Damon Knight—helped her to refine her craft. In fact, it was at the Clarion Workshop that she sold her first two stories. Butler herself has since become not only a major science fiction author, but an important African-American and feminist writer as well. She skillfully examines in her work issues involving race and gender in a manner that enhances her solid use of plotting and characterization. Her major science fiction series features the Patternist stories (dealing with superhuman telepaths), which includes her first novel, Patternmaster *(1976), as well as* Mind of My Mind *(1977),* Survivor *(1978),* Wild Seed *(1980), and* Clay's Ark *(1984). Butler has also authored another science fiction series, the Xenogenesis stories, featuring* Dawn: Xenogenesis *(1987),* Adulthood Rites: Xenogenesis *(1988), and* Imago *(1989). Her recently published novel,* Parable of the Sower *(1993), is a major contribution to the genre of dystopian literature.*

Butler has won a number of prestigious awards, including the Hugo Award, Nebula Award, and Locus Award for her novelette, "Bloodchild" (1984), which was anthologized in her book, Bloodchild and Other Stories *(1995). She won her first Hugo Award (in 1984) for the short story, "Speech Sounds," which was initially published in the mid-December 1983 issue of* Isaac Asimov's Science Fiction Magazine *(and later collected in* Bloodchild and Other Stories*). In "Speech Sounds," Butler writes elegantly of a post-apocalyptic Los Angeles where people have lost the ability to speak or to read. It is based, in part, on a real episode in Butler's life, during which she witnessed a bloody fight on a bus. Butler says of this episode, "I sat where I was [on the bus], more depressed than ever, hating the whole hopeless, stupid business and wondering whether the human species would ever grow up enough to learn to communicate without using fists of one kind or another." Her resulting bleak—yet compassionate and hopeful—tale of an intelligent woman's quest for meaning in a desolate life (a life in which most human intelligence has been lost) has become a major classic of contemporary science fiction.*

Speech Sounds

There was trouble aboard the Washington Boulevard bus. Rye had expected trouble sooner or later in her journey. She had put off going until loneliness and hopelessness drove her out. She believed she might have one group of relatives left alive—a brother and his two children twenty miles away in Pasadena. That was a day's journey one-way, if she were lucky. The unexpected arrival of the bus as she left her Virginia Road home had seemed to be a piece of luck—until the trouble began.

Two young men were involved in a disagreement of some kind, or, more likely, a misunderstanding. They stood in the aisle, grunting and gesturing at each other, each in his own uncertain T stance as the bus lurched over the potholes. The driver seemed to be putting some effort into keeping them off balance. Still, their gestures stopped just short of contact—mock punches, hand games of intimidation to replace lost curses.

People watched the pair, then looked at one another and made small anxious sounds. Two children whimpered.

Rye sat a few feet behind the disputants and across from the back door. She watched the two carefully, knowing the fight would begin when someone's nerve broke or someone's hand slipped or someone came to the end of his limited ability to communicate. These things could happen anytime.

One of them happened as the bus hit an especially large pothole and one man, tall, thin, and sneering, was thrown into his shorter opponent.

Instantly, the shorter man drove his left fist into the disintegrating sneer. He hammered his larger opponent as though he neither had nor needed any weapon other than his left fist. He hit quickly enough, hard enough to batter his opponent down before the taller man could regain his balance or hit back even once.

People screamed or squawked in fear. Those nearby scrambled to get out of the way. Three more young men roared in excitement and gestured wildly. Then, somehow, a second dispute broke out between two of these three—probably because one inadvertently touched or hit the other.

As the second fight scattered frightened passengers, a woman shook the driver's shoulder and grunted as she gestured toward the fighting.

The driver grunted back through bared teeth. Frightened, the woman drew away.

Rye, knowing the methods of bus drivers, braced herself and held on to the crossbar of the seat in front of her. When the driver hit the brakes, she was ready and the combatants were not. They fell over seats and onto screaming passengers, creating even more confusion. At least one more fight started.

The instant the bus came to a full stop, Rye was on her feet, pushing the back door. At the second push, it opened and she jumped out, holding her pack in one arm. Several other passengers followed, but some stayed on the bus. Buses were so rare and irregular now, people rode when they could, no matter what. There might not be another bus today—or tomorrow. People started walking, and if they saw a bus they flagged it down. People making intercity trips like Rye's from Los Angeles to Pasadena made plans to camp out, or risked seeking shelter with locals who might rob or murder them.

The bus did not move, but Rye moved away from it. She intended to wait until the trouble was over and get on again, but if there was shooting, she wanted the protection of a tree. Thus, she was near the curb when a battered blue Ford on the other side of the street made a U-turn and pulled up in front of the bus. Cars were rare these days—as rare as a severe shortage of fuel and of relatively unimpaired mechanics could make them. Cars that still ran were as likely to be used as weapons as they were to serve as transportation. Thus, when the driver of the Ford beckoned to Rye, she moved away warily. The driver got out—a big man, young, neatly bearded with dark, thick hair. He wore a long overcoat and a look of wariness that matched Rye's. She stood several feet from him, waiting to see what he would do. He looked at the bus, now rocking with the combat inside, then at the small cluster of passengers who had gotten off. Finally he looked at Rye again.

She returned his gaze, very much aware of the old forty-five automatic her jacket concealed. She watched his hands.

He pointed with his left hand toward the bus. The dark-tinted windows prevented him from seeing what was happening inside.

His use of the left hand interested Rye more than his obvious question. Left-handed people tended to be less impaired, more reasonable and comprehending, less driven by frustration, confusion, and anger.

She imitated his gesture, pointing toward the bus with her own left hand, then punching the air with both fists.

The man took off his coat revealing a Los Angeles Police Department uniform complete with baton and service revolver.

Rye took another step back from him. There was no more LAPD, no more *any* large organization, governmental or private. There were neighborhood patrols and armed individuals. That was all.

The man took something from his coat pocket, then threw the coat into the car. Then he gestured Rye back, back toward the rear of the bus. He had something made of plastic in his hand. Rye did not understand what he wanted until he went to the rear door of the bus and beckoned her to stand there. She obeyed mainly out of curiosity. Cop or not, maybe he could do something to stop the stupid fighting.

He walked around the front of the bus, to the street side where the driver's window was open. There, she thought she saw him throw something into the bus. She was still trying to peer through the tinted glass when people began stumbling out the rear door, choking and weeping. Gas.

Rye caught an old woman who would have fallen, lifted two little children down when they were in danger of being knocked down and trampled. She could see the bearded man helping people at the front door. She caught a thin old man shoved out by one of the combatants. Staggered by the old man's weight, she was barely able to get out of the way as the last of the young men pushed his way out. This one, bleeding from nose and mouth, stumbled into another, and they grappled blindly, still sobbing from the gas.

The bearded man helped the bus driver out through the front door, though the driver did not seem to appreciate his help. For a moment, Rye thought there would be another fight. The bearded man stepped back and watched the driver gesture threateningly, watched him shout in wordless anger.

The bearded man stood still, made no sound, refused to respond to clearly obscene gestures. The least impaired people tended to do this—stand back unless they were physically threatened and let those with less control scream and jump around. It was as though they felt it beneath them to be as touchy as the less comprehending. This was an attitude of superiority, and that was the way people like the bus driver perceived it. Such "superiority" was frequently punished by beatings, even by death. Rye had had close calls of her own. As a result, she never went unarmed. And in this world where the only likely common language was body language, being armed was often enough. She had rarely had to draw her gun or even display it.

The bearded man's revolver was on constant display. Apparently that was enough for the bus driver. The driver spat in disgust, glared at the bearded man for a moment longer, then strode back to his gas-filled bus. He stared at it for a moment, clearly wanting to get in, but the gas was still too strong. Of the windows, only his tiny driver's window actually opened. The front door was open, but the rear door would not stay open unless someone held it. Of course, the air conditioning had failed long ago. The bus would take some time to clear. It was the driver's property, his livelihood. He had pasted old magazine pictures of items he would accept as fare on its sides. Then he would use what he collected to feed his family or to trade. If his bus did not run, he did not eat. On the other hand, if the inside of his bus was torn apart by senseless fighting, he would not eat very well either. He was apparently unable to perceive this. All he could see was that it would be some time before he could use his bus again. He shook his fist at the bearded man and shouted. There seemed to be words in his shout, but Rye could not understand them. She did not know whether this was his fault or hers. She had heard so little coherent human speech for the past three years, she was no longer certain how well she recognized it, no longer certain of the degree of her own impairment.

The bearded man sighed. He glanced toward his car, then beckoned to Rye. He was ready to leave, but he wanted something from her first. No. No, he wanted her to leave with him. Risk getting into his car when, in spite of his uniform, law and order were nothing—not even words any longer.

She shook her head in a universally understood negative, but the man continued to beckon.

She waved him away. He was doing what the less impaired rarely did—drawing potentially negative attention to another of his kind. People from the bus had begun to look at her.

One of the men who had been fighting tapped another on the arm, then pointed from the bearded man to Rye, and finally held up the first two fingers of his right hand as though giving two-thirds of a Boy Scout salute. The gesture was very quick, its meaning obvious even at a distance. She had been grouped with the bearded man. Now what?

The man who had made the gesture started toward her.

She had no idea what he intended, but she stood her ground. The man was half a foot taller than she was and perhaps ten years younger. She did not imagine she could outrun him. Nor did she expect anyone to help her if she needed help. The people around her were all strangers.

She gestured once—a clear indication to the man to stop. She did not intend to repeat the gesture. Fortunately, the man obeyed. He gestured obscenely and several other men laughed. Loss of verbal language had spawned a whole new set of obscene gestures. The man, with stark simplicity, had accused her of sex with the bearded man and had suggested she accommodate the other men present—beginning with him.

Rye watched him wearily. People might very well stand by and watch if he tried to rape her. They would also stand and watch her shoot him. Would he push things that far?

He did not. After a series of obscene gestures that brought him no closer to her, he turned contemptuously and walked away.

And the bearded man still waited. He had removed his service revolver, holster and all. He beckoned again, both hands empty. No doubt his gun was in the car and within easy reach, but his taking it off impressed her. Maybe he was all right. Maybe he was just alone. She had been alone herself for three years. The illness had stripped her, killing her children one by one, killing her husband, her sister, her parents.

The illness, if it was an illness, had cut even the living off from one another. As it swept over the country, people hardly had time to lay blame on the Soviets (though they were falling silent along with the rest of the world), on a new virus, a new pollutant, radiation, divine retribution. . . . The illness was stroke-swift in the way it cut people down and strokelike in some of its effects. But it was highly specific. Language was always lost or severely impaired. It was never regained. Often there was also paralysis, intellectual impairment, death.

Rye walked toward the bearded man, ignoring the whistling and applauding of two of the young men and their thumbs-up signs to the bearded man. If he had smiled at them or acknowledged them in any way, she would almost certainly have changed her mind. If she had let herself think of the possible deadly consequences of getting into a stranger's car, she would have changed her mind. Instead, she thought of the man who lived across the street from her. He rarely washed since his bout with the illness. And he had gotten into the habit of urinating wherever he happened to be. He had two women already—one tending each of his large gardens. They put up with him in exchange for his protection. He had made it clear that he wanted Rye to become his third woman.

She got into the car and the bearded man shut the door. She watched as he walked around to the driver's door—watched for his sake because his gun was on the seat beside her. And the bus driver and a pair of young men had come a few steps closer. They did nothing, though, until the bearded man was in the car. Then one of them threw a rock. Others followed his example, and as the car drove away, several rocks bounced off harmlessly.

When the bus was some distance behind them, Rye wiped sweat from her forehead and longed to relax. The bus would have taken her more than halfway to Pasadena. She would have had only ten miles to walk. She wondered how far she would have to walk now—and wondered if walking a long distance would be her only problem.

At Figuroa and Washington where the bus normally made a left turn, the bearded man stopped, looked at her, and indicated that she should choose a direction. When she directed him left and he actually turned left, she began to relax. If he was willing to go where she directed, perhaps he was safe.

As they passed blocks of burned, abandoned buildings, empty lots, and wrecked or stripped cars, he slipped a gold chain over his head and handed it to her. The pendant attached to it was a smooth, glassy, black rock. Obsidian. His name might be Rock or Peter or Black, but she decided to think of him as Obsidian. Even her sometimes useless memory would retain a name like Obsidian.

She handed him her own name symbol—a pin in the shape of a large golden stalk of wheat. She had bought it long before the illness and the silence began. Now she wore it, thinking it was as close as she was likely to come to Rye. People like Obsidian who had not known her before probably thought of her as Wheat. Not that it mattered. She would never hear her name spoken again.

Obsidian handed her pin back to her. He caught her hand as she reached for it and rubbed his thumb over her calluses.

He stopped at First Street and asked which way again. Then, after turning right as she had indicated, he parked near the Music Center. There, he took a folded paper from the dashboard and unfolded it. Rye recognized it as a street map, though the writing on it meant nothing to her. He flattened the map, took her hand again, and put her index finger on one spot. He touched her, touched himself, pointed toward the floor. In effect, "We are here." She knew he wanted to know where she was going. She wanted to tell him, but she shook her head sadly. She had lost reading and writing. That was her most serious impairment and her most painful. She had taught history at UCLA. She had done freelance writing. Now she could not even read her own manuscripts. She had a houseful of books that she could neither read nor bring herself to use as fuel. And she had a memory that would not bring back to her much of what she had read before.

She stared at the map, trying to calculate. She had been born in Pasadena, had lived for fifteen years in Los Angeles. Now she was near L.A. Civic Center. She knew the relative positions of the two cities, knew streets, directions, even knew to stay away from freeways, which might be blocked by wrecked cars and destroyed overpasses. She ought to know how to point out Pasadena even though she could not recognize the word.

Hesitantly, she placed her hand over a pale orange patch in the upper right corner of the map. That should be right. Pasadena.

Obsidian lifted her hand and looked under it, then folded the map and put it back on the dashboard. He could read, she realized belatedly. He could probably write, too. Abruptly, she hated him—deep, bitter hatred. What did literacy mean to him—a grown man who played cops and robbers? But he was literate and she was not. She never would be. She felt sick to her stomach with hatred, frustration, and jealousy. And only a few inches from her hand was a loaded gun.

She held herself still, staring at him, almost seeing his blood. But her rage crested and ebbed and she did nothing.

Obsidian reached for her hand with hesitant familiarity. She looked at him. Her face had already revealed too much. No person still living in what was left of human society could fail to recognize that expression, that jealousy.

She closed her eyes wearily, drew a deep breath. She had experienced longing for the past, hatred of the present, growing hopelessness, purposelessness, but she had never experienced such a powerful urge to kill another person. She had left her home, finally, because she had come near to killing herself. She had found no reason to stay alive. Perhaps that was why she had gotten into Obsidian's car. She had never before done such a thing.

He touched her mouth and made chatter motions with thumb and fingers. Could she speak?

She nodded and watched his milder envy come and go. Now both had admitted what it was not safe to admit, and there had been no violence. He tapped his mouth and forehead and shook his head. He did not speak or comprehend spoken language. The illness had played with them, taking away, she suspected, what each valued most.

She plucked at his sleeve, wondering why he had decided on his own to keep the LAPD alive with what he had left. He was sane enough otherwise. Why wasn't he at home raising corn, rabbits, and children? But she did not know how to ask. Then he put his hand on her thigh and she had another question to deal with.

She shook her head. Disease, pregnancy, helpless, solitary agony . . . no.

He massaged her thigh gently and smiled in obvious disbelief.

No one had touched her for three years. She had not wanted anyone to touch her. What kind of world was this to chance bringing a child into even if the father were willing to stay and help raise it? It was too bad, though. Obsidian could not know how attractive he was to her—young, probably younger than she was, clean, asking for what he wanted rather than demanding it. But none of that mattered. What were a few moments of pleasure measured against a lifetime of consequences?

He pulled her closer to him and for a moment she let herself enjoy the closeness. He smelled good—male and good. She pulled away reluctantly.

He sighed, reached toward the glove compartment. She stiffened, not knowing what to expect, but all he took out was a small box. The writing on it meant nothing to her. She did not understand until he broke the seal, opened the box, and took out a condom. He looked at her, and she first looked away in surprise. Then she giggled. She could not remember when she had last giggled.

He grinned, gestured toward the backseat, and she laughed aloud. Even in her teens, she had disliked backseats of cars. But she looked around at the empty streets and ruined buildings, then she got out and into the backseat. He let her put the condom on him, then seemed surprised at her eagerness.

Sometime later, they sat together, covered by his coat, unwilling to become clothed near strangers again just yet. He made rock-the-baby gestures and looked questioningly at her.

She swallowed, shook her head. She did not know how to tell him her children were dead.

He took her hand and drew a cross in it with his index finger, then made his baby-rocking gesture again.

She nodded, held up three fingers, then turned away, trying to shut out a sudden flood of memories. She had told herself that the children growing up now were to be pitied. They would run through the downtown canyons with no real memory of what the buildings had been or even how they had come to be. Today's children gathered books as well as wood to be burned as fuel. They ran through the streets chasing one another and hooting like chimpanzees. They had no future. They were now all they would ever be.

He put his hand on her shoulder, and she turned suddenly, fumbling for his small box, then urging him to make love to her again. He could give her forgetfulness and pleasure. Until now, nothing had been able to do that. Until now, every day had brought her closer to the time when she would do what she had left home to avoid doing: putting her gun in her mouth and pulling the trigger.

She asked Obsidian if he would come home with her, stay with her.

He looked surprised and pleased once he understood. But he did not answer at once. Finally, he shook his head as she had feared he might. He was probably having too much fun playing cops and robbers and picking up women.

She dressed in silent disappointment, unable to feel any anger toward him. Perhaps he already had a wife and a home. That was likely. The illness had been harder on men than on women—had killed more men, had left male survivors more severely impaired. Men like Obsidian were rare. Women either settled for less or stayed alone. If they found an Obsidian, they did what they could to keep him. Rye suspected he had someone younger, prettier keeping him.

He touched her while she was strapping her gun on and asked with a complicated series of gestures whether it was loaded.

She nodded grimly.

He patted her arm.

She asked once more if he would come home with her, this time using a different series of gestures. He had seemed hesitant. Perhaps he could be courted.

He got out and into the front seat without responding.

She took her place in front again, watching him. Now he plucked at his uniform and looked at her. She thought she was being asked something but did not know what it was.

He took off his badge, tapped it with one finger, then tapped his chest. Of course.

She took the badge from his hand and pinned her wheat stalk to it. If playing cops and robbers was his only insanity, let him play. She would take him, uniform and all. It occurred to her that she might eventually lose him to someone he would meet as he had met her. But she would have him for a while.

He took the street map down again, tapped it, pointed vaguely northeast toward Pasadena, then looked at her.

She shrugged, tapped his shoulder, then her own, and held up her index and second fingers tight together, just to be sure.

He grasped the two fingers and nodded. He was with her.

She took the map from him and threw it onto the dashboard. She pointed back southwest—back toward home. Now she did not have to go to Pasadena. Now she could go on having a brother there and two nephews—three right-handed males. Now she did not have to find out for certain whether she was as alone as she feared. Now she was not alone.

Obsidian took Hill Street south, then Washington west, and she leaned back, wondering what it would be like to have someone again. With what she had scavenged, what she had preserved, and what she grew, there was easily enough food for them. There was certainly room enough in a four-bedroom house. He could move his possessions in. Best of all, the animal across the street would pull back and possibly not force her to kill him.

Obsidian had drawn her closer to him, and she had put her head on his shoulder when suddenly he braked hard, almost throwing her off the seat. Out of the corner of her eye, she saw that someone had run across the street in front of the car. One car on the street and someone had to run in front of it.

Straightening up, Rye saw that the runner was a woman, fleeing from an old frame house to a boarded-up storefront. She ran silently, but the man who followed her a moment later shouted what sounded like garbled words as he ran. He had something in his hand. Not a gun. A knife, perhaps.

The woman tried a door, found it locked, looked around desperately, finally snatched up a fragment of glass broken from the storefront window. With this she turned to face her pursuer. Rye thought she would be more likely to cut her own hand than to hurt anyone else with the glass.

Obsidian jumped from the car, shouting. It was the first time Rye had heard his voice—deep and hoarse from disuse. He made the same sound over and over the way some speechless people did, "Da, da, da!"

Rye got out of the car as Obsidian ran toward the couple. He had drawn his gun. Fearful, she drew her own and released the safety. She looked around to see who else might be attracted to the scene. She saw the man glance at Obsidian, then suddenly lunge at the woman. The woman jabbed his face with her glass, but he caught her arm and managed to stab her twice before Obsidian shot him.

The man doubled, then toppled, clutching his abdomen. Obsidian shouted, then gestured Rye over to help the woman.

Rye moved to the woman's side, remembering that she had little more than bandages and antiseptic in her pack. But the woman was beyond help. She had been stabbed with a long, slender boning knife.

She touched Obsidian to let him know the woman was dead. He had bent to check the wounded man who lay still and also seemed dead. But as Obsidian looked around to see what Rye wanted, the man opened his eyes. Face contorted, he seized

Obsidian's just-holstered revolver and fired. The bullet caught Obsidian in the temple and he collapsed.

It happened just that simply, just that fast. An instant later, Rye shot the wounded man as he was turning the gun on her.

And Rye was alone—with three corpses.

She knelt beside Obsidian, dry-eyed, frowning, trying to understand why everything had suddenly changed. Obsidian was gone. He had died and left her—like everyone else.

Two very small children came out of the house from which the man and woman had run—a boy and girl perhaps three years old. Holding hands, they crossed the street toward Rye. They stared at her, then edged past her and went to the dead woman. The girl shook the woman's arm as though trying to wake her.

This was too much. Rye got up, feeling sick to her stomach with grief and anger. If the children began to cry, she thought she would vomit.

They were on their own, those two kids. They were old enough to scavenge. She did not need any more grief. She did not need a stranger's children who would grow up to be hairless chimps.

She went back to the car. She could drive home, at least. She remembered how to drive.

The thought that Obsidian should be buried occurred to her before she reached the car, and she did vomit.

She had found and lost the man so quickly. It was as though she had been snatched from comfort and security and given a sudden, inexplicable beating. Her head would not clear. She could not think.

Somehow, she made herself go back to him, look at him. She found herself on her knees beside him with no memory of having knelt. She stroked his face, his beard. One of the children made a noise and she looked at them, at the woman who was probably their mother. The children looked back at her, obviously frightened. Perhaps it was their fear that reached her finally.

She had been about to drive away and leave them. She had almost done it, almost left two toddlers to die. Surely there had been enough dying. She would have to take the children home with her. She would not be able to live with any other decision. She looked around for a place to bury three bodies. Or two. She wondered if the murderer were the children's father. Before the silence, the police had always said some of the most dangerous calls they went out on were domestic disturbance calls. Obsidian should have known that—not that the knowledge would have kept him in the car. It would not have held her back either. She could not have watched the woman murdered and done nothing.

She dragged Obsidian toward the car. She had nothing to dig with her, and no one to guard for her while she dug. Better to take the bodies with her and bury them next to her husband and her children. Obsidian would come home with her after all.

When she had gotten him onto the floor in the back, she returned for the woman. The little girl, thin, dirty, solemn, stood up and unknowingly gave Rye a gift. As Rye began to drag the woman by her arms, the little girl screamed, "No!"

Rye dropped the woman and stared at the girl.

"No!" the girl repeated. She came to stand beside the woman. "Go away!" she told Rye.

"Don't talk," the little boy said to her. There was no blurring or confusing of sounds. Both children had spoken and Rye had understood. The boy looked at the dead murderer and moved further from him. He took the girl's hand. "Be quiet," he whispered.

Fluent speech! Had the woman died because she could talk and had taught her children to talk? Had she been killed by a husband's festering anger or by a stranger's jealous rage? And the children . . . they must have been born after the silence. Had the disease run its course, then? Or were these children simply immune? Certainly they had had time to fall sick and silent. Rye's mind leaped ahead. What if children of three or fewer years were safe and able to learn language? What if all they needed were teachers? Teachers and protectors.

Rye glanced at the dead murderer. To her shame, she thought she could understand some of the passions that must have driven him, whomever he was. Anger, frustration, hopelessness, insane jealousy . . . how many more of him were there—people willing to destroy what they could not have?

Obsidian had been the protector, had chosen that role for who knew what reason. Perhaps putting on an obsolete uniform and patrolling the empty streets had been what he did instead of putting a gun into his mouth. And now that there was something worth protecting, he was gone.

She had been a teacher. A good one. She had been a protector, too, though only of herself. She had kept herself alive when she had no reason to live. If the illness let these children alone, she could keep them alive.

Somehow she lifted the dead woman into her arms and placed her on the backseat of the car. The children began to cry, but she knelt on the broken pavement and whispered to them, fearful of frightening them with the harshness of her long unused voice.

"It's all right," she told them. "You're going with us, too. Come on." She lifted them both, one in each arm. They were so light. Had they been getting enough to eat?

The boy covered her mouth with his hand, but she moved her face away. "It's all right for me to talk," she told him. "As long as no one's around, it's all right." She put the boy down on the front seat of the car and he moved over without being told to, to make room for the girl. When they were both in the car, Rye leaned against the window, looking at them, seeing that they were less afraid now, that they watched her with at least as much curiosity as fear.

"I'm Valerie Rye," she said, savoring the words. "It's all right for you to talk to me."

—1983

C R I T I C A L   B I B L I O G R A P H Y

Aldiss, Brian W. *Billion Year Spree: The True History of Science Fiction.* Garden City: Doubleday, 1973.

——. *Trillion Year Spree: The History of Science Fiction.* New York: Atheneum, 1986.

Amis, Kingsley. *New Maps of Hell: A Survey of Science Fiction.* New York: Arno Press, 1975.

Antczak, Janice. *Science Fiction: The Mythos of a New Romance.* New York: Neal-Schuman, 1985.

Barron, Neil, ed. *Anatomy of Wonder/Science Fiction.* New York: Bowker, 1976.

Bretnor, Reginald. *Science Fiction, Today and Tomorrow: A Discursive Symposium.* New York: Harper & Row, 1974.

Clareson, Thomas D. *Science Fiction Criticism: An Annotated Checklist.* Kent: Kent State UP, 1972.

——, ed. *SF: The Other Side of Realism.* Bowling Green: BGSU Popular P, 1971.

——. *Voices for the Future: Essays on Major Science Fiction Writers.* Bowling Green: BGSU Popular P, 1976.

Clure, John, and Peter Nicholls. *The Encyclopedia of Science Fiction.* New York: St. Martin's Press, 1993.

Evans, Christopher. *Writing Science Fiction.* New York: St. Martin's Press, 1988.

Gunn, James, ed. *The New Encyclopedia of Science Fiction.* New York: Viking, 1988.

——. *The Road to Science Fiction: From Gilgamesh to Wells.* New York: Mentor, 1977.

——. *The Road to Science Fiction #2: From Wells to Heinlein.* New York: Mentor, 1979.

——. *The Road to Science Fiction #3: From Heinlein to Here.* New York: Mentor, 1979.

——. *The Road to Science Fiction: From Here to Forever.* New York: Mentor, 1982.

Ketterer, David. *New Worlds for Old: The Apocalyptic Imagination, Science Fiction, and American Literature.* Bloomington: Indiana UP, 1974.

Lundwall, Sam J. *Science Fiction: What It's All About.* New York: Ace Books, 1971.

Moskowitz, Sam. *Explorers of the Infinite: Shapers of Science Fiction.* Cleveland: World Publishing, 1963.

Parrinder, Patrick. *Science Fiction: Its Criticism and Teaching.* London: Methuen, 1980.

Philmus, Robert M. *Into the Unknown: The Evolution of Science Fiction from Francis Godwin to H. G. Wells.* Berkeley: U of California P, 1970.

Pringle, David. *Science Fiction: The 100 Best Novels—An English-Language Selection, 1949–1984.* London: Xanadu, 1985.

Roberts, Robin. *A New Species: Gender and Science in Science Fiction.* Urbana: U of Illinois P, 1993.

Rose, Mark, ed. *Science Fiction: A Collection of Critical Essays.* Englewood Cliffs: Prentice-Hall, 1976.

Rottensteiner, Franz. *The Science Fiction Book: An Illustrated History.* New York: Seabury, 1975.

Scholes, Robert, and Eric S. Rabkin. *Science Fiction: History, Science, Vision.* New York: Oxford, 1977.

Searles, Baird. *A Reader's Guide to Science Fiction.* New York: Avon, 1979.

Stableford, Brian M. *Scientific Romance in Britain, 1890–1950.* London: Fourth Estate, 1985.

Wolfe, Gary K. *The Known and the Unknown: The Iconography of Science Fiction.* Kent: Kent State UP, 1979.

Wollheim, Donald A. *The Universe Makers: Science Fiction Today.* New York: Harper & Row, 1971.

4

DETECTIVE FICTION

Some say the tale of murder is as ancient as the Bible, dating back to Cain's killing of his brother, one of our oldest stories about hot-blooded (or is it cold-blooded?) killing and the dire social repercussions that follow. Others claim the psychology of murder was never better depicted in narrative form than in William Shakespeare's classic tragedy, *Macbeth* (First Folio, 1623). Some two hundred years later, British author James Hogg examined the sociopathic psychology of murder in his novel, *The Private Memoirs and Confessions of a Justified Sinner* (1824), as did Charles Brockden Brown, America's first professional author and the writer who, in his novel *Wieland* (1798), created one of America's first fictional mass-murderers. Yet, these few examples reveal just the tip of the literary iceberg. In addition to murder, detective fiction encompasses theft, rape, robbery, prostitution, gambling, adultery and myriad other expressions of human vice.

Modern detective fiction, as a readily designated story type, dates from Edgar Allan Poe's "The Murders in the Rue Morgue," first published in 1841. Poe's major achievement—in this bizarre tale of two baffling murders and their subsequent solution—was to structure crime fiction into a predictable formula that would eventually inspire many authors throughout the nineteenth and twentieth centuries in both Europe and America. Thus, we can credit Poe with the invention of the modern detective hero and the "locked room" mystery, conventional features of the detective story that endure to the present day.

Because Edgar Allan Poe has often been identified as creating the modern detective story, American and European readers generally assume detective fiction is an invention of the Western cultural tradition. Author and diplomat Robert van Gulik (1910–1967) reminds us in his popular Judge Dee detective stories that this is an erroneous assumption. In his preface to his 1949 translation of an anonymous eighteenth-century Chinese detective novel (van Gulik's title, *Dee Goong An: Three Murder Cases Solved by Judge Dee*), van Gulik claims the origins of the detective novel in China go back as far as the early seventeenth century, some 240 years before Poe published "The Murders in the Rue Morgue." Van Gulik also states in his preface that the Chinese detective novel "reached its greatest development" in the eighteenth and nineteenth centuries. Judge Dee, who figures as the protagonist of van Gulik's translation, was an actual person named Dee Jen-djieh, a famous magistrate who served during the T'ang Dynasty in seventh-century China. Judge Dee's exploits became the stuff of legend in Chinese culture and later provided a significant source for the developing Chinese detective novel.

Through the years since Poe's landmark creation, detective fiction has encompassed the most diverse assemblage of heroes in all of popular fiction. Interested readers can find stories featuring lawyer detectives (Erle Stanley Gardner's Perry Mason), priest detectives (G. K. Chesterton's Father Brown), cop detectives (Georges Simenon's Inspector Jules Maigret), armchair detectives (Baroness Orczy's the Old Man in the Corner), vigilante detectives (Walter B. Gibson's The Shadow), medieval detectives (Ellis Peters's Brother Cadfael), snobbish detectives (S. S. Van Dine's Philo Vance), nerd detectives (Jacques Futrelle's Thinking Machine), science fiction detectives (Larry Niven's Gil Hamilton), Hollywood detectives (Stuart Kaminsky's Toby Peters), nameless detectives (Bill Pronzini's Nameless Detective), magician detectives (Clayton Rawson's Great Merlini), and medical detectives (Edward Hoch's Dr. Sam Hawthorne), to list but a few examples.

The short stories presented in this chapter span the vast spectrum of the detective fiction genre. Edgar Allan Poe's "The Murders in the Rue Morgue"—featuring the eccentric, yet brilliant, C. Auguste Dupin—formulated many of the genre's most recognizable conventions. Arthur Conan Doyle's Sherlock Holmes, the world-famous sleuth in "The Musgrave Ritual," helped to establish the international popularity of the detective story and provided an important archetype for the story form. The golden age of classic, or British, detective fiction is represented by Agatha Christie's "The Tuesday Night Club" and Dorothy L. Sayers's "Absolutely Elsewhere," while Dashiell Hammett's "Too Many Have Lived" and Raymond Chandler's "Blackmailers Don't Shoot" offer two fine examples of the Depression era "hard-boiled" school of American detective fiction. Marcia Muller's "The Place That Time Forgot" illustrates a contemporary example of the "hard-boiled" private investigator story (featuring a female hard-boiled detective rather than a male "gumshoe"). And the remaining stories—Tony Hillerman's "Chee's Witch" and Walter Mosley's "The Watts Lions"—illustrate several fine examples of ethnic detective heroes. The two crucial elements, however, that all of these marvelous tales of crime and detection have in common are their artistry and entertainment value, which are testaments to the talent of the authors.

EDGAR ALLAN POE
1809-1849

*Many historians of crime fiction consider Edgar Allan Poe's "The Murders
in the Rue Morgue" to be the first example of the modern detective story.
Poe created this new genre of fiction by updating the European Gothic horror story. Poe's forte had always been horror, and, in many ways, "The
Murders in the Rue Morgue" reads like a Gothic horror tale. The gruesome
murders would certainly qualify as a motif of the Gothic narrative, as
would the story's peculiar cast of characters. A "grotesque mansion"—a
common Gothic image—even serves as the rented home for the narrator
and his sagacious associate, Monsieur C. Auguste Dupin. Poe transforms
this particular tale of Gothic horror into a detective story by having Dupin
provide a rational solution to Madame L'Espanaye's and her daughter
Mademoiselle Camille L'Espanaye's bizarre murders—a solution that is
arrived at by the observation of clues and by the process of Dupin's logical
analysis.*

*Prior to publishing "The Murders in the Rue Morgue," Poe experimented
with creating puzzles and solutions to puzzles in his writing, as evidenced
in sketches such as "Maelzel's Chess-Player" (1836). His somewhat lengthy
preamble in "The Murders in the Rue Morgue," for example, which defines
"the higher powers of the reflective intellect," illustrates his fascination with
the intellectual process of puzzle solving. "The Murders in the Rue Morgue,"
initially appearing in the April 1841 issue of* Graham's Magazine, *is only the
first of the three tales that features Poe's brilliant, yet eccentric, protagonist
Dupin, the other two being "The Mystery of Marie Rogêt" (1842/1843) and
"The Purloined Letter" (1844). So impressive a character is Dupin that he
served in years to come as the model for the classic literary detective, influ-
encing the creation of such notable detective heroes as Arthur Conan
Doyle's Sherlock Holmes, Agatha Christie's Hercule Poirot, and Dorothy L.
Sayers's Lord Peter Wimsey, among many others. In addition, "The Murders
in the Rue Morgue" established the prototype for the "locked room" mystery, a category of detective fiction that features a murder, or other serious
crime, that has been committed in a locked room setting. Poe's invention of
the "locked room" mystery was later imitated and perfected by such masters of classic detective fiction as John Dickson Carr and Clayton Rawson.*

THE MURDERS IN THE RUE MORGUE

*What song the Syrens sang, or what name Achilles assumed when he hid
himself among women, although puzzling questions, are not beyond all
conjecture.*

—SIR THOMAS BROWNE

The mental features discoursed of as the analytical, are, in themselves, but little
susceptible of analysis. We appreciate them only in their effects. We know of them,
among other things, that they are always to their possessor, when inordinately pos-

sessed, a source of the liveliest enjoyment. As the strong man exults in his physical ability, delighting in such exercises as call his muscles into action, so glories the analyst in that moral activity which *disentangles*. He derives pleasure from even the most trivial occupations bringing his talent into play. He is fond of enigmas, of conundrums, hieroglyphics; exhibiting in his solutions of each a degree of *acumen* which appears to the ordinary apprehension præternatural. His results, brought about by the very soul and essence of method, have, in truth, the whole air of intuition.

The faculty of re-solution is possibly much invigorated by mathematical study, and especially by that highest branch of it which, unjustly, and merely on account of its retrograde operations, has been called, as if *par excellence,* analysis. Yet to calculate is not in itself to analyze. A chess-player, for example, does the one, without effort at the other. It follows that the game of chess, in its effects upon mental character, is greatly misunderstood. I am not now writing a treatise, but simply prefacing a somewhat peculiar narrative by observations very much at random; I will, therefore, take occasion to assert that the higher powers of the reflective intellect are more decidedly and more usefully tasked by the unostentatious game of draughts than by the elaborate frivolity of chess. In this latter, where the pieces have different and *bizarre* motions, with various and variable values, what is only complex, is mistaken (a not unusual error) for what is profound. The *attention* is here called powerfully into play. If it flag for an instant, an oversight is committed, resulting in injury or defeat. The possible moves being not only manifold, but involute, the chances of such oversights are multiplied; and in nine cases out of ten, it is the more concentrative rather than the more acute player who conquers. In draughts, on the contrary, where the moves are *unique* and have but little variation, the probabilities of inadvertence are diminished, and the mere attention being left comparatively unemployed, what advantages are obtained by either party are obtained by superior *acumen*. To be less abstract, let us suppose a game of draughts where the pieces are reduced to four kings, and where, of course, no oversight is to be expected. It is obvious that here the victory can be decided (the players being at all equal) only by some *recherché* movement, the result of some strong exertion of the intellect.

Deprived of ordinary resources, the analyst throws himself into the spirit of his opponent, identifies himself therewith, and not unfrequently sees thus, at a glance, the sole methods (sometimes indeed absurdly simple ones) by which he may seduce into error or hurry into miscalculation.

Whist has long been known for its influence upon what is termed the calculating power; and men of the highest order of intellect have been known to take an apparently unaccountable delight in it, while eschewing chess as frivolous. Beyond doubt there is nothing of a similar nature so greatly tasking the faculty of analysis. The best chess-player in Christendom *may* be little more than the best player of chess; but proficiency in whist implies capacity for success in all these more important undertakings where mind struggles with mind. When I say proficiency, I mean that perfection in the game which includes a comprehension of *all* the sources whence legitimate advantage may be derived. These are not only manifold, but multiform, and lie frequently among recesses of thought altogether inaccessible to the ordinary understanding. To observe attentively is to remember distinctly; and, so far, the concentrative chess-player will do very well at whist; while the rules of Hoyle (themselves based upon the mere mechanism of the game) are sufficiently and generally comprehensible. Thus to have a retentive memory, and proceed by "the book" are points commonly regarded as the sum total of good playing. But it is in matters beyond the limits of mere rule that the skill of the analyst is evinced. He makes, in silence, a host of observations and inferences. So, perhaps, do his companions; and the difference in the extent of the information obtained, lies not so much in the validity of the inference as in the quality of the observation. The necessary knowledge is that of *what* to observe. Our player confines himself not at all; nor, because the game is the object, does he reject deductions from things external to the game. He examines the countenance of his partner, comparing it carefully with that of each of his opponents. He considers the mode of assorting the cards in each hand; often counting trump by trump, and honor by honor, through the glances bestowed by their holders upon each. He notes every variation of face as the play progresses, gathering a fund of thought from the differences in the expression of certainty, of surprise, of triumph, or chagrin. From the manner of gathering up a trick he judges whether the person taking it, can make another in the suit. He recognizes what is played through feint, by the manner with which it is thrown upon the table. A casual or inadvertent word; the accidental dropping or turning of a card, with the accompanying anxiety or carelessness in regard to its concealment; the counting of the tricks, with the order of their arrangement; embarrassment, hesitation, eagerness, or trepidation—all afford, to his apparently intuitive perception, indications of the true state of affairs. The first two or three rounds having been played, he is in full possession of the contents of each hand, and thenceforward puts down his cards with as absolute a precision of purpose as if the rest of the party had turned outward the faces of their own.

The analytical power should not be confounded with simple ingenuity; for while the analyst is necessarily ingenious, the ingenious man is often remarkably incapable of analysis. The constructive or combining power, by which ingenuity is usually manifested, and to which the phrenologists (I believe erroneously) have assigned a separate organ, supposing it a primitive faculty, has been so frequently seen in those whose intellect bordered otherwise upon idiocy, as to have attracted general observation among writers on morals. Between ingenuity and the analytic ability there exists a difference far greater, indeed, than that between the fancy and the imagination, but of a character very strictly analogous. It will be found, in fact, that the ingenious are always fanciful, and the *truly* imaginative never otherwise than analytic.

The narrative which follows will appear to the reader somewhat in the light of a commentary upon the propositions just advanced.

Residing in Paris during the spring and part of the summer of 18—, I there became acquainted with a Monsieur C. Auguste Dupin. This young gentleman was of an excellent, indeed of an illustrious family, but, by a variety of untoward events, had been reduced to such poverty that the energy of his character succumbed beneath it, and he ceased to bestir himself in the world, or to care for the retrieval of his fortunes. By courtesy of his creditors, there still remained in his possession a small remnant of his patrimony; and, upon the income arising from this, he managed, by means of a rigorous economy, to procure the necessities of life, without troubling himself about its superfluities. Books, indeed, were his sole luxuries, and in Paris these are easily obtained.

Our first meeting was at an obscure library in the Rue Montmartre, where the accident of our both being in search of the same very rare and very remarkable volume, brought us into closer communion. We saw each other again and again. I was deeply interested in the little family history which he detailed to me with all that candor which a Frenchman indulges whenever mere self is the theme. I was astonished, too, at the vast extent of his reading; and, above all, I felt my soul enkindled within me by the wild fervor, and the vivid freshness of his imagination. Seeking in Paris the objects I then sought, I felt that the society of such a man would be to me a treasure beyond price; and this feeling I frankly confided to him. It was at length arranged that we should live together during my stay in the city; and as my worldly circumstances were somewhat less embarrassed than his own, I was permitted to be at the expense of renting, and furnishing in a style which suited the rather fantastic gloom of our common temper, a time-eaten and grotesque mansion, long deserted through superstitions into which we did not inquire, and tottering to its fall in a retired and desolate portion of the Faubourg St. Germain.

Had the routine of our life at this place been known to the world, we should have been regarded as madmen—although, perhaps, as madmen of a harmless nature. Our seclusion was perfect. We admitted no visitors. Indeed the locality of our retirement had been carefully kept a secret from my own former associates; and it had been many years since Dupin had ceased to know or be known in Paris. We existed within ourselves alone.

It was a freak of fancy in my friend (for what else shall I call it?) to be enamored of the night for her own sake; and into this *bizarrerie*, as into all his others, I quietly fell; giving myself up to his wild whims with a perfect *abandon*. The sable divinity would not herself dwell with us always; but we could counterfeit her presence. At the first dawn of the morning we closed all the massy shutters of our old building; lighted a couple of tapers which, strongly perfumed, threw out only the ghastliest and feeblest of rays. By the aid of these we then busied our souls in dreams—reading, writing, or conversing, until warned by the clock of the advent of the true Darkness. Then we sallied forth into the streets, arm in arm, continuing the topics of the day, or roaming far and wide until a late hour, seeking, amid the wild lights and shadows of the populous city, that infinity of mental excitement which quiet observation can afford.

At such times I could not help remarking and admiring (although from his rich ideality I had been prepared to expect it) a peculiar analytic ability in Dupin. He seemed, too, to take an eager delight in its exercise—if not exactly in its display—and did not hesitate to confess the pleasure thus derived. He boasted to me, with a low chuckling laugh, that most men, in respect to himself, wore windows in their bosoms, and was wont to follow up such assertions by direct and very startling proofs of his intimate knowledge of my own. His manner at these moments was frigid and abstract; his eyes were vacant in expression; while his voice, usually a rich tenor, rose into a treble which would have sounded petulant but for the deliberateness and entire distinctness of the enunciation. Observing him in these moods, I often dwelt meditatively upon the old philosophy of the Bi-Part Soul, and amused myself with the fancy of a double Dupin—the creative and the resolvent.

Let it not be supposed, from what I have just said, that I am detailing any mystery, or penning any romance. What I have described in the Frenchman was merely the result of an excited, or perhaps of a diseased, intelligence. But of the character of his remarks at the periods in question an example will best convey the idea.

We were strolling one night down a long dirty street, in the vicinity of the Palais Royal. Being both, apparently, occupied with thought, neither of us had spoken a syllable for fifteen minutes at least. All at once Dupin broke forth with these words:

"He is a very little fellow, that's true, and would do better for the *Théâtre des Variétés.*"

"There can be no doubt of that," I replied, unwittingly, and not at first observing (so much had I been absorbed in reflection) the extraordinary manner in which the speaker had chimed in with my meditations. In an instant afterward I recollected myself, and my astonishment was profound.

"Dupin," said I, gravely, "this is beyond my comprehension. I do not hesitate to say that I am amazed, and can scarcely credit my senses. How was it possible you should know I was thinking of——?" Here I paused, to ascertain beyond a doubt whether he really knew of whom I thought.

"——of Chantilly," said he, "why do you pause? You were remarking to yourself that his diminutive figure unfitted him for tragedy."

This was precisely what had formed the subject of my reflections. Chantilly was a *quondam* cobbler of the Rue St. Denis, who, becoming stage-mad, had attempted the *rôle* of Xerxes, in Crébillon's tragedy so called, and been notoriously Pasquinaded for his pains.

"Tell me, for Heaven's sake," I exclaimed, "the method—if method there is—by which you have been enabled to fathom my soul in this matter." In fact, I was even more startled than I would have been willing to express.

"It was the fruiterer," replied my friend, "who brought you to the conclusion that the mender of soles was not of sufficient height for Xerxes *et id genus omne.*"

"The fruiterer!—you astonish me—I know no fruiterer whomsoever."

"The man who ran up against you as we entered the street—it may have been fifteen minutes ago."

I now remembered that, in fact, a fruiterer, carrying upon his head a large basket of apples, had nearly thrown me down, by accident, as we passed from the Rue C——into the thoroughfare where we stood; but what this had to do with Chantilly I could not possibly understand.

There was not a particle of *charlatânerie* about Dupin. "I will explain," he said, "and that you may comprehend all clearly, we will first retrace the course of your meditations, from the moment in which I spoke to you until that of the *rencontre* with the fruiterer in question. The larger links of the chain run thus—Chantilly, Orion, Dr. Nichols, Epicurus, Stereotomy, the street stones, the fruiterer."

There are few persons who have not, at some period of their lives, amused themselves in retracing the steps by which particular conclusions of their own minds have been attained. The occupation is often full of interest; and he who attempts it for the first time is astonished by the apparently illimitable distance and incoherence between the starting-point and the goal. What, then, must have been my amazement, when I heard the Frenchman speak what he had just spoken, and when I could not help acknowledging that he had spoken the truth. He continued:

"We had been talking of horses, if I remember aright, just before leaving the Rue C——. This was the last subject we discussed. As we crossed into this street, a fruiterer, with a large basket upon his head, brushing quickly past us, thrust you upon a pile of paving-stones collected at a spot where the causeway is undergoing repair. You stepped upon one of the loose fragments, slipped, slightly strained your ankle, appeared vexed or sulky, muttered a few words, turned to look at the pile, and then proceeded in silence. I was not particularly attentive to what you did; but observation has become with me, of late, a species of necessity.

"You kept your eyes upon the ground—glancing, with a petulant expression, at the holes and ruts in the pavement (so that I saw you were still thinking of the stones), until we reached the little alley called Lamartine, which has been paved, by way of experiment, with the overlapping and riveted blocks. Here your countenance brightened up, and, perceiving your lips move, I could not doubt that you murmured the word 'stereotomy,' a term very affectedly applied to this species of pavement. I knew that you could not say to yourself 'stereotomy' without being brought to think of atomies, and thus of the theories of Epicurus; and since, when we discussed this subject not very long ago, I mentioned to you how singularly, yet with how little notice, the vague guesses of that noble Greek had met with confirmation in the late nebular cosmogony, I felt that you could not avoid casting your eyes upward to the great *nebula* in Orion, and I certainly expected that you would do so. You did look up; and I was now assured that I had correctly followed your steps. But in that bitter *tirade* upon Chantilly, which appeared in yesterday's 'Musée,' the satirist, making some disgraceful allusions to the cobbler's change of name upon assuming the buskin, quoted a Latin line about which we have often conversed. I mean the line

Perdidit antiquum litera prima sonum.

I had told you that this was in reference to Orion, formerly written Urion; and, from certain pungencies connected with this explanation, I was aware that you could not have forgotten it. It was clear, therefore, that you would not fail to combine the two ideas of Orion and Chantilly. That you did combine them I saw by the character of the smile which passed over your lips. You thought of the poor cobbler's immolation. So far, you had been stooping in your gait; but now I saw you draw yourself up to your full height. I was then sure that you reflected upon the diminutive figure of Chantilly. At this point I interrupted your meditations to remark that as, in fact, he *was* a very little fellow—that Chantilly—he would do better at the *Théâtre des Variétés."*

Not long after this, we were looking over an evening edition of the *Gazette des Tribunaux*, when the following paragraphs arrested our attention.

"EXTRAORDINARY MURDERS.—This morning, about three o'clock, the inhabitants of the Quartier St. Roch were roused from sleep by a succession of terrific shrieks, issuing, apparently, from the fourth story of a house in the Rue Morgue, known to be in the sole occupancy of one Madame L'Espanaye, and her daughter, Mademoiselle Camille L'Espanaye. After some delay, occasioned by a fruitless attempt to procure admission in the usual manner, the gateway was broken in with a crowbar, and eight or ten of the neighbors entered, accompanied by two *gendarmes.* By this time the cries had ceased; but, as the party rushed up the first flight of stairs, two or more rough voices, in angry contention, were distinguished, and seemed to proceed from the upper part of the house. As the second landing was reached, these sounds, also, had ceased, and every thing remained perfectly quiet. The party spread themselves, and hurried from room to room. Upon arriving at a large back chamber in the fourth story (the door of which, being found locked, with the key inside, was forced open), a spectacle presented itself which struck every one present not less with horror than with astonishment.

"The apartment was in the wildest disorder—the furniture broken and thrown about in all directions. There was only one bedstead; and from this the bed had been removed, and thrown into the middle of the floor. On a chair lay a razor, besmeared with blood. On the hearth were two or three long and thick tresses of gray human hair, also dabbled with blood, and seeming to have been pulled out by the roots. Upon the floor were found four Napoleons, an ear-ring of topaz, three large silver spoons, three smaller of *métal d'Alger,* two bags, containing nearly four thousand francs in gold. The drawers of a *bureau,* which stood in one corner, were open, and had been, apparently, rifled, although many articles still remained in them. A small iron safe was discovered under the *bed* (not under the bedstead). It was open, with the key still in the door. It had no contents beyond a few old letters, and other papers of little consequence.

"Of Madame L'Espanaye no traces were here seen; but an unusual quantity of soot being observed in the fire-place, a search was made in the chimney, and (horrible to relate!) the corpse of the daughter, head downward, was dragged therefrom; it having been thus forced up the narrow aperture for a considerable distance. The body was quite warm. Upon examining it, many excoriations were perceived, no doubt occasioned by the violence with which it had been thrust up and disengaged. Upon the face were many severe scratches, and, upon the throat, dark bruises, and deep indentations of finger nails, as if the deceased had been throttled to death.

"After a thorough investigation of every portion of the house without farther discovery, the party made its way into a small paved yard in the rear of the building, where lay the corpse of the old lady, with her throat so entirely cut that, upon an attempt to raise her, the head fell off. The body, as well as the head, was fearfully mutilated—the former so much so as scarcely to retain any semblance of humanity.

"To this horrible mystery there is not as yet, we believe, the slightest clue."

The next day's paper had these additional particulars:

"The Tragedy in the Rue Morgue.—Many individuals have been examined in relation to this most extraordinary and frightful affair," [the word *"affaire"* has not yet, in France, that levity of import which it conveys with us] "but nothing whatever has transpired to throw light upon it. We give below all the material testimony elicited.

"Pauline Dubourg, laundress, deposes that she has known both the deceased for three years, having washed for them during that period. The old lady and her daughter seemed on good terms—very affectionate toward each other. They were excellent pay. Could not speak in regard to their mode or means of living. Believe that Madame L. told fortunes for a living. Was reputed to have money put by. Never met any person in the house when she called for the clothes or took them home. Was sure that they had no servant in employ. There appeared to be no furniture in any part of the building except in the fourth story.

"Pierre Moreau, tobacconist, deposes that he has been in the habit of selling small quantities of tobacco and snuff to Madame L'Espanaye for nearly four years. Was born in the neighborhood, and has always resided there. The deceased and her daughter had occupied the house in which the corpses were found, for more than six years. It was formerly occupied by a jeweller, who under-let the upper rooms to various persons. The house was the property of Madame L., who became dissatisfied with the abuse of the premises by her tenant, and moved into them herself, refusing to let any portion. The old lady was childish. Witness had seen the daughter some five or six times during the six years. The two lived an exceedingly retired life—were reputed to have money. Had heard it said among the neighbors that Madame L. told fortunes—did not believe it. Had never seen any person enter the door except the old lady and her daughter, a porter once or twice, and a physician some eight or ten times.

"Many other persons, neighbors, gave evidence to the same effect. No one was spoken of as frequenting the house. It was not known whether there were any living connections of Madame L. and her daughter. The shutters of the front windows were seldom opened. Those in the rear were always closed, with the exception of the large back room, fourth story. The house was a good house—not very old.

"*Isidore Musèt, gendarme,* deposes that he was called to the house about three o'clock in the morning, and found some twenty or thirty persons at the gateway, endeavoring to gain admittance. Forced it open, at length, with a bayonet—not with a crowbar. Had but little difficulty in getting it open, on account of its being a double or folding gate, and bolted neither at bottom nor top. The shrieks were continued until the gate was forced—and then suddenly ceased. They seemed to be screams of some person (or persons) in great agony—were loud and drawn out, not short and quick. Witness led the way up stairs. Upon reaching the first landing, heard two voices in loud and angry contention—the one a gruff voice, the other much shriller—a very strange voice. Could distinguish some words of the former, which was that of a Frenchman. Was positive that it was not a woman's voice. Could distinguish the words '*sacré*' and '*diable.*' The shrill voice was that of a foreigner. Could not be sure whether it was the voice of a man or of a woman. Could not make out what was said, but believed the language to be Spanish. The state of the room and of the bodies was described by this witness as we described them yesterday.

"*Henri Duval,* a neighbor, and by trade a silver-smith, deposes that he was one of the party who first entered the house. Corroborates the testimony of Musèt in general. As soon as they forced an entrance, they re-closed the door, to keep out the crowd, which collected very fast, notwithstanding the lateness of the hour. The shrill voice, this witness thinks, was that of an Italian. Was certain it was not French. Could not be sure that it was a man's voice. It might have been a woman's. Was not acquainted with the Italian language. Could not distinguish the words, but was convinced by the intonation that the speaker was an Italian. Knew Madame L. and her daughter. Had conversed with both frequently. Was sure that the shrill voice was not that of either of the deceased.

"——*Odenheimer, restaurateur.*——This witness volunteered his testimony. Not speaking French, was examined through an interpreter. Is a native of Amsterdam. Was passing the house at the time of the shrieks. They lasted for several minutes—probably ten. They were long and loud—very awful and distressing. Was one of those who entered the building. Corroborated the previous evidence in every respect but one. Was sure that the shrill voice was that of a man—of a Frenchman. Could not distinguish the words uttered. They were loud and quick—unequal—spoken apparently in fear as well as in anger. The voice was harsh—not so much shrill as harsh. Could not call it a shrill voice. The gruff voice said repeatedly, '*sacré,*' '*diable,*' and once '*mon Dieu.*'

"*Jules Mignaud,* banker, of the firm of Mignaud et Fils, Rue Deloraine. Is the elder Mignaud. Madame L'Espanaye had some property. Had opened an account with his banking house in the spring of the year— (eight years previously). Made frequent deposits in small sums. Had checked for nothing until the third day before her death, when she took out in person the sum of 4000 francs. This sum was paid in gold, and a clerk sent home with the money.

"*Adolphe Le Bon,* clerk to Mignaud et Fils, deposes that on the day in question, about noon, he accompanied Madame L'Espanaye to her residence with the 4000 francs, put up in two bags. Upon the door being opened, Mademoiselle L. appeared and took from his hands one of the bags, while the old lady relieved him of the other. He then bowed and departed. Did not see any person in the street at the time. It is a by-street—very lonely.

"*William Bird,* tailor, deposes that he was one of the party who entered the house. Is an Englishman. Has lived in Paris two years. Was one of the first to ascend the stairs. Heard the voices in contention. The gruff voice was that of a Frenchman. Could make out several words, but cannot now remember all. Heard distinctly '*sacré*' and '*mon Dieu.*' There was a sound at the moment as if of several persons struggling—a scraping and scuffling sound. The shrill voice was very loud—louder than the gruff one. Is sure that it was not the voice of an Englishman. Appeared to be that of a German. Might have been a woman's voice. Does not understand German.

"Four of the above-named witnesses, being recalled, deposed that the door of the chamber in which was found the body of Mademoiselle L. was locked on the inside when the party reached it. Every thing was perfectly silent—no groans or noises of any kind. Upon forcing the door no person was seen. The windows, both of the back and front room, were down and firmly fastened from within. A door between the two rooms was closed but not locked. The door leading from the front room into the passage was locked, with the key on the inside. A small room in the front of the house, on the fourth story, at the head of the passage, was open, the door being ajar. This room was crowded with old beds, boxes, and so forth. These were carefully removed and searched. There was not an inch of any portion of the house which was not carefully searched. Sweeps were sent up and down the chimneys.

"The house was a four-story one, with garrets *(mansardes).* A trapdoor on the roof was nailed down very securely—did not appear to have been opened for years. The time elapsing between the hearing of the voices in contention and the breaking open of the room door was variously stated by the witnesses. Some made it as short as three minutes—some as long as five. The door was opened with difficulty.

"*Alfonzo Garcio,* undertaker, deposes that he resides in the Rue Morgue. Is a native of Spain. Was one of the party who entered the house. Did not proceed upstairs. Is nervous, and was apprehensive of the consequences of agitation. Heard the voices in contention. The gruff voice was that of a Frenchman. Could not distinguish what was said. The shrill voice was that of an Englishman—is sure of this. Does not understand the English language, but judges by the intonation.

"*Alberto Montani,* confectioner, deposes that he was among the first to ascend the stairs. Heard the voices in question. The gruff voice was that of a Frenchman. Distinguished several words. The speaker appeared to be expostulating. Could not make out the words of the shrill voice. Spoke quick and unevenly. Thinks it the voice of a Russian. Corroborates the general testimony. Is an Italian. Never conversed with a native of Russia.

"Several witnesses, recalled, here testified that the chimneys of all the rooms on the fourth story were too narrow to admit the passage of a human being. By 'sweeps' were meant cylindrical sweeping-brushes, such as are employed by those who clean chimneys. These brushes were passed up and down every flue in the house. There is no back passage by which any one could have descended while the party proceeded up stairs. The body of Mademoiselle L'Espanaye was so firmly wedged in the chimney that it could not be got down until four or five of the party united their strength.

"*Paul Dumas,* physician, deposes that he was called to view the bodies about daybreak. They were both then lying on the sacking of the bedstead in the chamber where Mademoiselle L. was found. The corpse of the young lady was much bruised and excoriated. The fact that it had been thrust up the chimney would sufficiently account for these appearances. The throat was greatly chafed. There were several deep scratches just below the chin, together with a series of livid spots which were evidently the impression of fingers. The face was fearfully discolored, and the eyeballs protruded. The tongue had been partially bitten through. A large bruise was discovered upon the pit of the stomach, produced, apparently, by the pressure of a knee. In the opinion of M. Dumas, Mademoiselle L'Espanaye had been throttled to death by some person or persons unknown. The corpse of the mother was horribly mutilated. All the bones of the right leg and arm were more or less shattered. The left *tibia* much splintered, as well as all the ribs of the left side.

Whole body dreadfully bruised and discolored. It was not possible to say how the injuries had been inflicted. A heavy club of wood, or a broad bar of iron—a chair—any large, heavy, and obtuse weapon would have produced such results, if wielded by the hands of a very powerful man. No woman could have inflicted the blows with any weapon. The head of the deceased, when seen by witness, was entirely separated from the body, and was also greatly shattered. The throat had evidently been cut with some very sharp instrument—probably with a razor.

"*Alexandre Etienne,* surgeon, was called with M. Dumas to view the bodies. Corroborated the testimony, and the opinions of M. Dumas.

"Nothing further of importance was elicited, although several other persons were examined. A murder so mysterious, and so perplexing in all its particulars, was never before committed in Paris—if indeed a murder has been committed at all. The police are entirely at fault—an unusual occurrence in affairs of this nature. There is not, however, the shadow of a clew apparent."

The evening edition of the paper stated that the greatest excitement still continued in the Quartier St. Roch—that the premises in question had been carefully re-searched, and fresh examinations of witnesses instituted, but all to no purpose. A post-script, however, mentioned that Adolphe Le Bon had been arrested and imprisoned—although nothing appeared to criminate him beyond the facts already detailed. Dupin seemed singularly interested in the progress of this affair—at least so I judged from his manner, for he made no comments. It was only after the announcement that Le Bon had been imprisoned, that he asked me my opinion respecting the murders.

I could merely agree with all Paris in considering them an insoluble mystery. I saw no means by which it would be possible to trace the murderer.

"We must not judge of the means," said Dupin, "by this shell of an examination. The Parisian police, so much extolled for *acumen,* are cunning, but no more. There is no method in their proceedings, beyond the method of the moment. They make a vast parade of measures; but, not unfrequently, these are so ill-adapted to the objects proposed, as to put us in mind of Monsieur Jourdain's calling for his *robe-de-chambre—pour mieux entendre la musique.* The results attained by them are not unfrequently surprising, but, for the most part, are brought about by simple diligence and activity. When these qualities are unavailing, their schemes fail. Vidocq, for example, was a good guesser, and a persevering man. But, without educated thought, he erred continually by the very intensity of his investigations. He impaired his vision by holding the object too close. He might see, perhaps, one or two points with unusual clearness, but in so doing he, necessarily, lost sight of the matter as a whole. Thus there is such a thing as being too profound. Truth is not always in a well. In fact, as regards the more important knowledge, I do believe that she is invariably superficial. The depth lies in the valleys where we seek her, and not upon the mountain-tops where she is found. The modes and sources of this kind of error are well typified in the contemplation of the heavenly bodies. To look at a star by glances—to view it in a sidelong way, by turning toward it the exterior portions of the *retina* (more susceptible of feeble impressions of light than the interior), is to behold the star distinctly—is to have the best appreciation of its lustre—a lustre which grows dim just in proportion as we turn our vision *fully* upon it. A greater number of rays actually fall upon the eye in the latter case, but in the former, there is the more refined capacity for comprehension. By undue profundity we perplex and enfeeble thought; and it is possible to make even Venus herself vanish from the firmament by a scrutiny too sustained, too concentrated, or too direct.

"As for these murders, let us enter into some examinations for ourselves, before we make up an opinion respecting them. An inquiry will afford us amusement," [I thought this an odd term, so applied, but said nothing] "and besides, Le Bon once rendered me a service for which I am not ungrateful. We will go and see the premises with our own eyes. I know G——, the Prefect of Police, and shall have no difficulty in obtaining the necessary permission."

The permission was obtained, and we proceeded at once to the Rue Morgue. This is one of those miserable thoroughfares which intervene between the Rue Richelieu and the Rue St. Roch. It was late in the afternoon when we reached it, as this quarter is at a great distance from that in which we resided. The house was readily found; for there were still many persons gazing up at the closed shutters, with an objectless curiosity, from the opposite side of the way. It was an ordinary Parisian house, with a gateway, on one side of which was a glazed watch-box, with a sliding panel in the window, indicating a *loge de concierge.* Before going in we walked up the street, turned down an alley, and then, again turning, passed in the rear of the building—Dupin, meanwhile, examining the whole neighborhood, as well as the house, with a minuteness of attention for which I could see no possible object.

Retracing our steps we came again to the front of the dwelling, rang, and, having shown our credentials, were admitted by the agents in charge. We went up stairs—into the chamber where the body of Mademoiselle L'Espanaye had been found, and where both the deceased still lay. The disorders of the room had, as usual, been suffered to exist. I saw nothing beyond what had been stated in the *Gazette des Tribunaux.* Dupin scrutinized every thing—not excepting the bodies of the victims. We then went into the other rooms, and into the yard; a *gendarme* accompanying us throughout. The examination occupied us until dark, when we took our departure. On our way home my companion stepped in for a moment at the office of one of the daily papers.

I have said that the whims of my friend were manifold, and that *Je les ménagais:*—for this phrase there is no English equivalent. It was his humor, now, to decline all conversation on the subject of the murder, until about noon the next day. He then asked me, suddenly, if I had observed any thing *peculiar* at the scene of the atrocity.

There was something in his manner of emphasizing the word *"peculiar,"* which caused me to shudder, without knowing why.

"No, nothing *peculiar,*" I said; "nothing more, at least, than we both saw stated in the paper."

"The *Gazette,*" he replied, "has not entered, I fear, into the unusual horror of the thing. But dismiss the idle opinions of this print. It appears to me that this mystery is considered insoluble, for the very reason which should cause it to be regarded as easy of solution—I mean for the *outré* character of its features. The police are confounded by the seeming absence of motive—not for the murder itself—but for the atrocity of the murder. They are puzzled, too, by the seeming impossibility of reconciling the voices heard in contention, with the facts that no one was discovered up stairs but the assassinated Mademoiselle L'Espanaye, and that there were no means of egress without the notice of the party ascending. The wild disorder of the room; the corpse thrust, with the head downward, up the chimney; the frightful mutilation of the body of the old lady; these considerations, with those just mentioned, and others which I need not mention, have sufficed to paralyze the powers, by putting completely at fault the boasted *acumen,* of the government agents. They have fallen into the gross but common error of confounding the unusual with the abstruse. But it is by these deviations from the plane of the ordinary, that reason feels its way, if at all, in its search for the true. In investigations such as we are now pursuing, it should not be so much asked 'what has occurred,' as 'what has occurred that has never occurred before.' In fact, the facility with which I shall arrive, or have arrived, at the solution of this mystery, is in the direct ratio of its apparent insolubility in the eyes of the police."

I stared at the speaker in mute astonishment.

"I am now awaiting," continued he, looking toward the door of our apartment— "I am now awaiting a person who, although perhaps not the perpetrator of these butcheries, must have been in some measure implicated in their perpetration. Of the worst portion of the crimes committed, it is probable that he is innocent. I hope that I am right in this supposition; for upon it I build my expectation of reading the entire riddle. I look for the man here—in this room—every moment. It is true that he may not arrive; but the probability is that he will. Should he come, it will be necessary to detain him. Here are pistols; and we both know how to use them when occasion demands their use."

I took the pistols, scarcely knowing what I did, or believing what I heard, while Dupin went on, very much as if in a soliloquy. I have already spoken of his abstract manner at such times. His discourse was addressed to myself; but his voice, although by no means loud, had that intonation which is commonly employed in speaking to some one at a great distance. His eyes, vacant in expression, regarded only the wall.

"That the voices heard in contention," he said, "by the party upon the stairs, were not the voices of the women themselves, was fully proved by the evidence. This relieves us of all doubt upon the question whether the old lady could have first destroyed the daughter, and afterward have committed suicide. I speak of this point chiefly for the sake of method; for the strength of Madame L'Espanaye would have been utterly unequal to the task of thrusting her daughter's corpse up the chimney as it was found; and the nature of the wounds upon her own person entirely precludes the idea of self-destruction. Murder, then, has been committed by some third party; and the voices of this third party were those heard in contention. Let me now advert—not to the whole testimony respecting these voices—but to what was *peculiar* in that testimony. Did you observe any thing peculiar about it?"

I remarked that, while all the witnesses agreed in supposing the gruff voice to be that of a Frenchman, there was much disagreement in regard to the shrill, or, as one individual termed it, the harsh voice.

"That was the evidence itself," said Dupin, "but it was not the peculiarity of the evidence. You have observed nothing distinctive. Yet there *was* something to be observed. The witnesses, as you remark, agreed about the gruff voice; they were here unanimous. But in regard to the shrill voice, the peculiarity is—not that they disagreed—but that, while an Italian, an Englishman, a Spaniard, a Hollander, and a Frenchman attempted to describe it, each one spoke of it as that *of a foreigner.* Each is sure that it was not the voice of one of his own countrymen. Each likens it—not to the voice of an individual of any nation with whose language he is conversant— but the converse. The Frenchman supposes it the voice of a Spaniard, and 'might have distinguished some words *had he been acquainted with the Spanish.'* The Dutchman maintains it to have been that of a Frenchman; but we find it stated that *'not understanding French this witness was examined through an interpreter.'* The Englishman thinks it the voice of a German, and *'does not understand German.'* The Spaniard 'is sure' that it was that of an Englishman, but 'judges by the intonation' altogether, *'as he has no knowledge of the English.'* The Italian believes it the voice of a Russian, but *'has never conversed with a native of Russia.'* A second Frenchman differs, moreover, with the first, and is positive that the voice was that of an Italian; but, *not being cognizant of that tongue,* is, like the Spaniard, 'convinced by the into- nation.' Now, how strangely unusual must that voice have really been, about which such testimony as this *could* have been elicited!—in whose *tones,* even, denizens of the five great divisions of Europe could recognize nothing familiar! You will say that it might have been the voice of an Asiatic—of an African. Neither Asiatics nor Africans abound in Paris; but, without denying the inference, I will now merely call your attention to three points. The voice is termed by one witness 'harsh rather than shrill.' It is represented by two others to have been 'quick and *unequal.'* No words— no sounds resembling words—were by any witness mentioned as distinguishable.

"I know not," continued Dupin, "what impression I may have made, so far, upon your own understanding; but I do not hesitate to say that legitimate deductions even from this portion of the testimony—the portion respecting the gruff and shrill voices—are in themselves sufficient to engender a suspicion which should give direction to all farther progress in the investigation of the mystery. I said 'legitimate deductions'; but my meaning is not thus fully expressed. I designed to imply that the deductions are the *sole* proper ones, and that the suspicion arises *inevitably* from them as the single result. What the suspicion is, however, I will not say just yet. I merely wish you to bear in mind that, with myself, it was sufficiently forcible to give a definite form—a certain tendency—to my inquiries in the chamber.

"Let us now transport ourselves, in fancy, to this chamber. What shall we first seek here? The means of egress employed by the murderers. It is not too much to say that neither of us believe in præternatural events. Madame and Mademoiselle L'Espanaye were not destroyed by spirits. The doers of the deed were material and escaped materially. Then how? Fortunately there is but one mode of reasoning upon the point, and that mode *must* lead us to a definite decision. Let us examine, each by each, the possible means of egress. It is clear that the assassins were in the room where Mademoiselle L'Espanaye was found, or at least in the room adjoining, when the party ascended the stairs. It is, then, only from these two apartments that we have to seek issues. The police have laid bare the floors, the ceiling, and the masonry of the walls, in every direction. No *secret* issues could have escaped their vigilance. But, not trusting to *their* eyes, I examined with my own. There were, then, *no* secret issues. Both doors leading from the rooms into the passage were securely locked, with the keys inside. Let us turn to the chimneys. These, although of ordi- nary width for some eight or ten feet above the hearths, will not admit, throughout their extent, the body of a large cat. The impossibility of egress, by means already stated, being thus absolute, we are reduced to the windows. Through those of the front room no one could have escaped without notice from the crowd in the street. The murderers *must* have passed, then, through those of the back room. Now, brought to this conclusion in so unequivocal a manner as we are, it is not our part, as reasoners, to reject it on account of apparent impossibilities. It is only left for us to prove that these apparent 'impossibilities' are, in reality, not such.

"There are two windows in the chamber. One of them is unobstructed by furniture, and is wholly visible. The lower portion of the other is hidden from view by the head of the unwieldy bedstead which is thrust close up against it. The former was found securely fastened from within. It resisted the utmost force of those who endeavored to raise it. A large gimlet-hole had been pierced in its frame to the left, and a very stout nail was found fitted therein, nearly to the head. Upon examining the other window, a similar nail was seen similarly fitted in it; and a vigorous attempt to raise this sash failed also. The police were now entirely satisfied that egress had not been in these directions. And, *therefore,* it was thought a matter of supererogation to withdraw the nails and open the windows.

"My own examination was somewhat more particular, and was so for the reason I have just given—because here it was, I knew, that all apparent impossibilities *must* be proved to be not such in reality.

"I proceeded to think thus—*a posteriori.* The murderers *did* escape from one of these windows. This being so, they could not have refastened the sashes from the inside, as they were found fastened;—the consideration which put a stop, through its obviousness, to the scrutiny of the police in this quarter. Yet the sashes *were* fastened. They *must,* then, have the power of fastening themselves. There was no escape from this conclusion. I stepped to the unobstructed casement, withdrew the nail with some difficulty, and attempted to raise the sash. It resisted all my efforts, as I had anticipated. A concealed spring must, I now knew, exist; and this corroboration of my idea convinced me that my premises, at least, were correct, however mysterious still appeared the circumstances attending the nails. A careful search soon brought to light the hidden spring. I pressed it, and, satisfied with the discovery, forbore to upraise the sash.

"I now replaced the nail and regarded it attentively. A person passing out through this window might have reclosed it, and the spring would have caught—but the nail could not have been replaced. The conclusion was plain, and again narrowed in the field of my investigations. The assassins *must* have escaped through the other window. Supposing, then, the springs upon each sash to be the same, as was probable, there *must* be found a difference between the nails, or at least between the modes of their fixture. Getting upon the sacking of the bedstead, I looked over the head-board minutely at the second casement. Passing my hand down behind the board, I readily discovered and pressed the spring, which was, as I had supposed, identical in character with its neighbor. I now looked at the nail. It was as stout as the other, and apparently fitted in the same manner—driven in nearly up to the head.

"You will say that I was puzzled; but, if you think so, you must have misunderstood the nature of the inductions. To use a sporting phrase, I had not been once 'at fault.' The scent had never for an instant been lost. There was no flaw in any link of the chain. I had traced the secret to its ultimate result,—and that result was *the nail.* It had, I say, in every respect, the appearance of its fellow in the other window;

but this fact was an absolute nullity (conclusive as it might seem to be) when compared with the consideration that here, at this point, terminated the clew. 'There *must* be something wrong,' I said, 'about the nail.' I touched it; and the head, with about a quarter of an inch of the shank, came off in my fingers. The rest of the shank was in the gimlet-hole, where it had been broken off. The fracture was an old one (for its edges were incrusted with rust), and had apparently been accomplished by the blow of a hammer, which had partially imbedded, in the top of the bottom sash, the head portion of the nail. I now carefully replaced this head portion in the indentation whence I had taken it, and the resemblance to a perfect nail was complete—the fissure was invisible. Pressing the spring, I gently raised the sash for a few inches; the head went up with it, remaining firm in its bed. I closed the window, and the semblance of the whole nail was again perfect.

"This riddle, so far, was now unriddled. The assassin had escaped through the window which looked upon the bed. Dropping of its own accord upon his exit (or perhaps purposely closed), it had become fastened by the spring; and it was the retention of this spring which had been mistaken by the police for that of the nail,—farther inquiry being thus considered unnecessary.

"The next question is that of the mode of descent. Upon this point I had been satisfied in my walk with you around the building. About five feet and a half from the casement in question there runs a lightning-rod. From this rod it would have been impossible for any one to reach the window itself, to say nothing of entering it. I observed, however, that the shutters of the fourth story were of the peculiar kind called by Parisian carpenters *ferrades*—a kind rarely employed at the present day, but frequently seen upon very old mansions at Lyons and Bordeaux. They are in the form of an ordinary door (a single, not a folding door), except that the lower half is latticed or worked in open trellis—thus affording an excellent hold for the hands. In the present instance these shutters are fully three feet and a half broad. When we saw them from the rear of the house, they were both about half open—that is to say, they stood off at right angles from the wall. It is probable that the police, as well as myself, examined the back of the tenement; but, if so, in looking at these *ferrades* in the line of their breadth (as they must have done), they did not perceive this great breadth itself, or, at all events, failed to take it into due consideration. In fact, having once satisfied themselves that no egress could have been made in this quarter, they would naturally bestow here a very cursory examination. It was clear to me, however, that the shutter belonging to the window at the head of the bed, would, if swung fully back to the wall, reach to within two feet of the lightning-rod. It was also evident that, by exertion of a very unusual degree of activity and courage, an entrance into the window, from the rod, might have been thus effected. By reaching to the distance of two feet and a half (we now suppose the shutter open to its whole extent) a robber might have taken a firm grasp upon the trellis-work. Letting go, then, his hold upon the rod, placing his feet securely against the wall, and springing boldly from it, he might have swung the shutter so as to close it, and, if we imagine the window open at the time, might even have swung himself into the room.

"I wish you to bear especially in mind that I have spoken of a *very* unusual degree of activity as requisite to success in so hazardous and so difficult a feat. It is my design to show you first, that the thing might possibly have been accomplished:—but, secondly and *chiefly,* I wish to impress upon your understanding the *very extraordinary*—the almost præternatural character of that agility which could have accomplished it.

"You will say, no doubt, using the language of the law, that to make out my case, I should rather undervalue than insist upon a full estimation of the activity required in this matter. This may be the practice in law, but it is not the usage of reason. My ultimate object is only the truth. My immediate purpose is to lead you to place in juxtaposition, that *very unusual* activity of which I have just spoken, with that *very peculiar* shrill (or harsh) and *unequal* voice, about whose nationality no two persons could be found to agree, and in whose utterance no syllabification could be detected."

At these words a vague and half-formed conception of the meaning of Dupin flitted over my mind. I seemed to be upon the verge of comprehension, without power to comprehend—as men, at times, find themselves upon the brink of remembrance, without being able, in the end, to remember. My friend went on with his discourse.

"You will see," he said, "that I have shifted the question from the mode of egress to that of ingress. It was my design to convey the idea that both were effected in the same manner, at the same point. Let us now revert to the interior of the room. Let us survey the appearances here. The drawers of the bureau, it is said, had been rifled, although many articles of apparel still remained within them. The conclusion here is absurd. It is a mere guess—a very silly one—and no more. How are we to know that the articles found in the drawers were not all these drawers had originally contained? Madame L'Espanaye and her daughter lived an exceedingly retired life—saw no company—seldom went out—had little use for numerous changes of habiliment. Those found were at least of as good quality as any likely to be possessed by these ladies. If a thief had taken any, why did he not take the best—why did he not take all? In a word, why did he abandon four thousand francs in gold to encumber himself with a bundle of linen? The gold *was* abandoned. Nearly the whole sum mentioned by Monsieur Mignaud, the banker, was discovered, in bags, upon the floor. I wish you therefore, to discard from your thoughts the blundering idea of *motive,* engendered in the brains of the police by that portion of the evidence which speaks of money delivered at the door of the house. Coincidences ten times as remarkable as this (the delivery of the money, and murder committed within three days upon the party receiving it), happen to all of us every hour of our lives, without attracting even momentary notice. Coincidences, in general, are great stumbling-blocks in the way of that class of thinkers who have been educated to know nothing of the theory of probabilities—that theory to which the most glorious objects of human research are indebted for the most glorious of illustration. In the present instance, had the gold been gone, the fact of its delivery three days before would have formed something more than a coincidence. It would have been corroborative of this idea of motive. But, under the real circumstances of the case, if we are to suppose gold the motive of this outrage, we must also imagine the perpetrator so vacillating an idiot as to have abandoned his gold and his motive together.

"Keeping now steadily in mind the points to which I have drawn your attention—that peculiar voice, that unusual agility, and that startling absence of motive in a murder so singularly atrocious as this—let us glance at the butchery itself. Here is a woman strangled to death by manual strength, and thrust up a chimney head downward. Ordinary assassins employ no such mode of murder as this. Least of all, do they thus dispose of the murdered. In the manner of thrusting the corpse up the chimney, you will admit that there was something *excessively outré*—something altogether irreconcilable with our common notions of human action, even when we suppose the actors the most depraved of men. Think, too, how great must have been that strength which could have thrust the body *up* such an aperture so forcibly that the united vigor of several persons was found barely sufficient to drag it *down!*

"Turn, now, to other indications of the employment of a vigor most marvellous. On the hearth were thick tresses—very thick tresses—of gray human hair. These had been torn out by the roots. You are aware of the great force necessary in tearing thus from the head even twenty or thirty hairs together. You saw the locks in question as well as myself. Their roots (a hideous sight!) were clotted with fragments of the flesh of the scalp—sure token of the prodigious power which had been exerted in uprooting perhaps half a million of hairs at a time. The throat of the old lady was not merely cut, but the head absolutely severed from the body: the instrument was a mere razor. I wish you also to look at the *brutal* ferocity of these deeds. Of the bruises upon the body of Madame L'Espanaye I do not speak. Monsieur Dumas, and his worthy coadjutor Monsieur Etienne, have pronounced that they were inflicted by some obtuse instrument; and so far these gentlemen are very correct. The obtuse instrument was clearly the stone pavement in the yard, upon which the victim had fallen from the window which looked in upon the bed. This idea, however simple it may now seem, escaped the police for the same reason that the breadth of the shutters escaped them—because, by the affair of the nails, their perceptions had been hermetically sealed against the possibility of the windows having ever been opened at all.

"If now, in addition to all these things, you have properly reflected upon the odd disorder of the chamber, we have gone so far as to combine the ideas of an agility astounding, a strength superhuman, a ferocity brutal, a butchery without motive, a *grotesquerie* in horror absolutely alien from humanity, and a voice foreign in tone to the ears of men of many nations, and devoid of all distinct or intelligible syllabification. What result, then, has ensued? What impression have I made upon your fancy?"

I felt a creeping of the flesh as Dupin asked me the question. "A madman," I said, "has done this deed—some raving maniac, escaped from a neighboring *Maison de Santé.*"

"In some respects," he replied, "your idea is not irrelevant. But the voices of madmen, even in their wildest paroxysms, are never found to tally with that peculiar voice heard upon the stairs. Madmen are of some nation, and their language, however incoherent in its words, has always the coherence of syllabification. Besides, the hair of a madman is not such as I now hold in my hand. I disentangled this little tuft from the rigidly clutched fingers of Madame L'Espanaye. Tell me what you can make of it."

"Dupin!" I said, completely unnerved; "this hair is most unusual—this is no *human* hair."

"I have not asserted that it is," said he; "but before we decide this point, I wish you to glance at the little sketch I have here traced upon this paper. It is a *facsimile* drawing of what has been described in one portion of the testimony as 'dark bruises and deep indentations of finger nails' upon the throat of Mademoiselle L'Espanaye, and in another (by Messrs. Dumas and Etienne) as a 'series of livid spots, evidently the impression of fingers.' You will perceive," continued my friend, spreading out the paper upon the table before us, "that this drawing gives the idea of a firm and fixed hold. There is no *slipping* apparent. Each finger has retained—possibly until the death of the victim—the fearful grasp by which it originally imbedded itself.

Attempt, now, to place all your fingers, at the same time, in the respective impressions as you see them."

I made the attempt in vain.

"We are possibly not giving this matter a fair trial," he said. "The paper is spread out upon a plane surface; but the human throat is cylindrical. Here is a billet of wood, the circumference of which is about that of the throat. Wrap the drawing around it, and try the experiment again."

I did so; but the difficulty was even more obvious than before. "This," I said, "is the mark of no human hand."

"Read now," replied Dupin, "this passage from Cuvier."

It was a minute anatomical and generally descriptive account of the large fulvous Ourang-Outang of the East Indian Islands. The gigantic stature, the prodigious strength and activity, the wild ferocity, and the imitative propensities of these mammalia are sufficiently well known to all. I understood the full horrors of the murder at once.

"The description of the digits," said I, as I made an end of the reading, "is in exact accordance with this drawing. I see that no animal but an Ourang-Outang, of the species here mentioned, could have impressed the indentations as you have traced them. This tuft of tawny hair, too, is identical in character with that of the beast of Cuvier. But I cannot possibly comprehend the particulars of this frightful mystery. Besides, there were *two* voices heard in contention, and one of them was unquestionably the voice of a Frenchman."

"True; and you will remember an expression attributed almost unanimously, by the evidence, to this voice,—the expression, *'mon Dieu!'* This, under the circumstances, has been justly characterized by one of the witnesses (Montani, the confectioner) as an expression of remonstrance or expostulation. Upon these two words, therefore, I have mainly built my hopes of a full solution of the riddle. A Frenchman was cognizant of the murder. It is possible—indeed it is far more than probable—that he was innocent of all participation in the bloody transactions which took place. The Ourang-Outang may have escaped from him. He may have traced it to the chamber; but, under the agitating circumstances which ensued, he could never have recaptured it. It is still at large. I will not pursue these guesses—for I have no right to call them more—since the shades of reflection upon which they are based are scarcely of sufficient depth to be appreciable by my own intellect, and since I could not pretend to make them intelligible to the understanding of another. We will call them guesses, then, and speak of them as such. If the Frenchman in question is indeed, as I suppose, innocent of this atrocity, this advertisement, which I left last night, upon our return home, at the office of *Le Monde* (a paper devoted to the shipping interest, and much sought by sailors), will bring him to our residence."

He handed me a paper, and I read thus:

"CAUGHT—*In the Bois de Boulogne, early in the morning of the* ——*inst.* (the morning of the murder), *a very large, tawny Ourang-Outang of the Bornese species. The owner (who is ascertained to be a sailor, belonging to a Maltese vessel) may have the animal again, upon identifying it satisfactorily, and paying a few charges arising from its capture and keeping. Call at No.* —— *Rue*——, *Faubourg St. Germain—au troisième.*"

"How was it possible," I asked, "that you should know the man to be a sailor, and belonging to a Maltese vessel?"

"I do *not* know it," said Dupin. "I am not *sure* of it. Here, however, is a small piece of ribbon, which from its form, and from its greasy appearance, has evidently been used in tying the hair in one of those long *queues* of which sailors are so fond. Moreover, this knot is one which few besides sailors can tie, and is peculiar to the Maltese. I picked the ribbon up at the foot of the lightning-rod. It could not have belonged to either of the deceased. Now if, after all, I am wrong in my induction from this ribbon, that the Frenchman was a sailor belonging to a Maltese vessel, still I can have done no harm in saying what I did in the advertisement. If I am in error, he will merely suppose that I have been misled by some circumstance into which he will not take the trouble to inquire. But if I am right, a great point is gained. Cognizant although innocent of the murder, the Frenchman will naturally hesitate about replying to the advertisement—about demanding the Ourang-Outang. He will reason thus:—'I am innocent; I am poor; my Ourang-Outang is of great value—to one in my circumstances a fortune of itself—why should I lose it through idle apprehensions of danger? Here it is, within my grasp. It was found in the Bois de Boulogne—at a vast distance from the scene of that butchery. How can it ever be suspected that a brute beast should have done the deed? The police are at fault—they have failed to procure the slightest clew. Should they even trace the animal, it would be impossible to prove me cognizant of the murder, or to implicate me in guilt on account of that cognizance. Above all, *I am known.* The advertiser designates me as the possessor of the beast. I am not sure to what limit his knowledge may extend. Should I avoid claiming a property of so great value, which it is known that I possess, I will render the animal at least, liable to suspicion. It is not my policy to attract attention either to myself or to the beast. I will answer the advertisement, get the Ourang-Outang, and keep it close until this matter has blown over.'"

At this moment we heard a step upon the stairs.

"Be ready," said Dupin, "with your pistols, but neither use them nor show them until at a signal from myself."

The front door of the house had been left open, and the visitor had entered, without ringing, and advanced several steps upon the staircase. Now, however, he seemed to hesitate. Presently we heard him descending. Dupin was moving quickly to the door, when we again heard him coming up. He did not turn back a second time, but stepped up with decision, and rapped at the door of our chamber.

"Come in," said Dupin, in a cheerful and hearty tone.

A man entered. He was a sailor, evidently,—a tall, stout, and muscular-looking person, with a certain dare-devil expression of countenance, not altogether unprepossessing. His face, greatly sunburnt, was more than half hidden by whisker and *mustachio.* He had with him a huge oaken cudgel, but appeared to be otherwise unarmed. He bowed awkwardly, and bade us "good evening," in French accents, which, although somewhat Neufchatelish, were still sufficiently indicative of a Parisian origin.

"Sit down, my friend," said Dupin. "I suppose you have called about the Ourang-Outang. Upon my word, I almost envy you the possession of him; a remarkably fine, and no doubt a very valuable animal. How old do you suppose him to be?"

The sailor drew a long breath, with the air of a man relieved of some intolerable burden, and then replied, in an assured tone:

"I have no way of telling—but he can't be more than four or five years old. Have you got him here?"

"Oh, no; we had no conveniences for keeping him here. He is at a livery stable in the Rue Dubourg, just by. You can get him in the morning. Of course you are prepared to identify the property?"

"To be sure I am, sir."

"I shall be sorry to part with him," said Dupin.

"I don't mean that you should be at all this trouble for nothing, sir," said the man. "Couldn't expect it. I am very willing to pay a reward for the finding of the animal—that is to say, any thing in reason."

"Well," replied my friend, "that is all very fair, to be sure. Let me think!—what should I have? Oh! I will tell you. My reward shall be this. You shall give me all the information in your power about these murders in the Rue Morgue."

Dupin said the last words in a very low tone, and very quietly. Just as quietly, too, he walked toward the door, locked it, and put the key in his pocket. He then drew a pistol from his bosom and placed it, without the least flurry, upon the table.

The sailor's face flushed up as if he were struggling with suffocation. He started to his feet and grasped his cudgel; but the next moment he fell back into his seat, trembling violently, and with the countenance of death itself. He spoke not a word. I pitied him from the bottom of my heart.

"My friend," said Dupin, in a kind tone, "you are alarming yourself unnecessarily—you are indeed. We mean you no harm whatever. I pledge you the honor of a gentleman, and of a Frenchman, that we intend you no injury. I perfectly well know that you are innocent of the atrocities in the Rue Morgue. It will not do, however, to deny that you are in some measure implicated in them. From what I have already said, you must know that I have had means of information about this matter—means of which you could never have dreamed. Now the thing stands thus. You have done nothing which you could have avoided—nothing, certainly, which renders you culpable. You were not even guilty of robbery, when you might have robbed with impunity. You have nothing to conceal. You have no reason for concealment. On the other hand, you are bound by every principle of honor to confess all you know. An innocent man is now imprisoned, charged with that crime of which you can point out the perpetrator."

The sailor had recovered his presence of mind, in a great measure, while Dupin uttered these words; but his original boldness of bearing was all gone.

"So help me God!" said he, after a brief pause, "I *will* tell you all I know about this affair;—but I do not expect you to believe one half I say—I would be a fool indeed if I did. Still, I *am* innocent, and I will make a clean breast if I die for it."

What he stated was, in substance, this. He had lately made a voyage to the Indian Archipelago. A party, of which he formed one, landed at Borneo, and passed into the interior on an excursion of pleasure. Himself and a companion had captured the Ourang-Outang. This companion dying, the animal fell into his own exclusive possession. After great trouble, occasioned by the intractable ferocity of his captive during the home voyage, he at length succeeded in lodging it safely at his own residence in Paris, where, not to attract toward himself the unpleasant curiosity of his neighbors, he kept it carefully secluded, until such time as it should recover from a wound in the foot, received from a splinter on board ship. His ultimate design was to sell it.

Returning home from some sailors' frolic on the night, or rather in the morning, of the murder, he found the beast occupying his own bedroom, into which it had broken from a closet adjoining, where it had been, as was thought, securely confined. Razor in hand, and fully lathered, it was sitting before a looking-glass, attempting the operation of shaving, in which it had no doubt previously watched its master through the keyhole of the closet. Terrified at the sight of so dangerous a weapon in the possession of an animal so ferocious, and so well able to use it, the man, for some moments, was at a loss what to do. He had been accustomed, however, to quiet the creature, even in its fiercest moods, by the use of a whip, and to this he now resorted. Upon sight of it, the Ourang-Outang sprang at once through the door of the chamber, down the stairs, and thence, through a window, unfortunately open, into the street.

The Frenchman followed in despair; the ape, razor still in hand, occasionally stopping to look back and gesticulate at his pursuer, until the latter had nearly come up with it. It then again made off. In this manner the chase continued for a long time. The streets were profoundly quiet, as it was nearly three o'clock in the morning. In passing down an alley in the rear of the Rue Morgue, the fugitive's attention was arrested by a light gleaming from the open window of Madame L'Espanaye's chamber, in the fourth story of her house. Rushing to the building, it perceived the lightning-rod, clambered up with inconceivable agility, grasped the shutter, which was thrown fully back against the wall, and, by its means, swung itself directly upon the headboard of the bed. The whole feat did not occupy a minute. The shutter was kicked open again by the Ourang-Outang as it entered the room.

The sailor, in the meantime, was both rejoiced and perplexed. He had strong hopes of now recapturing the brute, as it could scarcely escape from the trap into which it had ventured, except by the rod, where it might be intercepted as it came down. On the other hand, there was much cause for anxiety as to what it might do in the house. This latter reflection urged the man still to follow the fugitive. A lightning-rod is ascended without difficulty, especially by a sailor; but, when he had arrived as high as the window, which lay far to his left, his career was stopped; the most that he could accomplish was to reach over so as to obtain a glimpse of the interior of the room. At this glimpse he nearly fell from his hold through excess of horror. Now it was that those hideous shrieks arose upon the night, which had startled from slumber the inmates of the Rue Morgue. Madame L'Espanaye and her daughter, habited in their night clothes, had apparently been occupied in arranging some papers in the iron chest already mentioned, which had been wheeled into the middle of the room. It was open, and its contents lay beside it on the floor. The victims must have been sitting with their backs toward the window; and, from the time elapsing between the ingress of the beast and the screams, it seems probable that it was not immediately perceived. The flapping-to of the shutter would naturally have been attributed to the wind.

As the sailor looked in, the gigantic animal had seized Madame L'Espanaye by the hair (which was loose, as she had been combing it), and was flourishing the razor about her face, in imitation of the motions of a barber. The daughter lay prostrate and motionless; she had swooned. The screams and struggles of the old lady (during which the hair was torn from her head) had the effect of changing the probably pacific purposes of the Ourang-Outang into those of wrath. With one determined sweep of its muscular arm it nearly severed her head from her body. The sight of blood inflamed its anger into phrensy. Gnashing its teeth, and flashing fire from its eyes, it flew upon the body of the girl, and imbedded its fearful talons in her throat, retaining its grasp until she expired. Its wandering and wild glances fell at this moment upon the head of the bed, over which the face of its master, rigid with horror, was just discernible. The fury of the beast, who no doubt bore still in mind the dreaded whip, was instantly converted into fear. Conscious of having deserved pun-ishment, it seemed desirous of concealing its bloody deeds, and skipped about the chamber in an agony of nervous agitation; throwing down and breaking the furni-ture as it moved, and dragging the bed from the bedstead. In conclusion, it seized first the corpse of the daughter, and thrust it up the chimney, as it was found; then that of the old lady, which it immediately hurled through the window headlong.

As the ape approached the casement with its mutilated burden, the sailor shrank aghast to the rod, and, rather gliding than clambering down it, hurried at once home—dreading the consequences of the butchery, and gladly abandoning, in his terror, all solicitude about the fate of the Ourang-Outang. The words heard by the party upon the staircase were the Frenchman's exclamations of horror and affright, commingled with the fiendish jabberings of the brute.

I have scarcely any thing to add. The Ourang-Outang must have escaped from the chamber, by the rod, just before the breaking of the door. It must have closed the window as it passed through it. It was subsequently caught by the owner him-self, who obtained for it a very large sum at the *Jardin des Plantes*. Le Bon was instantly released, upon our narration of the circumstances (with some comments from Dupin) at the *bureau* of the Prefect of Police. This functionary, however well disposed to my friend, could not altogether conceal his chagrin at the turn which affairs had taken, and was fain to indulge in a sarcasm or two about the propriety of every person minding his own business.

"Let him talk," said Dupin, who had not thought it necessary to reply. "Let him discourse; it will ease his conscience. I am satisfied with having defeated him in his own castle. Nevertheless, that he failed in the solution of this mystery, is by no means that matter for wonder which he supposes it; for, in truth, our friend the Prefect is somewhat too cunning to be profound. In his wisdom is no *stamen*. It is all head and no body, like the pictures of the Goddess Laverna—or, at best, all head and shoulders, like a codfish. But he is a good creature after all. I like him especially for one master stroke of cant, by which he has attained his reputation for ingenu-ity. I mean the way he has *'de nier ce qui est, et d'expliquer ce qui n'est pas.'"*

—1841

ARTHUR CONAN DOYLE

1859-1930

The world's most famous literary detective, as everyone knows, is Arthur Conan Doyle's master sleuth, Sherlock Holmes. Doyle patterned Holmes after Poe's Dupin: both detectives employ a detailed and systematic method of observation as part of their criminal investigations and use deductive reasoning to solve seemingly baffling crimes. Dupin and Holmes also both possess eccentric personalities; they are quite different from us, in many ways our intellectual superiors, yet in some ways our emotional inferiors.

In Doyle's "The Musgrave Ritual," for example, we learn from Dr.

*Rousseau—Nouvelle Héloise.

Watson that Holmes is an untidy roommate. His apartment at 221B Baker Street is unkempt, to say the least—he keeps his pipe tobacco in a Persian slipper, his chemicals laying about, and his documents scattered everywhere. When in "one of his queer humors," Holmes even engages in a highly unusual form of indoor target practice. These small touches, brief insights into Holmes's sometimes peculiar behavior, help make the otherwise superhuman Great Detective believable. Holmes may be brilliant, but we can identify with his idiosyncrasies and eccentricities.

Of course, with all of the critical attention paid over the years to Sherlock Holmes (he is one of the most written-about characters in all of literature), it is easy to forget his notable creator. Arthur Conan Doyle was born in Edinburgh, Scotland and attended medical school at Edinburgh University where one of his instructors, Dr. Joseph Bell, displayed astounding powers of observation and thus became a model for Doyle's Sherlock Holmes. After trying his hand at private practice, Doyle decided to become a full-time writer in 1891. A prolific and popular author, he published in a wide variety of literary genres—from historical romances to science fiction. Despite his creation of a character such as Holmes, who is the supreme rationalist, Doyle himself became, during his lifetime, a vocal advocate for spiritualism, a position that sometimes caused him professional embarrassment. However, Sherlock Holmes remains his most successful literary creation. Doyle published four Sherlock Holmes novels, A Study in Scarlet *(1888), the adventure that introduced Holmes,* The Sign of Four *(1890),* The Hound of the Baskervilles *(1902), and* The Valley of Fear *(1914); and he published five Sherlock Holmes short story collections,* The Adventures of Sherlock Holmes *(1892),* The Memoirs of Sherlock Holmes *(1894),* The Return of Sherlock Holmes *(1905),* His Last Bow: Some Reminiscences of Sherlock Holmes *(1917), and* The Case-Book of Sherlock Holmes *(1927).*

Doyle was not overjoyed about Holmes's tremendous popularity. He felt that writing the Holmes stories distracted him from working on more serious literary projects, such as his historical novels. At one point in the Sherlock Holmes series, he even tried to kill the Great Detective (in "The Final Problem"), but his shocked readers forced Doyle to bring the legendary Holmes back to life.

"The Musgrave Ritual" is one of the earlier Sherlock Holmes stories, first published in the May 1893 issue of The Strand Magazine *and collected in Doyle's second Holmes anthology,* The Memoirs of Sherlock Holmes. *This narrative effectively illustrates how the popular detective story functions as a metaphoric puzzle that requires solving. An actual puzzle called the Musgrave Ritual, in fact, is the literal key in Doyle's tale to both a possible murder and a fabulous treasure, a key that only Sherlock Holmes can decipher.*

THE MUSGRAVE RITUAL

An anomaly which often struck me in the character of my friend Sherlock Holmes was that, although in his methods of thought he was the neatest and most methodical of mankind, and although also he affected a certain quiet primness of dress, he was none the less in his personal habits one of the most untidy men that ever drove a fellow-lodger to distraction. Not that I am in the least conventional in that respect myself. The rough-and-tumble work in Afghanistan, coming on the top of a natural Bohemianism of disposition, has made me rather more lax than befits a medical man. But with me there is a limit, and when I find a man who keeps his cigars in the coal-scuttle, his tobacco in the toe end of a Persian slipper, and his unanswered correspondence transfixed by a jack-knife into the very centre of his wooden mantel-piece, then I begin to give myself virtuous airs. I have always held, too, that pistol practice should distinctly be an open-air pastime; and when Holmes in one of his queer humours would sit in an armchair, with his hair-trigger and a hundred Boxer cartridges, and proceed to adorn the opposite wall with a patriotic V. R. done in bullet-pocks, I felt strongly that neither the atmosphere nor the appearance of our room was improved by it.

Our chambers were always full of chemicals and of criminal relics, which had a way of wandering into unlikely positions, and of turning up in the butterdish, or in even less desirable places. But his papers were my great crux. He had a horror of destroying documents, especially those which were connected with his past cases, and yet it was only once in every year or two that he would muster energy to docket and arrange them, for as I have mentioned somewhere in these incoherent memoirs, the outbursts of passionate energy when he performed the remarkable feats with which his name is associated were followed by reactions of lethargy, during which he would lie about with his violin and his books, hardly moving, save from the sofa to the table. Thus month after month his papers accumulated, until every corner of the room was stacked with bundles of manuscript which were on no account to be burned, and which could not be put away save by their owner.

One winter's night, as we sat together by the fire, I ventured to suggest to him that as he had finished pasting extracts into his commonplace book he might employ the next two hours in making our room a little more habitable. He could not deny the justice of my request, so with a rather rueful face he went off to his bed-room, from which he returned presently pulling a large tin box behind him. This he placed in the middle of the floor, and squatting down upon a stool in front of it he threw back the lid. I could see that it was already a third full of bundles of paper tied up with red tape into separate packages.

"There are cases enough here, Watson," said he, looking at me with mischievous eyes. "I think that if you knew all that I had in this box you would ask me to pull some out instead of putting others in."

"These are the records of your early work, then?" I asked. "I have often wished that I had notes of those cases."

"Yes, my boy; these were all done prematurely before my biographer had come to glorify me." He lifted bundle after bundle in a tender, caressing sort of way. "They are not all successes, Watson," said he, "but there are some pretty little problems among them. Here's the record of the Tarleton murders and the case of Vamberry, the wine merchant, and the adventure of the old Russian woman, and the singular affair of the aluminum crutch, as well as a full account of Ricoletti of the club foot and his abominable wife. And here—ah, now! this really is something a little *recherché.*"

He dived his arm down to the bottom of the chest, and brought up a small wooden box, with a sliding lid, such as children's toys are kept in. From within he produced a crumpled piece of paper, an old-fashioned brass key, a peg of wood with a ball of string attached to it, and three rusty old discs of metal.

"Well, my boy, what do you make of this lot?" he asked, smiling at my expression.

"It is a curious collection."

"Very curious, and the story that hangs round it will strike you as being more curious still."

"These relics have a history, then?"

"So much so that they *are* history."

"What do you mean by that?"

Sherlock Holmes picked them up one by one, and laid them along the edge of the table. Then he reseated himself in his chair, and looked them over with a gleam of satisfaction in his eyes.

"These," said he, "are all that I have left to remind me of the episode of the Musgrave Ritual."

I had heard him mention the case more than once, though I had never been able to gather the details.

"I should be so glad," said I, "if you would give me an account of it."

"And leave the litter as it is?" he cried mischievously. "Your tidiness won't bear much strain, after all, Watson. But I should be glad that you should add this case to your annals, for there are points in it which make it quite unique in the criminal records of this or, I believe, of any other country. A collection of my trifling achievements would certainly be incomplete which contained no account of this very singular business.

"You may remember how the affair of the *Gloria Scott,* and my conversation with the unhappy man, whose fate I told you of, first turned my attention in the direction of the profession which has become my life's work. You see me now when my name has become known far and wide, and when I am generally recognized both by the public and by the offficial force as being a final court of appeal in doubtful cases. Even when you knew me first, at the time of the affair which you have commemorated in *A Study in Scarlet,* I had already established a considerable, though not a very lucrative connection. You can hardly realize, then, how difficult I found it at first, and how long I had to wait before I succeeded in making any headway.

"When I first came up to London I had rooms in Montague Street, just round the corner from the British Museum, and there I waited, filling in my too abundant leisure time by studying all those branches of science which might make me more efficient. Now and again cases came in my way, principally through the introduction of old fellow students, for during my last years at the university there was a good deal of talk there about myself and my methods. The third of these cases was that of the Musgrave Ritual, and it is to the interest which was aroused by that singular chain of events, and the large issues which proved to be at stake, that I trace my first stride towards the position which I now hold.

"Reginald Musgrave had been in the same college as myself, and I had some slight acquaintance with him. He was not generally popular among the undergraduates, though it always seemed to me that what was set down as pride was really an attempt to cover extreme natural diffidence. In appearance he was a man of an exceedingly aristocratic type, thin, high-nosed, and large-eyed, with languid and yet courtly manners. He was indeed a scion of one of the very oldest families in the kingdom, though his branch was a cadet one which had separated from the northern Musgraves some time in the sixteenth century, and had established itself in western Sussex, where the manor house of Hurlstone is perhaps the oldest inhabited building in the county. Something of his birthplace seemed to cling to the man, and I never looked at his pale, keen face, or the poise of his head, without associating him with grey archways and mullioned windows and all the venerable wreckage of a feudal keep. Now and again we drifted into talk, and I can remember that more than once he expressed a keen interest in my methods of observation and inference.

"For four years I had seen nothing of him, until one morning he walked into my room in Montague Street. He had changed little, was dressed like a young man of fashion—he was always a bit of a dandy—and preserved the same quiet, suave manner which had formerly distinguished him.

"'How has all gone with you, Musgrave?' I asked, after we had cordially shaken hands.

"'You probably heard of my poor father's death,' said he. 'He was carried off about two years ago. Since then I have, of course, had the Hurlstone estates to manage, and as I am member for the district as well, my life has been a busy one; but I understand, Holmes, that you are turning to practical ends those powers with which you used to amaze us.'

"'Yes,' said I, 'I have taken to living by my wits.'

"'I am delighted to hear it, for your advice at present would be exceedingly valuable to me. We have had some very strange doings at Hurlstone, and the police have been able to throw no light upon the matter. It is really the most extraordinary and inexplicable business.'

"You can imagine with what eagerness I listened to him, Watson, for the very chance for which I had been panting during all those months of inaction seemed to have come within my reach. In my inmost heart I believed that I could succeed where others failed, and now I had the opportunity to test myself.

"'Pray let me have the details,' I cried.

"Reginald Musgrave sat down opposite me, and lit the cigarette which I had pushed towards him.

"'You must know,' said he, 'that though I am a bachelor I have to keep up a considerable staff of servants at Hurlstone, for it is a rambling old place, and takes a good deal of looking after. I preserve, too, and in the pheasant months I usually have a house party, so that it would not do to be short-handed. Altogether there are eight maids, the cook, the butler, two footmen, and a boy. The garden and the stables, of course, have a separate staff.

"'Of these servants the one who had been longest in our service was Brunton, the butler. He was a young schoolmaster out of place when he was first taken up by my father, but he was a man of great energy and character, and he soon became quite invaluable in the household. He was a well-grown, handsome man, with a splendid forehead, and though he has been with us for twenty years he cannot be more than forty now. With his personal advantages and his extraordinary gifts, for he can speak several languages and play nearly every musical instrument, it is wonderful that he should have been satisfied so long in such a position, but I suppose that he was comfortable and lacked energy to make any change. The butler of Hurlstone is always a thing that is remembered by all who visit us.

"'But this paragon has one fault. He is a bit of a Don Juan, and you can imagine that for a man like him it is not a very difficult part to play in a quiet country district.

"'When he was married it was all right, but since he has been a widower we have had no end of trouble with him. A few months ago we were in hopes that he was about to settle down again, for he became engaged to Rachel Howells, our second housemaid, but he has thrown her over since then and taken up with Janet Tregellis, the daughter of the head gamekeeper. Rachel, who is a very good girl, but of an excitable Welsh temperament, had a sharp touch of brain fever, and goes about the house now—or did until yesterday—like a black-eyed shadow of her former self. That was our first drama at Hurlstone, but a second one came to drive it from our minds, and it was prefaced by the disgrace and dismissal of butler Brunton.

"'This was how it came about. I have said that the man was intelligent, and this very intelligence has caused his ruin, for it seems to have led to an insatiable curiosity about things which did not in the least concern him. I had no idea of the lengths to which this would carry him until the merest accident opened my eyes to it.

"'I have said that the house is a rambling one. One day last week—on Thursday night, to be more exact—I found that I could not sleep, having foolishly taken a cup of strong *café noir* after my dinner. After struggling against it until two in the morning I felt that it was quite hopeless, so I rose and lit the candle with the intention of continuing a novel which I was reading. The book, however, had been left in the billiard-room, so I pulled on my dressing-gown and started off to get it.

"'In order to reach the billiard-room I had to descend a flight of stairs, and then to cross the head of the passage which led to the library and the gun-room. You can imagine my surprise when as I looked down this corridor I saw a glimmer of light coming from the open door of the library. I had myself extinguished the lamp and closed the door before coming to bed. Naturally, my first thought was of burglars. The corridors at Hurlstone have their walls largely decorated with trophies of old weapons. From one of these I picked a battle-axe, and then, leaving my candle behind me, I crept on tip-toe down the passage and peeped in at the open door.

"'Brunton, the butler, was in the library. He was sitting, fully dressed, in an easy chair, with a slip of paper, which looked like a map, upon his knee, and his forehead sunk forward upon his hand in deep thought. I stood, dumb with astonishment, watching him from the darkness. A small taper on the edge of the table shed a feeble light, which sufficed to show me that he was fully dressed. Suddenly, as I looked, he rose from his chair, and walking over to a bureau at the side, he unlocked it and drew out one of the drawers. From this he took a paper, and, returning to his seat, he flattened it out beside the taper on the edge of the table, and began to study it with minute attention. My indignation at this calm examination of our family documents overcame me so far that I took a step forward, and Brunton, looking up, saw me standing in the doorway. He sprang to his feet, his face turned livid with fear, and he thrust into his breast the chart-like paper which he had been originally studying.

"'"So!" said I, "this is how you repay the trust which we have reposed in you! You will leave my service tomorrow."

"'He bowed with the look of a man who is utterly crushed, and slunk past me without a word. The taper was still on the table, and by its light I glanced to see what the paper was which Brunton had taken from the bureau. To my surprise it was nothing of any importance at all, but simply a copy of the questions and answers in the singular old observance called the Musgrave Ritual. It is a sort of ceremony peculiar to our family, which each Musgrave for centuries past has gone through on his coming of age—a thing of private interest, and perhaps of some little importance to the archaeologist, like our own blazonings and charges, but of no practical use whatever.'

"'We had better come back to the paper afterwards,' said I.

"'If you think it really necessary,' he answered, with some hesitation. 'To continue my statement, however, I re-locked the bureau, using the key which Brunton had left, and I had turned to go, when I was surprised to find that the butler had returned and was standing before me.

"'"Mr. Musgrave, sir," he cried, in a voice which was hoarse with emotion, "I can't bear disgrace, sir. I've always been proud above my station in life, and disgrace would kill me. My blood will be on your head, sir—it will, indeed—if you drive me to despair. If you cannot keep me after what has passed, then for God's sake let me give you notice and leave in a month, as if of my own free will. I could stand that, Mr. Musgrave, but not to be cast out before all the folk that I know so well."

"'"You don't deserve much consideration, Brunton," I answered. "Your conduct has been most infamous. However, as you have been a long time in the family, I have no wish to bring public disgrace upon you. A month, however, is too long. Take yourself away in a week, and give what reason you like for going."

"'"Only a week, sir?" he cried in a despairing voice. "A fortnight—say at least a fortnight."

"'"A week," I repeated, "and you may consider yourself to have been very leniently dealt with."

"'He crept away, his face sunk upon his breast, like a broken man, while I put out the light and returned to my room.

"'For two days after this Brunton was most assiduous in his attention to his duties. I made no allusion to what had passed, and waited with some curiosity to see how he would cover his disgrace. On the third morning, however, he did not appear, as was his custom, after breakfast to receive my instructions for the day. As I left the dining-room I happened to meet Rachel Howells, the maid. I have told you that she had only recently recovered from an illness, and was looking so wretchedly pale and wan that I remonstrated with her for being at work.

"'"You should be in bed," I said. "Come back to your duties when you are stronger."

"'She looked at me with so strange an expression that I began to suspect that her brain was affected.

"'"I am strong enough, Mr. Musgrave," said she.

"'"We will see what the doctor says," I answered. "You must stop work now, and when you go downstairs just say that I wish to see Brunton."

"'"The butler is gone," said she.

"'"Gone! Gone where?"

"'"He is gone. No one has seen him. He is not in his room. Oh, yes, he is gone— he is gone!" She fell back against the wall with shriek after shriek of laughter, while I, horrified at this sudden hysterical attack, rushed to the bell to summon help. The girl was taken to her room, still screaming and sobbing, while I made inquiries about Brunton. There was no doubt about it that he had disappeared. His bed had not been slept in; he had been seen by no one since he had retired to his room the night before; and yet it was difficult to see how he could have left the house, as both windows and doors were found to be fastened in the morning. His clothes, his watch, and even his money were in his room—but the black suit which he usually wore was missing. His slippers, too, were gone, but his boots were left behind. Where, then, could butler Brunton have gone in the night, and what could have become of him now?

"'Of course we searched the house from cellar to garret, but there was no trace of him. It is as I have said a labyrinth of an old house, especially the original wing, which is now practically uninhabited, but we ransacked every room and attic without discovering the least sign of the missing man. It was incredible to me that he could have gone away leaving all his property behind him, and yet where could he be? I called in the local police, but without success. Rain had fallen on the night before, and we examined the lawn and the paths all round the house, but in vain. Matters were in this state when a new development quite drew our attention away from the original mystery.

"'For two days Rachel Howells had been so ill, sometimes delirious, sometimes hysterical, that a nurse had been employed to sit up with her at night. On the third night after Brunton's disappearance, the nurse, finding her patient sleeping nicely, had dropped into a nap in the armchair, when she woke in the early morning to find the bed empty, the window open, and no signs of the invalid. I was instantly aroused, and with the two footmen started off at once in search of the missing girl. It was not difficult to tell the direction which she had taken, for, starting from under her window, we could follow her footmarks easily across the lawn to the edge of the mere, where they vanished, close to the gravel path which leads out of the grounds. The lake there is eight feet deep, and you can imagine our feelings when we saw that the trail of the poor demented girl came to an end at the edge of it.

"'Of course, we had the drags at once, and set to work to recover the remains; but no trace of the body could we find. On the other hand, we brought to the surface an object of a most unexpected kind. It was a linen bag, which contained within it a mass of old rusted and discoloured metal and several dull-coloured pieces of pebble or glass. This strange find was all that we could get from the mere, and although we made every possible search and inquiry yesterday, we know nothing of the fate either of Rachel Howells or Richard Brunton. The county police are at their wits' end, and I have come up to you as a last resource.'

"You can imagine, Watson, with what eagerness I listened to this extraordinary sequence of events, and endeavoured to piece them together, and to devise some common thread upon which they might all hang.

"The butler was gone. The maid was gone. The maid had loved the butler, but had afterwards had cause to hate him. She was of Welsh blood, fiery and passionate. She had been terribly excited immediately after his disappearance. She had flung into the lake a bag containing some curious contents. These were all factors which had to be taken into consideration, and yet none of them got quite to the heart of the matter. What was the starting-point of this chain of events? There lay the end of this tangled line.

"'I must see that paper, Musgrave,' said I, 'which this butler of yours thought it worth his while to consult, even at the risk of the loss of his place.'

"'It is rather an absurd business, this Ritual of ours,' he answered, 'but it has at least the saving grace of antiquity to excuse it. I have a copy of the questions and answers here, if you care to run your eye over them.'

"He handed me the very paper which I have here, Watson, and this is the strange catechism to which each Musgrave had to submit when he came to man's estate. I will read you the questions and answers as they stand:

"'Whose was it?

"'His who is gone.

"'Who shall have it?

"'He who will come.

"'What was the month?

"'The sixth from the first.

"'Where was the sun?

"'Over the oak.

"'Where was the shadow?

"'Under the elm.

"'How was it stepped?

"'North by ten and by ten, east by five and by five, south by two and by two, west by one and by one, and so under.

"'What shall we give for it?

"'All that is ours.

"'Why should we give it?

"'For the sake of the trust.'

"'The original has no date, but is in the spelling of the middle of the seventeenth century,' remarked Musgrave. 'I am afraid, however, that it can be of little help to you in solving this mystery.'

"'At least,' said I, 'it gives us another mystery, and one which is even more interesting than the first. It may be that the solution of the one may prove to be the solution of the other. You will excuse me, Musgrave, if I say that your butler appears to me to have been a very clever man, and to have had a clearer insight than ten generations of his masters.'

"'I hardly follow you,' said Musgrave. 'The paper seems to me to be of no practical importance.'

"'But to me it seems immensely practical, and I fancy that Brunton took the same view. He had probably seen it before that night on which you caught him.'

"'It is very possible. We took no pains to hide it.'

"'He simply wished, I should imagine, to refresh his memory upon that last occasion. He had, as I understand, some sort of map or chart which he was comparing with the manuscript, and which he thrust into his pocket when you appeared?'

"'That is true. But what could he have to do with this old family custom of ours, and what does this rigmarole mean?'

"'I don't think that we should have much difficulty in determining that,' said I. 'With your permission we will take the first train down to Sussex and go a little more deeply into the matter upon the spot.'

"The same afternoon saw us both at Hurlstone. Possibly you have seen pictures and read descriptions of the famous old building, so I will confine my account of it to saying that it is built in the shape of an L, the long arm being the more modern portion, and the shorter the ancient nucleus from which the other has developed. Over the low, heavy-lintelled door, in the centre of this old part, is chiselled the date 1607, but experts are agreed that the beams and stone-work are really much older than this. The enormously thick walls and tiny windows of this part had in the last century driven the family into building the new wing, and the old one was used now as a storehouse and a cellar when it was used at all. A splendid park, with fine old timber, surrounded the house, and the lake, to which my client had referred, lay close to the avenue, about two hundred yards from the building.

"I was already firmly convinced, Watson, that there were not three separate mysteries here, but one only, and that if I could read the Musgrave Ritual aright, I should hold in my hand the clue which would lead me to the truth concerning both the butler Brunton, and the maid Howells. To that, then, I turned all my energies. Why should this servant be so anxious to master this old formula? Evidently because he saw something in it which had escaped all those generations of country squires, and from which he expected some personal advantage. What was it, then, and how had it affected his fate?

"It was perfectly obvious to me on reading the Ritual that the measurements must refer to some spot to which the rest of the document alluded, and that if we could find that spot we should be in a fair way towards knowing what the secret was which the old Musgraves had thought it necessary to embalm in so curious a fashion. There were two guides given us to start with, an oak and an elm. As to the oak, there could be no question at all. Right in front of the house, upon the left-hand side of the drive, there stood a patriarch among oaks, one of the most magnificent trees that I have ever seen.

"'That was there when your Ritual was drawn up?' said I, as we drove past it.

"'It was there at the Norman Conquest, in all probability,' he answered. 'It has a girth of twenty-three feet.'

"Here was one of my fixed points secured.

"'Have you any old elms?' I asked.

"'There used to be a very old one over yonder, but it was struck by lightning ten years ago, and we cut down the stump.'

"'You can see where it used to be?'

"'Oh, yes.'

"'There are no other elms?'

"'No old ones, but plenty of beeches.'

"'I should like to see where it grew.'

"We had driven up in a dog-cart, and my client led me away at once, without our entering the house, to the scar on the lawn where the elm had stood. It was nearly midway between the oak and the house. My investigation seemed to be progressing.

"'I suppose it is impossible to find out how high the elm was?' I asked.

"'I can give you it at once. It was sixty-four feet.'

"'How do you come to know it?' I asked in surprise.

"'When my old tutor used to give me an exercise in trigonometry it always took the shape of measuring heights. When I was a lad I worked out every tree and building on the estate.'

"This was an unexpected piece of luck. My data were coming more quickly than I could have reasonably hoped.

"'Tell me,' I asked, 'did your butler ever ask you such a question?'

"Reginald Musgrave looked at me in astonishment. 'Now that you call it to my mind,' he answered, 'Brunton—did ask me about the height of the tree some months ago, in connection with some little argument with the groom.'

"This was excellent news, Watson, for it showed me that I was on the right road. I looked up at the sun. It was low in the heavens, and I calculated that in less than an hour it would lie just above the topmost branches of the old oak. One condition mentioned in the Ritual would then be fulfilled. And the shadow of the elm must mean the farther end of the shadow, otherwise the trunk would have been chosen as the guide. I had then to find where the far end of the shadow would fall when the sun was just clear of the oak."

"That must have been difficult, Holmes, when the elm was no longer there."

"Well, at least, I knew that if Brunton could do it, I could also. Besides, there was no real difficulty. I went with Musgrave to his study and whittled myself this peg, to which I tied this long string, with a knot at each yard. Then I took two lengths of a fishing-rod, which came to just six feet, and I went back with my client to where the elm had been. The sun was just grazing the top of the oak. I fastened the rod on end, marked out the direction of the shadow, and measured it. It was nine feet in length.

"Of course, the calculation now was a simple one. If a rod of six feet threw a shadow of nine, a tree of sixty-four feet would throw one of ninety-six feet, and the line of one would of course be the line of the other. I measured out the distance, which brought me almost to the wall of the house, and I thrust a peg into the spot. You can imagine my exultation, Watson, when within two inches of my peg I saw a conical depression in the ground. I knew that it was the mark made by Brunton in his measurements, and that I was still upon his trail.

"From this starting point I proceeded to step, having first taken the cardinal points by my pocket compass. Ten steps with each foot took me along parallel with the wall of the house, and again I marked my spot with a peg. Then I carefully paced off five to the east and two to the south. It brought me to the very threshold of the old door. Two steps to the west meant now that I was to go two paces down the stone-flagged passage, and this was the place indicated by the Ritual.

"Never have I felt such a cold chill of disappointment, Watson. For a moment it seemed to me that there must be some radical mistake in my calculations. The setting sun shone full upon the passage floor, and I could see that the old foot-worn grey stones, with which it was paved, were firmly cemented together, and had certainly not been moved for many a long year. Brunton had not been at work here. I tapped upon the floor, but it sounded the same all over, and there was no sign of any crack or crevice. But fortunately, Musgrave, who had begun to appreciate the meaning of my proceedings, and who was now as excited as myself, took out his manuscript to check my calculations.

"'"And under," he cried: "You have omitted the 'and under.'"

"I had thought that it meant that we were to dig, but now, of course, I saw at once that I was wrong. 'There is a cellar under this, then?' I cried.

"'Yes, and as old as the house. Down here, through this door.'

"We went down a winding stone stair, and my companion, striking a match, lit a large lantern which stood on a barrel in the corner. In an instant it was obvious that we had at last come upon the true place, and that we had not been the only people to visit the spot recently.

"It had been used for the storage of wood, but the billets, which had evidently been littered over the floor, were now piled at the sides so as to leave a clear space in the middle. In this space lay a large and heavy flagstone, with a rusted iron ring in the centre, to which a thick shepherd's check muffler was attached.

"'By Jove!' cried my client, 'that's Brunton's muffler. I have seen it on him, and could swear to it. What has the villain been doing here?'

"At my suggestion a couple of the county police were summoned to be present, and I then endeavoured to raise the stone by pulling on the cravat. I could only move it slightly, and it was with the aid of one of the constables that I succeeded at last in carrying it to one side. A black hole yawned beneath, into which we all peered, while Musgrave, kneeling at the side, pushed down the lantern.

"A small chamber about seven feet deep and four feet square lay open to us. At one side of this was a squat, brass-bound, wooden box, the lid of which was hinged upwards, with this curious, old-fashioned key projecting from the lock. It was furred outside by a thick layer of dust, and damp and worms had eaten through the wood so that a crop of living fungi was growing on the inside of it. Several discs of metal—

old coins apparently—such as I hold here, were scattered over the bottom of the box, but it contained nothing else.

"At the moment, however, we had no thought for the old chest, for our eyes were riveted upon that which crouched beside it. It was the figure of a man, clad in a suit of black, who squatted down upon his hams with his forehead sunk upon the edge of the box and his two arms thrown out on each side of it. The attitude had drawn all the stagnant blood to the face, and no man could have recognized that distorted, liver-coloured countenance; but his height, his dress, and his hair were all sufficient to show my client, when we had drawn the body up, that it was indeed his missing butler. He had been dead some days, but there was no wound or bruise upon his person to show how he had met his dreadful end. When his body had been carried from the cellar we found ourselves still confronted with a problem which was almost as formidable as that with which we had started.

"I confess that so far, Watson, I had been disappointed in my investigation. I had reckoned upon solving the matter when once I had found the place referred to in the Ritual; but now I was there, and was apparently as far as ever from knowing what it was which the family had concealed with such elaborate precautions. It is true that I had thrown a light upon the fate of Brunton, but now I had to ascertain how that fate had come upon him, and what part had been played in the matter by the woman who had disappeared. I sat down upon a keg in the corner and thought the whole matter carefully over.

"You know my methods in such cases, Watson: I put myself in the man's place, and having first gauged his intelligence, I try to imagine how I should myself have proceeded under the same circumstances. In this case the matter was simplified by Brunton's intelligence being quite first rate, so that it was unnecessary to make any allowance for personal equation, as the astronomers have dubbed it. He knew that something valuable was concealed. He had spotted the place. He found that the stone which covered it was just too heavy for a man to move unaided. What would he do next? He could not get help from outside, even if he had someone whom he could trust, without the unbarring of doors, and considerable risk of detection. It was better, if he could, to have his helpmate inside the house. But whom could he ask? This girl had been devoted to him. A man always finds it hard to realize that he may have finally lost a woman's love, however badly he may have treated her. He would try by a few attentions to make his peace with the girl Howells, and then would engage her as his accomplice. Together they would come at night to the cellar, and their united force would suffice to raise the stone. So far I could follow their actions as if I had actually seen them.

"But for two of them, and one a woman, it must have been heavy work, the raising of that stone. A burly Sussex policeman and I had found it no light job. What would they do to assist them? Probably what I should have done myself. I rose and examined carefully the different billets of wood which were scattered round the floor. Almost at once I came upon what I expected. One piece, about 3 ft in length, had a marked indentation at one end, while several were flattened at the sides as if they had been compressed by some considerable weight. Evidently, as they had dragged the stone up they had thrust the chunks of wood into the chink, until at last, when the opening was large enough to crawl through, they would hold it open by a billet placed lengthwise, which might very well become indented at the lower end, since the whole weight of the stone would press it down on to the edge of the other slab. So far I was still on safe ground.

"And now, how was I to proceed to reconstruct this midnight drama? Clearly only one could get into the hole, and that one was Brunton. The girl must have waited above. Brunton then unlocked the box, handed up the contents, presumably—since they were not to be found—and then—and then what happened?

"What smouldering fire of vengeance had suddenly sprung into flame in this passionate Celtic woman's soul when she saw the man who had wronged her— wronged her perhaps far more than we suspected—in her power? Was it a chance that the wood had slipped and that the stone had shut Brunton into what had become his sepulchre? Had she only been guilty of silence as to his fate? Or had some sudden blow from her hand dashed the support away and sent the slab crashing down into its place. Be that as it might, I seemed to see that woman's figure, still clutching at her treasure-trove, and flying wildly up the winding stair with her ears ringing perhaps with the muffled screams from behind her, and with the drumming of frenzied hands against the slab of stone which was choking her faithless lover's life out.

"Here was the secret of her blanched face, her shaken nerves, her peals of hysterical laughter on the next morning. But what had been in the box? What had she done with that? Of course, it must have been the old metal and pebbles which my client had dragged from the mere. She had thrown them in there at the first opportunity, to remove the last trace of her crime.

"For twenty minutes I had sat motionless thinking the matter out. Musgrave still stood with a very pale face swinging his lantern and peering down into the hole.

"'These are coins of Charles I,' said he, holding out the few which had been left in the box. 'You see we were right in fixing our date for the Ritual.'

"'We may find something else of Charles I,' I cried, as the probable meaning of the first two questions of the Ritual broke suddenly upon me. 'Let me see the contents of the bag which you fished from the mere.'

"We ascended to his study, and he laid the débris before me. I could understand his regarding it as of small importance when I looked at it, for the metal was almost black, and the stones lustreless and dull. I rubbed one of them on my sleeve, however, and it glowed afterwards like a spark, in the dark hollow of my hand. The metal-work was in the form of a double-ring, but it had been bent and twisted out of its original shape.

"'You must bear in mind,' said I, 'that the Royal party made headway in England even after the death of the King, and that when they at last fled they probably left many of their most precious possessions buried behind them, with the intention of returning for them in more peaceful times.'

"'My ancestor, Sir Ralph Musgrave, was a prominent Cavalier, and the right-hand man of Charles II in his wanderings,' said my friend.

"'Ah, indeed!' I answered. 'Well, now, I think that really should give us the last link that we wanted. I must congratulate you on coming into the possession, though in rather a tragic manner, of a relic which is of great intrinsic value, but of even greater importance as an historical curiosity.'

"'What is it, then?' he gasped in astonishment.

"'It is nothing less than the ancient crown of the Kings of England.'

"'The crown!'

"'Precisely. Consider what the Ritual says. How does it run? "Whose was it?" "His who is gone." That was after the execution of Charles. Then, "Who should have it?" "He who will come." That was Charles II, whose advent was already foreseen. There can, I think, be no doubt that this battered and shapeless diadem once encircled the brows of the Royal Stuarts.'

"'And how came it in the pond?'

"'Ah, that is a question that will take some time to answer,' and with that sketched out the whole long chain of surmise and of proof which I had constructed. The twilight had closed in and the moon was shining brightly in sky before my narrative was finished.

"'And how was it, then, that Charles did not get his crown when he returned?' asked Musgrave, pushing back the relic into its linen bag.

"'Ah, there you lay your finger upon the one point which we shall probably never be able to clear up. It is likely that the Musgrave who held the secret died in the interval, and by some oversight left this guide to his descendant without explaining the meaning of it. From that day to this it has been handed down from father to son, until at last it came within reach of a man who tore its secret out of it and lost his life in the venture.'

"And that's the story of the Musgrave Ritual, Watson. They have the crown down at Hurlstone—though they had some legal bother, and a considerable sum to pay before they were allowed to retain it. I am sure that if you mentioned my name they would be happy to show it to you. Of the woman nothing was ever heard, and the probability is that she got away out of England and carried herself and the memory of her crime to some land beyond the seas."

—1893

A G A T H A   C H R I S T I E
1890-1976

Devon-born Agatha Christie ranks as one of the most admired authors of British crime fiction. Her many novels and short story collections continue to enjoy renewed popularity with each new generation of devoted readers. Her work has been translated into numerous languages worldwide and has been frequently adapted for television and film. Her first novel, The Mysterious Affair at Styles *(1920), introduced one of crime fiction's most popular detective heroes, the prim yet brilliant little Belgian, Hercule Poirot. Poirot was featured in a great number of Christie's novels, but many readers agree his most famous case is* The Murder of Roger Ackroyd *(1926), a controversial story that helped establish Christie's international reputation as a first-class writer of mystery fiction. Some critics argue that* The Murder of Roger Ackroyd *does not "play fair" with the reader (a fundamental requirement for the classic detective story), but the novel's undeniably inventive resolution would soon become a trademark of the typical Christie mystery. Regarding her use of setting in her stories, Christie felt equally comfortable employing either the English country manor house or the exotic foreign locale. Though her books often dealt with murder, they generally lack the violence commonly associated with American "hard-boiled" crime fiction. Christie's extensive knowledge of poisons (derived from her work as a Voluntary Aid Detachment nurse during World War I) served her well in the plotting of her intricate mysteries. Other popular detective heroes created by Christie's fertile imagination include Superintendent Battle, whose first published adventure was* The Secret of Chimneys *(1925); the team of Tuppence and Tommy Beresford, who first appeared in* The Secret Adversary *(1922); Colonel Race, first seen in* The Man in the Brown Suit *(1924); and Jane Marple. (Christie also wrote under the "Mary Westmacott" pseudonym.)*

The Murder at the Vicarage (1930) was the first novel to feature Miss Marple. Over the years, Christie's elderly sleuth appeared in a number of adventures, such as The Body in the Library *(1942),* The Moving Finger *(1943),* A Murder Is Announced *(1950),* They Do It with Mirrors *(1952), and* Nemesis *(1971), to name just a few titles. In Miss Marple's final case,* Sleeping Murder *(1976), Christie brings to a close the exploits of one of her most memorable detectives. What makes Miss Marple such an interesting sleuth is her deceptive appearance. She does not look or act like a detective. She, instead, appears quite innocuous, more like someone's grandmother. But housed beneath the "piled-up masses . . . of snowy hair" there exists a mind possessing a razor sharp intellect, a keen understanding of human nature, and an unmatched ability to solve the most puzzling of mysteries.*

The introductory tale in the anthology entitled The Thirteen Problems *(1932; U.S. title:* The Tuesday Club Murders, *1933), "The Tuesday Night Club" is the first of a group of loosely connected short stories that highlights Miss Marple's phenomenal ability as an "armchair detective." The assortment of people who comprise this informal "club" of self-defined sleuths represents a spectrum of middle-class British society, from the clergyman to the solicitor. At the conclusion of the story, after each member of the "Tuesday Night Club," in round-robin fashion, offers his or her solution to the question of Mrs. Jones's murder, it is the unobtrusive Miss Marple (she of the "gentle smile" and "kindly" faded blue eyes) who provides the only correct solution to Sir Henry Clithering's baffling crime. What training has allowed Miss Marple such a perceptive understanding of the criminal mind? She even solves this mystery for us by stating early in "The Tuesday Night Club" that "living all these years in St. Mary Mead does give one an insight into human nature."*

THE TUESDAY NIGHT CLUB

"Unsolved Mysteries."

Raymond West blew out a cloud of smoke and repeated the words with a kind of deliberate self-conscious pleasure.

"Unsolved mysteries."

He looked round him with satisfaction. The room was an old one with broad black beams across the ceiling and it was furnished with good old furniture that belonged to it. Hence Raymond West's approving glance. By profession he was a writer and he liked the atmosphere to be flawless. His Aunt Jane's house always pleased him as the right setting for her personality. He looked across the hearth to where she sat erect in the big grandfather chair. Miss Marple wore a black brocade dress, very much pinched in round the waist. Mechlin lace was arranged in a cascade down the front of the bodice. She had on black lace mittens, and a black lace cap surmounted the piled-up masses of her snowy hair. She was knitting—something white and soft and fleecy. Her faded blue eyes, benignant and kindly, surveyed her nephew and her nephew's guests with gentle pleasure. They rested first on Raymond himself, self-consciously debonair, then on Joyce Lemprière, the artist, with her close-cropped black head and queer hazel-green eyes, then on that well-groomed man of the world, Sir Henry Clithering. There were two other people in the room, Dr. Pender, the elderly clergyman of the parish, and Mr. Petherick, the solicitor, a dried-up little man with eyeglasses which he looked over and not through. Miss Marple gave a brief moment of attention to all these people and returned to her knitting with a gentle smile upon her lips.

Mr. Petherick gave the dry little cough with which he usually prefaced his remarks.

"What is that you say, Raymond? Unsolved mysteries? Ha—and what about them?"

"Nothing about them," said Joyce Lemprière. "Raymond just likes the sound of the words and of himself saying them."

Raymond West threw her a glance of reproach at which she threw back her head and laughed.

"He is a humbug, isn't he, Miss Marple?" she demanded. "You know that, I am sure."

Miss Marple smiled gently at her but made no reply.

"Life itself is an unsolved mystery," said the clergyman gravely.

Raymond sat up in his chair and flung away his cigarette with an impulsive gesture.

"That's not what I mean. I was not talking philosophy," he said. "I was thinking of actual bare prosaic facts, things that have happened and that no one has ever explained."

"I know just the sort of thing you mean, dear," said Miss Marple. "For instance Mrs. Carruthers had a very strange experience yesterday morning. She bought two gills of pickled shrimps at Elliot's. She called at two other shops and when she got home she found she had not got the shrimps with her. She went back to the two shops she had visited but these shrimps had completely disappeared. Now that seems to me very remarkable."

"A very fishy story," said Sir Henry Clithering gravely.

"There are, of course, all kinds of possible explanations," said Miss Marple, her cheeks growing slightly pinker with excitement. "For instance, somebody else—"

"My dear Aunt," said Raymond West with some amusement, "I didn't mean that sort of village incident. I was thinking of murders and disappearances—the kind of thing that Sir Henry could tell us about by the hour if he liked."

"But I never talk shop," said Sir Henry modestly. "No, I never talk shop."

Sir Henry Clithering had been until lately Commissioner of Scotland Yard.

"I suppose there are a lot of murders and things that never are solved by the police," said Joyce Lemprière.

"That is an admitted fact, I believe," said Mr. Petherick.

"I wonder," said Raymond West, "what class of brain really succeeds best in unravelling a mystery? One always feels that the average police detective must be hampered by lack of imagination."

"That is the layman's point of view," said Sir Henry drily.

"You really want a committee," said Joyce, smiling. "For psychology and imagination go to the writer—"

She made an ironical bow to Raymond but he remained serious.

"The art of writing gives one an insight into human nature," he said gravely. "One sees, perhaps, motives that the ordinary person would pass by."

"I know, dear," said Miss Marple, "that your books are very clever. But do you think that people are really so unpleasant as you make them out to be?"

"My dear Aunt," said Raymond gently, "keep your beliefs. Heaven forbid that *I* should in any way shatter them."

"I mean," said Miss Marple, puckering her brow a little as she counted the stitches in her knitting, "that so many people seem to me not to be either bad or good, but simply you know, very silly."

Mr. Petherick gave his dry little cough again.

"Don't you think, Raymond," he said, "that you attach too much weight to imagination? Imagination is a very dangerous thing, as we lawyers know only too well. To be able to sift evidence impartially, to take the facts and look at them as facts— that seems to me the only logical method of arriving at the truth. I may add that in my experience it is the only one that succeeds."

"Bah!" cried Joyce, flinging back her black head indignantly. "I bet I could beat you all at this game. I am not only a woman—and say what you like, women have an intuition that is denied to men—I am an artist as well. I see things that you don't. And then, too, as an artist I have knocked about among all sorts and conditions of people. I know life as darling Miss Marple here cannot possibly know it."

"I don't know about that, dear," said Miss Marple. "Very painful and distressing things happen in villages sometimes."

"May I speak?" said Dr. Pender smiling. "It is the fashion nowadays to decry the clergy, I know, but we hear things, we know a side of human character which is a sealed book to the outside world."

"Well," said Joyce, "it seems to me we are a pretty representative gathering. How would it be if we formed a Club? What is today? Tuesday? We will call it The Tuesday Night Club. It is to meet every week, and each member in turn has to propound a problem. Some mystery of which they have personal knowledge, and to which, of course, they know the answer. Let me see, how many are we? One, two, three, four, five. We ought really to be six."

"You have forgotten me, dear," said Miss Marple, smiling brightly.

Joyce was slightly taken aback, but she concealed the fact quickly.

"That would be lovely, Miss Marple," she said. "I didn't think you would care to play."

"I think it would be very interesting," said Miss Marple, "especially with so many clever gentlemen present. I am afraid I am not clever myself, but living all these years in St. Mary Mead does give one an insight into human nature."

"I am sure your cooperation will be very valuable," said Sir Henry, courteously.

"Who is going to start?" said Joyce.

"I think there is no doubt as to that," said Dr. Pender, "when we have the great good fortune to have such a distinguished man as Sir Henry staying with us—"

He left his sentence unfinished, making a courtly bow in the direction of Sir Henry.

The latter was silent for a minute or two. At last he sighed and recrossed his legs and began:

"It is a little difficult for me to select just the kind of thing you want, but I think, as it happens, I know of an instance which fits these conditions very aptly. You may have seen some mention of the case in the papers of a year ago. It was laid aside at the time as an unsolved mystery, but, as it happens, the solution came into my hands not very many days ago.

"The facts are very simple. Three people sat down to a supper consisting, amongst other things, of tinned lobster. Later in the night, all three were taken ill, and a doctor was hastily summoned. Two of the people recovered, the third one died."

"Ah!" said Raymond approvingly.

"As I say, the facts as such were very simple. Death was considered to be due to ptomaine poisoning, a certificate was given to that effect, and the victim was duly buried. But things did not rest at that."

Miss Marple nodded her head.

"There was talk, I suppose," she said, "there usually is."

"And now I must describe the actors in this little drama. I will call the husband and wife Mr. and Mrs. Jones, and the wife's companion Miss Clark. Mr. Jones was a traveller for a firm of manufacturing chemists. He was a good-looking man in a kind of coarse, florid way, aged about fifty. His wife was a rather commonplace woman, of about forty-five. The companion, Miss Clark, was a woman of sixty, a stout cheery woman with a beaming rubicund face. None of them, you might say, very interesting.

"Now the beginning of the troubles arose in a very curious way. Mr. Jones had been staying the previous night at a small commercial hotel in Birmingham. It happened that the blotting paper in the blotting book had been put in fresh that day, and the chambermaid, having apparently nothing better to do, amused herself by studying the blotter in the mirror just after Mr. Jones had been writing a letter there. A few days later there was a report in the papers of the death of Mrs. Jones as the result of eating tinned lobster, and the chambermaid then imparted to her fellow servants the words that she had deciphered on the blotting pad. They were as follows: 'Entirely dependent on my wife . . . when she is dead I will . . . hundreds and thousands . . .'

"You may remember that there had recently been a case of a wife being poisoned by her husband. It needed very little to fire the imagination of these maids. Mr. Jones had planned to do away with his wife and inherit hundreds of thousands of pounds! As it happened one of the maids had relations living in the small market town where the Joneses resided. She wrote to them, and they in return wrote to her. Mr. Jones, it seemed, had been very attentive to the local doctor's daughter, a good-looking young woman of thirty-three. Scandal began to hum. The Home Secretary was petitioned. Numerous anonymous letters poured into Scotland Yard all accusing Mr. Jones of having murdered his wife. Now I may say that not for one moment did we think there was anything in it except idle village talk and gossip. Nevertheless, to quiet public opinion an exhumation order was granted. It was one of these cases of popular superstition based on nothing solid whatever, which proved to be so suprisingly justified. As a result of the autopsy sufficient arsenic was found to make it quite clear that the deceased lady had died of arsenical poisoning. It was for Scotland Yard working with the local authorities to prove how that arsenic had been administered, and by whom."

"Ah!" said Joyce. "I like this. This is the real stuff."

"Suspicion naturally fell on the husband. He benefited by his wife's death. Not to the extent of the hundreds of thousands romantically imagined by the hotel chambermaid, but to the very solid amount of £8000. He had no money of his own apart from what he earned, and he was a man of somewhat extravagant habits with a partiality for the society of women. We investigated as delicately as possible the rumour of his attachment to the doctor's daughter; but while it seemed clear that there had been a strong friendship between them at one time, there had been a most abrupt break two months previously, and they did not appear to have seen each other since. The doctor himself, an elderly man of a straightforward and unsuspicious type, was dumbfounded at the result of the autopsy. He had been called in about midnight to find all three people suffering. He had realized immediately the serious condition of Mrs. Jones, and had sent back to his dispensary for some opium pills, to allay the pain. In spite of all his efforts, however, she succumbed, but not for a moment did he suspect that anything was amiss. He was convinced that her death was due to a form of botulism. Supper that night had consisted of tinned lobster and salad, trifle and bread and cheese. Unfortunately none of the lobster remained—it had all been eaten and the tin thrown away. He had interrogated the young maid, Gladys Linch. She was terribly upset, very tearful and agitated, and he found it hard to get her to keep to the point, but she declared again and again that the tin had not been distended in any way and that the lobster had appeared to her in a perfectly good condition.

"Such were the facts we had to go upon. If Jones had feloniously administered arsenic to his wife, it seemed clear that it could not have been done in any of the things eaten at supper, as all three persons had partaken of the meal. Also—another point—Jones himself had returned from Birmingham just as supper was being brought in to table, so that he would have had no opportunity of doctoring any of the food beforehand."

"What about the companion," asked Joyce—"the stout woman with the good-humoured face?"

Sir Henry nodded.

"We did not neglect Miss Clark, I can assure you. But it seemed doubtful what motive she could have had for the crime. Mrs. Jones left her no legacy of any kind and the net result of her employer's death was that she had to seek for another situation."

"That seems to leave her out of it," said Joyce thoughtfully.

"Now one of my inspectors soon discovered a significant fact," went on Sir Henry. "After supper on that evening Mr. Jones had gone down to the kitchen and had demanded a bowl of corn-flour for his wife, who had complained of not feeling well. He had waited in the kitchen until Gladys Linch prepared it, and then carried it up to his wife's room himself. That, I admit, seemed to clinch the case."

The lawyer nodded.

"Motive," he said, ticking the point off on his fingers. "Opportunity. As a traveller for a firm of druggists, easy access to the poison."

"And a man of weak moral fibre," said the clergyman.

Raymond West was staring at Sir Henry.

"There is a catch in this somewhere," he said. "Why did you not arrest him?"

Sir Henry smiled rather wryly.

"That is the unfortunate part of the case. So far all had gone swimmingly, but now we come to the snags. Jones was not arrested because on interrogating Miss Clark she told us that the whole of the bowl of corn-flour was drunk not by Mrs. Jones but by her.

"Yes, it seems that she went to Mrs. Jones's room as was her custom. Mrs. Jones was sitting up in bed and the bowl of corn-flour was beside her.

"'I am not feeling a bit well, Milly,' she said. 'Serves me right, I suppose, for touching lobster at night. I asked Albert to get me a bowl of corn-flour, but now that I have got it I don't seem to fancy it.'

"'A pity,' commented Miss Clark—'it is nicely made too, no lumps. Gladys is really quite a nice cook. Very few girls nowadays seem to be able to make a bowl of corn-flour nicely. I declare I quite fancy it myself, I am that hungry.'

"'I should think you were with your foolish ways,' said Mrs. Jones.

"I must explain," broke off Sir Henry, "that Miss Clark, alarmed at her increasing stoutness, was doing a course of what is popularly known as 'banting.'

"'It is not good for you, Milly, it really isn't,' urged Mrs. Jones. 'If the Lord made you stout he meant you to be stout. You drink up that bowl of corn-flour. It will do you all the good in the world.'

"And straight away Miss Clark set to and did in actual fact finish the bowl. So, you see, that knocked our case against the husband to pieces. Asked for an explanation of the words on the blotting book Jones gave one readily enough. The letter, he explained, was in answer to one written from his brother in Australia who had applied to him for money. He had written, pointing out that he was entirely dependent on his wife. When his wife was dead he would have control of money and would assist his brother if possible. He regretted his inability to help but pointed out that there were hundreds and thousands of people in the world in the same unfortunate plight."

"And so the case fell to pieces?" said Dr. Pender.

"And so the case fell to pieces," said Sir Henry gravely. "We could not take the risk of arresting Jones with nothing to go upon."

There was a silence and then Joyce said, "And that is all, is it?"

"That is the case as it has stood for the last year. The true solution is now in the hands of Scotland Yard, and in two or three days' time you will probably read of it in the newspapers."

"The true solution," said Joyce thoughtfully. "I wonder. Let's all think for five minutes and then speak."

Raymond West nodded and noted the time on his watch. When the five minutes were up he looked over at Dr. Pender.

"Will you speak first?" he said.

The old man shook his head. "I confess," he said, "that I am utterly baffled. I can but think that the husband in some way must be the guilty party, but how he did it I cannot imagine. I can only suggest that he must have given her the poison in some way that has not yet been discovered, although how in that case it should have come to light after all this time I cannot imagine."

"Joyce?"

"The companion!" said Joyce decidedly. "The companion every time! How do we know what motive she may have had? Just because she was old and stout and ugly it doesn't follow that she wasn't in love with Jones herself. She may have hated the wife for some other reason. Think of being a companion—always having to be pleasant and agree and stifle yourself and bottle yourself up. One day she couldn't bear it any longer and then she killed her. She probably put the arsenic in the bowl of corn-flour and all that story about eating it herself is a lie."

"Mr. Petherick?"

The lawyer joined the tips of his fingers together professionally. "I should hardly like to say. On the facts I should hardly like to say."

"But you have got to, Mr. Petherick," said Joyce. "You can't reserve judgment and say 'without prejudice,' and be legal. You have got to play the game."

"On the facts," said Mr. Petherick, "there seems nothing to be said. It is my private opinion, having seen, alas, too many cases of this kind, that the husband was guilty. The only explanation that will cover the facts seems to be that Miss Clark for some reason or other deliberately sheltered him. There may have been some financial arrangement made between them. He might realize that he would be suspected, and she, seeing only a future of poverty before her, may have agreed to tell the story of drinking the corn-flour in return for a substantial sum to be paid to her privately. If that was the case it was of course most irregular. Most irregular indeed."

"I disagree with you all," said Raymond. "You have forgotten the one important factor in the case. *The doctor's daughter.* I will give you my reading of the case. The tinned lobster was bad. It accounted for the poisoning symptoms. The doctor was sent for. He finds Mrs. Jones, who has eaten more lobster than the others, in great pain, and he sends, as you told us, for some opium pills. He does not go himself, he sends. Who will give the messenger the opium pills? Clearly his daughter. Very likely she dispenses his medicines for him. She is in love with Jones and at this moment all the worst instincts in her nature rise and she realizes that the means to procure his freedom are in her hands. The pills she sends contain pure white arsenic. That is my solution."

"And now Sir Henry, tell us," said Joyce eagerly.

"One moment," said Sir Henry, "Miss Marple has not yet spoken."

"Dear, dear," she said. "I have dropped another stitch. I have been so interested in the story. A sad case, a very sad case. It reminds me of old Mr. Hargraves who lived up at the Mount. His wife never had the least suspicion—until he died, leaving all his money to a woman he had been living with and by whom he had had five children. She had at one time been their housemaid. Such a nice girl, Mrs. Hargraves always said—thoroughly to be relied upon to turn the mattresses every day—except Fridays, of course. And there was old Hargraves keeping this woman in a house in the neighbouring town and continuing to be a Churchwarden and to hand round the plate every Sunday."

"My dear Aunt Jane," said Raymond with some impatience. "What have dead and gone Hargraves got to do with the case?"

"This story made me think of him at once," said Miss Marple. "The facts are so very alike, aren't they? I suppose the poor girl has confessed now and that is how you know, Sir Henry."

"What girl?" said Raymond. "My dear Aunt, what *are* you talking about?"

"That poor girl, Gladys Linch, of course—the one who was so terribly agitated when the doctor spoke to her—and well she might be, poor thing. I hope that wicked Jones is hanged, I am sure, making that poor girl a murderess. I suppose they will hang her too, poor thing."

"I think, Miss Marple, that you are under a slight misapprehension," began Mr. Petherick.

But Miss Marple shook her head obstinately and looked across at Sir Henry.

"I am right, am I not? It seems so clear to me. The hundreds and thousands—and the trifle—I mean, one cannot miss it."

"What about the trifle and the hundreds and thousands?" cried Raymond.

His aunt turned to him.

"Cooks nearly always put hundreds and thousands on trifle, dear," she said.

"Those little pink and white sugar things. Of course when I heard that they had had trifle for supper and that the husband had been writing to someone about hundreds and thousands, I naturally connected the two things together. That is where the arsenic was—in the hundreds and thousands. He left it with the girl and told her to put it on the trifle."

"But that is impossible," said Joyce quickly. "They all ate the trifle."

"Oh, no," said Miss Marple. "The companion was banting, you remember. You never eat anything like trifle if you are banting; and I expect Jones just scraped the hundreds and thousands off his share and left them at the side of his plate. It was a clever idea, but a very wicked one."

The eyes of the others were all fixed upon Sir Henry.

"It is a very curious thing," he said slowly, "but Miss Marple happens to have hit upon the truth. Jones had got Gladys Linch into trouble, as the saying goes. She was nearly desperate. He wanted his wife out of the way and promised to marry Gladys when his wife was dead. He doctored the hundreds and thousands and gave them to her with instructions how to use them. Gladys Linch died a week ago. Her child died at birth and Jones had deserted her for another woman. When she was dying she confessed the truth."

There was a few moments' silence and then Raymond said:

"Well, Aunt Jane, this is one up to you. I can't think how on earth you managed to hit upon the truth. I should never have thought of the little maid in the kitchen being connected with the case."

"No, dear," said Miss Marple, "but you don't know as much of life as I do. A man of that Jones's type—coarse and jovial. As soon as I heard there was a pretty young girl in the house I felt sure that he would not have left her alone. It is all very distressing and painful, and not a very nice thing to talk about. I can't tell you the shock it was to Mrs. Hargraves, and a nine days' wonder in the village."

—1932

DASHIELL HAMMETT
1894-1961

Samuel Dashiell Hammett is generally regarded as perhaps the single most influential author of the "hard-boiled" school of American detective fiction. Raymond Chandler, in fact, credited Hammett with helping to create this type of detective story, and Erle Stanley Gardner, author of the famous Perry Mason series, called Hammett a genius. Hammett's brand of "hard-boiled" "tough guy" fiction found its cultural origins during the Prohibition era in America, when the American public became fascinated with the glamorous crime bosses of the 1920s, and gangsters such as Al "Scarface" Capone became nationally recognized figures. Crime, itself, had left the urban ghettos to become part of American mainstream culture. People thought it exciting to drink illegal liquor in forbidden "speak-easies." Mob violence was front-page news, and mob language became adopted as part of the nation's vernacular. Fact eventually made its way into fiction; the "tough guy" lingo of the street was adopted by Hammett (and others) in their work as part of a new type of fiction intended to make the tale of crime and detection more realistic.

Born in St. Mary's County, Maryland, Hammett worked at a variety of occupations—from freight clerk to stevedore—before landing a job with the Pinkerton Detective Agency. Over the next several years, Hammett's experience laboring as a private investigator would later provide him with useful material for his writing. Hammett also worked as an advertising copywriter from 1922 to 1927, and published his first novel, Red Harvest, *serially in the American pulp magazine,* Black Mask, *in 1927 (this novel was later revised and published in 1929 as a book). He served in the U.S. Ambulance Corps from 1918 to 1919, and he returned to duty during the Second World War in the U.S. Army Signal Corps. Beginning in 1937, Hammett became involved with left-wing political organizations and, in 1951, during the McCarthy era, he was jailed for contempt of Congress.*

Though Hammett was not a prolific writer, his "hard-boiled" style influenced many other authors, from Raymond Chandler to Sara Paretsky. He published his first story, "The Road Home," in the December 1922 issue of Black Mask, *under the "Peter Collinson" pseudonym, but his most famous detective protagonist for that magazine was the Continental Op, the private investigator who is featured in* Red Harvest *and* The Dain Curse *(1929). Other Hammett novels include* The Glass Key *(1931),* The Thin Man *(1934), and his single finest work,* The Maltese Falcon *(1930).* The Maltese Falcon *is arguably the best "hard-boiled" detective novel ever written, and it was filmed several times by Hollywood, the most famous version being director John Huston's 1941 motion picture starring Mary Astor, Peter Lorre, Sydney Greenstreet, and Humphrey Bogart as the crafty gumshoe, Sam Spade.*

Sam Spade is also the detective hero in the short story, "Too Many Have Lived," which was published in the October 1932 issue of American Magazine *and later was anthologized in the Hammett collection,* The Adventures of Sam Spade and Other Stories *(1944; also titled* A Man Called Spade, *1945). Those easily-recognizable storytelling qualities that made Hammett's brand of "hard-boiled" detective fiction so appealing to his many readers also appear in this tale—such features as a rapidly paced plot, sparse, effectively-used language, and a tough guy hero who is as street-wise as they come.*

TOO MANY HAVE LIVED

The man's tie was as orange as a sunset. He was a large man, tall and meaty, without softness. The dark hair parted in the middle, flattened to his scalp, his firm, full cheeks, the clothes that fit him with noticeable snugness, even the small, pink ears flat against the sides of his head—each of these seemed but a differently colored part of the same, smooth surface. His age could have been thirty-five or forty-five.

He sat beside Samuel Spade's desk, leaning forward a little over his Malacca stick, and said, "No. I want you to find out what happened to him. I hope you never find him." His protuberant green eyes stared solemnly at Spade.

Spade rocked back in his chair. His face—given a not unpleasantly satanic cast by the v's of his bony chin, mouth, nostrils, and thickish brows—was as politely interested as his voice. "Why?"

The green-eyed man spoke quietly, with assurance: "I can talk to you, Spade. You've the sort of reputation I want in a private detective. That's why I'm here."

Spade's nod committed him to nothing.

The green-eyed man said, "And any fair price is all right with me."

Spade nodded as before. "And with me," he said, "but I've got to know what you want to buy. You want to find out what's happened to this—uh—Eli Haven, but you don't care what it is?"

The green-eyed man lowered his voice, but there was no other change in his mien: "In a way I do. For instance, if you found him and fixed it so he stayed away for good, it might be worth more money to me."

"You mean even if he didn't want to stay away?"

The green-eyed man said, "Especially."

Spade smiled and shook his head. "Probably not enough more money—the way you mean it." He took his long, thick-fingered hands from the arms of his chair and turned their palms up. "Well, what's it all about, Colyer?"

Colyer's face reddened a little, but his eyes maintained their unblinking cold stare. "This man's got a wife. I like her. They had a row last week and he blew. If I can convince her he's gone for good, there's a chance she'll divorce him."

"I'd want to talk to her," Spade said. "Who is this Eli Haven? What does he do?"

"He's a bad egg. He doesn't do anything. Writes poetry or something."

"What can you tell me about him that'll help?"

"Nothing Julia, his wife, can't tell you. You're going to talk to her." Colyer stood up. "I've got connections. Maybe I can get something for you through them later . . ."

A small-boned woman of twenty-five or -six opened the apartment door. Her powder-blue dress was trimmed with silver buttons. She was full-bosomed but slim, with straight shoulders and narrow hips, and she carried herself with a pride that would have been cockiness in one less graceful.

Spade said, "Mrs. Haven?"

She hesitated before saying "Yes."

"Gene Colyer sent me to see you. My name's Spade. I'm a private detective. He wants me to find your husband."

"And have you found him?"

"I told him I'd have to talk to you first."

Her smile went away. She studied his face gravely, feature by feature, then she said, "Certainly," and stepped back, drawing the door back with her.

When they were seated in facing chairs in a cheaply furnished room overlooking a playground where children were noisy, she asked, "Did Gene tell you why he wanted Eli found?"

"He said if you knew he was gone for good maybe you'd listen to reason."

She said nothing.

"Has he ever gone off like this before?"

"Often."

"What's he like?"

"He's a swell man," she said dispassionately, "when he's sober; and when he's drinking he's all right except with women and money."

"That leaves him a lot of room to be all right in. What does he do for a living?"

"He's a poet," she replied, "but nobody makes a living at that."

"Well?"

"Oh, he pops in with a little money now and then. Poker, races, he says. I don't know."

"How long've you been married?"

"Four years, almost"—she smiled mockingly.

"San Francisco all the time?"

"No, we lived in Seattle the first year and then came here."

"He from Seattle?"

She shook her head. "Some place in Delaware."

"What place?"

"I don't know."

Spade drew his thickish brows together a little. "Where are you from?"

She said sweetly, "You're not hunting for me."

"You act like it," he grumbled. "Well, who are his friends?"

"Don't ask me!"

He made an impatient grimace. "You know some of them," he insisted.

"Sure. There's a fellow named Minera and a Louis James and somebody he calls Conny."

"Who are they?"

"Men," she replied blandly. "I don't know anything about them. They phone or drop by to pick him up, or I see him around town with them. That's all I know."

"What do they do for a living? They can't all write poetry."

She laughed. "They could try. One of them, Louis James, is a—a member of Gene's staff, I think. I honestly don't know any more about them than I've told you."

"Think they'd know where your husband is?"

She shrugged. "They're kidding me if they do. They still call up once in a while to see if he's turned up."

"And these women you mentioned?"

"They're not people I know."

Spade scowled thoughtfully at the floor, asked, "What'd he do before he started not making a living writing poetry?"

"Anything—sold vacuum cleaners, hoboed, went to sea, dealt blackjack, railroaded, canning houses, lumber camps, carnivals, worked on a newspaper—anything."

"Have any money when he left?"

"Three dollars he borrowed from me."

"What'd he say?"

She laughed. "Said if I used whatever influence I had with God while he was gone he'd be back at dinnertime with a surprise for me."

Spade raised his eyebrows. "You were on good terms?"

"Oh, yes. Our last fight had been patched up a couple of days before."

"When did he leave?"

"Thursday afternoon; three o'clock, I guess."

"Got any photographs of him?"

"Yes." She went to a table by one of the windows, pulled a drawer out, and turned towards Spade again with a photograph in her hand.

Spade looked at the picture of a thin face with deep-set eyes, a sensual mouth, and a heavily lined forehead topped by a disorderly mop of coarse blond hair.

He put Haven's photograph in his pocket and picked up his hat. He turned towards the door, halted. "What kind of poet is he? Pretty good?"

She shrugged. "That depends on who you ask."

"Any of it around here?"

"No." She smiled. "Think he's hiding between pages?"

"You never can tell what'll lead to what. I'll be back some time. Think things over and see if you can't find some way of loosening up a little more. 'By."

He walked down Post Street to Mulford's book store and asked for a volume of Haven's poetry.

"I'm sorry," the girl said. "I sold my last copy last week"—she smiled—"to Mr. Haven himself. I can order it for you."

"You know him?"

"Only through selling his books."

Spade pursed his lips, asked, "What day was it?" He gave her one of his business cards. "Please. It's important."

She went to a desk, turned the pages of a red-bound sales-book, and came back to him with the book open in her hand. "It was last Wednesday," she said, "and we delivered it to a Mr. Roger Ferris, 1981 Pacific Avenue."

"Thanks a lot," he said.

Outside, he hailed a taxicab and gave the driver Mr. Roger Ferris's address . . .

The Pacific Avenue house was a four-story, graystone one set behind a narrow strip of lawn. The room into which a plump-faced maid ushered Spade was large and high-ceiled.

Spade sat down, but when the maid had gone away he rose and began to walk around the room. He halted at a table where there were three books. One of them had a salmon-colored jacket on which was printed in red an outline drawing of a bolt of lightning striking the ground between a man and a woman, and in black the words *Colored Light, by Eli Haven.*

Spade picked up the book and went back to his chair.

There was an inscription on the flyleaf—heavy, irregular characters written with blue ink:

> *To good old Buck, who knew his colored lights,*
> *in memory of them there days.*
>
> *Eli*

Spade turned pages at random and idly read a verse:

> STATEMENT
> *Too many have lived*
> *As we live*
> *For our lives to be*
> *Proof of our living.*
> *Too many have died*
> *As we die*
> *For their deaths to be*
> *Proof of our dying.*

He looked up from the book as a man in dinner clothes came into the room. He was not a tall man, but his erectness made him seem tall even when Spade's six feet and a fraction of an inch were standing before him. He had bright blue eyes undimmed by his fifty-some years, a sunburned face in which no muscle sagged, a smooth, broad forehead, and thick, short, nearly white hair. There was dignity in his countenance, and amiability.

He nodded at the book Spade still held. "How do you like it?"

Spade grinned, said, "I guess I'm just a mug," and put the book down. "That's what I came to see you about, though, Mr. Ferris. You know Haven?"

"Yes, certainly. Sit down, Mr. Spade." He sat in a chair not far from Spade's. "I knew him as a kid. He's not in trouble, is he?"

Spade said, "I don't know. I'm trying to find him."

Ferris spoke hesitantly: "Can I ask why?"

"You know Gene Colyer?"

"Yes." Ferris hesitated again, then said, "This is in confidence. I've a chain of picture houses through northern California, you know, and a couple of years ago when I had some labor trouble I was told that Colyer was the man to get in touch with to have it straightened out. That's how I happened to meet him."

"Yes," Spade said dryly. "A lot of people happen to meet Gene that way."

"But what's he got to do with Eli?"

"Wants him found. How long since you've seen him?"

"Last Thursday he was here."

"What time did he leave?"

"Midnight—a little after. He came over in the afternoon around half past three. We hadn't seen each other for years. I persuaded him to stay for dinner—he looked pretty seedy—and lent him some money."

"How much?"

"A hundred and fifty—all I had in the house."

"Say where he was going when he left?"

Ferris shook his head. "He said he'd phone me the next day."

"Did he phone you the next day?"

"No."

"And you've known him all his life?"

"Not exactly, but he worked for me fifteen or sixteen years ago when I had a carnival company—Great Eastern and Western Combined Shows—with a partner for a while and then by myself, and I always liked the kid."

"How long before Thursday since you'd seen him?"

"Lord knows," Ferris replied. "I'd lost track of him for years. Then, Wednesday, out of a clear sky, that book came, with no address or anything, just that stuff written in the front, and the next morning he called me up. I was tickled to death to know he was still alive and doing something with himself. So he came over that afternoon and we put in about nine hours straight talking about old times."

"Tell you much about what he'd been doing since then?"

"Just that he'd been knocking around, doing one thing and another, taking the breaks as they came. He didn't complain much; I had to make him take the hundred and fifty."

Spade stood up. "Thanks ever so much, Mr. Ferris. I—"

Ferris interrupted him: "Not at all, and if there's anything I can do, call on me."

Spade looked at his watch. "Can I phone my office to see if anything's turned up?"

"Certainly; there's a phone in the next room, to the right."

Spade said "Thanks" and went out. When he returned he was rolling a cigarette. His face was wooden.

"Any news?" Ferris asked.

"Yes. Colyer's called the job off. He says Haven's body's been found in some bushes on the other side of San Jose, with three bullets in it." He smiled, adding mildly, "He *told* me he might be able to find out something through his connections . . ."

Morning sunshine, coming through the curtains that screened Spade's office windows, put two fat, yellow rectangles on the floor and gave everything in the room a yellow tint.

He sat at his desk, staring meditatively at a newspaper. He did not look up when Effie Perine came in from the outer office.

She said, "Mrs. Haven is here."

He raised his head then and said, "That's better. Push her in."

Mrs. Haven came in quickly. Her face was white and she was shivering in spite of her fur coat and the warmth of the day. She came straight to Spade and asked, "Did Gene kill him?"

Spade said, "I don't know."

"I've got to know," she cried.

Spade took her hands. "Here, sit down." He led her to a chair. He asked, "Colyer tell you he'd called the job off?"

She stared at him in amazement. "He what?"

"He left word here last night that your husband had been found and he wouldn't need me any more."

She hung her head and her words were barely audible. "Then he did."

Spade shrugged. "Maybe only an innocent man could've afforded to call it off then, or maybe he was guilty, but had brains enough and nerve enough to—"

She was not listening to him. She was leaning towards him, speaking earnestly: "But, Mr. Spade, you're not going to drop it like that? You're not going to let him stop you?"

While she was speaking his telephone bell rang. He said, "Excuse me," and picked up the receiver. "Yes? . . . Uh-huh . . . So?" He pursed his lips. "I'll let you know." He pushed the telephone aside slowly and faced Mrs. Haven again. "Colyer's outside."

"Does he know I'm here?" she asked quickly.

"Couldn't say." He stood up, pretending he was not watching her closely. "Do you care?"

She pinched her lower lip between her teeth, said "No" hesitantly.

"Fine. I'll have him in."

She raised a hand as if in protest, then let it drop, and her white face was composed. "Whatever you want," she said.

Spade opened the door, said, "Hello, Colyer. Come on in. We were just talking about you."

Colyer nodded and came into the office holding his stick in one hand, his hat in the other. "How are you this morning, Julia? You ought to've phoned me. I'd've driven you back to town."

"I—I didn't know what I was doing."

Colyer looked at her for a moment longer, then shifted the focus of his expressionless green eyes to Spade's face. "Well, have you been able to convince her I didn't do it?"

"We hadn't got around to that," Spade said. "I was just trying to find out how much reason there was for suspecting you. Sit down."

Colyer sat down somewhat carefully, asked, "And?"

"And then you arrived."

Colyer nodded gravely. "All right, Spade," he said; "you're hired again to prove to Mrs. Haven that I didn't have anything to do with it."

"Gene!" she exclaimed in a choked voice and held her hands out toward him appealingly. "I don't think you did—I don't want to think you did—but I'm so afraid." She put her hands to her face and began to cry.

Colyer went over to the woman. "Take it easy," he said. "We'll kick it out together."

Spade went into the outer office, shutting the door behind him.

Effie Perine stopped typing a letter.

He grinned at her, said, "Somebody ought to write a book about people some-time—they're peculiar," and went over to the water bottle. "You've got Wally Kellogg's number. Call him up and ask him where I can find Tom Minera."

He returned to the inner office.

Mrs. Haven had stopped crying. She said, "I'm sorry."

Spade said, "It's all right." He looked sidewise at Colyer. "I still got my job?"

"Yes." Colyer cleared his throat. "But if there's nothing special right now, I'd bet-ter take Mrs. Haven home."

"OK, but there's one thing: According to the *Chronicle,* you identified him. How come you were down there?"

"I went down when I heard they'd found a body," Colyer replied deliberately. "I told you I had connections. I heard about the body through them."

Spade said, "All right; be seeing you," and opened the door for them.

When the corridor door closed behind them, Effie Perine said, "Minera's at the Buxton on Army Street."

Spade said, "Thanks." He went into the inner office to get his hat. On his way out he said, "If I'm not back in a couple of months tell them to look for my body there . . ."

Spade walked down a shabby corridor to a battered green door marked "411." The murmur of voices came through the door, but no words could be distinguished. He stopped listening and knocked.

An obviously disguised male voice asked, "What is it?"

"I want to see Tom. This is Sam Spade."

A pause, then: "Tom ain't here."

Spade put a hand on the knob and shook the frail door. "Come on, open up," he growled.

Presently the door was opened by a thin, dark man of twenty-five or -six who tried to make his beady dark eyes guileless while saying, "I didn't think it was your voice at first." The slackness of his mouth made his chin seem even smaller than it was. His green-striped shirt, open at the neck, was not clean. His gray pants were carefully pressed.

"You've got to be careful these days," Spade said solemnly, and went through the doorway into a room where two men were trying to seem uninterested in his arrival.

One of them leaned against the window sill filing his fingernails. The other was tilted back in a chair with his feet on the edge of a table and a newspaper spread between his hands. They glanced at Spade in unison and went on with their occupations.

Spade said cheerfully, "Always glad to meet any friends of Tom Minera's."

Minera finished shutting the door and said awkwardly, "Uh—yes—Mr. Spade, meet Mr. Conrad and Mr. James."

Conrad, the man at the window, made a vaguely polite gesture with the nail file in his hand. He was a few years older than Minera, of average height, sturdily built, with a thick-featured, dull-eyed face.

James lowered his paper for an instant to look coolly, appraisingly at Spade and say, "How'r'ye, brother?" Then he returned to his reading. He was as sturdily built as Conrad, but taller, and his face had a shrewdness the other's lacked.

"Ah," Spade said, "and friends of the late Eli Haven."

The man at the window jabbed a finger with his nail file, and cursed it bitterly. Minera moistened his lips, and then spoke rapidly, with a whining note in his voice: "But on the level, Spade, we hadn't none of us seen him for a week."

Spade seemed mildly amused by the dark man's manner.

"What do you think he was killed for?"

"All I know is what the paper says: His pockets was all turned inside out and there wasn't as much as a match on him." He drew down the ends of his mouth. "But far as I know he didn't have no dough. He didn't have none Tuesday night."

Spade, speaking softly, said, "I hear he got some Thursday night."

Minera, behind Spade, caught his breath audibly.

James said, "I guess you ought to know. I don't."

"He ever work with you boys?"

James slowly put aside his newspaper and took his feet off the table. His interest in Spade's question seemed great enough, but almost impersonal. "Now what do you mean by that?"

Spade pretended surprise. "But you boys must work at something?"

Minera came around to Spade's side. "Aw, listen, Spade," he said. "This guy Haven was just a guy we knew. We didn't have nothing to do with rubbing him out; we don't know nothing about it. You know we—"

Three deliberate knocks sounded at the door.

Minera and Conrad looked at James, who nodded, but by then Spade, moving swiftly, had reached the door and was opening it.

Roger Ferris was there.

Spade blinked at Ferris, Ferris at Spade. Then Ferris put out his hand and said, "I *am* glad to see you."

"Come on in," Spade said.

"Look at this, Mr. Spade." Ferris's hand trembled as he took a slightly soiled envelope from his pocket.

Ferris's name and address were typewritten on the envelope. There was no postage stamp on it. Spade took out the enclosure, a narrow slip of cheap white paper, and unfolded it. On it was typewritten:

You had better come to Room No 411 Buxton Hotel on Army St at 5 p.m. this afternoon on account of Thursday night.

There was no signature.

Spade said, "It's a long time before five o'clock."

"It is," Ferris agreed with emphasis. "I came as soon as I got that. It was Thursday night Eli was at my house."

Minera was jostling Spade, asking, "What is all this?"

Spade held the note up for the dark man to read. He read it and yelled, "Honest, Spade, I don't know nothing about that letter."

"Does anybody?" Spade asked.

Conrad said "No" hastily.

James said, "What letter?"

Spade looked dreamily at Ferris for a moment, then said, as if speaking to himself, "Of course, Haven was trying to shake you down."

Ferris's face reddened. "What?"

"Shake-down," Spade repeated patiently; "money, blackmail."

"Look here, Spade," Ferris said earnestly; "you don't really believe what you said? What would he have to blackmail me on?"

"'To good old Buck'"—Spade quoted the dead poet's inscription—"'who knew his colored lights, in memory of them there days.'" He looked somberly at Ferris from beneath slightly raised brows. "What colored lights? What's the circus and carnival slang term for kicking a guy off a train while it's going? Red-lighting. Sure, that's it—red lights. Who'd you red-light, Ferris, that Haven knew about?"

Minera went over to a chair, sat down, put his elbows on his knees, his head between his hands, and stared blankly at the floor. Conrad was breathing as if he had been running.

Spade addressed Ferris: "Well?"

Ferris wiped his face with a handkerchief, put the handkerchief in his pocket, and said simply, "It was a shake-down."

"And you killed him."

Ferris's blue eyes, looking into Spade's yellow-gray ones, were clear and steady, as was his voice. "I did not," he said. "I swear I did not. Let me tell you what happened. He sent me the book, as I told you, and I knew right away what that joke he wrote in the front meant. So the next day, when he phoned me and said he was coming over to talk over old times and to try to borrow some money for old times' sake, I knew what he meant again, and I went down to the bank and drew out ten thousand dollars. You can check that up. It's the Seamen's National."

"I will," Spade said.

"As it turned out, I didn't need that much. He wasn't very big-time, and I talked him into taking five thousand. I put the other five back in the bank next day. You can check that up."

"I will," Spade said.

"I told him I wasn't going to stand for any more taps, this five thousand was the first and last. I made him sign a paper saying he'd helped in the—in what I'd done—and he signed it. He left sometime around midnight, and that's the last I ever saw of him."

Spade tapped the envelope Ferris had given him. "And how about this note?"

"A messenger boy brought it at noon, and I came right over. Eli had assured me he hadn't said anything to anybody, but I didn't know. I had to face it, whatever it was."

Spade turned to the others, his face wooden. "Well?"

Minera and Conrad looked at James, who made an impatient grimace and said, "Oh, sure, we sent him the letter. Why not? We was friends of Eli's, and we hadn't been able to find him since he went to put the squeeze to this baby, and then he turns up dead, so we kind of like to have the gent come over and explain things."

"You knew about the squeeze?"

"Sure. We was all together when he got the idea."

"How'd he happen to get the idea?" Spade asked.

James spread the fingers of his left hand. "We'd been drinking and talking—you know the way a bunch of guys will, about all they'd seen and done—and he told a yarn about once seeing a guy boot another off a train into a cañon, and he happens to mention the name of the guy that done the booting—Buck Ferris. And somebody says, 'What's this Ferris look like?' Eli tells him what he looked like then, saying he ain't seen him for fifteen years; and whoever it is whistles and says, 'I bet that's the Ferris that owns about half the movie joints in the state. I bet you he'd give something to keep that back trail covered!'

"Well, the idea kind of hit Eli. You could see that. He thought a little while and then he got cagey. He asked what this movie Ferris's first name is, and when the other guy tells him, 'Roger,' he makes out he's disappointed and says, 'No, it ain't him. His first name was Martin.' We all give him the ha-ha and he finally admits he's thinking of seeing the gent, and when he called me up Thursday around noon and says he's throwing a party at Pogey Hecker's that night, it ain't no trouble to figure out what's what."

"What was the name of the gentleman who was red-lighted?"

"He wouldn't say. He shut up tight. You couldn't blame him."

"Uh-huh," Spade agreed.

"Then nothing. He never showed up at Pogey's. We tried to get him on the phone around two o'clock in the morning, but his wife said he hadn't been home, so we stuck around till four or five and then decided he had given us a run-around, and made Pogey charge the bill to him, and beat it. I ain't seen him since—dead or alive."

Spade said mildly, "Maybe. Sure you didn't find Eli later that morning, take him riding, swap him bullets for Ferris's five thou, dump him in the—?"

A sharp double knock sounded on the door.

Spade's face brightened. He went to the door and opened it.

A young man came in. He was very dapper, and very well proportioned. He wore a light topcoat and his hands were in its pockets. Just inside the door he stepped to the right, and stood with his back to the wall. By that time another young man was coming in. He stepped to the left. Though they did not actually look alike, their common dapperness, the similar trimness of their bodies, and their almost identical positions—backs to wall, hands in pockets, cold, bright eyes studying the occupants of the room—gave them, for an instant, the appearance of twins.

Then Gene Colyer came in. He nodded at Spade, but paid no attention to the others in the room, though James said, "Hello, Gene."

"Anything new?" Colyer asked Spade.

Spade nodded. "It seems this gentleman" —he jerked a thumb at Ferris—"was—"

"Any place we can talk?"

"There's a kitchen back here."

Colyer snapped a "Smear anybody that pops" over his shoulder at the two dapper young men and followed Spade into the kitchen. He sat on the one kitchen chair and stared with unblinking green eyes at Spade while Spade told him what he had learned.

When the private detective had finished, the green-eyed man asked, "Well, what do you make of it?"

Spade looked thoughtfully at the other. "You've picked up something. I'd like to know what it is."

Colyer said, "They found the gun in a stream a quarter of a mile from where they found him. It's James's—got the mark on it where it was shot out of his hand once in Vallejo."

"That's nice," Spade said.

"Listen. A kid named Thurber says James comes to him last Wednesday and gets him to tail Haven. Thurber picks him up Thursday afternoon, puts him in at Ferris's, and phones James. James tells him to take a plant on the place and let him know where Haven goes when he leaves, but some nervous woman in the neighborhood puts in a rumble about the kid hanging around, and the cops chase him along about ten o'clock."

Spade pursed his lips and stared thoughtfully at the ceiling.

Colyer's eyes were expressionless, but sweat made his round face shiny, and his voice was hoarse. "Spade," he said, "I'm going to turn him in."

Spade switched his gaze from the ceiling to the protuberant green eyes.

"I've never turned in one of my people before," Colyer said, "but this one goes. Julia's *got* to believe I hadn't anything to do with it if it's one of my people and I turn him in, hasn't she?"

Spade nodded slowly. "I think so."

Colyer suddenly averted his eyes and cleared his throat. When he spoke again it was curtly: "Well, he goes."

Minera, James, and Conrad were seated when Spade and Colyer came out of the kitchen. Ferris was walking the floor. The two dapper young men had not moved.

Colyer went over to James. "Where's your gun, Louis?" he asked.

James moved his right hand a few inches towards his left breast, stopped it, and said, "Oh, I didn't bring it."

With his gloved hand—open—Colyer struck James on the side of the face, knocking him out of his chair.

James straightened up, mumbling, "I didn't mean nothing." He put a hand to the side of his face. "I know I oughtn't't've done it, Chief, but when he called up and said he didn't like to go up against Ferris without something and didn't have any of his own, I said, 'All right,' and sent it over to him."

Colyer said, "And you sent Thurber over to him, too."

"We were just kind of interested in seeing if he did go through with it," James mumbled.

"And you couldn't't've gone there yourself, or sent somebody else?"

"After Thurber had stirred up the whole neighborhood?"

Colyer turned to Spade. "Want us to help you take them in, or want to call the wagon?"

"We'll do it regular," Spade said, and went to the wall telephone. When he turned away from it his face was wooden, his eyes dreamy. He made a cigarette, lit it, and said to Colyer, "I'm silly enough to think your Louis has got a lot of right answers in that story of his."

James took his hand down from his bruised cheek and stared at Spade with astonished eyes.

Colyer growled, "What's the matter with you?"

"Nothing," Spade said softly, "except I think you're a little too anxious to slam it on him." He blew smoke out. "Why, for instance, should he drop his gun there when it had marks on it that people knew?"

Colyer said, "You think he's got brains."

"If these boys killed him, knew he was dead, why do they wait till the body's found and things are stirred up before they go after Ferris again? What'd they turn his pockets inside out for if they hijacked him? That's a lot of trouble and only done by folks that kill for some other reason and want to make it look like robbery." He shook his head. "You're too anxious to slam it on them. Why should they—?"

"That's not the point right now," Colyer said. "The point is, why do you keep saying I'm too anxious to slam it on him?"

Spade shrugged. "Maybe to clear yourself with Julia as soon as possible and as clear as possible, maybe even to clear yourself with the police, and then you've got clients."

Colyer said, "What?"

Spade made a careless gesture with his cigarette. "Ferris," he said blandly. "He killed him, of course."

Colyer's eyelids quivered, though he did not actually blink.

Spade said, "First, he's the last person we know of who saw Eli alive, and that's always a good bet. Second, he's the only person I talked to before Eli's body turned up who cared whether I thought they were holding out on me or not. The rest of you just thought I was hunting for a guy who'd gone away. He knew I was hunting for a man he'd killed, so he had to put himself in the clear. He was even afraid to throw that book away, because it had been sent up by the book store and could be traced, and there might be clerks who'd seen the inscription. Third, he was the only one who thought Eli was just a sweet, clean, lovable boy—for the same reasons. Fourth, that story about a blackmailer showing up at three o'clock in the afternoon, making an easy touch for five grand, and then sticking around till midnight is just silly, no matter how good the booze was. Fifth, the story about the paper Eli signed is still worse, though a forged one could be fixed up easy enough. Sixth, he's got the best reason of anybody we know for wanting Eli dead."

Colyer nodded slowly. "Still—"

"Still nothing," Spade said. "Maybe he did the ten-thousand-out-five-thousand-back trick with his bank, but that was easy. Then he got this feeble-minded blackmailer in his house, stalled him along until the servants had gone to bed, took the borrowed gun away from him, shoved him downstairs into his car, took him for a ride—maybe took him already dead, maybe shot him down there by the bushes—frisked him clean to make identification harder and to make it look like robbery, tossed the gun in the water, and came home—"

He broke off to listen to the sound of a siren in the street. He looked then, for the first time since he had begun to talk, at Ferris.

Ferris's face was ghastly white, but he held his eyes steady.

Spade said, "I've got a hunch, Ferris, that we're going to find out about that red-lighting job, too. You told me you had your carnival company with a partner for a while when Eli was working for you, and then by yourself. We oughtn't to have a lot of trouble finding out about your partner—whether he disappeared, or died a natural death, or is still alive."

Ferris had lost some of his erectness. He wet his lips and said, "I want to see my lawyer. I don't want to talk till I've seen my lawyer."

Spade said, "It's all right with me. You're up against it, but I don't like blackmailers myself. I think Eli wrote a good epitaph for them in that book back there—'Too many have lived.'"

—1932

RAYMOND CHANDLER
1888-1959

Raymond Chandler did not become a full-time professional writer until rel-atively late in life. Born in Chicago, Illinois, Chandler served in the Canadian Army and the Royal Air Force between 1917 and 1919. Before the First World War, he worked as a reporter for the London Daily Express *and the Bristol* Western Gazette, *and following the war, he eventually returned to newspaper work at the Los Angeles* Daily Express. *From 1922 to 1932, Chandler was employed as a bookkeeper and an auditor for the Dabney Oil Syndicate in Los Angeles, but when he lost his job during the lean years of the Great Depression, he turned to writing full time in 1933.*

Chandler subsequently became involved with the Black Mask *school of crime fiction.* Black Mask *was a long-running American pulp magazine— established in 1920 by H. L. Mencken and George Jean Nathan—that intro-duced to popular fiction the "hard-boiled" detective story. Carroll John Daly invented the "hard-boiled" detective story (so-called because, like an egg, the detective hero in this type of crime fiction becomes tougher as the pres-sure or "heat" increases) in the early 1920s, but the formula was later per-fected between the mid-1920s and the mid-1930s under the supervision of the* Black Mask's *most notable editor, "Captain" Joseph T. Shaw, and in the fiction of one of its most famous literary disciples, Dashiell Hammett, the creator of Sam Spade and the Continental Op. Raymond Chandler, who himself was a popular contributor to* Black Mask, *is considered (along with Hammett) as being an important author of "hard-boiled" crime fiction, which is sometimes also called "tough guy" or "P.I." (private eye) fiction. Chandler's most famous "hard-boiled" detective hero is Philip Marlowe, who is featured as the protagonist in every novel Chandler ever published, including* The Big Sleep *(1939), which was his first novel,* Farewell My Lovely *(1940),* The High Window *(1942),* The Lady in the Lake *(1943),* The Little Sister *(1949),* The Long Goodbye *(1953), and* Playback *(1958). Unlike Dorothy L. Sayers's version of the classic detective story, Chandler's "hard-boiled" detective fiction is less concerned with plot (which is sometimes con-voluted and unresolved in Chandler's novels) and more concerned with atmosphere and character psychology. And unlike Lord Peter Wimsey and his ilk, Marlowe is a member of the working class. He is less cerebral and more emotional than the classic detective hero, and is willing to resort to violence when necessary. Yet, he is always a man of honor, a "white knight" fighting evil in a corrupt (and corrupting) society.*

Chandler himself was a consummate literary craftsman, and his writ-ing reflects his love of language and subtle metaphor. His essay, "The Simple Art of Murder"—first published in the December 1944 issue of The Atlantic Monthly *and later reprinted in a revised form in* The Art of the Mystery Story *(1946) and in the Chandler collection,* The Simple Art of Murder *(1950)—offers his iconoclastic response to the artistic limitations and literary weaknesses found in the classical detective story. This essay remains, since its initial publication, one of the best critical discussions of the detective story and one of the most damning attacks of the type of detec-tive fiction popularized by Agatha Christie and Dorothy L. Sayers. Yet, Chandler is fundamentally wrong when he argues in this essay that*

Hammett is more "realistic" than his British counterparts. In many ways, the "hard-boiled" writing of Hammett (and Chandler) is as far from the real world as is Christie's or Sayers's classic detective story. Hammett's crime fiction merely appears more real, because it makes crime more "democratic," but it contains similar formulaic conventions and assumptions found in what Chandler disdainfully identifies as the "logic-and-deduction novel of detection."

"Blackmailers Don't Shoot"—initially appearing in the December 1933 issue of Black Mask *and reprinted in the anthology,* The Black Mask Boys *(1985), edited by William F. Nolan—was Chandler's first* Black Mask *story and the first story to feature Chandler's detective hero, Mallory (who was a prototype for Philip Marlowe). Mallory later appeared in one other tale, "Smart-Aleck Kill," which was also published in* Black Mask *(July 1934).*

The Simple Art of Murder

Fiction in any form has always intended to be realistic. Old-fashioned novels which now seem stilted and artificial to the point of burlesque did not appear that way to the people who first read them. Writers like Fielding and Smollett could seem realistic in the modern sense because they dealt largely with uninhibited characters, many of whom were about two jumps ahead of the police, but Jane Austen's chronicles of highly inhibited people against a background of rural gentility seem real enough psychologically. There is plenty of that kind of social and emotional hypocrisy around today. Add to it a liberal dose of intellectual pretentiousness and you get the tone of the book page in your daily paper and the earnest and fatuous atmosphere breathed by discussion groups in little clubs. These are the people who make best-sellers, which are promotional jobs based on a sort of indirect snob-appeal, carefully escorted by the trained seals of the critical fraternity, and lovingly tended and watered by certain much too powerful pressure groups whose business is selling books, although they would like you to think they are fostering culture. Just get a little behind in your payments and you will find out how idealistic they are.

The detective story for a variety of reasons can seldom be promoted. It is usually about murder and hence lacks the element of uplift. Murder, which is a frustration of the individual and hence a frustration of the race, may have, and in fact has, a good deal of sociological implication. But it has been going on too long for it to be news. If the mystery novel is at all realistic (which it very seldom is) it is written in a certain spirit of detachment; otherwise nobody but a psychopath would want to write it or read it. The murder novel has also a depressing way of minding its own business, solving its own problems and answering its own questions. There is nothing left to discuss, except whether it was well enough written to be good fiction, and the people who make up the half-million sales wouldn't know that anyway. The detection of quality in writing is difficult enough even for those who make a career of the job, without paying too much attention to the matter of advance sales.

The detective story (perhaps I had better call it that, since the English formula still dominates the trade) has to find its public by a slow process of distillation. That it does do this, and holds on thereafter with such tenacity, is a fact; the reasons for it are a study for more patient minds than mine. Nor is it any part of my thesis to maintain that it is a vital and significant form of art. There are no vital and significant forms of art; there is only art, and precious little of that. The growth of populations has in no way increased the amount; it has merely increased the adeptness with which substitutes can be produced and packaged.

Yet the detective story, even in its most conventional form, is difficult to write well. Good specimens of the art are much rarer than good serious novels. Rather second-rate items outlast most of the high velocity fiction, and a great many that should never have been born simply refuse to die at all. They are as durable as the statues in public parks and just about that dull.

This is very annoying to people of what is called discernment. They do not like it that penetrating and important works of fiction of a few years back stand on their special shelf in the library marked 'Best-sellers of Yesteryear', and nobody goes near them but an occasional shortsighted customer who bends down, peers briefly and hurries away; while old ladies jostle each other at the mystery shelf to grab off some item of the same vintage with a title like *The Triple Petunia Murder Case,* or *Inspector Pinchbottle to the Rescue.* They do not like it that 'really important books' get dusty on the reprint counter, while *Death Wears Yellow Garters* is put out in editions of fifty or one hundred thousand copies on the news-stands of the country, and is obviously not there just to say good-bye.

To tell you the truth, I do not like it very much myself. In my less stilted moments I too write detective stories, and all this immortality makes just a little too much competition. Even Einstein couldn't get very far if three hundred treatises of the high physics were published every year, and several thousand others in some form or other were hanging around in excellent condition, and being read too.

Hemingway says somewhere that the good writer competes only with the dead. The good detective story writer (there must after all be a few) competes not only with all the unburied dead but with all the hosts of the living as well. And on almost equal terms; for it is one of the qualities of this kind of writing that the thing that makes people read it never goes out of style. The hero's tie may be a little off the mode and the good grey inspector may arrive in a dogcart instead of a streamlined sedan with siren screaming, but what he does when he gets there is the same old fussing around with timetables and bits of charred paper and who trampled the jolly old flowering arbutus under the library window.

I have, however, a less sordid interest in the matter. It seems to me that production of detective stories on so large a scale, and by writers whose immediate reward is small and whose meed of critical praise is almost nil would not be possible at all if the job took any talent. In that sense the raised eyebrow of the critic and the shoddy merchandizing of the publisher are perfectly logical. The average detective story is probably no worse than the average novel, but you never see the average novel. It doesn't get published. The average—or only slightly above average—detective story does. Not only is it published but it is sold in small quantities to rental libraries, and it is read. There are even a few optimists who buy it at the full retail price of two dollars, because it looks so fresh and new, and there is a picture of a corpse on the cover.

And the strange thing is that this average, more than middling dull, pooped-out piece of utterly unreal and mechanical fiction is not terribly different from what are called the masterpieces of the art. It drags on a little more slowly, the dialogue is a little greyer, the cardboard out of which the characters are cut is a shade thinner, and the cheating is a little more obvious; but it is the same kind of book. Whereas the good novel is not at all the same kind of book as the bad novel. It is about entirely different things. But the good detective story and the bad detective story are about exactly the same things, and they are about them in very much the same way. (There are reasons for this too, and reasons for the reasons; there always are.)

I suppose the principal dilemma of the traditional or classic or straight-deductive or logic-and-deduction novel of detection is that for any approach to perfection it demands a combination of qualities not found in the same mind. The cool-headed constructionist does not also come across with lively characters, sharp dialogue, a sense of pace and an acute use of observed detail. The grim logician has as much atmosphere as a drawing-board. The scientific sleuth has a nice new shiny laboratory, but I'm sorry I can't remember the face. The fellow who can write you a vivid and colourful prose simply won't be bothered with the coolie labour of breaking down unbreakable alibis.

The master of rare knowledge is living psychologically in the age of the hoop skirt. If you know all you should know about ceramics and Egyptian needlework, you don't know anything at all about the police. If you know that platinum won't melt under about 2,800 degrees Fahrenheit by itself, but will melt at the glance of a pair of deep blue eyes when put close to a bar of lead, then you don't know how men make love in the twentieth century. And if you know enough about the elegant *flânerie* of the pre-war French Riviera to lay your story in that locale, you don't know that a couple of capsules of barbitol small enough to be swallowed will not only not kill a man—they will not even put him to sleep if he fights against them.

Every detective story writer makes mistakes, and none will ever know as much as he should. Conan Doyle made mistakes which completely invalidated some of his stories, but he was a pioneer, and Sherlock Holmes after all is mostly an attitude and a few dozen lines of unforgettable dialogue. It is the ladies and gentlemen of what Mr. Howard Haycraft (in his book *Murder for Pleasure)* calls the Golden Age of detective fiction that really get me down. This age is not remote. For Mr. Haycraft's purpose it starts after the First World War and lasts up to about 1930. For all practical purposes it is still here. Two-thirds or three-quarters of all the detective stories published still adhere to the formula the giants of this era created, perfected, polished and sold to the world as problems in logic and deduction.

These are stern words, but be not alarmed. They are only words. Let us glance at one of the glories of the literature, an acknowledged masterpiece of the art of fooling the reader without cheating him. It is called *The Red House Mystery,* was written by A. A. Milne, and has been named by Alexander Woollcott (rather a fast man with a superlative) 'One of the three best mystery stories of all time.' Words of that size are not spoken lightly. The book was published in 1922, but is quite timeless, and might as easily have been published in July 1939, or, with a few slight changes, last week. It ran thirteen editions and seems to have been in print, in the original format, for about sixteen years. That happens to few books of any kind. It is an agreeable book, light, amusing in the *Punch* style, written with a deceptive smoothness that is not so easy as it looks.

It concerns Mark Ablett's impersonation of his brother Robert, as a hoax on his friends. Mark is the owner of the Red House, a typical laburnum-and-lodge-gate English country house, and he has a secretary who encourages him and abets him in this impersonation, because the secretary is going to murder him, if he pulls it off. Nobody around the Red House has ever seen Robert, fifteen years absent in

Australia, known to them by repute as a no-good. A letter from Robert is talked about, but never shown. It announces his arrival, and Mark hints it will not be a pleasant occasion. One afternoon, then, the supposed Robert arrives, identifies him-self to a couple of servants, is shown into the study, and Mark (according to testi-mony at the inquest) goes in after him. Robert is then found dead on the floor with a bullet-hole in his face, and of course Mark has vanished into thin air. Arrive the police, suspect Mark must be the murderer, remove the debris and proceed with the investigation, and in due course, with the inquest.

Milne is aware of one very difficult hurdle and tries as well as he can to get over it. Since the secretary is going to murder Mark once he has established himself as Robert, the impersonation has to continue on and fool the police. Since, also, every-body around the Red House knows Mark intimately, disguise is necessary. This is achieved by shaving off Mark's beard, roughening his hands ('not the manicured hands of a gentleman'—testimony) and the use of a gruff voice and rough manner.

But this is not enough. The cops are going to have the body and the clothes on it and whatever is in the pockets. Therefore none of this must suggest Mark. Milne therefore works like a switch engine to put over the motivation that Mark is such a thoroughly conceited performer that he dresses the part down to the socks and underwear (from all of which the secretary has removed the maker's labels), like a ham blacking himself all over to play Othello. If the reader will buy this (and the sales record shows he must have) Milne figures he is solid. Yet, however light in tex-ture the story may be, it is offered as a problem of logic and deduction.

If it is not that, it is nothing at all. There is nothing else for it to be. If the situa-tion is false, you cannot even accept it as a light novel, for there is no story for the light novel to be about. If the problem does not contain the elements of truth and plausibility, it is no problem; if the logic is an illusion, there is nothing to deduce. If the impersonation is impossible once the reader is told the conditions it must ful-fil, then the whole thing is a fraud. Not a deliberate fraud, because Milne would not have written the story, if he had known what he was up against. He is up against a number of deadly things, none of which he even considers. Nor, apparently, does the casual reader, who wants to like the story, hence takes it at its face value. But the reader is not called upon to know the facts of life; it is the author who is the expert in the case. Here is what this author ignores:

1. The coroner holds formal jury inquest on a body for which no legally compe-tent identification is offered. A coroner, usually in a big city, will sometimes hold inquest on a body that *cannot* be identified, if the record of such an inquest has or may have a value (fire, disaster, evidence of murder, etc.). No such reason exists here, and there is no one to identify the body. A couple of witnesses said the man said he was Robert Ablett. This is mere presumption, and has weight only if nothing conflicts with it. Identification is a condition precedent to an inquest. Even in death a man has a right to his own identity. The coroner will, wherever humanly possible, enforce that right. To neglect it would be a violation of his office.
2. Since Mark Ablett, missing and suspected of the murder, cannot defend him-self, all evidence of his movements before and after the murder is vital (as also whether he has money to run away on); yet all such evidence is given by the man closest to the murder, and is without corroboration. It is automatically suspect until proved true.

3. The police find by direct investigation that Robert Ablett was not well thought of in his native village. Somebody there must have known him. No such person was brought to the inquest. (The story couldn't stand it.)

4. The police know there is an element of threat in Robert's supposed visit, and that it is connected with the murder must be obvious to them. Yet they make no attempt to check Robert in Australia, or find out what character he had there, or what associates, or even if he actually came to England, and with whom. (If they had, they would have found out he had been dead three years.)

5. The police surgeon examines the body, with a recently shaved beard (exposing unweathered skin), artificially roughened hands, yet the body of a wealthy, soft-living man, long resident in a cool climate. Robert was a rough individual and had lived fifteen years in Australia. That is the surgeon's information. It is impossible he would have noticed nothing to conflict with it.

6. The clothes are nameless, empty, and have had the labels removed. Yet the man wearing them asserted an identity. The presumption that he was not what he said he was is overpowering. Nothing whatever is done about this peculiar circumstance. It is never even mentioned as being peculiar.

7. A man is missing, a well-known local man, and a body in the morgue closely resembles him. It is impossible that the police should not at once eliminate the chance that the missing man *is* the dead man. Nothing would be easier than to prove it. Not even to think of it is incredible. It makes idiots of the police, so that a brash amateur may startle the world with a fake solution.

The detective in the case is an insouciant amateur named Anthony Gillingham, a nice lad with a cheery eye, a cosy little flat in London, and that airy manner. He is not making any money on the assignment, but is always available when the local gendarmerie loses its notebook. The English police seem to endure him with their customary stoicism; but I shudder to think of what the boys down at the Homicide Bureau in my city would do to him.

There are less plausible examples of the art than this. In *Trent's Last Case* (often called 'the perfect detective story') you have to accept the premiss that a giant of international finance, whose lightest frown makes Wall Street quiver like a chihuahua, will plot his own death so as to hang his secretary, and that the secretary when pinched will maintain an aristocratic silence; the old Etonian in him maybe. I have known relatively few international financiers, but I rather think the author of this novel has (if possible) known fewer.

There is one by Freeman Wills Crofts (the soundest builder of them all when he doesn't get too fancy) wherein a murderer by the aid of make-up, split-second timing, and some very sweet evasive action, impersonates the man he has just killed and thereby gets him alive and distant from the place of crime. There is one of Dorothy Sayers' in which a man is murdered alone at night in his house by a mechanically released weight which works because he always turns the radio on at just such a moment, always stands in just such a position in front of it, and always bends over just so far. A couple of inches either way and the customers would get a rain check. This is what is vulgarly known as having God sit in your lap; a murderer who needs that much help from Providence must be in the wrong business.

And there is a scheme of Agatha Christie's featuring M. Hercule Poirot, that ingenious Belgian who talks in a literal translation of schoolboy French, wherein, by duly messing around with his 'little grey cells', M. Poirot decides that nobody on a certain sleeper could have done the murder alone, therefore everybody did it together, breaking the process down into a series of simple operations, like assembling an egg-beater. This is the type that is guaranteed to knock the keenest mind for a loop. Only a halfwit could guess it.

There are much better plots by these same writers and by others of their school. There may be one somewhere that would really stand up under close scrutiny. It would be fun to read it, even if I did have to go back to page 47 and refresh my memory about exactly what time the second gardener potted the prize-winning tea-rose begonia. There is nothing new about these stories and nothing old. The ones I mention are all English only because the authorities (such as they are) seem to feel the English writers had an edge in this dreary routine, and that the Americans (even the creator of Philo Vance—probably the most asinine character in detective fiction) only made the Junior Varsity.

This, the classic detective story, has learned nothing and forgotten nothing. It is the story you will find almost any week in the big shiny magazines, handsomely illustrated, and paying due deference to virginal love and the right kind of luxury goods. Perhaps the tempo has become a trifle faster, and the dialogue a little more glib. There are more frozen daiquiris and stingers ordered, and fewer glasses of crusty old port; more clothes by *Vogue,* and décors by *House Beautiful,* more chic, but not more truth. We spend more time in Miami hotels and Cape Cod summer colonies and go not so often down by the old grey sundial in the Elizabethan garden.

But fundamentally it is the same careful grouping of suspects, the same utterly incomprehensible trick of how somebody stabbed Mrs. Pottington Postlethwaite III with the solid platinum poniard just as she flatted on the top note of the Bell Song from *Lakmé* in the presence of fifteen ill-assorted guests; the same ingénue in fur-trimmed pyjamas screaming in the night to make the company pop in and out of doors and ball up the timetable; the same moody silence next day as they sit around sipping Singapore slings and sneering at each other, while the flatfeet crawl to and fro under the Persian rugs, with their derby hats on.

Personally I like the English style better. It is not quite so brittle, and the people, as a rule, just wear clothes and drink drinks. There is more sense of background, as if Cheesecake Manor really existed all around and not just the part the camera sees; there are more long walks over the downs and the characters don't all try to behave as if they had just been tested by MGM. The English may not always be the best writers in the world, but they are incomparably the best dull writers.

There is a very simple statement to be made about all these stories: they do not really come off intellectually as problems, and they do not come off artistically as fiction. They are too contrived, and too little aware of what goes on in the world. They try to be honest, but honesty is an art. The poor writer is dishonest without knowing it, and the fairly good one can be dishonest because he doesn't know what to be honest about. He thinks a complicated murder scheme which baffled the lazy reader, who won't be bothered itemizing the details, will also baffle the police, whose business is with details.

The boys with their feet on the desks know that the easiest murder case in the world to break is the one somebody tried to get very cute with; the one that really bothers them is the murder somebody only thought of two minutes before he pulled it off. But if the writers of this fiction wrote about the kind of murders that happen, they would also have to write about the authentic flavour of life as it is lived. And since they cannot do that, they pretend that what they do is what should be done. Which is begging the question—and the best of them know it.

In her introduction to the first *Omnibus of Crime,* Dorothy Sayers wrote: "It [the detective story] does not, and by hypothesis never can, attain the loftiest level of literary achievement." And she suggested somewhere else that this is because it is a "literature of escape" and not "a literature of expression." I do not know what the loftiest level of literary achievement is: neither did Aeschylus or Shakespeare; neither does Miss Sayers. Other things being equal, which they never are, a more powerful theme will provoke a more powerful performance. Yet some very dull books have been written about God, and some very fine ones about how to make a living and stay fairly honest. It is always a matter of who writes the stuff, and what he has in him to write it with.

As for literature of expression and literature of escape, this is critics' jargon, a use of abstract words as if they had absolute meanings. Everything written with vitality expresses that vitality; there are no dull subjects, only dull minds. All men who read escape from something else into what lies behind the printed page; the quality of the dream may be argued, but its release has become a functional necessity. All men must escape at times from the deadly rhythm of their private thoughts. It is part of the process of life among thinking beings. It is one of the things that distinguish them from the three-toed sloth; he apparently—one can never be quite sure—is perfectly content hanging upside down on a branch, and not even reading Walter Lippmann. I hold no particular brief for the detective story as the ideal escape. I merely say that *all* reading for pleasure is escape, whether it be Greek, mathematics, astronomy, Benedetto Croce, or The Diary of the Forgotten Man. To say otherwise is to be an intellectual snob, and a juvenile at the art of living.

I do not think such considerations moved Miss Dorothy Sayers to her essay in critical futility.

I think what was really gnawing at her mind was the slow realization that her kind of detective story was an arid formula which could not even satisfy its own implications. It was second-grade literature because it was not about the things that could make first-grade literature. If it started out to be about real people (and she could write about them—her minor characters show that), they must very soon do unreal things in order to form the artificial pattern required by the plot. When they did unreal things, they ceased to be real themselves. They became puppets and cardboard lovers and papier-mâché villains and detectives of exquisite and impossible gentility.

The only kind of writer who could be happy with these properties was the one who did not know what reality was. Dorothy Sayers' own stories show that she was annoyed by this triteness; the weakest element in them is the part that makes them detective stories, the strongest the part which could be removed without touching the "problem of logic and deduction." Yet she could not or would not give her characters their heads and let them make their own mystery. It took a much simpler and more direct mind than hers to do that.

In *The Long Week-end,* which is a drastically competent account of English life and manners in the decade following the First World War, Robert Graves and Alan Hodge gave some attention to the detective story. They were just as traditionally English as the ornaments of the Golden Age, and they wrote of the time in which these writers were almost as well known as any writers in the world. Their books in one form or another sold into the millions, and in a dozen languages. These were the people who fixed the form and established the rules and founded the famous Detection Club, which is a Parnassus of English writers of mystery. Its roster includes practically every important writer of detective fiction since Conan Doyle.

But Graves and Hodge decided that during this whole period only one first-class writer had written detective stories at all. An American, Dashiell Hammett. Traditional or not, Graves and Hodge were not fuddy-duddy connoisseurs of the second-rate; they could see what went on in the world and that the detective story of their time didn't; and they were aware that writers who have the vision and the ability to produce real fiction do not produce unreal fiction.

How original a writer Hammett really was, it isn't easy to decide now, even if it mattered. He was one of a group, the only one who achieved critical recognition, but not the only one who wrote or tried to write realistic mystery fiction. All literary movements are like this; some one individual is picked out to represent the whole movement; he is usually the culmination of the movement. Hammett was the ace performer, but there is nothing in his work that is not implicit in the early novels and short stories of Hemingway.

Yet for all I know, Hemingway may have learned something from Hammett, as well as from writers like Dreiser, Ring Lardner, Carl Sandburg, Sherwood Anderson and himself. A rather revolutionary debunking of both the language and material of fiction had been going on for some time. It probably started in poetry; almost everything does. You can take it clear back to Walt Whitman, if you like. But Hammett applied it to the detective story, and this, because of its heavy crust of English gentility and American pseudo-gentility, was pretty hard to get moving.

I doubt that Hammett had any deliberate artistic aims whatever; he was trying to make a living by writing something he had first-hand information about. He made some of it up; all writers do; but it had a basis in fact; it was made up out of real things. The only reality the English detection writers knew was the conversational accent of Surbiton and Bognor Regis. If they wrote about dukes and Venetian vases, they knew no more about them out of their own experience than the well-heeled Hollywood character knows about the French Modernists that hang in his Bel-Air château or the semi-antique Chippendale-cum-cobbler's-bench that he uses for a coffee table. Hammett took murder out of the Venetian vase and dropped it into the alley; it doesn't have to stay there for ever, but it was a good idea to begin by getting as far as possible from Emily Post's idea of how a well-bred débutante gnaws a chicken wing.

Hammett wrote at first (and almost to the end) for people with a sharp, aggressive attitude to life. They were not afraid of the seamy side of things; they lived there. Violence did not dismay them; it was right down their street. Hammett gave murder back to the kind of people that commit it for reasons, not just to provide a corpse; and with the means at hand, not with handwrought duelling pistols, curare, and tropical fish. He put these people down on paper as they are, and he made them talk and think in the language they customarily used for these purposes.

He had style, but his audience didn't know it, because it was in a language not supposed to be capable of such refinements. They thought they were getting a good meaty melodrama written in the kind of lingo they imagined they spoke themselves. It was, in a sense, but it was much more. All language begins with speech, and the speech of common men at that, but when it develops to the point of becoming a literary medium it only looks like speech. Hammett's style at its worst was almost as formalized as a page of *Marius the Epicurean;* at its best it could say almost anything. I believe this style, which does not belong to Hammett or to anybody, but is the American language (and not even exclusively that any more), can say things he did not know how to say or feel the need of saying. In his hands it had no overtones, left no echo, evoked no image beyond a distant hill.

Hammett is said to have lacked heart, yet the story he thought most of himself is the record of a man's devotion to a friend. He was spare, frugal, hard-boiled, but he did over and over again what only the best writers can ever do at all. He wrote scenes that seemed never to have been written before.

With all this he did not wreck the formal detective story. Nobody can; production demands a form that can be produced. Realism takes too much talent, too much knowledge, too much awareness. Hammett may have loosened it up a little here, and sharpened it a little there. Certainly all but the stupidest and most meretricious writers are more conscious of their artificiality than they used to be. And he demonstrated that the detective story can be important writing. *The Maltese Falcon* may or may not be a work of genius, but an art which is capable of it is not "by hypothesis" incapable of anything. Once a detective story can be as good as this, only the pedants will deny that it *could* be even better.

Hammett did something else, he made the detective story fun to write, not an exhausting concatenation of insignificant clues. Without him there might not have been a regional mystery as clever as Percival Wilde's *Inquest,* or an ironic study as able as Raymond Postgate's *Verdict of Twelve,* or a savage piece of intellectual double-talk like Kenneth Fearing's *The Dagger of the Mind,* or a tragi-comic idealization of the murderer as in Donald Henderson's *Mr. Bowling Buys a Newspaper,* or even a gay and intriguing Hollywoodian gambol like Richard Sale's *Lazarus No. 7.*

The realistic style is easy to abuse: from haste, from lack of awareness, from inability to bridge the chasm that lies between what a writer would like to be able to say and what he actually knows how to say. It is easy to fake; brutality is not strength, flipness is not wit, edge-of-the-chair writing can be as boring as flat writing; dalliance with promiscuous blondes can be very dull stuff when described by goaty young men with no other purpose in mind than to describe dalliance with promiscuous blondes. There has been so much of this sort of thing that if a character in a detective story says 'Yeah,' the author is automatically a Hammett imitator.

And there are still quite a few people around who say that Hammett did not write detective stories at all, merely hard-boiled chronicles of mean streets with a perfunctory mystery element dropped in like the olive in a martini. These are the flustered old ladies—of both sexes (or no sex) and almost all ages—who like their murders scented with magnolia blossoms and do not care to be reminded that murder is an act of infinite cruelty, even if the perpetrators sometimes look like playboys or college professors or nice motherly women with softly greying hair.

There are also a few badly scared champions of the formal or the classic mystery who think no story is a detective story which does not pose a formal and exact problem and arrange the clues around it with neat labels on them. Such would point out, for example, that in reading *The Maltese Falcon* no one concerns himself with who killed Spade's partner, Archer (which is the only formal problem of the story) because the reader is kept thinking about something else. Yet in *The Glass Key* the reader is constantly reminded that the question is who killed Taylor Henry, and exactly the same effect is obtained; an effect of movement, intrigue, cross-purposes and the gradual elucidation of character, which is all the detective story has any right to be about anyway. The rest is spillikins in the parlour.

But all this (and Hammett too) is for me not quite enough. The realist in murder writes of a world in which gangsters can rule nations and almost rule cities, in which hotels and apartment houses and celebrated restaurants are owned by men who made their money out of brothels, in which a screen star can be the finger man for a mob, and the nice man down the hall is a boss of the numbers racket; a world where a judge with a cellar full of bootleg liquor can send a man to jail for having a pint in his pocket, where the mayor of your town may have condoned murder as an instrument of money-making, where no man can walk down a dark street in safety because law and order are things we talk about but refrain from practising; a world where you may witness a hold-up in broad daylight and see who did it, but you will fade quickly back into the crowd rather than tell anyone, because the hold-up men may have friends with long guns, or the police may not like your testimony, and in any case the shyster for the defence will be allowed to abuse and vilify you in open court, before a jury of selected morons, without any but the most perfunctory interference from a political judge.

It is not a very fragrant world, but it is the world you live in, and certain writers with tough minds and a cool spirit of detachment can make very interesting and even amusing patterns out of it. It is not funny that a man should be killed, but it is sometimes funny that he should be killed for so little, and that his death should be the coin of what we call civilization. All this still is not quite enough.

In everything that can be called art there is a quality of redemption. It may be pure tragedy, if it is high tragedy, and it may be pity and irony, and it may be the raucous laughter of the strong man. But down these mean streets a man must go who is not himself mean, who is neither tarnished nor afraid. The detective in this kind of story must be such a man. He is the hero, he is everything. He must be a complete man and a common man and yet an unusual man. He must be, to use a rather weathered phrase, a man of honour, by instinct, by inevitability, without thought of it, and certainly without saying it. He must be the best man in his world and a good enough man for any world. I do not care much about his private life; he is neither a eunuch nor a satyr; I think he might seduce a duchess and I am quite sure he would not spoil a virgin; if he is a man of honour in one thing, he is that in all things.

He is a relatively poor man, or he would not be a detective at all. He is a common man or he could not go among common people. He has a sense of character, or he would not know his job. He will take no man's money dishonestly and no man's insolence without a due and dispassionate revenge. He is a lonely man and his pride is that you will treat him as a proud man or be very sorry you ever saw him. He talks as the man of his age talks, that is, with rude wit, a lively sense of the grotesque, a disgust for sham, and a contempt for pettiness.

The story of this man's adventure in search of a hidden truth, and it would be no adventure if it did not happen to a man fit for adventure. He has a range of awareness that startles you, but it belongs to him by right, because it belongs to the world he lives in. If there were enough like him, I think the world would be a very safe place to live in, and yet not too dull to be worth living in.

—1944

BLACKMAILERS DON'T SHOOT

The man in the powder-blue suit—which wasn't powder-blue under the lights of the Club Bolivar—was tall, with wide-set gray eyes, a thin nose, a jaw of stone. He had a rather sensitive mouth. His hair was crisp and black, ever so faintly touched with gray, as by an almost diffident hand. His clothes fitted him as though they had a soul of their own, not just a doubtful past. His name happened to be Mallory.

He held a cigarette between the strong, precise fingers of one hand. He put the other hand flat on the white tablecloth and said:

"The letters will cost you ten grand, Miss Farr. That's not too much."

He looked at the girl opposite him very briefly; then he looked across empty tables toward the heart-shaped space of floor where the dancers prowled under shifting colored lights.

They crowded the customers around the dance floor so closely that the perspiring waiters had to balance themselves like tightrope walkers to get between the tables. But near where Mallory sat were only four people.

A slim, dark woman was drinking a highball across the table from a man whose fat red neck glistened with damp bristles. The woman stared into her glass morosely and fiddled with a big silver flask in her lap. Farther along two bored, frowning men smoked long thin cigars, without speaking to each other.

Mallory said thoughtfully: "Ten grand does it nicely, Miss Farr."

Rhonda Farr was very beautiful. She was wearing, for this occasion, all black, except a collar of white fur, light as thistledown, on her evening wrap. Except also a white wig which, meant to disguise her, made her look very girlish. Her eyes were cornflower blue, and she had the sort of skin an old rake dreams of.

She said nastily, without raising her head: "That's ridiculous."

"Why is it ridiculous?" Mallory asked, looking mildly surprised and rather annoyed.

Rhonda Farr lifted her face and gave him a look as hard as marble. Then she picked a cigarette out of a silver case that lay open on the table and fitted it into a long slim holder, also black. She went on:

"The love letters of a screen star? Not so much anymore. The public has stopped being a sweet old lady in long lace panties."

A light danced contemptuously in her purplish-blue eyes. Mallory gave her a hard look.

"But you came here to talk about them quick enough," he said, "with a man you never heard of."

She waved the cigarette holder and said: "I must have been nuts."

Mallory smiled with his eyes, without moving his lips. "No, Miss Farr. You had a damn good reason. Want me to tell you what it is?"

Rhonda Farr looked at him angrily. Then she looked away, almost appeared to forget him. She held up her hand, the one with the cigarette holder, looked at it, posing. It was a beautiful hand, without a ring. Beautiful hands are as rare as jacaranda trees in bloom, in a city where pretty faces are as common as runs in dollar stockings.

She turned her head and glanced at the stiff-eyed woman, beyond her toward the mob around the dance floor. The orchestra went on being saccharine and monotonous.

"I loathe these dives," she said thinly. "They look as if they only existed after dark, like ghouls. The people are dissipated without grace, sinful without irony." She lowered her hand to the white cloth. "Oh yes, the letters, what makes them so dangerous, blackmailer?"

Mallory laughed. He had a ringing laugh with a hard quality in it, a grating sound. "You're good," he said. "The letters are not so much perhaps. Just sexy tripe. The memoirs of a schoolgirl who's been seduced and can't stop talking about it."

"That's lousy," Rhonda Farr said in a voice like iced velvet.

"It's the man they're written to that makes them important," Mallory said coldly. "A racketeer, a gambler, a fast-money boy. And all that goes with it. A guy you couldn't be seen talking to—and stay in the cream."

"I don't talk to him, blackmailer. I haven't talked to him in years. Landrey was a pretty nice boy when I knew him. Most of us have something behind us we'd rather not go into. In my case it *is* behind."

"Oh yes? Make mine strawberry," Mallory said with a sudden sneer. "You just got through asking him to help you get your letters back."

Her head jerked. Her face seemed to come apart, to become merely a set of features without control. Her eyes looked like the prelude to a scream—but only for a second.

Almost instantly she got her self-control back. Her eyes were drained of color, almost as gray as his own. She put the black cigarette holder down with exaggerated care, laced her fingers together. The knuckles looked white.

"You know Landrey that well?" she said bitterly.

"Maybe I just get around, find things out. . . . Do we deal, or do we just go on snarling at each other?"

"Where did you get the letters?" Her voice was still rough and bitter.

Mallory shrugged. "We don't tell things like that in our business."

"I had a reason for asking. Some other people have been trying to sell me these same damned letters. That's why I'm here. It made me curious. But I guess you're just one of them trying to scare me into action by stepping the price."

Mallory said: "No, I'm on my own."

She nodded. Her voice was scarcely more than a whisper. "That makes it nice. Perhaps some bright mind thought of having a private edition of my letters made. Photostats . . . Well, I'm not paying. It wouldn't get me anywhere. I don't deal, blackmailer. So far as I'm concerned, you can go out some dark night and jump off the dock with your lousy letters!"

Mallory wrinkled his nose, squinted down it with an air of deep concentration. "Nicely put, Miss Farr. But it doesn't get us anywhere."

She said deliberately: "It wasn't meant to. I could put it better. And if I'd thought to bring my little pearl-handled gun, I could say it with slugs and get away with it! But I'm not looking for that kind of publicity."

Mallory held up two lean fingers and examined them critically. He looked amused, almost pleased. Rhonda Farr put her slim hand up to her white wig, held it there a moment, and dropped it.

A man sitting at a table some way off got up at once and came toward them.

He came quickly, walking with a light, lithe step and swinging a soft black hat against his thigh. He was sleek in dinner clothes.

While he was coming Rhonda Farr said: "You didn't expect me to walk in here alone, did you? Me, I don't go to nightclubs alone."

Mallory grinned. "You shouldn't ought to have to, baby," he said dryly.

The man came up to the table. He was small, neatly put together, dark. He had a little black mustache, shiny like satin, and the clear pallor that Latins prize above rubies.

With a smooth gesture, a hint of drama, he leaned across the table and took one of Mallory's cigarettes out of the silver case. He lit it with a flourish.

Rhonda Farr put her hand to her lips and yawned. She said, "This is Erno, my bodyguard. He takes care of me. Nice, isn't it?"

She stood up slowly. Erno helped her with her wrap. Then he spread his lips in a mirthless smile, looked at Mallory, said:

"Hello, baby."

He had dark, almost opaque eyes with hot lights in them.

Rhonda Farr gathered her wrap about her, nodded slightly, sketched a brief sarcastic smile with her delicate lips, and turned off along the aisle between the tables. She went with her head up and proud, her face a little tense and wary, like a queen in jeopardy. Not fearless, but disdaining to show fear. It was nicely done.

The two bored men gave her an interested eye. The dark woman brooded glumly over the task of mixing herself a highball that would have floored a horse. The man with the fat sweaty neck seemed to have gone to sleep.

Rhonda Farr went up the five crimson-carpeted steps to the lobby, past a bowing headwaiter. She went through looped-back gold curtains, and disappeared.

Mallory watched her out of sight, then he looked at Erno. He said: "Well, punk, what's on your mind?"

He said it insultingly, with a cold smile. Erno stiffened. His gloved left hand jerked the cigarette that was in it so that some ash fell off.

"Kiddin' yourself, baby?" he inquired swiftly.

"About what, punk?"

Red spots came into Erno's pale cheeks. His eyes narrowed to black slits. He moved his ungloved right hand a little, curled the fingers so that the small pink nails glittered. He said thinly:

"About some letters, baby. Forget it! It's out, baby, out!"

Mallory looked at him with elaborate, cynical interest, ran his fingers through his crisp black hair. He said slowly: "Perhaps I don't know what you mean, little one."

Erno laughed. A metallic sound, a strained deadly sound. Mallory knew that kind of laugh; the prelude to gun music in some places. He watched Erno's quick little right hand. He spoke raspingly.

"On your way, red hot. I might take a notion to slap that fuzz off your lip."

Erno's face twisted. The red patches showed startlingly in his cheeks. He lifted the hand that held his cigarette, lifted it slowly, and snapped the burning cigarette straight at Mallory's face. Mallory moved his head a little, and the white tube arced over his shoulder.

There was no expression on his lean, cold face. Distantly, dimly, as though another voice spoke, he said:

"Careful, punk. People get hurt for things like that."

Erno laughed the same metallic, strained laugh. "Blackmailers don't shoot, baby," he snarled. "Do they?"

"Beat it, you dirty little wop!"

The words, the cold sneering tone, stung Erno to fury. His right hand shot up like a striking snake. A gun whisked into it from a shoulder holster. Then he stood motionless, glaring. Mallory bent forward a little, his hands on the edge of the table, his fingers curled below the edge. The corners of his mouth sketched a dim smile.

There was a dull screech, not loud, from the dark woman. The color drained from Erno's cheeks, leaving them pallid, sunk in. In a voice that whistled with fury he said:

"Okay, baby. We'll go outside. March, you—!"

One of the bored men three tables away made a sudden movement of no significance. Slight as it was it caught Erno's eye. His glance flickered. Then the table rose into his stomach, knocked him sprawling.

It was a light table, and Mallory was not a lightweight. There was a complicated thudding sound. A few dishes clattered, some silver. Erno was spread on the floor with the table across his thighs. His gun settled a foot from his clawing hand. His face was convulsed.

For a poised instant of time it was as though the scene were imprisoned in glass and would never change. Then the dark woman screeched again, louder. Everything became a swirl of movement. People on all sides came to their feet. Two waiters put their arms straight up in the air and began to spout violent Neapolitan. A moist, overdriven bus-boy charged up, more afraid of the headwaiter than of sudden death. A plump, reddish man with corn-colored hair hurried down steps, waving a bunch of menus.

Erno jerked his legs clear, weaved to his knees, snatched up his gun. He swiveled, spitting curses. Mallory, alone, indifferent in the center of the babble, leaned down and cracked a hard fist against Erno's flimsy jaw.

Consciousness evaporated from Erno's eyes. He collapsed like a half-filled sack of sand.

Mallory observed him carefully for a couple of seconds. Then he picked his cigarette case up off the floor. There were still two cigarettes in it. He put one of them between his lips, put the case away. He took some bills out of his trouser pocket, folded one lengthwise, and poked it at a waiter.

He walked away without haste, toward the five crimson-carpeted steps and the entrance.

The man with the fat neck opened a cautious and fishy eye. The drunken woman staggered to her feet with a cackle of inspiration, picked up a bowl of ice cubes in her thin jeweled hands, and dumped it on Erno's stomach, with fair accuracy.

Mallory came out from under the canopy with his soft hat under his arm. The doorman looked at him inquiringly. He shook his head and walked a little way down the curving sidewalk that bordered the semicircular private driveway. He stood at the edge of the curbing, in the darkness, thinking hard. After a little while an Isotta-Fraschini went by him slowly.

It was an open phaeton, huge even for the calculated swank of Hollywood. It glittered like a Ziegfeld chorus as it passed the entrance lights, then it was all dull gray and silver. A liveried chauffeur sat behind the wheel as stiff as a poker, with a peaked cap cocked rakishly over one eye. Rhonda Farr sat in the backseat, under the half-deck, with the rigid stillness of a wax figure.

The car slid soundlessly down the driveway, passed between a couple of squat stone pillars, and was lost among the lights of the boulevard. Mallory put on his hat absently.

Something stirred in the darkness behind him, between tall Italian cypresses. He swung around, looked at faint light on a gun barrel.

The man who held the gun was very big and broad. He had a shapeless felt hat on the back of his head, and an indistinct overcoat hung away from his stomach. Dim light from a high-up, narrow window outlined bushy eyebrows, a hooked nose. There was another man behind him.

He said: "This is a gun, buddy. It goes boom-boom, and guys fall down. Want to try it?"

Mallory looked at him emptily and said: "Grow up, flattie! What's the act?"

The big man laughed. His laughter had a dull sound, like the sea breaking on rocks in a fog. He said with heavy sarcasm:

"Bright boy has us spotted, Jim. One of us must look like a cop." He eyed Mallory, and added: "Saw you pull a rod on a little guy inside. Was that nice?"

Mallory tossed his cigarette away, watched it arc through the darkness. He said carefully:

"Would twenty bucks make you see it some other way?"

"Not tonight, mister. Most any other night, but not tonight."

"A C note?"

"Not even that, mister."

"That," Mallory said gravely, "must be damn tough."

The big man laughed again, came a little closer. The man behind him lurched out of the shadows and planted a soft fattish hand on Mallory's shoulder. Mallory slid sidewise, without moving his feet. The hand fell off. He said:

"Keep your paws off me, gumshoe!"

The other man made a snarling sound. Something swished through the air. Something hit Mallory very hard behind his left ear. He went to his knees. He kneeled swaying for a moment, shaking his head violently. His eyes cleared. He could see the lozenge design in the sidewalk. He got to his feet again rather slowly.

He looked at the man who had blackjacked him and cursed him in a thick dull voice, with a concentration of ferocity that set the man back on his heels with his slack mouth working like melting rubber.

The big man said: "Damn your soul, Jim! What in hell'd you do that for?"

The man called Jim put his soft fat hand to his mouth and gnawed at it. He shuffled the blackjack into the side pocket of his coat.

"Forget it!" he said. "Let's take the —— and get on with it. I need a drink."

He plunged down the walk. Mallory turned slowly, followed him with his eyes, rubbing the side of his head. The big man moved his gun in a businesslike way and said:

"Walk, buddy. We're takin' a little ride in the moonlight."

Mallory walked. The big man fell in beside him. The man called Jim fell in on the other side. He hit himself hard in the pit of the stomach, said:

"I need a drink, Mac. I've got the jumps."

The big man said peacefully: "Who don't, you poor egg?"

They came to a touring car that was double-parked near the squat pillars at the edge of the boulevard. The man who had hit Mallory got in behind the wheel. The big man prodded Mallory into the backseat and got in beside him. He held his gun across his big thigh, tilted his hat a little further back, and got out a crumpled pack of cigarettes. He lit one carefully, with his left hand.

The car went out into the sea of lights, rolled east a short way, then turned south down the long slope. The lights of the city were an endless glittering sheet. Neon signs glowed and flashed. The languid ray of a searchlight prodded about among high faint clouds.

"It's like this," the big man said, blowing smoke from his wide nostrils. "We got you spotted. You were tryin' to peddle some phony letters to the Farr twist."

Mallory laughed shortly, mirthlessly. He said: "You flatties give me an ache."

The big man appeared to think it over, staring in front of him. Passing electroliers threw quick waves of light across his broad face. After a while he said:

"You're the guy, all right. We got to know these things in our business."

Mallory's eyes narrowed in the darkness. His lips smiled. He said: "What business, copper?"

The big man opened his mouth wide, shut it with a click. He said:

"Maybe you better talk, bright boy. Now would be a hell of a good time. Jim and me ain't tough to get on with, but we got friends who ain't so dainty."

Mallory said: "What would I talk about, Lieutenant?"

The big man shook with silent laughter, made no answer. The car went past the oil well that stands in the middle of La Cienega Boulevard, then turned off on to a quiet street fringed with palm trees. It stopped halfway down the block, in front of an empty lot. Jim cut the motor and the lights. Then he got a flat bottle out of the door pocket and held it to his mouth, sighed deeply, passed the bottle over his shoulder.

The big man took a drink, waved the bottle, said:

"We got to wait here for a friend. Let's talk. My name's Macdonald—detective bureau. You was tryin' to shake the Farr girl down. Then her protection stepped in front of her. You bopped him. That was a nice routine and we liked it. But we didn't like the other part."

Jim reached back for the whiskey bottle, took another drink, sniffed at the neck, said: "This liquor is lousy."

Macdonald went on: "We was stashed out for you. But we don't figure your play out in the open like that. It don't listen."

Mallory leaned an arm on the side of the car and looked out and up at the calm, blue, star-spattered sky. He said:

"You know too much, copper. And you didn't get your dope from Miss Farr. No screen star would go to the police on a matter of blackmail."

Macdonald jerked his big head around. His eyes gleamed faintly in the dark interior of the car.

"We didn't say how we got our dope, bright boy. So you *was* tryin' to shake her down, huh?"

Mallory said gravely: "Miss Farr is an old friend of mine. Somebody is trying to blackmail her, but not me. I just have a hunch."

Macdonald said swiftly: "What the wop pull a gun on you for?"

"He didn't like me," Mallory said in a bored voice. "I was mean to him."

Macdonald said: "Horsefeathers!" He rumbled angrily. The man in the front seat said: "Smack him in the kisser, Mac. Make the —— like it!"

Mallory stretched his arms downward, twisting his shoulders like a man cramped from sitting. He felt the bulge of his Luger under his left arm. He said slowly, wearily:

"You said I was trying to peddle some phony letters. What makes you think the letters would be phony?"

Macdonald said softly: "Maybe we know where the right ones are."

Mallory drawled: "That's what I thought, copper," and laughed.

Macdonald moved suddenly, jerked his balled fist up, hit him in the face, but not very hard. Mallory laughed again, then he touched the bruised place behind his ear with careful fingers.

"That went home, didn't it?" he said.

Macdonald swore dully. "Maybe you're just a bit too damn smart, bright boy. I guess we'll find out after a while."

He fell silent. The man in the front seat took off his hat and scratched at a mat of gray hair. Staccato horn blasts came from the boulevard a half-block away. Headlights streamed past the end of the street. After a time a pair of them swung around in a wide curve, speared white beams along below the palm trees. A dark bulk drifted down the half-block, slid to the curb in front of the touring car. The lights went off.

A man got out and walked back. Macdonald said: "Hi, Slippy. How'd it go?"

The man was a tall thin figure with a shadowy face under a pulled-down cap. He lisped a little when he spoke. He said:

"Nothin' to it. Nobody got mad."

"Okay," Macdonald grunted. "Ditch the hot one and drive this heap."

Jim got into the back of the touring car and sat on Mallory's left, digging a hard elbow into him. The lanky man slid under the wheel, started the motor, and drove back to La Cienega, then south to Wilshire, then west again. He drove fast and roughly.

They went casually through a red light, passed a big movie palace with most of its lights out and its glass cashier's cage empty; then through Beverly Hills, over interurban tracks. The exhaust got louder on a long hill with high banks paralleling the road. Macdonald spoke suddenly:

"Hell, Jim, I forgot to frisk this baby. Hold the gun a minute."

He leaned in front of Mallory, close to him, blowing whiskey breath in his face. A big hand went over his pockets, down inside his coat around the hips, up under his left arm. It stopped there a moment, against the Luger in the shoulder holster. It went on to the other side, went away altogether.

"Okay, Jim. No gun on bright boy."

A sharp light of wonder winked into being deep in Mallory's brain. His eyebrows drew together. His mouth felt dry.

"Mind if I light up a cigarette?" he asked, after a pause.

Macdonald said with mock politeness: "Now why would we mind a little thing like that, sweetheart?"

The apartment house stood on a hill above Westward Village, and was new and rather cheap-looking. Macdonald and Mallory and Jim got out in front of it, and the touring car went on around the corner, disappeared.

The three men went through a quiet lobby past a switchboard where no one sat at the moment, up to the seventh floor in the automatic elevator. They went along a corridor, stopped before a door. Macdonald took a loose key out of his pocket, unlocked the door. They went in.

It was a very new room, very bright, very foul with cigarette smoke. The furniture was upholstered in loud colors, the carpet was a mess of fat green and yellow lozenges. There was a mantel with bottles on it.

Two men sat at an octagonal table with tall glasses at their elbows. One had red hair, very dark eyebrows, and a dead white face with deep-set dark eyes. The other one had a ludicrous big bulbous nose, no eyebrows at all, hair the color of the inside of a sardine can. This one put some cards down slowly and came across the room with a wide smile. He had a loose, good-natured mouth, an amiable expression.

"Have any trouble, Mac?" he said.

Macdonald rubbed his chin, shook his head sourly. He looked at the man with the nose as if he hated him. The man with the nose went on smiling. He said:

"Frisk him?"

Macdonald twisted his mouth to a thick sneer and stalked across the room to the mantel and the bottles. He said in a nasty tone:

"Bright boy don't pack a gun. He works with his head. He's smart."

He recrossed the room suddenly and smacked the back of his rough hand across Mallory's mouth. Mallory smiled thinly, did not stir. He stood in front of a big bile-colored davenport spotted with angry-looking red squares. His hands hung down at his sides, and cigarette smoke drifted up from between his fingers to join the haze that already blanketed the rough, arched ceiling.

"Keep your pants on, Mac," the man with the nose said. "You've done your act. You and Jim check out now. Oil the wheels and check out."

Macdonald snarled: "Who you givin' orders to, big shot? I'm stickin' around till this chiseler gets what's coming to him, Costello."

The man called Costello shrugged his shoulders briefly. The red-haired man at the table turned a little in his chair and looked at Mallory with the impersonal air of a collector studying an impaled beetle. Then he took a cigarette out of a neat black case and lit it carefully with a gold lighter.

Macdonald went back to the mantel, poured some whiskey out of a square bottle into a glass, and drank it raw. He leaned, scowling, with his back to the mantel.

Costello stood in front of Mallory, cracking the joints of long, bony fingers.

He said: "Where do you come from?"

Mallory looked at him dreamily and put his cigarette in his mouth. "McNeil's Island," he said with vague amusement.

"How long since?"

"Ten days."

"What were you in for?"

"Forgery." Mallory gave the information in a soft, pleased voice.

"Been here before?"

Mallory said: "I was born here. Didn't you know?"

Costello's voice was gentle, almost soothing. "No-o, I didn't know that," he said. "What did you come for—ten days ago?"

Macdonald heaved across the room again, swinging his thick arms. He slapped Mallory across the mouth a second time, leaning past Costello's shoulder to do it. A red mark showed on Mallory's face. He shook his head back and forth. Dull fire was in his eyes.

"Jeeze, Costello, this crumb ain't from McNeil. He's ribbin' you." His voice blared. "Bright boy's just a cheap chiseler from Brooklyn or K. C.—one of those hot towns where the cops are all cripples."

Costello put a hand up and pushed gently at Macdonald's shoulder. He said: "You're not needed in this, Mac," in a flat, toneless voice.

Macdonald balled his fist angrily. Then he laughed, lunged forward, and ground his heel on Mallory's foot. Mallory said: "—— damn!" and sat down hard on the davenport.

The air in the room was drained of oxygen. Windows were in one wall only, and heavy net curtains hung straight and still across them. Mallory got out a handkerchief and wiped his forehead, patted his lips.

Costello said: "You and Jim check out, Mac," in the same flat voice.

Macdonald lowered his head, stared at him steadily through a fringe of eyebrow. His face was shiny with sweat. He had not taken his shabby, rumpled overcoat off. Costello didn't even turn his head. After a moment Macdonald barged back to the mantel, elbowed the gray-haired cop out of the way, and grabbed at the square bottle of Scotch.

"Call the boss, Costello," he blared over his shoulder. "You ain't got the brains for this deal. For —— sake do something besides talk!" He turned a little toward Jim, thumped him on the back, said sneeringly: "Did you want just one more drink, copper?"

"What did you come here for?" Costello asked Mallory again.

"Looking for a connection." Mallory stared up at him lazily. The fire had died out of his eyes.

"Funny way you went about it, boy."

Mallory shrugged. "I thought if I made a play, I might get in touch with the right people."

"Maybe you made the wrong kind of play," Costello said quietly. He closed his eyes and rubbed his nose with a thumbnail. "These things are hard to figure sometimes."

Macdonald's harsh voice boomed across the close room. "Bright boy don't make mistakes, mister. Not with his brains."

Costello opened his eyes and glanced back over his shoulder at the red-haired man. The red-haired man swiveled loosely in his chair. His right hand lay along his leg, slack, half closed. Costello turned the other way, looked straight at Macdonald.

"Move out!" he snapped coldly. "Move out now. You're drunk, and I'm not arguing with you."

Macdonald ground his shoulders against the mantel and put his hands in the side pockets of his suit coat. His hat hung formless and crumpled on the back of his big, square head. Jim, the gray-haired cop, moved a little away from him, stared at him strainedly, his mouth working.

"Call the boss, Costello!" Macdonald shouted. "You ain't givin' me orders. I don't like you well enough to take 'em."

Costello hesitated, then moved across to the telephone. His eyes stared at a spot high up on the wall. He lifted the instrument off the prongs and dialed with his back to Macdonald. Then he leaned against the wall, smiling thinly at Mallory over the cup. Waiting.

"Hello . . . yes . . . Costello. Everything's oke except Mac's loaded. He's pretty hostile . . . won't move out. Don't know yet . . . some out-of-town boy. Okay."

Macdonald made a motion, said: "Hold it . . ."

Costello smiled and put the phone aside without haste. Macdonald's eyes gleamed at him with a greenish fire. He spit on the carpet, in the corner between a chair and the wall. He said:

"That's lousy. Lousy. You can't dial Montrose from here." Costello moved his hands vaguely. The red-haired man got to his feet. He moved away from the table and stood laxly, tilting his head back so that the smoke from his cigarette rose clear of his eyes.

Macdonald rocked angrily on his heels. His jawbone was a hard white line against his flushed face. His eyes had a deep, hard glitter.

"I guess we'll play it this way," he stated. He took his hands out of his pockets in a casual manner, and his blued service revolver moved in a tight, businesslike arc.

Costello looked at the red-haired man and said: "Take him, Andy."

The red-haired man stiffened, spit his cigarette straight out from between his pale lips, flashed a hand up like lightning.

Mallory said: "Not fast enough. Look at this one."

He had moved so quickly and so little that he had not seemed to move at all. He leaned forward a little on the davenport. The long black Luger lined itself evenly on the red-haired man's belly.

The red-haired man's hand came down slowly from his lapel, empty. The room was very quiet. Costello looked once at Macdonald with infinite disgust, then he put his hands out in front of him, palms up, and looked down at them with a blank smile.

Macdonald spoke slowly, bitterly. "The kidnapping is one too many for me, Costello. I don't want any part of it. I'm takin' a powder from this toy mob. I took a chance that bright boy might side me."

Mallory stood up and moved sidewise toward the red-haired man. When he had gone about half the distance, the gray-haired cop, Jim, let out a strangled sort of yell and jumped for Macdonald, clawing at his pocket. Macdonald looked at him with quick surprise. He put his big left hand out and grabbed both lapels of Jim's overcoat tight together, high up. Jim flailed at him with both fists, hit him in the face twice. Macdonald drew his lips back over his teeth. Calling to Mallory, "Watch those birds," he very calmly laid his gun down on the mantel, reached down into the pocket of Jim's coat, and took out the woven leather blackjack. He said:

"You're a louse, Jim. You always were a louse."

He said it rather thoughtfully, without rancor. Then he swung the blackjack and hit the gray-haired man on the side of the head. The gray-haired man sagged slowly to his knees. He clawed freely at the skirts of Macdonald's coat. Macdonald stooped over and hit him again with the blackjack, in the same place, very hard.

Jim crumpled down sidewise and lay on the floor with his hat off and his mouth open. Macdonald swung the blackjack slowly from side to side. A drop of sweat ran down the side of his nose.

Costello said: "Rough boy, ain't you, Mac?" He said it dully, absently, as though he had very little interest in what went on.

Mallory went on toward the red-haired man. When he was behind him he said:

"Put the hands way up, wiper."

When the red-haired man had done this, Mallory put his free hand over his shoulder, down inside his coat. He jerked a gun loose from a shoulder holster and dropped it on the floor behind him. He felt the other side, patted pockets. He stepped back and circled to Costello. Costello had no gun.

Mallory went to the other side of Macdonald, stood where everyone in the room was in front of him. He said:

"Who's kidnapped?"

Macdonald picked up his gun and glass of whiskey. "The Farr girl," he said. "They got her on her way home, I guess. It was planned when they knew from the wop bodyguard about the date at the Bolivar. I don't know where they took her."

Mallory planted his feet wide apart and wrinkled his nose. He held his Luger easily, with a slack wrist. He said:

"What does your little act mean?"

Macdonald said grimly: "Tell me about yours. I gave you a break."

Mallory nodded, said: "Sure—for your own reasons. . . . I was hired to look for some letters that belong to Rhonda Farr." He looked at Costello. Costello showed no emotion.

Macdonald said: "Okay by me. I thought it was some kind of a plant. That's why I took the chance. Me, I want an out from this connection, that's all." He waved his hand around to take in the room and everything in it.

Mallory picked up a glass, looked into it to see if it was clean, then poured a little Scotch into it and drank it in sips, rolling his tongue around in his mouth.

"Let's talk about the kidnapping," he said. "Who was Costello phoning to?"

"Atkinson. Big Hollywood lawyer. Front for the boys. He's the Farr girl's lawyer, too. Nice guy, Atkinson. A louse."

"He in on the kidnapping?"

Macdonald laughed and said: "Sure."

Mallory shrugged, said: "It seems like a dumb trick—for him."

He went past Macdonald, along the wall to where Costello stood. He stuck the muzzle of the Luger against Costello's chin, pushed his head back against the rough plaster.

"Costello's a nice old boy," he said thoughtfully. "He wouldn't kidnap a girl. Would you, Costello? A little quiet extortion maybe, but nothing rough. That right, Costello?"

Costello's eyes went blank. He swallowed. He said between his teeth: "Can it. You're not funny."

Mallory said: "It gets funnier as it goes on. But perhaps you don't know it all."

He lifted the Luger and drew the muzzle down the side of Costello's big nose, hard. It left a white mark that turned to a red weal. Costello looked a little worried.

Macdonald finished pushing a nearly full bottle of Scotch into his overcoat pocket and said:

"Let me work on the ——!"

Mallory shook his head gravely from side to side, looking at Costello.

"Too noisy. You know how these places are built. Atkinson is the boy to see. Always see the head man—if you can get to him."

Jim opened his eyes. Flapped his hands on the floor, tried to get up. Macdonald lifted a large foot and planted it carelessly in the gray-haired man's face. Jim lay down again. His face was a muddy gray color.

Mallory glanced at the red-haired man and went over to the telephone stand. He lifted the instrument down and dialed a number awkwardly, with his left hand.

He said: "I'm calling the man who hired me. . . . He has a big fast car. . . . We'll put these boys in soak for a while."

Landrey's big black Cadillac rolled soundlessly up the long grade to Montrose. Lights shone low on the left, in the lap of the valley. The air was cool and clear, and the stars were very bright. Landrey looked back from the front seat, draped an arm over the back of the seat, a long black arm that ended in a white glove.

He said, for the third or fourth time: "So it's her own mouthpiece shaking her down. Well, well, well."

He smiled smoothly, deliberately. All his movements were smooth and deliberate. Landrey was a tall, pale man with white teeth and jet-black eyes that sparkled under the dome light.

Mallory and Macdonald sat in the backseat. Mallory said nothing; he stared out of the car window. Macdonald took a pull at his square bottle of Scotch, lost the cork on the floor of the car, and swore as he bent over to grope for it. When he found it he leaned back and looked morosely at Landrey's clear, pale face above the white silk scarf.

He said: "You still got that place on Highland Drive?"

Landrey said: "Yes, copper, I have. And it's not doin' so well."

Macdonald growled. He said: "That's a damn shame, Mr. Landrey." Then he put his head back against the upholstery and closed his eyes.

The Cadillac turned off the highway. The driver seemed to know just where he was going. He circled around into a landscaped subdivision of rambling elaborate homes. Tree frogs sounded in the darkness, and there was a smell of orange blossoms.

Macdonald opened his eyes and leaned forward. "The house on the corner," he told the driver.

The house stood well back from a wide curve. It had a lot of tiled roof, an entrance like a Norman arch, and wrought-iron lanterns lit on either side of the door. By the sidewalk there was a pergola covered with climbing roses. The driver cut his lights and drifted expertly up to the pergola.

Mallory yawned and opened the car door. Cars were parked along the street around the corner. The cigarette tips of a couple of lounging chauffeurs spotted the soft bluish dark.

"Party," he said. "That makes it nice."

He got out, stood a moment looking across the lawn. Then he walked over soft grass to a pathway of dull bricks spaced so that the grass grew between them. He stood between the wrought-iron lanterns and rang the bell.

A maid in cap and apron opened the door. Mallory said:

"Sorry to disturb Mr. Atkinson, but it's important. Macdonald is the name."

The maid hesitated, then went back into the house, leaving the front door open a crack. Mallory pushed it open carelessly, looked into a roomy hallway with Indian rugs on the floor and walls. He went in.

A few yards down the hallway a doorway gave on a dim room lined with books, smelling of good cigars. Hats and coats were spread around on the chairs. From the back of the house a radio droned dance music.

Mallory took his Luger out and leaned against the jamb of the door, inside.

A man in evening dress came along the hall. He was a plump man with thick white hair above a shrewd, pink, irritable face. Beautifully tailored shoulders failed to divert attention from rather too much stomach. His heavy eyebrows were drawn together in a frown. He walked fast and looked mad.

Mallory stepped out of the doorway and put his gun in Atkinson's stomach.

"You're looking for me," he said.

Atkinson stopped, heaved a little, made a choked sound in his throat. His eyes were wide and startled. Mallory moved the Luger up, put the cold muzzle into the flesh of Atkinson's throat, just above the V of his wing collar. The lawyer partly lifted one arm, as though to make a sweep of the gun. Then he stood quite still, holding the arm up in the air.

Mallory said: "Don't talk. Just think. You're sold out. Macdonald has ratted on you. Costello and two other boys are taped up at Westwood. We want Rhonda Farr."

Atkinson's eyes were dull blue, opaque, without interior light. The mention of Rhonda Farr's name did not seem to make much impression on him. He squirmed against the gun and said:

"Why do you come to me?"

"We think you know where she is," Mallory said tonelessly. "But we won't talk about it here. Let's go outside."

Atkinson jerked, sputtered. "No . . . no, I have guests."

Mallory said coldly: "The guest we want isn't here." He pressed on the gun.

A sudden wave of emotion went over Atkinson's face. He took a short step back and snatched at the gun. Mallory's lips tightened. He twisted his wrist in a tight circle, and the gun sight flicked across Atkinson's mouth. Blood came out on his lips. His mouth began to puff. He got very pale.

Mallory said: "Keep your head, fat boy, and you may live through the night."

Atkinson turned and walked straight out of the open door, swiftly, blindly.

Mallory took his arm and jerked him to the left, on to the grass. "Make it slow, mister," he said gratingly.

They rounded the pergola. Atkinson put his hands out in front of him and floundered at the car. A long arm came out of the open door and grabbed him. He went in, fell against the seat. Macdonald clapped a hand over his face and forced him back against the upholstery. Mallory got in and slammed the car door.

Tires squealed as the car circled rapidly and shot away. The driver drove a block before he switched the lights on again. Then he turned his head a little, said: "Where to, boss?"

Mallory said: "Anywhere. Back to town. Take it easy."

The Cadillac turned on to the highway again and began to drop down the long grade. Lights showed in the valley once more, little white lights that moved ever so slowly along the floor of the valley. Headlights.

Atkinson heaved up in the seat, got a handkerchief out and dabbed at his mouth. He peered at Macdonald and said in a composed voice:

"What's the frame, Mac? Shakedown?"

Macdonald laughed gruffly. Then he hiccuped. He was a little drunk. He said thickly:

"Hell, no. The boys hung a snatch on the Farr girl tonight. Her friends here don't like it. But you wouldn't know anything about it, would you, big shot?" He laughed again, jeeringly.

Atkinson said slowly: "It's funny . . . but I wouldn't." He lifted his white head higher, went on: "Who are these men?"

Macdonald didn't answer him. Mallory lit a cigarette, guarding the match flame with cupped hands. He said slowly:

"That's not important, is it? Either you know where Rhonda Farr was taken, or you can give us a lead. Think it out. There's lots of time."

Landrey turned his head and looked back. His face was a pale blur in the dark.

"It's not much to ask, Mr. Atkinson," he said gravely. His voice was cool, suave, pleasant. He tapped on the seatback with his gloved fingers.

Atkinson stared toward him for a while, then put his head back against the upholstery. "Suppose I don't know anything about it," he said wearily.

Macdonald lifted his hand and hit him in the face. The lawyer's head jerked against the cushions. Mallory said in a cold, unpleasant voice:

"A little less of your crap, copper."

Macdonald swore at him, turned his head away. The car went on.

They were down in the valley now. A three-colored airport beacon swung through the sky not far away. There began to be wooded slopes and little beginnings of valley between dark hills. A train roared down from the Newhall tunnel, gathered speed and went by with a long shattering crash.

Landrey said something to his driver. The Cadillac turned off on to a dirt road. The driver switched the lights off and picked his way by moonlight. The dirt road ended in a spot of dead brown grass with low bushes around it. There were old cans and torn discolored newspapers faintly visible on the ground.

Macdonald got his bottle out, hefted it, and gurgled a drink. Atkinson said thickly:

"I'm a bit faint. Give me one."

Macdonald turned, held the bottle out, then growled: "Aw, go to hell!" and put it away in his coat. Mallory took a flash out of the door pocket, clicked it on, and put the beam on Atkinson's face. He said:

"Talk, kidnapper."

Atkinson put his hands on his knees and stared straight at the beacon of the flashlight. His eyes were glassy and there was blood on his chin. He spoke:

"This is a frame by Costello. I don't know what it's all about. But if it's Costello, a man named Slippy Morgan will be in on it. He has a shack on the mesa by Baldwin Hills. They might have taken Rhonda Farr there."

He closed his eyes, and a tear showed in the glare of the flash. Mallory said slowly:

"Macdonald should know that."

Atkinson kept his eyes shut, said: "I guess so." His voice was dull and without any feeling.

Macdonald balled his fist, lurched sidewise, and hit him in the face again. The lawyer groaned, sagged to one side. Mallory's hand jerked; jerked the flash. His voice shook with fury. He said:

"Do that again and I'll put a slug in your guts, copper. So help me I will."

Macdonald rolled away, with a foolish laugh. Mallory snapped off the light. He said, more quietly:

"I think you're telling the truth, Atkinson. We'll case this shack of Slippy Morgan's."

The driver swung and backed the car, picked his way back to the highway again.

A white picket fence showed up for a moment before the headlights went off. Behind it on a rise the gaunt shapes of a couple of derricks groped toward the sky. The darkened car went forward slowly, stopped across the street from a small frame house. There were no houses on that side of the street, nothing between the car and the oil field. The house showed no light.

Mallory got to the ground and went across. A gravel driveway led along to a shed without a door. There was a touring car parked under the shed. There was thin worn grass along the driveway and a dull patch of something that had once been a lawn at the back. There was a wire clothesline and a small stoop with a rusted screen door. The moon showed all this.

Beyond the stoop there was a single window with the blind drawn; two thin cracks of light showed along the edges of the blind. Mallory went back to the car, walking on the dry grass and the dirt road surface without sound.

He said: "Let's go, Atkinson."

Atkinson got out heavily, stumbled across the street like a man half asleep. Mallory grabbed his arm sharply. The two men went up the wooden steps, crossed the porch quietly. Atkinson fumbled and found the bell. He pressed it. There was a dull buzz inside the house. Mallory flattened himself against the wall, on the side where he would not be blocked by the opening screen door.

Then the house door came open without sound, and a figure loomed behind the screen. There was no light behind the figure. The lawyer said mumblingly:

"It's Atkinson."

The screen hook was undone. The screen door came outward.

"What's the big idea?" said a lisping voice that Mallory had heard before.

Mallory moved, holding his Luger waist high. The man in the doorway whirled at him. Mallory stepped in on him swiftly, making a clucking sound with tongue and teeth, shaking his head reprovingly.

"You wouldn't have a gun, would you, Slippy?" he said, nudging the Luger forward. "Turn slow and easy, Slippy. When you feel something against your spine go on in, Slippy. We'll be right with you."

The lanky man put his hands up and turned. He walked back into the darkness, Mallory's gun in his back. A small living room smelled of dust and casual cooking. A door had light under it. The lanky man put one hand down slowly and opened the door.

An unshaded light bulb hung from the middle of the ceiling. A thin woman in a dirty white smock stood under it, limp arms at her sides. Dull colorless eyes brooded under a mop of rusty hair. Her fingers fluttered and twitched in involuntary contractions of the muscles. She made a thin plaintive sound, like a starved cat.

The lanky man went and stood against the wall on the opposite side of the room, pressing the palms of his hands against wallpaper. There was a fixed, meaningless smile on his face.

Landrey's voice said from behind: "I'll take care of Atkinson's pals."

He came into the room with a big automatic in his gloved hand. "Nice little home," he added pleasantly.

There was a metal bed in a corner of the room. Rhonda Farr was lying on it, wrapped to the chin in a brown army blanket. Her white wig was partly off her head and damp golden curls showed. Her face was bluish white, a mask in which the rouge and lip paint glared. She was snoring.

Mallory put his hand under the blanket, felt for her pulse. Then he lifted an eyelid and looked closely at the upturned pupil.

He said: "Doped."

The thin woman in the smock wet her lips. "A shot of M," she said in a slack voice. "No harm done, mister."

Atkinson sat down on a hard chair that had a dirty towel on the back of it. His dress shirt was dazzling under the unshaded light. The lower part of his face was smeared with dry blood. The lanky man looked at him contemptuously and patted the stained wallpaper with the flat of his hands. Then Macdonald came into the room.

His face was flushed and sweaty. He staggered a little and put a hand up along the door frame. "Hi ho, boys," he said vacantly. "I ought to rate a promotion for this."

The lanky man stopped smiling. He ducked sidewise very fast, and a gun jumped into his hand. Roar filled the room, a great crashing roar. And again a roar.

The lanky man's duck became a slide and the slide degenerated into a fall. He spread himself out on the bare carpet in a leisurely sort of way. He lay quite still, one half-open eye apparently looking at Macdonald. The thin woman opened her mouth wide, but no sound came out of it.

Macdonald put his other hand up to the door frame, leaned forward, and began to cough. Bright red blood came out on his chin. His hands came down the door frame slowly. Then his shoulder twitched forward; he rolled like a swimmer in a breaking wave and crashed. He crashed on his face, his hat still on his head, the mouse-colored hair at the nape of his neck showing below it in an untidy curl.

Mallory said: "Two down," and looked at Landrey with a disgusted expression. Landrey looked down at his big automatic and put it away out of sight, in the side pocket of his thin dark overcoat.

Mallory stooped over Macdonald, put a finger to his temple. There was no heartbeat. He tried the jugular vein with the same result. Macdonald was dead, and he still smelled violently of whiskey.

There was a faint trace of smoke under the light bulb, an acrid fume of powder. The thin woman bent forward at the waist and scrambled toward the door. Mallory jerked a hard hand against her chest and threw her back.

"You're fine where you are, sister," he snapped.

Atkinson took his hands off his knees and rubbed them together as if all the feeling had gone out of them. Landrey went over to the bed, put his gloved hand down, and touched Rhonda Farr's hair.

"Hello, baby," he said lightly. "Long time no see." He went out of the room, saying: "I'll get the car over on this side of the street."

Mallory looked at Atkinson. He said casually: "Who has the letters, Atkinson? The letters belonging to Rhonda Farr?"

Atkinson lifted his blank face slowly, squinted as though the light hurt his eyes. He spoke in a vague, far-off sort of voice.

"I—I don't know. Costello, maybe. I never saw them."

Mallory let out a short harsh laugh which made no change in the hard cold lines of his face. "Wouldn't it be funny as hell if that's true!" he said jerkily.

He stooped over the bed in the corner and wrapped the brown blanket closely around Rhonda Farr. When he lifted her she stopped snoring, but she did not wake.

A window or two in the front of the apartment house showed light. Mallory held his wrist up and looked at the curved watch on the inside of it. The faintly glowing hands were at half-past three. He spoke back into the car:

"Give me ten minutes or so. Then come on up. I'll fix the doors."

The street entrance to the apartment house was locked. Mallory unlocked it with a loose key, put it on the latch. There was a little light in the lobby, from one bulb in a floor lamp and from a hooded light above the switchboard. A wizened, white-haired little man was asleep in a chair by the switchboard, with his mouth open and his breath coming in long, wailing snores, like the sounds of an animal in pain.

Mallory walked up one flight of carpeted steps. On the second floor he pushed the button for the automatic elevator. When it came rumbling down from above, he got in and pushed the button marked "7." He yawned. His eyes were dulled with fatigue.

The elevator lurched to a stop, and Mallory went down the bright, silent corridor. He stopped at a gray olive wood door and put his ear to the panel. Then he fitted the loose key slowly into the lock, turned it slowly, moved the door back an inch or two. He listened again, went in.

There was light from a lamp with a red shade that stood beside an easy chair. A man was sprawled in the chair, and the light splashed on his face. He was bound at the wrists and ankles with strips of wide adhesive tape. There was a strip of adhesive across his mouth.

Mallory fixed the door latch and shut the door. He went across the room with quick silent steps. The man in the chair was Costello. His face was a purplish color above the white adhesive that plastered his lips together. His chest moved in jerks and his breath made a snorting noise in his big nose.

Mallory yanked the tape off Costello's mouth, put the heel of one hand on the man's chin, forced his mouth wide open. The cadence of the breathing changed a bit. Costello's chest stopped jerking, and the purplish color of his face faded to pallor. He stirred, made a groaning sound.

Mallory took an unopened pint bottle of rye off the mantel and tore the metal strip from the cap with his teeth. He pushed Costello's head far back, poured some whiskey into his open mouth, slapped his face hard. Costello choked, swallowed convulsively. Some of the whiskey ran out of his nostrils. He opened his eyes, focused them slowly. He mumbled something confused.

Mallory went through velour curtains that hung across a doorway at the inner end of the room, into a short hall. The first door led into a bedroom with twin beds. A light burned, and a man was lying bound on each of the beds.

Jim, the gray-haired cop, was asleep or still unconscious. The side of his head was stiff with congealed blood. The skin of his face was a dirty gray.

The eyes of the red-haired man were wide open, diamond bright, angry. His mouth worked under the tape, trying to chew it. He had rolled over on his side and almost off the bed. Mallory pushed him back toward the middle, said:

"Sorry, punk. It's all in the game."

He went back to the living room and switched on more light. Costello had struggled up in the easy chair. Mallory took out a pocket knife and reached behind him, sawed the tape that bound his wrists. Costello jerked his hands apart, grunted, and rubbed the backs of his wrists together where the tape had pulled hairs out. Then he bent over and tore tape off his ankles. He said:

"That didn't do me any good. I'm a mouth breather." His voice was loose, flat, and without cadence.

He got to his feet and poured two inches of rye into a glass, drank it at a gulp, sat down again and leaned his head against the high back of the chair. Life came into his face; glitter came into his washed-out eyes.

He said: "What's new?"

Mallory spooned at a bowl of water that had been ice, frowned, and drank some whiskey straight. He rubbed the left side of his head gently with his fingertips and winced. Then he sat down and lit a cigarette.

He said: "Several things. Rhonda Farr is home. Macdonald and Slippy Morgan got gunned. But that's not important. I'm after some letters you were trying to peddle to Rhonda Farr. Dig 'em up."

Costello lifted his head and grunted. He said: "I don't have the letters."

Mallory said: "Get the letters, Costello. Now." He sprinkled cigarette ash carefully in the middle of a green and yellow diamond in the carpet design.

Costello made an impatient movement. "I don't have them," he insisted. "Straight goods. I never saw them."

Mallory's eyes were slate-gray, very cold, and his voice was brittle. He said: "What you heels don't know about your racket is just pitiful. . . . I'm tired, Costello. I don't feel like an argument. You'd look lousy with that big beezer smashed over on one side of your face with a gun barrel."

Costello put his bony hand up and rubbed the reddened skin around his mouth where the tape had chafed it. He glanced down the room. There was a slight movement of the velour curtains across the end door, as though a breeze had stirred them. But there was no breeze. Mallory was staring down at the carpet.

Costello stood up from the chair, slowly. He said: "I've got a wall safe. I'll open it up."

He went across the room to the wall in which the outside door was, lifted down a picture, and worked the dial of a small inset circular safe. He swung the little round door open and thrust his arm into the safe.

Mallory said: "Stay just like that, Costello."

He stepped lazily across the room and passed his left hand down Costello's arm, into the safe. It came out again holding a small pearl-handled automatic. He made a sibilant sound with his lips and put the little gun into his pocket.

"Just can't learn, can you, Costello?" he said in a tired voice.

Costello shrugged, went back across the room. Mallory plunged his hands into the safe and tumbled the contents out on to the floor. He dropped on one knee. There were some long white envelopes, a bunch of clippings fastened with a paper clip, a narrow, thick checkbook, a small photograph album, an address book, some loose papers, some yellow bank statements with checks inside. Mallory spread one of the long envelopes carelessly, without much interest.

The curtains over the end door moved again. Costello stood rigid in front of the mantel. A gun came through the curtains in a small hand that was very steady. A slim body followed the hand, a white face with blazing eyes—Erno.

Mallory came to his feet, his hands breast high, empty.

"Higher, baby," Erno croaked. "Much higher, baby!"

Mallory raised his hands a little more. His forehead was wrinkled in a hard frown. Erno came forward into the room. His face glistened. A lock of oily black hair drooped over one eyebrow. His teeth showed in a stiff grin.

He said: "I think we'll give it to you right here, two-timer."

His voice had a questioning inflection, as if he waited for Costello's confirmation. Costello didn't say anything.

Mallory moved his head a little. His mouth felt very dry. He watched Erno's eyes, saw them tense. He said rather quickly:

"You've been crossed, mugg, but not by me."

Erno's grin widened to a snarl, and his head went back. His trigger finger whitened at the first joint. Then there was a noise outside the door, and it came open.

Landrey came in. He shut the door with a jerk of his shoulder and leaned against it, dramatically. Both his hands were in the side pockets of his thin dark overcoat. His eyes under the soft black hat were bright and devilish. He looked pleased. He moved his chin in the white silk evening scarf that was tucked carelessly about his neck. His handsome pale face was like something carved out of old ivory.

Erno moved his gun slightly and waited. Landrey said cheerfully:

"Bet you a grand you hit the floor first!"

Erno's lips twitched under his shiny little mustache. Two guns went off at the same time. Landrey swayed like a tree hit by a gust of wind; the heavy roar of his .45 sounded again, muffled a little by cloth and the nearness to his body.

Mallory went down behind the davenport, rolled, and came up with the Luger straight out in front of him. But Erno's face had already gone blank.

He went down slowly, his light body seemed to be drawn down by the weight of the gun in his right hand. He bent at the knees as he fell and slid forward on the floor. His back arched once and then went loose.

Landrey took his left hand out of his coat pocket and spread the fingers away from him as though pushing at something. Slowly and with difficulty he got the big automatic out of the other pocket and raised it inch by inch, turning on the balls of his feet. He swiveled his body toward Costello's rigid figure and squeezed the trigger again. Plaster jumped from the wall at Costello's shoulder.

Landrey smiled vaguely, said: "Damn!" in a soft voice. Then his eyes went up in his head and the gun plunged down from his nerveless fingers, bounded on the carpet. Landrey went down joint by joint, smoothly and gracefully, kneeled, swaying a moment before he melted over sidewise, spread himself on the floor almost without sound.

Mallory looked at Costello and said in a strained, angry voice: "Boy, are you lucky!"

The buzzer droned insistently. Three little lights glowed red on the panel of the switchboard. The wizened, white-haired little man shut his mouth with a snap and struggled sleepily upright.

Mallory jerked past him with his head turned the other way, shot across the lobby, out of the front door of the apartment house, down the three marble-faced steps, across the sidewalk and the street. The driver of Landrey's car had already stepped on the starter. Mallory swung in beside him, breathing hard, and slammed the car door.

"Get goin' fast!" he rasped. "Stay off the boulevard. Cops here in five minutes!"

The driver looked at him and said: "Where's Landrey? . . . I heard shootin'."

Mallory held the Luger up, said swiftly and coldly: "Move, baby!"

The gears went in; the Cadillac jumped forward; the driver took a corner recklessly, the tail of his eye on the gun.

Mallory said: "Landrey stopped lead. He's cold." He held the Luger up, put the muzzle under the driver's nose. "But not from my gun. Smell that, punk! It hasn't been fired!"

The driver said: "Jeeze!" in a shattered voice, swung the big car wildly, missing the curb by inches.

It was getting to be daylight.

Rhonda Farr said: "Publicity, darling. Just publicity. Any kind is better than none at all. I'm not so sure my contract is going to be renewed, and I'll probably need it."

She was sitting in a deep chair, in a large, long room. She looked at Mallory with lazy, indifferent purplish-blue eyes and moved her hand to a tall, misted glass. She took a drink.

The room was enormous. Mandarin rugs in soft colors swathed the floor. There was a lot of teakwood and red lacquer. Gold frames glinted high up on the walls, and the ceiling was remote and vague, like the dusk of a hot day. A huge carved radio gave forth muted and unreal strains.

Mallory wrinkled his nose and looked amused in a grim sort of way. He said: "You're a nasty little rat. I don't like you."

Rhonda Farr said: "Oh, yes, you do, darling. You're crazy about me."

She smiled and fitted a cigarette into a jade-green holder that matched her jade-green lounging pajamas. Then she reached out her beautifully shaped hand and pushed the button of a bell that was set into the top of a low nacre and teakwood table at her side. A silent, white-coated Japanese butler drifted into the room and mixed more highballs.

"You're a pretty wise lad, aren't you, darling?" Rhonda Farr said, when he had gone out again. "And you have some letters in your pocket you think are body and soul to me. Nothing like it, mister, nothing like it." She took a sip of the fresh highball. "The letters you have are phony. They were written about a month ago. Landrey never had them. He gave *his* letters back a long time ago. . . . What you have are just props." She put a hand to her beautifully waved hair. The experience of the previous night seemed to have left no trace on her.

Mallory looked at her carefully. He said: "How do you prove that, baby?"

"The notepaper—if I have to prove it. There's a little man down at Fourth and Spring who makes a study of that kind of thing."

Mallory said: "The writing?"

Rhonda Farr smiled dimly. "Writing's easy to fake, if you have plenty of time. Or so I'm told. That's my story anyhow."

Mallory nodded, sipped at his own highball. He put his hand into his inside breast pocket and took out a flat manila envelope, legal size. He laid it on his knee.

"Four men got gunned out last night on account of these phony letters," he said carelessly.

Rhonda Farr looked at him mildly. "Two crooks, a double-crossing policeman make three of them. I should lose my sleep over that trash! Of course, I'm sorry about Landrey."

Mallory said politely: "It's nice of you to be sorry about Landrey. Swell."

She said peacefully: "Landrey, as I told you once, was a pretty nice boy a few years ago, when he was trying to get into pictures. But he chose another business, and in that business he was bound to stop a bullet sometime."

Mallory rubbed his chin. He said: "It's funny he didn't remember he'd given you back your letters. Very funny."

"He wouldn't care, darling. He was that kind of actor, and he'd like the show. It gave him a chance for a swell pose. He'd like that terribly."

Mallory let his face get hard and disgusted. He said: "The job looked on the level to me. I didn't know much about Landrey, but he knew a good friend of mine in Chicago. He figured a way to the boys who were working on you, and I played his hunch. Things happened that made it easier—but a lot noisier."

Rhonda Farr tapped little bright nails against her little bright teeth. She said: "What are you back where you live, darling? One of those hoods they call private dicks?"

Mallory laughed harshly, made a vague movement, and ran his fingers through his crisp dark hair. "Let it go, baby," he said softly. "Let it go."

Rhonda Farr looked at him with a surprised glance, then laughed rather shrilly. "It gets mad, doesn't it?" she cooed. She went on, in a dry voice: "Atkinson has been bleeding me for years, one way and another. I fixed the letters up and put them where he could get hold of them. They disappeared. A few days afterward a man with one of those tough voices called up and began to apply the pressure. I let it ride. I figured I'd hang a pinch on Atkinson somehow, and our two reputations put together would be good for a write-up that wouldn't hurt me too much. But the thing seemed to be spreading out, and I got scared. I thought of asking Landrey to help me out. I was sure he would like it."

Mallory said roughly: "Simple, straightforward kid, ain't you? Like hell!"

"You don't know much about this Hollywood racket, do you, darling?" Rhonda Farr said. She put her head on one side and hummed softly. The strains of a dance band floated idly through the quiet air. "That's a gorgeous melody. . . . It's swiped from a Weber sonata. . . . Publicity has to hurt a bit out here. Otherwise nobody believes it."

Mallory stood up, lifting the manila envelope off his knee. He dropped it in her lap.

"Five grand these are costing you," he said.

Rhonda Farr leaned back and crossed her jade-green legs. One little green slipper fell off her bare foot to the rug, and the manila envelope fell down beside it. She didn't stir toward either one.

She said: "Why?"

"I'm a businessman, baby. I get paid for my work. Landrey didn't pay me. Five grand was the price. The price to him, and now the price to you."

She looked at him almost casually, out of placid, cornflower-blue eyes, and said: "No deal . . . blackmailer. Just like I told you at the Bolivar. You have all my thanks, but I'm spending my money myself."

Mallory said curtly: "This might be a damn good way to spend some of it."

He leaned over and picked up her highball, drank a little of it. When he put the glass down, he tapped the nails of two fingers against the side for a moment. A small tight smile wrinkled the corners of his mouth. He lit a cigarette and tossed the match into a bowl of hyacinths.

He said slowly: "Landrey's driver talked, of course. Landrey's friends want to see me. They want to know how come Landrey got rubbed out in Westwood. The cops will get around to me after a while. Someone is sure to tip them off. I was right beside four killings last night, and naturally I'm not going to run out on them. I'll probably have to spill the whole story. The cops will give you plenty of publicity, baby. Landrey's friends—I don't know what they'll do. Something that will hurt a lot, I should say."

Rhonda Farr jerked to her feet, fumbling with her toe for the green slipper. Her eyes had gone wide and startled.

"You'd . . . sell me out?" she breathed.

Mallory laughed. His eyes were bright and hard. He stared along the floor at a splash of light from one of the standing lamps. He said in a bored voice:

"Why the hell should I protect you? I don't owe you anything. And you're too damn tight with your dough to hire me. I haven't a record, but you know how the law boys love my sort. And Landrey's friends will just see a dirty plant that got a good lad killed. —— sake, why should I front for a chiseler like you, baby?"

He snorted angrily and flung his cigarette at the bowl of hyacinths. Red spots showed in his tanned cheeks.

Rhonda Farr stood quite still and shook her head slowly from side to side. She said: "No deal, blackmailer . . . no deal." Her voice was small and weak but her chin stuck out hard and brave.

Mallory reached out and picked up his hat. "You're a hell of a guy, baby," he said, grinning. "——! but you Hollywood frails must be hard to get on with!"

He leaned forward suddenly, put his left hand behind her head, and kissed her on the mouth hard. Then he flipped the tips of his fingers across her cheek.

"You're a nice kid—in some ways," he said. "And a fair liar. Just fair. You didn't fake any letters, baby. Atkinson wouldn't fall for a trick like that." Rhonda Farr stooped over, snatched the manila envelope off the rug, and tumbled out what was in it—a number of closely written gray pages, deckle-edged, with thin gold monograms. She stared down at them with quivering nostrils.

She said slowly: "I'll send you the money."

Mallory put his hand against her chin and pushed her head back.

He said rather gently:

"I was kidding you, baby. I have that bad habit. But there are two funny things about these letters. They haven't any envelopes, and there's nothing to show who they were written to—nothing at all. The second thing is, Landrey had them in his pocket when he was killed."

He nodded once, turned away. Rhonda Farr said sharply: "Wait!" Her voice was suddenly terrified. She flopped down into the chair, sat limp.

Mallory said: "It gets you when it's over, baby. Take a drink."

He went a little way down the room, turned his head. He said: "I have to go. Got a date with a big black spot. . . . Send me some flowers, baby. Wild, blue flowers, like your eyes."

He went out under an arch. A door opened and shut heavily. Rhonda Farr sat without moving for a long time.

Cigarette smoke laced the air. A group of people in evening clothes stood sipping cocktails at one side of a curtained opening that led to the gambling rooms. Beyond the curtains, light blazed down on one end of a roulette table.

Mallory put his elbows on the bar, and the bartender left two young girls in party gowns and slid a white towel along the polished wood toward him. He said:

"What'll it be, chief?"

Mallory said: "A small beer."

The bartender gave it to him, smiled, went back to the two girls. Mallory sipped the beer, made a face, and looked into the long mirror that ran all the way behind the bar and slanted forward a little, so that it showed the floor all the way over to the far wall. A door opened in the wall and a man in dinner clothes came through. He had a wrinkled brown face and hair the color of steel wool. He met Mallory's glance in the mirror and came across the room nodding.

He said, "I'm Mardonne. Nice of you to come." He had a soft, husky voice, the voice of a fat man, but he was not fat.

Mallory said: "It's not a social call."

Mardonne said: "Let's go up to my office."

Mallory drank a little more of the beer, made another face, and pushed the glass away from him across the bar top. They went through the door, up a carpeted staircase that met another staircase halfway up. An open door shone light on the landing. They went in where the light was.

The room had been a bedroom, and no particular trouble had been taken to make it over into an office. It had gray walls, two or three prints in narrow frames. There was a big filing cabinet, a good safe, chairs. A parchment-shaded lamp stood on a walnut desk. A very blond young man sat on a corner of the desk swinging one leg over the other. He was wearing a soft hat with a gay band.

Mardonne said: "All right, Henry. I'll be busy."

The blond young man got off the desk, yawned, put his hand to his mouth with an affected flirt of the wrist. There was a large diamond on one of his fingers. He looked at Mallory, smiled, went slowly out of the room, closing the door.

Mardonne sat down in a blue leather swivel chair. He lit a thin cigar and pushed a humidor across the grained top of the desk. Mallory took a chair at the end of the desk, between the door and a pair of open windows. There was another door, but the safe stood in front of it. He lit a cigarette, said:

"Landrey owed me some money. Five grand. Anybody here interested in paying it?"

Mardonne put his brown hands on the arms of his chair and rocked back and forth. "We haven't come to that," he said.

Mallory said: "Right. What have we come to?"

Mardonne narrowed his dull eyes. His voice was flat and without tone. "To how Landrey got killed."

Mallory put his cigarette in his mouth and clasped his hands together behind his head. He puffed smoke and talked through it at the wall above Mardonne's head.

"He crossed everybody up and then he crossed himself. He played too many parts and got his lines mixed. He was gun-drunk. When he got a rod in his hand he had to shoot somebody. Somebody shot back."

Mardonne went on rocking, said: "Maybe you could make it a little more definite."

"Sure . . . I could tell you a story . . . about a girl who wrote some letters once. She thought she was in love. They were reckless letters, the sort a girl would write who had more guts than was good for her. Time passed, and somehow the letters got on the blackmail market. Some workers started to shake the girl down. Not a high stake, nothing that would have bothered her, but it seems she liked to do things the hard way. Landrey thought he would help her out. He had a plan, and the plan needed a man who could wear a tux, keep a spoon out of a coffee cup, and wasn't known in this town. He got me. I run a small agency in Chicago."

Mardonne swiveled toward the open windows and stared out at the tops of some trees. "Private dick, huh?" he grunted impassively. "From Chicago."

Mallory nodded, looked at him briefly, looked back at the same spot on the wall. "And supposed to be on the level, Mardonne. You wouldn't think it from some of the company I've been keeping lately."

Mardonne made a quick impatient gesture, said nothing.

Mallory went on: "Well, I gave the job a tumble, which was my first and worst mistake. I was making a little headway when the shakedown turned into a kidnapping. Not so good. I got in touch with Landrey, and he decided to show with me. We found the girl without a lot of trouble. We took her home. We still had to get the letters. While I was trying to pry them loose from the guy I thought had them, one of the bad boys got in the back way and wanted to play with his gun. Landrey made a swell entrance, struck a pose, and shot it out with the hood, toe to toe. He stopped some lead. It was pretty, if you like that sort of thing, but it left me in a spot. So perhaps I'm prejudiced. I had to lam out and collect my ideas."

Mardonne's dull brown eyes showed a passing flicker of emotion. "The girl's story might be interesting, too," he said coolly.

Mallory blew a pale cloud of smoke. "She was doped and doesn't know anything. She wouldn't talk, if she did. And I don't know her name."

"I do," Mardonne said. "Landrey's driver also talked to me. So I won't have to bother you about that."

Mallory talked on, placidly. "That's the tale from the outside, without notes. The notes make it funnier—and a hell of a lot dirtier. The girl didn't ask Landrey for help, but he knew about the shakedown. He'd once had the letters, because they were written to him. His scheme to get on their trail was for me to make a wrong pass at the girl myself, make her think *I* had the letters, talk her into a meeting at a nightclub where we could be watched by the people who were working on her. She'd come, because she had that kind of guts. She'd be watched, because there would be an inside—maid, chauffeur, or something. The boys would want to know about me. They'd pick me up, and if I didn't get conked out of hand, I might learn who was who in the racket. Sweet setup, don't you think so?"

Mardonne said coldly: "A bit loose in places. . . . Go on talking."

"When the decoy worked, I knew it was fixed. I stayed with it, because for the time being I had to. After a while there was another sour play, unrehearsed this time. A big flattie who was taking graft money from the gang got cold feet and threw the boys for a loss. He didn't mind a little extortion, but a snatch was going off the deep end on a dark night. The break made things easier for me, and it didn't hurt Landrey any, because the flattie wasn't in on the clever stuff. The hood who got Landrey wasn't either, I guess. That one was just sore, thought he was being chiseled out of his cut."

Mardonne flipped his brown hands up and down on the chair arms, like a purchasing agent getting restless under a sales talk. "Were you supposed to figure things out this way?" he asked with a sneer.

"I used my head, Mardonne. Not soon enough, but I used it. Maybe I wasn't hired to think, but that wasn't explained to me, either. If I got wise, it was Landrey's hard luck. He'd have to figure an out to that one. If I didn't I was the nearest thing to an honest stranger he could afford to have around."

Mardonne said smoothly: "Landrey had plenty of dough. He had some brains. Not a lot, but some. He wouldn't go for a cheap shake like that."

Mallory laughed harshly: "It wasn't so cheap to him, Mardonne. He wanted the girl. She'd got away from him, out of his class. He couldn't pull himself up, but he could pull her down. The letters were not enough to bring her into line. Add a kidnapping and a fake rescue by an old flame turned racketeer, and you have a story no rag could be made to soft-pedal. If it was spilled, it would blast her right out of her job. *You* guess the price for not spilling it, Mardonne."

Mardonne said: "Uh-huh," and kept on looking out of the window.

Mallory said: "But all that's on the cuff, now. I was hired to get some letters, and I got them—out of Landrey's pocket when he was bumped. I'd like to get paid for my time."

Mardonne turned in his chair and put his hands flat on the top of the desk. "Pass them over," he said. "I'll see what they're worth to me."

Mallory let out another harsh laugh. His eyes got sharp and bitter. He said: "The trouble with you heels is that you can't figure anybody to be on the up and up. . . . The letters are withdrawn from circulation, Mardonne. They passed around too much and they wore out."

"It's a sweet thought," Mardonne sneered. "For somebody else. Landrey was my partner, and I thought a lot of him. . . . So you give the letters away, and I pay you dough for letting Landrey get gunned. I ought to write that one in my diary. My hunch is you've been paid plenty already—by Miss Rhonda Farr."

Mallory said, sarcastically: "I figured it would look like that to you. Maybe *you'd* like the story better this way. . . . The girl got tired of having Landrey trail her around. She faked some letters and put them where her smart lawyer could lift them, pass them along to a man who was running a strong-arm squad the lawyer used in his business sometimes. The girl wrote to Landrey for help and he got me. The girl got to me with a better bid. She hired me to put Landrey on the spot. I played along with him until I got him under the gun of a wiper that was pretending to make a pass at me. The wiper let him have it, and I shot the wiper with Landrey's gun, to make it look good. Then I had a drink and went home to get some sleep."

Mardonne leaned over and pressed a buzzer on the side of his desk. He said: "I like that one a lot better. I'm wondering if I could make it stick."

"You could try," Mallory said lazily. "I don't guess it would be the first lead quarter you've tried to pass."

The room door came open and the blond boy strolled in. His lips were spread in a pleased grin and his tongue came out between them. He had an automatic in his hand.

Mardonne said: "I'm not busy anymore, Henry."

The blond boy shut the door. Mallory stood up and backed slowly toward the wall. He said grimly:

"Now for the funny stuff, eh?"

Mardonne put brown fingers up and pinched the fat part of his chin. He said curtly:

"There won't be any shooting here. Nice people come to this house. Maybe you didn't spot Landrey, but I don't want you around. You're in my way."

Mallory kept on backing until he had his shoulders against the wall. The blond boy frowned, took a step toward him. Mallory said:

"Stay right where you are, Henry. I need room to think. You might get a slug into me, but you wouldn't stop my gun from talking a little. The noise wouldn't bother me at all."

Mardonne bent over his desk, looking sidewise. The blond boy slowed up. His tongue still peeped out between his lips. Mardonne said:

"I've got some C notes in the desk here. I'm giving Henry ten of them. He'll go to your hotel with you. He'll even help you pack. When you get on the train east he'll pass you the dough. If you come back after that, it will be a new deal—from a cold deck." He put his hand down slowly and opened the desk drawer.

Mallory kept his eyes on the blond boy. "Henry might make a change in the continuity," he said unpleasantly. "Henry looks kind of unstable to me."

Mardonne stood up, brought his hand from the drawer. He dropped a packet of notes on top of the desk. He said:

"I don't think so. Henry usually does what he is told."

Mallory grinned tightly. "Perhaps *that's* what I'm afraid of," he said. His grin got tighter still, and crookeder. His teeth glittered between his pale lips. "You said you thought a lot of Landrey, Mardonne. That's hooey. You don't care a thin dime about Landrey, now he's dead. You probably stepped right into his half of the joint, and nobody around to ask questions. It's like that in the rackets. You want me out because you think you can still peddle your dirt—in the right place—for more than this small-time joint would net in a year. But you can't peddle it, Mardonne. The market's closed. Nobody's going to pay you a plugged nickel either to spill it or not to spill it."

Mardonne cleared his throat softly. He was standing in the same position, leaning forward a little over the desk, both hands on top of it, and the packet of notes between his hands. He licked his lips, said:

"All right, mastermind. Why not?"

Mallory made a quick but expressive gesture with his right thumb.

"I'm the sucker in this deal. *You're* the smart guy. I told you a straight story the first time, and my hunch says Landrey wasn't in that sweet frame alone. You were in it up to your fat neck! . . . But you aced yourself backward when you let Landrey pack those letters around with him. The girl can talk now. Not a whole lot, but enough to get backing from an outfit that isn't going to scrap a million-dollar reputation because some cheap gambler wants to get smart. . . . If your money says different, you're going to get a jolt that'll have you picking your eye-teeth out of your socks. You're going to see the sweetest cover-up even Hollywood ever fixed."

He paused, flashed a quick glance at the blond boy. "Something else, Mardonne. When you figure on gunplay, get yourself a loogan that knows what it's all about. The gay caballero here forgot to thumb back his safety."

Mardonne stood frozen. The blond boy's eyes flinched down to his gun for a split second of time. Mallory jumped fast along the wall, and his Luger snapped into his hand. The blond boy's face tensed; his gun crashed. Then the Luger cracked, and a slug went into the wall beside the blond boy's gay felt hat. Henry faded down gracefully, squeezed lead again. The shot knocked Mallory back against the wall. His left arm went dead.

His lips writhed angrily. He steadied himself; the Luger talked twice, very rapidly.

The blond boy's gun arm jerked up and the gun sailed against the wall high up. His eyes widened; his mouth came open in a yell of pain. Then he whirled, wrenched the door open, and pitched straight out on the landing with a crash.

Light from the room streamed after him. Somebody shouted somewhere. A door banged. Mallory looked at Mardonne, saying evenly:

"Got me in the arm ——! I could have killed the ——four times!"

Mardonne's hand came up from the desk with a blued revolver in it. A bullet splashed into the floor at Mallory's feet. Mardonne lurched drunkenly, threw the gun away like something red hot. His hands groped high in the air. He looked scared stiff.

Mallory said: "Get in front of me, big shot! I'm moving out of here."

Mardonne came out from behind the desk. He moved jerkily, like a marionette. His eyes were as dead as stale oysters. Saliva drooled down his chin.

Something loomed in the doorway. Mallory heaved sidewise, firing blindly at the door. But the sound of the Luger was overborne by the terrific flat booming of a shotgun. Searing flame stabbed down Mallory's right side. Mardonne got the rest of the load.

He plunged to the floor on his face, dead before he landed.

A sawed-off shotgun dumped itself in through the open door. A thick-bellied man in shirt-sleeves eased himself down in the door frame, clutching and rolling as he fell. A strangled sob came out of his mouth, and blood spread on the pleated front of a dress shirt.

Sudden noise flared out down below. Shouting, running feet, a shrilling off-key laugh, a high sound that might have been a shriek. Cars started outside; tires screeched on the driveway. The customers were getting away. A pane of glass went out somewhere. There was a loose clatter of running feet on a sidewalk.

Across the lighted patch of landing nothing moved. The blond boy groaned softly, out there on the floor, behind the dead man in the doorway.

Mallory plowed across the room, sank into the chair at the end of the desk. He wiped sweat from his eyes with the heel of his gun hand. He leaned his ribs against the desk, panting, watching the door.

His left arm was throbbing now, and his right leg felt like the plagues of Egypt. Blood ran down his sleeve inside, down on his hand, off the tips of two fingers.

After a while he looked away from the door, at the packet of notes lying on the desk under the lamp. Reaching across, he pushed them into the open drawer with the muzzle of the Luger. Grinning with pain, he leaned far enough over to pull the drawer shut. Then he opened and closed his eyes quickly, several times, squeezing them tight together, then snapping them open wide. That cleared his head a little. He drew the telephone toward him.

There was silence below stairs now. Mallory put the Luger down, lifted the phone off the prongs and put it down beside the Luger.

He said out loud: "Too bad, baby. . . . Maybe I played it wrong after all. . . . Maybe the louse hadn't the guts to hurt you at that . . . well . . . there's got to be talking done now."

As he began to dial, the wail of a siren got louder coming up the long hill from Sherman. . . .

The uniformed officer behind the typewriter desk talked into a Dictaphone, then looked at Mallory and jerked his thumb toward a glass-paneled door that said: "Captain of Detectives. Private."

Mallory got up stiffly from a hard chair and went across the room, leaned against the wall to open the glass-paneled door, went on in.

The room he went into was paved with dirty brown linoleum, furnished with the peculiar sordid hideousness only municipalities can achieve. Cathcart, the captain of detectives, sat in the middle of it alone, between a littered rolltop desk that was not less than twenty years old and a flat oak table large enough to play Ping-Pong on.

Cathcart was a big shabby Irishman with a sweaty face and a loose-lipped grin. His white mustache was stained in the middle by nicotine. His hands had a lot of warts on them.

Mallory went towards him slowly, leaning on a heavy cane with a rubber tip. His right leg felt large and hot. His left arm was in a sling made from a black silk scarf. He was freshly shaved. His face was pale and his eyes were as dark as slate.

He sat down across the table from the captain of detectives, put his cane on the table, tapped a cigarette and lit it. Then he said casually:

"What's the verdict, chief?"

Cathcart grinned. "How you feel, kid? You look kinda pulled down."

"Not bad. A bit stiff."

Cathcart nodded, cleared his throat, fumbled unnecessarily with some papers that were in front of him. He said:

"You're clear. It's a lulu, but you're clear. Chicago gives you a clean sheet—damn clean. Your Luger got Mike Corliss, a two-time loser. I'm keepin' the Luger for a souvenir. Okay?"

Mallory nodded, said: "Okay. I'm getting me a twenty-five with copper slugs. A sharpshooter's gun. No shock effect, but it goes better with evening clothes."

Cathcart looked at him closely for a minute, then went on: "Mike's prints are on the shotgun. The shotgun got Mardonne. Nobody's cryin' about that much. The blond kid ain't hurt bad. That automatic we found on the floor had his prints, and that will take care of him for a while."

Mallory rubbed his chin slowly, wearily. "How about the others?"

The captain raised tangled eyebrows, and his eyes looked absent. He said: "I don't know of nothin' to connect you there. Do you?"

"Not a thing," Mallory said apologetically. "I was just wondering."

The captain said firmly: "Don't wonder. And don't get to guessin', if anybody should ask you. . . . Take that Baldwin Hills thing. The way we figure it, Macdonald got killed in the line of duty, takin' with him a dope peddler named Slippy Morgan. We have a tag out for Slippy's wife, but I don't guess we'll make her. Mac wasn't on the narcotic detail, but it was his night off and he was a great guy to gumshoe around on his night off. Mac loved his work."

Mallory smiled faintly, said politely: "Is that so?"

"Yeah," the captain said. "In the other one, it seems this Landrey, a known gambler—he was Mardonne's partner too. That's kind of a funny coincidence—went down to Westwood to collect dough from a guy called Costello that ran a book on the eastern tracks. Jim Ralston, one of our boys, went with him. Hadn't ought to, but he knew Landrey pretty well. There was a little trouble about the money. Jim got beaned with a blackjack, and Landrey and some little hood fogged each other. There was another guy there we don't trace. We got Costello, but he won't talk and we don't like to beat up an old guy. He's got a rap comin' on account of the blackjack. He'll plead, I guess."

Mallory slumped down in his chair until the back of his neck rested on top of it. He blew smoke straight up toward the stained ceiling. He said:

"How about night before last? Or was that the time the roulette wheel backfired and the trick cigar blew a hole in the garage floor?"

The captain of detectives rubbed both his moist cheeks briskly, then hauled out a very large handkerchief and snorted into it.

"Oh, that," he said negligently, "that wasn't nothin'. The blond kid—Henry Anson or something like that—says it was all his fault. He was Mardonne's bodyguard, but that didn't mean he could go shootin' anyone he might want to. That takes care of him, but we let him down easy for tellin' a straight story."

The captain stopped short and stared at Mallory hard-eyed. Mallory was grinning. "Of course if you don't *like* his story . . ." the captain went on coldly.

Mallory said: "I haven't heard it yet. I'm sure I'll like it fine."

"Okay," Cathcart rumbled, mollified. "Well, this Anson says Mardonne buzzed him in where you and the boss were talkin'. You was makin' a kick about something, maybe a crooked wheel downstairs. There was some money on the desk, and Anson got the idea it was a shake. You looked pretty fast to him, and not knowing you was a dick he gets kinda nervous. His gun went off. You didn't shoot right away, but the poor sap lets off another round and plugs you. Then, by —— you drilled him in the shoulder, as who wouldn't, only if it had been me, I'd of pumped his guts. Then the shotgun boy comes bargin' in, lets go without asking any questions, fogs Mardonne and stops one from you. We kinda thought at first the guy might of got Mardonne on purpose, but the kid says no, he tripped in the door comin' in. . . . Hell, we don't like for you to do all that shooting, you being a stranger and all that, but a man ought to have a right to protect himself against illegal weapons."

Mallory said gently: "There's the D.A. and the coroner. How about them? I'd kind of like to go back as clean as I came away."

Cathcart frowned down at the dirty linoleum and bit his thumb as if he liked hurting himself.

"The coroner don't give a damn about that trash. If the D.A. wants to get funny, I can tell him about a few cases his office didn't clean up so good."

Mallory lifted his cane off the table, pushed his chair back, put weight on the cane and stood up. "You have a swell police department here," he said. "I shouldn't think you'd have any crime at all."

He moved across toward the outer door. The captain said to his back:

"Goin' on to Chicago?"

Mallory shrugged carefully with his right shoulder, the good one. "I might stick around," he said. "One of the studios made me a proposition. Private extortion detail. Blackmail and so on."

The captain grinned heartily. "Swell," he said. "Eclipse Films is a swell outfit. They always been swell to me. . . . Nice easy work, blackmail. Oughtn't to run into any rough stuff."

Mallory nodded solemnly. "Just light work, chief. Almost effeminate, if you know what I mean."

He went on out, down the hall to the elevator, down to the street. He got into a taxi. It was hot in the taxi. He felt faint and dizzy going back to his hotel.

—1933

DOROTHY L. SAYERS
1893-1957

The golden age of detective fiction is generally thought to have existed during the decades that fell between the two World Wars. The classic detective story dominated this golden age period. Also called the British detective story—because many of the most successful authors who published classic detective fiction were British—this type of crime fiction polished and refined the earlier efforts of Poe and Doyle. The detective hero featured in the classic detective story often is an amateur sleuth. In addition, the classic detective hero tends to be an aristocrat, or, at the very least, a member of the upper class. The plot of the classic detective story is easily recognizable and highly formulaic. It highlights a puzzle-like mystery that demands a sense of "fair play" from its author, so that the reader is permitted the same opportunity as the detective hero to solve the mystery. The classic detective story typically downplays violence, instead viewing crime both as an abstract social aberration and as an opportunity for the detective hero to engage in an intellectual exercise in deductive reasoning.

A recognized master of the classic detective story is Dorothy L. Sayers. Born in Oxford, England, Sayers was an instructor of modern languages at a girls' school in Yorkshire from 1915 to 1917, and later worked as a writer for an advertising agency in London during the 1920s and early 1930s. Sayers's first novel, Whose Body?, *was published in 1923 and introduced one of crime fiction's great golden age detective heroes, Lord Peter Wimsey. Lord Peter was to be featured as the central protagonist in nearly all of Sayers's crime novels. Several of Lord Peter's more famous cases include* Clouds of Witness *(1926),* The Unpleasantness at the Bellona Club *(1928),* The Five Red Herrings *(1931),* Murder Must Advertise *(1933), and the Sayers novel that a number of readers consider to be the finest example of the classic detective story,* The Nine Tailors *(1934).*

Dorothy L. Sayers calls detective fiction the "art of framing lies," and follows this line of thinking well in her short story, "Absolutely Elsewhere," which was first published in the January 1934 issue of Mystery: the Illustrated Detective Magazine *as "Impossible Alibi," and which was later collected in her anthology,* In the Teeth of Evidence, and Other Stories *(1939). Sayers effectively manipulates the conventions of classic detective fiction in this tale, and the result of her efforts features a murder mystery that is strong on plot, sparse on characterization, and structured like a narrative puzzle. Regarding Mr. Grimbold's untimely death, one of the important questions Sayers presents to us in our reading of "Absolutely Elsewhere" is: Did the butler do it?*

ABSOLUTELY ELSEWHERE

Lord Peter Wimsey sat with Chief-Inspector Parker, of the C.I.D., and Inspector Henley, of the Baldock police, in the library at "The Lilacs."

"So you see," said Parker, "that all the obvious suspects were elsewhere at the time."

"What do you mean by 'elsewhere'?" demanded Wimsey, peevishly. Parker had hauled him down to Wapley, on the Great North Road, without his breakfast, and his temper had suffered. "Do you mean that they couldn't have reached the scene of the murder without travelling at over 186,000 miles a second? Because, if you don't mean that, they weren't absolutely elsewhere. They were only relatively and apparently elsewhere."

"For heaven's sake, don't go all Eddington. Humanly speaking, they were elsewhere, and if we're going to nail one of them we shall have to do it without going into their Fitzgerald contractions and coefficients of spherical curvature. I think, Inspector, we had better have them in one by one, so that I can hear all their stories again. You can check them up if they depart from their original statements at any point. Let's take the butler first."

The Inspector put his head out into the hall and said: "Hamworthy."

The butler was a man of middle age, whose spherical curvature was certainly worthy of consideration. His large face was pale and puffy, and he looked unwell. However, he embarked on his story without hesitation.

"I have been in the late Mr. Grimbold's service for twenty years, gentlemen, and have always found him a good master. He was a strict gentleman, but very just. I know he was considered very hard in business matters, but I suppose he had to be that. He was a bachelor, but he brought up his two nephews, Mr. Harcourt and Mr. Neville, and was very good to them. In his private life I should call him a kind and considerate man. His profession? Yes, I suppose you would call him a money-lender.

"About the events of last night, sir, yes. I shut up the house at 7:30 as usual. Everything was done exactly to time, sir,—Mr. Grimbold was very regular in his habits. I locked all the windows on the ground floor, as was customary during the winter months. I am quite sure I didn't miss anything out. They all have burglar-proof bolts and I should have noticed if they had been out of order. I also locked and bolted the front door and put up the chain."

"How about the conservatory door?"

"That, sir, is a Yale lock. I tried it, and saw that it was shut. No, I didn't fasten the catch. It was always left that way, sir, in case Mr. Grimbold had business which kept him in Town late, so that he could get in without disturbing the household."

"But he had no business in Town last night?"

"No, sir, but it was always left that way. Nobody could get in without the key, and Mr. Grimbold had that on his ring."

"Is there no other key in existence?"

"I believe"—the butler coughed—"I believe, sir, though I do not know, that there is *one*, sir,—in the possession of—of a lady, sir, who is at present in Paris."

"I see. Mr. Grimbold was about sixty years old, I believe. Just so. What is the name of this lady?"

"Mrs. Winter, sir. She lives at Wapley, but since her husband died last month, sir, I understand she has been residing abroad."

"I see. Better make a note of that, Inspector. Now, how about the upper rooms and the back door?"

"The upper-room windows were all fastened in the same way, sir, except Mr. Grimbold's bedroom and the cook's room and mine, sir; but they couldn't be reached without a ladder, and the ladder is locked up in the tool-shed."

"That's all right," put in Inspector Henley. "We went into that last night. The shed was locked and, what's more, there were unbroken cobwebs between the ladder and the wall."

"I went through all the rooms at half-past seven, sir, and there was nothing out of order."

"You may take it from me," said the Inspector, again, "that there was no interference with any of the locks. Carry on, Hamworthy."

"Yes, sir. While I was seeing to the house, Mr. Grimbold came down into the library for his glass of sherry. At 7:45 the soup was served and I called Mr. Grimbold to dinner. He sat at the end of the table as usual, facing the serving-hatch."

"With his back to the library door," said Parker, making a mark on a rough plan of the room, which lay before him. "Was that door shut?"

"Oh, yes, sir. All the doors and windows were shut."

"It looks a dashed draughty room," said Wimsey. "Two doors and a serving-hatch and two french windows."

"Yes, my lord; but they are all very well-fitting, and the curtains were drawn."

His lordship moved across to the connecting door and opened it.

"Yes," he said; "good and heavy and moves in sinister silence. I like these thick carpets, but the pattern's a bit fierce." He shut the door noiselessly and returned to his seat.

"Mr. Grimbold would take about five minutes over his soup, sir. When he had done, I removed it and put on the fish. I did not have to leave the room; everything comes through the serving-hatch. The wine—that is, the Chablis—was already on the table. That course was only a small portion of turbot, and would take Mr. Grimbold about five minutes again. I removed that, and put on the roast pheasant. I was just about to serve Mr. Grimbold with the vegetables, when the telephone-bell rang. Mr. Grimbold said: 'You'd better see who it is. I'll help myself.' It was not the cook's business, of course, to answer the telephone."

"Are there no other servants?"

"Only the woman who comes in to clean during the day, sir. I went out to the instrument, shutting the door behind me."

"Was that this telephone or the one in the hall?"

"The one in the hall, sir. I always used that one, unless I happened to be actually in the library at the time. The call was from Mr. Neville Grimbold in Town, sir. He and Mr. Harcourt have a flat in Jermyn Street. Mr. Neville spoke, and I recognised his voice. He said: 'Is that you, Hamworthy? Wait a moment. Mr. Harcourt wants you.' He put the receiver down and then Mr. Harcourt came on. He said: 'Hamworthy, I want to run down to-night to see my uncle, if he's at home.' I said: 'Yes, sir, I'll tell him.' The young gentlemen often come down for a night or two, sir. We keep their bedrooms ready for them. Mr. Harcourt said he would be starting at once and expected to get down by about half-past nine. While he was speaking I heard the big grandfather-clock up in their flat chime the quarters and strike eight, and immediately after, our own hall-clock struck, and then I heard the Exchange say 'Three minutes.' So the call must have come through at three minutes to eight, sir."

"Then there's no doubt about the time. That's a comfort. What next, Hamworthy?"

"Mr. Harcourt asked for another call and said: 'Mr. Neville has got something to say,' and then Mr. Neville came back to the 'phone. He said he was going up to Scotland shortly, and wanted me to send up a country suit and some stockings and shirts that he had left down here. He wanted the suit sent to the cleaner's first, and there were various other instructions, so that he asked for another three minutes. That would be at 8:03, sir, yes. And about a minute after that, while he was still speaking, the front-door bell rang. I couldn't very well leave the 'phone, so the caller had to wait, and at five past eight he rang the bell again. I was just going to ask Mr. Neville to excuse me, when I saw Cook come out of the kitchen and go through the hall to the front door. Mr. Neville asked me to repeat his instructions, and then the Exchange interrupted us again, so he rang off, and when I turned round I saw Cook just closing the library door. I went to meet her, and she said: 'Here's that Mr. Payne again, wanting Mr. Grimbold. I've put him in the library, but I don't like the looks of him.' So I said: 'All right; I'll fix him,' and Cook went back to the kitchen."

"One moment," said Parker. "Who's Mr. Payne?"

"He's one of Mr. Grimbold's clients, sir. He lives about five minutes away, across the fields, and he's been here before, making trouble. I think he owes Mr. Grimbold money, sir, and wanted more time to pay."

"He's here, waiting in the hall," added Henley.

"Oh?" said Wimsey. "The unshaven party with the scowl and the ash-plant, and the blood-stained coat?"

"That's him, my lord," said the butler. "Well, sir,"—he turned to Parker again, "I started to go along to the library, when it come over me sudden-like that I'd never taken in the claret—Mr. Grimbold would be getting very annoyed. So I went back to my pantry—you see where that is, sir,—and fetched it from where it was warming before the fire. I had a little hunt then for the salver, sir, till I found I had put down my evening paper on top of it, but I wasn't more than a minute, sir, before I got back into the dining-room. And then, sir"—the butler's voice faltered—"then I saw Mr. Grimbold fallen forward on the table, sir, all across his plate, like. I thought he must have been took ill, and I hurried up to him and found—I found he was dead, sir, with a dreadful wound in his back."

"No weapon anywhere?"

"Not that I could see, sir. There was a terrible lot of blood. It made me feel shockingly faint, sir, and for a minute I didn't hardly know what to do. As soon as I could think of anything, I rushed over to the serving-hatch and called Cook. She came hurrying in and let out an awful scream when she saw the master. Then I remembered Mr. Payne and opened the library door. He was standing there, and he began at once, asking how long he'd have to wait. So I said: 'Here's an awful thing! Mr. Grimbold has been murdered!' and he pushed past me into the dining-room, and the first thing he said was: 'How about those windows?' He pulled back the curtain of the one nearest the library, and there was the window standing open. 'This is the way he went,' he said, and started to rush out. I said, 'no, you don't'—thinking he meant to get away, and I hung on to him. He called me a lot of names, and then he said: 'Look here, my man, be reasonable. The fellow's getting away all this time. We must have a look for him.' So I said, 'Not without I go with you.' And he said, 'All right.' So I told Cook not to touch anything but to ring up the police, and Mr. Payne and I went out after I'd fetched my torch from the pantry."

"Did Payne go with you to fetch it?"

"Yes, sir. Well, him and me went out and we searched about in the garden, but we couldn't see any footprints or anything, because it's an asphalt path all round the house and down to the gate. And we couldn't see any weapon, either. So then he said: 'We'd better go back and get the car and search the roads,' but I said: 'No, he'll be away by then,' because it's only a quarter of a mile from our gate to the Great North Road, and it would take us five or ten minutes before we could start. So Mr. Payne said: 'Perhaps you're right,' and came back to the house with me. Well, then, sir, the constable came from Wapley, and after a bit, the Inspector here and Dr. Crofts from Baldock, and they made a search and asked a lot of questions, which I answered to the best of my ability, and I can't tell you no more, sir."

"Did you notice," asked Parker, "whether Mr. Payne had any stains of blood about him?"

"No, sir,—I can't say that he had. When I first saw him, he was standing in here, right under the light, and I think I should have seen it if there was anything, sir. I can't say fairer than that."

"Of course you've searched this room, Inspector, for bloodstains or a weapon or for anything such as gloves or a cloth, or anything that might have been used to protect the murderer from bloodstains?"

"Yes, Mr. Parker. We searched very carefully."

"Could anybody have come downstairs while you were in the dining-room with Mr. Grimbold?"

"Well, sir, I suppose they might. But they'd have to have got into the house before half-past seven, sir, and hidden themselves somewhere. Still, there's no doubt it might have happened that way. They couldn't come down by the back stairs, of course, because they'd have had to pass the kitchen, and Cook would have heard them, the passage being flagged, sir, but the front stairs—well, I don't know hardly what to say about that."

"That's how the man got in, depend upon it," said Parker. "Don't look so distressed, Hamworthy. You can't be expected to search all the cupboards in the house every evening for concealed criminals. Now I think I had better see the two nephews. I suppose they and their uncle got on together all right?"

"Oh, yes, sir. Never had a word of any sort. It's been a great blow to them, sir. They were terribly upset when Mr. Grimbold was ill in the summer—"

"He was ill, was he?"

"Yes, sir, with his heart, last July. He took a very bad turn, sir, and we had to send for Mr. Neville. But he pulled round wonderfully, sir,—only he never seemed to be quite such a cheerful gentleman afterwards. I think it made him feel he wasn't getting younger, sir. But I'm sure nobody ever thought he'd be cut off like this."

"How is his money left?" asked Parker.

"Well, sir, that I don't know. I believe it would be divided between the two gentlemen, sir—not but what they have plenty of their own. But Mr. Harcourt would be able to tell you, sir. He's the executor."

"Very well, we'll ask him. Are the brothers on good terms?"

"Oh, yes, indeed, sir. Most devoted. Mr. Neville would do anything for Mr. Harcourt—and Mr. Harcourt for him, I'm sure. A very pleasant pair of gentlemen, sir. You couldn't have nicer."

"Thanks, Hamworthy. That will do for the moment, unless anybody else has anything to ask?"

"How much of the pheasant was eaten, Hamworthy?"

"Well, my lord, not a great deal of it—I mean, nothing like all of what Mr. Grimbold had on his plate. But he'd ate some of it. It might have taken three or four minutes or so to eat what he had done, my lord, judging by what I helped him to."

"There was nothing to suggest that he had been interrupted, for example, by somebody coming to the windows, or of his having got up to let the person in?"

"Nothing at all, my lord, that I could see."

"The chair was pushed in close to the table when I saw him," put in the Inspector, "and his napkin was on his knees and the knife and fork lying just under his hands, as though he had dropped them when the blow came. I understand that the body was not disturbed."

"No, sir. I never moved it—except, of course, to make sure that he was dead. But I never felt any doubt of that, sir, when I saw that dreadful wound in his back. I just lifted his head and let it fall forward again, same as before."

"All right, then, Hamworthy. Ask Mr. Harcourt to come in."

Mr. Harcourt Grimbold was a brisk-looking man of about thirty-five. He explained that he was a stockbroker and his brother Neville an official in the Ministry of Public Health, and that they had been brought up by their uncle from the ages of eleven and ten respectively. He was aware that his uncle had had many business enemies, but for his own part he had received nothing from him but kindness.

"I'm afraid I can't tell you much about this terrible business, as I didn't get here till 9:45 last night, when, of course, it was all over."

"That was a little later than you hoped to be here?"

"Just a little. My tail-lamp went out between Welwyn Garden City and Welwyn, and I was stopped by a bobby. I went to a garage in Welwyn, where they found that the lead had come loose. They put it right, and that delayed me for a few minutes more."

"It's about forty miles from here to London?"

"Just over. In the ordinary way, at that time of night, I should reckon an hour and a quarter from door to door. I'm not a speed merchant."

"Did you drive yourself?"

"Yes. I have a chauffeur, but I don't always bring him down here with me."

"When did you leave London?"

"About 8:20, I should think. Neville went round to the garage and fetched the car as soon as he'd finished telephoning, while I put my toothbrush and so on in my bag."

"You didn't hear about the death of your uncle before you left?"

"No. They didn't think of ringing me up, I gather, till after I had started. The police tried to get Neville later on, but he'd gone round to the club, or something. I 'phoned him myself after I got here, and he came down this morning."

"Well, now, Mr. Grimbold, can you tell us anything about your late uncle's affairs?"

"You mean his will? Who profits, and that kind of thing? Well, I do, for one, and Neville, for another. And Mrs.—— Have you heard of a Mrs. Winter?"

"Something, yes."

"Well, she does, for a third. And then, of course, old Hamworthy gets a nice little nest-egg, and the cook gets something, and there is a legacy of £500 to the clerk at my uncle's London office. But the bulk of it goes to us and to Mrs. Winter. I know what you're going to ask—how much is it? I haven't the faintest idea, but I know it must be something pretty considerable. The old man never let on to a soul how much he really was worth, and we never bothered about it. I'm turning over a good bit, and Neville's salary is a heavy burden on a long-suffering public, so we only had a mild, academic kind of interest in the question."

"Do you suppose Hamworthy knew he was down for a legacy?"

"Oh, yes—there was no secret about that. He was to get £100 and a life-interest in £200 a year, provided, of course, he was still in my uncle's service when he—my uncle, I mean—died."

"And he wasn't under notice, or anything?"

"N-no. No. Not more than usual. My uncle gave everybody notice about once a month, to keep them up to the mark. But it never came to anything. He was like the Queen of Hearts in *Alice*—he never executed nobody, you know."

"I see. We'd better ask Hamworthy about that, though. Now, this Mrs. Winter. Do you know anything about her?"

"Oh, yes. She's a nice woman. Of course, she was Uncle William's mistress for donkey's years, but her husband was practically potty with drink, and you could scarcely blame her. I wired her this morning and here's her reply, just come."

He handed Parker a telegram, despatched from Paris, which read: "Terribly shocked and grieved. Returning immediately. Love and sympathy. Lucy."

"You are on friendly terms with her, then?"

"Good Lord, yes. Why not? We were always damned sorry for her. Uncle William would have taken her away with him somewhere, only she wouldn't leave Winter. In fact, I think they had practically settled that they were to get married now that Winter has had the grace to peg out. She's only about thirty-eight, and it's time she had some sort of show in life, poor thing."

"So, in spite of the money, she hadn't really very much to gain by your uncle's death?"

"Not a thing. Unless, of course, she wanted to marry somebody younger, and was afraid of losing the cash. But I believe she was honestly fond of the old boy. Anyhow, she couldn't have done the murder, because she's in Paris."

"H'm!" said Parker. "I suppose she is. We'd better make sure, though. I'll ring through to the Yard and have her looked out for at the ports. Is this 'phone through to the Exchange?"

"Yes," said the Inspector. "It doesn't have to go through the hall 'phone; they're connected in parallel."

"All right. Well, I don't think we need trouble you further, at the moment, Mr. Grimbold. I'll put my call through, and after that we'll send for the next witness. . . . Give me Whitehall 1212, please. . . . I suppose the time of Mr. Harcourt's call from town has been checked, Inspector?"

"Yes, Mr. Parker. It was put in at 7:57 and renewed at 8 o'clock and 8:03. Quite an expensive little item. And we've also checked up on the constable who spoke to him about his lights and the garage that put them right for him. He got into Welwyn at 9:05 and left again about 9:15. The number of the car is right, too."

"Well, he's out of it in any case, but it's just as well to check all we can. . . . Hullo, is that Scotland Yard? Put me through to Chief-Inspector Hardy. Chief-Inspector Parker speaking."

As soon as he had finished with his call, Parker sent for Neville Grimbold. He was rather like his brother, only a little slimmer and a little more suave in speech, as befitted a Civil Servant. He had nothing to add, except to confirm his brother's story and to explain that he had gone to a cinema from 8:20 to about 10 o'clock, and then on to his club, so that he had heard nothing about the tragedy till later in the evening.

The cook was the next witness. She had a great deal to say, but nothing very convincing to tell. She had not happened to see Hamworthy go to the pantry for the claret, otherwise she confirmed his story. She scouted the idea that somebody had been concealed in one of the upper rooms, because the daily woman, Mrs. Crabbe, had been in the house till nearly dinner-time, putting camphor-bags in all the wardrobes; and, anyhow, she had no doubt but what "that Payne" had stabbed Mr. Grimbold—"a nasty, murdering beast." After which, it only remained to interview the murderous Mr. Payne.

Mr. Payne was almost aggressively frank. He had been treated very harshly by Mr. Grimbold. What with exorbitant usury and accumulated interest added to the principal, he had already paid back about five times the original loan, and now Mr. Grimbold had refused him any more time to pay, and had announced his intention of foreclosing on the security, namely, Mr. Payne's house and land. It was all the more brutal because Mr. Payne had every prospect of being able to pay off the entire debt in six months' time, owing to some sort of interest or share in something or other which was confidently expected to turn up trumps. In his opinion, old Grimbold had refused to renew on purpose, so as to prevent him from paying—what *he* wanted was the property. Grimbold's death was the saving of the situation, because it would postpone settlement till after the confidently-expected trumps had turned up. Mr. Payne would have murdered old Grimbold with pleasure, but he hadn't done so, and in any case he wasn't the sort of man to stab anybody in the back, though, if the money-lender had been a younger man, he, Payne, would have been happy to break all his bones for him. There it was, and they could take it or leave it. If that old fool, Hamworthy, hadn't got in his way, he'd have laid hands on the murderer all right—if Hamworthy was a fool, which he doubted. Blood? yes, there was blood on his coat. He had got that in struggling with Hamworthy at the window. Hamworthy's hands had been all over blood when he made his appearance in the library. No doubt he had got it from the corpse. He, Payne, had taken care not to change his clothes, because, if he had done so, somebody would have tried to make out that he was hiding something. Actually, he had not been home, or asked to go home, since the murder. Mr. Payne added that he objected strongly to the attitude taken up by the local police, who had treated him with undisguised hostility. To which Inspector Henley replied that Mr. Payne was quite mistaken.

"Mr. Payne," said Lord Peter, "will you tell me one thing? When you heard the commotion in the dining-room, and the cook screaming, and so on, why didn't you go in at once to find out what was the matter?"

"Why?" retorted Mr. Payne. "Because I never heard anything of the sort, that's why. The first thing I knew about it was seeing the butler-fellow standing there in the doorway, waving his bloody hands about and gibbering."

"Ah!" said Wimsey. "I thought it was a good, solid door. Shall we ask the lady to go in and scream for us now, with the dining-room window open?"

The Inspector departed on this errand, while the rest of the company waited anxiously to count the screams. Nothing happened, however, till Henley put his head in and asked, what about it?

"Nothing," said Parker.

"It's a well-built house," said Wimsey. "I suppose any sound coming through the window would be muffled by the conservatory. Well, Mr. Payne, if you didn't hear the screams it's not surprising that you didn't hear the murderer. Are those all your witnesses, Charles? Because I've got to get back to London to see a man about a dog. But I'll leave you two suggestions with my blessing. One is, that you should look for a car, which was parked within a quarter of a mile of this house last night, between 7:30 and 8:15; the second is, that you should all come and sit in the dining-room to-night, with the doors and windows shut, and watch the french windows. I'll give Mr. Parker a ring about eight. Oh, and you might lend me the key of the conservatory door. I've got a theory about it."

The Chief Inspector handed over the key, and his lordship departed.

The party assembled in the dining-room was in no very companionable mood. In fact, all the conversation was supplied by the police, who kept up a chatty exchange of fishing reminiscences, while Mr. Payne glowered, the two Grimbolds smoked cigarette after cigarette, and the cook and the butler balanced themselves nervously on the extreme edges of their chairs. It was a relief when the telephone-bell rang.

Parker glanced at his watch as he got up to answer it. "Seven-fifty-seven," he observed, and saw the butler pass his handkerchief over his twitching lips. "Keep your eye on the windows." He went out into the hall.

"Hullo!" he said.

"Is that Chief-Inspector Parker?" asked a voice he knew well. "This is Lord Peter Wimsey's man speaking from his lordship's rooms in London. Would you hold the line a moment? His lordship wishes to speak to you."

Parker heard the receiver set down and lifted again. Then Wimsey's voice came through: "Hullo, old man? Have you found that car yet?"

"We've heard of *a* car," replied the Chief Inspector cautiously, "at a Road-House on the Great North Road, about five minutes' walk from the house."

"Was the number A B J 28?"

"Yes. How did you know?"

"I thought it might be. It was hired from a London garage at five o'clock yesterday afternoon and brought back just before ten. Have you traced Mrs. Winter?"

"Yes, I think so. She landed from the Calais boat this evening. So apparently she's O.K."

"I thought she might be. Now, listen. Do you know that Harcourt Grimbold's affairs are in a bit of a mess? He nearly had a crisis last July, but somebody came to his rescue—possibly Uncle, don't you think? All rather fishy, my informant saith. And I'm told, very confidentially, that he's got badly caught over the Biggars-Whitlow crash. But of course he'll have no difficulty in raising money now, on the strength of Uncle's will. But I imagine the July business gave Uncle William a jolt. I expect—"

He was interrupted by a little burst of tinkling music, followed by the eight silvery strokes of a bell.

"Hear that? Recognise it? That's the big French clock in my sitting-room. . . . What? All right, Exchange, give me another three minutes. Bunter wants to speak to you again."

The receiver rattled, and the servant's suave voice took up the tale.

"His lordship asks me to ask you, sir, to ring off at once and go straight into the dining-room."

Parker obeyed. As he entered the room, he got an instantaneous impression of six people, sitting as he had left them, in an expectant semi-circle, their eyes strained towards the french windows. Then the library door opened noiselessly and Lord Peter Wimsey walked in.

"Good God!" exclaimed Parker, involuntarily. "How did you get here?" The six heads jerked round suddenly.

"On the back of the light waves," said Wimsey, smoothing back his hair. "I have travelled eighty miles to be with you, at 186,000 miles a second."

"It was rather obvious, really," said Wimsey, when they had secured Harcourt Grimbold (who fought desperately) and his brother Neville (who collapsed and had to be revived with brandy). "It had to be those two; they were so very much elsewhere—almost absolutely elsewhere. The murder could only have been committed between 7:57 and 8:06, and there had to be a reason for that prolonged 'phone-call about something that Harcourt could very well have explained when he came. And the murderer had to be in the library before 7:57, or he would have been seen in the hall—unless Grimbold had let him in by the french window, which didn't appear likely.

"Here's how it was worked. Harcourt set off from Town in a hired car about six o'clock, driving himself. He parked the car at the Road-House, giving some explanation. I suppose he wasn't known there?"

"No; it's quite a new place; only opened last month."

"Ah! Then he walked the last quarter-mile on foot, arriving here at 7:45. It was dark, and he probably wore goloshes, so as not to make a noise coming up the path. He let himself into the conservatory with a duplicate key."

"How did he get that?"

"Pinched Uncle William's key off his ring last July, when the old boy was ill. It was probably the shock of hearing that his dear nephew was in trouble that caused the illness. Harcourt was here at the time—you remember it was only Neville that had to be 'sent for'—and I suppose Uncle paid up then, on conditions. But I doubt if he'd have done as much again—especially as he was thinking of getting married. And I expect, too, Harcourt thought that Uncle might easily alter his will after marriage. He might even have founded a family, and what would poor Harcourt do then, poor thing? From every point of view, it was better that Uncle should depart this life. So the duplicate key was cut and the plot thought out, and Brother Neville, who would 'do anything for Mr. Harcourt,' was roped in to help. I'm inclined to think that Harcourt must have done something rather worse than merely lose money, and Neville may have troubles of his own. But where was I?"

"Coming in at the conservatory door."

"Oh, yes—that's the way I came to-night. He'd take cover in the garden and would know when Uncle William went into the dining-room, because he'd see the library light go out. Remember, he knew the household. He came in, in the dark, locking the outer door after him, and waited by the telephone till Neville's call came through from London. When the bell stopped ringing, he lifted the receiver in the library. As soon as Neville had spoken his little piece, Harcourt chipped in. Nobody could hear him through these sound-proof doors, and Hamworthy couldn't possibly tell that his voice wasn't coming from London. In fact, it *was* coming from London, because, as the 'phones are connected in parallel, it could only come by way of the Exchange. At eight o'clock, the grandfather clock in Jermyn Street struck—further proof that the London line was open. The minute Harcourt heard that, he called on Neville to speak again, and hung up under cover of the rattle of Neville's receiver. Then Neville detained Hamworthy with a lot of rot about a suit, while Harcourt walked into the dining-room, stabbed his uncle and departed by the window. He had five good minutes in which to hurry back to his car and drive off—and Hamworthy and Payne actually gave him a few minutes more by suspecting and hampering one another."

"Why didn't he go back through the library and conservatory?"

"He hoped everybody would think that the murderer had come in by the window. In the meantime, Neville left London at 8:20 in Harcourt's car, carefully drawing the attention of a policeman and a garage man to the licence number as he passed through Welwyn. At an appointed place outside Welwyn he met Harcourt, primed him with his little story about tail-lights, and changed cars with him. Neville returned to town with the hired 'bus; Harcourt came back here with his own car. But I'm afraid you'll have a little difficulty in finding the weapon and the duplicate key and Harcourt's blood-stained gloves and coat. Neville probably took them back, and they may be anywhere. There's a good, big river in London."

—1934

TONY HILLERMAN

B. 1925

Tony Hillerman's mysteries are notable for several qualities: they are some of the best-written crime fiction novels appearing in today's genre, and they are distinguished by Hillerman's adept incorporation of Native American culture as part of his stories' plots and settings. He was born in Sacred Heart, Oklahoma, and attended a Native American boarding school for a number of years. He received a B.A. in journalism from University of Oklahoma in 1948 and an M.A. in English from the University of New Mexico in 1965. During World War II, Hillerman was awarded the Bronze Star, the Silver Star, and the Purple Heart for his distinguished military service. Following the war, Hillerman worked as a newspaper reporter and editor in the southwestern region of the United States. He turned to teaching journalism at the university level during the mid-1960s and began publishing crime fiction in the early 1970s. His two Navajo detective heroes are Joe Leaphorn—who appeared in The Blessing Way *(1970),* Dance Hall of the Dead *(1973), and* Listening Woman *(1978)—and Jim Chee of the Navajo Tribal Police—who appeared in* People of Darkness *(1980),* The Dark Wind *(1982), and* The Ghostway *(1984). Hillerman also featured both Leaphorn and Chee working together in several novels:* Skinwalkers *(1987),* A Thief of Time *(1988),* Talking God *(1989), and* Coyote Waits *(1990).*

Jimmy Chee is the detective protagonist in Hillerman's "Chee's Witch," originally published in 1986 as part of an original paperback anthology series, The New Black Mask, *that attempted to revive the type of crime fiction once featured in the famous pulp magazine. In "Chee's Witch," Hillerman skillfully offers his reader an insightful look at the complexities of Native American culture, a scrutiny that is housed within the formulaic frame of the police detective story. Jimmy Chee's understanding of the cultural definitions of witchcraft, as it is perceived by the various Navajo tribal clans, ultimately helps to provide an important key to the solution of the bizarre mystery surrounding Simon Begay.*

CHEE'S WITCH

Snow is so important to the Eskimos they have nine nouns to describe its variations. Corporal Jimmy Chee of the Navajo Tribal Police had heard that as an anthropology student at the University of New Mexico. He remembered it now because he was thinking of all the words you need in Navajo to account for the many forms of witchcraft. The word Old Woman Tso had used was "anti'l," which is the ultimate sort, the absolute worst. And so, in fact, was the deed which seemed to have been done. Murder, apparently. Mutilation, certainly, if Old Woman Tso had her facts right. And then if one believed all the mythology of witchery told among the fifty clans who comprised The People, there must also be cannibalism, incest, even necrophilia.

On the radio in Chee's pickup truck, the voice of the young Navajo reading a Gallup used-car commercial was replaced by Willie Nelson singing of trouble and a worried mind. The ballad fit Chee's mood. He was tired. He was thirsty. He was sticky with sweat. He was worried. His pickup jolted along the ruts in a windless heat, leaving a white fog of dust to mark its winding passage across the Rainbow Plateau. The truck was gray with it. So was Jimmy Chee. Since sunrise he had covered maybe two hundred miles of half-graded gravel and unmarked wagon tracks of the Arizona-Utah-New Mexico border country. Routine at first—a check into a witch story at the Tsossie hogan north of Teec Nos Pos to stop trouble before it started. Routine and logical. A bitter winter, a sand storm spring, a summer of rainless, desiccating heat. Hopes dying, things going wrong, anger growing, and then the witch gossip. The logical. A bitter winter, a sand storm spring, a summer awry. The trouble at the summer hogan of the Tsossies was a sick child and a water well that had turned alkaline—nothing unexpected. But you didn't expect such a specific witch. The skinwalker, the Tsossies agreed, was the City Navajo, the man who had come to live in one of the government houses at Kayenta. Why the City Navajo? Because everybody knew he was a witch. Where had they heard that, the first time? The People who came to the trading post at Mexican Water said it. And so Chee had driven westward over Tohache Wash, past Red Mesa and Rabbit Ears to Mexican Water. He had spent hours on the shady porch giving those who came to buy, and to fill their water barrels, and to visit, a chance to know who he was until finally they might risk talking about witchcraft to a stranger. They were Mud Clan, and Many Goats People, and Standing Rock Clan—foreign to Chee's own Slow Talking People—but finally some of them talked a little.

A witch was at work on the Rainbow Plateau. Adeline Etcitty's mare had foaled a two-headed colt. Hosteen Musket had seen the witch. He'd seen a man walk into a grove of cottonwoods, but when he got there an owl flew away. Rudolph Bisti's boys lost three rams while driving their flocks up into the Chuska high pastures, and when they found the bodies, the huge tracks of a werewolf were all around them. The daughter of Rosemary Nashibitti had seen a big dog bothering her horses and had shot at it with her .22 and the dog had turned into a man wearing a wolfskin and had fled, half running, half flying. The old man they called Afraid of His Horses had heard the sound of the witch on the roof of his winter hogan, and saw the dirt falling through the smoke hole as the skinwalker tried to throw in his corpse powder. The next morning the old man had followed the tracks of the Navajo Wolf for a mile, hoping to kill him. But the tracks had faded away. There was nothing very unusual in the stories, except their number and the recurring hints that the City Navajo was the witch. But then came what Chee hadn't expected. The witch had killed a man.

The police dispatcher at Window Rock had been interrupting Willie Nelson with an occasional blurted message. Now she spoke directly to Chee. He acknowledged. She asked his location.

"About fifteen miles south of Dennehotso," Chee said. "Homeward bound for Tuba City. Dirty, thirsty, hungry, and tired."

"I have a message."

"Tuba City," Chee repeated, "which I hope to reach in about two hours, just in time to avoid running up a lot of overtime for which I never get paid."

"The message is FBI Agent Wells needs to contact you. Can you make a meeting at Kayenta Holiday Inn at eight P.M.?"

"What's it about?" Chee asked. The dispatcher's name was Virgie Endecheenie, and she had a very pretty voice and the first time Chee had met her at the Window Rock headquarters of the Navajo Tribal Police he had been instantly smitten. Unfortunately, Virgie was a born-into Salt Cedar Clan, which was the clan of Chee's father, which put an instant end to that. Even thinking about it would violate the complex incest taboo of the Navajos.

"Nothing on what it's about," Virgie said, her voice strictly business. "It just says confirm meeting time and place with Chee or obtain alternate time."

"Any first name on Wells?" Chee asked. The only FBI Wells he knew was Jake Wells. He hoped it wouldn't be Jake.

"Negative on the first name," Virgie said.

"All right," Chee said. "I'll be there."

The road tilted downward now into the vast barrens of erosion which the Navajos call Beautiful Valley. Far to the west, the edge of the sun dipped behind a cloud—one of the line of thunderheads forming in the evening heat over the San Francisco Peaks and the Cococino Rim. The Hopis had been holding their Niman Kachina dances, calling the clouds to come and bless them.

Chee reached Kayenta just a little late. It was early twilight and the clouds had risen black against the sunset. The breeze brought the faint smells that rising humidity carries across desert country—the perfume of sage, creosote brush, and dust. The desk clerk said that Wells was in room 284 and the first name was Jake. Chee no longer cared. Jake Wells was abrasive but he was also smart. He had the best record in the special FBI Academy class Chee had attended, a quick, tough intelligence. Chee could tolerate the man's personality for a while to learn what Wells could make of his witchcraft puzzle.

"It's unlocked," Wells said. "Come on in." He was propped against the padded headboard of the bed, shirt off, shoes on, glass in hand. He glanced at Chee and then back at the television set. He was as tall as Chee remembered, and the eyes were just as blue. He waved the glass at Chee without looking away from the set. "Mix yourself one," he said, nodding toward a bottle beside the sink in the dressing alcove.

"How you doing, Jake?" Chee asked.

Now the blue eyes reexamined Chee. The question in them abruptly went away. "Yeah," Wells said. "You were the one at the Academy." He eased himself on his left elbow and extended a hand. "Jake Wells," he said.

Chee shook the hand. "Chee," he said.

Wells shifted his weight again and handed Chee his glass. "Pour me a little more while you're at it," he said, "and turn down the sound. "

Chee turned down the sound.

"About thirty percent booze," Wells demonstrated the proportion with his hands. "This is your district then. You're in charge around Kayenta? Window Rock said I should talk to you. They said you were out chasing around in the desert today. What are you working on?"

"Nothing much," Chee said. He ran a glass of water, drinking it thirstily. His face in the mirror was dirty—the lines around mouth and eyes whitish with dust. The sticker on the glass reminded guests that the laws of the Navajo Tribal Council prohibited possession of alcoholic beverages on the reservation. He refilled his own glass with water and mixed Wells's drink. "As a matter of fact, I'm working on a witchcraft case."

"Witchcraft?" Wells laughed. "Really?" He took the drink from Chee and examined it. "How does it work? Spells and like that?"

"Not exactly," Chee said. "It depends. A few years ago a little girl got sick down near Burnt Water. Her dad killed three people with a shotgun. He said they blew corpse powder on his daughter and made her sick."

Wells was watching him. "The kind of crime where you have the insanity plea."

"Sometimes," Chee said. "Whatever you have, witch talk makes you nervous. It happens more when you have a bad year like this. You hear it and you try to find out what's starting it before things get worse."

"So you're not really expecting to find a witch?"

"Usually not," Chee said.

"Usually?"

"Judge for yourself," Chee said. "I'll tell you what I've picked up today. You tell me what to make of it. Have time?"

Wells shrugged. "What I really want to talk about is a guy named Simon Begay." He looked quizzically at Chee. "You heard the name?"

"Yes," Chee said.

"Well, shit," Wells said. "You shouldn't have. What do you know about him?"

"Showed up maybe three months ago. Moved into one of those U.S. Public Health Service houses over by the Kayenta clinic. Stranger. Keeps to himself. From off the reservation somewhere. I figured you federals put him here to keep him out of sight."

Wells frowned. "How long you known about him?"

"Quite a while," Chee said. He'd known about Begay within a week after his arrival.

"He's a witness," Wells said. "They broke a car-theft operation in Los Angeles. Big deal. National connections. One of those where they have hired hands picking up expensive models and they drive 'em right on the ship and off-load in South America. This Begay is one of the hired hands. Nobody much. Criminal record going all the way back to juvenile, but all nickel-and-dime stuff. I gather he saw some things that help tie some big boys into the crime, so Justice made a deal with him."

"And they hide him out here until the trial?"

Something apparently showed in the tone of the question. "If you want to hide an apple, you drop it in with the other apples," Wells said. "What better place?"

Chee had been looking at Wells's shoes, which were glossy with polish. Now he examined his own boots, which were not. But he was thinking of Justice Department stupidity. The appearance of any new human in a country as empty as the Navajo Reservation provoked instant interest. If the stranger was a Navajo, there were instant questions. What was his clan? Who was his mother? What was his father's clan? Who were his relatives? The City Navajo had no answers to any of these crucial questions. He was (as Chee had been repeatedly told) unfriendly. It was quickly guessed that he was a "relocation Navajo," born to one of those hundreds of Navajo families in which the federal government had tried to reestablish forty years ago in Chicago, Los Angeles, and other urban centers. He was a stranger. In a year of witches, he would certainly be suspected. Chee sat looking at his boots, wondering if that was the only basis for the charge that City Navajo was a skinwalker. Or had someone seen something? Had someone seen the murder?

"The thing about apples is they don't gossip," Chee said.

"You hear gossip about Begay?" Wells was sitting up now, his feet on the floor.

"Sure," Chee said. "I hear he's a witch."

Wells produced a pro-forma chuckle. "Tell me about it," he said.

Chee knew exactly how he wanted to tell it. Wells would have to wait awhile before he came to the part about Begay. "The Eskimos have nine nouns for snow," Chee began. He told Wells about the variety of witchcraft on the reservations and its environs: about frenzy witchcraft, used for sexual conquests, of witchery distortions, of curing ceremonials, of the exotic two-heart witchcraft of the Hopi Fog Clan, of the Zuni Sorcery Fraternity, of the Navajo "chindi," which is more like a ghost than a witch, and finally of the Navajo Wolf, the anti'l witchcraft, the werewolves who pervert every taboo of the Navajo Way and use corpse powder to kill their victims.

Wells rattled the ice in his glass and glanced at his watch.

"To get to the part about your Begay," Chee said, "about two months ago we started picking up witch gossip. Nothing much, and you expect it during a drought. Lately it got to be more than usual." He described some of the tales and how uneasiness and dread had spread across the plateau. He described what he had learned today, the Tsossies's naming City Navajo as the witch, his trip to Mexican Water, of learning there that the witch had killed a man.

"They said it happened in the spring—couple of months ago. They told me the ones who knew about it were the Tso outfit." The talk of murder, Chee noticed, had revived Wells's interest. "I went up there," he continued, "and found the old woman who runs the outfit. Emma Tso. She told me her son-in-law had been out looking for some sheep, and smelled something, and found the body under some chamiso brush in a dry wash. A witch had killed him."

"How—"

Chee cut off the question. "I asked her how he knew it was a witch killing. She said the hands were stretched out like this." Chee extended his hands, palms up. "They were flayed. The skin was cut off the palms and fingers."

Wells raised his eyebrows.

"That's what the witch uses to make corpse powder," Chee explained. "They take the skin that has the whorls and ridges of the individual personality—the skin from the palms and the finger pads, and the soles of the feet. They take that, and the skin from the glans of the penis, and the small bones where the neck joins the skull, and they dry it, and pulverize it, and use it as poison."

"You're going to get to Begay any minute now," Wells said. "That right?"

"We got to him," Chee said. "He's the one they think is the witch. He's the City Navajo."

"I thought you were going to say that," Wells said. He rubbed the back of his hand across one blue eye. "City Navajo. Is it that obvious?"

"Yes," Chee said. "And then he's a stranger. People suspect strangers."

"Were they coming around him? Accusing him? Any threats? Anything like that, you think?"

"It wouldn't work that way—not unless somebody had someone in their family killed. The way you deal with a witch is hire a singer and hold a special kind of curing ceremony. That turns the witchcraft around and kills the witch."

Wells made an impatient gesture. "Whatever," he said. "I think something has made this Begay spooky." He stared into his glass, communing with the bourbon. "I don't know."

"Something unusual about the way he's acting?"

"Hell of it is I don't know how he usually acts. This wasn't my case. The agent who worked him retired or some damn thing, so I got stuck with being the delivery man." He shifted his eyes from glass to Chee. "But if it was me, and I was holed up here waiting, and the guy came along who was going to take me home again, then I'd be glad to see him. Happy to have it over with. All that."

"He wasn't?"

Wells shook his head. "Seemed edgy. Maybe that's natural, though. He's going to make trouble for some hard people."

"I'd be nervous," Chee said.

"I guess it doesn't matter much anyway," Wells said. "He's small potatoes. The guy who's handling it now in the U.S. Attorney's Office said it must have been a toss-up whether to fool with him at all. He said the assistant who handled it decided to hide him out just to be on the safe side."

"Begay doesn't know much?"

"I guess not. That, and they've got better witnesses."

"So why worry?"

Wells laughed. "I bring this sucker back and they put him on the witness stand and he answers all the questions with I don't know and it makes the USDA look like a horse's ass. When a U.S. Attorney looks like that, he finds an FBI agent to blame it on." He yawned. "Therefore," he said through the yawn, "I want to ask you what you think. This is your territory. You are the officer in charge. Is it your opinion that someone got to my witness?"

Chee let the question hang. He spent a fraction of a second reaching the answer, which was they could have if they wanted to try. Then he thought about the real reason Wells had kept him working late without a meal or shower. Two sentences in Wells's report. One would note that the possibility the witness had been approached had been checked with local Navajo Police. The next would report whatever Chee said next. Wells would have followed Federal Rule One—Protect Your Ass.

Chee shrugged. "You want to hear the rest of my witchcraft business?"

Wells put his drink on the lamp table and untied his shoe. "Does it bear on this?"

"Who knows? Anyway there's not much left. I'll let you decide. The point is we had already picked up this corpse Emma Tso's son-in-law found. Somebody had reported it weeks ago. It had been collected, and taken in for an autopsy. The word we got on the body was Navajo male in his thirties probably. No identification on him."

"How was this bird killed?"

"No sign of foul play," Chee said. "By the time the body was brought in, decay and the scavengers hadn't left a lot. Mostly bone and gristle, I guess. This was a long time after Emma Tso's son-in-law saw him."

"So why do they think Begay killed him?" Wells removed his second shoe and headed for the bathroom.

Chee picked up the telephone and dialed the Kayenta clinic. He got the night supervisor and waited while the supervisor dug out the file. Wells came out of the bathroom with his toothbrush. Chee covered the mouthpiece. "I'm having them read me the autopsy report," Chee explained. Wilson began brushing his teeth at the sink in the dressing alcove. The voice of the night supervisor droned into Chee's ear.

"That all?" Chee asked. "Nothing added on? No identity yet? Still no cause?"

"That's him," the voice said.

"How about shoes?" Chee asked. "He have shoes on?"

"Just a sec," the voice said. "Yep. Size ten D. And a hat, and . . ."

"No mention of the neck or skull, right? I didn't miss that? No bones missing?"

Silence. "Nothing about neck or skull bones."

"Ah," Chee said. "Fine. I thank you." He felt great. He felt wonderful. Finally things had clicked into place. The witch was exorcised. "Jake," he said. "Let me tell you a little more about my witch case."

Wells was rinsing his mouth. He spit out the water and looked at Chee, amused. "I didn't think of this before," Wells said, "but you really don't have a witch problem. If you leave that corpse a death by natural causes, there's no case to work. If you decide it's a homicide, you don't have jurisdiction anyway. Homicide on an

Indian reservation, FBI has jurisdiction." Wells grinned. "We'll come in and find your witch for you."

Chee looked at his boots, which were still dusty. His appetite had left him, as it usually did an hour or so after he missed a meal. He still hungered for a bath. He picked up his hat and pushed himself to his feet.

"I'll go home now," he said. "The only thing you don't know about the witch case is what I just got from the autopsy report. The corpse had his shoes on and no bones were missing from the base of the skull."

Chee opened the door and stood in it, looking back. Wells was taking his pajamas out of his suitcase. "So what advice do you have for me? What can you tell me about my witch case?"

"To tell the absolute truth, Chee, I'm not into witches," Wells said. "Haven't been since I was a boy."

"But we don't really have a witch case now," Chee said. He spoke earnestly. "The shoes were still on, so the skin wasn't taken from the soles of his feet. No bones missing from the neck. You need those to make corpse powder."

Wells was pulling his undershirt over his head. Chee hurried.

"What we have now is another little puzzle," Chee said. "If you're not collecting stuff for corpse powder, why cut the skin off this guy's hands?"

"I'm going to take a shower," Wells said. "Got to get my Begay back to L.A. tomorrow."

Outside the temperature had dropped. The air moved softly from the west, carrying the smell of rain. Over the Utah border, over the Cococino Rim, over the Rainbow Plateau, lightning flickered and glowed. The storm had formed. The storm was moving. The sky was black with it. Chee stood in the darkness, listening to the mutter of thunder, inhaling the perfume, exulting in it.

He climbed into the truck and started it. How had they set it up, and why? Perhaps the FBI agent who knew Begay had been ready to retire. Perhaps an accident had been arranged. Getting rid of the assistant prosecutor who knew the witness would have been even simpler—a matter of hiring him away from the government job. That left no one who knew this minor witness was not Simon Begay. And who was he? Probably they had other Navajos from the Los Angeles community stealing cars for them. Perhaps that's what had suggested the scheme. To most white men all Navajos looked pretty much alike, just as in his first years at college all Chee had seen in white men was pink skin, freckles, and light-colored eyes. And what would the imposter say? Chee grinned. He'd say whatever was necessary to cast doubt on the prosecution, to cast the fatal "reasonable doubt," to make—as Wells had put it— the U.S. District Attorney look like a horse's ass.

Chee drove into the rain twenty miles west of Kayenta. Huge, cold drops drummed on the pickup roof and turned the highway into a ribbon of water. Tomorrow the backcountry roads would be impassable. As soon as they dried and the washouts had been repaired, he'd go back to the Tsossie hogan, and the Tso place, and to all the other places from which the word would quickly spread. He'd tell the people that the witch was in custody of the FBI and was gone forever from the Rainbow Plateau.

−1986

MARCIA MULLER

B. 1944

Marcia Muller is part of the new American school of "hard-boiled" detective fiction. She was born in Detroit, Michigan, and after receiving her B.A. in English and M.A. in journalism from the University of Michigan, she held a variety of jobs before becoming a full-time writer in 1983. Muller is credited with inventing the female private investigator—a character named Sharon McCone. McCone appeared in Muller's first published novel, Edwin of the Iron Shoes *(1977) and has remained her most popular detective hero through the intervening years. A representative selection of novels in the Sharon McCone mystery series are* The Cheshire Cat's Eye *(1983),* Leave a Message for Willie *(1984),* Eye of the Storm *(1988),* Wolf in the Shadows *(1993), and* A Wild and Lonely Place *(1995).*

Other Muller series detective characters include Joanna Stark—a security specialist for art collections who is featured as a detective in The Cavalier in White *(1986),* There Hangs the Knife *(1988), and* Dark Star *(1989)—and Elena Oliverez—a curator working for the Museum of Mexican Arts in Santa Barbara, California and who also serves as an amateur sleuth in* The Tree of Death *(1983),* The Legend of the Slain Soldiers *(1985), and* Beyond the Grave *(co-written with her husband Bill Pronzini; 1986).*

In her essay, "Creating a Female Sleuth," published in the October 1978 issue of The Writer, *Muller effectively outlines her philosophy about writing detective fiction. She also describes the fascinating "nuts and bolts" operation that lies behind an author's creative process, such as the development of her detective hero's character and the structuring of her story's plot.*

The Sharon McCone short story entitled "The Place That Time Forgot" was originally published in the anthology, Sisters in Crime 2 *(1990), edited by Marilyn Wallace. In this somewhat offbeat tale, Muller provides us with a mystery that is both poignant and tragic. Muller intends her detective protagonist to function as an involved social worker, as well as a private investigator. Muller usually employs the traditional narrative frame of the P.I. story to discuss complex problems that exist in our society. For example, Muller's "The Place That Time Forgot" explores the acute emotional fallout that can result from a long-standing, estranged domestic relationship.*

CREATING A FEMALE SLEUTH

Several years ago, a friend handed me my first whodunit as I was about to embark on a long bus ride. I finished the book before I reached my destination and, upon arrival, went straight to the paperback racks for another. I was hooked.

In the years that followed, my puzzle-prone friends and I noticed that one figure was missing from the mystery scene. There were scores of male sleuths, both hard- and soft-boiled. There were old ladies with knitting needles and noses for secrets. There were even a few dedicated and hard-working policewomen. But nowhere, at that time, could we find a female private eye.

Obviously, I decided, if I wanted to read about such a character, I would first have to write about her.

The process of creating my sleuth, Sharon McCone, and plotting her first case—*Edwin of the Iron Shoes*—presented a number of technical problems. Because female sleuths are in themselves a rarity, my imaginary friend could not be too unusual or too much of a super-woman if modern readers—both male and female—were to identify with her. She also needed to have background that would make her choice of profession believable.

On the other hand, like all detectives, she had to be somewhat larger than life. She had to be the sort of person who would do things you and I might never dream of: stalk her quarry through the highways and byways of the city; stand her ground with hostile cops; grapple hand-to-hand with dangerous criminals.

In order to reconcile these seeming opposites, I chose to give Sharon a normal, perhaps pedestrian, family background and upbringing that produced a well-adjusted, uncomplicated adult. Sharon's problems are those we've all experienced at one time: an affectionate but nosy mother who, fortunately, lives 500 miles away; the frustration of not finding a decent job after graduating from college with a sociology major; the lack of an interesting man in one's life; too high a rent for too small a studio apartment.

Marital status, which affects a female investigator's freedom of movement far more than a male's, was easy to decide, particularly when the police lieutenant in charge of Sharon's first murder case turned out to be attractive, if a bit of a smart-aleck. Sharon is single.

For the background that would qualify her for a career as a private investigator, I chose department-store security, a relatively easy field to break into. Where else could a nice girl learn to fire a .38 Special or flip a grown man over with a judo hold? I decided that Sharon was bored with guarding dresses on the sales floor, had gone off to college, and then returned to investigative work when she realized the demand for sociologists was nil. Further training with a big security agency equipped her for a position as staff investigator at a San Francisco legal cooperative in time for her first big case.

With this plausible basis for my sleuth's choice of occupation and a number of down-to-earth character traits, I gave my imagination free rein. I wanted to make Sharon's physical attributes stand out in the reader's mind, and at the same time to avoid the old, overused mirror-on-the-wall device ("As I stood before the mirror and brushed my hair, I thought about the case and noticed gray strands among the black."). Therefore, I decided to make Sharon a person with Scotch-Irish ancestry, whose one-eighth Shoshone Indian blood dominates her appearance. Her unusual looks, coupled with her name, cause people to comment, "McCone? But you look like an Indian!"—and this enabled me to dispense with a great deal of description.

Larger than life

Now I was really getting into the larger-than-life qualities, or, more accurately, the larger-than-author traits. Sharon is much taller than I, so she can more easily wrestle with criminals. She never has to worry about her weight, presumably because she does not sit at a typewriter all day. She is more independent than the average soul, delights in asserting herself, and, of course, is much braver.

These admirable qualities were all very well to list, but the next problem was how to express them in action. When I began writing up her first case, I found my heroine in a given situation and asked myself: "All right, what would *I* do?" The answer, inevitably, was something like "Run." Since this was not working out, I conditioned myself to think of what I would do if I were brave, tall, an expert at judo, and so on, each time taking it a step farther. I discovered it was better to have Sharon act ridiculously brave, even foolhardy, and moderate her actions later, than to start off timidly, because a timid response to a situation was more difficult to correct in a rewrite.

Touchier yet was the problem of emotional balance: how was Sharon to deal with the rough situations that came up in the course of her work without sacrificing her femininity? The qualities of empathy and intuition would be great assets to her, because as a woman she might realize or even be told things that ordinary investigative methods would not turn up. Still, she couldn't cry at every bump and bruise, or lose her gun in her purse at the crucial moment. Again, I constantly had to consider what I would do if I were a trained professional, how I would condition and curb my natural responses. I constantly made adjustments for this balance in every draft of the novel, and am still making adjustments now, as I guide my sleuth through her second case.

A mechanical aid in getting acquainted with my character was writing the biographical sketch, a detailed run-down on Sharon's history, preferences and opinions from her own point of view. I wrote this in the first person, as if she were standing up to introduce herself to a group. Throughout the writing process, this "biography" was there to help refresh my memory as to details. It was no substitute, however, for getting to know my character through writing about her.

Two rules for plotting

Now that I had my sleuth, the next question was what kind of case she should solve. In short, what was my plot to be?

I had a setting I wanted to explore: an enclave of antique and junk shops, loosely based on several such areas in San Francisco, and I wanted to center on one particular shop containing an assortment of strange objects, including a department store mannequin named Edwin, who wore a pair of ornate iron shoes. I also had a problem for Sharon to solve: the dead body of the proprietor on the floor of the shop, with Edwin as the only witness to the murder.

With this in mind, I began to play the game of "what if." I started with the very obvious questions: What if the proprietor had a fortune in antiques hidden in the shop? What if she had a jealous lover? What if several powerful real-estate syndicates were after the land the shop was on? What if, beneath her ordinary exterior, the victim hid some criminal secret? The answers to these and other often laughable questions gave the basis for my solution.

Knowing my solution was the real key to a plot that held together. I needed to have some ending, however tentative, in mind at all times, or I couldn't plant clues or make my suspects act properly suspicious. Without a solution, I didn't know what the clues pointed to or why my characters needed to behave strangely. This has become my first unbreakable rule of plotting.

My second unbreakable rule, to keep the plot as flexible as possible, may sound like a direct contradiction to the first. I found, however, that I had to be willing to modify my original solution or even throw it out and replace it with another when characters and events indicated this was necessary.

For example, I reached a point in my whodunit where all the loose ends were tying up nicely. Everything pointed to my chosen killer, his motives were coming clear, and my sleuth had won over the nasty police lieutenant by her clever use of logic. Elated, I took a break to count pages and realized that I was only halfway through the book!

This is the kind of situation in which you need all the flexibility you can muster. I looked over what I had written and concluded that this would be not only a very short book, but also a very boring one. Everything pointed clearly to the killer. His motives were too pat and ordinary. I began once more to play "what if."

What if, at the height of his bedazzlement with Sharon's logic, the police lieutenant receives a phone call, and then smugly announces to her that the supposed murderer himself was dead? That he was knifed in his own apartment, in fact, and that the apartment had been searched?

Of course, the answer was that I had to get myself a new killer. What if the sleazy bail bondsman that the victim had been consorting with . . . ? The new solution was more interesting all around, and it gave me the extra pages I needed.

Plot control

This experience taught me the difficulty of keeping the plot of a whodunit in hand even after you think you know what it is. I had to keep track of events that happened weeks, even years, before my opening action, all of which led up to the initial crime. There were also facts that had to be withheld from the reader as long as possible, and clues the reader had to be given. A number of characters were engaged in suspicious activities that may or may not have had something to do with the murder. How was I to keep track of all this?

Several mechanical devices helped. The first, a sketch of what really happened, was like a well-detailed short story. I started at the beginning of my mystery, two years before the murder, when the antique shop proprietor needed a great deal more money than her shop could bring in. I followed the course of events from there to the day she ended up dead on the shop floor, and finally ended the sketch with the arrest of her killer. The sketch was available for reference as my plot unfolded and the past was explained. And, in accordance with the flexibility rule, it was discarded and rewritten when the solution changed.

A second device was the sketch of each main character. While not as detailed as the biography of the heroine, it contained much the same types of information: background, important life events, outstanding physical and personality traits. These sketches helped me keep the characters' motivations in mind and to keep details about their lives consistent.

The most useful device for plot control was my time chart. It took the form of a grid, with major characters plotted across the top and chapters or time frames plotted down the side; it covered the same period as the sketch of what really happened.

In the squares under each character on the chart, I noted what he or she was doing during every time period. In this way, I avoided such embarrassing situations as finding that the murderer was really with my detective when he was supposed to have been doing in his second victim. I usually plotted only three to five chapters ahead at a time, finding that the things characters said and did often suggested new complications or scenes. However, I imagine this type of chart could be adapted nicely to complete preplanning as well.

The rewrite was my final check of how well my plot hung together. This was when I went back and inserted clues I had forgotten, brought out necessary facets of a suspect's character, and smoothed over inconsistencies and cut and cleaned up style. My experience with rewrites has been rewarding: the wicked-looking bone-handled knife which, as the murder weapon, plays a large part in my whodunit, didn't even exist until the rewrite, when a critic friend pointed out that a small paring knife made a pretty silly instrument of violent death.

During the final typing of the manuscript, I checked and rechecked my clues. I believe in playing fair with the reader, and I wanted to make sure I'd given him every clue Sharon came across in solving the case. Rather than have Sharon say: "I realized something that told me who the killer was," I had her carry on a mental conversation with Edwin, the heavy-footed mannequin. At its end, she says: "Edwin, why didn't you tell me?" The conversation provides the reader with all the clues he needs to solve the murders along with Sharon. And I will be delighted to hear of readers who solve my whodunit ahead of my sleuth!

—1978

THE PLACE THAT TIME FORGOT

In San Francisco's Glen Park district there is a small building with the words GREEN-GLASS 5 & 10¢ STORE painted in faded red letters on its wooden facade. Broadleaf ivy grows in planter boxes below its windows and partially covers their dusty panes. Inside is a counter with jars of candy and bubble gum on top and cigars, cigarettes, and pipe tobacco down below. An old-fashioned jukebox—the kind with colored glass tubes—hulks against the opposite wall. The rest of the room is taken up by counters laden with merchandise that has been purchased at fire sales and manufacturers' liquidations. In a single shopping spree, it is possible for a customer to buy socks, playing cards, off-brand cosmetics, school supplies, kitchen utensils, sports equipment, toys, and light bulbs—all at prices of at least ten years ago.

It is a place forgotten by time, a fragment of yesterday in the midst of today's city.

I have now come to know the curious little store well, but up until one rainy Wednesday last March, I'd done no more than glance inside while passing. But that morning Hank Zahn, my boss at All Souls Legal Cooperative, had asked me to pay a call on its owner, Jody Greenglass. Greenglass was a client who had asked if Hank knew an investigator who could trace a missing relative for him. It didn't sound like a particularly challenging assignment, but my assistant, who usually handles routine work, was out sick. So at ten o'clock, I put on my raincoat and went over there.

When I pushed open the door I saw there wasn't a customer in sight. The interior was gloomy and damp; a fly buzzed fitfully against one of the windows. I was about to call out, thinking the proprietor must be beyond the curtained doorway at the rear, when I realized a man was sitting on a stool behind the counter. That was all he was doing—just sitting, his eyes fixed on the wall above the jukebox.

He was a big man, elderly, with a belly that bulged out under his yellow shirt and black suspenders. His hair and beard were white and luxuriant, his eyebrows startlingly black by contrast. When I said, "Mr. Greenglass?" he looked at me, and I saw an expression of deep melancholy.

"Yes?" he asked politely.

"I'm Sharon McCone, from All Souls Legal Cooperative."

"Ah, yes. Mr. Zahn said he would send someone."

"I understand you want to locate a missing relative."

"My granddaughter."

"If you'll give me the particulars, I can get on it right away." I looked around for a place to sit, but didn't see any chairs.

Greenglass stood. "I'll get you a stool." He went toward the curtained doorway, moving gingerly, as if his feet hurt him. They were encased in floppy slippers.

While I waited for him, I looked up at the wall behind the counter and saw it was plastered with faded pieces of slick paper that at first I took to be playbills. Upon closer examination I realized they were sheet music, probably of forties and fifties vintage. Their artwork was of that era anyway: formally dressed couples performing intricate dance steps; showgirls in extravagant costumes; men with patent-leather hair singing their hearts out; perfectly coiffed women showing plenty of even, pearly white teeth. Some of the song titles were vaguely familiar to me: "Dreams of You," "The Heart Never Lies," "Sweet Mystique." Others I had never heard of.

Jody Greenglass came back with a wooden stool and set it on my side of the counter. I thanked him and perched on it, then took a pencil and notebook from my bag. He hoisted himself onto his own stool, sighing heavily.

"I see you were looking at my songs," he said.

"Yes. I haven't really seen any sheet music since my piano teacher gave up on me when I was about twelve. Some of those are pretty old, aren't they?"

"Not nearly as old as I am." He smiled wryly. "I wrote the first in thirty-nine, the last in fifty-three. Thirty-seven of them in all. A number were hits."

"*You* wrote them?"

He nodded and pointed to the credit line on the one closest to him: "Words and Music by Jody Greenglass."

"Well, for heaven's sake," I said. "I've never met a songwriter before. Were these recorded too?"

"Sure. I've got them all on the jukebox. Some good singers performed them—Como, Crosby." His smile faded. "But then, in the fifties, popular music changed. Presley, Holly, those fellows—that's what did it. I couldn't change with it. Luckily, I'd always had the store; music was more of a hobby for me. 'My Little Girl'"—he indicated a sheet with a picture-pretty toddler on it—"was the last song I ever sold. Wrote it for my granddaughter when she was born in fifty-three. It was *not* a big hit."

"This is the granddaughter you want me to locate?"

"Yes. Stephanie Ann Weiss. If she's still alive, she's thirty-seven now."

"Let's talk about her. I take it she's your daughter's daughter."

"My daughter Ruth's. I only had the one child."

"Is your daughter still living?"

"I don't know." His eyes clouded. "There was a . . . an estrangement. I lost track of both of them a couple of years after Stephanie was born."

"If it's not too painful, I'd like to hear about that."

"It's painful, but I can talk about it." He paused, thoughtful. "It's funny. For a long time it didn't hurt, because I had my anger and disappointment to shield myself. But those kinds of emotions can't last without fuel. Now that they're gone, I hurt as much as if it happened yesterday. That's what made me decide to try to make amends to my granddaughter."

"But not your daughter too?"

He made a hand motion as if to erase the memory of her. "Our parting was too bitter; there are some things that can't be atoned for, and frankly, I'm afraid to try. But Stephanie—if her mother hasn't completely turned her against me, there might be a chance for us."

"Tell me about this parting."

In a halting manner that conveyed exactly how deep his pain went, he related his story.

Jody Greenglass had been widowed when his daughter was only ten and had raised the girl alone. Shortly after Ruth graduated from high school, she married the boy next door. The Weiss family had lived in the house next to Greenglass's Glen Park cottage for close to twenty years, and their son, Eddie, and Ruth were such fast childhood friends that a gate was installed in the fence between their adjoining backyards. Jody, in fact, thought of Eddie as his own son.

After their wedding the couple moved north to the small town of Petaluma, where Eddie had found a good job in the accounting department of one of the big egg hatcheries. In 1953, Stephanie Ann was born. Greenglass didn't know exactly when or why they began having marital problems; perhaps they hadn't been ready for parenthood, or perhaps the move from the city to the country didn't suit them. But by 1955, Ruth had divorced Eddie and taken up with a Mexican national named Victor Rios.

"I like to think I'm not prejudiced," Greenglass said to me. "I've mellowed with the years, I've learned. But you've got to remember that this was the mid-fifties. Divorce wasn't all that common in my circle. And people like us didn't even marry outside our faith, much less form relationships out of wedlock with those of a different race. Rios was an illiterate laborer, not even an American citizen. I was shocked that Ruth was living with this man, exposing her child to such a situation."

"So you tried to stop her."

He nodded wearily. "I tried. But Ruth wasn't listening to me anymore. She'd always been such a good girl. Maybe that was the problem—she'd been *too* good and it was her time to rebel. We quarreled bitterly, more than once. Finally I told her that if she kept on living with Rios, she and her child would be dead to me. She said that was just fine with her. I never saw or heard from her again."

"Never made any effort to contact her?"

"Not until a couple of weeks ago. I nursed my anger and bitterness, nursed them well. But then in the fall I had some health problems—my heart—and realized I'd be leaving this world without once seeing my grown-up granddaughter. So when I was back on my feet again, I went up to Petaluma, checked the phone book, asked around their old neighborhood. Nobody remembered them. That was when I decided I needed a detective."

I was silent, thinking of the thirty-some years that had elapsed. Locating Stephanie Ann Weiss—or whatever name she might now be using—after all that time would be difficult. Difficult, but not impossible, given she was still alive. And certainly more challenging than the job I'd initially envisioned.

Greenglass seemed to interpret my silence as pessimism. He said, "I know it's been a very long time, but isn't there something you can do for me? I'm seventy-eight years old; I want to make amends before I die."

I felt the prickle of excitement that I often experience when faced with an out-of-the-ordinary problem. I said, "I'll try to help you. As I said before, I can get on it right away."

I gathered more information from him—exact spelling of names, dates—then asked for the last address he had for Ruth in Petaluma. He had to go in the back of the store where, he explained, he now lived, to look it up. While he did so, I wandered over to the jukebox and studied the titles of the 78s. There was a basket of metal slugs on top of the machine, and on a whim I fed it one and punched out selection E-3, "My Little Girl." The somewhat treacly lyrics boomed forth in a smarmy baritone; I could understand why the song hadn't gone over in the days when America was gearing up to feverishly embrace the likes of Elvis Presley. Still, I had to admit the melody was pleasing—downright catchy, in fact. By the time Greenglass returned with the address, I was humming along.

Back in my office at All Souls, I set a skiptrace in motion, starting with an inquiry to my friend Tracy at the Department of Motor Vehicles regarding Ruth Greenglass, Ruth Weiss, Ruth Rios, Stephanie Ann Weiss, Stephanie Ann Rios, or any variant thereof. A check with directory assistance revealed that neither woman currently had a phone in Petaluma or the surrounding communities. The Petaluma Library had nothing on them in their reverse street directory. Since I didn't know either woman's occupation, professional affiliations, doctor, or dentist, those avenues were closed to me. Petaluma High School would not divulge information about graduates, but the woman in Records with whom I spoke assured me that no one named Stephanie Weiss or Stephanie Rios had attended during the mid- to late-sixties. The county's voter registration had a similar lack of information. The next line of inquiry to pursue while waiting for a reply from the DMV was vital statistics—primarily marriage licenses and death certificates—but for those I would need to go to the Sonoma County Courthouse in Santa Rosa. I checked my watch, saw it was only a little after one, and decided to drive up there.

Santa Rosa, some fifty miles north of San Francisco, is a former country town that has risen to the challenge of migrations from the crowded communities of the Bay Area and become a full-fledged city with a population nearing a hundred thousand. Testimony to this is the new County Administration Center on its outskirts, where I found the Recorder's Office housed in a building on the aptly named Fiscal Drive.

My hour-and-a-half journey up there proved well worth the time: the clerk I dealt with was extremely helpful, the records easily accessed. Within half an hour, for a nominal fee, I was in possession of a copy of Ruth Greenglass Weiss's death certificate. She had died of cancer at Petaluma General Hospital in June of 1974; her next of kin was shown as Stephanie Ann Weiss, at an address on Bassett Street in Petaluma. It was a different address than the last one Greenglass had had for them.

The melody of "My Little Girl" was still running through my head as I drove back down the freeway to Petaluma, the southernmost community in the county. A picturesque river town with a core of nineteenth-century business buildings, Victorian homes, and a park with a bandstand, it is surrounded by little hills—which is what the Indian word *petaluma* means. The town used to be called the Egg Basket of the World, because of the proliferation of hatcheries such as the one where Eddie Weiss worked, but since the decline of the egg- and chicken-ranching businesses, it has become a trendy retreat for those seeking to avoid the high housing costs of San Francisco and Marin. I had friends there—people who had moved up from the city for just that reason—so I knew the lay of the land fairly well.

Bassett Street was on the older west side of town, far from the bland, treeless tracts that have sprung up to the east. The address I was seeking turned out to be a small white frame bungalow with a row of lilac bushes planted along the property line on either side. Their branches hung heavy with as yet unopened blossoms; in a few weeks the air would be sweet with their perfume.

When I went up on the front porch and rang the bell, I was greeted by a very pregnant young woman. Her name, she said, was Bonita Clark; she and her husband Russ had bought the house two years before from some people named Berry. The Berrys had lived there for at least ten years and had never mentioned anyone named Weiss.

I hadn't really expected to find Stephanie Weiss still in residence, but I'd hoped the present owner could tell me where she had moved. I said, "Do you know anyone on the street who might have lived here in the early seventies?"

"Well, there's old Mrs. Caubet. The pink house on the corner with all the rosebushes. She's lived here forever."

I thanked her and went down the sidewalk to the house she'd indicated. Its front yard was a thicket of rosebushes whose colors ranged from yellows to reds to a particularly beautiful silvery purple. The rain had stopped before I'd reached town, but not all that long ago; the roses' velvety petals were beaded with droplets.

Mrs. Caubet turned out to be a tall, slender woman with sleek gray hair, vigorous-looking in a blue sweatsuit and athletic shoes. I felt a flicker of amusement when I first saw her, thinking of how Bonita Clark had called her "old," said she'd lived there "forever." Interesting, I thought, how one's perspective shifts. . . .

Yes, Mrs. Caubet said after she'd examined my credentials, she remembered the Weisses well. They'd moved to Bassett Street in 1970. "Ruth was already ill with the cancer that killed her," she added. "Steff was only seventeen, but so grown-up, the way she took care of her mother."

"Did either of them ever mention a man named Victor Rios?"

The woman's expression became guarded. "You say you're working for Ruth's father?"

"Yes."

She looked thoughtful, then motioned at a pair of white wicker chairs on the wraparound porch. "Let's sit down."

We sat. Mrs. Caubet continued to look thoughtful, pleating the ribbing on the cuff of her sleeve between her fingers. I waited.

After a time she said, "I wondered if Ruth's father would ever regret disowning her."

"He's in poor health. It's made him realize he doesn't have much longer to make amends."

"A pity that it took until now. He's missed a great deal because of his stubbornness. I know; I'm a grandparent myself. And I'd like to put him in touch with Steff, but I don't know what happened to her. She left Petaluma six months after Ruth died."

"Did she say where she planned to go?"

"Just something about getting in touch with relatives. By that I assumed she meant her father's family in the city. She promised to write, but she never did, not even a Christmas card."

"Will you tell me what you remember about Ruth and Stephanie? It may give me some sort of lead, and besides, I'm sure my client will want to know about their lives after his falling-out with Ruth."

She shrugged. "It can't hurt. And to answer your earlier question, I have heard of Victor Rios. He was Ruth's second husband; although the marriage was a fairly long one, it was not a particularly good one. When she was diagnosed as having cancer, Rios couldn't deal with her illness, and he left her. Ruth divorced him, took back her first husband's name. It was either that, she once told me, or Greenglass, and she was even more bitter toward her father than toward Rios."

"After Victor Rios left, what did Ruth and Stephanie live on? I assume Ruth couldn't work."

"She had some savings—and, I suppose, alimony."

"It couldn't have been much. Jody Greenglass told me Rios was an illiterate laborer."

Mrs. Caubet frowned. "That's nonsense! He must have manufactured the idea, out of prejudice and anger at Ruth for leaving her first husband. He considered Eddie Weiss a son, you know. It's true that when Ruth met Rios, he didn't have as good a command of the English language as he might, but he did have a good job at Sunset Line and Twine. They weren't rich, but I gather they never lacked for the essentials."

It made me wonder what else Greenglass had manufactured. "Did Ruth ever admit to living with Rios before their marriage?"

"No, but it wouldn't have surprised me. She always struck me as a nonconformist. And that, of course, would better explain her father's attitude."

"One other thing puzzles me," I said. "I checked with the high school, and they have no record of Stephanie attending."

"That's because she went to parochial school. Rios was Catholic, and that's what he wanted. Ruth didn't care either way. As it was, Steff dropped out in her junior year to care for her mother. I offered to arrange home care so she might finish her education—I was once a social worker and knew how to go about it—but Steff said no. The only thing she really missed about school, she claimed, was choir and music class. She had a beautiful singing voice."

So she'd inherited her grandfather's talent, I thought. A talent I was coming to regard as considerable, since I still couldn't shake the lingering melody of "My Little Girl."

"How did Stephanie feel about her grandfather? And Victor Rios?" I asked.

"I think she was fond of Rios, in spite of what he'd done to her mother. Her feelings toward her grandfather I'm less sure of. I do remember that toward the end Steff had become very like her mother; observing that alarmed me somewhat."

"Why?"

"Ruth was a very bitter woman, totally turned in on herself. She had no real friends, and she seemed to want to draw Steff into a little circle from which the two of them could fend off the world together. By the time Steff left Petaluma she'd closed off, too, withdrawn from what few friends she'd been permitted. I'd say such bitterness in so young a woman is cause for alarm, wouldn't you?"

"I certainly would. And I suspect that if I do find her, it's going to be very hard to persuade her to reconcile with her grandfather."

Mrs. Caubet was silent for a moment, then said, "She might surprise you."

"Why do you say that?"

"It's just a feeling I have. There was a song Mr. Greenglass wrote in celebration of Steff's birth. Do you know about it?"

I nodded.

"They had a record of it. Ruth once told me that it was the only thing he'd ever given them, and she couldn't bear to take that away from Steff. Anyway, she used to play it occasionally. Sometimes I'd go over there, and Steff would be humming the melody while she worked around the house."

That didn't mean much, I thought. After all, I've been mentally humming it since that morning.

When I arrived back in the city I first checked at All Souls to see if there had been a response to my inquiry from my friend at the DMV. There hadn't. Then I headed for Glen Park to break the news about his daughter's death to Jody Greenglass, as well as to get some additional information.

This time there were a few customers in the store: a young couple poking around in Housewares; an older woman selecting some knitting yarn. Greenglass sat at his customary position behind the counter. When I gave him the copy of Ruth's death certificate, he read it slowly, then folded it carefully and placed it in his shirt pocket. His lips trembled inside his nest of fluffy white beard, but otherwise he betrayed no emotion. He said, "I take it you didn't find Stephanie Ann at that address."

"She left about six months after Ruth died. A neighbor thought she might have planned to go to relatives. Would that be the Weisses, do you suppose?"

He shook his head. "Norma and Al died within months of each other in the mid-sixties. They had a daughter, name of Sandra, but she married and moved away before Eddie and Ruth did. To Los Angeles, I think. I've no idea what her husband's name might be."

"What about Eddie Weiss—what happened to him?"

"I didn't tell you?"

"No."

"He died a few months after Ruth divorced him. Auto accident. He'd been drinking. Damned near killed his parents, following so close on the divorce. That was when Norma and Al stopped talking to me; I guess they blamed Ruth. Things got so uncomfortable there on the old street that I decided to come to live here at the store."

The customer who had been looking at yarn came up, her arms piled high with heather-blue skeins. I stepped aside so Greenglass could ring up the sale, glanced over my shoulder at the jukebox, then went up to it and played "My Little Girl" again. As the mellow notes poured from the machine, I realized that what had been running through my head all day was not quite the same. Close, very close, but there were subtle differences.

And come to think of it, why should the song have made such an impression, when I'd only heard it once? It was catchy, but there was no reason for it to haunt me as it did.

Unless I'd heard something like it. Heard it more than once. And recently . . .

I went around the counter and asked Greenglass if I could use his phone. Dialed the familiar number of radio KSUN, the Light of the Bay. My former lover, Don Del Boccio, had just come into the studio for his six-to-midnight stint as disc jockey, heartthrob, and hero to half a million teenagers who have to be either hearing-impaired or brain-damaged, and probably both. Don said he'd be glad to provide expert assistance, but not until he got off work. Why didn't I meet him at his loft around twelve-thirty?

I said I would and hung up, thanking the Lord that I somehow manage to remain on mostly good terms with the men from whom I've parted.

Don said, "Hum it again."

"You know I'm tone-deaf."

"You have no vocal capabilities. You can distinguish tone, though. And I can interpret your warbling. Hum it."

We were seated in his big loft in the industrial district off Third Street, surrounded by his baby grand piano, drums, sound equipment, books, and—a recent acquisition—a huge aquarium of tropical fish. I'd taken a nap after going home from Greenglass's and felt reasonably fresh. Don—a big, easygoing man who enjoys his minor celebrity status and also keeps up his serious musical interests—was reasonably wired. We were drinking red wine and picking at a plate of antipasto he'd casually thrown together.

"Hum it," he said again.

I hummed, badly, my face growing hot as I listened to myself.

He imitated me—on key. "It's definitely not rock, not with that tempo. Soft rock? Possibly. There's something about it . . . that sextolet—"

"That what?"

"An irregular rhythmic grouping. One of the things that makes it stick in your mind. Folk? Maybe country. You say you think you've been hearing it recently?"

"That's the only explanation I can come up with for it sticking in my mind the way it has."

"Hmm. There's been some new stuff coming along recently, out of L.A. rather than Nashville, that might . . . You listen to a country station?"

"KNEW, when I'm driving sometimes."

"Disloyal thing."

"I never listened to KSUN much, even when we . . ."

Our eyes met and held. We were both remembering, but I doubted if the mental images were the same. Don and I are too different; that was what ultimately broke us up.

After a moment he grinned and said, "Well, no one over the mental age of twelve does. Listen, what I guess is that you've been hearing a song that's a variation on the melody of the original one. Which is odd, because it's an uncommon one to begin with."

"Unless the person who wrote the new song knew the old one."

"Which you tell me isn't likely, since it wasn't very popular. What is it you're investigating—a plagiarism case?"

I shook my head. If Jody Greenglass's last song had been plagiarized, I doubted it was intentional—at least not on the conscious level. I said, "Is it possible to track down the song, do you suppose?"

"Sure. Care to run over to the studio? I can do a scan on our library, see what we've got."

"But KSUN doesn't play anything except hard rock."

"No, but we get all sorts of promos, new releases. Let's give it a try."

"There you are," Don said. "'It Never Stops Hurting.' Steff Rivers. Atlas Records. Released last November."

I remembered it now, half heard as I'd driven the city streets with my old MG's radio tuned low. Understandable that for her professional name she'd Anglicized that of the only father figure she'd ever known.

"Play it again," I said.

Don pressed the button on the console and the song flooded the sound booth, the woman's voice soaring and clean. The lyrics were about grieving for a lost lover, but I thought I knew other experiences that had gone into creating the naked emotion behind them: the scarcely known father who had died after the mother left him; the grandfather who had rejected both mother and child; the stepfather who had been unable to cope with fatal illness and had run away.

When the song ended and silence filled the little booth, I said to Don, "How would I go about locating her?"

He grinned. "One of the Atlas reps just happens to be a good friend of mine. I'll give her a call in the morning, see what I can do."

The rain started again early the next morning. It made the coastal road that wound north on the high cliffs above the Pacific dangerously slick. By the time I arrived at the village of Gualala, just over the Mendocino County line, it was close to three and the cloud cover was beginning to break up.

The town, I found, was just a strip of homes and businesses between the densely forested hills and the sea. A few small shopping centers, some unpretentious eateries, the ubiquitous realty offices, a new motel, and a hotel built during the logging boom of the late 1800s—that was about it. It would be an ideal place, I thought, for retirees or starving artists, as well as a young woman seeking frequent escape from the pressures of a career in the entertainment industry.

Don's record-company friend had checked with someone she knew in Steff Rivers's producer's office to find out her present whereabouts, had sworn me to secrecy about where I'd received the information and given me an address. I'd pinpointed the turnoff from the main highway on a county map. It was a small lane that curved off toward the sea about a half mile north of town; the house at its end was actually a pair of A frames, weathered gray shingle, connected by a glassed-in walkway. Hydrangeas and geraniums bloomed in tubs on either side of the front door; a stained glass oval depicting a sea gull in flight hung in the window. I left the MG next to a gold Toyota sports car parked in the drive.

There was no answer to my knock. After a minute I skirted the house and went around back. The lawn there was weedy and uneven; it sloped down toward a low grapestake fence that guarded the edge of the ice-plant-covered bluff. On a bench in front of it sat a small figure wearing a red rain slicker, the hood turned up against the fine mist. The person was motionless, staring out at the flat, gray ocean.

When I started across the lawn, the figure turned. I recognized Steff Rivers from the publicity photo Don had dug out of KSUN's files the night before. Her hair was black and cut very short, molded to her head like a bathing cap; her eyes were large, long-lashed, and darkly luminous. In her strong features I saw traces of Jody Greenglass's.

She called out, "Be careful there. Some damn rodent has dug the yard up."

I walked cautiously the rest of the way to the bench.

"I don't know what's wrong with it," she said, gesturing at a hot tub on a deck opening off the glassed-in walkway of the house. "All I can figure is something's plugging the drain."

"I'm sorry?"

"Aren't you the plumber?"

"No."

"Oh. I knew she was a woman, and I thought . . . Who are you, then?"

I took out my identification and showed it to her. Told her why I was there.

Steff Rivers seemed to shrink inside her loose slicker. She drew her knees up and hugged them with her arms.

"He needs to see you," I concluded. "He wants to make amends."

She shook her head. "It's too late for that."

"Maybe. But he *is* sincere."

"Too bad." She was silent for a moment, turning her gaze back toward the sea. "How did you find me? Atlas and my agent know better than to give out this address."

"Once I knew Stephanie Weiss was Steff Rivers, it was easy."

"And how did you find *that* out?"

"The first clue I had was 'It Never Stops Hurting.' You adapted the melody of 'My Little Girl' for it."

"I what?" She turned her head toward me, features frozen in surprise. Then she was very still, seeming to listen to the song inside her head. "I guess I did. My God . . . I *did!*"

"You didn't do it consciously?"

"No. I haven't thought of that song in years. I . . . I broke the only copy of the record that I had the day my mother died." After a moment she added, "I suppose the son of a bitch will want to sue me."

"You know that's not so." I sat down beside her on the wet bench, turned my collar up against the mist. "The lyrics of that song say a lot about you, you know."

"Yeah—that everybody's left me or fucked me over as long as I've lived."

"Your grandfather wants to change that pattern. He wants to come back to you."

"Well, he can't. I don't want him."

A good deal of her toughness was probably real—would have to be, in order for her to survive in her business—but I sensed some of it was armor that she could don quickly whenever anything threatened the vulnerable core of her persona. I remained silent for a few minutes, wondering how to get through to her, watching the waves ebb and flow on the beach at the foot of the cliff. Eroding the land, giving some of it back again. Take and give, take and give . . .

Finally I asked, "Why were you sitting out here in the rain?"

"They said it would clear around three. I was just waiting. Waiting for something good to happen."

"A lot of good things must happen to you. Your career's going well. This is a lovely house, a great place to escape to."

"Yeah, I've done all right. 'It Never Stops Hurting' wasn't my first hit, you know."

"Do you remember a neighbor of yours in Petaluma—a Mrs. Caubet?"

"God! I haven't thought of her in years either. How is she?"

"She's fine. I talked with her yesterday. She mentioned your talent."

"Mrs. Caubet. Petaluma. That all seems so long ago."

"Where did you go after you left there?"

"To my Aunt Sandra, in L.A. She was married to a record-company flack. It made breaking in a little easier."

"And then?"

"Sandra died of a drug overdose. She found out that the bastard she was married to had someone else."

"What did you do then?"

"What do you think? Kept on singing and writing songs. Got married."

"And?"

"What the hell is this and-and-and? Why am I even talking to you?"

I didn't reply.

"All right. Maybe I need to talk to somebody. That didn't work out—the marriage, I mean—and neither did the next one. Or about a dozen other relationships. But things just kept clicking along with my career. The money kept coming in. One weekend a few years ago I was up here visiting friends at Sea Ranch. I saw this place while we were just driving around, and . . . now I live here when I don't have to be in L.A. Alone. Secure. Happy."

"Happy, Steff?"

"Enough." She paused, arms tightening around her drawn-up knees. "Actually, I don't think much about being happy anymore."

"You're a lot like your grandfather."

She rolled her eyes. "Here we go again!"

"I mean it. You know how he lives? Alone in the back of his store. He doesn't think much about being happy either."

"He still has that store?"

"Yes." I described it, concluding, "It's a place that's just been forgotten by time. *He's* been forgotten. When he dies there won't be anybody to care—unless you do something to change that."

"Well, it's too bad about him, but in a way he had it coming."

"You're pretty bitter toward someone you don't even know."

"Oh, I know enough about him. Mama saw to that. You think *I'm* bitter? You should have known her. She'd been thrown out by her own father, had two rotten marriages, and then she got cancer. Mama was a very bitter, angry woman."

I didn't say anything, just looked out at the faint sheen of sunlight that had appeared on the gray water.

Steff seemed to be listening to what she'd just said. "I'm turning out exactly like my mother, aren't I?"

"It's a danger."

"I don't seem to be able to help it. I mean, it's all there in that song. It never *does* stop hurting."

"No, but some things can ease the pain."

"The store—it's in the Glen Park district, isn't it?"

"Yes. Why?"

"I get down to the city occasionally."

"How soon can you be packed?"

She looked over her shoulder at the house, where she had been secure in her loneliness. "I'm not ready for that yet."

"You'll never be ready. I'll drive you, go to the store with you. If it doesn't work out, I'll bring you right back here."

"Why are you doing this? I'm a total stranger. Why didn't you just turn my address over to my grandfather, let him take it from there?"

"Because you have a right to refuse comfort and happiness. We all have that."

Steff Rivers tried to glare at me but couldn't quite manage it. Finally—as a patch of blue sky appeared offshore and the sea began to glimmer in the sun's rays—she unwrapped her arms from her knees and stood.

"I'll go get my stuff," she said.

—1990

WALTER MOSLEY

B. 1952

Despite its highly formulaic structure, the American "hard-boiled" private investigator story has proved itself to be one of the most flexible vehicles for social commentary in all of popular fiction. Walter Mosley, for example, illustrates in his best-selling "Easy" Rawlins series how effectively the crime story can be used to examine the contemporary African-American experi-ence. Introduced in Mosley's first novel, Devil in a Blue Dress *(1990), Easy Rawlins begins work as a private investigator in 1948, after he loses his job. Hired by a white man to find a blonde woman named Daphne Monet, Rawlins soon discovers (in typical "hard-boiled" detective fashion) that appearances can be deceiving, and he soon gets more than he bargained for in earning his hundred dollar quick-money fee. As in Chandler's Philip Marlowe novels, Rawlins's base of operation is Los Angeles. Rawlins's "City of Angels" features a postwar, African-American inner-city setting; that is, his is an underclass world that is all too often defined by racial prejudice and senseless violence. Subsequent Easy Rawlins mystery novels include* A Red Death *(1991),* White Butterfly *(1992),* Black Betty *(1994), and* A Little Yellow Dog: An Easy Rawlins Mystery *(1996).*

Mosley's work has earned both critical and commercial success. Born in Los Angeles and educated at the City College of New York, Mosley worked as a computer programmer before turning to writing full time. He is cur-rently regarded as an important rising star in the newest generation of "hard-boiled" detective story authors, having won the Private Eye Writers of America's Shamus Award in 1990 for Devil in a Blue Dress. *He has also been ranked as among the most important African-American literary voices of the 1990s. Mosley's legion of fans include President Bill Clinton, who has publicly stated that the Rawlins novels are his favorite crime fic-tion.*

Originally published in The New Mystery *(1993), edited by Jerome Charyn, the Easy Rawlins short story entitled "The Watts Lions" explores the bleak world of marital violence. Issues of good and evil, once so clearly defined in the detective fiction of Arthur Conan Doyle and Agatha Christie, in Mosley's capable hands become clouded and problematic. RayJohn's murderous anger about the rape of his daughter is understandable, but his violent treatment of his daughter and his wife is unjustified, even mon-strous. Rawlins himself, the reader learns in the story, is not without his prejudices. He accepts employment as a bodyguard in order to be admitted to an African-American professional businessman's club, so that he, too, can find some measure of social acceptance in the white man's Los Angeles of 1955. Rawlins learns the hard way, however, that the respectable Watts Lions he has been hired to protect are something less than respectable.*

THE WATTS LIONS

"If you don't help, Mr. Rawlins, that RayJohn gonna kill us all," Bigelow said. He was the largest of the men sitting before us.

"That's right!" Mr. Mink shouted. "We gotta have us some p'otection from that crazy man!" He wore white painter's overalls and smelled strongly of turpentine.

Bledsoe, the third man, said nothing.

At the desk next to mine Mofass lit a match on a piece of sandpaper nailed to the wall behind. In the flare his fat, black and deeply lined face shone like a hideous tiki mask.

"You mean Raymond Johns?" I asked.

"He's gonna kill us, Mr. Rawlins. He already got Ornin." Mr. Mink spoke loudly enough to be heard across a football field.

"He means Ornin Levesque," Mofass said. The cool smoke of his cigar broke in a wave across my desk.

I nodded. Mofass stifled a cough.

"Well?" Bigelow asked.

"Well what?"

"What can you do to help us?"

I took a beat-up Lucky from my breast pocket.

"Gimme a light, Mofass," I said. And while he struck another match and leaned across the span of our desks, I asked, "Why would RayJohn wanna kill Ornin Levesque?"

"'Cause he crazy, that's why!" Mr. Mink shouted.

"So go to the po-lice. It's they job t'catch killers. They do that kinda work fo' free."

"They been to the police, Mr. Rawlins," Mofass said. "But RayJohn moved out his house an' all the police said was that if he come around botherin' them again that they should call back then."

It was 1955 and the police weren't too worried about colored murders.

"Why would RayJohn wanna kill anybody? He ain't all that crazy," I said, but I knew that he was.

"He is now!" Mr. Mink squealed.

"Now I'm gonna ask you boys again," I said. "Why would this man wanna kill you?"

"We sinned against him," Bledsoe whispered. His quiet eyes were focused on a point far behind my head.

"Don't listen to him, Easy." Bigelow put up his hand like a boy in school. "He's so upset over this killin' that he's a li'l crazy hisself."

"That's alright," I said. "*You* tell me."

"We was mindin' our own business, man. We was at the Lions when he come bustin' in there . . ."

The Watts Lions was a social club that some colored "professionals" had formed. Electricians, plumbers, real estate men (like Mofass) and other tradesmen. They didn't want to hear from *street niggers* like me. Of course they didn't know that I owned more property than the three of them combined. Mofass represented my apartment buildings but I still pretended to be his "assistant."

". . . it was that Olson-Turpin fight," Bigelow was saying. "RayJohn said that he laid a bet on Olson wit' Ornin. Three hundred dollars at four to one."

"An' you didn't pay?" I asked.

"We thought he was lyin' at first!" Mr. Mink screamed. Maybe he thought that if he yelled loud enough I'd believe his lies. "An' then we thought that it was Ornin's bet! Why should we pay just 'cause Ornin lost a bet?"

I was wondering whether or not to call him a liar when the coughing started. Mofass had developed a smoker's cough over the years. I told him that all that smoke was going to kill him but he blamed his health on the smog. He hacked long and loud, sounding like an engine that wouldn't turn over.

"He intends t'kill them," Mofass whispered after a long while.

I motioned my head at Bigelow. "Who says?"

"He told us hisself when he come over to the Lions. Then they found Ornin . . ." Bigelow paused. He put his thumbs in the pockets of his vest and stared at the floor.

I knew what he saw there.

On page fourteen the *Examiner* had reported that Ornin Levesque was found tied up, naked and spread-eagled, on his own bed. His mouth was stuffed full with cotton balls and taped shut. The flesh from his belly had been stripped off while he was still alive and plastered to the wall over his head. I could imagine RayJohn, the Louisiana halfbreed, stripping off a patch of Ornin's stomach and then walking to the head of the bed where he held the flesh tight until the blood scabbed up enough to hold. All the while Ornin, in pain and fear, trying to rip free of the knots at his wrists and ankles.

Then RayJohn would pick up his straight razor and go back to his grisly revenge. The report said that Ornin died from a heart attack and not his wounds. Just another way of saying that he was scared to death.

"So what do you want from me?" I asked.

"Save us, man!" Mr. Mink begged. "Save my life. You know I got fam'ly t'look after."

"We know that you do . . ." Bigelow moved his hands around as if he were trying to pick words out of the air. "Things. Things to help people out when the cops cain't . . ."

"They need protection, Mr. Rawlins," Mofass wheezed. "An' they willin' t'pay off the bet now even if they didn't know 'bout it."

I shook my head and said, "I don't know. T'get me t'go up against RayJohn would cost you boys sumpin'."

"How much?" Bigelow said. He reached for his back pocket to show me that he was serious.

"I don't know." I rubbed my chin. "Maybe be a lifetime membership in the Lions."

The Watts Lions were all middle-class craftsmen and minor professionals. They could look at me, or the hundred thousand men just like me, and feel that they were better—superior.

They wore gold-plated rings with platinum-embossed onyx emblems of a roaring lion. They had the respect of churches and white businessmen. As a group they had climbed to a higher social level than any black people I'd known.

Everybody wanted something. Bigelow and Mink wanted to live a little longer. Bledsoe looked like he wanted his mother to slap his face and tell him that everything was okay. I wanted to share the knowledge of my success among the company of my peers.

"I thought you wanted money," Bigelow said.

"I don't need money that bad, man. Shit! Raymond Johns' one'a the baddest men in L.A. If you want me t'stop him you gotta be willin' to get up off'a that membership."

"Let's do it," Mr. Mink whispered.

"Okay," Bigelow answered. I could barely hear him.

Bledsoe didn't say a word.

"An' maybe you could come across wit' five hundred dollars too," I said.

"Fi'e hunnert!" Mr. Bigelow roared.

"Listen, man, I need a li'l stake t'pay my dues."

They both agreed. They weren't happy though. I wasn't either.

My friends would have called me a fool. Three men in mortal danger, telling me what anybody could see was a lie and there I was blinded by the offer of their company.

I made a few calls and then invited my clients to come downstairs. We left Mofass hucking phlegm and wiping his tongue with a stained handkerchief. Mofass' office was on Hooper at the time. The street was empty at two o'clock on a Tuesday afternoon.

It was a glorious November day. The clouds were piled high on a mild desert wind. All the smoke and smog had blown away. The mountains were so clear that I could almost see the craggy valleys and pointy pines. I imagined that I could even hear a branch cracking . . .

"Get'own! Get'own!" I shouted.

The shots were weak echoes in the air. They sounded harmless, like a car back-firing down a country road. Mr. Mink shouted in fear and then, again, in pain. A sliver of granite, or maybe a ricochet, whizzed past my face.

"Goddammit!" Bigelow yelled and suddenly there was a .44-caliber pistol in his outstretched hand. He was behind Mofass' Pontiac, firing blindly in any direction the shots might have come from.

Mr. Mink was holding his calf. Thick blood oozed between his fingers. I tried to squeeze behind a bright yellow fire hydrant. It wasn't much, but it was all I could do.

Bledsoe didn't jump or try to hide. He just fell to his knees and let his head sag down.

Bigelow had shot all his cartridges and wasn't moving to reload. The streets were quiet except for Mr. Mink's moaning.

I got up into a crouch and sidled behind the Pontiac with Bigelow.

"You think I got 'im?" the fat man asked.

"Only if he gonna laugh to death; lookin' at you shootin' at shadows."

I hugged the side of Mofass' green car and caught a distorted glimpse of myself in the chrome. I looked like a grounded fish sucking at air. My eyes were big enough to see behind my head.

After a minute I stood up, cautiously. Bledsoe got up too. His navy blue pants were torn. His sad expression and raggedy knees made him look more like a boy than a man.

"You okay?" I asked him.

He just looked at me, the tears brimming in his sad eyes.

People were peeping out of their windows by then. A few brave souls ventured to their front doors. I hustled my future club brothers into my car and drove off before RayJohn came back to finish the job.

"What are we gonna do, Easy?" Mr. Mink cried. "That crazy man must be fol-lowin' us."

"Don't worry, Mink. I got places for all y'all." I drove on wondering how RayJohn knew to stake out Mofass' place.

I took Mr. Mink out to Primo Pena's house in the barrio. Primo's wife Flower knew how to dress a flesh wound.

I left Bigelow with Andre Lavender who had moved to Compton with his wife Juanita and their five-year-old boy.

I kept Bledsoe with me till last because I was worried about him and because I thought he was the one of them who might tell me the truth.

"What's wrong with you, man?" I asked Bledsoe. We were going down Avalon, to the safest place I knew.

"Nuthin'." With his knees hidden under the shadow of the dashboard and his dark blue suit and tie, Bledsoe almost looked like the notary public he was supposed to be.

"Then why didn't you hide when RayJohn shot at us?"

"Lord'll call me when I suffered enough to his will."

Bledsoe was a slight man. His dark blue suit seemed to be draped over wire. The bones of his eyebrows and cheeks protruded while the rest of his face drew back; black parchment stretched on a skull. He tried to smile at me but that failed.

"You wanna tell me why RayJohn is after you boys, Bled?"

"I'd like to thank you, Mr. Easy Rawlins, for he'pin' us brothers," he answered, then he nodded to himself. "Yes, I'd like to thank you, Mr. Easy Rawlins."

"Are you okay, Bled?"

He nodded in answer.

It was five-thirty by the time we made it to John Mckenzie's bar.

The side entrance to Targets was in an alley off of Cyprus. I led Bledsoe by the arm into the crowded bar. When I pushed open the swinging door that led to the private part of John's place the stony-eyed bartender looked up, but when he saw me he just waved.

Bledsoe and I went up to the second floor where we came to a small room that was adorned with an army cot, a straight-backed wooden chair and a sink.

"You stay here," I told the sad-eyed man. "John will bring you anything you need. Just ask'im when he comes up." I pointed in his face. "Now I don't want you to go nowhere, an' don't call nobody neither. Just sit in this room. Do you understand me?"

He sat down on the bed and nodded. It felt like I was talking to a dog.

Targets was a small bar but it was popular among my crowd: immigrants from southern Texas and Louisiana. The room, built to hold ninety, was populated by at least two hundred and fifty souls. People were drinking and shouting, blowing smoke and swaying to the tinny phonograph sounds of Billie Holiday. A woman yelled as I pushed open the swinging door. John was in the center of the room forcing Cedric Waters back by the lapels of his jacket.

"I'm'a kill the mothahfuckah, John! Ain't nobody gonna stop me!"

"You ain't gonna kill'im here, Cedric," John said firmly.

I noticed Jackson Blue leaning at the far end of the bar. Even though Jackson was a small man he stood out because he was blacker than waxed coal.

"Yes I will!" Cedric shouted and at the same time he threw a wild punch at John's jaw. Unluckily for Cedric that blow landed true. John cocked his head with almost the look of surprise on his stone face. Then he hit Cedric with a short left jab.

Cedric collapsed as if some great magician had suddenly snatched the bones from his body.

"Get this man outta here!" John shouted. Cedric's friends dragged the comatose man away. John strode through the crowd back toward his place behind the bar.

I stopped him before he got back to work. I put my arm around his shoulder, restraining him in a friendly fashion, and spoke into his ear, "I need a li'l help fo'a couple'a days, John. I put Nathaniel Bledsoe in yo' extra room upstairs."

"What you want me to do with'im?"

"Give'im some food if he need it. An' if he leaves tell me 'bout it. I think Raymond Johns wanna kill'im."

John nodded and made back toward his bar. The prospect of RayJohn didn't scare him. He faced death nearly every day in his trade.

After John was situated behind the bar I went over to Jackson Blue. I pointed at Jackson's empty glass and John filled it with sour mash.

"Obliged to ya, Easy," Jackson said after he'd downed the shot.

I pointed again and John poured.

"You know anything 'bout Raymond Johns?" I asked.

"You don't wanna mess wit' that boy, Easy. RayJohn on the warpath."

"Over what?"

"Easy, you just bought me a drink. Why I wanna send you into pain?"

When John saw that we were talking he went away.

"I take care'a myself, Jackson. Just tell me what you know."

"Alright," the little man shrugged. "They sayin' RayJohn kilt Ornin Levesque. They say Ray ain't gonna rest till he get a couple'a more'a them Watts Lions."

"Anybody know why he killed Ornin?"

"One story is that he didn't pay on a bet."

"That true?"

"I don't hardly think so."

"No?"

"Uh-uh," Jackson shook his head. "The word is that RayJohn found out that them boys took advantage of his daughter, Reba. Raped her pretty good, I hear."

"That the truth, Jackson?"

"Well I don't rightly know, but I do know that it would take sumpin' like that t'get RayJohn that mad."

"You know where I can find Raymond?"

Jackson stuck out his bottom lip and shook his head. "Don't know, Easy. He's hidin'. But he's pretty well known down in the hobo jungle. When he ain't got no place t' stay, they say he gets a box down there."

"Where's Reba then?"

"She wit' Selma. They got a place down on Crenshaw." Jackson laughed. "You know Ray ain't lived wit' them in ten years, since Reba was five. I guess it takes a tragedy to bring a fam'ly back together."

The hobo jungle was a big empty lot behind Metropolitan High School, downtown. It was about four square blocks in area and undeveloped so the earth was soft enough for a man's back. The unfortunates who stayed there would go to the nearby Sears-Roebuck and find a cardboard box from a refrigerator or other large appliance and use that for their home.

I stood at the edge of the jungle at about midnight. Here and there faint lights outlined the cardboard structures but, by and large, the lot was dark.

"Hello, mister," someone said. It was a little man with a blanket wrapped around his shoulders. When he looked up his face was revealed in the faint light. He was a brown man. Not a Negro but a white man who had spent so much time outside that he had weathered. He was hunched over and barefoot. His left eye winked at odd intervals and a coarse dank odor hung around him.

"Got a quarter for an old soldier?" he asked and winked.

"Maybe," I said. That got him to smile. "I might even have a dollar."

That got him grinning, winking and smelling like a pig in shit.

"I'm lookin' fo' somebody," I said.

"No girls down here, mister. An' if there was you wouldn't want 'em."

"Lookin' for a man. A Negro, halfbreed. Raymond Johns is his name."

The derelict grinned. He had a full set of teeth. They were as brown as his skin.

"RayJohn's a regular down here," he said. "He stays over on the colored side mostly. I could show you."

He held his hand out courteously and I went before him.

We made our way between the tents and flat beds of cardboard. Here and there a hand or foot stuck out. The smell of urine was everywhere. I could hear men scratching and moaning, snoring and talking. One man must have had a woman in his box, either that or he was dreaming pretty good about one.

The brown man kept talking about RayJohn and what a nice guy he was and how much he could use that dollar.

"Yeah, I sure could, sure could use a little Tokay right now," he said. "Eighty-nine cents buys you a whole quart. Bet you RayJohn would like that. Yeah, I sure . . ."

It was because he stopped talking that I turned around. I saw a man to my left throw something that looked like a brass globe. Somebody shouted, "Get 'im!" I ducked under the missile and heard the groan of a man on the other side of me. Two hands grabbed my ankles. I swung my fist downward but I don't know if I hit him because a board split itself on my back right then. There were at least five men on me. I kept swinging but they were at close quarters with me so the blows I threw were pretty much useless. Then there came a bright pain in the middle of my forehead and, for a moment, darkness.

"I got it," the brown man shouted. Suddenly I could see him running toward the outskirts of the jungle. I moved to run after him but tripped over the box that the sounds of love came from. The box ripped open and an angry, naked white man swarmed out at me. I grabbed half the plank I'd been hit with and brandished it. That slowed his pace.

I said, "Hey, man, listen, I'm sorry."

The torn crate revealed a slim brown girl. The white man hesitated and then crawled back into the box with her, pulling the tatters of cardboard over them.

The thieves were gone. So was my wallet. Sixteen dollars, a social security card and my driver's license. I wasn't mad at being robbed. I was mad because I was a fool to be out there in the first place. I was a fool to protect rapists, to look for RayJohn. I was a fool to want to be a Watts Lion. Shit! I was a fool to be a black man in a white man's world.

Fool though I was I still rummaged around looking for the killer. I carried two half-pound stones, one in either hand, in case I was attacked again. But I went unmolested. I found the colored side of the jungle but RayJohn hadn't been there in weeks.

The next morning I checked on Bledsoe. He was in the same position he'd been in the night before; sitting on the cot and nodding. John told me he hadn't eaten but I didn't care if a rapist wanted to starve.

I drove out to Primo's next.

By then Primo and Flower had their dreamhouse. It was a two-story wood-frame house with a fake Victorian facade. Everywhere there were flowers. Roses, begonias, dahlias, asters, sweet pea vines on a trellis. Row after row of flowering bushes and trees.

I knew when I saw the police car parked across the street that Mr. Mink was dead. The policemen and a few civilians were in the Jewish graveyard that sat across from Primo's house. It was an old graveyard reflecting how the neighborhood had changed.

I walked in like the other curiosity seekers. Primo and I saw each other but we didn't talk. The short, stout Mexican looked at me apologetically.

Behind a great stone at the top of a hill they'd found Mr. Mink. His throat was slashed so terribly that the ligaments in his neck were severed. His head lay back from the open neck like the hinged lid of a trash can.

His clothes were torn and there were bruises on his face from the beating he got before he was killed. Flower's bandage was still wrapped around his calf.

The man climbing into the side window of the Lavender house wasn't tall but his short sleeves revealed the arms of a titan. I saw him reach to lift the window silently as I opened the car door. He raised his foot into the window as I raced as quietly as I could across Andre's lawn. It was just when RayJohn turned, his legs already in the house, that he saw me.

I grabbed his shirt and shin and yanked him from the house. He fell to the ground like a cat, rolling into his crouch. Then I hit RayJohn with a solid right hand.

I could have just as well socked a tree.

I saw RayJohn's fist coming but I didn't feel it. I was just opening my eyes, flat on my back, when I saw three things. The first was Ray standing over me still crouching, but this time he had the second thing I saw in his hand. That was a vicious-looking hunter's knife. Just when I knew that that knife would be my end I saw a big, fat, jiggly belly come running down the path to the side of the house. Then a yell full of fear and the belly collided with my death stroke.

RayJohn rolled away and kept on running. I watched him go down the street but I didn't go after him. We'd had our duel and I was a dead man. I even waved him good-bye.

"I'm cut!" Andre yelled. He stood there above me, nude to the waist and bleeding pretty well from his left forearm. Skinny little Juanita and porky Andre Jr. came to him and wrapped his wound in their own shirts. I wanted to get up and help but the strength had gone out of me.

When I knocked there was no answer so I began to work the lock with my pocket knife.

"Who's that?" a woman shouted when I almost had the door open.

"It's me, Selma, Easy Rawlins."

"Why you breakin' in my house, Easy?"

It wasn't really a house. It was a renovated storeroom above the rear of a pawnshop on Crenshaw Boulevard, but I said, "I'm tryin' t'keep some men from gettin' killed by that crazy old man'a yours."

The door opened a crack. Selma put her face there and I pushed my way in. She didn't fight it, just backed away hanging her head. Selma was a big woman. Rose-brown in color, she had Ethiopian features.

Reba was spread out on the couch. Her face bore the same marks as Mr. Mink. Bruises and cuts. Her hands were wrapped in blood-soaked gauze. Both eyes were swollen to slimy slits.

"Huh huh huh," she cried, a blind salamander dropped into the sun's harsh light.

"Shush now," Selma said, going to the girl, stroking her hair. "It's just Easy Rawlins. It's okay."

"They do this?" I asked.

"What you want, Easy?" Selma asked. I noticed that she had a mouse under her own eye.

"What happened to her?"

"Why? You wanna do sumpin' 'bout it? You wanna save her?"

"What happened?"

Reba moaned. She had her father's buff skin color and she was slight. I wondered that the violence perpetrated on that slim body didn't kill her.

"Shut up!" Selma said. She was talking to Reba. "Women get beat! Women get fucked! An' cryin' just make it worse!"

She kept stroking the girl tenderly as she ranted.

"You kept t'home wouldn't none'a this happened in the first place!" she cried. "But ain't no use in cryin' now!"

I noticed that the furniture in the house was overturned and that shards of broken plates littered the floor. On the far wall to my left someone had flung a plate of spaghetti. The red stain was scrawled over by drying pasta worms.

"Just shut up!" Selma told her daughter.

"Those men at the Lions do this?" I asked again.

"They did worse than that," a voice said.

I can't say that I was scared at that moment. I only feel fear when there is some chance that I might survive.

"I didn't know, RayJohn," I said to the man behind me.

"Daddy, no!" Reba cried.

"Get yo' ass outta here!" Selma stood in front of her daughter. She pushed her shoulders forward and put her hands behind her, wrapped in the folds of her house coat.

"Calm down now, baby. I'm just here fo' Easy. He's gonna take me into Targets so I can have a talk with Nathaniel Bledsoe."

"No, Daddy. Please . . ." Reba got up from the couch holding her hands in front of her.

Selma went right up to RayJohn and started shouting.

"Get the fuck outta my house, niggah! Get out! Ain't you hurt her enough!"

It came clear to me that RayJohn had somehow found out about what happened to his daughter and he'd beaten her for being raped.

"Get outta my way, Selma." RayJohn sounded calm, but it was the kind of calm that preceded violence.

She bulled against him with her chest and shouted curses in his face.

I was hoping that she'd back off because I felt pretty sure that I could get the help I needed to stop the maniac at Targets. But I had no desire to take him on trying to save Selma's life.

"I say get yo' ass outta here!" Selma yelled.

"I'm'a have t'hurt you girl. Stand back now."

"Hurt me! Okay! Yeah, hurt me! Put yo' coward's fist there!" Selma pointed at her own jaw. RayJohn obliged with a solid slap that would have killed a smaller woman, or man. But Selma simply listed to the side. She drove her hand deep into the pocket of her house coat. Reba cried, "Momma!" The flash of the steak knife disappeared instantly, deeply into RayJohn's chest. The surprise on his face would have been comical in the movies. Maybe if he wasn't surprised, if he had believed that a woman could fight to save her own, he might have survived. But while RayJohn was gaping that blade flashed four times, five, six. When he fell to the floor he was already dead. I didn't see any reason to pull her off.

Bledsoe sat with his back against the wall on the cot. He hugged his knees to his chest and nodded slightly.

I asked him, "Why?"

He smiled.

The police didn't take Selma to jail. When they saw Reba they figured that it was self-defense. I didn't argue with them.

"Why, man?" I asked again.

"What?" He grinned at me.

"You know, Bled. You the one called RayJohn an' told him 'bout Reba. You the one told 'im where t'find Biggs and Mink too. You the one had him waitin' outside Mofass' place. Had to be you."

"I told 'em when that girl started t'fightin' that it was wrong."

"They raped her, really?"

"She was playin' at first. It was late en' they had some drinks. But when Ornin started to pull at her dress she got scared. Then Bigelow exposed hisself . . . That ain't right." Bledsoe stared off into space again.

I don't know if they would have ever let me join the Watts Lions. I never asked. I went to the funerals though. Ornin Levesque and Gregory Mink were buried at the same service.

Raymond Johns was interred the next day. There were only four people there. Selma was dressed in a nice blue two-piece suit. Reba's eyes had opened like a newborn kitten's. I stayed in the back and watched Nathaniel Bledsoe with his arms around both ladies. I remember wondering which one he would marry.

—1993

CRITICAL BIBLIOGRAPHY

Allen, Dick, and David Chacko. *Detective Fiction: Crime and Compromise.* New York: Harcourt Brace Jovanovich, 1974.

Bargainnier, Earl F., ed. *10 Women of Mystery.* Bowling Green: BGSU Popular P, 1981.

——, ed. *Twelve Englishmen of Mystery.* Bowling Green: BGSU Popular P, 1984.

Cassiday, Bruce, ed. *Roots of Detection: The Art of Deduction Before Sherlock Holmes.* New York: Frederick Ungar, 1983.

DeAndrea, William L. *Encyclopedia Mysteriosa.* New York: Prentice Hall, 1994.

Dove, George N. *The Police Procedural.* Bowling Green: BGSU Popular P, 1982.

Geherin, David. *The American Private Eye: The Image in Fiction.* New York: Frederick Ungar, 1985.

——. *Sons of Sam Spade: The Private-Eye Novel in the 70s.* New York: Frederick Ungar, 1980.

Goulart, Ron. *The Dime Detectives.* New York: Mysterious Press, 1988.

Haycraft, Howard, ed. *The Art of the Mystery Story.* 1946; New York: Carroll & Graf, 1992.

——. *Murder for Pleasure: The Life and Times of the Detective Story.* 1941; New York: Carroll & Graf, 1984.

Henderson, Lesley, ed. *Twentieth-Century Crime and Mystery Writers.* 3rd ed. Chicago: St. James, 1991.

Hoppenstand, Gary, and Ray B. Browne, eds. *The Defective Detective in the Pulps.* Bowling Green: BGSU Popular P, 1983.

Jakubowski, Maxim, ed. *100 Great Detectives: or The Detective Directory.* New York: Carroll & Graf, 1991.

Keating, H. R. F. *The Bedside Companion to Crime.* New York: Mysterious Press, 1989.

Klein, Kathleen Gregory. *The Woman Detective: Gender & Genre.* 2nd ed. Urbana: U of Illinois P, 1995.

Mann, Jessica. *Deadlier Than the Male: An Investigation into Feminine Crime Writing.* Newton Abbot: David & Charles, 1981.

Marling, William. *The American Roman Noir: Hammett, Cain, and Chandler.* Athens: U of Georgia P, 1995.

Nolan, William F., ed. *The Black Mask Boys: Masters in the Hard-Boiled School of Detective Fiction.* New York: William Morrow, 1985.

Panek, LeRoy Lad. *An Introduction to the Detective Story.* Bowling Green: BGSU Popular P, 1987.

——. *Watteau's Shepherds: The Detective Novel in Britain, 1914–1940.* Bowling Green, BGSU Popular P, 1979.

Penzler, Otto, Chris Steinbrunner, and Marvin Lachman, eds. *Detectionary: A Biographical Dictionary of Leading Characters in Mystery Fiction.* Woodstock: Overlook Press, 1977.

Peterson, Audrey. *Victorian Masters of Mystery: From Wilkie Collins to Conan Doyle.* New York: Frederick Ungar, 1984.

Roberts, Garyn, ed. *A Cent a Story!: The Best from Ten Detective Aces.* Bowling Green: BGSU Popular P, 1986.

——. *Dick Tracy and American Culture: Morality and Mythology, Text and Context.* Jefferson: McFarland, 1993.

Steinbrunner, Chris, and Otto Penzler. *Encyclopedia of Mystery & Detection.* New York: McGraw-Hill, 1976.

Symons, Julian. *Bloody Murder: From the Detective Story to the Crime Novel.* New York: Mysterious Press, 1993.

5

ADVENTURE
FICTION

The adventure story may be one of the easiest categories of popular fiction for readers to recognize, yet it is also one of the hardest to define. Part of the problem in classifying the popular tale of adventure as a distinct (and distinctive) literary genre is that, unlike many of the other major popular fiction genres, it has few obvious definitional boundaries. In fact, the other genres of popular fiction may exhibit some elements commonly found in adventure fiction. Certain types of crime fiction, for example, such as the "hard-boiled" detective story, look a great deal like adventure fiction. Carroll John Daly, who invented the "hard-boiled" detective story in the American pulp magazines of the 1920s, wrote crime fiction that could easily pass for "shoot-em-up" Westerns. Replace Daly's urban settings for the frontier, clothe Daly's two-fisted detective hero, Race Williams, in traditional Western garb, alter Daly's tough-guy lingo in his detective fiction for the frontier vernacular common to the popular Western, and the distinctions between the crime story and the adventure story become transparent. The fact, however, that a particular tale possesses some narrative elements of adventure does not necessarily mean that it is an adventure story.

This being the case, the adventure story does possess a few readily identifiable characteristics that should be collectively present in order for a story to be classified as a discrete literary type. Perhaps the most important quality to be found in popular adventure fiction, as suggested by its name, is adventure. The adventure story, in fact, tends to de-emphasize the importance of characterization, while emphasizing the role of narrative action. Michael Crichton does not want detailed character descriptions or lengthy passages involving his protagonists' personal introspections to interfere with his skilled use of slam-bang action, so when writing his latest techno-thriller, Crichton sacrifices the one for the other. Crichton thus fabricates his heroes, Ian Malcolm and Sarah Harding in *The Lost World* (1995), from white cardboard, and his villain, Lewis Dodgson, from black cardboard, so as not to complicate or diminish the novel's nail-biting suspense. Crichton obviously prefers a brisk narrative pacing over characterization in his fiction, and such a choice has brought him much success on the international best-seller lists.

The adventure story also typically features a larger-than-life hero as its protagonist. Whether this hero is Edgar Rice Burroughs's Tarzan of the Apes, Ian Fleming's James Bond, or Baroness Orczy's Scarlet Pimpernel, the single defining quality evident in the actions of all the great adventure heroes is their ability to conquer their adversaries. This is the reason why the dramatic conflict in many adventure stories is structured as a series of traps and escapes. The adventure hero demonstrates great courage, strength, or intelligence by escaping imminent destruction at the hands of a villain or by a harsh environment. At a larger, thematic level, the adventure hero's conquest of danger becomes a symbolic conquest of human mortality. Death, ultimately, is the adventure hero's greatest foe, and when certain death is thwarted by the hero's actions in Clive Cussler's latest Dirk Pitt adventure, for example, we as readers celebrate with Pitt the temporary defeat of an otherwise implacable fate.

The origins of the adventure story in popular fiction may be located in the novels of British authors Daniel Defoe (1660–1731) and Walter Scott (1771–1832). Defoe, considered by historians of English literature to be an early inventor of the novel, helped to establish a number of the conventions found in the modern adventure story, as illustrated in works such as *Robinson Crusoe* (1719) and *Adventures of Captain Singleton* (1720). Defoe was among the first authors of fiction to use descriptive action as a crucial narrative device in the structuring of plot, which is also one of the defining characteristics of modern adventure fiction. In addition, some of Defoe's work features an adventure hero who facilitates or manages a story's narrative action. Walter Scott expanded upon Defoe's earlier efforts by combining historical fact with the writing of adventure fiction. Considered to be the inventor of the historical adventure novel, Scott's popular books, including *Waverley* (1814), *Rob Roy* (1817), and *Ivanhoe* (1819), established an ideological understanding of heroism and the hero's obligations to a chivalric code in the popular consciousness of his many readers. Scott's work influenced a considerable number of important nineteenth-century novelists, from James Fenimore Cooper in America, to Alexandre Dumas in France, to Robert Louis Stevenson in Scotland and England.

Collectively, all of the stories that can be considered adventure fiction, and, indeed, all of the stories collected in this chapter, have descended from these two basic traditions: Defoe's contemporary adventure story and Scott's historical adventure story. The popular adventure fiction reprinted in this chapter has been selected for several reasons—first, because these tales sample the work of some of the most commercially successful authors of the English language, and second, because these tales also embody the wide variety of contemporary and historical adventure stories.

Representing historical adventure fiction are Westerns written by three grand masters of the genre—Zane Grey's "From Missouri," Max Brand's "The Ghost," and

Louis L'Amour's "The Gift of Cochise." Also representing the historical adventure story are tales featuring three of the most famous adventure heroes of all time—H. Rider Haggard's Allan Quatermain in "Long Odds," Baroness Orczy's Scarlet Pimpernel in "Two Good Patriots," and Rafael Sabatini's Captain Blood in "The Treasure Ship." Assembled from the general category of contemporary adventure fiction are stories highlighting other great adventure heroes, such as Edgar Rice Burroughs's Tarzan of the Apes in the jungle adventure, "The Battle for Teeka," and Ian Fleming's James Bond in the spy adventure, "From a View to a Kill." And exemplifying the soldier-of-fortune adventure are Rudyard Kipling's "The Man Who Would Be King" and Jack London's "The Taste of the Meat." All of these distinctive, yet thematically related, tales of adventure fiction epitomize what is one of the most entertaining—and least critically understood—genres of popular fiction.

H. RIDER HAGGARD
1856-1925

The modern adventure story in popular fiction begins with H. Rider Haggard's publication of King Solomon's Mines *(1885). This exotic tale of three intrepid explorers who traverse the proverbial heart of Africa and discover the legendary diamond mines of King Solomon has enjoyed much success over the past century in numerous reprintings and translations.* King Solomon's Mines—*along with Haggard's other adventure romance,* She *(1887)—inspired an entire generation of popular writers, such as Edgar Rice Burroughs, Arthur Conan Doyle, and A. Merritt, and created numerous literary conventions in adventure and fantasy fiction, like the often-imitated "lost world" adventure. Along with contemporary Rudyard Kipling, Haggard's great success at writing exciting "blood and thunder" yarns established him as a household name during the late Victorian period in English literature. Interestingly, Haggard's defense of the adventure romance in his essay, "About Fiction," published in the February 1887 issue of* The Contemporary Review, *created quite a stir among literary critics of the period because of his pointed attack against the naturalistic school of fiction then in vogue. During the remainder of his career as a popular writer, Haggard's work was vilified by those critics who were offended by his ill-timed remarks in "About Fiction." The controversy that resulted from this essay represents one of the earliest hostile debates between the advocates of popular fiction and those of "elite" fiction.*

Born in Bradenham, Norfolk, England, H. Rider Haggard trained to be a lawyer. He eventually relocated to South Africa, where he served as secretary, from 1875 until 1877, to Sir Henry Bulwer, the Lieutenant-Governor of Natal, and later, worked on the staff of Sir Theophilus Shepstone, the Special Commissioner in the Transvaal. His experiences in Africa during this period of his life eventually were to provide him with background material for a number of his novels. Haggard returned to England in 1879, where he tried his hand at politics among other occupations. He published his first novel, Dawn, *in 1884, but it was not until the publication of* King Solomon's Mines *and* She *that he achieved his reputation as a topflight author of adventure romances. Agriculture was also among Haggard's many interests, and he wrote several books about the topic, including* A Farmer's Year *(1899) and* A Gardener's Year *(1905). He was knighted in England in 1912.*

"Long Odds" is one of Haggard's handful of short tales featuring his fearless hunter and adventure seeker, Allan Quatermain. It first appeared in the February 1886 issue of Macmillan's Magazine *and later was reprinted in* Allan's Wife *(1889). Haggard, in fact, wrote an entire series of Quatermain adventures, beginning with* King Solomon's Mines *and continuing in* Allan Quatermain *(1887),* The Treasure of the Lake *(1926),* The Ancient Allan *(1920), and* Allan and the Ice Gods *(1927), among others. In developing Allan Quatermain as a series hero, Haggard initially made the same misstep as did American author James Fenimore Cooper when Cooper began writing his Leather-Stocking frontier novels. Cooper and Haggard introduced their respective heroes in the twilight years of the characters' lives. Cooper's Natty Bumppo, when the reader first meets him in* The Pioneers *(1823), is an old frontiersman. When first seen in* King Solomon's Mines, *Haggard's Quatermain, is also a grizzled, veteran hunter who is then killed off in Haggard's sequel,* Allan Quatermain. *Because popular demand compelled both Cooper and Haggard to return to the literary environs of Natty Bumppo and Allan Quatermain, each author had to reconstruct distinctly unromantic protagonists into more youthful, and hence more appealing, heroes. Thus, in Cooper's second published Leather-Stocking novel,* The Last of the Mohicans *(1826), and in Haggard's third published Quatermain novel,* Maiwa's Revenge *(1888), this somewhat inadvertent process of rejuvenation became an unplanned metaphor representing the adventure hero's ongoing triumph over death.*

Haggard successfully borrowed narrative elements from the earlier literary efforts of Daniel Defoe in creating his Quatermain stories. Defoe's Robinson Crusoe *is a believable hero, and the reader will note in "Long Odds" that Haggard deliberately masks Quatermain's heroism in rather plain packaging. Quatermain's physical appearance is decidedly unheroic, as are his occasional irrational actions and sometimes frequent expressions of fear during the course of his wondrous adventures. Indeed, what made the Quatermain series so appealing to a Victorian audience was Haggard's decision to assemble his hero from common fabric, which thus made the character more accessible to middle-class readers. When the common Quatermain becomes entangled in uncommon exploits, the thematic contrast is striking. In "Long Odds," for example, the story opens in the comfortable setting of Quatermain's home in Yorkshire, before transporting the reader to the exotic wilds of Haggard's Africa.*

About Fiction

The love of romance is probably coeval with the existence of humanity. So far as we can follow the history of the world we find traces of it and its effects among every people, and those who are acquainted with the habits and ways of thought of savage races will know that it flourishes as strongly in the barbarian as in the cultured breast. In short, it is like the passions, an innate quality of mankind. In modern England this love is not by any means dying out, as must be clear, even to that class of our fellow-countrymen who, we are told, are interested in nothing but politics and religion. A writer in the *Saturday Review* computed not long ago that the yearly output of novels in this country is about eight hundred; and probably he was within the mark. It is to be presumed that all this enormous mass of fiction finds a market of some sort, or it would not be produced. Of course a large quantity of it is brought into the world at the expense of the writer, who guarantees or deposits his thirty or sixty pounds, which in the former case he is certainly called upon to pay, and in the latter he never sees again. But this deducted, a large residue remains, out of which a profit must be made by the publisher, or he would not publish it. Now, most of this crude mass of fiction is worthless. If three-fourths of it were never put into print the world would scarcely lose a single valuable idea, aspiration, or amusement. Many people are of opinion in their secret hearts that they could, if they thought it worth while to try, write a novel that would be very good indeed, and a large number of people carry this opinion into practice without scruple or remorse. But as a matter of fact, with the exception of perfect sculpture, really good romance writing is perhaps the most difficult art practised by the sons of men. It might even be maintained that none but a great man or woman can produce a *really* great work of fiction. But great men are rare, and great works are rarer still, because all great men do not write. If, however, a person is intellectually a head and shoulders above his or her fellows, that person is *primâ facie* fit and able to write a good work. Even then he or she may not succeed, because in addition to intellectual pre-eminence, a certain literary quality is necessary to the perfect flowering of the brain in books. Perhaps, therefore, the argument would stand better conversely. The writer who can produce a noble and lasting work of art is of necessity a great man, and one who, had fortune opened to him any of the doors that lead to material grandeur and to the busy pomp of power, would have shown that the imagination, the quick sympathy, the insight, the depth of mind, and the sense of order and proportion which went to constitute the writer would have equally constituted the statesman or the general. It is not, of course, argued that only great writers should produce books, because if this was so publishing as a trade would come to an end, and Mudie would be obliged to put up his shutters. Also there exists a large class of people who like to read, and to whom great books would scarcely appeal. Let us imagine the consternation of the ladies of England if they were suddenly forced to an exclusive fare of George Eliot and Thackeray! But it *is* argued that a large proportion of the fictional matter poured from the press into the market is superfluous, and serves no good purpose. On the contrary, it serves several distinctly bad ones. It lowers and vitiates the public taste, and it obscures the true ends of fiction. Also it brings the high and honourable profession of authorship into contempt and disrepute, for the general public, owing perhaps to the comparative poverty of literary men, has never yet quite made up its mind as to the status of their profession. Lastly, this over-production stops the sale of better work without profiting those who are responsible for it.

The publication of inferior fiction can, in short, be of no advantage to any one, except perhaps the proprietors of circulating libraries. To the author himself it must indeed be a source of nothing but misery, bitterness, and disappointment, for only those who have written one can know the amount of labour involved in the production of even a bad book. Still, the very fact that people can be found to write and publishers to publish to such an unlimited extent, shows clearly enough the enormous appetite of readers, who are prepared, like a diseased ostrich, to swallow stones, and even carrion, rather than not get their fill of novelties. More and more, as what we call culture spreads, do men and women crave to be taken out of themselves. More and more do they long to be brought face to face with Beauty, and stretch out their arms towards that vision of the Perfect, which we only see in books and dreams. The fact that we, in these latter days, have as it were macadamized all the roads of life does not make the world softer to the feet of those who travel through it. There are now royal roads to everything, lined with staring placards, whereon he who runs may learn the sweet uses of advertisement; but it is dusty work to follow them, and some may think that our ancestors on the whole found their voyaging a shadier and fresher business. However this may be, a weary public calls continually for books, new books to make them forget, to refresh them, to occupy minds jaded with the toil and emptiness and vexation of our competitive existence.

In some ways this demand is no doubt a healthy sign. The intellect of the world must be awakening when it thus cries aloud to be satisfied. Perhaps it is not a good thing to read nothing but three-volumed novels of an inferior order, but it, at any rate, shows the possession of a certain degree of intelligence. For there still exists among us a class of educated people, or rather of people who have had a certain sum of money spent upon their education, who are absolutely incapable of reading *anything,* and who never do read anything, except, perhaps, the reports of famous divorce cases and the spiciest paragraphs in Society papers. It is not their fault; they are very often good people enough in their way; and as they go to church on Sundays, and pay their rates and taxes, the world has no right to complain of them. They are born without intellects, and with undeveloped souls, that is all, and on the whole they find themselves very comfortable in that condition. But this class is getting smaller, and all writers have cause to congratulate themselves on the fact, for the dead wall of its crass stupidity is a dreadful thing to face. Those, too, who begin by reading novels may end by reading Milton and Shakespeare. Day by day the mental area open to the operations of the English-speaking writer grows larger. At home the Board schools pour out their thousands every year, many of whom have acquired a taste for reading, which, when once it has been born, will, we may be sure, grow apace. Abroad the colonies are filling up with English-speaking people, who, as they grow refined and find leisure to read, will make a considerable call upon the literature of their day. But by far the largest demand for books in the English tongue comes from America, with its reading population of some forty millions. Most of the books patronized by this enormous population are stolen from English authors, who, according to American law, are outcasts, unentitled to that protection to the work of their brains and the labour of their hands which is one of the foundations of common morality. Putting aside this copyright question, however (and, indeed, it is best left undiscussed), there may be noted in passing two curious results which are being brought about in America by this wholesale perusal of English books. The first of these is that the Americans are destroying their own literature, that cannot live in the face of the unfair competition to which it is subjected. It will be noticed that since piracy, to use the politer word, set in with its present severity, America has scarcely produced a writer of the first class—no one, for instance, who can be compared to Poe, or Hawthorne, or Longfellow. It is not, perhaps, too rash a prophecy to say that, if piracy continues, American literature proper will shortly be chiefly represented by the columns of a very enterprising daily press. The second result of the present state of affairs is that the whole of the

American population, especially the younger portion of it, must be in course of thorough impregnation with English ideas and modes of thought as set forth by English writers. We all know the extraordinary effect books read in youth have upon the fresh and imaginative mind. It is not too much to say that many a man's whole life is influenced by some book read in his teens, the very title of which he may have forgotten. Consequently, it would be difficult to overrate the effect that must be from year to year produced upon the national character of America by the constant perusal of books born in England. For it must be remembered that for every reader that a writer of merit finds in England, he will find three in America.

In the face of this constant and ever-growing demand at home and abroad writers of romance must often find themselves questioning their inner consciousness as to what style of art it is best for them to adopt, not only with the view of pleasing their readers, but in the interests of art itself. There are several schools from which they may choose. For instance, there is that followed by the American novelists. These gentlemen, as we know, declare that there are no stories left to be told, and certainly, if it may be said without disrespect to a clever and laborious body of writers, their works go far towards supporting the statement. They have developed a new style of romance. Their heroines are things of silk and cambric, who soliloquize and dissect their petty feelings, and elaborately review the feeble promptings which serve them for passions. Their men—well, they are emasculated specimens of an overwrought age, and, with culture on their lips, and emptiness in their hearts, they dangle round the heroines till their three-volumed fate is accomplished. About their work is an atmosphere like that of the boudoir of a luxurious woman, faint and delicate, and suggesting the essence of white rose. How different is all this to the swiftness, and strength, and directness of the great English writers of the past. Why,

"The surge and thunder of the Odyssey"

is not more widely separated from the tinkling of modern society verses, than the laboured nothingness of this new American school of fiction from the giant life and vigour of Swift and Fielding, and Thackeray and Hawthorne. Perhaps, however, it is the art of the future, in which case we may hazard a shrewd guess that the literature of past ages will be more largely studied in days to come than it is at present.

Then to go from Pole to Pole, there is the Naturalistic school, of which Zola is the high priest. Here things are all the other way. Here the chosen function of the writer is to

"Paint the mortal shame of nature with the living hues of art."

Here are no silks and satins to impede our vision of the flesh and blood beneath, and here the scent is patchouli. Lewd, and bold, and bare, living for lust and lusting for this life and its good things, and naught beyond, the heroines of realism dance, with Bacchanalian revellings, across the astonished stage of literature. Whatever there is brutal in humanity—and God knows that there is plenty—whatever there is that is carnal and filthy, is here brought into prominence, and thrust before the reader's eyes. But what becomes of the things that are pure and high—of the great aspirations and the lofty hopes and longings, which *do,* after all, play their part in our human economy, and which it is surely the duty of a writer to call attention to and nourish according to his gifts?

Certainly it is to be hoped that this naturalistic school of writing will never take firm root in England, for it is an accursed thing. It is impossible to help wondering if its followers ever reflect upon the mischief that they must do, and, reflecting, do not shrink from the responsibility. To look at the matter from one point of view only, Society has made a rule that for the benefit of the whole community individuals must keep their passions within certain fixed limits, and our social system is so arranged that any transgression of this rule produces mischief of one sort or another, if not actual ruin, to the transgressor. Especially is this so if she be a woman. Now, as it is, human nature is continually fretting against these artificial bounds, and especially among young people it requires considerable fortitude and self-restraint to keep the feet from wandering. We all know, too, how much this sort of indulgence depends upon the imagination, and we all know how easy it is for a powerful writer to excite it in that direction. Indeed, there could be nothing *more* easy to a writer of any strength and vision, especially if he spoke with an air of evil knowledge and intimate authority. There are probably several men in England at this moment who, if they turned their talents to this bad end, could equal, if not outdo, Zola himself, with results that would shortly show themselves in various ways among the population. Sexual passion is the most powerful lever with which to stir the mind of man, for it lies at the root of all things human; and it is impossible to over-estimate the damage that could be worked by a single English or American writer of genius, if he grasped it with a will. "But," say these writers, "our aim is most moral; from Nana and her kith and kin may be gathered many a virtuous lesson and example." Possibly this is so, though as I write the words there rises in my mind a recollection of one or two French books where—but most people have seen such books. Besides, it is not so much a question of the object of the school as of the fact that it continually, and in full and luscious detail, calls attention to erotic matters. Once start the average mind upon this subject, and it will go down the slope of itself. It is useless afterwards to turn round and say that, although you cut loose the cords of decent reticence which bound the fancy, you intended that it should run *uphill* to the white heights of virtue. If the seed of eroticism is sown broadcast its fruit will be according to the nature of the soil it falls on, but fruit it must and will. And however virtuous may be the aims with which they are produced, the publications of the French Naturalistic school are such seed as was sown by that enemy who came in the night season.

In England, to come to the third great school of fiction, we have as yet little or nothing of all this. Here, on the other hand, we are at the mercy of the Young Person, and a dreadful nuisance most of us find her. The present writer is bound to admit that, speaking personally and with humility, he thinks it a little hard that all fiction should be judged by the test as to whether or no it is suitable reading for a girl of sixteen. There are plenty of people who write books for little girls in the schoolroom; let the little girls read them, and leave the works written for men and women to their elders. It may strike the reader as inconsistent, after the remarks made above, that a plea should now be advanced for greater freedom in English literary art. But French naturalism is one thing, and the unreal, namby-pamby nonsense with which the market is flooded here is quite another. Surely there is a middle path! Why do *men* hardly ever read a novel? Because, in ninety-nine cases out of a hundred, it is utterly false as a picture of life; and, failing in that, it certainly does not take ground as a work of high imagination. The ordinary popular English novel represents life as it is considered desirable that schoolgirls should suppose it to be.

Consequently it is for the most part rubbish, without a spark of vitality about it, for no novel written on those false lines will live. Also, the system is futile as a means of protection, for the young lady, wearied with the account of how the good girl who jilted the man who loved her when she was told to, married the noble lord, and lived in idleness and luxury for ever after, has only to turn to the evening paper to see another picture of existence. Of course, no humble producer of fiction, meant to interest through the exercise of the intelligence rather than through the senses, can hope to compete with the enthralling details of such cases as that of Lord Colin Campbell and Sir Charles Dilke. That is the naturalism of this country, and, like all filth, its popularity is enormous, as will be shown by the fact that the circulation of one evening paper alone was, I believe, increased during the hearing of a recent case by 60,000 copies nightly. Nor would any respectable author wish to compete with this. But he ought, subject to proper reservations and restraints, to be allowed to picture life as life is, and men and women as they are. At present, if he attempts to do this, he is denounced as immoral; and perchance the circulating library, which is curiously enough a great power in English literature, suppresses the book in its fear of losing subscriptions. The press, too—the same press that is so active in printing "full and special" reports—is very vigilant in this matter, having the Young Person continually before its eyes. Some time ago one of the London dailies reviewed a batch of eight or nine books. Of these reviews nearly every one was in the main an inquiry into the moral character of the work, judged from the standpoint of the unknown reviewer. Of their literary merits little or nothing was said. Now, the question that naturally arose in the mind of the reader of these notices was—Is the novelist bound to inculcate any particular set of doctrines that may at the moment be favoured by authority? If that is the aim and end of his art, then why is he not paid by the State like any other official? And why should not the principle be carried further? Each religion and every sect of each religion might retain their novelist. So might the Blue Ribbonites, and the Positivists, and the Purity people, and the Social Democrats, and others without end. The results would be most enlivening to the general public. Then, at any rate, the writer would be sure of the approbation of his own masters; as it is, he is at the mercy of every unknown reviewer, some of whom seem to have peculiar views—though, not to make too much of the matter, it must be remembered that the ultimate verdict is with the public.

Surely, what is wanted in English fiction is a higher ideal and more freedom to work it out. It is impossible, or, if not impossible, it requires the very highest genius, such as, perhaps, no writers possess to-day, to build up a really first-class work without the necessary materials in their due proportion. As it is, in this country, while crime may be used to any extent, passion in its fiercer and deeper forms is scarcely available, unless it is made to receive some conventional sanction. For instance, the right of dealing with bigamy is by custom conceded to the writer of romance, because in cases of bigamy vice has received the conventional sanction of marriage. True, the marriage is a mock one, but such as it is, it provides the necessary cloak. But let him beware how he deals with the same subject when the sinner of the piece has not added a sham or a bigamous marriage to his evil doings, for the book will in this case be certainly called immoral. English life is surrounded by conventionalism, and English fiction has come to reflect the conventionalism, not the life, and has in consequence, with some notable exceptions, got into a very poor way, both as regards art and interest.

If this moderate and proper freedom is denied to imaginative literature alone among the arts (for, though Mr. Horsley does not approve of it, sculptors may still model from the naked), it seems probable that the usual results will follow. There will be a great reaction, the Young Person will vanish into space and be no more seen, and Naturalism in all its horror will take its root among us. At present it is only in the French tongue that people read about the inner mysteries of life in brothels, or follow the interesting study of the passions of senile and worn-out debauchees. By-and-by, if liberty is denied, they will read them in the English. Art in the purity of its idealized truth should resemble some perfect Grecian statue. It should be cold but naked, and looking thereon men should be led to think of naught but beauty. Here, however, we attire Art in every sort of dress, some of them suggestive enough in their own way, but for the most part in a pinafore. The difference between literary Art, as the present writer submits it ought to be, and the Naturalistic Art of France is the difference between the Venus of Milo and an obscene photograph taken from the life. It seems probable that the English-speaking people will in course of time have to choose between the two.

But however this is—and the writer only submits an opinion—one thing remains clear, fiction à l'Anglaise becomes, from the author's point of view, day by day more difficult to deal with satisfactorily under its present conditions. This age is not a romantic age. Doubtless under the surface human nature is the same to-day as it was in the time of Rameses. Probably, too, the respective volumes of vice and virtue are, taking the altered circumstances into consideration, much as they were then or at any other time. But neither our good nor our evil doing is of an heroic nature, and it is things heroic and their kin and not petty things that best lend themselves to the purposes of the novelist, for by their aid he produces his strongest effects. Besides, if by chance there is a good thing on the market it is snapped up by a hundred eager newspapers, who tell the story, whatever it may be, and turn it inside out, and draw morals from it till the public loathes its sight and sound. Genius, of course, can always find materials wherewith to weave its glowing web. But these remarks, it is scarcely necessary to explain, are not made from that point of view, for only genius can talk of genius with authority, but rather from the humbler standing-ground of the ordinary conscientious labourer in the field of letters, who, loving his art for her own sake, yet earns living by following her, and is anxious to continue to do so with credit to himself. Let genius, if genius there be, come forward and speak on its own behalf! But if the reader is inclined to doubt the proposition that novel writing is becoming every day more difficult and less interesting, let him consult his own mind, and see how many novels proper among the hundreds that have been published within the last five years, and which deal in any way with every day contemporary life, have excited his profound interest. The present writer can at the moment recall but two—one was called "My Trivial Life and Misfortunes," by an unknown author, and the other, "The Story of a South African Farm," by Ralph Iron. But then neither of these books if examined into would be found to be a novel such as the ordinary writer produces once or twice a year. Both of them are written from within, and not from without; both convey the impression of being the outward and visible result of inward personal suffering on the part of the writer, for in each the key-note is a note of pain. Differing widely from the ordinary run of manufactured books, they owe their chief interest to a certain atmosphere of spiritual intensity, which could not in all probability be even approximately reproduced. Another recent work of the same powerful class, though of more painful detail, is called "Mrs. Keith's Crime." It is, however, almost impossible to conceive their respective authors producing a second "Trivial Life and Misfortunes" or a further edition of the crimes of Mrs. Keith. These books were written from the heart. Next time their authors write it will probably be from the head and not from the heart, and they must then come down to the use of the dusty materials which are common to us all.

There is indeed a refuge for the less ambitious among us, and it lies in the paths and calm retreats of pure imagination. Here we may weave our humble tale, and point our harmless moral without being mercilessly bound down to the prose of a somewhat dreary age. Here we may even—if we feel that our wings are strong enough to bear us in that thin air—cross the bounds of the known, and, hanging between earth and heaven, gaze with curious eyes into the great profound beyond. There are still subjects that may be handled *there* if the man can be found bold enough to handle them. And, although some there be who consider this a lower walk in the realms of fiction, and who would probably scorn to become a "mere writer of romances," it may be urged in defence of the school that many of the most lasting triumphs of literary art belong to the producers of purely romantic fiction, witness the "Arabian Nights," "Gulliver's Travels," "The Pilgrim's Progress," "Robinson Crusoe," and other immortal works. If the present writer may be allowed to hazard an opinion, it is that, when Naturalism has had its day, when Mr. Howells ceases to charm, and the Society novel is utterly played out, the kindly race of men in their latter as in their earlier developments will still take pleasure in those works of fancy which appeal, not to a class, or a nation, or even to an age, but to all time and humanity at large.

—1887

LONG ODDS

The story which is narrated in the following pages came to me from the lips of my old friend Allan Quatermain, or Hunter Quatermain, as we used to call him in South Africa. He told it to me one evening when I was stopping with him at the place he bought in Yorkshire. Shortly after that, the death of his only son so unsettled him that he immediately left England, accompanied by two companions, his old fellow-voyagers, Sir Henry Curtis and Captain Good, and has now utterly vanished into the dark heart of Africa. He is persuaded that a white people, of which he has heard rumours all his life, exists somewhere on the highlands in the vast, still unexplored interior, and his great ambition is to find them before he dies. This is the wild quest upon which he and his companions have departed, and from which I shrewdly suspect they never will return. One letter only have I received from the old gentleman, dated from a mission station high up the Tana, a river on the east coast, about three hundred miles north of Zanzibar. In it he says that they have gone through many hardships and adventures, but are alive and well, and have found traces which go far towards making him hope that the results of their wild quest may be a "magnificent and unexampled discovery." I greatly fear, however, that all he has discovered is death; for this letter came a long while ago, and nobody has heard a single word of the party since. They have totally vanished.

It was on the last evening of my stay at his house that he told the ensuing story to me and Captain Good, who was dining with him. He had eaten his dinner and drunk two or three glasses of old port, just to help Good and myself to the end of the second bottle. It was an unusual thing for him to do, for he was a most abstemious man, having conceived, as he used to say, a great horror of drink from observing its effects upon the class of colonists—hunters, transport riders and others—amongst whom he had passed so many years of his life. Consequently the good wine took more effect on him than it would have done on most men, sending a little flush into his wrinkled cheeks, and making him talk more freely than usual.

Dear old man! I can see him now, as he went limping up and down the vestibule, with his grey hair sticking up in scrubbing-brush fashion, his shrivelled yellow face, and his large dark eyes, that were as keen as any hawk's, and yet soft as a buck's. The whole room was hung with trophies of his numerous hunting expeditions, and he had some story about every one of them, if only he could be got to tell it. Generally he would not, for he was not very fond of narrating his own adventures, but to-night the port wine made him more communicative.

"Ah, you brute!" he said, stopping beneath an unusually large skull of a lion, which was fixed just over the mantelpiece, beneath a long row of guns, its jaws distended to their utmost width. "Ah, you brute! you have given me a lot of trouble for the last dozen years, and will, I suppose to my dying day."

"Tell us the yarn, Quatermain," said Good. "You have often promised to tell me, and you never have."

"You had better not ask me to," he answered, "for it is a longish one."

"All right," I said, "the evening is young, and there is some more port."

Thus adjured, he filled his pipe from a jar of coarse-cut Boer tobacco that was always standing on the mantelpiece, and still walking up and down the room, began—

"It was, I think, in the March of '69 that I was up in Sikukuni's country. It was just after old Sequati's time, and Sikukuni had got into power—I forget how. Anyway, I was there. I had heard that the Bapedi people had brought down an enormous quantity of ivory from the interior, and so I started with a waggon-load of goods, and came straight away from Middelburg to try and trade some of it. It was a risky thing to go into the country so early, on account of the fever; but I knew that there were one or two others after that lot of ivory, so I determined to have a try for it, and take my chance of fever. I had become so tough from continual knocking about that I did not set it down at much.

"Well, I got on all right for a while. It is a wonderfully beautiful piece of bush veldt, with great ranges of mountains running through it, and round granite koppies starting up here and there, looking out like sentinels over the rolling waste of bush. But it is very hot—hot as a stew-pan—and when I was there that March, which, of course, is autumn in this part of Africa, the whole place reeked of fever. Every morning, as I trekked along down by the Oliphant River, I used to creep from the waggon at dawn and look out. But there was no river to be seen—only a long line of billows of what looked like the finest cotton wool tossed up lightly with a pitchfork. It was the fever mist. Out from among the scrub, too, came little spirals of vapour, as though there were hundreds of tiny fires alight in it—reek rising from thousands of tons of rotting vegetation. It was a beautiful place, but the beauty was the beauty of death; and all those lines and blots of vapour wrote one great word across the surface of the country, and that word was 'fever.'

"It was a dreadful year of illness that. I came, I remember, to one little kraal of Knobnoses, and went up to it to see if I could get some *maas,* or curdled butter-milk, and a few mealies. As I drew near I was struck with the silence of the place. No children began to chatter, and no dogs barked. Nor could I see any native sheep or cattle. The place, though it had evidently been inhabited of late, was as still as the bush round it, and some guinea-fowl got up out of the prickly pear bushes right at the kraal gate. I remember that I hesitated a little before going in, there was such an air of desolation about the spot. Nature never looks desolate when man has not yet laid his hand upon her breast; she is only lonely. But when man has been, and has passed away, then she looks desolate.

"Well, I passed into the kraal, and went up to the principal hut. In front of the hut was something with an old sheep-skin *kaross* thrown over it. I stooped down and drew off the rug, and then shrank back amazed, for under it was the body of a young woman recently dead. For a moment I thought of turning back, but my curiosity overcame me; so going past the dead woman, I went down on my hands and knees and crept into the hut. It was so dark that I could not see anything, though I could smell a great deal, so I lit a match. It was a 'tandstickor' match, and burnt slowly and dimly, and as the light gradually increased I made out what I took to be a family of people, men, women, and children, fast asleep. Presently it burnt up brightly, and I saw that they too, five of them altogether, were quite dead. One was a baby. I dropped the match in a hurry, and was making my way from the hut as quick as I could go, when I caught sight of two bright eyes staring out of a corner. Thinking it was a wild cat, or some such animal, I redoubled my haste, when suddenly a voice near the eyes began first to mutter, and then to send up a succession of awful yells.

"Hastily I lit another match, and perceived that the eyes belonged to an old woman, wrapped up in a greasy leather garment. Taking her by the arm, I dragged her out, for she could not, or would not, come by herself, and the stench was overpowering me. Such a sight as she was—a bag of bones, covered over with black, shrivelled parchment. The only white thing about her was her wool, and she seemed to be pretty well dead except for her eyes and her voice. She thought that I was a devil come to take her, and that is why she yelled so. Well, I got her down to the waggon, and gave her a 'tot' of Cape smoke, and then, as soon as it was ready, poured about a pint of beef-tea down her throat, made from the flesh of a blue vilderbeeste I had killed the day before, and after that she brightened up wonderfully. She could talk Zulu—indeed, it turned out that she had run away from Zululand in T'Chaka's time—and she told me that all the people whom I had seen had died of fever. When they had died the other inhabitants of the kraal had taken the cattle and gone away, leaving the poor old woman, who was helpless from age and infirmity, to perish of starvation or disease, as the case might be. She had been sitting there for three days among the bodies when I found her. I took her on to the next kraal, and gave the headman a blanket to look after her, promising him another if I found her well when I came back. I remember that he was much astonished at my parting with two blankets for the sake of such a worthless old creature. 'Why did I not leave her in the bush?' he asked. Those people carry the doctrine of the survival of the fittest to its extreme, you see.

"It was the night after I had got rid of the old woman that I made my first acquaintance with my friend yonder," and he nodded towards the skull that seemed to be grinning down at us in the shadow of the wide mantelshelf. "I had trekked from dawn till eleven o'clock—a long trek—but I wanted to get on, and had turned the oxen out to graze, sending the voorlooper to look after them, my intention being to inspan again about six o'clock, and trek with the moon till ten. Then I got into the waggon and had a good sleep till half-past two or so in the afternoon, when I rose and cooked some meat, and had my dinner, washing it down with a pannikin of black coffee—for it was difficult to get preserved milk in those days. Just as I had finished, and the driver, a man called Tom, was washing up the things, in comes the young scoundrel of a voorlooper driving one ox before him.

"'Where are the other oxen?' I asked.

"'Koos!' he said, 'Koos! the other oxen have gone away. I turned my back for a minute, and when I looked round again they were all gone except Kaptein, here, who was rubbing his back against a tree.'

"'You mean that you have been asleep, and let them stray, you villain. I will rub your back against a stick,' I answered, feeling very angry, for it was not a pleasant prospect to be stuck up in that fever trap for a week or so while we were hunting for the oxen. 'Off you go, and you too, Tom, and mind you don't come back till you have found them. They have trekked back along the Middelburg Road, and are a dozen miles off by now, I'll be bound. Now, no words; go both of you.'

"Tom, the driver, swore, and caught the lad a hearty kick, which he richly deserved, and then, having tied old Kaptein up to the disselboom with a reim, they took their assegais and sticks, and started. I would have gone too, only I knew that somebody must look after the waggon, and I did not like to leave either of the boys with it at night. I was in a very bad temper, indeed, although I was pretty well used to these sort of occurrences, and soothed myself by taking a rifle and going to kill something. For a couple of hours I poked about without seeing anything that I could get a shot at, but at last, just as I was again within seventy yards of the waggon, I put up an old Impala ram from behind a mimosa thorn. He ran straight for the waggon, and it was not till he was passing within a few feet of it that I could get a decent shot at him. Then I pulled, and caught him half-way down the spine. Over he went, dead as a door-nail, and a pretty shot it was, though I ought not to say it. This little incident put me into rather a better humour, especially as the buck had rolled right against the after-part of the waggon, so I had only to gut him, fix a reim round his legs, and haul him up. By the time I had done this the sun was down, and the full moon was up, and a beautiful moon it was. And then there came that wonderful hush which sometimes falls over the African bush in the early hours of the night. No beast was moving, and no bird called. Not a breath of air stirred the quiet trees, and the shadows did not even quiver, they only grew. It was very oppressive and very lonely, for there was not a sign of the cattle or the boys. I was quite thankful for the society of old Kaptein, who was lying down contentedly against the disselboom, chewing the cud with a good conscience.

"Presently, however, Kaptein began to get restless. First he snorted, then he got up and snorted again. I could not make it out, so like a fool I got down off the waggon-box to have a look round, thinking it might be the lost oxen coming.

"Next instant I regretted it, for all of a sudden I heard a roar and saw something yellow flash past me and light on poor Kaptein. Then came a bellow of agony from the ox, and a crunch as the lion put his teeth through the poor brute's neck, and I began to understand what had happened. My rifle was in the waggon, and my first thought being to get hold of it, I turned and made a bolt for the box. I got my foot up on the wheel and flung my body forward on to the waggon, and there I stopped as if I were frozen, and no wonder, for as I was about to spring up I heard the lion behind me, and next second I felt the brute, ay, as plainly as I can feel this table. I felt him, I say, sniffing at my left leg that was hanging down.

"My word! I did feel queer; I don't think that I ever felt so queer before. I dared not move for the life of me, and the odd thing was that I seemed to lose power over my leg, which developed an insane sort of inclination to kick out of its own mere motion—just as hysterical people want to laugh when they ought to be particularly solemn. Well, the lion sniffed and sniffed, beginning at my ankle and slowly nosing away up to my thigh. I thought that he was going to get hold then, but he did not. He only growled softly, and went back to the ox. Shifting my head a little I got a full view of him. He was about the biggest lion I ever saw, and I have seen a great many, and he had a most tremendous black mane. What his teeth were like you can see— look there, pretty big ones, ain't they? Altogether he was a magnificent animal, and as I lay sprawling on the fore tongue of the waggon, it occurred to me that he would look uncommonly well in a cage. He stood there by the carcass of poor Kaptein, and deliberately disembowelled him as neatly as a butcher could have done. All this while I dared not move, for he kept lifting his head and keeping an eye on me as he licked his bloody chops. When he had cleaned Kaptein out he opened his mouth and roared, and I am not exaggerating when I say that the sound shook the waggon. Instantly there came back an answering roar.

"'Heavens!' I thought, 'there is his mate.'

"Hardly was the thought out of my head when I caught sight in the moonlight of the lioness bounding along through the long grass, and after her a couple of cubs about the size of mastiffs. She stopped within a few feet of my head, and stood, waved her tail, and fixed me with her glowing yellow eyes; but just as I thought that it was all over she turned and began to feed on Kaptein, and so did the cubs. There were the four of them within eight feet of me, growling and quarrelling, rending and tearing, and crunching poor Kaptein's bones; and there I lay shaking with terror, and the cold perspiration pouring out of me, feeling like another Daniel come to judgment in a new sense of the phrase. Presently the cubs had eaten their fill, and began to get restless. One went round to the back of the waggon and pulled at the Impala buck that hung there, and the other came round my way and commenced the sniffing game at my leg. Indeed, he did more than that, for, my trouser being hitched up a little, he began to lick the bare skin with his rough tongue. The more he licked the more he liked it, to judge from his increased vigour and the loud purring noise he made. Then I knew that the end had come, for in another second his file-like tongue would have rasped through the skin of my leg—which was luckily pretty tough—and have drawn the blood, and then there would be no chance for me. So I just lay there and thought of my sins, and prayed to the Almighty, and reflected that after all life was a very enjoyable thing.

"Then of a sudden I heard a crashing of bushes and the shouting and whistling of men, and there were the two boys coming back with the cattle, which they had found trekking along all together. The lions lifted their heads and listened, then bounded off without a sound—and I fainted.

"The lions came back no more that night, and by the next morning my nerves had got pretty straight again; but I was full of wrath when I thought of all that I had gone through at the hands, or rather noses, of those four brutes, and of the fate of my after-ox Kaptein. He was a splendid ox, and I was very fond of him. So wroth was I that like a fool I determined to attack the whole family of them. It was worthy of a greenhorn out on his first hunting trip; but I did it nevertheless. Accordingly after breakfast, having rubbed some oil upon my leg, which was very sore from the cub's tongue, I took the driver, Tom, who did not half like the business, and having armed myself with an ordinary double No. 12 smoothbore, the first breechloader I ever had, I started. I took the smoothbore because it shot a bullet very well; and my experience has been that a round ball from a smoothbore is quite as effective against a lion as an express bullet. The lion is soft, and not a difficult animal to finish if you hit him anywhere in the body. A buck takes far more killing.

"Well, I started, and the first thing I set to work to do was to try to discover whereabouts the brutes lay up for the day. About three hundred yards from the waggon was the crest of a rise covered with single mimosa trees, dotted about in a park-like fashion, and beyond this lay a stretch of open plain running down to a dry pan, or waterhole, which covered about an acre of ground, and was densely clothed with reeds, now in the sere and yellow leaf. From the further edge of this pan the ground sloped up again to a great cleft, or nullah, which had been cut out by the action of the water, and was pretty thickly sprinkled with bush, amongst which grew some large trees, I forget of what sort.

"It at once struck me that the dry pan would be a likely place to find my friends in, as there is nothing a lion is fonder of than lying up in reeds, through which he can see things without being seen himself. Accordingly thither I went and prospected. Before I had got half-way round the pan I found the remains of a blue vilderbeeste that had evidently been killed within the last three or four days and partially devoured by lions; and from other indications about I was soon assured that if the family were not in the pan that day they spent a good deal of their spare time there. But if there, the question was how to get them out; for it was clearly impossible to think of going in after them unless one was quite determined to commit suicide. Now there was a strong wind blowing from the direction of the waggon, across the reedy pan towards the bush-clad kloof or donga, and this first gave me the idea of firing the reeds, which, as I think I told you, were pretty dry. Accordingly Tom took some matches and began starting little fires to the left, and I did the same to the right. But the reeds were still green at the bottom, and we should never have got them well alight had it not been for the wind, which grew stronger and stronger as the sun climbed higher, and forced the fire into them. At last, after half-an-hour's trouble, the flames got a hold, and began to spread out like a fan, whereupon I went round to the further side of the pan to wait for the lions, standing well out in the open, as we stood at the copse to-day where you shot the woodcock. It was a rather risky thing to do, but I used to be so sure of my shooting in those days that I did not so much mind the risk. Scarcely had I got round when I heard the reeds parting before the onward rush of some animal. 'Now for it,' said I. On it came. I could see that it was yellow, and prepared for action, when instead of a lion out bounded a beautiful reit bok which had been lying in the shelter of the pan. It must, by the way, have been a reit bok of a peculiarly confiding nature to lay itself down with the lion, like the lamb of prophesy, but I suppose the reeds were thick, and that it kept a long way off.

"Well, I let the reit bok go, and it went like the wind, and kept my eyes fixed upon the reeds. The fire was burning like a furnace now; the flames crackling and roaring as they bit into the reeds, sending spouts of fire twenty feet and more into the air, and making the hot air dance above in a way that was perfectly dazzling. But the reeds were still half green, and created an enormous quantity of smoke, which came rolling towards me like a curtain, lying very low on account of the wind. Presently, above the crackling of the fire, I heard a startled roar, then another and another. So the lions were at home.

"I was beginning to get excited now, for, as you fellows know, there is nothing in experience to warm up your nerves like a lion at close quarters, unless it is a wounded buffalo; and I became still more so when I made out through the smoke that the lions were all moving about on the extreme edge of the reeds. Occasionally they would pop their heads out like rabbits from a burrow, and then, catching sight of me standing about fifty yards away, draw them back again. I knew that it must be getting pretty warm behind them, and that they could not keep the game up for long; and I was not mistaken, for suddenly all four of them broke cover together, the old black-maned lion leading by a few yards. I never saw a more splendid sight in all my hunting experience than those four lions bounding across the veldt, over-shadowed by the dense pall of smoke and backed by the fiery furnace of the burning reeds.

"I reckoned that they would pass, on their way to the bushy kloof, within about five and twenty yards of me, so, taking a long breath, I got my gun well on to the lion's shoulder—the black-maned one—so as to allow for an inch or two of motion, and catch him through the heart. I was on, dead on, and my finger was just beginning to tighten on the trigger, when suddenly I went blind—a bit of reed-ash had drifted into my right eye. I danced and rubbed, and succeeded in clearing it more or less just in time to see the tail of the last lion vanishing round the bushes up the kloof.

"If ever a man was mad I was that man. It was too bad; and such a shot in the open! However, I was not going to be beaten, so I just turned and marched for the kloof. Tom, the driver, begged and implored me not to go, but though as a general rule I never pretend to be very brave (which I am not), I was determined that I would either kill those lions or they should kill me. So I told Tom that he need not come unless he liked, but I was going; and being a plucky fellow, a Swazi by birth, he shrugged his shoulders, muttered that I was mad or bewitched, and followed doggedly in my tracks.

"We soon reached the kloof, which was about three hundred yards in length and but sparsely wooded, and then the real fun began. There might be a lion behind every bush—there certainly were four lions somewhere; the delicate question was, where. I peeped and poked and looked in every possible direction, with my heart in my mouth, and was at last rewarded by catching a glimpse of something yellow moving behind a bush. At the same moment, from another bush opposite me out burst one of the cubs and galloped back towards the burnt pan. I whipped round and let drive a snap shot that tipped him head over heels, breaking his back within two inches of the root of the tail, and there he lay helpless but glaring. Tom afterwards killed him with his assegai. I opened the breech of the gun and hurriedly pulled out the old case, which, to judge from what ensued, must, I suppose, have burst and left a portion of its fabric sticking to the barrel. At any rate, when I tried to get in the new cartridge it would only enter half-way; and—would you believe it?—this was the moment that the lioness, attracted no doubt by the outcry of her cub, chose to put in an appearance. There she stood, twenty paces or so from me, lashing her tail and looking just as wicked as it is possible to conceive. Slowly I stepped backwards, trying to push in the new case, and as I did so she moved on in little runs, dropping down after each run. The danger was imminent, and the case would not go in. At the moment I oddly enough thought of the cartridge maker, whose name I will not mention, and earnestly hoped that if the lion got *me* some condign punishment would overtake *him*. It would not go in, so I tried to pull it out. It would not come out either, and my gun was useless if I could not shut it to use the other barrel. I might as well have had no gun.

"Meanwhile I was walking backward, keeping my eye on the lioness, who was creeping forward on her belly without a sound, but lashing her tail and keeping her eye on me; and in it I saw that she was coming in a few seconds more. I dashed my wrist and the palm of my hand against the brass rim of the cartridge till the blood poured from them—look, there are the scars of it to this day!"

Here Quatermain held up his right hand to the light and showed us four or five white cicatrices just where the wrist is set into the hand.

"But it was not of the slightest use," he went on; "the cartridge would not move. I only hope that no other man will ever be put in such an awful position. The lioness gathered herself together, and I gave myself up for lost, when suddenly Tom shouted out from somewhere in my rear—

"'You are walking on to the wounded cub; turn to the right.'

"I had the sense, dazed as I was, to take the hint, and slewing round at right-angles, but still keeping my eyes on the lioness, I continued my backward walk.

"To my intense relief, with a low growl she straightened herself, turned, and bounded further up the kloof.

"'Come on, Macumazahn,' said Tom, 'let's get back to the waggon.'

"'All right, Tom,' I answered. 'I will when I have killed those three other lions,' for by this time I was bent on shooting them as I never remember being bent on anything before or since. 'You can go if you like, or you can get up a tree.'

"He considered the position a little, and then he very wisely got up a tree. I wish that I had done the same.

"Meanwhile I had found my knife, which had an extractor in it, and succeeded after some difficulty in pulling out the cartridge which had so nearly been the cause of my death, and removing the obstruction in the barrel. It was very little thicker than a postage-stamp; certainly not thicker than a piece of writing-paper. This done, I loaded the gun, bound a handkerchief round my wrist and hand to staunch the flowing of the blood, and started on again.

"I had noticed that the lioness went into a thick green bush, or rather cluster of bushes, growing near the water, about fifty yards higher up, for there was a little stream running down the kloof, and I walked towards this bush. When I got there, however, I could see nothing, so I took up a big stone and threw it into the bushes. I believe that it hit the other cub, for out it came with a rush, giving me a broadside shot, of which I promptly availed myself, knocking it over dead. Out, too, came the lioness like a flash of light, but quick as she went I managed to put the other bullet into her ribs, so that she rolled right over three times like a shot rabbit. I instantly got two more cartridges into the gun, and as I did so the lioness rose again and came crawling towards me on her fore-paws, roaring and groaning, and with such an expression of diabolical fury on her countenance as I have not often seen. I shot her again through the chest, and she fell over on to her side quite dead.

"That was the first and last time that I ever killed a brace of lions right and left, and, what is more, I never heard of anybody else doing it. Naturally I was considerably pleased with myself, and having again loaded up, I went on to look for the black-maned beauty who had killed Kaptein. Slowly, and with the greatest care, I proceeded up the kloof, searching every bush and tuft of grass as I went. It was wonderfully exciting work, for I never was sure from one moment to another but that he would be on me. I took comfort, however, from the reflection that a lion rarely attacks a man—rarely, I say; sometimes he does, as you will see—unless he is cornered or wounded. I must have been nearly an hour hunting after that lion. Once I thought I saw something move in a clump of tambouki grass, but I could not be sure, and when I trod out the grass I could not find him.

"At last I worked up to the head of the kloof, which made a *cul-de-sac*. It was formed of a wall of rock about fifty feet high. Down this rock trickled a little waterfall, and in front of it, some seventy feet from its face, rose a great piled-up mass of boulders, in the crevices and on the top of which grew ferns, grasses, and stunted bushes. This mass was about twenty-five feet high. The sides of the kloof here were also very steep. Well, I came to the top of the nullah and looked all round. No signs of the lion. Evidently I had either overlooked him further down or he had escaped right away. It was very vexatious; but still three lions were not a bad bag for one gun before dinner, and I was fain to be content. Accordingly I departed back again, making my way round the isolated pillar of boulders, beginning to feel, as I did so, that I was pretty well done up with excitement and fatigue, and should be more so before I had skinned those three lions. When I had got, as nearly as I could judge, about eighteen yards past the pillar or mass of boulders, I turned to have another look round. I have a pretty sharp eye, but I could see nothing at all.

"Then, on a sudden, I saw something sufficiently alarming. On the top of the mass of boulders, opposite to me, standing out clear against the rock beyond, was the huge black-maned lion. He had been crouching there, and now arose as though by magic. There he stood lashing his tail, just like a living reproduction of the animal on the gateway of Northumberland House that I have seen in a picture. But he did not stand long. Before I could fire—before I could do more than get the gun to my shoulder—he sprang straight up and out from the rock, and driven by the impetus of that one mighty bound came hurtling through the air towards me.

"Heavens! how grand he looked, and how awful! High into the air he flew, describing a great arch. Just as he touched the highest point of his spring I fired. I did not dare to wait, for I saw that he would clear the whole space and land right upon me. Without a sight, almost without aim, I fired, as one would fire a snap shot at a snipe. The bullet told, for I distinctly heard its thud above the rushing sound caused by the passage of the lion through the air. Next second I was swept to the ground (luckily I fell into a low, creeper-clad bush, which broke the shock), and the lion was on the top of me, and the next those great white teeth of his had met in my thigh—I heard them grate against the bone. I yelled out in agony, for I did not feel in the least benumbed and happy, like Dr. Livingstone—whom, by the way, I knew very well—and gave myself up for dead. But suddenly, at that moment, the lion's grip on my thigh loosened, and he stood over me, swaying to and fro, his huge mouth, from which the blood was gushing, wide opened. Then he roared, and the sound shook the rocks.

"To and fro he swung, and then the great head dropped on me, knocking all the breath from my body, and he was dead. My bullet had entered in the centre of his chest and passed out on the right side of the spine about half way down the back.

"The pain of my wound kept me from fainting, and as soon as I got my breath I managed to drag myself from under him. Thank heavens, his great teeth had not crushed my thigh-bone; but I was losing a great deal of blood, and had it not been for the timely arrival of Tom, with whose aid I loosed the handkerchief from my wrist and tied it round my leg, twisting it tight with a stick, I think that I should have bled to death.

"Well, it was a just reward for my folly in trying to tackle a family of lions single-handed. The odds were too long. I have been lame ever since, and shall be to my dying day; in the month of March the wound always troubles me a great deal, and every three years it breaks out raw.

"I need scarcely add that I never traded the lot of ivory at Sikukuni's. Another man got it—a German—and made five hundred pounds out of it after paying expenses. I spent the next month on the broad of my back, and was a cripple for six months after that. And now I've told you the yarn, so I will have a drop of Hollands and go to bed. Good-night to you all, good-night!"

—1886

RUDYARD KIPLING
1865-1936

Rudyard Kipling was born in Bombay, India, and raised, when he reached the age of five, in Southsea, England. After attending what was basically a military college in Devon, Kipling returned to India to work as a newspaperman. Following his journalistic period in India, Kipling returned to London in 1889 and subsequently lived for a time in the United States during the 1890s (when his two famous Jungle Books were published), and in various locales in England afterwards. In 1907, he won the Nobel Prize for literature.

*Along with his good friend H. Rider Haggard, Kipling was the most popular author of the adventure story during the late Victorian period in England. Both Kipling and Haggard helped to reinforce with their readers an unwavering belief in British imperialism (which functioned as a crucial motif in their work). But whereas Haggard specialized in writing longer fiction like novels, Kipling preferred writing short stories and poetry. He only published a handful of novels, yet two of these—*Captains Courageous *(1897) and* Kim *(1901)—represent some of his finest work. A review of Kipling's abundant body of short fiction reveals that his best tales are adventure stories. In particular, eighteen short stories written as a series featuring Kipling's notorious Soldiers Three (Learoyd, Mulvaney, and Ortheris of the British Army serving in India) have been praised for their sense of dramatic pace and humor by Kipling's many readers and vilified for their imperialistic zeal by Kipling's critics. These eighteen tales were anthologized in five collections:* Plain Tales from the Hills *(1888),* Soldiers Three *(1888),* Life's Handicap *(1891),* Many Inventions *(1893), and* Actions and Reactions *(1909). Kipling was also quite adept at writing adventure fiction for children, his most notable efforts in this area being his two Jungle Book anthologies,* The Jungle Book *(1894) and* The Second Jungle Book *(1895). Edgar Rice Burroughs, in his popular Tarzan stories, borrowed from and elaborated upon Kipling's depiction of the feral child protagonist, Mowgli, in the Jungle Books.*

"Literature" (a speech delivered at the Royal Academy Dinner on May 6, 1906) reveals Kipling's understanding of the powerful "magic" contained in words and stories, and the honored role storytelling possesses in human society. "The Man Who Would Be King" (first published in the 1888 edition of The Phantom Rickshaw and Other Tales) *is generally regarded as Kipling's single best adventure story. Detailing the exploits of two soldiers-of-fortune—who travel to the exotic land of Kafiristan to become king—this yarn is both riveting in its portrayal of Peachey Carnehan's and Daniel Dravot's ambitious scheme for power and tragic in its depiction of a fantastic dream realized, then lost. Like some of Kipling's other writings, "The Man Who Would Be King" has been attacked by Kipling's detractors for its overtly imperialistic and racist sentiments, but as adventure fiction, it has few equals. In 1975, it was released as a motion picture directed by John Huston and starring Sean Connery and Michael Caine.*

LITERATURE

A great, and I frankly admit, a somewhat terrifying, honour has come to me; but I think, compliments apart, that the most case-hardened worker in letters, speaking to such an assembly as this, must recognise the gulf that separates even the least of those who do things worthy to be written about from even the best of those who have written things worthy of being talked about.

There is an ancient legend which tells us that when a man first achieved a most notable deed he wished to explain to his Tribe what he had done. As soon as he began to speak, however, he was smitten with dumbness, he lacked words, and sat down. Then there arose—according to the story—a masterless man, one who had taken no part in the action of his fellow, who had no special virtues, but who was afflicted—that is the phrase—with the magic of the necessary word. He saw; he told; he described the merits of the notable deed in such a fashion, we are assured, that the words "became alive and walked up and down in the hearts of all his hearers." Thereupon, the Tribe seeing that the words were certainly alive, and fearing lest the man with the words would hand down untrue tales about them to their children, took and killed him. But, later, they saw that the magic was in the words, not in the man.

We have progressed in many directions since the time of this early and destructive criticism, but, so far, we do not seem to have found a sufficient substitute for the necessary word as the final record to which all achievement must look. Even to-day, when all is done, those who have done it must wait until all has been said by the masterless man with the words. It is certain that the overwhelming bulk of those words will perish in the future as they have perished in the past; but it is true that a minute fraction will continue to exist, and by the light of these words, and by that light only, will our children be able to judge of the phases of our generation. Now we desire beyond all things to stand well with our children; but when our story comes to be told we do not know who will have the telling of it. We are too close to the tellers; there are many tellers and they are all talking together; and, even if we know them, we must not kill them. But the old and terrible instinct which taught our ancestors to kill the original storyteller warns us that we shall not be far wrong if we challenge any man who shows signs of being afflicted with the magic of the necessary word. May not this be the reason why, without any special legislation on its behalf, Literature has always stood a little outside the law as the one calling that is absolutely free—free in the sense that it needs no protection? For instance, if, as occasionally happens, a Judge makes a bad law, or a surgeon a bad operation, or a manufacturer makes bad food, criticism upon their actions is by law and custom confined to comparatively narrow limits. But if a man, as occasionally happens, makes a book, there is no limit to the criticism that may be directed against it. And this is perfectly as it should be. The world recognises that little things like bad law, bad surgery, and bad food, affect only the cheapest commodity that we know about—human life. Therefore, in these circumstances, men can afford to be swayed by pity for the offender, by interest in his family, by fear, or loyalty, or respect for the organisation he represents, or even by a desire to do him justice. But when the question is of words—words that may become alive and walk up and down in the hearts of the hearers—it is then that this world of ours, which is disposed to take an interest in its future, feels instinctively that it is better that a thousand innocent people should be punished rather than that one guilty word should be preserved, carrying that which is an untrue tale of the Tribe. The chances, of course, are almost astronomically remote that any given tale will survive for so long as it takes an oak to grow to timber size. But that guiding instinct warns us not to trust to chance a matter of the supremest concern. In this durable record, if anything short of indisputable and undistilled truth be seen there, we all feel, "How shall our achievements profit us?" The Record of the Tribe is its enduring literature.

The magic of Literature lies in the words, and not in any man. Witness, a thousand excellent, strenuous words can leave us quite cold or put us to sleep, whereas a bare half-hundred words breathed upon by some man in his agony, or in his exaltation, or in his idleness, ten generations ago, can still lead whole nations into and out of captivity, can open to us the doors of the three worlds, or stir us so intolerably that we can scarcely abide to look at our own souls. It is a miracle—one that happens very seldom. But secretly each one of the masterless men with the words has hope, or has had hope, that the miracle may be wrought again through him.

And why not? If a tinker in Bedford gaol; if a pamphleteering shopkeeper, pilloried in London; if a muzzy Scot; if a despised German Jew; or a condemned French thief, or an English Admiralty official with a taste for letters can be miraculously afflicted with the magic of the necessary word, why not any man at any time? Our world, which is only concerned in the perpetuation of the record, sanctions that hope just as kindly and just as cruelly as Nature sanctions love.

All it suggests is that the man with the Words shall wait upon the man of achievement, and step by step with him try to tell the story to the Tribe. All it demands is that the magic of every word shall be tried out to the uttermost by every means, fair or foul, that the mind of man can suggest. There is no room, and the world insists that there shall be no room, for pity, for mercy, for respect, for fear, or even for loyalty between man and his fellow-man, when the record of the Tribe comes to be written. That record must satisfy, at all costs to the word and to the man behind the word. It must satisfy alike the keenest vanity and the deepest self-knowledge of the present; it must satisfy also the most shameless curiosity of the future. When it has done this it is literature of which it will be said, in due time, that it fitly represents its age. I say in due time because ages, like individuals, do not always appreciate the merits of a record that purports to represent them. The trouble is that one always expects just a little more out of a thing than one puts into it. Whether it be an age or an individual, one is always a little pained and a little pessimistic to find that all one gets back is just one's bare deserts. This is a difficulty old as literature.

A little incident that came within my experience a while ago shows that that difficulty is always being raised by the most unexpected people all about the world. It happened in a land where the magic of words is peculiarly potent and far-reaching, that there was a Tribe that wanted rain, and the rain-doctors set about getting it. To a certain extent the rain-doctors succeeded. But the rain their magic brought was not a full driving downpour that tells of large prosperity; it was patchy, local, circumscribed, and uncertain. There were unhealthy little squalls blowing about the country and doing damage. Whole districts were flooded out by waterspouts, and other districts annoyed by trickling showers, soon dried by the sun. And so the Tribe went to the rain-doctors, being very angry, and they said, "What is this rain that you make? You did not make rain like this in the time of our fathers. What have you been doing?" And the rain-doctors said, "We have been making our proper magic. Supposing you tell us what you have been doing lately?" And the Tribe said, "Oh, our head-men have been running about hunting jackals, and our little people have been running about chasing grasshoppers! What has that to do with your rain-making?" "It has everything to do with it," said the rain-doctors. "Just as long as your head-men run about hunting jackals, and just as long as your little people run about chasing grasshoppers, just so long will the rain fall in this manner."

—1906

THE MAN WHO WOULD BE KING

"Brother to a Prince and fellow to a beggar if he be found worthy."

The Law, as quoted, lays down a fair conduct of life, and one not easy to follow. I have been fellow to a beggar again and again under circumstances which prevented either of us finding out whether the other was worthy. I have still to be brother to a Prince, though I once came near to kinship with what might have been a veritable King and was promised the reversion of a Kingdom—army, law-courts, revenue and policy all complete. But, to-day, I greatly fear that my King is dead, and if I want a crown I must go and hunt it for myself.

The beginning of everything was in a railway train upon the road to Mhow from Ajmir. There had been a Deficit in the Budget, which necessitated traveling, not Second-class, which is only half as dear as First-class, but by Intermediate, which is very awful indeed. There are no cushions in the Intermediate class, and the population are either Intermediate, which is Eurasian, or native, which for a long night journey is nasty, or Loafer, which is amusing though intoxicated. Intermediates do not patronize refreshment-rooms. They carry their food in bundles and pots, and buy sweets from the native sweet meat-sellers, and drink the roadside water. That is why in the hot weather Intermediates are taken out of the carriages dead, and in all weathers are most properly looked down upon.

My particular Intermediate happened to be empty till I reached Nasirabad, when a huge gentleman in shirt-sleeves entered, and, following the custom of Intermediates, passed the time of day. He was a wanderer and a vagabond like myself, but with an educated taste for whiskey. He told tales of things he had seen and done, of out-of-the-way corners of the Empire into which he had penetrated, and of adventures in which he risked his life for a few days' food. "If India was filled with men like you and me, not knowing more than the crows where they'd get their next day's rations, it isn't seventy millions of revenue the land would be paying—it's seven hundred millions," said he; and as I looked at his mouth and chin I was disposed to agree with him. We talked politics—the politics of Loaferdom that sees things from the underside where the lath and plaster is not smoothed off—and we talked postal arrangements because my friend wanted to send a telegram back from the next station to Ajmir, which is the turning-off place from the Bombay to the Mhow line as you travel westward. My friend had no money beyond eight annas which he wanted for dinner, and I had no money at all, owing to the hitch in the Budget before mentioned. Further, I was going into a wilderness where, though I should resume touch with the Treasury, there were no telegraph offices. I was, therefore, unable to help him in any way.

"We might threaten a Station-master, and make him send a wire on tick," said my friend, " but that'd mean inquiries for you and for me, and I've got my hands full these days. Did you say you are traveling back along this line within any days?"

"Within ten," I said.

"Can't you make it eight?" said he. "Mine is rather urgent business."

"I can send your telegram within ten days if that will serve you," I said.

"I couldn't trust the wire to fetch him now I think of it. It's this way. He leaves Delhi on the 23d for Bombay. That means he'll be running through Ajmir about the night of the 23d."

"But I'm going into the Indian Desert," I explained.

"Well *and* good," said he. "You'll be changing at Marwar Junction to get into Jodhpore territory—you must do that—and he'll be coming through Marwar Junction in the early morning of the 24th by the Bombay Mail. Can you be at Marwar Junction on that time? 'Twon't be inconveniencing you because I know that there's precious few pickings to be got out of these Central India States—even though you pretend to be correspondent of the *Backwoodsman.*"

"Have you ever tried that trick?" I asked.

"Again and again, but the Residents find you out, and then you get escorted to the Border before you've time to get your knife into them. But about my friend here. I *must* give him a word o' mouth to tell him what's come to me or else he won't know where to go. I would take it more than kind of you if you was to come out of Central India in time to catch him at Marwar Junction, and say to him:—'He has gone South for the week.' He'll know what that means. He's a big man with a red beard, and a great swell he is. You'll find him sleeping like a gentleman with all his luggage round him in a Second-class compartment. But don't you be afraid. Slip down the window, and say:—'He has gone South for the week,' and he'll tumble. It's only cutting your time of stay in those parts by two days. I ask you as a stranger—going to the West," he said, with emphasis.

"Where have *you* come from?" said I.

"From the East," said he, "and I am hoping that you will give him the message on the Square—for the sake of my Mother as well as your own."

Englishmen are not usually softened by appeals to the memory of their mothers, but for certain reasons, which will be fully apparent, I saw fit to agree.

"It's more than a little matter," said he, "and that's why I ask you to do it—and now I know that I can depend on you doing it. A Second-class carriage at Marwar Junction, and a red-haired man asleep in it. You'll be sure to remember. I get out at the next station, and I must hold on there till he comes or sends me what I want."

"I'll give the message if I catch him," I said, "and for the sake of your Mother as well as mine I'll give you a word of advice. Don't try to run the Central India States just now as the correspondent of the *Backwoodsman*. There's a real one knocking about here, and it might lead to trouble."

"Thank you," said he, simply, "and when will the swine be gone? I can't starve because he's ruining my work. I wanted to get hold of the Degumber Rajah down here about his father's widow, and give him a jump."

"What did he do to his father's widow then?"

"Filled her up with red pepper and slippered her to death as she hung from a beam. I found that out myself and I'm the only man that would dare going into the State to get hush-money for it. They'll try to poison me, same as they did in Chortumna when I went on the loot there. But you'll give the man at Marwar Junction my message?"

He got out at a little roadside station, and I reflected. I had heard, more than once, of men personating correspondents of newspapers and bleeding small Native States with threats of exposure, but I had never met any of the caste before. They lead a hard life, and generally die with great suddenness. The Native States have a wholesome horror of English newspapers, which may throw light on their peculiar methods of government, and do their best to choke correspondents with champagne, or drive them out of their mind with four-in-hand barouches. They do not understand that nobody cares a straw for the internal administration of Native States so long as oppression and crime are kept within decent limits, and the ruler is not drugged, drunk, or diseased from one end of the year to the other. Native States were created by Providence in order to supply picturesque scenery, tigers, and tall-writing. They are the dark places of the earth, full of unimaginable cruelty, touching the Railway and the Telegraph on one side, and, on the other, the days of Harun-al-Raschid. When I left the train I did business with divers Kings, and in eight days passed through many changes of life. Sometimes I wore dress-clothes and consorted with Princes and Politicals, drinking from crystal and eating from silver. Sometimes I lay out upon the ground and devoured what I could get, from a plate made of a flapjack, and drank the running water, and slept under the same rug as my servant. It was all in the day's work.

Then I headed for the Great Indian Desert upon the proper date, as I had promised, and the night Mail set me down at Marwar Junction, where a funny little, happy-go-lucky, native-managed railway runs to Jodhpore. The Bombay Mail from Delhi makes a short halt at Marwar. She arrived as I got in, and I had just time to hurry to her platform and go down the carriages. There was only one Second-class on the train. I slipped the window and looked down upon a flaming red beard, half covered by a railway rug. That was my man, fast asleep, and I dug him gently in the ribs. He woke with a grunt and I saw his face in the light of the lamps. It was a great and shining face.

"Tickets again?" said he.

"No," said I. "I am to tell you that he is gone South for the week. He is gone South for the week!"

The train had begun to move out. The red man rubbed his eyes. "He has gone South for the week," he repeated. "Now that's just like his impidence. Did he say that I was to give you anything?—'Cause I won't."

"He didn't," I said, and dropped away, and watched the red lights die out in the dark. It was horribly cold because the wind was blowing off the sands. I climbed into my own train—not an Intermediate Carriage this time—and went to sleep.

If the man with the beard had given me a rupee I should have kept it as a memento of a rather curious affair. But the consciousness of having done my duty was my only reward.

Later on I reflected that two gentlemen like my friends could not do any good if they foregathered and personated correspondents of newspapers, and might, if they "stuck up" one of the little rat-trap states of Central India or Southern Rajputana, get themselves into serious difficulties. I therefore took some trouble to describe them as accurately as I could remember to people who would be interested in deporting them: and succeeded, so I was later informed, in having them headed back from the Degumber borders.

Then I became respectable, and returned to an Office where there were no Kings and no incidents except the daily manufacture of a newspaper. A newspaper office seems to attract every conceivable sort of person, to the prejudice of discipline. Zenana-mission ladies arrive, and beg that the Editor will instantly abandon all his duties to describe a Christian prize-giving in a back-slum of a perfectly inaccessible village; Colonels who have been overpassed for commands sit down and sketch the outline of a series of ten, twelve, or twenty-four leading articles on Seniority *versus* Selection; missionaries wish to know why they have not been permitted to escape from their regular vehicles of abuse and swear at a brother-missionary under special patronage of the editorial We; stranded theatrical companies troop up to explain that they cannot pay for their advertisements, but on their return from New Zealand or Tahiti will do so with interest; inventors of patent punkah-pulling machines, carriage couplings and unbreakable swords and axle-trees call with specifications in their pockets and hours at their disposal; tea-companies enter and elaborate their prospectuses with the office pens; secretaries of ball-committees clamor to have the glories of their last dance more fully expounded; strange ladies rustle in and say—"I want a hundred lady's cards printed *at once,* please," which is manifestly part of an Editor's duty; and every dissolute ruffian that ever tramped the Grand Trunk Road makes it his business to ask for employment as a proofreader. And, all the time, the telephone-bell is ringing madly, and Kings are being killed on the Continent, and Empires are saying—"You're another," and Mister Gladstone is calling down brimstone upon the British Dominions, and the little black copy-boys are whining, *"kaa-pi chay-ha-yeh"* (copy wanted) like tired bees, and most of the paper is as blank as Modred's shield.

But that is the amusing part of the year. There are other six months wherein none ever come to call, and the thermometer walks inch by inch up to the top of the glass, and the office is darkened to just above reading-light, and the press machines are red-hot of touch, and nobody writes anything but accounts of amusements in the Hill-stations or obituary notices. Then the telephone becomes a tinkling terror, because it tells you of the sudden deaths of men and women that you knew intimately, and the prickly-heat covers you as with a garment, and you sit down and write:—"A slight increase of sickness is reported from the Khuda Janta Khan District. The outbreak is purely sporadic in its nature, and, thanks to the energetic efforts of the District authorities, is now almost at an end. It is, however, with deep regret we record the death, etc."

Then the sickness really breaks out, and the less recording and reporting the better for the peace of the subscribers. But the Empires and the Kings continue to divert themselves as selfishly as before, and the Foreman thinks that a daily paper really ought to come out once in twenty-four hours, and all the people at the Hill-stations in the middle of their amusements say:—"Good gracious! Why can't the paper be sparkling? I'm sure there's plenty going on up here."

That is the dark half of the moon, and, as the advertisements say, "must be experienced to be appreciated."

It was in that season, and a remarkably evil season, that the paper began running the last issue of the week on Saturday night, which is to say Sunday morning, after the custom of a London paper. This was a great convenience, for immediately after the paper was put to bed, the dawn would lower the thermometer from 96° to almost 84° for half an hour, and in that chill—you have no idea how cold is 84° on the grass until you begin to pray for it—a very tired man could set off to sleep ere the heat roused him.

One Saturday night it was my pleasant duty to put the paper to bed alone. A King or courtier or a courtesan or a community was going to die or get a new Constitution, or do something that was important on the other side of the world, and the paper was to be held open till the latest possible minute in order to catch the telegram. It was a pitchy black night, as stifling as a June night can be, and the *loo,* the red-hot wind from the westward, was booming among the tinder-dry trees and pretending that the rain was on its heels. Now and again a spot of almost boiling water would fall on the dust with the flop of a frog, but all our weary world knew that was only pretence. It was a shade cooler in the press-room than the office, so I sat there, while the type ticked and clicked, and the night-jars hooted at the windows, and the all but naked compositors wiped the sweat from their foreheads and called for water. The thing that was keeping us back, whatever it was, would not come off, though the *loo* dropped and the last type was set, and the whole round earth stood still in the choking heat, with its finger on its lip, to wait the event. I drowsed, and wondered whether the telegraph was a blessing, and whether this dying man, or struggling people, was aware of the inconvenience the delay was causing. There was no special reason beyond the heat and worry to make tension, but, as the clock hands crept up to three o'clock and the machines spun their fly-wheels two and three times to see that all was in order, before I said the word that would set them off, I could have shrieked aloud.

Then the roar and rattle of the wheels shivered the quiet into little bits. I rose to go away, but two men in white clothes stood in front of me. The first one said:—"It's him!" The second said:—"So it is!" And they both laughed almost as loudly as the machinery roared, and mopped their foreheads. "We see there was a light burning across the road and we were sleeping in that ditch there for coolness, and I said to my friend here, The office is open. Let's come along and speak to him as turned us back from the Degumber State," said the smaller of the two. He was the man I had met in the Mhow train, and his fellow was the red-bearded man of Marwar Junction. There was no mistaking the eyebrows of the one or the beard of the other.

I was not pleased, because I wished to go to sleep, not to squabble with loafers. "What do you want?" I asked.

"Half an hour's talk with you cool and comfortable, in the office," said the red-bearded man. "We'd *like* some drink—the Contrack doesn't begin yet, Peachey, so you needn't look—but what we really want is advice. We don't want money. We ask you as a favor, because you did us a bad turn about Degumber."

I led from the press-room to the stifling office with the maps on the walls, and the red-haired man rubbed his hands. "That's something like," said he. "This was the proper shop to come to. Now, Sir, let me introduce to you Brother Peachey Carnehan, that's him, and Brother Daniel Dravot, that is *me,* and the less said about our professions the better, for we have been most things in our time. Soldier, sailor, compositor, photographer, proof-reader, street-preacher, and correspondents of the *Backwoodsman* when we thought the paper wanted one. Carnehan is sober, and so am I. Look at us first and see that's sure. It will save you cutting into my talk. We'll take one of your cigars apiece, and you shall see us light."

I watched the test. The men were absolutely sober, so I gave them each a tepid peg.

"Well *and* good," said Carnehan of the eyebrows, wiping the froth from his moustache. "Let me talk now, Dan. We have been all over India, mostly on foot. We have been boiler-fitters, engine-drivers, petty contractors, and all that, and we have decided that India isn't big enough for such as us."

They certainly were too big for the office. Dravot's beard seemed to fill half the room and Carnehan's shoulders the other half, as they sat on the big table. Carnehan continued:—"The country isn't half worked out because they that governs it won't let you touch it. They spend all their blessed time in governing it, and you can't lift a spade, nor chip a rock, nor look for oil, nor anything like that without all the Government saying—'Leave it alone and let us govern.' Therefore, such as it is, we will let it alone, and go away to some other place where a man isn't crowded and can come to his own. We are not little men, and there is nothing that we are afraid of except Drink, and we have signed a Contrack on that. *Therefore,* we are going away to be Kings."

"Kings in our own right," muttered Dravot.

"Yes, of course," I said. "You've been tramping in the sun, and it's a very warm night, and hadn't you better sleep over the notion? Come to-morrow."

"Neither drunk nor sunstruck," said Dravot. "We have slept over the notion half a year, and require to see Books and Atlases, and we have decided that there is only one place now in the world that two strong men can Sar-a-*whack*. They call it Kafiristan. By my reckoning it's the top right-hand corner of Afghanistan, not more than three hundred miles from Peshawur. They have two and thirty heathen idols there, and we'll be the thirty-third. It's a mountaineous country, and the women of those parts are very beautiful."

"But that is provided against in the Contrack," said Carnehan. "Neither Women nor Liqu-or, Daniel."

"And that's all we know, except that no one has gone there, and they fight, and in any place where they fight a man who knows how to drill men can always be a King. We shall go to those parts and say to any King we find—'D' you want to vanquish your foes?' and we will show him how to drill men; for that we know better than anything else. Then we will subvert that King and seize his Throne and establish a Dy-nasty."

"You'll be cut to pieces before you're fifty miles across the Border," I said. "You have to travel through Afghanistan to get to that country. It's one mass of mountains and peaks and glaciers, and no Englishman has been through it. The people are utter brutes, and even if you reached them you couldn't do anything."

"That's more like," said Carnehan. "If you could think us a little more mad we would be more pleased. We have come to you to know about this country, to read a book about it, and to be shown maps. We want you to tell us that we are fools and to show us your books." He turned to the bookcases.

"Are you at all in earnest?" I said.

"A little," said Dravot, sweetly. "As big a map as you have got, even if it's all blank where Kafiristan is, and any books you've got. We can read, though we aren't very educated."

I uncased the big thirty-two-miles-to-the-inch map of India, and two smaller Frontier maps, hauled down volume INF-KAN of the *Encyclopædia Brittanica,* and the men consulted them.

"See here!" said Dravot, his thumb on the map. "Up to Jagdallak, Peachey and me know the road. We was there with Roberts's Army. We'll have to turn off to the right at Jagdallak through Laghmann territory. Then we get among the hills—fourteen thousand feet—fifteen thousand—it will be cold work there, but it don't look very far on the map."

I handed him Wood on the *Sources of the Oxus.* Carnehan was deep in the *Encyclopædia.*

"They're a mixed lot," said Dravot, reflectively; "and it won't help us to know the names of their tribes. The more tribes the more they'll fight, and the better for us. From Jagdallak to Ashang. H'mm!"

"But all the information about the country is as sketchy and inaccurate as can be," I protested. "No one knows anything about it really. Here's the file of the *United Services' Institute.* Read what Bellew says."

"Blow Bellew!" said Carnehan. "Dan, they're an all-fired lot of heathens, but this book here says they think they're related to us English."

I smoked while the men pored over *Raverty, Wood,* the maps and the *Encyclopædia.*

"There is no use your waiting," said Dravot, politely. "It's about four o'clock now. We'll go before six o'clock if you want to sleep, and we won't steal any of the papers. Don't you sit up. We're two harmless lunatics, and if you come, to-morrow evening, down to the Serai we'll say good-bye to you."

"You *are* two fools," I answered. "You'll be turned back at the Frontier or cut up the minute you set foot in Afghanistan. Do you want any money or a recommendation down-country? I can help you to the chance of work next week."

"Next week we shall be hard at work ourselves, thank you," said Dravot. "It isn't so easy being a King as it looks. When we've got our Kingdom in going order we'll let you know, and you can come up and help us to govern it."

"Would two lunatics make a Contrack like that?" said Carnehan, with subdued pride, showing me a greasy half-sheet of note-paper on which was written the following. I copied it, then and there, as a curiosity:

> *This Contract between me and you persuing witnesseth in the name of God—Amen and so forth.*
>
> (One)   *That me and you will settle this matter together: i.e., to be Kings of Kafiristan.*
>
> (Two)   *That you and me will not, while this matter is being settled, look at any Liquor, nor any Woman, black, white or brown, so as to get mixed up with one or the other harmful.*

(Three)   *That we conduct ourselves with dignity and discretion, and if one*
            of us gets into trouble the other will stay by him.
          Signed by you and me this day.
            Peachey Taliaferro Carnehan.
            Daniel Dravot.
            Both Gentlemen at Large.

"There was no need for the last article," said Carnehan, blushing modestly; "but it looks regular. Now you know the sort of men that loafers are—we *are* loafers, Dan, until we get out of India—and *do* you think that we would sign a Contrack like that unless we was in earnest? We have kept away from the two things that make life worth having."

"You won't enjoy your lives much longer if you are going to try this idiotic adventure. Don't set the office on fire," I said, "and go away before nine o'clock."

I left them still poring over the maps and making notes on the back of the "Contrack." "Be sure to come down to the Serai to-morrow," were their parting words.

The Kumharsen Serai is the great four-square sink of humanity where the strings of camels and horses from the North load and unload. All the nationalities of Central Asia may be found there, and most of the folk of India proper. Balkh and Bokhara there meet Bengal and Bombay, and try to draw eye-teeth. You can buy ponies, turquoises, Persian pussy-cats, saddlebags, fat-tailed sheep and musk in the Kumharsen Serai, and get many strange things for nothing. In the afternoon I went down there to see whether my friends intended to keep their word or were lying about drunk.

A priest attired in fragments of ribbons and rags stalked up to me, gravely twisting a child's paper whirligig. Behind him was his servant bending under the load of a crate of mud toys. The two were loading up two camels, and the inhabitants of the Serai watched them with shrieks of laughter.

"The priest is mad," said a horse-dealer to me. "He is going up to Kabul to sell toys to the Amir. He will either be raised to honor or have his head cut off. He came in here this morning and has been behaving madly ever since."

"The witless are under the protection of God," stammered a flat-cheeked Usbeg in broken Hindi. "They foretell future events."

"Would they could have foretold that my caravan would have been cut up by the Shinwaris almost within shadow of the Pass!" grunted the Eusufzai agent of a Rajputana trading-house whose goods had been feloniously diverted into the hands of other robbers just across the Border, and whose misfortunes were the laughing-stock of the bazar. "Ohé, priest, whence come you and whither do you go?"

"From Roum have I come," shouted the priest, waving his whirligig; "from Roum, blown by the breath of a hundred devils across the sea! O thieves, robbers, liars, the blessing of Pir Khan on pigs, dogs, and perjurers! Who will take the Protected of God to the North to sell charms that are never still to the Amir? The camels shall not gall, the sons shall not fall sick, and the wives shall remain faithful while they are away, of the men who give me place in their caravan. Who will assist me to slipper the King of the Roos with a golden slipper with a silver heel? The protection of Pir Khan be upon his labors!" He spread out the skirts of his gaberdine and pirouetted between the lines of tethered horses.

"There starts a caravan from Peshawur to Kabul in twenty days, *Huzrut*," said the

Eusufzai trader. "My camels go therewith. Do thou also go and bring us good-luck."

"I will go even now!" shouted the priest. "I will depart upon my winged camels, and be at Pashawur in a day! Ho! Hazar Mir Khan," he yelled to his servant, "drive out the camels, but let me first mount my own."

He leaped on the back of his beast as it knelt, and, turning round to me, cried:— "Come thou also, Sahib, a little along the road, and I will sell thee a charm—an amulet that shall make thee King of Kafiristan."

Then the light broke upon me, and I followed the two camels out of the Serai till we reached open road and the priest halted.

"What d' you think o' that?" said he in English. "Carnehan can't talk their patter, so I've made him my servant. He makes a handsome servant. 'Tisn't for nothing that I've been knocking about the country for fourteen years. Didn't I do that talk neat? We'll hitch on to a caravan at Peshawur till we get to Jagdallak, and then we'll see if we can get donkeys for our camels, and strike into Kafiristan. Whirligigs for the Amir, O Lor! Put your hand under the camel-bags and tell me what you feel."

I felt the butt of a Martini, and another and another.

"Twenty of 'em," said Dravot, placidly. "Twenty of 'em, and ammunition to correspond, under the whirligigs and the mud dolls."

"Heaven help you if you are caught with those things!" I said. "A Martini is worth her weight in silver among the Pathans."

"Fifteen hundred rupees of capital—every rupee we could beg, borrow, or steal— are invested on these two camels," said Dravot. "We won't get caught. We're going through the Khaiber with a regular caravan. Who'd touch a poor mad priest?"

"Have you got everything you want?" I asked, overcome with astonishment.

"Not yet, but we shall soon. Give us a memento of your kindness, *Brother.* You did me a service yesterday, and that time in Marwar. Half my Kingdom shall you have, as the saying is." I slipped a small charm compass from my watch-chain and handed it up to the priest.

"Good-bye," said Dravot, giving me hand cautiously. "It's the last time we'll shake hands with an Englishman these many days. Shake hands with him, Carnehan," he cried, as the second camel passed me.

Carnehan leaned down and shook hands. Then the camels passed away along the dusty road, and I was left alone to wonder. My eye could detect no failure in the disguises. The scene in Serai attested that they were complete to the native mind. There was just the chance, therefore, that Carnehan and Dravot would be able to wander through Afghanistan without detection. But, beyond, they would find death, certain and awful death.

Ten days later a native friend of mine, giving me the news of the day from Peshawur, wound up his letter with:—"There has been much laughter here on account of a certain mad priest who is going in his estimation to sell petty gauds and insignificant trinkets which he ascribes as great charms to H. H. the Amir of Bokhara. He passed through Peshawur and associated himself to the Second Summer caravan that goes to Kabul. The merchants are pleased because through superstition they imagine that such mad fellows bring good-fortune."

The two, then, were beyond the Border. I would have prayed for them, but, that night, a real King died in Europe, and demanded an obituary notice.

The wheel of the world swings through the same phases again and again. Summer passed and winter thereafter, and came and passed again. The daily paper continued and I with it, and upon the third summer there fell a hot night, a night-issue, and a strained waiting for something to be telegraphed from the other side of the world, exactly as had happened before. A few great men had died in the past two years, the machines worked with more clatter, and some of the trees in the Office garden were a few feet taller. But that was all the difference.

I passed over to the press-room, and went through just such a scene as I have already described. The nervous tension was stronger than it had been two years before, and I felt the heat more acutely. At three o'clock I cried, "Print off," and turned to go, when there crept to my chair what was left of a man. He was bent into a circle, his head was sunk between his shoulders, and he moved his feet one over the other like a bear. I could hardly see whether he walked or crawled—this rag-wrapped, whining cripple who addressed me by name, crying that he was come back. "Can you give me a drink?" he whimpered. "For the Lord's sake, give me a drink!"

I went back to the office, the man following with groans of pain, and I turned up the lamp.

"Don't you know me?" he gasped, dropping into a chair, and he turned his drawn face, surmounted by a shock of grey hair, to the light.

I looked at him intently. Once before had I seen eyebrows that met over the nose in an inch-broad black band, but for the life of me I could not tell where.

"I don't know you," I said, handing him the whiskey. "What can I do for you?"

He took a gulp of the spirit raw, and shivered in spite of the suffocating heat.

"I've come back," he repeated; "and I was the King of Kafiristan—me and Dravot—crowned Kings we was! In this office we settled it—you setting there and giving us the books. I am Peachey—Peachey Taliaferro Carnehan, and you've been setting here ever since—O Lord!"

I was more than a little astonished, and expressed my feelings accordingly.

"It's true," said Carnehan, with a dry cackle, nursing his feet, which were wrapped in rags. "True as gospel. Kings we were, with crowns upon our heads—me and Dravot—poor Dan—oh, poor, poor Dan, that would never take advice, not though I begged of him!"

"Take the whiskey," I said, "and take your own time. Tell me all you can recollect of everything from beginning to end. You got across the border on your camels, Dravot dressed as a mad priest and you his servant. Do you remember that?"

"I ain't mad—yet, but I shall be that way soon. Of course I remember. Keep looking at me, or maybe my words will go all to pieces. Keep looking at me in my eyes and don't say anything."

I leaned forward and looked into his face as steadily as I could. He dropped one hand upon the table and I grasped it by the wrist. It was twisted like a bird's claw, and upon the back was a ragged, red, diamond-shaped scar.

"No, don't look there. Look at *me*," said Carnehan.

"That comes afterward, but for the Lord's sake don't distrack me. We left with that caravan, me and Dravot playing all sorts of antics to amuse the people we were with. Dravot used to make us laugh in the evenings when all the people was cooking their dinners—cooking their dinners, and . . . what did they do then? They lit little fires with sparks that went into Dravot's beard, and we all laughed—fit to die. Little red fires they was, going into Dravot's big red beard—so funny." His eyes left mine and he smiled foolishly.

"You went as far as Jagdallak with that caravan," I said, at a venture, "after you had lit those fires. To Jagdallak, where you turned off to try to get into Kafiristan."

"No, we didn't neither. What are you talking about? We turned off before Jagdallak, because we heard the roads was good. But they wasn't good enough for our two camels—mine and Dravot's. When we left the caravan, Dravot took off all his clothes and mine too, and said we would be heathen, because the Kafirs didn't allow Mohammedans to talk to them. So we dressed betwixt and between, and such a sight as Daniel Dravot I never saw yet nor expect to see again. He burned half his beard, and slung a sheep-skin over his shoulder, and shaved his head into patterns. He shaved mine, too, and made me wear outrageous things to look like a heathen. That was in a most mountaineous country, and our camels couldn't go along any more because of the mountains. They were tall and black, and coming home I saw them fight like wild goats—there are lots of goats in Kafiristan. And these mountains, they never keep still, no more than the goats. Always fighting they are, and don't let you sleep at night."

"Take some more whiskey," I said, very slowly. "What did you and Daniel Dravot do when the camels could go no further because of the rough roads that led into Kafiristan?"

"What did which do? There was a party called Peachey Taliaferro Carnehan that was with Dravot. Shall I tell you about him? He died out there in the cold. Slap from the bridge fell old Peachey, turning and twisting in the air like a penny whirligig that you can sell to the Amir.—No; they was two for three ha'pence, those whirligigs, or I am much mistaken and woful sore. And then these camels were no use, and Peachey said to Dravot—'For the Lord's sake, let's get out of this before our heads are chopped off,' and with that they killed the camels all among the mountains, not having anything in particular to eat, but first they took off the boxes with the guns and the ammunition, till two men came along driving four mules. Dravot up and dances in front of them, singing,—'Sell me four mules.' Says the first man,—'If you are rich enough to buy, you are rich enough to rob;' but before ever he could put his hand to his knife, Dravot breaks his neck over his knee, and the other party runs away. So Carnehan loaded the mules with the rifles that was taken off the camels, and together we starts forward into those bitter cold mountaineous parts, and never a road broader than the back of your hand."

He paused for a moment, while I asked him if he could remember the nature of the country through which he had journeyed.

"I am telling you as straight as I can, but my head isn't as good as it might be. They drove nails through it to make me hear better how Dravot died. The country was mountaineous and the mules were most contrary, and the inhabitants was dispersed and solitary. They went up and up, and down and down, and that other party, Carnehan, was imploring of Dravot not to sing and whistle so loud, for fear of bringing down the tremenjus avalanches. But Dravot says that if a King couldn't sing it wasn't worth being King, and whacked the mules over the rump, and never took no heed for ten cold days. We came to a big level valley all among the mountains, and the mules were near dead, so we killed them, not having anything in special for them or us to eat. We sat upon the boxes, and played odd and even with the cartridges that was jolted out.

"Then ten men with bows and arrows ran down that valley, chasing twenty men with bows and arrows, and the row was tremenjus. They was fair men—fairer than you or me—with yellow hair and remarkable well built. Says Dravot, unpacking the guns—'This is the beginning of the business. We'll fight for the ten men,' and with that he fires two rifles at the twenty men, and drops one of them at two hundred yards from the rock where we was sitting. The other men began to run, but Carnehan and Dravot sits on the boxes picking them off at all ranges, up and down the valley. Then we goes up to the ten men that had run across the snow too, and they fires a footy little arrow at us. Dravot he shoots above their heads and they all falls down flat. Then he walks over them and kicks them, and then he lifts them up and shakes hands all round to make them friendly like. He calls them and gives them the boxes to carry, and waves his hand for all the world as though he was King already. They takes the boxes and him across the valley and up the hill into a pine wood on the top, where there was half a dozen big stone idols. Dravot he goes to the biggest—a fellow they call Imbra—and lays a rifle and a cartridge at his feet, rubbing his nose respectful with his own nose, patting him on the head, and saluting in front of it. He turns round to the men and nods his head, and says,—'That's all right. I'm in the know too, and all these old jim-jams are my friends.' Then he opens his mouth and points down it, and when the first man brings him food, he says—'No;' and when the second man brings him food, he says—'No;' but when one of the old priests and the boss of the village brings him food, he says—'Yes;' very haughty, and eats it slow. That was how we came to our first village, without any trouble, just as though we had tumbled from the skies. But we tumbled from one of those damned rope-bridges, you see, and you couldn't expect a man to laugh much after that."

"Take some more whiskey and go on," I said. "That was the first village you came into. How did you get to be King?"

"I wasn't King," said Carnehan. "Dravot he was the King, and a handsome man he looked with the gold crown on his head and all. Him and the other party stayed in that village, and every morning Dravot sat by the side of old Imbra, and the people came and worshipped. That was Dravot's order. Then a lot of men came into the valley, and Carnehan and Dravot picks them off with the rifles before they knew where they was, and runs down into the valley and up again the other side, and finds another village, same as the first one, and the people all falls down flat on their faces, and Dravot says,—'Now what is the trouble between you two villages?' and the people points to a woman, as fair as you or me, that was carried off, and Dravot takes her back to the first village and counts up the dead—eight there was. For each dead man Dravot pours a little milk on the ground and waves his arms like a whirligig and 'That's all right,' says he. Then he and Carnehan takes the big boss of each village by the arm and walks them down into the valley and shows them how to scratch a line with a spear right down the valley, and gives each a sod of turf from both sides o' the line. Then all the people comes down and shouts like the devil and all, and Dravot says,—'Go and dig the land, and be fruitful and multiply,' which they did, though they didn't understand. Then we asks the names of things in their lingo—bread and water and fire and idols and such, and Dravot leads the priest of each village up to the idol, and says he must sit there and judge the people, and if anything goes wrong he is to be shot.

"Next week they was all turning up the land in the valley as quiet as bees and much prettier, and the priests heard all the complaints and told Dravot in dumb show what it was about. 'That's just the beginning,' says Dravot. 'They think we're Gods.' He and Carnehan picks out twenty good men and shows them how to click off a rifle, and form fours, and advance in line, and they was very pleased to do so, and clever to see the hang of it. Then he takes out his pipe and his baccy-pouch and leaves one at one village and one at the other, and off we two goes to see what was to be done in the next valley. That was all rock, and there was a little village there, and Carnehan says,—'Send 'em to the old valley to plant,' and takes 'em there and gives 'em some land that wasn't took before. They were a poor lot, and we blooded 'em with a kid before letting 'em into the new Kingdom. That was to impress the people, and then they settled down quiet, and Carnehan went back to Dravot who had got into another valley, all snow and ice and most mountaineous. There was no people there and the Army got afraid, so Dravot shoots one of them, and goes on till he finds some people in a village, and the Army explains that unless the people wants to be killed they had better not shoot their little matchlocks; for they had matchlocks. We makes friends with the priest and I stays there alone with two of the Army, teaching the men how to drill, and a thundering big Chief comes across the snow with kettle-drums and horns twanging, because he heard there was a new God kicking about. Carnehan sights for the brown of the men half a mile across the snow and wings one of them. Then he sends a message to the Chief that, unless he wished to be killed, he must come and shake hands with me and leave his arms behind. The chief comes alone first, and Carnehan shakes hands with him and whirls his arms about, same as Dravot used, and very much surprised that Chief was, and strokes my eyebrows. Then Carnehan goes alone to the Chief, and asks him in dumb show if he had an enemy he hated. 'I have,' says the Chief. So Carnehan weeds out the pick of his men, and sets the two of the Army to show them drill and at the end of two weeks the men can manœuvre about as well as Volunteers. So he marches with the Chief to a great big plain on the top of a mountain, and the Chief's men rushes into a village and takes it; we three Martinis firing into the brown of the enemy. So we took that village too, and I gives the Chief a rag from my coat and says, 'Occupy till I come:' which was scriptural. By way of a reminder, when me and the Army was eighteen hundred yards away, I drops a bullet near him standing on the snow, and all the people falls flat on their faces. Then I sends a letter to Dravot, wherever he be by land or by sea."

At the risk of throwing the creature out of train I interrupted,—"How could you write a letter up yonder?"

"The letter?—Oh!—The letter! Keep looking at me between the eyes, please. It was a string-talk letter, that we'd learned the way of it from a blind beggar in the Punjab."

I remember that there had once come to the office a blind man with a knotted twig and a piece of string which he wound round the twig according to some cypher of his own. He could, after the lapse of days or hours, repeat the sentence which he had reeled up. He had reduced the alphabet to eleven primitive sounds; and tried to teach me his method, but failed.

"I sent that letter to Dravot," said Carnehan; "and told him to come back because this Kingdom was growing too big for me to handle, and then I struck for the first valley, to see how the priests were working. They called the village we took along with the Chief, Bashkai, and the first village we took, Er-Heb. The priests at Er-Heb was doing all right, but they had a lot of pending cases about land to show me, and some men from another village had been firing arrows at night. I went out and looked for that village and fired four rounds at it from a thousand yards. That used all the cartridges I cared to spend, and I waited for Dravot, who had been away two or three months, and I kept my people quiet.

"One morning I heard the devil's own noise of drums and horns, and Dan Dravot marches down the hill with his Army and a tail of hundreds of men, and, which was the most amazing—a great gold crown on his head. 'My Gord, Carnehan,' says Daniel, 'this is a tremenjus business, and we've got the whole country as far as it's worth having. I am the son of Alexander by Queen Semiramis, and you're my younger brother and a God too! It's the biggest thing we've ever seen. I've been marching and fighting for six weeks with the Army, and every footy little village for fifty miles has come in rejoiceful; and more than that, I've got the key of the whole show, as you'll see, and I've got a crown for you! I told 'em to make two of 'em at a place called Shu, where the gold lies in the rock like suet in mutton. Gold I've seen, and turquoise I've kicked out of the cliffs, and there's garnets in the sands of the river, and here's a chunk of amber that a man brought me. Call up all the priests and, here, take your crown.'

"One of the men opens a black hair bag and I slips the crown on. It was too small and too heavy, but I wore it for the glory. Hammered gold it was—five pound weight, like a hoop of a barrel.

"'Peachey,' says Dravot, 'we don't want to fight no more. The Craft's the trick so help me!' and he brings forward that same Chief that I left at Bashkai—Billy Fish we called him afterward, because he was so like Billy Fish that drove the big tank-engine at Mach on the Bolan in the old days. 'Shake hands with him,' says Dravot, and I shook hands and nearly dropped, for Billy Fish gave me the Grip. I said nothing, but tried him with the Fellow Craft Grip. He answers, all right, and I tried the Master's Grip, but that was a slip. 'A Fellow Craft he is!' I says to Dan. 'Does he know the word?' 'He does,' says Dan, 'and all the priests know. It's a miracle! The Chiefs and the priests can work a Fellow Craft Lodge in a way that's very like ours, and they've cut the marks on the rocks, but they don't know the Third Degree, and they've come to find out. It's Gord's Truth. I've known these long years that the Afghans knew up to the Fellow Craft Degree, but this is a miracle. A God and a Grand-Master of the Craft am I, and a Lodge in the Third Degree I will open, and we'll raise the head priests and the Chiefs of the villages.'

"'It's against all the law,' I says, 'holding a Lodge without warrant from any one; and we never held office in any Lodge.'

"'It's a master-stroke of policy,' says Dravot. 'It means running the country as easy as a four wheeled bogy on a down grade. We can't stop to inquire now, or they'll turn against us. I've forty Chiefs at my heel, and passed and raised according to their merit they shall be. Billet these men on the villages and see that we run up a Lodge of some kind. The temple of Imbra will do for the Lodge-room. The women must make aprons as you show them. I'll hold a levee of Chiefs to-night and Lodge to-morrow.'

"I was fair run off my legs, but I wasn't such a fool as not to see what a pull this Craft business gave us. I showed the priests' families how to make aprons of the degrees, but for Dravot's apron the blue border and marks was made of turquoise lumps on white hide, not cloth. We took a great square stone in the temple for the Master's chair, and little stones for the officers' chairs, and painted the black pavement with white squares, and did what we could to make things regular.

"At the levee which was held that night on the hillside with big bonfires, Dravot gives out that him and me were Gods and sons of Alexander, and Past Grand-Masters in the Craft, and was come to make Kafiristan a country where every man should eat in peace and drink in quiet, and specially obey us. Then the Chiefs come round to shake hands, and they was so hairy and white and fair it was just shaking hands with old friends. We gave them names according as they was like men we had known in India—Billy Fish, Holly Dilworth, Pikky Kergan that was Bazar-master when I was at Mhow, and so on and so on.

"*The* most amazing miracle was at Lodge next night. One of the old priests was watching us continuous, and I felt uneasy, for I knew we'd have to fudge the Ritual, and I didn't know what the men knew. The old priest was a stranger come in from beyond the village of Bashkai. The minute Dravot puts on the Master's apron that the girls had made for him, the priest fetches a whoop and a howl, and tries to over-turn the stone that Dravot was sitting on. 'It's all up now,' I says. 'That comes of meddling with the Craft without warrant!' Dravot never winked an eye, not when ten priests took and tilted over the Grand-Master's chair—which was to say the stone of Imbra. The priest begins rubbing the bottom end of it to clear away the black dirt, and presently he shows all the other priests the Master's Mark, same as was on Dravot's apron, cut into the stone. Not even the priests of the temple of Imbra knew it was there. The old chap falls flat on his face at Dravot's feet and kisses 'em. 'Luck again,' says Dravot, across the Lodge to me, 'they say it's the missing Mark that no one could understand the why of. We're more than safe now.' Then he bangs the butt of his gun for a gavel and says:—'By virtue of the authority vested in me by my own right hand and the help of Peachey, I declare myself Grand-Master of all Freemasonry in Kafiristan in this the Mother Lodge o' the country, and King of Kafiristan equally with Peachey!' At that he puts on his crown and I puts on mine—I was doing Senior Warden—and we opens the Lodge in most ample form. It was a amazing miracle! The priests moved in Lodge through the first two degrees almost without telling, as if the memory was coming back to them. After that, Peachey and Dravot raised such as was worthy—high priests and Chiefs of far-off villages. Billy Fish was the first, and I can tell you we scared the soul out of him. It was not in any way according to Ritual, but it served our turn. We didn't raise more than ten of the biggest men because we didn't want to make the Degree common. And they was clamoring to be raised.

"'In another six months,' says Dravot, 'we'll hold another Communication and see how you are working.' Then he asks them about their villages, and learns that they was fighting one against the other and were fair sick and tired of it. And when they wasn't doing that they was fighting with the Mohammedans. 'You can fight those when they come into our country,' says Dravot. 'Tell off every tenth man of your tribes for a Frontier guard, and send two hundred at a time to this valley to be drilled. Nobody is going to be shot or speared any more so long us he does well, and I know that you won't cheat me because you're white people—sons of Alexander—and not like common, black Mohammedans. You are *my* people and by God,' says he, running off into English at the end—'I'll make a damned fine Nation of you, or I'll die in the making!'

"I can't tell all we did for the next six months because Dravot did a lot I couldn't see the hang of, and he learned their lingo in a way I never could. My work was to help the people plough, and now and again go out with some of the Army and see what the other villages were doing, and make 'em throw rope-bridges across the ravines which cut up the country horrid. Dravot was very kind to me, but when he walked up and down in the pine wood pulling that bloody red beard of his with both fists I knew he was thinking plans I could not advise him about, and I just waited for orders.

"But Dravot never showed me disrespect before the people. They were afraid of me and the Army, but they loved Dan. He was the best of friends with the priests and the Chiefs; but any one could come across the hills with a complaint and Dravot would hear him out fair, and call four priests together and say what was to be done. He used to call in Billy Fish from Bashkai, and Pikky Kergan from Shu, and an old Chief we called Kafuzelum—it was like enough to his real name—and hold councils with 'em when there was any fighting to be done in small villages. That was his Council of War, and the four priests of Bashkai, Shu, Khawak, and Madora was his Privy Council. Between the lot of 'em they sent me, with forty men and twenty rifles, and sixty men carrying turquoises, into the Ghorband country to buy those hand-made Martini rifles, that come out of the Amir's workshops at Kabul, from one of the Amir's Herati regiments that would have sold the very teeth out of their mouths for turquoises.

"I stayed in Ghorband a month, and gave the Governor there the pick of my baskets for hush-money, and bribed the Colonel of the regiment some more, and, between the two and the tribes-people, we got more than a hundred hand-made Martinis, a hundred good Kohat Jezails that'll throw to six hundred yards, and forty man-loads of very bad ammunition for the rifles. I came back with what I had, and distributed 'em among the men that the Chiefs sent to me to drill. Dravot was too busy to attend to those things, but the old Army that we first made helped me, and we turned out five hundred men that could drill, and two hundred that knew how to hold arms pretty straight. Even those cork-screwed, hand-made guns was a miracle to them. Dravot talked big about powder-shops and factories, walking up and down in the pine wood when the winter was coming on.

"'I won't make a Nation,' says he. 'I'll make an Empire! These men aren't niggers; they're English! Look at their eyes—look at their mouths. Look at the way they stand up. They sit on chairs in their own houses. They're the Lost Tribes, or something like it, and they've grown to be English. I'll take a census in the spring if the priests don't get frightened. There must be a fair two million of 'em in these hills. The villages are full o' little children. Two million people—two hundred and fifty thousand fighting men—and all English! They only want the rifles and a little drilling. Two hundred and fifty thousand men, ready to cut in on Russia's right flank when she tries for India! Peachey man,' he says, chewing his beard in great hunks, 'we shall be Emperors—Emperors of the Earth! Rajah Brooke will be a suckling to us. I'll treat with the Viceroy on equal terms. I'll ask him to send me twelve picked English— twelve that I know of—to help us govern a bit. There's Mackray, Sergeant-pensioner at Segowli—many's the good dinner he's given me, and his wife a pair of trousers. There's Donkin, the Warder of Tounghoo Jail; there's hundreds that I could lay my hand on if I was in India. The Viceroy shall do it for me. I'll send a man through in the spring for those men, and I'll write for a dispensation from the Grand Lodge for what I've done as Grand-Master. That—and all the Sniders that'll be thrown out when the native troops in India take up the Martini. They'll be worn smooth, but they'll do for fighting in these hills. Twelve English, a hundred thousand Sniders run through the Amir's country in driblets—I'd be content with twenty thousand in one year—and we'd be an Empire. When everything was shipshape, I'd hand over the crown—this crown I'm wearing now—to Queen Victoria on my knees, and she'd say: "Rise up, Sir Daniel Dravot." Oh, it's big! It's big, I tell you! But there's so much to be done in every place—Bashkai, Khawak, Shu, and everywhere else.'

"'What is it?' I says. 'There are no more men coming in to be drilled this autumn. Look at those fat, black clouds. They're bringing the snow.'

"'It isn't that,' says Daniel, putting his hand very hard on my shoulder; 'and I don't wish to say anything that's against you, for no other living man would have followed me and made me what I am as you have done. You're a first-class Commander-in-Chief, and the people know you; but—it's a big country, and somehow you can't help me, Peachey, in the way I want to be helped.'

"'Go to your blasted priests, then!' I said, and I was sorry when I made that remark, but it did hurt me sore to find Daniel talking so superior when I'd drilled all the men, and done all he told me.

"'Don't let's quarrel, Peachey,' says Daniel, without cursing. 'You're a King too, and the half of this Kingdom is yours; but can't you see, Peachey, we want cleverer men than us now—three or four of 'em, that we can scatter about for our Deputies. It's a hugeous great State, and I can't always tell the right thing to do, and I haven't time for all I want to do, and here's the winter coming on and all.' He put half his beard into his mouth, and it was as red us the gold of his crown.

"'I'm sorry, Daniel,' says I. 'I've done all I could. I've drilled the men and shown the people how to stack their oats better; and I've brought in those tinware rifles from Ghorband—but I know what you're driving at. I take it Kings always feel oppressed that way.'

"'There's another thing too,' says Dravot walking up and down. 'The winter's coming and these people won't be giving much trouble, and if they do we can't move about. I want a wife.'

"'For Gord's sake leave the women alone!' I says. 'We've both got all the work we can, though I *am* a fool. Remember the Contrack, and keep clear o' women.'

"'The Contrack only lasted till such time as we was Kings; and Kings we have been these months past,' says Dravot, weighing his crown in his hand. 'You go get a wife too, Peachey—a nice, strappin', plump girl that'll keep you warm in the winter. They're prettier than English girls, and we can take the pick of 'em. Boil 'em once or twice in hot water, and they'll come as fair as chicken and ham.'

"'Don't tempt me!' I says. 'I will not have any dealings with a woman not till we are a dam' side more settled than we are now. I've been doing the work o' two men, and you've been doing the work o' three. Let's lie off a bit, and see if we can get some better tobacco from Afghan country and run in some good liquor; but no women.'

"'Who's talking o' *women?*' says Dravot. 'I said *wife*—a Queen to breed a King's son for the King. A Queen out of the strongest tribe, that'll make them your blood-brothers, and that'll lie by your side and tell you all the people thinks about you and their own affairs. That's what I want.'

"'Do you remember that Bengali woman I kept at Mogul Serai when I was a plate-layer?' says I. 'A fat lot o' good she was to me. She taught me the lingo and one or two other things; but what happened? She ran away with the Station Master's servant and half my month's pay. Then she turned up at Dadur Junction in tow of a half-caste, and had the impidence to say I was her husband—all among the drivers in the running-shed!'

"'We've done with that,' says Dravot. 'These women are whiter than you or me, and a Queen I will have for the winter months.'

"'For the last time o' asking, Dan, do *not*,' I says 'It'll only bring us harm. The Bible says that Kings ain't to waste their strength on women, 'specially when they've got a new raw Kingdom to work over.'

"'For the last time of answering I will,' said Dravot, and he went away through the pine-trees looking like a big red devil. The low sun hit his crown and beard on one side and the two blazed like hot coals.

"But getting a wife was not as easy as Dan thought. He put it before the Council, and there was no answer till Billy Fish said that he'd better ask the girls. Dravot damned them all round. 'What's wrong with me?' he shouts, standing by the idol Imbra. 'Am I a dog or am I not enough of a man for your wenches? Haven't I put the shadow of my hand over this country? Who stopped the last Afghan raid?' It was me really, but Dravot was too angry to remember. 'Who brought your guns? Who repaired the bridges? Who's the Grand-Master of the sign cut in the stone?' and he thumped his hand on the block that he used to sit on in Lodge, and at Council, which opened like Lodge always. Billy Fish said nothing and no more did the others. 'Keep your hair on, Dan,' said I; 'and ask the girls. That's how it's done at Home, and these people are quite English.'

"'The marriage of the King is a matter of State,' says Dan, in a white-hot rage, for he could feel, I hope, that he was going against his better mind. He walked out of the Council-room, and the others sat still, looking at the ground.

"'Billy Fish,' says I to the Chief of Bashkai, 'what's the difficulty here? A straight answer to a true friend.' 'You know,' says Billy Fish. 'How should a man tell you who know everything? How can daughters of men marry Gods or Devils? It's not proper.'

"I remembered something like that in the Bible; but if, after seeing us as long as they had, they still believed we were Gods, it wasn't for me to undeceive them.

"'A God can do anything,' says I. 'If the King is fond of a girl he'll not let her die.' 'She'll have to,' said Billy Fish. 'There are all sorts of Gods and Devils in these mountains, and now and again a girl marries one of them and isn't seen any more. Besides, you two know the Mark cut in the stone. Only the Gods know that. We thought you were men till you showed the sign of the Master.'

"I wished then that we had explained about the loss of the genuine secrets of a Master-Mason at the first go-off; but I said nothing. All that night there was a blowing of horns in a little dark temple half-way down the hill, and I heard a girl crying fit to die. One of the priests told us that she was being prepared to marry the King.

"'I'll have no nonsense of that kind,' says Dan. 'I don't want to interfere with your customs, but I'll take my own wife.' 'The girl's a little bit afraid,' says the priest. 'She thinks she's going to die, and they are a-heartening of her up down in the temple.'

"'Hearten her very tender, then,' says Dravot, 'or I'll hearten you with the butt of a gun so that you'll never want to be heartened again.' He licked his lips, did Dan, and stayed up walking about more than half the night, thinking of the wife that he was going to get in the morning. I wasn't any means comfortable, for I knew that dealings with a woman in foreign parts, though you was a crowned King twenty times over, could not but be risky. I got up very early in the morning while Dravot was asleep, and I saw the priests talking together in whispers, and the Chiefs talking together too, and they looked at me out of the corners of their eyes.

"'What is up, Fish?' I says to the Bashkai man, who was wrapped up in his furs and looking splendid to behold.

"'I can't rightly say,' says he; 'but if you can induce the King to drop all this nonsense about marriage, you'll be doing him and me and yourself a great service.'

"'That I do believe,' says I. 'But sure, you know, Billy, as well as me, having fought against and for us, that the King and me are nothing more than two of the finest men that God Almighty ever made. Nothing more, I do assure you.'

"'That may be,' says Billy Fish, 'and yet I should be sorry if it was.' He sinks his head upon his great fur cloak for a minute and thinks. 'King,' says he, 'be you man or God or Devil, I'll stick by you to-day. I have twenty of my men with me, and they will follow me. We'll go to Bashkai until the storm blows over.'

"A little snow had fallen in the night, and everything was white except the greasy fat clouds that blew down and down from the north. Dravot came out with his crown on his head, swinging his arms and stamping his feet, and looking more pleased than Punch.

"'For the last time, drop it, Dan,' says I, in a whisper. 'Billy Fish here says that there will be a row.'

"'A row among my people!' says Dravot. 'Not much. Peachey, you're a fool not to get a wife too. Where's the girl?' says he, with a voice as loud as the braying of a jackass. 'Call up all the Chiefs and priests, and let the Emperor see if his wife suits him.'

"There was no need to call any one. They were all there leaning on their guns and spears round the clearing in the centre of the pine wood. A deputation of priests went down to the little temple to bring up the girl, and the horns blew up fit to wake the dead. Billy Fish saunters round and gets as close to Daniel as he could, and behind him stood his twenty men with matchlocks. Not a man of them under six feet. I was next to Dravot, and behind me was twenty men of the regular Army. Up comes the girl, and a strapping wench she was, covered with silver and turquoises but white as death, and looking back every minute at the priests.

"'She'll do,' said Dan, looking her over. 'What's to be afraid of, lass? Come and kiss me.' He puts his arm round her. She shuts her eyes, gives a bit of a squeak, and down goes her face in the side of Dan's flaming red beard.

"'The slut's bitten me!' says he, clapping his hand to his neck, and, sure enough, his hand was red with blood. Billy Fish and two of his matchlock-men catches hold of Dan by the shoulders and drags him into the Bashkai lot, while the priests howls in their lingo,—'Neither God nor Devil but a man!' I was all taken aback, for a priest cut at me in front, and the Army behind began firing into the Bashkai men.

"'God A-mighty!' says Dan. 'What is the meaning o' this?'

"'Come back! Come away!' says Billy Fish. 'Ruin and Mutiny is the matter. We'll break for Bashkai if we can.'

"I tried to give some sort of orders to my men—the men o' the regular Army—but it was no use, so I fired into the brown of 'em with an English Martini and drilled three beggars in a line. The valley was full of shouting, howling creatures, and every soul was shrieking, 'Not a God nor a Devil but only a man!' The Bashkai troops stuck to Billy Fish all they were worth, but their matchlocks wasn't half as good as the Kabul breech-loaders, and four of them dropped. Dan was bellowing like a bull, for he was very wrathy; and Billy Fish had a hard job to prevent him running out at the crowd.

"'We can't stand,' says Billy Fish. 'Make a run for it down the valley! The whole place is against us.' The matchlock-men ran, and we went down the valley in spite of Dravot's protestations. He was swearing horribly and crying out that he was a King. The priests rolled great stones on us, and the regular Army fired hard, and there wasn't more than six men, not counting Dan, Billy Fish, and Me, that came down to the bottom of the valley alive.

"Then they stopped firing and the horns in the temple blew again. 'Come away—for Gord's sake come away!' says Billy Fish. 'They'll send runners out to all the villages before ever we get to Bashkai. I can protect you there, but I can't do anything now.'

"My own notion is that Dan began to go mad in his head from that hour. He stared up and down like a stuck pig. Then he was all for walking back alone and killing the priests with his bare hands; which he could have done. 'An Emperor am I,' says Daniel, 'and next year I shall be a Knight of the Queen.'

"'All right, Dan,' says I; 'but come along now while there's time.'

"'It's your fault,' says he, 'for not looking after your Army better. There was mutiny in the midst, and you didn't know—you damned engine-driving, plate-laying, missionary's-pass-hunting hound!' He sat upon a rock and called me every foul name he could lay tongue to. I was too heart-sick to care, though it was all his foolishness that brought the smash.

"'I'm sorry, Dan,' says I, 'but there's no accounting for natives. This business is our Fifty-Seven. Maybe we'll make something out of it yet, when we've got to Bashkai.'

"'Let's get to Bashkai, then,' says Dan, 'and, by God, when I come back here again I'll sweep the valley so there isn't a bug in a blanket left!'

"We walked all that day, and all that night Dan was stumping up and down on the snow, chewing his beard and muttering to himself.

"'There's no hope o' getting clear,' said Billy Fish. 'The priests will have sent runners to the villages to say that you are only men. Why didn't you stick on as Gods till things was more settled? I'm a dead man,' says Billy Fish, and he throws himself down on the snow and begins to pray to his Gods.

"Next morning we was in a cruel bad country—all up and down, no level ground at all, and no food either. The six Bashkai men looked at Billy Fish hungry-wise as if they wanted to ask something, but they said never a word. At noon we came to the top of a flat mountain all covered with snow, and when we climbed up into it, behold, there was an Army in position waiting in the middle!

"'The runners have been very quick,' says Billy Fish, with a little bit of a laugh. 'They are waiting for us.'

"Three or four men began to fire from the enemy's side, and a chance shot took Daniel in the calf of the leg. That brought him to his senses. He looks across the snow at the Army, and sees the rifles that we had brought into the country.

"'We're done for,' says he. 'They are Englishmen, these people,—and it's my blasted nonsense that has brought you to this. Get back, Billy Fish, and take your men away; you've done what you could, and now cut for it. Carnehan,' says he, 'shake hands with me and go along with Billy. Maybe they won't kill you. I'll go and meet 'em alone. It's me that did it. Me, the King!'

"'Go!' says I. 'Go to Hell, Dan. I'm with you here. Billy Fish, you clear out, and we two will meet those folk.'

"'I'm a Chief,' says Billy Fish, quite quiet. 'I stay with you. My men can go.'

"The Bashkai fellows didn't wait for a second word but ran off, and Dan and Me and Billy Fish walked across to where the drums were drumming and the horns were horning. It was cold—awful cold. I've got that cold in the back of my head now. There's a lump of it there."

The punkah-coolies had gone to sleep. Two kerosene lamps were blazing in the office, and the perspiration poured down my face and splashed on the blotter as I leaned forward. Carnehan was shivering, and I feared that his mind might go. I wiped my face, took a fresh grip of the piteously mangled hands, and said:—"What happened after that?"

The momentary shift of my eyes had broken the clear current.

"What was you pleased to say?" whined Carnehan. "They took them without any sound. Not a little whisper all along the snow, not though the King knocked down the first man that set hand on him—not though old Peachey fired his last cartridge into the brown of 'em. Not a single solitary sound did those swines make. They just closed up tight, and I tell you their furs stunk. There was a man called Billy Fish, a good friend of us all, and they cut his throat, Sir, then and there, like a pig; and the King kicks up the bloody snow and says:—'We've had a dashed fine run for our money. What's coming next?' But Peachey, Peachey Taliaferro, I tell you, Sir, in confidence as betwixt two friends, he lost his head, Sir. No, he didn't neither. The King lost his head, so he did, all along o' one of those cunning rope-bridges. Kindly let me have the paper-cutter, Sir. It tilted this way. They marched him a mile across that snow to a rope-bridge over a ravine with a river at the bottom. You may have seen such. They prodded him behind like an ox. 'Damn your eyes!' says the King. 'D'you suppose I can't die like a gentleman?' He turns to Peachey—Peachey that was crying like a child. 'I've brought you to this, Peachey,' says he. 'Brought you out of your happy life to be killed in Kafiristan, where you was late Commander-in-Chief of the Emperor's forces. Say you forgive me, Peachey.' 'I do,' says Peachey. 'Fully and freely do I forgive you, Dan,' 'Shake hands, Peachey,' says he. 'I'm going now.' Out he goes, looking neither right nor left, and when he was plumb in the middle of those dizzy dancing ropes, 'Cut, you beggars,' he shouts; and they cut, and old Dan fell, turning round and round and round twenty thousand miles, for he took half an hour to fall till he struck the water, and I could see his body caught on a rock with the gold crown close beside.

"But do you know what they did to Peachey between two pine trees? They crucified him, Sir, as Peachey's hand will show. They used wooden pegs for his hands and his feet; and he didn't die. He hung there and screamed, and they took him down next day, and said it was a miracle that he wasn't dead. They took him down—poor old Peachey that hadn't done them any harm—that hadn't done them any. . . ."

He rocked to and fro and wept bitterly, wiping his eyes with the back of his scarred hands and moaning like a child for some ten minutes.

"They was cruel enough to feed him up in the temple, because they said he was more of a God than old Daniel that was a man. Then they turned him out on the snow, and told him to go home, and Peachey came home in about a year, begging along the roads quite safe: for Daniel Dravot he walked before and said:—'Come along, Peachey. It's a big thing we're doing.' The mountains they danced at night, and the mountains they tried to fall on Peachey's head, but Dan he held up his hand, and Peachey came along bent double. He never let go of Dan's hand, and he never let go of Dan's head. They gave it to him as a present in the temple, to remind him not to come again, and though the crown was pure gold, and Peachey was starving, never would Peachey sell the same. You knew Dravot, Sir! You knew Right Worshipful Brother Dravot! Look at him now!"

He fumbled in the mass of rags round his bent waist; brought out a black horse-hair bag embroidered with silver thread; and shook therefrom on to my table—the dried, withered head of Daniel Dravot! The morning sun that had long been paling the lamps struck the red beard and blind sunken eyes; struck, too, a heavy circlet of gold studded with raw turquoises, that Carnehan placed tenderly on the battered temples.

"You behold now," said Carnehan, "the Emperor in his habit as he lived—the King of Kafiristan with his crown upon his head. Poor old Daniel that was a monarch once!"

I shuddered, for, in spite of defacements manifold, I recognized the head of the man of Marwar Junction. Carnehan rose to go. I attempted to stop him. He was not fit to walk abroad. "Let me take away the whiskey, and give me a little money," he gasped. "I was a King once. I'll go to the Deputy Commissioner and ask to set in the Poorhouse till I get my health. No, thank you, I can't wait till you get a carriage for me. I've urgent private affairs—in the south—at Marwar."

He shambled out of the office and departed in the direction of the Deputy Commissioner's house. That day at noon I had occasion to go down the blinding hot Mall, and I saw a crooked man crawling along the white dust of the roadside, his hat in his hand, quavering dolorously after the fashion of street-singers at Home. There was not a soul in sight, and he was out of all possible earshot of the houses. And he sang through his nose, turning his head from right to left:

> "The Son of Man goes forth to war,
>   A golden crown to gain;
> His blood-red banner streams afar—
>   Who follows in his train?"

I waited to hear no more, but put the poor wretch into my carriage and drove him off to the nearest missionary for eventual transfer to the Asylum. He repeated the hymn twice while he was with me whom he did not in the least recognize, and I left him singing it to the missionary.

Two days later I inquired after his welfare of the Superintendent of the Asylum.

"He was admitted suffering from sunstroke. He died early yesterday morning," said the Superintendent. "Is it true that he was half an hour bareheaded in the sun at midday?"

"Yes," said I, "but do you happen to know if he had anything upon him by any chance when he died?"

"Not to my knowledge," said the Superintendent.

And there the matter rests.

—1888

JACK LONDON
1876-1916

Jack London was a prolific author, who, during his relatively brief life, published widely in subjects ranging from social criticism, to science fiction, to adventure fiction. Along with Ambrose Bierce and Bret Harte, London became both a popular international writer and a major voice in the American West Coast literary community. Born in San Francisco, California, the young London pursued a variety of occupations, including a brief stint in 1891 as an oyster pirate. He completed his public school education in 1895, but only attended the University of California for a single semester. In 1897, London traveled to the Yukon as part of the Klondike gold rush, leaving the Yukon in 1898 to become a full-time writer. He subsequently developed a reputation as one of America's foremost authors of *popular adventure fiction. His most famous adventure novels—*The Call of the Wild *(1903),* The Sea-Wolf *(1904), and* White Fang *(1906)—continue to enjoy lasting popularity with contemporary readers. London, in fact, attempted to live a life as exciting as that of any of his fictional protagonists. Adventurer, world traveler, war correspondent, and seaman, Jack London became all of these before his untimely death in 1916.*

"The Taste of the Meat" (first published in the June, 1911 issue of Cosmopolitan Magazine *and later reprinted, in 1912, as the opening chapter in London's episodic novel,* Smoke Bellew*) features an important theme common in London's popular fiction. The protagonist Kit Bellew's transformation from a useless, "Lord-Fauntleroyish" dandy to a tough-as-nails adventurer represents London's own beliefs about the manly virtues of the rugged life. Like Edgar Rice Burroughs, London enjoyed placing his heroes in a Darwinian "survival of the fittest" contest. When Kit Bellew (the passive, citified writer) becomes "Smoke" Bellew (the robust adventurer), the name change embodies the character's physical metamorphosis. Smoke Bellew has not only survived the grueling ordeal of his "masculine vacation" in the Klondike, he has triumphed spiritually because of his newfound liberation from his past in San Francisco. By the conclusion of London's story, the out of shape tenderfoot is now a reborn man, one who has enjoyed his "taste of meat" and wants more.*

THE TASTE OF THE MEAT

In the beginning he was Christopher Bellew. By the time he was at college he had become Chris Bellew. Later, in the Bohemian crowd of San Francisco, he was called Kit Bellew. And in the end he was known by no other name than Smoke Bellew. And this history of the evolution of his name is the history of his evolution. Nor would it have happened had he not had a fond mother and an iron uncle, and had he not received a letter from Gillet Bellamy.

"I have just seen a copy of *The Billow*," Gillet wrote from Paris. "Of course O'Hara will succeed with it. But he's missing some tricks." Here followed details in the improvement of the budding society weekly. "Go down and see him. Let him think they're your own suggestions. Don't let him know they're from me. If you do, he'll make me Paris correspondent, which I can't afford, because I'm getting real money for my stuff from the big magazines. Above all, don't forget to make him fire that dub who's doing the musical and art criticism. Another thing. San Francisco has always had a literature of her own. But she hasn't any now. Tell him to kick around and get some gink to turn out a live serial, and to put into it the real romance and glamour and color of San Francisco."

And down to the office of *The Billow* went Kit Bellew faithfully to instruct. O'Hara listened. O'Hara debated. O'Hara agreed. O'Hara fired the dub who wrote criticisms. Further, O'Hara had a way with him, the very way that was feared by Gillet in distant Paris. When O'Hara wanted anything, no friend could deny him. He was sweetly and compellingly irresistible. Before Kit Bellew could escape from the office, he had become an associate editor, had agreed to write weekly columns of criticism till some decent pen was found, and had pledged himself to write a weekly instalment of ten thousand words on the San Francisco serial—and all this without pay. *The Billow* wasn't paying yet, O'Hara explained; and just as convincingly had he exposited that there was only one man in San Francisco capable of writing the serial and that man Kit Bellew.

"Oh, Lord, I'm the gink!" Kit had groaned to himself afterward on the narrow stairway.

And thereat had begun his servitude to O'Hara and the insatiable columns of *The Billow.* Week after week he held down an office chair, stood off creditors, wrangled with printers, and turned out twenty-five thousand words of all sorts. Nor did his labors lighten. *The Billow* was ambitious. It went in for illustration. The processes were expensive. It never had any money to pay Kit Bellew, and by the same token it was unable to pay for any additions to the office staff. Luckily for Kit, he had his own income. Small it was, compared with some, yet it was large enough to enable him to belong to several clubs and maintain a studio in the Latin quarter. In point of fact, since his associate-editorship, his expenses had decreased prodigiously. He had no time to spend money. He never saw the studio any more, nor entertained the local Bohemians with his famous chafing-dish suppers. Yet he was always broke, for *The Billow,* in perennial distress, absorbed his cash as well as his brains. There were the illustrators, who periodically refused to illustrate; the printers, who periodically refused to print; and the office-boy, who frequently refused to officiate. At such times O'Hara looked at Kit, and Kit did the rest.

When the steamship *Excelsior* arrived from Alaska, bringing the news of the Klondike strike that set the country mad, Kit made a purely frivolous proposition.

"Look here, O'Hara," he said. "This gold rush is going to be big—the days of '49 over again. Suppose I cover it for *The Billow?* I'll pay my own expenses."

O'Hara shook his head. "Can't spare you from the office, Kit. Then there's that serial. Besides, I saw Jackson not an hour ago. He's starting for the Klondike tomorrow, and he's agreed to send a weekly letter and photos. I wouldn't let him get away till he promised. And the beauty of it is that it doesn't cost us anything."

The next Kit heard of the Klondike was when he dropped into the club that afternoon and in an alcove off the library encountered his uncle.

"Hello, avuncular relative," Kit greeted, sliding into a leather chair and spreading out his legs. "Won't you join me?"

He ordered a cocktail, but the uncle contented himself with the thin native claret he invariably drank. He glanced with irritated disapproval at the cocktail and on to his nephew's face. Kit saw a lecture gathering.

"I've only a minute," he announced hastily. "I've got to run and take in that Keith exhibition at Ellery's and do half a column on it."

"What's the matter with you?" the other demanded. "You're pale. You're a wreck."

Kit's only answer was a groan.

"I'll have the pleasure of burying you. I can see that."

Kit shook his head sadly. "No destroying worm, thank you. Cremation for mine."

John Bellew came of the old hard and hardy stock that had crossed the plains by ox-team in the fifties, and in him was this same hardness and the hardness of a childhood spent in the conquering of a new land. "You're not living right, Christopher. I'm ashamed of you."

"Primrose path, eh?" Kit chuckled.

The older man shrugged his shoulders.

"Shake not your gory locks at me, avuncular. I wish it were the primrose path. But that's all cut out. I have no time."

"Then what in—?"

"Overwork."

John Bellew laughed harshly and incredulously.

"Honest."

Again came the laughter.

"Men are the products of their environment," Kit proclaimed, pointing at the other's glass. "Your mirth is thin and bitter as your drink."

"Overwork!" was the sneer. "You never earned a cent in your life."

"You bet I have, only I never got it. I'm earning five hundred a week right now, and doing four men's work."

"Pictures that won't sell? Or—er—fancy work of some sort? Can you swim?"

"I used to."

"Sit a horse?"

"I have essayed that adventure."

John Bellew snorted his disgust. "I'm glad your father didn't live to see you in all the glory of your gracelessness," he said. "Your father was a man, every inch of him. Do you get it? A man. I think he'd have whaled all this musical and artistic tom foolery out of you."

"Alas! these degenerate days," Kit sighed.

"I could understand it, and tolerate it," the other went on savagely, "if you succeeded at it. You've never earned a cent in your life, nor done a tap of man's work. What earthly good are you, anyway? You were well put up, yet even at university you didn't play football. You didn't row. You didn't—"

"I boxed and fenced—some."

"When did you box last?"

"Not since, but I was considered an excellent judge of time and distance, only I was—er—"

"Go on."

"Considered desultory."

"Lazy, you mean."

"I always imagined it was an euphemism."

"My father, sir, your grandfather, old Isaac Bellew, killed a man with a blow of his fist when he was sixty-nine years old."

"The man?"

"No, you graceless scamp! But you'll never kill a mosquito at sixty-nine."

"The times have changed, O my avuncular! They send men to prison for homicide now."

"Your father rode one hundred and eighty-five miles, without sleeping, and killed three horses."

"Had he lived to-day he'd have snored over the same course in a Pullman."

The older man was on the verge of choking with wrath, but swallowed it down and managed to articulate, "How old are you?"

"I have reason to believe—"

"I know. Twenty-seven. You finished college at twenty-two. You've dabbled and played and frilled for five years. Before God and man, of what use are you? When I was your age I had one suit of underclothes. I was riding with the cattle in Coluso. I was hard as rocks, and I could sleep on a rock. I lived on jerked beef and bear-meat.

I am a better man physically right now than you are. You weigh about one hundred and sixty-five. I can throw you right now, or thrash you with my fists."

"It doesn't take a physical prodigy to mop up cocktails or pink tea," Kit murmured deprecatingly. "Don't you see, my avuncular, the times have changed. Besides, I wasn't brought up right. My dear fool of a mother—"

John Bellew started angrily.

"—as you once described her, was too good to me, kept me in cotton wool and all the rest. Now, if when I was a youngster I had taken some of those intensely masculine vacations you go in for—I wonder why you didn't invite me sometimes? You took Hal and Robbie all over the Sierras and on that Mexico trip."

"I guess you were too Lord-Fauntleroyish."

"Your fault, avuncular, and my dear—er—mother's. How was I to know the hard? I was only a chee-ild. What was there left but etchings and pictures and fans? Was it my fault that I never had to sweat?"

The older man looked at his nephew with unconcealed disgust. He had no patience with levity from the lips of softness. "Well, I'm going to take another one of those what you call masculine vacations. Suppose I asked you to come along?"

"Rather belated, I must say. Where is it?"

"Hal and Robert are going in to Klondike, and I'm going to see them across the pass and down to the lakes, then return—"

He got no further, for the young man had sprung forward and gripped his hand. "My preserver!"

John Bellew was immediately suspicious. He had not dreamed the invitation would be accepted. "You don't mean it?" he said.

"When do we start?"

"It will be a hard trip. You'll be in the way."

"No, I won't. I'll work. I've learned to work since I went on *The Billow*."

"Each man has to take a year's supplies in with him. There'll be such a jam the Indian packers won't be able to handle it. Hal and Robert will have to pack their outfits across themselves. That's what I'm going along for—to help them pack. If you come you'll have to do the same."

"Watch me."

"You can't pack," was the objection.

"When do we start?"

"To-morrow."

"You needn't take it to yourself that your lecture on the hard has done it," Kit said, at parting. "I just had to get away, somewhere, anywhere, from O'Hara."

"Who is O'Hara? A Jap?"

"No; he's an Irishman, and a slave-driver, and my best friend. He's the editor and proprietor and all-round big squeeze of *The Billow*. What he says goes. He can make ghosts walk."

That night Kit Bellew wrote a note to O'Hara. "It's only a several weeks' vacation," he explained. "You'll have to get some gink to dope out instalments for that serial. Sorry, old man, but my health demands it. I'll kick in twice as hard when I get back."

Kit Bellew landed through the madness of the Dyea beach congested with the thousand-pound outfits of thousands of men. This immense mass of luggage and food, flung ashore in mountains by the steamers, was beginning slowly to dribble up the Dyea Valley and across Chilkoot. It was a portage of twenty-eight miles, and could be accomplished only on the backs of men. Despite the fact that the Indian packers had jumped the freight from eight cents a pound to forty, they were swamped with the work, and it was plain that winter would catch the major portion of the outfits on the wrong side of the divide.

Tenderest of the tenderfeet was Kit. Like many hundreds of others, he carried a big revolver swung on a cartridge-belt. Of this his uncle, filled with memories of old lawless days, was likewise guilty. But Kit Bellew was romantic. He was fascinated by the froth and sparkle of the gold rush, and viewed its life and movement with an artist's eye. He did not take it seriously. As he said on the steamer, it was not his funeral. He was merely on a vacation, and intended to peep over the top of the pass for a "look see" and then return.

Leaving his party on the sand to wait for the putting ashore of the freight, he strolled up the beach toward the old trading-post. He did not swagger, though he noticed that many of the be-revolvered individuals did. A strapping, six-foot Indian passed him, carrying an unusually large pack. Kit swung in behind, admiring the splendid calves of the man, and the grace and ease with which he moved along under his burden. The Indian dropped his pack on the scales in front of the post, and Kit joined the group of admiring gold-rushers who surrounded him. The pack weighed one hundred and twenty-five pounds, which fact was uttered back and forth in tones of awe. It was going some, Kit decided, and he wondered if he could lift such a weight, much less walk off with it.

"Going to Lake Linderman with it, old man?" he asked.

The Indian, swelling with pride, grunted an affirmative.

"How much you make that one pack?"

"Fifty dollars."

Here Kit slid out of the conversation. A young woman, standing in the doorway, had caught his eye. Unlike other women landing from the steamers, she was neither short-skirted not bloomer-clad. She was dressed as any woman traveling anywhere would be dressed. What struck him was the justness of her being there, a feeling that somehow she belonged. Moreover, she was young and pretty. The bright beauty and color of her oval face held him, and he looked overlong—looked till she resented, and her own eyes, long lashed and dark, met his in cool survey. From his face, they traveled in evident amusement down to the big revolver at his thigh. Then her eyes came back to his, and in them was amused contempt. It struck him like a blow. She turned to the man beside her and indicated Kit. The man glanced him over with the same amused contempt.

"Chekako," the girl said.

The man, who looked like a tramp in his cheap overalls and dilapidated woolen jacket, grinned dryly, and Kit felt withered, though he knew not why. But anyway she was an unusually pretty girl, he decided, as the two moved off. He noted the way of her walk, and recorded the judgment that he would recognize it after the lapse of a thousand years.

"Did you see that man with the girl?" Kit's neighbor asked him excitedly. "Know who he is?"

Kit shook his head.

"Cariboo Charley. He was just pointed out to me. He struck it big on Klondike. Old-timer. Been on the Yukon a dozen years. He's just come out."

"What does 'chekako' mean?" Kit asked.

"You're one; I'm one," was the answer.

"Maybe I am, but you've got to search me. What does it mean?"

"Tenderfoot."

On his way back to the beach, Kit turned the phrase over and over. It rankled to be called tenderfoot by a slender chit of a woman. Going into a corner among the heaps of freight, his mind still filled with the vision of the Indian with the redoubtable pack, Kit essayed to learn his own strength. He picked out a sack of flour which he knew weighed an even hundred pounds. He stepped astride it, reached down, and strove to get it on his shoulder. His first conclusion was that one hundred pounds were real heavy. His next was that his back was weak. His third was an oath, and it occurred at the end of five futile minutes, when he collapsed on top of the burden with which he was wrestling. He mopped his forehead, and across a heap of grub-sacks saw John Bellew gazing at him, wintry amusement in his eyes.

"God!" proclaimed that apostle of the hard. "Out of our loins has come a race of weaklings. When I was sixteen I toyed with things like that."

"You forget, avuncular," Kit retorted, "that I wasn't raised on bear-meat."

"And I'll toy with it when I'm sixty."

"You've got to show me."

John Bellew did. He was forty-eight, but he bent over the sack, applied a tentative, shifting grip that balanced it, and with a quick heave stood erect, the sack of flour on his shoulder.

"Knack, my boy, knack—and a spine."

Kit took off his hat reverently. "You're a wonder, avuncular, a shining wonder. D' ye think I can learn the knack?"

John Bellew shrugged his shoulders. "You'll be hitting the back trail before we get started."

"Never you fear," Kit groaned. "There's O'Hara, the roaring lion, down there. I'm not going back till I have to."

Kit's first pack was a success. Up to Finnegan's Crossing they had managed to get Indians to carry the twenty-five-hundred-pound outfit. From that point their own backs must do the work. They planned to move forward at the rate of a mile a day. It looked easy—on paper. Since John Bellew was to stay in camp and do the cooking, he would be unable to make more than an occasional pack; so to each of the three young men fell the task of carrying eight hundred pounds one mile each day. If they made fifty-pound packs, it meant a daily walk of sixteen miles loaded and of fifteen miles light—"Because we don't back-trip the last time," Kit explained the pleasant discovery. Eighty-pound packs meant nineteen miles travel each day; and hundred-pound packs meant only fifteen miles.

"I don't like walking," said Kit. "Therefore I shall carry one hundred pounds." He caught the grin of incredulity on his uncle's face, and added hastily: "Of course I shall work up to it. A fellow's got to learn the ropes and tricks. I'll start with fifty."

He did, and ambled gaily along the trail. He dropped the sack at the next camp-site and ambled back. It was easier than he had thought. But two miles had rubbed off the velvet of his strength and exposed the underlying softness. His second pack was sixty-five pounds. It was more difficult, and he no longer ambled. Several times, following the custom of all packers, he sat down on the ground, resting the pack behind him on a rock or stump. With the third pack he became bold. He fastened the straps to a ninety-five-pound sack of beans and started. At the end of a hundred yards he felt that he must collapse. He sat down and mopped his face.

"Short hauls and short rests," he muttered. "That's the trick."

Sometimes he did not make a hundred yards, and each time he struggled to his feet for another short haul the pack became undeniably heavier. He panted for breath, and the sweat streamed from him. Before he had covered a quarter of a mile he stripped off his woolen shirt and hung it on a tree. A little later he discarded his hat. At the end of half a mile he decided he was finished. He had never exerted himself so in his life, and he knew that he was finished. As he sat and panted, his gaze fell upon the big revolver and the heavy cartridge-belt.

"Ten pounds of junk!" he sneered, as he unbuckled it.

He did not bother to hang it on a tree, but flung it into the underbrush. And as the steady tide of packers flowed by him, up trail and down, he noted that the other tenderfeet were beginning to shed their shooting-irons.

His short hauls decreased. At times a hundred feet was all he could stagger, and then the ominous pounding of his heart against his eardrums and the sickening totteriness of his knees compelled him to rest. And his rests grew longer. But his mind was busy. It was a twenty-eight-mile portage, which represented as many days, and this by all accounts was the easiest part of it. "Wait till you get to Chilkoot," others told him as they rested and talked, "where you climb with hands and feet."

"They ain't going to be no Chilkoot," was his answer. "Not for me. Long before that I'll be at peace in my little couch beneath the moss."

A slip and a violent, wrenching effort at recovery frightened him. He felt that everything inside him had been torn asunder.

"If ever I fall down with this on my back, I'm a goner," he told another packer.

"That's nothing," came the answer. "Wait till you hit the Canyon. You'll have to cross a raging torrent on a sixty-foot pine-tree. No guide-ropes, nothing, and the water boiling at the sag of the log to your knees. If you fall with a pack on your back, there's no getting out of the straps. You just stay there and drown."

"Sounds good to me," he retorted; and out of the depths of his exhaustion he almost meant it.

"They drown three or four a day there," the man assured him. "I helped fish a German out of there. He had four thousand in greenbacks on him."

"Cheerful, I must say," said Kit, battling his way to his feet and tottering on.

He and the sack of beans became a perambulating tragedy. It reminded him of the old man of the sea who sat on Sindbad's neck. And this was one of those intensely masculine vacations, he meditated. Compared with it, the servitude to O'Hara was sweet. Again and again he was nearly seduced by the thought of abandoning the sack of beans in the brush and of sneaking around the camp to the beach and catching a steamer for civilization.

But he didn't. Somewhere in him was the strain of the hard, and he repeated over and over to himself that what other men could do he could. It became a nightmare chant, and he gibbered it to those that passed him on the trail. At other times, resting, he watched and envied the stolid, mule-footed Indians that plodded by under heavier packs. They never seemed to rest, but went on and on with a steadiness and certitude that were to him appalling.

He sat and cursed—he had no breath for it when under way—and fought the temptation to sneak back to San Francisco. Before the mile pack was ended he ceased cursing and took to crying. The tears were tears of exhaustion and of disgust with self. If ever a man was a wreck, he was. As the end of the pack came in sight, he strained himself in desperation, gained the camp-site, and pitched forward on his face, the beans on his back. It did not kill him, but he lay for fifteen minutes before he could summon sufficient shreds of strength to release himself from the straps.

Then he became deathly sick, and was so found by Robbie, who had similar troubles of his own. It was this sickness of Robbie that braced Kit up.

"What other men can do we can do," he told Robbie, though down in his heart he wondered whether or not he was bluffing.

"And I am twenty-seven years old and a man," he privately assured himself many times in the days that followed. There was need for it. At the end of a week, though he had succeeded in moving his eight hundred pounds forward a mile a day, he had lost fifteen pounds of his own weight. His face was lean and haggard. All resilience had gone out of his body and mind. He no longer walked, but plodded. And on the back-trips, traveling light, his feet dragged almost as much as when he was loaded.

He had become a work animal. He fell asleep over his food, and his sleep was heavy and beastly, save when he was aroused, screaming with agony, by the cramps in his legs. Every part of him ached. He tramped on raw blisters; yet even this was easier than the fearful bruising his feet received on the water-rounded rocks of the Dyea Flats, across which the trail led for two miles. These two miles represented thirty-eight miles of traveling. His shoulders and chest, galled by the pack-straps, made him think, and for the first time with understanding, of the horses he had seen on city streets.

When they had moved the outfit across the foot-logs at the mouth of the Canyon, they made a change in their plans. Word had come across the pass that at Lake Linderman the last available trees for building boats were being cut. The two cousins, with tools, whipsaw, blankets, and grub on their backs, went on, leaving Kit and his uncle to hustle along the outfit. John Bellew now shared the cooking with Kit, and both packed shoulder to shoulder. Time was flying, and on the peaks the first snow was falling. To be caught on the wrong side of the pass meant a delay of nearly a year. The older man put his iron back under a hundred pounds. Kit was shocked, but he gritted his teeth and fastened his own straps to a hundred pounds. It hurt, but he had learned the knack, and his body, purged of all softness and fat, was beginning to harden up with lean and bitter muscle. Also, he observed and devised. He took note of the head-straps worn by the Indians and manufactured one for himself which he used in addition to the shoulder-straps. It made things easier, so that he began the practise of piling any light, cumbersome piece of luggage on top. Thus he was soon able to bend along with a hundred pounds in the straps, fifteen or twenty more lying loosely on top the pack and against his neck, an ax or a pair of oars in one hand, and in the other the nested cooking-pails of the camp.

But work as they would, the toil increased. The trail grew more rugged; their packs grew heavier; and each day saw the snow-line dropping down the mountains, while freight jumped to sixty cents. No word came from the cousins beyond, so they knew they must be at work chopping down the standing trees and whipsawing them into boat-planks. John Bellew grew anxious. Capturing a bunch of Indians back-tripping from Lake Linderman, he persuaded them to put their straps on the outfit. They charged thirty cents a pound to carry it to the summit of Chilkoot, and it nearly broke him. As it was, some four hundred pounds of clothes-bags and camp outfit were not handled. He remained behind to move it along, despatching Kit with the Indians. At the summit Kit was to remain, slowly moving his ton until overtaken by the four hundred pounds with which his uncle guaranteed to catch him.

Kit plodded along the trail with his Indian packers. In recognition of the fact that it was to be a long pack, straight to the top of Chilkoot, his own load was only eighty pounds. The Indians plodded under their loads, but it was a quicker gait than he had practised. Yet he felt no apprehension, and by now had come to deem himself almost the equal of an Indian.

At the end of a quarter of a mile he desired to rest. But the Indians kept on. He stayed with them, and kept his place in the line. At the half-mile he was convinced that he was incapable of another step, yet he gritted his teeth, kept his place, and at the end of the mile was amazed that he was still alive. Then, in some strange way, came the thing called second wind, and the next mile was almost easier than the first. The third mile nearly killed him, but, though half delirious with pain and fatigue, he never whimpered. And then, when he felt he must surely faint, came the rest. Instead of sitting in the straps, as was the custom of the white packers, the Indians slipped out of the shoulder- and head-straps and lay at ease, talking and smoking. A full half-hour passed before they made another start. To Kit's surprise, he found himself a fresh man, and "long hauls and long rests" became his newest motto.

The pitch of Chilkoot was all he had heard of it, and many were the occasions when he climbed with hands as well as feet. But when he reached the crest of the divide in the thick of a driving snow-squall, it was in the company of his Indians, and his secret pride was that he had come through with them and never squealed and never lagged. To be almost as good as an Indian was a new ambition to cherish.

When he had paid off the Indians and seen them depart, a stormy darkness was falling, and he was left alone, a thousand feet above timber-line, on the backbone of a mountain. Wet to the waist, famished and exhausted, he would have given a year's income for a fire and a cup of coffee. Instead, he ate half a dozen cold flapjacks and crawled into the folds of the partly unrolled tent. As he dozed off he had time for only one fleeting thought, and he grinned with vicious pleasure at the picture of John Bellew in the days to follow, masculinely back-tripping his four hundred pounds up Chilkoot. As for himself, even though burdened with two thousand pounds, he was bound down the hill.

In the morning, stiff from his labors and numb with the frost, he rolled out of the canvas, ate a couple of pounds of uncooked bacon, buckled the straps on a hundred pounds, and went down the rocky way. Several hundred yards beneath, the trail led across a small glacier and down to Crater Lake. Other men packed across the glacier. All that day he dropped his packs at the glacier's upper edge, and by virtue of the shortness of the pack, he put his straps on one hundred and fifty pounds each load. His astonishment at being able to do it never abated. For two dollars he bought from an Indian three leathery sea-biscuits, and out of these, and a huge quantity of raw bacon, made several meals. Unwashed, unwarmed, his clothing wet with sweat, he slept another night in the canvas.

In the early morning he spread a tarpaulin on the ice, loaded it with three-quarters of a ton, and started to pull. Where the pitch of the glacier accelerated, his load likewise accelerated, overran him, scooped him in on top, and ran away with him.

A hundred packers, bending under their loads, stopped to watch him. He yelled frantic warnings, and those in his path stumbled and staggered clear. Below, on the lower edge of the glacier, was pitched a small tent, which seemed leaping toward him, so rapidly did it grow larger. He left the beaten track where the packers' trail swerved to the left, and struck a patch of fresh snow. This arose about him in frosty smoke, while it reduced his speed. He saw the tent the instant he struck it, carrying away the corner guys, bursting in the front flaps, and fetching up inside, still on top of the tarpaulin and in the midst of his grub-sacks. The tent rocked drunkenly, and in the frosty vapor he found himself face to face with a startled young woman who was sitting up in her blankets—the very one who had called him a tenderfoot at Dyea.

"Did you see my smoke?" he queried cheerfully.

She regarded him with disapproval.

"Talk about your magic carpets!" he went on.

Her coolness was a challenge. "It was a mercy you did not overturn the stove," she said.

He followed her glance and saw a sheet-iron stove and a coffee-pot, attended by a young squaw. He sniffed the coffee and looked back to the girl.

"I'm a chekako," he said.

Her bored expression told him that he was stating the obvious. But he was unabashed.

"I've shed my shooting-irons," he added.

Then she recognized him, and her eyes lighted. "I never thought you'd get this far," she informed him.

Again, and greedily, he sniffed the air. "As I live, coffee!" He turned and directly addressed her: "I'll give you my little finger—cut it off right now; I'll do anything; I'll be your slave for a year and a day or any other old time, if you'll give me a cup out of that pot."

And over the coffee he gave his name and learned hers—Joy Gastell. Also, he learned that she was an old-timer in the country. She had been born in a trading-post on the Great Slave, and as a child had crossed the Rockies with her father and come down to the Yukon. She was going in, she said, with her father, who had been delayed by business in Seattle and who had then been wrecked on the ill-fated *Chanter* and carried back to Puget Sound by the rescuing steamer.

In view of the fact that she was still in her blankets, he did not make it a long conversation, and, heroically declining a second cup of coffee, he removed himself and his heaped and shifted baggage from her tent. Further, he took several conclusions away with him: she had a fetching name and fetching eyes; could not be more than twenty, or twenty-one or two; her father must be French; she had a will of her own; temperament to burn; and she had been educated elsewhere than on the frontier.

Over the ice-scoured rocks and above the timberline, the trail ran around Crater Lake and gained the rocky defile that led toward Happy Camp and the first scrub-pines. To pack his heavy outfit around would take days of heart-breaking toil. On the lake was a canvas boat employed in freighting. Two trips with it, in two hours, would see him and his ton across. But he was broke, and the ferryman charged forty dollars a ton.

"You've got a gold-mine, my friend, in that dinky boat," Kit said to the ferryman. "Do you want another gold-mine?"

"Show me," was the answer.

"I'll sell it to you for the price of ferrying my outfit. It's an idea, not patented, and you can jump the deal as soon as I tell you it. Are you game?"

The ferryman said he was, and Kit liked his looks.

"Very well. You see that glacier. Take a pick-ax and wade into it. In a day you can have a decent groove from top to bottom. See the point? The Chilkoot and Crater Lake Consolidated Chute Corporation, Limited. You can charge fifty cents a hundred, get a hundred tons a day, and have no work to do but collect the coin."

Two hours later, Kit's ton was across the lake and he had gained three days on himself. And when John Bellew overtook him, he was well along toward Deep Lake, another volcanic pit filled with glacial water.

The last pack, from Long Lake to Linderman, was three miles, and the trail, if trail it could be called, rose up over a thousand-foot hogback, dropped down a scramble of slippery rocks, and crossed a wide stretch of swamp. John Bellew remonstrated when he saw Kit rise with a hundred pounds in the straps and pick up a fifty-pound sack of flour and place it on top of the pack against the back of his neck.

"Come on, you chunk of the hard," Kit retorted. "Kick in on your bear-meat fodder and your one suit of underclothes."

But John Bellew shook his head. "I'm afraid I'm getting old, Christopher."

"You're only forty-eight. Do you realize that my grandfather, sir, your father, old Isaac Bellew, killed a man with his fist when he was sixty-nine years old?"

John Bellew grinned and swallowed his medicine.

"Avuncular, I want to tell you something important. I was raised a Lord Fauntleroy, but I can out-pack you, outwalk you, put you on your back, or lick you with my fists right now."

John Bellew thrust out his hand and spoke solemnly. "Christopher, my boy, I believe you can do it. I believe you can do it with that pack on your back at the same time. You've made good, boy, though it's too unthinkable to believe."

Kit made the round trip of the last pack four times a day, which is to say that he daily covered twenty-four miles of mountain climbing, twelve miles of it under one hundred and fifty pounds. He was proud, hard, and tired, but in splendid physical condition. He ate and slept as he had never eaten and slept in his life, and as the end of the work came in sight, he was almost half sorry.

One problem bothered him. He had learned that he could fall with a hundred-weight on his back and survive; but he was confident that if he fell with that additional fifty pounds across the back of his neck, it would break it clean. Each trail through the swamp was quickly churned bottomless by the thousands of packers, who were compelled continually to make new trails. It was while pioneering such a new trail that he solved the problem of the extra fifty.

The soft, lush surface gave way under him, he floundered, and pitched forward on his face. The fifty pounds crushed his face into the mud and went clear without snapping his neck. With the remaining hundred pounds on his back, he arose on hands and knees. But he got no farther. One arm sank to the shoulder, pillowing his cheek in the slush. As he drew this arm clear, the other sank to the shoulder. In this position it was impossible to slip the straps, and the hundred-weight on his back would not let him rise. On hands and knees, sinking first one arm and then the other, he made an effort to crawl to where the small sack of flour had fallen. But he exhausted himself without advancing, and so churned and broke the grass surface that a tiny pool of water began to form in perilous proximity to his mouth and nose.

He tried to throw himself on his back with the pack underneath, but this resulted in sinking both arms to the shoulders and gave him a foretaste of drowning. With exquisite patience, he slowly withdrew one sucking arm and then the other and rested them flat on the surface for the support of his chin. Then he began to call for help. After a time he heard the sound of feet sucking through the mud as some one advanced from behind.

"Lend a hand, friend," he said. "Throw out a life-line or something."

It was a woman's voice that answered, and he recognized it.

"If you'll unbuckle the straps I can get up."

The hundred pounds rolled into the mud with a soggy noise, and he slowly gained his feet.

"A pretty predicament," Miss Gastell laughed, at sight of his mud-covered face.

"Not at all," he replied airily. "My favorite physical-exercise stunt. Try it some time. It's great for the pectoral muscles and the spine." He wiped his face, flinging the slush from his hand with a snappy jerk.

"Oh!" she cried in recognition. "It's Mr.—ah Mr. Smoke Bellew."

"I thank you gravely for your timely rescue and for that name," he answered. "I have been doubly baptized. Henceforth I shall insist always on being called Smoke Bellew. It is a strong name, and not without significance."

He paused, and then voice and expression became suddenly fierce.

"Do you know what I'm going to do?" he demanded. "I'm going back to the States. I am going to get married. I am going to raise a large family of children. And then, as the evening shadows fall, I shall gather those children about me and relate the sufferings and hardships I endured on the Chilkoot Trail. And if they don't cry— I repeat, if they don't cry, I'll lambaste the stuffing out of them."

The arctic winter came down apace. Snow that had come to stay lay six inches on the ground, and the ice was forming in quiet ponds, despite the fierce gales that blew. It was in the late afternoon, during a lull in such a gale, that Kit and John Bellew helped the cousins load the boat and watched it disappear down the lake in a snow-squall.

"And now a night's sleep and an early start in the morning," said John Bellew. "If we aren't storm-bound at the summit we'll make Dyea to-morrow night, and if we have luck in catching a steamer we'll be in San Francisco in a week."

"Enjoyed your vacation?" Kit asked absently.

Their camp for that last night at Linderman was a melancholy remnant. Everything of use, including the tent, had been taken by the cousins. A tattered tarpaulin, stretched as a wind-break, partially sheltered them from the driving snow. Supper they cooked on an open fire in a couple of battered and discarded camp utensils. All that was left them were their blankets and food for several meals.

Only once during supper did Kit speak. "Avuncular," he said, "after this I wish you'd call me Smoke. I've made some smoke on this trail, haven't I?"

A few minutes later he wandered away in the direction of the village of tents that sheltered the gold-rushers who were still packing or building their boats. He was gone several hours, and when he returned and slipped into his blankets John Bellew was asleep.

In the darkness of a gale-driven morning, Kit crawled out, built a fire in his stocking feet, by which he thawed out his frozen shoes, then boiled coffee and fried bacon. It was a chilly, miserable meal. As soon as it was finished, they strapped their blankets. As John Bellew turned to lead the way toward the Chilkoot Trail, Kit held out his hand.

"Good-by, avuncular," he said.

John Bellew looked at him and swore in his surprise.

"Don't forget, my name's Smoke," Kit chided.

"But what are you going to do?"

Kit waved his hand in a general direction northward over the storm-lashed lake. "What's the good of turning back after getting this far?" he asked. "Besides, I've got my taste of meat, and I like it. I'm going on."

"You're broke," protested John Bellew. "You have no outfit."

"I've got a job. Behold your nephew, Christopher Smoke Bellew! He's got a job. He's a gentleman's man. He's got a job at a hundred and fifty per month and grub. He's going down to Dawson with a couple of dudes and another gentleman's man—camp-cook, boatman, and general all-round hustler. And O'Hara and *The Billow* can go to the devil. Good-by."

But John Bellew was dazed, and could only mutter, "I don't understand."

"They say the bald-face grizzlies are thick in the Yukon Basin," Kit explained. "Well, I've got only one suit of underclothes, and I'm going after the bear-meat, that's all."

—1911

EDGAR RICE BURROUGHS

1875-1950

No other American author had a greater impact on the development of popular fiction during the early decades of the twentieth century than did Edgar Rice Burroughs. Specifically, in the categories of adventure fiction, science fiction, and fantasy, Burroughs established many of the popular literary conventions that were widely imitated by a number of his contemporaries. His Tarzan of the Apes adventures created what is perhaps the world's most recognizable fictional hero, while his John Carter of Mars adventures have become for many readers an all-time favorite fantasy series. Burroughs also developed several other popular fantasy and science fiction series, including the Pellucidar stories and the Carson of Venus stories.

Edgar Rice Burroughs was born in Chicago, Illinois. He enlisted in the U.S. Army in 1896, serving with the Seventh Cavalry. Following his discharge from the Army in 1897, and up until 1908, Burroughs worked as a railroad policeman, a construction worker, a salesman, and an accountant (among other occupations). In 1911, he began writing two novels that were to change his life, A Princess of Mars and Tarzan of the Apes. A Princess of Mars, the first novel in the John Carter of Mars series, was initially published as a six-part serial in 1912 (appearing in the American pulp magazine, The All-Story, with a different title, Under the Moons of Mars), followed in the same year by the publication of Tarzan of the Apes in The All-Story. For Burroughs, who up to this point had experienced some difficulty holding a steady job, the sudden financial success he experienced writing fiction convinced him to turn professional. Eventually, he was to become one of the most commercially successful writers of his era.

Burroughs's literary efforts were prolific and varied. In addition to publishing extensively in the fantasy and science fiction genres, he also wrote humor, popular melodrama, historical fiction, and, perhaps most significantly, adventure fiction. His Tarzan of the Apes series proved to be among his most popular works, and he returned time and again throughout his life to writing about this character. Between 1912 and 1941, Burroughs published twenty-four Tarzan books (plus two books for juvenile readers), including The Return of Tarzan *(1913)*, The Son of Tarzan *(1915-1916)*, Tarzan and the Jewels of Opar *(1916)*, Tarzan and the Lion Man *(1933-1934), and* Tarzan's Quest *(1935-1936). "The Battle for Teeka" is one of an interconnected collection of twelve short stories that comprises the sixth Tarzan book,* Jungle Tales of Tarzan *(hardcover publication, 1919). It was originally published in the June 1917 issue of* The Blue Book Magazine *under the general, serialized title,* The New Stories of Tarzan *(1916-1917).*

In the Jungle Tales of Tarzan, *Burroughs documents Tarzan's childhood, before Tarzan became the Lord of the Jungle, borrowing heavily from folklore, mythology, and literary sources in his construction of the character. For example, Tarzan is a feral child—an orphaned infant who is, by birth, the British nobleman, Lord Greystoke, yet who is "adopted" and raised by savage apes in Africa. (This feral upbringing places Tarzan in the same mythological company as Romulus and Remus, the legendary founders of Rome, and in the same literary company as Mowgli from Rudyard Kipling's* Jungle Books.) *In addition, the adolescent Tarzan is a trickster character, an archetypal figure typically found in various world religions. Burroughs, in fact, uses Tarzan's love of practical jokes as the dramatic catalyst for a number of his youthful adventures. As did Jack London, Burroughs set many of his stories within a Darwinian context that emphasizes the "survival of the fittest." Since Tarzan is both clever and strong, he triumphs over his primitive environment, literally becoming the leader of the tribe of fierce apes that have adopted him. Burroughs thus intends Tarzan to represent humanity's triumph over savagery. Be warned that the version of Tarzan in film and television is not the same as the character portrayed in Burroughs's fiction. Burroughs's Tarzan is, paradoxically, both more civilized and more violent than are his various counterparts as depicted in the other mass media.*

THE BATTLE FOR TEEKA

The day was perfect. A cool breeze tempered the heat of the equatorial sun. Peace had reigned within the tribe for weeks and no alien enemy had trespassed upon its preserves from without. To the ape-mind all this was sufficient evidence that the future would be identical with the immediate past—that Utopia would persist.

The sentinels, now from habit become a fixed tribal custom, either relaxed their vigilance or entirely deserted their posts, as the whim seized them. The tribe was far scattered in search of food. Thus may peace and prosperity undermine the safety of the most primitive community even as it does that of the most cultured.

Even the individuals became less watchful and alert, so that one might have thought Numa and Sabor and Sheeta entirely deleted from the scheme of things. The shes and the balus roamed unguarded through the sullen jungle, while the greedy males foraged far afield, and thus it was that Teeka and Gazan, her balu, hunted upon the extreme southern edge of the tribe with no great male near them.

Still farther south there moved through the forest a sinister figure—a huge bull ape, maddened by solitude and defeat. A week before he had contended for the kingship of a tribe far distant, and now battered, and still sore, he roamed the wilderness an outcast. Later he might return to his own tribe and submit to the will of the hairy brute he had attempted to dethrone; but for the time being he dared not do so, since he had sought not only the crown but the wives, as well, of his lord and master. It would require an entire moon at least to bring forgetfulness to him he had wronged, and so Toog wandered a strange jungle, grim, terrible, hate-filled.

It was in this mental state that Toog came unexpectedly upon a young she feeding alone in the jungle—a stranger she, lithe and strong and beautiful beyond compare. Toog caught his breath and slunk quickly to one side of the trail where the dense foliage of the tropical underbrush concealed him from Teeka while permitting him to feast his eyes upon her loveliness.

But not alone were they concerned with Teeka—they roved the surrounding jungle in search of the bulls and cows and balus of her tribe, though principally for the bulls. When one covets a she of an alien tribe one must take into consideration the great, fierce, hairy guardians who seldom wander far from their wards and who will fight a stranger to the death in protection of the mate or offspring of a fellow, precisely as they would fight for their own.

Toog could see no sign of any ape other than the strange she and a young balu playing near by. His wicked, bloodshot eyes half closed as they rested upon the charms of the former—as for the balu, one snap of those great jaws upon the back of its little neck would prevent it from raising any unnecessary alarm.

Toog was a fine, big male, resembling in many ways Teeka's mate, Taug. Each was in his prime, and each was wonderfully muscled, perfectly fanged and as horrifyingly ferocious as the most exacting and particular she could wish. Had Toog been of her own tribe, Teeka might as readily have yielded to him as to Taug when her mating time arrived; but now she was Taug's and no other male could claim her without first defeating Taug in personal combat. And even then Teeka retained some rights in the matter. If she did not favor a correspondent, she could enter the lists with her rightful mate and do her part toward discouraging his advances, a part, too, which would prove no mean assistance to her lord and master, for Teeka, even though her fangs were smaller than a male's, could use them to excellent effect.

Just now Teeka was occupied in a fascinating search for beetles, to the exclusion of all else. She did not realize how far she and Gazan had become separated from the balance of the tribe, nor were her defensive senses upon the alert as they should have been. Months of immunity from danger under the protecting watchfulness of the sentries, which Tarzan had taught the tribe to post, had lulled them all into a sense of peaceful security based on that fallacy which has wrecked many enlightened communities in the past and will continue to wreck others in the future—that because they have not been attacked they never will be.

Toog, having satisfied himself that only the she and her balu were in the immediate vicinity, crept stealthily forward. Teeka's back was toward him when he finally rushed upon her; but her senses were at last awakened to the presence of danger and she wheeled to face the strange bull just before he reached her. Toog halted a few paces from her. His anger had fled before the seductive feminine charms of the stranger. He made conciliatory noises—a species of clucking sound with his broad, flat lips—that were, too, not greatly dissimilar to that which might be produced in an osculatory solo.

But Teeka only bared her fangs and growled. Little Gazan started to run toward his mother, but she warned him away with a quick "Kreeg-ah!" telling him to run high into a tall tree. Evidently Teeka was not favorably impressed by her new suitor.

Toog realized this and altered his methods accordingly. He swelled his giant chest, beat upon it with his calloused knuckles and swaggered to and fro before her.

"I am Toog," he boasted. "Look at my fighting fangs. Look at my great arms and my mighty legs. With one bite I can slay your biggest bull. Alone have I slain Sheeta. I am Toog. Toog wants you." Then he waited for the effect, nor did he have long to wait. Teeka turned with a swiftness which belied her great weight and bolted in the opposite direction. Toog, with an angry growl, leaped in pursuit; but the smaller, lighter female was too fleet for him. He chased her for a few yards and then, foaming and barking, he halted and beat upon the ground with his hard fists.

From the tree above him little Gazan looked down and witnessed the stranger bull's discomfiture. Being young, and thinking himself safe above the reach of the heavy male, Gazan screamed an ill-timed insult at their tormentor. Toog looked up. Teeka had halted at a little distance—she would not go far from her balu; that Toog quickly realized and as quickly determined to take advantage of. He saw that the tree in which the young ape squatted was isolated and that Gazan could not reach another without coming to earth. He would obtain the mother through her love for her young.

He swung himself into the lower branches of the tree. Little Gazan ceased to insult him; his expression of deviltry changed to one of apprehension, which was quickly followed by fear as Toog commenced to ascend toward him. Teeka screamed to Gazan to climb higher, and the little fellow scampered upward among the tiny branches which would not support the weight of the great bull; but nevertheless Toog kept on climbing. Teeka was not tearful. She knew that he could not ascend far enough to reach Gazan, so she sat at a little distance from the tree and applied jungle opprobrium to him. Being a female, she was a past master of the art.

But she did not know the malevolent cunning of Toog's little brain. She took it for granted that the bull would climb as high as he could toward Gazan and then, finding that he could not reach him, resume his pursuit of her, which she knew would prove equally fruitless. So sure was she of the safety of her balu and her own ability to take care of herself that she did not voice the cry for help which would soon have brought the other members of the tribe flocking to her side.

Toog slowly reached the limit to which he dared risk his great weight to the slender branches. Gazan was still fifteen feet above him. The bull braced himself and seized the main branch in his powerful hands, then he commenced shaking it vigorously. Teeka was appalled. Instantly she realized what the bull purposed. Gazan clung far out upon a swaying limb. At the first shake he lost his balance, though he did not quite fall, clinging still with his four hands; but Toog redoubled his efforts; the shaking produced a violent snapping of the limb to which the young ape clung. Teeka saw all too plainly what the outcome must be and forgetting her own danger in the depth of her mother love, rushed forward to ascend the tree and give battle to the fearsome creature that menaced the life of her little one.

But before ever she reached the bole, Toog had succeeded, by violent shaking of the branch, to loosen Gazan's hold. With a cry the little fellow plunged down through the foliage, clutching futilely for a new hold, and alighted with a sickening thud at his mother's feet, where he lay silent and motionless. Moaning, Teeka stooped to lift the still form in her arms; but at the same instant Toog was upon her.

Struggling and biting she fought to free herself; but the giant muscles of the great bull were too much for her lesser strength. Toog struck and choked her repeatedly until finally, half unconscious, she lapsed into quasi submission. Then the bull lifted her to his shoulder and turned back to the trail toward the south from whence he had come.

Upon the ground lay the quiet form of little Gazan. He did not moan. He did not move. The sun rose slowly toward meridian. A mangy thing, lifting its nose to scent the jungle breeze, crept through the underbrush. It was Dango, the hyena. Presently its ugly muzzle broke through some near-by foliage and its cruel eyes fastened upon Gazan.

Early that morning, Tarzan of the Apes had gone to the cabin by the sea, where he passed many an hour at such times as the tribe was ranging in the vicinity. On the floor lay the skeleton of a man—all that remained of the former Lord Greystoke—lay as it had fallen some twenty years before when Kerchak, the great ape, had thrown it, lifeless, there. Long since had the termites and the small rodents picked clean the sturdy English bones. For years Tarzan had seen it lying there, giving it no more attention than he gave the countless thousand bones that strewed his jungle haunts. On the bed another, smaller, skeleton reposed and the youth ignored it as he ignored the other. How could he know that the one had been his father, the other his mother? The little pile of bones in the rude cradle, fashioned with such loving care by the former Lord Greystoke, meant nothing to him—that one day that little skull was to help prove his right to a proud title was as far beyond his ken as the satellites of the suns of Orion. To Tarzan they were bones—just bones. He did not need them, for there was no meat left upon them, and they were not in his way, for he knew no necessity for a bed, and the skeleton upon the floor he easily could step over.

Today he was restless. He turned the pages first of one book and then of another. He glanced at pictures which he knew by heart, and tossed the books aside. He rummaged for the thousandth time in the cupboard. He took out a bag which contained several small, round pieces of metal. He had played with them many times in the years gone by; but always he replaced them carefully in the bag, and the bag in the cupboard, upon the very shelf where first he had discovered it. In strange ways did heredity manifest itself in the ape-man. Come of an orderly race, he himself was orderly without knowing why. The apes dropped things wherever their interest in them waned—in the tall grass or from the high-flung branches of the trees. What they dropped they sometimes found again, by accident; but not so the ways of Tarzan. For his few belongings he had a place and scrupulously he returned each thing to its proper place when he was done with it. The round pieces of metal in the little bag always interested him. Raised pictures were upon either side, the meaning of which he did not quite understand. The pieces were bright and shiny. It amused him to arrange them in various figures upon the table. Hundreds of times had he played thus. Today, while so engaged, he dropped a lovely yellow piece—an English sovereign—which rolled beneath the bed where lay all that was mortal of the once beautiful Lady Alice.

True to form, Tarzan at once dropped to his hands and knees and searched beneath the bed for the lost gold piece. Strange as it might appear, he had never before looked beneath the bed. He found the gold piece, and something else he found, too—a small wooden box with a loose cover. Bringing them both out he returned the sovereign to its bag and the bag to its shelf within the cupboard; then he investigated the box. It contained a quantity of cylindrical bits of metal, cone-shaped at one end and flat at the other, with a projecting rim. They were all quite green and dull, coated with years of verdigris.

Tarzan removed a handful of them from the box and examined them. He rubbed one upon another and discovered that the green came off, leaving a shiny surface for two-thirds of their length and a dull gray over the cone-shaped end. Finding a bit of wood he rubbed one of the cylinders rapidly and was rewarded by a lustrous sheen which pleased him.

At his side hung a pocket pouch taken from the body of one of the numerous black warriors he had slain. Into this pouch he put a handful of the new playthings, thinking to polish them at his leisure; then he replaced the box beneath the bed, and finding nothing more to amuse him, left the cabin and started back in the direction of the tribe.

Shortly before he reached them he heard a great commotion ahead of him—the loud screams of shes and balus, the savage, angry barking and growling of the great bulls. Instantly he increased his speed, for the "Kreeg-ahs" that came to his ears warned him that something was amiss with his fellows.

While Tarzan had been occupied with his own devices in the cabin of his dead sire, Taug, Teeka's mighty mate, had been hunting a mile to the north of the tribe. At last, his belly filled, he had turned lazily back toward the clearing where he had last seen the tribe and presently commenced passing its members scattered alone or in twos or threes. Nowhere did he see Teeka or Gazan, and soon he began inquiring of the other apes where they might be; but none had seen them recently.

Now the lower orders are not highly imaginative. They do not, as you and I, paint vivid mental pictures or things which might have occurred, and so Taug did not now apprehend that any misfortune had overtaken his mate and their offspring—he merely knew that he wished to find Teeka that he might lie down in the shade and have her scratch his back while his breakfast digested; but though he called to her and searched for her and asked each whom he met, he could find no trace of Teeka, nor of Gazan either.

He was beginning to become peeved and had about made up his mind to chastise Teeka for wandering so far afield when he wanted her. He was moving south along a game trail, his calloused soles and knuckles giving forth no sound, when he came upon Dango at the opposite side of a small clearing. The eater of carrion did not see Taug, for all his eyes were for something which lay in the grass beneath a tree—something upon which he was sneaking with the cautious stealth of his breed.

Taug, always cautious himself, as it behooves one to be who fares up and down the jungle and desires to survive, swung noiselessly into a tree, where he could have a better view of the clearing. He did not fear Dango; but he wanted to see what it was that Dango stalked. In a way, possibly, he was actuated as much by curiosity as by caution.

And when Taug reached a place in the branches from which he could have an unobstructed view of the clearing he saw Dango already sniffing at something directly beneath him—something which Taug instantly recognized as the lifeless form of his little Gazan.

With a cry so frightful, so bestial, that it momentarily paralyzed the startled Dango, the great ape launched his mighty bulk upon the surprised hyena. With a cry and a snarl, Dango, crushed to earth, turned to tear at his assailant; but as effectively might a sparrow turn upon a hawk. Taug's great, gnarled fingers closed upon the hyena's throat and back, his jaws snapped once on the mangy neck, crushing the vertebrae, and then he hurled the dead body contemptuously aside.

Again he raised his voice in the call of the bull ape to its mate, but there was no reply; then he leaned down to sniff at the body of Gazan. In the breast of this savage, hideous beast there beat a heart which was moved, however slightly, by the same emotions of paternal love which affect us. Even had we no actual evidence of this, we must know it still, since only thus might be explained the survival of the human race in which the jealousy and selfishness of the bulls would, in the earliest stages of the race, have wiped out the young as rapidly as they were brought into the world had not God implanted in the savage bosom that paternal love which evidences itself most strongly in the protective instinct of the male.

In Taug the protective instinct was not alone highly developed; but affection for his offspring as well, for Taug was an unusually intelligent specimen of these great, man-like apes which the natives of the Gobi speak of in whispers; but which no white man ever had seen, or, if seeing, lived to tell of until Tarzan of the Apes came among them.

And so Taug felt sorrow as any other father might feel sorrow at the loss of a little child. To you little Gazan might have seemed a hideous and repulsive creature, but to Taug and Teeka he was as beautiful and as cute as is your little Mary or Johnnie or Elizabeth Ann to you, and he was their firstborn, their only balu, and a he—three things which might make a young ape the apple of any fond father's eye.

For a moment Taug sniffed at the quiet little form. With his muzzle and his tongue he smoothed and caressed the rumpled coat. From his savage lips broke a low moan; but quickly upon the heels of sorrow came the overmastering desire for revenge.

Leaping to his feet he screamed out a volley of "Kreeg-ahs," punctuated from time to time by the blood-freezing cry of an angry, challenging bull—a rage-mad bull with the blood lust strong upon him.

Answering his cries came the cries of the tribe as they swung through the trees toward him. It was these that Tarzan heard on his return from his cabin, and in reply to them he raised his own voice and hurried forward with increased speed until he fairly flew through the middle terraces of the forest.

When at last he came upon the tribe he saw their members gathered about Taug and something which lay quietly upon the ground. Dropping among them, Tarzan approached the center of the group. Taug was still roaring out his challenges; but when he saw Tarzan he ceased and stooping picked up Gazan in his arms and held him out for Tarzan to see. Of all the bulls of the tribe, Taug held affection for Tarzan only. Tarzan he trusted and looked up to as one wiser and more cunning. To Tarzan he came now—to the playmate of his balu days, the companion of innumerable battles of his maturity.

When Tarzan saw the still form in Taug's arms, a low growl broke from his lips, for he too loved Teeka's little balu.

"Who did it?" he asked. "Where is Teeka?"

"I do not know," replied Taug. "I found him lying here with Dango about to feed upon him; but it was not Dango that did it—there are no fang marks upon him."

Tarzan came closer and placed an ear against Gazan's breast. "He is not dead," he said. "Maybe he will not die." He pressed through the crowd of apes and circled once about them, examining the ground step by step. Suddenly he stopped and placing his nose close to the earth sniffed. Then he sprang to his feet, giving a peculiar cry. Taug and the others pressed forward, for the sound told them that the hunter had found the spoor of his quarry.

"A stranger bull has been here," said Tarzan. "It was he that hurt Gazan. He has carried off Teeka."

Taug and the other bulls commenced to roar and threaten; but they did nothing.

Had the stranger bull been within sight they would have torn him to pieces; but it did not occur to them to follow him.

"If the three bulls had been watching around the tribe this would not have happened," said Tarzan. "Such things will happen as long as you do not keep the three bulls watching for an enemy. The jungle is full of enemies, and yet you let your shes and your balus feed where they will, alone and unprotected. Tarzan goes now—he goes to find Teeka and bring her back to the tribe."

The idea appealed to the other bulls. "We will all go," they cried.

"No," said Tarzan, "you will not all go. We cannot take shes and balus when we go out to hunt and fight. You must remain to guard them or you will lose them all."

They scratched their heads. The wisdom of his advice was dawning upon them, but at first they had been carried away by the new idea—the idea of following up an enemy offender to wrest his prize from him and punish him. The community instinct was ingrained in their characters through ages of custom. They did not know why they had not thought to pursue and punish the offender—they could not know that it was because they had as yet not reached a mental plane which would permit them to work as individuals. In times of stress, the community instinct sent them huddling into a compact herd where the great bulls, by the weight of their combined strength and ferocity, could best protect them from an enemy. The idea of separating to do battle with a foe had not yet occurred to them—it was too foreign to custom, too inimical to community interests; but to Tarzan it was the first and most natural thought. His senses told him that there was but a single bull connected with the attack upon Teeka and Gazan. A single enemy did not require the entire tribe for his punishment. Two swift bulls could quickly overhaul him and rescue Teeka.

In the past no one ever had thought to go forth in search of the shes that were occasionally stolen from the tribe. If Numa, Sabor, Sheeta or a wandering bull ape from another tribe chanced to carry off a maid or a matron while no one was looking, that was the end of it—she was gone, that was all. The bereaved husband, if the victim chanced to have been mated, growled around for a day or two and then, if he were strong enough, took another mate within the tribe, and if not, wandered far into the jungle on the chance of stealing one from another community.

In the past Tarzan of the Apes had condoned this practice for the reason that he had had no interest in those who had been stolen; but Teeka had been his first love and Teeka's balu held a place in his heart such as a balu of his own would have held. Just once before had Tarzan wished to follow and revenge. That had been years before when Kulonga, the son of Mbonga, the chief, had slain Kala. Then, single-handed, Tarzan had pursued and avenged. Now, though to a lesser degree, he was moved by the same passion.

He turned toward Taug. "Leave Gazan with Mumga," he said. "She is old and her fangs are broken and she is no good; but she can take care of Gazan until we return with Teeka, and if Gazan is dead when we come back," he turned to address Mumga, "I will kill you, too."

"Where are we going?" asked Taug.

"We are going to get Teeka," replied the ape-man, "and kill the bull who has stolen her. Come!"

He turned again to the spoor of the stranger bull, which showed plainly to his trained senses, nor did he glance back to note if Taug followed. The latter laid Gazan in Mumga's arms with a parting: "If he dies Tarzan will kill you," and he followed after the brown-skinned figure that already was moving at a slow trot along the jungle trail.

No other bull of the tribe of Kerchak was so good a trailer as Tarzan, for his trained senses were aided by a high order of intelligence. His judgment told him the natural trail for a quarry to follow, so that he need but note the most apparent marks upon the way, and today the trail of Toog was as plain to him as type upon a printed page to you or me.

Following close behind the lithe figure of the ape-man came the huge and shaggy bull ape. No words passed between them. They moved as silently as two shadows among the myriad shadows of the forest. Alert as his eyes and ears, was Tarzan's patrician nose. The spoor was fresh, and now that they had passed from the range of the strong ape odor of the tribe he had little difficulty in following Toog and Teeka by scent alone. Teeka's familiar scent spoor told both Tarzan and Taug that they were upon her trail, and soon the scent of Toog became as familiar as the other.

They were progressing rapidly when suddenly dense clouds overcast the sun. Tarzan accelerated his pace. Now he fairly flew along the jungle trail, or, where Toog had taken to the trees, followed nimbly as a squirrel along the bending, undulating pathway of the foliage branches, swinging from tree to tree as Toog had swung before them; but more rapidly because they were not handicapped by a burden such as Toog's.

Tarzan felt that they must be almost upon the quarry, for the scent spoor was becoming stronger and stronger, when the jungle was suddenly shot by livid lightning, and a deafening roar of thunder reverberated through the heavens and the forest until the earth trembled and shook. Then came the rain—not as it comes to us of the temperate zones, but as a mighty avalanche of water—a deluge which spills tons instead of drops upon the bending forest giants and the terrified creatures which haunt their shade.

And the rain did what Tarzan knew that it would do—it wiped the spoor of the quarry from the face of the earth. For a half hour the torrents fell—then the sun burst forth, jeweling the forest with a million scintillant gems; but today the ape-man, usually alert to the changing wonders of the jungle, saw them not. Only the fact that the spoor of Teeka and her abductor was obliterated found lodgment in his thoughts.

Even among the branches of the trees there are well-worn trails, just as there are trails upon the surface of the ground; but in the trees they branch and cross more often, since the way is more open than among the dense undergrowth at the surface. Along one of these well-marked trails Tarzan and Taug continued after the rain had ceased, because the ape-man knew that this was the most logical path for the thief to follow; but when they came to a fork, they were at a loss. Here they halted, while Tarzan examined every branch and leaf which might have been touched by the fleeing ape.

He sniffed the bole of the tree, and with his keen eyes he sought to find upon the bark some sign of the way the quarry had taken. It was slow work and all the time, Tarzan knew, the bull of the alien tribe was forging steadily away from them—gaining precious minutes that might carry him to safety before they could catch up with him.

First along one fork he went, and then another, applying every test that his wonderful junglecraft was cognizant of; but again and again he was baffled, for the scent had been washed away by the heavy downpour, in every exposed place. For a half hour Tarzan and Taug searched, until at last upon the bottom of a broad leaf,

Tarzan's keen nose caught the faint trace of the scent spoor of Toog, where the leaf had brushed a hairy shoulder as the great ape passed through the foliage.

Once again the two took up the trail, but it was slow work now and there were many discouraging delays when the spoor seemed lost beyond recovery. To you or me there would have been no spoor, even before the coming of the rain, except, possibly, where Toog had come to earth and followed a game trail. In such places the imprint of a huge handlike foot and the knuckles of one great hand were sometimes plain enough for an ordinary mortal to read. Tarzan knew from these and other indications that the ape was yet carrying Teeka. The depth of the imprint of his feet indicated a much greater weight than that of any of the larger bulls, for they were made under the combined weight of Toog and Teeka, while the fact that the knuckles of but one hand touched the ground at any time showed that the other hand was occupied in some other business—the business of holding the prisoner to a hairy shoulder. Tarzan could follow, in sheltered places, the changing of the burden from one shoulder to another, as indicated by the deepening of the foot imprint upon the side of the load, and the changing of the knuckle imprints from one side of the trail to the other.

There were stretches along the surface paths where the ape had gone for considerable distances entirely erect upon his hind feet—walking as a man walks; but the same might have been true of any of the great anthropoids of the same species, for, unlike the chimpanzee and the gorilla, they walk without the aid of their hands quite as readily as with. It was such things, however, which helped to identify to Tarzan and to Taug the appearance of the abductor, and with his individual scent characteristic already indelibly impressed upon their memories, they were in a far better position to know him when they came upon him, even should he have disposed of Teeka before, than is a modern sleuth with his photographs and Bertillon measurements, equipped to recognize a fugitive from civilized justice.

But with all their high-strung and delicately attuned perceptive faculties the two bulls of the tribe of Kerchak were often sore pressed to follow the trail at all, and at best were so delayed that in the afternoon of the second day, they still had not overhauled the fugitive. The scent was now strong, for it had been made since the rain, and Tarzan knew that it would not be long before they came upon the thief and his loot. Above them, as they crept stealthily forward, chattered Manu, the monkey, and his thousand fellows; squawked and screamed the brazen-throated birds of plumage; buzzed and hummed the countless insects amid the rustling of the forest leaves, and, as they passed, a little gray-beard, squeaking and scolding upon a swaying branch, looked down and saw them. Instantly the scolding and squeaking ceased, and off tore the long-tailed mite as though Sheeta, the panther, had been endowed with wings and was in close pursuit of him. To all appearances he was only a very much frightened little monkey, fleeing for his life—there seemed nothing sinister about him.

And what of Teeka during all this time? Was she at last resigned to her fate and accompanying her new mate in the proper humility of a loving and tractable spouse? A single glance at the pair would have answered these questions to the utter satisfaction of the most captious. She was torn and bleeding from many wounds, inflicted by the sullen Toog in his vain efforts to subdue her to his will, and Toog too was disfigured and mutilated; but with stubborn ferocity, he still clung to his now useless prize.

On through the jungle he forced his way in the direction of the stamping ground of his tribe. He hoped that his king would have forgotten his treason; but if not he was still resigned to his fate—any fate would be better than suffering longer the sole companionship of this frightful she, and then, too, he wished to exhibit his captive to his fellows. Maybe he could wish her on the king—it is possible that such a thought urged him on.

At last they came upon two bulls feeding in a parklike grove—a beautiful grove dotted with huge boulders half embedded in the rich loam—mute monuments, possibly, to a forgotten age when mighty glaciers rolled their slow course where now a torrid sun beats down upon a tropic jungle.

The two bulls looked up, baring long fighting fangs, as Toog appeared in the distance. The latter recognized the two as friends. "It is Toog," he growled. "Toog has come back with a new she."

The apes waited his nearer approach. Teeka turned a snarling, fanged face toward them. She was not pretty to look upon, yet through the blood and hatred upon her countenance they realized that she was beautiful, and they envied Toog—alas! they did not know Teeka.

As they squatted looking at one another there raced through the trees toward them a long-tailed little monkey with gray whiskers. He was a very excited little monkey when he came to a halt upon the limb of a tree directly overhead.

"Two strange bulls come," he cried. "One is a Mangani, the other a hideous ape without hair upon his body. They follow the spoor of Toog. I saw them."

The four apes turned their eyes backward along the trail Toog had just come; then they looked at one another for a minute. "Come," said the larger of Toog's two friends, "we will wait for the strangers in the thick bushes beyond the clearing."

He turned and waddled away across the open place, the others following him. The little monkey danced about, all excitement. His chief diversion in life was to bring about bloody encounters between the larger denizens of the forest, that he might sit in the safety of the trees and witness the spectacles. He was a glutton for gore, was this little, whiskered, gray monkey, so long as it was the gore of others—a typical fight fan was the graybeard.

The apes hid themselves in the shrubbery beside the trail along which the two stranger bulls would pass. Teeka trembled with excitement. She had heard the words of Manu, and she knew that the hairless ape must be Tarzan, while the other was, doubtless, Taug. Never, in her wildest hopes, had she expected succor of this sort. Her one thought had been to escape and find her way back to the tribe of Kerchak; but even this had appeared to her practically impossible, so closely did Toog watch her.

As Taug and Tarzan reached the grove where Toog had come upon his friends, the ape scent became so strong that both knew the quarry was but a short distance ahead. And so they went even more cautiously, for they wished to come upon the thief from behind if they could and charge him before he was aware of their presence. That a little gray-whiskered monkey had forestalled them they did not know, nor that three pairs of savage eyes were already watching their every move and waiting for them to come within reach of itching paws and slavering jowls.

On they came across the grove, and as they entered the path leading into the dense jungle beyond, a sudden "Kreeg-ah!" shrilled out close before them—a "Kreeg-ah" in the familiar voice of Teeka. The small brains of Toog and his companions had not been able to foresee that Teeka might betray them, and now that she had, they went wild with rage. Toog struck the she a mighty blow that felled her, and then the three rushed forth to do battle with Tarzan and Taug. The little monkey danced upon his perch and screamed with delight.

And indeed he might well be delighted, for it was a lovely fight. There were no preliminaries, no formalities, no introductions—the five bulls merely charged and clinched. They rolled in the narrow trail and into the thick verdure beside it. They bit and clawed and scratched and struck, and all the while they kept up the most frightful chorus of growlings and barkings and roarings. In five minutes they were torn and bleeding, and the little graybeard leaped high, shrilling his primitive bravos; but always his attitude was "thumbs down." He wanted to see something killed. He did not care whether it were friend or foe. It was blood he wanted—blood and death.

Taug had been set upon by Toog and another of the apes, while Tarzan had the third—a huge brute with the strength of a buffalo. Never before had Tarzan's assailant beheld so strange a creature as this slippery, hairless bull with which he battled. Sweat and blood covered Tarzan's sleek, brown hide. Again and again he slipped from the clutches of the great bull, and all the while he struggled to free his hunting knife from the scabbard in which it had stuck.

At length he succeeded—a brown hand shot out and clutched a hairy throat, another flew upward clutching the sharp blade. Three swift, powerful strokes and the bull relaxed with a groan, falling limp beneath his antagonist. Instantly Tarzan broke from the clutches of the dying bull and sprang to Taug's assistance. Toog saw him coming and wheeled to meet him. In the impact of the charge, Tarzan's knife was wrenched from his hand and then Toog closed with him. Now was the battle even—two against two—while on the verge, Teeka, now recovered from the blow that had felled her, slunk waiting for an opportunity to aid. She saw Tarzan's knife and picked it up. She never had used it, but knew how Tarzan used it. Always had she been afraid of the thing which dealt death to the mightiest of the jungle people with the ease that Tantor's great tusks deal death to Tantor's enemies.

She saw Tarzan's pocket pouch torn from his side, and with the curiosity of an ape, that even danger and excitement cannot entirely dispel, she picked this up, too.

Now the bulls were standing—the clinches had been broken. Blood streamed down their sides—their faces were crimsoned with it. Little graybeard was so fascinated that at last he had even forgotten to scream and dance; but sat rigid with delight in the enjoyment of the spectacle.

Back across the grove Tarzan and Taug forced their adversaries. Teeka followed slowly. She scarce knew what to do. She was lame and sore and exhausted from the frightful ordeal through which she had passed, and she had the confidence of her sex in the prowess of her mate and the other bull of her tribe—they would not need the help of a she in their battle with these two strangers.

The roars and screams of the fighters reverberated through the jungle, awakening the echoes in the distant hills. From the throat of Tarzan's antagonist had come a score of "Kreeg-ahs!" and now from behind came the reply he had awaited. Into the grove, barking and growling, came a score of huge bull apes—the fighting men of Toog's tribe.

Teeka saw them first and screamed a warning to Tarzan and Taug. Then she fled past the fighters toward the opposite side of the clearing, fear for a moment claiming her. Nor can one censure her after the frightful ordeal from which she was still suffering.

Down upon them came the great apes. In a moment Tarzan and Taug would be torn to shreds that would later form the *pièce de résistance* of the savage orgy of a Dum-Dum. Teeka turned to glance back. She saw the impending fate of her defenders and there sprang to life in her savage bosom the spark of martyrdom, that some common forbear had transmitted alike to Teeka, the wild ape, and the glorious women of a higher order who have invited death for their men. With a shrill scream she ran toward the battlers who were rolling in a great mass at the foot of one of the huge boulders which dotted the grove; but what could she do? The knife she held she could not use to advantage because of her lesser strength. She had seen Tarzan throw missiles, and she had learned this with many other things from her childhood playmate. She sought for something to throw and at last her fingers touched upon the hard objects in the pouch that had been torn from the ape-man. Tearing the receptacle open, she gathered a handful of shiny cylinders—heavy for their size, they seemed to her, and good missiles. With all her strength she hurled them at the apes battling in front of the granite boulder.

The result surprised Teeka quite as much as it did the apes. There was a loud explosion, which deafened the fighters, and a puff of acrid smoke. Never before had one there heard such a frightful noise. Screaming with terror, the stranger bulls leaped to their feet and fled back toward the stamping ground of their tribe, while Taug and Tarzan slowly gathered themselves together and arose, lame and bleeding, to their feet. They, too, would have fled had they not seen Teeka standing there before them, the knife and the pocket pouch in her hands.

"What was it?" asked Tarzan.

Teeka shook her head. "I hurled these at the stranger bulls," and she held forth another handful of the shiny metal cylinders with the dull gray, cone-shaped ends.

Tarzan looked at them and scratched his head.

"What are they?" asked Taug.

"I do not know," said Tarzan. "I found them."

The little monkey with the gray beard halted among the trees a mile away and huddled, terrified, against a branch. He did not know that the dead father of Tarzan of the Apes, reaching back out of the past across a span of twenty years, had saved his son's life.

Nor did Tarzan, Lord Greystoke, know it either.

—1917

BARONESS ORCZY
1865-1947

We seek him here, we seek him there,
Those Frenchies seek him everywhere.
Is he in heaven?—Is he in hell?
That demmed, elusive Pimpernel?

The poem above is reprinted from one of the most popular historical adventures of all time, Baroness Orczy's The Scarlet Pimpernel *(1905), the novel that introduces the infamous rogue hero, the Scarlet Pimpernel. Set in 1792 during the Reign of Terror following the French Revolution,* The Scarlet

Pimpernel *details the exploits of British nobleman, Sir Percy Blakeney, who dedicates his life to saving captured French aristocrats who are otherwise doomed to be executed by zealous revolutionaries and "Madame la Guillotine." As the Scarlet Pimpernel, Sir Percy smuggles aristocrats from their French prisons to asylum in England, all under the nose of the villainous French agent, Chauvelin. Orczy's mix of history, romance, and adventure was a commercially successful one, and her blue-blooded hero was paid the highest of compliments by being frequently imitated. Many popular historical adventures, such as Johnston McCulley's* The Mark of Zorro *(1924, originally published in magazine serial form, in 1919, as* The Curse of Capistrano) *and Rafael Sabatini's* Captain Blood: His Odyssey *(1922), among numerous others, owe a debt of gratitude to Orczy's* The Scarlet Pimpernel. *Orczy herself borrowed freely from Walter Scott, Alexandre Dumas, and Robert Louis Stevenson in writing her historical romances. But her skilled refinement of the trickster hero figure in her development of Sir Percy's character (that is, the protagonist who adopts an alter ego identity to combat injustice) became such a compelling motif in dime novel and pulp magazine adventure fiction that it continues to be used in many contemporary popular culture narratives, like superhero comic books. Bruce Wayne's Batman, for example, is an obvious first cousin to Orczy's Scarlet Pimpernel.*

Baroness (Emma Magdalena Rosalia Maria Josefa Barbara) Orczy was born in Tarna-Ors, Hungary, and educated in Brussels, Paris, and London. She attended both the West London School of Art and the Heatherley School of Art, and her work was exhibited at the Royal Academy in London. Orczy also wrote prodigiously. Her best fiction includes her series featuring The Old Man in the Corner, one of the crime genre's most famous "armchair" detectives, and her collection of interrelated short stories, Lady Molly of Scotland Yard *(1910), featuring an early version of the female sleuth. Orczy mainly published historical fiction and melodrama. Her most notable literary creation—the Scarlet Pimpernel—was also the protagonist of a long-running series of novels that includes* The Elusive Pimpernel *(1908),* Lord Tony's Wife: An Adventure of the Scarlet Pimpernel *(1917), and* Sir Percy Hits Back: An Adventure of the Scarlet Pimpernel *(1927). "Two Good Patriots" is reprinted from* The League of the Scarlet Pimpernel *(1919).*

TWO GOOD PATRIOTS

Being the deposition of citizeness Fanny Roussell, who was brought up, together with her husband, before the Tribunal of the Revolution on a charge of treason—both being subsequently acquitted.

My name is Fanny Roussell, and I am a respectable married woman, and as good a patriot as any of you sitting there.

Aye, and I'll say it with my dying breath, though you may send me to the guillotine . . . as you probably will, for you are all thieves and murderers, every one of you, and you have already made up your minds that I and my man are guilty of having sheltered that accursed Englishman whom they call the Scarlet Pimpernel . . . and of having helped him to escape.

But I'll tell you how it all happened, because, though you call me a traitor to the people of France, yet am I a true patriot and will prove it to you by telling you exactly how everything occurred, so that you may be on your guard against the cleverness of that man, who, I do believe, is a friend and confederate of the devil . . . else how could he have escaped that time?

Well! it was three days ago, and as bitterly cold as anything that my man and I can remember. We had no travellers staying in the house, for we are a good three leagues out of Calais, and too far for the folk who have business in or about the harbour. Only at midday the coffee-room would get full sometimes with people on their way to or from the port.

But in the evenings the place was quite deserted, and so lonely that at times we fancied that we could hear the wolves howling in the forest of St. Pierre.

It was close on eight o'clock, and my man was putting up the shutters, when suddenly we heard the tramp of feet on the road outside, and then the quick word, "Halt!"

The next moment there was a peremptory knock at the door. My man opened it, and there stood four men in the uniform of the 9th Regiment of the Line . . . the same that is quartered at Calais. The uniform, of course, I knew well, though I did not know the men by sight.

"In the name of the People and by the order of the Committee of Public Safety!" said one of the men, who stood in the forefront, and who, I noticed, had a corporal's stripe on his left sleeve.

He held out a paper, which was covered with seals and with writing, but as neither my man nor I can read, it was no use our looking at it.

Hercule—that is my husband's name, citizens—asked the corporal what the Committee of Public Safety wanted with us poor *hôteliers* of a wayside inn.

"Only food and shelter for tonight for me and my men," replied the corporal, quite civilly.

"You can rest here," said Hercule, and he pointed to the benches in the coffee-room, "and if there is any soup left in the stockpot, you are welcome to it."

Hercule, you see, is a good patriot, and he had been a soldier in his day. . . . No! no . . . do not interrupt me any of you . . . you would only be saying that I ought to have known . . . but listen to the end.

"The soup we'll gladly eat," said the corporal very pleasantly. "As for shelter . . . well! I am afraid that this nice warm coffee-room will not exactly serve our purpose. We want a place where we can lie hidden, and at the same time keep a watch on the road. I noticed an outhouse as we came. By your leave we will sleep in there."

"As you please," said my man curtly.

He frowned as he said this, and it suddenly seemed as if some vague suspicion had crept into Hercule's mind.

The corporal, however, appeared unaware of this, for he went on quite cheerfully:

"Ah! that is excellent! *Entre nous,* citizen, my men and I have a desperate customer to deal with. I'll not mention his name, for I see you have guessed it already. A small red flower, what? . . . Well, we know that he must be making straight for the port of Calais, for he has been traced through St. Omer and Ardres. But he cannot possibly enter Calais city tonight, for we are on the watch for him. He must seek shelter somewhere for himself and any other aristocrat he may have with him, and, bar this house, there is no other place between Ardres and Calais where he can get it. The night is bitterly cold, with a snow blizzard raging round. I and my men have been detailed to watch this road, other patrols are guarding those that lead toward Boulogne and to Gravelines; but I have an idea, citizen, that our fox is making for Calais, and that to me will fall the honour of handing that tiresome scarlet flower to the Public Prosecutor *en route* for Madame la Guillotine."

Now I could not really tell you, citizens, what suspicions had by this time entered Hercule's head or mine; certainly what suspicions we did have were still very vague.

I prepared the soup for the men and they ate it heartily, after which my husband led the way to the outhouse where we sometimes stabled a traveller's horse when the need arose.

It is nice and dry, and always filled with warm, fresh straw. The entrance into it immediately faces the road; the corporal declared that nothing would suit him and his men better.

They retired to rest apparently, but we noticed that two men remained on the watch just inside the entrance, whilst the two others curled up in the straw.

Hercule put out the lights in the coffee-room, and then he and I went upstairs— not to bed, mind you—but to have a quiet talk together over the events of the past half-hour.

The result of our talk was that ten minutes later my man quietly stole down-stairs and out of the house. He did not, however, go out by the front door, but through a back way which, leading through a cabbage-patch and then across a field, cuts into the main road some two hundred metres higher up.

Hercule and I had decided that he would walk the three leagues into Calais, despite the cold, which was intense, and the blizzard, which was nearly blinding, and that he would call at the post of *gendarmerie* at the city gates, and there see the officer in command and tell him the exact state of the case. It would then be for that officer to decide what was to be done; our responsibility as loyal citizens would be completely covered.

Hercule, you must know, had just emerged from our cabbage-patch on to the field when he was suddenly challenged:

"*Qui va là?*"

He gave his name. His certificate of citizenship was in his pocket; he had noth-ing to fear. Through the darkness and the veil of snow he had discerned a small group of men wearing the uniform of the 9th Regiment of the Line.

"Four men," said the foremost of these, speaking quickly and commandingly, "wearing the same uniform that I and my men are wearing . . . have you seen them?"

"Yes," said Hercule hurriedly.

"Where are they?"

"In the outhouse close by."

The other suppressed a cry of triumph.

"At them, my men!' he said in a whisper, "and you, citizen, thank your stars that we have not come too late."

"These men . . ." whispered Hercule. "I had my suspicions."

"Aristocrats, citizen," rejoined the commander of the little party, "and one of them is that cursed Englishman—the Scarlet Pimpernel."

Already the soldiers, closely followed by Hercule, had made their way through our cabbage-patch back to the house.

The next moment they had made a bold dash for the barn. There was a great deal of shouting, a great deal of swearing and some firing, whilst Hercule and I, not a little frightened, remained in the coffee-room, anxiously awaiting events.

Presently the group of soldiers returned, not the ones who had first come, but the others. I noticed their leader, who seemed to be exceptionally tall.

He looked very cheerful, and laughed loudly as he entered the coffee-room. From the moment that I looked at his face I knew, somehow, that Hercule and I had been fooled, and that now, indeed, we stood eye to eye with that mysterious personage who is called the Scarlet Pimpernel.

I screamed, and Hercule made a dash for the door; but what could two humble and peaceful citizens do against this band of desperate men, who held their lives in their own hands? They were four and we were two, and I do believe that their leader has supernatural strength and power.

He treated us quite kindly, even though he ordered his followers to bind us down to our bed upstairs, and to tie a cloth round our mouths so that our cries could not be distinctly heard.

Neither my man nor I closed an eye all night, of course, but we heard the miscreants moving about in the coffee-room below. But they did no mischief, nor did they steal any of the food or wines.

At daybreak we heard them going out by the front door, and their footsteps disappearing toward Calais. We found their discarded uniforms lying in the coffee-room. They must have entered Calais by daylight, when the gates were opened—just like other peaceable citizens. No doubt they had forged passports, just as they had stolen uniforms.

Our maid-of-all-work released us from our terrible position in the course of the morning, and we released the soldiers of the 9th Regiment of the Line, whom we found bound and gagged, some of them wounded, in the outhouse.

That same afternoon we were arrested, and here we are, ready to die if we must, but I swear that I have told you the truth, and I ask you, in the name of justice, if we have done anything wrong, and if we did not act like loyal and true citizens, even though we were pitted against an emissary of the devil?

—1919

MAX BRAND
1892-1944

Max Brand is the nom de plume of Frederick Faust, an amazingly prolific author of popular fiction who wrote under some twenty-one pseudonyms in a variety of genres. Faust, as "Max Brand," was the author of numerous slam-bang action Westerns, and he dominated this type of story in the American pulp magazines. His productivity was simply astonishing. Biographer William F. Nolan reports in Max Brand: Western Giant *(BGSU Popular Press, 1985) that during a three-year period in the early 1930s, Faust wrote over five millions words of fiction. Nolan states that Faust produced some 170 Western novels under his "Max Brand" pseudonym, as well as enough short stories to compile an additional fifty books.*

Frederick Faust was born in Seattle, Washington. At an early age, he expressed an interest in classical mythology and literature; he later attended the University of California at Berkeley, where he refined his writing skills. He failed to graduate because of a dispute with the university administration. During the Second World War, Faust served as a war correspondent in Italy, where he died during the battle for the town, Santa Maria Infante, in early May of 1944.

In 1917, Faust published his first Max Brand story, "Mr. Cinderella," in the June 23 issue of the American pulp magazine, All -Story Weekly. *During those embryonic decades of the Western tale's development in the first half of the twentieth century, Max Brand and Zane Grey were among the most successful and influential authors working in the genre. Included among Max Brand's best-known works are* Destry Rides Again *(1930), which was made into a popular Western film in 1939 starring James Stewart and Marlene Dietrich, and the Silvertip novels—*Silvertip *(1942),* Silvertip's Strike *(1942), and* Silvertip's Trap *(1943), among others—featuring the Western hero, Jim Silver.*

"The Ghost" is one of Brand's earliest published stories, originally appearing in the May 3, 1919 issue of All-Story Weekly. *Though Faust's Max Brand Westerns are sometimes attacked by critics as being mere pulp hack writing, "The Ghost" reveals Faust's great skill at plotting, as well as his proficiency in developing frontier humor.*

THE GHOST

The gold strike which led the fortune-hunters to Murrayville brought with them the usual proportion of bad men and outlaws. Three months after the rush started a bandit appeared so consummate in skill and so cool in daring that all other offenders against the law disappeared in the shade of his reputation. He was a public dread. His comings were unannounced; his goings left no track. Men lowered their voices when they spoke of him. His knowledge of affairs in the town was so uncanny that people called him the "Ghost."

The stages which bore gold to the railroad one hundred and thirty miles to the south left at the most secret hours of the night, but the Ghost knew. Once he "stuck up" the stage not a mile from town while the guards were still occupied with their flasks of snake-bite. Again, when the stage rolled on at midday, eighty miles south of Murrayville, and the guards nodded in the white-hot sun, the Ghost rose from behind a bush, shot the near-leader, and had the cargo at his mercy in thirty seconds.

He performed these feats with admirable *finesse*. Not a single death lay charged to his account, for he depended upon surprise rather than slaughter. Yet so heavy was the toll he exacted that the miners passed from fury to desperation.

They organized a vigilance committee. They put a price on his head. Posses scoured the region of his hiding-place, Hunter's Cañon, into which he disappeared when hard pressed, and left no more trace than the morning mist which the sun disperses. A hundred men combed the myriad recesses of the cañon in vain. Their efforts merely stimulated the bandit.

While twoscore men rode almost within calling distance, the Ghost appeared in the moonlight before Pat McDonald and Peters and robbed them of eighteen pounds of gold-dust which they carried in their belts. When the vigilance committee got word of this insolent outrage they called a mass-meeting so large that even drunken Geraldine was enrolled.

Never in the history of Murrayville had there been so grave and dry-throated an affair. William Collins, the head of the vigilantes, addressed the assembly. He rehearsed the list of the Ghost's outrages, pointed out that what the community needed was an experienced man-hunter to direct their efforts, and ended by asking Silver Pete to stand up before them. After some urging Pete rose and stood beside Collins, with his hat pushed back from his gray and tousled forelock and both hands tugging at his cartridge-belt.

"Men," went on Collins, placing one hand on the shoulder of the man-killer, "we need a leader who is a born and trained fighter, a man who will attack the Ghost with system and never stop after he takes up the trail. And I say the man we need is Silver Pete!"

Pete's mouth twitched back on one side into the faint semblance of a grin, and he shrugged off the patronizing hand of the speaker. The audience stirred, caught each other with side-glances, and then stared back at Silver Pete. His reputation gave even Murrayville pause, for his reputed killings read like the casualty list of a battle.

"I repeat," said Collins, after the pause, in which he allowed his first statement to shudder its way home, "that Silver Pete is the man for us. I've talked it over with him before this, and he'll take the job, but he needs an inducement. Here's the reward I propose for him or for any other man who succeeds in taking the Ghost prisoner or in killing him. We'll give him any loot which may be on the person of the bandit. If the Ghost is disposed of in the place where he has cached his plunder, the finder gets it all. It's a high price to pay, but this thing has to be stopped. My own opinion is that the Ghost is a man who does his robbing on the side and lives right here among us. If that's the case, we'll leave it to Silver Pete to find him out, and we'll obey Pete's orders. He's the man for us. He's done work like this before. He has a straight eye, and he's fast with his six-gun. If you want to know Pete's reputation as a fighting man—"

"He'll tell you himself," said a voice, and a laugh followed.

Silver Pete scowled in the direction of the laugh, and his right hand caressed the butt of his gun, but two miners rose from the crowd holding a slender fellow between them.

"It's only Geraldine," said one of them. "There ain't no call to flash your gun, Pete."

"Take the drunken fool away," ordered Collins angrily. "Who let him in here? This is a place for men and not for girl-faced clowns!"

"Misher Collins," said Geraldine, doffing his broad-brimmed hat and speaking with a thick, telltale accent—"Misher Collins, I ask your pardon, shir."

He bowed unsteadily, and his hat brushed the floor.

"I plumb forgot I was in church with Silver Pete for a preacher!" he went on.

The audience turned their heads and chuckled deeply.

"Take him out, will you?" thundered Collins. "Take him out, or I'll come down there and kick him out myself!"

The two men at Geraldine's side turned him about and led him toward the door. Here he struggled away from his guides. "Misher Collins!" he cried in a voice half-whining and half-anger, "if I capture the Ghost do *I* get the loot?"

A yell of laughter drowned the reply, and Geraldine staggered from the room.

"What do you say, men?" roared Collins, enraged by these repeated interruptions. "Is Silver Pete the man for us?"

There was no shout of approval but a deep muttering of consent.

"I'd hire the devil himself," murmured one man, "if he'd get rid of the Ghost."

"All right," said Collins, and he turned to Pete. "You're in charge here, and it's up to you to tell us what to do. You're the foreman, and we're all in your gang."

The crowd was delighted, for Pete, finding himself deserted before the mass of waiting men, shifted uneasily from one foot to the other and kept changing the angle of the hat upon his mop of gray hair.

"Speech!" yelled a miner. "Give us a speech, Pete!" Silver Pete favored the speaker with a venomous scowl.

"Speech nothin'," he answered. "I ain't here to talk. I ain't no gossipin' bit of calico. I got a hunch my six-gun'll do my chatterin' for me."

"But what do you want us to do, Pete?" asked Collins. "How are we going to help you?"

"Sit tight and chaw your own tobacco," he said amiably. "I don't want no advice. There's been too many posses around these diggin's. Maybe I'll start and hunt the Ghost by myself. Maybe I won't. If I want help I'll come askin' it."

As a sign that the meeting had terminated he pulled his hat farther down over his eyes, hitched his belt, and stalked through the crowd without looking to either side.

Thereafter Murrayville saw nothing of him for a month, during which the Ghost appeared five times and escaped unscathed. The community pondered and sent out to find Pete, but the search was vain. There were those who held that he must have been shot down in his tracks by the Ghost, and even now decorated some lank hillside. The majority felt that having undertaken his quest alone Pete was ashamed to appear in the town without his victim.

On the subject of the quest Geraldine composed a ballad which he sang to much applause in the eight saloons of the town. It purported to be the narrative of Silver Pete's wanderings in search of the Ghost. In singing it Geraldine borrowed a revolver and belt from one of the bystanders, pushed back his hat and roughed up his hair, and imitated the scowling face of Pete so exactly that his hearers fairly wept with pleasure. He sang his ballad to the tune of "Auld Lang Syne," and the sad narrative concluded with a wailing stanza:

> "I don't expect no bloomin' tears;
> The only thing I ask
> Is something for a monument
> In the way of a whisky flask."

Geraldine sang himself into popularity and many drinks with his song, and for the first time the miners began to take him almost seriously. He had appeared shortly after old John Murray struck gold six months before, a slender man of thirty-five, with a sadly drooping mouth and humorous eyes.

He announced himself as Gerald Le Roy Witherstone, and was, of course, immediately christened "Geraldine."

Thereafter he wandered about the town, with no apparent occupation except to sing for his drinks in the saloons. Hitherto he had been accepted as a harmless and amusing man-child, but his ballad gave him at once an Homeric repute, particularly when men remembered that the song was bound to come sooner or later to the ear of Silver Pete.

For the time being Pete was well out of ear-shot. After the meeting, at which he was installed chief manhunter of the community, he spent most of the evening equipping himself for the chase. Strangely enough, he did not hang a second revolver to his belt nor strap a rifle behind his saddle; neither did he mount a fleet horse. To pursue the elusive Ghost he bought a dull-eyed mule with a pendulous lower lip. On the mule he strapped a heavy pack which consisted chiefly of edibles, and in the middle of the night he led the mule out of Murrayville in such a way as to evade observation. Once clear of the town he headed straight for Hunter's Cañon.

Once inside the mouth of the cañon he began his search. While he worked he might have been taken for a prospector, for there was not a big rock in the whole course of the cañon which he did not examine from all sides. There was not a gully running into Hunter's which he did not examine carefully. He climbed up and down the cliffs on either side as if he suspected that the Ghost might take to wings and fly up the sheer rock to a cave.

The first day he progressed barely a half-mile. The second day he covered even less ground. So his search went on. In the night he built a fire behind a rock and cooked. Through four weeks his labor continued without the vestige of a clue to reward him. Twice during that time he saw posses go thundering through the valley and laughed to himself. They did not even find him, and yet he was making no effort to elude them. What chance would they have of surprising the Ghost?

This thought encouraged him, and he clung to the invisible trail, through the day and through the night, with the vision of the outlaw's loot before him. He ran out of bacon. Even his coffee gave out. For ten days he lived on flour, salt, and water, and then, as if this saintly fast were necessary before the vision, Pete saw the Ghost.

It was after sunset, but the moon was clear when he saw the fantom rider race along the far side of the valley. The turf deadened the sound of the horse's hoofs, and, like another worldly apparition, the Ghost galloped close to the wall of the valley—and disappeared.

Peter rubbed his eyes and looked again. It give him a queer sensation, as if he had awakened suddenly from a vivid dream, for the horse, with its rider, had vanished into thin air between the eyes of Peter and the sheer rock of the valley wall. A little shudder passed through his body, and he cursed softly to restore his courage.

Yet the dream of plunder sent his blood hotly back upon its course. He carefully observed the marks which should guide him to the point on the rock at which the rider disappeared. He hobbled the mule, examined his revolver, and spun the cylinder, and then started down across the cañon.

He had camped upon high ground, and his course led him on a sharp descent to the stream which cut the heart of the valley. Here, for two hundred yards, trees and the declivity of the ground cut off his view, but when he came to the higher ground again he found that he had wandered only a few paces to the left of his original course.

The wall of the valley was now barely fifty yards away, and as nearly as he could reckon the landmarks, the point at which the rider vanished was at or near a shrub which grew close against the rock. For an instant Pete thought that the tree might be a screen placed before the entrance of a cave. Yet the rider had made no pause to set aside the screen. He walked up to it and peered beneath the branches. He even fumbled at the base of the trunk, to make sure that the roots actually entered the earth. After this faint hope disappeared, Pete stepped back and sighed. His reason vowed that it was at this point that the horse turned to air, and Pete's was not a nature which admitted the supernatural.

He turned to the left and walked along the face of the cliff for fifty paces. It was solid rock. A chill like a moving piece of ice went up Pete's back.

He returned to the shrub and passed around it to the right.

At first he thought it merely the black shadow of the shrub. He stepped closer and then crouched with his revolver raised, for before him opened a crevice directly behind the shrub. It was a trifle over six feet high and less than half that in width; a man could walk through that aperture and lead a horse. Pete entered the passage with cautious steps.

Between each step he paused and listened. He put forth a foot and felt the ground carefully with it, for fear of a pebble which might roll beneath his weight, or a twig which might snap. His progress was so painfully slow that he could not even estimate distances in the pitch-dark. The passage grew higher and wider—it turned sharply to the right—a faint light shone.

Pete crouched lower and the grin of expectancy twisted at his lips. At every step, until this moment; he had scarcely dared to breathe, for fear of the bullet which might find him out. Now all the advantage was on his side. Behind him was the dark. Before him was the light which must outline, however faintly, the figure of any one who lurked in wait. With these things in mind he went on more rapidly. The passage widened again and turned to the left. He peered cautiously around the edge of rock and looked into as comfortable a living-room as he had ever seen.

The rock hung raggedly from the top of the cave, but the sides were smooth from the action of running water through long, dead ages. The floor was of level-packed gravel. Silver Pete remained crouched at the sharp angle of the passage until he heard the stamp and snort of a horse. It gave him heart and courage to continue the stealthy progress, inch by inch, foot by foot, pace by pace toward the light, and as he stole forward more and more of the cave developed before him.

A tall and sinewy horse was tethered at one end, and at the opposite side sat a man with his back to Pete, who leveled his revolver and drew a bead on a spot between the shoulder blades. Yet he did not fire, for the thought came to him that if it were an honor to track the Ghost to his abode and kill him, it would be immortal glory to bring back the bandit alive, a concrete testimony to his own prowess.

Once more that catlike progress began until he could see that the Ghost sat on his saddle in front of a level-topped boulder in lieu of a table. The air was filled with the sweet savor of fried bacon and coffee. Pete had crawled to the very edge of the cave when the horse threw up its head and snorted loudly. The Ghost straightened and tilted back his head to listen.

"Up with yer hands!" snarled Silver Pete.

He had his bead drawn and his forefinger tightened around the trigger, but the Ghost did not even turn. His hands raised slowly above his shoulders to the level of his head and remained there.

"Stand up!" said Pete, and rose himself from the ground, against which he had flattened himself. For if the Ghost had decided to try a quick play with his gun the shot in nine cases out of ten would travel breast-high.

"Turn around!" ordered Pete, feeling more and more sure of himself as he studied the slight proportions of the outlaw.

The Ghost turned and showed a face with a sad mouth and humorous eyes.

"By God!" cried Silver Pete, and took a pace back which brought his shoulders against the wall of rock, "Geraldine!"

If the Ghost had had his gun on his hip he could have shot Pete ten times during that moment of astonishment, but his belt and revolver hung on a jutting rock five paces away. He dropped his hands to his hips and smiled at his visitor.

"When they put you on the job, Pete," he said, "I had a hunch I should beat it."

At this inferred compliment the twisted smile transformed one side of Silver Pete's face with sinister pleasure, but there was still wonder in his eyes.

"Damn me, Geraldine," he growled, "I can't believe my eyes!"

Geraldine smiled again.

"Oh, it's me, all right," he nodded. "You got me dead to rights, Pete. What do you think the boys will do with me?"

"And you're—the Ghost?" sighed Silver Pete, pushing back his hat as though to give his thoughts freer play. He had met many a man of grim repute along the "border," but never such nonchalance as he found in the Ghost.

"What'll they do with you?" he repeated, "I dunno. You ain't plugged nobody, Geraldine. I reckon they'll ship you South and let the sheriff handle you. Git away from that gun."

For Geraldine had stepped back with apparent unconcern until he stood within a yard of his revolver. He obeyed the orders with unshaken good humor, but it seemed to Silver Pete that a yellow light gleamed for an instant in the eyes of the Ghost. It was probably only a reflection from the light of the big torch that burned in a corner of the cave.

"Gun?" grinned Geraldine. "Say, Pete, do you think I'd try and gunplay while *you* have the drop on me?"

He laughed.

"Nope," he went on. "If you was one of those tin-horn gunmen from the town over yonder, I'd lay you ten to one I could drill you and make a getaway, but you ain't one of them, Pete, and, seeing it's you, I ain't going to try no funny stuff. I don't hanker after no early grave, Pete!"

This tribute set a placid glow of satisfaction in Pete's eyes.

"Take it from me, Geraldine," he said, "you're wise. But there ain't no need for you to get scared of me so long as you play the game square and don't try no fancy moves. Now show me where you got the loot stowed and show it quick. If you don't—"

The threat was unfinished, for Geraldine nodded.

"Sure I'll show it to you, Pete," he said. "I know when I got a hand that's worth playing, and I ain't a guy to bet a measly pair of treys against a full house. Take a slant over there behind the rock and you'll find it all."

He indicated a pile of stones of all sizes which lay heaped in a corner. Pete backed toward it with his eye still upon the Ghost. A few kicks scattered the rocks and exposed several small bags. When he stirred these with his foot their weight was eloquent, and the gun-fighter's smile broadened.

"Think of them tin-horns," he said, "that offered all your pickings to the man that got you dead or alive, Geraldine!"

The Ghost sighed.

"Easy pickings," he agreed. "No more strong-arm work for you, Pete!"

The jaw of Silver Pete set sternly again.

"Lead your hoss over here," he said, "and help me stow this stuff in the saddlebags. And if you make a move to get the hoss between me and you—"

The Ghost grinned in assent, saddled his mount, and led him to Pete. Then in obedience to orders he unbuckled the slicker strapped behind the saddle and converted it into a strong bag which easily held the bags of loot. It made a small but ponderous burden, and he groaned with the effort as he heaved it up behind the saddle and secured it. Pete took the bridle and gestured at the Ghost with the revolver.

"Now git your hands up over your head agin, Geraldine," he said, "and go out down the tunnel about three paces ahead of me."

"Better let me take the torch," suggested the Ghost, "it'll show us the way."

Pete grunted assent, and Geraldine, on his way toward the torch, stopped at the boulder to finish off his coffee. He turned to Pete with the cup poised at his lips.

"Say, Pete," he said genially. "Anything wrong with a cup of coffee and a slice of bacon before we start back?"

"By God, Geraldine," grinned the gun-fighter, "you're a cool bird, but your game is too old!"

Nevertheless his very soul yearned toward the savor of bacon and coffee.

"Game?" repeated the Ghost, who caught the gleam of Pete's eye. "What game? I say let's start up the coffee-pot and the frying-pan. I can turn out flapjacks browner than the ones mother used to make, Pete!"

Pete drew a great breath, for the taste of his flour and water diet of the past few days was sour in his mouth.

"Geraldine," he said at last, "it's a go! But if you try any funny passes I ain't going to wait for explanations. Slide out the chow!"

He rolled a large stone close to the boulder which served as dining-table to the bandit, and sat down to watch the preparations. The Ghost paid little attention to him, but hummed as he worked. Soon a fire snapped and crackled. The coffee can straddled one end of the fire; the frying-pan occupied the other. While the bacon fried he mixed self-rising pancake flour in a tin plate, using water from a tiny stream which trickled down from the rocks at one side of the cave, disappearing again through a fissure in the floor. Next he piled the crisp slices of bacon on a second tin plate and used the fried-out fat to cook the flapjacks.

"What I can't make out," said Geraldine, without turning to his guest, "is why you'd do this job for those yellow livers over in the town."

Pete moved the tip of his tongue across his lips, for his mouth watered in anticipation.

"Why, you poor nut," he answered compassionately, "I ain't working for them. I'm working for the stuff that's up there behind the saddle."

Geraldine turned on him so suddenly that Pete tightened his grip upon the revolver, but the Ghost merely stared at him.

"Say," he grinned at last, "have you got a hunch they'll really let you walk off with all that loot?"

The face of the gunman darkened.

"I sure think they'll *let* me," he said with a sinister emphasis. "That was the way they talked."

Geraldine sighed in apparent bewilderment, but turned back to his work without further comment. In a few moments he rose with the plates of bacon and flapjacks piled on his left arm and the can of coffee in his right hand. He arranged them on the boulder before Silver Pete, and then sat on his heels on the other side of the big stone. The gun-fighter laid his revolver beside his tin cup and attacked the food with the will of ten. Yet even while he ate the eye which continually lingered on the Ghost noted that the latter stared at him with a curious and almost pitying interest. He came to a pause at last, with a piece of bacon folded in a flapjack.

"Look here," he said, "just what were you aiming at a while ago?"

Geraldine shrugged his shoulders and let his eye wander away as though the subject embarrassed him.

"Damn it!" said Pete with some show of anger, "don't go staring around like a cross-eyed girl. What's biting you?"

"It ain't my business," he said. "As long as I'm done for, I don't care what they do to you."

He stopped and drummed his finger-tips against his chin while he scowled at Pete.

"If it wasn't for you I'd be a free bird," he went on bitterly. "Do you think I'm goin' to weep any of the salt and briny for you, what?"

"Wha'd'ya mean?" Pete blurted. "D'ya mean to say them quitters are going to double-cross me?"

The Ghost answered nothing, but the shrug of his shoulders was eloquent. Pete started up with his gun in his hand.

"By God, Geraldine," he said, "you ain't playin' fair with me! Look what I done for you. Any other man would of plugged you the minute they seen you, but here I am lettin' you walk back safe and sound—treating you as if you was my own brother, almost!"

He hesitated a trifle over this simile. Legend told many things of what Silver Pete had done to his own brother. Nevertheless, Geraldine met his stare with an eye full as serious.

"I'm going to do it," he said in a low voice, as if talking to himself. "Just because you come out here and caught me like a man there ain't no reason I should stand by and see you made a joke of. Pete, I'm going to tell you!"

Pete settled back on his stone with his fingers playing nervously about the handle of his gun.

"Make it short, Geraldine," he said with an ominous softness. "Tell me what the wall-eyed cayuses figure on doin'!"

The Ghost studied him as if he found some difficulty in opening his story in a delicate manner.

"Look here, Pete," he said at last. "There ain't no getting out of it that some of the things you've done read considerable different from Bible stories."

"Well?" snarled Silver Pete.

"Well," said the Ghost, "those two-card Johnnies over to town know something of what you've done, and they figure to double-cross you."

He paused, and in the pause Pete's mouth twitched so that his teeth glinted yellow.

"Anybody could say that," he remarked. "What's your proof?"

"Proof?" echoed the Ghost angrily. "Do you think I'm telling you this for fun? No, Pete," he continued with a hint of sadness in his voice, "it's because I don't want to see those guys do you dirt. You're a real man and they're only imitation-leather. The only way they're tough is their talk."

"Damn them!" commented Pete.

"Well," said Geraldine, settling into the thread of his narrative, "they knew that once you left the town on this job you wouldn't come back until you had the Ghost. Then when you started they got together and figured this way. They said you was just a plain man-killer and that you hadn't any more right to the reward than the man in the moon. So they figured that right after you got back with the Ghost, dead or alive, they'd have the sheriff pay you a little visit and stick you in the coop. They've raked up plenty of charges against you, Peter."

"What?" asked Pete hoarsely.

The Ghost lowered his voice to an insinuating whisper.

"One thing is this. They say that once you went prospecting with a guy called Red Horry. Horace was his right name."

Silver Pete shifted his eyes and his lips fixed in a sculptured grin.

"They say that you went with him and that you was pals together for months at a time. They say once you were bit by a rattler and Red Horry stuck by you and saved you and hunted water for you and cared for you like a baby. They say you got well and went on prospecting together and finally he struck a mine. It looked rich. Then one day you come back to Truckee and say that Red Horry got caught in a landslide and was killed and you took the mine. And they say that two years later they found a skeleton, and through the skull, right between the eyes, was a little round hole, powerful like a hole made by a .45. They say—"

"They lie!" yelled Silver Pete, rising. "And you lie like the rest of them. I tell you it was—it was—"

"Huh!" said Geraldine, shrugging away the thought with apparent scorn. "Of course they lie. Nobody could look at you and think you'd plug a pal—not for nothing."

Pete dropped back to his stone.

"Go on," he said. "What else do they say?"

"I don't remember it all," said the Ghost, puckering his brows with the effort of recollection, "but they got it all planned out when you come back with the loot they'll take it and split it up between them—one-third to Collins, because he made the plan first.

"They even made up a song about you," went on Geraldine, "and the song makes a joke out of you all the way through, and it winds up like this—you're supposed to be talking, see?

> *"I don't expect no bloomin' tears;*
> *The only thing I ask*
> *Is something for a monument*
> *In the way of a whisky flask."*

"Who made up the song, Geraldine?" asked Pete.

"I dunno," answered the Ghost. "I reckon Collins had a hand in it."

"Collins," repeated the gun-fighter. "It sounds like him. I'll get him first!"

"And it was Collins," went on the Ghost, leaning a little forward across the boulder, while he lowered his voice for secrecy. "It was Collins who got them to send out three men to watch you from a distance. They was to trail you and see that if you ever got to the Ghost you didn't make off with the loot without showing up in town. Ever see anybody trailing you, Pete?"

The gun-fighter flashed a glance over his shoulder toward the dark and gaping opening of the passage from the cave. Then he turned back to the Ghost.

"I never thought of it," he whispered. "I didn't know they was such skunks. But, by God, they won't ever see the money! I'll take it and line out for new hunting grounds."

"And me?" asked the Ghost anxiously.

"You?" said Silver Pete, and the whisper made the words trebly sinister. "I can't leave you free to track me up, can I? I'll just tie you up and leave you here."

"To starve?" asked the Ghost with horror.

"You chose your own house," said Pete, "an' now I reckon it's good enough for you to live in it."

"But what'll you do if they're following you up?" suggested the Ghost. "What'll you do if they've tracked you here and the sheriff with them? What if they get you for Red Horry?"

The horse had wandered a few paces away. Now its hoof struck a loose pebble which turned with a crunching sound like a footfall.

"My God!" yelled the Ghost, springing up and pointing toward the entrance passage, "they've got you, Pete!"

The gun-fighter whirled to his feet, his weapon poised and his back to the Ghost. Geraldine drew back his arm and lunged forward across the boulder. His fist thudded behind Silver Pete's ear. The revolver exploded and the bullet clicked against a rock, while Pete collapsed upon his face, with his arms spread out crosswise. The Ghost tied his wrists behind his back with a small piece of rope. Silver Pete groaned and stirred, but before his brain cleared his ankles were bound fast and drawn up to his wrists, so that he lay trussed and helpless. The Ghost turned him upon one side and then, strangely enough, set about clearing up the tinware from the boulder. This he piled back in its niche after he had rinsed it at the runlet of water. A string of oaths announced the awakening of Silver Pete. Geraldine went to him and leaned over his body.

Pete writhed and cursed, but Geraldine kneeled down and brushed the sand out of the gun-fighter's hair and face. Then he wiped the blood from a small cut on his chin where his face struck a rock when he fell.

"I have to leave you now, Pete," he said, rising from this work of mercy. "You've been good company, Pete, but a little of you goes a long way."

He turned and caught his horse by the bridle.

"For God's sake!" groaned Silver Pete, and Geraldine turned. "Don't leave me here to die by inches. I done some black things, Geraldine, but never nothing as black as this. Take my own gun and pull a bead on me and we'll call everything even."

The Ghost smiled on him.

"Think it over, Pete," he said. "I reckon you got enough to keep your mind busy. So-long!"

He led his horse slowly down the passage, and the shouts and pleadings of Silver Pete died out behind him. At the mouth of the passage his greatest shout rang no louder than the hum of a bee.

Grimly silent was the conclave in Billy Hillier's saloon. That evening, while the sunset was still red in the west, the Ghost had stopped the stage scarcely a mile from Murrayville, shot the sawed-off shotgun out of the very hands of the only guard who dared to raise a weapon, and had taken a valuable packet of the "dust." They sent out a posse at once, which rode straight for Hunter's Cañon, and arrived there just in time to see the fantom horseman disappear in the mouth of the ravine. They had matched speed with that rider before, and they gave up the vain pursuit. That night they convened in Hillier's, ostensibly to talk over new plans for apprehending the outlaw, but they soon discovered that nothing new could be said. Even Collins was silent, twisting his glass of whisky between his fingers and scowling at his neighbors along the bar.

It was small wonder, therefore, if not a man smiled when a singing voice reached them from a horseman who cantered down the street:

> *"I don't expect no bloomin' tears;*
> *The only thing I ask*
> *Is something for a monument*
> *In the way of a whisky flask."*

The sound of the gallop died out before the saloon, the door opened, and Geraldine staggered into the room, carrying a small but apparently ponderous burden in his arms. He lifted it to the bar which creaked under the weight.

"Step up and liquor!" cried Geraldine in a ringing voice. "I got the Ghost!"

A growl answered him. It was a topic over which they were not prepared to laugh.

"Get out and tell that to your hoss, son," said one miner. "We got other things to think about than your damfoolery."

"Damfoolery?" echoed Geraldine. "Step up and look at the loot! Dust, boys, real dust!"

He untied the mouth of a small buckskin bag and shoved it under the nose of the man who had spoken to him. The latter jumped back with a yell and regarded Geraldine with fascinated eyes.

"By God, boys," he said, "it *is* dust!"

Geraldine fought off the crowd with both hands.

"All mine!" he cried. "Mine, boys! You voted the loot to the man who caught the Ghost!"

"And where's the Ghost?" asked several men together.

"Geraldine," said Collins, pushing through the crowd, "if this is another joke we'll hang you for it!"

"It's too heavy for a joke," grinned Geraldine. "I'll put the loot in your hands, Collins, and when I show you the Ghost I'll ask for it again."

Collins caught his shoulder in a strong grasp.

"Honest to God?" he asked. "Have you got him?"

"I have," said Geraldine, "and I'll give him to you on one ground."

"Out with it," said Collins.

"Well," said Geraldine, "when you see him you'll recognize him. He's been one of us!"

"I knew it," growled Collins; "some dirty dog that lived with us and knifed us in the back all the time."

"But, remember," said Geraldine, "he never shot to kill, and that's why you sha'n't string him up. Is it a bargain?"

"It's a bargain," said Collins, "we'll turn him over to the sheriff. Are you with me, boys?"

They yelled their agreement, and in thirty seconds every man who had a horse was galloping after Collins and Geraldine. At the shrub beside the wall of the valley Geraldine drew rein, and they followed him in an awed and breathless body into the passage.

"I went out scouting on my own hook," explained Geraldine, as he went before them, "and I saw the Ghost ride down the cañon and disappear in here. I followed him."

"Followed up this passage all alone?" queried Collins.

"I did," said Geraldine.

"And what did you do to him?"

"You'll see in a minute. There was only one shot fired, and it came from his gun."

They turned the sharp angle and entered the lighted end of the passage. In another moment they crowded into the cave and stood staring at the tightly bound figure of Silver Pete. His eyes burned furiously into the face of Geraldine. The men swarmed about his prostrate body.

"Untie his feet, boys," said Collins, "and we'll take him back. Silver Pete, you can thank your lucky stars that Geraldine made us promise to turn you over to the law."

"How did you do it?" he continued, turning to Geraldine.

"I'm not very handy with a gun," said the Ghost, "so I tackled him with my fists. Look at that cut on his jaw. That's where I hit him!"

A little murmur of wonder passed around the group. One of them cut the rope which bound Pete's ankles together, and two more dragged him to his feet.

"Stand up like a man, Pete," said Collins, "and thank Geraldine for not cutting out your rotten heart!"

But Silver Pete, never moving his eyes from the face of the Ghost, broke into a long and full-throated laugh.

"Watch him, boys!" called Collins sharply. "He's going looney! Here, Jim, grab on that side and I'll take him here. Now start down the tunnel."

Yet, as they went forward, the rumbling laugh of the gun-fighter broke out again and again.

"I got to leave you here," said the Ghost, when they came out from the mouth of the passage. "My way runs east, and I got a date at Tuxee for to-night. I'll just trouble you for that there slicker with the dust in it, Collins."

Without a word the vigilance men unstrapped the heavy packet which he had tied behind his saddle. He fastened it behind Geraldine's saddle and then caught him by the hand.

"Geraldine," he said, "you're a queer cuss! We haven't made you out yet, but we're going to take a long look at you when you come back to Murrayville to-morrow."

"When I come back," said Geraldine, "you can look at me as long as you wish."

His eyes changed, and he laid a hand on Collins's shoulder.

"Take it from me," he said softly, "you've given me your word that the boys won't do Pete dirt. Remember, he never plugged any of you. He's got his hands tied now, Collins, and if any of the boys try fancy stunts with him—maybe I'll be making a quick trip back from Tuxee. Savvy?"

His eyes held Collins for the briefest moment, and then he swung into his saddle and rode east with the farewell yells of the posse ringing after him. By the time they were in their saddles Geraldine had topped a hill several hundred yards away and his figure was black against the moon. A wind from the east blew back his song to them faintly:

> "I don't expect no bloomin' tears;
> The only thing I ask
> Is something for a monument
> In the way of a whisky flask."

"Look at him, boys," said Collins, turning in his saddle. "If it wasn't for what's happened to-night, I'd lay ten to one that that was the Ghost on the wing for his hiding-place!"

—1919

ZANE GREY
1872-1939

Along with Owen Wister (1860–1938), Zane Grey is often credited with help-ing to create many of the conventions of the twentieth-century American Western. He was also one of the first popular Western writers to publish out-side of the dime novels, discovering great success in the "slick" magazines such as Ladies' Home Journal *and* McCall's.

Born in Zanesville, Ohio, Grey was offered an athletic scholarship in baseball at the University of Pennsylvania, where he graduated with his D.D.S. in 1896. He practiced dentistry in New York City from 1896 to 1903, and in 1907, Grey visited the American West with "Buffalo" Jones. This expedition became the basis for his book, The Last of the Plainsmen, *pub-lished in 1908. He traveled widely—from Arizona and New Mexico to Cuba and Mexico—before settling in California in 1918. He published his first sketch, "A Day on the Delaware (Tales of Fresh Water Fishing)," in the May 1902 issue of* Recreation, *and his first book,* Betty Zane *(part of his Ohio River Trilogy), in 1903. Grey's success as a popular novelist began with* The Heritage of the Desert *(1910), which was followed by the classic,* Riders of the Purple Sage *(1912). Listed among Grey's many Westerns are* The Rustlers of Pecos County *(1914),* The Lone Star Ranger *(1915),* Western Union *(1939), and* Captives of the Desert *(1952). Grey also published a number of books and short sketches about fishing, one of his great loves.*

Grey is among the most prolific and commercially successful of popular Western writers. His fiction is distinguished by its combination of romance and adventure. In particular, Grey's literary strengths are his descriptions of frontier settings and his blending of romantic love with thrilling action. "I have loved the West for its vastness, its contrasts, its beauty and color and life," Grey once wrote, "and for the fact that I have seen how it developed great men and women who died unknown and unsung."

"From Missouri," first published in the July 1926 issue of McCall's, *offers a fine example of Grey's romantic (and romanticized) Western, told pri-marily from a woman's point-of-view.*

FROM MISSOURI

With jingling spurs a tall cowboy stalked out of the post office to confront three punchers who were just then crossing the wide street from the saloon opposite.

"Look heah," he said, shoving a letter under their noses. "Which one of you long-horns wrote her again?"

From a gay, careless trio his listeners suddenly looked blank, then intensely curi-ous. They stared at the handwriting on the letter.

"Tex, I'm a son-of-a-gun if it ain't from Missouri!" exclaimed Andy Smith, his lean red face bursting into a smile.

"It shore is," declared Nevada.

"From Missouri!" echoed Panhandle Hanes.

"Well?" asked Tex, almost with a snort.

The three cowboys drew back to look from Tex to one another, and then back at Tex.

"It's from *her*," went on Tex, his voice hushing on the pronoun. "You all know that handwritin'. Now how about this deal? We swore none of us would write to this schoolmarm. But some one of you has double-crossed the outfit."

Loud and simultaneous protestations of innocence arose from them. But it was evident that Tex did not trust them, and that they did not trust him or each other.

"Say, boys," said Panhandle suddenly. "I see Beady Jones in here lookin' darn sharp at us. Let's get off in the woods somewhere."

"Back to the bar," said Nevada. "I reckon we'll all need bracers."

"Beady!" exclaimed Tex as they turned across the street. "He could be to blame as much as any of us. An' he was still at Stringer's when we wrote the first letter."

"Shore. It'd be more like Beady," said Nevada. "But Tex, your mind ain't workin'. Our lady friend from Missouri wrote before without gettin' any letter from us."

"How do we know thet?" asked Tex suspiciously. "Shore the boss' typewriter is a puzzle, but it could hide tracks. Savvy, pards?"

"Doggone it, Tex, you need a drink," said Panhandle peevishly.

They entered the saloon and strode up to the bar, where from all appearances Tex was not the only one to seek artificial strength. Then they repaired to a corner, where they took seats and stared at the letter Tex threw down before them.

"From Missouri, all right," said Panhandle, studying the postmark. "Kansas City, Missouri."

"It's her writin'," said Nevada, in awe. "Shore I'd know that out of a million letters."

"Ain't you goin' to read it to us?" asked Andy Smith.

"Mr. Frank Owens," said Tex, reading from the address on the letter. "Springer's Ranch, Beacon, Arizona. . . . Boys, this Frank Owens is all of us."

"Huh! Mebbe he's a darn sight more," added Andy.

"Looks like a lowdown trick we're to blame for," resumed Tex, seriously shaking his hawklike head. "Heah we reads in a Kansas City paper about a schoolteacher wantin' a job out in dry Arizona. An' we writes her an' gets her ararin' to come. Then when she writes and tells us she's *not over forty*—then we quits like yellow coyotes. An' we four anyhow shook hands on never writin' her agin. Well, somebody did, an' I reckon you all think me as big a liar as I think you are. But that ain't the point. Heah's another letter to Mr. Owens an' I'll bet my saddle it means trouble."

Tex impressively spread out the letter and read laboriously:

Kansas City, Mo.
June 15

Dear Mr. Owens:

 Your last letter has explained away much that was vague and perplexing in your other letters.

 It has inspired me with hope and anticipation. I shall not take time now to express my thanks, but hasten to get ready to go west. I shall leave tomorrow and arrive at Beacon on June 19, at 4:30 P.M. You see I have studied the timetable.

Yours very truly,
Jane Stacey

Profound silence followed Tex's reading of the letter. The cowboys were struck completely dumb. Then suddenly Nevada exploded:

"My Gawd, fellers, today's the nineteenth!"

"Well, Springer needs a schoolmarm at the ranch," finally spoke up the more practical Andy. "There's half a dozen kids growin' up without schoolin', not to talk about other ranches. I heard the boss say so himself."

Tex spoke up. "I've an idea. It's too late now to turn this poor schoolmarm back. An' somebody'll have to meet her. You all come with me. I'll get a buckboard. I'll meet the lady and do the talkin'. I'll let her down easy. And if I cain't head her back to Missouri we'll fetch her out to the ranch an' then leave it up to Springer. Only we won't tell her or him or anybody who's the real Frank Owens."

"Tex, that ain't so plumb bad," said Andy admiringly.

"What I want to know is who's goin' to do the talkin' to the boss," asked Panhandle. "It mightn't be so hard to explain now. But after drivin' up to the ranch with a woman! You all know Springer's shy. Young an' rich, like he is, an' a bachelor—he's been fussed over so he's plumb afraid of girls. An' here you're fetchin' a middle-aged schoolmarm who's romantic an' mushy!—My Gawd; . . . I say send her home on the next train."

"Pan, you're wise as far as horses an' cattle goes, but you don't know human nature, an' you're dead wrong about the boss," said Tex. "We're in a bad fix, I'll admit. But I lean more to fetchin' the lady up than sendin' her back. Somebody down Beacon way would get wise. Mebbe the schoolmarm might talk. She'd shore have cause. An' suppose Springer hears about it—that some of us or all of us has played a lowdown trick on a woman. He'd be madder at that than if we fetched her up.

"Likely he'll try to make amends. The boss may be shy on girls but he's the squarest man in Arizona. My idea is that we'll deny any of us is Frank Owens, and we'll meet Miss—Miss—what was her name?—Miss Jane Stacey and fetch her up to the ranch, an' let her do the talkin' to Springer."

During the next several hours while Tex searched the town for a buckboard and team he could borrow, the other cowboys wandered from the saloon to the post office and back again, and then to the store, the restaurant and back again, and finally settled in the saloon.

When they emerged some time later they were arm in arm, and far from steady on their feet. They paraded up the one main street of Beacon, not in the least conspicuous on a Saturday afternoon. As they were neither hilarious nor dangerous, nobody paid any particular attention to them. Springer, their boss, met them, gazed at them casually, and passed by without sign of recognition. If he had studied the boys closely he might have received an impression that they were clinging to a secret, as well as to each other.

In due time the trio presented themselves at the railroad station. Tex was there, nervously striding up and down the platform, now and then looking at his watch. The afternoon train was nearly due. At the hitching rail below the platform stood a new buckboard and a rather spirited team of horses.

The boys, coming across the wide square, encountered this evidence of Tex's extremity, and struck a posture before it.

"Livery shtable outfit, my gosh," said Andy.

"Shon of a gun if it ain't," added Panhandle with a huge grin.

"This here Tex spendin' his money royal," agreed Nevada.

Then Tex saw them. He stared. Suddenly he jumped straight up. Striding to the edge of the platform, with face red as a beet, he began to curse them.

"Whash masher, ole pard?" asked Andy, who appeared a little less stable than his two comrades.

Tex's reply was another volley of expressive profanity. And he ended with: "—you all yellow quitters to get drunk and leave me in the lurch. But you gotta get away from here. I shore won't have you about when the train comes in."

"But pard, we jist want to shee you meet our Jane from Missouri," said Andy.

"If you all ain't a lot of fourflushers I'll eat my chaps!" burst out Tex hotly.

Just then a shrill whistle announced the arrival of the train.

"You can sneak off now," he went on, "an' leave me to face the music. I always knew I was the only gentleman in Springer's outfit."

The three cowboys did not act upon Tex's sarcastic suggestion, but they hung back, looking at once excited and sheepish and hugely delighted.

The long gray dusty train pulled into the station and stopped with a complaining of brakes. There was only one passenger for Springer—a woman—and she alighted from the coach near where the cowboys stood waiting. She wore a long linen coat and a brown veil that completely hid her face. She was not tall and she was much too slight for the heavy valise the porter handed down to her.

Tex strode swaggeringly toward her.

"Miss—Miss Stacey, ma'am?" he asked, removing his sombrero.

"Yes," she replied. "Are you Mr. Owens?"

Evidently the voice was not what Tex had expected and it disconcerted him.

"No, ma'am, I—I'm not Mister Owens," he said. "Please let me take your bag . . . I'm Tex Dillon, one of Springer's cowboys. An' I've come to meet you—and fetch you out to the ranch."

"Thank you, but I—I expected to be met by Mr. Owens," she replied.

"Ma'am, there's been a mistake—I've got to tell you—there ain't any Mister Owens," blurted out Tex manfully.

"Oh!" she said, with a little start.

"You see, it was this way," went on the confused cowboy. "One of Springer's cowboys—not me—wrote them letters to you, signin' his name Owens. There ain't no such named cowboy in this whole country. Your last letter—an' here it is—fell into my hands—all by accident, ma'am, it shore was. I took my three friends heah—I took them into my confidence. An' we all came down to meet you."

She moved her head and evidently looked at the strange trio of cowboys Tex pointed out as his friends. They shuffled forward, not too eagerly, and they still held on to each other. Their condition, not to consider their state of excitement, could not have been lost even upon a tenderfoot from Missouri.

"Please return my—my letter," she said, turning again to Tex, and she put out a small gloved hand to take it from him. "Then—there is no Mr. Frank Owens?"

"No ma'am, there shore ain't," said Tex miserably.

"Is there—no—no truth in his—is there no schoolteacher wanted here?" she faltered.

"I think so, ma'am," he replied. "Springer said he needed one. That's what started us answerin' the advertisement an' the letters to you. You can see the boss an'—an' explain. I'm shore it will be all right. He's one swell feller. He won't stand for no joke on a poor old schoolmarm."

In his bewilderment Tex had spoken his thoughts, and his last slip made him look more miserable than ever, and made the boys appear ready to burst.

"Poor old schoolmarm!" echoed Miss Stacey. "Perhaps the deceit has not been wholly on one side."

Whereupon she swept aside the enveloping veil to reveal a pale yet extremely pretty face. She was young. She had clear gray eyes and a sweet sensitive mouth. Little curls of chestnut hair straggled down from under her veil. And she had tiny freckles.

Tex stared at this lovely apparition.

"But you—you—the letter says she wasn't over forty," he exclaimed.

"She's not," rejoined Miss Stacey curtly.

Then there were visible and remarkable indication of a transformation in the attitude of the cowboy. But the approach of a stranger suddenly seemed to paralyze him. The newcomer was very tall. He strolled up to them. He was booted and spurred. He halted before the group and looked expectantly from the boys to the strange young woman and back again. But for the moment the four cowboys appeared dumb.

"Are—are you Mr. Springer?" asked Miss Stacey.

"Yes," he replied, and he took off his sombrero. He had a deeply tanned frank face and keen blue eyes.

"I am Jane Stacey," she explained hurriedly. "I'm a schoolteacher. I answered an advertisement. And I've come from Missouri because of letters I received from a Mr. Frank Owens, of Springer's Ranch. This young man met me. He has not been very—explicit. I gather there is no Mr. Owens—that I'm the victim of a cowboy joke . . . But he said that Mr. Springer wouldn't stand for a joke on a poor old schoolmarm."

"I sure am glad to meet you, Miss Stacey," said the rancher, with an easy Western courtesy that must have been comforting to her. "Please let me see the letters."

She opened a handbag, and searching in it, presently held out several letters. Springer never even glanced at his stricken cowboys. He took the letters.

"No, not that one," said Miss Stacey, blushing scarlet. "That's one I wrote to Mr. Owens, but didn't mail. It's—hardly necessary to read that."

While Springer read the others she looked at him. Presently he asked her for the letter she had taken back. Miss Stacey hesitated, then refused. He looked cool, serious, businesslike. Then his keen eyes swept over the four ill-at-ease cowboys.

"Tex, are you Mr. Frank Owens?" he asked sharply.

"I—shore—ain't," gasped Tex.

Springer asked each of the other boys the same question and received decidedly maudlin but negative answers. Then he turned to the girl.

"Miss Stacey, I regret to say that you are indeed the victim of a lowdown cowboy trick," he said. "I'd apologize for such heathen if I knew how. All I can say is I'm sorry."

"Then—then there isn't any school to teach—any place for me—out here?" she asked, and there were tears in her eyes.

"That's another matter," he said, with a pleasant smile. "Of course there's a place for you. I've wanted a schoolteacher for a long time. Some of the men out at the ranch have kids and they sure need a teacher badly."

"Oh, I'm—so glad," she murmured, in evident relief. "I was afraid I'd have to go all the way back. You see I'm not so strong as I used to be—and my doctor advised a change of climate—dry Western air."

"You don't look sick," he said, with his keen eyes on her. "You look very well to me."

"Oh, indeed, but I'm not very strong," she said quickly. "But I must confess I wasn't altogether truthful about my age."

"I was wondering about that," he said, gravely. There seemed just a glint of a twinkle in his eye. "Not over forty."

Again she blushed and this time with confusion.

"It wasn't altogether a lie. I was afraid to mention that I was only—young. And I wanted to get the position so much. . . . I'm a good—a competent teacher, unless the scholars are too grown up."

"The scholars you'll have at my ranch are children," he replied. "Well, we'd better be starting if we are to get there before dark. It's a long ride."

A few weeks altered many things at Springer's Ranch. There was a marvelous change in the dress and deportment of the cowboys when off duty. There were some clean and happy and interested children. There was a rather taciturn and lonely young rancher who was given to thoughtful dreams and whose keen blue eyes kept watch on the little adobe schoolhouse under the cottonwoods. And in Jane Stacey's face a rich bloom and tan had begun to drive out the city pallor.

It was not often that Jane left the schoolhouse without meeting one of Springer's cowboys. She met Tex most frequently, and according to Andy, that fact was because Tex was foreman and could send the boys off to the end of the range when he had the notion.

One afternoon Jane encountered the foreman. He was clean-shaven, bright and eager, a superb figure of a man. Tex had been lucky enough to have a gun with him one day when a rattlesnake had frightened the schoolteacher and he had shot the reptile. Miss Stacey had leaned against him in her fright; she had been grateful; she had admired his wonderful skill with a gun and had murmured that a woman always would be safe with such a man. Thereafter Tex packed his gun, unmindful of the ridicule of his rivals.

"Miss Stacey, come for a little ride, won't you?" he asked eagerly.

The cowboys had already taught her how to handle a horse and to ride; and if all they said of her appearance and accomplishment were true she was indeed worth watching.

"I'm sorry," said Jane. "I promised Nevada I'd ride with him today."

"I reckon Nevada is miles and miles up the valley by now," replied Tex. "He won't be back till long after dark."

"But he made an engagement with me," protested the schoolmistress.

"An' shore he has to work. He's ridin' for Springer, an' I'm foreman of this ranch," said Tex.

"You sent him off on some long chase," said Jane severely. "Now didn't you?"

"I shore did. He comes crowin' down to the bunkhouse—about how he's goin' to ride with you an' how we all are not in the runnin'."

"Oh! he did—And what did you say?"

"I says, 'Nevada, I reckon there's a steer mired in the sand up in Cedar Wash. You ride up there and pull him out.'"

"And then what did he say?" inquired Jane curiously.

"Why, Miss Stacey, shore I hate to tell you. I didn't think he was so—so bad. He just used the most awful language as was ever heard on this here ranch. Then he rode off."

"But was there a steer mired up in the wash?"

"I reckon so," replied Tex, rather shamefacedly. "Most always is one."

Jane let scornful eyes rest upon the foreman. "That was a mean trick," she said.

"There's been worse done to me by him, an' all of them. An' all's fair in love an' war . . . Will you ride with me?"

"No."

"Why not?"

"Because I think I'll ride off alone up Cedar Wash and help Nevada find that mired steer."

"Miss Stacey, you're shore not goin' to ride off alone. Savvy that."

"Who'll keep me from it?" demanded Jane with spirit.

"I will. Or any of the boys, for that matter, Springer's orders."

Jane started with surprise and then blushed rosy red. Tex, also, appeared confused at his disclosure.

"Miss Stacey, I oughtn't have said that. It slipped out. The boss said we needn't tell you, but you were to be watched an' taken care of. It's a wild range. You could get lost or thrown from a hoss."

"Mr. Springer is very kind and thoughtful," murmured Jane.

"The fact is, this ranch is a different place since you came," went on Tex as if suddenly emboldened. "An' this beatin' around the bush doesn't suit me. All the boys have lost their heads over you."

"Indeed? How flattering!" said Jane, with just a hint of mockery. She was fond of all her admirers, but there were four of them she had not yet forgiven.

The tall foreman was not without spirit. "It's true all right, as you'll find out pretty quick," he replied. "If you had any eyes you'd see that cattle raisin' on this ranch is about to halt till somethin' is decided. Why, even Springer himself is sweet on you!"

"How dare you!" flashed Jane, blushing furiously.

"I ain't afraid to tell the truth," said Tex stoutly. "He is. The boys all say so. He's grouchier than ever. He's jealous. Lord! he's jealous! He watches you—"

"Suppose I told him you had dared to say such things?" interrupted Jane, trembling on the verge of a strange emotion.

"Why, he'd be tickled to death. He hasn't got nerve enough to tell you himself."

Jane shook her head, but her face was still flushed. This cowboy, like all his comrades, was hopeless. She was about to change the topic of conversation when Tex suddenly took her into his arms. She struggled—and fought with all her might. But he succeeded in kissing her cheek and then the tip of her ear. Finally she broke away from him.

"Now—" she panted. "You've done it—you've insulted me! Now I'll never ride with you again—never even speak to you."

"Shore I didn't insult you," replied Tex. "Jane—won't you marry me?"

"No."

'Won't you be my sweetheart—till you care enough to—to—"

"No."

"But, Jane, you'll forgive me, an' be good friends with me again?"

"Never!"

Jane did not mean all she said. She had come to understand these men of the range—their loneliness—their hunger for love. But in spite of her sympathy and affection she needed sometimes to appear cold and severe with them.

"Jane, you owe me a great deal—more than you got any idea of," said Tex seriously.

"How so?"

"Didn't you ever guess about me?"

"My wildest flight at guessing would never make anything of you, Texas Jack."

"You'd never have been here but for me," he said solemnly.

Jane could only stare at him.

"I meant to tell you long ago. But I shore didn't have the nerve. Jane I—I was that there letter-writin' feller. I wrote them letters you got. I am Frank Owens."

"No!" exclaimed Jane.

She was startled. That matter of Frank Owens had never been cleared up to her satisfaction. It had ceased to rankle within her breast, but it had never been completely forgotten. She looked up earnestly into the big fellow's face. It was like a mask. But she saw through it. He was lying. He was brazen. Almost, she thought, she saw a laugh deep in his eyes.

"I shore am that lucky man who found you a job when you was sick an' needed a change . . . An' that you've grown so pretty an' so well you owe all to me."

"Tex, if you really were Frank Owens, *that* would make a great difference; indeed I do owe him everything, I would—but I don't believe you are he."

"It's shore honest Gospel fact," declared Tex. "I hope to die if it ain't!"

Jane shook her head sadly at his monstrous prevarication. "I don't believe you," she said, and left him standing there.

It might have been coincidence that the next few days both Nevada and Panhandle waylaid the pretty schoolteacher and conveyed to her intelligence by divers and pathetic arguments the astounding fact that each was none other than Mr. Frank Owens. More likely, however, was it attributable to the unerring instinct of lovers who had sensed the importance and significance of this mysterious correspondent's part in bringing health and happiness into Jane Stacey's life. She listened to them with both anger and amusement at their deceit, and she had the same answer for both. "I don't believe you."

Because of these clumsy machinations of the cowboys, Jane had begun to entertain some vague, sweet, and disturbing suspicions of her own as to the identity of that mysterious cowboy, Frank Owens.

It came about that a dance was to be held at Beacon during the late summer. The cowboys let Jane know that it was something she could not very well afford to miss. She had not attended either of the cowboy dances which had been given since her arrival. This next one, however, appeared to be an annual affair, at which all the ranching fraternity for miles around would be attending.

Jane, as a matter of fact, was wild to go. However, she felt that she could not accept the escort of any one of her cowboy admirers without alienating the others. And she began to have visions of this wonderful dance fading away without a chance of her attending, when Springer accosted her one day.

"Who's the lucky cowboy to take you to our dance?" he asked.

"He seems to be as mysterious and doubtful as Mr. Frank Owens," replied Jane.

"Oh, you still remember him," said the rancher, his keen dark eyes quizzically on her.

"Indeed I do," sighed Jane.

"Too bad! He was a villain . . . But you don't mean you haven't been asked to go?"

"They've all asked me. That's the trouble."

"I see. But you mustn't miss it. It'd be pleasant for you to meet some of the ranchers and their wives. Suppose you go with me?"

"Oh, Mr. Springer, I—I'd be delighted," replied Jane.

Jane's first sight of that dance hall astonished her. It was a big barnlike room, crudely raftered and sided, decorated with colored bunting which took away some of the bareness. The oil lamps were not bright, but there were plenty of them hung in brackets around the room. The volume of sound amazed her. Music and the trample of boots, gay laughter, the deep voices of men and the high-pitched voices of the children—all seemed to merge into a loud, confused uproar. A swaying, wheeling horde of dancers circled past her.

"Sure it's something pretty fine for old Bill Springer to have the prettiest girl here," her escort said.

"Thank you—but, Mr. Springer—I can easily see that you were a cowboy before you became a rancher," she replied archly.

"Sure I was. And that you will be dead sure to find out," he laughed. "Of course I could never compete with—say—Frank Owens. But let's dance. I shall have little enough of you in this outfit."

So he swung her into the circle of dancers. Jane found him easy to dance with, though he was far from expert. It was a jostling mob, and she soon acquired a conviction that if her gown did outlast the entire dance her feet never would. Springer took his dancing seriously and had little to say. She felt strange and uncertain with him. Presently she became aware of the cessation of hum and movement. The music had stopped.

"That sure was the best dance I ever had," said Springer, with a glow of excitement on his dark face. "An' now I must lose you to this outfit just coming."

Manifestly he meant his cowboys, Tex, Nevada, Panhandle, and Andy, who were presenting themselves four abreast shiny of hair and face.

"Good luck," he whispered. "If you get into a jam, let me know."

What he meant quickly dawned upon Jane. Right then it began. She saw there was absolutely no use in trying to avoid or refuse these young men. The wisest and safest course was to surrender, which she did.

"Boys, don't all talk at once. I can dance with only one of you at a time. So I'll take you in alphabetical order. I'm a poor old schoolmarm from Missouri, you know. It'll be Andy, Nevada, Panhandle, and Tex."

Despite their protests she held rigidly to this rule. Each one of the cowboys took shameless advantage of his opportunity. Outrageously as they all hugged her, Tex was the worst offender. She tried to stop dancing, but he carried her along as if she had been a child. He was rapt, and yet there seemed a devil in him.

"Tex—how dare—you!" she panted, when at last the dance ended.

"Well, I reckon I'd about dare anythin' for you, Jane," he replied, towering over her.

"You ought to be—ashamed," she went on. "I'll not dance with you again."

"Aw, now," he pleaded.

"I won't, Tex, so there. You're no gentleman."

"Ahuh!" he retorted, drawing himself up stiffly. "All right I'll go out an' get drunk, an' when I come back I'll clean out this hall so quick that you'll get dizzy watchin'."

"Tex! Don't go," she called hurriedly, as he started to stride away. "I'll take that back. I will give you another dance—if you promise to—to behave."

With this hasty promise she got rid of him, and was carried off by Mrs. Hartwell to be introduced to the various ranchers and their wives, and to all the girls and their escorts. She found herself a center of admiring eyes. She promised more dances than she could ever hope to remember or keep.

Her next partner was a tall handsome cowboy named Jones. She did not know quite what to make of him. But he was an unusually good dancer, and he did not hold her in such a manner that she had difficulty in breathing. He talked all the time. He was witty and engaging, and he had a most subtly flattering tongue. Jane could not fail to grasp that he might even be more outrageous than Tex, but at least he did not make love to her with physical violence.

She enjoyed that dance and admitted to herself that the singular forceful charm about this Mr. Jones was appealing. If he was a little too bold of glance and somehow too primitively self-assured and debonair, she passed it by in the excitement and joy of the hour, and in the conviction that she was now a long way from Missouri. Jones demanded, rather than begged for, another dance, and though she laughingly explained her predicament in regard to partners he said he would come after her anyhow.

Then followed several dances with new partners, and Jane became more than ever the center of attraction. It all went to the schoolteacher's head like wine. She was having a perfectly wonderful time. Jones claimed her again, in fact whirled her away from the man to whom she was talking and out on the floor. Twice again before the supper hour at midnight she found herself dancing with Jones. How he managed it she did not know. He just took her, carrying her off by storm.

She did not awaken to this unpardonable conduct of hers until she suddenly recalled that a little before she had promised Tex his second dance, and then she had given it to Jones, or at least had danced it with him. But, after all, what could she do when he had walked right off with her? It was a glimpse of Tex's face, as she whirled past in Jones' arms, that filled Jane with sudden remorse.

Then came the supper hour. It was a gala occasion, for which evidently the children had heroically kept awake. Jane enjoyed the children immensely. She sat with the numerous Hartwells, all of whom were most pleasantly attentive to her. Jane wondered why Mr. Springer did not put in an appearance, but considered his absence due to numerous duties on the dance committee!

When the supper hour ended and the people were stirring about the hall again, and the musicians were turning up, Jane caught sight of Andy. He looked rather pale and almost sick. Jane tried to catch his eye, but failing that she went to him.

"Andy, please find Tex for me. I owe him a dance, and I'll give him the very first, unless Mr. Springer comes for it."

Andy regarded her with an aloofness totally new to her.

"Well, I'll tell him. But I reckon Tex ain't presentable just now. An' all of us boys are through dancin' for tonight."

"What's happened?" asked Jane, swift to divine trouble.

"There's been a little fight."

"Oh, no!" cried Jane. "Who? Why?—Andy, please tell me."

"Well, when you cut Tex's dance for Beady Jones, you shore put our outfit in bad," replied Andy coldly. "At that there wouldn't have been anything come of it here if Beady Jones hadn't got to shootin' off his chin. Tex slapped his face an' that shore started a fight. Beady licked Tex, too, I'm sorry to say. He's a pretty bad hombre, Beady is, an' he's bigger'n Tex. Well, we had a hell of a time keepin' Nevada out of it. That would have been a worse fight. I'd like to have seen it. But we kept them apart till Springer come out. An' what the boss said to that outfit was sure aplenty.

"Beady Jones kept talkin' back, nastylike—you know he was once foreman for us—till Springer got good an' mad. An' he said: 'Jones, I fired you once because you were a little too slick for our outfit, an' I'll tell you this, if it come to a pinch I'll give you the damnedest thrashin' any smart-aleck cowboy ever got.' . . . Judas, the boss was riled. It sort of surprised me, an' tickled me pink. You can bet that shut Beady Jones's loud mouth and mighty quick!"

After his rather lengthy speech, Andy left her unceremoniously standing there alone. She was not alone long, but it was long enough for her to feel a rush of bitter dissatisfaction with herself.

Jane looked for Springer, hoping yet fearing he would come to her. But he did not. She had another uninterrupted dizzy round of dancing until her strength completely failed. By four o'clock she was scarcely able to walk. Her pretty dress was torn and mussed; her white stockings were no longer white; her slippers were worn ragged. And her feet were dead. She dragged herself to a chair where she sat looking on, and trying to keep awake. The wonderful dance that had begun so promisingly had ended sadly for her.

At length the exodus began, though Jane did not see many of the dancers leaving. She went out to be received by Springer, who had evidently made arrangements for their leaving. He seemed decidedly cool to the remorseful Jane.

All during the long ride to the ranch he never addressed her or looked toward her. Daylight came, appearing cold and gray to Jane. She felt as if she wanted to cry.

Springer's sister and the matronly housekeeper were waiting for them, with a cherry welcome, and an invitation to a hot breakfast.

Presently Jane found herself momentarily alone with the taciturn rancher.

"Miss Stacey," he said, in a voice she had never heard, "your crude flirting with Beady Jones made trouble for the Springer outfit last night."

"Mr. Springer!" she exclaimed, her head going up.

"Excuse me," he returned, in a cutting, dry tone that recalled Tex. After all, this Westerner was still a cowboy, just exactly like those who rode for him, only a little older, and therefore more reserved and careful of his speech. "If it wasn't that—then you sure appeared to be pretty much taken with Mr. Beady Jones."

"If that was anybody's business, it might have appeared so," she cried, tingling all over with some feeling which she could not control.

"Sure. But are you denying it?" he asked soberly, eyeing her with a grave frown and obvious disapproval. It was this more than his question that roused hot anger and contrariness in Jane.

"I admired Mr. Jones very much," she replied haughtily. "He was a splendid dancer. He did not maul me like a bear. I really had a chance to breathe during my dances with him. Then too he could talk. He was a gentleman."

Springer bowed with dignity. His dark face paled. It dawned upon Jane that the situation had become serious for everyone concerned. She began to repent her hasty pride.

"Thanks," he said. "Please excuse my impertinence. I see you have found your Mr. Frank Owens in this cowboy Jones, and it sure is not my place to say any more."

"But—but—Mr. Springer—" faltered Jane, quite unstrung by the rancher's amazing speech.

However, he merely bowed again and left her. Jane felt too miserable and weary for anything but rest and a good cry. She went to her room, and flinging off her hateful finery, she crawled into bed, and buried her head in her pillow.

About mid-afternoon Jane awakened greatly refreshed and relieved and strangely repentant. She invaded the kitchen, where the goodnatured housekeeper, who had become fond of her, gave her some wild-turkey sandwiches and cookies and sweet rich milk. While Jane appeased her hunger the woman gossiped about the cowboys and Springer, and the information she imparted renewed Jane's concern over the last night's affair.

From the kitchen Jane went out into the courtyard, and naturally, as always, gravitated toward the corrals and barns. Springer appeared in company with a rancher Jane did not know. She expected Springer to stop her for a few pleasant words as was his wont. This time, however, he merely touched his sombrero and passed on. Jane felt the incident almost as a slight. And it hurt.

As she went on down the land she became very thoughtful. A cloud suddenly had appeared above the horizon of her happy life there at the Springer ranch. It did not seem to her that what she had done deserved the change in everyone's attitude. The lane opened out onto a wide square, around which were the gates to the corrals, the entrances to several barns, the forge, granaries, and the commodious bunkhouse of the cowboys.

Jane's sharp eyes caught sight of the boys before they saw her. But when she looked up again every broad back was turned. They allowed her to pass without any apparent knowledge of her existence. This obvious snub was unprecedented. It offended her bitterly. She knew that she was being unreasonable, but could not or would not help it. She strolled on down to the pasture gate and watched the colts and calves.

Upon her return she passed even closer to the cowboys. But again they apparently did not see her. Jane added resentment to her wounded vanity and pride. Yet even then a still small voice tormented and accused her. She went back to her room, meaning to read or sew, or prepare school work. But instead she sat down in a chair and burst into tears.

Next day was Sunday. Heretofore every Sunday had been a full day for Jane. This one, however, bade fair to be an empty one. Company came as usual, neighbors from nearby ranches. The cowboys were off duty and other cowboys came over to visit them.

Jane's attention was attracted by sight of a superb horseman riding up the lane to the ranch house. He seemed familiar, somehow, but she could not place him. What a picture he made as he dismounted slick and shiny, booted and spurred, to doff his huge sombrero! Jane heard him ask for Miss Stacey. Then she recognized him. Beady Jones! She was at once horrified and yet attracted to this cowboy. She remembered how he had asked if he might call Sunday and she had certainly not refused to see him. But for him to come here after the fight with Tex and the bitter scene with Springer!

It seemed almost an unparalleled affront. What manner of man was this cowboy Jones? He certainly did not lack courage. But more to the point what idea he had of her? Jane rose to the occasion. She had let herself in for this, and she would see it through, come what might. Looming disaster stimulated her. She would show these indifferent, deceitful, fire-spirited, incomprehensible cowboys! She would let Springer see that she had indeed taken Beady Jones for Mr. Frank Owens.

With this thought in mind, Jane made her way down to the porch to greet her cowboy visitor. She made herself charming and gracious, and carried off the embarrassing situation—for Springer was present—just as if it were the most natural thing in the world. And she led Jones to one of the rustic benches farther down the porch.

Obvious, indeed, was it in all his actions that young Jones felt he had made a conquest. He was the most forceful and bold person Jane had ever met, quite incapable of appreciating her as a lady. It was not long before he was waxing ardent. Jane had become accustomed to the sentimental talk of cowboys, but this fellow was neither amusing nor interesting. He was dangerous. When she pulled her hand, by main force, free from his, and said she was not accustomed to allow men such privileges, he grinned at her like the handsome devil he was. Her conquest was only a matter of time.

"Sure, sweetheart, you have missed a heap of fun," Beady Jones said. "An' I reckon I'll have to break you in."

Jane could not really feel insulted at this brazen, conceited fool, but she certainly could feel enraged with herself. Her instant impulse was to excuse herself and abruptly leave him. But Springer was close by. She had caught his dark, speculative, covert glances. And the cowboys were at the other end of the long porch. Jane feared another fight. She had brought this situation upon herself, and she must stick it out. The ensuing hour was an increasing torment.

At last it seemed to her that she could not bear the false situation any longer. And when Jones again importuned her to meet him out on horseback some time, she stooped to deception to end the interview. She really did not concentrate her attention on his plan or really take stock of what she was agreeing to do, but she got rid of him with ease and dignity in the presence of Springer and the others. After that she did not have the courage to stay out there and face them, and stole off to the darkness and loneliness of her room.

The school teaching went on just the same, and the cowboys thawed out perceptibly, and Springer returned somewhat to his friendly manner, but Jane missed something from her work and in them, and her heart was sad the way everything was changed. Would it ever be the same again? What had happened? She had only been an emotional little tenderfoot, unused to Western ways. After all, she had not failed, at least in gratitude and affection, though now it seemed they would never know.

There came a day, when Jane rode off toward the hills. She forgot the risk and all of the admonitions of the cowboys. She wanted to be alone to think.

She rode fast until her horse was hot and she was out of breath. Then she slowed down. The foothills seemed so close now. But they were not really close. Still she could smell the fragrant dry cedar aroma on the air.

Then for the first time she looked back toward the ranch. It was a long way off—ten miles—a mere green spot in the gray. Suddenly she caught sight of a horseman coming. As usual, some one of the cowboys had observed her, let her think she had slipped away, and was now following her. Today it angered Jane. She wanted to be alone. She could take care of herself. And as was unusual with her, she used her quirt on the horse. He broke into a gallop.

She did not look back again for a long time. When she did it was to discover that the horseman had not only gained, but was now quite close to her. Jane looked intently, but she could not recognize the rider. Once she imagined it was Tex and again Andy. It did not make any difference which one of the cowboys it was. She was angry, and if he caught up with her he would be sorry.

Jane rode the longest and fastest race she had ever ridden. She reached the low foothills, and without heeding the fact that she might speedily become lost, she entered the cedars and began to climb.

What was her amazement when she heard a thud of hoofs and crackling of branches in the opposite direction from which she was expecting her pursuer, and saw a rider emerge from the cedars and trot his horse toward her. Jane needed only a second glance to recognize Beady Jones. Surely she had met him by chance. Suddenly she knew he was not the pursuer she had been so angrily aware of. Jones's horse was white. That checked her mounting anger.

Jones rode straight at her, and as he came close Jane saw his bold tanned face and gleaming eyes. Instantly she realized that she had been mad to ride so far into the wild country, to expose herself to something from which the cowboys on the ranch had always tried to save her.

"Howdy, sweetheart," sang out Jones, in his cool, devil-may-care way. "Reckon it took you a long time to make up your mind to meet me as you promised."

"I didn't ride out to meet you, Mr. Jones," said Jane spiritedly. "I know I agreed to something or other, but even then I didn't mean it."

"Yes, I had a hunch you were just playin' with me," he said darkly, riding his white mount right up against her horse.

He reached out a long gloved hand and grasped her arm.

"What do you mean, sir?" demanded Jane, trying to wrench her arm free.

"Shore I mean a lot," he said grimly. "You stood for the lovemakin' of that Springer outfit. Now you're goin' to get a taste of somethin' not quite so easy."

"Let go of me—you—you utter fool!" cried Jane, struggling fiercely. She was both furious and terrified. But she seemed to be a child in the grasp of a giant.

"Hell! Your fightin' will only make it more interestin'. Come here, you sassy little cat."

And he lifted her out of her saddle over onto his horse in front of him. Jane's mount, that had been frightened and plunging, ran away into the cedars. Then Jones proceeded to embrace Jane. She managed to keep her mouth from contact with his, but he kissed her face and neck, kisses that seemed to fill her with shame and disgust.

"Jane, I'm ridin' out of this country for good," he said. "An' I've just been waitin' for this chance. You bet you'll remember Beady Jones."

Jane realized that Jones would stop at nothing. Frantically she fought to get away from him, and to pitch herself to the ground. She screamed. She beat and tore at him. She scratched his face till the blood flowed. And as her struggles increased with her fright, she gradually slipped down between him and the pommel of his saddle, with head hanging down on one side and her feet on the other. This position was awkward and painful, but infinitely preferable to being crushed in his arms. He was riding off with her as if she had been a half-empty sack.

Suddenly Jane's hands, while trying to hold on to something to lessen the severe jolting her position was giving her, came in contact with Jones's gun. Dare she draw it and try to shoot him? Then all at once her ears filled with the approaching gallop of another horse. Inverted as she was, she was able to see and recognize Springer riding directly at Jones and yelling hoarsely.

Next she felt Jones's hand jerk at his gun. But Jane had hold of it, and suddenly her little hands had the strength of steel. The fierce energy with which Jones was wrestling to draw his gun threw Jane from the saddle. And when she dropped clear of the horse the gun came with her.

"Hands up, Beady!" she heard Springer call out, as she lay momentarily face down in the dust. Then, she struggled to her knees, and crawled to get away from the danger of the horses' hoofs. She still clung to the heavy gun. And when breathless and almost collapsing she fell back on the ground, she saw Jones with his hands above his head and Springer on foot with leveled gun.

"Sit tight, cowboy," ordered the rancher, in a hard tone. "It'll take damn little more to make me bore you."

Then while still covering Jones, evidently ready for any sudden move, Springer spoke again.

"Jane, did you come out here to meet this cowboy?" he asked.

"Oh, no! How can you ask that?" cried Jane, almost sobbing.

"She's a liar, boss," spoke up Jones coolly. "She let me make love to her. An' she agreed to ride out an' meet me. Well it shore took her a spell, an' when she did come she was shy on the lovemakin'. I was packin' her off to scare some sense into her when you rode in."

"Beady, I know your way with women. You can save your breath, for I've a hunch you're going to need it."

"Mr. Springer," faltered Jane, getting to her knees. "I—I was foolishly attracted to this cowboy—at first. Then—that Sunday after the dance when he called on me at the ranch—I saw through him then. I heartily despised him. To get rid of him I did say I'd meet him. But I never meant to. Then I forgot all about it. Today I rode alone for the first time. I saw someone following me and thought it must be Tex or one of the boys. Finally I waited, and presently Jones rode up to me . . . And, Mr. Springer, he—he grabbed me off my horse—and handled me shamefully. I fought him with all my might, but what could I do?"

Springer's face changed markedly during Jane's long explanation. Then he threw his gun on the ground in front of Jane.

"Jones, I'm going to beat you within an inch of your life," he said grimly; and leaping at the cowboy, he jerked him out of the saddle and sent him sprawling on the ground. Next Springer threw aside his sombrero, his vest, his spurs. But he kept on his gloves. The cowboy rose to one knee, and he measured the distance between him and Springer, and then the gun that lay on the ground. Suddenly he sprang toward it. Springer intercepted him with a powerful kick that tripped Jones and laid him flat.

"Jones, you're sure about as lowdown as they come," he said, in a tone of disgust. "I've got to be satisfied with beating you when I ought to kill you!"

"Ahuh! Well, boss, it ain't any safe bet that you can do either," cried Beady Jones sullenly, as he got up.

As they rushed together Jane had wit enough to pick up the gun, and then with it and Jones's, to get back a safe distance. She wanted to run away out of sight. But she could not keep her fascinated gaze from the combatants. Even in her distraught condition she could see that the cowboy, young and active and strong as he was, could not hold his own with Springer. They fought all over the open space, and crashed into the cedars and out again. The time came when Jones was on the ground about as much as he was erect. Bloody, dishevelled, beaten, he kept on trying to stem the onslaught of blows.

Suddenly he broke off a dead branch of cedar, and brandishing it rushed at the rancher. Jane uttered a cry, closed her eyes, and sank to the ground. She heard fierce muttered imprecations and savage blows. When at length she opened her eyes again, fearing something dreadful, she saw Springer erect, wiping his face with the back of one hand and Jones lying on the ground.

Then Jane saw him go to his horse, untie a canteen from the saddle, remove his bloody gloves, and wash his face with a wet scarf. Next he poured some water on Jones's face.

"Come on, Jane," he called. "I reckon it's all over."

He tied the bridle of Jones's horse to a cedar, and leading his own animal turned to meet Jane.

"I want to compliment you on getting that cowboy's gun," he said warmly. "But for that there'd sure have been something bad. I'd have had to kill him, Jane. . . . Here, give me the guns. . . . You poor little tenderfoot from Missouri. No, not tenderfoot any longer. You became a Westerner today."

His face was bruised and cut, his clothes dirty and bloody, but he did not appear the worse for such a desperate fight. Jane found her legs scarcely able to support her, and she had apparently lost her voice.

"Let me put you on my saddle till we find your horse," he said, and lifted her lightly as a feather to a seat crosswise in the saddle. Then he walked with a hand on the bridle.

Jane saw him examining the ground, evidently searching for horse tracks. "Here we are." And he led off in another direction through the cedars. Soon Jane saw her horse, calmly nibbling at the bleached grass.

Springer stood beside her with a hand on her horse. He looked frankly into her face. The keen eyes were softer than usual. He looked so fine and strong and splendid that she found herself breathing with difficulty. She was afraid of her betraying eyes and looked away.

"When the boys found out that you were gone, they all saddled up to find you," he said. "But I asked them if they didn't think the boss ought to have one chance. So they let me come."

Right about then something completely unforeseen happened to Jane's heart. She was overwhelmed by a strange happiness that she knew she ought to hide, but could not. She could not speak. The silence grew. She felt Springer there, but she could not look at him.

"Do you like it out here in the West?" he asked presently.

"Oh, I love it! I'll never want to leave it," she replied impulsively.

"I reckon I'm glad to hear you say that."

Then there fell another silence. He pressed closer to her and seemed now to be leaning against the horse. She wondered if he heard the thunderous knocking of her heart against her side.

"Will you be my wife an' stay here always?" he asked simply. "I'm in love with you. I've been lonely since my mother died. . . . You'll sure have to marry some of us. Because, as Tex says, if you don't, ranchin' can't go on much longer. These boys don't seem to get anywhere with you. Have I any chance—Jane?"

He possessed himself of her gloved hand and gave her a gentle tug. Jane knew it was gentle because she scarcely felt it. Yet it had irresistible power. She was swayed by that gentle pull. She moved into his arms.

A little later he smiled at her and said, "Jane, they call me Bill for short. Same as they call me boss. But my two front names are Frank Owens."

"Oh!" cried Jane. "Then you—"

"Yes, I'm the guilty one," he said happily. "It happened this way. My bedroom, you know is next to my office. I often heard the boys pounding the typewriter. I had a hunch they were up to some trick. So I spied upon them—heard about Frank Owens and the letters to the little schoolmarm. At Beacon I got the postmistress to give me your address. And, of course, I intercepted some of your letters. It sure has turned out great."

"I—I don't know about you or those terrible cowboys," said Jane dubiously. "How did *they* happen on the name Frank Owens?"

"That's sure a stumper. I reckon they put a job up on me."

"Frank—tell me—did *you* write the—the love letters?" she asked appealingly. "There were two kinds of letters. That's what I never could understand."

"Jane, I reckon I did," he confessed. "Something about your little notes made me fall in love with you clear back there in Missouri. Does that make it all right?"

"Yes, Frank, I reckon it does—now," she said.

"Let's ride back home and tell the boys," said Springer gayly. "The joke's sure on them. I've corralled the little 'under-forty schoolmarm from Missouri.'"

−1926

R A F A E L   S A B A T I N I

1875-1950

Rafael Sabatini was a historian and a best-selling author of the historical novel who revived the sagging popularity of historical fiction between the World Wars. He also ranks with C. S. Forester and Patrick O'Brian as one of the most skilled practitioners of the sea adventure story. Sabatini's fiction is distinguished by its use of richly detailed historical backgrounds and its incorporation of swashbuckling adventure. His most successful "costume epics" include The Sea-Hawk *(1915),* Scaramouche: A Romance of the French Revolution *(1921), and* The Black Swan *(1932).*

*Sabatini was born in Jesi, Italy, to Italian and English parents, and was educated in Switzerland and Portugal. He was skilled at many languages, including English, Spanish, Portuguese, French, German, and Italian. His varied interests in reading and writing eventually led him to a career as an author of historical biography, as well as historical fiction. His efforts at biography—*The Life of Cesare Borgia of France *(1911),* Torquemada and the Spanish Inquisition *(1913), and* Heroic Lives *(1934)—firmly established his reputation as a first-rate historian.*

*Sabatini's Captain Blood series is among his most popular historical fiction. He published three books featuring the heroic exploits of the infamous pirate captain—*Captain Blood: His Odyssey *(1922),* Captain Blood Returns *(also titled* The Chronicles of Captain Blood, *1931), and* The Fortunes of Captain Blood *(1936)—and they remain among the finest sea adventure stories ever written.* Warner Brothers Studios filmed Sabatini's *Captain Blood (starring Errol Flynn and directed by Michael Curtiz) in 1935. This movie solidified the popularity of the pirate film genre and encouraged Hollywood to produce many imitations, some more successful than others.*

"The Treasure Ship," reprinted from Captain Blood Returns *(a "novel" comprised of loosely connected short fiction), illustrates Sabatini's formidable knowledge of the sea battle tactics of the period. The tale, in addition, depicts Sabatini's colorful use of descriptive language and his equally colorful portrayal of the dashing British surgeon-turned-pirate, Captain Peter Blood, one of the greatest heroes in all of adventure fiction.*

THE TREASURE SHIP

It was a saying of Captain Blood's that the worth of a man manifests itself not so much in the ability to plan great undertakings as in the vision which perceives opportunity and the address which knows how to seize it.

He had certainly displayed these qualities in possessing himself of that fine Spanish ship the Cinco Llagas and he had displayed them again in foiling the designs of that rascally buccaneer Captain Easterling to rob him of that noble vessel.

Meanwhile, his own and his ship's near escape made it clear to all who followed him that there was little safety for them in Tortuga waters, and little trust to be placed in buccaneers. At a general council held that same afternoon in the ship's waist, Blood propounded the simple philosophy that when a man is attacked he must either fight or run.

"And since we are in no case to fight when attacked, as no doubt we shall be, it but remains to play the coward's part if only so that we may survive to prove ourselves brave men some other day."

They agreed with him. But whilst the decision to run was taken, it was left to be determined later whither they should repair. At the moment all that mattered was to get away from Tortuga and the further probable attentions of Captain Easterling.

Thus it fell out that, in the dead of the following night, which if clear was moonless, the great frigate, which once had been the pride of the Cadiz shipyards, weighed anchor as quietly as such an operation might be performed. With canvas spread to the faint favouring breeze from the shore and with the ebb tide to help the manœuvre, the Cinco Llagas stood out to sea. If groan of windlass, rattle of chain, and creak of blocks had betrayed the action to Easterling aboard the Bonaventure, a cable's length away, it was not in Easterling's power to thwart Blood's intention. At least three quarters of his rascally crew were in the taverns ashore, and Easterling was not disposed to attempt boarding operations with the remnant of his men, even though that remnant outnumbered by two to one the hands of the Cinco Llagas. Moreover, even had his full complement of two hundred been aboard, Easterling would still have offered no opposition to that departure. Whilst in Tortuga waters he might have attempted to get possession of the Cinco Llagas quietly and by strategy, not even his recklessness could consider seizing her violently by force in such a sanctuary, especially as the French Governor, Monsieur d'Ogeron, appeared to be friendly disposed towards Blood and his fellow fugitives.

Out on the open sea it would be another matter; and the tale he would afterwards tell of the manner in which the Cinco Llagas should have come into his possession would be such as no one in Cayona would be in a position to contradict.

So Captain Easterling suffered Peter Blood to depart unhindered, and was well content to let him go. Nor did he display any undue and betraying haste to follow. He made his preparations with leisureliness, and did not weigh anchor until the afternoon of the morrow. He trusted his wits to give him the direction Blood must take and depended upon the greater speed of the Bonaventure to overhaul him before he should have gone far enough for safety. His reasoning was shrewd enough. Since he knew that the Cinco Llagas was not victualled for a long voyage, there could be no question yet of any direct attempt to sail for Europe. First she must be equipped, and since to equip her Blood dared approach no English or Spanish settlement, it followed that he would steer for one of the neutral Dutch colonies, and there take his only remaining chance. Nor was Blood likely without experienced pilotage to venture among the dangerous reefs of the Bahamas. It was therefore an easy inference that his destination would be the Leeward Islands with intent to put in at San Martin, Saba, or Santa Eustacia. Confident, then, of overtaking him before he could make the nearest of those Dutch settlements, two hundred leagues away, the pursuing Bonaventure steered an easterly course along the northern shores of Hispaniola.

Things, however, were not destined to be so simple as Easterling conjectured. The wind, at first favourable, veered towards evening to the east, and increased throughout the night in vehemence; so that by dawn—an angry dawn with skies ominously flushed—the Bonaventure had not merely made no progress, but had actually drifted some miles out of her course. Then the wind shifted to the south towards noon, and it came on to blow harder than ever. It blew up a storm from the Caribbean, and for twenty-four hours the Bonaventure rode it out with bare yards and hatches battened against the pounding seas that broke athwart her and tossed her like a cork from trough to crest.

It was fortunate that the burly Easterling was not only a stout fighter, but also an able seaman. Under his skilled handling, the Bonaventure came through the ordeal unscathed, to resume the chase when at last the storm had passed and the wind had settled to a steady breeze from the south-west. With crowded canvas the sloop now went scudding through the heaving seas which the storm had left.

Easterling heartened his followers with the reminder that the hurricane which had delayed them must no less have delayed the Cinco Llagas; that, indeed, considering the lubbers who handled the erstwhile Spanish frigate, it was likely that the storm had made things easier for the Bonaventure.

What exactly the storm had done for them they were to discover on the following morning, when off Cape Engaño they sighted a galleon which at first, in the distance, they supposed to be their quarry, but which very soon they perceived to be some other vessel. That she was Spanish was advertised not only by her towering build, but by the banner of Castile which she flew beneath the Crucifix at the head of her mainmast. On the yards of this mainmast all canvas was close-reefed, and under the spread of only fore-sail mizzen and sprit, she was labouring clumsily towards the Mona Passage with the wind on her larboard quarter.

The sight of her in her partially maimed condition stirred Easterling like a hound at sight of a deer. For the moment the quest of the Cinco Llagas was forgotten. Here was more immediate prey and of a kind to be easily reduced.

At the poop rail he bawled his orders rapidly. In obedience the decks were cleared with feverish speed and the nettings spread from stem to stern to catch any spars that might be shot down in the approaching action. Chard, Easterling's lieutenant, a short, powerful man, who was a dullard in all things save the handling of a ship and the wielding of a cutlass, took the helm. The gunners at their stations cleared the leaden aprons from the touch-holes and swung their glowing matches, ready for the word of command. For however disorderly and unruly Easterling's crew might be at ordinary times, it knew the need for discipline when battle was to be joined.

Watchful on the poop the buccaneer captain surveyed the Spaniard upon which he was rapidly bearing down, and observed with scorn the scurry of preparation on her decks. His practised eye read her immediate past history at a glance, and his harsh, guttural voice announced what he read to Chard who stood below him at the whipstaff.

"She would be homing for Spain when the hurricane caught her. She's sprung her mainmast and likely suffered other damage besides, and she's beating back to San Domingo for repairs." Easterling laughed in his throat and stroked his dense black beard. The dark, bold eyes, in his great red face glinted wickedly. "Give me a homing Spaniard, Chard. There'll be treasure aboard that hulk. By God, we're in luck at last."

He was, indeed. It had long been his grievance, and the true reason of his coveting the Cinco Llagas, that his sloop the Bonaventure was unequal to tackling the real prizes of the Caribbean. And he would never have dared to attack this heavily armed galleon but that in her crippled condition she was unable to manœuvre so as to bring her guns to bear upon his flanks.

She gave him now a broadside from her starboard quarter, and by doing so sealed her own doom. The Bonaventure, coming head on, presented little target, and save for a round shot in her forecastle took no damage. Easterling answered the fire with the chasers on his prow, aiming high, and sweeping the Spaniard's decks. Then, nimbly avoiding her clumsy attempt to go about and change their relative positions, the Bonaventure was alongside on the quarter of her empty guns. There was a rattling, thudding jar, a creak of entangled rigging, a crack and clatter of broken spars, and the thud of grapnels rending into the Spaniard's timbers to bind her fast, and then, tight-locked, the two vessels went drifting down wind, whilst the buccaneers, led by the colossal Easterling, and after discharging a volley of musketry, swarmed like ants over the Spaniard's bulwarks. Two hundred of them there were, fierce fellows in loose leathern breeches, some with shirts as well, but the majority naked to the waist, and by that brown muscular nakedness the more terrific of aspect.

To receive them stood a bare fifty Spaniards in corselet and morion, drawn up in the galleon's waist as if upon parade, with muskets calmly levelled and a hawk-faced officer in a plumed hat commanding them.

The officer spoke an order, and a volley from the muskets momentarily checked the assault. Then, like an engulfing wave, the buccaneer mob went over the Spanish soldiers, and the ship, the Santa Barbara, was taken.

There was not perhaps upon the seas at the time a more cruel, ruthless man than Easterling; and those who sailed with him adopted, as men will, their captain's standard of ferocity. Brutally they exterminated the Spanish soldiery, heaving the bodies overboard, and as brutally they dealt with those manning the guns on the main deck below, although these unfortunates readily surrendered in the vain hope of being allowed to keep their lives.

Within ten minutes of the invasion of the Santa Barbara there remained alive upon her of her original crew only the captain, Don Ildefonso de Paiva, whom Easterling had stunned with the butt of a pistol, the navigating officer, and four deck hands, who had been aloft at the moment of boarding. These six Easterling spared for the present because he accounted that they might prove useful.

Whilst his men were busy in the shrouds about the urgent business of disentangling and where necessary repairing, the buccaneer captain began upon the person of Don Ildefonso the investigation of his capture.

The Spaniard, sickly and pallid and with a lump on his brow where the pistol-butt had smitten him, sat on a locker in the handsome, roomy cabin, with pinioned wrists, but striving, nevertheless, to preserve the haughty demeanour proper to a gentleman of Castile in the presence of an impudent sea-robber. Thus, until Easterling, towering over him, savagely threatened to loosen his tongue by the artless persuasions of torture. Then Don Ildefonso, realizing the futility of resistance, curtly answered the pirate's questions. From these answers and his subsequent investigations, Easterling discovered his capture to exceed every hope he could have formed. There had fallen into his hands—which of late had known so little luck—one of those prizes which had been the dream of every sea-rover since the days of Francis Drake. The Santa Barbara was a treasure-ship from Porto Bello, laden with gold and silver which had been conveyed across the Isthmus from Panama. She had put forth under the escort of three strong ships of war, with intent to call at San Domingo to revictual before crossing to Spain. But in the recent storm which had swept the Caribbean she had been separated from her consorts, and with damaged mainmast had been driven through the Mona Passage by the gale. She had been beating back for San Domingo in the hope of rejoining there her escort or else awaiting there another fleet for Spain.

The treasure in her hold was computed by Easterling, when his gleaming eyes came to consider those ingots, at between two and three hundred thousand pieces of eight. It was a prize such as does not come the way of a pirate twice in his career, and it meant fortune for himself and those who sailed with him.

Now the possession of fortune is inevitably attended by anxiety, and Easterling's besetting anxiety at the moment was to convey his prize with all possible speed to the security of Tortuga.

From his own sloop he took two score men to form a prize crew for the Spaniard, and himself remained aboard her because he could not suffer himself to be parted from the treasure. Then, with damage hurriedly repaired, the two ships went about, and started upon their voyage. Progress was slow, the wind being none too favourable and the Santa Barbara none too manageable, and it was past noon before they had Cape Raphael once more abeam. Easterling was uneasy in this near proximity to Hispaniola, and was for taking a wide sweep that would carry them well out to sea when from the crow's nest of the Santa Barbara came a hail, and a moment later the object first espied by the lookout was visible to them all.

There, rounding Cape Raphael, not two miles away, and steering almost to meet them, came a great red ship under full sail. Easterling's telescope confirmed at once what the naked eye had led him incredulously to suspect. This vessel was the Cinco Llagas, the original object of his pursuit, which in his haste he must have outsailed.

The truth was that, overtaken by the storm as they approached Samana, Jeremy Pitt, who navigated the Cinco Llagas, had run for the shelter of Samana Bay, and under the lee of a headland had remained snug and unperceived to come forth again when the gale had spent itself.

Easterling, caring little how the thing had happened, perceived in this sudden and unexpected appearance of the Cinco Llagas a sign that Fortune, hitherto so niggardly, was disposed now to overwhelm him with her favours. Let him convey himself and the Santa Barbara's treasure aboard that stout red ship, and in strength he could make good speed home.

Against a vessel so heavily armed and so undermanned as the Cinco Llagas there could be no question of any but boarding tactics, and it did not seem to Captain Easterling that this should offer much difficulty to the swifter and more easily handled Bonaventure, commanded by a man experienced in seamanship and opposed by a lubberly follower who was by trade a surgeon.

So Easterling signalled Chard to be about the easy business, and Chard, eager enough to square accounts with the man who once already had done them the injury of slipping like water through their fingers, put the helm over and ordered his men to their stations.

Captain Blood, summoned from the cabin by Pitt, mounted the poop, and tele-scope in hand surveyed the activities aboard his old friend the Bonaventure. He remained in no doubt of their significance. He might be a surgeon, but hardly a lub-berly one as Chard so rashly judged him. His service under de Ruyter, in those ear-lier adventurous days when medicine was neglected by him, had taught him more of fighting tactics than Easterling had ever known. He was not perturbed. He would show these pirates how he had profited by the lessons learnt under that great admiral.

Just as for the Bonaventure it was essential to employ boarding tactics, so for the Cinco Llagas it was vital to depend on gunfire. For with no more than twenty men in all, she could not face the odds of almost ten to one, as Blood computed them, of a hand-to-hand engagement. So now he ordered Pitt to put down the helm, and, keeping as close to the wind as possible, to steer a course that would bring them on to the Bonaventure's quarter. To the main deck below he ordered Ogle, that sometime gunner of the King's Navy, taking for his gun crew all but six of the hands who would be required for work above.

Chard perceived at once the aim of the manœuvre and swore through his teeth, for Blood had the weather gauge of him. He was further handicapped by the fact that, since the Cinco Llagas was to be captured for their own purposes, it must be no part of his work to cripple her by gunfire before attempting to board. Moreover, he perceived the risk to himself of the attempt, resulting from the longer range and heavier calibre of the guns of the Cinco Llagas, if she were resolutely handled. And there appeared to be no lack of resolution about her present master.

Meanwhile, the distance between the ships was rapidly lessening, and Chard realized that unless he acted quickly he would be within range with his flank exposed. Unable to bring his ship any closer to the wind, he went about on a south-easterly course with intent to circle widely and so get to windward of the Cinco Llagas.

Easterling, watching the manœuvre from the deck of the Santa Barbara, and not quite understanding its purpose, cursed Chard for a fool. He cursed him the more virulently when he saw the Cinco Llagas veer suddenly to larboard and follow as if giving chase. Chard, however, welcomed this, and taking in sail allowed the other to draw closer. Then, with all canvas spread once more, the Bonaventure was off with the wind on her quarter to attempt her circling movement.

Blood understood, and took in sail in his turn, standing so that as the Bonaventure turned north she must offer him her flank within range of his heavy guns. Hence Chard, to avoid this, must put up his helm and run south once more.

Easterling watched the two ships sailing away from him in a succession of such manœuvres for position, and purple with rage demanded of Heaven and Hell whether he could believe his eyes, which told him only that Chard was running away from the lubberly leech. Chard, however, was far from any such intention. With mas-terly patience and self-control he awaited his chance to run in and grapple. And with equal patience and doggedness Blood saw to it that he should be given no such chance.

In the end it became a question of who should commit the first blunder, and it was Chard who committed it. In his almost excessive anxiety to avoid coming broadside on with the Cinco Llagas, he forgot the chasers on her beak-head, and at last in playing for position allowed her to come too near. He realized his blunder when those two guns roared suddenly behind him and the shot went tearing through his shrouds. It angered him, and in his anger he replied with his stern chasers; but their inferior calibre left their fire ineffective. Then, utterly enraged, he swung the Bonaventure about, so as to put a broadside athwart the hawse of the other, and by crippling her sailing powers lay her at the mercy of his boarders.

The heavy groundswell, however, combined with the length of the range utterly to defeat his object, and his broadside thundered forth in impotence to leave a cloud of smoke between himself and the Cinco Llagas. Instantly Blood swung broadside on, and emptied his twenty larboard guns into that smoke cloud, hoping to attain the Bonaventure's exposed flank beyond. The attempt was equally unsuccessful, but it served to show Chard the mettle of the man he was engaging, a man with whom it was not safe to take such chances. Nevertheless, one more chance he took, and went briskly about, so as to charge through the billowing smoke, and so bear down upon the other ship before she could suspect the design. The manœuvre, however, was too protracted for success. By the time the Bonaventure was upon her fresh course, the smoke had dispersed sufficiently to betray her tactics to Blood, and the Cinco Llagas, lying well over to larboard, was ripping through the water at twice the speed of the Bonaventure now ill-served by the wind.

Again Chard put the helm over and raced to intercept the other and to get to windward of her. But Blood, now a mile away, and with a safety margin of time, went about and returned so as to bring his starboard guns to bear at the proper moment. To elude this, Chard once more headed south and presented no more than his counter as a target.

In this manner the two vessels worked gradually away until the Santa Barbara, with the raging, blaspheming Easterling aboard, was no more than a speck on the northern horizon; and still they were as far as ever from joining battle.

Chard cursed the wind which favoured Captain Blood, and cursed Captain Blood who knew so well how to take and maintain the advantage of his position. The lubberly surgeon appeared possessed of perfect understanding of the situation and uncannily ready to meet each move of his opponent. Occasional shots continued to be exchanged by the chasers of each vessel, each aiming high so as to damage the other's sailing powers, yet, at the long range separating them, without success.

Peter Blood at the poop rail, in a fine back-and-breast and cap of black damascened steel, which had been the property of the original Spanish commander of the Cinco Llagas, was growing weary and anxious. To Hagthorpe similarly armed beside him, to Wolverstone whom no armour aboard would fit, and to Pitt at the whipstaff, immediately below, he confessed it in the tone of his question:

"How long can this ducking and dodging continue? And however long it continues what end can it have but one? Sooner or later the wind will drop or veer, or else it's ourselves will drop from sheer weariness. When that happens, we'll be at that scoundrel's mercy."

"There's always the unexpected," said young Pitt.

"Why, so there is, and I thank you for reminding me of it, Jerry. Let's put our hopes in it, for all that I can't see whence it's to come."

It was coming at that moment and coming quickly, although Blood was the only one of them who recognized it when he saw it. They were standing in towards the land at the end of a long westerly run, when round the point of Espada, less than a mile away, a towering, heavily armed ship came sailing as close to the wind as she dared, her ports open and the mouths of a score of guns gaping along her larboard flank, the banner of Castile flapping aloft in the breeze.

At sight of this fresh enemy of another sort, Wolverstone loosed an oath that sounded like a groan.

"And that's the end of us!" he cried.

"I'm by no means sure, now, that it may not be the beginning," Blood answered him, with something that sounded like laughter in his voice, which when last heard had been jaded and dispirited. And his orders, flowing fast, showed clearly what was in his mind. "Run me the flag of Spain aloft, and bid Ogle empty his chasers at the Bonaventure as we go about."

As Pitt put the helm over, and, with straining cordage and creaking blocks the Cinco Llagas swung slowly round, the gold and scarlet banner of Castile broke bravely from her main truck. An instant later the two guns on her forecastle thundered forth, ineffectually in one way but very effectually in another. Their fire conveyed very plainly to the Spanish newcomer that here he beheld a compatriot ship in pursuit of an English rover.

Explanations, no doubt, must follow, especially if upon the discovery of the identity of the Cinco Llagas the Spaniards should happen to be already acquainted with her recent history. But that could not come until they had disposed of the Bonaventure, and Blood was more than content to let the future take care of itself.

Meanwhile, the Spanish ship, a guarda-costa from San Domingo, which whilst on patrol had been attracted beyond the Point of Espada by the sound of gunfire out at sea, behaved precisely as was to be expected. Even without the flag now floating at her masthead, the Spanish origin of the Cinco Llagas was plain to read in the lines of her; that she was engaged with this equally obvious English sloop was no less plain. The guarda-costa went into the fight without a moment's hesitation and loosed a broadside at the Bonaventure as she was in the act of going about to escape this sudden and unforeseen peril.

Chard raged like a madman as the sloop shuddered under blows at stem and stern and her shattered bowsprit hung in a tangle of cordage athwart her bows. In his frenzy he ordered the fire to be returned, and did some damage to the guarda-costa, but not of a kind to impair her mobility. The Spaniard, warming to the battle, went about so as to pound the sloop with her starboard guns, and Chard, having lost his head by now, swung round also so as to return or even anticipate that fire.

Not until he had done so did it occur to him that with empty guns he was helplessly vulnerable to an onslaught from the Cinco Llagas. For Blood, too, espying the opportunity whilst yet it was shaping, had gone about, drawn level, and hurled at him the contents of his heavy artillery. That broadside at comparatively short range swept his deck, shattered the windows of the coach, and one well-placed shot opened a wound in the bows of the Bonaventure almost on the waterline, through which the sea rushed into the hold at every roll of the crippled vessel.

Chard realized that he was doomed, and his bitterness was deepened by perception of the misapprehension at the root of his destruction. He saw the Spanish flag at the masthead of the Cinco Llagas, and grinned in livid malice.

On a last inspiration, he struck his colours in token of surrender. It was his forlorn hope that the guarda-costa, accepting this, and ignorant of his strength in men, would rush in to grapple him, in which case he would turn the tables on the Spaniards and, possessing himself of the guarda-costa, might yet come out of the adventure with safety and credit.

But the vigilant Captain Blood guessed if not the intention at least the possibility, as well as the alternative possibility of explanations dangerous to himself from the captured Chard to the Spanish commander. To provide against either danger, he sent for Ogle, and under his instructions that skilful gunner crashed a thirty-two-pound shot into the Bonaventure's waterline amidships, so as to supplement the leakage already occurring forward.

The captain of the guarda-costa may have wondered why his compatriot should continue to fire upon a ship that had struck her colours, but the circumstance would hardly seem to him suspicious, although it might be vexatious, for its consequence appeared to be the inevitable destruction of a vessel which might yet have been turned to account.

As for Chard, he had no time for speculations of any kind. The Bonaventure was now making water so fast that his only hope of saving the lives of himself and his men lay in attempting to run her aground before she sank. So he headed her for the shoals at the foot of the Point of Espada, thanking God that she might now run before the wind, although at an ominously diminishing speed, despite the fact that the buccaneers heaved their cannon overboard to lighten her as they went. She grounded at last in the shallows, with the seas breaking over her stern- and forecastles which alone remained above water. These and the shrouds were now black with the men who had climbed to safety. The guarda-costa stood off with idly flapping sails, waiting, her captain wondering to behold the Cinco Llagas half a mile away already heading northwards.

Aboard her presently, Captain Blood was inquiring of Pitt if a knowledge of Spanish signals was included in his lore of the sea, and if so would he read the signals that the guarda-costa was flying. The young shipmaster confessed that it was not, and expressed the opinion that as a consequence they had but escaped the frying-pan to fall into the fire.

"Now here's a lack of faith in Madam Fortune," said Blood. "We'll just be dipping our flag in salute to them, to imply that we've business elsewhere, and be off to attend to it. We look like honest Spaniards. Even through a telescope in this Spanish armour, Hagthorpe and I must look like a pair of dons. Let's go and see how it's faring with the ingenious Easterling. I'm thinking the time has come to improve our acquaintance with him."

The guarda-costa, if surprised at the unceremonious departure of the vessel she had assisted in the destruction of that pirate sloop, cannot have suspected her bona-fides. Either taking it for granted that she had business elsewhere, or else because too intent upon making prisoners of the crew of the Bonaventure, she made no attempt to follow.

And so it fell out that some two hours later, Captain Easterling, waiting off the coast between Cape Raphael and Cape Engaño, beheld to his stupefaction and horror the swift approach of Peter Blood's red ship. He had listened attentively and in some uneasiness to the distant cannonade, but he had assumed its cessation to mean that the Cinco Llagas was taken. The sight now of that frigate, sailing briskly, jauntily, and undamaged, defied belief. What had happened to Chard? There was no sign of him upon the sea. Could he have blundered so badly as to have allowed Captain Blood to sink him?

Speculation on this point was presently quenched by speculation of an infinitely graver character. What might be this damned doctor-convict's present intention? If Easterling had been in case to board him, he would have known no apprehension, for even his prize crew on the Santa Barbara outnumbered Blood's men by more than two to one. But the crippled Santa Barbara could never be laid board and board with the Cinco Llagas unless Blood desired it, and if Blood meant mischief as a result of what had happened with the Bonaventure, the Santa Barbara must lie at the mercy of his guns.

The reflection, vexatious enough in itself, was maddening to Easterling when he considered what he carried under hatches. Fortune, it now began to seem, had not favoured him at all. She had merely mocked him by allowing him to grasp something which he could not hold.

But this was by no means the end of his vexation. For now, as if the circumstances in themselves had not been enough to enrage a man, his prize crew turned mutinous. Led by a scoundrel named Gunning, a man almost as massive and ruthless as Easterling himself, they furiously blamed their captain and his excessive and improvident greed for the peril in which they found themselves, a peril of death or capture embittered by the thought of the wealth they held. With such a prize in his hands, Easterling should have taken no risks. He should have kept the Bonaventure at hand for protection and paid no heed to the empty hulk of the Cinco Llagas. This they told him in terms of fiercest vituperation, whose very justice left him without answer other than insults, which he liberally supplied.

Whilst they wrangled, the Cinco Llagas drew nearer, and now Easterling's quartermaster called his attention to the signals she was flying. These demanded the immediate presence aboard her of the commander of the Santa Barbara.

Easterling was taken with panic. The high colour receded from his cheeks, his heavy lips grew purple. He vowed that he would see Doctor Blood in hell before he went.

His men assured him that they would see him in hell, and shortly, if he did not go.

Gunning reminded him that Blood could not possibly know what the Santa Barbara carried, and that therefore it should be possible to cozen him into allowing her to go her ways without further molestation.

A gun thundered from the Cinco Llagas, to send a warning shot across the bows of the Santa Barbara. That was enough. Gunning thrust the quartermaster aside, and himself seized the helm and put it over, so that the ship lay hove to, as a first intimation of compliance. After that the buccaneers launched the cockboat and a half-dozen of them swarmed down to man her, whilst, almost at pistol-point, Gunning compelled Captain Easterling to follow them.

When presently he climbed into the waist of the Cinco Llagas where she lay hove to, a cable's length away across the sunlit waters, there was hell in his eyes and terror in his soul. Straight and tall, in Spanish corselet and headpiece, the despised doctor stood forward to receive him. Behind him stood Hagthorpe and a half-score of his followers. He seemed to smile.

"At last, Captain, ye stand where ye have so long hoped to stand: on the deck of the Cinco Llagas."

Easterling grunted ragefully for only answer to this raillery. His great hands twitched as if he would have them at his Irish mocker's throat. Captain Blood continued to address him.

"It's an ill thing, Captain, to attempt to grasp more than you can comfortably hold. Ye'll not be the first to find himself empty-handed as a consequence. That was a fine fast-sailing sloop of yours, the Bonaventure. Ye should have been content. It's a pity that she'll sail no more; for she's sunk, or will be entirely at high water." Abruptly he asked: "How many hands are with you?"—and he had to repeat the question before he was sullenly answered that forty men remained aboard the Santa Barbara.

"What boats does she carry?"

"Three with the cock-boat."

"That should be enough to accommodate your following. Ye'll order them into those boats at once if you value their lives, for in fifteen minutes from now I shall open fire on the ship and sink her. This because I can spare no men for a prize crew, nor can I leave her afloat to be repossessed by you and turned to further mischief."

Easterling began a furious protest that was mixed with remonstrances of the peril to him and his of landing on Hispaniola. Blood cropped it short.

"Ye're receiving such mercy as you probably never showed to any whom ye compelled to surrender. Ye'ld best profit by my tenderness. If the Spaniards on Hispaniola spare you when you land there, you can get back to your hunting and boucanning, for which ye're better fitted than the sea. Away with you now."

But Easterling did not at once depart. He stood with feet planted wide, swaying on his powerful legs, clenching and unclenching his hands. At last he took his decision.

"Leave me that ship, and in Tortuga, when I get there, I'll pay you fifty thousand pieces of eight. That's better nor the empty satisfaction of turning us adrift."

"Away with you!" was all that Blood answered him, his tone more peremptory.

"A hundred thousand!" cried Easterling.

"Why not a million?" wondered Blood. "It's as easily promised, and the promise as easily broken. Oh, I'm like to take your word, Captain Easterling, as like as I am to believe that ye command such a sum as a hundred thousand pieces of eight."

Easterling's baleful eyes narrowed. Behind his black beard his thick lips tightened. Almost they smiled. Since there was nothing to be done without disclosures, nothing should be done at all. Let Blood sink a treasure which in any case must now be lost to Easterling. There was in the thought a certain bitter negative satisfaction.

"I pray that we may meet again, Captain Blood," he said, falsely, grimly unctuous. "I'll have something to tell you then that'll make you sorry for what you do now."

"If we meet again, I've no doubt the occasion will be one for many regrets. Good-day to you, Captain Easterling. Ye've just fifteen minutes, ye'll remember."

Easterling sneered and shrugged, and then abruptly turned and climbed down to the rocking boat that awaited him below.

When he came to announce Blood's message to his buccaneers, they stormed and raged so fiercely at the prospect of thus being cheated of everything that they could be heard across the water aboard the Cinco Llagas, to the faintly scornful amusement of Blood, who was far from suspecting the true reason of all this hubbub.

He watched the lowering of the boats, and was thereafter amazed to see the decks of the Santa Barbara empty of that angry, vociferous mob. The buccaneers had gone below before leaving, each man intent upon taking as much of the treasure as he could carry upon his person. Captain Blood became impatient.

"Pass the word down to Ogle to put a shot into her forecastle. Those rogues need quickening."

The roar of the gun, and the impact of the twenty-four-pound shot as it smashed through the timbers of the high forward structure, brought the buccaneers swarming upon deck again and thence to the waiting boats with the speed of fear. Yet a certain order they preserved for their safety's sake, for in the sea that was running, the capsizing of a boat would have been an easy matter.

They pushed off; their wet oars flashed in the sunlight, and they began to draw away towards the promontory not more than two miles to windward. Once they were clear, Blood gave the word to open fire, when Hagthorpe clutched his arm.

"Wait, man! Wait! Look! There's someone still aboard her."

Surprised, Blood looked, first with his naked eye, then through his telescope. He beheld a bareheaded gentleman in corselet and thigh-boots, who clearly was no buccaneer of the kind that sailed with Easterling, and who stood on the poop frantically waving a scarf. Blood was quick to guess his identity.

"It'll be one of the Spaniards who were aboard when Easterling took the ship and whose throat he forgot to cut."

He ordered a boat to be launched and sent six men with Dyke, who had some knowledge of Spanish, to bring the Spaniard off.

Don Ildefonso, who, callously left to drown in the doomed ship, had worked himself free of the thong that bound his wrists, stood in the forechains to await the coming of that boat. He was quivering with excitement at this deliverance of himself and the vessel in his charge with her precious freight; a deliverance which he regarded as little short of miraculous. For like the guarda-costa, Don Ildefonso, even if he had not recognized the Spanish lines of this great ship which had come so unexpectedly to the rescue, must have been relieved of all doubt by the flag of Spain which had been allowed to remain floating at the masthead of the Cinco Llagas.

So with speech bubbling eagerly out of him in that joyous excitement of his, the Spanish commander poured into the ears of Dyke, when the boat brought up alongside, the tale of what had happened to them and what they carried. Because of this, it was necessary that they should lend him a dozen men so that with the six now under hatches on the Santa Barbara he might bring his precious cargo safely into San Domingo.

To Dyke this was an amazing and exciting narrative. But he did not on that account lose grip of his self-possession. Lest too much Spanish should betray him to Don Ildefonso, he took refuge in curtness.

"Bueno," said he. "I'll inform my captain." Under his breath he ordered his men to push off and head back for the Cinco Llagas.

When Blood heard the tale and had digested his amazement, he laughed.

"So this is what that rogue would have told me if ever we met again. 'Faith, it's a satisfaction to be denied him."

Ten minutes later the Cinco Llagas lay board and board with the Santa Barbara.

In the distance Easterling and his men, observing the operation, rested on their oars to stare and mutter. They saw themselves cheated of even the meagre satisfaction for which they had looked in the sinking of an unsuspected treasure. Easterling burst into fresh profanity.

"It'll be that damned Spaniard I forgot in the cabin who'll ha' blabbed of the gold. Oh, 'sdeath! This is what comes o' being soft-hearted. If only I'd cut his throat now . . ."

Meanwhile, to Don Ildefonso, who had been able to make nothing of this boarding manœuvre, Captain Blood, save for the light eyes in his bronzed face, looking every inch a Spaniard, and delivering himself in the impeccable Castilian of which he was master, was offering explanations.

He was unable to spare a crew to man the Santa Barbara, for his own following was insufficient. Nor dared he leave her afloat, since in that case she would be repossessed by the abominable pirates whom he had constrained to abandon her. It remained, therefore, before scuttling her only to transship the treasure with which Don Ildefonso informed him she was laden. At the same time he would be happy to offer Don Ildefonso and his six surviving hands the hospitality of the Cinco Llagas as far as Tortuga, or, if Don Ildefonso preferred it, as seemed probable, Captain Blood would seize a favourable moment for allowing them to take one of his boats and land themselves upon the coast of Hispaniola.

Now this speech was the most amazing thing that had yet happened to Don Ildefonso in that day of amazements.

"Tortuga!" he exclaimed. "Tortuga! You sail to Tortuga, do you say? But what to do there? In God's name, who are you, then? What are you?"

"As for who I am, I am called Peter Blood. As for what I am, faith, I scarce know myself."

"You are English!" cried the Spaniard in sudden horror of partial understanding.

"Ah, no. That, at least, I am not." Captain Blood drew himself up with great dignity. "I have the honour to be Irish."

"Ah, bah! Irish or English, it is all one."

"Indeed and it is not. There's all the difference in the world between the two."

The Spaniard looked at him with angry eyes. His face was livid, his mouth scornful. "English or Irish, the truth is you are just a cursed pirate."

Blood looked wistful. He fetched a sigh. "I'm afraid you are right," he admitted. "It's a thing I've sought to avoid. But what am I to do now, when Fate thrusts it upon me in this fashion, and insists that I make so excellent a beginning?"

—1931

LOUIS L'AMOUR
1908-1988

The all-time best-selling author of frontier and Western fiction is Louis L'Amour. Born in Jamestown, North Dakota, L'Amour pursued a wide variety of occupations—from longshoreman to miner—and served in the U.S. Army from 1942 to 1946. He published his first novel, Westward the Tide, *in 1950, but it was his novel,* Hondo (1953), *that made his reputation as a first-rate Western writer. L'Amour authored many novels and short stories over the course of the next four decades; a significant number of these were Westerns, but some included historical fiction, detective fiction, and thrillers. He also wrote a lengthy series of popular Western novels featuring the exploits of the Sackett family, including* The Daybreakers (1960), Lando (1962), Sackett's Gold (1977), *and* Jubal Sackett (1985). *In addition, L'Amour published fiction under several pseudonyms. As "Tex Burns," he wrote four Hopalong Cassidy novels during the early 1950s, and as "Jim Mayo," he published two Western novels in the mid-1950s.*

"The Gift of Cochise"—which first appeared in the July 5, 1952 issue of Collier's *and was later collected in L'Amour's first anthology,* War Party (1975)—*is an excellent example of L'Amour's great skill as a popular storyteller. It was the basis for the 1953 film,* Hondo, *starring John Wayne, and it also became the foundation upon which L'Amour developed his 1953 nov-*

elization of the movie, still considered by many of L'Amour's readers to be his finest work. Despite the brevity of "The Gift of Cochise," L'Amour captures, in this engaging tale, many of those elements that not only made the Western a popular literary genre, but also made L'Amour one of a handful of the world's most commercially successful writers. Sometimes criticized for being overly formulaic, L'Amour's Western fiction is nevertheless characterized by his effectively sparse use of language and his skilled manipulation of narrative action. In contrast to the romanticized Westerns of Zane Grey, for example, L'Amour's Western adventures tend to be more realistically depicted. Typically, characters in L'Amour's Westerns are rugged men and women who are in fierce conflict with a frequently hostile, yet beautiful, American frontier.

THE GIFT OF COCHISE

Tense, and white to the lips, Angie Lowe stood in the door of her cabin with a double-barreled shotgun in her hands. Beside the door was a Winchester '73, and on the table inside the house were two Walker Colts.

Facing the cabin were twelve Apaches on ragged calico ponies, and one of the Indians had lifted his hand palm outward. The Apache sitting the white-splashed bay pony was Cochise.

Beside Angie were her seven-year-old son Jimmy and her five-year-old daughter Jane.

Cochise sat his pony in silence; his black, unreadable eyes studied the woman, the children, the cabin, and the small garden. He looked at the two ponies in the corral and the three cows. His eyes strayed to the small stack of hay cut from the meadow, and to the few steers farther up the canyon.

Three times the warriors of Cochise had attacked this solitary cabin and three times they had been turned back. In all, they had lost seven men, and three had been wounded. Four ponies had been killed. His braves reported that there was no man in the house, only a woman and two children, so Cochise had come to see for himself this woman who was so certain a shot with a rifle and who killed his fighting men.

These were some of the same fighting men who had outfought, outguessed and outrun the finest American army on record, an army outnumbering the Apaches by a hundred to one. Yet a lone woman with two small children had fought them off, and the woman was scarcely more than a girl. And she was prepared to fight now. There was a glint of admiration in the old eyes that appraised her. The Apache was a fighting man, and he respected fighting blood.

"Where is your man?"

"He has gone to El Paso." Angie's voice was steady, but she was frightened as she had never been before. She recognized Cochise from descriptions, and she knew that if he decided to kill or capture her it would be done. Until now, the sporadic attacks she had fought off had been those of casual bands of warriors who raided her in passing.

"He has been gone a long time. How long?"

Angie hesitated, but it was not in her to lie. "He has been gone four months."

Cochise considered that. No one but a fool would leave such a woman, or such fine children. Only one thing could have prevented his return. "Your man is dead," he said.

Angie waited, her heart pounding with heavy, measured beats. She had guessed long ago that Ed had been killed but the way Cochise spoke did not imply that Apaches had killed him, only that he must be dead or he would have returned.

"You fight well," Cochise said. "You have killed my young men."

"Your young men attacked me." She hesitated then added, "They stole my horses."

"Your man is gone. Why do you not leave?"

Angie looked at him with surprise. "Leave? Why, this is my home. This land is mine. This spring is mine. I shall not leave."

"This was an Apache spring," Cochise reminded her reasonably.

"The Apache lives in the mountains," Angie replied. "He does not need this spring. I have two children, and I do need it."

"But when the Apache comes this way, where shall he drink? His throat is dry and you keep him from water."

The very fact that Cochise was willing to talk raised her hopes. There had been a time when the Apache made no war on the white man. "Cochise speaks with a forked tongue," she said. "There is water yonder." She gestured toward the hills, where Ed had told her there were springs. "But if the people of Cochise come in peace they may drink at this spring."

The Apache leader smiled faintly. Such a woman would rear a nation of warriors. He nodded at Jimmy. "The small one—does he also shoot?"

"He does," Angie said proudly, "and well, too!" She pointed at an upthrust leaf of prickly pear. "Show them, Jimmy."

The prickly pear was an easy two hundred yards away, and the Winchester was long and heavy, but he lifted it eagerly and steadied it against the doorjamb as his father had taught him, held his sight an instant, then fired. The bud on top of the prickly pear disintegrated.

There were grunts of appreciation from the dark-faced warriors. Cochise chuckled.

"The little warrior shoots well. It is well you have no man. You might raise an army of little warriors to fight my people."

"I have no wish to fight your people," Angie said quietly. "Your people have your ways, and I have mine. I live in peace when I am left in peace. I did not think," she added with dignity, "that the great Cochise made war on women!"

The Apache looked at her, then turned his pony away. "My people will trouble you no longer," he said. "You are the mother of a strong son."

"What about my two ponies?" she called after him. "Your young men took them from me."

Cochise did not turn or look back, and the little cavalcade of riders followed him away. Angie stepped back into the cabin and closed the door. Then she sat down abruptly, her face white, the muscles in her legs trembling.

When morning came, she went cautiously to the spring for water. Her ponies were back in the corral. They had been returned during the night.

Slowly, the days drew on. Angie broke a small piece of the meadow and planted it. Alone, she cut hay in the meadow and built another stack. She saw Indians several times, but they did not bother her. One morning, when she opened the door, a quarter of antelope lay on the step, but no Indian was in sight. Several times, during the weeks that followed, she saw moccasin tracks near the spring.

Once, going out at daybreak, she saw an Indian girl dipping water from the spring. Angie called to her, and the girl turned quickly, facing her. Angie walked toward her, offering a bright red silk ribbon. Pleased at the gift, the Apache girl left.

And the following morning there was another quarter of antelope on her step—but she saw no Indian.

Ed Lowe had built the cabin in West Dog Canyon in the spring of 1871, but it was Angie who chose the spot, not Ed. In Santa Fe they would have told you that Ed Lowe was good-looking, shiftless and agreeable. He was, also, unfortunately handy with a pistol.

Angie's father had come from County Mayo to New York and from New York to the Mississippi, where he became a tough, brawling river boatman. In New Orleans, he met a beautiful Cajun girl and married her. Together, they started west for Santa Fe, and Angie was born en route. Both parents died of cholera when Angie was fourteen. She lived with an Irish family for the following three years, then married Ed Lowe when she was seventeen.

Santa Fe was not good for Ed, and Angie kept after him until they started south. It was Apache country, but they kept on until they reached the old Spanish ruin in West Dog. Here there were grass, water, and shelter from the wind.

There was fuel, and there were pinions and game. And Angie, with an Irish eye for the land, saw that it would grow crops.

The house itself was built on the ruins of the old Spanish building, using the thick walls and the floor. The location had been admirably chosen for defense. The house was built in a corner of the cliff, under the sheltering overhang, so that approach was possible from only two directions, both covered by an easy field of fire from the door and windows.

For seven months, Ed worked hard and steadily. He put in the first crop, he built the house, and proved himself a handy man with tools. He repaired the old plow they had bought, cleaned out the spring, and paved and walled it with slabs of stone. If he was lonely for the carefree companions of Santa Fe, he gave no indication of it. Provisions were low, and when he finally started off to the south, Angie watched him go with an ache in her heart.

She did not know whether she loved Ed. The first flush of enthusiasm had passed, and Ed Lowe had proved something less than she had believed. But he had tried, she admitted. And it had not been easy for him. He was an amiable soul, given to whittling and idle talk, all of which he missed in the loneliness of the Apache country. And when he rode away, she had no idea whether she would ever see him again. She never did.

Santa Fe was far and away to the north, but the growing village of El Paso was less than a hundred miles to the west, and it was there Ed Lowe rode for supplies and seed.

He had several drinks—his first in months—in one of the saloons. As the liquor warmed his stomach, Ed Lowe looked around agreeably. For a moment, his eyes clouded with worry as he thought of his wife and children back in Apache country, but it was not in Ed Lowe to worry for long. He had another drink and leaned on the bar, talking to the bartender. All Ed had ever asked of life was enough to eat, a horse to ride, an occasional drink, and companions to talk with. Not that he had anything important to say. He just liked to talk.

Suddenly a chair grated on the floor, and Ed turned. A lean, powerful man with a shock of uncut black hair and a torn, weather-faded shirt stood at bay. Facing him across the table were three hard-faced young men, obviously brothers.

Ches Lane did not notice Ed Lowe watching from the bar. He had eyes only for the men facing him. "You done that deliberate!" The statement was a challenge.

The broad-chested man on the left grinned through broken teeth. "That's right, Ches. I done it deliberate. You killed Dan Tolliver on the Brazos."

"He made the quarrel." Comprehension came to Ches. He was boxed, and by three of the fighting, blood-hungry Tollivers.

"Don't make no difference," the broad-chested Tolliver said. "Who sheds a Tolliver's blood, by a Tolliver's hand must die!'"

Ed Lowe moved suddenly from the bar. "Three to one is long odds," he said, his voice low and friendly. "If the gent in the corner is willin', I'll side him."

Two Tollivers turned toward him. Ed Lowe was smiling easily, his hand hovering near his gun. "You stay out of this!" one of the brothers said harshly.

"I'm in," Ed replied. "Why don't you boys light a shuck?"

"No, by—!" The man's hand dropped for his gun, and the room thundered with sound.

Ed was smiling easily, unworried as always. His gun flashed up. He felt it leap in his hand, saw the nearest Tolliver smashed back, and he shot him again as he dropped. He had only time to see Ches Lane with two guns out and another Tolliver down when something struck him through the stomach and he stepped back against the bar, suddenly sick.

The sound stopped, and the room was quiet, and there was the acrid smell of powder smoke. Three Tollivers were down and dead, and Ed Lowe was dying. Ches Lane crossed to him.

"We got 'em," Ed said, "we sure did. But they got me."

Suddenly his face changed. "Oh Lord in heaven, what'll Angie do?" And then he crumpled over on the floor and lay still, the blood staining his shirt and mingling with the sawdust.

Stiff-faced, Ches looked up. "Who was Angie?" he asked.

"His wife," the bartender told him. "She's up northeast somewhere, in Apache country. He was tellin' me about her. Two kids, too."

Ches Lane stared down at the crumpled, used-up body of Ed Lowe. The man had saved his life.

One he could have beaten, two he might have beaten; three would have killed him. Ed Lowe, stepping in when he did, had saved the life of Ches Lane.

"He didn't say where?"

"No."

Ches Lane shoved his hat back on his head. "What's northeast of here?"

The bartender rested his hands on the bar. "Cochise," he said. . . .

For more than three months, whenever he could rustle the grub, Ches Lane quartered the country over and back. The trouble was, he had no lead to the location of Ed Lowe's homestead. An examination of Ed's horse revealed nothing. Lowe had bought seed and ammunition, and the seed indicated a good water supply, and the ammunition implied trouble. But in the country there was always trouble.

A man had died to save his life, and Ches Lane had a deep sense of obligation. Somewhere that wife waited, if she was still alive, and it was up to him to find her and look out for her. He rode northeast, cutting for sign, but found none. Sandstorms had wiped out any hope of back-trailing Lowe. Actually, West Dog Canyon was more east than north, but this he had no way of knowing.

North he went, skirting the rugged San Andreas Mountains. Heat baked him hot, dry winds parched his skin. His hair grew dry and stiff and alkali-whitened. He rode north, and soon the Apaches knew of him. He fought them at a lonely water hole, and he fought them on the run. They killed his horse, and he switched his saddle to the spare and rode on. They cornered him in the rocks, and he killed two of them and escaped by night.

They trailed him through the White Sands, and he left two more for dead. He fought fiercely and bitterly, and would not be turned from his quest. He turned east through the lava beds and still more east to the Pecos. He saw only two white men, and neither knew of a white woman.

The bearded man laughed harshly. "A woman alone? She wouldn't last a month! By now the Apaches got her, or she's dead. Don't be a fool! Leave this country before you die here."

Lean, wind-whipped and savage, Ches Lane pushed on. The Mescaleros cornered him in Rawhide Draw and he fought them to a standstill. Grimly, the Apaches clung to his trail.

The sheer determination of the man fascinated them. Bred and born in a rugged and lonely land, the Apaches knew the difficulties of survival; they knew how a man could live, how he must live. Even as they tried to kill this man, they loved him, for he was one of their own.

Lane's jeans grew ragged. Two bullet holes were added to the old black hat. The slicker was torn; the saddle, so carefully kept until now, was scratched by gravel and brush. At night he cleaned his guns and by day he scouted the trails. Three times he found lonely ranch houses burned to the ground, the buzzard- and coyote-stripped bones of their owners lying nearby.

Once he found a covered wagon, its canvas flopping in the wind, a man lying sprawled on the seat with a pistol near his hand. He was dead and his wife was dead, and their canteens rattled like empty skulls.

Leaner every day, Ches Lane pushed on. He camped one night in a canyon near some white oaks. He heard a hoof click on stone and he backed away from his tiny fire, gun in hand.

The riders were white men, and there were two of them. Joe Tompkins and Wiley Lynn were headed west, and Ches Lane could have guessed why. They were men he had known before, and he told them what he was doing.

Lynn chuckled. He was a thin-faced man with lank yellow hair and dirty fingers. "Seems a mighty strange way to get a woman. There's some as comes easier."

"This ain't for fun," Ches replied shortly. "I got to find her."

Tompkins stared at him. "Ches, you're crazy! That gent declared himself in of his own wish and desire. Far's that goes, the gal's dead. No woman could last this long in Apache country."

At daylight, the two men headed west, and Ches Lane turned south.

Antelope and deer are curious creatures, often led to their death by curiosity. The longhorn, soon going wild on the plains, acquires the same characteristic. He is essentially curious. Any new thing or strange action will bring his head up and his ears alert. Often a longhorn, like a deer, can be lured within a stone's throw by some queer antic, by a handkerchief waving, by a man under a hide, by a man on foot.

This character of the wild things holds true of the Indian. The lonely rider who fought so desperately and knew the desert so well soon became a subject of gossip among the Apaches. Over the fires of many a rancheria they discussed this strange rider who seemed to be going nowhere, but always riding, like a lean wolf dog on a trail. He rode across the mesas and down the canyons; he studied sign at every water hole; he looked long from every ridge. It was obvious to the Indians that he searched for something—but what?

Cochise had come again to the cabin in West Dog Canyon. "Little warrior too small," he said, "too small for hunt. You join my people. Take Apache for man."

"No." Angie shook her head. "Apache ways are good for the Apache, and the white man's ways are good for white men—and women."

They rode away and said no more, but that night, as she had on many other nights after the children were asleep, Angie cried. She wept silently, her head pillowed on her arms. She was as pretty as ever, but her face was thin, showing the worry and struggle of the months gone by, the weeks and months without hope.

The crops were small but good. Little Jimmy worked beside her. At night, Angie sat alone on the steps and watched the shadows gather down the long canyon, listening to the coyotes yapping from the rim of the Guadalupes, hearing the horses blowing in the corral. She watched, still hopeful, but now she knew that Cochise was right: Ed would not return.

But even if she had been ready to give up this, the first home she had known, there could be no escape. Here she was protected by Cochise. Other Apaches from other tribes would not so willingly grant her peace.

At daylight she was up. The morning air was bright and balmy, but soon it would be hot again. Jimmy went to the spring for water, and when breakfast was over, the children played while Angie sat in the shade of a huge old cottonwood and sewed. It was a Sunday, warm and lovely. From time to time, she lifted her eyes to look down the canyon, half smiling at her own foolishness.

The hard-packed earth of the yard was swept clean of dust; the pans hanging on the kitchen wall were neat and shining. The children's hair had been clipped, and there was a small bouquet on the kitchen table.

After a while, Angie put aside her sewing and changed her dress. She did her hair carefully, and then, looking in her mirror, she reflected with sudden pain that she *was* pretty, and that she was only a girl.

Resolutely, she turned from the mirror and, taking up her Bible, went back to the seat under the cottonwood. The children left their playing and came to her, for this was a Sunday ritual, their only one. Opening the Bible, she read slowly,

". . . though I walk through the valley of the shadow of death, I will fear no evil; for thou art with me; thy rod and thy staff, they comfort me. Thou preparest a table before me in the presence of mine enemies: thou . . ."

"Mommy." Jimmy tugged at her sleeve. "Look!"

Ches Lane had reached a narrow canyon by midafternoon and decided to make camp. There was small possibility he would find another such spot, and he was dead tired, his muscles sodden with fatigue. The canyon was one of those unexpected gashes in the cap rock that gave no indication of its presence until you came right on it. After some searching, Ches found a route to the bottom and made camp under a wind-hollowed overhang. There was water, and there was a small patch of grass.

After his horse had a drink and a roll on the ground, it began cropping eagerly at the rich, green grass, and Ches built a smokeless fire of some ancient driftwood in the canyon bottom. It was his first hot meal in days, and when he had finished he put out his fire, rolled a smoke, and leaned back contentedly.

Before darkness settled, he climbed to the rim and looked over the country. The sun had gone down, and the shadows were growing long. After a half hour of study, he decided there was no living thing within miles, except for the usual desert life. Returning to the bottom, he moved his horse to fresh grass, then rolled in his blanket. For the first time in a month, he slept without fear.

He woke up suddenly in the broad daylight. The horse was listening to something, his head up. Swiftly, Ches went to the horse and led it back under the overhang. Then he drew on his boots, rolled his blankets, and saddled the horse. Still he heard no sound.

Climbing the rim again, he studied the desert and found nothing. Returning to his horse, he mounted up and rode down the canyon toward the flatland beyond. Coming out of the canyon mouth, he rode right into the middle of a war party of more than twenty Apaches—invisible until suddenly they stood up behind rocks, their rifles leveled. And he didn't have a chance.

Swiftly, they bound his wrists to the saddle horn and tied his feet. Only then did he see the man who led the party. It was Cochise.

He was a lean, wiry Indian of past fifty, his black hair streaked with gray, his features strong and clean-cut. He stared at Lane, and there was nothing in his face to reveal what he might be thinking.

Several of the younger warriors pushed forward, talking excitedly and waving their arms. Ches Lane understood some of it, but he sat straight in the saddle, his head up, waiting. Then Cochise spoke and the party turned, and, leading his horse, they rode away.

The miles grew long and the sun was hot. He was offered no water and he asked for none. The Indians ignored him. Once a young brave rode near and struck him viciously. Lane made no sound, gave no indication of pain. When they finally stopped, it was beside a huge anthill swarming with big red desert ants.

Roughly, they quickly untied him and jerked him from his horse. He dug in his heels and shouted at them in Spanish: "The Apaches are women! They tie me to the ants because they are afraid to fight me!"

An Indian struck him, and Ches glared at the man. If he must die, he would show them how it should be done. Yet he knew the unpredictable nature of the Indian, of his great respect for courage.

"Give me a knife, and I'll kill any of your warriors!"

They stared at him, and one powerfully built Apache angrily ordered them to get on with it. Cochise spoke, and the big warrior replied angrily.

Ches Lane nodded at the anthill. "Is this the death for a fighting man? I have fought your strong men and beaten them. I have left no trail for them to follow, and for months I have lived among you, and now only by accident have you captured me. Give me a knife," he added grimly, "and I will fight *him!*" He indicated the big, black-faced Apache.

The warrior's cruel mouth hardened, and he struck Ches across the face.

The white man tasted blood and fury. "Woman!" Ches said. "Coyote! You are afraid!" Ches turned on Cochise, as the Indians stood irresolute. "Free my hands and let me fight!" he demanded. "If I win, let me go free."

Cochise said something to the big Indian. Instantly, there was stillness. Then an Apache sprang forward and, with a slash of his knife, freed Lane's hands. Shaking loose the thongs, Ches Lane chafed his wrists to bring back the circulation. An Indian threw a knife at his feet. It was his own bowie knife.

Ches took off his riding boots. In sock feet, his knife gripped low in his hand, its cutting edge up, he looked at the big warrior.

"I promise you nothing," Cochise said in Spanish, "but an honorable death."

The big warrior came at him on cat feet. Warily, Ches circled. He had not only to defeat this Apache but to escape. He permitted himself a side glance toward his horse. It stood alone. No Indian held it.

The Apache closed swiftly, thrusting wickedly with the knife. Ches, who had learned knife-fighting in the bayou country of Louisiana, turned his hip sharply, and the blade slid past him. He struck swiftly, but the Apache's forward movement deflected the blade, and it failed to penetrate. However, as it swept up between the Indian's body and arm, it cut a deep gash in the warrior's left armpit.

The Indian sprang again, like a clawing cat, streaming blood. Ches moved aside, but a backhand sweep nicked him, and he felt the sharp bite of the blade. Turning, he paused on the balls of his feet.

He had had no water in hours. His lips were cracked. Yet he sweated now, and the salt of it stung his eyes. He stared into the malevolent black eyes of the Apache, then moved to meet him. The Indian lunged, and Ches sidestepped like a boxer and spun on the ball of his foot.

The sudden side step threw the Indian past him, but Ches failed to drive the knife into the Apache's kidney when his foot rolled on a stone. The point left a thin red line across the Indian's back. The Indian was quick. Before Ches could recover his balance, he grasped the white man's knife wrist. Desperately, Ches grabbed for the Indian's knife hand and got the wrist, and they stood there straining, chest to chest.

Seeing his chance, Ches suddenly let his knees buckle, then brought up his knee and fell back, throwing the Apache over his head to the sand. Instantly, he whirled and was on his feet, standing over the Apache. The warrior had lost his knife, and he lay there, staring up, his eyes black with hatred.

Coolly, Ches stepped back, picked up the Indian's knife, and tossed it to him contemptuously. There was a grunt from the watching Indians, and then his antagonist rushed. But loss of blood had weakened the warrior, and Ches stepped in swiftly, struck the blade aside, then thrust the point of his blade hard against the Indian's belly.

Black eyes glared into his without yielding. A thrust, and the man would be disemboweled, but Ches stepped back. "He is a strong, man," Ches said in Spanish. "It is enough that I have won."

Deliberately, he walked to his horse and swung into the saddle. He looked around, and every rifle covered him.

So he had gained nothing. He had hoped that mercy might lead to mercy, that the Apache's respect for a fighting man would win his freedom. He had failed. Again they bound him to his horse, but they did not take his knife from him.

When they camped at last, he was given food and drink. He was bound again, and a blanket was thrown over him. At daylight they were again in the saddle. In Spanish he asked where they were taking him, but they gave no indication of hearing. When they stopped again, it was beside a pole corral, near a stone cabin.

When Jimmy spoke, Angie got quickly to her feet. She recognized Cochise with a start of relief, but she saw instantly that this was a war party. And then she saw the prisoner.

Their eyes met and she felt a distinct shock. He was a white man, a big, unshaven man who badly needed both a bath and a haircut, his clothes ragged and bloody. Cochise gestured at the prisoner.

"No take Apache man, you take white man. This man good for hunt, good for fight. He strong warrior. You take 'em."

Flushed and startled, Angie stared at the prisoner and caught a faint glint of humor in his dark eyes.

"Is this here the fate worse than death I hear tell of?" he inquired gently.

"Who are you?" she asked, and was immediately conscious that it was an extremely silly question.

The Apaches had drawn back and were watching curiously. She could do nothing for the present but accept the situation. Obviously they intended to do her a kindness, and it would not do to offend them. If they had not brought this man to her, he might have been killed.

"Name's Ches Lane, ma'am," he said. "Will you untie me? I'd feel a lot safer."

"Of course." Still flustered, she went to him and untied his hands. One Indian said something, and the others chuckled; then, with a whoop, they swung their horses and galloped off down the canyon.

Their departure left her suddenly helpless, the shadowy globe of her loneliness shattered by this utterly strange man standing before her, this big, bearded man brought to her out of the desert.

She smoothed her apron, suddenly pale as she realized what his delivery to her implied. What must he think of her? She turned away quickly. "There's hot water," she said hastily, to prevent his speaking. "Dinner is almost ready."

She walked quickly into the house and stopped before the stove, her mind a blank. She looked around her as if she had suddenly waked up in a strange place. She heard water being poured into the basin by the door, and heard him take Ed's razor. She had never moved the box. To have moved it would—

"Sight of work done here, ma'am."

She hesitated, then turned with determination and stepped into the doorway. "Yes, Ed—"

"You're Angie Lowe."

Surprised, she turned toward him, and recognized his own startled awareness of her. As he shaved, he told her about Ed, and what had happened that day in the saloon.

"He—Ed was like that. He never considered consequences until it was too late."

"Lucky for me he didn't."

He was younger looking with his beard gone. There was a certain quiet dignity in his face. She went back inside and began putting plates on the table. She was conscious that he had moved to the door and was watching her.

"You don't have to stay," she said. "You owe me nothing. Whatever Ed did, he did because he was that kind of person. You aren't responsible."

He did not answer, and when she turned again to the stove, she glanced swiftly at him. He was looking across the valley.

There was a studied deference about him when he moved to a place at the table. The children stared, wide-eyed and silent; it had been so long since a man sat at this table.

Angie could not remember when she had felt like this. She was awkwardly conscious of her hands, which never seemed to be in the right place or doing the right things. She scarcely tasted her food, nor did the children.

Ches Lane had no such inhibitions. For the first time, he realized how hungry he was. After the half-cooked meat of lonely, trailside fires, this was tender and flavored. Hot biscuits, desert honey . . . Suddenly he looked up, embarrassed at his appetite.

"You were really hungry," she said.

"Man can't fix much, out on the trail."

Later, after he'd got his bedroll from his saddle and unrolled it on the hay in the barn, he walked back to the house and sat on the lowest step. The sun was gone, and they watched the cliffs stretch their red shadows across the valley. A quail called plaintively, a mellow sound of twilight.

"You needn't worry about Cochise," she said. "He'll soon be crossing into Mexico."

"I wasn't thinking about Cochise."

That left her with nothing to say, and she listened again to the quail and watched a lone bright star in the sky.

"A man could get to like it here," he said quietly.

—1952

IAN FLEMING
1908-1964

Ian Fleming's James Bond is the most popular secret agent hero in all of spy fiction. Introduced in Fleming's first published novel, Casino Royale *(1953), Bond epitomizes the ultimate escapist hero in the literature of espionage. He is suave, cool under pressure, a connoisseur of the good life, a consummate British gentleman (at least in Fleming's view), adept at violence, and equally adept at seduction of the opposite sex. The popularity of James Bond was so great in the 1960s that it extended well beyond the realm of the paperback best-seller. Fleming's master spy appeared in both television and the cinema, eventually becoming one of the longest-running and most successful series characters in motion picture history. Indeed, numerous Bond imitations saturated American popular culture during this period, from the* I Spy *and* The Man from U.N.C.L.E. *television programs to the* Matt Helm *and* Our Man Flint *movie series parodies.*

Ian Fleming was born in London, England, and was educated at Eton, the Royal Military Academy at Sandhurst, Tennerhof in the Austrian Alps, the University of Munich, and the University of Geneva in Switzerland. He eventually found employment at the Reuters news agency, but then switched careers from journalism to business in order to secure a better income. At the start of the Second World War, Fleming joined the staff of Admiral John Godfrey, the director of British Naval Intelligence, as his personal assistant and was commissioned in the Naval Reserve as a lieutenant. He eventually achieved the rank of commander. Fleming's experiences in military intelligence work provided him with essential background materials for his James Bond adventures. Following the war, Fleming became the manager of the Kemsley newspapers' foreign news service.

When Fleming decided to try his hand at writing novels, he selected the espionage genre. Prior to Fleming's significant literary contributions, the spy story in popular fiction had evolved along two distinctly separate paths since the publication of James Fenimore Cooper's The Spy *in 1821, the novel generally regarded as establishing the genre. The first, and more respected, category of espionage fiction highlighted realism. Erskine Childers's* The Riddle of the Sands *(1903), Joseph Conrad's* The Secret Agent *(1907), W. Somerset Maugham's Ashenden stories, and the fiction of Eric Ambler, Graham Greene, and John le Carré epitomized the realistic spy story. The second category of espionage fiction, as it developed in the American pulp magazines during the 1930s, featured fantastic plots and larger-than-life heroes. Pulp series titles like* Operator #5 *and* Secret Agent X *published numerous apocalyptic adventures specializing in bizarre villains bent on world domination or world destruction.*

What Fleming accomplished in the creation of his James Bond series was the combination of the realistic and the fantastic spy story. The "pulp" element in the Bond adventures is made readily evident by Fleming's incorporation of incredible plots and villains in his stories. Hugo Drax, Bond's adversary in Moonraker *(1955), for example, plans to destroy London with a rocket. The evil Doctor No, Fleming's "yellow peril" variant of the mad scientist stereotype, schemes to disrupt the development of the U.S. missile program in* Doctor No *(1958).* Goldfinger *conspires to rob the gold reserve at Fort Knox in* Goldfinger *(1959), while Blofeld threatens the political stability of Western governments with stolen nuclear weapons in* Thunderball *(1961). Yet, even though some critics may upbraid the Bond adventures as being too unrealistic, Fleming does incorporate much in his writing to enhance verisimilitude, including such narrative particulars as the detailed description of food or the specific representation of an exotic locale.*

"From a View to a Kill" certainly utilizes both the realistic and the fantastic. Note how Fleming contrasts Bond's pedestrian views of Paris in the story with the incredible events surrounding the assassination of the SHAPE dispatch courier. Originally developed by Fleming as one of several story outlines for a proposed James Bond television series for CBS that was never produced, "From a View to a Kill" was later rewritten as a short story and anthologized for publication in Fleming's For Your Eyes Only *(1960). The James Bond motion picture "adaptation"—*A View to a Kill—*was released in 1985, bearing little in common with Fleming's original story other than a similar title. It starred Roger Moore as the daring secret agent.*

FROM A VIEW TO A KILL

The eyes behind the wide black rubber goggles were cold as flint. In the howling speed-turmoil of his motorbike, a BSAM 20 doing seventy, they were the only quiet things in the hurtling flesh and metal. Protected by the glass of the goggles, they stared fixedly ahead from just above the center of the handlebars, and their dark, unwavering focus was that of gun-muzzles. Below the goggles, the wind had got into the face through the mouth and had wrenched the lips back into a square grin that showed big tombstone teeth and strips of whitish gum. On both sides of the grin the cheeks had been blown out by the wind into pouches that fluttered slightly. To right and left of the hurtling face under the crash helmet, the black gauntlets, brokenwristed at the controls, looked like the attacking paws of a big animal.

The man was dressed in the uniform of a dispatch-rider in the Royal Corps of Signals, and his machine, painted olive green, was, with certain modifications to the valves and the carburetor and the removal of some of the silencer baffles to give more speed, identical with a standard British Army machine. There was nothing in the man or his equipment to suggest that he was not what he appeared to be, except a fully loaded Luger by a clip to the top of the petrol tank.

It was seven o' clock on a May morning, and the dead straight road through the forest glittered with the tiny luminous mist of spring. On both sides of the road the moss- and flower-carpeted depths between the great oak trees held the theatrical enchantment of the royal forests of Versailles and Saint-Germain. The road was D98, a secondary road serving local traffic in the Saint-Germain area, and the motorcyclist had just passed beneath the Paris-Mantes Autoroute already thundering with commuter traffic for Paris. He was heading north toward Saint-Germain and there was no one else in sight in either direction, except, perhaps half a mile ahead, an almost identical figure—another Royal Corps dispatch-rider. He was a younger, slimmer man and he sat comfortably back on his machine, enjoying the morning and keeping his speed to around forty. He was well on time and it was a beautiful day. He wondered whether to have his eggs fried or scrambled when he got back to HQ around eight.

Five hundred yards, four hundred, three, two, one. The man coming up from behind slowed to fifty. He put his right gauntlet up to his teeth and pulled it off. He stuffed the gauntlet between the buttons of his tunic and reached down and unclipped the gun.

By now he must have been big in the driving-mirror of the young man ahead, for suddenly the young man jerked his head around, surprised to find another dispatch-rider on his run at that time of the morning. He expected that it would be an American or perhaps French military police. It might be anyone from the eight NATO nations that made up the staff of SHAPE, but when he recognized the uniform of the Corps he was astonished and delighted. Who the hell could it be? He raised a cheerful right thumb in recognition and cut his speed to thirty, waiting for the other man to drift up alongside. With one eye on the road ahead and the other on the approaching silhouette in the mirror, he ran through the names of the British riders in the Special Service Transportation Unit at Headquarters Command. Albert, Sid, Wally—might be Wally, same thick build. Good show! He'd be able to pull his leg about that little frog bit in the canteen. Louise, Elise, Lise—what the hell was her name?

The man with the gun had slowed. Now he was fifty yards away. His face, undistorted by the wind, had set into blunt, hard, perhaps Slav lines. A red spark burned behind the black, aimed muzzles of the eyes. Forty yards, thirty. A single magpie flew out of the forest ahead of the young dispatch-rider. It fled clumsily across the road into the bushes behind a Michelin sign that said that Saint-Germain was one kilometer to go. The young man grinned and raised an ironical finger in salute and self-protection—"One magpie is sorrow."

Twenty yards behind him the man with the gun took both hands off the handlebars, lifted the Luger, rested it carefully on his left forearm, and fired one shot.

The young man's hands whipped off his controls and met across the center of his backward-arching spine. His machine veered across the road, jumped a narrow ditch, and plowed into a patch of grass and lilies of the valley. There it rose up on its screaming back wheel and slowly crashed backward on top of its dead rider. The BSA coughed and kicked and tore at the young man's clothes and at the flowers, and then lay quiet.

The killer executed a narrow turn and stopped with his machine pointing back the way he had come. He stamped down the wheelrest, pulled his machine up onto it, and walked in among the wild flowers under the trees. He knelt down beside the dead man and brusquely pulled back an eyelid. Just as roughly he tore the black leather dispatch-case off the corpse and ripped open the buttons of the tunic and removed a battered leather wallet. He wrenched a cheap wristwatch so sharply off the left wrist that the chrome expanding bracelet snapped in half. He stood up and slung the dispatch-case over his shoulder. While he stowed the wallet and the watch away in his tunic pocket he listened. There were only forest sounds and the slow tick of hot metal from the crashed BSA. The killer retraced his steps to the road. He walked slowly, scuffing leaves over the tire marks in the soft earth and moss. He took extra trouble over the deep scars in the ditch and the grass verge, and then stood beside his motorcycle and looked back toward the lily-of-the-valley patch. Not bad! Probably only the police dogs would get it, and, with ten miles of road to cover, they would be hours, perhaps days—plenty long enough. The main thing in these jobs was to have enough safety margin. He could have shot the man at forty yards, but he had preferred to get to twenty. And taking the watch and the wallet had been nice touches—pro touches.

Pleased with himself, the man heaved his machine off its rest, vaulted smartly into the saddle, and kicked down on the starter. Slowly, so as not to show skid marks, he accelerated away back down the road, and in a minute or so he was doing seventy again and the wind had redrawn the empty turnip-grin across his face.

Around the scene of the killing, the forest, which had held its breath while it was done, slowly began to breathe again.

James Bond had his first drink of the evening at Fouquet's. It was not a solid drink. One cannot drink seriously in French cafés. Out of doors on a pavement in the sun is no place for vodka or whisky or gin. A *fine à l'eau* is fairly serious, but it intoxicates without tasting very good. A *quart de champagne* or a *champagne à l'orange* is all right before luncheon, but in the evening one *quart* leads to another *quart,* and a bottle of indifferent champagne is a bad foundation for the night. Pernod is possible, but it should be drunk in company, and anyway Bond had never liked the stuff because its licorice taste reminded him of his childhood. No, in cafés you have to drink the least offensive of the musical-comedy drinks that go with them, and Bond always had the same thing, an Americano—bitter Campari, Cinzano, a large slice of lemon peel, and soda. For the soda he always stipulated Perrier, for in his opinion expensive soda water was the cheapest way to improve a poor drink.

When Bond was in Paris he invariably stuck to the same addresses. He stayed at the Terminus Nord, because he liked station hotels and because this was the least pretentious and most anonymous of them. He had luncheon at the Café de la Paix, the Rotonde, or the Dôme, because the food was good enough and it amused him to watch the people. If he wanted a solid drink he had it at Harry's Bar, both because of the solidity of the drinks and because, on his first ignorant visit to Paris at the age of sixteen, he had done what Harry's advertisement in the *Continental Daily Mail* had told him to do and had said to his taxi-driver, "Sank Roo Doe Noo." That had started one of the memorable evenings of his life, culminating in the loss, almost simultaneously, of his virginity and his notecase. For dinner, Bond went to one of the great restaurants—Véfour, the Caneton, Lucas-Carton, or the Cochon d'Or. These he considered, whatever Michelin might say about the Tour d'Argent, Maxim's, and the like, to have somehow avoided the tarnish of the expense account and the dollar. Anyway, he preferred their cooking. After dinner he generally went to the Place Pigalle to see what would happen to him. When, as usual, nothing did, he would walk home across Paris to the Gare du Nord and go to bed.

Tonight Bond decided to tear up this dusty address book and have himself an old-fashioned ball. He was on his way through Paris after a dismally failed assignment on the Austro-Hungarian border. It had been a question of getting a certain Hungarian out. Bond had been sent from London specially to direct the operation over the head of Station V. This had been unpopular with the Vienna Station. There had been misunderstandings—willful ones. The man had been killed in the frontier minefield. There would have to be a Court of Inquiry. Bond was due back at his London headquarters on the following day to make his report, and the thought of it all depressed him. Today had been so beautiful—one of those days when you almost believe that Paris is beautiful and gay—and Bond had decided to give the town just one more chance. He would somehow find himself a girl who was a real girl, and he would take her to dinner at some make-believe place in the Bois like the Armenonville. To clean the money-look out of her eyes—for it would certainly be there—he would as soon as possible give her fifty thousand francs. He would say to her, "I propose to call you Donatienne, or possibly Solange, because these are names that suit my mood and the evening. We knew each other before and you lent me this money because I was in a jam. Here it is, and now we will tell each other what we have been doing since we last met in Saint-Tropez just a year ago. In the meantime, here is the menu and the wine list and you must choose what will make you happy and fat." And she would look relieved at not having to try any more, and she would laugh and say, "But, James, I do not want to be fat." And there they would be, started on the myth of "Paris in the Spring," and Bond would stay sober and be interested in her and everything she said. And, by God, by the end of the evening it would not be his fault if it transpired that there was in fact no shred of stuffing left in the hoary old fairy tale of "A good time in Paris."

Sitting in Fouquet's, waiting for his Americano, Bond smiled at his vehemence. He knew that he was only playing at this fantasy for the satisfaction of launching a last kick at a town he had cordially disliked since the war. Since 1945, he had not had a happy day in Paris. It was not that the town had sold its body. Many towns have done that. It was its heart that was gone—pawned to the tourists, pawned to the Russians and Rumanians and Bulgars, pawned to the scum of the world who had gradually taken the town over. And, of course, pawned to the Germans. You could see it in the people's eyes—sullen, envious, ashamed. Architecture? Bond glanced across the pavement at the shiny black ribbons of cars off which the sun glinted painfully. Everywhere it was the same as in the Champs-Elysées. There were only two hours in which you could even see the town—between five and seven in the morning. After seven it was engulfed in a thundering stream of black metal with which no beautiful buildings, no spacious, tree-lined boulevards, could compete.

The waiter's tray clattered down on the marble-topped table. With a slick one-handed jerk that Bond had never been able to copy, the waiter's bottle-opener prised the cap off the Perrier. The man slipped the tab under the ice-bucket, said a mechanical *"Voilà, m'sieur,"* and darted away. Bond put ice into his drink, filled it to the top with soda, and took a long pull at it. He sat back and lit a Laurens *jaune.* Of course the evening would be a disaster. Even supposing he found the girl in the next hour or so, the contents would certainly not stand up to the wrapping. On closer examination she would turn out to have the heavy, dank, wide-pored skin of the bourgeois French. The blond hair under the rakish velvet beret would be brown at the roots and as coarse as piano wire. The peppermint on the breath would not conceal the midday garlic. The alluring figure would be intricately scaffolded with wire and rubber. She would be from Lille and she would ask him if he was American. And—Bond smiled to himself—she or her *maquereau* would probably steal his notecase. *La ronde!* He would be back where he came in. More or less, that was. Well, to hell with it!

A battered black Peugeot 403 broke out of the center stream of traffic, cut across the inside line of cars, and pulled in to double park at the curb. There was the usual screaming of brakes, hooting, and yelling. Quite unmoved, a girl got out of the car and, leaving the traffic to sort itself out, walked purposefully across the sidewalk. Bond sat up. She had everything, but absolutely everything that belonged in his fantasy. She was tall, and although her figure was hidden by a light raincoat, the way she moved and the way she held herself promised that it would be beautiful. The face had the gaiety and bravado that went with her driving, but now there was impatience in the compressed lips and the eyes fretted as she pushed diagonally through the moving crowd on the pavement.

Bond watched her narrowly as she reached the edge of the tables and came up the aisle. Of course it was hopeless. She was coming to meet someone—her lover. She was the sort of woman who always belongs to somebody else. She was late for him. That's why she was in such a hurry. What damnable luck—right down to the long blond hair under the rakish beret! And she was looking straight at him. She was smiling . . . !

Before Bond could pull himself together, the girl had come up to his table and had drawn out a chair and sat down.

She smiled rather tautly into his startled eyes. "I'm sorry I'm late, and I'm afraid we've got to get moving at once. You're wanted at the office." She added under her breath, "Crash dive."

Bond jerked himself back to reality. Whoever she was, she was certainly from "the firm." "Crash dive" was a slang expression the Secret Service had borrowed from the Submarine Service. It meant bad news—the worst. Bond dug into his pockets and slid some coins over the tab. He said, "Right. Let's go," and got up and followed her down through the tables and across to her car. It was still obstructing the inner lane of traffic. Any minute now there would be a policeman. Angry faces glared at them as they climbed in. The girl had left the engine running. She banged the gears into second and slid out into the traffic.

Bond looked sideways at her. The pale skin was velvet. The blond hair was silk— to the roots. He said, "Where are you from and what's it all about?"

She said, concentrating on the traffic, "From the Station. Grade two assistant, Number 765 on duty, Mary Ann Russell off. I've no idea what it's all about. I just saw the signal from HQ—personal from M to Head of Station. Most Immediate and all that. He was to find you at once and if necessary use the Deuxième to help. Head of F said you always went to the same places when you were in Paris, and I and another girl were given a list." She smiled. "I'd only tried Harry's Bar, and after Fouquet's I was going to start on the restaurants. It was marvelous picking you up like that." She gave him a quick glance. "I hope I wasn't very clumsy."

Bond said, "You were fine. How were you going to handle it if I'd had a girl with me?"

She laughed. "I was going to do much the same except call you 'sir.' I was only worried about how you'd dispose of the girl. If she started a scene I was going to offer to take her home in my car and for you to take a taxi."

"You sound pretty resourceful. How long have you been in the Service?"

"Five years. This is my first time with a station."

"How do you like it?"

"I like the work all right. The evenings and days off drag a bit. It's not easy to make friends in Paris without"—her mouth turned down with irony—"without all the rest. I mean," she hastened to add, "I'm not a prude and all that, but somehow the French make the whole business such a bore. I mean I've had to give up taking the Métro or buses. Whatever time of day it is, you end up with your behind black and blue." She laughed. "Apart from the boredom of it and not knowing what to say to the man, some of the pinches really hurt. It's the limit. So to get around I bought this car cheap, and other cars seem to keep out of my way. As long as you don't catch the other driver's eye, you can take on even the meanest of them. They're afraid you haven't seen them. And they're worried by the bashed-about look of the car. They give you a wide berth."

They had come to the Rond Point. As if to demonstrate her theory, she tore round it and went straight at the line of traffic coming up from the Place de la Concorde. Miraculously it divided and let her through into the Avenue Matignon.

Bond said, "Pretty good. But don't make it a habit. There may be some French Mary Anns about."

She laughed. She turned into the Avenue Gabrielle and pulled up outside the Paris headquarters of the Secret Service. "I only try that sort of maneuver in the line of duty."

Bond got out and came round to her side of the car. He said, "Well, thanks for picking me up. When this whirl is over, can I pick you up in exchange? I don't get the pinches, but I'm just as bored in Paris as you are."

Her eyes were blue and wide apart. They searched his. She said seriously, "I'd like that. The switchboard here can always find me."

Bond reached in through the window and pressed the hand on the wheel. He said, "Good," and turned and walked quickly in through the archway.

Wing Commander Rattray, Head of Station F, was a fattish man with pink cheeks and fair hair brushed straight back. He dressed in a mannered fashion with turned-back cuffs and double slits to his coat, bow ties and fancy waistcoats. He made a good-living, wine-and-food-society impression in which only the slow, rather cunning blue eyes struck a false note. He chain-smoked Gauloises and his office stank of them. He greeted Bond with relief. "Who found you?"

"Russell. At Fouquet's. Is she new?"

"Six months. She's a good one. But take a pew. There's the hell of a flap on and I've got to brief you and get you going." He bent to his intercom and pressed down a switch. "Signal to M, please. Personal from Head of Station. 'Located 007 briefing now.' Okay?" He let go the switch.

Bond pulled a chair over by the open window to keep away from the fog of Gauloise. The traffic on the Champs-Elysées was a soft roar in the background. Half an hour before he had been fed up with Paris, glad to be going. Now he hoped he would be staying.

Head of F said, "Somebody got our dawn dispatch-rider from SHAPE to the Saint-Germain Station yesterday morning. The weekly run from the SHAPE Intelligence Division with the Summaries, Joint Intelligence papers, Iron Curtain Order of Battle—all the top gen. One shot in the back. Took his dispatch-case and his wallet and watch."

Bond said, "That's bad. No chance that it was an ordinary hold-up? Or do they think the wallet and watch were cover?"

"SHAPE Security can't make up their minds. On the whole they guess it was cover. Seven o'clock in the morning's a rum time for a hold-up. But you can argue it out with them when you get down there. M's sending you as his personal representative. He's worried as hell. Apart from the loss of the Intelligence dope, their I. people have never liked having one of our stations outside the reservation, so to speak. For years they've been trying to get the Saint-Germain unit incorporated in the SHAPE Intelligence set-up. But you know what M is, independent old devil. He's never been happy about NATO Security. Why, right in the SHAPE Intelligence Division there are not only a couple of Frenchmen and an Italian, but the head of their Counterintelligence and Security section is a German!"

Bond whistled.

"The trouble is that this damnable business is all SHAPE needs to bring M to heel. Anyway, he says you're to get down there right away. I've fixed up clearance for you. Got the passes. You're to report to Colonel Schreiber, Headquarters Command Security Branch. American. Efficient chap. He's been handling the thing from the beginning. As far as I can gather, he's already done just about all there was to be done."

"What's he done? What actually happened?"

Head of F picked up a map from his desk and walked over with it. It was the big-scale Michelin *Environs de Paris.* He pointed with a pencil. "Here's Versailles, and here, just north of the park, is the big junction of the Paris-Mantes and the Versailles Autoroutes. A couple of hundred yards north of that, on N184, is SHAPE. Every Wednesday, at seven in the morning, a Special Services dispatch-rider leaves SHAPE with the weekly intelligence stuff I told you about. He has to get to this little village called Fourqueux, just outside Saint-Germain, deliver his stuff to the duty officer at our HQ, and report back to SHAPE by seven-thirty. Rather than go through all this built-up area, for security reasons his orders are to take this N307 to Saint-Nom, turn right-handed onto D98, and go under the Autoroute and through the Forest of Saint-Germain. The distance is about twelve kilometers, and, taking it easy, he'll do the trip in under a quarter of an hour. Well, yesterday it was a corporal from the Corps of Signals, good solid man called Bates, and when he hadn't reported back to SHAPE by seven-forty-five they sent another rider to look for him. Not a trace, and he hadn't reported at our HQ. By eight-fifteen the Security Branch was on the job, and by nine the roadblocks were up. The police and the Deuxième were told and search parties got under way. The dogs found him, but not till the evening around six, and by that time if there had been any clues on the road they'd been wiped out by the traffic." Head of F handed the map to Bond and walked back to his desk. "And that's about the lot, except that all the usual steps have been taken—frontiers, ports, airdromes and so forth. But that sort of thing won't help. If it was a professional job, whoever did it could have had the stuff out of the country by midday or into an embassy in Paris inside an hour."

Bond said impatiently, "Exactly! And so what the hell does M expect me to do? Tell SHAPE Security to do it all over again, but better? This sort of thing isn't my line at all. Bloody waste of time."

Head of F smiled sympathetically. "Matter of fact I put much the same point of view to M over the scrambler. Tactfully. The old man was quite reasonable. Said he wanted to show SHAPE he was taking the business just as seriously as they were. You happened to be available and more or less on the spot, and he said you had the sort of mind that might pick up the invisible factor. I asked him what he meant, and he said that at all closely guarded headquarters there's bound to be an invisible man, a man everyone takes so much for granted that he just isn't noticed—gardener, window-cleaner, postman. I said that SHAPE had thought of that, and that all those sort of jobs were done by enlisted men. M told me not to be so literal-minded and hung up."

Bond laughed. He could see M's frown and hear the crusty voice. He said, "All right, then. I'll see what I can do. Who do I report back to?"

"Here. M doesn't want the Saint-Germain unit to get involved. Anything you have to say I'll put straight on the printer to London. But I may not be available when you call up. I'll make someone your duty officer and you'll be able to get them any time in the twenty-four hours. Russell can do it. She picked you up. She might as well carry you. Suit you?"

"Yes," said Bond. "That'll be all right."

The battered Peugeot, commandeered by Rattray, smelled of her. There were bits of her in the glove compartment—half a packet of Suchard milk chocolate, a twist of paper containing bobby pins, a paperback John O'Hara, a single black suede glove. Bond thought about her as far as the Etoile and then closed his mind to her and pushed the car along fast through the Bois. Rattray had said it would take about fifteen minutes at fifty. Bond said to halve the speed and double the time and to tell Colonel Schreiber that he would be with him by nine-thirty. After the Porte de Saint-Cloud there was little traffic, and Bond held seventy on the Autoroute until the second exit road came up on his right and there was the red arrow for SHAPE. Bond turned up the slope and onto N184. Two hundred yards farther, in the center of the road, was the traffic policeman Bond had been told to look out for. The policeman waved him in through the big gates on the left and he pulled up at the first checkpoint. A gray-uniformed American policeman hung out of the cabin and glanced at his pass. He was told to pull inside and hold it. Now a French policeman took his pass, noted the details on a printed form clipped to a board, gave him a large plastic windshield number, and waved him on. As Bond pulled into the car park, with theatrical suddenness a hundred arc-lights blazed and lit up the acre of low-lying hutments in front of him as if it were day. Feeling naked, Bond walked across the open gravel beneath the flags of the NATO countries and ran up the four shallow steps to the wide glass doors that gave entrance to the Supreme Headquarters Allied Forces Europe. Now there was the main Security desk. American and French military police again checked his pass and noted the details. He was handed over to a red-capped British MP and led off down the main corridor past endless office doors.

They bore no names but the usual alphabetical abracadabra of all headquarters. One said COMSTRIKFLTLANT AND SACLANT LIAISON TO SACEUR. Bond asked what it meant. The military policeman, either ignorant or, more probably, security-minded, said stolidly, "Couldn't rightly say, sir."

Behind a door that said COLONEL G. A. SCHREIBER, CHIEF OF SECURITY, HEADQUARTERS COMMAND, was a ramrod-straight middle-aged American with graying hair and the politely negative manner of a bank manager. There were several family photographs in silver frames on his desk and a vase containing one white rose. There was no smell of tobacco smoke in the room. After cautiously amiable preliminaries, Bond congratulated the colonel on his security. He said, "All these checks and double checks don't make it easy for the opposition. Have you ever lost anything before, or have you ever found signs of a serious attempt at a *coup?*"

"No to both questions, Commander. I'm quite satisfied about Headquarters. It's only the outlying units that worry me. Apart from this section of your Secret Service, we have various detached signal units. Then, of course, there are the Home Ministries of fourteen different nations. I can't answer for what may leak from those quarters."

"It can't be an easy job," agreed Bond. "Now, about this mess. Has anything else come up since Wing Commander Rattray spoke to you last?"

"Got the bullet. Luger. Severed the spinal cord. Probably fired at around thirty yards, give or take ten yards. Assuming our man was riding a straight course, the bullet must have been fired from dead astern on a level trajectory. Since it can't have been a man standing in the road, the killer must have been moving in or on some vehicle."

"So your man would have seen him in the driving-mirror?"

"Probably."

"If your riders find themselves being followed, do they have any instructions about taking evasive action?"

The colonel smiled lightly. "Sure. They're told to go like hell."

"And at what speed did your man crash?"

"Not fast, they think. Between twenty and forty. What are you getting at, Commander?"

"I was wondering if you'd decided whether it was a pro or an amateur job. If your man wasn't trying to get away, and assuming he saw the killer in his mirror, which I agree is only a probability, that suggests that he accepted the man on his tail as a friend rather than foe. That could mean some sort of a disguise that would fit in with the set-up here—something your man would accept even at that hour of the morning."

A small frown had been gathering across Colonel Schreiber's smooth forehead. "Commander"—there was an edge of tension in the voice—"we have, of course, been considering every angle of this case, including the one you mention. At midday yesterday the commanding general declared emergency in this matter, standing security and security ops committees were set up, and from that moment on every angle, every hint of a clue, has been systematically run to earth. And I can tell you, Commander"—the colonel raised one well-manicured hand and let it descend in soft emphasis on his blotting-pad—"any man who can come up with an even remotely original idea on this case will have to be closely related to Einstein. There is nothing, repeat nothing, to go on in this case whatsoever."

Bond smiled sympathetically. He got to his feet. "In that case, Colonel, I won't waste any more of your time this evening. If I could just have the minutes of the various meetings to bring myself up to date, and if one of your men could show me the way to the canteen and my quarters . . ."

"Sure, sure." The colonel pressed a bell. A young crew-cutted aide came in. "Proctor, show the commander to his room in the VIP wing, would you, and then take him along to the bar and the canteen." He turned to Bond. "I'll have those papers ready for you after you've had a meal and a drink. They'll be in my office. They can't be taken out, of course, but you'll find everything to hand next door, and Proctor will be able to fill you in on anything that's missing." He held out his hand. "Okay? Then we'll meet again in the morning."

Bond said good night and followed the aide out. As he walked along the neutral-painted, neutral-smelling corridors, he reflected that this was probably the most hopeless assignment he had ever been on. If the top security brains of fourteen countries were stumped, what hope had he got? By the time he was in bed that night, in the Spartan luxury of the visitors' overnight quarters, Bond had decided he would give it a couple more days—largely for the sake of keeping in touch with Mary Ann Russell for as long as possible—and then chuck it. On this decision he fell immediately into a deep and untroubled sleep.

Not two but four days later, as the dawn came up over the Forest of Saint-Germain, James Bond was lying along the thick branch of an oak tree, keeping watch over a small empty glade that lay deep among the trees bordering D98, the road of the murder.

He was dressed from head to foot in parachutists' camouflage—green, brown, and black. Even his hands were covered with the stuff, and there was a hood over his head with slits cut for the eyes and mouth. It was good camouflage, which would be still better when the sun was higher and the shadows blacker, and from anywhere on the ground, even directly below the high branch, he could not be seen.

It had come about like this. The first two days at SHAPE had been the expected waste of time. Bond had achieved nothing except to make himself mildly unpopular with the persistence of his double-checking questions. On the morning of the third day he was about to go and say his good-byes when he had a telephone call from the colonel. "Oh, Commander, thought I'd let you know that the last team of police dogs got in late last night—your idea that it might be worthwhile covering the whole forest. Sorry"—the voice sounded unsorry—"but negative, absolutely negative."

"Oh. My fault for the wasted time." As much to annoy the colonel as anything, Bond said, "Mind if I have a talk with the handler?"

"Sure, sure. Anything you want. By the way, Commander, how long are you planning to be around? Glad to have you with us for as long as you like. But it's a question of your room. Seems there's a big party coming in from Holland in a few days' time. Top-level staff course or something of the kind, and Admin says they're a bit pushed for space."

Bond had not expected to get on well with Colonel Schreiber and he had not done so. He said amiably, "I'll see what my chief has to say and call you back, Colonel."

"Do that, would you." The colonel's voice was equally polite, but the manners of both men were running out and the two receivers broke the line simultaneously.

The chief handler was a Frenchman from the Landes. He had the quick, sly eyes of a poacher. Bond met him at the kennels, but the handler's proximity was too much for the Alsatians, and to get away from the noise he took Bond into the duty-room, a tiny office with binoculars hanging from pegs, and waterproofs, gumboots, dog-harness, and other gear stacked round the walls. There were a couple of deal chairs and a table covered with a large-scale map of the Forest of Saint-Germain. This had been marked off into penciled squares. The handler made a gesture over the map. "Our dogs covered it all, monsieur. There is nothing there."

"Do you mean to say they didn't check once?"

The handler scratched his head. "We had trouble with a bit of game, monsieur. There was a hare or two. A couple of foxes' earths. We had quite a time getting them away from a clearing near the Carrefour Royal. They probably still smelled the gypsies."

"Oh." Bond was only mildly interested. "Show me. Who were these gypsies?"

The handler pointed daintily with a grimy little finger. "These are the names from the old days. Here is the Etoile Parfaite, and here, where the killing took place, is the Carrefour des Curieux. And here, forming the bottom of the triangle, is the Carrefour Royal. It makes," he added dramatically, "a cross with the road of death." He took a pencil out of his pocket and made a dot just off the crossroads. "And this is the clearing, monsieur. There was a gypsy caravan there for most of the winter. They left last month. Cleaned the place up all right, but, for the dogs, their scent will hang about there for months."

Bond thanked him and, after inspecting and admiring the dogs and making some small talk about the handler's profession, he got into the Peugeot and went off to the *gendarmerie* in Saint-Germain. Yes, certainly they had known the gypsies. Real Romany-looking fellows. Hardly spoke a word of French, but they had behaved themselves. There had been no complaints. Six men and two women. No. No one had seen them go. One morning they just weren't there any more. Might have been gone a week for all one knew. They had chosen an isolated spot.

Bond took the D98 through the forest. When the great Autoroute bridge showed up a quarter of a mile ahead over the road, Bond accelerated and then switched off the engine and coasted silently until he came to the Carrefour Royal. He stopped and got out of the car without a sound, and, feeling rather foolish, softly entered the forest and walked with great circumspection toward where the clearing would be. Twenty yards inside the trees he came to it. He stood in the fringe of bushes and trees and examined it carefully. Then he walked in and went over it from end to end.

The clearing was about as big as two tennis courts and floored in thick grass and moss. There was one large patch of lilies of the valley and, under the bordering trees, a scattering of bluebells. To one side there was a low mound, perhaps a tumulus, completely surrounded and covered with brambles and brier roses now thickly in bloom. Bond walked round this and gazed in among the roots, but there was nothing to see except the earthy shape of the mound.

Bond took one last look around and then went to the corner of the clearing that would be nearest to the road. Here there was easy access through the trees. Were there traces of a path, a slight flattening of the leaves? Not more than would have been left by the gypsies or last year's picnickers. On the edge of the road there was a narrow passage between two trees. Casually Bond bent to examine the trunks. He stiffened and dropped to a crouch. With a fingernail he delicately scraped away a narrow sliver of caked mud. It hid a deep scratch in the tree-trunk. He caught the scraps of mud in his free hand. He now spat and moistened the mud and carefully filled up the scratch again. There were three camouflaged scratches on one tree and four on the other. Bond walked quickly out of the trees onto the road. His car had stopped on a slight slope leading down under the Autoroute bridge. Although there was some protection from the boom of the traffic on the Autoroute, Bond pushed the car, jumped in, and engaged the gears only when he was well under the bridge.

And now Bond was back in the clearing, above it, and he still did not know if his hunch had been right. It had been M's dictum that had put him on the scent—if it was a scent—and the mention of the gypsies. "It was the gypsies the dogs smelled. . . . Most of the winter . . . they went last month. No complaints. . . . One morning they just weren't there any more." The invisible factor. The invisible man. The people who are so much part of the background that you don't know if they're there or not. Six men and two girls, and they hardly spoke a word of French. Good cover, gypsies. You could be a foreigner and yet not a foreigner, because you were only a gypsy. Some of them had gone off in the caravan. Had some of them stayed, built themselves a hideout during the winter, a secret place from which the hijacking of the top-secret dispatches had been the first sortie? Bond had thought he was building fantasies until he found the scratches, the carefully camouflaged scratches, on the two trees. They were just at the height where, if one was carrying any kind of cycle, the pedals might catch against the bark. It could all be a pipedream, but it was good enough for Bond. The only question in his mind was whether these people had made a one-time-only coup or whether they were so confident of their security that they would try again. He confided only in Station F. Mary Ann Russell told him to be careful. Head of F, more constructively, ordered his unit at Saint-Germain to cooperate. Bond said good-by to Colonel Schreiber and moved to a camp-bed in the unit's HQ—an anonymous house in an anonymous village back street. The unit had provided the camouflage outfit, and the four Secret Service men who ran the unit had happily put themselves under Bond's orders. They realized as well as Bond did that if Bond managed to wipe the eye of the whole security machine of SHAPE, the Secret Service would have won a priceless feather in its cap *vis-à-vis* the SHAPE high command, and M's worries over the independence of his unit would be gone forever.

Bond, lying along the oak branch, smiled to himself. Private armies, private wars. How much energy they siphoned off from the common cause, how much fire they directed away from the common enemy!

Six-thirty. Time for breakfast. Cautiously Bond's right hand fumbled in his clothing and came up to the slit of his mouth. Bond made the glucose tablet last as long as possible and then sucked another. His eyes never left the glade. The red squirrel that had appeared at first light and had been steadily eating away at young beech shoots ever since ran a few feet nearer to the rose bushes on the mound, picked up something, and began turning it in its paws and nibbling at it. Two wood-pigeons that had been noisily courting among the thick grass started to make clumsy, fluttering love. A pair of hedge-sparrows went busily on collecting bits and pieces for a nest they were tardily building in a thorn bush. The fat thrush finally located its worm and began pulling at it, legs braced. Bees clustered thick among the roses on the mound, and from where he was, perhaps twenty yards away from and above the mound, Bond could just hear their summery sound. It was a scene from a fairy tale—the roses, the lilies of the valley, the birds, and the great shafts of sunlight lancing down through the tall trees into the pool of glistening green. Bond had climbed to his hideout at four in the morning and he had never examined so closely or for so long the transition from night to a glorious day. He suddenly felt rather foolish. Any moment now and some damned bird would come and sit on his head.

It was the pigeons that gave the first alarm. With a loud clatter they took off and dashed into the trees. All the birds followed, and the squirrel. Now the glade was quite quiet except for the soft hum of the bees. What had sounded the alarm? Bond's heart began to thump. His eyes hunted, quartering the glade for a clue. Something was moving among the roses. It was a tiny movement, but an extraordinary one. Slowly, inch by inch, a single thorny stem, an unnaturally straight and rather thick one, was rising through the upper branches. It went on rising until it was a clear foot above the bush. Then it stopped. There was a solitary pink rose at the tip of the stem. Separated from the bush, it looked unnatural, but only if one happened to have watched the whole process. At a casual glance it was a stray stem and nothing else. Now, silently, the petals of the rose seemed to swivel and expand, the yellow pistils drew aside, and sun glinted on a glass lens the size of a shilling. The lens seemed to be looking straight at Bond, but then very, very slowly, the rose-eye began to turn on its stem and continued to turn until the lens was again looking at Bond and the whole glade had been minutely surveyed. As if satisfied, the petals softly swiveled to cover the eye, and very slowly the single rose descended to join the others.

Bond's breath came out with a rush. He momentarily closed his eyes to rest them. Gypsies! If that piece of machinery was any evidence, inside the mound, deep down in the earth, was certainly the most professional left-behind spy unit that had ever been devised, far more brilliant than anything England had prepared to operate in the wake of a successful German invasion, far better than what the Germans themselves had left behind in the Ardennes. A shiver of excitement and anticipation—almost of fear—ran down Bond's spine. So he had been right! But what was to be the next act?

Now, from the direction of the mound, came a thin, high-pitched whine, the sound of an electric motor at very high revs. The rose bush trembled slightly. The bees took off, hovered, and settled again. Slowly a jagged fissure formed down the center of the big bush and smoothly widened. Now the two halves of the bush were opening like double doors. The dark aperture broadened until Bond could see the roots of the bush running into the earth on both sides of the opening doorway. The whine of machinery was louder, and there was a glint of metal from the edges of the curved doors. It was like the opening of a hinged Easter egg. In a moment the two segments stood apart and the two halves of the rose bush, still alive with bees, were splayed wide open. Now the inside of the metal caisson that supported the earth and the roots of the bush was naked to the sun. There was a glint of pale electric light from the dark aperture between the curved doors. The whine of the motor had stopped. A head and shoulders appeared, and then the rest of the man. He climbed softly out and crouched, looking sharply round the glade. There was a gun—a Luger—in his hand. Satisfied, he turned and gestured into the shaft. The head and shoulders of a second man appeared. He handed up three pairs of what looked like snowshoes and ducked out of sight. The first man selected a pair and knelt and strapped them over his boots. Now he moved about more freely, leaving no footprints, for the grass flattened only momentarily under the wide mesh and then rose slowly again. Bond smiled to himself. Clever bastards!

The second man emerged. He was followed by a third. Between them they manhandled a motorcycle out of the shaft and stood holding it slung between them by harness webbing while the first man, who was clearly the leader, knelt and strapped the snowshoes under their boots. Then, in single file, they moved off through the trees toward the road. There was something extraordinarily sinister about the way they softly high-stepped along through the shadows, lifting and carefully placing each big webbed foot in turn.

Bond let out a long sigh of released tension and laid his head softly down on the branch to relax the strain in his neck muscles. So that was the score! Even the last small detail could now be added to the file. While the two underlings were dressed in gray overalls, the leader was wearing the uniform of the Royal Corps of Signals, and his motorcycle was an olive-green BSAM 20 with a British Army registration number on its petrol tank. No wonder the SHAPE dispatch-rider had let him get within range. And what did the unit do with its top-secret booty? Probably radioed the cream of it out at night. Instead of the periscope, a rose-stalked aerial would rise up from the bush, the pedal generator would get going deep down under the earth, and off would go the high speed cipher groups. Ciphers? There would be many good enemy secrets down that shaft if Bond could round up the unit when it was outside the hideout. And what a chance to feed back phony intelligence to GRU, the Soviet Military Intelligence Apparat, which was presumably the control! Bond's thoughts raced.

The two underlings were coming back. They went into the shaft, and the rose bush closed over it. The leader with his machine would be among the bushes on the verge of the road. Bond glanced at his watch. Six-fifty-five. Of course! He would be waiting to see if a dispatch-rider came along. Either he did not know the man he had killed was doing a weekly run, which was unlikely, or he was assuming that SHAPE would now change the routine for additional security. These were careful people. Probably their orders were to clean up as much as possible before the summer came and there were too many holiday-makers about in the forest. Then the unit might be pulled out and put back again in the winter. Who could say what the long-term plans were? Sufficient that the leader was preparing for another kill.

The minutes ticked by. At seven-ten the leader reappeared. He stood in the shadow of a big tree at the edge of the clearing and whistled once on a brief, high, birdlike note. Immediately the rose bush began to open and the two underlings came out and followed the leader back into the trees. In two minutes they were back with the motorcycle slung between them. The leader, after a careful look around to see that they had left no traces, followed them down into the shaft, and the two halves of the rose bush closed swiftly behind him.

Half an hour later life had started up in the glade again. An hour later still, when the high sun had darkened the shadows, James Bond silently edged backward along his branch, dropped softly onto a patch of moss behind some brambles, and melted carefully back into the forest.

That evening Bond's routine call to Mary Ann Russell was a stormy one. She said, "You're crazy. I'm not going to let you do it. I'm going to get Head of F to ring up Colonel Schreiber and tell him the whole story. This is SHAPE's job. Not yours."

Bond said sharply, "You'll do nothing of the sort. Colonel Schreiber says he's perfectly happy to let me make a dummy run tomorrow morning instead of the duty dispatch-rider. That's all he needs to know at this stage. Reconstruction of the crime sort of thing. He couldn't care less. He's practically closed the file on this business. Now, be a good girl and do as you're told. Just put my report on the printer to M. He'll see the point of me cleaning this thing up. He won't object."

"Damn M! Damn you! Damn the whole silly Service!" There were angry tears in the voice. "You're just a lot of children playing at red Indians. Taking these people on by yourself! It's—it's showing off. That's all it is. Showing off."

Bond was beginning to get annoyed. He said, "That's enough, Mary Ann. Put that report on the printer. I'm sorry, but it's an order."

There was resignation in the voice. "Oh, all right. You don't have to pull your rank on me. But don't get hurt. At least you'll have the boys from the local Station to pick up the bits. Good luck."

"Thanks, Mary Ann. And will you have dinner with me tomorrow night? Some place like Armenonville. Pink champagne and gypsy violins. Paris-in-the-spring routine."

"Yes," she said seriously. "I'd like that. But then take care all the more, would you? Please?"

"Of course I will. Don't worry. Good night."

"Night."

Bond spent the rest of the evening putting a last high polish on his plans and giving a final briefing to the four men from the Station.

It was another beautiful day. Bond, sitting comfortably astride the throbbing BSA waiting for the take-off, could hardly believe in the ambush that would now be waiting for him just beyond the Carrefour Royal. The corporal from the Signal Corps who had handed him his empty dispatch-case and was about to give him the signal to go said, "You look as if you'd been in the Royal Corps all your life, sir. Time for a haircut soon, I'd say, but the uniform's bang on. How d'you like the bike, sir?"

"Goes like a dream. I'd forgotten what fun these damned things are."

"Give me a nice little Austin A40 any day, sir." The corporal looked at his watch. "Seven o'clock just coming up." He held up his thumb. "Okay."

Bond pulled the goggles down over his eyes, lifted a hand to the corporal, kicked the machine into gear, and wheeled off across the gravel and through the main gates.

Off 184 and onto 307, through Bailly and Noisy-le-Roi, and there was the straggle of Saint-Nom. Here he would be turning sharp right onto D198—the *route de la mort,* as the handler had called it. Bond pulled into the grass verge and once more looked to the long-barrel .45 Colt. He put the warm gun back against his stomach and left the jacket button undone. On your marks! Get set . . . !

Bond took the sharp corner and accelerated up to fifty. The viaduct carrying the Paris Autoroute loomed up ahead. The dark mouth of the tunnel beneath it opened and swallowed him. The noise of his exhaust was gigantic, and for an instant there was a tunnel smell of cold and damp. Then he was out in the sunshine again and immediately across the Carrefour Royal. Ahead the oily tarmac glittered dead straight for two miles through the enchanted forest, and there was a sweet smell of leaves and dew. Bond cut his speed to forty. The driving-mirror by his left hand shivered slightly with his speed. It showed nothing but an empty unfurling vista of road between lines of trees that curled away behind him like a green wake. No sign of the killer. Had he taken fright? Had there been some hitch? But then there was a tiny black speck in the center of the convex glass—a midge that became a fly and then a bee and then a beetle. Now it was a crash helmet bent low over handlebars between two big black paws. God, he was coming fast! Bond's eyes flickered from the mirror to the road ahead and back to the mirror. When the killer's right hand went for his gun . . . !

Bond slowed—thirty-five, thirty, twenty. Ahead the tarmac was smooth as metal. A last quick look in the mirror. The right hand had left the handlebars. The sun on the man's goggles made huge fiery eyes below the rim of the crash helmet. Now! Bond braked fiercely and skidded the BSA through forty-five degrees, killing the engine. He was not quite quick enough on the draw. The killer's gun flared twice, and a bullet tore into the saddle springs beside Bond's thigh. But then the Colt spoke its single word, and the killer and his BSA, as if lassoed from within the forest, veered crazily off the road, leaped the ditch, and crashed head on into the trunk of a beech. For a moment the tangle of man and machinery clung to the broad trunk, and then, with a metallic death-rattle, toppled backward into the grass.

Bond got off his machine and walked over to the ugly twist of khaki and smoking steel. There was no need to feel for a pulse. Wherever the bullet had struck, the crash helmet had smashed like an eggshell. Bond turned away and thrust his gun back into the front of his tunic. He had been lucky. It would not do to press his luck. He got on the BSA and accelerated back down the road.

He leaned the BSA up against one of the scarred trees just inside the forest and walked softly through to the edge of the clearing. He took up his stand in the shadow of the big beech. He moistened his lips and gave, as near as he could, the killer's bird-whistle. He waited. Had he got the whistle wrong? But then the bush trembled and the high, thin whine began. Bond hooked his right thumb through his belt within inches of his gun-butt. He hoped he would not have to do any more killing. The two underlings had not seemed to be armed. With any luck they would come quietly.

Now the curved doors were open. From where he was, Bond could not see down the shaft, but within seconds the first man was out and putting on his snowshoes, and the second followed. Snowshoes! Bond's heart missed a beat. He had forgotten them! They must be hidden back in the bushes. Blasted fool! Would they notice?

The two men came slowly toward him, delicately placing their feet. When he was about twenty feet away, the leading man said something softly in what sounded like Russian. When Bond did not reply, the two men stopped in their tracks. They stared at him in astonishment, waiting perhaps for the answer to a password. Bond sensed trouble. He whipped out his gun and moved toward them, crouching. "Hands up." He gestured with the muzzle of the Colt. The leading man shouted an order and threw himself forward. At the same time the second man made a dash back toward the hideout. A rifle boomed from among the trees and the man's right leg buckled under him. The men from the Station broke cover and came running. Bond fell to one knee and clubbed upward with his gun-barrel at the hurtling body. It made contact, but then the man was on him. Bond saw fingernails flashing toward his eyes, ducked, and ran into an uppercut. Now a hand was at his right wrist and his gun was being slowly turned on him. Not wanting to kill, he had kept the safety catch up. He tried to get his thumb to it. A boot hit him in the side of the head, and he let the gun go and fell back. Through a red mist he saw the muzzle of the gun pointing at his face. The thought flashed through his mind that he was going to die—die for showing mercy! . . .

Suddenly the gun-muzzle had gone and the weight of the man was off him. Bond got to his knees and then to his feet. The body, spread-eagled in the grass beside him, gave a last kick. There were bloody rents in the back of the dungarees. Bond looked around. The four men from the station were in a group. Bond undid the strap of his crash helmet and rubbed the side of his head. He said, "Well, thanks. Who did it?"

Nobody answered. The men looked embarrassed.

Bond walked toward them, puzzled. "What's up?"

Suddenly Bond caught a trace of movement behind the men. An extra leg showed—a woman's leg. Bond laughed out loud. The men grinned sheepishly and looked behind them. Mary Ann Russell, in a brown shirt and black jeans, came out from behind them with her hands up. One of the hands held what looked like a .22 target pistol. She brought her hands down and tucked the pistol into the top of her jeans. She came up to Bond. She said anxiously, "You won't blame anybody, will you? I just wouldn't let them leave this morning without me." Her eyes pleaded. "Rather lucky I did come, really. I mean, I just happened to get to you first. No one wanted to shoot for fear of hitting you."

Bond smiled into her eyes. He said, "If you hadn't come, I'd have had to break that dinner date." He turned back to the men, his voice businesslike. "All right. One of you take the motorbike and report the gist of this to Colonel Schreiber. Say we're waiting for his team before we take a look at the hide-out. And would he include a couple of anti-sabotage men. That shaft may be boobytrapped. All right?"

Bond took the girl by the arm. He said, "Come over here. I want to show you a bird's nest."

"Is that an order?"

"Yes."

—1960

CRITICAL BIBLIOGRAPHY

Cawelti, John G., and Bruce A. Rosenberg. *The Spy Story*. Chicago: U of Chicago P, 1987.

Dinan, John A. *The Pulp Western: A Popular History of the Western Fiction Magazine in America*. San Bernardino: Borgo Press, 1983.

Fisher, Margery. *The Bright Face of Danger*. Boston: Horn Book, 1986.

Green, Martin. *Dreams of Adventure, Deeds of Empire*. New York: Basic Books, 1979.

——. *The Great American Adventure*. Boston: Beacon, 1984.

——. *Seven Types of Adventure Tale: An Etiology of a Major Genre*. University Park: Pennsylvania State UP, 1991.

Howe, Susanne. *Novels of Empire*. New York: Columbia UP, 1949.

Jones, Daryl. *The Dime Novel Western*. Bowling Green: BGSU Popular P, 1978.

Jones, Robert Kenneth. *The Lure of Adventure*. Mercer Island: Starmont House, 1989.

McCormick, Donald, and Katy Fletcher. *Spy Fiction: A Connoisseur's Guide*. New York: Facts on File, 1990.

Milne, Gordon. *Ports of Call: A Study of the American Nautical Novel*. Lanham: UP of America, 1986.

Orel, Harold. *The Historical Novel from Scott to Sabatini: Changing Attitudes toward a Literary Genre, 1814–1920*. New York: St. Martin's Press, 1995.

Rovin, Jeff. *Adventure Heroes: Legendary Characters from Odysseus to James Bond*. New York: Facts on File, 1994.

Sampson, Robert. *Deadly Excitements: Shadows and Phantoms*. Bowling Green: BGSU Popular P, 1989.

——. *Yesterday's Faces: A Study of Series Characters in the Early Pulp Magazines (Vol. 1)—Glory Figures*. Bowling Green: BGSU Popular P, 1983.

——. *Yesterday's Faces: A Study of Series Characters in the Early Pulp Magazines (Vol. 2)—Strange Days*. Bowling Green: BGSU Popular P, 1984.

——. *Yesterday's Faces: A Study of Series Characters in the Early Pulp Magazines (Vol. 3)—From the Dark Side*. Bowling Green: BGSU Popular P, No copyright date listed.

——. *Yesterday's Faces: A Study of Series Characters in the Early Pulp Magazines (Vol. 4)—The Solvers*. Bowling Green: BGSU Popular P, 1987.

——. *Yesterday's Faces: A Study of Series Characters in the Early Pulp Magazines (Vol. 5)—Dangerous Horizons*. Bowling Green: BGSU Popular P, 1991.

——. *Yesterday's Faces: A Study of Series Characters in the Early Pulp Magazines (Vol. 6)—Violent Lives*. Bowling Green: BGSU Popular P, 1993.

Shaw, Harry E. *The Forms of Historical Fiction: Sir Walter Scott and His Successors*. Ithaca: Cornell UP, 1983.

Street, Brian V. *The Savage in Literature: Representations of "Primitive" Society in English Fiction, 1858–1920*. London: Routledge & Kegan Paul, 1975.

Taves, Brian. *The Romance of Adventure: The Genre of Historical Adventure Movies*. Jackson: UP of Mississippi, 1993.

Tuska, Jon, and Vicki Piekarski, eds. *Encyclopedia of Frontier and Western Fiction*. New York: McGraw-Hill, 1983.

Van Hise, James, ed. *Pulp Heroes of the Thirties*. Yucca Valley: Midnight Graffiti, 1994.

Wright, Will. *Sixguns and Society: A Structural Study of the Western*. Berkeley: U of California P, 1975.

Zweig, Paul. *The Adventurer*. New York: Basic Books, 1974.

CRITICAL PERSPECTIVES ON POPULAR FICTION

The study of popular culture at the university level is a fairly recent development. Along with Russel B. Nye, Ray B. Browne has spearheaded the push to legitimize popular culture studies in academic circles. Browne created The Popular Culture Association (an international organization of teachers and scholars that sponsors an annual national convention), and he established, in the early 1970s, the only Popular Culture Studies department in the country at Bowling Green State University in Ohio. He founded the *Journal of Popular Culture* and the Popular Press, both major publishing venues, and he is the prolific author of numerous book-length popular culture monographs, including *Challenges in American Culture* (1970), *Popular Culture and the Expanding Consciousness* (1973), *Theories & Methodologies in Popular Culture* (1975), and *Heroes and Humanities: Detective Fiction and Culture* (1986). Browne's essay, "Popular Culture—New Notes Toward a Definition," provides one of the finest general working definitions of popular culture. It also discusses the relationship between folk, popular, and elite cultures, and it argues that popular culture has a history predating the origins of the Industrial Revolution and mass produced culture. Popular fiction, Browne would agree, is an important part of our society's popular culture.

The foremost scholar of formula fiction is John G. Cawelti. Author of such works as *Apostles of the Self-Made Man* (1965), *The Six-Gun Mystique* (1971), *Adventure, Mystery, and Romance: Formula Stories as Art and Popular Culture* (1976), and *The*

Spy Story (co-authored with Bruce A. Rosenberg, 1987), Cawelti's scholarly investigations into popular literary formulas, such as the Western, have profoundly influenced the direction of formula studies over the past several decades. Cawelti was one of the first to recognize the cultural and artistic values of popular formulas. His essay, "The Concept of Formula in the Study of Popular Literature," outlines a detailed examination of the dynamic relationship between culture and popular literary formula.

The remaining essays in this section illustrate a variety of theory-based, critical investigations of popular fiction. Each essay features a particular methodological approach to an analysis of a specific genre of popular fiction. Arthur Asa Berger offers a psychological scrutiny of the horror story in *"Frankenstein:* The Modern Prometheus." Linda Barlow and Jayne Ann Krentz, in "Beneath the Surface: The Hidden Codes of Romance," utilize a structuralist approach to the study of the popular romance, while Gail Landsman employs a mythological discussion of speculative fiction in her essay, "Science Fiction: The Rebirth of Mythology." Ernest Mandel applies an ideological review of crime fiction in "A Marxist Interpretation of the Crime Story," and Jane Tompkins provides a feminist reading of the Western in "Women and the Language of Men."

Collectively, all of these essays demonstrate that popular fiction can be studied in much the same way as elite literature, and that our understanding and appreciation of popular fiction can be enhanced by the use of traditional cultural and literary theoretical approaches.

RAY B. BROWNE

POPULAR CULTURE—NEW NOTES TOWARD A DEFINITION

Popular Culture, in its simplest definition, is the way of life we inherit from the generations before us, use ourselves, and pass on to our followers. It is our attitudes, habits and actions: how we act and why we act the way we do; what we eat, wear; our buildings, roads and means of travel; our entertainments, sports; our politics, religion, medical practices; our beliefs and activities and what shapes and controls them. It is, in other words, the world we live in.

Popular culture is the culture of the people, of *all* the people, as distinguished from a select, small elite group. It is also the dominant culture of minorities—of ethnic, social, religious, or financial minorities—simply because their way of life is, by and large, not accepted into the elite culture of the dominant group. As the way of life of a people, popular culture has existed since the most primitive times, when it was simple and uncomplicated. It has obviously become more complex and sophisticated as means of communicating and ways of life have developed.

Although popular culture has existed as long as people have, the concentrated and widespread academic study of people's ways—even among anthropologists and sociologists—is a recent development. As such, today, of course, definitions differ somewhat as to what popular culture really is. In the recent past, many people have felt that popular culture is mass culture—that is, the common culture of the masses of people—and therefore it could develop only after the eighteenth century, when rapid means of producing the printed word came into being. Though this attitude has some validity and appeal, it may be too narrow in concept and too short in time-span to be sufficiently comprehensive. The development of rapid means of printing and distribution led to a faster way of disseminating people's culture than had existed before, to be sure, and the very means of distribution increasingly created its own culture. But before this phenomenon people had had much culture in common; nowadays we call that "folk culture."

Folk culture traditionally had to a certain extent been individual and community oriented. Individual artisans and artists developed their own aspects of culture and folk community life evolved its own characteristics. Both aspects often were of necessity units unto themselves. After the eighteenth century, with the invention of movable type and rapid printing presses "folk culture" underwent some drastic changes. Wide and rapid dissemination of cultural phenomena forced former folk communities to become parts of a larger world, and mixing the cultures made them more similar. The development of machines to mass produce thousands or millions of articles has had a dramatic and lasting influence. The means of dissemination always influences, or controls, the material being disseminated. Technology, of whatever degree of sophistication, holds our way of life in an iron grip. So, through the years, newspapers, magazines, radio, television and movies, as well as the numerous other means of communication, have demanded and worked best with a certain sameness in the material being communicated. This sameness created patterns of expectancy and understanding that appealed to a majority of the intended audience, all of which make dissemination easier and more profitable.

This is not to say, of course, that in this new mix of culture, folk life has disappeared. On the contrary, folk culture is still important—though on a modified scale—and remains very much alive. Folklorists recognize that old definitions of the field of their interests were too narrow and inflexible in the past and needed to be broadened, as indeed they have been.

Another conventional way to define popular culture is to distinguish among three areas of society—the elite, the mass and the folk. In such an arrangement, generally speaking, the elite and the folk each constitute roughly ten percent of society, each on opposite ends of the social and education line. Such a division leaves approximately 80 per cent of society for what many people call "mass" or "popular" culture. Such a distinction must be generalized and indeed might be somewhat artificial and arbitrary, since, in the anthropological sense of the term, virtually all people of a nation live in the same kind of life, are acted on by the same ways of behavior; they experience the same buildings, use the same kinds of transportation, hear the same music on radio, television or in public performances, see the same movies and television programs, attend the same sports events, eat at the same kinds of restaurants, etc. Thus Americans live an *American way of life,* English have an English way of life, Eskimoes have their own way of life; though an alien looking down from another planet would clearly tend to group all people on Earth as living substantially the same kind of life. Many people like to view mass and popular culture as one and the same and as the massive section lost between elite and folk cultures. This large field of phenomena was possible only after the development of rapid means of disseminating culture such as the electronic media.

There is, of course, more to popular culture than that which is distributed by the electronic media, though they surely have a major impact. Popular culture consists of our patterns of thought and behavior, our educational system, what we study and why and how.

A series of graphs might be useful at this time to show the interrelatedness among the various aspects of culture. Traditionally cultures have been tiered according to degrees of sophistication, with the elite being on top and the folk on the bottom (fig. 1). Folklore scholars, however, finally tired of having their field of interest always relegated to the lowest, and inferior, level, and have quite properly insisted that all cultures draw from and feed into folk patterns (fig. 2). Figure 1 is false therefore because "elite" culture is not "higher" and "superior" to folk; in fact, at least in an anthropological and scholarly sense, it is only different. To change the figure from a vertical scaling to a horizontal and thus to demonstrate that neither is "superior" to the other but merely different is a more proper delineation. To a large extent, however, even figure 2 is artificial because the solid lines separating the "three" cultures seem to mark clear and distinct separations one from another, when in fact even the most casual observation of society reveals that there are not hard and fast lines separating one from the other; in fact all three—elite, popular and folk—exist pretty much at the same time in the same place (with noticeable shadings of differences). Perhaps the most revealing metaphor for culture is a flattened ellipse or a lens (the CBS logo is a good model) with elite and folk cultures on either end, both looking fundamentally alike in many ways and both having some characteristics in common. In the center, largest in bulk by far is popular culture, with no lines separating one from the other, only degrees of emphasis. Popular culture therefore consists of all the aspects of civilization that make up a way of life.

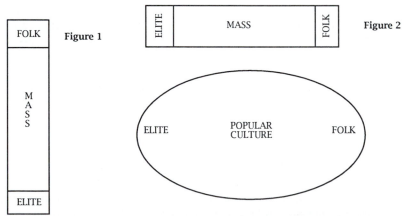

Figure 3

If people's popular culture consists of a total way of life, it would seem obvious that it is necessary that we understand this culture if we are to understand our country, our way of life, if we are to understand ourselves, if, in other words, we are to be "educated" in any sense of the word. The controversy of what constitutes a proper education is old and is yet very much unsettled, especially in these days when many people advocate a trip "back to basics." Socrates held to the injunction "Know thyself." Plato, following hard on Socrates' counsel, was all for educating out of the context of life, for dealing only in the ideal, for despising the common people—whom he called the oxen of the world—and their way of life. The same attitude was voiced in the eighteenth century by the Englishman Edmund Burke. Burke, as every student of American history remembers, had been a friend of the American Revolution, but he condemned the French—and all the masses—as the "swinish multitude" when they tried to throw off their monarch's yoke. Burke's attitude was condemned by the American patriot Tom Paine and though it is still held by many this attitude has been gradually ground away throughout the history of this country. In fact, it seems obvious that the democratic way of life demands respect for and understanding of a *total people's culture.* The Declaration of Independence proclaimed the fact and the Bill of Rights guaranteed it.

Americans generally have always been a practical people, and most realize that one must train for life as we lead it. It is not proper for people to be educated for life as it might have been or might become, or as we wish ideally it were. One makes more progress toward improving the conditions of life if he recognizes where reality begins and sets out to work from that point, not from some idealized position where he is not and cannot ever be. Many Americans therefore think that the old Socratic injunction of "Know thyself," must be modified to read "Know yourself in your surroundings."

Commenting on the change in people's attitudes toward popular culture, Irving Wallace, present-day author of half a dozen bestselling novels and co-editor of, among various books, *The People's Almanac* (1976) and *The Book of Lists* (1977), observed, "The relationship between the critical community and the popular author has changed in recent years. Some critics are honest enough to respect public taste, or at least be curious about it and treat it seriously." Concerning his own purposes in writing, Wallace said, "I write to explore other human beings, the human condition, through my own psyche and within my own limitations."

Ross Macdonald, contemporary creator of the great detective Lew Archer, commented, somewhat on the same subject as Wallace's, on the value of popular culture in our society. "We learn to see reality through the popular arts we create and patronize. That's what they're for. That's why we love them." And Irving Wallace, again, attested to the power of the popular arts as model when he commented: "I was always going to be a writer. But if I ever faltered in my singleminded ambition, then surely there was popular art to influence me in my ambition and prop me up and carry me along."

The value of popular culture as a window to the human condition is timeless. Perhaps because it is less artful, less altered by the alchemy of the artist, popular culture is often a more truthful picture of what the people were thinking and doing at any given time than artistic creations are. In other words, a catalogue of what Athenians in Socrates' time were wearing, eating, drinking, joking about, how they were reacting to sports, their sex habits, their whole mode of life, might be more revealing of the real Athens than the philosophy of Socrates is. They surely would be more *important.* Realizing the value of these documents of everyday life, Thomas Jefferson commented ". . . It is the duty of every good citizen to use all the opportunities which occur to him for preserving documents relating to the history of our country."

Jefferson might wisely have expanded his call to collect documents to include the preservation of all kinds of artifacts. If, for example, one wants to understand

Shakespeare's plays fully, he studies outside the dramas, in what was going on in London at the time, the attitude of the people toward England's kings and queens, toward war, housing, poverty, foreigners, etc.

If one wants to understand eighteenth-century America he must read the old broadsides, sing the contemporary songs, investigate the wills and inventories of holdings, get as much into the lifestyle as possible, investigate all kinds of records.

In order to understand George Washington, for example, one needs to visit Mt. Vernon and while there study deeply the physical setting in which the man lived and worked: the house, the furniture, the geography of the surrounding houses, the slave culture, modes of transportation, distance, the music that was a part of the daily household. And the visitor must visit and examine the artifacts in the museum—the clothing, the trinkets, items of daily living; why, for example, was the set of dental equipment used on slaves' teeth composed of five iron instruments, probably made by the local blacksmith and easily bent, while Mr. Washington's set was of eight stainless steel instruments that probably could easily be used by dentists today? These artifacts tell us much, if only we learn to read and understand them, if we will listen to their stories.

If a picture is worth a thousand words, a museum is worth a million words, or a hundred books. And actually living the life—though the effort is to a large extent make-believe—is worth millions of words more. Thus one learns much from visiting restored historical communities and living museums and seeing how people actually dressed, behaved, talked in different times. Such communities are travels in time just like present-day travels in geography, and just as valuable.

In order to understand present-day life, the place of the sports hero in our financial and cultural hierarchy, for example, obviously one must understand the setting. The weakness of many interpretations of life comes from the fact that the person doing the interpretation uses an artificial and half-complete setting.

Society cannot comfortably exist without heroes and heroines. The electronic media create and discard heroes so fast that they must always have new ones ready to be brought forward. A study of this need and process tells us much about ourselves. For example, on June 18, 1983 when Sally Ride became the first American woman astronaut she was flung into the heroic mold and immortality because America needed a female in their hall of heroes, at a time when they, especially women, seemed to be fewer than they had been in the past. It will be interesting to see how Ride is built up and into what proportions and how long she will last. The electronic media create and burn out heroes and heroines rapidly. This is a process that we need to understand.

Such an attitude about the value of understanding everyday things is generally appreciated by the public, though often it is minimized by the academic, the so-called intellectual, because he or she is biased. For a long time intellectuals have been fond of quoting the old saying that one never went broke underestimating the intelligence of the American public. But is such a statement valid or is it the rankest snobbery? Is it for or against democracy? In America the answer obviously is of the greatest importance because it cuts to the heart of our political beliefs.

But one should not act under the false assumption that one's attitude toward the elite or the democratic should dictate whether or not the person wants to know about and understand all aspects of culture. One should always make a distinction between studying cultural phenomena in order to understand them and actually approving of or participating in them. For example, we do not have to engage in professional sports, or approve of them, in order to be interested in them or to want to understand their place in society; one does not even have to own a set to realize that television has a great impact on our lives, and to realize that he or she needs to comprehend this phenomenon. In understanding one does not have to love—or to hate. *Understanding* is the goal. Then one can shape one's life according to his or her likes or dislikes. But understanding is or should be requisite.

What, then, is the role of the intelligent and educated citizen in society? How does one start on the road to education? American education is, and perhaps always should be, in a state of crisis and consequently always debated. This means that we should try to understand, then act. We should not be afraid to examine our assumptions. To this end Raymond Williams, a noted British critic, has stated:

> The human crisis is always a crisis of understanding; what we genuinely understand we can do. . . . There are ideas, and ways of thinking, with the seeds of life in them, and there are others, perhaps deep in our minds, with the seeds of general death. Our measure of success in recognizing these kinds, and in naming them making possible their common recognition, may be literally the measure of the future.

Toward better preparing the citizen for life, the critics, Stuart Hall and Paddy Whannel pointed out an important value in popular culture, aside from its enjoyable aspect:

> Perhaps the most significant connection between popular art and high art is to be seen in the way popular work helps the serious artist to focus the actual world, to draw upon common types, to sharpen his observations and to detach the large but hidden movements of society. New art forms frequently arise when profound modifications are taking place in social life and in the 'structure of feeling' in the society. Often this change is first recorded in popular work, and new popular themes and conventions are devised to deal with them, or to express them.

In other words, it could be argued that in the arts the forms and shapes, and ideas, that last, come up from the people, or at least last longest among them.

Lewis Mumford, one of the keener minds of our day, observed that education should be looked upon as a "lifelong transformation of the human personality, in which every aspect of life plays a part." In other words, these individuals, and many others like them, are saying that a person owes it to himself to develop his learning as much as possible, and this learning should include the popular culture.

Perhaps a word of caution might be necessary. Educators who insist that popular culture should be studied emphasize that it should be a supplement to not a substitute for the so-called classics of culture and civilization. Although for too long popular culture was excluded from the ordinary fare of education and should now be included, the more traditional materials—where their validity can be demonstrated and proved—should be retained. Popular culture should be studied to more nearly round out—to deepen and to enrich—at least portions of the more conventional curriculum. Education is too important to settle for anything less.

JOHN G. CAWELTI

THE CONCEPT OF FORMULA IN THE STUDY OF POPULAR LITERATURE

The growing interest among humanistic scholars and teachers in popular culture is one of the more exciting academic trends of the present day. This field of study represents a great expansion in the range of human expression and activity subjected to the scrutiny of historians and scholars of the arts. Consequently one of the central problems in giving some shape to our inquiries into popular culture has been the need for analytical concepts which might enable us to find our way through the huge amount of material which is the potential subject-matter of studies in popular culture. Moreover, we badly need some way of relating the various perspectives, historical, psychological, sociological and aesthetic which are being used in the investigation of such phenomena as the Western, the spy story, pop music, the comic strip, film and TV.

To some extent, students of popular culture have simply applied to a wider range of materials the historical and critical methods of traditional humanistic scholarship. This practice has led to more complex analyses of such popular forms as the detective story and richer, more carefully researched accounts of the development of various popular traditions. Approaching the materials of popular culture with the traditional arsenal of humanistic disciplines is certainly a necessary first step. Nonetheless, the analysis of popular culture is somewhat different from that of the fine arts. When we are studying the fine arts, we are essentially interested in the unique achievement of the individual artist, while in the case of popular culture, we are dealing with a product that is in some sense collective. Of course it is possible to study the fine arts as collective products just as it is possible to examine individual works of popular culture as unique artistic creations. In the former case, the present discussion should apply with some qualifications to the fine arts, while in the latter, the traditional methods of humanistic scholarship are obviously the most appropriate, with some allowance for the special aesthetic problems of the popular arts.

Students of popular culture have defined the field in terms of several different concepts. When scholars were first interesting themselves in dime novels, detective stories, etc. they thought of them as subliterature. This concept reflected the traditional qualitative distinction between high culture and mass culture. Unfortunately it was really too vague to be of much analytical use. Even if one could determine where literature left off and subliterature began, a distinction that usually depended on the individual tastes of the inquirer, the term suggested only that the object of study was a debased form of something better. Like many concepts that have been applied to the study of popular culture, the idea of subliterature inextricably confused normative and descriptive problems.

Four additional concepts have come into fairly wide use in recent work: a) the analysis of cultural themes; b) the concept of medium; c) the idea of myth; and d) the concept of formula. I would like to deal briefly with the first three, mainly by way of getting to a fuller discussion of what I consider the most promising concept of all.

The analysis of cultural, social, or psychological themes is certainly a tried and true method of dealing with popular culture. In essence, what the analyst does is to determine what themes appear most often or most prominently in the works under analysis and to group different works according to the presence or absence of the themes he is interested in. Unfortunately, there is a certain vagueness about the concept of theme. Such various things as the ideal of progress, the oedipal conflict, racism, and innocence have all been treated as themes. In effect, a theme turns out to be any prominent element or characteristic of a group of works which seems to have some relevance to a social or cultural problem. Though the vagueness of the concept can be cleared up when the investigator defines the particular theme or set of themes he is interested in, the concept of theme still seems inadequate because it depends on the isolation of particular elements from a total structure. This not only tends to oversimplify the works under investigation, but to lead to the kind of falsifying reduction that translates one kind of experience into another. Thus, a story of a certain kind becomes a piece of social rhetoric or the revelation of an unconscious urge. No doubt a story is or can be these things and many others, but to treat it as if it were only one or another social or psychological function is too great a reduction. What we need is a concept that will enable us to deal with the total structure of themes and its relationship to the story elements in the complete work.

The concept of medium has become notorious through the fascinating theories of Marshall McLuhan, Walter Ong and others who insist that medium rather than content or form as we have traditionally understood them ought to be the focus of our cultural analyses. This concept seems to have a particular application to studies in popular culture because many of the works we are concerned with are transmitted through the new electric media which McLuhan sees as so different from the Gutenberg galaxy, the media associated with print. The concept of medium is an important one and McLuhan is doubtless correct that it has been insufficiently explored in the past, but I am not persuaded that more sophisticated studies of the nature of media will do away with the need for generalizations about content. I am sure that we will need to revise many of our notions about where medium leaves off and content begins as the new studies in media progress, but for the present, I would like to forget about the idea of medium altogether with the explanation that I'm concerned with a different kind of problem, the exploration of the content of the popular media.

One more distinction along these lines is necessary. In this paper I will be concerned primarily with stories and with understanding the various cultural significances of these stories. While a large proportion of popular culture can be defined as stories of different kinds, this is certainly not an exhaustive way of defining popular culture. Just as there are the other arts than fiction, so there are works of popular culture which do not tell stories. With additional qualifications the concepts I am seeking to define are applicable to the analysis of other expressions of popular culture than those embodied in stories, but to keep my task as simple as possible, I have chosen to limit myself to the discussion of stories.

The most important generalizing concept which has been applied to cultural studies in recent years is that of myth. Indeed, it could be argued that the concept of formula which I will develop in the course of this paper is simply another variation of the idea of myth. But if this is the case, I would argue that distinctions between meanings of the concept of myth are worth making and naming, for many different meanings can be ascribed to the term. In fact, the way in which some people use the term myth hardly separates it from the concept of theme, as when we talk about the myth of progress or the myth of success. There is also another common meaning of the term which further obfuscates its use, namely myth as a common belief which is demonstrably false as in the common opposition between myth and reality. Thus, when a critic uses the term myth one must first get clear whether he means to say that the object he is describing is a false belief, or simply a belief, or something still more complicated like an archetypal pattern. Moreover, because of the special connection of the term myth with a group of stories which have survived from ancient cultures, particularly the Greco-Roman, the scholar who uses the concept in the analysis of contemporary popular culture sometimes finds himself drawn into another kind of reductionism which takes the form of statements like the following: "the solution of the paradox of James Bond's popularity may be, not in considering the novels as thrillers, but as something very different, as historic epic and romance, based on the stuff of myth and legend." But if the retelling of myth is what makes something popular why on earth didn't Mr. Fleming simply retell the ancient myths.

Because of this great confusion about the term myth, I propose to develop another concept which I think I can define more clearly and then to differentiate this concept from that of myth, thereby giving us two more clearly defined generalizing concepts to work with. Let me begin with a kind of axiom or assumption which I hope I can persuade you to accept without elaborate argumentation: all cultural products contain a mixture of two kinds of elements: conventions and inventions. Conventions are elements which are known to both the creator and his audience beforehand—they consist of things like favorite plots, stereotyped characters, accepted ideas, commonly known metaphors and other linguistic devices, etc. Inventions, on the other hand, are elements which are uniquely imagined by the creator such as new kinds of characters, ideas, or linguistic forms. Of course it is difficult to distinguish in every case between conventions and inventions because many elements lie somewhere along a continuum between the two poles. Nonetheless, familiarity with a group of literary works will usually soon reveal what the major conventions are and therefore, what in the case of an individual work is unique to that creator.

Convention and invention have quite different cultural functions. Conventions represent familiar shared images and meanings and they assert an ongoing continuity of values; inventions confront us with a new perception or meaning which we have not realized before. Both these functions are important to culture. Conventions help maintain a culture's stability while inventions help it respond to changing circumstances and provide new information about the world. The same thing is true on the individual level. If the individual does not encounter a large number of conventionalized experiences and situations, the strain on his sense of continuity and identity will lead to great tensions and even to neurotic breakdowns. On the other hand, without new information about his world, the individual will be increasingly unable to cope with it and will withdraw behind a barrier of conventions as some people withdraw from life into compulsive reading of detective stories.

Most works of art contain a mixture of convention and invention. Both Homer and Shakespeare show a large proportion of conventional elements mixed with inventions of great genius. Hamlet, for example, depends on a long tradition of stories of revenge, but only Shakespeare could have invented a character who embodies so many complex perceptions of life that every generation is able to find new ways of viewing him. So long as cultures were relatively stable over long periods of time and homogeneous in their structure, the relation between convention and invention in works of literature posed relatively few problems. Since the Renaissance, however, modern cultures have become increasingly heterogeneous and pluralistic in their structure and discontinuous in time. In consequence, while public communications have become increasingly conventional in order to be understood by an extremely broad and diverse audience, the intellectual elites have placed ever higher valuation on invention out of a sense that rapid cultural changes require continually new perceptions of the world. Thus we have arrived at a situation in which the model great work of literature is Joyce's *Finnegans Wake,* a creation which is almost as far as possible along the continuum toward total invention as it is possible to go without leaving the possibility of shared meanings behind. At the same time, there has developed a vast amount of literature characterized by the highest degree of conventionalization.

This brings us to an initial definition of formula. A formula is a conventional system for structuring cultural products. It can be distinguished from form which is an invented system of organization. Like the distinction between convention and invention, the distinction between formula and form can be best envisaged as a continuum between two poles, one pole is that of a completely conventional structure of conventions—an episode of the Lone Ranger or one of the Tarzan books comes close to this pole; the other end of the continuum is a completely original structure which orders inventions—*Finnegans Wake* is perhaps the best example of this, though one might also cite such examples as Resnais' film *Last Year at Marienbad,* T. S. Eliot's poem *The Waste Land,* or Becket's play *Waiting for Godot.* All of these works not only manifest a high degree of invention in their elements but unique organizing principles. *The Waste Land* makes the distinction even sharper for that poem contains a substantial number of conventional elements—even to the point of using quotations from past literary works—but these elements are structured in such a fashion that a new perception of familiar elements is forced upon the reader.

I would like to emphasize that the distinction between form and formula as I am using it here is a descriptive rather than a qualitative one. Though it is likely for a number of reasons that a work possessing more form than formula will be a greater work, we should avoid this easy judgment in our study of popular culture. In distinguishing form from formula we are trying to deal with the relationship between the work and its culture, and not with its artistic quality. Whether or not a different set of aesthetic criteria are necessary in the judgment of formula as opposed to formulaic works is an important and interesting question, but necessarily the subject of another series of reflections.

We can further differentiate the conception of formula by comparing it to genre and myth. Genre, in the sense of tragedy, comedy, romance, etc., seems to be based on a difference between basic attitudes or feelings about life. I find Northrop Frye's suggestion that the genres embody fundamental archetypal patterns reflecting stages of the human life cycle, a very fruitful idea here. In Frye's sense of the term genre and myth are universal patterns of action which manifest themselves in all human cultures. Following Frye, let me briefly suggest a formulation of this kind— genre can be defined as a structural pattern which embodies a universal life pattern or myth in the materials of language; formula, on the other hand, is a cultural pattern; it represents the way in which a culture has embodied both mythical archetypes and its own preoccupations in narrative form.

An example will help clarify this distinction. The western and the spy story can both be seen as embodiments of the archetypal pattern of the hero's quest which Frye discusses under the general heading of the mythos of romance. Or if we prefer psychoanalytic archetypes these formulas embody the Oedipal myth in fairly explicit fashion, since they deal with the hero's conquest of a dangerous and powerful figure. However, though we can doubtless characterize both Western and spy stories in terms of these universal archetypes, they do not account for the basic and important differences in setting, characters, and action between the Western and the spy story. These differences are clearly cultural and they reflect the particular preoccupations and needs of the time in which they were created and the group which created them: the Western shows its nineteenth century American origin while the spy story reflects the fact that it is largely a twentieth century British creation. Of course, a formula articulated by one culture can be taken over by another. However, we will often find important differences in the formula as it moves from one culture or from one period to another. For example, the gunfighter western of the 1950s is importantly different from the cowboy romances of Owen Wister and Zane Grey, just as the American spy stories of Donald Hamilton differ from the British secret agent adventures of Eric Ambler and Graham Greene.

The cultural nature of formulas suggests two further points about them. First, while myths, because of their basic and universal nature turn up in many different manifestations, formulas, because of their close connection to a particular culture and period of time, tend to have a much more limited repertory of plots, characters, and settings. For example, the pattern of action known generally as the Oedipus myth can be discerned in an enormous range of stories from Oedipus Rex to the latest Western. Indeed, the very difficulty with this myth as an analytical tool is that it is so universal that it hardly serves to differentiate one story from another. Formulas, however, are much more specific: Westerns must have a certain kind of setting, a particular cast of characters, and follow a limited number of lines of action. A Western that does not take place in the West, near the frontiers, at a point in history when social order and anarchy are in tension, and that does not involve some form of pursuit, is simply not a Western. A detective story that does not involve the solution of a mysterious crime is not a detective story. This greater specificity of plot, character, and setting reflects a more limited framework of interests, values, and tensions that relate to culture rather than to the generic nature of man.

The second point is a hypothesis about why formulas come into existence and enjoy such wide popular use. Why of all the infinite possible subjects for fictions do a few like the adventures of the detective, the secret agent, and the cowboy so dominate the field.

I suggest that formulas are important because they represent syntheses of several important cultural functions which, in modern cultures, have been taken over by the popular arts. Let me suggest just one or two examples of what I mean. In earlier more homogeneous cultures religious ritual performed the important function of articulating and reaffirming the primary cultural values. Today, with cultures composed of a multiplicity of differing religious groups, the synthesis of values and their reaffirmation has become an increasingly important function of the mass media and the popular arts. Thus, one important dimension of formula is social or cultural ritual. Homogeneous cultures also possessed a large repertory of games and songs which all members of the culture understood and could participate in both for a sense of group solidarity and for personal enjoyment and recreation.

Today, the great spectator sports provide one way in which a mass audience can participate in games together. Artistic formulas also fulfill this function in that they constitute entertainments with rules known to everyone. Thus, a very wide audience can follow a Western, appreciate its fine points and vicariously participate in its pattern of suspense and resolution. Indeed one of the more interesting ways of defining a Western is as a game: a Western is a three-sided game played on a field where the middle line is the frontier and the two main areas of play are the settled town and the savage wilderness. The three sides are the good group of townspeople who stand for law and order, but are handicapped by lack of force; the villains who reject law and order and have force; and the hero who has ties with both sides. The object of the game is to get the hero to lend his force to the good group and to destroy the villain. Various rules determine how this can be done; for example, the hero cannot use force against the villain unless strongly provoked. Also like games, the formula always gets to its goal. Someone must win, and the story must be resolved.

This game dimension of formulas has two aspects. First, there is the patterned experience of excitement, suspense, and release which we associate with the functions of entertainment and recreation. Second, there is the aspect of play as ego-enhancement through the temporary resolution of inescapable frustrations and tensions through fantasy. As Piaget sums up this aspect of play:

> Conflicts are foreign to play, or, if they do occur, it is so that the ego may be freed from them by compensation or liquidation whereas serious activity has to grapple with conflicts which are inescapable. The conflict between obedience and individual liberty is, for example, the affliction of childhood [and we might note a key theme of the Western] and in real life the only solutions to this conflict are submission, revolt, or cooperation which involves some measure of compromise. In play, however, the conflicts are transposed in such a way that the ego is revenged, either by suppression of the problem or by giving it an acceptable solution . . . it is because the ego dominates the whole universe in play that it is freed from conflict.

Thus, the game dimension of formula is a culture's way of simultaneously entertaining itself and of creating an acceptable pattern of temporary escape from the serious restrictions and limitations of human life. In formula stories, the detective always solves the crime, the hero always determines and carries out true justice, and the agent accomplishes his mission or at least preserves himself from the omnipresent threats of the enemy.

Finally, formula stories seem to be one way in which the individuals in a culture act out certain unconscious or repressed needs, or express in an overt and symbolic fashion certain latent motives which they must give expression to, but cannot face openly. This is the most difficult aspect of formula to pin down. Many would argue that one cannot meaningfully discuss latent contents or unconscious motives beyond the individual level or outside of the clinical context. Certainly it is easy to generate a great deal of pseudo-psychoanalytic theories about literary formulas and to make deep symbolic interpretations which it is clearly impossible to substantiate convincingly. However, though it may be difficult to develop a reliable method of analysis of this aspect of formulas, I am convinced that the Freudian and Jungian insight that recurrent myths and stories embody a kind of collective dreaming process is essentially correct and has an important application on the cultural as well as the universal level, that is, that the idea of a collective dream applies to formula as well as to myth. But there is no doubt that we need to put much more thought into the relation between these additional dimensions of formula and their basic character as narrative and dramatic constructions.

My argument, then, is that formula stories like the detective story, the Western, the seduction novel, the biblical epic, and many others are structures of narrative conventions which carry out a variety of cultural functions in a unified way. We can best define these formulas as principles for the selection of certain plots, characters, and settings, which possess in addition to their basic narrative structure the dimensions of collective ritual, game and dream. To analyze these formulas we must first define them as narrative structures of a certain kind and then investigate how the additional dimensions of ritual, game and dream have been synthesized into the particular patterns of plot, character and setting which have become associated with the formula. Once we have understood the way in which particular formulas are structured, we will be able to compare them, and also to relate them to the cultures which use them. By these methods I feel that we will arrive at a new understanding of the phenomena of popular literature and new insights into the patterns of culture. The point where we begin to get new insights into culture is where we start to ask how the culture has integrated the different dimensions of game, ritual and dream into a work of art. Can we state the structural principles which govern this integration? If we can do this, we can learn much about how a culture resolves its intrinsic conflicts of value and attitude, how it anneals psychic and social tensions which beset it and therefore something of how it achieves that sense of shared acceptance of life without which a culture cannot long endure.

THE PSYCHOANALYTIC APPROACH
TO THE HORROR STORY

There is much in the adventure story, the horror story, or the tale of romance that connects our world of dreams with our conscious, day-to-day lives. The suave James Bond, for example, has been defined by both his admirers and detractors as being a character who represents nothing more than pure male wish fulfillment. Barbara Cartland's numerous best-selling romance novels, her critics claim, reveal little else but young women's adolescent fantasies about love and marriage. Indeed, for better or worse, popular fiction is the literature of escapism, and an examination of the relationship between the field of psychoanalysis and the various genres of popular storytelling may say a great deal about the social functions of both.

Sigmund Freud was one of the pioneers who initially mapped the terrain of the human mind. In his study, The Interpretation of Dreams *(1899), Freud developed a new theory about the connection between conscious and unconscious thought. Dreams, Freud argued, were the means by which the individual's unconscious could be accessed and evaluated. One of Freud's most important disciples, Carl Jung, applied his own version of Freudian analysis to an examination of literature, art, and cultural myth, and from*

Jung's groundbreaking efforts there developed the school of psychoanalytic criticism in the field of literary studies. Listed among Jung's numerous writings about psychology are The Theory of Psychoanalysis *(1915),* Psychology of the Unconscious *(1916),* Psychological Types *(1921), and* The Undiscovered Self *(1958).*

Jung defined the human mind as being composed of the conscious and the unconscious. He further divided the unconscious into two areas: the personal unconscious and the collective unconscious. According to Jung, the collective unconscious is the repository of the entire human experience (the racial memories of all members of all societies, if you will), and archetypes (certain universal patterns of human behavior and experience) define people's collective unconscious (and, by extension, the way people think and act in society). Jung's efforts influenced an entire generation of literary critics, ranging from Northrop Frye and his own theory of archetypal criticism (and the monomyth) to Joseph Campbell and his comparative approach to the study of world mythologies.

Arthur Asa Berger's essay, "Frankenstein: The New Prometheus" *(published as a chapter in* Popular Culture Genres: Theories and Texts, *1992), provides a reading of Mary Shelley's* Frankenstein *that discusses the psychological role of monsters in horror fiction. Part of the psychology of horror fiction, Berger argues, is the oppositional relationship between symbolic polarities of life and death.*

ARTHUR ASA BERGER

FRANKENSTEIN: THE NEW PROMETHEUS

The Creation of the Novel

The details involving the creation of the book, *Frankenstein,* are almost as incredible as the creation of the central character of the book. The being created by Dr. Victor Frankenstein and commonly known as Frankenstein most certainly is one of the most famous creatures, monsters, nightmare figures—call him or it what you will—in all literature, a figure who has a remarkable hold on our imaginations. (Although unnamed in the book, the monster has come, in popular usage, to be known as Frankenstein. Thus we have films with titles such as *Bride of Frankenstein* that adopt this convention.)

Why the monster is so resonant is something of an enigma. The quotation by Mays refers to the Faust myth and to Milton's *Paradise Lost,* which deal with, among other things, our desire for immortality. In Paradise, Adam and Eve were immortal; it was only after they tasted of the tree of knowledge that they were expelled and became mortal.

Frankenstein was written by Mary Shelley, a nineteen-year-old woman, at the suggestion of the poet Byron. Byron proposed that he, Shelley (a famous poet), Shelley's wife, and a friend, a Dr. Polidori, amuse themselves by each writing a "macabre" story to help pass the time during a summer they were all spending together in Switzerland. The book was published in 1818, which means that Dr. Frankenstein's monster has been scaring the devil out of people for more than 170 years. Mary Shelley described what was on her mind in creating the book in a preface she wrote to the 1831 edition.

> I busied myself *to think of a story* . . . which would speak to the mysterious fears of our nature, and awaken thrilling horror—one to make the reader dread to look round, to curdle the blood and quicken the beatings of the heart. (1967, p. v)

Her words speak very graphically to one of the main functions of horror literature—to provide thrills and to scare people by connecting to various morbid residues in our psyches.

The Creation of the Monster

Why is it that Frankenstein's monster has become so important a figure? Why is it that he dominates our imagination so powerfully? What is it that gives this gigantic, eight-foot figure, created out of dead flesh and yet alive, so much cultural resonance?

The monster is a figure who mediates between dominant oppositions in the book and in the human mind—between life and death. Frankenstein's monster is dead flesh that, somehow, is given the spark of life and, as such, a creature that transcends life and death.

As the monster's creator, Dr. Frankenstein says, in describing his feelings about the creature:

> No one can conceive of the variety of feelings which bore me onwards, like a hurricane, in the first enthusiasm of success. Life and death appeared to me ideal bounds, which I should first break through, and pour a torrent of light into our dark world. A new species would bless me as its creator and source; many happy and excellent natures would owe their being to me. No father could claim the gratitude of his child so completely as I should deserve theirs. Pursuing these reflections, I thought that if I could bestow animation upon lifeless matter, I might in process of time . . . renew life where death had apparently devoted the body to corruption. (1967, pp. 38, 39)

There is a tragic irony in the story for Frankenstein's creation *becomes* a monster who kills everyone his creator loves and wreaks havoc on a world that abhors and shuns him.

Frankenstein's creation turns out to be a monster, it might be argued, by chance and a decent case might be made that he is, in reality, an heroic figure who is driven to commit his crimes by a sense of rejection and alienation. To the extent that he is dead flesh come alive in a world where that never happens, he is one more alien figure from the world of science fiction, which is one reason, as I suggested in my chapter on this subject, some critics see horror as a subgenre of science fiction.[1]

The monster is repudiated by everyone because he is unnatural, because he inspires revulsion, representing as he does the violation of divine law, which tells us that man must not create life, that we must not tamper with natural processes in this area, and that if we do, things will turn out terribly.

The monster, we must remember, did not create himself. In a sense, he is the victim of Dr. Frankenstein's transgressions—of society's inability to see this creature as a new Adam. Thus the monster is justified, in a sense, when he pleads with Dr. Frankenstein, his creator, for understanding.

> Oh, Frankenstein, be not equitable to every other and trample upon me alone, to whom thy justice, and even thy clemency and affection is most due. Remember that I am thy creature; and I ought to be thy Adam, but I am rather the fallen angel who thou drivest from joy for no misdeed. Everywhere I see bliss, from which I alone am irrevocably excluded. I was benevolent and good; misery made me a fiend. Make me happy, and I shall again be virtuous. (1967, p. 84)

This and various other entreaties Frankenstein's creation makes fall on deaf ears and, as a result, he turns against his creator and everyone else. He is, I would argue, as much a victim as a monster, and his definition of himself as "monster" is one that society places upon him and which, ultimately, he comes to accept.

His monsterhood raises an interesting question. What is a monster? From a sociological perspective, one must be labeled a monster and treated as one by others to be confirmed in one's role. In his case, it was the sins of his creator, Dr. Frankenstein, that were visited upon him that led to his becoming a monster and, once confirmed as such, acting accordingly.

Oppositions in the Novel

The selections I have quoted establish the nature of the story. There is a binary opposition that informs the novel—the opposition between life and death. The monster transcends them, and this gives him an anxiety-provoking status. Human beings, we know, are either alive or dead. They are born, live, and die. Frankenstein is something that, somehow, is dead and yet alive, a creature who is the result of meddling by his creator in "realms reserved for God." The monster violates the logical exclusions, alive or dead, and reflecting our deepest fears and anxieties, escapes the control of his creator.

In the natural realm, control is not too great a problem, for all living things eventually die. But what do we do with monsters who are dead, yet somewhat alive? Let us look at this life versus death polarity and the extensions that come from it (Table 1).

These two oppositions reflect the boundaries within which human beings live. The monster's role, however, was to destroy these boundaries in that he represented both life and death, which is reflected in Table 2.

The monster, created from parts of dead bodies, is lifeless matter that somehow, magically, becomes animated. He is not the result of sexual relations between two human beings, the development of an egg into an embryo and the embryo into human form, but is, instead, the result of perverted knowledge, intruding into bounds beyond man's understanding. Dr. Frankenstein, in a sense, can be seen as challenging God and the natural forces of the universe, and suffers grievously for his transgressions.

TABLE 1 Life and Death Polarities

Life	Death
Creation (sex)	Destruction
Naturally born	Naturally died
Growth	Decay
Change	Permanence
Controlled by man (social animal)	Controlled by God (the soul)
Outside: light, air, sun	Inside: dark, putrid
Unitary: from an embryo	Decomposition
Feeling	Insensate

The novel is informed by irony. Dr. Frankenstein's creation is not his Adam, but, instead, a fallen angel—in part because of Victor Frankenstein's refusal to make a companion for his creation. Instead of a "new species to bless its creator," Dr. Frankenstein produces the instrument of his own destruction.

On Monsters and the Psyche

One of the reasons creatures like Frankenstein's monster and other monsters excite and intrigue people is because they wonder what it would be like to be "out of control" the way monsters are—to escape from all the inhibitions society places upon us and, somehow, let ourselves go and do whatever we want to do. Most of us have strong super-egos that inhibit us, but the idea of being powerful, of allowing our impulses free reign, appeals to us while, at the same time, it frightens us.

In *The Strategy of Desire,* Ernest Dichter (a psychologist who developed the science of motivation research for advertisers) makes some interesting points about how people react to monsters.

> He argues that the inability of society to act quickly to control these monsters is really a consequence of society's own guilt. And this guilt is the result of four factors:

TABLE 2 Life Versus Monster Polarity

Life	Monster (Life and Death)
Naturally born	Unnaturally born
Created from living body	Created from dead flesh
Insider: accepted	Outsider: rejected
Sex good: life from life	Sex bad: cannot have life from death
Live but slowly dying	Dead but living
Natural human form	Unnatural human form
Lives in society	Solitary, alien figure
Controlled by society	Not controlled by society
Good	Evil
Outside world: sun, air	Inside world: laboratory, darkness
Beautiful	Ugly

1. A feeling of sharing the responsibility for the creations of these creatures.
2. An expression of a failure to act on the recognition of the essential humanity of these creatures.
3. The feeling that "there, but for the grace of God, go I."
4. Society's recognition of the monster in itself. "How like myself that monster really is." (1960, pp. 196, 197)

One of the problems these monsters create for us is that we do not know where to locate the evil. Is the monster in the creator of the monster or in the monster himself? We solve this problem, Dichter suggests, by having the monster go out of control, thus locating the evil in the monster and making it acceptable to do away with him.

We can attack the monster and experience a kind of guilt-free aggression against an obviously horrible creature that needs to be destroyed. We do not blame Dr. Frankenstein (or the creators of other monsters) for creating someone or something that can go out of control; instead, we blame the monsters, who can be seen, in this respect, as victims of their creators and society. In this regard, consider the monster's touching entreaty to his creator.

> Believe me, Frankenstein, I was benevolent; my soul glowed with love and humanity; but am I not alone, miserably alone? You, my creator, abhor me; what hope can I gather from your fellow creatures, who owe me nothing? They spurn and hate me. . . . Shall I not then hate them who abhor me? I will keep no terms with my enemies. (1967, p. 84)

But Victor Frankenstein shows no *compassion,* the word used by his creation, who then becomes a destructive monster.

On the Psychology of Horror

The oppositions found in *Frankenstein* provide insights into the nature of horror. The book is a classic horror story, which was written for one basic purpose—to scare people. But what is horror? Mary Shelley offers us some insights in her description of a nightmare she had, which, she tells us, led to the creation of the book. She writes:

> I saw—with shut eyes, but acute mental vision—I saw the pale student of unhallowed arts kneeling beside the thing he had put together. I saw the hideous phantasm of a man stretched out, and then, on the working of some powerful engine, show signs of life and stir with an uneasy, half-vital motion. Frightful must it be, for supremely frightful would be the effect of any human endeavor to mock the stupendous mechanism of the Creator of the world. His success would terrify the artist; he would rush away from his odious handwork, horror-stricken. (1967, p. xv)

One aspect of horror, from Mary Shelley's perspective, is ugliness and the grotesque. Horror is also connected with nightmare visions of something dead that, somehow, lives—something that has power but no humanity. The monster, who escapes Dr. Frankenstein's control, is really a mirror of him, for he has searched for knowledge beyond human boundaries and, in that respect, escaped the control of God. Dr. Frankenstein's hubris is reflected in his monster's destructiveness.

Horror is different from terror, which we may describe as an extreme form of fear. Horror involves something more diffuse, a sense of anxiety and dread, tied to the unknown. The significance of the monster is that he (it?) calls forth latent, submerged, morbid, unconscious anxieties in people—he is a nightmare creature who speaks to our secret fears and evokes dread, disgust, fright, and similar feelings in us.

There is, I should point out, a strong Oedipal element in the story (though in a somewhat unnatural form). *Frankenstein* is, after all, a story about a "son" who destroys his "father" (we can substitute creature and creator here). And like the child who must be socialized, must learn language and customs, the monster, a new Prometheus, undergoes the same process of development. When first created, the creature is mute and ignorant. By chance, he has the good fortune to be able to observe a family and gain knowledge about mankind and society, and his development mirrors the development of children, with one major difference. He learns purely by observation, not being able to participate in society.

He is an Adamic figure and he becomes society's stepchild, driven by his terrible loneliness to revenge. "I am miserable," the monster tells his creator, pleading with him for a partner to share his loneliness, "and they shall share my wretchedness." Then he adds, pleading with Dr. Frankenstein:

> Yet it is in your power to recompense me and deliver them from an evil which it only remains for you to make so great, that not only you and your family, but thousands of others, shall be swallowed up in the whirlwinds of its rage. (1967, p. 84)

The monster was not created as an evil thing and was not an evil being at first. He became evil because he was rejected by his creator, shunned by society and denied the one favor he asked—a partner with whom to live so as to avoid what is suggested to be the worst of all curses, loneliness.

Conclusions

The monster, who in popular usage bears his creator's name, is a symbol of incredible resonance. Our interest in horror may reflect our fascination with the mysteries of creation at a time when traditional religions are losing their appeal for many people. In a sense, horror might be seen as a functional alternative to traditional religion (and a reversal of many of its values). *Frankenstein* (and texts in the horror genre) may be seen as a symbol of our desire to escape from the confines of human rationality, a "normal" life and the numerous burdens and limitations that society imposes on us.

The story is also a parable about the evolution of humanity and a warning about the danger of overreaching knowledge. Part of the monster's power, as a symbolic figure, probably stems from the strong Oedipal component of the story—a son who kills (by breaking his heart) his father and all those he loves, and in a vengeance driven fury, wreaks terror on society—until, as the book concludes, he leaps upon a raft of ice that is borne away by waves "and lost in darkness and distance" (1967, p. 206).

From a Freudian psychoanalytic perspective, there may also be an element of castration anxiety (and other disguised and perhaps repressed sexual aspects) to horror stories—that scare the hell out of people (and in films generate almost hysterical screaming at times) yet are eventually resolved in an acceptable manner, with the triumph of good over evil. Whatever the case, horror stories have a curious appeal to us and represent one of the most popular genres of books and films, for reasons which I hope I have helped, to some measure, explain.

Note

1. In the introduction to the Bantam edition of the book, Robert Donald Spector makes this point. He argues that *Frankenstein* ties the gothic romance to modern science and created a "robot" book. (See Scholes, 1967.)

THE STRUCTURALIST APPROACH TO THE ROMANCE STORY

Perhaps no other type of prose lends itself more to structural analysis than does popular fiction. Indeed, the various major genres of popular fiction—such as the horror or the mystery tale—are constructed of a wide range of highly codified literary formulas that define the way in which authors write their stories. S. S. Van Dine, for example, when devising one of his elegant detective tales, followed a precise narrative pattern that dictated everything from his plots to his characters. Van Dine resisted violating the formula of the classic detective story, because the formula proved itself quite successful with his devoted audience. Structured formulas also create and fulfill readers' expectations. When we buy a Western at the local bookstore, we expect certain established conventions to be present in that Western. The story should be set in the American frontier during the nineteenth century, and it should feature characters and dramatic conflicts consistent with that historic place and period. To read a Western in which Martians land and invade Tombstone, Arizona during the gunfight at the OK Corral would violate (and subsequently undermine) reader expectations. Finally, the structured predictability of formula and genre promotes the sale and distribution of popular fiction. When we walk into our local book store wanting to purchase the new Stephen King horror novel, we know we'll find it in the horror section. And when King proves that genre fiction can become best-selling fiction, publishers take notice and encourage other authors to duplicate King's formula. The dynamic relationship among the writer, the audience, and the publisher of popular fiction is founded entirely on structured predictability.

As a field of literary analysis, structuralism evolved from structural linguistics, or the study of how languages provide meaning. Structuralism offers a scientific method for the examination of literature that attempts to discover meaning from its overall structure, in the similar way that meaning is deciphered from the grammatical units of a sentence. Important structural theorists include Roland Barthes (Elements of Semiology, trans. 1967), *Claude Lévi-Strauss* (Structural Anthropology, trans. 1968), *and Vladimir Propp* (The Morphology of the Folktale, 1968). *Structuralist analysis encompasses the related field of semiotics, the science of identifying the meaning of signs in our culture. Thus, using semi-*

otics theory, a particular story is perceived as housing a group of signs or symbols that, when properly decoded and evaluated, reveal its cultural significance.

Linda Barlow and Jayne Ann Krentz, in their essay "Beneath the Surface: The Hidden Codes of Romance," apply a structuralist analysis to the best-selling romance. Their argument suggests that those critics who are hostile to the romance story are "unable to interpret the conventional language of the genre or to recognize in that language the symbols, images, and allusions that are the fundamental stuff of romance."

LINDA BARLOW AND JAYNE ANN KRENTZ

BENEATH THE SURFACE: THE HIDDEN CODES OF ROMANCE

Townsfolk called him devil. For dark and enigmatic Julian, Earl of Ravenwood, was a man with a legendary temper and a first wife whose mysterious death would not be forgotten. Some said the beautiful Lady Ravenwood had drowned herself in the black, murky waters of Ravenwood Pond. Others whispered of foul play and the devil's wrath.

Now country-bred Sophy Dorring is about to become Ravenwood's new bride. Drawn to his masculine strength and the glitter of desire that burned in his emerald eyes, the tawny-haired lass had her own reasons for agreeing to a marriage of convenience . . . Sophy Dorring intended to teach the devil to love.

back cover copy for Seduction, *by Jayne Ann Krentz writing as Amanda Quick, Bantam, 1990.*

It is difficult to explain the appeal of romance novels to people who don't read them. Outsiders tend to be unable to interpret the conventional language of the genre or to recognize in that language the symbols, images, and allusions that are the fundamental stuff of romance. Moreover, romance writers are consistently attacked for their use of this language by critics who fail to fathom its complexities. In a sense, romance writers are writing in a code clearly understood by readers but opaque to others.

The author of a romance novel and her audience enter into a pact with one another. The reader trusts the writer to create and recreate for her a vision of a fictional world that is free of moral ambiguity, a larger-than-life domain in which such ideals as courage, justice, honor, loyalty, and love are challenged and upheld. It is an active, dynamic realm of conflict and resolution, evil and goodness, darkness and light, heroes and heroines, and it is a familiar world in which the roads are well-traveled and the rules are clear. The romance writer gives form and substance to this vision by locking it in language, and the romance reader yields herself to this alternative world in the act of reading, allowing the narrative to engage her mind and her emotions and to provide her with a certain intensity of experience. She knows that certain expectations will be met and that certain conventions will not be violated.

How does the romance writer construct this fictional universe? By means of the figurative language she chooses to employ—rich, evocative diction that is heavy-laden with familiar symbols, images, metaphors, paradoxes, and allusions to the great mythical traditions that reach from ancient Greece to Celtic Britain to the American West. Through this language she creates the plots, characters, and settings that evoke the vision and transport the reader into the landscape of romance.

Because the figurative language, allusions, and plot elements of the best-loved stories are so familiar and accessible, romance writers are often criticized for the lack of originality of our plots (which are regarded as contrived and formulaic) and the excessive lushness or lack of subtlety of our language. In other words, we are condemned for making use of the very codes that are most vital to our genre.

But these codes, familiar though they may be, are extremely powerful. Contained within them is a collection of subtle feminine voices, part myth, part fantasy, part reality, messages that have been passed down from one generation of women to the next. The voices arise from deep within our collective feminine psyche and consciousness, and we suspect that most women have access to them, however strongly they have been defended against or denied.

What are these messages? They include the celebration of feminine wisdom and power. Celebration of female ability to share, empathize, and communicate on the deepest levels. Celebration of the integration of male and female, both within the psyche and in society. Celebration of the reconciling power of love to heal, to renew, to affirm, and to create new life. And finally, celebration of the feminine ability to do battle on the most mythical planes of existence where emotions rise to epic levels, and to temper and transform all this energy in such a way that it is brought down to human levels by the marriage at the end of the book.

Romance novels are often criticized for certain plot elements that occur over and over in the genre—spirited young women forced into marriage with mysterious earls and heroes with dark and dangerous pasts who are bent upon vengeance rather than love. It is possible to write a romance that does not utilize these elements; indeed, it's done all the time. But the books that hit the bestseller lists are invariably those with plots that place an innocent young woman at risk with a powerful, enigmatic male. Her future happiness and *his* depend upon her ability to teach him how to love.

Writers in the genre know that the plot elements that lend themselves to such clashes are those which force the hero and heroine into a highly charged emotional situation which neither can escape without sacrificing his or her agenda: forced marriage, vengeance, kidnapping, and so forth. Such situations effectively ensure intimacy while establishing clear battle lines. They produce conflicts with stakes that are particularly important to women. They promise the possibility of a victory that romance readers find deeply satisfying: a victory that is an affirmation of life, a victory that fuses male and female.

The plot devices in romance novels are based on paradoxes, opposites, and the threat of danger. The more strongly emphasized the contrasts between hero and heroine are, the more the confrontations between the two take on a sense of the heroic. In many cases the heroine must do battle with a hero whose mythical resonance is that of the devil himself. She is light, he is darkness; she is hope, he is despair. The love that develops between them is the mediating, reconciling force.

These heroic quests are often carried out against a lush setting which subtly deepens the sense of danger by presenting yet another contrast. Dark menace can walk through a dazzling ballroom. The devil can pass in high society.

Stories that utilize these elements have always been wildly popular. After being used and reused for centuries, certain plot devices have become associated with an elaborate set of emotional and intellectual responses in the minds of both romance writers and romance readers. When she sits down to pen a novel, the romance writer takes this web of responses for granted. She knows the conventions, she understands the layers of meaning that certain words, phrases, and plot elements have accumulated through the years, and she knows how these meanings have been shaped and refined for romance. She can be confident that her readers also understand these subtleties. The worldwide popularity of romance novels is testimony to the way the familiar codes are universally recognized by women as cues for their deepest thoughts, dreams, and fantasies.

Most of the emotional and intellectual responses generated by romance plot devices are rendered complex by their paradoxical nature: marriages that are simultaneously real and false (the marriage of convenience); heroes who also function as villains; victories that are acts of surrender; seductions in which one is both seducer and seduced; acts of vengeance that conflict with acts of love. Such contradictory elements must be integrated in a happy ending for a romance novel to be deemed successful.

It is the promise of integration and reconciliation which captures the reader's imagination. She is reminded of this tacit contract between herself and the author every time she picks up a book, reads the back cover copy, and registers such code phrases as "a lust for vengeance," "a hunter stalking his prey," "marriage of convenience," "teach the devil to love." Drawing on her own emotional and intellectual background, both inside and outside the romance genre, she responds to these code phrases with lively interest and anticipation as she looks forward to the pleasurable reading experience the novel promises.

The concept of being forced to marry the devil, for instance, resonates with centuries of history, myth, and legend. Both reader and writer understand the allusions. They have knowledge on the subject of devils and demons that is wide ranging, gleaned from philosophy, theology, psychology, and literature, knowledge that encompasses many conflicting facts and cultural traditions. Both reader and writer also have a vast acquaintance with the devil-heroes who appear in romance novels, since there is a time-honored tradition of heroines sent on quests to encounter and transform these masculine creatures of darkness.

When the romance reader picks up a book that describes a marriage of convenience to such a devil-hero, she understands she is being promised a tale that will deliver a strong sense of emotional risk and at the same time resolve paradoxes and integrate opposites. The happy ending will be especially satisfying because it will have been preceded by several exciting clashes between the heroine and her beloved adversary.

To make such clashes work, the hero must be a worthy and suitably dangerous opponent, a larger-than-life male imbued with great power and a mysterious past. He will not run from the coming battle. Recognizing the allusions that testify to his mythic nature, the reader mentally girds herself for the fray when she reads the code words—phrases such as "townsfolk called him devil" on the back of the book. She glories in the expectation of the complex warfare she—in her imaginative identification with the characters—will soon wage. If the romance is well done, she will find herself plunged into a combat in which she will fight on both sides. The romance novel will be a chess game in which the reader simultaneously plays the white and the black, a medieval joust in which she rides both horses into the lists.

Such fantasies are exquisitely subtle and require that the reader be an active participant. She will enjoy the combat, relish the danger, and, perhaps most intriguing, exercise the full range of her options. This, by the way, is one of the true joys of romance fantasies. The reader knows that in the conflict between hero and heroine the heroine will never have to pull her punches. She won't have to worry—as many modern women do in their everyday lives—about being too assertive, too aggressive, too verbally direct because this hero is as strong as she is. He is a worthy opponent, a mythic beast who is her heroic complement. He has been variously described as a devil, a demon, a tiger, a hawk, a pirate, a bandit, a potentate, a hunter, a warrior. He is definitely *not* the boy next door.

Indeed, he's a man in every sense of the word, and for most women the word *man* reverberates with thousands of years of connotative meanings which touch upon everything from sexual prowess, to the capacity for honor and loyalty, to the ability to protect and defend the family unit. He is no weakling who will run away or turn to another woman when the conflict between himself and the heroine flares. Instead, he will be forced in the course of the plot to prove his commitment to the relationship, and, unlike many men in the real world, he will pass this test magnificently.

Should the book fail to deliver on its implied promise, should the writer be unable to create the fantasy satisfactorily, make it accessible, and achieve the integration of opposites that results in a happy ending, the reader will consider herself cheated. The happy ending in a romance novel is far more significant than it might appear to those who do not understand the codes. It requires that the final union of male and female be a fusing of contrasting elements: heroes who are gentled by love yet who lose none of their warrior qualities in the process and heroines who conquer devils without sacrificing their femininity. It requires a quintessentially female kind of victory, one in which neither side loses, one which produces a whole that is stronger than either of its parts. It requires that the hero acknowledge the heroine's heroic qualities in both masculine and feminine terms. He must recognize and admire her sense of honor, courage, and determination as well as her traditionally female qualities of gentleness and compassion. And it requires a sexual bonding that transcends the physical, a bond that reader and writer know can never be broken.

Thus, as the romance novel ends, the contrasting elements in the plot are entirely fused and reconciled. Male and female are integrated. The heroine's quest is won. She has succeeded in shining light into the darkness surrounding the hero. She has taught the devil to love.

Nothing about the romance genre is more reviled by literary critics and, indeed, by the public at large, than the conventional diction of romance. Descriptive passages are regularly culled from romance novels and read aloud with great glee and mockery by everybody from college professors to talk show hosts. You would think that we romance novelists—who, like anyone else, cringe at the thought of being made the object of ridicule on national TV—would have the wit to clean up our act. After all, we are talented professionals. We're quite capable of choosing other, more subtle, less effusive forms of narrative and discourse. Yet we persist in penning sentences like "Caught up in the tender savagery of love . . . she saw him, felt him, *knew* him in a manner that, for an instant, transcended the physical. It was as if their souls yearned toward each other, and in a flash of glory, merged and became one" (Barlow, *Fires of Destiny*).

Why? Are we woefully derivative and unoriginal? Do our editors force us to write this way? Do we all have access to some sort of romance writers' phrase book to which we constantly refer? Are we incapable of expressing ourselves in any other manner?

The answer, of course, is none of the above. We write this way because we know that this is the language which best serves our purposes as romance authors. This is the language that, for romance novels, *works.* Why? Because the language of romance most effectively carries and reinforces the essential messages that we, consciously or unconsciously, are endeavoring to convey.

In our genre (and in others, we believe), stock phrases and literary figures are regularly used to evoke emotion. This is not well understood by critics of these genres. Romance readers have a keyed-in response to certain words and phrases (the sardonic lift of the eyebrows, the thundering of the heart, the penetrating glance, the low murmur or sigh). Because of their past reading experiences, readers associate certain emotions—anger, fear, passion, sorrow—with such language and expect to feel the same responses each time they come upon such phrases. This experience can be quite intense, yet, at the same time, the codes that evoke the dramatic illusion also maintain it *as* illusion (not delusion—romance readers do not confuse fantasy with reality). Encountering the familiar language, the reader responds emotionally to the characters, settings, and events in the *fictional* world of romance. And although what she feels is her own internal experience, it is something that can be shared with millions of other women around the world, so the commonality of the experience is appealing, too.

But the reader's pleasure is not purely emotional. She also responds on an intellectual level. Because the language of romance is more lushly symbolic and metaphorical than ordinary discourse, the reader is stimulated not only to feel, but also to analyze, interpret, and understand. Surveys of romance readers have consistently shown that these women are more highly educated and well-read than detractors have assumed, a fact which should be evident to anyone studying the mythological traditions underpinning the language of romance. When the heroine of Judith McNaught's *Whitney My Love* attends a ball costumed as Proserpina and meets a black-cloaked man whom she regards as "satanic" in appearance, the reader is expected to recognize the myth that is being alluded to and to identify this dark god as the novel's hero. Later in the novel when the heroine is forcibly carried off by this man, the reader understands that the story is following a map laid down by a far more ancient tale.

What exactly *is* the language of romance? For the purpose of discussion, we have decided to examine two forms of discourse: romantic dialogue and romantic description.

Dialogue in a romance novel serves a larger purpose than simply to provide exposition and demonstrate character. What is said between the hero and the heroine is often the primary battlefield for the conflicts between them. Provocative, confrontational dialogue has been the hallmark of the adversarial relationship that exists between the two major characters ever since the earliest days of romance narrative. It is Jane Eyre's verbal impertinence that calls her to the attention of her employer, Mr. Rochester, who notes in one of their first conversations, "Ah! By my word! there is something singular about you . . . when one asks you a question, or makes a remark to which you are obliged to reply, you rap out a round rejoinder, which, if not blunt, is at least brusque." She is not his equal in terms of fortune or circumstance, but Jane proves early on that she is very much his equal in verbal acuity and assertiveness.

Such is also the case in *Pride and Prejudice,* in which Elizabeth Bennet's growing attraction for Mr. Darcy is based not only upon her "fine eyes," but also upon her ready wit. The opportunity to engage in verbal sparring is rarely declined by the heroines of romance since it is far more likely to be her words than her beauty that win her the love she most desires. Romances are full of heroes who eschew the company of beautiful but insipid women who would rather fawn than fight. Indeed, heroes of romance *enjoy* the duel of wits. Frequently they take the heroine's words to heart, changing in response to her stated criticisms. The heroine's words are her most potent weapon. It is Elizabeth's scathing refusal of his marriage proposal that forces Darcy to reevaluate his own behavior and relinquish the worst aspects of his pride; it is Cathy's overheard comment about Heathcliff's unsuitability as a husband that drives him from Wuthering Heights and inspires him to educate and improve himself.

In modern stories heroines continue to charm, provoke, and challenge their lovers with their conversation. After only one spirited dialogue with Whitney Stone, the heroine of Judith McNaught's *Whitney My Love,* the Duke of Claymore is inspired to court her. "She had a sense of humor, an irreverent contempt for the absurd, that matched his own. She was warm and witty and elusive as a damned butterfly. She would never bore him as other women had."

In real life women often complain about the reluctance of their male partners to engage in meaningful dialogue, but in the world of romantic fantasy heroes willingly participate in verbal discussions. They fence, they flirt, they express their anger, they talk out the confounding details of their relationships with the heroine. No hero of romance will ever respond to the eternal feminine query, "What's wrong?" with the word, "Nothing." He will tell her what's wrong; they will argue about it, perhaps, but they will be communicating, and eventually, as they resolve their various conflicts, the war of words will end. One of the most significant victories the heroine achieves at the close of the novel is that the hero is able to express his love for her *not only physically but also verbally.* Don't just show me, tell me, is one of the prime messages that every romance hero must learn. Romance heroines, like women the world over, need to hear the words, and the dialogue of romance provides them with this welcome opportunity.

Our second form of discourse, romantic description, is frequently denounced by critics as being overly florid. But effusive imagery has a purpose. As we have already noted, the primary task of the romance writer is to create for her readers a vision of an alternative world and to give mythical dimension to its landscape and characters. Piling on the detail by means of a generous use of the romance codes is an effective way to achieve this goal. Lush use of symbols, metaphors, and allusion is emotionally powerful as well as mythologically evocative. It is the verbal equivalent of putting a person or an action under a microscope. Horror genre novelists like Stephen King use this technique to describe, for example, a murdered corpse, shocking the reader into a visceral response to the graphic horrors of death. Romance writers use the same technique in sensual love scenes to draw the reader into the landscape and to solidify her identification with the lovers by evoking within her some of the same emotions they are experiencing. The codes transport her to the world of romance and make her feel, briefly, as if she is a participant in the ancient dramas being enacted there.

The physical characteristics of the hero and heroine are presented in considerable detail, and phrases such as "his lean, hard thighs," "her sparkling, emerald eyes," "his penetrating glance," "her prim features were softened by a generous lower lip" are standard fare in romance. Many such codes reverberate with allusions to mythical archetypes: "He was leaning against the cold stone wall, regarding her steadily with a slight smile on his narrow, sensual lips. *Devil,* she thought" (Barlow, *Siren's Song).* And, from the hero in the same book: "Faerie music, he thought, listening to a low-toned feminine voice caressing the words of a ballad . . . this lovely Siren must be she."

A careful analysis of the physical description in most romance novels will demonstrate that, from a large lexicon of common descriptive codes, authors consciously or unconsciously choose those that best illustrate the particular archetypes with which they are working. Heroes associated with demons, the devil, the dark gods, and vampires tend to be dark-haired, with eyes that are luminous, piercing, penetrating, fierce, fiery, and so forth. Blond heroes are less common, but there is usually a fallen-angel quality about them.

In the passage of sample back cover copy at the beginning of this essay, the description of the hero is a blatant evocation of the Hades-Persephone myth. *Ravenwood* is dark and enigmatic, with the glittering eyes that one might expect to be attributed to the devil. He is clearly linked with the death god. Having drowned in the black, murky waters of a pond, the first Lady Ravenwood is a permanent shade in the underworld, and it is hinted that her husband may have been responsible.

Sophy is, in many ways, his opposite. Described as country bred, she is fresh and innocent. Like Persephone of the myth, she is drawn into a marriage that she does not, at first, desire. Her tawny hair, the color of wheat, evokes her role as the daughter of Demeter, the great earth goddess of the harvest, spring, fertility. Thus the descriptive language sets up one of the oldest and best-loved of romantic conflicts: the mythical battle of death and life, despair and hope, eternal darkness and everlasting light.

The individual words employed in the passage are highly connotative. Adjectives include such words as black, legendary, mysterious, beautiful, murky, country-bred, emerald, tawny-haired, and masculine. Verbs include whispered, drowned, drawn, burned, teach, love. Nouns include devil, wrath, waters, bride, lass, strength, desire, foul play, and marriage of convenience. Such language is emotionally loaded. Each word conjures up vivid images in the minds of the readers, and the combination of so many evocative phrases in a short passage of prose creates for the reader a dynamic, multi-layered intellectual and emotional gestalt.

Is it possible to do away with such language and still retain the romance? Suppose we tried to rewrite the passage in nonfigurative language. It might come out something like this:

His acquaintances regard Julian, the Earl of Ravenwood, as neurotic. He's an odd character with a belligerent temperament, whose first wife drowned in the family swimming pool. Some believe she committed suicide, others think he murdered her.

Sophy Dorring, an unsophisticated young woman, is engaged to Julian. Strongly attracted to him, she overcomes her initial reluctance to marry and sets her own agenda for their relationship: to help her husband get in touch with his emotions.

Same story, different language. But what a difference. By expressing the same ideas in ordinary discourse, we sacrifice the fantasy, the mythical elements, and that sense of magnificent opposition between two powerful but opposing forces. The problems of the hero and heroine are reduced to the mundane. Such diction might be deemed appropriate for the writer of mainstream fiction, but it is worthless to the romance novelist.

Another interesting detail about romantic description is the use of paradoxical elements, echoing the heavy use of paradoxical plot devices. Although the hero is more commonly associated with darkness, hardness, strength, roughness, and evil, and the heroine with light, softness, vulnerability, gentleness, and good, there are elements of strength in the heroine and softness in the hero. "A mouth that smiled easily was counterbalanced by the firm angles of her nose and jaw" (Krentz, *Affair of Honor*). "His eyes were large, brown, and dramatic . . . heavily fringed with dark lashes and arched with delicate brows that might have appeared too feminine had the rest of his features not been so uncompromisingly male" (Barlow, *Siren's Song*). Or, as the hero of Amanda Quick's *Seduction* notes about the heroine, "beneath that sweet, demure facade, she had a streak of willful pride."

The reason for this type of description is to distract the reader from the fantasy elements of the story long enough to remind her of the underlying reality of the hero's and heroine's characters. The hero is not really such a bad guy, the reader divines. And the heroine is much tougher and more self-sufficient than she initially appears.

Paradoxical words and phrases like "fierce pleasure" and "tender command" (from *Seduction*) are also used to depict the dynamics of the developing relationship. Frequently, the romance heroine is described as a "willing captive" to the "tender violence" of the hero's lovemaking. Detractors of the genre tend to quote such phrases to bolster their view that romance writers are doing a disservice to their sisters by perpetuating the myth that women enjoy rape. In reality, the rape of the heroine by the hero is rarely, if ever, seen in today's romance novel. Readers do not take such passages literally; indeed, the very use of paradox makes a literal interpretation impossible. The words "captive" and "violence" remind the reader of the ancient *fantasy* underpinning such tales—the Hades-Persephone myth, for example—while the function of the words "willing" and "tender" is to clue the reader in to the *reality* of the characters' lovemaking, which is consensual and loving.

The use of paradox also serves to hint at the perfect reconciliation that will occur at the end of the romance novel. This will be possible because each of the main characters is, in addition to being the embodiment of an ancient myth, a whole person, integrated and autonomous, with various strengths and weaknesses. When these two individuals come together, they create a union that is both mythological and real, a union that celebrates the power of the female to heal and civilize the male.

In conclusion, we suggest that in order to understand the appeal of romance fiction, one must be sensitive to the subtle codes, contained in figurative language and in plot, that point toward a uniquely feminine sharing of a common emotional and intellectual heritage. Dedicated romance readers, long accustomed to responding to these cues, perceive the hidden meanings intuitively and find through them an intimacy with other women all over the world. It is our sex, after all, that excels at reconciliation and intimacy. Recent works on the differences between men and women, whether these be biological, psychological, or linguistic, suggest that women's particular expertise seems to be our ability to form significant relationships with the men, women, and children in our lives and to anchor and hold these relationships together. The messages contained in romance fiction, the language in which these messages are conveyed, and the intense experience induced by the act of reading itself tend to support and reflect this essential feminine concern. Like a secret handshake, the codes make the reader feel that she is part of a group. They increase her feelings of connection to other women who share her most intimate thoughts, dreams, and fantasies.

In general, women tend to be less afraid than men to blend our voices with others. Women who write romance don't seek autonomy in our story-telling. We don't seek a distinctive voice (although most writers have one). Instead, in telling stories and using language that we *know* are beloved of women all over the world, we are validating each other. We are articulating the feelings and fantasies of our sisters who cannot, or choose not to, write them down. Their voices ring out, through us, as strongly as our own.

It may well be that the use of the romance codes are more important to the success of a particular romance novel than are the usual elements upon which fiction is judged—the logic and cleverness of the plot, the development of the characters, or the vigor and originality of the author's voice. It's interesting to note that what is usually regarded as "good" prose style—presupposing the value of the original, individual voice over the value of merged voices—is not necessary for the writing of romance. This is true because in romance novels the shared experience is more valuable than the independent one.

Is it possible that accepted literary standards of excellence are essentially patriarchal in nature? We propose this as a matter for further debate and discussion. Are there any differences between what men and women generally regard as acceptable prose style? Who made the rules that all serious writers are supposed to have internalized? "Get rid of every adjective and adverb," a male colleague advised me after reading a draft of my latest manuscript. He also advised the use of shorter sentences. Lean and spare, short and terse. No emotion.

But why, for example, must we show and not tell? Women *enjoy* the telling. We value the exploration of emotion in verbal terms. We are not as interested in action as we are in depth of emotion. And we like the emotion to be clear and authoritative, not vague or overly subtle the way it often seems to be in male discourse.

Why do many of us who write romance feel a defiant pleasure as we compose our "bad" prose? Are we really a bunch of silly, incompetent, unoriginal writers, or are we thumbing our noses at the literary establishment while continuing to use the sort of diction that not only works best in our genre, but satisfies our most deep-seated fantasies on a subtle and profound level?

This is a subject upon which a good deal more could be written, and we hope, through this essay, to stimulate such debate. The greatest challenge for the romance writer working today is to excite and delight our readers while, at the same time, fulfilling their expectations. It has been our experience that this is best achieved by making full use of the codes and conventions that have served us well for centuries, codes that are universally recognized by our sisters in every nation and culture, codes that celebrate the most enduring myths of feminine consciousness.

THE MYTHOLOGICAL APPROACH TO SPECULATIVE FICTION

The new "mythology" of our post-industrial society is to be found in popular fiction. In fact, popular fiction is quite similar in structure to oral folklore. When regarding how the process of storytelling functions, both popular fiction and folklore (as mythology) possess formulaic patterns that are utilized for specific purposes. The predictability of the tall tale in folklore is paralleled by the predictability of an Arthur Conan Doyle Sherlock Holmes story. The tall tale and the Holmes story, by virtue of their respective formulas, provide a recognizable narrative context for listener and reader. In addition, the heroes of ancient legend and classical mythology are yet present in our popular fiction of today. Homer's trickster warrior, Odysseus, for example, is embodied in Edgar Rice Burroughs's trickster Lord of the Jungle, Tarzan. The demigod, Hercules, appears as Doc Savage, the Man of Bronze, in the American adventure pulp magazines of the 1930s and 1940s. And, the community authorship found in participatory folklore is quite similar to the mass market readership of the best-selling novel. Both print and nonprint media place their emphasis on audience, and each rely on including as wide an involved membership as possible.

Thus, an effective way to discuss the social function of popular fiction is to analyze it as mythology. One of the most respected scholars of comparative mythology, Joseph Campbell, in works such as The Hero with a Thousand Faces *(1949) and* Myths to Live By *(1972), helped to define the various applications of mythological analysis to contemporary culture. The American frontier, in particular, has proved itself a fit topic for mythological analysis. Scholars who have studied the function of myth and archetype in the literature and culture of the American frontier include Henry Nash Smith, author of* Virgin Land: The American West as Symbol and Myth *(1950), and Richard Slotkin, author of a trilogy of myth/symbol criticism—* Regeneration Through Violence: The Mythology of the American Frontier, 1600-1860 *(1973),* The Fatal Environment: The Myth of the Frontier in the Age of Industrialization, 1800-1890 *(1985), and* Gunfighter Nation: The Myth of the Frontier in Twentieth-Century America *(1992).*

The opportunities associated with space exploration, as we enter the twenty-first century, provide us with a new mythology as well as a new frontier. In the essay, "Science Fiction: The Rebirth of Mythology," Gail Landsman argues that modern-day society has stripped us of our defining myths and that scientific progress and rationalism have denied us the therapeutic benefits of a powerful mythological belief system. Landsman contends that science fiction and fantasy have constructed a new mythology, one that relates the future with the present in the similar way that traditional mythology related the past with the present.

GAIL LANDSMAN

SCIENCE FICTION:
THE REBIRTH OF MYTHOLOGY

One of the most striking peculiarities of our Western culture is that in the entire history of man's cultural and religious development, it alone lacks a mythology. We often pride ourselves on the absence of such irrationality in our society, yet we suffer unspeakable pain and intolerable emptiness as the price of its loss. Indeed, despite our pleas for rationalism, our calls for progress, our conviction in the "scientific explanation," our need for mythology is so great, so compelling, that we have forced our culture to provide us with a new mythology—and this modern mythology is taking form in the literature of science fiction.

Myth functions, according to anthropologist Clifford Geertz, at the margins of man's understanding—at the limits of his analytic capacities, at the limits of his powers of endurance, and at the limits of his moral insight. The second and third of these limits involve the problem of suffering, which through mythology becomes a matter not of avoiding suffering, but of somehow making suffering bearable, supportable,—something, as we say, sufferable.

The incomprehensibility of suffering is a theme tackled by many science fiction writers, among them Kurt Vonnegut. In his *Slaughterhouse Five,* he uses speculative fantasy to bring himself and his readers to face and understand the fact of the Dresden holocaust. Like myth, he seeks not to avoid suffering, but to somehow make it understandable, sufferable. In an article, "Science Fiction—The Modern Mythology," Willis McNelly proposes that because we live in an increasingly technological age, science fiction has become "a contemporary form of Eliot's objective correlative," enabling us to face problems we cannot otherwise face directly, permitting us to comprehend the tragic consequences of our misuse of science. McNelly contends that to enable himself and his readers to cope with these matters, even if only stoically, Vonnegut invents (or reinvents) the planet Tralfamadore, whose inhabitants see time as discontinuous, with all moments eternally present. The "hero," Billy Pilgrim, is kidnapped one night by Tralfamadorians on a flying saucer, and placed in a zoo on the planet. He writes of his experiences:

> The most important thing I learned on Tralfamadore was that when a person dies he only appears to die. He is still very much alive in the past, so it is very silly for people to cry at his funeral. All moments, past, present and future, always have existed, always will exist. . . . It is just an illusion we have here on Earth that one moment follows another one, like beads on a string, and that once a moment is gone it is gone forever.
>
> When a Tralfamadorian sees a corpse, all he thinks is that the dead person is in bad condition in that particular moment, but that the same person is just fine in plenty of other moments. Now when I myself hear that somebody is dead, I simply shrug and say what the Tralfamadorians say about dead people, which is "So it goes."[1]

And "so it goes." These words, McNelly says,

become a fatalistic chant, a dogmatic utterance, to permit Vonnegut himself to endure. In creating Tralfamadore, Vonnegut is suggesting that cyclic time or the eternal present will enable himself and mankind to accept the unacceptable. The sin of Dresden is so great that it will require an eternity to expiate. But eternity is not available to all men—only to the Tralfamadorians and the Pilgrim soul of man, and Vonnegut has, out of his science-fiction heritage, created both.[2]

Cruelty and suffering surely have always existed, and simultaneously mythology has existed to enable man to face this suffering and yet to still endure. But Western man, at the same time that he repudiated and "freed" himself from mythology, also opened the way for himself to create unprecedented tools of destruction—manifested in such things as the fire-bombing of Dresden. The adoption of a scientific over a mythological perspective thus has placed man in a unique dilemma—his science has destroyed man's traditional means for coping with the problem of evil and suffering, while at the same time it has created a vast new level of inhumanity for man to confront and come to grips with. Eliot Rosewater, in essence, is expressing this dilemma when he remarks to Billy Pilgrim that "everything there was to know about life was in *The Brothers Karamazov,* by Feodor Dostoevsky. 'But that isn't *enough* anymore,' said Rosewater."[3]

And so because modern man's inhumanity has come to the point where it cannot be understood directly, Vonnegut invents mythological, science-fictional devices to express it tangentially—flying saucers, alternate universes, time travel, etc. Billy's conception of time becomes the only perspective which will allow Vonnegut, and with him Western man, to face Dresden, and yet to still go on and find meaning and love in life. Speculative fantasy has thus performed the role of mythology.

In order to understand why Western culture has forced us to recreate a mythology, and why our new mythology takes the form it does, we must first understand some of the basic differences between the concepts and perspectives which govern our own lives, and those which characterize other cultures.

In a scheme proposed by anthropologist Robert N. Bellah,[4] our culture can be viewed as the temporary end product of an evolutionary process of religious symbol transformation. At one end of the continuum is "primitive" society, at the other, "modern"; at one end life is lived in an atmosphere known as cosmological monism, at the other in cosmological dualism. Primitive culture, according to Bellah, is oriented to a single cosmos. In such religious systems there is what Peacock and Kirsch[5] refer to as a union of the actual and the cosmic. In contrast to the vast gap existing between "God" and man in Western societies, what we would call the primitives' gods are on relatively the same level as their mortals. This is seen no more clearly than in the Trickster myths of various North American Indian tribes, in which the Creator is portrayed as a foolish rogue.

Primitive mythology is distinctive in "the very high degree to which the mythical world is related to the detailed features of the actual world" as well as the fluidity of its organization. "Both the particularity and the fluidity, then," Bellah says, "help account for the hovering closeness of the world of myth to the actual world."[6] This correlation between the mythical world and the actual one is very specific in many cases; indeed, virtually every mountain, rock and tree is explained in terms of the actions of mythical beings.

W. E. Stanner, in his study of aboriginal culture in Australia, further expresses the primitive's atmosphere of cosmological monism.

> The truth of it seems to be that man, society, and nature and past, present, and future are at one together within a unitary system of such a kind that its ontology cannot illumine minds too much under the influence of humanism, rationalism, and science. One cannot easily, in the mobility of modern life and thought, grasp the vast institutions of stability and permanence, and of life and man, at the heart of aboriginal ontology.[7]

Our culture is at the polar opposite from this sense of cosmic unity. We are the latest stage of a process tending (in Bellah's words) "in the direction of a more differentiated, comprehensive, and in Weber's sense, more rationalized formulations.[8] It is these characteristics of our culture which place "science fiction" and fantasy in a separate category from other literature, and therefore which account for definitions of s-f (such as Alexei and Cory Panshin's) as literature of "crucial removal from the mimetic world." For in the primitive's life there is only *one* world, with natural and supernatural, "real" and fantastical, all intertwined. It is only our culture which isolates so drastically the "real" from the mystical.

These "more rationalized formulations," this "disenchantment" of the world has had numerous consequences for us, not the least of which is Nietzsche's "crisis of our time." Our rationalism has created a scientific perspective, it has repudiated the notion of any supernatural intelligence governing the world, and has stripped us of our "illusions" and visions. Our literature reflects these conceptions. (One need only read a few books written by American Indians in the early 1900's—the Hopi Talayesva, or the Oglala Sioux prophet Black Elk—to grasp the comparison.) The magician in modern literature has become the chemist or biologist, and apparitions that were once believed to be authentic visions are now explained by neurosis and schizophrenia. In a study of the supernatural in fiction, Dr. Peter Penzoldt remarks that

> science not only furnishes us with extraordinary situations, but also gives us an excellent excuse for believing anything however incredible. We are inclined to think nowadays that nothing is outside its range, and we seek to invest its laws with those supernatural qualities that our sophisticated imagination can no longer attribute to ghosts and goblins. Science itself must offer a compensation for the imaginary world it has destroyed.[9]

It appears that man needs irrationality, a sense of the mystical, to give life meaning. Primitive man attributes a status of power (shaman) to one who has plunged into the abyss and returned, to the man who has gone mad in the bush and who in this way has seen the wholeness and truth in life. The experience is somewhat like stepping into Vonnegut's chrono-synclastic infundibulum—a terribly dangerous atmosphere full of the infinite seemingly contradictory truths that exist in the universe. To have had such a vision or madness in primitive culture is to have found wisdom: in modern society it is generally referred to as insanity.

Yet there are those that desperately feel the need, in our technological society, to experience this state of insanity, these alternate conceptions. Science fiction, among other devices, provides a certain medium for such experiences. In accounting for Kurt Vonnegut's appeal to the counter-culture, Leslie Fiedler asserts that it is partly the fact that structurally, archetypically speaking, the space-odyssey is the same thing as the "trip"; and that having chosen the mode of science fiction, Vonnegut has subscribed to a mythology otherwise sustained by smoking grass or dropping LSD, or, for that matter, simply sitting half-stunned before the late, late show on TV. In a certain sense, it can be said that the taking of drugs is a technological substitute for a special kind of literature, for fantasy—an attempt to substitute chemistry for words.[10]

Stripped of any mythology we can believe in, we are left with only artificial substitutes. And so perhaps this is where science fiction comes in—as compensation for the imaginary world our culture has destroyed for us, as an attempt to recreate the mythology we have lost.

Both mythology and speculative fantasy are artistic forms subject to condescension and paternalism. Writing of aboriginal mythology, Stanner remarks that

> European minds are made uneasy by the facts that the stories are quite plainly preposterous; are often a mass of internal contradictions; are encrusted by superstitious fancies about magic, sorcery, hobgoblins, and superhuman heroes, and lack of the kind of theme and structure—in other words, the "story" element—for which we look. Many of us cannot help feeling that such things can only be the products of absurdly ignorant credulity and a lower order of mentality. This is to fall victim to a facile fallacy.[11]

Similarly, science fiction is often referred to as "escape literature," mere pleasure reading, but certainly not high art. One reason for such criticism of s-f is that writing style and technique is often poorer in science fiction than in mainstream literature. Yet this can be accounted for by the primacy in speculative fantasy, as in myth, of the *idea.* In the Zuni creation myth, for example, the particular plot and characterizations are of much less significance than the concept of the earth as mother, at whose breast we (people, the four-leggeds, the winged ones, and the grasses) shall suck throughout our lives.

Similarly, in Frank Herbert's *Dune,* the plot is flawed with loopholes and clichés, while the idea of adherence to ecology is vividly portrayed. Perhaps the "idea as hero" is best seen in Isaac Asimov's *Foundation*—the concept of psychohistory carries the book, with little help from characters such as Limmar Ponyets or Hober Mallow or Eskel Gorov, other than that they are where they are when they should be according to Hari Seldon's plan. For a reader attuned to mainstream fiction with emphasis on character development, *Foundation* (with its *idea* development) is quite alien. Even in a work written with superb command of language and exceptional coherence of plot such as George Orwell's *1984,* the idea reigns supreme. It is the efficiency and effects of totalitarianism which are expressed; it is O'Brien's words to Winston that remain in the reader's mind: "If you want a picture of the future, imagine a boot stamping on a human face—forever."

The primacy of the idea in speculative fantasy means that a good science fiction story usually will sound good in paraphrase. Similarly primitive myths are never written down, but passed on (paraphrased) from one to another. Different versions of the myth might exist even within the same society (as one person's paraphrase of a story differs in details from another's), but the essence, the idea, remains.

The effect of the "idea as hero" and of the somewhat easy passage of story from one to another help account for mythology's role of relating man to his universe. The primitive lives in a state Stanner calls the "'Every-when"—it is a stable world containing past, present and future. It presents no cosmic duality, no distinction between what is and what ought to be, and thus no outstanding drive to progress or change or manipulate. Primitive life is thus present-oriented, and its mythology defines and justifies man as he is today as the direct result of events in "the beginning." Thus myth is an explanation of how, through the deeds of supernatural beings in the nebulous "pre-now," a reality came into existence. In the Zuni creation myth, for example again, Awonawilono transformed himself into the Sun, and out of his own substance he produced two seeds with which he impregnated the Great Waters. Under the warmth of the Creator's light, the waters grew continually to finally become Earth-Mother and Sky-Father. From the sexual union of these two, life was engendered and all forms of beings were held within the body, in the four wombs, of the earth-mother. Such a description of the beginning orients the Zuni to his universe; he knows his place and his relationship to all—son of earth, brother to all life.

Western society, on the other hand, is future-oriented. Largely deriving its character from the Protestant heritage, our culture is devoted to the concepts of progress and change. Whereas primitive man, living in a stable and generally unchanging culture, judges his actions and makes his decisions on the basis of precedent set "in the beginning," modern man judges his behavior and approaches decisions on the basis of how they will affect his future. Thus for a future-oriented culture, science fiction, with its setting most often in the future, is well-adapted for a modern culture's mythology. The list of speculative fantasy taking place somewhere in the future is endless—*Foundation, Martian Chronicles, A Canticle for Leibowitz, Brave New World, The Demolished Man,* etc., etc. . . . So while primitive mythology's portrayal of the past largely determines behavior in the present, it is our view of the future, often expressed in science fiction, which helps determine our behavior in the present. Because we believed in robots as they were presented in Buck Rogers and other early SF, Donald Wolheim contends in *The Universe Makers,* we created robots. And as for space flight and rockets, Wolheim asserts that "science fiction and its followers can truly claim the right to say we started it and we pushed it through."

Not only does science fiction's portrayal of the future encourage certain behavior now, it also, like mythology's depiction of the past, relates us to our present universe. Vonnegut's *The Sirens of Titan,* for example, uses the medium of the future to tell man that his place in the universe is ridiculous, absurd, and unexplainable. For man to search for the answer, the purpose of his life, is not only painful but futile according to Vonnegut's myth. Man's purpose in life is only, at best, to love what is around him (and of course to laugh at his plight). Orwell's *1984* is another example of science fiction using a future setting to portray the present state of man. Our vision of what humanity may become in the *future* helps us to recognize what man is now, just as mythology's depiction of the *past* relates primitive man to his present condition.

One reason myth is capable of expressing human nature and the functioning of the cosmos is because it can isolate characteristics and tendencies, and then extend them, presenting them in what we would call a "larger than life" representation. Surely a novel like Orwell's *1984* shares this capacity with mythology. Ray Bradbury also employs this technique in *Fahrenheit 451*. The characterization of Mildred Montag is an extension of traits Bradbury has observed in the modern world—the longing to abandon reality by means of mechanical wonders.

Orwell uses an exaggerated depiction of the future; Bradbury, numerous technical innovations on the verge of being created now (the Seashell radio, three-wall television, etc.). Yet neither the future nor scientific inventions need be employed in speculative fantasy to isolate and project the workings of the universe and mankind. Perhaps *Gulliver's Travels* is the best example of fantasy performing this function of mythology, with an absence of any "science." In a way that mimetic fiction could not, Swift portrays man's pettiness through the Lilliputians who are not only physically small, but mentally and emotionally small to the extent that they would fight over which end to crack an egg; man's notion of science for science's sake, through the research of the Academy of Lagado where men pursue useless endeavors while the people starve; as well as man's greed through the exaggerated characterizations of the Yahoos.

In such a way, Swift, Bradbury, Orwell, as other science fiction writers, use symbolism to much the same effect as primitive mythology.

> Abstract principles, precepts, and moral judgments are more easily felt and understood, and more highly valued, when met in a human being endowed with a symbolic form that expresses them. . . . (Mythical) symbols are not truly rational for they do not refer to meanings that belong to the ordinary workaday world or to referential and scientific concepts. They are "evocative," which is to say, nonrational, expressive, and emotional. . . . Such symbols condense and evoke in an effective manner not possible without symbols.[12]

Ours is a culture dominated by "referential and scientific concepts," marked by a poverty of "evocative, nonrational, and emotional" symbols. For this reason we live in a desensitized atmosphere. And so the western world has gone far toward destroying us. Its rationalism has stripped us of our life-giving visions and illusions, and inflicted upon mankind seemingly unbearable indignities, incomprehensible suffering. Yet in leaving us with such vast emptiness it has also allowed us a means for filling (or perhaps half-filling) this void. It has, through the literature of speculative fantasy, returned to us our lost mythology.

Notes

1. Kurt Vonnegut, Jr., *Slaughterhouse Five* (Delacorte Press, 1969), p. 23.
2. Willis McNelly, "Science Fiction—The Modern Mythology." *America,* September 5, 1970), p. 126.
3. Kurt Vonnegut. p. 87.
4. Robert Bellah, "Religious Evolution." in Lessa and Vogt (eds.) *Reader in Comparative Religion* (New York: Harper and Row, 1965).
5. James Peacock and A. Thomas Kirsch, *The Human Direction* (New York: Appleton-Century-Crofts, 1970).
6. Bellah. p. 77.
7. W. E. H. Stanner, "The Dreaming." in Lessa and Vogt (eds.), *Reader in Comparative Religion* (New York: Harper and Row, 1965), p. 160.
8. Bellah. p. 77.

9. Dr. Peter Penzoldt, *The Supernatural in Fiction* (New York: Humanities Press, 1965), p. 50.

10. Leslie Fiedler, "The Divine Stupidity of Kurt Vonnegut." *Esquire* (September 1970).

11. Stanner. p. 162.

12. William Lessa. Lessa and Vogt (eds.), *Readers in Comparative Religion* (New York: Harper and Row, 1965), p. 203.

A MARXIST APPROACH TO THE CRIME STORY

The single quality that is common to all forms of popular fiction is its commercial value. The marketplace defines how a popular story is written, how it is produced, how it is distributed, how it is sold, and how it is consumed. Certain types of genre fiction, at various historical moments, achieve great popularity with a readership, only to forfeit it later when that readership loses interest. The crime stories of E. W. Hornung, for example, featuring the amateur "cracksman," Raffles, during the late Victorian and Edwardian periods enjoyed a comparable level of popularity to Arthur Conan Doyle's Sherlock Holmes adventures. Both Raffles and Holmes appeared in similar popular serial magazines, and both attracted the same enthusiastic audience. But, following the decline of the fiction serial periodical, Doyle's Holmes persisted in attracting new, avid readers (in the trade hardcover and paperback markets) throughout the twentieth century, while Hornung's Raffles faded in popularity, becoming, over time, little more than historical curiosity. The Holmes stories continued to sell, and thus remained in print. The Raffles stories did not sell, and thus disappeared into relative obscurity. This example illustrates how popular fiction is defined as commodity. And as commodity, the study of popular fiction readily lends itself to Marxist analysis.

In the essay, "Debaten ueber Pressfreiheit," Karl Marx wrote: "The writer must, naturally, make a living in order to exist and write, but he must not exist and write in order to make a living." Marx—co-author (with Friedrich Engels) of the "Manifesto of the Communist Party" (first English translation, 1850) and other works defining the Communist movement during the nineteenth century in Europe—did not approve of commercial fiction, of fiction defined as commodity. A number of neo-Marxist critics have also attacked the commercial function of popular fiction, perceiving this type of story as bourgeoisie, capitalist ideology. Perhaps the foremost Marxist literary critic is Georg Lukács, author of The Historical Novel *(1962), and* The Meaning of Contemporary Realism *(1963).*

Ernest Mandel's essay, "A Marxist Interpretation of the Crime Story," which is a chapter from his book-length study, Delightful Murder: A Social History of the Crime Story *(1984), offers a Marxist reading of detective fiction, one that effectively analyzes the formula crime story as ideology. As Mandel argues in his essay: "Bourgeois rationality [in the detective story] is a cheater's rationality. The 'best man' never wins; the richest does. Private property, law and order, must triumph, regardless of the cost in human life and misery."*

ERNEST MANDEL

A MARXIST INTERPRETATION OF THE CRIME STORY

Preoccupation with death is as old as humanity. Death, like labor, is our inevitable fate. But it is a natural fatality mediated by social conditions determined by particular socio-economic structures. The causes of death, and its moment, depend upon social conditions to a large extent. Infant mortality and life expectancy have varied widely throughout history, and so have ideas about death. The social history of death is a precious source of information about the social history of life.

The development of commodity production and the emergence of generalized commodity production, or capitalism, have profoundly altered attitudes toward death. In primitive societies and in class societies still based essentially on the production of use-values, death is seen as a result of nature, as something for which people have to prepare themselves, aided by the attention of their families and the social groups within which they are integrated. Hence respect for elders and the culture of ancestors, which is part of an attempt to accept death as a natural end of life.

In societies based upon the production and circulation of exchange-values, competition between individuals reigns supreme. People are judged not for the maturity of their experience or for their strength of character, but for their performance in the rat race. Older people are therefore considered a burden, increasingly useless, inasmuch as they do not hold jobs and earn money. Protection of the old becomes increasingly de-personalized, anonymous, and taken over by bureaucratic apparatuses.

Because of the changed fate of the elderly, the altered relation between the individual and the community, and the absolute rule of value and money, capital and wealth, the alienated human being in bourgeois society is obsessed with the integrity of the body, indispensable instrument of labor and earning. Hence a much greater obsession with death. Hence also the view that death is a catastrophic accident and not an inevitable conclusion of life. Indeed, accidents are a rising cause of death statistically: road accidents, wars, the "diseases of civilization." Accidental death has taken the place of ontological death in the bourgeois consciousness of death, and certainly in the ideology of death.[1]

Boileau and Narcejac maintain that fear is at the root of the ideology of the detective novel. But fear, in particular fear of death, is as old as humanity. It cannot explain why the crime story did not originate in the fifth century BC or during the Renaissance. The crime story requires a particular kind of fear of death, one that clearly has its roots in the conditions of bourgeois society. Obsession with death seen as an accident leads to obsession with violent death, and hence to obsession with murder, with crime.

Traditionally, preoccupation with death treats it as an anthropological question (magic, theology, philosophy) or as an individual tragedy (institutionalized religion, literature, psychology). With the advent of the detective story as a specific literary genre, a significant break in that tradition occurs. Death—and more particularly murder—is at the very center of the crime story. There is hardly one without violent death. But death in the crime story is not treated as a human fate, or as a tragedy. It becomes an object of enquiry. It is not lived, suffered, feared or fought against. It becomes a corpse to be dissected, a thing to be analyzed. Reification of death is at the very heart of the crime story.

This phenomenon of the reification of death in the crime story amounts to the replacement of preoccupation with human destiny by preoccupation with crime. . . . [T]his is the line that divides the murders occurring in great literature—from Sophocles to Shakespeare, Stendhal, Goethe, Dostoevsky, Dreiser—from those occurring in crime stories. Preoccupation with crime, however, is preoccupation with certain objective rules, with law and order, with *individual* security, the safety of someone's (or some family's) personal fate in a limited portion of life (by definition, subjects like wars, revolutions and depressions fall outside the purview of this sort of security). Preoccupation with crime and personal security leads inevitably to a Manichaean polarization. Personal security is good by definition; an attack against it is evil by nature. Psychological analysis, the complexity and ambiguity of human motives and behavior, has no place within that Manichaeanism. The crime story is based upon the mechanical, formal division of the characters into two camps: the bad (the criminals) and the good (the detective and the more or less inefficient police).

The extreme polarization of the universe of the crime story, however, is accompanied by a de-personalization of good and evil, one that is part and parcel of the de-humanization of death. Good and evil are not embodied in real human beings, in real complex personalities. There is no battle of passions and wills, only a clash of wits, analytical as opposed to precautionary cleverness. Clues have to be *discovered* because tracks have been *covered*. Instead of human conflict, there is competition between abstract intelligences. This competition is like that of the marketplace, where what is involved is a struggle over cost-prices and sales-prices, and not between complex human beings. That reification of conflict reflects the reification of death as a reification of human fate.

Of course, such reification is not purely negative. In feudal and despotic societies, torture was the main means of "proving" crimes and unmasking criminals. Innocents died under torture in horrible pain. By formalizing the process of proof-gathering, submitting it to rules based on the principles of bourgeois values, nineteenth-century criminal justice meant a historical step forward for human liberty, however limited and contradictory a step it may have been. To characterize that advance as hypocritical is to close one's eyes to the obvious fact that the elimination of torture is a key conquest of the bourgeois-democratic revolution, one that socialists do not reject but must defend and integrate into the socialist revolution and the building of socialism.

By replacing scholastic disputes with clue-gathering in the process of crime-detection, by replacing confessions extracted under torture with formalized proof acceptable in court as the basis of a verdict of guilty, science at least partially supplants magic, rationality at least partially supplants irrationality. In that sense, as Ernst Bloch has pointed out, the detective story reflects and summarizes the historical progress won by the revolutionary bourgeoisie, for obvious reasons of self-defence and self-interest.

But rationality and rationalism are not identical. Reified rationality is incompletely and therefore insufficiently rational. It cannot grasp or explain the human condition in its totality, but artificially breaks it up into separate compartments:

economic, political (citizen), cultural, sexual, moral, psychological, religious. Criminals are the products of their drives, the heroes products of their search for justice (or for order). Within such a formalized context, it is impossible to understand, or even to pose, the way the criminal and detective alike, along with crime and justice, prison and property, are products of the same society, of a specific stage of social development. Crime and the detecting of crime are not only reified, but also made banal and without problems. They are taken for granted, outside the specific social context and concrete historical development that have created them.

Bourgeois rationalism is always a combination of rationality and irrationality, and it produces a growing trend toward overall irrationality. That is why the detective story, while placing analytical intelligence and scientific clue-gathering at the heart of crime detection, often resorts to blind passions, crazy plots, and references to magic, if not to clinical madness, in order to "explain" why criminals commit crimes. Conan Doyle himself symbolizes that contradiction by his rising concern for the supernatural, which moved him, late in life, to write a book seeking to prove the existence of fairies. Even if individual passion were the dominant motive for crime, there would still be the question of why a given social context produces more and more madness while another does not—a question the classical detective story never raises.

The very structure of the classical detective novel reflects this combination. As Professor [S.] Dresden pointed out in the Dutch study *Marionettenspel met de Dood*, such a novel moves at two levels of reality simultaneously.[3] On the one hand, everything must look as real and matter-of-fact as possible. Exact time is always mentioned, precise locations offered, sometimes complete with maps and other sketches. The actions of the characters are described in the most minute detail, as are their clothes and physical appearance. At the same time, everything is shrouded in ambiguity and mystery. Sinister shadows lurk in the background. People are not what they seem. Unreality constantly takes over from reality. Simenon brings out this contrast—and combination—in two telling sentences: "Maigret watched the passers-by and told himself that Paris was peopled by mysterious and elusive beings that you come across only rarely, in the course of some tragedy." "It was good to come back to the voice of Mrs. Maigret, to the smell of the flat, with the furniture and objects in their place."

Disorder being brought into order, order falling back into disorder; irrationality upsetting rationality, rationality restored after irrational upheavals: that is what the ideology of the crime novel is all about.

It is no accident that this classical detective story developed primarily in the Anglo-Saxon countries. One of the central characteristics of the prevailing ideology in Britain and the United States during the latter half of the nineteenth century and the early years of the twentieth was the absence, or at least extreme debility, of concepts of class struggle as tools for the interpretation of social phenomena. (In Britain, this represented a regression compared with earlier periods.) This reflected the stability of bourgeois society and the self-confidence of the ruling class. The intelligentsia in general, and authors of books in particular, whether socially critical or conservative, assumed that this stability was a fact of life.

In these circumstances, it was natural for them to assimilate revolt against the social order into criminal activity, to identify the rebellious proletariat with the "criminal classes" (an expression that crops up repeatedly in popular Anglo-Saxon detective stories). What began as natural soon acquired a social function, and an effective one at that. In France, by contrast, although academics writing for an exclusively bourgeois audience might use such a phrase, the lower-middle classes and literate workers who made up the mass audience of the popular novel, would certainly not have accepted such notions after experiences like the 1848 revolution or the Paris Commune. Just because the class struggle was sharper and more politicized in France than in the Anglo-Saxon countries, it was far more difficult, and therefore far less effective and thus less widely practiced, to criminalize class conflict or to subsume it under individual conflicts.

It is interesting to note that in Germany and Japan "serious" detective stories began to sink national roots only after the Second World War (with authors such as Hansjörg Martin, Thomas Andresen, Friedhelm Werremaier, Richard Hey, Irène Rodrian, and Ky), although J. D. H. Temme had written many kinds of crime stories in the 1860s.[2] Only at that point in history bourgeois ideology in its purest sense became all-pervasive. But in both cases, momentous social upheavals—war, defeat, foreign occupation and spectacular economic expansion in its wake—made it impossible to write stories with an atmosphere of secular order and normality. The context of crime is wealth and business, sometimes with a modestly critical social dimension.

Significantly, the criminals in most of these novels are themselves entrepreneurs and corporation managers. Their motive is nearly always greed or the pressure of financial difficulties.

A substantial anthology of Latin American mystery stories, edited by Donald Yates, *Latin Blood: The Best Crime and Detective Stories of South America,* was published in 1972. The Dutch author Erik Lankester has doubled the input in his *Zuidamerikaanse Misdaadverhalen* (1982), including such famous writers as [Jorge Luis] Borges, [Julio] Cortazar, Gabriel Garcia Marquez, Ben Traven, who have all dabbled in crime stories.

While the criminalization of the lower classes is a special feature of the more trivial Anglo-Saxon detective novels, it is not unusual to find middle-class, and even wealthy, murderers in the classical crime stories of the twenties and thirties (Agatha Christie's novels, for example). The key point is not the class origin of the murderer, but his presentation as a social misfit, a "bounder" who violates the norms of the ruling class and must be punished for that very reason.

Likewise, it is only partially correct to assimilate the British and American traditions of the mystery novel. In Britain, rising capitalism was integrated with a consolidated state, the product of a protracted historical development and combined, as concerns the social superstructure, with many remnants of semi-feudal superstructure. Hence the general atmosphere of class divisions accepted by consensus in the classical British detective story, an acceptance expressed even at the level of language. Violence, absent from the center of the social scene, is pushed to the periphery (the colonies, Ireland, working-class slums). The state is relatively weak, the London police unarmed, because of the apparent stability of society. To some extent, this was a false impression, but it did determine the way ruling ideology reflected British reality, and thus the framework within which the detective novel developed in Britain.

When the center of world capitalism shifted from Britain to the United States, the international system had already ceased expanding and had begun its decline, although US capitalism continued to expand. The growth of American capitalism was therefore accompanied by declining faith in bourgeois values, although up to 1929, if not 1945, they remained more widely accepted in American society than in less stable and wealthy capitalist countries.

But this decline was combined with a different historical tradition, a different form of integration of the capitalist order and the bourgeois state. Just because American capitalism was the "purest" in the world (once slavery was abolished), with no semi-feudal remnants and no hierarchical order of pre-capitalist origin, prevailing social values were less deeply anchored in tradition and less thoroughly internalized by the population. The bourgeoisie was much less respectful of its own state.

Corruption, violence, and crime were evident not only in the periphery of American society, but in its very center. Where the British civil service was a genuine servant of bourgeois society and the successful British politician was seen as a public sage, the American civil service was regarded as virtually useless throughout the nineteenth century, and successful politicians were seen as crooks. From the outset then, the American crime story presented crime as far more completely integrated into society as a whole than the British did.

The theme is still the clash between individual interests and passions, but the events of the novels are less artificial, less tangential to the bourgeois order as a whole, than in the British mystery story. Passion, greed, power, envy, jealousy and property do not merely set individual against individual, but increasingly involve conflicts between individuals and groups or families, and even revolts against class conformism. Crime becomes a means by which to climb the social ladder, or to remain a capitalist despite financial disasters. It is the road from threatened hell to paradise regained. It is the nightmare that stalks the American dream as the shadow stalks the body. The differences between Dashiell Hammett, Raymond Chandler, Ross Macdonald and even Ellery Queen on the one hand and Agatha Christie, Dorothy Sayers, Anthony Berkeley and John Dickson Carr on the other originate in this specificity of bourgeois society in the United States.

Nevertheless, the common ideology of the original and classical detective story in Britain, the United States, and the countries of the European continent remains quintessentially bourgeois. Reified death; formalized crime-detection oriented toward proof acceptable in courts of justice operating according to strictly defined rules; the pursuit of the criminal by the hero depicted as a battle between brains; human beings reduced to "pure" analytical intelligence, partial, fragmented rationality elevated to the status of an absolute guiding principle of human behavior; individual conflicts used as a generalized substitute for conflicts between social groups and layers—all this is bourgeois ideology *par excellence,* a striking synthesis of human alienation in bourgeois society.

It plays a powerful integrative role among all but extremely critical and sophisticated readers. It suggests to them that individual passions, drives and greed, and the social order itself—bourgeois society—have to be accepted as such regardless of shortcomings and injustices, and that those who catch criminals and deliver them to law-enforcement agencies, the courts, and the gallows or electric chair are serving the interests of the immense majority of the citizenry. The class nature of the state, property, law and justice remains completely obscured. Total irrationality combined with partial rationality, condensed expression of bourgeois alienation, rules supreme. The detective story is the realm of the happy ending. The criminal is always caught. Justice is always done. Crime never pays. Bourgeois legality, bourgeois values, bourgeois society, always triumph in the end. It is soothing, socially integrating literature, despite its concern with crime, violence and murder.

S. Vestdijk has called attention to the similarities and dissimilarities of the detective story and the game of chess. In both cases we have a limited number of players and strictly conventional rules, which are mechanical and purely rational in nature; both are deterministic, each move determined by the previous ones and leading to the next. But the differences are no less striking. In chess, the winner is the one who really manifests superior rational skill and memory (although capacity for concentration and absence of nervous over-reaction and anxiety also play a role in determining the winner). In the classical detective story, on the other hand, the winner is predetermined by the author. Like the hunted fox, the criminal never wins. It is not fair play, but fake play under the guise of fair play. It is a game with loaded dice. Bourgeois rationality is a cheater's rationality. The "best man" never wins; the richest does. Private property, law and order, must triumph, regardless of the cost in human life and misery. For the "survival of the fittest" (meaning the richest) to be disguised as fair play, the detective must be a super-brain, and the predetermined winner must appear as the best player.

Many crime-story writers began as "mechanical writers" churning the stuff out for a pittance paid by pulp magazines. But the inner drive that moved them to write was anything but mechanical. In his biography of the creator of Sherlock Holmes, *Portrait of an Artist: Conan Doyle,* Julian Symons points out that the decent, law-abiding, patriotic, and typically Victorian bourgeois Conan Doyle invented a hero with quite the opposite personality: a brainy, Bohemian, violin-playing drug addict. He suggests that there were really two Conan Doyles: "Behind the beefy face and rampant moustaches lurked another figure, hurt, perplexed and uncomforting."

Edgar Allan Poe's early writing was dominated by his tormented anxiety and hallucinations, which prevented him from conducting a normal life and earning a normal living. Suddenly he got a job as editor of the popular journal *Graham's* in Philadelphia. For the only time of his life he was better off. He desperately wanted to keep that job. Was that the drive that transformed his gothic-romantic writing into the pure rationalism of *The Murders in the Rue Morgue?* This is at least the hypothesis of the literary historian Howard Haycraft in *The Life and Times of the Detective Story.* We see the parallel with the older Thomas De Quincey, whose hallucinations are twisted into reasonable logic and persiflage in his *Murder considered as one of the Fine Arts.*

In James Brabazon's biography of Dorothy Sayers, we learn of an obviously frustrated woman unable to have a normal relationship with a man of her own intellectual and moral standard and therefore projecting herself (Miss Harriet) and her fantasy Ideal Companion (Lord Peter Wimsey) into her books.

The case of Georges Simenon is even clearer. He has said that he was very religious up to the age of 13, even wanting to become a priest. Then, with his first sexual encounter, "I saw that all that about guilt and sin was nonsense. I found out that all the sins I'd heard about were not sins at all." (Interview in *The Sunday Times,* 16 May 1982.) When we read his poignant autobiography, *Mémoires Intimes,* we discover a deeply unhappy and guilt-ridden man. He boasts of having slept with ten thousand women, eight thousand of them prostitutes, but he has obviously been unable to establish real human relationships in the first place with women. ("The more ordinary a woman is, the more one can consider her as 'woman,' the more the act takes on significance.") He is aware of having made his family deeply unhappy by his extravagance, drunkenness, and egoism, and he feels at least some guilt for the suicide of his daughter Marie-Jo.

Yet Inspector Maigret is the most ordinary of petty-bourgeois citizens, happy to return to his wife after a fair day's work for a fair day's pay, someone who would never dream of visiting a prostitute, let alone thousands of them. The life the author believes he would like to have lived is in his books. But how sincere is that belief? For after he had made some money (not necessarily millions), he did, after all, have a choice. And he was weak enough to choose wrongly, not only from the point of view of social morality, but also from the point of view of personal happiness. As he himself explained to the Paris daily *Le Monde* (13 November 1981): "It's life that keeps me going. . . . I have seen misery close up, in slums throughout the world. I have seen the rich, and participated in their orgies." But that was not really unavoidable, was it? It was a result of uncontrolled drives, which he continued to suffer, for which he felt deep guilt, and which he tried to sublimate in his books.

Graham Greene is the writer most conscious of the motives that make him write. As the conservative German historian Joachim Fest pointed out *(Frankfurter Allgemeine Zeitung,* 10 April 1982), behind his books stands "the need to escape the tedium of life, the monotony suffered as pain, and to escape it through experience of fear and of extreme risk."[3] Here we find escapist literature, which helps the reader to endure the ills of bourgeois society, corresponding to the author's own need to escape, both through actual life (Greene's travelling and spying adventures) and through his writings. In his autobiography *Ways of Escape,* Greene writes: "Sometimes I ask myself how all those who cannot write, compose, or paint are capable of escaping the absurdity, the sadness, and the panic fear which characterize the human condition."

Adam Hall makes his hero Quiller, the technocratic spy, into a faceless operative like those employed by a great corporation, institution or government. He draws a picture of total alienation. Reading his speech to a potential recruit, we are left with the question: is this only Quiller's universe, or does it reflect the author's own inner despair?

> You've got to learn to cross the line and live your life outside society[!], shut yourself away from people, cut yourself off. Values are different out there. Let a man show friendship for you and you've got to deny him, mistrust him, suspect him, and nine times out of ten you'll be wrong but it's the tenth time that'll save you from a dirty death in a cheap hotel because you'd opened the door to a man you thought was a friend. Out there you'll be alone and you'll have no one you can trust, not even the people who are running you. Not even me. If you make the wrong kind of mistake at the wrong time in the wrong place, and it looks like you're fouling up the mission or exposing the Bureau, they'll throw you to the dogs. And so will I.

We've come a long way from the famous Raymond Chandler formula about the quality of the lone detective walking down the streets.

Umberto Eco, who became interested in the crime novel through semiotics, tries to throw more light on his own inner motives for writing the famous detective story *The Name of the Rose.* He actually suggests that he was moved by the desire to murder a monk, which seized him in March 1978 (precisely!). Indeed, if it would be so easy to psychoanalyze oneself, a whole profession would soon be out of business.

Jack London provides the most fascinating and moving of cases. On the eve of his tragic suicide in 1916 he had almost finished one of the most amazing crime stories of all time. *Assassination Bureau Ltd* is the only truly philosophical crime novel. It is a battle of wits between two individuals who represent opposite trends in philosophy and in the radical movement. One embodies the attempt to eliminate social evil by the murder of evil individuals; the other one looks for a solution to the social question through self-organization and self-emancipation of the oppressed.

London starts from that elementary debate between the Nietzschean organizer of the Assassination Bureau and his Marxist nemesis (who is also the lover of the murderer's daughter) and proceeds to peel off layer after layer of subtle analysis. The head of the Assassination Bureau makes fun of the inefficiency of the traditional anarcho-terrorists. He actually tries to build a "perfect organization" and in so doing comes strikingly close to becoming a Zinovievist ideological forerunner of Stalin. Some of his philosopher-murderers stick to rigid moral principles which they refuse to violate, even if it costs them their lives; but at the same time they murder for money. The Marxist hero, on the other hand, is somewhat like an anti-hero—a rich individualist who ends up by destroying the Assassination Bureau's chief while desperately trying to save him. He is unable to formulate or see through his own motives except that of general respect for the sanctity of human life, though that does not prevent him from killing a dozen people! But more than the fanatically principled assassin, it is he who is the genuine idealist and who is completely uninterested in money.

All the debates, adventures and increasing suspense of this significant novel take place against the background of Jack London's premonition of the decline of capitalism into barbarism, his hatred of exploitation and injustice, his abhorrence of war and his identification with the "people of the abyss," which makes him in Trotsky's eyes, one of the greatest revolutionary thinkers of this century. But these agonizing reappraisals also reflect London's torment which in the end led to his suicide. He was unable to decide on a political course of action; he failed to live in conformity with his own convictions; and his desperate quest for personal happiness, which he so movingly projects onto several of his novels' heroes, also ended in failure.

Notes

1. Our Swiss friend Marc Perrenoud has worked out the first attempt at a Marxist analysis of humanity's relation with death (Marx: *la Mort et les Autres*, mimeographed manuscript). For two recent books about the social history of death see Michel Vovelle, *La Mort et l'Occident de 1300 à nos jours* (Paris: [Gallimard], 1983) and Philippe Ariès, *L'Homme devant la Mort* (Paris: [Editions du Souil], 1977).

2. The Japanese detective story originated with Edogawa Rampo in the 1920s *(Nisen Doka,* "The Two-Sen Copper Coin," 1923), but really developed after World War Two: 14 million copies of crime stories were sold in the mid-sixties, 20 million in the mid-seventies. Apart from Rampo, the main authors are Seicho Matsumoto, Masahi Yokomizo *(The Honjin Murder Case,* 1947), Yoh Sano, and Shizuko Tatsuki *(The Passed Death).* All these references come from Ellery Queen, *Japanese Golden Dozen: The Detective Story World in Japan,* Charles E. Tuttle, Tokyo 1972.

3. On this psychopathology of violence, note this passage from Jack Higgins' thriller *Solo* (Pan, London, 1980-1) [New York: Stein and Day, 1980]:

"Rules of the game. They weren't the target."

"The game?" Morgan said, "And what game would that be?"

"You should know. You have been playing it long enough. The most exciting game in the world, with your own life as the ultimate stake. Can you honestly tell me anything else you've done that offered quite the same kick?"

"You're mad," Morgan said.

Mikali looked fairly surprised. "Why? I used to do the same things in uniform and they gave me medals for it. Your own position exactly. When you look in the mirror it's me you see."

Mikali is a famous concert pianist and a psychopathological killer. Morgan is a highly placed army officer and something of a psychopathological killer too.

THE FEMINIST APPROACH
TO THE WESTERN

Historically, women have had great influence in shaping the various genres of popular fiction. The novelist, Ann Radcliffe, for example, by moving The Mysteries of Udolpho *(as well as her other fiction) away from Horace Walpole's Gothic model, helped to develop a new popular genre, the romance story. The young Mary Shelley invented modern science fiction in her novel,* Frankenstein, *while authors like Agatha Christie and Dorothy L. Sayers defined the golden age of classic detective fiction. Women authors of popular domestic melodrama, such as E. D. E. N. Southworth and Harriet Beecher Stowe, were primarily responsible for transforming book publishing from a cottage industry to a commercially lucrative business. Women readers, as well as women writers, over the years have also had a significant impact on the evolution of popular fiction. Indeed, depending on which demographic statistical analysis you read, all agree on one point: women constitute the vast majority of book buyers.*

Regrettably, many studies of popular fiction (and literature in general) tend only to discuss the work of male writers, while ignoring the vast and significant contributions of women. Survey the research of American pulp magazine scholarship and you'll discover numerous monographs discussing the "hard-boiled" detective fiction of Dashiell Hammett and Raymond Chandler, the science fiction of Robert A. Heinlein, the adventure fiction of Edgar Rice Burroughs, or the Western fiction of Max Brand. Yet nothing is published about the pulp magazine romances or their authors. In fact, the romance pulps were high volume, high profit publications that frequently helped to bankroll many other less profitable pulps. Thus, the story of popular fiction is only half told when, by intent or by default, it neglects what women have accomplished, both as writers and as readers.

Feminist literary criticism attempts to tell the rest of this important story. Critical studies such as Elaine Showalter's A Literature of Their Own: British Women Novelists from Brontë to Lessing *(1978) and Sandra M. Gilbert's and Susan Gubar's* The Madwoman in the Attic: The Woman Writer and the Nineteenth-Century Literary Imagination *(1979) have rede-*

*fined the historic and artistic role women have played in the culture of lit-
erature. Jane Tompkins, one of the leading scholars of reader response theory, is also one of the foremost contemporary feminist critics of literature.
In her essay, "Women and the Language of Men," which appeared as a
chapter in her book-length study,* West of Everything: The Inner Life of
Westerns *(1992), Tompkins addresses the relationship between gender and
language in the popular Western, arguing that language use is perceived as
being emotional and feminine, and thus inferior, while lack of emotion and
reticence of speech are perceived as being masculine qualities, and thus
superior. In fact, Tompkins's analysis of gender imagery in the Western can
be applied usefully to other types of popular adventure fiction as well.*

JANE TOMPKINS

WOMEN AND THE LANGUAGE OF MEN

Fear of losing his identity drives a man west, where the harsh conditions of life
force his manhood into being. Into this do-or-die, all-or-nothing world we step when
we read this passage from Louis L'Amour's novel *Radigan* (1958), where a woman
about to be attacked by a gunman experiences a moment of truth:

> She had never felt like this before, but right now she was backed up
> against death with all the nonsense and the fancy words trimmed away.
> The hide of the truth was peeled back to expose the bare, quivering raw
> flesh of itself, and there was no nonsense about it. She had been taught
> the way a lady should live, and how a lady should act, and it was all good
> and right and true . . . but out here on the mesa top with a man hunting
> her to put her back on the grass it was no longer the same. . . . There are
> times in life when the fancy words and pretty actions don't count for
> much, when it's blood and death and a cold wind blowing and a gun in the
> hand and you know suddenly you're just an animal with guts and blood
> that wants to live, love and mate, and die in your own good time. (144-45)

L'Amour lays it on the line. Faced with death, we learn the truth about life. And
the truth is that human nature is animal. When your back is to the wall you find out
that what you want most is not to save your eternal soul—if it exists—but to live, in
the body. For truth is flesh, raw and quivering, with the hide peeled back. All else is
nonsense. The passage proposes a set of oppositions fundamental to the way the
Western thinks about the world. There are two choices: either you can remain in a
world of illusions, by which is understood religion, culture, and class distinctions, a
world of fancy words and pretty actions, of "manners for the parlor and the ball
room, and . . . womanly tricks for courting"; or you can face life as it really is—blood,
death, a cold wind blowing, and a gun in the hand. These are the classic oppositions
from which all Westerns derive their meaning: parlor versus mesa, East versus West,

woman versus man, illusion versus truth, words versus things. It is the last of these oppositions I want to focus on now because it stands for all the rest.

But first a warning. What is most characteristic of these oppositions is that as soon as you put pressure on them they break down. Each time one element of a pair is driven into a corner, it changes shape and frequently turns into its opposite. It's as if the genre's determination to have a world of absolute dichotomies ensures that interpenetration and transmutation will occur. For instance, when Burt Lancaster, playing Wyatt Earp in *Gunfight at the OK Corral,* declares toward the beginning of the movie, "I've never needed anybody in my life and I sure don't need Doc Holliday," the vehemence of his claim to autonomy virtually guarantees that it will be undermined. And sure enough, by the time the showdown arrives you can hardly tell him and Kirk Douglas (playing Doc) apart: they dress alike, walk alike, talk alike, and finally they fight side by side as brothers. Two who started out as opposites—gambler versus sheriff, drunken failure versus respected citizen, rake versus prude—have become indistinguishable.

Westerns strive to depict a world of clear alternatives—independence versus connection, anarchy versus law, town versus desert—but they are just as compulsively driven to destroying these opposites and making them contain each other.

So it is with language. Westerns distrust language. Time and again they set up situations whose message is that words are weak and misleading, only actions count; words are immaterial, only objects are real. But the next thing you know, someone is using language brilliantly, delivering an epigram so pithy and dense it might as well be a solid thing. In fact, Westerns go in for their own special brand of the bon mot, seasoned with skepticism and fried to a turn. The product—chewy and tough— is recognizable anywhere:

> Cow's nothin' but a heap o' trouble tied up in a leather bag.
>
> *The Cowboys,* 1972

> A human rides a horse until he's dead and then goes on foot. An Indian rides him another 20 miles and then eats him.
>
> *The Searchers,* 1956

> A Texan is nothin' but a human man way out on a limb.
>
> *The Searchers*

> Kansas is all right for men and dogs but it's pretty hard on women and horses.
>
> *The Santa Fe Trail,* 1940

> God gets off at Leavenworth, and Cyrus Holliday drives you from there to the devil.
>
> *The Santa Fe Trail*

> There ain't no Sundays west of Omaha.
>
> *The Cowboys*

> This is hard country, double hard.
>
> *Will Penny,* 1968

> When you boil it all down, what does a man really need? Just a smoke and a cup of coffee.
>
> *Johnny Guitar,* 1954

In the end you end up dyin' all alone on a dirty street. And for what? For nothin'.

High Noon, 1952

You can't serve papers on a rat, baby sister. You gotta kill 'em or let 'em be.

True Grit, 1969

He wasn't a good man, he wasn't a bad man, but Lord, he was a *man.*

The Ballad of Cable Hogue, 1969

Some things a man has to do, so he does 'em.

Winchester '73, 1950

Only a man who carries a gun ever needs one.

Angel and the Bad Man, 1947

Mr. Grimes: "God, dear God."
Yaqui Joe: "He won't help you."

100 Rifles, 1969

You haven't gotten tough, you've just gotten miserable.

Cowboy, 1958

The sayings all have one thing in common: they bring you down. Like the wisdom L'Amour offers his female protagonist out on the mesa top, these gritty pieces of advice challenge romantic notions. Don't call on God; he's not there. Think you're tough? You're just miserable. What do you die for? Nothin'. The sayings puncture big ideas and self-congratulation; delivered with perfect timing, they land like stones from a slingshot and make a satisfying thunk.

For the Western is at heart antilanguage. Doing, not talking, is what it values. And this preference is connected to its politics, as a line from L'Amour suggests: "A man can . . . write fine words, or he can do something to hold himself in the hearts of the people" (*Treasure Mountain*, 1972). "Fine words" are contrasted not accidentally with "the hearts of the people." For the men who are the Western's heroes don't have the large vocabularies an expensive education can buy. They don't have time to read that many books. Westerns distrust language in part because language tends to be wielded most skillfully by people who possess a certain kind of power: class privilege, political clout, financial strength. Consequently, the entire enterprise is based on a paradox. In order to exist, the Western has to use words or visual images, but these images are precisely what it fears. As a medium, the Western has to pretend that it doesn't exist at all, its words and pictures, just a window on the truth, not really there.

So the Western's preferred parlance ideally consists of abrupt commands: "Turn the wagon. Tie 'em up short. Get up on the seat" *(Red River)*; "Take my horse. Good swimmer. Get it done, boy" *(Rio Grande*, 1950). Or epigrammatic sayings of a strikingly aggressive sort: "There's only one thing you gotta know. Get it out fast and put it away slow" *(Man Without a Star)*; "When you pull a gun, kill a man" *(My Darling Clementine)*. For the really strong man, language is a snare; it blunts his purpose and diminishes his strength. When Joey asks Shane if he knows how to use a rifle, Shane answers, and we can barely hear him, "Little bit." The understatement and the clipping off of the indefinite article are typical of the minimalist language Western heroes speak, a desperate shorthand, comic, really, in its attempt to communicate without using words.

Westerns are full of contrasts between people who spout words and people who act. At the beginning of Sam Peckinpah's *The Wild Bunch* a temperance leader harangues his pious audience; in the next scene a violent bank robbery makes a shambles of their procession through town. The pattern of talk canceled by action always delivers the same message: language is false or at best ineffectual; only actions are real. When heroes talk, it *is* action: their laconic put-downs cut people off at the knees. Westerns treat salesmen and politicians, people whose business is language, with contempt. Braggarts are dead men as soon as they appear. When "Stonewall" Tory, in *Shane,* brags that he can face the Riker gang any day, you know he's going to get shot; it's Shane, the man who clips out words between clenched teeth, who will take out the hired gunman.

The Western's attack on language is wholesale and unrelenting, as if language were somehow tainted in its very being. When John Wayne, in John Ford's *The Searchers,* rudely tells an older woman who is taking more than a single sentence to say something, "I'd be obliged, ma'am if you would get to the point," he expresses the genre's impatience with words as a way of dealing with the world. For while the woman is speaking, Indians are carrying a prisoner off. Such a small incident, once you unpack it, encapsulates the Western's attitude toward a whole range of issues:

1. Chasing Indians—that is, engaging in aggressive physical action—is doing something, while talking about the situation is not.
2. The reflection and negotiation that language requires are gratuitous, even pernicious.
3. The hero doesn't need to think or talk; he just *knows.* Being the hero, he is in a state of grace with respect to the truth.

In a world of bodies true action must have a physical form. And so the capacity for true knowledge must be based in physical experience. John Wayne playing Ethan Edwards in *The Searchers* has that experience and knows what is right because, having arrived home after fighting in the Civil War, he better than anyone else realizes that life is "blood and death and a cold wind blowing and a gun in the hand." In such a world, language constitutes an inferior kind of reality, and the farther one stays away from it the better.

Language is gratuitous at best; at worst it is deceptive. It takes the place of things, screens them from view, creates a shadow world where anything can be made to look like anything else. The reason no one in the Glenn Ford movie *Cowboy* can remember the proper words for burying a man is that there aren't any. It is precisely *words* that cannot express the truth about things. The articulation of a creed in the Western is a sign not of conviction but of insincerity. The distaste with which John Wayne says, "The Lord giveth, the Lord taketh away," as he buries a man in *Red River,* not only challenges the authority of the Christian God but also expresses disgust at all the trappings of belief: liturgies, litanies, forms, representations, all of which are betrayals of reality itself.

The features I am describing here, using the abstract language the Western shuns, are dramatically present in a movie called *Dakota Incident* (1956), whose plot turns in part on the bootlessness of words and, secondarily, on the perniciousness of money (another system of representation the Western scorns). Near the beginning, a windbag senator, about to depart on the stage from a miserable town called Christian Flats, pontificates to a crowd that has gathered to watch a fight, "There's no problem that can't be solved at a conference table," adding, "Believe me, gentle-men, I know whereof I speak." The next minute, two gunfights break out on Main Street; in one of them the hero shoots and kills his own brother.

The theme of loquacity confounded by violence, declared at the outset, replays itself at the end when the main characters have been trapped by some Indians in a dry creek bed. The senator has been defending the Indians throughout, saying that they're misunderstood, have a relationship with the land, and take from the small end of the horn of plenty. Finally, when he and the others are about to die of thirst, he goes out to parley with the Indians. He makes a long and rather moving speech about peace and understanding, and they shoot him; he dies clawing at the arrow in his chest.

In case we hadn't already gotten the point about the ineffectuality of language, we get it now. But no sooner is the point made than the movie does an about-face. The other characters start saying that the senator died for what he believed, that he was wrong about the Indians "but true to himself." They say that perhaps his words "fell on barren ground: the Indians and us." And the story ends on a note of peaceful cooperation between whites and Indians (after the attacking Indians have been wiped out), with talk about words of friendship falling on fertile ground.

Language is specifically linked in this movie to a belief in peace and cooperation as a way of solving conflicts. And though it's made clear from the start that only wimps and fools believe negotiation is the way to deal with enemies (the movie was made in 1956 during the Cold War), that position is abandoned as soon as "our side" wins. *Dakota Incident* is not the only Western to express this ambivalent attitude toward language and the peace and harmony associated with it. Such ambivalence is typical, but it is always resolved in the end. Language gets its day in court, and then it is condemned.

When John Wayne's young protégé in *The Searchers,* for example, returns to his sweetheart after seven years, he's surprised to learn that she hasn't been aware of his affection. "But I always loved you," he protests. "I thought you knew that with-out me havin' to say it." For a moment here, John Ford seems to be making fun of the idea that you can communicate without language, gently ridiculing the young man's assumption that somehow his feelings would be known although he had never articulated them. But his silence is vindicated ultimately when the girl he loves, who was about to marry another man, decides to stick with him. The cowboy hero's taciturnity, like his awkward manners around women and inability to dance, is only superficially a flaw; actually, it's proof of his manhood and trueheartedness. In Westerns silence, sexual potency, and integrity go together.

Again, in *My Darling Clementine* Ford seems to make an exception to the inter-diction against language. When Victor Mature, playing Doc Holliday, delivers the "To be or not to be" speech from *Hamlet,* taking over from the drunken actor who has forgotten his lines, we are treated to a moment of verbal enchantment. The beauty and power of the poetry are recognized even by the hero, Wyatt Earp (played by Henry Fonda), who appreciates Shakespeare and delivers a long soliloquy himself over the grave of his brother. But when the old actor who has been performing locally leaves town, he tricks the desk clerk into accepting his signature on a bill in place of money. The actor, like the language he is identified with, is a lovable old fraud, wonderfully colorful and entertaining, but not, finally, to be trusted.

The position represented by language, always associated with women, religion, and culture, is allowed to appear in Westerns and is accorded a certain plausibility and value. It functions as a critique of force and, even more important, as a symbol of the peace, harmony, and civilization that force is invoked in order to preserve. But in the end, that position is deliberately proven wrong—massively, totally, and unequivocally—with pounding hooves, thundering guns, blood and death. Because the genre is in revolt against a Victorian culture where the ability to manipulate language confers power, the Western equates power with "not-language." And not-language it equates with being male.

In his book *Phallic Critiques* (1984) Peter Schwenger has identified a style of writing he calls "the language of men," a language that belongs to what he terms the School of Virility, starting with Jack London and continuing through Ernest Hemingway to Norman Mailer and beyond. Infused with colloquialism, slang, choppy rhythms, "bitten-off fragments," and diction that marks the writer as "tough," this language is pitted against itself *as* language, and devoted to maintaining, in Schwenger's terminology, "masculine reserve."

Drawing on Octavio Paz's definition of the *macho* as a "hermetic being, closed up in himself" ("women are inferior beings because, in submitting, they open themselves up"), Schwenger shows the connections these authors make among speaking, feeling, and feminization. "It is by talking," he writes, "that one opens up to another person and becomes vulnerable. It is by putting words to an emotion that it becomes feminized. As long as the emotion itself is restrained, held back, it hardly matters what the emotion itself is; it will retain a male integrity." Thus, "not talking is a demonstration of masculine control over emotion" (43-45).

Control is the key word here. Not speaking demonstrates control not only over feelings but over one's physical boundaries as well. The male, by remaining "hermetic," "closed up," maintains the integrity of the boundary that divides him from the world. (It is fitting that in the Western the ultimate loss of that control takes place when one man puts holes in another man's body.) To speak is literally to open the body to penetration by opening an orifice; it is also to mingle the body's substance with the substance of what is outside it. Finally, it suggests a certain incompleteness, a need to be in relation. Speech relates the person who is speaking to other people (as opposed to things); it requires acknowledging their existence and, by extension, their parity. If "to become a man," as Schwenger says, "must be finally to attain the solidity and self-containment of an object," "an object that is self-contained does not have to open itself up in words." But it is not so much the vulnerability or loss of dominance that speech implies that makes it dangerous as the reminder of the speaker's own interiority.

The interdiction masculinity imposes on speech arises from the desire for complete objectivization. And this means being conscious of nothing, not knowing that one has a self. To be a man is not only to be monolithic, silent, mysterious, impenetrable as a desert butte, it is to *be* the desert butte. By becoming a solid object, not only is a man relieved of the burden of relatedness and responsiveness to others, he is relieved of consciousness itself, which is to say, primarily, consciousness *of* self.

At this point, we come upon the intersection between the Western's rejection of language and its emphasis on landscape. Not fissured by self-consciousness, nature is what the hero aspires to emulate: perfect being-in-itself. This is why John Wayne was impatient with the woman who took longer than a sentence to speak her mind. As the human incarnation of nature, he neither speaks nor listens. He is monumentality in motion, propelling himself forward by instinct, no more talkable to than a river or an avalanche, and just as good company.

> WOMAN   That's a pretty dog.
> MAN   (No response)
> WOMAN   Well, it's got a pretty coat.
> MAN   (Silence)

The foregoing account of the Western's hostility to language refers to a mode of behavior—masculine behavior for the most part—that has left an indelible mark on the experience of practically every person who has lived in this country in the twentieth century. I mean the linguistic behavior of men toward women, particularly in domestic situations.

> He finds it very difficult to talk about his personal feelings, and intimidates me into not talking either. He also finds it very difficult to accept my affection. . . . I become angry that his need to be unemotional is more important than my need to have an outward show of love. Why do I always have to be the one that is understanding? (18)

> When I was married, it was devastatingly lonely—I wanted to die—it was just so awful being in love with someone who . . . never talked to me or consulted me. . . . (23)

> My husband grew up in a very non-emotional family and it took a long time for me to make him understand that it's a good thing to let people (especially the ones you love) know how you feel. (18)

> The relationship did not fill my deepest needs for closeness, that's why I'm no longer in it. I did share every part of myself with him but it was never mutual. (19)

> The loneliness comes from knowing you can't contact another person's feelings or actions, no matter how hard you try. (23)

> If I could change one thing—it would be to get him to be more expressive of his emotions, his wants, needs. I most criticize him for not telling me what he wants or how he feels. He denies he feels things when his non-verbals indicate he does feel them. (21)

The quotations come from Shere Hite's *Women and Love: A Cultural Revolution in Progress* (1987). I quote them here because I want to make clear that the Western's hatred of language is not a philosophical matter only; it has codified and sanctioned the way several generations of men have behaved verbally toward women in American society. Young boys sitting in the Saturday afternoon darkness could not ride horses or shoot guns, but they could talk. Or rather, they could learn how to keep silent. The Western man's silence functions as a script for behavior; it expresses and authorizes a power relation that reaches into the furthest corners of domestic and social life. The impassivity of male silence suggests the inadequacy of female verbalization, establishes male superiority, and silences the one who would engage in conversation. Hite comments:

> We usually don't want to see . . . non-communication or distancing types
> of behavior as expressing attitudes of inequality or superiority, as signs of
> a man not wanting to fraternize (sororize?) with someone of lower status.
> This is too painful. And yet, many men seem to be asserting superiority by
> their silences and testy conversational style with women. Thus, not talk-
> ing to a woman on an equal level can be a way for a man to dominate a
> relationship. . . . (25)

For a man to speak of his inner feelings not only admits parity with the person
he is talking to, but it jeopardizes his status as potent being, for talk dissipates
presence, takes away the mystery of an ineffable self which silence preserves.
Silence establishes dominance at the same time as it protects the silent one from
inspection and possible criticism by offering nothing for the interlocutor to grab
hold of. The effect, as in the dialogue about the dog quoted above, is to force the
speaker into an ineffectual flow of language which tries to justify itself, achieve significance, make an impression by additions which only diminish the speaker's force
with every word.

When Matthew Garth returns to his hotel room at the end of *Red River,* he acts
the part of silent conqueror to perfection. The heroine, who has been waiting for
him, warns him that his enemy is on the way to town. The film has her babble nervously about how she came to be there, how she found out about the danger, how
there's no way he can escape, no way to stop his enemy, nothing anyone can do,
nothing she can do. As he looks down at her, not hearing a thing she says, her words
spill out uncontrollably, until finally she says, "Stop me, Matt, stop me." He puts his
hand over her mouth, then kisses her. The fade-out that immediately follows suggests that the heroine, whose name is Tess Millay, is getting laid.

The scene invites diametrically opposed interpretations. From one point of view,
what happens is exactly right: the desire these characters feel for each other yearns
for physical expression. Nonverbal communication, in this case sex, is entirely
appropriate. But the scene gets to this point at the woman's expense.

Tess is the same character who, earlier in the film, had been shot by an arrow
and had it removed without batting an eyelash, had seduced the young man with
her arm in a sling, and had refused a proposition from his enemy. In this scene she
is totally undercut. As her useless verbiage pours out, she falls apart before our
eyes, a helpless creature who has completely lost control of herself and has to beg
a man to stop her.

> When I feel insecure, I need to talk about things a lot. It sometimes wor-
> ries me that I say the same things over and over. (19)

> I can be an emotional drain on my husband if I really open up. (19)

Hite notes that women feel ashamed of their need to talk, blaming themselves
and making excuses for the silence of men. "My husband grew up in a very non-
emotional family." The heroine of *Red River* cares so much about the hero that her
words pour out in a flood of solicitude. But instead of seeing this as a sign of love,
the film makes her anxiety look ridiculous and even forces *her to* interpret it this
way.

Tess Millay's abject surrender to the hero's superiority at the end of *Red River* is a supreme example of woman's introjection of the male attitude toward her. She sees herself as he sees her, silly, blathering on about manly business that is none of her concern, and beneath it all really asking for sex. The camera and the audience identify with the hero, while the heroine dissolves into a caricature of herself. Sex joins here with blood and death and a cold wind blowing as the only true reality, extinguishing the authority of women and their words.

Someone might argue that all the Western is doing here is making a case for non-verbal communication. If that were true, so much the better. But, at least when it comes to the relations between men and women, the Western doesn't aim to com-municate at all. The message, in the case of Tess Millay, as in the case of women in Westerns generally, is that there's nothing *to* them. They may seem strong and resilient, fiery, and resourceful at first, but when push comes to shove, as it always does, they crumble. Even Marian, Joe Starret's wife in *Shane,* one of the few women in Western films who, we are made to feel, is also substantial as a person, dissolves into an ineffectual harangue at the end, unsuccessfully pleading with her man not to go into town to get shot. When the crunch comes, women shatter into words.

A classic moment of female defeat appears in Owen Wister's *The Virginian,* which set the pattern for the Western in the twentieth century. In the following pas-sage, Molly, the heroine, is vanquished by the particular form of male silence that her cowboy lover practices. The Virginian has just passed his mortal enemy on the road with drawn pistol and without a word. But when Molly tries to get him to talk about it and "ventures a step inside the border of his reticence," he turns her away:

> She looked at him, and knew that she must step outside his reticence again. By love and her surrender to him their positions had been exchanged. . . . She was no longer his half-indulgent, half-scornful supe-rior. Her better birth and schooling that had once been weapons to keep him at a distance, to bring her off victorious in their encounters, had given way before the onset of the natural man himself. She knew her cow-boy lover, with all that he lacked, to be more than ever she could be, with all that she had. He was her worshipper still, but her master, too. Therefore now, against the baffling smile he gave her, she felt powerless. (256)

Wister makes explicit the connection between the Virginian's mastery over Molly and his reticence, his conversational droit du seigneur. Like L'Amour, Wister sees the relationship between men and women as a version of the East–West, parlor–mesa, word–deed opposition. Molly is identified by her ties to the East, her class background, her education, but most of all by her involvement in language. Words are her work and her pleasure and the source of her power. She teaches them in school and keeps company with them in books, but they cannot protect her from "the onset of the natural man himself." The man's sheer physical presence is stronger than language, and so words are finally the sign of Molly's—and all women's—inferiority.

This is what lies behind the strange explanation the Virginian offers Molly of his relationship to the villain, Trampas. He says that he and Trampas just lie in wait for each other, hating each other in silence, always ready to draw. Then he tells a story about a women's temperance meeting he once overheard while staying at a hotel. "Oh, heavens. Well, I couldn't change my room and the hotel man, he apologized to me next mawnin'. Said it didn't surprise him the husbands drank some" (259). Then, reverting to himself and Trampas, the Virginian remarks, "We were not a bit like a temperance meetin'" (259).

The temperance ladies talk and talk; that is *all* they do. It never comes to shooting. Meanwhile, they drive their husbands crazy with their cackle. Drive them to drink, which dulls the feelings men can't talk about. So the Virginian and Trampas (the enemy he passes on the road) hardly exchange a word. They cannot communicate; therefore, they will kill each other someday. Their silence signals their seriousness, their dignity and reality, and the inevitability of their conflict. Silence is a sign of mastery, and goes along with a gun in the hand. They would rather die than settle the argument by talking to each other.

Why does the Western harbor such animus against women's words? Why should it be so extreme and unforgiving? Is it because, being the weaker sex physically, women must use words as their chief weapon, and so, if men are to conquer, the gun of women's language must be emptied? Or is it because, having forsworn the solace of language, men cannot stand to see women avail themselves of it because it reminds them of their own unverbalized feelings? Hite remarks:

> It could be argued that, if men are silent, they are not trying to dominate women; rather, they are trapped in their own silence (and their own pain), unable to talk or communicate about feelings, since this is such forbidden behavior for them. (25)

If Hite has guessed correctly, men's silence in Westerns is the counterpart of women's silence; that is, it is the silence of an interior self who has stopped trying to speak and has no corresponding self to talk to. Its voice is rarely heard, since it represents the very form of interior consciousness the genre wishes to stamp out. But it does burst out occasionally. In *The Virginian* it speaks in the form of a song, roared out by the rebellious cowhands who are getting drunk in a caboose on their way back to the ranch where the Virginian is taking them. They sing:

> "I'm wild and woolly, and full of fleas;
> I'm hard to curry above the knees;
> I'm a she-wolf from Bitter Creek, and
> It's my night to ho-o-wl—"

The wolf bitch inside men, what would it sound like if they ever let it out? What would it say? The silence of this inner voice, its muteness, keeps the woman's voice, its counterpart, from being heard. It is replaced by the narrative of the gunfight, the range war, the holdup, the chase. By the desert. The Western itself is the language of men, what they do vicariously, instead of speaking.

I used to keep a photograph of the young John Wayne posted on my bulletin board. He has on a cowboy hat, and he is even then developing a little of that inimitable cowboy squint so beloved of millions. But he has not yet gotten the cowboy face, the leathery wall of noncommunication written over by wrinkles, speaking pain and hardship and the refusal to give in to them, speaking the determination to tough it out against all odds, speaking the willingness to be cruel in return for cruelty, and letting you know, beyond all shadow of a doubt, who's boss.

The other expression, the expression of the young John Wayne, is tender, and more than a little wistful; it is delicate and incredibly sensitive. Pure and sweet; shy, really, and demure.

Where is she, this young girl that used to inhabit John Wayne's body along with the Duke? I think of the antiwar song from the sixties, "Where have all the young girls gone?" and the answer comes back, "Gone to young men every one," and the young men in the song are gone to battle and the soldiers to the graveyard. How far is it from the death of the young girl in John Wayne's face to the outbreak of war? How far is it from the suppression of language to the showdown on Main Street? In *The Virginian* Wister suggests that the silence that reigns between the hero and the villain guarantees that one will kill the other someday. And still he ridicules women's language.

The Western hero's silence symbolizes a massive suppression of the inner life. And my sense is that this determined shutting down of emotions, this cutting of the self off from contact with the interior well of feeling, exacts its price in the end. Its equivalent: the force of the bullets that spew forth from the guns in little orgasms of uncontained murderousness. Its trophy: the bodies in the dust. Its victory: the silence of graves. Its epitaph: that redundant sign that keeps on appearing in *Gunfight at the OK Corral*—BOOT HILL GRAVEYARD TOMBSTONE.

Why does the Western hate women's language? I argued earlier that the Western turned against organized religion and the whole women's culture of the nineteenth century and all the sermons and novels that went with them; the rejection took place in the name of purity, of a truth belied by all these trappings, something that could not be stated. But perhaps the words the Western hates stand as well for inner confusion. A welter of thoughts and feelings, a condition of mental turmoil that is just as hateful as the more obvious external constraints of economics, politics, and class distinctions. Women, like language, remind men of their own interiority; women's talk evokes a whole network of familial and social relationships and their corollaries in the emotional circuitry. What men are fleeing in Westerns is not only the cluttered Victorian interior but also the domestic dramas that go on in that setting, which the quotations from Shere Hite recall. The gesture of sweeping the board clear may be intended to clear away the reminders of emotional entanglements that cannot be dealt with or faced. Men would rather die than talk, because talking might bring up their own unprocessed pain or risk a dam burst that would undo the front of imperturbable superiority. It may be the Western hero flees into the desert seeking there what Gretel Ehrlich has called "the solace of open spaces," a place whose physical magnificence and emptiness are the promise of an inward strength and quietude. "Where seldom is heard a discouraging word, and the skies are not cloudy all day."

CRITICAL BIBLIOGRAPHY

Bakhtin, Mikhail. *The Dialogic Imagination: Four Essays*. Ed. Michael Holquist. Austin: U of Texas P, 1981.

Bann, Stephen and John E. Bowlt, eds. *Russian Formalism*. Edinburgh: Scottish Academic Press, 1973.

Barthes, Roland. *Critical Essays*. Evanston: Northwestern UP, 1972.

——. *Elements of Semiology*. London: Jonathan Cape, 1967.

——. *The Pleasures of the Text*. New York: Hill & Wang, 1975.

Baxandall, Lee and Stefan Morawski. *Marx and Engels on Literature and Art*. New York: International General, 1973.

Bleich, David. *Subjective Criticism*. Baltimore: Johns Hopkins UP, 1978.

Bloom, Harold. *The Anxiety of Influence: A Theory of Poetry*. New York: Oxford UP, 1973.

——. *A Map of Misreading*. New York: Oxford UP, 1975.

Browne, Ray B. *Popular Culture and the Expanding Consciousness*. New York: Wiley, 1973.

——. *Theories & Methodologies in Popular Culture*. Bowling Green: BGSU Popular P, 1975.

Campbell, Joseph. *The Hero With a Thousand Faces*. New York: Pantheon Books, 1949.

——. *The Masks of God*. New York: Viking Press, 1959.

——. *Myths to Live By*. New York: Viking Press, 1972.

Cawelti, John G. *Adventure, Mystery, and Romance: Formula Stories As Art and Popular Culture*. Chicago: U of Chicago P, 1976.

——. *The Six-Gun Mystique*. Bowling Green: BGSU Popular P, 1971.

Chatman, Seymour. *Story and Discourse: Narrative Structure in Fiction and Film*. Ithaca: Cornell UP, 1978.

Davis, Robert Con, ed. *Contemporary Literary Criticism: Modernism through Poststructuralism*. White Plains: Longman, 1986.

Derrida, Jacques. *Of Grammatology*. Baltimore: Johns Hopkins UP, 1976.

Donovan, Josephine. *Feminist Literary Criticism: Explorations in Theory*. Lexington: UP of Kentucky, 1975.

Eagleton, Mary, ed. *Feminist Literary Theory: A Reader*. Oxford: Blackwell, 1986.

Eagleton, Terry. *Literary Theory: An Introduction*. Oxford: Blackwell, 1983.

Eco, Umberto. *The Role of the Reader: Explorations in the Semiotics of Texts*. Bloomington: Indiana UP, 1979.

Ehrmann, Jacques, ed. *Structuralism*. Garden City: Anchor Books, 1970.

Fish, Stanley. *Is There a Text in This Class?: The Authority of Interpretive Communities*. Cambridge: Harvard UP, 1980.

Foucault, Michel. *Language, Counter-Memory, Practice: Selected Essays and Interviews*. Ed. D. F. Bouchard. Ithaca: Cornell UP, 1977.

Freud, Sigmund. *Introductory Lectures on Psycho-Analysis*. London: Allen & Unwin, 1922.

Frye, Northrop. *Anatomy of Criticism: Four Essays*. Princeton: Princeton UP, 1957.

Gilbert, Sandra M. and Susan Gubar. *The Madwoman in the Attic: The Woman Writer and the Nineteenth-Century Literary Imagination*. New Haven: Yale UP, 1979.

Harari, Josué V., ed. *Textual Strategies: Perspectives in Post-Structuralist Criticism*. Ithaca: Cornell UP, 1979.

Holland, Norman N. *The Dynamics of Literary Response*. New York: Oxford UP, 1968.

Innis, Robert E., ed. *Semiotics: An Introductory Anthology*. Bloomington: Indiana UP, 1985.

Iser, Wolfgang. *The Act of Reading: A Theory of Aesthetic Response*. Baltimore: Johns Hopkins UP, 1978.

Jacobus, Mary, ed. *Women Writing and Writing About Women*. New York: Barnes & Noble, 1979.

Jameson, Fredric. *The Political Unconscious: Narrative as a Socially Symbolic Act*. Ithaca: Cornell UP, 1981.

Johnson, Barbara. *The Critical Difference: Essays in the Contemporary Rhetoric of Reading*. Baltimore: Johns Hopkins UP, 1980.

Jung, C. G. *Analytical Psychology: Its Theory and Practice*. New York: Pantheon Books, 1968.

——. *The Archetypes and the Collective Unconscious*. New York: Pantheon Books, 1959.

Lemon, Lee T. and Marion J. Reis, eds. *Russian Formalist Criticism: Four Essays*. Lincoln: U of Nebraska P, 1965.

Lévi-Strauss, Claude. *Structural Anthropology*. London: Allen Lane, 1968.

Lodge, David, ed. *20th-Century Literary Criticism*. London: Longman, 1972.

Lukács, Georg. *The Historical Novel*. London: Merlin Press, 1962.

——. *Writer and Critic and Other Essays*. London: Merlin Press, 1970.

Marx, Leo. *The Machine in the Garden: Technology and the Pastoral Ideal in America*. New York: Oxford UP, 1964.

Matejka, Ladislav and Krystyna Pomorska, eds. *Readings in Russian Poetics: Formalist and Structuralist Views*. Cambridge: MIT Press, 1971.

Propp, Vladimir. *The Morphology of the Folktale*. Austin: U of Texas P, 1968.

Ryan, Michael. *Marxism and Deconstruction: A Critical Articulation*. Baltimore: Johns Hopkins UP, 1982.

Said, Edward W. *The World, the Text, and the Critic*. Cambridge: Harvard UP, 1983.

Sartre, Jean-Paul. *What is Literature?* New York: Philosophical Library, 1949.

Showalter, Elaine. *A Literature of Their Own: British Women Novelists from Brontë to Lessing*. Princeton: Princeton UP, 1977.

——. *The New Feminist Criticism: Essays on Women, Literature, and Theory*. New York: Pantheon Books, 1985.

Slote, Bernice. *Myth and Symbol: Critical Approaches and Applications*. Lincoln: U of Nebraska P, 1963.

Slotkin, Richard. *Regeneration Through Violence: The Mythology of the American Frontier, 1600–1860*. Middletown: Wesleyan UP, 1973.

Smith, Henry Nash. *Virgin Land: The American West as Symbol and Myth*. Cambridge: Harvard UP, 1950.

Suleiman, Susan and Inge Crosman, eds. *The Reader in the Text: Essays on Audience and Interpretation*. Princeton: Princeton UP, 1980.

Todorov, Tzvetan. *The Fantastic: A Structural Approach to a Literary Genre*. Ithaca: Cornell UP, 1975.

Tompkins, Jane, ed. *Reader-Response Criticism: From Formalism to Post-Structuralism*. Baltimore: Johns Hopkins UP, 1980.

SELECTED GENRE FILMOGRAPHY

Horror

Film Title	Director	Year of Release
The Cabinet of Dr. Caligari	Robert Wiene	1919
Nosferatu	F. W. Murnau	1922
The Phantom of the Opera	Rupert Julian	1925
The Cat and the Canary	Paul Leni	1927
Dracula	Tod Browning	1931
Frankenstein	James Whale	1931
Freaks	Tod Browning	1932
The Mummy	Karl Freund	1932
Vampyr	Carl Theodor Dreyer	1932
King Kong	Merian C. Cooper Ernest B. Schoedsack	1933
Mystery of the Wax Museum	Michael Curtiz	1933
The Black Cat	Edgar G. Ulmer	1934
Bride of Frankenstein	James Whale	1935
The Hunchback of Notre Dame	William Dieterle	1939
Dr. Jekyll and Mr. Hyde	Victor Fleming	1941
The Wolf Man	George Waggner	1941
Cat People	Jacques Tourneur	1942
The Uninvited	Lewis Allen	1944
The Thing (From Another World)	Christian Nyby	1951
Creature From the Black Lagoon	Jack Arnold	1954
Them!	Gordon Douglas	1954
Godzilla, King of the Monsters	Terry Morse Inoshiro Honda	1956
Invasion of the Body Snatchers	Don Siegel	1956
Curse of the Demon	Jacques Tourneur	1958
The Fly	Kurt Neumann	1958
Horror of Dracula	Terence Fisher	1958
House on Haunted Hill	William Castle	1958
Psycho	Alfred Hitchcock	1960
The Innocents	Jack Clayton	1961
The Birds	Alfred Hitchcock	1963
The Haunting	Robert Wise	1963
Night of the Living Dead	George A. Romero	1968
Rosemary's Baby	Roman Polanski	1968
The Exorcist	William Friedkin	1973
The Texas Chainsaw Massacre	Tobe Hooper	1974
Jaws	Steven Spielberg	1975
Carrie	Brian De Palma	1976
The Omen	Richard Donner	1976
Halloween	John Carpenter	1978
Alien	Ridley Scott	1979
Friday the 13th	Sean S. Cunningham	1980
The Shining	Stanley Kubrick	1980
Poltergeist	Tobe Hooper	1982
The Evil Dead	Sam Raimi	1983
Gremlins	Joe Dante	1984
A Nightmare on Elm Street	Wes Craven	1984
Hellraiser	Clive Barker	1987
The Lost Boys	Joel Schumacher	1987
Near Dark	Kathryn Bigelow	1987
Bram Stoker's Dracula	Francis Ford Coppola	1992
Interview with the Vampire: The Vampire Chronicles	Neil Jordan	1994

Romance

The Sheik	George Melford	1921
It Happened One Night	Frank Capra	1934
Bringing Up Baby	Howard Hawks	1939
Gone with the Wind	Victor Fleming	1939
Wuthering Heights	William Wyler	1939
The Philadelphia Story	George Cukor	1940
Forever Amber	Otto Preminger	1947
Roman Holiday	William Wyler	1953
Sabrina	Billy Wilder	1954
An Affair to Remember	Leo McCarey	1957
Gigi	Vincente Minnelli	1958
Pillow Talk	Michael Gordon	1959
Some Like It Hot	Billy Wilder	1959
Breakfast at Tiffany's	Blake Edwards	1961
West Side Story	Robert Wise Jerome Robbins	1961
Cleopatra	Joseph L. Mankiewicz	1963
Barefoot in the Park	Gene Saks	1967
The Graduate	Mike Nichols	1967
The Taming of the Shrew	Franco Zeffirelli	1967
Romeo and Juliet	Franco Zeffirelli	1968
Love Story	Arthur Hiller	1970
The Way We Were	Sydney Pollack	1973
Annie Hall	Woody Allen	1977
The Goodbye Girl	Herbert Ross	1977
Heaven Can Wait	Warren Beatty Buck Henry	1978
Manhattan	Woody Allen	1979
Somewhere in Time	Jeannot Szwarc	1980
An Officer and a Gentleman	Taylor Hackford	1982
Murphy's Romance	Martin Ritt	1985
Moonstruck	Norman Jewison	1987
Big	Penny Marshall	1988
Look Who's Talking	Amy Heckerling	1989
Pretty Woman	Garry Marshall	1990
The Age of Innocence	Martin Scorsese	1993
Benny & Joon	Jeremiah Chechik	1993
Sleepless in Seattle	Nora Ephron	1993

Science Fiction and Fantasy

A Trip to the Moon	Georges Mèliès	1902
The Lost World	Harry Hoyt	1925
Metropolis	Fritz Lang	1926
Things to Come	William Cameron Menzies	1936
The Wizard of Oz	Victor Fleming	1939
The Thief of Bagdad	Ludwig Berger et. al.	1940
Destination Moon	Irving Pichel	1950
The Day the Earth Stood Still	Robert Wise	1951
The Thing (From Another World)	Christian Nyby	1951
When Worlds Collide	Rudolph Matė	1951
The 5,000 Fingers of Dr. T.	Roy Rowland	1953
Invaders From Mars	William Cameron Menzies	1953
War of the Worlds	Byron Haskin	1953
20,000 Leagues Under the Sea	Richard Fleischer	1954
Earth vs. the Flying Saucers	Fred F. Sears	1956
Forbidden Planet	Fred McLeod Wilcox	1956
20 Million Miles to Earth	Nathan Juran	1957
The Blob	Irvin S. Yeaworth, Jr.	1958
The 7th Voyage of Sinbad	Nathan Juran	1958
Journey to the Center of the Earth	Henry Levin	1959
The Time Machine	George Pal	1960
Mysterious Island	Cy Endfield	1961
Jason and the Argonauts	Don Chaffey	1963
Robinson Crusoe on Mars	Byron Haskin	1964
7 Faces of Dr. Lao	George Pal	1964
Fantastic Voyage	Richard Fleischer	1966
Fahrenheit 451	Francois Truffaut	1967
Barbarella	Roger Vadim	1968
Planet of the Apes	Franklin J. Schaffner	1968
The Illustrated Man	Jack Smight	1969
Colossus: The Forbin Project	Joseph Sargent	1970
The Andromeda Strain	Robert Wise	1971
A Clockwork Orange	Stanley Kubrick	1971
The Omega Man	Boris Sagal	1971
Silent Running	Douglas Trumbull	1971
THX-1138	George Lucas	1971
Soylent Green	Richard Fleischer	1973
Westworld	Michael Crichton	1973
Dark Star	John Carpenter	1974
The Land That Time Forgot	Kevin Connor	1975
Close Encounters of the Third Kind	Steven Spielberg	1977
Star Wars	George Lucas	1977
The Lord of the Rings	Ralph Bakshi	1978
Alien	Ridley Scott	1979
Star Trek: The Motion Picture	Robert Wise	1979
The Empire Strikes Back	Irvin Kershner	1980
Clash of the Titans	Desmond Davis	1981
Dragonslayer	Matthew Robbins	1981
Blade Runner	Ridley Scott	1982
E.T. The Extra-Terrestrial	Steven Spielberg	1982
Tron	Steven Lisberger	1982
The Dark Crystal	Jim Henson	1983
Return of the Jedi	Richard Marquand	1983
The NeverEnding Story	Wolfgang Petersen	1984
Starman	John Carpenter	1984
The Terminator	James Cameron	1984
Back To the Future	Robert Zemeckis	1985
Cocoon	Ron Howard	1985
Legend	Ridley Scott	1985
Aliens	James Cameron	1986
Alien Nation	Graham Baker	1988
Willow	Ron Howard	1988
The Abyss	James Cameron	1989
The Adventures of Baron Munchausen	Terry Gilliam	1989
Terminator 2: Judgement Day	James Cameron	1991
Alien3	David Fincher	1992

Detective and Crime

Bulldog Drummond	F. Richard Jones	1929
The Greene Murder Case	Frank Tuttle	1929
Little Caesar	Mervyn LeRoy	1930
Raffles	Harry D'Arrast	1930
The Black Camel	Hamilton MacFadden	1931
M	Fritz Lang	1931
Arsene Lupin	Jack Conway	1932
Scarface	Howard Hawks	1932
Sherlock Holmes	William K. Howard	1932
The Kennel Murder Case	Michael Curtiz	1933
The Thin Man	W. S. Van Dyke	1934
The Case of the Lucky Legs	Archie Mayo	1935
G Men	William Keighley	1935
The Lone Wolf Returns	Roy William Neill	1935
Think Fast, Mr. Moto	Norman Foster	1937
The Saint in New York	Ben Holmes	1938
The Hound of the Baskervilles	Sidney Lanfield	1939
The Letter	William Wyler	1940
The Maltese Falcon	John Huston	1941
Sherlock Holmes and the Secret Weapon	Roy William Neill	1942
This Gun for Hire	Frank Tuttle	1942
Double Indemnity	Billy Wilder	1944
Laura	Otto Preminger	1944

And Then There Were None	René Clair	1945
Detour	Edgar G. Ulmer	1945
Scarlet Street	Fritz Lang	1945
The Big Sleep	Howard Hawks	1946
The Blue Dahlia	George Marshall	1946
The Killers	Robert Siodmak	1946
The Postman Always Rings Twice	Tay Garnett	1946
Key Largo	John Huston	1948
The Naked City	Jules Dassin	1948
Rope	Alfred Hitchcock	1948
White Heat	Raoul Walsh	1949
D.O.A.	Rudolph Maté	1950
Detective Story	William Wyler	1951
I, the Jury	Harry Essex	1953
Rear Window	Alfred Hitchcock	1954
To Catch a Thief	Alfred Hitchcock	1955
Witness for the Prosecution	Billy Wilder	1957
Touch of Evil	Orson Welles	1958
Vertigo	Alfred Hitchcock	1958
Anatomy of a Murder	Otto Preminger	1959
Cape Fear	J. Lee Thompson	1962
Harper	Jack Smight	1966
Bonnie and Clyde	Arthur Penn	1967
In the Heat of the Night	Norman Jewison	1967
Bullitt	Peter Yates	1968
Cotton Comes to Harlem	Ossie Davis	1970
Dirty Harry	Don Siegel	1971
Klute	Alan J. Pakula	1971
The Godfather	Francis Ford Coppola	1972
The Long Goodbye	Robert Altman	1973
Chinatown	Roman Polanski	1974
Death Wish	Michael Winner	1974
Murder on the Orient Express	Sidney Lumet	1974
The Seven Percent Solution	Herbert Ross	1976
The Late Show	Robert Benton	1977
Coma	Michael Crichton	1978
Death on the Nile	John Guillermin	1978
Body Heat	Lawrence Kasdan	1981
Thief	Michael Mann	1981
Dead Men Don't Wear Plaid	Carl Reiner	1982
Once Upon a Time in America	Sergio Leone	1984
Jagged Edge	Richard Marquand	1985
Black Widow	Bob Rafelson	1986
Blue Velvet	David Lynch	1986
The Name of the Rose	Jean-Jacques Annaud	1986
Wise Guys	Brian DePalma	1986
Fatal Attraction	Adrian Lyne	1987
Lethal Weapon	Richard Donner	1987
The Untouchables	Brian DePalma	1987
Sea of Love	Harold Becker	1989
Dick Tracy	Warren Beatty	1990
GoodFellas	Martin Scorsese	1990
The Grifters	Stephen Frears	1990
Presumed Innocent	Alan J. Pakula	1990
V. I. Warshawski	Jeff Kanew	1991
Basic Instinct	Paul Verhoeven	1992
The Firm	Sydney Pollack	1993
Manhattan Murder Mystery	Woody Allen	1993
The Pelican Brief	Alan J. Pakula	1993
Pulp Fiction	Quentin Tarantino	1994

Adventure, Western, and Spy

Spies	Fritz Lang	1928
The Mask of Fu Manchu	Charles Brabin	1932
Treasure Island	Victor Fleming	1934
Captain Blood	Michael Curtiz	1935
The Scarlet Pimpernel	Harold Young	1935
The Charge of the Light Brigade	Michael Curtiz	1936
The Prisoner of Zenda	John Cromwell	1937
The Adventures of Robin Hood	Michael Curtiz William Keighley	1938
Beau Geste	William Wellman	1939
The Four Feathers	Zoltan Korda	1939
Gunga Din	George Stevens	1939
Stagecoach	John Ford	1939
The Mark of Zorro	Rouben Mamoulian	1940
The Sea Hawk	Michael Curtiz	1940
The Westerner	William Wyler	1940
The Sea Wolf	Michael Curtiz	1941
To Have and Have Not	Howard Hawks	1944
My Darling Clementine	John Ford	1946
Notorious	Alfred Hitchcock	1946
Captain From Castile	Henry King	1947
She Wore a Yellow Ribbon	John Ford	1949
The Third Man	Carol Reed	1949
Twelve O'Clock High	Henry King	1949
King Solomon's Mines	Compton Bennet Andrew Marton	1950
The African Queen	John Huston	1951
High Noon	Fred Zinnemann	1952
Scaramouche	George Sidney	1952
The Snows of Kilimanjaro	Henry King	1952
The Searchers	John Ford	1956
North by Northwest	Alfred Hitchcock	1959
Rio Bravo	Howard Hawks	1959
Spartacus	Stanley Kubrick	1960
The Guns of Navarone	J. Lee Thompson	1961
Dr. No	Terence Young	1962
Hatari!	Howard Hawks	1962
How the West Was Won	John Ford Henry Hathaway George Marshall	1962
The 300 Spartans	Rudolph Maté	1962
55 Days at Peking	Nicholas Ray	1963
Goldfinger	Guy Hamilton	1964
A Fistful of Dollars	Sergio Leone	1964
Zulu	Cy Endfield	1964
She	Robert Day	1965

The Spy Who Came In From the Cold	Martin Ritt	1965
Funeral in Berlin	Guy Hamilton	1966
The Professionals	Richard Brooks	1966
Torn Curtain	Alfred Hitchcock	1966
Butch Cassidy and the Sundance Kid	George Roy Hill	1969
True Grit	Henry Hathaway	1969
Where Eagles Dare	Brian G. Hutton	1969
The Wild Bunch	Sam Peckinpah	1969
Little Big Man	Arthur Penn	1970
Patton	Franklin Schaffner	1970
Rio Lobo	Howard Hawks	1970
The Day of the Jackal	Fred Zinnemann	1973
Enter the Dragon	Robert Clouse	1973
The Three Musketeers	Richard Lester	1974
Doc Savage: The Man of Bronze	Michael Anderson	1975
The Man Who Would Be King	John Huston	1975
Royal Flash	Richard Lester	1975
Three Days of the Condor	Sydney Pollack	1975
The Eagle Has Landed	John Sturges	1977
Superman	Richard Donner	1978
Riddle of the Sands	Tony Maylam	1979
Eye of the Needle	Richard Marquand	1981
Raiders of the Lost Ark	Steven Spielberg	1981
Firefox	Clint Eastwood	1982

First Blood	Ted Kotcheff	1982
High Road to China	Brian G. Hutton	1983
Indiana Jones and the Temple of Doom	Steven Spielberg	1984
Missing In Action	Joseph Zito	1984
Romancing the Stone	Robert Zemeckis	1984
The Goonies	Richard Donner	1985
Firewalker	J. Lee Thompson	1986
The Golden Child	Michael Ritchie	1986
Platoon	Oliver Stone	1986
Bloodsport	Newt Arnold	1987
Die Hard	John McTiernan	1988
Batman	Tim Burton	1989
Indiana Jones and the Last Crusade	Steven Spielberg	1989
Dances With Wolves	Kevin Costner	1990
The Hunt for Red October	John McTiernan	1990
Quigley Down Under	Simon Wincer	1990
The Russia House	Fred Schepisi	1990
Thelma & Louise	Ridley Scott	1991
The Last of the Mohicans	Michael Mann	1992
Patriot Games	Phillip Noyce	1992
Shining Through	David Seltzer	1992
Under Siege	Andrew Davis	1992
Unforgiven	Clint Eastwood	1992
Universal Soldier	Roland Emmerich	1992
Hard Target	John Woo	1993
Jurassic Park	Steven Spielberg	1993
Last Action Hero	John McTiernan	1993
On Deadly Ground	Steven Seagal	1994
True Lies	James Cameron	1994

CREDITS

INDEX OF AUTHORS AND TITLES